Handbook of Minority Aging

Keith E. Whitfield, PhD, is vice provost for Academic Affairs, professor of Psychology and Neuroscience, codirector of the Center on Biobehavioral Health Disparities Research, and senior fellow, Center for the Study of Aging and Human Development, Duke University. He has received numerous awards and honors including the 2010 Distinguished Mentorship in Gerontology Award, the 2007 Leadership Award, GSA Task Force on Minority Issues, and the Allen L. Edwards Endowed Lecturer, Department of Psychology, University of Washington, Seattle. Dr. Whitfield has received or been a part of grants totaling more than 10 million dollars, authored over 115 professional articles, 30 book chapters, and coedited four books, among other accomplishments. His research involves the study of individuals and twins to examine individual variability in later life. His "Baltimore Study of Black Aging (BSBA)" has operated for more than 13 years and includes multiple studies of the relationship between cognition, health, and psychosocial factors. Dr. Whitfield has also developed a twin study of health and psychosocial factors related to health called the Carolina African American Twin Study of Aging (CAATSA). CAATSA is one of the largest in-person studies of adult African American twins. He has served as a member and chair of a number of NIH study sections. He was a member of the National Research Council/National Academy of Sciences "Aging Mind" and "Research Agenda for the Social Psychology of Aging" committees and the Institute of Medicine committee's report on "Assessing Interactions Among Social, Behavioral, and Genetic Factors on Health." He is a member of the National Advisory Board for the Center for Urban African American Aging Research at the University of Michigan, the Advisory Board for Institute on Aging at Wayne State University, the Data Monitoring Board for the National Healthy Aging Trends Study, and served a term on the Board of Scientific Counselors for the National Institute on Aging.

Tamara A. Baker, PhD, is associate professor in the School of Aging Studies at the University of South Florida. She is a Gerontological Society of America Fellow, the current chair of the Gerontological Society of America's Task Force on Minority Issues, and has been recognized by the National Institutes of Health as a promising scholar in the area of pain research. Her research has been published in several high-impact scientific journals and has been featured in a number of venues such as the *New York Times*. Dr. Baker is the recipient of federal funding from the National Institute on Aging (NIA), the National Cancer Institute (NCI), and the National Institute of Arthritis and Musculoskeletal and Skin Disorders (NIAMS). She has authored 45 selected publications, with more than 80 invited presentations nationally and internationally on her research on health and aging among diverse race and ethnic populations. Dr. Baker currently serves on the editorial board of *The Gerontologist*, is on the National Advisory Committee for the Cornell-Columbia Edward R. Roybal Center (Translational Research Institute on Pain in Later Life [TRIPLL]), and has served on the Advisory Council for the West Central Florida Area Agency on Aging. Dr. Baker's research focuses on the behavioral and psychosocial predictors and outcomes of chronic pain and disease in older adults from diverse race and ethnic populations. She also has a particular interest in examining health disparities and disparities in chronic pain management among older community-dwelling adults. Dr. Baker has an ongoing project examining psychological, social, and cultural factors influencing cancer pain management in older adults.

About the Associate Editors

Cleopatra M. Abdou, PhD, received her PhD in social and health psychology from UCLA in 2008. She completed a postdoctoral fellowship in social epidemiology and population health at the University of Michigan as a Robert Wood Johnson Foundation Health and Society Scholar in 2010. In 2010, Dr. Abdou joined the faculty in the University of Southern California's Davis School of Gerontology and Department of Psychology. Dr. Abdou conducts interdisciplinary experimental and survey research to investigate how society, culture, stress, and positive resources interact to affect health, well-being, and broader aging processes over the individual life span and across multiple generations. Dr. Abdou's research focuses on African Americans, Arabs, and Latinos in the United States and North Africans globally. Her research has been funded by the National Science Foundation, the National Institutes of Health, the Robert Wood Johnson Foundation, the Michigan Center for Integrative Approaches to Health Disparities, and Advancing Scholarship in the Humanities and Social Sciences. Dr. Abdou was the 2012 recipient of the Junior Scientist Award from the National Institute of Standards and Technology's U.S.–Egypt Joint Fund for Science & Technology. Three questions guide her research program: (a) How do demands for successful physical and psychological adaptation vary in diverse populations and contexts? (b) How do these challenges become embedded in biology in order to produce the stark health inequalities that characterize most societies around the globe? and (c) What are the capabilities of cultural and other nonmaterial resources to buffer the health consequences of social inequality, thereby reducing health disparities within and between nations? As part of her empirical research, Dr. Abdou examines broader theoretical and measurement issues surrounding conceptual and operational distinctions between the constructs of culture and several social identities, including nationality, race, ethnicity, and social status. Dr. Abdou developed the Culture and Social Identity Health Theory to direct these efforts. In addition to publishing in psychology, medicine, and public health journals, Dr. Abdou is the author of *Healthy Egypt*.

Jacqueline L. Angel, PhD, is currently a professor of Public Affairs and Sociology and a faculty affiliate at the Population Research Center and LBJ School Center for Health and Social Policy at the University of Texas (UT) at Austin. Prior to joining the UT faculty, she did her postdoctoral training at Rutgers State University of New Jersey in mental health services research and the Pennsylvania State University Program in Demography of Aging. Her research addresses the relationships linking family structures, inequality, and health across the life course, including a special focus on older Hispanics. Some of her recent publications include *Aging, Health, and Longevity in the Mexican-Origin Population*, coedited with Fernando Torres-Gil and Kyriakos Markides; *Handbook of the Sociology of Aging* with Rick Settersten; and *Hispanic Families at Risk: The New Economy, Work, and the Welfare State*, coauthored with Ronald Angel. Dr. Angel is a fellow of the Behavioral and Social Sciences section of the Gerontological Society of America (GSA) and a senior fellow at the Sealy Center on Aging, UTMB School of Medicine.

Letha A. Chadiha, PhD, MSW, is professor of Social Work at the University of Michigan, Ann Arbor, and codirector of the Community Core in the Michigan Center for Urban African American Aging Research at the University of Michigan and Wayne State University. Her research focuses on the mental health and social functioning of African American female caregivers assisting older African Americans and the recruitment of older African Americans in health-related research.

Kerstin Gerst-Emerson, PhD, received her PhD in Gerontology from the University of Massachusetts Boston in 2008. She joined the University of Georgia's Institute of Gerontology in August 2010 as an assistant professor. Prior to her faculty appointment, she worked for 2 years as a postdoctoral fellow at the Sealy Center on Aging at the University of Texas Medical Branch, where she studied the health of older Hispanics. Before pursuing a career in academics, Dr. Gerst-Emerson worked as a policy analyst for Thomson-Medstat where she researched long-term care issues in the United States and produced policy reports for the Centers for Medicare and Medicaid Services. As a gerontologist interested in aging and health, her research uses large secondary data analyses to explore minority aging issues in the United States. Her research includes exploring the impact of immigration on mental health, as well as the influence of neighborhood characteristics on physical and mental health outcomes. Currently Dr. Gerst-Emerson is studying disability incidence among elders living in Mexico in comparison to elders living in the United States. She has presented her research findings at national and international conferences and has given invited lectures on topics related to diversity and health within an aging population.

James S. Jackson, PhD, is the Daniel Katz Distinguished University Professor of Psychology, Professor of Afroamerican and African Studies, and Director of the Institute for Social Research, all at the University of Michigan. His research focuses on issues of racial and ethnic influences on life course development, attitude change, reciprocity, social support, and coping and health among blacks in the diaspora. He is past Director of the Center for Afroamerican and African Studies and past national President of the Association of Black Psychologists. He is a fellow of the Gerontological Society of America, the Society of Experimental Social Psychology, the American Psychological Association, the Association of Psychological Sciences, AAAS, and the W.E.B. Du Bois Fellow of the American Academy of Political and Social Science. He received numerous awards, including the Distinguished Career Contributions to Research Award of the Society for the Psychological Study of Ethnic Minority Issues, the James McKeen Cattell Fellow Award for Distinguished Career Contributions in Applied Psychology of the American Psychological Association, and the Medal for Distinguished Contributions in Biomedical Sciences of the New York Academy of Medicine. He is the President of the Consortium of Social Science Associations. He is a member of the Institute of Medicine and a fellow of the American Academy of Arts and Sciences. He is currently directing the most extensive social, political behavior, and mental and physical health surveys on the African American and Black Caribbean populations ever conducted. He serves on several Boards for the National Research Council and the National Academies of Science and is a founding member of the new "Aging Society Research Network" of the MacArthur Foundation.

Kyriakos S. Markides, PhD, received his PhD in Sociology in 1976 from Louisiana State University. He is currently the Annie and John Gnitzinger Distinguished Professor of Aging and director of the Division of Sociomedical Sciences, Department of Preventive Medicine and Community Health at the University of Texas Medical Branch in Galveston. Dr. Markides is the editor of the *Journal of Aging and Health,* which he founded in 1989. He is the author or coauthor of over 325 publications, most of which are on aging and health issues in the Mexican American population as well as minority aging issues in general. His research has been funded continuously by the National Institutes of Health since 1980. He is currently principal investigator of the *Hispanic EPESE* (Established Population for the Epidemiological Study of the Elderly), a longitudinal study of the health of 3952 older Mexican Americans from the five southwestern states. Dr. Markides is credited with coining the term "Hispanic Epidemiological Paradox" (with J. Coreil), which is currently the leading theme in Hispanic health. He is also the editor of the *Encyclopedia of Health and Aging,* published by SAGE Publications in 2007. The Institute for Scientific Information (ISA) has listed Dr. Markides among the most highly cited social scientists in the world. Dr. Markides is the 2006 recipient of the Distinguished Mentorship Award of the Gerontological Society of America, and the 2009 Distinguished Professor Award in Gerontology and Geriatrics from UCLA. He was also the inaugural recipient of the Pearmain Prize for outstanding service to the field of aging from the Roybal Institute on Aging at the University of Southern California. The prize was awarded in February 2010.

Philip A. Rozario, PhD, MSW, received his PhD in Social Work in 2002 from Washington University in St. Louis. He is currently associate professor and director of the PhD program at Adelphi University School of Social Work. Dr. Rozario serves on the editorial boards of several peer-reviewed journals, including the *Journal of Family Issues, Health and Social Work, Asia Pacific Journal of Social Work and Development*, and *Journal of Gerontological Social Work*. He has published in the areas of productive aging, the well-being of the African American female caregiver, successful aging for chronically ill older adults, and service utilization of depressed older adults. More recently, his scholarly interest has been in the implementation and impact of family responsibility law on social service practice in Singapore, especially in the face of a rapidly aging society and a privatized old age security system. Dr. Rozario is a John A. Hartford faculty scholar in Geriatric Social Work, and in 2010, he was elected a Gerontological Society of America Fellow.

Roland J. Thorpe, Jr., PhD, is an associate scientist in the Department of Health Policy and Management at The Johns Hopkins Bloomberg School of Public Health, and the Research, Education, and Training director, and director of the Program for Research on Men's Health in the Hopkins Center for Health Disparities Solutions. He is also a visiting research fellow in the Center on Biobehavioral Research on Health Disparities at Duke University. Dr. Thorpe completed a 3-year postdoctoral fellowship in Gerontology and Health Disparities in the Division of Geriatrics and Gerontology at Johns Hopkins University School of Medicine in 2007. Dr. Thorpe is a social epidemiologist and gerontologist whose research agenda focuses on ascertaining potentially malleable social, biobehavioral, and environmental factors that underlie racial and SES disparities in function and health among community-dwelling middle- to old-age adults. Dr. Thorpe's work has been supported by the Johns Hopkins Urban Health Institute, National Institute on Aging, Eunice Kennedy Shriver National Institute of Child Health and Human Development, and the National Center for Minority Health and Health Disparities of the National Institutes of Health.

Handbook of Minority Aging

EDITORS
Keith E. Whitfield, PhD and Tamara A. Baker, PhD

ASSOCIATE EDITORS
**Cleopatra M. Abdou, PhD, Jacqueline L. Angel, PhD,
Letha A. Chadiha, PhD, MSW,
Kerstin Gerst-Emerson, PhD, James S. Jackson, PhD,
Kyriakos S. Markides, PhD,
Philip A. Rozario, PhD, MSW, and
Roland J. Thorpe, Jr., PhD**

SPRINGER PUBLISHING COMPANY
NEW YORK

Springer Publishing Company, LLC
11 West 42nd Street
New York, NY 10036
www.springerpub.com

Acquisitions Editor: Sheri W. Sussman
Production Editor: Joseph Stubenrauch
Composition: Newgen Imaging

ISBN: 978–0-8261–0963-7
e-book ISBN: 978–0-8261–0964-4

13 14 15 / 5 4 3 2 1

The author and the publisher of this Work have made every effort to use sources believed to be reliable to provide information that is accurate and compatible with the standards generally accepted at the time of publication. The author and publisher shall not be liable for any special, consequential, or exemplary damages resulting, in whole or in part, from the readers' use of, or reliance on, the information contained in this book. The publisher has no responsibility for the persistence or accuracy of URLs for external or third-party Internet websites referred to in this publication and does not guarantee that any content on such websites is, or will remain, accurate or appropriate.

Library of Congress Cataloging-in-Publication Data
Handbook of minority aging / editors, Keith E. Whitfield, Tamara A. Baker; volume associate editors, Cleopatra M. Abdou ... [et al.].
    p. ; cm.
  Includes bibliographical references and index.
  ISBN 978-0-8261-0963-7 — ISBN 978-0-8261-0964-4 (e-book)
  I. Baker, Tamara A. II. Whitfield, Keith E., 1962-
  [DNLM: 1. Aging--psychology—United States. 2. Aging—ethnology—United States. 3. Minority Groups—United States. WT 145]
  RA564.8
  362.60973—dc23
                                                                                         2013010799

Printed in the United States of America by Bradford and Bigelow.

To my parents, Lt. Col. Glenn T. Whitfield (1937–2012) and Barbara Whitfield; my wife Dr. Linda M. Burton—KEW

To the two loves of my life: Landon and Sydney; Dr. Nathan Thomas; my 90-year-old grandmother Elizabeth Eley; and my parents Dr. Hollie Baker, Sr., and Clara E. Baker (1943–2007)—TAB

To those giants in the field of minority aging that have come before us—you know who you are—and to the future generations in the field of minority aging.

Contents

Contributors

Cleopatra M. Abdou, PhD
Leonard Davis School of Gerontology
Department of Psychology
University of Southern California
Los Angeles, CA

Sawsan Abdulrahim, PhD
Department of Health Promotion and
    Community Health
American University of Beirut
Beirut, Lebanon

Adrienne T. Aiken-Morgan, PhD
Social Science Research Institute
Duke University
Durham, NC

Kristine J. Ajrouch, PhD
Departments of Sociology, Anthropology,
    and Criminology
Eastern Michigan University
Ypsilanti, MI

Jacqueline L. Angel, PhD
Department of Sociology
University of Texas at Austin
Austin, TX

Ronald J. Angel, PhD
Department of Sociology
University of Texas at Austin
Austin, TX

A. E. Benjamin, PhD
Department of Social Welfare
UCLA Luskin School of Public Affairs
Los Angeles, CA

Maciej S. Buchowski, PhD
Department of Medicine
Vanderbilt University
Nashville, TN

Karen Bullock, PhD
Department of Social Work
North Carolina State University
Raleigh, NC

Jeffrey A. Burr, PhD
Department of Gerontology
University of Massachusetts, Boston
Boston, MA

Linda M. Chatters, PhD
School of Social Work
School of Public Health
Institute for Social Research
University of Michigan
Ann Arbor, MI

Letha A. Chadiha, PhD, MSW
School of Social Work
University of Michigan
Ann Arbor, MI

Hongtu Chen, PhD
Department of Psychiatry
Harvard Medical School
Boston, MA

Namkee G. Choi, PhD
School of Social Work
University of Texas at Austin
Austin, TX

Peggye Dilworth-Anderson, PhD
Department of Health Policy and
    Management
Gillings School of Global Public Health
University of North Carolina–Chapel Hill
Chapel Hill, NC

Christopher Edwards, PhD
Department of Psychiatry
Duke University Medical Center
Durham, NC

Irma T. Elo, MPA, PhD
Department of Sociology
Population Studies Center
University of Pennsylvania
Philadelphia, PA

Marvella E. Ford, PhD
Cancer Disparities
Hollings Cancer Center;
Department of Public Health Sciences
Medical University of South Carolina
Charleston, SC

Kerstin Gerst-Emerson, PhD
Institute of Gerontology
Department of Health Policy &
    Management
University of Georgia
Athens, GA

Teresa Ghilarducci, PhD
Department of Economics
The New School for Social Research
New York, NY

Subharati Ghosh, PhD, MSW
Lurie Institute for Disability Policy
Heller School for Social Policy and
    Management
Brandeis University
Waltham, MA

Jodi K. Hall, EdD
Department of Social Work
North Carolina State University
Raleigh, NC

Elise Hernandez, BS
Department of Psychology
School of Social Work
University of Michigan
Ann Arbor, MI

Tandrea S. Hilliard, MPH
Department of Health Policy and
    Management
Gillings School of Global Public Health
University of North Carolina–
    Chapel Hill
Chapel Hill, NC

Robert A. Hummer, BA, MA, PhD
Population Research Center
Department of Sociology
University of Texas at Austin
Austin, TX

Emily S. Ihara, PhD, MSW
Department of Social Work
George Mason University
Fairfax, VA

James S. Jackson, PhD
Institute for Social Research
University of Michigan
Ann Arbor, MI

Verna M. Keith, PhD
Race and Ethnic Studies Institute
Texas A&M University
College Station, TX

Jessica A. Kelley-Moore, PhD
Department of Sociology
Case Western Reserve University
Cleveland, OH

Monica T. Leach, EdD
Department of Social Work
North Carolina State University
Raleigh, NC

Sue Levkoff, ScD, SM, MSW
College of Social Work
University of South Carolina
Columbia, SC

Karen D. Lincoln, BA, MSW, MA, PhD
Edward R. Roybal Institute of Aging
School of Social Work
University of Southern California
Los Angeles, CA

Sandy Magaña, PhD, MSW
Departments of Disability and
    Human Development and
    Occupational Therapy
University of Illinois at Chicago
Chicago, IL

Kyriakos S. Markides, PhD
Department of Preventive Medicine and
    Community Health
University of Texas Medical Branch
Galveston, TX

Philip McCallion, PhD, MSW
School of Social Welfare
University at Albany
State University of New York
Albany, NY

Neil K. Mehta, PhD
Department of Global Health
Emory University
Atlanta, GA

Jennifer E. Melvin, MA
Department of Sociology
University of Texas at Austin
Austin, TX

Toni P. Miles, MD, PhD
Institute of Gerontology, Epidemiology, and
    Biostatistics
College of Public Health
University of Georgia
Athens, GA

Nancy Morrow-Howell, PhD, MSW
George Warren Brown School of
    Social Work
Washington University in St. Louis
St. Louis, MO

Emily J. Nicklett, PhD, MSW
School of Social Work
University of Michigan
Ann Arbor, MI

Ann W. Nguyen, BA, MSW
School of Social Work
Department of Psychology
University of Michigan
Ann Arbor, MI

Martha Norton, MA
Environment & Health Group, Inc.
Cambridge, MA

D. Imelda Padilla-Frausto, MPH
Department of Community Health Sciences
UCLA Center for Health Policy Research
UCLA Fielding School of Public Health
Los Angeles, CA

Melanie A. Paige, BA
General Internal Medicine
Duke University Medical Center
Durham, NC

M. Paige Powell, PhD
Department of Health Systems Management
    and Policy
University of Memphis
Memphis, TN

James S. Powers, MD
Department of Medicine
Vanderbilt University
Nashville, TN

Rohit Pradhan, PhD
Department of Health Policy and Management
University of Arkansas for Medical Sciences
Little Rock, AR

Karen Richman, PhD
Academic Programs
Institute for Latino Studies
University of Notre Dame
Notre Dame, IN

Marta B. Rodríguez-Galán, PhD
Department of Sociology
St. John Fisher College
Rochester, NY

Ronica N. Rooks, PhD, MA
Department of Health and Behavioral Sciences
University of Colorado, Denver
Denver, CO

Caroline Rosenthal Gelman, PhD, MSW
Silberman School of Social Work
Hunter College
City University of New York
New York, NY

Philip A. Rozario, PhD, MSW
School of Social Work
Adelphi University
Garden City, NY

Brittany Rudinica, MSW
UCLA Luskin School of Public Affairs
University of California, Los Angeles
Los Angeles, CA

Joelle Saad-Lessler, PhD
Schwartz Center for Economic Policy Analysis
The New School for Social Research
New York, NY

Connor M. Sheehan, BA, MA
Population Research Center
Department of Sociology
University of Texas at Austin
Austin, TX

Mohamad A. Sidani, MD, MS
Department of Family and Community
    Medicine
Meharry Medical College
Nashville, TN

Matthew Lee Smith, PhD, MPH, CHES
Department of Health Promotion and
    Behavior
College of Public Health
University of Georgia
Athens, GA

Kimberly N. Spencer-Suarez, MSW
School of Social Work
Columbia University
New York, NY

Nikkil Sudharsanan, MPH
Department of Global Health
Emory University
Atlanta, GA

Harry Owen Taylor, MPH, MSW
George Warren Brown School of Social Work
Washington University in St. Louis
St. Louis, MO

Robert Joseph Taylor, PhD, MSW
School of Social Work
Institute for Social Research
University of Michigan
Ann Arbor, MI

Roland J. Thorpe, Jr., PhD
Hopkins Center for Health
    Disparities Solutions
Department of Health Policy and Management
Johns Hopkins Bloomberg School of Public
    Health
Baltimore, MD

Catherine J. Tompkins, PhD, MSW
Department of Social Work
George Mason University
Fairfax, VA

Fernando Torres-Gil, PhD, MSW
UCLA Luskin School of Public Affairs
University of California, Los Angeles
Los Angeles, CA

Steven P. Wallace, PhD
Department of Community Health
    Sciences
UCLA Center for Health Policy
    Research
UCLA Fielding School of Public
    Health
Los Angeles, CA

Yi Wang, MSW
George Warren Brown School of Social
    Work
Washington University in St. Louis
St. Louis, MO

Ying-Ting Wang, MA
Population Research Center
Department of Sociology
University of Texas at Austin
Austin, TX

Robert Weech-Maldonado, PhD
Department of Health Services
    Administration
University of Alabama at
    Birmingham
Birmingham, AL

Keith E. Whitfield, PhD
Department of Psychology and
    Neuroscience
Duke University
Durham, NC

Preface

Over the last 25 years, there has been a growing emphasis in the field of gerontology to study issues related to diversity across racial and ethnic groups. This has resulted in a clear need for an organized review focusing on the scientific advances of the aged from diverse race and ethnic populations, while enhancing conceptual and theoretical models within and across varying ethnic and race groups.

The growing need to better understand the aging process across race and ethnic groups garnered support from the Gerontological Society of America (GSA), thus commencing the Task Force on Minority Issues in Gerontology (TFMIG; circa 1987). The TFMIG has had a substantial and established history in addressing issues pertinent to minority aging and to members of the GSA. The editors of this volume have each served as chair of this important group (TFMIG), and heard from its membership of the need for a comprehensive volume devoted to emergent issues surrounding the aging process of diverse race and ethnic groups.

To meet this challenge, one of the goals of this volume, established by the editors, was to create a multidisciplinary review of literature on minority aging. Realizing the magnitude of this challenge, leaders in the field of gerontology were enlisted to recruit contributing authors with the knowledge and insight on matters most pertinent to understanding the changing demographic structure of the older adult population. This effort resulted in a volume that provides a progressive and multidisciplinary compendium of research pertaining to aging among diverse racial and ethnic populations in the United States. It is the only book to focus on paramount public health, social, behavioral, and biological concerns as they relate to the needs of older minorities. The text distills the most important advances in the science of minority aging and incorporates the evidence of scholars in gerontology, anthropology, psychology, public health, sociology, social work, biology, medicine, and nursing. Additionally, the book incorporates the work of both established and emerging scholars to provide the broadest possible knowledge base on the needs of and concerns for this rapidly growing population.

The chapters focus on an array of subject areas that are recognized as being critical to understanding the well-being of minority elders. These include sociology (Medicare, socioeconomic status [SES], work and retirement, social networks, context/neighborhood, ethnography, gender, demographics), psychology (cognition, stress, mental health, personality, sexuality, religion, neuroscience, discrimination), medicine/nursing/public health (mortality and morbidity, disability, health disparities, long-term care, genetics, dietary issues, health interventions, physical functioning), social work (caregiving, housing, social services, end-of-life care), and many other topics. The book focuses on the needs of four major race and ethnic groups: Asian/Pacific Islander, Hispanic/Latino, black/African American, and Native American. This comprehensive sourcebook also includes both inter- and intra-race and ethnic group research for insights regarding minority aging.

These well-written examinations of issues central to the study of minority aging create an incredible review of the available scholarship on a broad range of topics. In reading the chapters, it also becomes apparent that there are racial and ethnic groups, as well as topics, that have been examined less than others. Scholarship on minority aging has focused more on black–white comparisons than information on other groups. Thus, current and impending changes in the demographics of older populations will hopefully challenge scholars to increase our knowledge on the life course and aging issues pertinent to Hispanics, Asians, Native Americans, and other cultural groups. The future for bringing our knowledge of these understudied groups, in line with the needs and impact they will have on society, will be the challenge of future generations of scholars. The associate editorial teams reflect junior/senior scholar pairing designed to help promote and mentor the next generation of scholars. Their leadership has been significant and important for both the development of this volume and the future of minority aging science.

PART I

PSYCHOLOGY OF MINORITY AGING

CHAPTER 1

Introduction: Psychology—Rising as a Discipline to Meet the Challenges of an Aging, Increasingly Diverse Society

Cleopatra M. Abdou and James S. Jackson

Although Part I focuses on psychology as a discipline, minority aging research during the last several decades has revealed the need for multidisciplinary and intersectional conceptual and research approaches. As noted elsewhere in this book, increased longevity and reduced fertility is creating a unique demographic transition, especially in advanced industrial countries. Between 2030 and 2050 there will be more individuals over the age of 60 than under 15 years of age (Rowe & Berkman, 2009). This change in the fundamental nature of the age pyramid provides stark evidence, especially in advanced industrial nations, that reduced death by childbirth and infectious diseases, better control of chronic illnesses, and reduced rates of infant mortality are changing our notions of what is possible for the individual lifespan. These demographic changes will create many new challenges for individuals, families, and governments (Robinson, Novelli, Pearson, & Norris, 2007; Rowe & Berkman, 2009). Also significant in the changing age demographics in the United States is the increase in the numbers and types of ethnic and racial minority groups. This increase is due to the same population-level fertility and longevity forces as well as to increased immigration (Antonucci & Jackson, 2010). A significant proportion of individuals from these racial and ethnic minority groups have distinct lifespan histories and life course experiences that unfortunately are associated with early disadvantage, resulting in pronounced inequalities, particularly in later life (Govia, Jackson, & Sellers, 2011; Jackson & Govia, 2009; Jackson, Govia, & Sellers, 2010).

The chapters in this part do not focus on all ethnic or cultural groups. We realize that, to some degree, ethnicity is an important source of diversity and meaning in the lives of all aging individuals, including non-Hispanic whites (Govia et al., 2011). Because of the growing proportions of ethnic and racial minorities among American older adults (Aiken-Morgan, Whitfield, & Paige, this part), however, we focus our attention on ethnic minority groups of color. Their historical relative deprivation, in comparison to non-Hispanic white ethnic elders, differentially shapes the nature of their aging experiences (Jackson, Brown, Antonucci, & Daatland, 2005). Despite such profound differences, there has been a neglect of research on ethnic groups of color (Lincoln, this part). Ethnicity, national origin, and culture, in fact, all play important roles in aging-related processes (Abdou, this part). In addition, it is increasingly apparent that other social group memberships (e.g., gender and socioeconomic status) also contribute significantly to aging processes. In fact, many of these factors operate in parallel, interact, or intersect with race and ethnicity to influence the aging process (Abdou, this part).

Our previous work has suggested the need for a greater consideration of cross-racial/ethnic and cross-national perspectives in aging research (e.g., Brown, Jackson, & Faison, 2006; Markides, Liang, & Jackson, 1990). We have suggested that the infusion of racial and ethnic content into theory and research designs can have positive effects on the health and well-being of all population groups (Jackson, 2000); this is especially true given the current and predicted rise in the proportions of groups of color, relative to whites, in all age ranges in the United States. We have also suggested the need to disentangle the constructs of minority group, race, ethnicity, and culture (Abdou, this part; Abdou et al., 2010; Abdou, Dominguez, & Myers, 2013; Jackson, Antonucci, & Gibson, 1990; Jackson et al., 2005).

It is evident that contexts—social, material, environmental, and historical—as well as cohort and period influences are vital in studying and understanding aging-related psychological processes among the increasing proportions of groups and individuals of color in the United States. In addition, a life course perspective (i.e., the consideration of historical, cohort, and early experience factors that influence the life situations of individuals over time) provides the necessary framing for viewing human development; this is true for all population groups, and especially for racial and ethnic minorities. For this same reason, the current book on aging includes consideration of birth outcomes and early development as bases for understanding psychological development over the lifespan. Similarly, as we have suggested earlier, the development of more encompassing models of aging is best accomplished by first understanding the ways in which race, ethnicity, and culture contribute to human developmental and aging-related processes. Finally, intersectionality theory and research provides a useful framework for understanding the ways in which social inequalities and status-based advantages contextualize individual lifespan development (Govia et al., 2011). Recent research reveals how the different social identities that individuals hold are implicated in different psychological and health outcomes (e.g., Bowleg, 2008; Cole, 2009; Sen, Iyer, & Mukherjee, 2009; Settles, Navarette, Pagano, Abdou, & Sidanius, 2010; Warner, 2008). In Chapter 2, Abdou explicitly proposes the Culture and Social Identity Health Theory (CSIH) as an encompassing approach for examining the independent and interdependent influences of culture and social identities on development and health. As noted in CSIH, intersectionality theory and research do not presume that social identities are hierarchically ordered, and they also do not assume commonalities in the outcomes of individuals who share specific social identities, such as all African Americans, Latinos, females, or even all elderly (Govia et al., 2011).

One of the principal ways in which intersectionality theory and research can be used to understand how social inequalities contextualize and affect development across the individual lifespan is by considering the subjective identities that arise from specific intergenerational positioning, time periods, and generational cohorts. These subjective identities can be considered social locations that function in much the same way as the identities that are traditionally explored within intersectionality theory (i.e., racial and ethnic group membership, gender, sexuality, and age). Disciplines such as public health, epidemiology, and sociology contribute substantially to the empirical research focused on the role of social inequalities and advantages in how people change, or remain the same, throughout their individual life spans. Suggestions have been made recently to develop theoretical frameworks that anchor race and culture in discussions about biological and social functioning, and how these, in turn, affect health across the lifespan (Govia et al., 2011; Griffin & Jackson, 2010; Jackson & Govia, 2009). Nevertheless, we believe that psychology is a critical linchpin in understanding how individuals and groups actively address the structural and interpersonal barriers to group and individual mobility and progress (Jackson, Govia, & Sellers, 2010). This individual, agency-based viewpoint is an important aspect of a positive psychology perspective on human development and posits that racial and ethnic groups of color are not merely passive recipients of the destructive forces of discrimination, maltreatment, and structural disadvantage; but, instead, are active agents who interact with family, friends, and religious institutions in positive and productive ways to combat their unequal statuses and live their best lives (Abdou, this part; Chatters, Nguyen, & Taylor, this part; Franklin & Jackson, 1990; Lincoln, this part).

Collectively, the chapters in this part provide an illustration of the complexities involved in studying ethnic and racial influences on psychosocial processes and how they are intimately tied to physical outcomes in later life. Although selective, since no one set of papers can address the entire landscape of this large and complex topic, the chapters in this part provide a broad sampling of recent thinking and research on this important set of issues. Chapters addressing personality development over the life course and serious mental disorders would have added to the coverage of psychology in aging-related processes among ethnic and racial minority groups. Notably, all of the chapters in this part, either explicitly or implicitly, adopt a life course perspective (Antonucci & Jackson, 2010). They emphasize, in particular, a bio-behavioral framework, implicating the critical intersections among genetic, environmental, and social group influences from conception to death, which produce the individual trajectories and risks for psychological and physical morbidity and mortality at different points in the individual life course (Whitfield, 2005).

Abdou's chapter (this part) makes the strong case for a cradle-to-grave conceptualization of aging, as well as for the need for more explicit theory of how culture, race, ethnicity, and other aspects of identity exert their influences on lifespan processes. She concludes that there is greater need for research on social integration, group belongingness, and the role of culture as a positive nonmaterial resource. Lincoln (this part) analyses this theme in a thorough review of social relationships and health and how these connections differ by race and ethnicity. She concludes with a call for more research on the nature and processes of social support, especially on how these processes may differ with complex interactions of culture, race, ethnicity, immigration status, and socioeconomic positioning. Working with related themes, Keith (this part) addresses the explicit role of stress, discrimination, and coping resources among racial and ethnic minorities. Situating her review within the stress process literature, she focuses on discrimination as a mundane, yet potent, stressor that makes a significant contribution to psychological and physical health disparities. She concludes with a call for further research on environmental influences as well as greater attention to how discrimination interacts with other daily stressors in creating observed health disparities among minorities. Aiken-Morgan, Whitfield, and Paige (this part) focus their attention on cognitive aging and especially on the ways in which ethnicity and racial group membership may mediate the nature of cognitive declines. They conclude that there is ample evidence of the importance of cognitive decline among racial and ethnic groups and call for greater attention to variations in the process of mild cognitive impairment and dementia among these groups of color. No section on psychology could be complete without a discussion of religion and spirituality among racial and ethnic minorities. Chatters and colleagues (this part) address the nature and role of spirituality and religion in psychological, social, and physical health among African American, Asian American, and Hispanic/Latino groups. They particularly attend to the complex positive and negative influences of religiosity and spirituality on important life outcomes. They conclude with a call for more nuanced research on this important context of aging in diverse groups, particularly research involving greater attention to the social and psychological contexts of identity, social connections, and relationships.

CONCLUSIONS

In summary, this part focuses on the age, gender, socioeconomic, cultural, and racial and ethnic graded influences on life course development that eventuate in unequal burdens of psychological and physical health morbidity and mortality for certain groups in late life. A key feature of these chapters is that they reveal the appropriateness and need for a life course framework, encompassing the intersections of genetics, intrapersonal characteristics, socialization, and cumulative life experiences and risks on the fundamental nature of lifespan development, especially psychological development.

There are several major issues that need to be addressed in future research in this area. Perhaps, the most pressing is the development of sound theory and theoretically guided empirical studies. For example, the study of social inequalities during the individual life course is called to move from an outcome-oriented perspective to a process-oriented perspective relative to the influence of racial and ethnic group memberships, and to develop and test a series of theory-driven premises and hypotheses. Theoretical frameworks like CSIH may provide critical guidance for moving the field in this direction.

A related issue is that there are few theoretically guided empirical tests of longitudinal and multilevel models of how social inequalities affect individual lifespan development. With a few exceptions, such as studies that attempt to capture the ways in which contexts affect intelligence in infancy and early childhood, there are few studies that integrate an understanding of the role of social inequalities (Antonucci & Jackson, 2010). There are also few theoretically guided empirical tests of intra- and intergenerational processes that are implicit in models of social inequalities in development across the life course. Generational processes are clearly implicated in ideas about the cyclical nature of poverty and health behaviors that are intricately linked with environmental factors and social influence (e.g., Adler & Stewart, 2010; Govia et al., 2011). These processes and dynamics need to be explored even more urgently given the demographic shifts contributing to our coming aging and increasingly diverse society (Rowe & Berkman, 2009). These demographic shifts will fundamentally alter intergenerational dynamics. Consequently, the psychological, social, and health implications of these changed intergenerational relationships need to be investigated (Antonucci & Jackson, 2010).

Another issue is that in-depth examinations of groups within countries are needed. Such examinations will shed light on conundrums that still exist in the health disparities literature, such as why ethnic disparities that disadvantage blacks and other minorities exist for psychological distress and depressive symptoms, but may actually be reversed for more serious mental and psychiatric disorders, such that, unexpectedly, whites are worse off in terms of psychopathology than blacks and other minorities (Jackson, Knight, & Rafferty, 2010). Other issues that these in-depth examinations can highlight include how self- versus other-constructions of racial group membership (i.e., how we self-identify racially versus how others are likely to categorize us) affect experiences of discrimination and other types of stressors as well as broader health outcomes. Finally, more cross-national comparisons are needed to investigate how social inequalities throughout the individual life course function in different national, cultural, and political settings (Govia et al., 2011).

REFERENCES

Abdou, C. M., Dominguez, T. P., & Myers, H. F. (2013). Maternal familism predicts birthweight and asthma symptoms by age three. *Social Science & Medicine, 76*, 28–38. doi:10.1016/j.socscimed.2012.07.041

Abdou, C. M., Dunkel Schetter, C., Campos, B., Hilmert, C. J., Dominguez, T. P., Hobel, C. J.,…Sandman, C. (2010). Communalism predicts prenatal affect, stress, and physiology better than ethnicity and socioeconomic status. *Cultural Diversity & Ethnic Minority Psychology, 16*, 395–403. doi:10.1037/a0019808

Adler, N. E., & Stewart, J. (2010). Health disparities across the lifespan: Meaning, methods, and mechanisms. *Annals of the New York Academy of Sciences, 1186*, 5–23. doi:10.1111/j.1749–6632.2009.05337.x

Antonucci, T. C., & Jackson, J. S. (2010). Introduction: A life-course framework for understanding late life health inequalities. In T. C. Antonucci & J. S. Jackson (Eds.), *Annual Review of Geriatrics and Gerontology: Vol. 29, 2009. Life-course perspectives on late life health inequalities* (pp. xvii–xxxi). New York, NY: Springer.

Bowleg, L. (2008). When Black + lesbian + woman ≠ Black lesbian woman: The methodological challenges of qualitative and quantitative intersectionality research. *Sex Roles, 59*, 312–325. doi:10.1007/s11199–008-9400-z

Brown, E., Jackson, J. S., & Faison, N. (2006). The work and retirement experiences of aging black Americans. In J. B. James & P. Wink (Eds.), *The crown of life: Dynamics of the early post-retirement period* (pp. 39–60). New York, NY: Springer.

Cole, E. R. (2009). Intersectionality and research in psychology. *American Psychologist, 64*, 170–180. doi:10.1037/a0014564

Franklin, A. J., & Jackson, J. S. (1990). Factors contributing to positive mental health among black Americans. In D. Smith-Ruiz (Ed.), *Handbook of black mental health and mental disorder among black Americans* (pp. 291–307). Westport, CT: Greenwood Press.

Govia, I. O., Jackson, J. S., & Sellers, S. L. (2011). Social inequalities. In K. L. Fingerman, C. A. Berg, T. C. Antonucci, & J. Smith (Eds.), *Handbook of life-span development* (pp. 727–744). New York, NY: Springer.

Griffin, T. M., & Jackson, J. S. (2010). Racial differences. In I. B. Weiner & W. E. Craighead (Eds.), *The Corsini encyclopedia of psychology* (4th ed., Vol. 4, pp. 1411–1413). New York, NY: Wiley.

Jackson, J. S. (Ed.). (2000). *New directions: African Americans in a diversifying nation*. Washington, DC: National Policy Association.

Jackson, J. S., Antonucci, T. C., & Gibson, R. C. (1990). Cultural, racial, and ethnic minority influences on aging. In J. E. Birren, & K. W. Schaie (Eds.), *Handbook of the psychology of aging* (3rd ed., pp. 103–123). New York, NY: Academic Press.

Jackson, J. S., Brown, E., Antonucci, T. C., & Daatland, S. O. (2005). Ethnic diversity in aging, multicultural societies. In M. L. Johnson, V. L. Bengston, P. G. Coleman, & T. B. L. Kirkwood (Eds.), *The Cambridge handbook of age and aging* (pp. 476–481). Cambridge, UK: Cambridge University Press.

Jackson, J. S., & Govia, I. O. (2009). Quality of life for ethnic and racial minority elders in the 21st century: Setting a research agenda. In P. Sanford & T. C. Nelson (Eds.), *Diversity and aging in the 21st century: Let the dialogue begin* (pp. 148–169). Washington, DC: AARP.

Jackson, J. S., Govia, I. O., & Sellers, S. L. (2010). Race and ethnic influences over the life-course. In R. H. Binstock & L. K. George (Eds.), *Handbook of aging and the social sciences* (7th ed., pp. 91–103). New York, NY: Academic Press.

Jackson, J. S., Knight, K. M., & Rafferty, J. A. (2010). Race and unhealthy behaviors: Chronic stress, the HPA Axis, and physical and mental health disparities over the life course. *American Journal of Public Health, 100*, 933–939. doi:10.2105/AJPH.2008.143446

Markides, K. S., Liang, J., & Jackson, J. S. (1990). Race, ethnicity, and aging: Conceptual and methodological issues. In R. H. Binstock & L. K. George (Eds.), *Handbook of aging and the social sciences* (3rd ed., pp. 112–129). San Diego, CA: Academic Press.

Robinson, M., Novelli, W., Pearson, C., & Norris, L. (Eds.). (2007). *Global health & global aging*. New York, NY: John Wiley & Sons.

Rowe, J., & Berkman, L. (2009, June 2). Investing over the life-course: A winning strategy [Web log post]. *The Huffington Post*. Retrieved from http://www.huffingtonpost.com/john-rowe/investing-over-the-life-c_b_210391.html

Sen, G., Iyer, A., & Mukherjee, C. (2009). A methodology to analyse the intersections of social inequalities in health. *Journal of Human Development and Capabilities: A Multi-Disciplinary Journal for People-Centered Development, 10*, 397–415. doi:10.1080/19452820903048894

Settles, I. H., Navarette, C. D., Pagano, S. J., Abdou, C. M., & Sidanius, J. (2010). Racial identity and depression among African American women. *Cultural Diversity and Ethnic Minority Psychology, 16*, 248–255. doi:10.1037/a0016442

Warner, L. R. (2008). A best practices guide to intersectional approaches in psychological research. *Sex Roles, 59*, 454–463. doi: 10.1007/S11199-008-9504-5

Whitfield, K. E. (2005). Studying biobehavioral aspects of health among older adult minorities. *Journal of Urban Health, 82*(2 Suppl 3), iii103–110.

CHAPTER 2

Minority Aging Before Birth and Beyond: Life Span and Intergenerational Adaptation Through Positive Resources

Cleopatra M. Abdou

Minority status—whether based on ethnicity, gender, socioeconomic status (SES), citizenship, religion, or other factors—is a robust determinant of health, well-being, and success across the life span and intergenerationally. Nevertheless, we know from substantial unexplained variance in minority outcomes and within-group variability that this picture is complex and nuanced, and that our understanding is incomplete in costly ways. We also know that thriving often emerges in the face of adversity, yet research on when and how minorities thrive despite the adversity of lower social status is inadequate.

An integrative approach to the psychological study of minority populations and the reduction of health disparities through positive nonmaterial resources is presented in this chapter. It first provides a brief introduction to positive psychology and to the concept of early life origins of disease, highlighting the value of integrating these seemingly disparate literatures as a lens for studying health and broader aging processes among minority populations. These integrated themes are then linked to consideration of cultural determinants of health and broader aging processes. Specifically, the case for why we might expect culture to be important for health and for reducing status-based health inequalities is discussed, analyzing the case of infant mortality to illustrate this point. The example of infant mortality was selected because it is a critical intergenerational health outcome with important implications for the health and aging potential of future generations. Nevertheless, it should be noted that other outcomes across the life span—including educational outcomes, mental health, and life expectancy—would have illustrated this point equally well.

Next, a three-layered approach to uncovering positive insights into life span and intergenerational minority health is taken. First, the Culture and Social Identity Health Theory (CSIH), a theoretical framework for examining independent and interactive effects of culture and social identities on health, is introduced. Second, the CSIH framework is used to create the context for a discussion of the theoretical, methodological, and practical differences between studies that equate ethnic differences and cultural differences and those that distinguish the effects of ethnicity or social status on health from the effects of culture on health. Third, three specific research questions implied by CSIH as critical to understanding minority health are discussed, highlighting the potential of cultural resources to buffer the health consequences of lower social status and, thereby, to reduce ethnic and socioeconomic disparities. These questions are as follows: (a) What are the unique challenges or sources of stress faced by minorities? (b) How do these challenges become embedded in biology to produce the stark ethnic and socioeconomic health inequalities that characterize our society? And (c) what are the capabilities of nonmaterial resources—particularly cultural resources—to buffer these inequalities, and thereby reduce health disparities? Finally, the chapter closes with recommendations for future research, including a call for the formal development of a minority positive psychology research area.

The theoretical and methodological ideas presented in this chapter build on the work of many others and draw from several disciplines that complement and enrich psychological perspectives, including sociology, epidemiology, and, to a lesser degree, medicine and anthropology. Although the chapter highlights the literature on African Americans and Latinos living in the United States, other traditionally recognized but understudied U.S. ethnic groups, including Asians and Native Americans—as well as one U.S. ethnic group still largely overlooked in social and health sciences research, namely Arabs—are addressed where possible. In some cases, minority groups are discussed relative to the social majority, white Americans or Caucasians; in other cases, multiple minority groups are discussed comparatively; and, in still other cases, single minority groups are highlighted with an emphasis on sources of important within-group heterogeneity—an approach that is both increasingly called for in the literature (Abdou, Dominguez, & Myers, 2013; Abdou, Dunkel Schetter, Campos, et al., 2010; Abdou, Dunkel Schetter, Jones, et al., 2010; Betancourt & López, 1993) and increasingly supported by the complexity of empirical findings on population health and health disparities (Abdou, Dunkel Schetter, Campos, et al., 2010; Abdou et al., 2013; Jackson, Knight, & Rafferty, 2010; Markides & Coreil, 1986; Mezuk et al., 2010; Miniño & Murphy, 2012; Whitfield, Allaire, Belue, & Edwards, 2008).

TOWARD A POSITIVE MINORITY PSYCHOLOGY OF HUMAN LIFE-SPAN DEVELOPMENT

Positive psychology has been defined as the science of strengths, or the science of what makes life worth living and of what is working for individuals, families, communities, and society more broadly (Seligman & Csikszentmihalyi, 2000). Positive psychology is relevant to health and development—particularly physiological and psychological adaptation to stress—across the life span, and even across multiple generations among humans in general and among minority populations in particular.

The now well-documented Epidemiological Paradox and increasingly popular cultural resource–health hypothesis are suggestive of positive psychology at work in the lives of minority populations (James, 1993; Markides & Coreil, 1986). They are also suggestive of specific avenues for formally applying positive psychology to the study of minority health and health disparities. It is plausible that nonmaterial cultural resources are among those factors beyond traditional, objective measures of SES, and even subjective measures of social status, that either have direct positive impacts on health or moderate the negative health consequences of lower SES and related psychological and physiological stressors.

EARLY LIFE ORIGINS OF HEALTH AND AGING

Increasing attention is given to the idea that aging begins before birth. Currently, there is compelling evidence, from both animal and human studies, to support the fact that our stress responses and many of the diseases that we experience as adults are programmed during critical developmental phases in utero and in early childhood (Barker, Bagby, & Hanson, 2006; Mazumder, Almond, Park, Crimmins, & Finch, 2010). Among the terms that have become attached to this phenomenon are the Barker Hypothesis (Paneth & Susser, 1995), fetal

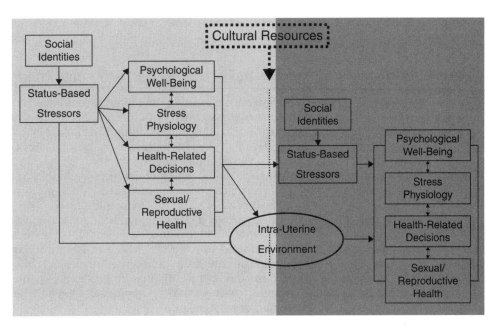

FIGURE 2.1 Aging Before Birth and Beyond Conceptual Model.

Double-sided arrows denote bidirectional relationships; single-sided arrows denote unidirectional associations. Social identities (e.g., ethnicity, SES, gender, immigration status) determine exposure to status-based stressors (e.g., unsafe neighborhoods, discrimination, acculturative stress). Exposure to status-based stressors impacts health, including psychological well-being (e.g., depression and anxiety), stress physiology (e.g., cortisol, blood pressure, hippocampal volume), and sexual/reproductive health (e.g., sexually transmitted infections, fertility, pregnancy outcomes, infant mortality). The transition from the lighter to darker shade of gray in the background indicates a generational shift. The intrauterine environment (**oval**) is the first link between generations. Social identities, exposure to status-based stressors, and health are transmitted between generations biologically in utero and, later, socially. Cultural resources (**dotted-line box at top**) may moderate the health consequences of minority status within and between generations.

programming (Godfrey & Barker, 2001), and perinatal programming (Plagemann & Harder, 2009). The Barker Hypothesis is named after David Barker, a pioneer in this area of research in human models. The term perinatal programming is commonly used in studies involving nonhuman primates and other animal models (e.g., Coe & Lubach, 2008). In addition to the importance of the early part of the individual life span for lifelong health and broader aging processes, the life spans of previous generations also matter for the health and aging potential of subsequent generations (Geronimus et al., 2010; Hilmert et al., 2008).

Figure 2.1 depicts a conceptual model of "aging before birth and beyond," proposed as an organized conceptual framework for more explicitly extending the idea of early life programming to the domain of aging across the individual life span and into subsequent generations. This conceptual model also accounts for the effects of culture and minority status and how they interact to affect the aging process both within and across generations.

MINORITY HEALTH AND HEALTH DISPARITIES

Health inequalities are the result of unique challenges to successful psychological and physiological adaptation faced by minority group members (Williams, Neighbors, & Jackson, 2003). Although the stress and coping literatures are largely built on majority (middle-class Anglo) experiences, the suggestion that minority groups face unique challenges to successful adaptation has existed for centuries (Frank, 1790; Myers, 2009; Williams et al., 2003). It is evident, in easily measurable terms, that a disproportionate burden of poverty is among such challenges and also inflames the conditions surrounding most other psychological and physiological challenges (Adler et al., 1994; Chen, 2004; Gallo, Espinosa de los Monteros, & Shivpuri, 2009). As a result, we have come to understand minority health primarily as a socioeconomic issue.

THE UNIQUE STRESS AND COPING CONTEXT FACED BY MINORITY POPULATIONS

Over and above socioeconomic factors, however, minority populations face unique contextual, psychological, and physiological pressures associated with lower social status (Mays, Cochran, & Barnes, 2007; Settles, Navarette, Pagano, Abdou, & Sidanius, 2010; Zeki al Hazourri et al., 2011). A broad and pervasive implication that emerges repeatedly in the minority health research literature is that the negative messages communicated about certain groups via popular media, interpersonal interaction, and exposure to a lack of diversity in desirable institutions that represent opportunity and affluence can become embedded in biology through pathways other than equal access or SES (Borrell et al., 2010; Dominguez, Strong, Krieger, Gillman, & Rich-Edwards, 2009). For example, mixed-methods research (i.e., quantitative and qualitative; Abdou, Dunkel Schetter, Jones, et al., 2010; Dominguez et al., 2009), particularly community-based participatory studies, conducted with African American, Latino, and other minority communities, has provided a glimpse into how social structures leave biological imprints through inadequate health information and discriminatory experiences with the medical community (Abdou, Dunkel Schetter, Jones, et al., 2010; Dominguez, Dunkel Schetter, Glynn, Hobel, & Sandman, 2008; Dominguez et al., 2009).

Finally, as suggested by the phenomenon of early life programming, the psychological and physiological tolls of minority status can be passed down through generations. In a longitudinal prospective study of pregnancy, Hilmert et al. (2008) found that the combination of high chronic stress and elevated blood pressure was twice as common in African American women compared to white American women, resulting in the lowest birthweights in the sample (Hilmert et al., 2008), with low birthweight and the related outcome of preterm birth having a host of potential long-term physical, emotional, cognitive, and economic costs (Behrman & Butler, 2007; Hodek, von der Schulenburg, & Mittendorf, 2011; Lu & Halfon, 2003). Findings such as these highlight the long-term intergenerational costs, not only of adverse reproductive outcomes, but also of the social stratification that contributes to them.

Taken together, these diverse literatures suggest that minorities will, and do, face a broad range of unique social, psychological, and physiological—in addition to socioeconomic—challenges to successful adaptation during the individual life course and across multiple generations. Moreover, these challenges have significant short- and long-term mental and physical health consequences in addition to economic and other social consequences.

ECONOMICS, HEALTH, AND HAPPINESS

It is evident without a doubt that health and well-being are economic issues. In fact, the SES–health gradient is among the most documented findings in the social and health sciences, including among gerontological research. With the exception of a few diseases, there is a clear, graded positive association between SES and health, such that morbidity and mortality decrease in proportion to increases in socioeconomic resources (Adler et al., 1994; Hayward, Crimmins, Miles, & Yu, 2000). This same pattern is true of the association between wealth and well-being worldwide, with those countries possessing the greatest wealth enjoying greater health, including lower infant mortality rates and longer life expectancies, and also greater overall levels of happiness (Myers, 2000).

It follows logically from this, then, that non-white ethnic groups would have poorer health and be less happy, because they generally have a much smaller share of wealth, both within the United States and throughout the world. Given this very clear pattern that our economic situation largely dictates, how healthy and happy we are likely to be (Coburn, 2004; Myers, 2000), and given the likelihood that social hierarchy will persist (Sidanius & Pratto, 1999), what is it that facilitates human adaptability and thriving, both physiologically and psychologically, among people of lower social status, including in ethnic minority populations?

THE CASE OF U.S. INFANT MORTALITY AND WITHIN-GROUP VARIABILITY

A closer look at infant mortality patterns in the United States may shed new light on this question. Infant mortality refers to death within the first year of life. This, in and of itself, is an important health outcome, but the national rate of infant mortality is also significant because it is considered the most stringent indicator of the health of a country. It also serves as a very concrete marker by which to compare the health of populations both within and between nations (Coburn, 2004). Thus, if we take a look at infant mortality rates around the world, we can see that, overall, poorer countries carry a much higher burden of infant mortality. This is as we would expect based on what we know about the robustly established SES–health gradient.

Importantly, though, the United States has an unexpectedly high infant death rate for an industrialized nation, with more than six deaths for every 1,000 babies born alive (Mathews, Miniño, Osterman, Strobino, & Guyer, 2011). This rate puts the United States near Croatia and behind Cuba as a country overall (Central Intelligence Agency, 2008). If we take an even closer look at U.S. rates, however, what we clearly see is that infant mortality among African Americans, in particular, is alarmingly high. With a rate of 12.67 infant deaths per every 1,000 live births, the African American infant mortality rate is more than two times the national average (Mathews et al., 2011). If the United States were judged by this rate alone, we would rank among developing countries in the Caribbean and the Asian portion of the Middle East (Central Intelligence Agency, 2008).

Moreover, based on the rates observed for aggregated racial and ethnic categories in the United States, it is very easy to conclude that, other than African Americans and Native Americans, Americans are doing pretty well in terms of infant mortality rates (Miniño & Murphy, 2012), but let us examine this assumption more closely. In actuality, the broad social categories that we use to group people, particularly minority populations—including "American" or "Latino American"—distort the nuances of health inequalities. What emerges when we disaggregate the two categories "American" and "Latino American," for instance, is a very different picture—a picture that seems to be important, but, as yet, is not well understood.

In fact, Americans who are immigrants (i.e., Americans who were born outside of the United States) are less likely than their U.S.-born counterparts to experience infant mortality in the United States (Miniño & Murphy, 2012)—a pattern that challenges our understanding of the robust SES–health gradient described earlier, because these same immigrants generally have fewer material resources than their U.S.-born counterparts. There is an even more complex picture to speak of within the "Latino" category than the one just described in the "American" category. This category combines some of the lowest U.S. infant mortality rates of all Americans, a rate of 4.90 per 1,000 births among Cubans and 4.76 per 1,000 births among Central and South Americans; the fairly low rate of 5.58 per 1,000 births among Mexicans; and the third highest burden of infant mortality in America, which is among Puerto Ricans, at a rate of 7.29 per 1,000 births (Mathews & MacDorman, 2012). On average, these Latino subgroups share the common experience of relative economic disadvantage in America—even Cubans, despite their apparent greater affluence in certain regions of the United States (e.g., South Florida)—so material resources are not likely to account for these differences (Zambrana & Dorrington, 1998).

THE SES–HEALTH GRADIENT: WHAT IT DOES AND DOES NOT EXPLAIN

Clearly, although we have amassed a great deal of empirical evidence on the contribution of socioeconomic inequality to poor health (Adler et al., 1994; Crimmins, Hayward, & Seeman, 2004), the case of infant mortality illustrates that this association is less reliable among minority groups. Corroborating evidence comes from other, broader patterns in the literature. First, many ethnic differences in health persist even after accounting for SES (Adler & Snibbe, 2003; Shiono, Rauh, Park, Lederman, & Zuskar, 1997). Second, the slope of the SES–health gradient can differ for majority and minority groups, with the health consequences of lower SES more pronounced for minorities and the health benefits of higher SES, in some cases, blunted for these same groups (Abdou, Dunkel Schetter, Campos, et al., 2010; Collins, Herman, & David, 1997). Third, the overall SES–health gradient is less reliable for minority groups (Morales, Lara, Kington, Valdez, & Escarce, 2002). In fact, as in the case of infant mortality, some minorities (often those who are less acculturated, or have adopted American culture to a lesser degree; Lara, Gamboa, Kahramanian, Morales, & Hayes Bautista, 2005) thrive despite lower SES, with health comparable to, or even better than, the average American—a pattern first documented among Latinos (the Hispanic Paradox; Markides & Coreil, 1986) and increasingly documented in other ethnic groups (now commonly referred to as the Epidemiological Paradox; Morales et al., 2002).

Let us now return to the example of the "Latino" category to make this more concrete. Cubans, Mexicans, and Puerto Ricans all share the common experience of relative economic disadvantage in the United States, as mentioned earlier (Zambrana & Dorrington, 1998). They also share the experience of being Latino. What they do not share is the experience of this unexpected health advantage (Markides & Eschbach, 2005). Then, if being Latino is a culture rather than an ethnicity, we would have to conclude that culture will not protect your health—at least if you are Latino. However, this conclusion appears to be inaccurate for some Latino groups. One plausible explanation, then, is that, on average, Cubans possess a cultural advantage that Puerto Ricans do not, which means that Cubans and Puerto Ricans probably have different cultures (or at least some critical cultural differences) despite their shared ethnicity and their similar relative socioeconomic position.

But if this is not a story about economics, then what could it be?

THE EPIDEMIOLOGICAL PARADOX, POSITIVE PSYCHOLOGY, AND A PROCESS-ORIENTED VIEW OF MINORITY HEALTH

Several explanations for the Epidemiological Paradox have been put forth that are consistent with the idea that positive resources can protect health even in the face of socioeconomic disadvantage and other forms of status-based stress. One such hypothesis is that cultural resources protect the health of minorities by intercepting stress exposure and/or buffering the health effects of stress exposure (Campos et al., 2008; Morales et al., 2002). This hypothesis is popular perhaps because it is optimistic and, more practically, is suggestive of prevention and intervention strategies that might be employed at the level of individuals, families, and larger communities.

Importantly, however, there is very little empirical research that directly evaluates this cultural resource hypothesis (Abdou, Dunkel Schetter, Campos, et al., 2010; Abdou et al., 2013; Betancourt & López, 1993). Instead, group membership is a routine explanation for group differences. Similarly, group differences are often labeled cultural differences—that is, without examining anything "cultural" beyond ethnic identification itself (Betancourt & López, 1993). Circular explanations for health inequality are symptoms of insufficient operational—not conceptual—distinctions in scientific research. There is widespread transdisciplinary agreement that attitudes, beliefs, and behaviors, both at the individual and the aggregate level, make up culture (Dressler, 2004; Oyserman & Uskul, 2008; Triandis, 1984). However, the social groupings that describe people, such as female (gender), college educated (SES), or Latino (ethnicity), are better described as what social psychologists refer to as social identities (Tajfel & Turner, 1986). Culture and ethnicity (a social identity), therefore, are different things. Still, quantitative health research often treats social identities and culture as interchangeable. Just as culture and social identities can be distinguished as concepts, they can be distinguished as measured variables. They also differ in what they teach us about the health of individuals and populations. Social identities provide categories for organizing and describing people. Measured cultural variables tell us something about the cognitive processes, affect, behaviors, and/or relational styles that create, modify, or mediate differences.

In sum, culture can be thought of as the socially shaped cognitive filter by which we evaluate and attach meaning to life experiences and that is reflected in attitudes, beliefs, and behaviors (Baltes, 1997; Triandis, 1984). Social identity, however, is constructed through identification with social groupings, such as female (gender), college educated (SES), Asian American (ethnicity and nationality), or Black (race; Tajfel & Turner, 1986). Although there is a tendency in quantitative research to think of social identities and culture interchangeably, they differ in important ways, including in what they can teach us about social and psychological phenomena, that are intimately tied to the aging process at all life stages. Uncovering social identity (e.g., ethnic, socioeconomic, gender) differences in health and related psychosocial phenomena is a critical descriptive process. Nevertheless, the study of culture has the potential to specify pathways (e.g., particular worldviews, behaviors) to differences and, critically, to thriving.

Keeping these distinctions in mind, it is possible to directly evaluate whether cultural resources, in fact, lead to better health among minorities despite objectively challenging circumstances. The CSIH, introduced below, outlines these distinctions and provides a guiding framework for testing the individual and joint effects of culture and social identity (specifically, ethnicity and SES) on health. CSIH's application is illustrated by reviewing studies that directly evaluate the cultural resource–health hypothesis.

DIFFERENTIATING SOCIAL IDENTITIES AND CULTURES

We now know that the broad social groupings that are commonly referred to as "cultures" in the scientific literature, and even in mainstream society, more accurately represent aspects of our social identities, or the ways that we define ourselves based on membership in widely recognized social groups (Oyserman, Harrison, & Bybee, 2001; Tajfel & Turner, 1986). The most easily recognized social identity groups include ethnicity and gender, because these are highly visible aspects of a person, but social identities also include potentially less-apparent factors as well, such as how educated we are, whether we are immigrants, and even our religious faith and sexual orientation. What constitutes our social identities can be distinguished from what constitutes our cultures, then; and this is a critical distinction (Abdou, Dunkel Schetter, Campos, et al., 2010; Abdou et al., 2013).

CULTURE: CONCEPTUAL VERSUS OPERATIONAL DEFINITIONS

If *culture* is what can be summarized as the socially shaped cognitive filter that we use to make sense of the world around us and our places in it, then it becomes apparent that, although our membership in particular social groups may make us more likely to make sense of the world in a certain way, that group membership in and of itself is not culture, just as skin color and language, in and of themselves, are not cultures. Instead, attitudes, beliefs, and values are the substance of culture (Rohner, 1984). In fact, these are virtually unanimously agreed-upon elements of culture across disciplines (e.g., Baltes, 1997; Triandis, 1984), although disciplines do vary in terms of conceptualizing these elements of culture at the individual versus group level (Dressler & Bindon, 2000; Greenfield & Suzuki, 1998).

The challenge, though, is that especially in largely quantitative disciplines—gerontology and psychology included—there is a substantial disconnect between the way that culture is conceptualized, on the one hand, and the way that it is measured, on the other. We agree that values and beliefs are the substance of culture, but when we set out to study culture, what we tend to measure is ethnicity, and sometimes we get a little closer by also measuring socioeconomic context and immigration factors. However, as previously mentioned, these are also aspects of our social identities rather than cultures in and of themselves (Abdou, Dunkel Schetter, Campos, et al., 2010; Abdou et al., 2013).

It is clear that the operationalization of culture is a central issue here. Up until this point, this discussion has focused primarily on what culture is not. The recommendation in the literature is to directly measure indicators of culture that map directly onto the widely accepted conceptual definitions of culture outlined above (Betancourt & López, 1993; Greenfield & Suzuki, 1998; Markus, 2008; Oyserman, Coon, & Kemmelmeier, 2002). In other words, studies of cultural differences should examine the specific cultural elements hypothesized to be relevant to the process and/or outcome of interest (Betancourt & López, 1993).

THE CULTURE AND SOCIAL IDENTITY HEALTH THEORY

If the health consequences of minority status can be diminished for people who are less acculturated (the process of adopting a majority culture; Morales et al., 2002), a phenomenon commonly attributed to nonmaterial cultural resources (Abdou, Dunkel Schetter, Campos, et al., 2010; Abdou et al., 2013), there is potentially great scientific and practical value in increasing the understanding of these processes and making the theoretical and methodological distinctions necessary to do so. Emerging research directly evaluates the hypothesis that cultural resources promote thriving by linking specific cultural orientations to health, and by distinguishing the effects of culture from the effects of related, often conflated, constructs, including social identities (e.g., Abdou, Dunkel Schetter, Campos, et al., 2010; Abdou et al., 2013; Betancourt & López, 1993).

The body of work described below, in its nascent stages, is guided by CSIH, which comprises four premises concerning the interrelations among culture, social identities, and health: (a) social identities impose powerful constraints on culture by making certain beliefs, attitudes, and experiences more salient; (b) culture can have direct effects on health that are independent of links to social identity; (c) culture often exerts its effects on health by moderating social identity-based disparities, or operating synergistically with social identities to impact outcomes; and (d) intrapersonal (e.g., individual and collective self-esteem) and interpersonal (e.g., discrimination) processes underlie both cultural and social identity effects on health. Each of these premises maps directly onto the previous discussion of infant mortality patterns in the United States, but additional examples from existing research will be used to illustrate each of the four CSIH premises.

It is important to begin by noting the limits of the CSIH theory. The focus of CSIH is the downstream effects of social identities and culture on the health of individuals, families, and broader social groups. It is critical to emphasize that the processes predicted by this theory do not operate in isolation and are largely produced by higher order societal factors, which continue to warrant public attention, scientific resources, and intervention at multiple levels, including public policy.

CSIH Premise I

Premise 1 of CSIH is that social identities and culture are related, though not interchangeable, constructs. They are related, at least in part, because social identities such as ethnicity, SES, and gender impose powerful constraints on our cultural orientations by making particular experiences more or less salient for us, but also by affecting our ability to enact our cultural preferences. For instance, the social identity of being female tends to make the experience of caretaking more salient and, as a result, makes having a collectivistic or interdependent relational style more likely (Gaines et al., 1997). The idea of tend and befriend (Taylor, 2006) suggests that women are more likely to engage in affiliative behavior, as opposed to fighting or fleeing, during times of stress. This is posited as an adaptive reaction, which increases the likelihood of survival of offspring. Importantly, however, having multidimensional social identities, as we all do, complicates matters; and it may be that environmental and other contextual factors increase the likelihood that certain aspects of social identities trump others. In support of this notion, a mixed-methods community-based participatory research study conducted with disadvantaged African American and Latino parents living in Los Angeles showed that mothers do tend to engage in affiliative behavior under times of stress more often than fathers, but that living in unsafe environments resulted in more independent behavior among both mothers and fathers (Abdou, Dunkel Schetter, Jones, et al., 2010).

CSIH Premise II

Building on the idea that social identities and culture are related yet distinct, Premise 2 of CSIH suggests that culture can exert effects on health that are independent of its ties to social identities. For example, an Internet-based study conducted by Settles and colleagues (2010) found that cultural pride was associated with less depression among African American women, and this relationship held across diverse socioeconomic backgrounds and life stages. Replicating this pattern in terms of mental health outcomes as well as expanding to physiological outcomes, a study of stress and pregnancy outcomes showed that the cultural resource of communalism was a more robust predictor of prenatal mental health than ethnicity, childhood SES, and adult SES (Abdou, Dunkel Schetter, Campos, et al., 2010). Notably, this pattern also seems to extend beyond the individual life span and diverse life stages. A study examined the intergenerational health effects of the cultural resource of maternal familism as compared to the relative contributions of ethnicity and life-span family socioeconomic position in a large sample of African American, Latina, and white American mothers (Abdou et al., 2013). Findings demonstrated that culture—in this case, familism endorsed by mothers on giving birth—was positively associated with infant birthweight and negatively associated with related asthma risk three years later net of the effects of social identity (operationalized as ethnicity and life-span family socioeconomic position).

CSIH Premise III

Premise 3 of CSIH suggests that culture may also moderate the effects of social identities on health. For instance, what we see in the Epidemiological Paradox literature is that minorities can have health comparable to, or even better than, in some cases, majority group members—presumably when cultural resources are present. This appears to be the case even, or maybe *especially*, when economic disadvantage is also present; therefore, in such cases, both ethnic and socioeconomic effects on health are moderated by nonmaterial cultural resources. In fact, the communalism and familism studies touched on earlier directly test this CSIH premise. The cultural resource of communalism interacted with ethnicity, childhood SES, and adult SES, resulting in lower prenatal blood pressure among African American women and women having experienced socioeconomic disadvantage at some point over their life course (Abdou, Dunkel Schetter, Campos, et al., 2010). In this study, all ethnic and socioeconomic health disparities observed in the full sample and among participants with lower communalism disappeared among women with higher communalism. As prenatal health effects of communalism were not explained by depressive symptoms at study entry, perceived availability of social support, self-esteem, optimism, mastery, or pregnancy-specific factors, the authors concluded that the cultural resource of communalism influenced health independently of links to other personal and social resources in addition to economic resources (Abdou, Dunkel Schetter, Campos, et al., 2010). Similarly, in addition to direct independent effects on birthweight and childhood asthma symptoms three years later, maternal familism interacted with life-span family socioeconomic position, such that higher maternal familism eliminated the large disparity in childhood asthma symptoms among participants with lower life-span family socioeconomic position. As seen in the previous study, this resulted in significant reductions in the socioeconomic disparities in childhood asthma symptoms initially observed in the overall sample (Abdou et al., 2013).

CSIH Premise IV

A premise implicit in CSIH, of course, is that social identities are directly related to health. The example that we all know too well is that ethnicity and SES are strong predictors of health and result in marked disparities, as countless studies have shown (Crimmins et al., 2004). With this link in mind, the fourth and final premise of CSIH is that the health effects of social identity and culture are mediated by both intrapersonal (i.e., relating to the self; e.g., self-esteem, stereotype threat) and interpersonal (i.e., relating to others; e.g., social support, discrimination) processes (Markus & Wurf, 1987; Settles et al., 2010). Intrapersonal processes, here, are intended to encompass things happening inside the body, including epigenetic processes like perinatal programming and broader psychophysiological responses to the physical and social environments. Illustratively, Kershaw and colleagues (2010) found that health-relevant coping behaviors largely mediate the association between lower SES and clinically elevated C-reactive protein levels, a marker of systemic inflammation that has been linked to cardiovascular disease (National Heart, Lung, and Blood Institute, 2006).

Similarly, both quantitative and qualitative studies of socioeconomically diverse African American mothers are suggestive of additional processes—beyond health behaviors—whereby lower status becomes embedded in biology, potentially resulting in this kind of higher allostatic load or accelerated aging (Dominguez et al., 2009; Geronimus et al., 2010). These studies suggest that the social identity of being both African American and female becomes embedded in biology through repeated experiences with overt as well as more subtle discrimination, which takes the form of negative expectations about stereotypical behavior, and, in turn, becomes heavily internalized (Mays et al., 2007; Nuru-Jeter et al., 2009; Woods-Giscombé & Lobel, 2008). African American women in general, and particularly African American mothers, encounter such stereotypes and negative expectations in medical settings, especially when seeking prenatal care, and also in day-to-day life while doing simple things that many of us take for granted (e.g., shopping; enrolling children in activities; and requesting more information about something to inform decisions, including health-related decisions; Hackett & Byars, 1996). Because minority women may find themselves actively trying to counter stereotypes, ruminating over negative interpersonal experiences that might very plausibly be attributable to race and worrying about when they might experience them again or, worse, when their children will experience them, such interpersonal and intrapersonal processes affect the health and well-being of minority women in ways that they are consciously aware of and can articulate very clearly (Abdou, Dunkel Schetter, Jones, et al., 2010).

CURRENT KNOWLEDGE OF POSITIVE NONMATERIAL RESOURCES AND PRACTICAL IMPLICATIONS

Research on the potential of cultural and social resources to enhance mental and physical health and other important life outcomes, such as academic achievement and professional success, is relatively young. More work on this topic is underway, but what we do know so far is that social integration is critical (Berkman, Glass, Brisette, & Seeman, 2000); that feeling a part of a substantive and meaningful social network that one can call on, both during times of celebration and times of hardship, is critical for health and well-being. An important feature of social networks is that they serve as potential sources of different types of social support, including emotional/informational, tangible (e.g., money, housing, or other material goods), affectionate, and positive social interaction (Sherbourne & Stewart, 1991). Perceived availability of social support helps to foster a sense of security, efficacy, and probably also serenity in individuals, groups, and even society more broadly. In fact, walking through life feeling as though support is available should we need it seems to matter more than whether those support systems are actually accessed.

Communalism, or a sense of interconnectedness with other people, as well as familism, or a strong connection with family, also seem to enhance mental and physical health, even independently of links to social support (Abdou, Dunkel Schetter, Campos, et al., 2010; Abdou et al, 2013; Campos et al., 2008). This is true at all stages of the life course—from infancy to childhood, to parenthood, to retirement, and through the end of life. Communalism seems to encompass greater belief in the goodness of other people and value placed on interpersonal harmony, both of which can contribute to positive and nurturing interpersonal relationships (Abdou, Dunkel Schetter, Campos, et al., 2010). Again, relationships with other people seem to be the key to all forms of resource, even those resources that originate internally (e.g., self-esteem). Although the investment in people that often accompanies a communal orientation is not without costs (literally and figuratively), emerging research in this area seems to suggest that the benefits of a communal approach to life outweighs the costs. For racial, ethnic, cultural, sexual, or other minorities, a feeling of belonging within both majority and minority groups and society more broadly also seems to be beneficial for a wide range of life outcomes (e.g., Fingerhut, Peplau, & Ghavami, 2005; Settles et al., 2010). While straddling multiple cultures comes with its own unique set of stressors, the benefits of this social flexibility—often referred to as being bicultural or culturally integrated—generally appear, again, to outweigh the costs (LaFromboise, Coleman, & Gerton, 1993).

For racial and/or ethnic minorities, including African, Arab, Asian, Latino, and Native Americans, and immigrants of all backgrounds, being bicultural can mean having both a strong minority identity as well as a strong mainstream American identity. Having a deep sense of cultural pride and participating in cultural customs is often a part of having a strong ethnic identity (Landrine & Klonoff, 1996; Roberts et al., 1999). Placing a high degree of respect and value on our own ethnic and/or racial groups has also been shown to be associated with better self-esteem and to protect against depression (Settles et al., 2010). Also, because individuals are not immune to societal beliefs about different groups of people (i.e., stereotypes), believing that American society at large holds the groups to which we belong in high regard seems to be important for self-concept, well-being, and health over time (Mays et al., 2007; Settles et al., 2010). The presidential election of Barack Obama in 2008, and re-election in 2012, may have afforded African Americans, and possibly other minorities, the strongest sense in history thus far of being both accepted and valued by broader society, both nationally and globally. Finally, any and all measures taken by a society to equalize access to the type of wisdom that is handed down through families and valuable social networks, to education and information, to opportunity, to health care, to safety and peace, to autonomy and space (both mental and physical), and to dignity will improve the lives of individuals. Even small individual gains may amount to sweeping social change at the collective population level.

CONCLUSION AND DIRECTIONS FOR FUTURE RESEARCH

This chapter reviews factors beyond ethnicity and SES that account for majority–minority differences in health, focusing on those that contribute to thriving among minorities. The ideas presented here expand perspectives on minority health in three ways. First, they connect the positive psychology literature to the issue of minority health. Second, they highlight the positive potential of culture in attenuating health inequalities, particularly when environments are otherwise low in resources. Third, they demonstrate the theoretical and practical need to differentiate—not only conceptually but also operationally—between the construct of culture and the social categories of ethnicity and SES as well as other social identities, including age and gender.

Additional research is needed, particularly with populations that have been traditionally overlooked in minority health and health disparities research. This includes Arab Americans, who typically face lower status in the United States and throughout much of the world on the basis of ethnicity, race, SES, religion, and language, among other factors. Additional research consisting of quantitative and qualitative data collection methods, comprehensive measures of culture, and larger, disaggregated ethnic subgroups is also needed to advance knowledge of cultural determinants of health as well as of the related theoretical and measurement issues discussed throughout this chapter. Further, additional research is needed to evaluate the applicability of findings, such as those demonstrating the capability of nonmaterial cultural resources to reduce health disparities, to diverse contexts and populations elsewhere in the world, including within the context of poverty in the developing world as well as within contexts in which lower social status is associated with threats to livelihood in addition to unfair treatment and systematic disadvantage.

The discussion presented in this chapter has considerable theoretical and methodological relevance to diverse disciplines. Apart from psychology and aging, these include social epidemiology, population health, sociology, and anthropology. A primary contribution of this chapter is that it demonstrates the importance of distinguishing, not just conceptually but also operationally, the construct of culture from the related constructs of ethnicity, acculturation, and socioeconomic context. Finally, CSIH and the related ideas presented here are consistent with ongoing calls in the literature to distinguish complex sociocultural constructs, including ethnicity, SES, and culture, and to directly take into account how they interact with one another (e.g., Betancourt & López, 1993; Markus, 2008) to arrive at a more complete and nuanced understanding of health among individuals and populations within the United States and throughout the world. Direct examination of cultural factors, and how they interact with sociodemographic and other contextual factors, highlights important sources of within-group variability and provides a more nuanced understanding of health disparities and how they might be reduced, particularly in resource-poor environments. These findings may suggest demand for individual, family, and community-level interventions that promote health across multiple generations through maintenance or cultivation of nonmaterial resources.

In sum, emerging research demonstrates that there is substantial cultural heterogeneity within broad social groupings that we often refer to as cultures, such as ethnic groups and social classes. In addition, it appears that cultural resources often covary with material resources. A commonly held belief is that cultural orientations, including relational perspectives such as communalism and familism, are differentially distributed by ethnicity. However, as others have suggested, SES seems to be a better predictor of cultural orientation than ethnicity alone, and the interaction of SES and ethnicity an even better predictor (Betancourt & López, 1993). Although the likelihood of possessing cultural resources is bound by SES and, to some degree, ethnicity, the emerging picture is that their health benefits are not. In fact, the effects of cultural resources appear to be most pronounced in contexts lacking other forms of capital. A related point is that the health benefits of nonmaterial cultural resources also appear to be distinct from the health effects of other personal (e.g., well-being) and social (e.g., social support) resources in addition to status-based resources, such as socioeconomic resources (e.g., childhood and/or adulthood SES; Abdou, Dunkel Schetter, Campos, et al., 2010; Abdou et al., 2013). Finally, the ideas and literature discussed here hint at the intriguing possibility that cultural resources may aid in the reduction of persistent ethnic and socioeconomic inequalities in health and well-being. Cultural resources seem to benefit not only the health of foreign-born Americans, as is commonly suggested in the Epidemiological Paradox literature, but also that of U.S.-born Americans, especially those of lower social status, including African Americans, Latinos, and people of lower childhood and adulthood SES. Just as we look to other nations for clues on how to improve quality of life, it appears that different cultural orientations within U.S. borders have much to teach us about being happy and living well.

ACKNOWLEDGMENT

I am grateful to Dr. Christine Dunkel Schetter for her comments on this work at various stages and to the Abdou USC Human Flourishing Research Lab, including Jessica Gonzalez, Kyrstin Harris, and Kezia Rusli, for technical assistance with the preparation of this manuscript.

REFERENCES

Abdou, C. M., Dominguez, T. P., & Myers, H. F. (2013). Maternal familism predicts birthweight and asthma symptoms by age three. *Social Science & Medicine, 76*, 28–38. doi:10.1016/j.socscimed.2012.07.041

Abdou, C. M., Dunkel Schetter, C., Campos, B., Hilmert, C. J., Dominguez, T. P., Hobel, C. J.,...Sandman, C. (2010). Communalism predicts maternal affect, stress, and physiology better than ethnicity and socioeconomic status. *Cultural Diversity and Ethnic Minority Psychology, 16*, 395–403. doi:10.1037/a0019808

Abdou, C. M., Dunkel Schetter, C., Jones, F., Roubinov, D., Tsai, S., Jones, L.,...Hobel, C. J. (2010). Community perspectives: Mixed-methods investigation of culture, stress, resilience, and health. *Ethnicity and Disease, 20* (1 Supplement 2), 41–48.

Adler, N. E., Boyce, T., Chesney, M. A., Cohen, S., Folkman, S., Kahn, R. L., & Syme, S. L. (1994). Socioeconomic status and health: The challenge of the gradient. *American Psychologist, 49*, 15–24.

Adler, N. E., & Snibbe, A. C. (2003). The role of psychosocial processes in explaining the gradient between socioeconomic status and health. *Current Directions in Psychological Science, 12*, 119–123.

Baltes, P. B. (1997). On the incomplete architecture of human ontogeny: Selection, optimization, and compensation as foundation of developmental theory. *American Psychologist, 52*, 366–380.

Barker, D. J., Bagby, S. P., & Hanson, M. A. (2006). Mechanisms of disease: *In utero* programming in the pathogenesis of hypertension. *Nature Reviews Nephrology, 2*, 700–707. doi:10.1038/ncpneph0344

Behrman, R. E., & Butler, A. S. (Eds.). (2007). *Preterm birth: Causes, consequences, and prevention.* Washington, DC: The National Academies Press.

Berkman, L. F., Glass, T., Brisette, I., & Seeman, T. E. (2000). From social integration to health: Durkheim in the new millenium. *Social Science & Medicine, 51*, 843–857.

Betancourt, H., & López, S. R. (1993). The study of culture, ethnicity, and race in American psychology. *American Psychologist, 48*, 629–637.

Borrell, L. N., Diez Roux, A. V., Jacobs, D. R., Jr., Shea, S., Jackson, S. A., Shrager, S., & Blumenthal, R. S. (2010). Perceived racial/ethnic discrimination, smoking and alcohol consumption in the MultiEthnic Study of Atherosclerosis (MESA). *Preventive Medicine, 51*, 307–312. doi:10.1016/j.ypmed.2010.05.017

Campos, B., Dunkel Schetter, C., Abdou, C. M., Hobel, C. J., Glynn, L. M., & Sandman, C. A. (2008). Familialism, social support, and stress: Positive implications for pregnant Latinas. *Cultural Diversity and Ethnic Minority Psychology, 14*, 155–162. doi:10.1037/1099–9809.14.2.155

Central Intelligence Agency. (2008). *The CIA world factbook 2009.* New York, NY: Skyhorse.

Chen, E. (2004). Why socioeconomic status affects the health of children: A psychosocial perspective. *Current Directions in Psychological Science, 13*, 112–115. doi:10.1111/j.0963–7214.2004.00286.x

Coburn, D. (2004). Beyond the income inequality hypothesis: Class, neo-liberalism, and health inequalities. *Social Science & Medicine, 58*, 41–56.

Coe, C. L., & Lubach G. R. (2008). Fetal programming: Prenatal origins of health and illness. *Current Directions in Psychological Science, 17*, 36–41.

Collins, J. W., Jr., Herman, A. A., & David, R. J. (1997). Very-low-birthweight infants and income incongruity among African American and white parents in Chicago. *American Journal of Public Health, 87*, 414–417.

Crimmins, E. M., Hayward, M. D., & Seeman, T. E. (2004). Race/ethnicity, socioeconomic status, and health. In N. B. Anderson, R. A. Bulatao, & B. Cohen (Eds.), *Critical perspectives on racial and ethnic differences in health in late life* (pp. 310–352). Washington, DC: National Research Council of the National Academies.

Dominguez, T. P., Dunkel-Schetter, S. C., Glynn, L. M., Hobel, C., & Sandman, C. A. (2008). Racial differences in birth outcomes: The role of general, pregnancy, and racism stress. *Health Psychology, 27*, 194–203. doi:10.1037/0278–6133.27.2.194

Dominguez, T. P., Strong, E. F., Krieger, N., Gillman, M. W., & Rich-Edwards, J. W. (2009). Differences in the self-reported racism experiences of US-born and foreign-born Black pregnant women. *Social Science and Medicine, 69*, 258–265. doi:10.1016/j.socscimed.2009.03.022

Dressler, W. W. (2004). Culture and the risk of disease. *British Medical Bulletin, 69*, 21–31.

Dressler, W. W., & Bindon, J. R. (2000). The health consequences of cultural consonance: Cultural dimensions of lifestyle, social support and arterial blood pressure in an African American community. *American Anthropologist, 102*, 244–260.

Fingerhut, A. W., Peplau, L. A., & Ghavami, N. (2005). A dual-identity framework for understanding lesbian experience. *Psychology of Women Quarterly, 29*, 129–139. doi:10.1111/j.1471–6402.2005.00175.x

Frank, J. P. (1790). *The people's misery, mother of diseases* (An address, delivered in 1790 by Johann Peter Frank, translated from Latin with an introduction by Henry E. Sigerist). Baltimore, MD: The Johns Hopkins University Press. (Reprinted from *Bulletin of the History of Medicine*, Vol. IX, No. 1, January 1941.)

Gaines, S. O., Jr., Marelich, W. D., Bledsoe, K. L., Steers, W. N., Henderson, M. C., Granrose, C. S.,… Page, M. S. (1997). Links between race/ethnicity and cultural values as mediated by racial/ethnic identity and moderated by gender. *Journal of Personality and Social Psychology, 72*, 1460–1476. doi:10.1037/0022-3514.72.6.1460

Gallo, L. C., Espinosa de los Monteros, K., & Shivpuri, S. (2009). Socioeconomic status and health: What is the role of reserve capacity? *Current Directions in Psychological Science, 18*, 269–274.

Geronimus, A. T., Hicken, M. T., Pearson, J. A., Seashols, S. J., Brown, K. L., & Dawson Cruz, T. (2010). Do US black women experience stress-related accelerated biological aging? A novel theory and first population-based test of black-white differences in telomere length. *Human Nature: An Interdisciplinary Biosocial Perspective, 21*(1), 19–38. doi:10.1007/s12110–010-9078–0

Godfrey, K. M., & Barker, D. J. P. (2001). Fetal programming and adult health. *Public Health Nutrition, 4,* 611–624. doi:10.1079/PHN2001145

Greenfield, P. M., & Suzuki, L. K. (1998). Culture and human development: Implications for parenting, education, pediatrics and mental health. In I. E. Sigel & K. A. Renninger (Eds.), *Handbook of child psychology, Vol. 4, child psychology in practice* (5th ed., pp. 1059–1109). New York, NY: Wiley.

Hackett, G., & Byars, A. M. (1996). Social cognitive theory and the career development of African American women. *The Career Development Quarterly, 44,* 322–340. doi:10.1002/j.2161–0045.1996.tb00449.x

Hayward, M. D., Crimmins, E. M., Miles, T. P., & Yu, Y. (2000). The significance of socioeconomic status in explaining the racial gap in chronic health conditions. *American Sociological Review, 65,* 910–930.

Hilmert, C. J., Dunkel Schetter, C., Dominguez, T. P., Abdou, C., Hobel, C. J., Glynn, L., & Sandman, C. (2008). Stress and blood pressure during pregnancy: Racial differences and associations with birthweight. *Psychosomatic Medicine, 70,* 57–64.

Hodek, J.-M., von der Schulenburg, J.-M., & Mittendorf, T. (2011). Measuring economic consequences of preterm birth—Methodological recommendations for the evaluation of personal burden on children and their caregivers. *Health Economics Review, 1,* 1–10.

Jackson, J. S., Knight, K. M., & Rafferty, J. A. (2010). Race and unhealthy behaviors: Chronic stress, the HPA axis, and physical and mental health disparities over the life course. *American Journal of Public Health, 100,* 933–939. doi:10.2105/AJPH.2008.143446

James, S. A. (1993). Racial and ethnic differences in infant mortality and low birth weight: A psychosocial critique. *Annals of Epidemiology, 3,* 130–136.

Kershaw, K. N., Mezuk, B., Abdou, C. M., Rafferty, J. A., & Jackson, J. S. (2010). Socioeconomic position, health behaviors, and C-reactive protein: A moderated-mediation analysis. *Health Psychology, 29,* 307–316. doi:10.1037/a0019286

LaFromboise, T., Coleman, H. L., & Gerton, J. (1993). Psychological impact of biculturalism: Evidence and theory. *Psychological Bulletin, 114,* 395–412.

Landrine, H., & Klonoff, E. A. (1992). Culture and health-related schemas: A review and proposal for interdisciplinary integration. *Health Psychology, 11,* 267–276. doi:10.1037/0278–6133.11.4.267

Lara, M., Gamboa, C., Kahramanian, M. I., Morales, L. S., & Hayes Bautista, D. E. (2005). Acculturation and Latino health in the United States: A review of the literature and its sociopolitical context. *Annual Review of Public Health, 26,* 367–397. doi:10.1146/annurev.publhealth.26.021304.144615

Lu, M. C., & Halfon, N. (2003). Racial and ethnic disparities in birth outcomes: A life-course perspective. *Maternal and Child Health Journal, 7,* 13–30.

Markides, K. S., & Coreil, J. (1986). The health of Hispanics in the Southwestern United States—An Epidemiological Paradox. *Public Health Reports, 101,* 253–265.

Markides, K., & Eschbach, K. (2005). Aging, migration, and mortality: Current status of research on the Hispanic paradox. *The Journals of Gerontology, Series B: Social Sciences and Psychological Sciences, 60,* 68–75.

Markus, H. R. (2008). Pride, prejudice, and ambivalence: Toward a unified theory of race and ethnicity. *American Psychologist, 63,* 651–670. doi:10.1037/0003–066X.63.8.651

Markus, H., & Wurf, E. (1987). The dynamic self-concept: A social psychological perspective. *Annual Review of Psychology, 38,* 299–337.

Mathews, T. J., & MacDorman, M. F. (2012). *Infant mortality statistics from the 2008 period linked birth/infant death data set* (National vital statistics reports; Vol. 60, No. 5). Hyattsville, MD: National Center for Health Statistics.

Mathews, T. J., Miniño, A. M., Osterman, M. J. K., Strobino, D. M., & Guyer, B. (2011). Annual summary of vital statistics: 2008. *Pediatrics, 127,* 146–157. doi:10.1542/peds.2010–3175

Mays, V. M., Cochran, S. D., & Barnes, N. W. (2007). Race, race-based discrimination, and health outcomes among African Americans. *Annual Review of Psychology, 58,* 201–225. doi:10.1146/annurev.psych.57.102904.190212

Mazumder, B., Almond, D., Park, K., Crimmins, E. M., & Finch, C. E. (2010). Lingering prenatal effects of the 1918 influenza pandemic on cardiovascular disease. *Journal of Developmental Origins of Health and Disease, 1*, 26–34.

Mezuk, B., Rafferty, J. A., Kershaw, K. N., Hudson, D., Abdou, C. M., Lee, H.,...Jackson, J.S. (2010). Reconsidering the role of social disadvantage in physical and mental health: Stressful life events, health behaviors, race, and depression. *American Journal of Epidemiology, 172*, 1238–1249. doi:10.1093/aje/kwq283

Miniño, A. L., & Murphy, S. L. (2012, July). Death in the United States, 2010. *NCHS data brief* (No. 99). Hyattsville, MD: National Center for Health Statistics.

Morales, L. S., Lara, M., Kington, R. S., Valdez, R. O., & Escarce, J. J. (2002). Socioeconomic, cultural, and behavioral factors affecting Hispanic health outcomes. *Journal of Health Care for the Poor and Underserved, 13*, 477–503.

Myers, D. G. (2000). The funds, friends, and faith of happy people. *American Psychologist, 55*, 56–67.

Myers, H. F. (2009). Ethnicity and socio-economic status-related stresses in context: An integrative review and conceptual model. *Journal of Behavioral Medicine, 32*, 9–19.

National Heart, Lung, and Blood Institute. (2006, July). *NHLBI workshop report: C-Reactive protein: Basic and clinical research needs*. Retrieved from http://www.nhlbi.nih.gov/meetings/workshops/crp/report.htm

Nuru-Jeter, A., Dominguez, T. P., Hammond, W. P., Leu, J., Skaff, M., Egerton, S.,...Braveman, M. (2009). "It's the skin you're in": African-American women talk about their experiences of racism. An exploratory study to develop measures of racism for birth outcome studies. *Maternal and Child Health Journal, 13*, 29–39. doi:10.1007/s10995–008-0357-x

Oyserman, D., Coon, H. M., & Kemmelmeier, M. (2002). Rethinking individualism and collectivism: Evaluation of theoretical assumptions and meta-analyses. *Psychological Bulletin, 128*, 3–72.

Oyserman, D., Harrison, K., & Bybee, D. (2001). Can racial identity be promotive of academic efficacy? *International Journal of Behavioral Development, 25*, 379–385. doi:10.1080/01650250042000401

Oyserman, D., & Uskul, A. (2008). Individualism and collectivism: Societal-level processes with implications for individual-level and society-level outcomes. In F. J. R. van de Vijver, D. A. van Hemert, & Y. H. Poortinga (Eds.), *Multilevel analysis of individuals and cultures* (pp. 145–173). Mahwah, NJ: Erlbaum.

Paneth, N., & Susser, M. (1995). Early origin of coronary heart disease (the "Barker Hypothesis"). *British Medical Journal, 310*, 411–412.

Plagemann, A., & Harder, T. (2009). Hormonal programming in perinatal life: Leptin and beyond. *The British Journal of Nutrition, 101*, 151–152. doi:10.1017/S0007114508024021

Roberts, R. E., Phinney, J. S., Masse, L. C., Chen, Y. R., Roberts, C. R., & Romero, A. (1999). The structure of ethnic identity of young adolescents from diverse ethnocultural groups. *The Journal of Early Adolescence, 19*, 301–322.

Rohner, R. (1984). Toward a conception of culture for cross-cultural psychology. *Journal of Cross-Cultural Psychology, 15*, 111–138. doi:10.1177/0022002184015002002

Seligman, M. E., & Csikszentmihalyi, M. (2000). Positive psychology: An introduction. *American Psychologist, 55*, 5–14.

Settles, I. H., Navarette, C. D., Pagano, S. J., Abdou, C. M., & Sidanius, J. (2010). Racial identity and depression among African American women. *Cultural Diversity and Ethnic Minority Psychology, 16*, 248–255. doi:10.1037/a0016442

Sherbourne, C. D., & Stewart, A. L. (1991). The MOS Social Support Survey. *Social Science and Medicine, 32*, 705–714.

Shiono, P. H., Rauh, V. A., Park, M., Lederman, S. A., & Zuskar, D. (1997). Ethnic differences in birthweight: The role of lifestyle and other factors. *American Journal of Public Health, 87*, 787–793.

Sidanius, J., & Pratto, F. (1999). *Social Dominance Theory*. New York, NY: Cambridge University Press.

Tajfel, H., & Turner, J. C. (1986). The social identity theory of inter-group behavior. In S. Worchel & W. G. Austin (Eds.), *Psychology of Intergroup Relations* (pp. 7–24). Chicago, IL: Nelson-Hall.

Taylor, S. E. (2006). Tend and befriend: Biobehavioral bases of affiliation under stress. *Current Directions in Psychological Science, 15*, 273–277.

Triandis, H. C. (1984). *Culture and Social Behavior*. New York, NY: McGraw-Hill.

Whitfield, K. E., Allaire, J. C., Belue, R., & Edwards, C. L. (2008). Are comparisons the answer to understanding behavioral aspects of aging in racial and ethnic groups? *Journal of Gerontology: Psychological Sciences, 63B,* 301–308.

Williams, D. R., Neighbors, H. W., & Jackson, J. S. (2003). Racial/ethnic discrimination and health: Findings from community studies. *American Journal of Public Health, 93,* 200–208.

Woods-Giscombé, C. L., & Lobel, M. (2008). Race and gender matter: A multidimensional approach to conceptualizing and measuring stress in African American women. *Cultural Diversity and Ethnic Minority Psychology, 14,* 173–182. doi:10.1037/1099–9809.14.3.173

Zambrana, R. E., & Dorrington, C. (1998). Economic and social vulnerability of Latino children and families by subgroup: Implications for child welfare. *Child Welfare, 77,* 5–27.

Zeki al Hazzouri, A., Haan, M. N., Osypuk, T., Abdou, C., Hinton, L., & Aiello, A. E. (2011). Neighborhood socioeconomic context ands cognitive decline among older Mexican Americans: Results from the Sacramento Area Latino Study on Aging. *American Journal of Epidemiology, 174,* 423–431. doi:10.1093/aje/kwr095

CHAPTER 3

Social Relationships and Health Among Minority Older Adults

Karen D. Lincoln

Social relationships are an important predictor of health and psychological well-being across the life course (Bowlby, 1969; Watzlawick, Beavin, & Jackson, 1967). Although social interactions decrease in later life (Bowling, Grundy, & Farquhar, 1995; Field & Minkler, 1988; Lee & Markides, 1990; Palmore, 1981; van Willigen, Chadha, & Kedia, 1995), life satisfaction and subjective well-being are maintained or improved (Baltes & Carstensen, 1996) and physical and mental health are protected when older adults have access to or are involved in supportive networks.

The latest U.S. Census Bureau brief on data from the 2010 Census shows that older adults overall are increasing faster than younger populations (U.S. Census, 2010), resulting in a dependency ratio that is projected to increase from 67 to 85 between 2010 and 2050. Substantively, there will be a potential burden on those in the working-age population to care for the growing number of older adults. This is especially true among minority populations who tend to rely heavily on informal sources of support for their day-to-day needs rather than formal care (e.g., nursing homes, long-term care facilities).

The projected substantial increase in the older adult population during the next four decades potentially means longer lives, better health, and more active life styles for older adults than previous generations. However, many minority older adults will face the continued challenges of declining functional status due to physical and mental health conditions over the course of their lives. For example, evidence indicates that African American baby boomers are no better off than their parents or grandparents (Hughes & O'Rand, 2004). Thus, successful "aging in place" for minority older adults presents challenges to policy makers and programs, such as Social Security and Medicare, and will also place huge demands on providers of formal support including social services and health care. However, the demands will be even greater for families who have traditionally been the "safety net" by providing the much needed informal social support to their aging family members.

Despite volumes of research on social support among older adults, many questions of conceptual, methodological, and theoretical importance remain. This is especially the case for older racial and ethnic minorities. The widely accepted but more recently challenged belief that some groups, such as African Americans and immigrants, receive more social support from their networks than other groups has major implications for policies that affect long-term health care, poverty, and social insurance, particularly among populations with limited resources. Moreover, questions remain about the mechanisms that link social support with physical and mental health among older adults in general and minority populations in particular (Uchino, 2006).

This chapter discusses current thinking in the field of social support and social relationships, and physical and mental health among older racial and ethnic minorities. Since African Americans and to some extent Latinos are the racial/ethnic minority groups most often featured in the social support research, the literature on these groups will be highlighted. However, literature on other ethnic/minority older adults that should be highlighted in future research such as Asians/Pacific Islanders and American Indians/Alaska Natives will be discussed where available. First, methodological perspectives on social support and social relationships will be presented. Second, a review of the social support and physical and mental health research will be highlighted, followed by research on negative interaction and a discussion of research on immigration and social support. Finally, biological and psychosocial mechanisms underlying the relationship between social support and physical and mental health will be highlighted, followed by directions for future research.

METHODOLOGICAL APPROACHES

Social support, as a field of study, rose to prominence in the early 1970s and ushered in a groundswell of articles and books dealing with this topic. The burgeoning literature resulted in a plethora of definitions of the term. The term "social support" usually refers to a process of interaction or exchange between individuals and significant others. Studies of race and social support among older adults have typically used a comparative approach—most often comparing African Americans to non-Hispanic whites. This research has yielded critical insights about social support in diverse communities. However, these studies have invariably treated racial groups as homogeneous categories rather than fully examining the heterogeneity within these categories. That is to say, data on social support and physical and mental health from previous gerontological studies have focused on narrow dimensions of race and ethnicity with just a few exceptions (Aranda & Lincoln, 2011; Lincoln et al., 2010; Merz & Consedine, 2009). As a result, our understanding of social support is limited to racial differences (primarily black–white) in types of support (e.g., emotional, informational, instrumental), sources of support (e.g., family, friends, neighbors, church members), functional aspects (e.g., emotional support, sense of acceptance, or belonging), and structural aspects (e.g., size, density, frequency of contact) of support as a protection against stress and poor physical and mental health outcomes.

Findings from these comparative studies of race indicate that African Americans have smaller networks compared to non-Hispanic whites, but that blacks have more frequent contact and exchanges and are more geographically proximal to their network members than whites (Ajrouch, Antonucci, & Janevic, 2001). African Americans also have more emotionally close social partners and are more likely to include extended kin networks as social resources than are whites (Hogan, Eggebeen, & Clogg, 1993). Moreover, the principle of substitution, a phenomenon in which nieces and nephews serve as children when an older person is childless (Luckey, 1994; Perry & Johnson, 1994), is more prevalent among African Americans than among whites (Johnson & Barer, 1990; Troll, 1994).

To move the study of race and social support among older adults further, it is important to consider racial, ethnic, and cultural variation to explain observed differences both within and between groups. To this end, some scholars have engaged in research that builds upon and advances previous empirical research on social support and physical and mental health by taking into account variations in race, ethnicity, and immigration status and how these factors influence social relationships among diverse populations. This work highlights the heterogeneity within and between groups as well as important similarities and differences within older racial and ethnic minority populations (Aranda & Lincoln, 2011; Lincoln et al., 2010; Merz & Consedine, 2009). Some of this research will be highlighted later in this chapter.

SOCIAL SUPPORT AND PHYSICAL AND MENTAL HEALTH

Most empirical studies on social support among older racial and ethnic minority adults explore the association between social support and both physical and mental health. A review of this broad literature during several decades primarily highlights the health restorative role of social support networks; that is, their ability to meet basic human needs for social contact, assistance, and affirmation.

The quality and quantity of social support have been consistently linked to a host of diverse outcomes among older adults, including mortality (Berkman & Syme, 1994), depression (Lincoln et al., 2010; Travis, Lyness, Shields, King, & Cox, 2004; Wethington & Kessler, 1986), and anxiety (Lincoln et al., 2010; Mehta et al., 2004) as well as a host of physical health problems, including heart disease (Kristenson et al., 1998) and rheumatoid arthritis (Krol, Sanderman, & Suurmeijer, 1993). Miller et al. (2009) identified low levels of social support as the most important risk factor for depression among middle-aged and older African Americans even after adjusting for such covariates as medications, environmental factors (e.g., home and neighborhood conditions), functional status (e.g., physical disability), biomedical factors (e.g., blood pressure, weight, chronic conditions), and health service utilization characteristics.

There is a particularly strong link between social support and mental health, especially depression (Lincoln et al., 2010) and depressive symptoms (Chou, 1999; Cohen & Wills, 1985; Newsom & Schulz, 1996). Study findings suggest that subjective evaluations of supportive encounters may be more strongly related to mental health than are objective markers of social support such as frequency of contact with others (Jang, Haley, Small, & Mortier, 2002; Krause, 1995). Further, satisfaction with one's social support has been shown to be inversely related to future depression in older adults (Krause, Liang, & Yatomi, 1989). Studies among older African Americans, in particular, indicate that social support is protective against a host of physical and mental health outcomes, including depression (Lincoln, Chatters, & Taylor, 2005; Miller et al., 2004), anxiety (Lincoln et al., 2010), and diabetes self-management (Tang, Brown, Funnell, & Anderson, 2008).

Although studies comparing older African Americans to non-Hispanic whites comprise a majority of the social support literature, a number of studies are suggestive of the possible association between social support, physical and mental health among diverse groups. Studies on Latino family networks indicate that older Latinos have strong bonds with family members and higher levels of interaction with their adult children, especially in times of need (Aranda & Knight, 1997; Aranda & Miranda, 1997; Mui, 1996; Sotomayor & Randolph, 1988).

However, others report potential areas of negative familial relationships such as social isolation (Barrio, 2007), caregiver burden (Adams, Aranda, Kemp, & Takagi, 2002; Hinton, Haan, Geller, & Mungas, 2003), and abuse (Cardona, Meyer, Schiamberg, & Post, 2007). These studies are suggestive of possible mechanisms whereby stress is linked to mental health, both positively and negatively, within the Latino population. Aranda and Lincoln (2011) provide one of the few, if not only, empirical investigations of negative interaction and mental health among older Latinos. Findings from their study indicated that financial stress exerted a major influence on the respondents' psychological well-being regardless of the positive or negative aspects of social relationships of older Latinos. An examination of nativity revealed that older Latinos who were born in the United States reported fewer sources of negative interaction compared with their immigrant counterparts. Although not the principal focus of the analysis, this finding is consistent with socioemotional selectivity theory, which suggests that as people grow older, they discontinue those relationships that are bothersome while maintaining those ties that are emotionally rewarding and supportive (Carstensen, Isaacowitz, & Charles, 1999). This finding is also consistent with family solidarity theory's notion of "generational stake" (Bengtson, Burton, & Mangen, 1985), in which older people become more invested in their family relationships and tend to view them more positively. Accordingly, older Latinos' perceptions of family relationships may not be mirrored in objective circumstances regarding negative interaction. Whether real or perceived, these findings indicate that reports of negative interaction with family are lower for older U.S.-born Latinos.

Research among Asian Americans is much more limited compared to other racial/ethnic minorities. Much of this work focuses on Asian immigrants. Available studies among older

Asians indicate that social support, particularly from family, is a mechanism that is used heavily to prevent, or deal with, adverse stressful situations (Mui & Kang, 2006; Shibusawa & Mui, 2001). Research on Asian families suggests that, unlike many white older adults who prefer to live alone and be independent whenever possible (Johnson & Barer, 1997; Silverstein & Litwak, 1993), Asian older adults tend to live with their adult children, who provide a considerable amount of emotional and instrumental support to their aging parents (Hooyman & Kiyak, 2011; Mui, Burnette, & Chen, 2001; Mui & Kang, 2006). Within this population, there is still an expectation that their adult children will be available and live in proximity should there be a need to provide assistance (Mui & Kang, 2006). This unique living arrangement may reflect the fact that children of immigrant parents often act as brokers between a confined ethnic community and the wider mainstream society. Much of this research has established that such a level of support is associated with lower levels of psychological distress and depression (Han, Kim, Lee, Pistulka, & Kim, 2007; Mui & Kang, 2006). However, findings that social support is unrelated to depression among older Asians (Han et al., 2007) highlight the need to consider heterogeneity within Asian populations and types and sources of social support. For example, Han et al. (2007) found a significant association between perceived social support and depression among a sample of older Korean respondents; however, satisfaction with support received and the size of a person's network were unrelated to depression. Non-kin should also be considered as sources of social support for older adults, as suggested by the findings of one study by Gellis (2003). Gellis found that Vietnamese immigrants who had non-kin (nonethnic) social support networks from the broader community had lower levels of depressive symptoms compared to those who had networks primarily comprising family members. In contrast, support from kinship networks was associated with higher levels of depressive symptoms. Studies conducted among the general population of Asian Americans (e.g., young and old) indicate that during times of stress, Asian Americans are less likely than non-Hispanic whites to seek emotional support, advice, and help from members of their social network (Kim, Sherman, Ko, & Taylor, 2006). Asian Americans are reportedly more concerned with the negative implications of asking for help, including the risk of burdening others, disrupting the harmony of the group, making the problem worse, or bringing shame to oneself or one's family.

Older Koreans reportedly have a deeply seated Korean cultural value of "saving face" (i.e., not talking badly about one's family member, especially one's children) as well as a traditional parenting style often described as "devoted" and "sacrificing." Today's Korean elderly in their sixties and seventies are particularly prone to practicing these cultural values, since their priority has been to provide a better life to their next generation, due in part to the historical context of Japanese colonization in the 1940s and the Korean war in the 1950s, through which they lived. Consequently, null effects of social support on physical and mental health outcomes should be considered within a cultural context. Additionally, immigration status should also be taken into account in the social support–health relationship.

NEGATIVE INTERACTION

The wealth of studies on social support among minority older adults has much to offer with respect to understanding the correlates of emotional support and patterns of assistance. However, the overwhelming majority of this research focuses on the positive aspects of social relationships with only a limited amount of work examining the correlates of negative interaction, especially among minority older adults. Negative interaction refers to unpleasant social exchanges between individuals who are perceived by the recipient as unsupportive, critical, manipulative, demanding, or otherwise inconsequential to their needs. Negative interactions, unfortunately, are an inevitable consequence of involvement in social networks (Lincoln, 2000). A growing body of literature indicates that positive and negative aspects of social relationships are distinctive social occurrences, and that negative interactions are, themselves, an important predictor of psychological functioning among African Americans (Lincoln, Chatters, Taylor, & Jackson, 2007; Lincoln, Taylor, et al., 2003). Scholars from various fields have used the concept of ambivalence to better understand the quality of family relationships by incorporating both positive and negative elements in a single study (Connidis & McMullin, 2002; Fingerman,

Hay, & Birditt, 2004; Lüscher & Pillemer, 1998; Uchino, Holt-Lunstad, Uno, & Flinders, 2001). Findings from this work demonstrate that positive and negative interactions are built into the nature and structure of family relationships (Lincoln, Taylor, Chatters, & Jackson, 2012).

Studies of negative interaction provide important insight into the complex nature of social relationships and how social ties can be both a source of support and stress (Lakey, Tardiff, & Drew, 1994; Okun & Keith, 1998; Swindle, Heller, & Frank, 2000). Most of the work in this area focuses on the predictive nature of negative interactions with respect to mental health outcomes, with a smaller body of work examining physical health outcomes (Krause, 2005). Findings from this work indicate that negative interactions are a direct source of stress that are associated with negative affect (Newsom, Nishishiba, Morgan, & Rook, 2003), depression (Rook, 1984), heightened physiological reactivity (King, Atienza, Castro, & Collins, 2002), heightened susceptibility to infectious disease (Cohen, Doyle, Skoner, Rabin, & Gwaltney, 1997), declines in physical functioning (Seeman & Chen, 2002), and mortality (Tanne, Goldbourt, & Medalie, 2004). Studies of negative interaction have much to offer with respect to revealing additional linkages between social relationships and well-being among older racial/ethnic minorities. Psychoimmunological research in the area of negative interaction and mental health is more limited compared with research focused on physical health outcomes. However, studies in the behavior and social sciences and gerontology, in particular those that conceptualize negative interaction as a chronic stressor, provide strong evidence linking negative interaction to mental health and psychiatric disorders.

Interpersonal stress, like negative interactions, arouses more distress in individuals than do other types of stress (Zautra, Burleson, Matt, Roth, & Burrows, 1994). This persists over a longer period of time (Bolger, DeLongis, Kessler, & Schilling, 1989) compared to many other types of stressors, which tend to dissipate more quickly. In addition to their direct effects, negative interactions may have indirect effects on physical and mental health by hindering goal-directed activity, eroding perceived self-efficacy, disrupting problem-solving, posing a threat to self-esteem, and interfering with the use of resources like mental health services. Empirical findings indicate that negative interactions may also exacerbate the effects of other types of stressors on mental health (Kiecolt-Glaser, Dyer, & Shuttleworth, 1988; Lincoln et al., 2005). Despite the deleterious effects of negative interaction on well-being, very few studies of negative interaction focus on older racial and ethnic minorities. Lincoln (2003, 2005, 2007, 2010, 2011, 2012) is one of few, if not the only scholar who has systematically examined negative interaction among black Americans. The work by Lincoln and her colleagues has identified demographic and family correlates of negative interaction (some of these findings are discussed below). Findings from this work also provide some evidence that negative interactions increase levels of psychological distress (Lincoln, Chatters, & Taylor, 2003) and depressive symptoms (Lincoln et al., 2005) by eroding feelings of personal control and mastery. Additional evidence indicates that negative interactions do not embody the same level of threat to mental health for African Americans as they do for non-Hispanic whites (Lincoln et al., 2003). This work further suggests that the role of social support networks as a protective or risk factor for depression varies across diverse populations.

CORRELATES OF NEGATIVE INTERACTION

Few studies investigate the correlates of negative interaction among diverse older adult populations (Lincoln, Taylor, & Chatters, 2003). Available research, however, does provide some information about the factors that have some predictive power with respect to negative exchanges with network members.

Empirical evidence indicates that negative interactions vary as a function of gender, such that women are more likely than men to experience negative interactions with members of their social network (Okun & Keith, 1998; Rook, 1984; Schuster, Kessler, & Aseltine, 1990). Apparently, women's more frequent involvement in social networks increases their risk of exposure to negative interactions. In addition, minority persons of advanced age are less likely to report experiencing negative interactions (Akiyama, Antonucci, Takahashi, & Lagfahl, 2003; Lincoln, Taylor, & Chatters, 2003).

Findings for the relationship between marital status and negative interactions are complex. Marriage represents a primary and intimate personal relationship that is a source of long-term support. The benefits of marriage presumably stem from the enhanced feelings of social support, belonging, and attachment that are related to higher states of well-being among those who are married (House, Umberson, & Landis, 1988). However, there are emotional costs associated with all relationships, including marriage. Studies of negative interactions within marital relationships provide evidence of their more potent impact on mental health outcomes compared to supportive exchanges (Horwitz, McLaughlin, & White, 1998). Studies that include both married and unmarried respondents in the sample report mixed results, with some studies finding no effects of marital status on exposure to negative interactions (e.g., Stephens, Kinney, Norris, & Ritchie, 1987) and others reporting higher levels of negative interaction among the unmarried (Lincoln et al., 2003).

Social relationships are important contexts for the exchange of support, regardless of the level of socioeconomic status. However, the effects of socioeconomic status (e.g., education and income) on negative interactions have not been extensively studied. Available studies are inconsistent with respect to education, with some reporting no effects of education (Pagel, Erdly, & Becker, 1987; Rook, 1984) and others finding that more education is associated with more negative interactions (Lincoln, Taylor, & Chatters, 2003). The effects of income are less clear due to the dearth of studies that investigate this factor.

Research that examines negative interactions among African Americans exclusively, highlights important points of divergence from studies of the general population. For example, gender was not a strong predictor of negative interactions among a sample of older African Americans once personality and family contact factors were taken into account (Lincoln, Taylor, & Chatters, 2003). Education was found to be positively associated with negative interactions. Specifically, older African Americans with more education were more likely to report negative interactions with relatives and friends. Consistent with previous research, however, African Americans who were married and had children reported fewer negative interactions with members of their social network (Lincoln, Taylor, & Chatters, 2003).

IMMIGRATION AND SOCIAL SUPPORT

Few studies of older racial and ethnic minorities in the United States examine the influence of immigration on social support networks. However, available studies indicate that social support is indeed altered by the immigration experience. The process of cultural transmutation, whereby one shifts back and forth between the customs and cultural practices of two cultures, can result in the erosion of strong family and social ties among immigrants. As a result of immigration, individuals may experience social mobility and changes in family structure, as well as the disaggregation of family and friend networks and the formation of new social networks, all of which amounts to a stressful process of loss and gain. Unfortunately, there are few formal empirical tests of the role of family ties as a resiliency factor for physical and mental health among older Latino, Asian, and black Caribbean immigrants, in particular. Most of the work on social support and black immigrants in particular, are ethnographic studies of younger populations that focus on the role of social networks in providing economic aid (Bashi, 2007) and continuity in ethnic identity (Waters, 1999).

Available studies on Asian and Latino immigrants report beneficial effects of social support on well-being (Cruza-Guet, Spokane, Caskie, Brown, & Szapocznik, 2008; Hurh & Kim, 1990; Min, Moon, & Lubben, 2005; Shin, 1994). However, we know less, comparatively, about the social networks of Caribbean blacks in the United States. We know from ethnographic studies and conceptual work that family and kinship relationships are instrumental for ethnic identity formation (Waters, 1999), preservation of cultural values and traits, and social support and assistance patterns (Bashi, 2007). Further, family and kinship relationships and networks are involved in all stages of the migration process. Migration decisions for Caribbean blacks often depend on their connections to existing social networks in the United States (Curran & Saguy, 2001). These social networks are vital for preventing social isolation and exclusion, buffering economic hardships associated with immigration, and defining and reaffirming a transnational Caribbean ethnic identity. The social networks of Caribbean blacks have also been credited with facilitating immigrant groups' abilities to create niches in housing and labor markets, start their own businesses, financially shore up network members who need assistance, and offer co-residence to help other immigrants establish themselves immediately following migration (Gilbertson & Gurak, 1992; Massey, 1986; Waldinger, 1996; Waters, 1999). Immigrant networks also provide nonmaterial social support, encouragement, and reinforce cultural practices (Glick, 1999; Ho, 1993; Kuo & Tsai, 1986; Levitt, 1999; Tilly & Brown, 1967).

Empirical findings from a recent study of the demographic and family correlates of social support among African Americans and Caribbean blacks report similar demographic correlates of social support for these two groups (Lincoln, Taylor, Chatters, & Jackson, 2012). However, distinct differences were found in social support when family variables were considered. African Americans and Caribbean blacks who indicated that they were subjectively closer to their families received more emotional support and experienced fewer negative interactions. However, Caribbean blacks, overall, had less frequent interactions with their family members compared to African Americans, which is likely a reflection of the fact that contemporary Caribbean black families often have high levels of geographic dispersion (i.e., transnational families). It is not unusual for Caribbean black families who reside in Brooklyn to also have relatives in Florida, Toronto, Montreal, and London, as well as their country of origin (Olwig, 2001; Plaza, 2000). Consequently, geographic dispersion may, to some degree, reduce levels of family interaction. However, frequency of contact with family was not associated with social support or negative interaction with family among Caribbean blacks, suggesting that a lower level of family interaction, itself, does not reduce the frequency of emotional support received or negative interactions experienced by Caribbean blacks. However, frequency of interaction with family was associated with the receipt of social support and more frequent experiences of negative interaction among African Americans, which most likely reflects the fact that African Americans are more likely to live in close proximity to their family members.

MECHANISMS LINKING SOCIAL RELATIONSHIPS TO PHYSICAL AND MENTAL HEALTH

Many have speculated about the psychosocial and psychological mechanisms whereby social support affects mental health outcomes. For example, perceived social support in particular may reduce older adults' depression or anxiety over time because believing that emotional or tangible support is available if needed may cause people to spend less time worrying about life's problems and daily hassles (Peirce, Frone, Russell, Cooper, & Mudar, 2000). In addition, perceived support may enhance emotional functioning by promoting less threatening interpretations of adverse events and more effective coping strategies (Cohen & Wills, 1985). Comparatively, studies of negative interaction are not as developed as the social support research. However, a few studies have identified psychosocial factors such as personal control and mastery, which help shed some light on how negative interaction might be linked to mental health among African Americans, in particular (Lincoln, Chatters & Taylor, 2003; Lincoln et al., 2005). However, in a study of older Latinos, problem-solving and avoidance coping styles did not mediate the relationship between social support, negative interaction and depression (Aranda & Lincoln, 2011).

Research examining the potential biological mechanisms responsible for the epidemiological links between social support and multiple aspects of physical and mental health outcomes has characterized the potential mechanisms responsible for these relationships. Uchino's (2006) review of epidemiologic studies provides strong and ample evidence linking social support to morbidity and mortality through changes in cardiovascular, neuroendocrine, and immune function. Findings from several cross-sectional and prospective studies indicate that social support is associated with better health and physiological profiles characterized by reduced levels of blood pressure, cardiovascular reactivity, stress hormones, and immune system dysfunction. Social support is thought to confer a health advantage, in part, because it "buffers" the potentially harmful influences of stress-induced cardiovascular reactivity by decreasing deleterious cardiovascular and neuroendocrine changes during stress (usually indexed by blood pressure or heart rate). This is particularly the case among older adults

(Ong & Allaire, 2005; Uchino, Cacioppo, Malarkey, Glaser, & Kiecolt-Glaser, 1995; Uchino, Holt-Lunstad, Uno, & Betancourt, 1999). Studies adjusting for some of these effects, however, indicate that the benefit of support is not entirely explained by these factors (Uchino, Cacioppo, & Kiecolt-Glaser, 1996). For example, strong networks and supportive relationships may foster better health behaviors, or healthier individuals may attract and have the resources to engage in more social interactions and activities. In addition, social support might buffer stress responses by rendering an individual's cognitive appraisals of stressful events as less harmful and threatening (Cohen, 1988) and these altered appraisals, in turn, lessen physiological responses (Seeman, Singer, Ryff, Dienberg Love, & Levy-Storms, 2002). Because greater frequency, intensity, and duration of cardiovascular responses to life's many challenges have been linked to acceleration of the onset and progression of coronary artery disease, hypertension (Sherwood & Turner, 1992), and coronary heart disease (Seeman et al., 2002), these support-mediated decrements in reactivity may be one way that better relationships foster healthier cardiovascular outcomes.

One study investigated the relationship between brief warm social and physical contact among cohabiting couples and blood pressure reactivity to stress in a sample of African American and non-Hispanic white adults (Grewen, Davenport, & Light, 2010). Findings indicated that a brief positive interaction with a spouse or partner (10-minute period of hand-holding while viewing a romantic video, followed by a 20-second hug with their partner) reduced subsequent blood pressure and heart rate responses to a stressful interpersonal event compared with those who rested alone before the event. Furthermore, findings indicated that African Americans conferred a greater benefit of social support in the form of warm contact on reactivity to stress compared to whites.

Regarding neuroendocrine function, there is some evidence that social support is associated with lower plasma and urinary catecholamine levels (Flemming, Baum, Gisriel, & Gatchel, 1982; Grewen, Girdler, Amico, & Light, 2005; Seeman, Berkman, Blazer, & Rowe, 1994). Studies that have measured salivary cortisol over several time points have found a consistent link between social support and lower overall cortisol levels (Heinrichs, Baumgartner, Kirschbaum, & Ehlert, 2003; Milagros, King, Ma, & Reed, 2004; Olga and Steptoe, 2001; Turner-Cobb, Sephton, Koopman, Blake-Mortimer, & Spiegel, 2000).

Finally, social support may influence physical health via the immune system. Some of the strongest associations reported are for a link between social support and better immune function, especially in older adults (Uchino et al., 1996). This association is particularly noteworthy because the risk of cancer increases with age and infectious diseases are a leading cause of death in older individuals (Effros & Walford, 1987).

This research is quite promising and provides much insight into how social support is linked to health outcomes. However, the biological mechanisms explaining the link between social support and physical health outcomes have been largely unexplored among older racial and ethnic minority groups. Available studies of minority older adults tend to focus on behavioral mechanisms rather than biological mechanisms. For example, studies among minority older adults, specifically, report positive associations between social support and physical activity. One study found that social support from family and friends for physical activity was associated with higher levels of physical activity for African American, Hispanic, and American Indian/Alaska Native women age 40 and over (with a significant portion of the sample being older than 65 years; Eyler et al., 1999). This study also reported more support for physical activity from family among Hispanic and American Indian/Alaska Native women compared to African American and non-Hispanic white women. However, support from friends was higher among the minority women compared to non-Hispanic white women. Social support for physical activity is important for health among older adults in particular because it lowers the risk of cardiovascular disease (Blair, Kohl, & Barlow, 1993; Paffenbarger, Wing, & Hyde, 1978; United States Department of Health and Human Services, 1996), hypertension (Folsom et al., 1990; Paffenbarger, Jung, Leung, & Hyde, 1991; Stamler et al., 1989), diabetes mellitus (Helmrich, Ragland, Leung, & Paffenbarger, 1991; Kaye, Folsom, Sprafka, & Prineas, 1991; Manson et al., 1991, 1995), reduces the risk of certain types of cancer (Bernstein, Henderson, Hanisch, Sullivan-Halley, & Ronald, 1994; Lee, Paffenbarger, & Hsieh, 1991; Vena,

Graham, Zielezny, Brasure, & Swanson, 1987), and lowers the risk of osteoporosis (Chow, Harrison, Brown, & Hajek, 1986; Dalsky et al., 1988).

Another study examined psychosocial and behavioral predictors of inflammation (a risk factor for cardiovascular disease) in middle-aged and older adults (age 50–67 years; McDade, Louise, & Cacioppo, 2006). The distribution of C-reactive protein (CRP) concentration was significantly higher for both African Americans and Latinos compared with non-Hispanic whites, suggesting a higher risk for cardiovascular disease (CVD) for African Americans and Latinos. However, social support was neither significantly predictive of CRP, nor did social support moderate the associations of other psychosocial variables, such as stress and depressive symptoms, on CRP.

It might very well be that the biological and physiological mechanisms that explain the link between social support and physical health also explain the link between social support and mental health. However, few studies of social support and mental health examine these mechanisms among the general population or among minority older adults more specifically.

CONCLUSION AND FUTURE DIRECTIONS

Social support is beneficial for the overall well-being of older minority adults. There is also evidence suggesting that negative interactions pose significant risk to the physical and mental health of minority older adults. However, questions remain regarding the relationship between social relationships and health among minority older adults. For example, the association between social support, negative interaction, and physical/mental health among foreign-born populations, Asian Americans, and Native Americans is unclear. Research findings indicate that Asian Americans are less likely than non-Hispanic whites to seek social support in times of stress (Kim, Sherman, & Taylor, 2008). The extent to which immigration status and level of acculturation explain this finding remains an empirical question that should be investigated. In addition, whether this relationship is sustained when negative interaction and social support are simultaneously examined remains unclear. Given the more potent impact of negative interaction on physical and mental health for some groups, it is unclear whether low levels of social support, high levels of negative interaction, or some combination of the two increases or reduces the risk for physical and mental health problems.

In light of findings indicating that negative interaction does not have the same effect on the mental health of African Americans as it does for non-Hispanic whites (Lincoln et al., 2003), studies that examine the extent to which negative interaction poses a risk for the physical/ mental health of diverse populations of older adults, as well as the extent to which social support mitigates the effect of negative interaction on outcomes are needed. Few studies examine the effect of immigration on social networks. As stated above, we know from ethnographic studies that social networks provide economic aid, continuity in ethnic identity, and other assistance associated with settlement in the United States. However, the impact of immigration on the informal social support networks of older racial and ethnic minority immigrants is unclear. Immigration disrupts social support networks and there is scant information regarding how changes in social networks and relationships facilitate or hinder the mental health of older minority immigrants. Studies in these areas will shed new light on the relationship between social support, negative interaction, and physical/mental health risk within and between populations who demonstrate a wide range of diversity across a number of sociodemographic categories. Findings from this work will also enhance our understanding of how social support operates in relation to other protective and risk factors and health outcomes, and how and why the combination of high levels of negative interaction and low levels of social support may be especially problematic for some older adults but not for others.

There are several interesting new directions in recent research that may facilitate the goal of developing a theory of social support and moving studies of social support forward. First, a thorough examination of possible intervening factors among minority older adults can help us understand the mechanisms whereby social support operates to influence particular outcomes. Studies that examine the influence of biological and psychosocial factors are promising.

However, very few studies focus on older minority adults. Understanding the intervening mechanisms and supportive processes is a crucial next step to building theory in this area.

Figure 3.1 illustrates several pathways linking social support (and negative interaction) to physical and mental health. Of central importance to the model is that the links between social support and physical/mental health are hypothesized to be mediated through relevant psychosocial, health behavioral, and biological processes. However, it is important to keep in mind that these mediating factors represent just a few levels of analysis in the complex link between social relationships and physical/mental health. There is a pressing need to also identify processes and mechanisms impacting the association between social support and physical/mental health at other levels of analysis. Although not depicted in the figure, structural factors, such as the built environment and the physical characteristics of neighborhoods, influence the availability of support as well as support seeking for older adults (Clarke & George, 2005; Frank, Andresen, & Schmid, 2004; Kim & Kaplan, 2004; Leyden, 2003; Rohrer, Pierce, & Denison, 2004; Szapocznik et al., 2006).

Despite the growing body of research on the built environment and health and wellness, few studies have examined these relationships among minority older adults. One study examined the association between the built environment, perceived social support, and psychological distress among older Latinos (70 years and older; Brown et al., 2009). Findings indicated that features of the built environment were associated with perceived social support and psychological distress. Specifically, older adults who lived on blocks with greater proportions of frontage that included porches, stoops, and buildings above-grade (buildings that "sat" at least 12 in. above the level of the sidewalk) reported higher levels of social support. Older adults who lived on blocks with greater proportions of window area and/or greater low sill height and who had ground floor parking reported lower levels of social support. Consistent with other study findings, low levels of perceived social support was associated with psychological distress for this sample.

Returning to the conceptual model depicted in Figure 3.1, it does take into account the fact that the structure, function, and quality of social relationships are influenced by demographic factors including race, gender, income, education, and immigration history. As mentioned above, there are several demographic correlates to negative interaction. This is also true for social support, with gender (Lincoln, Taylor, & Chatters, 2003; Lu, 1995), age (Lansford,

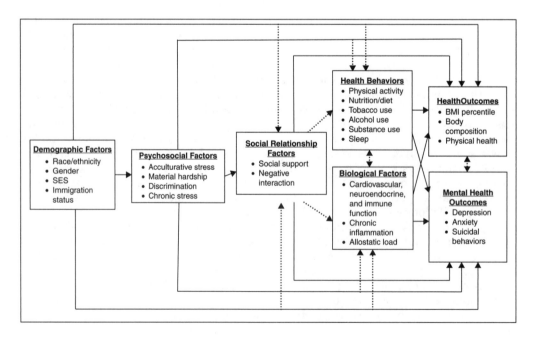

FIGURE 3.1 Potential Pathways Linking Social Relationships to Health and Mental Health.

Sherman, & Antonucci, 1998), marital status (Chatters, Taylor, & Neighbors, 1989; Lincoln, Taylor, & Chatters, 2003; Moore, 1990; Pugliesi & Shook, 1998; Taylor, 1986), socioeconomic position (SEP; Eggebeen & Hogan, 1990; Jayakody, 1998), and immigration status (Min, Moon, & Lubben, 2005) being differentially associated with the receipt and perceptions of social support among different groups of minority older adults.

To recap, a wealth of previous research, some of which has been discussed in this chapter, indicates that stress (due to economic, social, and environmental factors) increases one's risk for chronic health conditions and mental health problems. Social support is an effective coping resource that reduces the impact of stress on these outcomes. However, the mechanisms whereby social support reduces the negative effects of social stress are unclear. Further, evidence suggests that individuals who occupy lower SEPs as measured by minority status, income, and gender, may be disadvantaged with respect to the recruitment and effective utilization of supportive ties, as well as increased exposure to stress and conflictual relationships. The conceptual model depicted in Figure 3.1 specifies several pathways whereby social relationships—both positive and negative—might operate in the presence of stress to influence physical health and mental health outcomes among minority older adults.

SEP might increase exposure to stressful situations such as discrimination or acculturative stress, while at the same time, impacting social support by either reducing or increasing it. Higher levels of exposure to social stress and less access to support can increase one's risk for physical and mental health problems via health behaviors and biological mechanisms. Specifically, trajectories of health behaviors and stress unfold over the life course. Individuals who are chronically confronted with stressful conditions in daily life sometimes engage in health-compromising but often pleasurable behaviors that help to alleviate immediate symptoms of stress (Kuntsche, Knibbe, Gmel, & Engels, 2005; Lawlor, Frankel, Shaw, Ebrahim, & Smith, 2003; Ng & Jeffery, 2003) but contribute to morbidity and mortality in the longer term. High levels of perceived stress are associated with smoking initiation (Byrne & Mazanov, 2003), increased smoking levels (Colby et al., 1994), less successful smoking cessation attempts (Chassin, Presson, Rose, Sherman, & Prost, 2002), drinking alcohol more often and in heavier quantities (Cooper, Russell, & George, 1988), increased problem drinking (Grunberg, Moore, Anderson-Connolly, & Greenberg, 1999), and less frequent physical activity (Boutelle, Murray, Jeffery, Hennrikus, & Lando, 2000; Kouvonen et al., 2005). Health behavior change in response to stress has been seen in children and adolescents (Kassel, Stroud, & Paronis, 2003; Stunkard, Faith, & Allison, 2003). However, very little, if any, research exists among minority older adults. Findings from previous work indicate that high levels of perceived stress are associated with less frequent physical activity (Nguyen-Michel, Unger, Hamilton, & Spruijt-Metz, 2006) and emotional eating (Nguyen-Rodriguez, Chou, Unger, & Spruijt-Metz, 2008; Nguyen-Rodriguez, Unger, & Spruijt-Metz, 2009), especially sweet energy-dense foods, among minority females (Nguyen-Michel, Unger, &, Spruijt-Metz, 2007). Some behaviors, including dietary practices and physical activity patterns, develop throughout childhood and are culturally sustained, while others, such as smoking and alcohol consumption, typically begin in adolescence or early adulthood. Some behaviors, such as drinking, smoking, and exercise, are most prevalent in early adulthood and become less prevalent with advancing age (Vierck & Hodges, 2003). While there may be some stability in health behaviors over time, significant stressful life events may trigger significant change in certain health behaviors (Rosenbloom & Whittington, 1993; Schone & Weinick, 1998; Wilcox et al., 2003). A life course perspective should be used to direct attention to stress exposure. High levels of stress in childhood may set a trajectory of stress into motion that reverberates throughout the adult life course, having a cumulative effect on health over time (Ferraro & Kelley-Moore, 2003; Hayward & Gorman, 2004) and culminating in increased morbidity or mortality in late life. These relationships should be investigated in future research, particularly in light of epidemiologic study findings indicating that 61% of black women and 37% of Mexican American women 60 years and older are overweight or obese (Center for Disease Control and Prevention, 2009; Ogden, Carroll, McDowell, & Flegal, 2007).

In addition to the association between biological factors and social support previously discussed, disparities researchers have noted that SEP is an overriding determinant of health status and health disparities in the U.S. because it affects stress exposures, risk behaviors, physical constitution, and other direct or contributory causes of disease (Kaufman & Cooper, 1999; Krieger, Rowley, Herman, Avery, & Phillips, 1993) via biological processes. Heightened levels of cortisol have been found to promote weight gain, with a particular impact on increased visceral adiposity (Ottosson, Lönnroth, Björntorp, & Edén, 2000; Pasquali et al., 2002), particularly in the presence of specific stressors. Stress in combination with poor dietary and exercise habits is exacerbated by an obesogenic environment (Baker, Schootman, Barnidge, & Kelly, 2006; Block & Kouba, 2006; Burdette & Whitaker, 2004; Franco, Diez Roux, Glass, Caballero, & Brancati, 2008; Powell, Slater, Mirtcheva, Bao, & Chaloupka, 2007; Small & McDermott, 2006; Sturm & Datar, 2005; Zenk et al., 2006), which leads to accumulation of visceral fat and inflammatory state. These broad causal factors structure daily social experiences and lifestyles at the micro level of personal social support networks and interpersonal relationships at the meso level of neighborhood and community, and at the nexus with health care and other social services (Vega & Sribney, 2005). Cumulative adversity derived from these exposures is associated with higher allostatic load across the life course, potentially affecting the hypothalamic-pituitary-adrenal axis (HPA), thereby contributing to neuroendocrine and metabolic derangement (Marmot, 2006). If unchecked through exogenous or endogenous (biochemical) interventions, over time these biologic set points may be altered and can ultimately result in chronic conditions and mental health disorder. These potentially adverse processes interacting in a biochemical milieu may produce a propensity to inflammation and oxidative stress with resulting heightened risk of obesity, CVD, heart disease, stroke, and diabetes (Bjorntorp, 1997; McEwen, Magarinos, & Reagan, 2002; Wolkowitz, Epel, Reus, & Mellon, 2010). However, the long range of social environmental exposure effects on biological systems among minority older adults have not been carefully examined. A rich body of stress process research has compellingly demonstrated the independent and additive effects of cumulative stress exposure on physical and mental health, and has identified social support as an important coping resource that affords protection against or increased risk for these adverse outcomes (Billings & Moos, 1982; Pearlin & Schooler, 1978; Turner & Avison, 2003).

Research designs have advanced from the cross-sectional correlational research that characterized early studies (Heller & Swindle, 1983) to longitudinal designs (Barnes, Mendes de Leon, Bienias, & Evans, 2004). The relatively underexplored questions concerning the effects of SEP, stress, health behaviors, biological factors, and social support on well-being over the life span should be examined in future longitudinal studies. Stressors, such as financial problems and death of a loved one, are generally assumed to result in support mobilization rather than erosion or withdrawal. However, acute stressors are more likely to result in support mobilization in the short run, whereas chronic stressors may entail serious costs to the social network and thus erode support over time. More research is needed to clarify and understand these relationships.

Most studies view social support primarily as an individual-level or interpersonal construct. Community psychologists, however, have identified the need for studies that treat social support as a system- or community-level phenomenon that promotes social integration and perceptions of support. A focus on system- and community-level factors is consistent with a sociological approach to the study of interactions among people and how social contexts influence these relationships. One example of this approach involves studies of social support in religious settings. Although this literature is not well developed among older minorities, findings to date indicate that people who are members of formal religious organizations receive a sizable amount of emotional and tangible assistance (Taylor, Chatters, & Levin, 2004) from their fellow congregants. Most of this work has been conducted using older African American samples. However, more work is needed that includes other racial and ethnic groups and immigrants as well as studies that examine the role of spirituality, which might be more relevant than religion for some older ethnic groups. In addition to this line of research, more information is needed about the role of clergy and religious/spiritual leaders in facilitating social support among parishioners and followers. Research findings indicate that some people are more likely to consult members of the clergy than professional helpers (Taylor, Chatters, & Levin, 2004). However, more research is needed to understand what clergy and religious/spiritual leaders actually do to assist their older congregants, whether they act as a conduit to professional helpers, or if it is the types of problems they confront.

More discussion on policy implications of social support is needed. The widely accepted but often challenged belief that older racial and ethnic minority adults receive more social support than their non-Hispanic white counterparts has major implications for policies that affect long-term health care, poverty, and social insurance, particularly among populations with limited resources. For example, empirical findings indicate that older African Americans have smaller social networks (compared to whites; Barnes et al., 2004) but have a higher proportion of kin in their social networks (Ajrouch, Antonucci, & Janevic, 2001). Whereas negative exchanges might be relatively uncommon among more distal network members (e.g., coworkers, neighbors) where few resources are transferred, they have been found to be fairly common among family members and when extensive support is provided. Consequently, some older minority adults might be more vulnerable to conflict within their networks and have limitations in the availability or range of supportive resources compared to those with more multiplex networks (e.g., family, friends, neighbors, coworkers).

Another promising new direction for future research is the use of computers and the Internet to provide and receive social support. This area of study views computer-mediated support groups as weak tie networks that have the potential to provide support to those individuals who have limited or restricted opportunities to engage in supportive exchanges. Persons with functional limitations or loss of mobility, illness, advanced age, time constraints due to competing demands (e.g., caring for a disabled, aging, or ill family member), or who simply prefer social contact or discussing personal problems via cyberspace rather than face-to-face might benefit from this form of support.

While social media use has grown dramatically across all age groups, older users have been especially enthusiastic recently about embracing new networking tools. Empirical findings indicate that social networking use among Internet users ages 50 and older has nearly doubled, from 22% to 42% over the past year (Madden, 2010). Although email continues to be the primary way that older users maintain contact with friends, families, and colleagues, many users now rely on social network platforms such as Facebook and LinkedIn, to help manage their daily communications, sharing links, photos, videos, news, and status updates with a growing network of contacts. Although minorities, in general, are steadily gaining access to and using the Internet, there are disparities in access and use among older minority adults. For example, just 11% of African Americans age 65 and over reported using the Internet in 2003, compared to 22% of white seniors (Fox, 2004). By comparison, 7% of African American older adults went online in 2000. African Americans as a group lag behind whites when it comes to Internet access, but the difference is most stark in the 55 and over population. In 2003, 58% of whites between 55 and 64 years old had Internet access compared to just 22% of African Americans.

Findings for older Latinos are slightly better. However, disparities still exist. Twenty-one percent of English-speaking Hispanics age 65 and over reported using the Internet in 2003, which is statistically equal to the 22% of non-Hispanic white older adults who had access. However, there are disparities among the younger population; 32% of English-speaking Hispanics age 55–64 reported having Internet access in 2003, compared to 58% of non-Hispanic whites in that age group.

Research in this area is in its infancy and competing claims have been presented in the literature regarding the impact of Internet use on social support, with some studies suggesting that Internet use increases social interaction and support (Shaw & Gant, 2002), while others suggest that it leads to decreased interaction and support, or has no effect (Noel & Epstein, 2003). There is some disagreement as to whether the Internet has a positive or negative impact on social connection and well-being for older adults, in particular. Clearly, more work is needed in this area to determine who uses, who benefits, who has access, and what are the motives for using this form of exchange, as well as whether it is a replacement or supplement to face-to-face interactions.

The past few decades have made strides in clarifying the theoretical construct of social support and for establishing how it is associated with different facets of social life among older minority adults. As more systematic research continues, future research will provide a more nuanced and contextualized understanding of the promise and limits of social support for these populations.

REFERENCES

Adams, B., Aranda, M., Kemp, B., & Takagi, K. (2002). Ethnic and gender differences in distress among Anglo American, African American, Japanese American, and Mexican American spousal caregivers of persons with dementia. *Journal of Clinical Geropsychology, 8*(4), 279–301.

Ajrouch, K. J., Antonucci, T. C. & Janevic, M. R. (2001). Social networks among blacks and whites: The interaction between race and age. *Journals of Gerontology: Social Sciences, 56*(2), S112–S118.

Akiyama, H., Antonucci, T., Takahashi, K., & Langfahl, E. S. (2003). Negative interactions in close relationships across the life span. *Journal of Gerontology: Psychological Sciences, 58*(2), 70–79.

Aranda, M. P., & Knight, B. G. (1997). The influence of ethnicity and culture on the caregiver stress and coping process: A sociocultural review and analysis. *The Gerontologist, 37*(3), 342–354.

Aranda, M. P., & Lincoln, K. (2011). Financial strain, negative interaction, coping styles, and mental health among low-income Latinos. *Race and Social Problems, 3*(4), 280–297.

Aranda, M. P., & Miranda, M. R. (1997). Hispanic aging, social support, and mental health: Does acculturation make a difference? In K. S. Markides & M. R. Miranda (Eds.), Minorities, Aging, and Health (pp. 271–294). Thousand Oaks, CA: Sage.

Baker, E. A., Schootman, M., Barnidge, E., & Kelly, C. (2006). The role of race and poverty in access to foods that enable individuals to adhere to dietary guidelines. *Preventing Chronic Disease, 3*(3), A76.

Baltes, M. M., & Carstensen, L. L. (1996). The process of successful ageing. *Ageing and Society, 16*(4), 397–422.

Barnes, L. L., Mendes de Leon, C. F., Bienias, J. L., & Evans, D. A. (2004). A longitudinal study of Black-White differences in social resources. *Journals of Gerontology: Social Sciences, 59*(3), S146–S153.

Barrio, C. A. (2007). Assessing suicide risk in children: Guidelines for developmentally appropriate interviewing. *Journal of Mental Health Counseling, 29*(1), 50–66.

Bashi, V. F. (2007). *Survival of the knitted: Immigrant social networks in a stratified world.* Stanford, CA: Stanford University Press.

Bengtson, V. L., Burton, L., & Mangen, D. J. (1985). Generations, cohorts, and relations between age groups. In R. H. Binstock & E. Shanas (Eds.), *Handbook of aging and the social sciences* (2nd ed., pp. 304–338). New York, NY: Van Nostrand Reinhold.

Berkman, L. F., & Syme, S. L. (1994). Social networks, host resistance, and mortality: A nine year follow-up study of Alameda County residents. In A. Steptoe & J. Wardle (Eds.), *Psychosocial processes and health: A reader* (pp. 43–67). New York, NY: Cambridge University Press.

Bernstein, L., Henderson, B. E., Hanisch, R., Sullivan-Halley, J., & Ronald, K. R. (1994). Physical exercise and reduced risk of breast cancer in young women. *Journal of the National Cancer Institute, 86*(18), 1403–1408.

Billings, A. C., & Moos, R. H. (1982). Psychosocial theory and research on depression: An integrative framework and review. *Clinical Psychology Review, 2*(2), 213–237.

Bjorntorp, P. (1997). Body fat distribution, insulin resistance, and metabolic diseases. *Nutrition, 13*(9), 795–803.

Blair, S. N., Kohl, H. W., & Barlow, C. E. (1993). Physical activity, physical fitness, and all-cause mortality in women: Do women need to be active? *Journal of American College of Nutrition, 12*(4), 368–371.

Block, D., & Kouba, J. A (2006). Comparison of the availability and affordability of a market basket in two communities in the Chicago area. *Public Health Nutrition, 9*(7), 837–845.

Bolger, N., DeLongis, A., Kessler, R. C., & Schilling, E. A. (1989). Effects of daily stress on negative mood. *Journal of Personality and Social Psychology, 57*(5), 808–818.

Boutelle, K. N., Murray, D. M., Jeffery, R. W., Hennrikus, D. J., & Lando, H. A. (2000). Associations between exercise and health behaviors in a community sample of working adults. *Preventive Medicine, 30*(3), 217–224.

Bowlby, J. (1969). Attached and loss: Volume I. *Attachment.* New York, NY: Basic Books.

Bowling, A., Grundy, E., & Farquhar, M. (1995). Changes in network composition among the very old living in inner London. *Journal of Cross-cultural Gerontology, 10*(4), 331–337.

Brown, S. C., Mason, C. A., Spokane, A. R., Cruza-Guel, M. C., Lopez, B., & Szapocznik, J. (2009). The relationship of neighborhood climate to perceived social support and mental health in older Hispanic immigrants in Miami, Florida. *Journal of Aging and Health, 21*(3), 431–459.

Burdette, H. L., & Whitaker, R. C. (2004). Neighborhood playgrounds, fast food restaurants, and crime: Relationships to overweight in low-income preschool children. *Preventive Medicine, 38*(1), 57–63.

Byrne, D. G., & Mazanov, J. (2003). Adolescent stress and future smoking behavior: A prospective investigation. *Journal of Psychosomatic Research, 54*(4), 313–321.

Cardona, J. R. P., Meyer, E., Schiamberg, L., & Post, L. (2007). Elder abuse and neglect in Latino families: An ecological and culturally relevant theoretical framework for clinical practice. *Family Process, 46*(4), 451–470.

Carstensen, L. L., Isaacowitz, D. M., & Charles, S. T. (1999). Taking time seriously: A theory of socioemotional selectivity. *American Psychologist, 54*(3), 165–181.

Centers for Disease Control and Prevention. (2009). National Center for Health Statistics (NCHS). National Health and Nutrition Examination Survey, 2009. http://www.cdc.gov/nchs/nhanes/nhanes_questionnaires.htm

Chassin, L., Presson, C., Rose, J., Sherman, S. J., & Prost, J. (2002). Parental smoking cessation and adolescent smoking. *Journal of Pediatric Psychology, 27*(6), 485–96.

Chatters, L. M., Taylor, R. J., & Neighbors, H. W. (1989). Size of the informal helper network mobilized in response to serious personal problems. *Journal of Marriage and the Family, 51*(3), 667–676.

Chou, K. L. (1999). Social support and subjective well-being among Hong Kong Chinese young adults. *Journal of Genetic Psychology, 160*(3), 319–331.

Chow, R. K., Harrison, J. E., Brown, C. F., & Hajek, V. (1986). Physical fitness effect on bone mass in postmenopausal women. *Archives of Physical Medicine and Rehabilitation, 67*(4), 231–234.

Clarke, P., & George, L. K. (2005). The role of the built environment in the disablement process. *American Journal of Public Health, 95*(11), 1933–1939.

Cohen, S. (1988). Psychosocial models of the role of social support in the etiology of physical disease. *Health Psychology, 7*(3), 269–297.

Cohen, S., & Wills, T. A. (1985). Stress, social support and the buffering hypothesis. *Psychological Bulletin, 98*(2), 310–357.

Cohen, S., Doyle, W. J., Skoner, D. P., Rabin, B. S., & Gwaltney, J. M. (1997). Social ties and susceptibility to the common cold. *Journal of the American Medical Association, 277*(24), 1940–1944.

Colby, S. M., Rohsenow, D. J., Sirota, A. D., Abrams, D. B., Niaura, R. S., & Monti, P. M. (1994, June). Alcoholics' beliefs about quitting smoking during alcohol treatment: Do they make a difference? In P. M. Monti & D. B. Abrams, (Eds.), *Alcohol and nicotine dependence: Biobehavioral mechanism, treatment and policy implications*. Symposium presented at the Annual Meeting of the Research Society on Alcoholism, Maui, HI.

Connidis, I. A., & McMullin, J. A. (2002). Ambivalence, family ties, and doing sociology. *Journal of Marriage and Family, 64*(3), 595–601.

Cooper, M. L., Russell, M., & George, W. H. (1988). Coping, expectancies, and alcohol abuse: A test of social learning formulations. *Journal of Abnormal Psychology, 97*(2), 218–230.

Cruza-Guet, M. C., Spokane, A. R., Caskie, G. I. L., Brown, S. C., & Szapocznik, J. (2008). The relationship between social support and psychological distress among Hispanic elders in Miami, Florida. *Journal of Counseling Psychology, 55*(4), 427–441.

Curran, S. R., & Saguy, A. C. (2001). Migration and cultural change: A role for gender and social networks. *Journal of International Women's Studies, 2*(3), 54–77.

Dalsky, G. P., Stocke, K. S., Ehsani, A. A., Slatopolsky, E., Lee, W. C., & Birge, S. J. (1988). Weight-bearing exercise training and lumber bone mineral content in postmenopausal women. *Annals of Internal Medicine, 108*(6), 824–828.

Effros, R. B., & Walford, R. L. (1987). Neonatal T cells as a model system to study the possible in vitro senescence of lymphocytes. *Experimental Gerontology, 22*(5), 307–316.

Eggebeen, D. J., & Hogan, D. P. (1990). Giving between generations in American families. *Human Nature, 1*(3), 211–232.

Eyler, A. A., Brownson, R. C., Donatelle, R. J., King, A. C., Brown, D., & Sallis, J. F. (1999). Physical activity social support and middle- and older-aged minority women: Results from a US survey. *Social Science & Medicine, 49*(6), 781–789.

Ferraro, K., & Kelley-Moore, J. A. (2003). Cumulative disadvantage and health: Long-term consequences of obesity? *American Sociological Review, 68*(5), 707–729.

Field, D., & Minkler, M. (1988). Continuity and change in social support between young-old and old-old or very-old age. *Journal of Gerontology: Psychological Sciences, 43*(4), 100–106.

Fingerman, K. L., Hay, E. L., & Birditt, K. S. (2004). The best of ties, the worst of ties: Close, problematic, and ambivalent social relationships. *Journal of Marriage and Family, 66*(3), 792–808.

Flemming, R., Baum, A., Gisriel, M. M., & Gatchel, R. J. (1982). Mediating influences of social support on stress at Three Mile Island, *Journal of Human Stress, 8*(3), 14–23.

Folsom, A. R., Prineas, R. J., Kaye, S. A., & Munger, R. G. (1990). Incidence of hypertension and stroke in relation to body fat distribution and other risk factors in older women. *Stroke, 21*, 701–706.

Franco, M., Diez Roux, A. V., Glass, T. A., Caballero, B., & Brancati, F. L. (2008). Neighborhood characteristics and availability of healthy foods in Baltimore. *American Journal of Preventive Medicine, 35*(6), 561–567.

Frank, L. D., Andresen, M. A., & Schmid, T. L. (2004). Obesity relationships with community design, physical activity, and time spent in cars. *American Journal of Preventive Medicine, 27*(2), 87–96.

Gellis, Z. D. (2003). Kin and nonkin social supports in a community sample of Vietnamese immigrants. *Social Work, 48*(2), 248–258.

Gilbertson, G., & Gurak, D. T. (1992). Household transitions in the migrations of Dominicans and Columbians to New York, *International Migration Review, 26*(1), 22–45.

Glick, J. E. (1999). Economic support from and to extended kin: A comparison of Mexican Americans and Mexican Immigrants. *International Migration Review, 33*(3), 745–765.

Grewen, K. M., Davenport, R. E., & Light, K. C. (2010). An investigation of plasma and salivary oxytocin responses in breast and formula-feeding mothers of infants, *Psychophysiology, 47*(4), 625–632.

Grewen, K. M., Girdler, S. S., Amico, J., & Light, K. C. (2005). Oxytocin, cortisol, norepinephrine, and blood pressure before and after warm partner contact. *Psychosomatic Medicine, 67*(4), 531–538.

Grunberg, L., Moore, S., Anderson-Connolly, R., & Greenberg, E. (1999). Work stress and self-reported alcohol use: The moderating role of escapist reasons for drinking. *Journal of Occupational Health Psychology, 4*(1), 29–36.

Han, H. R., Kim, M., Lee, H. B., Pistulka, G., & Kim, K. B. (2007). Correlates of depression in the Korean American elderly: Focusing on personal resources of social support. *Journal of Cross Cultural Gerontology, 22*(1), 115–127.

Hayward, M. D., & Gorman, B. (2004). The long arm of childhood: The influence of early-life social conditions on men's mortality. *Demography, 41*(1), 87–107.

Heinrichs, M., Baumgartner, T., Kirschbaum, C., & Ehlert, U. (2003). Social support and oxytocin interact to suppress cortisol and subjective responses to psychosocial stress. *Biological Psychiatry, 54*(12), 1389–1398.

Heller, K., & Swindle, R. (1983). Social networks, perceived social support, and coping with stress. In R. D. Felner, L. A. Jason, J. Moritsugu, & S. S. Faber (Eds.), *Preventive psychology, research and practice in community intervention* (pp. 87–103). New York: Pergamon.

Helmrich, S., Ragland, D., Leung, R., & Paffenbarger, R. J. (1991). Physical activity and reduced occurence of non-insulin dependent diabetes mellitus. *New England Journal of Medicine, 325*, 147–152.

Hinton, L., Haan, M., Geller, S., & Mungas, D. (2003). Neuropsychiatric symptoms in Latino elders with dementia or cognitive impairment without dementia and factors that modify their association with caregiver depression. *The Gerontologist, 43*(5), 669–677.

Ho, C. G. T. (1993). The internationalization of kinship and the feminization of Caribbean migration: The case of Afro-Trinidadian immigrants in Los Angeles. *Human Organization, 52*(1), 32–40.

Hogan, D. P., Eggebeen, D. J., & Clogg, C. C. (1993). The structure of intergenerational exchanges in American families. *American Journal of Sociology, 98*(6), 1428–1458.

Hooyman, N. R., & Kiyak, H. A. (2011). *Social gerontology: A multidisciplinary perspective* (9th ed.). Boston: Allyn & Bacon.

Horwitz, A. V., McLaughlin, J., & White, H. R. (1998). How the negative and positive aspects of part-ner relationships affect the mental health of young married persons. *Journal of Health and Social Behavior, 39*(2), 124–136.

House, J. S., Umberson, D., & Landis, K. R. (1988). Structures and processes of social support. *Annual Review of Sociology, 14*, 293–318.

Hughes, M. E., & O'Rand, A. M. (2004). *The Lives and Times of the Baby Boomers*. Census 2000 Russell Sage Foundation and the Population Reference Bureau.

Hurh, M. H., & Kim, K. C. (1990). Correlates of Korean immigrants' mental health. *Journal of Nervous and Mental Disease, 178*(11), 703–711.

Jang, Y., Haley, W. E., Small, B. J., & Mortier, J. A. (2002). The role of mastery and social resources in the associations between disability and depression in later life. *The Gerontologist, 42*(6), 807–813.

Jayakody, R. (1998). Race differences in intergenerational financial assistance. *Journal of Family Issues, 19*(5), 508–533.

Johnson, C. L., & Barer, B. M. (1990). Families and networks among older inner-city blacks. *The Gerontologist, 30*(6), 726–733.

Johnson, C. L., & Barer, B. M. (1997). *Life beyond 85 years: The aura of survivorship*. New York, NY: Springer.

Kassel, J. D., Stroud, L. R., & Paronis, C. A. (2003). Smoking, stress, and negative affect: Correlation, cau-sation, and context across stages of smoking. *Psychological Bulletin, 129*(2), 270–304.

Kaufman, J. S., & Cooper, R. S. (1999). Seeking causal explanations in social epidemiology. *American Journal of Epidemiology, 150*(2), 113–120.

Kaye, S. A., Folsom, A. R., Sprafka, J. M., & Prineas, R. J. (1991). Increased incidence of diabetes mellitus in relation to abdominal adiposity in older women. *Journal of Clinical Epidemiology, 44*(3), 329–334.

Kiecolt-Glaser, J. K., Dyer, C. S., & Shuttleworth, E. C. (1988). Upsetting social interactions and distress among Alzheimer's disease family care-givers: A replication and extension. *American Journal of Community Psychology, 16*(6), 825–837.

Kim, H. S., Sherman, D. K., & Taylor, S. E. (2008). Culture and social support. *American Psychologist, 63*(6), 518–526.

Kim, H. S., Sherman, D. K., Ko, D., & Taylor, S. E. (2006). Pursuit of comfort and pursuit of harmony: Culture, relationships, and social support seeking. *Personality and Social Psychology Bulletin, 32*(12), 1595–1607.

Kim, J., & Kaplan, R. (2004). Physical and psychological factors in sense of community: New Urbanist Kentlands and nearby Orchard Village. *Environment and Behavior, 36*(3), 313–340.

King, A. C., Atienza, A., Castro, C., & Collins, R. (2002). Physiological and affective responses to fam-ily caregiving in the natural setting in wives versus daughters. *International Journal of Behavioral Medicine, 9*(3), 176–194.

Kouvonen, A., Kivimaki, M., Elovainio, M., Virtanen, M., Linna, A., & Vahtera, J. (2005). Job strain and leisure-time physical activity in female and male public sector employees. *Preventive Medicine, 41*(2), 532–539.

Krause, N. (1995). Religiosity and self-esteem among older adults. *Journal of Gerontology: Psychological Sciences, 50*(5), 236–246.

Krause, N. (2005). Negative interaction and heart disease in late life: Exploring variations by socioeco-nomic status. *Journal of Aging Health, 17*(1), 28–55.

Krause, N., Liang, J., & Yatomi, N. (1989). Satisfaction with social support and depressive symptoms: A panel analysis. *Psychology and Aging, 4*(1), 88–97.

Krieger, N., Rowley, D. L., Herman, A. A., Avery, B., & Phillips, M. T. (1993). Racism, sexism, and social class: Implications for studies of health, disease, and well-being. *American Journal of Preventive Medicine, 9*(6 Suppl), 82–122.

Kristenson, M., Orth-Gomer, K., Kucinskiene, Z., Bergdahl, B., Calkauskas, H., Balinkyniene, I., & Olsson, A. G. (1998). Attenuated cortisol response to a standardized stress test in Lithuanian versus Swedish men: The Livicordia study. *International Journal of Behavioral Medicine, 5*(1), 17–30.

Krol, B., Sanderman, R., & Suurmeijer, T. P. (1993). Social support, rheumatoid arthritis and quality of life: Concepts, measurement and research. *Patient Education & Counseling, 20*(2–3), 101–120.

Kuntsche, E., Knibbe, R., Gmel, G., & Engels, R. (2005). Why do young people drink? A review of drinking motives. *Clinical Psychology Review, 25*(7), 841–861.

Kuo, W. H., & Tsai, Y. M. (1986). Social networking, hardiness and immigrant's mental health. *Journal of Health and Social Behavior, 27*(2), 133–149.

Lakey, B., Tardiff, T. A., & Drew, J. B. (1994). Negative social interactions: Assessment and relations to social support, cognition and psychological distress. *Journal of Social and Clinical Psychology, 13*(1), 42–62.

Lansford, J. E., Sherman, A. M., & Antonucci, T. C. (1998). Satisfaction with social networks: An examination of socioemotional selectivity theory across cohorts. Psychology and Aging, 13(4), 544–552.

Lawlor, D. A., Frankel, S., Shaw, M., Ebrahim, S., & Smith, G. D. (2003). Smoking and ill health: Does lay epidemiology explain the failure of smoking cessation programs among deprived populations? *Journal of Public Health, 93,* 266–270.

Lee, D. J., & Markides, K. S. (1990). Activity and mortality among aged persons over an eight-year period. *Journal of Gerontology, 45*(1), S39-S42.

Lee, I. M., Paffenbarger, R. S., Jr., & Hsieh, C. C. (1991). Physical activity and risk of developing colorectal cancer among college alumni. *Journal of the National Cancer Institute, 83*(18), 1324–1329.

Levitt, P. (1999). Social remittances: A local-level, migration-driven form of cultural diffusion. *International Migration Review, 32*(4), 926–949.

Leyden, K. M. (2003). Social capital and the built environment: The importance of walkable neighborhoods. *American Journal of Public Health, 93*(9), 1546–1551.

Lincoln, K. D. (2000). Social support, negative social interactions, and psychological well-being. *Social Service Review, 74*(2), 231–252.

Lincoln, K. D., Chatters, L. M., & Taylor, R. J. (2003). Psychological distress among Black and White Americans: Differential effects of social support, negative interaction and personal control. *Journal of Health and Social Behavior, 44*(3), 390–407.

Lincoln, K. D., Chatters, L. M., & Taylor, R. J. (2005). Social support, traumatic events and depressive symptoms among African Americans. *Journal of Marriage and Family, 67*(3), 754–766.

Lincoln, K. D., Chatters, L. M., Taylor, R. J., & Jackson, J. S. (2007). Profiles of depressive symptoms among African Americans and Caribbean Blacks. *Social Science & Medicine, 65*(2), 200–213.

Lincoln, K. D., Taylor, R. J., Bullard, K. M., Chatters, L. M., Himle, J. A., Woodward, A. T., & Jackson, J. S. (2010). Emotional support, negative interaction and DSM IV lifetime disorders among older African Americans: Findings from the National Survey of American Life (NSAL). *International Journal of Geriatric Psychiatry, 25*(6), 612–621.

Lincoln, K. D., Taylor, R. J., & Chatters, L. M. (2003). Correlates of emotional support and negative interaction among older black Americans. *Journals of Gerontology: Social Sciences, 58B*(4), S225–S233.

Lincoln, K. D., Taylor, R. J., Chatters, L. M., & Jackson, J. S. (2012). Correlates of negative interaction and social support among African Americans and Black Caribbeans. *Journal of Family Issues.*

Lu, L. (1995). The relationship between subjective well-being and psychosocial variables in Taiwan. *Journal of Social Psychology, 135*(3), 351–357.

Luckey, I. (1994). African American elders: The support network of generational kin. *Families in Society: The Journal of Contemporary Human Services, 75*(2), 82–89.

Lüscher, K., & Pillemer, K. (1998). Intergenerational ambivalence: A new approach to the study of parent-child relations in later life. *Journal of Marriage and Family, 60*(2), 413–425.

Manson, J. E., Stampfer, M. J., Colditz, G. A., Willett, W. C., Rosner, B., Hennekens, C. H.,...Krolewski, A. S. (1991). Physical activity and incidence of non-insulin dependent diabetes mellitus in women. *The Lancet, 338,* 774–778.

Manson, J. E., WIllett, W. C., Stampfer, M. J., Colditz G. A., Hynter, D. J., Hankinson, S. E.,...Speizer, F. E. (1995). Body weight and mortality among women. *New England Journal of Medicine, 333,* 677–685.

Marmot, M. G. (2006). Status syndrome: A challenge to medicine. *Journal of the American Medical Association, 295*(11), 1304–1307.

Massey, D. S. (1986). The settlement process among Mexican migrants to the United States. *American Sociological Review, 51*(5), 670–684.

McDade, T. W., Louise, C. H., & Cacioppo, J. T. (2006). Psychosocial and behavioral predictors of inflammation in middle-aged and older adults: The Chicago health, aging, and social relations study, *Psychosomatic Medicine, 68*(3), 376–381.

McEwen, B. S., Magarinos, A. M., & Reagan, L. P. (2002). Studies of hormone action in the hippocampal formation: Possible relevance to depression and diabetes. *Journal of Psychosomatic Research, 53*(4), 883–890.

Mehta, K. M., Simonsick, E. M., Penninx, B., Schulz, R., Rubin, S. M., Satterfield, S., & Yaffe, K. (2004). Prevalence and correlates of anxiety symptoms in well-functioning older adults: Findings from the Healthy Aging and Body Composition Study. *Journal of the American Geriatric Society, 12,* 265–271.

Merz, E-M, & Consedine, N. S. (2009). The association of family support and well-being in later life depends on adult attachment style. *Attachment and Human Development, 11*(2), 203–221.

Milagros, C. R., King, J., Ma, Y., & Reed, G. W. (2004). Stress, social support, and cortisol: Inverse associations? *Behavioral medicine, 30*(1), 11–21.

Miller, G. E., Chen, E., Fok, A. K., Walker, H., Lim, A., Nicholls, E. F.,…Kobor, M. S. (2009). Low early-life social class leaves a biological residue manifested by decreased glucocorticoid and increased proinflammatory signaling. *Proceeding of the National Academy of Sciences of the United States of America, 106*(34), 14716–14721.

Miller, D. K., Malmstrom, T. K., Joshi, S., Andresen, E. M., Morely, J. E., & Wolinsky, F. D. (2004). Clinically relevant levels of depressive symptoms in community-dwelling middle-aged African Americans. *Journal of the American Geriatric Society, 52*(5), 741–748.

Min, J. W., Moon, A., & Lubben, J. E. (2005). Determinants of psychological distress over time among older Korean immigrants and non-Hispanic white elders: Evidence from a two-wave panel study. *Aging & Mental Health, 9*(3), 210–222.

Moore, G. (*1990*). Structural determinants of men's and women's personal networks. *American Sociological Review, 55*(5), 726–735.

Mui, A. C. (1996). Correlates of psychological distress among Mexican, Cuban, and Puerto Rican elders living in the USA. *Journal of Cross-Cultural Gerontology, 11*(2), 131–147.

Mui, A. C., & Kang, S. Y. (2006). Acculturation stress and depression among Asian immigrant elders. *Social Work, 51*(3), 243–255.

Mui, A. C., Burnette, D., & Chen, L. M. (2001). Cross-cultural assessment of geriatric depression: A review of the CES-D and the GDS. *Journal of Mental Health and Aging, 7*(1), 137–164.

Newsom, J. T, & Schulz, R. (1996). Social support as a mediator in the relation between functional status and quality of life in older adults. *Psychology and Aging, 11*(1), 34–44.

Newsom, J. T., Nishishiba, M., Morgan, D. L., & Rook, K. S. (2003). The relative importance of three domains of positive and negative social exchanges: A longitudinal model with comparable measures. *Psychology and Aging, 18*(4), 746–754.

Ng, D. M., & Jeffery, R. W. (2003). Relationships between perceived stress and health behaviors in a sample of working adults. *Health Psychology, 22*(6), 638–642.

Nguyen-Rodriguez, S. T., Chou, C. P., Unger, J. B., & Spruijt-Metz, D. (2008). BMI as a moderator of perceived stress and emotional eating in adolescents, *Eating Behaviors, 9*(2), 238–246.

Nguyen-Rodriguez, S. T., Unger, J. B., & Spruijt-Metz, D. (2009). Psychological determinants of emotional eating in adolescence. *Journal of Treatment & Prevention, 17*(3), 211–224.

Nguyen-Michel, S. T., Unger, J. B., Hamilton, J., & Spruijt-Metz, D. (2006). Associations between physical activity and perceived stress/hassles in college students. *General Psychology, 22*(3), 179–188.

Nguyen-Michel, S. T., Unger, J. B., & Spruijt-Metz, D. (2007). Dietary correlates of emotional eating in adolescence. *Appetite, 49*(2), 494–499.

Noel, J. G., & Epstein, J. (2003) Social support and health among senior Internet users: Results of an online survey. *Journal of Technology in Human Services, 21*(3), 35–54.

Ogden, C. L., Carroll, M. D., McDowell, M. A., & Flegal, K. M. (2007). *Obesity among adults in the United States: No statistically significant change since 2003–2004.* Hyattsville, Maryland: U.S. Department of Health and Human Services, Center for Disease Control and Prevention, National Center for Health Statistics; November 2007. NCHS Data Brief.

Okun, M. A., & Keith, V. M. (1998). Effects of positive and negative social exchanges with various sources on depressive symptoms in younger and older adults. *Journal of Gerontology, 53*(1), 4–20.

Olga, E., & Steptoe, A. (2001). Social support at work, heart rate, and cortisol: A self-monitoring study. *Journal of Occupational Health Psychology, 6*(4), 361–370.

Olwig, K. F. (2001). New York as a locality in a global family network. In N. Foner (Ed.), *Islands in the City: West Indian Migration to New York* (pp. 142–160). Berkeley, CA: University of California Press.

Ong, A. D., & Allaire, J. (2005). Cardiovascular intraindividual variability in later life: The influence of social connectedness and positive emotions. *Psychology and Aging, 20*(3), 476–485.

Ottosson, M., Lönnroth, P., Björntorp, P., & Edén, S. (2000). Effects of cortisol and growth hormone on lipolysis in human adipose tissue. *The Journal of Clinical Endocrinology & Metabolism, 85*(2), 799–803.

Paffenbarger, R. S., Jr., Wing, A. L., & Hyde, R. T. (1978). Physical activity as an index of heart attack risk in college alumni. *American Journal of Epidemiology, 108*(3), 161–175.

Paffenbarger, R. S., Jr., Jung, D. L., Leung, R. W., & Hyde, R. T. (1991). Physical activity and hypertension: An epidemiological view. *Annals of Medicine, 23*(3), 319–327.

Pagel, M. D., Erdly, W. W., & Becker, J. (1987). Social networks: We get by with (and in spite of) a little help from our friends. *Journal of Personality and Social Psychology, 53*(4), 793–804.

Palmore, E. (1981). The facts on aging quiz: Part two. *The Gerontologist, 21*(4), 431–437.

Pasquali, R., Vicennati, V., & Gambineri, A. (2002). Adrenal and gonadal function in obesity. *Journal of Endocrinological Investigation, 25*(10), 893–898.

Pearlin, L. I., & Schooler, C. (1978). The structure of coping. *Journal of Health and Social Behavior, 19*(1), 2–21.

Peirce, R. S., Frone, M. R., Russell, M., Cooper, M. L., & Mudar, P. (2000). A longitudinal model of social contact, social support, depression, and alcohol use. *Health Psychology, 19*(1), 28–38.

Perry, C. M., & Johnson, C. L. (1994). Families and support networks among African American oldest-old. *International Journal of Aging and Human Development, 38*(1), 41–50.

Fox, S. (2004). *Older Americans and the Internet.* Director of Research, March 25, 2004; Pew Research Center, Washington, DC. http://www.pewinternet.org/~/media//Files/Reports/2004/PIP_Seniors_Online_2004.pdf.pdf

Madden, M. (2010). *Older adults and social media: Social networking use among those ages 50 and older nearly doubled over the past year.* Senior Research Specialist, August 27, 2010; Pew Research Center, Washington, DC. http://pewinternet.org/Reports/2010/Older-Adults-and-Social-Media.aspx

Plaza, D. (2000). Transnational grannies: The changing family responsibilities of elderly African Caribbean-born women resident in Britain. *Social Indicators Research, 51*(1), 75–105.

Powell, L. M., Slater, S., Mirtcheva, D., Bao, Y., & Chaloupka, F. J. (2007). Food store availability and neighborhood characteristics in the United States. *Preventive Medicine, 44*(3), 189–195.

Pugliesi, K., & Shook, S. L. (1998). Gender, ethnicity, and network characteristics: Variation in social support resources. *Sex Roles, 38*(1), 215–238.

Rohrer, J., Pierce, J. R., Jr., & Denison, A. (2004). Walkability and self-rated health in primary care patients. *BMC Family Practice, 5*(1), 29.

Rook, K. S. (1984). The negative side of social interaction: Impact on psychological well-being. *Journal of Personality and Social Psychology, 46*(5), 1097–1108.

Rosenbloom, C. A., & Whittington, F. (1993). The effects of bereavement on eating behaviors and nutrient intakes in elderly widowed persons. *Journal of Gerontology, 48*(4), S223–S229.

Schone, B. S., & Weinick, R. M. (1998). Health-related behaviors and the benefits of marriage for elderly persons. *The Gerontologist, 38*(5), 618–627.

Schuster, T. L., Kessler, R. C., & Aseltine, R. H. (1990). Supportive interactions, negative interactions and depressed mood. *American Journal of Community Psychology, 18*(3), 423–438.

Seeman, T. E., Berkman, L. F., Blazer, D., & Rowe, J. W. (1994). Social ties and support and neuroendocrine function: The MacArthur Studies of Successful Aging. *Annals of Behavioral Medicine, 16*(2), 95–106.

Seeman, T., & Chen, X. (2002). Risk and protective factors for physical functioning in older adults with and without chronic conditions. *Journal of Gerontology: Social Sciences, 57*(3), S135–S144.

Seeman, T., Singer, B., Ryff, C., Dienberg Love, G., & Levy-Storms, L. (2002). Social relationships, gender, and allostatic load across two age cohorts. *Psychosomatic Medicine, 64*(3), 395–406.

Shaw, L. H., & Gant, L. M. (2002). In defense of the Internet: The relationship between Internet communication and depression, loneliness, self-esteem, and perceived social support. *Cyberpsychology & Behavior, 5*(2), 157–171.

Sherwood, A., & Turner, J. (1992). A conceptual and methodological overview of cardiovascular reactivity research. In J. Turner, A. Sherwood, & K. Light (Eds.), *Individual differences in cardiovascular response to stress* (pp. 3–32). New York, NY: Plenum.

Shibusawa, T., & Mui, A. C. (2001). Stress, coping, and depression among Japanese American elders. *Journal of Gerontological Social Work, 36*(1–2), 63–81.

Shin, K. R. (1994). Psychosocial predictors of depressive symptoms in Korean American women in New York City. *Women & Health, 21*(1), 73–82.

Silverstein, M., & Litwak, E. (1993). A task-specific typology of intergenerational family structure in later life. *The Gerontologist, 33*(2), 258–264.

Small, M. L., & McDermott, M. (2006). The presence of organizational resources in poor urban neighborhoods: An analysis of average and contextual effects. *Social Forces, 84*(3), 1697–1724.

Sotomayor, M., & Randolph, S. (1988). A preliminary review of caregiving issues and the Hispanic family. In M. Sotomayor & H. Curiel (Eds.), *Hispanic elderly: A cultural signature* (pp. 137–160). Edinburg, TX: Pan American University Press.

Stamler, R., Stamler, J., Gosch, F. C., Civinelli, J., Fishman, J., McKeever, P., ... Dyer, A. R. (1989). Primary prevention of hypertension by nutritional-hygienic means: Final report of a randomized controlled trial. *Journal of the American Medical Association, 262*(13), 1801–1807.

Stephens, M. A., Kinney, J. M., Norris, V. K., & Ritchie, S. W. (1987). Social networks as assets and liabilities in recovery from stroke by geriatric patients. *Psychology and Aging, 2*(2), 125–129.

Stunkard, A. J., Faith, M. S., & Allison, K. C. (2003). Depression and obesity. *Biological Psychiatry, 54*(3), 330–337.

Sturm, R., & Datar, A. (2005). Body mass index in elementary school children, metropolitan area food prices and food outlet density. *Public Health, 119*(12), 1059–1068.

Swindle, R., Heller, K., & Frank, M. (2000). Differentiating the effects of positive and negative social transactions in HIV illness. *Journal of Community Psychology, 28*(1), 35–50.

Szapocznik, J., Lombard, J., Martinez, F., Mason, C. A., Gorman-Smith, D., Plater-Zyberk, E., ... Spokane, A. (2006). The impact of the built environment on children's school grades: The role of diversity of use in a Hispanic neighborhood. *American Journal of Community Psychology, 38*(3–4), 299–310.

Tang, T. S., Brown, M. B., Funnell, M. M., & Anderson, R. M. (2008). Social support, quality of life, and self-care behaviors among African Americans with type 2 diabetes. *The Diabetes Educator, 34*(2), 266–276.

Tanne, D., Goldbourt, U., & Medalie, J. H. (2004). Perceived family difficulties and prediction of 23-year stroke mortality among middle-aged men. *Cerebrovascular Diseases, 18*(4), 277–282.

Taylor, R. J. (1986). Receipt of support from family among Black Americans: Demographic and familial differences. *Journal of Marriage and the Family, 48*(1), 6–77.

Taylor, R. J., Chatters, L. M., & Levin, J. (2004). *Religion in the lives of African Americans: social, psychological, and health perspectives.* California: Sage.

Tilly, C., & Brown, C. H. (1967). On uprooting, kinship and the auspices of migration. *International Journal of Comparative Sociology, 8*, 139–164.

Travis, L. A., Lyness, J. M., Shields, C. G., King, D. A., & Cox, C. (2004). Social support, depression, and functional disability in older adult primary-care patients. *American Journal of Geriatric Psychiatry, 12*(3), 265–271.

Troll, L. E. (1994). Family-embedded vs. family-deprived oldest-old: A study of contrasts. *International Journal of Aging and Human Development, 38*(1), 51–63.

Turner, R. J., & Avison, W. R. (2003). Status variations in stress exposure: Implications for the interpretation of research on race, socioeconomic status, and gender. *Journal of Health and Social Behavior, 44*(4), 488–505.

Turner-Cobb, J. M., Sephton, S. E., Koopman, C., Blake-Mortimer, J., & Spiegel, D. (2000). Social support and salivary cortisol in women with metastatic breast cancer. *Psychosomatic Medicine, 62*(3), 337–345.

U.S. Census. *Age and sex composition, 2010.* 2010 Census briefs. May, 2011. U.S. Department of Commerce Economics and Statistics Administration U.S. Census Bureau, Washington, DC.

Uchino, B. N. (2006). Social support and health: A review of physiological processes potentially underlying links to disease outcomes. *Journal of Behavioral Medicine, 29*(4), 377–387.

Uchino, B. N., Cacioppo, J. T., & Kiecolt-Glaser, J. K. (1996). The relationship between social support and physiological processes: A review with emphasis on underlying mechanisms and implications for health. *Psychological Bulletin, 119*(3), 488–531.

Uchino, B. N., Cacioppo, J. T., Malarkey, W., Glaser, R., & Kiecolt-Glaser, J. K. (1995). Appraisal support predicts age-related differences in cardiovascular function in women. *Health Psychology, 14*(6), 556–562.

Uchino, B. N., Holt-Lunstad, J., Uno, D., & Betancourt, R. (1999). Social support and age-related differences in cardiovascular function: An examination of potential mediators. *Annals of Behavioral Medicine, 21*(2), 135–142.

Uchino, B. N., Holt-Lunstad, J., Uno, D., & Flinders, J. B. (2001). Heterogeneity in the social networks of young and older adults: Prediction of mental health and cardiovascular reactivity during acute stress. *Journal of Behavioral Medicine, 24*(4), 361–382.

United States Department of Health and Human Services. (1996). *Physical activity and health: A report of the surgeon general.* Atlanta, GA: U.S. Department of Health and Human Services, Centers for Disease Control and Prevention, National Center for Chronic Disease Prevention and Health Promotion.

van Willigen, J., Chadha, N. K., & Kedia, S. (1995). Personal networks and sacred texts: Social aging in Delhi, India. *Journal of Cross-Cultural Gerontology, 10*(3), 175–198.

Vega, W. A., & Sribney, W. M. (2005). Seeking care for alcohol problems: Patterns of need and treatment among Mexican origin adults in central California. *Alcoholism Treatment Quarterly, 23*(2–3), 29–50.

Vena, J. E., Graham, S., Zielezny, M., Brasure, J., & Swanson, M. (1987). Occupational exercise and risk of cancer, *American Journal of Clinical Nutrition, 45*(1), 318–327.

Vierck, E., & Hodges, K. (2003). Aging: Demographics, health and health services. Westport, CT: Greenwood Press.

Waldinger, R. (1996). *Still the promised city? African Americans and new immigrants in postindustrial New York.* Cambridge, MA: Harvard University Press.

Waters, M. (1999). *Black identities.* Cambridge, MA: Harvard University Press.

Watzlawick, P., Beavin, J. H., & Jackson, D. D. (1967). *Pragmatics of human communication: A study of interactional patterns, pathologies & paradoxes.* New York, NY: Norton.

Wethington, E. & Kessler, R. C. (1986). Perceived support, received support and adjustment to stressful events. *Journal of Health and Social Behavior, 27*(1), 78–89.

Wilcox, S., Evenson, K. R., Aragaki, A., Wassertheil-Smoller, S., Mouton, C. P., & Loevinger, B. L. (2003). The effects of widowhood on physical and mental health, health behaviors, and health outcomes: The Women's Health Initiative. *Health Psychology, 22*(5), 513–522.

Wolkowitz, O. M., Epel, E. S., Reus, V. I., & Mellon, S. H. (2010). Depression gets old fast: Do stress and depression accelerate cell aging? *Depress Anxiety, 27*(4), 327–338.

Zautra, A. J., Burleson, M. H., Matt, K. S., Roth, S., & Burrows, L. (1994). Interpersonal stress, depression, and disease activity in rheumatoid arthritis and osteoarthritis patients. *Health Psychology, 13*(2), 139–148.

Zenk, S. N., Schulz, A. J., Israel, B. A., James, S. A., Bao, S., & Wilson, M. L. (2006). Fruit and vegetable access differs by community racial composition and socioeconomic position in Detroit, Michigan. *Ethnicity & Disease, 16*(1), 275–280.

CHAPTER 4

Religion and Spirituality Among Older African Americans, Asians, and Hispanics

Linda M. Chatters, Ann W. Nguyen,
and Robert Joseph Taylor

Religion and spirituality have a long research tradition in gerontology in their own right and in regard to issues such as social role engagement, psychological well-being, physical and mental health, and coping with life stressors and losses (Koenig, King, & Carson, 2012; Levin, 1994). Religious and spiritual frameworks address essential questions of the meaning of life and purpose, especially in the face of the personal and social losses associated with aging. Religious concerns are especially salient for older adults and members of racial and ethnic minority groups who are more likely than younger persons and non-Hispanic whites to affiliate with a religious tradition and have high rates of religious behaviors and sentiments (Krause, 2010; Levin, Taylor, & Chatters, 1994; Pew Forum on Religion & Public Life, 2008; Taylor, Chatters, Jayakody, & Levin, 1996). For racial/ethnic minority older adults, religion and spirituality embody values, beliefs, and behaviors that are culturally congruent, occur within the context of familiar and trusted social relationships and communities, and represent distinctive cultural resources that provide social, psychological, and material benefits to adherents. These benefits are particularly important for foreign-born elderly who, because of linguistic barriers and acculturative (relocation) stress, may be at greater risk for social isolation and poor functioning (Kang, Domanski, & Moon, 2009; Mui & Kang, 2006). Finally, religion and spirituality is particularly beneficial to persons who are socially marginalized, integrate religion into their lives to a significant degree, and use religious beliefs and practices to manage stressful situations (Ellison & Taylor, 1996; Pargament, 2002)—circumstances that often characterize the racial and ethnic minority elderly.

This chapter is a selective review of research on religion and spirituality across three groups of racial and ethnic minority older adults—African American, Asian American, and Hispanic/Latino. We employ a definition of religion similar to Koenig et al. (2012) who indicate that "'religion'...involves beliefs, practices, and rituals related to the sacred....religion originates in an established tradition that arises out of a community with common beliefs and practices (page 37)." Defining "spirituality" is a more difficult task, given changes over time in its meaning and imprecision in its conceptualization and measurement (see Koenig et al.,

2012 for an extended discussion). Nonetheless, spirituality is important for appreciating those faith traditions with distinctive emphases on transcendent states, as well as the beliefs and devotional practices that focus on explicitly spiritual content.

In reviewing this diverse literature, several caveats are necessary. Research on religion and spirituality is predominated by studies of Christian, non-Hispanic whites, whereas investigations focusing on racial/ethnic minorities and adherents of non-Christian faith traditions and spiritual practices are limited in overall numbers, scope, and depth. Available studies do not always stratify analyses by age, or focus specifically on older adults. Furthermore, study samples are often designated by pan-ethnic labels (i.e., Hispanic, Asian American) without reference to differences by country of origin/ancestry (e.g., Mexico vs. Puerto Rico) that are consequential for religion/spirituality. To the degree possible, this discussion identifies the specific subgroups (e.g., Mexican American, Puerto Rican) that comprise the different racial/ethnic populations that are examined. Methodological challenges in this research area include differences in sample sizes and types (e.g., national studies, community samples, clinical studies) and in the analysis strategies used (i.e., bivariate, multivariate analyses) across studies. Finally, this brief summary can only touch upon the theoretical frameworks of mechanisms and pathways linking religion/spirituality and health and well-being outcomes (see Chatters, 2000; Koenig, McCullough, & Larson, 2001; Koenig et al., 2012) and the distinctive historical and sociocultural context of religion/spirituality for each group; readers are referred to other works cited in this chapter for in-depth discussions.

The chapter has three sections corresponding to each racial/ethnic group examined. For each, we first discuss major denomination and faith traditions, as well as information about types and patterns of participation and their sociodemographic correlates. Second, we examine informal social support provisions within faith communities and the types of assistance exchanged. In this regard, ethnic and immigrant churches are especially important in establishing a sense of community and providing important social welfare and civic functions for immigrant groups. Religion and spirituality, through a variety of psychosocial mechanisms and pathways (e.g., social support, behavioral proscriptions), are thought to have largely beneficial impacts on physical and mental health. Accordingly, the third section examines associations between religion, spirituality and physical/mental health, and psychological well-being. Following this, in the fourth section, we focus on religious coping strategies—using religious cognitions, behaviors, and resources to manage the perception, occurrence or consequences of threatening events—and their sociodemographic correlates and relationships with health and well-being. The chapter concludes with a discussion of gaps in the literature on religion and spirituality and identifies priority areas for future research within and across diverse groups of racial and ethnic minority elderly.

AFRICAN AMERICAN ELDERS

Distribution and Patterns

A tradition of research documents the historical and cultural significance of religion and spirituality for African American elderly (Billingsley, 1999; Lincoln & Mamiya, 1990). National surveys and polls of the U.S. population indicate that African Americans have the highest levels of religious involvement (Newport, 2006; Pew Forum on Religion & Public Life, 2008), are most likely to report a formal religious affiliation, and are least likely to be unaffiliated. Even among unaffiliated African Americans, 89% indicate that they are either very or somewhat religious (Taylor, 1988). Overall, 60% of African Americans are affiliated with the historically black denominations, whereas roughly 20% are members of predominately white denominations. African American elderly have higher rates of involvement across all forms of religious participation (e.g., organizational involvement, devotional behaviors, religious identification, and salience) than their white counterparts (Krause 2010; Krause & Chatters, 2005; Levin et al., 1994; Taylor et al., 1996; Taylor, Chatters, & Jackson, 2007a). Fifty-two percent of African American elders are Baptist, 9% identify as Methodist, 7% are Pentecostal, and 6% report being Catholic. Twenty-one percent of African Americans elders report other denominations and religions, whereas 5% indicate no religious affiliation (Taylor et al., 2007a). With respect to spirituality, African American elders are more likely than older whites to view spirituality as being important in their lives and to identify as being spiritual (Taylor et al., 2007a). Across all age ranges, African Americans are more likely than older whites to indicate that they are "both religious *and* spiritual," while being less likely to indicate that they are "spiritual only" or "neither religious nor spiritual" (Chatters et al., 2008).

For the African American elderly population, those who are older (Chatters & Taylor, 1989; Levin et al., 1994; Taylor et al., 2004), Southerners (Taylor, Chatters, Bullard, Wallace, & Jackson, 2009; Taylor, Chatters, & Jackson, 2007a; Taylor, Chatters, & Levin, 2004), and who are married (Taylor et al., 2007a; Taylor et al., 2009) report higher rates of religion and spirituality. Although older African American women have overall higher rates of religiosity and spirituality (Chatters, Levin, & Taylor, 1992; Levin et al., 1994; Taylor et al., 2004; Taylor et al., 2009), older men report spending more time in ancillary church activities and roles (e.g., maintenance of church property), indicating a male advantage for specific types of religious time use (Taylor et al., 2009). Findings for socioeconomic status are mixed: income is positively associated with service attendance and education is positively related to reading religious materials (Taylor et al., 2007a). However, both are negatively associated with subjective religiosity and spirituality and felt importance of religion, indicating that elders of lower income and education are more likely to invest in religious identities (Newport, 2006; Taylor et al., 2007a).

In a study of the full adult age range, African Americans were the most likely to report that spirituality is important in their lives and view themselves as being spiritual (self-defined), followed by Caribbean blacks and non-Hispanic whites (Taylor, Chatters, & Jackson, 2009). Being older, female, married, a Southerner, having more years of formal education, and identifying as Pentecostal was associated with higher levels of the importance of spirituality among African Americans. Similarly, age, gender, education, marital status, and denomination were associated with self-descriptions as a spiritual person.

Black Caribbeans are an important, but often unrecognized, ethnic subgroup of the black American population (Logan & Deane, 2003), whose diverse religious beliefs and practices are a central component of both their life experiences and their immigration histories (Bashi, 2007). Two articles provide a comprehensive overview of religious participation among older black Caribbeans (Taylor et al., 2007a, 2007b). Although black Caribbean elders' patterns of religious involvement are similar to that of native-born African Americans, overall they have different denominational profiles and are less likely to affiliate with Baptist (23%) and Methodist (5%) denominations, while being more likely to affiliate with Catholic (18%), Episcopalian (4%), and Pentecostal (11%) traditions or to have no affiliation (8%; Taylor et al., 2007a). Older Caribbean blacks and African Americans are both noted to have high rates of religious participation and spirituality, but black Caribbean elders are less likely to indicate that they are an official member of a church (Taylor et al., 2007a). Women and married persons show higher rates of service attendance and devotional behaviors than men and unmarried persons. Older black Caribbeans with more years of education are more likely to attend services than those with less education, whereas lower income elderly participate in church activities and nonorganizational behaviors (prayer, religious reading) at higher rates and report greater subjective religiosity than their higher income counterparts. Older black Caribbeans who immigrated less than 35 years ago have higher levels of religious participation than those born in the United States, and persons of Jamaican heritage participate in congregational activities more frequently than those from other English-speaking countries. These findings suggest that factors related to country of origin and immigration history may be important in shaping distinctive religious profiles among older black Caribbeans.

Communities and Social Networks

The black Church is a central institution within African American communities and a significant source of support (Lincoln & Mamiya, 1990). Formally organized initiatives and programs, assistance from clergy, and informal social networks within the black Church play a vital role in sustaining human, social, and political capital within African American communities (Billingsley, 1999; Chatters et al., 2011; Taylor & Chatters, 1986a, 1986b, 1988; Taylor et al., 2004; Walls, 1992). Roughly, six in ten African American elderly report assistance from church-based social support networks, such as direct aid and services (e.g., help during illness, monetary loans, transportation), socioemotional support (e.g., companionship, prayer), and cognitive aid (e.g., advice and information), as the most common types of aid (Morrison, 1991; Taylor & Chatters, 1986a). Morrison (1991) found that elderly African Americans who are ill received support in the form of visitations by clergy or laypersons, help with chores, small cash gifts, transportation to church or medical services, and provision of recorded sermons. For physically healthy African American elders, small, primary groups, such as choirs and men's fellowship groups provided social support rather than the congregation as a whole. For older African Americans, family provides more overall support than church members (Walls & Zarit, 1991), as well as more emotional versus instrumental support, whereas church members provide more instrumental as opposed to emotional support (Walls, 1992). In a study of older adults, older age was positively associated with receiving church support for older persons with adult children, but was negatively associated among childless elderly, indicating the importance of children in the church support relationship (Taylor & Chatters, 1986a). Although African Americans typically receive both family support and assistance from church-based networks (Taylor & Chatters, 1986a, 1986b), older persons are more likely than their younger counterparts to report not receiving help from either group or relying exclusively on church networks (Chatters, Taylor, Lincoln, & Schroepfer, 2002).

In terms of racial comparisons, older African Americans are more likely than older whites to both give and receive social support, exchange greater amounts of social support, and to anticipate receiving more support from church members (Krause, 2002, 2010; Krause, 2011; Krause & Bastida, 2011e). Intensive social support exchanges, in part, reflect the fact that religious and secular functions within black churches are closely aligned with one another (Lincoln & Mamiya, 1990). For example, black elders are more likely than white elders to indicate that their secular social support network is significantly influenced by social relationships maintained in their church (Krause, 2011). Features of older African Americans' religious involvement (i.e., high levels of religious attendance and membership, Baptist affiliation, involvement in church-based support networks, attitudes concerning the importance of church), reflect a distinctive social context that is associated with higher amounts of assistance (Krause, 2002, 2008b; Taylor et al., 1996; Taylor & Chatters, 1986b; Taylor & Chatters, 1988; Taylor, Lincoln, & Chatters, 2005). Further, those with extensive church-based ties and involvement (e.g., formal membership, regular attendance) benefit most from church support networks (Krause, 2002).

In addition to congregational support, older African Americans regard clergy as important sources of assistance (Chatters et al., 2011; Taylor et al., 2004; Taylor, Ellison, Chatters, Levin, & Lincoln, 2000). Clergy typically have long-standing relationships with congregants characterized by high levels of authority, esteem, and interpersonal trust (Taylor et al., 2000), similar worldviews and perspectives, and familiarity with the social conditions and life circumstances facing congregants (Kramer et al., 2007). Pastors and ministers are important members of African American communities and are instrumental in providing counseling, resources, and assistance to congregants to address a range of personal challenges including family/marital difficulties, economic problems, and substance abuse (Bohnert et al., 2010; Taylor et al., 2004). For example, African American adults 30 years of age and above were more likely than persons 18 to 29 years to contact clergy for personal problems; however, controls for denomination eliminated this effect (Chatters et al., 2011). African Americans have more contact with clergy than do whites (Krause, 2008b) and older African Americans receive more emotional and tangible support from their pastors and anticipated receiving more support than older whites and Mexican Americans (Krause & Bastida, 2011e).

Religious institutions occupy a prominent role in black Caribbean communities (Maynard-Reid, 2000; McAlister, 1998; Waters, 1999) by providing social supports for individuals and families and assisting in the migration and resettlement process of recent arrivals. Many black Caribbeans belong to ethnically identified churches that, in addition to providing spiritual support and tangible assistance to members, function to enhance social relationships and connections with other immigrants and reinforce a sense of ethnic identity (Waters, 1999).

Health and Well-Being

A large body of research across different data collections and designs (e.g., clinical samples, surveys, and epidemiological studies) and within diverse study populations confirms that religion is associated with physical and mental health and well-being (see reviews by Chatters, 2000; Koenig et al., 2012). Religious differences are evident in a diverse set of physical health outcomes, disease states, and health status indicators, as well as mental health, psychological well-being, lifestyle behaviors, and care utilization (Taylor et al., 2004). Explanations for religion–health linkages focus on behavioral and psychosocial mechanisms, including promotion of healthy behaviors and lifestyles, social support, and prosocial behaviors within religious institutions (Ellison & Levin, 1998; Taylor & Chatters 1988); religious coping strategies that alleviate stress (Pargament, 1997; Pargament, Smith, Koenig, & Perez, 1998); and beliefs/worldviews that promote a sense of identity, coherence, and meaning (Ellison & Levin, 1998). Moreover, because religion is multidimensional (e.g., denomination, attendance, devotional behaviors), different forms of involvement may demonstrate distinct functional relationships (e.g., protective, resource mobilization) with health measures and outcomes (see Chatters, 2000; Ellison & Levin, 1998; Koenig et al., 2012 for reviews). Associations in which religious factors are linked with better mental and physical health suggest that religion has preventive or protective effects. For example, among African American elderly, service attendance is associated with greater levels of life satisfaction (Levin, Chatters, & Taylor, 1995), self-rated health (Levin & Chatters, 1998), and a reduced likelihood of lifetime mood disorders (Chatters et al., 2008a). In contrast, negative associations between religion and health may suggest that (a) religious factors are, in fact, deleterious to health and well-being (Mochon, Norton, & Ariely, 2011; Pargament, 1999) or (b) that religious activities (e.g., resource mobilization) increase when people are attempting to cope with problem situations (e.g., stressors, poor health). For example, older adults may increase their devotional behaviors (e.g., reading religious materials and prayer) when faced with a chronic health problem, yielding a negative relationship between religion and health status. One recent study of lifetime prevalence of obsessive-compulsive disorder (OCD) among African Americans (Himle, Taylor, & Chatters, 2012) found that religious factors had different relationships to OCD; frequent service attendance was negatively associated with OCD prevalence, whereas Catholic affiliation and religious coping (prayer when dealing with stressful situations) were positively associated. Notably, older persons were significantly less likely to have OCD.

A recent study (Taylor, Chatters, & Joe, 2011) investigated the relationship between religious involvement and suicidal risk (lifetime prevalence of suicide ideation and attempts) among African Americans and black Caribbeans. For both groups, religious involvement was largely protective of suicidal ideation and attempts. Looking to God for strength, comfort, and guidance was protective against suicidal attempts and ideation, whereas stating that prayer is important in stressful situations was associated with higher levels of ideation for both groups and higher attempts among black Caribbeans. Similarly, recent studies of religion and *DSM-IV* 12-month and lifetime depression (Taylor, Chatters, & Abelson, 2012) also indicate that among African Americans, religious involvement is protective of depression.

Studies of religion and health among older African Americans indicate that better physical and mental health is associated with attendance, strength of affiliation, religious coping, and devotional behaviors (Ellison & Gay, 1990; Ferraro & Koch, 1994; Koenig et al., 1992; Levin & Chatters, 1998; Levin et al., 1995; Musick, 1996). Religion is also associated with poorer health in several studies (Ellison, 1995; Ferraro & Koch, 1994), likely reflecting the use of religion as a coping process. Religion also offsets or counterbalances the impact of negative events and stressors on measures of personal well-being and psychological distress, often through mediating constructs like optimism, self-esteem, and control perceptions (Krause, 1992; Krause & Tran, 1989).

Religion–health research has focused specific attention on features of church-based social support networks. Church-based social support has direct and mediated effects on a variety of health and psychosocial outcomes, such as self-rated health (Krause, 2006a), life satisfaction and well-being (Krause, 2004, 2008b), health care use (Krause, 2010), and lower mortality rates (Krause, 2006b). Among African American elders, church-based social support is associated with higher levels of psychological well-being and life satisfaction (Krause, 2010; Walls, 1992; Walls & Zarit, 1991), counteracts the harmful effect of financial strain on self-rated health (Krause, 2006a), and is associated with the use of religious coping strategies (Krause, 2004; Krause, 2010). Krause (2002) demonstrated that church-based emotional support is indirectly associated with optimism by way of contributing to a greater sense of closeness to God, which is linked to optimism. Optimism is also associated with better health. Compared to older whites, older African Americans are more likely to benefit from the indirect effects of church-based social support on health and well-being. Finally, Krause, Shaw, and Liang (2011) found that church-based support promotes healthy lifestyles for older African Americans (but not older whites), but specifically among those who feel strongly connected to their congregation. Church member support for healthy lifestyles was more important than either support from secular social network members or formal programs offered by the church in adopting healthy lifestyles.

Chatters and associates (Chatters, Taylor, Lincoln, Nguyen, & Joe, 2011) provided the first examination of the relationship between church support and lifetime prevalence of suicidal ideation and attempts. Subjective closeness to church members (an indicator of the degree to which individuals feel a sense of belonging with this social group) was inversely related to suicidal ideation, suggesting that it may prevent suicidal ideations. However, frequency of interaction with church members was positively associated with suicidal attempts. Although counterintuitive, this finding is consistent with the Resource Mobilization or Stressor Response model of religion and health (Ellison & Levin, 1998; Levin & Chatters, 2008), which hypothesizes that adversity may prompt individuals to seek assistance from their support networks. Within this context, persons who have previously attempted suicide may be more likely to interact with church members as a means of mobilizing their support resources as part of ongoing efforts to cope with difficult circumstances.

In addition to the noted benefits of social interactions within the church social support network, church life can also involve negative social interactions that have harmful effects on health and well-being (Ellison, Zhang, Krause, & Marcum, 2009; Krause, 2008a; Krause, Ellison, & Wulff, 1998). Krause and Bastida (2011e) found that elderly African Americans are more likely to encounter negative interactions with clergy and other congregants than elderly whites and Mexican Americans. Interestingly, although negative interactions inevitably arise as common features of social interactions within the church, they do not appear to have a detrimental effect on the health and well-being of older African Americans.

Religious and Spiritual Coping

Religious/spiritual coping is a multidimensional construct involving behaviors (e.g., individual prayer, devotional reading), attitudes and beliefs (e.g., efficacy of prayer in stressful situations), and psychological states (e.g., hope, personal efficacy) that have diverse impacts on the stress and coping process (Chatters et al., 2008; Koenig et al., 2001, 2012; Pargament, 1997, 1999; Taylor et al., 2004). Religious and spiritual coping is reflected in the stress and coping process in various ways (Ellison & Levin, 1998), including the reframing and reappraisal of the nature of problem situations, efforts to regulate emotional responses, enhancement of personal coping resources (i.e., efficacy, control perceptions), mobilization and use of social resources (e.g., social support, role modeling), and development of beneficial personal beliefs (e.g., hope, optimism).

As a group, African Americans are more likely than non-Hispanic whites to endorse and use religious and spiritual coping strategies (e.g., prayer, other spiritual practices) for acute and chronic health concerns (Chatters, Taylor, Jackson, & Lincoln, 2008; Gillum & Griffith, 2010; Mansfield, Mitchell, & King, 2002) in response to specific mood, anxiety, or substance disorders (Woodward et al., 2009) and for decisions concerning medical treatment (Johnson, Elbert-Avila, & Tulsky, 2005; True et al., 2005). Overall, 90% of African Americans and black Caribbeans indicate that prayer is an important source of coping when dealing with stress and that they rely on God for strength, support, and guidance (Chatters et al., 2008). Among African Americans, religious coping is unrelated to age, but is more common among women,

Southerners, married persons, and those with fewer years of education (Chatters et al., 2008). Furthermore, persons with lower levels of personal mastery and who face health problems and bereavement are more likely to use religious coping (Ellison & Taylor, 1996), and religious coping is perceived as being effective in reducing stress and worry (Jones, et al., 2006; Taylor, Lincoln, & Chatters, 2005).

Older African Americans engage in religious coping more frequently than older whites (Dilworth-Anderson, Williams, & Gibson, 2002; Krause & Chatters, 2005; Taylor et al., 2007a), and use religious resources and strategies in response to stressful events and to manage problematic life situations (Chatters et al., 2008; Ellison & Taylor, 1996), such as health problems (Dunn & Horgas, 2000; Mansfield et al., 2002; McAuley, Pecchioni, & Grant, 2000; Yeates et al., 2002), caregiving strains (Dilworth-Anderson et al., 2002; Miltiades & Pruchno, 2002; Taylor et al., 2007a; Wood & Parham, 1990), bereavement (Robinson, Thiel, Backus, & Meyer, 2006), and interpersonal problems (Taylor et al., 2004).

Notwithstanding the positive aspects of religious coping, there are circumstances in which religious coping is potentially detrimental (Pargament, 1997). Religious coping strategies that inhibit help-seeking behaviors and encourage exclusive treatment by clergy or lay religious/spiritual advisors may prevent or delay use of professional helpers (Chatters, 2000; Taylor et al., 2004), resulting in delays in receiving medical attention or diagnosis and treatment of a health problem, for instance, delays in breast cancer screening and treatment (Pargament, 1997). Furthermore, negative religious coping (Pargament, 1997) characterized by spiritual discontent, anger at God, punishing God reappraisals, and spiritual struggle are associated with negative health and well-being outcomes (Koenig et al., 2012). Clearly, religious coping is an important and central resource in handling life problems; however, under particular circumstances, it may be detrimental to the health and well-being of older African Americans.

ASIAN AMERICAN ELDERS

Distribution and Patterns

Currently, persons of Chinese, Asian Indian, Filipino, Vietnamese, Koreans, and Japanese descent account for 85% of the Asian American population (Hoeffel, Rastogi, Kim, & Shahid, 2012). Given these different ethnic and national origin subgroups, religious and spiritual traditions within the Asian American population are particularly diverse. Denominational profiles for Asian Americans reflect the religious/spiritual traditions of specific ethnic subgroups, as well as differential immigration patterns and trends from within specific countries. From 1990 to 2008, the percentage of Asian Americans reporting Christian denominations (e.g., Catholic, mainline Christian) has declined, whereas those reporting Eastern religions (e.g., Buddhist, Hindu, Taoist, Baha'i, Shintoist, Zoroastrian, Sikh) has increased (American Religious Identification Survey [ARIS], 2008). Overall, roughly 45% of Asian Americans identify as Christians (17% each reporting Catholic or Evangelical Christian), 23% indicate Buddhist or Muslim, and 3% identify other religions/faiths (Pew Forum on Religion & Public Life, 2008). Moreover, compared to other racial/ethnic groups Asians have the largest percentage (27%) of persons who indicate they are "Nones" (i.e., atheist, agnostic, secular, or humanist; ARIS, 2009).

Communities and Social Networks

Religious institutions (e.g., churches, temples) serve many important functions for Asian American immigrants. By linking immigrants to established social and community networks in the United States, worship communities facilitate immigrants' transition to a new environment and culture (i.e., as cultural brokers; Hagan & Ebaugh, 2003). Churches and their congregational support networks provide immigrants with information, as well as emotional and instrumental support that are crucial for negotiating unfamiliar environments. Immigrant churches reproduce and reinforce immigrants' home cultures, values, and religious practices, thereby providing a sense of identity and familiarity (Hagan & Ebaugh, 2003; Hirschman,

2004). For these reasons, worship communities and their members play a major role in immigrants' adaptation.

The immigrant church is a place where elderly Chinese Americans socialize with one another and develop a social support network outside of their families (Zhang & Zhan, 2009). Given their relative social isolation, many older immigrants rely on family as their only source of social support. Therefore, the elderly may have no alternative sources of support if they experience conflict with family members or if adult children are unable to provide the emotional support and care they need. Religious service attendance and participation in other activities (e.g., fellowship groups) at places of worship help elderly congregants develop social relationships and supportive ties outside of their families. Worship services and other activities (traditional holidays and observances) organized by the church are delivered in a manner that is congruent with congregants' culture (e.g., pastors of the same background and program and services in Chinese) and traditions. In addition, church-sponsored community centers provide social services, respite from their familial responsibilities, and additional opportunities for elders to socialize. Finally, for many older immigrants, the church reaffirms ethnic and cultural identities that are jeopardized in relocating to the United States (i.e., acculturative stress), fosters a sense of belonging, and helps them cope with life stressors.

Health and Well-Being

Elderly Asian Americans who are more religious report lower levels of depression and less negative affect than those who are less religious, whether measured by stated importance of religion in one's life, participation in organizational (e.g., service attendance) and nonorganizational religious activities (e.g., private prayers), or religious coping (Diwan, Jonnalagadda, & Balaswamy, 2004; Mui & Kang, 2006; Pang, 1998, 2000; Roh, 2010). Religion is also associated with perceptions of well-being among aging Asian Americans (Iwamasa & Iwasaki, 2011; Park, Roh, & Yeo, 2011; Pincharoen & Congdon, 2003). Japanese American elders report that religion and faith bring them inner peace and happiness (Iwamasa & Iwasaki, 2011), whereas Thai elderly indicate that connecting with religious resources (i.e., attending temple) helps them achieve comfort and security, peace of mind, harmony, acceptance, and meaning in life, which is viewed as a way to maintain health in later life (Pincharoen & Congdon, 2003). Finally, religiosity is positively correlated with life satisfaction among elderly Korean immigrants (Park et al., 2011).

Religious and Spiritual Coping

Asian American elders recognize religion as an important psychological resource for coping with life stressors. Asian Indian elderly report that religion imparts meaning and purpose to stressful life events (i.e., reframing) and, in turn, minimizes the negative impact of these situations (Diwan et al., 2004). Among Thai elderly, religious practices provide a sense of comfort and security about the future, which helps them maintain harmony and manage stress (Pincharoen & Congdon, 2003). In addition to Buddhist teachings and meditation, Thai elderly immigrants report that attending temple helped them cope with depression (Soonthornchaiya & Dancy, 2006). Participants noted that the temple was a sacred and peaceful space that calmed them and helped them find inner peace. In a similar vein, older Korean immigrants following the Taoist teaching of nondoing (i.e., nonaction that allows the passage of time and space alone to resolve problems) helped participants cope with life stressors and depression (Pang, 1998). Elderly Korean Americans who hold specific religious beliefs (e.g., good deeds rewarded and the existence of heaven) tend to be more resilient and better able to adapt and cope with major losses (e.g., death or divorce). Moreover, their religion and beliefs help them find meaning in life, which is linked to lower levels of death anxiety (Kim, 2008). Finally, a small study of elderly Chinese American immigrants (Lee & Chan, 2009) indicated that religious and spiritual traditions (Christianity, Buddhist, Confucian, Taoist) and beliefs (filial piety) were important for coping with life difficulties (e.g., chronic health problems) and maintaining family relationships.

HISPANIC AMERICAN ELDERS

Distribution and Patterns

Religion and spirituality are important concerns within the Hispanic population (Arredondo, Elder, Ayala, Campbell, & Baquero, 2005; Kaiser Family Foundation-Pew Hispanic Center, 2002; Pew Forum on Religion & Public Life, 2007). Within this diverse group, specific religious practices and spiritual beliefs (e.g., religiously oriented suffering) reflect the complex interplay between cultural traditions and values (e.g., collectivist and communal orientation) and contemporaneous events and processes, such as country of origin, nativity, and immigration experiences (Krause, 2012b; Krause & Bastida, 2009c; Pew Forum on Religion & Public Life, 2007). Hispanics as a group are more likely than non-Hispanic whites to view religion as being important, attend church at least weekly, and report use of intercessory prayer (Gillum & Griffith, 2010; Kaiser Family Foundation-Pew Hispanic Center, 2002). With respect to denomination, the Hispanic population overall is predominately Catholic (68%), with roughly 20% identifying as Protestants (Pew Forum on Religion & Public Life, 2007). Other religious traditions include other Christian denominations (<3%), other faiths (<1%), seculars (8%), and the unaffiliated (8%). Interestingly, recent data indicate significant growth in the percentage of Hispanics who characterize themselves as "nones" (atheist, agnostic, secular, humanist; ARIS, 2008).

Denominational affiliation among Hispanics is associated with social characteristics, such as country of origin, nativity, education and income, and primary language (Pew Forum on Religion & Public Life, 2007). For example, Hispanics of Mexican ancestry and the foreign born are more likely to identify as Catholic, whereas Puerto Ricans and native-born Hispanics are more likely to identify as evangelical Protestants, mainline Protestants, and secular. Thirty-nine percent of Hispanic Christians describe themselves as evangelical or "born again," including 28% of Catholics and 70% of non-Catholic Christians. Furthermore, Hispanics who identify as evangelical or other Christian traditions have higher rates of church attendance, daily prayer, and indicate that religion is "very important" in their lives (see Perl, Greely, & Gray, 2006, and Pew Forum on Religion & Public Life, 2007, for in-depth discussion of Hispanic denominational affiliation). Nativity differences indicate that foreign-born Hispanics are more likely than their native-born counterparts to view religion as being important and to attend weekly religious services (Kaiser Family Foundation-Pew Hispanic Center, 2002). Hispanics as a group and especially those foreign-born are more likely than African Americans and non-Hispanic whites to view religious institutions favorably (Kaiser Family Foundation-Pew Hispanic Center, 2002).

Among older adults, Mexican Americans engage in prayer (for oneself and for others) more often than do whites (Krause, 2012b); older Hispanics are more devout with respect to religious belief and practices and are more likely to be Catholic than their younger counterparts (NORC & AP-Univsion, 2010). Among older Mexican Americans, the oldest old have stronger beliefs in the efficacy of prayer, pray more often, and have higher God-mediated control perceptions, but attend services less often (Krause & Bastida, 2011c). Finally, gender differences indicate that elderly Latino women are more religious than men and are more likely to attend Mass and other religious events (Beyene, Becker, & Mayen, 2002). Similarly, older Mexican American men are less likely than women to pray (Krause & Bastida, 2011c).

Communities and Social Networks

Churches not only fulfill religious and spiritual needs, but are also important ethnically identified institutions (i.e., ethnic churches) in which support networks and social relationships are developed and maintained. Church networks provide various types of assistance (e.g., instrumental, emotional) within the context of a community of individuals with similar social characteristics, values, and beliefs. Information on the correlates of church-based support indicates that among older Mexican Americans, men and women are comparable in terms of social support exchanges with church members (Krause & Hayward, in press). However, men appear to benefit more than women in terms of their sense of connection to the congregation. Mexican American elders who attend services frequently receive higher levels of emotional and spiritual support from church members (Krause & Bastida, 2010; Krause, 2011; Krause & Bastida, 2011a). Frequent attendance affords more opportunities to build and strengthen relationships with others, which, in turn, foster higher levels of social integration within these networks. In addition to the tangible assistance provided (e.g., monetary, in-kind services), support exchanges enhance levels of social cohesion and connection with the church (Krause & Bastida, 2011a; Krause & Hayward, in press).

Health and Well-Being

A collection of early studies exploring associations between religion and spirituality and health and well-being among elderly Mexican Americans found positive associations between service attendance and self-rated health and life satisfaction (Levin & Markides, 1985), as well as longitudinal associations between service attendance and life satisfaction (Markides, 1983; Markides, Levin, & Ray, 1987). A recent longitudinal study (four waves of data) of cognitive decline among older Mexican Americans found that those attending religious services (i.e., social engagement) monthly, weekly, and more than weekly had slower rates of cognitive decline than did nonattenders. Controls for age, baseline cognitive functioning, functional disability, and sensory impairments partially explained, but did not eliminate this effect (Hill, Burdette, Angel, & Angel, 2006).

Krause and colleagues' work focuses on theoretically derived conceptual models of religion, well-being, and intervening psychosocial factors. In a study of religion, financial strain, and life satisfaction among older Mexican Americans, formal church involvement (service attendance and Bible study) was associated with a greater sense of religious meaning, which, in turn, was associated with higher life satisfaction (Krause & Bastida, 2011d). Financial strain limited elders' involvement in formal activities at the church, resulting in a diminished sense of religious meaning. In other words, financial strain indirectly impacts older Mexican American congregants' sense of religious meaning and life satisfaction through decreased participation in informal church activities. In addition, those receiving spiritual support from other congregants were more likely to report that their faith helps them better understand themselves and others, feel more grateful to God, and have a strong sense of religious meaning (Krause, 2012a).

Older Mexican Americans' feelings of closeness to God (Krause & Bastida, 2011b) and beliefs regarding the efficacy of prayers to the Virgin Mary and saints are associated with an optimistic outlook on life and more positive perceptions of health (Krause & Bastida, 2011c). Beliefs in prayer efficacy are associated with more frequent prayer that, in turn, is related to greater God-mediated control beliefs (for solving problems and attaining life goals) that are associated with greater optimism and better self-rated health. Further, research by Krause and associates demonstrates the interconnections between religious practices (e.g., service attendance, devotional behaviors), social integration, support within the church, personal control, and self-rated health. Older Mexican Americans who believe in the importance of the practice of "making mandas" (i.e., requests to a religious figure on the promise to perform a religious act) report a higher sense of personal control and better self-rated health than those who regard this ritual as less important (Krause & Bastida, 2010). The underlying pathways indicate that church attendance and receiving spiritual support are associated with felt importance of making mandas, which indirectly influences self-rated health by increasing a sense of personal control. Similarly, a sense of belonging to one's congregation is also related to an increased sense of personal control among elderly Mexican Americans, which, in turn, is associated with positive ratings of self-rated health (Krause & Bastida, 2011a).

Religious and Spiritual Coping

Older Hispanics employ a variety of religious and spiritual strategies and practices to cope with life problems. As a group, they are more likely than non-Hispanic whites to use prayer for health reasons, but less likely to report using other spiritual practices (i.e., meditation), to address health issues (Gillum & Griffith, 2010). Among Latino elderly, women are more likely than men to state that they rely on their faith to cope with life stressors (Beyene et al., 2002). Older Mexican American women are more likely than men to search for something positive in personal suffering, indicate a close relationship with God (Krause & Bastida, 2011b), and have a higher sense of prayer efficacy and God-mediated control (Krause & Bastida, 2011c). Older Mexican Americans with lower levels of education are more likely to both search for positive meaning in suffering and suffer in silence, whereas elders who were born in Mexico are more likely to suffer in silence and are less likely to search for positive meaning in suffering and indicate a close relationship with God. Finally, the practice of making mandas does not vary by age, gender, or marital status; however, older Mexican Americans with fewer years of education are more likely to engage in this religious ritual (Krause & Bastida, 2010).

Krause and associates' work on religious coping among older Mexican Americans illustrates the complex interrelationships between religious beliefs and behaviors, psychosocial factors, and ethnically derived coping strategies. Older Mexican Americans use religiously oriented suffering as a coping resource by searching for religious meaning in negative events and identifying positive aspects of their suffering (Krause & Bastida, 2009a; Krause & Bastida, 2011b). Although positive suffering is related to both positive and negative self-evaluations of health, its relationship to positive self-rated health is more robust (Krause & Bastida, 2011b). More importantly, for older Mexican Americans, the pain and suffering experienced by Divine figures (Jesus, the Virgin Mary) is an integral part of religious life, has a central role in religious worship, and is associated with stronger religious faith and positive psychosocial factors such as optimism and better self-assessed health (Krause & Bastida, 2009a, 2011b).

In contrast, suffering in silence, as a distinct coping strategy, was associated with poorer self-rated health. Through experiencing their own pain and suffering, elders emulated the experiences of Jesus and deepened their faith in God through awareness of their need for God and instilling gratefulness for what God has done for them. Pain and suffering also helps individuals understand lessons taught in the New Testament and allow people who have sinned to return to their faith. Some older Mexican Americans report positive aspects to pain and suffering by promoting empathy for other's difficulties. Pain and suffering is also regarded as empowering when understood in reference to Jesus and the Virgin Mary, who were able to overcome their own pain and suffering. Finally, pain and suffering provides an opportunity to atone for a person's misdeeds.

Older Mexican Americans also report that contact with deceased loved ones is useful in coping with life stressors (Krause & Bastida, 2009b, in press). Characteristics of these interactions vary greatly from one person to another; some individuals report being able to directly see the dead while others are only able to hear, feel, or smell deceased loved ones. Contact with the dead facilitates the grieving process by allowing mourners to express their thoughts, feelings, and concerns to the deceased, including interacting with the deceased for help with their own problems. Maintaining contact with the dead also allays concerns about what has happened to loved ones and helps ease concerns about the uncertainty of death and transition to the next life. A recent study (Krause, 2012b) examined the relationships between praying for others and depressed affect and somatic symptoms of depression among older Mexican Americans living in distressed neighborhoods. Praying for others appeared to moderate the negative effect of living in poor neighborhood conditions on depressive symptoms; those who do not pray for others were more likely to experience greater depressed affect.

In addition to the positive effects on physical and mental health and well-being, religion and spirituality can have negative impacts (e.g., negative interactions, guilt, religious doubt, negative religious coping) as well (Pargament, 1997). Among older Mexican Americans, both religious doubt (e.g., about religious teachings, God's personal involvement) and greater financial difficulty were associated with more frequent symptoms of depressed cognition and more somatic depressive symptoms. Further, religious doubt exacerbated the negative effect of financial strain on depressed affect and somatic symptoms (Krause, 2012b).

CHAPTER SUMMARY AND CONCLUSIONS

Racial and ethnic minority elderly derive meaning from religion and spirituality, and these affiliations, behaviors, and resources are unique reflections of their cultural/ethnic backgrounds and life experiences (i.e., immigration, nativity). Moreover, in many instances, aspects of religion and spirituality are important for offsetting the disadvantaged economic, social, and health circumstances (e.g., high rates of poverty and low levels of education, poorer health) facing many racial/ethnic minority elderly. Worship communities and their social networks provide supportive relationships and resources that address elders' physical, spiritual, and psychosocial needs, as well as promote a sense of identity and community. Finally, a diversity of faith traditions religious/spiritual beliefs, practices, and coping strategies are associated with the physical/mental health and well-being of older ethnic/racial minority elders.

Several methodological and substantive issues are noted in relation to religion and spirituality among ethnic and racial minority elderly. First, there is significant variation in the quantity and types of studies (qualitative and quantitative studies) available across racial/ethnic minority groups. Research on African American and Hispanic American elderly (mainly Mexican American) is the most numerous and well developed, and includes a relatively large body of research employing sophisticated conceptual, methodological, and analytic approaches among representative samples of older adults.

Second, this literature review clearly illustrates that religion and spirituality are diverse constructs comprising multiple dimensions. Although this is a well-recognized fact among religion researchers, several studies continue to rely on sole measures such as service attendance to represent religious involvement in its entirety; in some cases, attendance is used as a measure of "spirituality." A comprehensive understanding of religion and spirituality, their distribution and correlates, and relationships to health and social outcomes require that the field move toward a systematic appreciation of these constructs in their entirety, as well as their relationships to specific outcomes. Several articles and books discuss the theoretical frameworks, mechanisms, and pathways linking religion/spirituality to health and well-being outcomes (see Chatters, 2000; Ellison & Levin, 1998; Koenig et al., 2012).

Third, religion and spirituality are dynamic and influenced by one's background and culture of origin, as well as contemporary events (e.g., immigration experiences). Consequently, minority elderly differ from the majority population, not only in relation to their racial and ethnic group membership, but in their religious faith and spiritual practices as well. This is even the case for religious traditions that are nominally identical (e.g., Mexican and Irish Catholics). At present, the vast majority of studies of religion in the United States focus on non-Hispanic whites who identify as Christian. Continuing investigations among ethnic and racial minority elderly will add immeasurably to the diversity of this literature and deepen our understanding of religion and spirituality in relation to the health and well-being of older populations.

Fourth, studies that focus on the social patterning of religion and spirituality (e.g., race, gender, and socioeconomic position) and incorporate a comparative approach address important theoretically informed questions concerning group differences (e.g., gender differentials). However, a broader approach to understanding religion and spirituality focuses attention on both comparisons across racial and ethnic minority elderly, as well as differences within these groups. Country and culture of origin differences are of particular importance in examining within group variability among ethnic (e.g., Hispanic) and racial minority (e.g., Asian) elderly. Unfortunately, common usage of pan-ethnic labels (e.g., Asian, Hispanic/Latino/a) subsumes and effectively obscures distinct ethnic and national origin groups and cultural experiences that are consequential for understanding religion and spirituality. Furthermore, to a large extent, research on religion and spirituality among ethnic and racial minority elderly focuses on recent immigrants (first- and second-generation immigrants). As a consequence, the experiences of ethnic/racial minority elderly (e.g., Americans of Mexican, Japanese, and Chinese ancestry) whose families date back to several generations of U.S. citizens are effectively rendered invisible (i.e., the "perpetual stranger" phenomenon).

A more nuanced understanding of racial/ethnic group differences requires an appreciation of the social context of religion/spirituality practices for particular groups, as well as the specific meanings attached to these phenomena for racial and ethnic minority elderly.

For example, ethnic group differences in rates of service attendance have more meaning if we know the overall normative expectations for attendance (e.g., daily, weekly, or monthly) for each group and whether worship is traditionally performed in a religious (i.e., church, temple) or household setting. In each of the groups examined in this chapter, aspects of religion and spirituality were intimately aligned with issues of individual and religious identity and social connection and relationship—whether it involved social reciprocity with co-religionists or communication with deceased relatives. Understanding the social meanings of "making mandas" for Mexican American elderly (Krause & Bastida, 2010) can help us to appreciate the significance of this practice and understand how it relates to issues of religious identity, social connection and reciprocity, spiritual support, and feelings of control and health.

Further, because religious communities comprise different individuals with diverse characteristics, within-group diversity is important as well. As noted previously, religion and spirituality have special significance for those who are socially marginalized, integrate religion in their lives, and use religion/spirituality to manage stressful situations (Ellison & Taylor, 1996; Krause, 2002; Pargament, 2002). Conversely, for various reasons, not all ethnic/ racial minority elderly will participate in or experience the benefits of religion and spiritual pursuits. Understanding why this is the case is important for fully appreciating the correlates, functions, and roles of religion for elderly adults.

Finally, a fuller appreciation of religion and spirituality for ethnic and racial minority elderly requires that our research engage questions involving the social context and meaning of religion/spirituality for diverse groups of elders. Continuing growth in the racial and ethnic composition of the United States and in the elderly population requires that we understand not only the pattern and distribution of religion and spirituality, but also the social context and implications of religious diversity for the health and social well-being of elders.

REFERENCES

American Religious Identification Survey. (2009). *Summary report.* In B. A. Kosmin & A. Keysar, PIs. Hartford, CT: Trinity College.

Arredondo, E. M., Elder, J. P., Ayala, G. X., Campbell, N. R., & Baquero, B. (2005). Is church attendance associated with Latinas' health practices and self-reported health? *American Journal of Health Behavior, 29*(6), 502–11.

Bashi, V. (2007). *Survival of the knitted: Immigrant social networks in a stratified world.* Stanford, CA: Stanford University Press.

Beyene, Y., Becker, G., & Mayen, N. (2002). Perception of aging and sense of well-being among Latino elderly. *Journal of Cross-Cultural Gerontology, 17*(2), 155–172.

Billingsley, A. (1999). *Mighty like a river: The Black Church and social reform.* New York: Oxford University Press.

Bohnert, A. S. B., Perron, B. E., Jarman, C. N., Vaughn, M. G., Chatters, L. M., & Taylor, R. J. (2010). Use of clergy services among individuals seeking treatment for alcohol use problems. *American Journal of Addictions, 19*(4), 345–351.

Chatters, L. M. (2000). Religion and health: Public health research and practice. *Annual Review of Public Health, 21*, 335–367.

Chatters, L. M., Bullard, K. M., Taylor, R. J., Woodward, A. T., Neighbors, H. W., & Jackson, J. S. (2008). Religious participation and DSM-IV disorders among older African Americans: Findings from the National Survey of American Life (NSAL). *American Journal of Geriatric Psychiatry, 16*, 957–965.

Chatters, L. M., Levin, J. S., & Taylor, R. J. (1992). Antecedents and dimensions of religious involvement among older black adults. *Journal of Gerontology: Social Sciences, 47*, S269–S278.

Chatters, L. M., Mattis, J. S., Taylor, R. J., Woodward, A. T., Neighbors, H. W., & Grayman, N. (2011). Use of ministers for a serious personal problem among African Americans. *American Journal of Orthopsychiatry, 81*(1), 118–127.

Chatters, L. M., & Taylor, R. J. (1989). Age differences in religious participation among Black adults. *Journals of Gerontology: Social Sciences, 44*, S183–S189.

Chatters, L. M., Taylor, R. J., Jackson, J. S., & Lincoln, K. D. (2008). Religious coping among African Americans, Caribbean Blacks and Non-Hispanic Whites. *Journal of Community Psychology, 36*(3), 371–386.

Chatters, L. M., Taylor, R. J., Lincoln, K. D., Nguyen, A., & Joe, S. (2011). Church-based social support and suicidality among African Americans and Black Caribbeans. *Archives of Suicide Research, 15,* 337–353.

Chatters, L. M., Taylor, R. J., Lincoln, K. D., & Schroepfer, T. (2002). Patterns of informal support from family and church members among African Americans. *Journal of Black Studies, 33*(1), 66–85.

Dilworth-Anderson, P., Williams, I. C., & Gibson, B. (2002). Issues of race, ethnicity, and culture in caregiving research: A twenty-year review (1980–2000). *The Gerontologist, 42,* 237–272.

Diwan, S., Jonnalagadda, S. S., & Balaswamy, S. (2004). Resources predicting positive and negative affect during the experience of stress: A study of older Asian Indian immigrants in the United States. *The Gerontologist, 44*(5), 605–614.

Dunn, K. S., & Horgas, A. L. (2000). The prevalence of prayer as a spiritual self-care modality in elders. *Journal of Holistic Nursing, 18*(4), 337–351.

Ellison, C. G. (1995). Race, religious involvement and depressive symptomatology in a southeastern U.S. community. *Social Science and Medicine, 40,* 1561–1572.

Ellison, C. G., & Gay, D. A. (1990). Region, religious commitment, and life satisfaction among black Americans. *Sociological Quarterly, 31,* 123–147.

Ellison, C. G., & Levin, J. S. (1998). The religion-health connection: Evidence, theory and future directions. *Health Education and Behavior, 25,* 700–720.

Ellison, C. G., & Taylor, R. J. (1996). Turning to prayer: Social and situational antecedents of religious coping among African Americans. *Review of Religious Research, 38*(2), 111–131.

Ellison, C. G., Zhang, W., Krause, N., & Marcum, J. P. (2009). Does negative interaction in the church increase depression? Longitudinal findings from the Presbyterian Panel Survey. *Sociology of Religion, 70,* 409–431.

Ferraro, K. F., & Koch, J. R. (1994). Religion and health among black and white adults: Examining social support and consolation. *Journal for the Scientific Study of Religion, 33,* 362–375.

Gillum, F., & Griffith, D. M. (2010). Prayer and spiritual practices for health reasons among American adults: The role of race and ethnicity. *Journal of Religion and Health, 49*(3), 283–295.

Hagan, J., & Ebaugh, H. R. (2003). Calling upon the sacred: Migrants' use of religion in the migration process. *International Migration Review, 37*(4), 1145–1162.

Hill, T., Burdette, A., Angel, J., & Angel, R. (2006). Religious attendance and cognitive functioning among older Mexican Americans. *Journal of Gerontology: Psychological Sciences, 61B,* P3–P9.

Himle, J. A., Taylor, R. J., & Chatters, L. M. (2012). Religious involvement and prevalence of DSM-IV Diagnosed OCD among African Americans and Black Caribbeans. *Journal of Anxiety Disorders, 26,* 502–510.

Hirschman, C. (2004). The role of religion in the origins and adaptation of immigrant groups in the United States. *International Migration Review, 38*(3), 1206–1233.

Hoeffel, E. M., Rastogi, S., Kim, M. O., & Shahid, H. (2012). The Asian Population: 2010. 2010 Census Briefs, C2010BR-11. Retrieved from http://www.census.gov/prod/cen2010/briefs/c2010br-11.pdf

Iwamasa, G. Y., & Iwasaki, M. (2011). A new multidimensional model of successful aging: Perceptions of Japanese American older adults. *Journal of Cross-Cultural Gerontology, 26*(3), 261–278.

Johnson, K. S., Elbert-Avila, K. I., & Tulsky, J. A. (2005). The influence of spiritual beliefs and practices on the treatment preferences of African Americans: A review of the literature. *Journal of the American Geriatric Society, 53,* 711–719.

Jones, R. A., Utz, S., Wenzel, J., Steeves, R., Hinton, I., Andrews, D.,…Oliver, N. (2006). Use of complementary and alternative therapies by rural African Americans with Type 2 Diabetes. *Alternative Therapies, 12*(5), 34–38.

Kaiser Family Foundation-Pew Hispanic Center. (2002). *National Survey of Latinos.* Washington, DC: Henry J. Kaiser Family Foundation, Menlo Park, California and Pew Hispanic Center.

Kang, S., Domanski, M. D., & Moon, S. S. (2009): Ethnic enclave resources and predictors of depression among Arizona's Korean immigrant elders, Journal of Gerontological Social Work, 52:5, 489–502.

Kim, H. H. (2008). Impact of spirituality and religion on attitudes toward death and dying among Korean seniors living in Chicago. (Doctoral dissertation). Retrieved from ProQuest Dissertations and Theses database.

Koenig, H. G., Cohen, H. J., Blazer, D. G., et al. (1992), Religious coping and depression in elderly, hospitalized medically ill men. Am J Psychiatry 149(12):1693–1700.

Koenig, H., King, D. A., & Carson, V. B. (2012). *Handbook of religion and health* (Second ed.). New York, NY: Oxford University Press.

Koenig, H., McCullough, M., & Larson, D. (2001). *Handbook of religion and health*. New York, NY: Oxford University Press.

Kramer, T. L., Blevins, D., Miller, T. L., Phillips, M. M., Davis, V., & Burris, B. (2007). Ministers' perceptions of depression: A model to understand and improve care. *Journal of Religion and Health, 46*(1), 123–139.

Krause, N. (1992). Stress, religiosity, and psychological well-being among older blacks. *Journal of Aging and Health, 4*, 412–439.

Krause, N. (2002). Church-based social support and health in old age: Exploring variations by race. *The Journals of Gerontology Series B: Psychological Sciences and Social Sciences, 57*(6), S332–S347.

Krause, N. (2004). Common facets of religion, unique facets of religion, and life satisfaction among older African Americans. *The Journals of Gerontology Series B: Psychological Sciences and Social Sciences, 59*(2), S109–S117.

Krause, N. (2006a). Exploring the stress-buffering effects of church-based and secular social support on self-rated health in late life. *The Journals of Gerontology Series B: Psychological Sciences and Social Sciences, 61*(1), S35–S43.

Krause, N. (2006b). Church-based social support and mortality. *The Journals of Gerontology: Social Sciences, 61B*, S140–S146.

Krause, N. (2008a). *Aging in the church: How social relationship affect health*. West Conshohocken, PA: Templeton Foundation Press.

Krause, N. (2008b). The social foundation of religious meaning in life. *Research on Aging, 30*(4), 395–427.

Krause, N. (2010). The social milieu of the church and religious coping responses: A longitudinal investigation of older Whites and older Blacks. *International Journal for the Psychology of Religion, 20*(2), 109–129.

Krause, N. (2011). Do church-based social relationships influence social relationships in the secular world? *Mental Health, Religion & Culture, 14*(9), 877–897.

Krause, N. (2012a). Feelings of gratitude toward God among older Whites, older African Americans, and older Mexican Americans. *Research on Aging, 34*, 156–173.

Krause, N. (2012b). Religious doubt, financial strain, and depressive symptoms among older Mexican Americans. *Mental Health, Religion & Culture, 15*, 335–348.

Krause, N., & Bastida, E. (2009a). Religion, suffering, and health among older Mexican Americans. *Journal of Aging Studies, 23*(2), 114–123.

Krause, N., & Bastida, E. (2009b). Exploring the interface between religion and contact with the dead among older Mexican Americans. *Review of Religious Research, 51*(1), 5–20.

Krause, N., & Bastida, E. (2009c). Core religious beliefs and providing support to others in late life. *Mental Health, Religion & Culture, 12*(1), 75–96.

Krause, N., & Bastida, E. (2010). Religion and health among older Mexican Americans: Exploring the influence of making mandas. *Journal of Religion and Health*. Advance online publication.

Krause, N., & Bastida, E. (2011a). Church-based social relationships, belonging, and health among older Mexican Americans. *Journal for the Scientific Study of Religion, 50*(2), 397–409.

Krause, N., & Bastida, E. (2011b). Religion, suffering, and self-rated health among older Mexican Americans. *The Journals of Gerontology Series B: Psychological Sciences and Social Sciences, 66*(2), 207.

Krause, N., & Bastida, E. (2011c). Prayer to the saints or the virgin and health among older Mexican Americans. *Hispanic Journal of Behavioral Sciences, 33*(1), 71–87.

Krause, N., & Bastida, E. (2011d). Financial strain, religious involvement, and life satisfaction among older Mexican Americans. *Research on Aging, 33*(4), 403–425.

Krause, N., & Bastida, E. (2011e). Social relationships in the church during late life: Assessing differences between African Americans, Whites, and Mexican Americans. *Review of Religious Research, 53*(1), 41–63.

Krause, N., & Bastida, E. (2012). Contact with the dead, religion, and death anxiety among older Mexican Americans. *Death Studies,36*(10), 932–948.

Krause, N., & Chatters, L. M. (2005). Exploring race differences in a multidimensional battery of prayer measures among older adults. *Sociology of Religion, 66*(1), 23–43.

Krause, N., Ellison, C. G., & Wulff, K. M. (1998). Church-based emotional support, negative interaction, and psychological well-being: Findings from a national sample of Presbyterians. *Journal for the Scientific Study of Religion, 37*, 725–741.

Krause, N., & Hayward, D. (2012, October). Church-based social support and a sense of belonging in a congregation among older Mexican Americans. *Review of Religious Research.* Adavance online publication.

Krause, N., Shaw, B., & Liang, J. (2011). Social relationships in religious institutions and healthy lifestyles. *Health Education & Behavior, 38*, 25–38.

Krause, N., & Tran, T. V. (1989). Stress and religious involvement among older blacks. *Journal of Gerontology, 44*, S4–13.

Lee, E. K., & Chan, K. (2009). Religious/spiritual and other adaptive coping strategies among Chinese American older immigrants. *Journal of Gerontological Social Work, 52*(5), 517–533.

Levin, J. S. (1994). Religion and health: Is there an association, is it valid, and is it causal? *Social Science and Medicine, 38*, 1475–1482.

Levin, J. S., & Chatters, L. M. (1998). Religion, health, and psychological well-being in older adults. *Journal of Aging and Health, 10*, 504–531.

Levin, J. S., & Chatters, L. M. (2008). Religion, aging, and health: Historical perspectives, current trends, and future directions. *Journal of Religion, Spirituality and Aging, 20*(1–2), 153–172.

Levin, J. S., Chatters, L. M., & Taylor, R. J. (1995). Religious effects on health and life satisfaction among Black Americans. *Journal of Gerontology: Social Sciences, 50B*, S154–S163.

Levin, J. S., & Markides, K. (1985). Religion and health in Mexican Americans. *Journal of Religion & Health, 24*(1), 60–69.

Levin, J. S., Taylor, R. J., & Chatters, L. M. (1994). Race and gender differences in religiosity among older adults: Findings from four national surveys. *Journals of Gerontology: Social Sciences, 49*, S137–S145.

Lincoln, C. E., & Mamiya, L. H. (1990). *The Black church in the African American experience.* Durham, NC: Duke University Press.

Logan, J. R., & Deane, G. (2003). Black diversity in metropolitan America. Report from the Mumford Center for Comparative Urban and Regional Research. Albany, NY: State University of New York. Retrieved from http://mumford1.dyndns.org/cen2000/BlackWhite/BlackDiversityReport/black-diversity01.htm

Mansfield, C. J., Mitchell, J., & King, D. E. (2002). The doctor as God's mechanic? Beliefs in the Southeastern United States. *Social Science and Medicine, 54*(3), 399–409.

Markides, K. (1983). Aging, religiosity and adjustment: A longitudinal analysis. *Journal of Gerontology, 38*, 621–625.

Markides, K., Levin, J., & Ray, L. (1987). Religion, aging and life satisfaction: An eight-year, three-wave, longitudinal study. *The Gerontologist, 27*, 660–665.

Maynard-Reid, P. U. (2000). *Diverse worship: African-American, Caribbean and Hispanic perspectives.* Downers Grove, IL: InterVarsity Press.

McAlister, E. (1998). The Madonna of 115th street revisited: Vodou and Haitian Catholicism in the age of transnationalism'. In R. S. Warner & J. G. Wittner (Eds.), *Gatherings in diaspora: religious communities and the new immigration*(pp. 123–160). Philadelphia, PA: Temple University Press.

McAuley, W. J., Pecchioni, L., & Grant, J. A. (2000). Personal accounts of the role of God in health and illness among older rural African American and White residents. *Journal of Cross-Cultural Gerontology, 15*, 13–35.

Miltiades, H., & Pruchno, R. (2002). The effect of religious coping on caregiving appraisals of mothers with developmental disabilities. *The Gerontologist, 42*, 82–91.

Mochon, D., Norton, M. I., & Ariely, D. (2011). Who benefits from religion? *Social Indicators Research, 101*, 1–15.

Morrison, J. (1991). The Black church as a support system for black elderly. *Journal of Gerontological Social Work, 17*(1–2), 105–120.

Mui, A. C., & Kang, S. Y. (2006). Acculturation stress and depression among Asian immigrant elders. *Social Work, 51*(3), 243–255.

Musick, M. A. (1996). Religion and subjective health among Black and White elders. *Journal of Health and Social Behavior, 37*, 221–237.

Newport, F. (2006, April 14). Mormons, Evangelical Protestants, Baptists top church attendance list. *Gallup Poll News Service*. Retrieved from http://www.gallup.com/poll/22414/mormons-evangel-ical-protestants-baptists-top-church-attendance-list.aspx

NORC & AP-Univsion. (2010). Associated Press-Univision Poll. Retrieved from http://surveys.ap.org/data%5CNORC%5CAP-Univision%20Topline_posting.pdf

Pang, K. Y. C. (1998). Symptoms of depression in elderly Korean immigrants: Narration and the healing process. *Culture, Medicine and Psychiatry, 22*(1), 93–122.

Pang, K. Y. (2000). *Virtuous transcendence: Self-cultivation and self–healing in Korean elderly immigrants*. New York, NY: Haworth Press.

Pargament, K. I. (1997). *The psychology of religion and coping: Theory, research, practice*. New York, NY: Guilford.

Pargament, K. I. (1999). The psychology of religion and spirituality? Yes and no. *International Journal for the Psychology of Religion, 9*, 3–16.

Pargament, K. I. (2002). The bitter and the sweet: An evaluation of the costs and benefits of religiousness. *Psychological Inquiry, 13*(3), 168–181.

Pargament, K. I., Smith, B. W., Koenig, H. G., & Perez, L. (1998). Patterns of positive and negative religious coping with major life stressors. *Journal for the Scientific Study of Religion, 37*, 710–724.

Park, J., Roh, S., & Yeo, Y. (2011). Religiosity, social support, and life satisfaction among elderly Korean immigrants. *The Gerontologist*. Advanced online publication.

Perl, P., Greely, J. Z., & Gray, M. M. (2006), What proportion of adult Hispanics are Catholic? A review of survey data and methodology. *Journal for the Scientific Study of Religion, 45*, 419–436.

Pew Forum on Religion & Public Life. (2007). *U.S. religious landscape: Religious beliefs & practices/social & political views*. Retrieved from http://religions.pewforum.org/pdf/report2-religious-landscape-study-full.pdf

Pew Forum on Religion & Public Life. (2008). U.S. religious landscape survey: Religious affiliation-diverse and dynamic. Washington, D.C.: Pew Research Center.

Pincharoen, S., & Congdon, J. G. (2003). Spirituality and health in older Thai persons in the United States. *Western Journal of Nursing Research, 25*(1), 93–108.

Robinson, M. R., Thiel, M. M., Backus, M. M., & Meyer, E. C. (2006). Matters of spirituality at the end of life in the pediatric intensive care unit. *Pediatrics, 118*(3), 719–729.

Roh, S. (2010). The impact of religion, spirituality, and social support on depression and life satisfaction among Korean immigrant older adults. (Doctoral dissertation) Retrieved from ProQuest Dissertations and Theses database. (UMI No. 3432768).

Soonthornchaiya, R., & Dancy, B. L. (2006). Perceptions of depression among elderly Thai immigrants. *Issues in Mental Health Nursing, 27*(6), 681–698.

Taylor, R. J. (1988). Correlates of religious non-involvement among Black Americans. *Review of Religious Research, 30*, 126–139.

Taylor, R. J., & Chatters, L. M. (1986a). Church-based informal support among elderly Blacks. *The Gerontologist, 26*(6), 637–642.

Taylor, R. J., & Chatters, L. M. (1986b). Patterns of informal support to elderly black adults: The role of family, friends, and church members. *Social Work, 31*, 432–438.

Taylor, R. J., & Chatters, L. M. (1988). Church members as a source of informal social support. *Review of Religious Research, 30*(2), 193–203.

Taylor, R. J., Chatters, L. M., & Abelson, J. M. (2012). Religious involvement and DSM IV 12 Month and lifetime major depressive disorder among African Americans. *Journal of Nervous and Mental Disease.*

Taylor, R. J., Chatters, L. M., Bullard, K. M., Wallace, J. M., & Jackson, J. S. (2009). Organizational religious behavior among older African Americans: Findings from the National Survey of American Life. *Research on Aging, 31*, 440–462.

Taylor, R. J., Chatters, L. M., & Jackson, J. S. (2007a). Religious and spiritual involvement among older African Americans, Caribbean Blacks and non-Hispanic Whites: Findings from the National Survey of American Life. *Journal of Gerontology: Social Sciences, 62*, S238–S250.

Taylor, R. J., Chatters, L. M., & Jackson, J. S. (2007b). Religious participation among older Black Caribbeans in the United States. *The Journals of Gerontology: Social Sciences, 62*, S251–S256.

Taylor, R. J., Chatters, L. M., & Jackson, J. S. (2009). Correlates of spirituality among African Americans and Caribbean Blacks in the United States: Findings from the National Survey of American Life. *Journal of Black Psychology, 35*, 317–342.

Taylor, R. J., Chatters, L. M., Jayakody, R. T., & Levin, J. S. (1996). Black and White differences in religious participation: A multi-sample comparison. *Journal for the Scientific Study of Religion, 35*, 403–410.

Taylor, R. J., Chatters, L. M., & Joe, S. (2011). Religious involvement and suicidal behavior among African Americans and Black Caribbeans. *Journal of Nervous and Mental Disease, 199*(7), 478–486.

Taylor, R. J., Chatters, L. M., & Levin, J. (2004). *Religion in the lives of African Americans.* Thousand Oaks, CA: Sage.

Taylor, R. J., Ellison, C. G., Chatters, L. M., Levin, J. S., & Lincoln, K. D. (2000). Mental health services within faith communities: The role of clergy in Black churches. *Social Work, 45*(1), 73–87.

Taylor, R. J., Lincoln, K. D., & Chatters, L. M. (2005). Supportive relationships with church members among African Americans. *Family Relations, 54*(4), 501–511.

True, G., Phipps, E. J., Leonard, E., Braitman, L. E., Harralson, T., Harris, D., & Tester, W. (2005). Treatment preferences and advance care planning at end of life: The role of ethnicity and spiritual coping in cancer patients. *Annals of Behavioral Medicine, 30*(2), 174–179.

Walls, C. T. (1992). The role of church and family support in the lives of older African Americans. *Generations, 16*(3), 33–36.

Walls, C. T., & Zarit, S. H. (1991). Informal support from black churches and the well-being of elderly blacks. *The Gerontologist, 31*(4), 490–495.

Waters, M. (1999). *Black identities: West Indian immigrant dreams and American realities.* New York: Russell Sage Foundation.

Wood, J. B., & Parham, I. A. (1990). Coping with perceived burden: Ethnic and cultural issues in Alzheimer's family caregiving. *Journal of Applied Gerontology, 9*, 325–339.

Woodward, A. T., Bullard, K. M., Taylor, R. J., Chatters, L. M., Baser, R. E., & Perron, B. E. (2009). Use of complementary and alternative medicines for mental and substance use disorders: A comparison of African Americans Black Caribbeans, and non-Hispanic Whites. *Psychiatric Services, 60*(10), 1342–1349.

Yeates, K. O., Taylor, H. G., Woodrome, S. E., Wade, S. L., Stancin, T., & Drotar, D. (2002). Race as a moderator of parent and family outcomes following pediatric traumatic brain injury. *Journal of Pediatric Psychology, 27*(4), 393–403.

Zhang, G., & Zhan, H. J. (2009). Beyond the Bible and the cross: A social and cultural analysis of Chinese elders' participation in Christian congregations in the United States. *Sociological Spectrum, 29*(2), 295–317.

CHAPTER 5

Stress, Discrimination, and Coping in Late Life

Verna M. Keith

A growing body of research documents racial and ethnic disparities in physical and mental health among older Americans (National Research Council, 2004). Racial and ethnic diversity in health among older Americans reflects a confluence of factors, including group differences in socioeconomic position, health risk behaviors, access to health care, general exposure to stressful life conditions, as well as the unique stressors that are associated with minority group status (Brondolo, Gallo, & Myers, 2009; Hayward, Crimmins, Miles, & Yu, 2000; Myers, 2009; Williams & Mohammed, 2009). Discrimination, unequal treatment, and discrepancies in access to valued resources based on ascribed social categories, such as race-ethnicity, is being pursued as a major social determinant of health (Pascoe & Richman, 2009). The interest in discrimination, particularly as it pertains to racial-ethnic differences in health, comes in large part from the inability of socioeconomic status (SES), considered a fundamental cause of health disparities (Link & Phelan, 1995), and the stress exposure associated with low SES to fully account for racial and ethnic inequalities in health (see Farmer & Ferraro 2005; Lantz, House, Mero, & Williams, 2005; Williams, Mohammed, Leavell, & Collins, 2010; Williams & Sternthal, 2010). This is not surprising given that minorities do not receive the same returns to socioeconomic achievement as compared to whites. Indeed, the disparity in health between African Americans and whites is often more pronounced at higher rather than lower SES levels (Farmer & Ferraro, 2005; Williams et al., 2010).

This chapter is situated within the larger stress process literature (Aneshensel, 1992; Pearlin, 1999) and reviews research on discrimination as a source of stress that is an influential determinant of racial and ethnic differences in the health status of older Americans. Research indicates that discrimination, together with other social stressors associated with disadvantaged social positions, alters mood and damages key physiological regulatory systems that accumulate during the life course to result in emotional problems, premature onset of chronic disease, accelerated disease progression, premature aging, and ultimately death among some minority group members (Geronimus, Hicken, Keene, & Bound, 2006; Jackson, Knight, & Rafferty, 2010; Lewis, Aiello, Leurgans, Kelly, & Barnes, 2009; Seeman et al., 2008). The stress process framework accommodates analyses of such disparities because it posits that exposure to discrimination and the availability of coping resources and repertoires are intertwined with race-ethnicity and SES; that achieved, SES is influenced by racialized institutional processes, such as residential segregation and place stratification, that result from historical relationships between racial and ethnic minorities and the larger society. These processes, in turn, shape opportunities for optimum health.

The chapter is divided into four major sections. The first section provides a brief overview of disparities in health among older Americans. The second discusses the biology of stress, elaborates on key elements of the general stress process framework, and highlights findings pertinent to the health of older minorities. The third section reviews the research on personally mediated discrimination and health that includes findings from both age-diverse samples and those specific to older adults. This section also addresses the literature on coping with discrimination and the contribution of institutionalized discrimination to health inequalities. The final section briefly addresses issues for future research.

HEALTH DISPARITIES IN LATE LIFE

Examining racial and ethnic differences across multiple indicators of morbidity, disability, and mortality among mid-life and late life adults, Hummer, Benjamins, and Rogers (2004) concluded that older African Americans and American Indians/Native Alaskans (AINAs) are in the poorest health, although they were cautious in drawing generalizations regarding AINAs due to exceptionally problematic data quality issues. Mortality is higher in these groups from birth until advanced age, 85 and older, when white American death rates become higher. This crossover phenomenon is widely believed to either reflect selective survival of the most physically hardy African Americans or misreporting of age. Importantly, there is a lack of consensus as to whether the crossover applies to disability and other health outcomes (Hummer et al., 2004; Jackson et al., 2011), suggesting that elderly blacks' and AINAs' survival advantage comes with the cost of lower quality of life. Other evidence also points to a black health disadvantage. Using 20 years of data, Farmer and Ferraro (2005) found that African Americans reported poorer self-rated health than whites, even after accounting for selective mortality from chronic disease, with the widest gap occurring at higher SES levels.

Older Asians and Pacific Islanders, considered collectively, have a mortality advantage over white Americans, with their higher death rates from stomach and liver cancer being offset by lower death rates from other causes (Hummer et al., 2004; Singh & Hiatt, 2006). Latinos, especially immigrants, appear to have a mortality advantage over white Americans. This unexpected combination of both lower mortality and lower SES is termed the Latino paradox. The paradox is hypothesized to reflect either a healthy immigrant effect, whereby those in good health are most likely to seek residence in a new country, or the salmon bias effect, whereby the seriously ill return to their native countries and are not counted in U.S. mortality statistics (Mutchler & Burr, 2011). In contrast to their favorable mortality, older Latinos have lower self-reported health, higher obesity and diabetes rates, and higher levels of disability than whites, which also points to an impaired quality of life (Markides, Salinas, & Wong, 2010; McGee, Liao, Cao, & Cooper, 1999).

The picture is more mixed for mental health. Some studies find that older African Americans report fewer, more, or similar levels of depressive symptoms than whites, but have similar or lower prevalence of major depressive disorder (George, 2011; Myers & Hwang, 2004). Jimenez, Algería, Chen, Chan, and Laderman (2010), using data from the Mental Health Collaborative Psychiatric Epidemiological studies, found no racial-ethnic differences in 12-month prevalence of mental disorders, but the prevalence of lifetime disorders was lower for Asian, African American, and Afro-Caribbean respondents than their white counterparts. In the case of the larger African American population, researchers have taken note of the seeming paradox of poorer physical health, but perhaps better mental health (Jackson et al., 2010). The paradox seems to extend to late-life African Americans and to other minorities.

Underlying these more general patterns in physical and mental health are complexities in the onset, prevalence, and progression of chronic disease that vary across gender, age (young vs. older late life), and socioeconomic position within and across groups (Hayward et al., 2000; Williams & Sternthal, 2010). As a result of increasing diversity through immigration, especially among Asians and Latinos, health is also shaped by nativity and, among immigrants, country of origin and duration of residence in the United States in ways that require frequent reconsideration of the existing knowledge base. For instance, the Latino mortality advantage varies by subgroup, age, and gender (Borrell & Lancet, 2011), and the healthy immigrant effect is not universal, especially among those arriving in the United States at midlife and older (Jackson, Forsythe-Brown, & Govia, 2007; Mutchler, Prakash, & Burr, 2007).

There is a pressing need to identify the factors contributing to the dissimilar health profiles observed in late life. Many of the racial and ethnic health disparities in late life arise from social inequalities in power and access to resources at earlier stages of the life course and are thus preventable and modifiable (Adler & Rehkopf, 2008; Williams et al., 2010). Prior research reveals that exposure to stressful life conditions is a key factor linking social inequalities and health.

STRESS AND HEALTH

The Stress Response

Stress, or the stress response, is a state of physiological or emotional arousal that challenges the adaptive capacity of individuals (Aneshensel, 1992; Cohen, Kessler, & Gordon, 1995). When individuals are confronted with physical or symbolic threats, the sympathetic nervous system (SNS) and the hypothalamic pituitary adrenal axis (HPA) trigger cascading biological processes (neural, neuroendocrine, and immune) that prepare the body for fight or flight, a process referred to as allostasis (Dallman & Hellhammer, 2011; McEwen & Stellar, 1993). These systems operate efficiently under conditions of short-term threat but may become inefficient under conditions of repeated or chronic threat. The repeated activation of inefficient allostatic responses can result in high allostatic load, a cumulative biological burden, or wear and tear on important body systems, which heightens the risk for disease (McEwen & Seeman, 1999), a process that Geronimus refers to as weathering (Geronimus, Hicken, Keene, & Bound, 2006).

The development of biomarkers that signal impaired functioning of physiological systems (e.g., C-reactive protein for the system controlling inflammation, cortisol for the endrocrine system, etc.) have made it possible for researchers to evaluate the impact of allostatic load on disease outcomes and to assess its implication for health disparities (Seeman et al., 2008). High allostatic load is linked to various health indicators including cardiovascular risk factors (e.g., hypertension, atherosclerosis), arthritis, diabetes, depression, and mortality (Mattei, Demissie, Falcon, Ordovas, & Tucker, 2010; McEwen, 2000; Seeman, Singer, Rowe, Horwitz, & McEwen, 1997). Important for health disparities are findings that low SES adults (Seeman et al., 2008) and racial/ethnic minorities (Finch, Do, Frank, & Seeman, 2009; Geronimus et al., 2006) carry a higher burden of allostatic load, indicating greater stress exposure. Time in the United States is also positively associated with higher allostatic burden among Latino immigrants (Finch et al., 2009; Kaestner, Pearson, Keene, & Geronimus, 2009), which is consistent with findings that immigrant health tends to erode with longer residence. Further, telomere length, a stress-related biomarker for cell aging, is shorter in mid-life African American women, suggesting that they age at an accelerated rate compared to white women. On average, black women in the study were 7.5 years biologically older than their counterparts (Geronimus et al., 2010). Although not conclusive, these studies point to a greater stress burden that may derive from membership in groups that are socially and economically disadvantaged in the United States.

The Stress Process Perspective

Scholars have long been interested in the social circumstances that provoke stress response and their connections to health outcomes. The stress process perspective (Pearlin, 1999), sometimes referenced as stress and coping, serves as the guiding framework in a large number of sociological and psychological studies, especially in mental health, and now anchors studies of discrimination. At its very basic, the framework incorporates three central concepts: stressors, coping, and the physical and mental health outcomes that result from the stress response.

Stressors are life adversities that provoke the stress response. Stressors arise from unexpected and often uncontrollable events, interpersonal interactions with others, and social roles, all of which are patterned by social hierarchies, such as race, gender, socioeconomic position (SEP), sexual orientation, and age (Aneshensel, 1992; Thoits, 1995). During the life course, individuals are at risk of experiencing a continuum of stressors, including discrete life-changing events (e.g., being fired or forced to retire), traumatic events (e.g., being physically attacked), and chronic strains that consist of enduring and persistent problems such as financial hardship (Wheaton & Montazer, 2010). The stress continuum is dynamic in that stressful events may transition into chronic strains, e.g., involuntary retirement may evolve into financial hardship due to inadequate resources and assets (Brown, 2009). Conversely, a chronic stressor may become a life event when the protracted illness of a family member ends in release through death. A major assumption of the framework is that subjective perceptions and appraisals of experiences as stressful are critical for their impact on health (Lazarus & Folkman, 1984). Thus, stress research privileges self-reported experiences, including those of discrimination.

Coping refers to behavioral strategies that individuals use to avoid, tolerate, manage, deny, or minimize the impact of stressors (Pearlin, 1999). Efforts to resolve stressful situations that involve direct confrontation and/or purposeful problem-solving is often termed problem-focused coping. Efforts that involve reinterpretation or denial of stressful situations are often referred to as emotion-focused or avoidance coping (Taylor & Stanton, 2007; Thoits, 1995). Social and psychological resources, such as social support and mastery/personal control, theorized to influence the selection of coping strategies, are frequently investigated (Taylor & Stanton, 2007; Thoits, 1995). The relationship among stressors, coping, and health may take different forms (Wheaton, 1985), but stress researchers are most interested in situations where resources and strategies act to buffer or mitigate the harmful effects of stressors. Buffering occurs, for instance, when network members mobilize to provide support to the stressed individual, which in turns dampens the stressor's impact, or when the coping resource is found to be more efficacious in mitigating the health-damaging effects among those experiencing high levels of stress than among those experiencing lower levels. Differences in coping aid in understanding why some individuals and groups are more or less reactive or vulnerable to stressors. Depending on the context, coping strategies and actions do not always alleviate the effects of stressors and may even be harmful to health, such as when supportive others become sources of stress (Okun & Keith, 1998; Taylor & Stanton, 2007).

The third concept, physical and mental health outcomes, represents the end products of the stress process. Stressful experiences may affect a broad range of health indicators as well as health-related behavioral risk factors—smoking, being overweight, and lack of exercise. In sum, the stress process perspective argues that when individuals are confronted with stressful life experiences and are unable to utilize coping resources and behaviors effectively to overcome these difficulties, they are likely to suffer both emotionally and physically.

The stress process framework is well suited to guiding research in racial and ethnic health disparities. One of its basic tenants is that stressors and coping are inextricably tied to social inequality such that stressors are more prevalent among socially disadvantaged groups, while their ability to cope with stressors is constrained. A large volume of literature finds, for instance, that greater exposure to stressors accounts, in part, for higher psychological distress and depression among socially disadvantaged groups, such as women, the unmarried, and individuals of lower SES (Thoits, 2010; Turner & Lloyd, 1999; Turner, Wheaton, & Lloyd, 1995). A body of work also finds that, independent of SES, stressful events and chronic strains are more prevalent among people of color, including the stressors associated with acculturation and racism (e.g., Brown & Gary, 1987; Finch, Frank, & Vega, 2004; Hatch & Dohrenwend, 2007; Jang & Chiriboga, 2010; Mui & Kang, 2006; Schulz et al., 2000; Sternthal, Slopen, & Williams, 2011). Coping resources such as social support, mastery, religious involvement, and John Henryism (a strong behavioral predisposition to engage in high-effort coping under extraordinary circumstances), have been found to be protective of mental health in minority populations (Ellison, Boardman, Williams, & Jackson, 2001; Krause & Bastida, 2011; Kiecolt, Hughes, & Keith, 2009; Lincoln, Chatters, & Taylor, 2003; Shibusawa & Mui, 2008). Although helpful in coping with stressors, these resources are generally, although not always, less available to the socially disadvantaged. For example, mastery or personal control, the belief that one can control events in one's life, is associated with more effective coping and more positive health outcomes. Yet, women, racial-ethnic minorities, and other disadvantaged groups tend to have lower levels of mastery (Mirowsky & Ross, 2003; Shaw & Krause, 2002). Lower levels of mastery derive from the experiences that come with having less power to execute plans and see them through (Pearlin, 1999).

Stressors in Late Life

Research reveals that chronic stressors are prevalent in late life as widowhood, retirement, and health-related dependency become increasingly common. Persistent, ongoing stressors pose a higher risk to health than eventful stressors among the elderly (Avison & Turner, 1988). Inadequate financial resources are a major source of chronic stress for minority elders, especially those who have spent their adult lives in the United States. A history of poor educational opportunities coupled with labor force discrimination means that current cohorts of minority elders are disproportionately more likely to have experienced unstable employment; underemployment; and jobs characterized by low wages, low autonomy, and hard physical labor; and to end their working lives with fewer retirement benefits and assets (Brown, 2009; Flippen & Tienda, 2000). For many African Americans and Latinos, and even for some older immigrants unable to find work after relocation (Zhang & Zhan 2009), the transition to nonworking status is aptly described as involuntary exit from the labor force rather than retirement. For these reasons, subjective financial hardship (e.g., not enough money at the end of the month) is often investigated in older minority groups. Research finds that subjective feelings of financial strain are associated with poorer self-rated health and higher mortality and depressive symptoms among older African Americans (Kahn & Pearlin, 2006; Szanton et al., 2008), and lower self-esteem and higher depressive symptoms among older adults of Mexican origin (Angel, Frisco, Angel, & Chiriboga, 2003; Black & Markides, 1999).

Findings are mixed with regard to whether the health of older minorities and whites are equally affected when they confront similar levels of financial hardship; that is, whether their health is equally likely to be compromised by such problems. An analysis of mortality during a five-year period found that older African American women in financial distress had lower survival rates than white women in similar circumstance (Szanton et al., 2008). In contrast, Kahn and Fazio (2005) found no differences between older African Americans and whites in responsiveness to financial strain across several physical health outcomes. Still other studies indicate that the degree to which older blacks and whites react to financial stress varies by the coping resource evaluated. Ulbrich and Warheit (1989) found that supportive friends buffered the effects of financial problems among older African Americans but not older whites, while supportive relatives were more important in coping with financial stress among low-income whites. Krause, in studies of religion and coping in older adults, found that support from fellow church members (2006) and praying for others (2003) reduced the impact of financial strain on self-rated health more for African Americans than whites. Overall, findings regarding the stress-buffering role of religion among the African American elderly are consistent with an expansive literature that attests to the powerful influence of religion in the lives of African Americans (Chatters, 2000; Ellison et al., 2001; Taylor, Chatters, Bullard, Wallace, & Jackson, 2009). Although the stress-buffering effects of religion are not as well researched among other minority elders, there is evidence that religious involvement is associated with better health among older Mexican American (Krause & Bastida, 2011) and older Chinese and Koreans (Lee, 2007; Zhang & Zhan, 2009).

Extending the Stress Process Framework: The Minority Stress Hypothesis

The minority status stress model argues that individuals occupying stigmatized statuses are exposed to unique stressors, including prejudice and unfair treatment that determine their chances to live healthy lives (Flores et al., 2008; Meyer, 2003). Although the model applies to all stigmatized statuses, it is especially pertinent to racial and ethnic minorities. Race/ethnic discrimination emanates from racism a system of ideologies and practices that hierarchically ranks some groups as superior to others and allocates societal resources accordingly (Williams & Mohammed, 2009). Discrimination, both at the personal and institutional levels, is common to the historical and contemporary experiences of visible minorities in the United States, with most having been deemed biologically and/or culturally inferior and subjected to violence at one time or another. Slavery and segregation left indelible marks on the African American community, including deeply embedded negative stereotypes and continuing inequities in education, employment, income, and wealth accumulation (Feagin, 2001). The history of Native Americans is characterized by conquest through war, broken treaties, the extinction of culture via Indian boarding schools, and forced evacuation to reservations located on inhospitable lands (Fenelon, 2007). Incorporated into the United States after the American war with Mexico and treated as conquered people on their own land, Mexican Americans faced segregation, prejudice, deportation in the 1930s, and other indignities that persist (Estrada, 2009; Feagin, 2001, p. 217–220). Many Mexican immigrants arrive in the United States without legal papers and are easy targets for labor exploitation. Current anti-immigrant sentiment and state-sanctioned tactics to guard the U.S. border makes both citizens and immigrants targets for arrest or deportation (Estrada, 2009). Asian history in the United States includes denial of citizenship and major state-sanctioned discrimination, such as internment of Japanese Americans during World War II (Gee, Ro, Shariff-Marco, & Chae, 2009). Asian Americans are still regarded by other Americans as "foreign," although Japanese and Chinese Americans have long had a presence in the United States. Social distance measures show that Asians are viewed as being different from whites on several indicators, such as "which group do you have the least in common with"—34% and 16% for Asian and African Americans, respectively (Gee et al., 2009). At the same time, they are labeled inappropriately as a "model minority," owing to their economic success. As the designated model for upward mobility, Asian Americans serve as scapegoats in the denial of systemic racism in the United States (Chou & Feagin, 2008). The model minority frame delegitimizes any claims of discrimination by them or any other minority group (Gee et al., 2009). In sum, all visible minorities are racialized, although to varying degrees.

Efforts to assess the minority stress hypothesis have proceeded in two directions. One line of research focuses on personally mediated discrimination, occurrences of unfair treatment in interpersonal interactions that the targets are aware of and directly experience. A second line of research attends to structural aspects of discrimination by investigating the effects of residential segregation patterns and neighborhood characteristics (e.g., SES, residential stability, crime, perceptions of disorder) on health at the individual level.

DISCRIMINATION AND HEALTH

Personally Mediated Experiences of Discrimination and Health

Personally mediated discrimination stems from interactions with others and consists of perceptions of actions involving exclusion, verbal slurs, slights, avoidance, and physical threats or harassment (Brondolo, Brady Ver Halen, Pencille, Beatty, & Contrada, 2011). Discrimination can occur in numerous settings including work, retail shopping, and medical encounters (Lawson, Rodgers-Rose, & Rajaram, 1999), and are humiliating, frustrating, and often anger provoking. Consistent with the minority stress hypothesis, evidence indicates that members of racial and ethnic minorities report more experiences of unfair treatment than the white majority. Kessler, Mickelson, and Williams (1999), in a national study of adults, found that about 49% of African Americans reported a lifetime occurrence of at least one of 11 acute discriminatory events such as not being hired for a job or being denied a bank loan, and nearly three fourths (71.3%) reported that they often or sometimes experienced chronic day-to-day discrimination such as being treated with less courtesy and being called derogatory names. Figures for white Americans were 31% and 24% for lifetime and day-to-day discrimination, respectively. Analyses from the National Latino and Asian American Study (NLAAS) revealed a prevalence rate of 30% among all Latinos, and 40% for Puerto Ricans, 16% for Cubans, and 34% for persons of Mexican origin (Pérez, Fortuna, & Alegría, 2008). Based on NLAAS data, Chae et al. (2008) found that 75% of Asians experienced unfair treatment, with 38% attributing discrimination to their ethnicity. Prevalence in the NLAAS ranged from 38% for Vietnamese to 61% for Chinese (Gee et al., 2009). Across a series of 13 studies drawn from convenience samples, Brondolo and colleagues found that 53% to 61% of African Americans, 51% to 54% of Latino(a)s, 28% of Chinese, 47% of Filipinos, 42% of Asian Indians, and 49% of Koreans reported that they were most likely to be targeted for discrimination by Whites (Brondolo et al., 2011).

Reviews of the literature (e.g., Araújo & Borrell, 2006; Gee et al., 2009; Harrell, Hall, & Taliaferro, 2003; Paradies, 2006; Williams & Mohammed, 2009) and a meta-analysis (Pascoe & Richman, 2009) conclude that perceived discrimination is injurious to health. These reviews reference multiple studies that vary in the health measure considered, number and location of respondents (e.g., national vs. local), and in the measure of discrimination employed. Measures have ranged from one-item indicators asking respondents whether they have ever experienced any discrimination, to more elaborate instruments that incorporate appraisals of how personally upsetting or stressful their experiences were and whether or not they were attributed to race or some other status characteristic (Krieger, 1999; Landrine & Klonoff, 1996; Williams, Yu, Jackson, & Anderson, 1997). A majority of studies reviewed find positive associations between discrimination and physical health indicators, including higher blood pressure, higher prevalence of chronic conditions, and self-rated health; mental health outcomes including depressive symptoms, PTSD and other psychiatric disorders, and general psychological distress; health-related behaviors, such as cigarette smoking and substance use; and health care utilization and satisfaction with care. Laboratory-based studies have also registered physiological and affective reactions in subjects, largely African Americans, when they are exposed to mental images or videotaped vignettes of racially biased behavior (Clark, 2004). The deleterious impact of interpersonal discrimination is most robust for mental health and self-rated health, and their association with discrimination is observed in all major groups, including American Indians (e.g., Whitbeck, McMorris, Hoyt, Stubben, & Lafromboise, 2002), Asians (e.g., Gee et al., 2009; Mossakowski, 2003), Latinos (e.g., Araújo & Borrell, 2006; Finch, Kolody, & Vega, 2000), and among African Americans and whites (e.g., Kessler et al., 1999; Schulz et al., 2000). Collectively, the literature points to personally mediated discrimination as a social stressor that constitutes an important social determinant of health disparities.

Research on the relationship between discrimination and health among older Americans is just beginning to appear in the literature. In age-diverse samples, the prevalence of reported discrimination is lowest among those ages 65 and older (e.g., Chae et al., 2008; Kessler et al., 1999; Pérez et al., 2008), perhaps because retirement and other role-related changes limit interaction with others and thus opportunities for inequitable treatment. While exposure to unfair treatment may be less common in old age, studies show that discrimination is nevertheless associated with elevated depressive symptoms and poorer subjective health ratings among mid-life and older African Americans, Latinos, whites, and Koreans (Ayalon & Gum, 2011; Barnes et al., 2004; Jang, Chiriboga, Kim, & Rhew, 2010; Luo, Xu, Granberg, & Wentworth, 2012), and with more negative affect among African Americans and whites (Bierman, 2006). Discrimination was associated with an increased likelihood of ever smoking or using alcohol in a sample of older Puerto Ricans (Todorova, Falcón, Lincoln, & Price, 2010). Among older African Americans, discrimination is also positively associated with higher diastolic blood pressure (Lewis, Barnes, et al., 2009), the stress marker C-reactive protein (Lewis, Aiello, et al., 2009), and coronary artery calcification (Lewis, Everson-Rose, et al., 2006), all of which are risk factors for cardiovascular disease.

Older African Americans generally report more discrimination than either European Americans or Latinos, but their health is not always as adversely impacted by it, suggesting that they are more effective in coping with unfair treatment. Ayalon and Gum (2011), for example, analyzed baseline data from the Health and Retirement survey and found that major discriminatory events were most strongly associated with depressive symptoms among whites followed by Latinos, but were not statistically significant for African Americans. In that same study, chronic discrimination was associated with more depressive symptoms and lowered life satisfaction in all three groups, but the effect was stronger for whites and Latinos. Similarly, an ongoing study of African American and white participants in the Chicago Health and Aging Project (CHAP) revealed that higher levels of perceived discrimination, particularly the type that entails personal rejection, was associated with higher mortality and depressive symptoms among both groups (Barnes et al., 2004, 2008). The impact of unfair treatment on depressive symptoms was similar for both groups, but discrimination had a more adverse effect on the mortality of whites. Aylon and Gum, as well as Barnes et al., speculate that African Americans, who have encountered discrimination throughout their lives, may be more accustomed to managing discrimination, or that African Americans who were less effective in coping with discrimination experienced mortality at earlier ages, leaving behind individuals who are more capable of managing unfair treatment. Whites, however, may have their first experience with discrimination as they reach mid-life and begin to experience age-based discrimination. While Latinos were most likely to attribute their experiences to age also, the discrimination measures did not address language discrimination and may thus have underestimated ethnic-related stressors in this population. Studies have established that poor English language proficiency and language-based discrimination are risk factors for poor mental and physical health outcomes (Black et al., 1998; Falcón & Tucker, 2000; Mui, Kang, Kang, & Domanski, 2007; Yoo, Gee, & Takeuchi, 2009). Further investigations are needed to evaluate explicitly the effects of language discrimination on the health of older immigrants and to disentangle these effects from other sources of discriminatory stress.

Perceived Discrimination and Coping

The pervasiveness of interpersonal acts of discrimination and their impact on the health of racial and ethnic minorities have prompted researchers to search for resources and strategies that are efficacious in coping with these experiences and thus protective of health. Several reviews of the literature have commented on the mixed, often contradictory, findings and concluded that resources and strategies more often than not fail to buffer or mitigate the deleterious effects of discrimination (Brondolo, Brady ver Halen, Pencille, Beatty, & Contrada, 2009; Paradies, 2006; Pascoe & Richman, 2009). In cases where buffering is supported, it varies by outcome and is found only under certain and unexpected conditions. For instance, in contrast to the general literature that finds emotional support to be more efficacious than other types of support in buffering stress, Finch and Vega (2003) found that it was instrumental support (e.g., someone to borrow money from) that buffered the effects of discrimination on the self-reported health of Mexican origin adults. Opposite to what is predicted by the stress process model, Clark's (2003) research revealed that social support mitigated the impact of discrimination on blood pressure, but only among those experiencing low levels of unfair treatment.

A number of studies have also investigated racial or ethnic identity as a coping resource that is potentially protective of mental health, theorizing that individuals are better equipped to manage discrimination if they take pride in their ethnic group, are acquainted with its history, and if race/ethnicity is a major part of their self-concept (Brondolo et al., 2009; Sellers, Caldwell, Schmeelk-Cone, & Zimmerman, 2003). This collective sense of belonging is hypothesized to protect health by instilling awareness that racism and discrimination are shared group experiences rather than a consequence of individual failings that, in turn, bolsters one's self image (Landrine & Klonoff, 1996). Similar to studies of social support, findings pertaining to the stress-buffering effects of ethnic identity are varied and often multifaceted. In a study of Filipino American adults, Mossakowski (2003) reported that ethnic identity buffered the impact of major discriminatory events, but not day-to-day chronic discrimination, on depressive symptoms, and a Whitbeck et al. (2002) study of discrimination and depressive symptoms among American Indian adults supported the buffering effects of engaging in traditional practices such as engaging in tribal games. A test of the identity profiles yielded by the Cross's nigrescence model indicated that black women holding multicultural attitudes were less depressed by stressful racist events (Jones, Cross, & DeFour, 2007). Similarly, Sellers and Shelton (2003) found that the mental health of African American college students was less affected by racial discrimination when they held nationalist ideologies and when they believed that other groups held blacks in low regard. Lee (2005) also found that having pride in one's group, but not other aspects of identity, were protective of Korean American college students' mental health. In a slight departure, Fischer and Shaw (1999) investigated the buffering effects of racial socialization, the beliefs and experiences about race and ethnicity that parents impart to their children, and found that African American college students who reported low levels of racial socialization also reported poorer mental health. In contrast to these protective effects, having a strong ethnic or racial identity has been found to actually exacerbate the negative effects of discrimination on mental health (Noh, Beiser, Kaspar, Hou, & Rummens, 1999; Sellers, Copeland-Linder, Martin, & Lewis, 2006; Yip, Gee, & Takeuchi, 2008).

The general consensus in the stress literature is that problem-focused coping is more conducive to good health than emotion-focused coping (Taylor & Stanton, 2007). Consequently, a handful of studies have sought to determine which is most valuable for health—responding to discriminatory experiences by confronting and expressing anger towards the perpetrator, or passive acceptance of the situation. Krieger (1990), in a study of African American women, and Krieger and Sidney (1996), in a study of African American and whites, found that blood pressure was lower in those who "did something about" discrimination than in those who responded passively. Noh et al. (1999) found support for the efficacy of both confrontational and passive coping among ethnic minority groups in Canada. Southeast Asian immigrants (mostly Chinese and Vietnamese) who reported passive responses to ethnic discrimination, forbearance, had fewer depressive symptoms. This relationship was more robust for those with strong ethnic identities. In contrast, Korean immigrants had fewer symptoms when they personally confronted perpetrators or took formal actions (e.g., reported the experience), especially if they were highly acculturated (Noh & Kaspar, 2003). Although both groups have a collectivist cultural orientation that is consistent with resolving difficulties through avoidance, the Southeast Asians were a newer immigrant group who had low English proficiency, less financial security, and may have been unaware of their right to protest their treatment. The research reinforced the long-standing notion that the efficacy of any antidiscrimination coping strategy is dependent upon the situation. Confrontation may not be a viable option when retaliation for doing so is likely (Brondolo et al., 2009).

Knowledge of how older adults cope with discrimination is extremely limited. Consistent with the general literature, there may be circumstances in which coping resources and strategies are likely to be more or less effective depending on circumstances and health outcomes. One promising avenue for further research is to focus on religious coping, which has been found be effective for late life adults in managing more general stressors. In one of the few studies that examined discrimination and coping among late life adults, Bierman (2006) reported that the impact of discrimination on negative affect, a construct that is similar to depressive symptoms, was less pronounced among African Americans who attended religious services. Identifying how individuals cope with racial-ethnic and other sources of discrimination and developing interventions at the interpersonal level, however, does not address the root causes of discrimination. Instead, such efforts place the burden on the individual and are directed toward finding ways in which individuals can successfully adjust to discriminatory encounters rather than eliminating the need for adjustment.

Institutional Discrimination, Residential Segregation, and Health

In addition to individual experiences of unfair treatment, discrimination occurs through institutional arrangements, practices, and policies that reproduce and reinforce racial and ethnic inequality. Residential segregation by race/ethnicity and social class represents a key dimension of institutional discrimination that contributes prominently to health disparities by shaping the social and physical environment where people of color reside (Williams & Collins, 2001). Segregation was created by and is sustained by real estate and mortgage lending practices that steer racial/ethnic minorities into particular neighborhoods (Osypuk & Acevedo-Garcia, 2010). Redlining, land use policies, suburbanization, and other processes result in concentrated poverty within these residential spaces (Wilson, 1987). In highly segregated and poor minority neighborhoods, opportunities for high-quality education are restricted by underfunded schools and unemployment; underemployment is also high, owing to the movement of jobs to suburban areas (Wilson 1987; 1996). High unemployment and low wages are linked to neighborhoods with higher crime and victimization rates, and with more single-parent households that tend to be financially disadvantaged (Williams & Collins, 2001; Wilson, 1987). Lack of political power and a lower tax base in these neighborhoods due to out-migration by the middle class is associated with disinvestment in infrastructure and services as evidenced by abandoned buildings, vacant lots, streets with poor lighting and in disrepair, graffiti, and limited recreational and health service providers (Ross & Mirowsky, 2001; Schulz, Williams, Israel, & Lempert, 2002). Living under such conditions can be highly stressful and health threatening (Schulz et al., 2000), especially for late-life adults who spend a good deal of their time within the confines of their communities (Krause, 1996). With the exception of American Indians living on reservations, African Americans experience the highest levels of residential segregation from the white majority, though levels are rising among Latinos and Asians owing to increases in immigration (Logan, Stults, & Farley, 2004). While lower income whites are more likely to live in economically mixed neighborhoods, minorities of color, especially African Americans, are more likely to live in neighborhoods where poverty rates are high even when they themselves are not poor (Patillo-McCoy, 1999).

A major question for researchers is whether or not living in these highly segregated and impoverished neighborhoods influences health independently of the individual characteristics (e.g., race and SES) of their inhabitants. A majority of studies find that segregation adversely impacts the health of African Americans, with the strongest effects being found for mortality (Kramer & Hogue, 2009). Protective effects are sometimes found, usually when segregation is measured using ethnic concentration (e.g., % black). Mortality was lower for older African American New Yorkers residing in predominantly black areas (≥75% black) than in predominantly white areas (≥75% white; Fang, Madhavan, Bosworth, & Alterman, 1998). Mortality was also lowest for African Americans residing in residentially stable Philadelphia neighborhoods with a high percentage of coethnics (Hutchinson et al., 2009). These "enclave" effects have also been found among older Mexican Americans in the Southwest in analyses of mortality (Eschbach, Ostir, Patel, Markides, & Goodwin, 2004), self-rated health (Patel, Eschbach, Rudkin, Peek, & Markides, 2003), and depressive symptoms (Gerst et al., 2011); and among Chinese Americans in Los Angeles in analyses of physical and mental health (Gee, 2002). Investigations that rely on the isolation index, a more robust measure of the extent to which minority group members are exposed to coethnics, have yielded more mixed results. Analysis of isolation among Puerto Ricans and Mexican Americans in Chicago revealed that segregation had no effect on depressive symptoms, physical symptoms, or disability among Puerto Ricans, but segregation was associated with higher levels of all three outcomes among Mexican Americans (Lee & Ferraro, 2007; Lee, 2009). It is not clear whether these inconsistent findings for Mexican Americans are due to differences in the geographical location, the measures used, or the age groups included. The effects of ethnic concentration, while informative, do not speak to the distribution of minority groups relative to their representation in the overall geographical area. Hence, living in a neighborhood that is 90% Mexican American in San Antonio, a predominately Mexican American metro area, may be different from living in a Little Rock neighborhood that is 50% Mexican American, where the group's presence is a smaller proportion of the total population. The latter may be an enclave while the former is not.

Several mechanisms are hypothesized to explain the connection between racially segregated neighborhoods and health outcomes. First, segregation together with concentrated poverty shape SES at the individual and household level through their effects on educational and income opportunities (Williams & Collins, 2001), and individual level SES is a major social determinant of health (Link & Phelan, 1995; Williams et al., 2010). Second, beyond these individual effects, researchers have established that living in socially and economically disadvantaged neighborhoods is independently associated with higher mortality (for review, see Nandi & Kawachi, 2011), higher psychological distress (Schulz et al., 2000), higher allostatic load (Schulz et al., 2012), and self-reported poor health (Wight et al., 2008; Zhang et al, 2010) for both minorities and nonminorities. Robert and Ruel's (2006) analyses of national data revealed that neighborhood SES helps explain older African Americans' higher prevalence of chronic conditions and poor self-rated health. Collectively, this body of work suggests that living in neighborhoods characterized by high poverty levels, high unemployment, low home ownership, a lower percentage of college graduates, and high levels of public assistance is not conducive to good health.

In seeking to identify aspects of economically disadvantaged neighborhoods that influence health, researchers have investigated constructs such as stress exposure, social connectedness, and collective efficacy, a concept that entails trust and willingness to take actions that maintain informal social control and mobilize resources for beneficial community outcomes. Much of this research has not addressed segregation and health explicitly, but is instructive. Stressors in the form of noise, vandalism, loitering, and crime undermine health by instilling fear and anxiety (Hill, Ross, & Angel, 2005; Ross & Mirowsky, 2001). For the elderly, exposure to such noxious environments may lead to social isolation. Studies of community-level social connectedness and collective efficacy have yielded mixed and unexpected findings for older adults. An analysis of midlife and older adults in Chicago found that reciprocity, trust, and civic participation were associated with lower mortality from heart disease and other causes (Lochner, Kawachi, Brennan, & Buka, 2003), though the effects were less consistent for African Americans. Collective efficacy was also associated with lower mortality among older Chicago residents diagnosed with serious illness, but surprisingly, high levels of social integration were a risk factor and were mediated by violence and victimization rates (Wen, Cagney, & Christakis, 2005). Other studies indicate that social support and networks do not mediate the association between neighborhood social cohesion and self-rated health (Wen, Hawkley, & Cacioppo, 2006), and that living in stable, but less affluent neighborhoods is detrimental to subjective health (Cagney, Browning, & Wen, 2005). These scholars draw on Wilson (1996) to speculate that in many impoverished communities stability and social integration processes do not reflect the kind of social organization hypothesized to enhance health, but instead reflect situations where residents are socially and economically isolated and face constrained mobility.

Residence in segregated neighborhoods, especially those that are impoverished, also affects health by undermining the ability of inhabitants to engage in health-enhancing behaviors. Finding a variety of nutritious foods at reasonable prices is problematic in many minority and new immigrant communities, owing to the scarcity of larger supermarkets and the prevalence of smaller grocery stores and fast food outlets, which are more likely to stock energy-dense foods (Kwate, 2008; Walker, Keane, & Burke, 2010). Comprised food environments have been linked to higher rates of obesity, diabetes, and hypertension (Diez Roux & Mair, 2010). Lack of access to convenient transportation compounds these problems, as residents may have to travel some distance to reach the better-stocked supermarkets (Morland, Wing, Diez Roux, & Poole, 2002). Tobacco and alcohol advertising target minorities (Muggli, Pollay, Lew, & Joseph, 2002) and minority neighborhoods (Morello-Frosch, Pastor, Porres, & Sadd, 2002), and alcohol is more available in these communities than in predominantly white areas (LaVeist & Wallace, 2000). Moreover, some research demonstrates a positive association between the availability of alcohol and crime victimization in low-income minority neighborhoods (Nielsen, Martinez, & Lee, 2005).

CONCLUSIONS

There is compelling evidence to suggest that racial/ethnic disparities in health among late-life adults stem, in part, from differential exposure and vulnerability to stressors that arise from inequalities in social and economic resources and opportunities. For U.S.-born minority elders, their current health status embodies a lifetime of greater exposure to financial hardship, personal experiences with discrimination, and a higher probability of living in racially and economically segregated communities that are inimical to physical and mental health. Immigrating to the United States in late life can also be stressful as family dynamics change, language limitations restrict social engagement, and there is a sudden transition to minority status (Zhang & Zhan, 2009).

As research on the contribution of stressors to racial/ethnic disparities in health among older Americans proceeds, a number of issues are in need of further elaboration. For instance, little is known about how personally mediated discrimination affects the health of elders in the context of other stressors such as financial hardship. Lacking also are investigations on the joint impact of perceived discrimination and residential segregation. One study of African American women found an inverse association between perceived discrimination and neighborhood racial composition (Hunt, Wise, Jipguep, Cozier, & Rosenberg, 2007). Such relationships should be evaluated using more formal measures of segregation, such as isolation and concentration, which take into account the contours of segregation across the entire geographical area (Kramer & Hogue, 2009). At present, much of the research on neighborhood effects focuses on charting social and economic characteristics that are damaging to health, but does not make the very important connection of how these neighborhood characteristics are connected to race-based segregation. There is much evidence to suggest that being poor in a racially segregated community carries greater health risk than being poor in more economically mixed communities.

Unpacking the contribution of discrimination and other stressors to health disparities will require longitudinal data that makes it possible to evaluate these processes over the life course. Late-life minorities represent the survivors of long-term stress exposure; their less resilient counterparts having succumbed to mortality at midlife and earlier ages. Life course research indicates that stress begins to take its toll early in life and is cumulative throughout. Long-term projects that are currently underway with children and adolescents offer the best opportunities for understanding health disparities.

REFERENCES

Adler, N. E., & Rehkopf, D. H. (2008). U.S. disparities in health: Descriptions, causes, and mechanisms. *Annual Review of Public Health, 29*, 235–252.

Aneshensel, C. S. (1992). Social stress: Theory and research. *Annual Review of Sociology, 18*, 15–38.

Angel, R. J., Frisco, M., Angel, J. L., & Chiriboga, D. A. (2003). Financial strain and health among elderly Mexican-origin individuals. *Journal of Health and Social Behavior, 44*(4), 536–551.

Araújo, B. Y., & Borrell, L. N. (2006). Understanding the link between discrimination, mental health outcomes, and life chances among Latinos. *Hispanic Journal of Behavioral Sciences, 28*, 245–266.

Avison, W. R., & Turner, R. J. (1988). Stressful life events and depressive symptoms: Disaggregating the effects of acute stressors and chronic strains. *Journal of Health and Social Behavior, 29*, 253–264.

Ayalon, L., & Gum, A. M. (2011). The relationships between major lifetime discrimination, everyday discrimination, and mental health in three racial and ethnic groups of older adults. *Aging & Mental Health, 15*(5), 587–594.

Barnes, L. L., de Leon, C. F., Lewis, T. T., Bienias, J. L., Wilson, R. S., & Evans, D. A. (2008). Perceived discrimination and mortality in a population-based study of older adults. *American Journal of Public Health, 98*(7), 1241–1247.

Barnes, L. L., Mendes De Leon, C. F., Wilson, R. S., Bienias, J. L., Bennett, D. A., & Evans, D. A. (2004). Racial differences in perceived discrimination in a community population of older blacks and whites. *Journal of Aging and Health, 16*(3), 315–337.

Bierman, A. (2006). Does religion buffer the effects of discrimination on mental health? Differing effects by race. *Journal for the Scientific Study of Religion, 45*, 551–565.

Black, S. A., & Markides, K. S. (1999). Depressive symptoms and mortality in older Mexican Americans. *Annals of Epidemiology, 9*(1), 45–52.

Black, S. A., Markides, K. S., & Miller, T. Q. (1998). Correlates of depressive symptomatology among older community-dwelling Mexican Americans: The Hispanic EPESE. *Journal of Gerontology, 53B*, S198–S208.

Borrell, L. N., & Lancet, E. A. (2011). Race/ethnicity and all-cause mortality in US adults: Revisiting the Hispanic paradox. *American Journal of Public Health, 102*(5), 836–843.

Brondolo, E., Gallo, L. C., & Myers, H. F. (2009). Race, racism and health: Disparities, mechanisms, and interventions. *Journal of Behavioral Medicine, 32*(1), 1–8.

Brondolo, E., Brady Ver Halen, N., Pencille, M., Beatty, D., & Contrada, R. J. (2009). Coping with racism: A selective review of the literature and a theoretical and methodological critique. *Journal of Behavioral Medicine, 32*(1), 64–88.

Brondolo, E., Brady ver Halen, N., Libby, D., & Pencille, M. (2011). Racism as a psychosocial stressor. In R. J. Contrada & A. Baum (Eds.), *The handbook of stress science: Biology, psychology, and health* (pp. 167–184). New York, NY: Springer.

Brown, D. R., & Gary, L. E. (1987). Stressful life events, social support networks, and the physical and mental health of urban black adults. *Journal of Human Stress, 13*(4), 165–174.

Brown, E. (2009). Work, retirement, race, and health disparities. In K. Warner-Schaie & H. I. Sterns (Series Eds.) and T. C. Antonucci & J. S. Jackson (Vol. Eds.), *Annual review of gerontology and geriatrics: Life-course perspectives on late-life health inequalities* (Vol. 29, pp. 233–249). New York, NY: Springer.

Cagney, K. A., Browning, C. R., & Wen, M. (2005). Racial disparities in self-rated health at older ages: What difference does the neighborhood make? *The Journals of Gerontology, 60*(4), S181–S190.

Chae, D. H., Takeuchi, D. T., Barbeau, E. M., Bennett, G. G., Lindsey, J., & Krieger, N. (2008). Unfair treatment, racial/ethnic discrimination, ethnic identification, and smoking among Asian Americans in the National Latino and Asian American Study. *American Journal of Public Health, 98*(3), 485–492.

Chatters, L. M. (2000). Religion and health: Public health research and practice. *Annual Review of Public Health, 21*, 335–367.

Chou, R. S., & Feagin, J. R. (2008). *The myth of the model minority: Asian Americans facing racism*. Boulder, CO: Paradigm.

Clark, R. (2003). Self-reported racism and social support predict blood pressure reactivity in Blacks. *Annals of Behavioral Medicine: A Publication of The Society of Behavioral Medicine, 25*(2), 127–136.

Clark, R. (2004). Significance of perceived racism: Toward understanding ethnic group disparities in health, the later years. In N. B. Anderson, R. A. Bulatao, & B. Cohen (Eds.), *Critical perspectives on racial and ethnic differences in health in late life* (pp. 540–566). Washington, DC: National Academy Press.

Cohen, S., Kessler, R. C., & Gordon, L. U. (1995). Strategies for measuring stress in psychiatric and physical disorders. In S. Cohen, R. C. Kessler, & L. U. Gordon (Eds.), *Measuring stress* (pp. 3–28). New York, NY: Oxford University Press.

Colen, C. G. (2011). Addressing racial disparities in health using life course perspectives: Toward a constructive criticism. *Du Bois Review, 8*, 79–94.

Dallman, M., & Hellhammer, D. (2011). Regulation of the hypothalmo-pituitary-adrenal axis, chronic stress, and energy. The role of brain networks. In R. J. Contrada & A. Baum (Eds.), *The handbook of stress science: Biology, psychology, and health* (pp. 11–36). New York, NY: Springer.

Diez Roux, A. V., & Mair, C. (2010). Neighborhoods and health. *Annals of the New York Academy of Sciences, 1186*, 125–145.

Ellison, C. G., Boardman, J. D., Williams, D. R., & Jackson, J. S. (2001). Religious involvement, stress, and mental health: Findings from the 1995 Detroit area. *Social Forces, 80*, 215–249.

Eschbach, K., Ostir, G. V., Patel, K. V., Markides, K. S., & Goodwin, J. S. (2004). Neighborhood context and mortality among older Mexican Americans: Is there a barrio advantage? *American Journal of Public Health, 94*(10), 1807–1812.

Estrada, A. L. (2009). Mexican Americans and historical trauma theory: A theoretical perspective: *Journal of Ethnicity in Substance Abuse, 8*, 330–340.

Farmer, M. M., & Ferraro, K. F. (2005). Are racial disparities in health conditional on socioeconomic status? *Social Science & Medicine, 60*(1), 191–204.

Feagin, J. R. (2001). *Racist America: Roots, current realities, & future reparations*. New York, NY: Routledge.

Fenelon, J. V. (2007). The struggle of indigenous Americans: A socio-historical view. In H. Kaplan (Series Ed.), H. Vera, & J. R. Feagin (Vol. Eds.), *Handbook of the sociology of racial and ethnic relations* (pp. 15–38). New York, NY: Springer.

Falcón, L. M., & Tucker, K. L. (2000). Prevalence and correlates of depressive symptoms among Hispanic elders in Massachusetts. *The journals of gerontology. Series B, Psychological Sciences and Social Sciences, 55*(2), S108–S116.

Fang, J., Madhavan, S., Bosworth, W., & Alderman, M. H. (1998). Residential segregation and mortality in New York City. *Social Science & Medicine, 47*(4), 469–476.

Finch, B. K., Do, P., Seeman, T., & Frank, R. (2009). Could "acculturation" effects be explained by latent health disadvantages among Mexican immigrants? *International Migration Review, 43*, 471–495.

Finch, B. K., Frank, R., & Vega, W. A. (2004). Acculturation and acculturation stress: A social-epidemiological approach to Mexican migrant farmworkers' health. *International Migration Review, 38*, 236–262.

Finch, B. K., Kolody, B., & Vega, W. A. (2000). Perceived discrimination and depression among Mexican-origin adults in California. *Journal of Health and Social Behavior, 41*(3), 295–313.

Finch, B. K., & Vega, W. A. (2003). Acculturation stress, social support, and self-rated health among Latinos in California. *Journal of Immigrant Health, 5*(3), 109–117.

Fischer, A. R., & Shaw, C. M. (1999). African Americans' mental health and perceptions of racist discrimination: The moderating effects of racial socialization experiences and self-esteem. *Journal of Counseling Psychology, 46*, 395–407.

Flippen, C., & Tienda, M. (2000). Pathways to retirement: Patterns of labor force participation and labor market exit among the pre-retirement population by race, Hispanic origin, and sex. *The Journals of Gerontology, 55*(1), S14–S27.

Flores, E., Tschann, J. M., Dimas, J. M., Bachen, E. A., Pasch, L. A., de Groat, C. L. (2008). Perceived discrimination, perceived stress, and mental and physical health among Mexican-Origin adults. *Hispanic Journal of Behavioral Sciences, 30*, 401–424.

Gee, G. C. (2002). A multilevel analysis of the relationship between institutional and individual racial discrimination and health status. *American Journal of Public Health, 92*(4), 615–623.

Gee, G. C., Ro, A., Shariff-Marco, S., & Chae, D. (2009). Racial discrimination and health among Asian Americans: Evidence, assessment, and directions for future research. *Epidemiologic Reviews, 31*, 130–151.

George, L. K. (2011). Social factors, depression, and aging. In R. H. Binstock & L. K. George (Eds.), *Handbook of aging and the social sciences* (7th ed., pp.149–162). Burlington, MA: Elsevier.

Geronimus, A. T., Hicken, M., Keene, D., & Bound, J. (2006). "Weathering" and age patterns of allostatic load scores among blacks and whites in the United States. *American Journal of Public Health, 96*(5), 826–833.

Geronimus, A. T., Hicken, M. T., Pearson, J. A., Seashols, S. J., Brown, K. L., & Cruz, T. D. (2010). Do US black women experience stress-related accelerated biological aging? A novel theory and first population-based test of black-white differences in telomere length. *Human Nature, 21*(1), 19–38.

Gerst, K., Miranda, P. Y., Eschbach, K., Sheffield, K. M., Peek, M. K., & Markides, K. S. (2011). Protective neighborhoods: Neighborhood proportion of Mexican Americans and depressive symptoms in very old Mexican Americans. *Journal of the American Geriatrics Society, 59*(2), 353–358.

Harrell, J. P., Hall, S., & Taliaferro, J. (2003). Physiological responses to racism and discrimination: An assessment of the evidence. *American Journal of Public Health, 93*(2), 243–248.

Hatch, S. L., & Dohrenwend, B. P. (2007). Distribution of traumatic and other stressful life events by race/ethnicity, gender, SES and age: A review of the research. *American Journal of Community Psychology, 40*(3–4), 313–332.

Hayward, M. D., Crimmins, E. M., Miles, T. P., & Yu, Y. (2000). The significance of socioeconomic status in explaining the racial gap in chronic health conditions. *American Sociological Review, 65*, 910–930.

Hill, T. D., Ross, C. E., & Angel, R. J. (2005). Neighborhood disorder, psychophysiological distress, and health. *Journal of Health and Social Behavior, 46*(2), 170–186.

Hummer, R. A., Benjamins, M. R., & Rogers, R. G. (2004). Racial and ethnic disparities in health and mortality among the U.S. elderly population. In N. B. Anderson, R. A. Bulatao, & B. Cohen (Eds.), *Critical perspectives on racial and ethnic differences in health in late life* (pp. 53–94). Washington, DC: National Academy Press.

Hunt, M. O., Wise, L. A., Jipguep, M., Cozier, Y. C., & Rosenberg, L. (2007). Neighborhood racial composition and perceptions of racial discrimination: Evidence from the Black Women's Health Study. *Social Psychology Quarterly, 70*, 272–289.

Hutchinson, R. N., Putt, M. A., Dean, L. T., Long, J. A., Montagnet, C. A., & Armstrong, K. (2009). Neighborhood racial composition, social capital and black all-cause mortality in Philadelphia. *Social Science & Medicine, 68*(10), 1859–1865.

Jackson, J. S., Forsythe-Brown, I., & Govia, I. O. (2007). Age cohort, ancestry, and immigrant generation influences in family relations and psychological wellbeing among black Caribbean family members. *Journal of Social Issues, 63*, 729–743.

Jackson, J. S., Govia, I. O., & Sellers, S. L. (2011). Racial and ethnic influences over the life course. In R. H. Binstock & L. K. George (Eds.), *Handbook of aging and the social sciences* (7th ed., pp. 91–103). Burlington, MA: Elsevier.

Jackson, J. S., Hudson, D., Kershaw, K., Mezuk, B., Rafferty, J., & Tuttle, K. K. (2011). Discrimination, chronic stress, and mortality among black Americans: A life course framework. In R. G. Rogers, & E. M. Crimmins (Eds.), *International handbook of adult mortality* (1st ed., pp. 311–328). New York, NY: Springer.

Jackson, J. S., Knight, K. M., & Rafferty, J. A. (2010). Race and unhealthy behaviors: Chronic stress, the HPA axis, and physical and mental health disparities over the life course. *American Journal of Public Health, 100*(5), 933–939.

Jang, Y., & Chiriboga, D. A. (2010). Living in a different world: Acculturative stress among Korean American elders. *The Journals of Gerontology, 65B*(1), 14–21.

Jang, Y., Chiriboga, D. A., Kim, G., & Rhew, S. (2010). Perceived discrimination in older Korean Americans. *Asian American Journal of Psychology, 1*(2), 129–135.

Jimenez, D. E., Alegría, M., Chen, C. N., Chan, D., & Laderman, M. (2010). Prevalence of psychiatric illnesses in older ethnic minority adults. *Journal of the American Geriatrics Society, 58*(2), 256–264.

Jones, H. L., Cross, W. E., Jr., & DeFour, D. C. (2007). Race-related stress, racial identity attitudes, and mental health among Black women. *Journal of Black Psychology, 33*, 208–231.

Kaestner, R., Pearson, J. A., Keene, D., & Geronimus, A. T. (2009). Stress, allostatic load and health of Mexican immigrants. *Social Science Quarterly, 90*(5), 1089–1111.

Kahn, J. R., & Fazio, E. M. (2005). Economic status over the life course and racial disparities in health. *The Journals of Gerontology, 60*, 76–84.

Kahn, J. R., & Pearlin, L. I. (2006). Financial strain over the life course and health among older adults. *Journal of Health and Social Behavior, 47*(1), 17–31.

Kessler, R. C., Mickelson, K. D., & Williams, D. R. (1999). The prevalence, distribution, and mental health correlates of perceived discrimination in the United States. *Journal of Health and Social Behavior, 40*(3), 208–230.

Kiecolt, K. J., Hughes, M., & Keith, V. M. (2009). Can a high sense of control and John Henryism be bad for mental health? *The Sociological Quarterly, 50*, 693–714.

Kramer, M. R., & Hogue, C. R. (2009). Is segregation bad for your health? *Epidemiologic Reviews, 31*, 178–194.

Krause, N. (1996). Neighborhood deterioration and self-rated health in later life. *Psychology and Aging, 11*(2), 342–352.

Krause, N. (2003). Praying for others, financial strain, and physical health status in late life. *Journal for the Scientific Study of Religion, 42*, 377–391.

Krause, N. (2006). Exploring the stress-buffering effects of church-based social support and secular social support on health in late life. *Journal of Gerontology: Social Sciences, 61B*, S35–S43.

Krause, N., & Ellison, C. G. (2003). Forgiveness by God, forgiveness of others, and psychological well-being in late life. *Journal for the Scientific Study of Religion, 42*(1), 77–94.

Krause, N., & Ellsion, C. G. (2007) Parental religious socialization practices and self-esteem in late life. *Review of Religious Research, 49*, 109–127.

Krause, N., & Bastida, E. (2011). Church-based social relationships, belonging, and health among older Mexican Americans. *Journal for the Scientific Study of Religion, 50*(2), 397–409.

Krieger, N. (1990). Racial and gender discrimination: Risk factors for high blood pressure? *Social Science & Medicine, 30*(12), 1273–1281.

Krieger, N. (1999). Embodying inequality: A review of concepts, measures, and methods for studying health consequences of discrimination. *International Journal of Health Services, 29*(2), 295–352.

Krieger, N., & Sidney, S. (1996). Racial discrimination and blood pressure: The CARDIA Study of young black and white adults. *American Journal of Public Health, 86*(10), 1370–1378.

Kwate, N. A. (2008). Fried chicken and fresh apples: Racial segregation as a fundamental cause of fast food density in black neighborhoods. *Health & Place, 14*, 32–44.

Landrine, H., & Klonoff, E. A. (1996). The schedule of racist events: A measure of racial discrimination and a study of its negative physical and mental health consequences. *Journal of Black Psychology, 22,* 144–168.

Lantz, P. M., House, J. S., Mero, R. P., & Williams, D. R. (2005). Stress, life events, and socioeconomic disparities in health: Results from the Americans' Changing Lives Study. *Journal of Health and Social Behavior, 46*(3), 274–288.

LaVeist, T. A., & Wallace, J. M. (2000). Health risk and inequitable distribution of liquor stores in African American neighborhood. *Social Science & Medicine, 51*(4), 613–617.

Lawson, E. J., Rodgers-Rose, L. F., & Rajaram, S. (1999). The psychosocial context of Black women's health. *Health Care for Women International, 20*(3), 279–289.

Lazarus, R. S. (1984). Puzzles in the study of daily hassles. *Journal of Behavioral Medicine, 7*(4), 375–389.

Lee, E. O. (2007). Religion and spirituality as predictors of well-being among Chinese American and Korean American older adults. *Journal of Religion, Spirituality & Aging, 19,* 77–100.

Lee, M. A., & Ferraro, K. F. (2007). Neighborhood residential segregation and physical health among Hispanic Americans: Good, bad, or benign? *Journal of Health and Social Behavior, 48*(2), 131–148.

Lee, M. A. (2009). Neighborhood residential segregation and mental health: A multilevel analysis on Hispanic Americans in Chicago. *Social Science & Medicine, 68*(11), 1975–1984.

Lee, R. M. (2005). Resilience against discrimination: Ethnic identity and other-group orientation as protective factors for Korean Americans. *Journal of Counseling Psychology, 52,* 36–44.

Lewis, T. T., Aiello, A. E., Leurgans, S., Kelly, J., & Barnes, L. L. (2010). Self-reported experiences of everyday discrimination are associated with elevated C-reactive protein levels in older African-American adults. *Brain, Behavior, and Immunity, 24*(3), 438–443.

Lewis, T. T., Barnes, L. L., Bienias, J. L., Lackland, D. T., Evans, D. A., & Mendes de Leon, C. F. (2009). Perceived discrimination and blood pressure in older African American and white adults. *The Journals of Gerontology, 64*(9), 1002–1008.

Lewis, T. T., Everson-Rose, S. A., Powell, L. H., Matthews, K. A., Brown, C., Karavolos, K.,... Wesley, D. (2006). Chronic exposure to everyday discrimination and coronary artery calcification in African-American women: The SWAN Heart Study. *Psychosomatic Medicine, 68*(3), 362–368.

Link, B. G., & Phelan, J. (1995). Social conditions as fundamental causes of disease. *Journal of Health and Social Behavior,* (Extra issue), 80–94.

Lincoln, K. D., Chatters, L. M., & Taylor, R. J. (2003). Psychological distress among black and white Americans: Differential effects of social support, negative interaction and personal control. *Journal of Health and Social Behavior, 44*(3), 390–407.

Lochner, K. A., Kawachi, I., Brennan, R. T., & Buka, S. L. (2003). Social capital and neighborhood mortality rates in Chicago. *Social Science & Medicine, 56*(8), 1797–1805.

Logan, J. R., Stults, B. J., & Farley, R. (2004). Segregation of minorities in the metropolis: Two decades of change. *Demography, 41*(1), 1–22.

Luo, Y., Xu, J., Granberg, E., & Wentworth, W. M. (2012). A longitudinal study of social status, perceived discrimination, and physical and emotional health among older adults. *Research on Aging, 34,* 275–301.

Markides, K. S., & Eschbach, K. (2011). Hispanic paradox in adult mortality in the United States. In R. G. Rogers & E. M. Crimmins (Eds.), *International handbook of adult mortality* (1st ed., pp. 227–240). New York, NY: Springer.

Markides, K. S., & Gerst, K. (2011). Immigration, aging, and health in the United States. In R. A. Settersten Jr. & J. L. Angels (Eds.), *Handbook of sociology of aging* (pp. 103–116). New York, NY: Springer Science and Business Media.

Markides, K. S., Salinas, J., & Wong, R. (2010). Ageing and health among Hispanic/Latinos in the Americas. In W. E. Dannefer & C. Philips (Eds.), *Handbook of social gerontology.* London, UK: Sage.

Mattei, J., Demissie, S., Falcon, L. M., Ordovas, J. M., & Tucker, K. (2010). Allostatic load is associated with chronic conditions in the Boston Puerto Rican Health Study. *Social Science & Medicine, 70*(12), 1988–1996.

McEwen, B. S. (2000). Allostasis and allostatic load: Implications for neuropsychopharmacology. *Neuropsychopharmacology, 22*(2), 108–124.

McEwen, B. S., & Seeman, T. (1999). Protective and damaging effects of mediators of stress. Elaborating and testing the concepts of allostasis and allostatic load. *Annals of the New York Academy of Sciences, 896,* 30–47.

McEwen, B. S., & Stellar, E. (1993). Stress and the individual. Mechanisms leading to disease. *Archives of Internal Medicine, 153*(18), 2093–2101.

McGee, D. L., Liao, Y., Cao, G., & Cooper, R. S. (1999). Self-reported health status and mortality in a multiethnic US cohort. *American Journal of Epidemiology, 149*(1), 41–46.

Mirowsky, J., & Ross, C. (2003). *Social causes of psychological distress.* Hawthorne, NY: Aldine de Gruyter.

Mossakowski, K. N. (2003). Coping with perceived discrimination: Does ethnic identity protect mental health? *Journal of Health and Social Behavior, 44*(3), 318–331.

Mui, A. C., & Kang, S. Y. (2006). Acculturation stress and depression among Asian immigrant elders. *Social Work, 51*(3), 243–255.

Mui, A. C., Kang, S. Y., Kang, D., & Domanski, M. D. (2007). English language proficiency and health-related quality of life among Chinese and Korean immigrant elders. *Health & Social Work, 32*(2), 119–127.

Mutchler, J. E., & Burr, J. A. (2011). Race, ethnicity, and aging. In R. A. Settersten Jr. & J. L. Angels (Eds.), *Handbook of Sociology of Aging* (pp. 83–101). New York, NY: Springer Science and Business Media.

Mutchler, J. E., Prakash, A., & Burr, J. A. (2007). The demography of disability and the effects of immigrant history: Older Asians in the United States. *Demography, 44*(2), 251–263.

Meyer, I. H. (2003). Prejudice, social stress, and mental health in lesbian, gay, and bisexual populations: Conceptual issues and research evidence. *Psychological Bulletin, 129*(5), 674–697.

Morello-Frosch, R., Pastor, M., Porras, C., & Sadd, J. (2002). Environmental justice and regional inequality in southern California: Implications for future research. *Environmental Health Perspectives, 110,* 149–154.

Morland, K., Wing, S., Diez Roux, A., & Poole, C. (2002). Neighborhood characteristics associated with the location of food stores and food service places. *American Journal of Preventive Medicine, 22*(1), 23–29.

Muggli, M. E., Pollay, R. W., Lew, R., & Joseph, A. M. (2002). Targeting of Asian Americans and Pacific Islanders by the tobacco industry: Results from the Minnesota Tobacco Document Depository. *Tobacco Control, 11*(3), 201–209.

Myers, H. F. (2009). Ethnicity- and socio-economic status-related stresses in context: An integrative review and conceptual model. *Journal of Behavioral Medicine, 32*(1), 9–19.

Myers, H. F., & Hwang, W. (2004). Cumulative psychosocial risks and resilience: A conceptual perspective on ethnic health disparities in late life. In N. B. Anderson, R. A. Bulatao, & B. Cohen (Eds.), *Critical perspectives on racial and ethnic differences in health in late life* (pp. 492–539). Washington, DC: National Academy Press.

Nandi, A., & Kawachi, I. (2011). Neighborhood effects on mortality. In R. G. Rogers & E. M. Crimmins (Eds.). *International handbook of adult mortality* (1st ed., pp. 413–438). New York, NY: Springer.

National Research Council. (2004). Critical Perspectives on Racial and Ethnic Differences in Health in Late Life. In N. B. Anderson, R. A. Bulato, & B. Cohen, (Eds.). *Panel on race, ethnicity, and health in later life. Committee on Population, Division of Behavioral and Social Sciences and Education.* Washington, DC: The National Academies Press.

Nielsen, A. L., Martinez, R., & Lee, M. T. (2005). Alcohol, ethnicity, and violence: The role of alcohol availability for Latino and Black aggravated assaults and robberies. *Sociological Quarterly, 46,* 479–502.

Noh, S., Beiser, M., Kaspar, V., Hou, F., & Rummens, J. (1999). Perceived racial discrimination, depression, and coping: A study of Southeast Asian refugees in Canada. *Journal of Health and Social Behavior, 40*(3), 193–207.

Noh, S., & Kaspar, V. (2003). Perceived discrimination and depression: Moderating effects of coping, acculturation, and ethnic support. *American Journal of Public Health, 93*(2), 232–238.

Okun, M. A., & Keith, V. M. (1998). Effects of positive and negative social exchanges with various sources on depressive symptoms in younger and older adults. *The Journals of Gerontology, 53*(1), P4–20.

Osypuk, T. L., & Acevedo-Garcia, D. (2010). Beyond individual neighborhoods: A geography of opportunity perspective for understanding racial/ethnic health disparities. *Health & Place, 16*(6), 1113–1123.

Paradies, Y. (2006). A systematic review of empirical research on self-reported racism and health. *International Journal of Epidemiology, 35*(4), 888–901.

Pascoe, E. A., & Smart Richman, L. (2009). Perceived discrimination and health: A meta-analytic review. *Psychological Bulletin, 135*(4), 531–554.

Patel, K. V., Eschbach, K., Rudkin, L. L., Peek, M. K., & Markides, K. S. (2003). Neighborhood context and self-rated health in older Mexican Americans. *Annals of Epidemiology, 13*, 620–628.

Patillo-McCoy, M. (1999) *Black picket fences: Privilege and peril among the black middle class.* Chicago, IL: University of Chicago Press.

Pearlin, L. I. (1999). The stress process revisited: Reflections on concepts and their interrelationships. In C. Aneshensel & J. Phelan (Eds.), *Handbook of the sociology of mental health* (pp. 395–415). New York, NY: Kulwer Ademic/Plenum.

Pérez, D. J., Fortuna, L., & Alegria, M. (2008). Prevalence and correlates of everyday discrimination among U.S. Latinos. *Journal of Community Psychology, 36*(4), 421–433.

Robert, S. A., & Ruel, E. (2006). Racial segregation and health disparities between Black and White older adults. *The Journals of Gerontology, 61*(4), S203–S211.

Ross, C. E., & Mirowsky, J. (2001). Neighborhood disadvantage, disorder, and health. *Journal of Health and Social Behavior, 42*(3), 258–276.

Schulz, A. J., Mentz, G., Lachance, L., Johnson, J., Gaines, C., & Israel, B. A. (2012). Associations between socioeconomic status and allostatic load: Effects of neighborhood poverty and tests of mediating pathways. *American Journal of Public Health, 102*(9), 1706–1714.

Schulz, A., Williams, D., Israel, B., Becker, A., Parker, E., James, S. A., & Jackson, J. (2000). Unfair treatment, neighborhood effects, and mental health in the Detroit metropolitan area. *Journal of Health and Social Behavior, 41*(3), 314–332.

Schulz, A. J., Williams, D. R., Israel, B. A., & Lempert, L. B. (2002). Racial and spatial relations as fundamental determinants of health in Detroit. *The Milbank Quarterly, 80*(4), 677–707.

Seeman, T., Merkin, S. S., Crimmins, E., Koretz, B., Charette, S., & Karlamangla, A. (2008). Education, income and ethnic differences in cumulative biological risk profiles in a national sample of US adults: NHANES III (1988–1994). *Social Science & Medicine, 66*(1), 72–87.

Seeman, T. E., Singer, B. H., Rowe, J. W., Horwitz, R. I., & McEwen, B. S. (1997). Price of adaptation–allostatic load and its health consequences. MacArthur studies of successful aging. *Archives of Internal Medicine, 157*(19), 2259–2268.

Sellers, R. M., Caldwell, C. H., Schmeelk-Cone, K. H., & Zimmerman, M. A. (2003). Racial identity, racial discrimination, perceived stress, and psychological distress among African American young adults. *Journal of Health and Social Behavior, 44*(3), 302–317.

Sellers, R. M., Copeland-Linder, N., Martin, P. P., & Lewis, R. L. (2006). Racial identity matters: The relationship between racial discrimination and psychological functioning in African American adolescents. *Journal of Research on Adolescence, 16*, 187–216.

Sellers, R. M., & Shelton, J. N. (2003). The role of racial identity in perceived racial discrimination. *Journal of Personality and Social Psychology, 84*(5), 1079–1092.

Shaw, B. A., & Krause, N. (2002). Exposure to physical violence during childhood, aging, and health. *Journal of Aging and Health, 14*(4), 467–494.

Shibusawa, T., & Mui, A. D. (2008). Stress, coping, and depression among Japanese American elders. *Journal of Gerontological Social Work, 36*, 63–81.

Singh, G. K., & Hiatt, R. A. (2006). Trends and disparities in socioeconomic and behavioural characteristics, life expectancy, and cause-specific mortality of native-born and foreign-born populations in the United States, 1979–2003. *International Journal of Epidemiology, 35*(4), 903–919.

Sternthal, M. J., Slopen, N., & Williams, D. R. (2011). Racial disparities in health: How much does stress really matter? *Du Bois Review, 8,* 95–113.

Szanton, S. L., Allen, J. K., Thorpe, R. J., Seeman, T., Bandeen-Roche, K., & Fried, L. P. (2008). Effect of financial strain on mortality in community-dwelling older women. *The Journals of Gerontology, 63*(6), S369–S374.

Taylor, R. J., Chatters, L. M., Bullard, K. M., Wallace, J. M., & Jackson, J. S. (2009). Organizational religious behavior among older African Americans: Findings from the National Survey of American Life. *Research on Aging, 31*(4), 440–462.

Taylor, S. E., & Stanton, A. L. (2007). Coping resources, coping processes, and mental health. *Annual Review of Clinical Psychology, 3,* 377–401.

Thoits, P. A. (1995). Stress, coping, and social support processes: Where are we? What next? *Journal of Health and Social Behavior,* (Extra issue), 53–79.

Thoits, P. A. (2010). Stress and health: Major findings and policy implications. *Journal of Health and Social Behavior, 51,* S41–S53.

Todorova, I. L., Falcón, L. M., Lincoln, A. K., & Price, L. L. (2010). Perceived discrimination, psychological distress and health. *Sociology of Health & Illness, 32*(6), 843–861.

Turner, R. J., & Lloyd, D. A. (1999). The stress process and the social distribution of depression. *Journal of Health and Social Behavior, 40*(4), 374–404.

Turner, R. J., Wheaton, B., & Lloyd, D. A. (1995). The epidemiology of social stress. *American Sociological Review, 60*(1), 104–125.

Ulbrich, P. M., & Warheit, G. J. (1989). Social support, stress, and psychological distress among older black and white adults. *Journal of Aging and Health, 1,* 286–305.

Walker, R. E., Keane, C. R., & Burke, J. G. (2010). Disparities and access to healthy food in the United States: A review of food deserts literature. *Health & Place, 16*(5), 876–884.

Wen, M., Cagney, K. A., & Christakis, N. A. (2005). Effect of specific aspects of community social environment on the mortality of individuals diagnosed with serious illness. *Social Science & Medicine, 61*(6), 1119–1134.

Wen, M., Hawkley, L. C., & Cacioppo, J. T. (2006). Objective and perceived neighborhood environment, individual SES and psychosocial factors, and self-rated health: An analysis of older adults in Cook County, Illinois. *Social Science & Medicine, 63*(10), 2575–2590.

Wheaton, B. (1985). Models for the stress-buffering functions of coping resources. *Journal of Health and Social Behavior, 26*(4), 352–364.

Wheaton, B., & Montazer, S. (2010). Stressors, stress, and distress. In T. L. Schied & T. N. Brown (Eds.), *A handbook for the study of mental health: Social contexts, theories, and systems* (2nd ed., pp.171–199). New York, NY: Cambridge University Press.

Whitbeck, L. B., McMorris, B. J., Hoyt, D. R., Stubben, J. D., & Lafromboise, T. (2002). Perceived discrimination, traditional practices, and depressive symptoms among American Indians in the upper midwest. *Journal of Health and Social Behavior, 43*(4), 400–418.

Wight, R. G., Cummings, J. R., Miller-Martinez, D., Karlamangla, A. S., Seeman, T. E., & Aneshensel, C. S. (2008). A multilevel analysis of urban neighborhood socioeconomic disadvantage and health in late life. *Social Science & Medicine, 66*(4), 862–872.

Williams, D. R., & Collins, C. (2001). Racial residential segregation: A fundamental cause of racial disparities in health. *Public Health Reports, 116*(5), 404–416.

Williams, D. R., & Mohammed, S. A. (2009). Discrimination and racial disparities in health: Evidence and needed research. *Journal of Behavioral Medicine, 32*(1), 20–47.

Williams, D. R., Mohammed, S. A., Leavell, J., & Collins, C. (2010). Race, socioeconomic status, and health: Complexities, ongoing challenges, and research opportunities. *Annals of the New York Academy of Sciences, 1186,* 69–101.

Williams, D. R., & Sternthal, M. (2010). Understanding racial-ethnic disparities in health: Sociological contributions. *Journal of Health and Social Behavior, 51,* S15–S27.

Williams, D. R., Yu, Y., Jackson, J. S., & Anderson, N. B. (1997). Racial Differences in Physical and Mental Health: Socio-economic Status, Stress and Discrimination. *Journal of Health Psychology, 2*(3), 335–351.

Wilson, W. J. (1987). Brachial plexus palsy in basic trainees. *Military Medicine, 152*(10), 519–522.

Wilson W. J. (1996). *When work disappears: The world of the new urban poor.* New York, NY: Alfred A. Knopf.

Yip, T., Gee, G. C., & Takeuchi, D. T. (2008). Racial discrimination and psychological distress: The impact of ethnic identity and age among immigrant and United States-born Asian adults. *Developmental Psychology, 44*(3), 787–800.

Yoo, H. C., Gee, G. C., & Takeuchi, D. (2009). Discrimination and health among Asian American immigrants: Disentangling racial from language discrimination. *Social Science & Medicine, 68*(4), 726–732.

Zhang, G., & Zhan, H. J. (2009). Beyond the bible and the cross: A social and cultural analysis of Chinese elders' participation in Christian congregations in the United States. *Sociological Spectrum, 29*, 295–317.

CHAPTER 6

Correlates of Cognitive Aging in Racial/Ethnic Minorities

Adrienne T. Aiken-Morgan, Keith E. Whitfield, and Melanie A. Paige

Despite the fact that for many years now the U.S. older adult population, specifically racial/ethnic minority older adults, has been projected to increase dramatically by 2050 (Angel & Hogan, 2004), there remains a dearth of information regarding the unique features of the cognitive aging process for most racial/ethnic minority groups. While the total number of non-Hispanic whites age 65 and older will double, the number of African Americans age 65 and older will more than triple, and the number of Hispanics will increase 11-fold (Angel & Hogan, 2004). The predicted demographic shift toward ethnic minorities representing a greater proportion of the U.S. total population has made the science of studying race an imperative priority in the agenda of those who study adulthood and aging. In fact, the National Institutes of Health have made several recent revisions to their guidelines for human subject treatment, and some of the central points of change in policy are the strong statements and rules about the necessity of the inclusion of minorities in federally funded research projects. Every application for National Institutes of Health funding must address the inclusion of minorities or face reviews that are less than favorable. Although these guidelines have led to an increase in the amount of research that includes ethnic groups other than Caucasians, often the results are not discussed relative to race so that insights into unique or pervasive factors that affect biology, psychology, and social factors in later life can be better understood.

The goal of the present chapter is to discuss the various factors that influence cognitive aging in racial/ethnic minority groups. Although most of the information in the literature is focused on African Americans and/or Hispanic groups, where available, we will provide information on Asians. Information on American Indian and Alaskan Natives is virtually nonexistent but represent groups that should be examined in future research on patterns of normal cognitive aging. Here, we start by discussing theoretical perspectives and research design in studying race. Next, we discuss the impact of health and social factors on minority cognitive aging, and finally, we consider mild cognitive impairment (MCI) in racial/ethnic minority groups. We hope to provide some examples of culturally appropriate models and suggest some of the ways in which minority populations provide an understanding of cognitive aging in unique ways.

STUDYING RACE AND COGNITION: THEORETICAL PERSPECTIVES
AND RESEARCH DESIGN

Historically, Caucasian groups have been used as the comparison group to which research findings on ethnic minority groups are compared (Whitfield, Allaire, Belue, & Edwards, 2008). When race has been included in the literature, it is usually presented as main effect findings, without regard to important interactions between race and other variables (e.g., health, income, education; Whitfield et al., 2000). Further understanding of understudied racial/ethnic groups offers the possibility to promote healthy aging for the entire nation. To advance the current knowledge regarding cognitive aging in minorities, appropriate research designs are vitally important. Although cross-group research has generated literature on cognitive aging in racial/ethnic minority groups, such as African Americans and Hispanics, it has not provided insights on the degree to which within-group variability contributes to observed differences between groups (see Burton & Bengston, 1982). For example, using current theories of late-life cognitive function, it might be expected that cognitive decline is a prevalent and pervasive change as part of the normal aging process in ethnic minority elders; nonetheless, research questions such as, "What patterns exist in the changes of cognitive abilities in older racial/ethnic minorities?" and, "What is the nature of variability in cognitive abilities among older racial/ethnic minorities?" have not been systematically addressed (Whitfield & Aiken-Morgan, 2008). Instead, past research on culture has focused on addressing the significant differences among various qualities of the different racial/ethnic groups. A large body of racially comparative research on elders has been generated due to researchers initially believing that the distinctive attributes of racial/ethnic minority elders (e.g., language, lifestyle, socioeconomic status [SES], and historical experiences in the United States) were best explained by comparative research. Furthermore, most cross-cultural research typically uses statistical analyses that only employ group mean comparison. One central assumption in these types of analyses is homogeneity of variance; however, meeting this assumption is challenging in cross-cultural comparisons of cognitive functioning due to the distinct heterogeneity within ethnic groups (Whitfield et al., 2008).

Contemporary researchers cite several limitations in these cross-ethnic comparisons, which preclude a full appreciation of the distinctiveness of the groups under study (Markides, Liang, & J. S. Jackson, 1990). One relevant example is combining various Hispanic and/or Latino subgroups (e.g., Mexican Americans, Latin Americans, and Puerto Ricans) into one group and comparing them to Caucasian groups. Each of these cultural subgroups reflects some unique and varying historical culture and level of assimilation, which may bear on cognitive processes affected by aging. To this end, advances in cognitive aging research must depart from the exclusive use of between-subject designs. Future research must consider the fact that the factors that account for between-group variability do not necessarily account for within-group variability (Whitfield & Baker-Thomas, 1999).

If we are to grasp a cross-cultural understanding of cognitive functioning, we must be willing to reconceptualize our approach. Specifically, ample evidence suggests significant individual differences in cognitive aging in studies of Caucasians (e.g., Rapp & Amaral, 1992). In particular, the rate of cognitive decline varies such that cognitive decline does not occur linearly (e.g., Schaie, 1990; Willis, 1991). Longitudinal investigations of cognitive abilities have shown that very few individuals exhibit decline in all or most abilities, with some cognitive abilities maintained well into late life (e.g., Hertzog & Schaie, 1988; Schaie, 1989b). Fluid cognitive abilities are thought to be innate and less influenced by culture or education; however, they are vulnerable to decline with advancing age (Horn, 1982; Horn & Cattell, 1966; Horn & Hofer, 1992; Schaie, 1989a). In contrast, crystallized abilities are thought to depend on and develop from cultural influences and to be resistant to changes with advancing age (e.g., Horn, 1985; Horn & Noll, 1997; Hertzog & Schaie, 1988; Kramer & Willis, 2002; Park, 2000; Salthouse, 1996; Singer, Verhaeghen, Ghisletta, Lindenberger, & Baltes, 2003). However, crystallized abilities have been shown to have steeper decrement after age 70.

Less evidence exists regarding how such individual differences manifest within ethnic minority groups. The impact of SES and cultural and contextual factors on cognitive abilities may combine to produce even greater within-group heterogeneity than between groups. It is likely inappropriate to use traditional measures designed to measure crystallized and fluid cognitive abilities in the study of older ethnic minorities because of the inherent nature of crystallized abilities (which are considered to be significantly influenced by culture [Cattell, 1963]). These measures were standardized on Caucasian populations, such that using them with other cultural groups should be done cautiously. Making between-group comparisons is not likely to be proper without first examining the various sources of within-group variability.

The cognitive skills and strategies that have been provided to older African Americans and other minorities in their educational training may not be adequately tapped by standard cognitive tests. Older African Americans seem to possess strengths for problem solving relevant to their personal history and experiences and possess yet-unidentified abilities that serve them well for tasks and challenges inherent to their environments (Whitfield, 1996). Conversely, there is a significant proportion of African Americans who perform comparable to Caucasians on standard psychometric tasks. Thus, as a basic starting point for understanding cognitive aging in African Americans, it is just as important and meaningful to understand what factors create variability within African Americans as it is to conduct between-group comparisons. In essence, a within-group strategy allows one to first compare apples to apples and not apples to oranges (Whitfield & Baker-Thomas, 1999).

FACTORS CONTRIBUTING TO COGNITIVE AGING IN MINORITY POPULATIONS

Possible differences in the sources of individual variability between racial/ethnic groups (social, psychological, health, etc.) restrict the ability to form assumptions of parallelism in cognitive functioning in late life, without empirical support. Thus, it is important to understand significant contributors to individual variation in cognitive aging within racial/ethnic groups, as mentioned earlier in this chapter. Whitfield (1996) discussed the lack of studies on cognitive aging that have included African Americans and described the challenge to define conceptual starting points for investigations of cognitive aging. Although numerous variables have been found to correlate with and account for performance in cognitive abilities in older adults (e.g., occupation, education, age, health, emotional status), he suggested two conceptual issues that have been important in past research on cognitive aging in Caucasians and of importance in past studies of African American elderly as starting points: (a) health and (b) social factors, such as SES. Growing evidence around these two broad categories of factors support this position.

Health

An important variable in examining minority cognitive aging, given the pervasive disparities in health status in this country, is physical health (Hudson & Whitfield, 2003; Whitfield & Hayward, 2003). Health problems have been shown to negatively influence cognitive functioning and are more prevalent in the elderly. In the current chapter, we will present evidence regarding the relationships between cognition and self-rated health, cardiovascular disease, hypertension, and mortality.

Self-Rated Health

There is a considerable body of research on self-rated health as a significant predictor of cognition (e.g., Aiken-Morgan, Sims, & Whitfield, 2010; Anstey, Luszcz, Giles, & Andrews, 2001; Field, Schaie, & Leino, 1988; Hultsch, Hammer, & Small, 1993; Perlmutter et al., 1988; Perlmutter & Nyquist, 1990; Salthouse, Kausler, & Saults, 1990; Whitfield et al., 1997), with the opposite being true as well (Leinonen, Heikkinen, & Jylhä, 2001). Specifically, Perlmutter and Nyquist (1990) found that self-reported health accounted for a significant proportion of the variance in Digit Span and fluid intelligence performance, even after age-related differences in health were statistically controlled. Anstey et al. (2001) found that poor performance on nearly all the cognitive variables included in their study was associated with mortality, but many of these effects were explained by measures of self-rated health and disease. So, even in contrast to mortality, self-rated health is a significant predictor of cognitive performance. Aiken-Morgan et al. (2010) also examined the influence of self-rated health on cognitive performance, and the findings, while mixed, showed that cardiovascular health status predicted performance on two of five California Verbal Learning Test indices (Short Delay Free Recall and Long Delay Free Recall) and Raven's Progressive Matrices. Aiken-Morgan et al. (2010) concluded that these findings suggest a positive relationship between number of self-reported cardiovascular health conditions and cognitive difficulties.

Cardiovascular Disease and Hypertension

Similar to self-rated health, cardiovascular health/disease and blood pressure/hypertension have been associated with poorer cognitive function. Much of the research on associations between cognition and hypertension has focused on neuropsychological assessments of cognition (Waldstein, Wendell, & Katzel, 2010; Waldstein, Wendell, Hosey, Seliger, & Katzel, 2010). In summary, this extensive body of research suggests that high blood pressure levels are adversely related to cognitive functioning, particularly when normotensives are compared with hypertensives. This relationship between hypertension and cognition has been recently examined both within African Americans (e.g., Izquierdo-Porrera & Waldstein, 2002) and across racial groups (Bohannon, Fillenbaum, Pieper, Hanlon, & Blazer, 2002) and similar results have been found. Thus, hypertension is an important risk factor for cardiovascular disease as well as cognitive functioning. Robbins, M. A. Elias, M. F. Elias, and Budge (2005) demonstrated inverse linear associations of blood pressure and cognitive functioning in both African Americans and Caucasians, with an even higher magnitude of association for African Americans. For the African American sample, pulse pressure was more strongly associated with Digit Symbol Substitution than for whites. Furthermore, systolic and diastolic blood pressure ratings were negatively associated with Digit Symbol Substitution and Similarities subtests (Robbins et al., 2005). In their examination of blood pressure and memory in African Americans, Whitfield et al. (2008) found significant regression effects for systolic blood pressure on Digit Symbol, Telephone Interview of Cognitive Status, and Immediate Recall on the Wechsler Logical Memory test. These findings added to the existing literature on the importance of blood pressure as a source of individual variability in cognitive aging among African Americans. In a longitudinal study of systolic blood pressure and cognitive decline in older Mexican Americans (Insel, Palmer, Stroup-Benham, Markides, & Espino, 2005), blood pressure did not predict cognition at baseline; however, changes in systolic blood pressure for normotensives predicted cognitive decline, even with covariate adjustment.

Cardiovascular disease has also been shown to have a negative impact on cognitive functioning (e.g., Ylikoski et al., 2000). Heart disease continues to be the leading cause of death in the United States (for a review, see Whitfield, Weidner, Clark, & Anderson, 2002). African Americans experience significantly higher age-adjusted mortality rates and poorer trends for coronary heart disease than Caucasians (e.g., Barnett & Halverson, 2001).

Mortality

A number of studies have examined the relationship between mortality and cognitive performance. In summary, research on mortality and cognition suggests that lower cognitive performance is associated with higher mortality risk in older adults (e.g., Deeg, Hofman, & van Zonneveld, 1990; Evans et al., 1991; Kliegel, Moor, & Rott, 2004; Liu, LaCroix, White, Kittner, & Wolf, 1990; Swan, Carmelli, & LaRue, 1995). Kliegel et al. (2004) analyzed cognitive change over a 1.5-year period, and their findings suggest that the terminal decline or drop in cognitive functioning decreases in very old age. Given the well-observed earlier mortality by African Americans compared with Caucasians (for a review, see Whitfield et al., 2002; Whitfield & Hayward, 2003), the impact of chronic conditions on cognitive aging among this vulnerable population may be significant.

One study of the association between cognition and mortality rates (Wilson, Barnes, Mendes de Leon, & Evans, 2009) found that better cognitive function was related to better mortality risk, even when controlling for health and lifestyle differences. This relationship between cognition and mortality risk did not vary between African Americans and whites in this large population-based sample. Furthermore, the relationship between mortality and cognition was stronger for older rather than younger individuals and more pronounced for perceptual speed.

Social Factors

Social and sociodemographic factors have potential direct and mediated effects on cognitive functioning. Mediated effects conceptually arise from measures of social support affecting health that also affect cognition. Previous research suggests that socioeconomic (SES) indicators are strong candidates for sources of direct effects on cognitive functioning. Both social support and SES play an important role in cognitive functioning in African Americans.

Social Support

Social support is broadly defined as the resources available through social ties to other individuals and groups (Billings & Moos, 1984; Lin, Simeone, Ensel, & Kuo, 1979). These resources may serve as buffers against the effects of stress (Caplan, 1974; Cassel, 1974; Cobbs, 1976; Payne & Jones, 1987) and/or ways of fulfilling basic human attachment needs (Barrera, 1981; Kahn & Antonucci, 1980; Unger & Wandersman, 1985). Previous literature on social support among African Americans has shown that this group experiences deficits in social networks but also benefits from compensatory effects of cultural factors, such as religion (J. S. Jackson, Antonucci, & Gibson, 1990). In an older African American sample, greater perceived, appraisal, tangible, self-esteem, and belonging support all predicted greater inhibition on the Stroop Color Test (Sims, Levy, Mwendwa, Callender, & Campbell, 2011). Greater tangible support predicted greater shifting ability on the Wisconsin Card Sorting Test.

J. S. Jackson et al. (1990) proposed that demographic variables of SES, marital status, age, and sex are particularly salient in the study of religious behavior in African Americans. For many older African Americans, the church serves as an alternative source of support to that of family and friends (Ortega, Crutchfield, & Rushing, 1983). Similarly, among Mexican Americans, religious attendance was found to be associated with a slower progression or rate of cognitive decline. Those who attend church weekly, more than weekly, and monthly have slower rates of cognitive decline (Hill, Burdette, Angel, & Angel, 2006). In another study of Spanish older adults, elders with poor social connections and those who were socially disengaged were at a greater risk for cognitive decline and dementia (Zunzunegui, Alvarado, Del Ser, & Otero, 2003). Formal participation in social activities protected against cognitive decline. Engagement with friends was a protective factor for women but not for men.

In an editorial review of the literature regarding religious involvement and cognitive aging, Hill (2008) discussed how religious involvement has been shown to be an important factor in cognitive impairment risk. Among Mexican Americans, religious attendance slowed rates of cognitive impairment, and those who attended church more often exhibited slower rates of cognitive decline (Hill, 2008). Additionally, prior work has indicated that social involvement and social ties stimulate healthy cognitive aging and protect against cognitive deterioration in old age. Activities such as singing, praying, reading, and having philosophical discussion could aid in preserving cognitive function. Finally, religious attendance may also aid in healthy cognitive functioning through the greater likelihood of being involved in health behaviors/activities that reduce the risk of cognitive impairment (Hill, 2008). Furthermore, in an empirical article, Hill and colleagues studied Mexican Americans and found religious attendance was associated with a slower cognitive decline. Participants who attend church weekly, more than weekly, and monthly had slower decline. Finally, their sample of Mexican Americans demonstrated a greater benefit of religious involvement/attendance than educational attainment with regard to healthy cognitive functioning.

Among older Asians, some findings reported in the current literature have been mixed regarding the relationship between social support and cognitive function. In one study (Okabayashi, Liang, Krause, Akiyama, & Sugisawa, 2004), social support received from one's child was associated with life satisfaction, depressive symptoms, and cognitive deficiency for all categories of marital status, with the exception of older married Japanese adults. There was no relationship between cognitive functioning and positive or negative social exchanges. In contrast, high cognitive functioning was positively related to increased social support, specifically for measures of marital status and perceived positive support from friends in a sample of older Taiwanese (Yeh, & Liu, 2003). Furthermore, in another study of older adults in Taiwan, engagement in social activities was associated with a reduced risk of cognitive decline, and those with high levels of social engagements were found to have the greatest benefit as it relates to cognition (Glei, Landau, Goldman, Chuang, Rodríguez, & Weinstein, 2005). Although Taiwanese older adults are more likely to live with their children and interact with family members, due to living in a family-centered culture, data from this study suggest that being involved with social activities outside of one's family may have a greater impact on healthy cognitive functioning than social relationships with family members and friends.

Social Support and Health

Individual variability in cognition may also be influenced by social factors that are related to health in African Americans and other racial/ethnic minority groups. The relationships between health and cognition involve various complexities, and several social and psychological factors both directly and indirectly influence them. For example, prior research discussed associations between cardiovascular health and social support in African Americans and concluded that social disorganization is related to elevated stroke mortality rates, individuals within cohesive families are at reduced risk for elevated blood pressure, and social ties and support play a positive role in reducing elevated blood pressure (J. J. Jackson, 1988; J. S. Jackson et al., 1990; James, 1984).

Social factors, such as social support (e.g., Cohen & Syme, 1985; Debnam, Holt, Clark, Roth, & Southward, 2012; Dressler, Dos Santos, & Viteri, 1986; House et al., 1988; Strogatz & James, 1986) and religious participation (Livingston, Levine, & Moore, 1991; Lee & Sharpe, 2007), have been found to be important predictors of health outcomes. In one recent study on health and social support, general social support in older African Americans had a positive influence on health behaviors, as it was associated positively with fruit and vegetable consumption and negatively associated with the amount of alcohol consumed (Debnam et al., 2012). There was no relationship found between general social support and engagement in physical activity. Furthermore, religious social support had a positive association with fruit and vegetable consumption, while emotional support received from church members was even more significantly associated with fruit and vegetable consumption than was general support, suggesting that religious support has a greater influence on health and dietary behaviors than general support (Debnam et al., 2012). Participants who reported having negative interactions with members of their church body or religious social network were more likely to consume heavy alcohol than participants who did not report any negative interactions (Debnam et al., 2012).

Lee and Sharpe (2007) found that African American older adults scored higher on levels of religiosity and spirituality on the multidimensional measures of religiousness and spirituality (MMRS) in the form of daily spiritual experiences and private religious practices relative to their white counterparts. African American older adults also reported higher levels of forgiveness, religious and spiritual coping, and religious support, identifying God as their primary means of social support (Lee & Sharpe, 2007). Rather than God, white older adults depended more on their friends, family, and professionals as a means of social support. The authors suggested that African American older adults may rely more on religious support and spiritual coping due to the historical lack of access to secular support and resources. In addition, their data suggested that having a personal relationship with God and using him as a means of spiritual support helps to alleviate and manage stress, which can be caused in part by limited socioeconomic resources (Lee & Sharpe, 2007). Finally, interviews revealed that prayer was heavily used to manage financial hardship, loss of a loved one, racism, and health issues and other problems. Participants also showed strong commitment to their communities and a strong unity with their church family and their personal connection and faith in God (Lee & Sharpe, 2007).

Sociodemographic Factors

Socioeconomic Status (SES)

SES as a composite variable is important in the study of cognitive aging. The variables typically included in the conceptualization of SES are education, employment, and income (see Gibson, 1993). Each of these variables is a significant factor in the study of cognition (e.g., Arbuckle, Gold, & Andres, 1986; Gribbon, Schaie, & Parham, 1980; Owens, 1966; Schaie, 1983). As a consequence, SES may account for significant proportions of variability in the performance of older racial/ethnic minorities on various cognitive tasks.

The Role of Education

Among the components of SES, education is likely the most integral to the study of cognition. The relationship between intellectual abilities and education has a long history (e.g., Birren & Morrison, 1961; Blum & Jarvik, 1974; Denney & Palmer, 1981; Green, 1969; Kesler, Denny, & Whitney, 1976; Ripple & Jaquish, 1981; Selzer & Denney, 1980). A measure of years of education or some assessment of educational attainment is common in most studies of cognition in the elderly. A general summary statement that can be made regarding this literature is the positive association between education level and performance on cognitive tasks. Nonetheless, it is not only the *quantity* of education that must be accounted for, but also the *quality* of the educational experience that is vital, particularly when making statements regarding the influence of education on cognitive aging in racial/ethnic minority elders (e.g., Manly et al., 1999; Manly, Jacobs, Touradji, Small, & Stern, 2002; Aiken-Morgan, Marsiske, & Whitfield, 2008). For example, in part as a function of differential access to education, it is well documented that African American elderly are more likely to have less formal education on average than elderly Caucasians (e.g., Harper & Alexander, 1990), and that many older Caucasians obtained a higher quantity and quality of education than most African Americans did during childhood (e.g., Beady & Hansel, 1981; Bruno & Doscher, 1981; Massey, Scott, & Dornbusch, 1975; Walker, 1996). In comparing Caucasians and African Americans with an eighth-grade education, the level of attainment may be the same, but the groups may possess different knowledge bases, skills, and learning strategies from which to perform psychometric or laboratory-based cognitive tests. These different skills likely contribute to differential outcomes or perceived deficits in performance on measures of cognitive ability. To highlight this point, Manly et al. (2002) observed race differences in neuropsychological test performance, but after adjusting the scores for Wide Range Achievement Test—3 reading scores, racial differences on several neuropsychological tests (except category fluency and a drawing measure) were nonsignificant.

This issue of educational quantity versus quality is one of the significant challenges in making cognitive performance comparisons between Caucasian and African American elderly. The existing childhood educational variability among African American elders is also an important factor that has not been an inherent element in discussions of the origins of racial differences in intellectual abilities. One of the results of African Americans being restricted in their access to formal education is that the "spoken word" or verbal communication of information through storytelling was heavily relied upon and is a major component of African American culture of obtaining general knowledge, as well as passing on family histories and legacies (Carlton-LaNey, 1992). There is great variability in how much families and individuals currently rely on storytelling to communicate information (this ability might be assessed using a measure of verbal memory), and this practice may be associated with education and variability in intellectual function among African Americans.

Furthermore, the history of the access to and attainment of quality education for African Americans in this country due to segregated schooling is noteworthy here. Prior to the Brown v. Board of Education ruling in 1954, education was segregated among races. The Brown v. Board of education ruling established desegregated schools in three cities: (a) New York;

(b) Washington, District of Columbia; and (c) Baltimore, Maryland. The purpose of the ruling was to make education equal for blacks and whites in the United States. Whitfield and Wiggins (2003), among others in the literature, have examined the effects of desegregation on education for African Americans, with the expectation that there should be a difference in cognitive aging between those who attended segregated schools and those who attended desegregated schools. To examine the potential influence of quality of education on cognitive aging among African Americans, Whitfield and Wiggins (2003) used one of the most common conceptualizations of cognition: fluid and crystallized abilities (Horn, 1982, 1986). The results of their study indicated that the desegregated school group had significantly higher mean cognitive scores compared with the segregated school group; nevertheless, after controlling for age and years of education, significant mean differences between the schooling groups for either the fluid or crystallized composite dimensions were attenuated. Additionally, no group differences on the specific measures of numerical concepts and inductive reasoning were found, but mean differences were found for measures of verbal meanings and spatial orientation. This study involved one of the first cohorts to attend desegregated schools. The cognitive aging advantages of improved educational quality associated with desegregation appear to have been diminished by negative aspects of the school environment, such as racism experienced by African American students. In light of this, any differences in school attendance might be observed only in future cohorts.

The Role of Language and Bilingualism

Language function is an important correlate of cognitive performance; in fact, dysfunction in language abilities, particularly difficulty in word naming and verbal fluency, is often associated with cognitive impairment and potential dementia (e.g., Alzheimer's disease [AD]). Thus, it is important in this chapter to discuss the role of language and bilingualism as it relates to minority cognitive aging. Overall, the literature on bilingualism and cognitive aging in racial/ethnic minority groups appears to be small; however, many conclusions can be drawn from existing research. To date, focus often has been on Spanish–English bilingualism when studying its influence on cognitive test performance. A salient issue concerning cognitive testing of nonnative English speakers is that traditional cognitive measures, even when translated into Spanish, do not function in the same way when administered to native Spanish speakers and have not always been validated for use in Hispanic/Latino populations. For example, in a study of measurement in invariance of neuropsychology tests in diverse older adults, English-speaking Hispanics performed better on tasks of verbal attention span than Spanish-speaking Hispanics; however, they did not perform as well as African Americans or Caucasians. English- and Spanish-speaking Hispanics both had better expected performance on visual attention as it relates to the attention/working memory dimension (Mungas, Widaman, Reed, & Tomaszewski Farias, 2011).

Regarding age effects, Gollan and colleagues (Gollan, Sandoval, & Salmon, 2011) found that older Spanish–English bilinguals had more error responses in their self-reported dominant language as compared to the younger Spanish–English bilingual group. Older adults self-reported lower spoken-language proficiency skills in each language as compared to younger bilinguals. Results suggested that the self-reported dominant language is more sensitive to age effects, because the very old group produced cross-language intrusion errors during the dominant language fluency task as compared to the old group.

Next, several studies have focused on the Boston Naming Test. Gollan et al. (2007) showed that Spanish–English balanced bilingual older adults, who scored similarly for each language on the Boston Naming Test, were able to name more pictures correctly than unbalanced older bilingual adults. Balanced bilingual older adults were able to benefit from the fact that scoring included words from either language and they were also able to benefit from pictures that had cognate names. Balanced bilinguals appeared to have cognitive benefits that unbalanced bilinguals do not enjoy. One study examined age differences in language switching using the Boston Naming Test (Hernandez, & Kohnert, 1999). They found that Spanish–English bilinguals had greater error rates and increased reaction times when naming pictures (Boston Naming Test) in the mixed condition of naming English and Spanish words within the same set of stimuli. This effect was only found for older adults. This finding did not hold true for bilingual younger adults. In the blocked condition of having to only name either English or Spanish words within the same set of stimuli, little to no differences were found in correct identification of pictures. It can be concluded that older adults have a harder time switching. Older adults who participated in the unpredictable mixed condition (having to switch back and forth between responding in English and Spanish randomly) had lower response times on the first trial after the switch as compared to their younger counterparts, suggesting that older adults are able to recover quicker from the effects of having to switch back and forth. However, older adults had more trouble responding fast to auditory cues when having to alternate between languages compared to the younger group.

Furthermore, in a study of language in cognitive impairment, Gollan et al. (2010) showed that AD may have a greater effect on an older adult's dominant language as opposed to the nondominant one. One explanation they provide is that this could be due to the fact that the dominant language usually contains richer semantic representations, and AD is thought to primarily affect semantic representations. For the Boston Naming Test, the naming score yielded the highest difference for those with and without AD when being tested in their dominant language. Older bilinguals with AD were just as likely as Spanish-dominant bilinguals (and more likely than English-dominant bilinguals) to name pictures in their dominant language, which they were unable to correctly name in their secondary language.

An additional study found that within the semantic category, bilingualism was a significant predictor of verbal fluency in older Hispanic bilinguals, although it did not play a role in performance on tests of phonemic verbal fluency or free spontaneous fluency (Rosselli et al., 2000). Bilinguals performed significantly worse on verbal fluency tasks of generating Spanish words from fruit categories and when having to generate English words from fruit and animal categories. Spanish monolinguals, English monolinguals, and bilinguals performed nearly identical when asked to produce words within phonemic categories (Rosselli et al., 2000). Bilinguals who learned English as a second language early in life and simultaneously maintained frequent use of both Spanish and English were found not to have suffered linguistic decline in the Spanish or English language. Those who learned English after the age of 12 performed significantly worse on the English repetition test and were unable to generate as many description words of a picture as compared to those who learned English before the age of 12.

More research is needed to further our understanding of bilingualism effects on cognitive aging, especially in other racial/ethnic groups, such as Asians and Asian Americans.

MILD COGNITIVE IMPAIRMENT (MCI) AND DEMENTIA

Thus far, our review of the literature in the current chapter has focused on nonpathological, or normal cognitive aging. Normal cognitive aging ends and impairment begins when cognitive performance is lower than to be expected based on age and education-corrected norms. There are many types of impairment that can result, including dementias and MCI. Dementia is a common disorder among the elderly population in the United States. Recent estimates suggest that AD, in particular, is the sixth leading cause of death in the United States and the fifth leading cause in Americans aged 65 and older (Thies & Bleiler, 2011). In the recent decades, research shifted to focus on MCI, the presumed precursor of AD and other types of dementia (Smith et al., 1996). Many classification terms have been used in the literature, but the term "mild cognitive impairment" has gained consensus (Albert, 2008). Prevalence rates for MCI range from 3% to 53.8%, but these depend on the diagnostic guidelines employed (Panza et al., 2005).

Broadly defined, MCI is the impairment of one or more cognitive domains in the context of intact functional abilities (i.e., activities of daily living and instrumental activities of daily living; Petersen et al., 2001). Despite the existing knowledge of progression from normal aging to MCI and/or AD, relatively few studies have focused on dementia in older African Americans (Whitfield, 2002) or Hispanics (Rose, 2005). However, as would be expected in light of the overwhelming support for worse cognitive performance among racial/ethnic minority older adults in comparison to whites, when minority groups have been included in studies of cognitive impairment and dementia, there is general evidence for higher risk and rates of cognitive impairment and dementia among non-white elders (Manly et al., 2008; Rose, 2005). A review of the current literature focusing on within-group analysis of MCI in African Americans shows in one study that (Unverzagt et al., 2011) the age-standardized, annual incidence of CIND (Cognitive Impairment, No Dementia)/MCI was 4.95%, with MCI rates increasing with age, history of head injury, and history of depression. More years of schooling were protective of cognitive function, and MCI rates did not vary substantially by sex. The authors concluded that risk factors of age and education suggest exposures or mechanisms at both ends of the life span may be important variables in onset of CIND/MCI. (Unverzagt et al., 2011). In another study (Gamaldo et al., 2010), approximately 22% of the African American sample was classi-fied as meeting criteria for MCI (i.e., 18% nonamnestic vs. 4% amnestic). Nonamnestic MCI participants were significantly older and had more years of education than cognitively nor-mal individuals. Many also had impairment in one cognitive domain, particularly language and executive function (Gamaldo et al., 2010). In a study of Mexican American older adults, moderate-severe cognitive impairment at baseline was a significant predictor of mortality after the 5th-year of the longitudinal study. Mild cognitive impairment predicted increased mortal-ity risk (Nguyen, Black, Ray, Espino, & Markides, 2003). In addition, decline of four or more points on the Mini-Mental State Examination was found to be associated with mortality as well (Nguyen et al., 2003). Finally, in a South Korean study of the MCI and dementia preva-lence (Kim et al., 2011), age-, gender-, education-, and urbanicity-standardized prevalence of dementia was estimated to be 8.1% for overall dementia and 24.1% for MCI. AD was the most prevalent dementia type diagnosed (5.7%), followed by vascular dementia (2.0%). Amnestic MCI (20.1%) was found to be more prevalent than nonamnestic MCI (4.0%) in this sample (Kim et al., 2011). Being older and male, lower education level, illiteracy, smoking, and head trauma or depression history were associated with higher dementia risk, whereas alcohol use and moderately intense exercise were associated with decreased dementia risk. The authors noted that the prevalence of dementia is expected to double every 20 years until 2050 in Korea, with AD accounting for increasingly more cases of dementia in the future (Kim et al., 2011).

While there remains a need for further research, there is literature to suggest that cogni-tive impairment plays a significant role in the health of American Indian and Alaska native older adults (e.g., Roman, Jervis, & Manson, 2012). Jervis and colleagues found a high rate of dementia and cognitive impairment while reviewing the medical records of older adults in a Northern Plains American Indian tribe nursing facility (Jervis, & Manson, 2007). Although 64% of residents were diagnosed with dementia, it is likely that dementia was underdiag-nosed for some residents due to low scores on the Cognitive Performance Scale and the Mini-Mental State Examination. MMSE scores were available for about half of the residents in the study and, generally speaking, these scores were on average much lower than the 17/30 cutoff score, which would indicate cognitive impairment. These residents reported higher levels of non-Alzheimer's Disease dementia than the national averages. Although dementia diagno-sis was fairly high, mediations to enhance cognition were rarely used. In another study of 140 older Northern Plains Native adults, 11% performed more than two standard deviations below performance expectations on the Mini-Mental State Exam, whereas 28% performed the same on the Mattis Dementia Rating Scale (Jervis, Beals, Fickenscher, & Arciniegas, 2007).

Between-group examinations of MCI in racially diverse groups have shown an increased mortality risk for people with MCI compared with cognitively intact individuals (Wilson, Aggarwal, et al., 2009). Specifically, the risk of death was increased by about 50% among those with MCI and was almost three times greater among those with AD. These effects were observed for both African Americans and whites and did not differ significantly by race. A similar effect was seen among participants with AD, but it was slightly stronger for African Americans (Wilson, Barnes, et al., 2009). Lee et al. (2012) found that in a mixed-race sample of participants diagnosed with MCI, the three-year decline in mean Telephone Interview for Cognitive Status (TICS) score was significantly higher among African Americans than non-African Americans, and in general estimating equation analyses, African Americans had a faster rate of cognitive decline. Finally, in a large, longitudinal study of Caribbean Hispanic, black, and non-Hispanic white subjects (Manly et al., 2008) 21% of normal elderly subjects progressed to MCI (annual incidence rate, 5.1%). The rate of progression from MCI to AD was 21.8% (annual incidence rate, 5.4%), while 47% remained unchanged, and 31% reverted to normal. Those with MCI were 2.8 times more likely to experience development of AD than normal elderly subjects. Regarding rates by racial/ethnic group, being black or Hispanic was associated with greater risk for MCI and AD relative to non-Hispanic white counterparts (Manly et al., 2008). In addition, older age and history of hypertension put individuals at greater risk of MCI, whereas older age, less than 12 years of education, and history of diabetes or stroke had greater AD risk (Manly et al., 2008).

Previous research studies have suggested that the measures used to identify cognitive impairments have not been validated for use in ethnic minorities and lead to overdiagnosis of dementia in such groups (Manly & Jacobs, 2002; Whitfield, 2002). Furthermore, many cognitive measures have normative data based on white/Caucasian groups, with little or no normative data based on minority groups, which fail to account for the unique sociocultural experiences of non-white groups. For example, Fillenbaum et al. (1990) showed that African American elders had higher rates of false-positives for dementia classification than Caucasians, when their cognitive scores were compared to the neurological gold standard of Diagnostic and Statistical Manual (DSM) III criteria and the guidelines of the National Institute of Neurological and Communicative Disorders and Stroke-Alzheimer's Disease and Related Disorders Association (NINCDS-ADRDA). Similarly, Gurland, Wilder, and Groxx (1992) demonstrated a higher false-positive rate for African American versus Caucasian older adults when comparisons between mental status screenings and a clinician's gold standard of clinical criteria.

Thus, there is a growing need for alternate ways to assess and diagnose cognitive impairment in African American and other racial/ethnic minority older adults.

CONCLUSION

The inclusion of racial/ethnic minorities in cognitive aging research challenges scientists to use appropriate research designs and broaden research questions by examining within-group variability to better describe our diverse aging population. Much work is needed to better understand the origins of differences between and within ethnic groups regarding cognitive function in late life. Not only is there a need for more research on minorities, but also the research needs to encompass ethnic groups besides African Americans and Hispanics, particularly Asians, Asian Americans, and Native Americans. Typically, these underserved populations are not included in studies with cognitive interests; thus, no questions about their cognitive function are posed.

One reason for this dearth of research on groups other than African Americans is the history of race and cognition in the United States. Historically, scholarship in the area of intelligence and general cognitive functioning has focused on how African Americans differed from the dominant, white/Caucasian majority group (e.g., Jensen, 1969). This history of race and intelligence has been the subject of much controversy and debate and a source of deep division in the United States for the better part of its history (Lind, 1995). The work of race theorists and eugenicists has always strived to scientifically prove the genetic inferiority of individuals of African descent relative to Caucasians/whites in intellectual function (Jones, 1995; Rosen & Lane, 1995).

Much research has been conducted in the last decades to dispute these racist claims. So why do differences in cognitive test performance persist? As this chapter has addressed, there is growing recognition that, across the lifespan, cultural and health factors have great importance in explaining performance gaps that remain.

Future research should continue to move beyond making racial/ethnic group comparisons and further the investigation of within-group individual differences concerning cognitive aging and its various correlates. In order for the field to be successful in studying various racial/ethnic groups, we must develop and validate cognitive measures that are appropriate for cross-cultural use. This will not be without challenges, as there is significant variation within groups, such as in Hispanics/Latinos, Asians, and Asian Americans, based on nationality and variation in language spoken. Nonetheless, this work is important if we are to fully understand and be prepared for the cognitive aging of our growing population of elders.

REFERENCES

Aiken-Morgan, A., Marsiske, M., & Whitfield, K. E. (2008). Characterizing and explaining differences in cognitive test performance between African American and European American older adults. *Experimental Aging Research, 34*(1), 80–100.

Aiken-Morgan, A. T., Sims, R. C., & Whitfield, K. E. (2010). Cardiovascular health and education as sources of individual variability in cognitive aging among African Americans. *Journal of Aging and Health, 22*(4), 477–503.

Albert, M. S. (2008). The neuropsychology of the development of Alzheimer's disease. In: F. I. M. Craik & S. Salthouse (Eds.), *The handbook of aging and cognition* (3rd ed., pp. 97–132). New York, NY: Psychology Press.

Angel, J., & Hogan, D. (2004). Population aging and diversity in a new era. In K. E. Whitfield (Ed.),*Closing the gap: Improving the health of minority elders in the new millennium* (pp. 1–12). Washington, DC: Gerontological Society of America.

Anstey, K. J., Luszcz, M. A., Giles, L. C., & Andrews, G. R. (2001). Demographic, health, cognitive, and sensory variables as predictors of mortality in very old adults. *Psychology and Aging, 16*(1), 3–11.

Arbuckle, T. Y., Gold, D., & Andres, D. (1986). Cognitive functioning of older people in relation to social and personality variables. *Psychology and Aging, 1*(1), 55–62.

Barnett, E., & Halverson, J. (2001). Local increases in coronary heart disease mortality among blacks and whites in the United States, 1985–1995. *American Journal of Public Health, 91*(9), 1499–1506.

Barrera, M. (1981). Social support in the adjustment of pregnant adolescents. In B. H. Gottlieb (Ed.), *Social networks and social support* (pp. 69–96). Beverly Hills, CA: Sage.

Beady, C. H., & Hansel, S. (1981). Teacher race and expectations for student achievement. *American Education Research Journal, 18*, 191–206.

Billings, A. G., & Moos, R. H. (1984). Coping, stress, and social resources among adults with unipolar depression. *Journal of Personality and Social Psychology, 46*(4), 877–891.

Birren, J. E., & Morrison, D. F. (1961). Analysis of the WAIS subtests in relation to age and education. *Journal of Gerontology, 16*, 363–369.

Blum, J. E., & Jarvik, L. F. (1974). Intellectual performance of octogenarians as a function of education and initial ability. *Human Development, 17*(5), 364–375.

Bohannon, A. D., Fillenbaum, G. G., Pieper, C. F., Hanlon, J. T., & Blazer, D. G. (2002). Relationship of race/ethnicity and blood pressure to change in cognitive function. *Journal of the American Geriatrics Society, 50*(3), 424–429.

Bruno, J. D., & Doscher, M. L. (1981). Contributing to the harms of racial isolation: Analysis of a quest for teacher transfer in a large urban school district. *Educational Administration Quarterly, 17*, 93–108.

Burton, L. M., & Bengston, V. L. (1982). Research in elderly minority communities: Problems and potentials. In R. C. Manuel (Ed.), *Minority aging: Sociological and social psychological issues* (pp. 215–222). Westport, CT: Greenwood Press.

Caplan, C. (1974). *Support systems and community mental health.* New York, NY: Behavioral.

Carlton-LaNey, I. (1992). Elderly black farm women: A population at risk. *Social Work, 37*(6), 517–523.

Cassel, J. (1974). Psychosocial processes and "stress": Theoretical formulation. *International Journal of Health Services: Planning, Administration, Evaluation, 4*(3), 471–482.

Cattell, R. B. (1963). Theory of fluid and crystallized intelligence: A critical experiment. *Journal of Educational Psychology, 54*, 1–22.

Cobbs, S. (1976). Social support as a moderator of life stress. *Psychosomatic Medicine, 38*, 300–314.

Cohen, S., & Syme, S. L. (1985). *Social support and health.* San Francisco, CA: Academic Press.

Debnam, K., Holt, C., Clark, E., Roth, D., & Southward, P. (2012). Relationship between religious social support and general social support with health behaviors in a national sample of African Americans. *Journal Of Behavioral Medicine, 35*(2), 179–189. doi:10.1007/s10865-011-9338-4

Deeg, D. J., Hofman, A., & van Zonneveld, R. J. (1990). The association between change in cognitive function and longevity in Dutch elderly. *American Journal of Epidemiology, 132*(5), 973–982.

Denney, N. W., & Palmer, A. M. (1981). Adult age differences on traditional and practical problem-solving measures. *Journal of Gerontology, 36*(3), 323–328.

Dressler, W. W., Dos Santos, J. E., & Viteri, F. E. (1986). Blood pressure, ethnicity, and psychosocial resources. *Psychosomatic Medicine, 48*(7), 509–519.

Evans, D. A., Smith, L. A., Scherr, P. A., Albert, M. S., Funkenstein, H. H., & Hebert, L. E. (1991). Risk of death from Alzheimer's disease in a community population of older persons. *American Journal of Epidemiology, 134*(4), 403–412.

Field, D., Schaie, K. W., & Leino, E. V. (1988). Continuity in intellectual functioning: The role of self-reported health. *Psychology and Aging, 3*(4), 385–392.

Fillenbaum, G., Heyman, A., Williams, K., Prosnitz, B., & Burchett, B. (1990). Sensitivity and specificity of standardized screens of cognitive impairment and dementia among elderly black and white community residents. *Journal of Clinical Epidemiology, 43*(7), 651–660.

Gamaldo, A. A., Allaire, J. C., Sims, R. C., & Whitfield, K. E. (2010). Assessing mild cognitive impairment among older African Americans. *International Journal of Geriatric Psychiatry, 25*(7), 748–755.

Gibson, R. C. (1993). The black American retirement experience. In J. S. Jackson, L. M. Chatters, & R. T. Taylor (Eds.), *Aging in black America* (pp. 277–300). Newbury Park, CA: Sage.

Glei, D. A., Landau, D. A., Goldman, N., Chuang, Y. L., Rodríguez, G., & Weinstein, M. (2005). Participating in social activities helps preserve cognitive function: An analysis of a longitudinal, population-based study of the elderly. *International Journal of Epidemiology, 34*(4), 864–871.

Gollan, T. H., Fennema-Notestine, C., Montoya, R. I., & Jernigan, T. L. (2007). The bilingual effect on Boston Naming Test performance. *Journal of the International Neuropsychological Society, 13*(2), 197–208.

Gollan, T. H., Salmon, D. P., Montoya, R. I., & da Pena, E. (2010). Accessibility of the nondominant language in picture naming: A counterintuitive effect of dementia on bilingual language production. *Neuropsychologia, 48*(5), 1356–1366.

Gollan, T. H., Sandoval, T., & Salmon, D. P. (2011). Cross-language intrusion errors in aging bilinguals reveal the link between executive control and language selection. *Psychological Science, 22*(9), 1155–1164.

Green, R. F. (1969). Age–intelligence relationship between ages sixteen and sixty-four: A rising trend. *Developmental Psychology, 34*, 404–414.

Gribbon, K., Schaie, K. W., & Parham, I. (1980). Complexity of life style and maintenance of intellectual abilities. *Journal of Social Issues, 36*, 47–67.

Gurland, B. J., Wilder, D. E., & Groxx, P. (1992). Screening scales for dementia: Toward reconciliation of conflicting cross-cultural findings. *International Journal of Geriatric Psychiatry, 7*, 105–113.

Harper, M. S., & Alexander, C. D. (1990). Profile of the Black elderly. In M. S. Harper (Ed.), *Minority aging: Essential curricula content for selected health and allied health professions* (pp. 193–222). Rockville, MD: U.S. Department of Health.

Hernandez, A. E., & Kohnert, K. J. (1999). Aging and language switching in bilinguals. *Aging, Neuropsychology & Cognition, 6*(2), 69–83.

Hertzog, C., & Schaie, K. W. (1988). Stability and change in adult intelligence: 2. Simultaneous analysis of longitudinal means and covariance structures. *Psychology and Aging, 3*(2), 122–130.

Hill, T. D. (2008). Religious involvement and healthy cognitive aging: Patterns, explanations, and future directions. *The Journals of Gerontology, 63*(5), 478–479.

Hill, T. D., Burdette, A. M., Angel, J. L., & Angel, R. J. (2006). Religious attendance and cognitive functioning among older Mexican Americans. *The Journals of Gerontology, 61*(1), P3–P9.

Horn, J. L. (1982). The theory of fluid and crystallized intelligence in relation to concepts of cognitive psychology and aging in adulthood. In F. I. M. Craik & S. Trehub (Eds.), *Aging and cognitive processes* (pp. 245–263). New York, NY: Plenum.

Horn, J. L. (1985). Remodeling old models of intelligence. In B. B. Wolman (Ed.), *Handbook of Intelligence* (pp. 267–300). New York: Wiley.

Horn, J. L. (1986). Intellectual ability concepts. In R. J. Sternberg (Ed.), *Advances in the psychology of human intelligence* (Vol. 3, pp. 35–78). Hillsdale, NJ: Lawrence Erlbaum.

Horn, J. L., & Cattell, R. B. (1966). Refinement and test of the theory of fluid and crystallized general intel-ligences. *Journal of Educational Psychology, 57*(5), 253–270.

Horn, J. L., & Hofer, S. M. (1992). Major abilities and development in the adult period. In R. J. Sternberg & C. A. Berg (Eds.), *Intellectual development* (pp. 44–99). New York, NY: Cambridge University Press.

Horn, J. L., & Noll, J. (1997). Human cognitive capabilities: Gf–Gc theory. In D. P. Flanagan, J. Genshaft, & P. L. Harrison (Eds.), *Contemporary intellectual assessment: Theories, tests, and issues* (pp. 53–91). New York, NY: Guilford Press.

House, J. S., Landis, K. R., & Umberson, D. (1988). Social relationships and health. *Science, 241*(4865), 540–545.

Hudson, R., & Whitfield, K. E. (2003). Health disparities. *Public Policy and Aging Report, 13*(3), 1–24.

Hultsch, D. F., Hammer, M., & Small, B. J. (1993). Age differences in cognitive performance in later life: Relationships to self-reported health and activity life style. *Journal of Gerontology, 48*(1), P1–11.

Insel, K. C., Palmer, R. F., Stroup-Benham, C. A., Markides, K. S., & Espino, D. V. (2005). Association between change in systolic blood pressure and cognitive decline among elderly Mexican Americans: Data from the Hispanic established population for epidemiology study of the elderly. *Experimental Aging Research, 31*(1), 35–54.

Izquierdo-Porrera, A. M., & Waldstein, S. R. (2002). Cardiovascular risk factors and cognitive function in African Americans. *The Journals of Gerontology, 57*(4), P377–P380.

Jackson, J. J. (1988). Social determinants of the health of aging Black populations in the United States. In J. Jackson (Ed.), *The black American elderly: Research on physical and psychosocial health* (pp. 69–98). New York, NY: Springer.

Jackson, J. S., Antonucci, T. C., & Gibson, R. C. (1990). Cultural, racial, and ethnic minority influences on aging. In J. E. Birren & K. W. Schaie (Eds.), *Handbook of the psychology of aging* (pp. 103–123). San Diego, CA: Academic Press.

James, S. A. (1984). Socioeconomic influences on coronary heart disease in black populations. *American Heart Journal, 108*(3 Pt 2), 669–672.

Jensen, A. (1969). How much can we boost IQ and scholastic achievement? *Harvard Educational Review, 39*(1), 1–123.

Jervis, L. L., Beals, J., Fickenscher, A., & Arciniegas, D. B. (2007). Performance on the mini-mental state examination and mattis dementia rating scale among older American Indians. *The Journal of Neuropsychiatry and Clinical Neurosciences, 19*(2), 173–178.

Jervis, L. L., & Manson, S. M. (2007). Cognitive impairment, psychiatric disorders, and problematic behaviors in a tribal nursing home. *Journal of Aging and Health, 19*(2), 260–274.

Kahn, R. L., & Antonucci, T. C. (1980). Convoys over the life course: Attachment, roles, and social sup-port. In P. Baltes & O. Brim (Eds.), *Life-span development and behavior* (pp. 253–286). New York, NY: Academic Press.

Jones, J. (1995). Back to the future with The Bell Curve: Jim Crow, slavery, and g. In S. Fraser (Ed.), *The bell curve wars: Race, intelligence and the future of America* (pp. 11–22). New York, NY: Basic Books.

Kesler, M. S., Denny, N. W., & Whitney, S. E. (1976). Factors influencing problem solving in middle aged and elderly adults. *Human Development,19*, 310–320.

Kim, K. W., Park, J. H., Kim, M. H., Kim, M. D., Kim, B. J., Kim, S. K.,…Cho, M. J. (2011). A nationwide survey on the prevalence of dementia and mild cognitive impairment in South Korea. *Journal of Alzheimer's Disease, 23*(2), 281–291.

Kliegel, M., Moor, C., & Rott, C. (2004). Cognitive status and development in the oldest old: A longitu-dinal analysis from the Heidelberg Centenarian Study. *Archives of Gerontology and Geriatrics, 39*(2), 143–156.

Kramer, A. F., & Willis, S. L. (2002). Enhancing the cognitive vitality of older adults. *Current Directions in Psychological Science, 11*, 173–177.

Lee, E., & Sharpe, T. (2007). Understanding religious/spiritual coping and support resources among African American older adults: A mixed-method approach. *Journal of Religion, Spirituality & Aging, 19*(3), 55–75.

Lee, H. B., Richardson, A. K., Black, B. S., Shore, A. D., Kasper, J. D., & Rabins, P. V. (2012). Race and cognitive decline among community-dwelling elders with mild cognitive impairment: Findings from the Memory and Medical Care Study. *Aging & Mental Health, 16*(3), 372–377.

Leinonen, R., Heikkinen, E., & Jylhä, M. (2001). A pattern of long-term predictors of health ratings among older people. *Aging, 13*(6), 454–464.

Lin, N., Simeone, R. S., Ensel, W. M., & Kuo, W. (1979). Social support, stressful life events, and illness: A model and an empirical test. *Journal of Health and Social Behavior, 20*(2), 108–119.

Lind, M. (1995). The brave new right. In S. Fraser (Ed.), *The bell curve wars: Race, intelligence and the future of America* (pp. 11–22). New York, NY: BasicBooks.

Liu, I. Y., LaCroix, A. Z., White, L. R., Kittner, S. J., & Wolf, P. A. (1990). Cognitive impairment and mortality: A study of possible confounders. *American Journal of Epidemiology, 132*(1), 136–143.

Livingston, I. L., Levine, D. M., & Moore, R. D. (1991). Social integration and black intraracial variation in blood pressure. *Ethnicity & Disease, 1*(2), 135–149.

Manly, J. J., Jacobs, D. M., Sano, M., Bell, K., Merchant, C. A., Small, S. A., & Stern, Y. (1999). Effect of literacy on neuropsychological test performance in nondemented, education-matched elders. *Journal of The International Neuropsychological Society, 5*(3), 191–202.

Manly, J. J., & Jacobs, D. M. (2002). Future directions in neuropsychological assessment with African Americans. In F. R. Ferraro (Eds.), *Minority and cross-cultural aspects of neuropsychological assessment* (pp. 79–96). Lisse, The Netherlands: Swets & Zeitlinger.

Manly, J. J., Jacobs, D. M., Touradji, P., Small, S. A., & Stern, Y. (2002). Reading level attenuates differences in neuropsychological test performance between African American and White elders. *Journal of the International Neuropsychological Society, 8*(3), 341–348.

Manly, J. J., Tang, M. X., Schupf, N., Stern, Y., Vonsattel, J. P., & Mayeux, R. (2008). Frequency and course of mild cognitive impairment in a multiethnic community. *Annals of Neurology, 63*(4), 494–506.

Markides, K. S., Liang, J., & Jackson, J. S. (1990). Race, ethnicity, and aging: Conceptual and methodological issues. In R. H. Binstock & L. K. George (Eds.), *Handbook of aging and social sciences* (pp. 112–129). New York, NY: Van Nostrand Reinhold.

Massey, G. C., Scott, M. V., & Dornbusch, S. M. (1975). Racism without racists: Institution racism in urban schools. *The Black Scholar, 7*, 10–19.

Mungas, D., Widaman, K. F., Reed, B. R., & Tomaszewski Farias, S. (2011). Measurement invariance of neuropsychological tests in diverse older persons. *Neuropsychology, 25*(2), 260–269.

Nguyen, H. T., Black, S. A., Ray, L. A., Espino, D. V., & Markides, K. S. (2003). Cognitive impairment and mortality in older Mexican Americans. *Journal of the American Geriatrics Society, 51*(2), 178–183.

Okabayashi, H., Liang, J., Krause, N., Akiyama, H., & Sugisawa, H. (2004). Mental health among older adults in Japan: Do sources of social support and negative interaction make a difference? *Social Science & Medicine, 59*(11), 2259–2270.

Ortega, S. T., Crutchfield, R. D., & Rushing, W. A. (1983). Race differences in elderly personal well-being: Friendship, family, and church. *Research on Aging, 5*, 101–118.

Owens, W. A. (1966). Age and mental abilities: A second adult follow-up. *Journal of Educational Psychology, 57*(6), 311–325.

Panza, F., D'Introno, A., Colacicco, A. M., Capurso, C., Del Parigi, A., Caselli, R. J.,…Solfrizzi, V. (2005). Current epidemiology of mild cognitive impairment and other predementia syndromes. *The American Journal of Geriatric Psychiatry, 13*(8), 633–644.

Park, D. C. (2000). The basic mechanisms accounting for age-related decline in cognitive function. In D. Park & N. Schwarz (Eds.), *Cognitive aging: A primer* (pp. 3–21). Philadelphia, PA: Taylor & Francis.

Payne, R. L., & Jones, G. J. (1987). Measurements and methodological issues in social support. In S. V. Kasl & C. L. Cooper (Eds.), *Stress and health: Issues in research methodology* (pp. 167–205). New York, NY: Wiley.

Perlmutter, M., Adams, C., Berry, J., Kaplan, M., Persons, D., & Verdonik, F. (1988). Memory and aging. In K. W. Schaie (Ed.), *Annual review of gerontology and geriatrics* (pp. 57–92). New York, NY: Springer.

Perlmutter, M., & Nyquist, L. (1990). Relationships between self-reported physical and mental health and intelligence performance across adulthood. *Journal of Gerontology, 45*(4), P145–P155.

Petersen, R. C., Doody, R., Kurz, A., Mohs, R. C., Morris, J. C., Rabins, P. V., . . . Winblad, B. (2001). Current concepts in mild cognitive impairment. *Archives of Neurology, 58*(12), 1985–1992.

Rapp, P. R., & Amaral, D. G. (1992). Individual differences in the cognitive and neurobiological consequences of normal aging. *Trends in Neurosciences, 15*(9), 340–345.

Ripple, R. E., & Jaquish, G. A. (1981). Fluency, flexibility, and originality in later adulthood. *Educational Gerontology, 7*, 1–10.

Robbins, M. A., Elias, M. F., Elias, P. K., & Budge, M. M. (2005). Blood pressure and cognitive function in an African-American and a Caucasian-American sample: The Maine-Syracuse Study. *Psychosomatic Medicine, 67*(5), 707–714.

Roman, S., Jervis, L. L., & Manson, S. M. (2012). Psychology of older American Indians and Alaska Natives: Strengths and challenges to maintaining mental health. In E. C. Chang, C. A. Downey, E. C. Chang, & C. A. Downey (Eds.), *Handbook of race and development in mental health* (pp. 127–146). New York, NY: Springer Science and Business Media.

Rose, K. M. (2005). Mild cognitive impairment in Hispanic Americans: An overview of the state of the science. *Archives of Psychiatric Nursing, 19*(5), 205–209.

Rosen, J., & Lane, C. (1995). The sources of The Bell Curve. In S. Fraser (Ed.), *The bell curve wars: Race, intelligence and the future of America* (pp. 11–22). New York, NY: BasicBooks.

Rosselli, M., Ardila, A., Araujo, K., Weekes, V. A., Caracciolo, V., Padilla, M., & Ostrosky-Solís, F. (2000). Verbal fluency and repetition skills in healthy older Spanish-English bilinguals. *Applied Neuropsychology, 7*(1), 17–24.

Salthouse, T. A. (1996). The processing-speed theory of adult age differences in cognition. *Psychological Review, 103*(3), 403–428.

Salthouse, T. A., Kausler, D. H., & Saults, J. S. (1990). Age, self-assessed health status, and cognition. *Journal of Gerontology, 45*(4), P156–P160.

Schaie, K. W. (1983). The Seattle longitudinal study: A twenty-one year exploration of psychometric intelligence in adulthood. In K. W. Schaie (Ed.), *Longitudinal studies of adult psychological development* (pp. 64–135). New York, NY: Guilford Press.

Schaie, K. W. (1989a). Individual differences in rate of cognitive change in adulthood. In V. L. Bengtson & K. W. Schaie (Eds.), *The course of later life: Research and reflections* (pp. 65–85). New York, NY: Springer.

Schaie, K. W. (1989b). Perceptual speed in adulthood: Cross-sectional and longitudinal studies. *Psychology and Aging, 4*(4), 443–453.

Schaie, K. W. (1990). Intellectual development in adulthood. In J. E. Birren & K. W. Schaie (Eds.), *Handbook of the psychology of aging* (pp. 291–310). San Diego, CA: Academic Press.

Sims, R. C., Levy, S. A., Mwendwa, D. T., Callender, C. O., & Campbell, A. L. (2011). The influence of functional social support on executive functioning in middle-aged African Americans. *Neuropsychology, Development, and Cognition, 18*(4), 414–431.

Selzer, S. C., & Denney, N. W. (1980). Conservation abilities in middle-aged and elderly adults. *International Journal of Aging & Human Development, 11*(2), 135–146.

Singer, T., Verhaeghen, P., Ghisletta, P., Lindenberger, U., & Baltes, P. B. (2003). The fate of cognition in very old age: Six-year longitudinal findings in the Berlin Aging Study (BASE). *Psychology and Aging, 18*(2), 318–331.

Smith, G. E., Petersen, R. C., Parisi, J. E., Ivnik, R. J., Kokmen, E., Tangalos, E. G., & Waring, S. (1996). Definition, course, and outcome of mild cognitive impairment. *Aging, Neuropsychology, and Cognition, 3*(2), 141–147.

Strogatz, D. S., & James, S. A. (1986). Social support and hypertension among blacks and whites in a rural, southern community. *American Journal of Epidemiology, 124*(6), 949–956.

Swan, G. E., Carmelli, D., & LaRue, A. (1995). Performance on the digit symbol substitution test and 5-year mortality in the Western Collaborative Group Study. *American Journal of Epidemiology, 141*(1), 32–40.

Thies, W., & Bleiler, L. (2011). Alzheimer's disease facts and figures. *Alzheimer's & Dementia, 7*(2), 208–244.

Unger, D. G., & Wandersman, L. P. (1985). Social support and adolescent mothers: Action research contributions to theory and application. *Journal of Social Issues, 41*, 29–43.

Unverzagt, F. W., Ogunniyi, A., Taler, V., Gao, S., Lane, K. A., Baiyewu, O., . . . Hall, K. S. (2011). Incidence and risk factors for cognitive impairment no dementia and mild cognitive impairment in African Americans. *Alzheimer Disease and Associated Disorders, 25*(1), 4–10.

Waldstein, S. R., Wendell, C., Hosey, M. M., Seliger, S. L., & Katzel, L. L. (2010). Cardiovascular disease and neurocognitive function. In C. L. Armstrong, L. Morrow, C. L. Armstrong, & L. Morrow (Eds.), *Handbook of medical neuropsychology: Applications of cognitive neuroscience* (pp. 69–99). New York, NY: Springer Science and Business Media.

Waldstein, S. R., Wendell, C., & Katzel, L. I. (2010). Hypertension and neurocognitive function in older adults: Blood pressure and beyond. *Annual Review of Gerontology & Geriatrics, 30*, 115–134.

Walker, V. S. (1996). *Their highest potential: An African American school community in the segregated south.* Chapel Hill, NC: University of North Carolina Press.

Whitfield, K. E. (1996). Studying cognition in older African Americans: Some conceptual considerations. *Journal of Aging and Ethnicity, 1*, 35–45.

Whitfield, K. E. (2002). Challenges in cognitive assessment of African Americans in research on Alzheimer disease. *Alzheimer Disease and Associated Disorders, 16*, S80–S81.

Whitfield, K. E., & Aiken-Morgan, A. (2008). Minority populations and cognitive aging. In S. Hofer & D. Alwin (Eds.), *Handbook on cognitive aging: Interdisciplinary perspectives* (pp. 384–397). San Francisco, CA: Sage.

Whitfield, K. E., Allaire, J. C., Belue, R., & Edwards, C. L. (2008). Are comparisons the answer to understanding behavioral aspects of aging in racial and ethnic groups? *The Journals of Gerontology, 63*(5), P301–P308.

Whitfield, K. E., & Baker-Thomas, T. (1999). Individual differences in aging minorities. *International Journal of Aging & Human Development, 48*(1), 73–79.

Whitfield, K. E., Fillenbaum, G. G., Pieper, C., Albert, M. S., Berkman, L. F., Blazer, D. G., . . . Seeman, T. (2000). The effect of race and health-related factors on naming and memory. The MacArthur Studies of Successful Aging. *Journal of Aging and Health, 12*(1), 69–89.

Whitfield, K., & Hayward, M. (2003). The landscape of health disparities in older adults. *Public Policy and Aging Report,13*(3).

Whitfield, K. E., Seeman, T. E., Miles, T. P., Albert, M. S., Berkman, L. F., Blazer, D. G., & Rowe, J. W. (1997). Health indices as predictors of cognition among older African Americans: MacArthur studies of successful aging. *Ethnicity & Disease, 7*(2), 127–136.

Whitfield, K. E., Weidner, G., Clark, R., & Anderson, N. B. (2002). Sociodemographic diversity and behavioral medicine. *Journal of Consulting and Clinical Psychology, 70*(3), 463–481.

Whitfield, K. E., & Wiggins, S. A. (2003). Educational influences on cognitive aging among African Americans: Quantity and quality. *Journal of Black Psychology, 2*, 275–291.

Willis, S. L. (1991). Cognition and everyday competence. In K. W. Schaie & M. F. Lawton (Eds.), *Annual review of gerontology and geriatrics* (Vol. 11, pp. 80–109). New York, NY: Springer.

Wilson, R. S., Aggarwal, N. T., Barnes, L. L., Bienias, J. L., Mendes de Leon, C. F., & Evans, D. A. (2009). Biracial population study of mortality in mild cognitive impairment and Alzheimer disease. *Archives of Neurology, 66*(6), 767–772.

Wilson, R. S., Barnes, L. L., Mendes de Leon, C. F., & Evans, D. A. (2009). Cognition and survival in a biracial urban population of old people. *Intelligence, 37*(6), 545–550.

Yeh, S. C., & Liu, Y. Y. (2003). Influence of social support on cognitive function in the elderly. *BMC Health Services Research, 3*(1), 9.

Ylikoski, R., Ylikoski, A., Raininko, R., Keskivaara, P., Sulkava, R., Tilvis, R., & Erkinjuntti, T. (2000). Cardiovascular diseases, health status, brain imaging findings and neuropsychological functioning in neurologically healthy elderly individuals. *Archives of Gerontology and Geriatrics, 30*(2), 115–130.

Zunzunegui, M. V., Alvarado, B. E., Del Ser, T., & Otero, A. (2003). Social networks, social integration, and social engagement determine cognitive decline in community-dwelling Spanish older adults. *The Journals of Gerontology, 58*(2), S93–S100.

PART II

PUBLIC HEALTH/BIOLOGY OF MINORITY AGING

CHAPTER 7

Introduction: Minorities, Aging, and Health

Kyriakos S. Markides and Kerstin Gerst-Emerson

Gerontologists have been giving increasing attention to the racial and ethnic diversity of the aged population in recent decades. Such interest is undoubtedly related to the rapid growth in the numbers and proportions of people of color and of non-European origins in the United States, Canada, Australia, the United Kingdom, as well as other European countries. This growth has been fueled primarily by rising numbers of immigrants from non-Western origins (Markides & Gerst, 2011). As immigrants tend to be mostly young, the percentage of older people in the populations continues to be overwhelmingly native white. In the United States, for example, more than 80% of persons 65 years and over are non-Hispanic whites. However, this figure is projected to drop to around 60% by the year 2050 as the ethnic and minority population experiences rapid aging (Markides & Gerst, 2011).

In the United States, the field of minority aging originated in attempts of certain advocacy groups to highlight the disadvantaged portion of elderly African Americans in the 1960s (Dowd & Bengtson, 1978). Primary focus was given to income, health, and housing. The "double jeopardy" hypothesis suggested that elderly African Americans were doubly disadvantaged by color and age. The notion that being black and old constituted a double disadvantage had a certain appeal to scholars and dominated the field from the mid-1970s through the 1980s (Dowd & Bengtson, 1978; Ferraro, 1987; Jackson, 1985; Markides, 1983; Markides, Liang, & Jackson, 1990; Mutchler & Burr, 2011). The double jeopardy hypothesis was placed in a multiple hierarchy stratification perspective that in addition to ethnic minority group status and age also includes gender and socioeconomic status (Bengtson, 1979). The double jeopardy hypothesis suggested that minority group disadvantages observed in middle age should become wider in older age (Dowd & Bengtson, 1978). While such a prediction made good intuitive sense, it failed empirically because of the absence of focus on age changes and a comparative life course perspective. Cross-sectional analyses showed, for example, that racial differentials in health in middle age declined in old age most likely because of greater selective survival among African Americans as illustrated by the racial mortality crossover phenomenon (Markides, Liang, & Jackson, 1990; Mutchler & Burr, 2011). If anything, the literature supported the "aging-as-leveler" hypothesis of declining racial differences in health and other quality of life indicators with age (Mutchler & Burr, 2011).

More recently, the double jeopardy and age-as-leveler hypotheses have evolved into the more fully developed cumulative advantage–disadvantage perspective (Dannefer, 2003;

Mutchler & Burr, 2011; O'Rand, 1996). A similar cumulative inequality perspective has also been advanced (Ferraro, Shippee, & Shafer, 2009). The basic notion summarizing these perspectives' hypotheses is that initial inequalities experienced in childhood in economic resources, health status, and other indicators of quality of life widen with age. As such, this perspective is more about advantage–disadvantage or inequality based on social and economic class than on ethnic minority group status (Dannefer, 1987; Mutchler & Burr, 2011). The applicability of the perspective to racial and ethnic differences was illustrated in several articles published in a special issue of *Research on Aging* edited by Lynch (2008). Relevant articles included were those of Shuey and Willson (2008); Taylor (2008); and Walesmann, Geronimus, and Gee (2008). These researchers argued that minority group members, especially African Americans, most Hispanics, and Native Americans, are more likely to be born into disadvantaged families and those early disadvantages tend to cumulate over time later in life. Such disadvantages are also observed in the area of health as illustrated by the above-referenced manuscripts.

Perhaps, a limitation of the above perspectives as they apply to the area of health has been the lack of attention to the rising numbers of immigrants in the United States, as well as other Western countries, who tend to be healthier on average than the native-born population (Biddle & McDonald, 2007; Cunningham, Ruben, & Vengat Narayan, 2008; Gee, Kobayashi, & Prus, 2004; Markides & Eschbach, 2005; Markides & Gerst, 2011; Stephen, Foote, Hendershot, & Schoenborn, 1994). It is generally agreed that the superior health of immigrants is mostly the result of health selection as well as better health behaviors. Yet, initial health advantages tend to disappear with time in the host country (Antecol & Bedard, 2006; Markides & Eschbach, 2005; Markides & Gerst, 2011; McDonald & Kennedy, 2004). Much of this research in the United States has focused primarily on Hispanics, the majority of whom are of Mexican origin. The so-called Hispanic Epidemiologic Paradox of relatively good health despite socioeconomic disadvantages has dominated the field of Hispanic/Latino health for more than two decades (Markides & Eschbach, 2011). We also believe that initially healthy Mexican immigrants reach old age in generally poor health and in a more disabled state than the general population (Markides & Gerst, 2011).

This part of the handbook focuses on aging and health issues in all of America's major minority populations including African Americans, Hispanics/Latinos, Asian Americans, as well as Native Americans. The chapters address the issues of health inequality and health advantage/disadvantage. In addition, they introduce relatively new areas of inquiry including long-term care, genetics, nutrition, health interventions, and health policy issues.

Mehta, Sudursanan, and Elo (Chapter 8) provide an overview of patterns, trends, and determinants of disability among older people in America's major race and ethnic groups. They find that Native Americans appear to report the highest disability levels, followed by African Americans born in the United States. They also show that U.S.-born Hispanics also report higher disability rates than non-Hispanic whites—a difference that is attributed to differences in educational attainment between the two groups. The authors find a foreign-born disability advantage among African Americans and Hispanics but not among Asian Americans. The latter is likely the result of the changing composition of Asian American immigrants. As has been suggested in the literature (see Markides, Eschbach, Ray, & Peek, 2007), most of the native-born older Asian Americans were of Japanese or Chinese origins, whereas approximately half of foreign-born older Asian Americans are Vietnamese, Filipino, or from other less-advantaged origins. Thus, lumping such diverse subgroups can lead to highly misleading results. With respect to trends, the authors find little evidence that African American to white disparities have changed between 2000 and 2010. In addition, there is some evidence to suggest that older Hispanic women seem to be getting worse off relative to non-Hispanic white women—a trend that might be associated by rising rates of obesity among Hispanics, including Hispanic immigrants (Singh, Siahpush, Hiatt, & Timsina, 2011). Thus, trends in obesity as well as other risk factors among race/ethnic groups need to be further investigated to lead to better predictions in future trends in disability and health in general among older people from diverse backgrounds.

Hummer, Melvin, Sheehan, and Wang (Chapter 9) provide an overview of our knowledge of race and ethnic differences in mortality and longevity. After reviewing historical and conceptual issues, the authors present mortality statistics for the major ethnic groups in comparison with non-Hispanic whites for ages 45 and above. They show that the rates for non-Hispanic blacks are the highest of any group through age 84 and fall below the rates for non-Hispanic whites at ages 85 and over. The latter is consistent with the long-observed mortality crossover phenomenon of lower mortality rates among blacks at advanced ages, which likely results from selective mortality (Masters, 2012). The authors conclude that while black/ white mortality differences have narrowed in recent years, blacks continue to have much higher mortality rates than whites.

The authors also show that official mortality rates for Hispanics/Latinos and Asian Americans are lower than those of non-Hispanic whites and blacks at every age and both genders. Rates for American Indians/Alaska Natives show that they generally have low mortality rates especially at advanced ages, but these will likely result from misclassification of ethnicity on Native American death certificates (Arias, Schauman, Sorlie, & Backlund, 2008). The authors show that survey-based mortality rates, which avoid the misclassification of ethnicity on death certificates, suggest that American Indians exhibit considerably less favorable mortality patterns than non-Hispanic whites. They suggest that we need to continue refining explanations for mortality differentials, including the advantageous rates for most Hispanics (Markides & Eschbach, 2011).

Whitfield, Ford, and Edwards (Chapter 10) undertake the difficult topic of the influence of genetics on health status in different racial/ethnic groups. As might have been predicted, much of the literature has focused on potential genetic differences between African Americans and whites related to such diseases as hypertension, sickle cell anemia, obesity, diabetes, and cancer. The authors are careful to point out that genes typically interact with behavioral and socioenvironmental factors to influence racial health disparities such as observed in hypertension at all adult ages. In addition to possible genetic factors, the literature has emphasized the influence of poverty and socioeconomic status as well as stressors associated with minority group status. The authors argue that interventions to reduce health disparities must focus on both social factors related to access to health care as well as genetic markers of disease that can be addressed with targeted therapies.

Buchowski, Sidani, and Powers (Chapter 11) focus on how diet and nutrition influence disease and health disparities. They suggest that nutritional intake and genetic factors play a role, but so do cultural and socioeconomic factors including education and income. Also important are environmental factors such as access to food stores and transportation, which are known to influence food availability and variety. The authors provide a useful overview of cultural patterns among African Americans, Hispanics/Latinos, and Native Americans. In addition, they review factors related to the traditional Mediterranean diet, Eastern and Central European diets, as well as Middle Eastern and Caribbean diets. The authors conclude by commenting on the importance of combining positive physical and dietary activity behaviors to address racial and ethnic health disparities attributed to dietary and other lifestyle factors.

Levkoff, Chen, and Norton (Chapter 12) outline two approaches to developing health interventions. The authors argue that the increasing sociodemographic diversity of the United States population, including the older segment, are making the issue of addressing cultural competence a complex challenge. In addition, there are individual and institutional barriers to health care delivery, including the underrepresentation of ethnic minority populations in clinical trials, resulting from a variety of logistical difficulties and other factors preventing participation. The authors propose that there are two typical solutions to developing and delivering culturally competent interventions to older people of ethnic minority backgrounds. First, there is the science to practice approach, which involves adapting principles of health care to culture-specific situations, while the practice to science approach involves adapting interventions to unique features of individual ethno-cultural groups. Either approach can be successful as illustrated by numerous examples from the literature.

Padilla-Frausto and Wallace (Chapter 13) provide an overview of issues related to long-term care among older people from diverse ethnic backgrounds. They suggest that the system of long-term care services is difficult to navigate, which causes problems of access for older people from minority populations as well as others from socioeconomically disadvantaged backgrounds. It is important, they argue, to further understand current and future changes in the sociodemographic characteristics of older people from diverse backgrounds to facilitate better access to long-term care services. Based on recent trends and projected sociodemographic trends, the prevalence of nursing home use among older African Americans will likely continue to increase. The same may be predicted for older Hispanics. Increases in nursing home use among minority populations are taking place at a time when nursing home use among older non-Hispanic whites have been declining (Fennell, Feng, Clark, & Mor, 2010), primarily because they have greater access to alternatives such as assisted living. The system of long-term care services will need to be restructured to take into account issues affecting minority populations such as health care coverage, housing and income supports, as well as cultural issues as filial piety and trust.

Miles and Smith (Chapter 14) address the issue of how health quality may very well influence health disparities affecting ethnic minority aging populations in the changing U.S. health care climate. They note that since the Affordable Healthcare Act (ACA) has been upheld by the Supreme Court, there is a need to focus on its implementation in a manner that helps reduce health disparities rather than cause them to widen. The authors argue that the ACA will provide opportunities to address health care quality gaps at the local delivery system level since the law includes mechanisms to address these gaps. There will be standardized protocols for assessing the quality of health care by consumers, which will provide opportunities for gerontologists to evaluate how health policy impacts minority aging disparities in the quality of health care.

CONCLUSION

The field of minorities, aging, and health has been dominated by a health inequality perspective that has been illustrated by the application of cumulative disadvantage/cumulative inequality theory. By and large, such a perspective is supported by data on African Americans and Native Americans in comparison to non-Hispanic whites. The situation of Hispanics and Asian Americans is different. The latter seem to be health advantaged by most indicators reflecting immigrant selection and favorable socioeconomic profiles. The situation of most Hispanics is rather complex. For example, they enjoy favorable mortality profiles owing to immigrant selection and positive health behaviors and social supports. Yet, there appears to be gradual decline in the immigrants' initial health advantages with aging and time in the United States, which fits under the cumulative disadvantage perspective but also under what has been called a negative acculturation perspective.

The following chapters address issues related to mortality and longevity, disability, long-term care, genetic factors, diet and nutrition, approaches to health interventions, and health policy. A complex picture of ethnic disadvantage and barriers to quality of health care emerges, along with numerous suggested lines of future research opportunities as well as social and health policy interventions.

REFERENCES

Antecol, H., & Bedard, K. (2006). Unhealthy assimilation: Why do immigrants converge to American health status levels? *Demography, 43*(2), 337–360.

Arias, F., Schauman, W. S., Sorlie, P. D., & Backlund, E. (2008). The validity of race and Hispanic origin reporting on death certificates in the United States. *Vital and Health Statistics, 2*(148), 1–24.

Bengtson, V. L. (1979). Ethnicity and aging: Problems and issues in current social science inquiry. In D. E. Gelfand & A. J. Kutzik (Eds.), *Ethnicity and aging: Theory, research and policy* (pp. 9–31). New York, NY: Springer.

Biddle, N. S., & McDonald, J. T. (2007). Health assimilation patterns amongst Australian immigrants. *The Economic Record, 83*(260), 16–30.

Cunningham, S. A., Ruben, J. D., & Vengat Narayan, K. M. (2008). Health of the foreign-born people in the United States: A review. *Health and Place, 14*, 623–635.

Dannefer, D. (2003). Cumulative advantage/disadvantage and the life course: Cross-fertilizing age and social science theory. *The Journals of Gerontology, 58*(6), S327–S337.

Dannefer, D. (1987). Aging as intracohort differentiation: Accentuation, the Matthew effect, and the life course. *Sociological Form, 2*, 211–236.

Dowd, J. J., & Bengtson, V. L. (1978). Aging in minority populations: An examination of the double jeopardy hypothesis. *Journal of Gerontology, 33*(3), 427–436.

Fennell, M. L., Feng, Z., Clark, M. A., & Mor, V. (2010). Elderly hispanics more likely to reside in poor-quality nursing homes. *Health Affairs, 29*(1), 65–73.

Ferraro, K. F. (1987). Double jeopardy to health for black older adults. *Journal of Gerontology, 42*, 528–533.

Ferraro, K. F., Shippee, T. P., & Schafer, M. H. 2009. Cumulative inequality theory for research on aging and the life course. In V. L. Bengtson, D. Gans, N. M. Putney, & M. Silverstein (Eds.), *Handbook of theories of aging* (pp. 413–434). New York, NY: Springer.

Gee, E. M., Kobayashi, K. M., & Prus, S. G. (2004). Examining the healthy immigrant effect in mid to later life; findings from the Canadian community health survey. *Canadian Journal of Aging, 23*, S61–S69.

Jackson, J. J. (1985). Race, national origin, ethnicity, and aging. In R. B. Binstock & E. Shanas (Eds.), *Handbook of aging and the social sciences* (pp. 264–303). New York, NY: Van Nostrand-Reinhold.

Lynch, S. (2008). Race, socioeconomic status and health in life course perspective: Introduction to the special issue. *Research on Aging, 30*, 127–136.

Markides, K. S. (1983). Minority aging. In M. W. Riley, B. B. Hess, & K. Bond (Eds.), *Aging in society: Reviews of recent literature* (pp. 115–137). Hillsdale, NJ: Erlbaum.

Markides, K. S., & Eschbach, K. (2005). Aging, migration, and mortality: Current status of research on the Hispanic paradox. *The Journals of Gerontology, 2*, 68–75.

Markides, K. S., Eschbach, K., Ray, L. A., & Peek, M. K. (2007). Census disability rates among older people by race/ethnicity and type of Hispanic origin. In J. L. Angel & K. E. Whitfield (Eds.), *The health of aging Hispanics: The Mexican-origin population* (pp. 26–39). New York, NY: Springer.

Markides, K. S., & Eschbach, K. (2011). Hispanic paradox in adult mortality in the United States. In R. G. Rogers & E. Crimmins (Eds.), *International handbook of adult mortality* (pp. 225–238). New York, NY: Springer.

Markides, K. S., & Gerst, K. (2011). Immigration, aging, and health in the United States. In R. A. Settersen & J. L. Angel (Eds.), *Handbook of the sociology of aging* (chapter 7, pp. 103–116). New York, NY: Springer.

Markides, K. S., Liang, J., & Jackson, J. S. (1990). Race, ethnicity and aging: Conceptual and methodological issues. In R. H. Binstock & L. K. George (Eds.), *Handbook of aging and the social sciences* (3rd ed.). San Diego, CA: Academic Press.

Masters, R. K. (2012). Uncrossing the U.S. black-white mortality crossover: The role of cohort forces in life course mortality risk. *Demography, 49*(3), 773–796.

McDonald, J. T., & Kennedy, S. (2004). Insights into the "healthy immigrant effect": Health status and health service use of immigrants to Canada. *Social Science & Medicine, 59*(8), 1613–1627.

Mutchler, J. A., & Burr, J. A. (2011). Race, ethnicity, and aging. In R. A. Settersen & J. L. Angel (Eds.), *Handbook of the sociology of aging* (chapter 6, pp. 83–101). New York, NY: Springer.

O'Rand, A. M. (1996). The precious and the precocious: Understanding cumulative disadvantage and cumulative advantage over the life course. *The Gerontologist, 36*(2), 230–238.

Shuey, K. M., & Willson, A. E. (2008). Cumulative disadvantage and black-white disparities in life-course health trajectories. *Research on Aging, 30*, 200–225.

Singh, G., Siahpush, M., Hiatt, R., & Timsina, T. (2011). Dramatic increases in obesity and overweight prevalence and body mass index among ethnic-immigrant and social class groups in the United States, 1976–2008. *Journal of Community Health, 36*(1), 94–110.

Stephen, E. H., Foote, K., Hendershot, G. E., & Schoenborn, C. A. (1994). Health of the foreign-born population: United States, 1987–1990. *Advanced Data from Vital and Health Statistics* (No. 241). Hyattsville, MD: National Center for Health Statistics.

Taylor, M. G. (2008). Timing accumulation, and the black/white disability gap in later life: A test of weathering. *Research on Aging, 30*, 226–250.

Walesmann, K. M., Geronimus, A. T., & Gee, G. C. (2008). Accumulating disadvantage over the life course: Evidence from a longitudinal study investigating the relationship between educational advantage in youth and health in middle age. *Research on Aging, 30*, 169–199.

CHAPTER 8

Race/Ethnicity and Disability Among Older Americans

Neil K. Mehta, Nikkil Sudharsanan, and Irma T. Elo

Disability is responsible for massive social and economic costs to individuals, families, and health care systems (Anderson, Wiener, Finkelstein, & Armour, 2011). It is a key indicator of population health and is measured, in some form, in most national health surveys, including data collected by the U.S. Census Bureau. Disability, like most health outcomes, varies considerably across demographic subgroups and understanding the sources of these differentials remains an area of active research. This chapter examines racial and ethnic differences in disability in the United States with a focus on their patterns, trends, and determinants.

We begin by presenting a conceptual framework for understanding the determinants of disability at the population level and among U.S. racial and ethnic groups. We next provide a review of recent evidence on racial and ethnic differences in disability, focusing on studies that have used data from nationally representative surveys and the U.S. census. We then focus on evidence for those aged 50 and above.

Our review of the literature indicated that little is known about patterns and trends in racial and ethnic differences in disability during the recent decade (2000–2010). Therefore, we also present empirical evidence from the National Health Interview Survey (NHIS). Although disability encompasses both cognitive and physical manifestations, our focus is on physical disability. Given the increasing number of foreign-born Americans, particular attention is given to the roles of migration and immigration status in influencing racial and ethnic differences in disability.

DISABILITY AND ITS DETERMINANTS

Disability can be succinctly defined as the difficulty or inability to perform activities across any domain of life, in a manner that affects expected social roles (Altman, 2001; Crimmins, 2004). Thus, unlike other health outcomes, disability is defined by both biological and social processes. For example, the biopsychosocial model of disability, advocated by the World Health Organization, conceptualizes disability as a function of both an individual's underlying health status and his/her social and physical environment (World Health Organization, 2002). Some researchers further distinguish between functional limitations and disability. In this context, functional limitation is defined as the inability to perform rudimentary physical or mental tasks, such as lifting, walking, climbing stairs, counting, and so on. The term "disability" in turn refers to occasions when these functional limitations hinder social roles (e.g., ability to work, shop, perform self-care tasks, etc.; Crimmins, 2004). Although we realize the importance of this distinction, our use of the term disability in this chapter encompasses functional limitations.

Similar to death, late-life disability is most proximately the result of numerous acute and chronic diseases (Verbrugge, Lepkowski, & Imanaka, 1989; Zhao, Ford, Li, Crews, & Mokdad, 2009). Thus, it is best considered as a global indicator of health status. Commonly cited causal conditions include diabetes, heart and lung problems, depression and other mental health conditions, hypertension, and nervous system conditions. Based on the 2005 to 2007 waves of the NHIS, Martin, Freedman, Schoeni, and Andreski (2010) concluded that musculoskeletal conditions (e.g., "arthritis or rheumatism" and "back or neck problem") were the most commonly cited conditions causing limitations in activities of daily living (ADL) and instrumental activities of daily living (IADL) among those aged 50 to 64 years. Similar findings were reported by Zhao, Ford, Li, Crews, and Mokdad (2009) using data from the 2005 behavioral risk factor surveillance system. In this study, disability was assessed by asking a question about activity limitations and was most highly associated with arthritis and stroke. The authors also reported a cumulative association between morbidities and disability in that disability risks were positively and linearly related to the number of conditions reported.

A growing body of literature in life course epidemiology and demography highlights the role of early life factors that may have indirect and direct effects on disability (Haas, 2008; Haas & Rohlfsen, 2010; Huang, Soldo, & Elo, 2011; Schoeni, Freedman, & Martin, 2008; Verbrugge & Jette, 1994). For example, poor health in infancy and childhood has been shown to be associated with lower adult socioeconomic attainment, which in turn has been hypothesized to influence disability in adulthood through a variety of mechanisms (e.g., ability to purchase medical care and environmental and stressful exposures; Schoeni et al., 2008). Recent research has also highlighted the role of childhood health in the risk of functional limitations in later life, net of lifetime socioeconomic attainment (Haas, 2008; Huang, Soldo, et al., 2011). Others have linked fetal undernutrition to the risk of chronic conditions, especially heart disease, in adulthood (Barker, 1993; Barker & Clark, 1997), although its role remains somewhat controversial (Kramer, 2000). During adulthood, health-related behaviors, such as smoking, physical activity, diet, and heavy use of alcohol, are considered to be major contributors to disability risks in later life (Buchner, 2012; Chakravarty et al., 2012; Vita, Terry, Hubert, & Fries, 1998).

RACIAL AND ETHNIC DIFFERENCES IN DISABILITY

Racial and ethnic differences in health are one of the most widely studied topics in U.S. health disparities research (Barker & Clark, 1997; Jones, LaVeist, & Lillie-Blanton, 1991). These disparities have their roots in the unequal distribution of economic resources and access to health care, racial discrimination, and residential segregation (Kramer, 2000). Most research on racial and ethnic disparities in disability has focused on differences between non-Hispanic blacks and non-Hispanic whites, although in recent years this literature has expanded to include Hispanics, Asian-origin populations, and Native Americans.

A discussion of racial/ethnic differences in disability must also consider the role of immigration. A substantial proportion of Hispanics and Asians, and an increasing proportion of the U.S. black population, is foreign born (Capps, McCabe, & Fix, 2012; Kent, 2007; Patten, 2012; Thomas, 2012). Thus, observed patterns of later-life disability in many minority populations are increasingly determined by factors that contribute to the health status of immigrant subgroups. The literature on the health of the foreign born in the United States highlights that with some exceptions (e.g, see Mehta & Elo, 2012), such as that the U.S. foreign-born population displays better health and lower mortality compared to U.S.-born whites and the U.S.-born population of the same race/ethnicity (Argeseanu Cunningham, Ruben, & Narayan, 2008; Frisbie, Cho, & Hummer, 2001; Markides, & Eschbach, 2005; Singh & Siahpush, 2002).

The finding of better health outcomes among the foreign born, the "healthy migrant hypothesis," is thought to be a function of positive health selection from the originating population (Jasso, Massey, Rosenzweig, & Smith, 2004) and return migration back to countries of origin when the immigrant's health deteriorates (Blue & Fenelon, 2011; Turra & Elo, 2008). At the same time, a body of research shows that an increased duration of U.S. residence among the foreign born is associated with deteriorating health conditions and narrowing of health differentials compared to the U.S.-born population (Antecol & Bedard, 2006; Cho, Frisbie, Hummer, & Rogers, 2004; Elo, Mehta, & Huang, 2011; Frisbie et al., 2001). One explanation for this finding is that acculturation leads to negative changes in health behaviors and diet as well as to the erosion of social and familial ties (e.g., Hummer et al., 1999; Mutchler, Burr & Prakash, 2007). If early life conditions influence adult health and disability, a life course framework would additionally suggest that factors in *both* the sending and receiving countries influence levels of late-life disability. However, much less is known about the role of conditions in sending countries. Depending on countries of origin, immigrants may have experienced poorer nutritional and disease environments early in life and more adverse general conditions compared to the U.S.-born population.

We next turn to a review of the literature on disability, focusing on each of the major U.S. racial and ethnic groups.

African Americans/Blacks

Numerous studies document higher levels of disability among non-Hispanic blacks compared to most other U.S. racial and ethnic groups (Arbeev, Butov, Manton, Sannikov, & Yashin, 2004; Kelley-Moore & Ferraro, 2004; Manton & Gu, 2001), perhaps with the exception of Native Americans (Altman & Rasch, 2003; Markides, Eschbach, Ray, & Peek, 2007). Little work has examined whether black–white differences in disability differ markedly by sex. Nevertheless, recent evidence, even if fairly limited, indicates that the black disadvantage in disability, assessed by both self-reported measures and performance tests of physical functioning, is more pronounced for women than for men, net of controls for socioeconomic status (SES) in a population-based urban sample of individuals of ages 65 and above (Mendes de Leon, Barnes, Bienias, Skarupski, & Evans, 2005). Similarly, Warner and Brown (2011) found, when examining age-related trajectories of self-reported functional limitations, that black women reported the highest levels of limitations and experienced the steepest declines in functioning between ages 50 and 70 compared to five other race-sex groups (white men, white women, Hispanic men, Hispanic women, black men). At the same time, whether black–white differences in disability vary by age among older adults remains unclear. Some prior studies report a black–white "crossover" in disability occurring at ages 80 and above (Clark, Maddox, & Steinhauser, 1993; Johnson, 2000), whereas other studies do not find evidence of a crossover (Kelley-Moore & Ferraro, 2004).

Explanations for the black–white differences in later life disability focus primarily on the more adverse *lifetime* social and economic disadvantages experienced by U.S.-born blacks compared to U.S.-born whites. For example, the cumulative disadvantage hypothesis highlights the accumulating effects of negative life events experienced by blacks and other socially disadvantaged groups at each stage of the life cycle (DiPrete & Eirich, 2006; Taylor, 2008). Using data from the health and retirement study (HRS), two recent studies examine the contribution of early life conditions to black–white disparities in late-life disability. Bowen (2009) investigated whether childhood SES, measured by parental education and occupation, predicted black–white differences in disability measured by ADL and IADL among individuals aged 50 and above. The author found that early life SES explained slightly less than one third of the black–white difference in late-life disability. These associations were also partly mediated by adult SES and health behaviors. Haas, Krueger, and Rohlfsen (2012), in turn, studied racial/ethnic and nativity differentials in objective measures of physical functioning (lung function measured by peak expiratory flow, grip strength, and gait speed) at ages 50 and above among non-Hispanic whites, blacks, and Hispanics. The U.S.-born blacks had significantly poorer lung function than U.S.-born non-Hispanic whites, a disadvantage that was narrowed by about 18% when controlled for parental education and childhood health. This differential was further reduced with controls for adult SES, although they remained statistically significant. Foreign-born blacks also had significantly poorer lung function compared to U.S.-born non-Hispanic whites with and without controls for early life conditions and adult SES. Similarly, U.S.- and foreign-born blacks had slower gait speed than U.S.-born non-Hispanic whites. Controls for early life conditions narrowed these differentials only slightly, with more substantial reduction in the disparity when adult SES was included in the model. The disparity remained significant for U.S.-born blacks only. There were no significant differences in grip strength among U.S.-born whites, U.S.-born blacks, and foreign-born blacks. Other research on the role of early life conditions points to findings that blacks born in the historically poor southern United States have worse health and disability profiles at older ages than blacks born elsewhere (Kington, Carlisle, McCaffrey, Myers, & Allen, 1998).

In addition to the role of early life exposures, many more studies have focused on the contribution of attained SES to black–white differences in late-life disability. Some of these studies find that black–white differences in disability are greatly reduced or eliminated after accounting for adult SES (Guralnik, Land, Blazer, Fillenbaum, & Branch, 1993; Kim & Miech, 2009; Liao, McGee, Cao, & Cooper, 1999; Louie & Ward, 2011). In contrast, other studies, including Haas et al. (2012), find that adult SES only partially explains black–white differentials in disability (Clark & Maddox, 1992; Clark et al., 1993; Warner & Brown, 2011). These contrasting findings are due, at least in part, to differences in measures of disability as well as adult SES.

As noted, the foreign-born population makes up an increasing proportion of various racial/ethnic groups in the United States largely due to changes in the immigration laws passed in the mid-1960s. As a result, the U.S. black population is also becoming increasingly heterogeneous, as a steady stream of black immigrants have arrived in the United States since the late 1960s. In 2005, foreign-born blacks made up a sizeable 8% of the U.S. black residents, up from less than 1% in 1960 (Kent, 2007; Trupin, Rice, & Max, 1995). In addition, approximately 3% of Hispanics identified as black in the 2010 Census of Population and Hispanic blacks constituted approximately 4% of the U.S. black population that year (Humes, Jones, & Ramirez, 2011). The vast majority of foreign-born blacks have come from the Caribbean, other regions of the Americas, and Africa.

Using data from the NHIS, Read and Emerson (2005) report that, on average, black immigrants report lower levels of activity limitations compared to native-born blacks (ages 18+). They also found that blacks born in Africa tended to report lower levels of limitations compared to blacks born in the West Indies, South America, and Europe. Elo et al. (2011) compared levels of disability among native- and foreign-born blacks using the 5% PUMS sample of the 2000 census (ages 25+). They distinguished foreign-born blacks both by region of birth and Hispanic ethnicity and found that all foreign-born black subgroups reported lower levels of disability compared to U.S.-born blacks among both men and women. Among the foreign born, African immigrants had lower levels of disability compared to non-Hispanic immigrants from the Caribbean, but these differences were largely explained by SES and the timing of immigration; African immigrants tend to be more recent arrivals. A noteworthy finding was that Hispanic blacks were worse off compared to their U.S.- and foreign-born non-Hispanic counterparts. Thus, Hispanic status among U.S. blacks appeared to signal a relatively disadvantaged position.

Hispanics

There has been a great deal of interest in the health of U.S. Hispanics given the population's rapid growth due to immigration primarily from Mexico, and also from the Caribbean and Latin America. In 2010, 37% of the U.S. Hispanic population was foreign born (Patten, 2012, Table 6). Interest in the health of Hispanics is further fueled by the desire to unravel factors that contribute to the "Hispanic health paradox," that is, the better-than-expected health among select Hispanic subgroups given their low SES. Most research on Hispanic health at middle and older ages has focused on mortality (Franzini, Ribble, & Keddie, 2001;

Markides & Eschbach, 2005; Markides, Rudkin, Angel, & Espino, 1997; Turra & Elo, 2008; Verbrugge et al., 1989), with fewer studies on disability.

Recent evidence, however, suggest that there is substantial variation in disability among the various Hispanic subgroups. Based on the 5% PUMS sample of the 2000 U.S. census, Markides et al. (2007), for example, documented substantial variation in levels of age-adjusted disability among multiple Hispanic-origin subgroups at ages 65 and above. Disability was measured based on at least one affirmative response to five measures of disability, including mental disability. Hispanic-origin status was identified on the basis of responses to questions on ancestry and country of birth. In sex-stratified analyses, the authors found that older Puerto Rican men and women reported the highest levels of disability. Mexican- and Dominican-origin men and women reported the next highest levels, followed by Cubans and Central and South Americans. Spanish-origin men and women reported the lowest levels of disability. Using the same data, Markides and Gerst (2011) further showed that foreign-born Hispanic men as a group had slightly lower levels of disability than U.S.-born Hispanic men as a group, but no foreign-born advantage was observed for women. The authors attributed this finding to differential migrant selectivity by gender such that foreign-born women were thought to be less selected for health than foreign-born men.

Warner and Brown (2011) similarly highlighted the disadvantaged position of Hispanic women using data from the HRS. These authors found that disparities in functional limitations between non-Hispanic whites and Mexican Americans were considerably stronger for women than for men. Functional limitations were measured by self-reported questions on mobility, strength, and upper- and lower-body functioning. This study did not differentiate Hispanics by place of birth, but the analyses adjusted for SES, foreign-born status, and other sociodemographic characteristics. Haas et al. (2012) also differentiated among foreign- and U.S.-born Hispanics in their analysis of functional limitations (lung function, grip strength, and gait speed) using the HRS. In this study, there was no statistically significant difference in lung function between U.S.-born whites and Hispanics, although foreign-born Hispanics had a significantly lower lung function than U.S.-born whites. This difference was reduced by 55% when adjusting for parental education and childhood health. With further adjustment for adult SES, both U.S.- and foreign-born Hispanics had now *significantly better* lung function than that of U.S.-born whites. Similar results were documented for gait speed, whereas both U.S.- and foreign-born Hispanics had significantly lower grip strength, although this difference was attenuated with the inclusion of childhood characteristics and adult SES.

Asians

The risk of disability among older Asians is an understudied area, despite the growth of this population subgroup in recent years due to increased volume of immigration from Asia to the United States. Like Hispanics, a large fraction of Asian Americans are foreign born. In 2010, 67% of U.S. Asians were foreign born (Patten, 2012, Table 6). In addition, there is growing diversity among the Asian population in the United States, including in their levels of disability.

Using data from the 2006 American community survey (ACS), Fuller-Thomson, Brennenstuhl, and Hurd (2011) compared the prevalence of functional and ADL limitations between non-Hispanic whites and those who reported an Asian racial background at ages 55 and above. They found that, collectively, Asians had lower levels of both types of disability than non-Hispanic whites. At the same time, they also documented large variation among the various Asian subgroups, with Hawaiians, Pacific Islanders, and Vietnamese reporting the highest levels of disability and Chinese and Japanese reporting the lowest levels. Disability prevalence among Asian Indians and Filipinos was intermediary among the various Asian subgroups. These findings were robust to controls for education, foreign-born status, timing of immigration among the foreign born, citizenship, and other sociodemographic characteristics. The authors did not separate the Asian racial groups by place of birth (i.e., foreign born vs. U.S. born).

In contrast, Mutchler, Prakash, and Burr (2007), using disability data from the 5% PUMS sample of the 2000 census at ages 65 and above, disaggregated Asian subgroups by nativity. Disability was assessed by asking questions about difficulty with physical tasks (walking, climbing stairs, reaching, lifting, or carrying), self-care (an ADL), and going outside alone (IADL). These authors found that U.S.-born Asians were generally better off with respect to disability than foreign-born Asians. U.S.-born Asians were also better off than non-Hispanic whites, but that foreign-born Asians were generally worse off compared to non-Hispanic whites. Thus, the authors concluded that there is limited evidence for an immigrant advantage in disability among the older Asian population. Another noteworthy finding from Mutchler, Burr, et al. (2007) is that among the foreign-born Asian subgroups, foreign-born Asian Indians had high levels of disability, a finding that is consistent with the high levels of cardiovascular and metabolic diseases thought to occur in migrant Asian Indian populations (Barnett et al., 2006; Kanaya et al., 2010; Misra et al., 2010; Mohanty, Woolhandler, Himmelstein, & Bor, 2005).

Another study examined educational gradients in disability, measured by ADLs, IADLs, and functional limitations, among foreign-born Asians aged 65 and above, using data from the 2006 American Community Survey (Lee, 2011). The author found educational gradients to be flatter among foreign-born Asians compared to U.S.-born non-Hispanic whites, a finding that has also been reported for foreign-born blacks and Hispanics (Elo et al., 2011; Goldman, Kimbro, Turra, & Pebley, 2006). The authors did not compare differences in educational gradients in disability between foreign- and U.S-born Asians.

Although individuals of Arab ancestries are usually not considered to be Asian and are seldom studied, a recent study using the 5% PUMS of the 2000 U.S. Census (Dallo, Al Snih, & Ajrouch, 2009) compared levels of disability among U.S.- and foreign-born individuals who identified as being from one of the Arab ancestries based on a question on ancestry and ethnic origin (for details about Arab ancestries see Brittingham, 2005). The authors found that foreign-born Arab Americans had significantly higher odds of reporting functional and ADL limitations than U.S.-born Arab Americans at ages 65 and above. Adjustment for English language ability fully explained these differences in functional limitations and approximately half of the difference in ADL disability. Therefore, the foreign-born advantage also seems absent among older Arab Americans.

In sum, the disability estimates for Asians living in the United States require further study. Nonetheless, studies that have distinguished among Asian subgroups generally reveal considerable heterogeneity among them, with individuals emigrating from Southeast Asia displaying the highest levels of physical disability (also see, Huang, Mehta, et al., 2011). We did not uncover any studies that examined life cycle determinants of disability among older Asian populations.

Native Americans

Very few studies have characterized disability levels among older Native Americans using large-scale and representative samples. Most studies examine a single tribe or region using data from the Indian health service (IHS), which provides the broadest picture of Native American health. However, the IHS data are thought to be representative of only about 60% of the Native American population (see Altman & Rasch, 2003, for a more detailed discussion of data coverage among Native Americans).

To overcome these data limitations, Altman and Rasch (2003) used the disability supplement of the NHIS to examine disability among a nationally representative sample of noninstitutionalized Native Americans of ages 18 and above. The authors classified Native Americans as those reporting American Indian, Eskimo, Aleut, or Native Hawaiian on the race question in the NHIS and included both Hispanics and non-Hispanics. In a multivariate analysis adjusting for demographic and socioeconomic characteristics, the authors found that Native Americans had significantly higher levels of functional, ADL, and IADL limitations compared to non-Hispanic whites and blacks. The authors did not examine disability by sex or age. They found, however, that removing Native Hawaiians from their classification of Native Americans resulted in similar findings, indicating that disability levels among Native Hawaiians were similar to those among American Indians and the other indigenous populations.

Evidence for high levels of disability among older Native Americans also comes from Markides et al.'s study (2007) described above. The authors investigated disability levels specifically among the Native American population at ages 65 and above using data from the 5% PUMS of the 2000 U.S. census, which covers both institutionalized and noninstitutionalized populations. The authors found that older non-Hispanic Native American men and women generally reported the highest levels of physical and mental disability compared to other racial and ethnic groups.

RACIAL AND ETHNIC DIFFERENCES IN DISABILITY IN THE NATIONAL HEALTH INTERVIEW SURVEY, 2000 TO 2010

Data and Measures

Data were pooled from the 2000 to 2010 waves of the NHIS to provide recent estimates of disability among U.S. racial/ethnic subgroups aged 50 to 84. The NHIS is a nationally representative household-based survey of the noninstitutionalized U.S. population (50 states and District of Columbia). It is carried out annually by the National Center for Health Statistics. Two measures of self-reported disability, that is, functional limitations and ADL limitations, were examined. For functional limitations, an indicator variable (0/1) based on whether a respondent reported difficulty in any of the following tasks was constructed: walking (1/4 mile), climbing stairs (10 steps without resting), reaching, and carrying (10 pounds). These items are based on the Nagi's scale of physical functioning (Nagi, 1991). Functional limitations were asked in the Sample Adult questionnaire of the NHIS, which is given to a subset of NHIS respondents. These data are entirely self-reported. For ADL limitations, our measure is based on the question: "Because of a physical, mental, or emotional problem, [does the respondent] need the help of other persons with personal care needs, such as eating, bathing, dressing, or getting around inside the house?" ADL limitations were asked of the entire sample and could be answered by a proxy member of the household.

The total sample size for those aged 50 to 84 in the 2000 to 2010 waves was 260,218, of whom 124,442 were given the Sample Adult questionnaire. After accounting for missing data and other exclusions our sample sizes were 247,794 and 118,861 for ADL and functional limitations, respectively.

Using questions on race and Hispanic ethnicity, we examined the following subgroups: non-Hispanic whites, non-Hispanic blacks, Hispanics (of any race), non-Hispanic Asians, and non-Hispanic Native Americans. Results for those who reported a race other than those listed above or those who reported multiple races were not included ($N = 2,170$). The Native American subgroup included those who reported American Indian/Alaskan Native on the race question. For clarity of presentation, we omit the term "non-Hispanic" from subsequent discussion.

With the exception of Native Americans, each minority group was also distinguished by place of birth (U.S. born vs. foreign born). We did not distinguish non-Hispanic whites by place of birth because the foreign born represent a small proportion of this population (5.0%). Nonetheless, recent work by Mehta and Elo (2012) shows very high levels of disability among a subgroup of non-Hispanic white immigrants from the former Soviet Union. As discussed above, disability levels vary among Hispanic and Asian subgroups and among foreign-born blacks. Due to sample size constraints, we limit our subgroup analysis to Hispanic subgroups, namely Mexicans, Puerto Ricans, and other Hispanics.

Statistical Analyses

A series of logistic regression models predicting each of the disability measures were estimated. As explanatory variables, we included age and educational attainment (less than high school, HS graduate/GED, some college/associates degree, bachelor's degree, graduate degree). We do not include income as an additional measure of SES because of the bidirectional relationships between income and health (Smith, 1999) and also the fact that many in the sample are in the retirement age. We also included region of residence (Northeast, South Midwest, and West), as the distribution of racial/ethnic subgroups vary by region and region is associated with levels of disability. In addition, we assessed whether there have been changes over time in race/ethnic differences in disability between 2000 and 2010. All multivariate models are adjusted for age, U.S. census region of residence (Northeast, North Central/Midwest, South, West), and a continuous term for survey year. We obtained NHIS data from the Integrated Health Interview Series from the University of Minnesota (Minnesota Population Center and State Health Access Data Assistance Center, 2012). NHIS-provided sampling weights were used and were adjusted according to recommended guidelines for pooled analyses (Minnesota Population Center and State Health Access Data Assistance Center, 2012).

Disability Prevalence by Race/Ethnicity and Nativity

Table 8.1 shows the age-adjusted prevalence estimates for each disability measure by sex and race/ethnicity. The overall prevalence of functional limitations was 28.2% (men) and 39.4% (women). The overall prevalence of ADL limitations was 2.3% (men) and 3.0%

TABLE 8.1 Percentage Reporting Functional Limitations and ADL Limitations by Race/Ethnicity and Nativity; Ages 50 to 84, 50 United States and District of Columbia

Race/Ethnicity and Nativity Group	FUNCTIONAL LIMITATIONS (N = 118,861)			ADL LIMITATIONS (N = 247,794)		
	N	Males (%)	Females (%)	N	Males (%)	Females (%)
Overall	118,861	28.2 (27.6, 28.7)	39.4 (38.9, 39.9)	247,794	2.3 (2.2, 2.4)	3.0 (2.9, 3.1)
Non-Hispanic whites	85,009	27.5 (26.9, 28.1)	37.9 (37.3, 38.5)	172,276	2.1 (2.0, 2.2)	2.6 (2.5, 2.8)
Native-born blacks	14,843	37.5 (36.1, 39.0)	51.6 (50.2, 53.0)	28,443	4.3 (3.9, 4.7)	5.8 (5.4, 6.2)
Foreign-born blacks	1,128	19.9 (15.2, 24.6)	39.6 (34.9, 44.3)	2,685	1.7 (0.5, 3.0)	3.5 (2.6, 4.5)
Native-born Hispanics	5,127	32.7 (30.1, 35.2)	45.7 (43.7, 47.7)	11,394	3.1 (2.5, 3.7)	4.9 (4.2, 5.5)
Foreign-born Hispanics	8,566	26.6 (24.6, 28.5)	41.3 (39.3, 43.3)	21,577	2.9 (2.5, 3.3)	3.9 (3.5, 4.2)
Native-born Asians	789	18.9 (12.9, 25.0)	25.9 (20.5, 31.2)	1,704	1.3 (0.6, 2.0)	2.1 (0.9, 3.3)
Foreign-born Asians	2,860	18.1 (15.5, 20.6)	30.1 (27.3, 32.8)	8,678	1.4 (1.0, 1.8)	2.5% (2.0, 3.1)
Native Americans	539	47.0 (39.9, 54.1)	52.1 (45.4, 58.9)	1,037	5.9 (2.9, 8.9)	5.8 (4.0, 7.7)

Notes: Results are age-adjusted using the following age groups: 50 to 59, 60 to 69, 70 to 79, and 80+. Ninty-five percent confidence intervals shown in parentheses. Sample characteristics are based on weighted data except for sample sizes.

Source: 2000 to 2010 National Health Interview Survey.

(women). The lower prevalence of ADL limitations is reflective of the severity of this disability measure relative to functional limitations. In general, women were more likely to report a disability compared to their male counterparts. Among the racial/ethnic and nativity groups, Native Americans generally reported the highest level of disability. For example, Native American men and women were 1.7 to 1.4 times as likely to report functional limitations compared to their white counterparts (47.0% vs. 27.5% for men and 52.1% vs. 37.9% for women) and over two times as likely to report an ADL limitation (5.9% vs. 2.1% for men and 5.8% vs. 2.6% among women). The next highest levels were reported by U.S.-born blacks followed by U.S.-born Hispanics. Foreign-born Hispanic men had levels comparable to that of white men, but foreign-born Hispanic women appeared worse off compared to white women. The lowest levels of reported disability were observed for U.S.- and foreign-born Asians.

Table 8.1 also highlights the migrant health advantage in that foreign-born groups generally reported lower levels of disability than their U.S.-born counterparts. This pattern was most evident among blacks and least evident among Asians. In fact, nativity differences among Asians were small and in some instances the foreign-born Asians appeared worse off compared to their U.S.-born counterparts. For example, foreign-born Asian women reported higher levels of functional limitations (30.1%) compared to U.S.-born Asian women (25.9%), although the difference was not statistically significant ($p = .18$). As indicated previously, a lack of a foreign-born advantage among Asians may be due to differences in the distribution of ancestral countries of origin among the U.S.- and foreign-born segments of the Asian population.

The Role of Educational Attainment

We next examined whether controlling for educational attainment modified the differences shown in Table 8.1. Odds ratios from logistic regression models predicting the two types of disability are shown in Figure 8.1. We combined both sexes because the overall conclusions did not vary substantively by sex. Model 1 of Figure 8.1 includes adjustments for age, sex, survey year, and U.S. census region of residence. Model 2 also adjusts for educational attainment.

We begin with findings for the U.S.-born groups. Educational attainment appears to explain only a relatively small component of differences in both functional and ADL limitations between U.S.-born blacks and whites. For example, in the models predicting a functional limitation, the odds ratio for U.S.-born blacks is only partially reduced from 1.70 ($p < .001$; model 1) to 1.44 ($p < .001$; model 2) when education is added to the model. Similarly, the inclusion of educational attainment reduces the odds ratio for U.S.-born blacks from 2.24 ($p < .001$; model 1) to 1.92 ($p < .001$; model 2) in the model predicting ADL limitations. Thus, although education is a significant predictor of disability, it explains only a small fraction of the excess risk of U.S.-born blacks compared to whites. Similarly, educational attainment explains only a portion of the difference in both types of disability between Native Americans and whites (Figure 8.1). However, educational attainment appears to play a larger explanatory role in observed disparities between U.S.-born Hispanics and whites. The odds ratios for U.S.-born Hispanics for functional limitations in Model 1 is 1.40 ($p < .001$) and it is reduced to 1.10 ($p < .05$) in Model 2. A similar pattern is observed in the models predicting ADL limitations. Finally, educational attainment did not explain the lower levels of disability among U.S.-born Asians compared to whites.

When the foreign-born subgroups are compared to whites, the inclusion of educational attainment does not appreciably change the odds ratios for foreign-born blacks and Asians. Educational attainment, however, appears to play a larger role for foreign-born Hispanics compared to whites. Once educational attainment is controlled for, the foreign-born Hispanics have significantly lower levels of activity limitations than whites and a similar level of ADL disability. This finding is perhaps due to the large difference in educational levels between these two groups. In our sample, nearly 60% of foreign-born Hispanics had less than a high school degree/GED, which was considerably higher than for any other racial/ethnic and nativity group. Only 14% of whites, for example, fell into this lowest educational group.

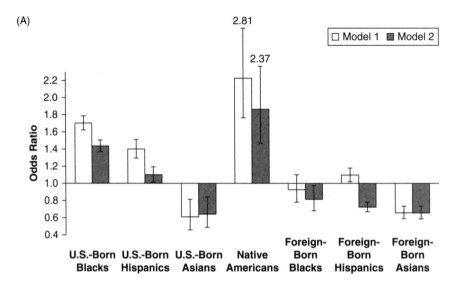

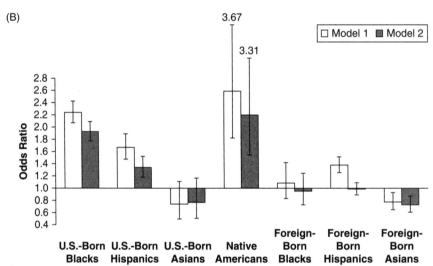

FIGURE 8.1 Odds Ratios for Functional and ADL Limitations; Ages 50 to 84, 50 United States and District of Columbia. (A) Functional Limitations (*N* = 118,861). (B) ADL Limitations (*N* = 247,794).

Notes: Reference group is non-Hispanic whites. Bars indicate 95% confidence intervals. Data reflect sample weighting. Model 1: Age, sex, U.S. census region of residence, and survey year. Model 2: Model 1 + educational attainment.

Source: 2000 to 2010 National Health Interview Survey.

Disability Among Hispanic Subgroups

As noted above, there is considerable interest in variations in health across Hispanic subgroups, particularly differences between Mexican-origin U.S. residents and other Hispanic subgroups. In Table 8.2, we present results from analyses restricted to Hispanics. U.S.-born Mexican Americans are the reference category. Table 8.2 shows odds ratios for Puerto Ricans, other U.S.-born Hispanics (non-Mexican and non-Puerto Rican), foreign-born Mexicans, and other foreign-born Hispanics. The vast majority of Puerto Ricans reported being born within the United States (including Puerto Rico). The few that reported being foreign-born were included in this group. The models shown in Table 8.2 were adjusted for age, sex, educational attainment, U.S. census region of residence, and survey year.

**TABLE 8.2 Odds Ratios for Functional and ADL Limitations for Hispanic Subgroups;
Ages 50 to 84, 50 United States and District of Columbia**

HISPANIC SUBGROUP	FUNCTIONAL LIMITATIONS	ADL LIMITATIONS
Puerto Ricans	1.03 (0.73, 1.47)	0.75 (0.45, 1.23)
Other U.S.-born Hispanics	1.09 (0.89, 1.34)	1.07 (0.78, 1.48)
Foreign-born Mexicans	0.66*** (0.58, 0.76)	0.72*** (0.60, 0.87)
Other foreign-born Hispanics	0.57*** (0.50, 0.66)	0.55*** (0.44, 0.67)

Notes: Reference group is U.S.-born Mexicans. Sample restricted to those reporting Hispanic ethnicity. Models are adjusted for age, sex, educational attainment, U.S. census region, and survey year. Ninty-five percent confidence intervals are shown in parentheses. N = 12,358 for functional limitation model and N = 30,307 for ADL limitation model. Data reflect sample weighting.

***p < .001

Source: 2000 to 2010 National Health Interview Survey.

The models for both measures of disability indicate no significant differences among the U.S.-born subgroups. Thus, we do not find evidence that Puerto Ricans, a group that is commonly thought to be disadvantaged in health relative to other Hispanics, are worse off at ages 50 and above than U.S.-born Mexican Americans net of controls for age, sex, educational attainment, U.S. region of residence, and survey year. Both disability models also highlight the foreign-born advantage among Hispanics in that those born in Mexico or other countries report lower levels of disability compared to U.S.-born Mexican Americans as well as other U.S.-born subgroups. The odds ratios for foreign-born Mexicans are 0.66 ($p < .001$) and 0.72 ($p < .001$) for functional and ADL limitations, respectively. Other foreign-born Hispanics appeared slightly better off than those born in Mexico for both measures of disability, although this comparison was only statistically significant for ADL limitations.

Trends in Racial/Ethnic Differences in Disability

Little is known about recent changes in race/ethnic differences in disability. We therefore examined changes over time in race/ethnic disparities focusing on differences between each minority group and whites. Using the pooled 2000 to 2010 NHIS sample, we estimated models that included an interaction between each race/ethnic category and survey year (whites were the omitted category). We then predicted the odds ratios at the beginning (2000) and end (2010) of the period. The p-values for these interaction terms indicate whether the trend for the minority group was statistically different ($p < .05$) from that of whites and therefore whether disparities were changing over time. We stratified the analysis by sex. Due to power constraints, we examined trends only for functional limitations, which are more prevalent than ADL limitations, and we did not disaggregate the race/ethnic groups by nativity or examine trends among Native Americans. The models adjusted for age, educational attainment, U.S. census region of residence, and migration status (U.S. born, immigrated less than 1 year ago, immigrated 1 to less than 5 years ago, immigrated 5 to less than 10 years ago, and immigrated 10 or more years ago). Migration status helps control for subgroup differences in the time of migration.

Results are shown in Figure 8.2. We found a statistically significant increase in the odds ratio for functional limitations among Hispanic women ($p = .03$ for the trend) such that Hispanic women seemed to be more disabled over time relative to white women. The predicted odds ratio for 2000 was 0.94 ($p = .30$), which increased to 1.17 ($p = .02$) by 2010. No trend was observed for Hispanic men. Among Asians, we find a statistically significant trend for men in that Asian men seemed to be less disabled over time relative to white men. In contrast, no significant trend was detected for Asian women. We did not detect any significant

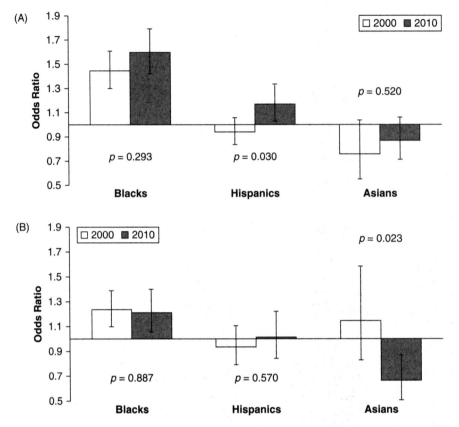

FIGURE 8.2 Changes Over Time in Odds Ratios for Functional Limitations; Ages 50 to 84, 50 United States and District of Columbia. (A) Female Functional Limitations. (B) Male Functional Limitations.

Notes: Reference group is non-Hispanic whites. Models adjust for age, educational attainment, U.S. census region of residence, migration status (U.S. born, immigrated less than 1 year ago, immigrated 1 to less than 5 years ago, immigrated 5 to less than 10 years ago, and immigrated 10 or more years ago), interactions between the race/ethnic categories, and survey year (main effects are included). *p*-values are for the trend (i.e., race/ethnic survey year interaction terms). Bars indicate 95% confidence intervals. Data reflect sample weighting.

Source: 2000 to 2010 National Health Interview Survey.

changes in disparities for black men and women compared to their white counterparts. Thus, it does not appear that black–white disparities in functional limitations have changed over the decade.

DISCUSSION

There is an ongoing interest in measuring and understanding the patterns and causes of racial/ethnic differences in disability in the United States. Our results contribute to the existing knowledge about these differences among older Americans for the recent 2000 to 2010 period. We find that Native Americans generally reported the highest levels of disability followed by U.S.-born blacks. We also find that U.S.-born Hispanics reported higher levels of disability compared to whites, but that this disparity is largely explained by educational differences between the two groups. In contrast, educational attainment only partially explains disparities between U.S.-born blacks and whites and between Native Americans and whites. Our analysis also highlights variations in the extent to which foreign-born populations are better off compared to their U.S.-born counterparts. Within the racial/ethnic groups, we find a foreign-born health advantage among blacks and Hispanics, but not among Asians.

Finally, our trend analysis reveals that there is little evidence that black–white disparities have changed in the last decade. Furthermore, we find some indication that Hispanic women are getting worse off over time relative to their white counterparts.

Among the U.S. born, an important area of further study is to uncover the factors that contribute to the relative disadvantage that we and others observe for blacks and Native Americans. Our measure of lifetime SES, namely educational attainment, explains only a small proportion of the disparity between these two groups and whites. Educational attainment is linked to the acquisition of a wide array of health-promoting resources such as higher incomes, increased knowledge about disease prevention, and more favorable social and psychological capacities (Elo, 2009). While educational attainment is an important indicator of SES and is set relatively early in life, it cannot fully capture the complex set of social and economic conditions experienced over the life course by various racial/ethnic groups (Kaufman, Cooper, & McGee, 1997; Link & Phelan, 1995; Williams & Jackson, 2005; Williams, Mohammed, Leavell, & Collins, 2010). Furthermore, it is seldom possible to include measures of the quality of education that various subgroups receive or to relate them to differing economic returns to schooling—factors that may contribute to racial/ethnic differences in health outcomes. Prior research further indicates that even among the highly educated, blacks report worse overall health and higher levels of stress compared to their white counterparts (Braveman & Barclay, 2009; Williams & Jackson, 2005). In addition, middle-class blacks tend to live in poorer and more highly segregated areas compared to middle-class whites, which may additionally contribute to poorer health outcomes among blacks than whites, independent of other factors (LeClere, Rogers, & Peters, 1997; Williams & Collins, 2001).

Less well understood are patterns of health among Native Americans. Residential context may also play a role in understanding levels of disability in this group. Altman and Rasch (2003) find that Native Americans living in rural areas show higher levels of disability compared to those living in urban areas and attribute this finding to the lack of comprehensive health care services in rural areas. As discussed above, adverse early life conditions for rural Native Americans may also play a role in their patterns of late-life disability independent of educational attainment, but to our knowledge their contribution has not been studied.

Our findings confirm the importance of accounting for nativity in studying racial/ethnic differentials in health and they are also consistent with prior studies by generally revealing lower levels of disability among the foreign-born groups compared to their U.S.-born counterparts. Exceptions to this pattern are found among Asian Americans. Among the Asian elderly, our results are consistent with prior findings, indicating little to no foreign-born advantage (Mutchler, Prakash, & Burr 2007). Indeed, both U.S.- and foreign-born Asians generally display the lowest levels of disability among all subgroups examined. The lack of a foreign-born advantage among Asians is partly reflective of the fact that the U.S.-born segment of this population has achieved a very high level of health. Another possible explanation is that the distribution of ancestral countries of origin among U.S.-born Asians differs from that of the countries of birth among foreign-born Asians. The U.S.-born and foreign-born Asians have very different cultures and lifetime exposures and experiences. For example, a large majority of U.S.-born Asians are of Japanese and Chinese ancestry, whereas foreign-born Asians are a much more heterogeneous group, with a larger representation of Southeast Asians and other groups at a higher risk of disability (Markides et al., 2007).

A fuller understanding of the life course determinants of late-life health among migrant populations would require information on conditions in the sending countries, health-related selective migration, and factors related to migrants' experiences in the United States. Data on early life conditions are sparse for the foreign born and we have little understanding on how exposures in the sending countries may influence disability risks at the older ages. In contrast, the role of health-selective migration and processes of acculturation after arrival in the United States has received considerable attention (e.g., see Jasso et al., 2004; Markides & Gerst, 2011).

We find little evidence to suggest that there are systematic changes over time in minority-white disparities in disability. Some caution should, however, be exercised in interpreting these results. First, the changing composition of each minority group with respect to country of birth may influence observed trends (although, we do adjust for timing of migration and U.S. birth status). This observation is most relevant for Hispanics and Asians, of whom a large proportion are foreign born, but also increasingly important for blacks due to rising immigration from Africa and the Caribbean. Second, we assess changes over a relatively short time period and thus the power to detect significant trends is limited. Nonetheless, our trend analysis does reveal a growing disadvantage of Hispanic women relative to white women in functional limitations. If confirmed in additional analyses, the reasons behind this trend are an important avenue for future research.

Rising obesity may play an important role in the findings for Hispanic women and for the trend in disability for all race/ethnic groups more generally. Obesity increases the risk of disability substantially (Alley & Chang, 2007; Seeman et al., 2010; Sturm, Ringel, & Andreyeva, 2004) and obesity disproportionately affects blacks and Hispanics (Flegal et al., 2010). The recent rise in obesity levels among young and middle-age adults suggests that obesity will play an important role in future patterns of disability among the elderly because its health effects are likely to accrue over a lifetime (Preston, Mehta, & Stokes, in press). Similar to the obesity trend in the United States, average body mass index in Latin America has risen rapidly (Finucane et al., 2011; Kain, Vio, & Albala, 2003). For example, recent data indicate that obesity levels among women in Mexico have reached levels similar to those of U.S. women (World Health Organization, 2002). It appears that migrants to the United States are "importing" their obesity, as evidenced by increasing obesity levels among immigrants recently arriving from Latin America (Singh Siahpush, Hiatt, & Timsina, 2011).

CONCLUSION

In summary, we reviewed the current evidence on racial/ethnic differences in disability among older Americans and presented new empirical evidence on recent levels and trends in disability from nationally representative data. We conclude that while overall patterns of racial/ethnic differences in disability are well documented, additional research into the causes of these differentials is warranted. Recent research has increasingly focused on life course determinants of disability and used models that attempt to quantify the relative importance of factors that occur at various stages in the life cycle (e.g., childhood vs. adulthood). Because information on early life conditions is not always readily available and is often based on a limited set of retrospectively reported measures, further progress in understanding their role remains challenging.

Another area where researchers can make important contributions is in the area of data quality. The vast majority of studies reviewed here rely on self-reported measures of disability because these are most readily available in large-scale, nationally representative surveys. It is reassuring that a number of studies find that self-reported measures of disability are valid measures of underlying physical health and future risks of mortality (Idler & Benyamini, 1997; Idler, Russell, & Davis, 2000; Kroenke et al., 2008; Lee, 2000; Wang & Satariano, 2007). Nonetheless, previous research also points to potential biases that may occur in comparing self-reported physical health measures across cultural and national groups (Carr, Gibson, & Robinson, 2001; Mathers, 2003; Murray & Chen, 1992; Sen, 2002). Thus, utilizing biological indicators and clinically based measures of physical performance and functioning are likely to be particularly valuable when comparing disability among diverse racial/ethnic groups and immigrants from varied countries of origin. In addition, there has been little work evaluating biases that may arise from differential selection into nursing homes and other institutional settings in studies that rely on data that sample only the noninstitutionalized U.S. population.

In addition, incorporating detailed information on lifetime histories of smoking, obesity, and other behavior-related attributes may prove useful in better explaining group differences in disability and that may be available from various data sources. For example, Ho and Elo (in press) highlight the role of differing cohort histories of smoking between blacks and whites and their role in explaining black–white mortality differentials using data from multiple sources. These types of analyses could be extended to disability and morbidity. Also, more detailed analyses examining disability and mortality simultaneously as well as racial/ethnic differences in the onset, progression, and recovery from disability will provide a more complete picture of health across racial/ethnic groups in late life.

REFERENCES

Alley, D. E., & Chang, V. W. (2007). The changing relationship of obesity and disability, 1988–2004. *JAMA, 298*(17), 2020–2027.

Altman , B. M. (2001). Disability, definitions, models, classification schemes, and applications. In G. L. Albrecht, K. D. Seelman, & M. Bury (Eds.), *Handbook of disability studies* (pp. 97–122). Thousand Oaks, CA: Sage.

Altman, B. M., & Rasch, E. K. (2003). Disability among native Americans. In S. B. Barbara, M. Altman, Gerry Hendershot, & Sheryl Larson (Eds.), *Using survey data to study disability: Results from the national health interview survey on disability* (pp. 299–326). London, UK: Elsevier.

Anderson, W. L., Wiener, J. M., Finkelstein, E. A., & Armour, B. S. (2011). Estimates of national health care expenditures associated with disability. *Journal of Disability Policy Studies, 21*(4), 230.

Antecol, H., & Bedard, K. (2006). Unhealthy assimilation: Why do immigrants converge to American health status levels? *Demography, 43*(2), 337–360.

Arbeev, K. G., Butov, A. A., Manton, K. G., Sannikov, I. A., & Yashin, A. I. (2004). Disability trends in gender and race groups of early retirement ages in the USA. *Sozial- und Präventivmedizin, 49*(2), 142–151.

Argeseanu Cunningham, S., Ruben, J. D., & Narayan, K. M. (2008). Health of foreign-born people in the United States: A review. *Health & Place, 14*(4), 623–635.

Barker, D. J. (1993). The intrauterine origins of cardiovascular disease. *Acta Paediatrica, 82*, 93–99; discussion 100.

Barker, D. J., & Clark, P. M. (1997). Fetal undernutrition and disease in later life. *Reviews of Reproduction, 2*(2), 105–112.

Barnett, A. H., Dixon, A. N., Bellary, S., Hanif, M. W., O'hare, J. P., Raymond, N. T., & Kumar, S. (2006). Type 2 diabetes and cardiovascular risk in the UK south Asian community. *Diabetologia, 49*(10), 2234–2246.

Blue, L., & Fenelon, A. (2011). Explaining low mortality among US immigrants relative to native-born Americans: The role of smoking. *International Journal of Epidemiology, 40*(3), 786–793.

Bowen, M. E. (2009). Childhood socioeconomic status and racial differences in disability: Evidence from the Health and Retirement Study (1998–2006). *Social Science & Medicine, 69*(3), 433–441.

Braveman, P., & Barclay, C. (2009). Health disparities beginning in childhood: A life-course perspective. *Pediatrics, 124*, S163–S175.

Brittingham, A., & De la Cruz, G. P. (2005). *We the people of Arab ancestry in the United States*: US Census Bureau.

Buchner, D. (2012). Physical activity and healthy aging. In *Physical Activity and Public Health Practice* (pp. 151–166). CRC Press.

Capps, R., McCabe, K., & Fix, M. (2012). Diverse streams: Black African migration to the United States. Washington, DC: Migration Policy Institute.

Carr, A. J., Gibson, B., & Robinson, P. G. (2001). Measuring quality of life: Is quality of life determined by expectations or experience? *British Medical Journal, 322*(7296), 1240–1243.

Chakravarty, E. F., Hubert, H. B., Krishnan, E., Bruce, B. B., Lingala, V. B., & Fries, J. F. (2012). Lifestyle risk factors predict disability and death in healthy aging adults. *The American Journal of Medicine, 125*(2), 190–197.

Cho, Y., Frisbie, W. P., Hummer, R. A., & Rogers, R. G. (2004). Nativity, duration of residence, and the health of Hispanic adults in the United States. *International Migration Review, 38*(1), 184–211.

Clark, D. O., & Maddox, G. L. (1992). Racial and social correlates of age-related changes in functioning. *Journal of Gerontology, 47*(5), S222–S232.

Clark, D. O., Maddox, G. L., & Steinhauser, K. (1993). Race, aging, and functional health. *Journal of Aging and Health, 5*(4), 536–553.

Crimmins, E. M. (2004). Trends in the health of the elderly. *Annual Review of Public Health, 25*, 79–98.

Dallo, F. J., Al Snih, S., & Ajrouch, K. J. (2009). Prevalence of disability among US- and foreign-born Arab Americans: Results from the 2000 US Census. *Gerontology, 55*(2), 153–161.

DiPrete, T. A., & Eirich, G. M. (2006). Cumulative advantage as a mechanism for inequality: A review of theoretical and empirical developments. *Annual Review of Sociology, 32*, 271–297.

Elo, I. T. (2009). Social class differentials in health and mortality: Patterns and explanations in comparative perspective. *Annual Review of Sociology, 35*(1), 553–572.

Elo, I. T., Mehta, N. K., & Huang, C. (2011). Disability among native-born and foreign-born blacks in the United States. *Demography, 48*(1), 241–265.

Finucane, M. M., Stevens, G. A., Cowan, M. J., Danaei, G., Lin, J. K., Paciorek, C. J.,...M. Ezzati. (2011). National, regional, and global trends in body-mass index since 1980: Systematic analysis of health examination surveys and epidemiological studies with 960 country-years and 9.1 million participants. *The Lancet, 377*(9765), 557–567.

Flegal, K. M., Carroll, M. D., Ogden, C. L., & Curtin, L. R. (2010). Prevalence and trends in obesity among US adults, 1999–2008. *The Journal of the American Medical Association, 303*(3), 235–241.

Franzini, L., Ribble, J. C., & Keddie, A. M. (2001). Understanding the Hispanic paradox. *Ethnicity & Disease, 11*(3), 496–518.

Frisbie, W. P., Cho, Y., & Hummer, R. A. (2001). Immigration and the health of Asian and Pacific Islander adults in the United States. *American Journal of Epidemiology, 153*(4), 372–380.

Fuller-Thomson, E., Brennenstuhl, S., & Hurd, M. (2011). Comparison of disability rates among older adults in aggregated and separate Asian American/Pacific Islander subpopulations. *American Journal of Public Health, 101*(1), 94–100.

Goldman, N., Kimbro, R. T., Turra, C. M., & Pebley, A. R. (2006). Socioeconomic gradients in health for white and Mexican-origin populations. *American Journal of Public Health, 96*(12), 2186–2193.

Guralnik, J. M., Land, K. C., Blazer, D., Fillenbaum, G. G., & Branch, L. G. (1993). Educational status and active life expectancy among older blacks and whites. *The New England Journal of Medicine, 329*(2), 110–116.

Haas, S. (2008). Trajectories of functional health: The "long arm" of childhood health and socioeconomic factors. *Social Science & Medicine, 66*(4), 849–861.

Haas, S., & Rohlfsen, L. (2010). Life course determinants of racial and ethnic disparities in functional health trajectories. *Social Science & Medicine, 70*(2), 240–250.

Haas, S. A., Krueger, P. M., & Rohlfsen, L. (2012). Race/ethnic and nativity disparities in later life physical performance: The role of health and socioeconomic status over the life course. *The Journals of Gerontology, 67*(2), 238–248.

Ho, J., & Elo, I. T. (in press). The contribution of smoking to black-white differences in mortality. *Demography.*

Huang, C., Mehta, N. K., Elo, I. T., Cunningham, S. A., Stephenson, R., Williamson, D. F., & Narayan, K. M. V. (2011). Region of birth and disability among recent US immigrants: Evidence from the 2000 Census. *Population Research and Policy Review, 30*(3), 399–418.

Huang, C., Soldo, B. J., & Elo, I. T. (2011). Do early-life conditions predict functional health status in adulthood? The case of Mexico. *Social Science & Medicine, 72*(1), 100–107.

Humes, K. R., Jones, N. A., & Ramirez, R. R. (2011). Overview of race and Hispanic origin: 2010. U.S. Census Bureau.

Hummer, R. A., Biegler, M., de Turk, R. G., Forbes, D., Frisbie, W. P., Hong, Y., & Pullum, S. G. (1999). Race/ethnicity, nativity, and infant mortality in the United States. *Social Forces, 77*(3), 1083–1117.

Idler, E. L., & Benyamini, Y. (1997). Self-rated health and mortality: A review of twenty-seven community studies. *Journal of Health and Social Behavior, 38*(1), 21–37.

Idler, E. L., Russell, L. B., & Davis, D. (2000). Survival, functional limitations, and self-rated health in the NHANES I Epidemiologic Follow-up Study, 1992. First National Health and Nutrition Examination Survey. *American Journal of Epidemiology, 152*(9), 874–883.

Jasso , G., Massey, D. S., Rosenzweig, M. S., & Smith, J. P. (2004). In *Immigrant Health, Selectivity and Acculturation.* EconWPA.

Johnson, N. E. (2000). The racial crossover in comorbidity, disability, and mortality. *Demography, 37*(3), 267–283.

Jones, C. P., LaVeist, T. A., & Lillie-Blanton, M. (1991). "Race" in the epidemiologic literature: An examination of the American Journal of Epidemiology, 1921–1990. *American Journal of Epidemiology, 134*(10), 1079–1084.

Kain, J., Vio, F., & Albala, C. (2003). Obesity trends and determinant factors in Latin America. *Cadernos De Saúde Pública, 19*, S77–S86.

Kanaya, A. M., Wassel, C. L., Mathur, D., Stewart, A., Herrington, D.,…Liu, K. (2010). Prevalence and correlates of diabetes in South Asian indians in the United States: Findings from the metabolic syndrome and atherosclerosis in South asians living in america study and the multi-ethnic study of atherosclerosis. *Metabolic Syndrome and Related Disorders, 8*(2), 157–164.

Kaufman, J. S., Cooper, R. S., & McGee, D. L. (1997). Socioeconomic status and health in blacks and whites: The problem of residual confounding and the resiliency of race. *Epidemiology, 8*(6), 621–628.

Kelley-Moore, J. A., & Ferraro, K. F. (2004). The black/white disability gap: Persistent inequality in later life? *The Journals of Gerontology, 59*(1), S34–S43.

Kent, M. M. (2007). Immigration and America's black population. *Population Bulletin, 62*(4), 1–16.

Kim, J., & Miech, R. (2009). The black-white difference in age trajectories of functional health over the life course. *Social Science & Medicine, 68*(4), 717–725.

Kington, R., Carlisle, D., McCaffrey, D., Myers, H., & Allen, W. (1998). Racial differences in functional status among elderly U.S. migrants from the South. *Social Science & Medicine, 47*(6), 831–840.

Kramer, M. S. (2000). Invited commentary: Association between restricted fetal growth and adult chronic disease: Is it causal? Is it important? *American Journal of Epidemiology, 152*(7), 605–608.

Kroenke, C. H., Kubzansky, L. D., Adler, N., & Kawachi, I. (2008). Prospective change in health-related quality of life and subsequent mortality among middle-aged and older women. *American Journal of Public Health, 98*(11), 2085–2091.

LeClere, F. B., Rogers, R. G., & Peters, K. D. (1997). Ethnicity and mortality in the United States: Individual and community correlates. *Social Forces, 76*(1), 169–198.

Lee, M. A. (2011). Disparity in disability between native-born non-Hispanic white and foreign-born Asian older adults in the United States: Effects of educational attainment and age at immigration. *Social Science & Medicine, 72*(8), 1249–1257.

Lee, Y. (2000). The predictive value of self assessed general, physical, and mental health on functional decline and mortality in older adults. *Journal of Epidemiology and Community Health, 54*(2), 123–129.

Liao, Y., McGee, D. L., Cao, G., & Cooper, R. S. (1999). Black-white differences in disability and morbidity in the last years of life. *American Journal of Epidemiology, 149*(12), 1097–1103.

Link, B. G., & Phelan, J. (1995). Social conditions as fundamental causes of disease. *Journal of Health and Social Behavior,* 80–94.

Louie, G. H., & Ward, M. M. (2011). Socioeconomic and ethnic differences in disease burden and disparities in physical function in older adults. *American Journal of Public Health, 101*(7), 1322–1329.

Manton, K. G., & Gu, X. (2001). Changes in the prevalence of chronic disability in the United States black and nonblack population above age 65 from 1982 to 1999. *Proceedings of the National Academy of Sciences of the United States of America, 98*(11), 6354–6359.

Markides, K. S., & Eschbach, K. (2005). Aging, migration, and mortality: Current status of research on the Hispanic paradox. *The Journals of Gerontology, 2,* 68–75.

Markides, K. S., Eschbach, K., Ray, L. A., & Peek, M. K. (2007). Census disability rates among older people by race/ethnicity and type O Hispanic origin. In J. L. Angel, & K. E. Whitfield (Eds.), *The health of aging Hispanics: The Mexican-origin population* (pp. 26–39). New York, NY: Springer.

Markides, K. S., & Gerst, K. (2011). Immigration, aging, and health in the United States. In R. A. Settersten, Jr., & J. L. Angel (Eds.), *Handbook of sociology of aging* (pp. 103–116).

Markides, K. S., Rudkin, L., Angel, J., & Espino, D. V. (1997). In L. G. Martin & B. J. Soldo (Eds.), *Health status of the hispanic elderly; racial and ethnic differences in the health of older Americans* (pp. 105–162). Washington, DC: National Academy Press.

Martin, L. G., Freedman, V. A., Schoeni, R. F., & Andreski, P. M. (2010). Trends in disability and related chronic conditions among people ages fifty to sixty-four. *Health Affairs, 29*(4), 725–731.

Mathers, C. D. (2003). Towards valid and comparable measurement of population health. *Bulletin of the World Health Organization, 81*(11), 787–788.

Mehta, N. K., & Elo, I. T. (2012). Migrant selection and the health of U.S. immigrants from the former Soviet Union. *Demography, 49*(2), 425–447.

Mendes de Leon, C. F., Barnes, L. L., Bienias, J. L., Skarupski, K. A., & Evans, D. A. (2005). Racial disparities in disability: Recent evidence from self-reported and performance-based disability measures in a population-based study of older adults. *The Journals of Gerontology Series B, 60*(5), S263–S271.

Minnesota Population Center and State Health Access Data Assistance Center. (2012). *Integrated health interview series: Version 5.0.* Retrieved from http://www.ihis.us.

Misra, R., Patel, T., Kotha, P., Raji, A., Ganda, O., Banerji, M.,... Balasubramanyam, A. (2010). Prevalence of diabetes, metabolic syndrome, and cardiovascular risk factors in US Asian Indians: Results from a national study. *Journal of Diabetes and its Complications, 24*(3), 145–153.

Mohanty, S. A., Woolhandler, S., Himmelstein, D. U., & Bor, D. H. (2005). Diabetes and cardiovascular disease among Asian Indians in the United States. *Journal of General Internal Medicine, 20*(5), 474–478.

Murray, C. J. L., & Chen, L. C. (1992). Understanding morbidity change. *Population and Development Review, 18*(3), 481–503.

Mutchler, J. E., Burr, J. A., & Prakash, A. (2007). The demography of disability and the effects of immigrant history: Older Asians in the United States. *Demography, 44*(2), 251–263.

Mutchler, J. E., Prakash, A., & Burr, J. A. (2007). The demography of disability and the effects of immigrant history: Older Asians in the United States. *Demography, 44*(2), 251–263.

Nagi, S. Z. (1991). Disability concepts revised: Implications for prevention. In A. M. Pope & A. R. Tarlov (Eds.), *Disability in America: Toward a national agenda for prevention* (pp. 309–339). Washington, DC: National Academy Press.

Patten, E. (2012). Statistical portrait of the foreign-born population in the United States, 2010. Retrieved from http://www.pewhispanic.org/2012/02/21/statistical-portrait-of-the-foreign-born-population-in-the-united-states-2010/#sub-menu.

Preston, S. H., Mehta, N. K., & Stokes, A. (in press). Modeling obesity histories in cohort analyses of health and mortality. *Epidemiology.*

Read, G. J., & Emerson, M. O. (2005). Racial context, black immigration and the U.S. black/white health disparity. *Social Forces, 84*(1), 181–199.

Schoeni, R. F., Freedman, V. A., & Martin, L. G. (2008). Why is late-life disability declining? *The Milbank Quarterly, 86*(1), 47–89.

Seeman, T. E., Merkin, S. S., Crimmins, E. M., & Karlamangla, A. S. (2010). Disability trends among older Americans: National health and nutrition examination surveys, 1988–1994 and 1999–2004. *American Journal of Public Health, 100*(1), 100–107.

Sen, A. (2002). Health: Perception versus observation. *British Medical Journal, 324*(7342), 860–861.

Singh, G., Siahpush, M., Hiatt, R., & Timsina, L. (2011). Dramatic increases in obesity and overweight prevalence and body mass index among ethnic-immigrant and social class groups in the United States, 1976–2008. *Journal of Community Health, 36*(1), 94–110.

Singh, G. K., & Siahpush, M. (2002). Ethnic-immigrant differentials in health behaviors, morbidity, and cause-specific mortality in the United States: An analysis of two national data bases. *Human Biology, 74*(1), 83–109.

Smith, J. P. (1999). Healthy bodies and thick wallets: The dual relation between health and economic status. *The Journal of Economic Perspectives, 13*(2), 144–166.

Sturm, R., Ringel, J. S., & Andreyeva, T. (2004). Increasing obesity rates and disability trends. *Health Affairs, 23*(2), 199–205.

Taylor, M. G. (2008). Timing, accumulation, and the black/white disability gap in later life. *Research on aging, 30*(2), 226–250.

Thomas, K. J. A. (2012). *Demographic profile of black Caribbean immigrants in the United States.* Washington, DC: Migration Policy Institute.

Trupin, L., Rice, D. P., & Max, W. (1995). *Who pays for the medical care of people with disabilities?*: U.S. Dept. of Education.

Turra, C. M., & Elo, I. T. (2008). The impact of Salmon bias on the hispanic mortality advantage: New evidence from social security data. *Population Research and Policy Review, 27*(5), 515–530.

Verbrugge, L. M., & Jette, A. M. (1994). The disablement process. *Social Science & Medicine, 38*(1), 1–14.

Verbrugge, L. M., Lepkowski, J. M., & Imanaka, Y. (1989). Comorbidity and its impact on disability. *The Milbank Quarterly, 67*(3–4), 450–484.

Vita, A. J., Terry, R. B., Hubert, H. B., & Fries, J. F. (1998). Aging, health risks, and cumulative disability. *The New England Journal of Medicine, 338*(15), 1035–1041.

Wang, C., & Satariano, W. A. (2007). Self-rated current and future health independently predict subsequent mortality in an aging population. *The Journals of Gerontology, 62*(12), 1428–1434.

Warner, D. F., & Brown, T. H. (2011). Understanding how race/ethnicity and gender define age-trajectories of disability: An intersectionality approach. *Social Science & Medicine, 72*(8), 1236–1248.

Williams, D. R., & Collins, C. (2001). Racial residential segregation: A fundamental cause of racial disparities in health. *Public Health Reports, 116*(5), 404–416.

Williams, D. R., & Jackson, P. B. (2005). Social sources of racial disparities in health. *Health Affairs, 24*(2), 325–334.

Williams, D. R., Mohammed, S. A., Leavell, J., & Collins, C. (2010). Race, socioeconomic status, and health: Complexities, ongoing challenges, and research opportunities. *Annals of the New York Academy of Sciences, 1186*, 69–101.

World Health Organization. (2002). Towards a common language for functioning, disability, and health ICF. Retrieved from http://www.who.int/classifications/icf/2010. WHO Global Infobase.

Zhao, G., Ford, E. S., Li, C., Crews, J. E., & Mokdad, A. H. (2009). Disability and its correlates with chronic morbidities among U.S. adults aged 50-<65 years. *Preventive Medicine, 48*(2), 117–121.

CHAPTER 9

Race/Ethnicity, Mortality, and Longevity

*Robert A. Hummer, Jennifer E. Melvin,
Connor M. Sheehan, and Ying-Ting Wang*

The topic of race/ethnic differences in U.S. mortality and longevity constitutes an important portion of the literature on minority aging. Because race/ethnic stratification results in highly inequitable resources across population subgroups, it is not surprising that U.S. society has long been characterized by mortality rate and longevity differentials as well. Thus, for example, there is a substantial literature dedicated to documenting and understanding the higher mortality rates and longevity disadvantage of non-Hispanic blacks compared to non-Hispanic whites (Geruso, 2012; Rogers, 1992; Satcher et al., 2005; Sloan, Ayyagari, Salm, & Grossman, 2010). Given the rapid changes in U.S. population composition, particularly since 1965, scholarly work in this area has also increasingly given attention to the mortality and longevity patterns of the Latino/Hispanic and Asian American and Pacific Islander populations (Hummer, Rogers, Nam, & LeClere, 1999; Markides & Eschbach, 2011; Singh & Miller, 2004); nonetheless, our understanding of mortality and longevity patterns for those groups lags well behind that of non-Hispanic blacks and non-Hispanic whites. Unfortunately, less attention is devoted to the population-based documentation and understanding of mortality and longevity among American Indians and Alaska Natives, particularly given their smaller population size relative to other U.S. minority groups and their extensive geographic and tribal heterogeneity.

This chapter has three aims. The first is to provide an overview of key theoretical considerations that are important to understanding mortality and longevity differences across groups. We briefly highlight the historical and social contexts as well as the life course processes that are most important in understanding patterns and trends of race/ethnicity, aging, and mortality/longevity in the United States. Second, we turn to documentation and gather data from recent official reports of U.S. mortality and longevity to summarize adult mortality and life expectancy differences across race/ethnic groups. This documentation focuses on five groups: non-Hispanic blacks, Hispanics, Asian Americans and Pacific Islanders, American Indians and Alaska Natives, and non-Hispanic whites (hereafter, blacks, Hispanics, Asian Americans, American Indians, and whites, respectively). Although we recognize substantial ethnic, cultural, socioeconomic, and geographic heterogeneity within each of these broad groups, data limitations restrict our analyses. The third aim is to provide a new empirical analysis of race/ethnicity and U.S. adult mortality risk, focusing on key demographic and socioeconomic factors that influence mortality differentials across groups. To accomplish this, we use data from the public National Health Interview Survey Linked Mortality Files (NHIS-LMF; Ingram, Lochner, & Cox, 2008; Lochner, Hummer, Bartee, Wheatcroft, & Cox, 2008). The concluding section focuses on the implications of work in this area for science and policy. We focus on critical research needs and on the ways that social and health policy might effectively influence future mortality and longevity trends for all race/ethnic subgroups in an increasingly diverse and aging society.

THEORETICAL CONSIDERATIONS

How might mortality and longevity differences across race/ethnic groups be best understood? Previous studies point toward two broad theoretical considerations that are critical to understanding mortality and longevity group differences and changes in such differences over time. Most often, these considerations cannot be adequately taken into account in the documentation and statistical modeling of race/ethnic differences in mortality/longevity because of limitations in the data sets that are available to study U.S. mortality differences and trends. Nonetheless, these considerations establish a context within which such differences can best be understood. The following subsections highlight those key theoretical considerations.

Historical and Social Context

Perhaps the most important, yet often ignored, issue in contemporary research on race/ethnicity and mortality/longevity is historical and social context. Recently, as an exception to this pattern, Hummer and Chinn (2011, p. 8; also see Hummer, 1996; Williams & Jackson, 2005; Williams & Sternthal, 2010) argue that understanding black–white differences in U.S. mortality rates cannot be successfully accomplished without attention to context:

> No analysis of mortality patterns and trends that contrasts African Americans with other racial/ethnic groups is sufficient without considering the impacts of institutional- and individual-level forms of discrimination on the African American population. Such discriminatory treatment first developed out of an ideology that justified the African slave trade and, while the forms of discrimination have shifted through the years and decades, the impact of such discrimination on the well-being of African Americans is still being felt…In contrast to African Americans, Whites in the United States have long enjoyed the privileges of living in a politically, culturally, and socioeconomically White-dominated society [Saenz & Morales, 2005]. With such privilege come numerous rewards that accrue throughout life and across generations.

Obviously, it is crucial that historical and social context be extended to all groups. Mortality and longevity patterns and trends for American Indians, Asian Americans, Hispanics, as well as all component subgroups that together comprise these broader groups, must be considered within the appropriate context for each group's social history. This historical and social phenomenon includes, but is not limited to, conquest and near genocide, immigrant selectivity, socioeconomic opportunity, immigrant refugee status, and many other factors specific to the social history of a group. Documenting patterns and trends in mortality/longevity without sensitivity and specificity to the historical and social context of the groups in question, while perhaps a valuable demographic or public health exercise, leaves the patterns and trends open for interpretation by readers who may not understand or even care about each group's particular social and historical context.

Specific to this chapter, it is evident that the experience and legacy of slavery, segregation, and continued discrimination in the housing, criminal justice, financial, education, political, and health care institutions has been particularly harmful for African Americans, even in the current era of legal equality (Gates, Jr. et al., 2012; Massey, 2007). It should be no surprise to students of social history, unfortunately, that mortality rates for blacks continue to be significantly higher than those of other U.S. race/ethnic groups. Although significant progress in various domains has been made since the Civil Rights Era of one-half century ago (Fischer & Hout, 2006; Gates, Jr. et al., 2012), much work remains to level the playing field for blacks (with whites) in all U.S. social institutions. Until that happens, it is unlikely that the mortality rates of blacks will match those of their more socially, economically, and politically advantaged counterparts. Perhaps most worrisome is the fact that the gap in wealth between the average black and white household grew fourfold between 1984 and 2007 (Shapiro, Meschede, & Sullivan, 2010). Indeed, wealth is a key marker of the intergenerational and life course accumulation of socioeconomic resources, and such widening inequality indicates that much work lies ahead with regard to the achievement of true racial equality in U.S. society.

It is also evident from decades of social science research that all of the minority groups discussed here have been subject to substantial discrimination and political, economic, and social disadvantages in U.S. society in comparison to whites (National Research Council, 2001, 2006; Saenz & Morales, 2005). The social history of the American Indian population, for example, is characterized by a tragic legacy of discrimination and near genocide. Perhaps the best example of their plight is their depopulation (through killing and disease) from an estimated 5 million around the year 1500 to a census count of just 237,000 in 1900 (Thornton, 1987). Fortunately, the resilient American Indian population has grown since then, due to both natural increase and evolving racial self-identification, with the 2010 U.S. Census enumerating 5.2 million people who identified as American Indian or Alaska Native, either alone or in combination with one or more other races. Of the 5.2 million total, 2.9 million (0.7% of the total U.S. population) identified as American Indian or Alaska Native alone (Norris, Vines, & Hoeffel, 2012). Despite substantial social and economic gains made by American Indians during the last few decades, they too remain well behind whites in the accumulation of socioeconomic resources that help facilitate healthy and long lives (Huyser, Sakamoto, & Takei, 2010). This socioeconomic disadvantage is particularly the case for American Indians and Alaska Natives who identify as American Indian or Alaska Native alone (Huyser et al., 2010), a subgroup that is more likely to live on designated reservations, tribal lands, or statistical areas than multiple-race American Indians (Norris et al., 2012).

The Asian American population has grown rapidly since changes in immigration laws in the 1960s; they currently comprise 5 percent of the U.S. population (Humes, Jones, & Ramirez, 2011). Nonetheless, Asian Americans trace their U.S. origins back well before the last five decades. Prior to 1965, the Asian American population was a relatively small group that originally immigrated to the U.S. due to the availability of low-wage jobs in the railroad, agriculture, manufacturing, and service sectors. They faced racial violence and severe racial discrimination throughout a majority of U.S. history, including the legal restriction of Chinese immigration (in 1882), the elimination of all Asian immigration (except for Filipinos) in 1924, and the interment of more than 100,000 Japanese Americans into camps during World War II (Xie & Goyette, 2005). In more recent decades, Asian American immigrants and their children have tended to be relatively well educated (Feliciano, 2005; Xie & Goyette, 2005), facilitating their socioeconomic incorporation into American society. This general characterization is, of course, overly simplistic because some subgroups of Asian Americans—particularly Vietnamese, Laotian, Cambodian, and Hmong—face significant socioeconomic and health disadvantages in the U.S. context (Frisbie, Cho, & Hummer, 2001; Xie & Goyette, 2005). Nonetheless, the positive health and educational selectivity of Asian immigrants (Akresh & Frank, 2008; Feliciano, 2005), along with the generally high levels of education attained by the U.S.-born children of Asian immigrants (Xie & Goyette, 2005), help provide a context for relatively low mortality and high longevity among this population in the contemporary United States.

Like Asian Americans, Hispanics are also a very diverse group, comprising of individuals tracing their roots to 20 different countries in Central America, South America, and Europe. Hispanics are also currently the largest U.S. minority group, accounting for more than 16 percent of the population (compared to blacks at 13 percent; Humes et al., 2011). Also similar to Asian Americans, Hispanics comprise a relatively small population that has lived in the United States for many generations and a much larger post-1965 immigrant stream, which further includes their relatively young children and grandchildren. The smaller Hispanic population living in the United States prior to the 1960s was largely Mexican, Puerto Rican, and Cuban in origin and faced severe social and economic discrimination, including being forced to attend segregated schools and live in segregated neighborhoods in some areas of the country (National Research Council, 2006). Post-1965, Hispanic immigrants have arrived from various countries (with Mexico being the most prominent sending country), and have arrived generally both healthier and more highly educated compared to those who did not migrate from the respective countries of origin (Akresh & Frank, 2008; Feliciano, 2005). However, Hispanic immigrants (particularly those from Mexico) have on average much lower educational attainment than other U.S. immigrant groups. Moreover, U.S.-born children and grandchildren of Hispanic immigrants have lower levels of education, live in households with lower income and substantially lower wealth than whites, and live in neighborhoods often highly segregated from more affluent Americans (Kochlar, 2004; National Research Council, 2006). The social context of Hispanics is also influenced by the undocumented status of perhaps 8 to 9 million immigrants in the United States, which poses risks for their health and well being because they necessarily live in the shadows of the American mainstream (National Research Council, 2006). Nevertheless, the Hispanic population is characterized by features that are particularly conducive to low mortality and long lives (e.g., positive immigrant selectivity on both health and education dimensions), as well as features that are strongly associated with high mortality rates and low life expectancy (e.g., a history of social and economic discrimination, an overall low level of education and socioeconomic status, and tenuous legal status among a sizable number of immigrants). It is no wonder, then, that Hispanic mortality patterns have long been difficult to both estimate and understand in the U.S. context, given the complex demographic and social history of this diverse group (Markides & Eschbach, 2005, 2011).

This brief discussion of the historical and social contexts that frame the mortality and longevity patterns for each broad minority group does not imply that all whites have been, or continue to be, equally privileged; that is clearly not the case. Indeed, members of national origin groups such as Italian, Irish, and Polish Americans were at one time highly disadvantaged and discriminated against, but their light skin tone facilitated their eventual entry into the white majority. Nor does it mean that whites necessarily have the lowest mortality rates and live the longest lives, on average; that too, is clearly not the case as we demonstrate below. However, on average, white Americans have been and continue to be characterized by political, economic, and social advantages that play out across the life course and that have the potential to influence, among many other things, their mortality rates and longevity patterns.

Life Course, Health, and Mortality

The understanding of race/ethnic patterns and trends of mortality and longevity must also consider the ways in which the life course unfolds in unique ways across groups. One important example is with regard to mortality selection and the changing composition of population groups by age. Most simply, group differences in mortality rates across the life course have the potential to seriously impact the health composition of the race/ethnic-specific populations that are alive at any specific age. For example, the comparison of mortality rates for two groups at age 90 may include one that has experienced high mortality rates throughout the life course and has just a small and highly select group of survivors remaining, while the second may have had low mortality rates throughout the life course and is characterized by a larger but less healthy group of remaining survivors. This example illustrates the classic issue of mortality selection that, at least in part, is thought to be responsible for the convergence and possible crossover of black and white mortality rates at around age 90 in the United States (Jackson et al., 2011; Masters, 2012; Nam, 1995; Preston & Elo, 2006). More broadly, any comparison of two or more mortality rates between race/ethnic groups at any specific age must consider that the populations being compared are (somewhat more or less) select subsets of the birth cohorts from which they originated.

A more substantive illustration of the importance of life course effects involves group differences in the aging process. Because of racial discrimination and related socioeconomic disadvantages, the average life course of black women and men has been hypothesized to be more stressful and thus unfold more quickly and, in terms of health, more deleteriously than the average life course of white women and men. Geronimus (1992) has termed this as the "weathering hypothesis." Jackson et al. (2011) more recently extended the idea of weathering to further include differential exposures of in-utero stress across race groups that, when combined with differential stress exposures during infancy, childhood, and young adulthood, go on to influence differential black and white mortality rates during the entire life course. Others (Kaestner, Pearson, Keene, & Geronimus, 2009; Powers, 2013) have recently extended the life course-based weathering framework to socially disadvantaged Hispanic populations in the attempt to place health and mortality trajectories of other population subgroups in a context that emphasizes the life course accumulation of advantages and/or disadvantages.

All told, the understanding of race/ethnic differences in mortality and longevity must be understood within a context that takes into account group differences in the life course experiences, stressors, and advantages/disadvantages that characterize diverse populations. Although a comprehensive statistical treatment of group-specific "life course effects" is not practical or feasible given the enormous data requirements of such an exercise, a theoretical framing emphasizing the differential life course trajectories (in historical and social context) of groups is a powerful way to think about and potentially explain the mortality differentials in question. Such framing should strongly emphasize how race/ethnic differences in socioeconomic status, even when poorly measured in many of the most commonly used mortality data sets, reflect differences in the intergenerational and life course accumulation of resources that are critical to living healthy and long lives in contemporary U.S. society (Hummer & Chinn, 2011).

DOCUMENTING RACE/ETHNIC DIFFERENCES IN ADULT MORTALITY

Data Quality Issues

The accurate documentation of mortality rates and levels of life expectancy by race/ethnicity is very challenging, even when broad groups are considered. Official U.S. vital statistics mortality rates are calculated through the tabulation of death certificates in the numerators and census counts (or intercensal estimates) in the denominators (Minino, Murphy, Xu, & Kochanek, 2011). Thus, the accuracy of official mortality rates depends on the completeness of counts and on the quality of demographic information (particularly age and race/ethnicity) in both the numerators and denominators of these rates. Given their dependence on mortality rates as inputs, race/ethnic-specific life tables (which provide us with life expectancy estimates) are highly sensitive to the quality of mortality rates (Arias, 2011).

Fortunately, researchers continue to closely monitor mortality data quality and, when possible, make informed adjustments in the numerators and/or denominators of the rates (Arias, Schauman, Sorlie, & Backlund, 2008; Arias, Eschbach, Schauman, Backlund, & Sorlie, 2010; Preston & Elo, 2006). One area of longstanding concern has been the quality of age reports in both numerator and denominator data, particularly among the elderly. Preston, Elo, and colleagues, for example, have consistently shown that official mortality rates among older (e.g., aged 85+) blacks are implausibly low due to age misreports on death certificates (Elo, 2001; Preston & Elo, 2006; Preston, Elo, Rosenwaike, & Hill, 1996).

A second issue of data quality concern involves numerator–denominator mismatches of race/ethnicity. Numerator data for mortality rates come from death certificates that are most often completed by funeral directors. Census-based denominator data, however, are usually reported by individuals or family members. Thus, there may be inconsistencies in reporting between the numerators and denominators that influence race/ethnic-specific mortality rates. For example, lacking information from available family members or on family history, a funeral director could identify a decedent as white when, in fact, that person had identified her- or himself while alive as American Indian. Indeed, studies of this phenomenon show that official death counts for Hispanics, Asian Americans, and American Indians in the numerator of mortality rates are most likely lower than what is actually the case, while those for blacks and whites are modestly higher than what is probably the case (Arias et al., 2010; Rosenberg et al., 1999; Stehr-Green, Bettles, & Robertson, 2002). Rates that are adjusted produce modestly higher mortality estimates for Asian Americans and Hispanics and much higher estimates for American Indians (Elo, Turra, Kestenbaum, & Ferguson, 2004; Lauderdale & Kestenbaum, 2002; Rosenberg et al., 1999; Stehr-Green et al., 2002). Using such adjustments, the U.S. government recently produced its first-ever official life tables for Hispanics (Arias, 2010). Notably, though, there are still no official life tables for the Asian American or American Indian populations. Moreover, official U.S. mortality rates by race/ethnicity are not adjusted for either race/ethnic mismatches or age misreports, so substantial skepticism in the interpretation of official vital statistics rates (to which we now turn) is warranted.

Race/Ethnicity and Age-Specific All-Cause Mortality: Official Estimates

Table 9.1 shows age- and sex-specific mortality rates (per 100,000 population), and death rate ratios for each of the five major race/ethnic groups under examination, drawn from the preliminary release of 2010 U.S. official mortality data (Murphy, Xu, & Kochanek, 2012). The death rate ratios use the age- and sex-specific mortality rates of whites, the nation's largest race/ethnic group, as the comparison. Careful documentation and understanding of mortality patterns across race/ethnic groups must also consider differentiation by age and gender. For example, summary measures of mortality (e.g., age-adjusted death rate) or longevity (e.g., life expectancy at birth) are insufficient in comprehensively documenting mortality patterns among population subgroups and differentials across subgroups; age- and sex-specific documentation is necessary. Thus, this section of the chapter uses data from the most recent official report of U.S. mortality to document and summarize age- and sex-specific mortality differences across the five major race/ethnic groups. We focus on ages 45 and above, since the middle (45–64) and older (65+) age groups together account for well over 90 percent of U.S. deaths (Xu, Kochanek, Murphy, & Tejada-Vera, 2010). It is to be noted that the rates depicted in Table 9.1 are not age-standardized within age categories; thus, race/ethnic differences in age structure could potentially influence the mortality comparisons if one race/ethnic group has an older age structure than another within specific age categories.

There are four important race/ethnic patterns to note in Table 9.1. Notably, the patterns are similar when looking at either females or males. First, death rates for blacks are the highest of any group through the age range of 75 to 84 years: black death rates are 40 to 60 percent higher than whites in the 45- to 54- and 55- to 64-year age groups, and 10 to 40 percent higher in the 65- to 74- and 75- to 84-year age groups. Moreover, the absolute mortality rate differences between blacks and whites (which are not specifically shown in Table 9.1, but are simply the age-specific mortality rates of whites subtracted from the age-specific mortality rates of blacks) increase up through the 65- to 74-year age group and then only decrease beginning with the 75- to 84-year age group. Thus, while black–white adult mortality differences have clearly narrowed since their most recent peak around 1990 (Harper, Lynch, Burris, & Davey-Smith, 2007; Hoyert, 2012), age-specific gaps remain very wide through at least age 85. That is, African Americans clearly continue to experience substantially higher adult mortality than all other major U.S. population groups. As such, an estimated 83,000 blacks experience premature mortality relative to whites on a yearly basis (Satcher et al., 2005), a majority of which is due to causes that are amenable to medical care or social policy interventions (Macinko & Elo, 2009).

Second, mortality rates among women and men aged 85+ are lower for blacks than for whites (but are still higher than the other three race/ethnic groups). The reasons for a black–white old age mortality crossover have long been debated (Nam, 1995). The first prominent explanation involves data quality issues that lead to the underestimation of black mortality rates at older ages (Preston & Elo, 2006). The second focuses on selective mortality; higher mortality among blacks throughout the life course results in a relatively healthy black subpopulation with relatively low mortality, particularly for heart disease, at the oldest ages

TABLE 9.1 Death Rates per 100,000 by Race/Ethnicity and Mortality Rate Ratios for Racial/Ethnic Minority Groups Compared With Non-Hispanic Whites, U.S. Adults Aged 45 and Above, Official (preliminary) Vital Statistics Mortality Data, 2010

SEX AND AGE GROUP	NON-HISPANIC BLACK		HISPANIC ORIGIN		ASIAN/PACIFIC ISLANDER		AMERICAN INDIAN/ALASKAN NATIVE		NON-HISPANIC WHITE	
	Death Rates	Death Rate ratios	Death Rates	Death Rate Ratios	Death Rates	Death Rate Ratios	Death Rates	Death Rate Ratios	Death Rates	Death Rate Ratios
Females										
45–54	496.3	1.61	193.7	0.63	127.9	0.42	325.5	1.06	307.4	1.00
55–64	995.0	1.58	449.8	0.71	298.8	0.47	622.7	0.99	630.9	1.00
65–74	2,062.9	1.34	1,084.6	0.71	788.5	0.51	1,478.2	0.96	1,534.3	1.00
75–84	4,663.9	1.10	3,066.4	0.73	2,445.2	0.58	3,362.5	0.80	4,228.4	1.00
85+	12,737.3	0.94	10,235.6	0.76	8,586.9	0.63	9,249.3	0.68	13,525.7	1.00
Males										
45–54	736.9	1.45	351.5	0.69	213.9	0.42	495.3	0.98	507.5	1.00
55–64	1,700.8	1.63	814.6	0.78	519.4	0.50	948.2	0.91	1,045.1	1.00
65–74	3,266.0	1.45	1,773.7	0.79	1,225.0	0.54	1,969.7	0.87	2,254.5	1.00
75–84	6,832.1	1.19	4,461.3	0.77	3,436.6	0.60	4,441.5	0.77	5,763.8	1.00
85+	14,947.1	0.95	11,775.6	0.75	10,822.7	0.69	10,240.5	0.65	15,796.1	1.00

Source: Adapted from Murphy et al. (2012).

(Eberstein, Nam, & Heyman, 2008; Lynch, Brown, & Harmsen, 2003). The most recent article on this topic strongly suggests that the black–white mortality crossover is the result of selective mortality among older birth cohorts of blacks and whites, but is also a phenomenon that will most likely not be experienced by more recent birth cohorts as the life course experiences of U.S. blacks and whites change in fundamental ways (Masters, 2012).

Third, Table 9.1 shows that the official mortality rates for Hispanics and Asian Americans are lower than those of whites and blacks in each of the age groups in the table. Asian American mortality is particularly low relative to the other groups in middle adulthood, and Asian American mortality rates remain 31 to 37 percent lower than whites even at ages 85 and above. Meanwhile, Hispanic mortality rates are generally 25 to 35 percent below those of whites (and even lower compared to blacks) in each age group. Again, though, these are unadjusted rates that, most importantly, do not account for the underreporting of deaths in the numerators for Hispanic and Asian American individuals (Arias et al., 2008).

Fourth, documented mortality rates for American Indians are similar to those of whites in the younger age groups and become progressively more and more advantaged compared to whites in the older age groups. For example, the rate ratio of American Indian-to-white mortality is 1.06 at age 45 to 54, but decreases to 0.68 at age group 85+. However, as noted above, a large number of deaths among American Indians are likely misclassified as white or black, particularly at the older ages (Arias et al., 2008; Stehr-Green et al., 2002). Thus, substantial caution in the interpretation of official American Indian mortality rates is warranted.

Cause of Death Patterns

Table 9.2 depicts cause-specific mortality differences across race/ethnic groups. Cause of death specification adds important detail to our understanding of group-specific mortality patterns. We again show data from an official U.S. vital statistics report (Heron, 2011), but issue further caution given the underestimation of mortality rates for Hispanics, Asian Americans and Pacific Islanders, and American Indians and Alaska Natives. The data are presented separately for women and men, as well as for the 45 to 54, 55 to 64, and 65+ age groups. We limit the analysis to the five leading causes of death for each specific age/sex group.

Several notable patterns of cause-specific mortality are highlighted. First, among adults aged 45 to 54 and 55 to 64, black women and men are characterized by much higher rates of the two leading causes of death, malignant neoplasms and heart disease, compared to the other groups. In most cases, mortality rates are 1.5 to 3 times higher among blacks for these causes in comparison to the other groups. On the contrary, Hispanics and Asian Americans exhibit the lowest rates of malignant neoplasms and heart disease in these age groups. As an illustrative example, estimated rates of heart disease mortality for 45- to 54-year-old men (per 100,000 population) are just 51.5 for Asian Americans and 73.3 for Hispanics, compared to 112.4 for American Indians, 121.6 for whites, and 222.4 for blacks.

A second clear pattern among younger (aged 45–54 and 55–64) adults is especially high mortality due to accidents and chronic liver disease and cirrhosis experienced by American Indians in comparison to the other groups. Among women aged 45 to 54, for example, mortality due to accidents is 1.5 to 5.5 times higher among American Indians than other groups and mortality due to liver disease and cirrhosis is 4.5 to 20 times as high compared to the other groups. Although rates for accidents and liver disease and cirrhosis are lower than those of heart disease and malignant neoplasms in these age groups, the significantly higher cause-specific levels among American Indians for these largely preventable causes is striking.

Third, diabetes mellitus becomes a top five cause of death for both women and men in the 55- to 64-year-old age group and is characterized by much higher rates among blacks and American Indians in comparison to the other groups. Unlike the patterns for both heart disease and malignant neoplasms, Hispanic women and men both exhibit much higher mortality rates for this cause at ages 55 to 64 in comparison to whites. Rates of diabetes mellitus for Asian American women and men are clearly the lowest of any group in this age range.

Fourth, while mortality rates for ages 65 and above are, as expected, far higher than those exhibited in the younger age categories, most of the cause-specific rates are lowest among

TABLE 9.2 Cause-Specific Mortality Rates per 100,000 by Race/Ethnicity for the Top Five Leading Causes of Death for Each Age/Sex Group, U.S. Adults Aged 45 and Above, Official Vital Statistics Mortality Data, 2007

SEX AND AGE GROUP	NON-HISPANIC BLACK	HISPANIC	ASIAN/PACIFIC ISLANDER	AMERICAN INDIAN	NON-HISPANIC WHITE
Females 45–54					
Malignant neoplasms	160.6	75.5	70.0	75.6	110.9
Heart disease	110.2	23.4	12.1	36.7	42.1
Accidents	29.3	14.7	7.9	46.6	31.0
Cerebrovascular	33.9	11.0	9.9	10.0	9.8
Chronic liver/cirrhosis	10.6	10.2	2.3	48.0	11.1
Females 55–64					
Malignant neoplasms	359.7	175.6	162.2	190.3	280.6
Heart disease	247.7	81.4	46.8	108.7	107.1
Lower respiratory	27.8	8.9	4.2	35.5	41.4
Diabetes mellitus	65.4	33.7	14.2	52.3	22.0
Cerebrovascular	60.0	25.4	25.2	23.7	22.1
Females 65+					
Heart disease	1331.5	780.6	569.5	627.5	1289.9
Malignant neoplasms	906.4	519.6	471.4	551.1	896.4
Cerebrovascular	357.6	205.3	219.7	188.3	346.0
Lower respiratory	133.0	97.7	63.8	176.7	301.2
Alzheimer's	174.0	113.7	66.8	93.4	264.3
Males 45–54					
Heart disease	222.4	73.3	51.5	112.4	121.6
Malignant neoplasms	183.6	74.2	73.4	78.3	116.8
Accidents	81.3	54.5	17.2	85.0	66.2
Suicide	*	13.1	11.0	17.8	32.6
Chronic liver/cirrhosis	23.4	38.5	7.0	73.5	26.0
Males 55–64					
Malignant neoplasms	558.0	221.9	190.0	264.5	357.6
Heart disease	527.7	201.9	131.5	235.8	276.6
Accidents	78.3	42.9	19.9	71.8	52.2
Lower respiratory	45.6	13.4	8.8	37.0	47.0
Diabetes mellitus	87.8	51.1	26.4	69.0	36.1
Males 65+					
Heart disease	1586.1	938.3	714.9	814.1	1465.7
Malignant neoplasms	1547.1	797.0	722.2	746.0	1299.4
Lower respiratory	240.3	145.4	123.4	212.2	353.8
Cerebrovascular	370.3	192.6	206.9	169.7	268.4
Diabetes mellitus	239.2	181.6	104.8	194.4	137.7

* Suicide was not a top 10 cause for non-Hispanic black men in this age group, thus the rate was not specified in the source publication.

Source: Adapted from Heron (2011).

Asian Americans, Hispanics, and American Indians and are highest among blacks and whites. Asian Americans, in particular, exhibit roughly 50 percent lower rates of heart disease and cancer mortality than either whites or blacks in this age group. Both Hispanic and American Indian women and men also exhibit lower heart disease and cancer mortality at ages 65 and above compared to whites and blacks. Again, though, mortality rates at these ages are likely to be underestimated for some minority groups, particularly American Indians. Indeed, in the Survey-Based Models section below, we provide strong evidence to support the fact that official mortality rates for American Indians are vastly underestimated; thus, much skepticism for the low rates of heart disease and cancer mortality among American Indian adults aged 65 and above is warranted.

Life Expectancy Estimates

Given the underestimation of mortality rates among several of the minority populations as noted above, official U.S. government life tables have largely been calculated and published only for the black and white populations. Recently, official life expectancy calculations have been extended to Hispanics (Arias, 2010). In Table 9.3, we show life expectancy estimates at ages 0, 45, 65, and 85 for the Hispanic, black, and white populations, as documented by the National Center for Health Statistics (2012; see www.cdc.gov/nchs/data/dvs/deaths_2009_release.pdf).

Given the mortality rate differences presented above, it is no surprise that Hispanic women and men have the highest estimated life expectancy at each age, whites generally have the second highest, and blacks have the lowest. Life expectancy at birth for black women is 3.8 years less than white women and 6.2 years less than Hispanic women, while life expectancy at birth for black men is 5.6 years less than white men and 8 years less than Hispanic men. In the late 1980s, black women and men exhibited life expectancies at birth that were 6 and 8.5 years less than white women and men, respectively, so the figures shown here indicate clear progress toward closing those gaps during the past 20 years (Harper et al., 2007; see also Harper, Rushani, & Kaufman, 2012). Nonetheless, the black–white gaps are still very wide, particularly among men, indicating much room for continued improvement among blacks (Harper et al., 2012; Hummer & Chinn, 2011). Moreover, life expectancy at birth for both blacks and whites lags well behind Hispanics, further indicating that both blacks and whites have potential for substantial gains.

Table 9.3 also indicates that race/ethnic gaps in life expectancy at age 85 are narrow: sex-specific race/ethnic differences at age 85 are 1 year or less, with black–white differences near 0. However, life expectancy differences at age 45 across groups, while somewhat smaller than at age 0, are wide. For example, life expectancy at age 45 for Hispanic men is 36.1 years, for white men is 33.9 years, and for black men is 29.9 years. This clearly indicates that excess mortality for whites compared to Hispanics and for blacks relative to both whites and Hispanics

TABLE 9.3 Life Expectancy at Selected Ages by Sex for Hispanics, Non-Hispanic Blacks, and Non-Hispanic Whites, United States, 2009

EXACT AGE IN YEARS	HISPANIC			NON-HISPANIC BLACK			NON-HISPANIC WHITE		
	Both Sexes	Male	Female	Both Sexes	Male	Female	Both Sexes	Male	Female
0	81.2	78.7	83.5	74.2	70.7	77.3	78.7	76.3	81.1
45	38.2	36.1	39.9	32.7	29.9	35.1	35.9	33.9	37.7
65	20.9	19.4	22.0	17.7	15.7	19.1	19.1	17.6	20.3
85	7.6	6.8	7.9	6.8	5.9	7.2	6.6	5.8	7.0

Source: National Center for Health Statistics (2011). 2009 Mortality Multiple Cause Micro-data Files. Retrieved at http://www.cdc.gov/nchs/data/dvs/deaths_2009_release.pdf.

is not just a function of higher mortality in the early life course; race/ethnic mortality differentials at ages 45 and above result in significant contemporary life expectancy disparities in middle and older adulthood as well.

RACE/ETHNICITY AND U.S. ADULT MORTALITY: SURVEY-BASED MODELS

Building on some of the theoretical considerations and resolving some of the weaknesses of official vital statistics data discussed above, this section employs a survey-based mortality data set to model contemporary race/ethnic differences in U.S. adult mortality. We use pooled data from 16 cross-sectional years (1989–2004) of the National Health Interview Survey, which have each been linked with the National Death Index through the end of 2006 to create the NHIS-LMF (Ingram et al., 2008; Lochner et al., 2008). The NHIS-LMF is *the* preeminent nationally representative, survey-based U.S. mortality data set because of its very large size, availability of mortality covariates, and high-quality linkages between the cross-sectional survey data and the follow-up mortality records (Rogers, Hummer, & Nam, 2000). Because the NHIS-LMF is survey-based and individuals or family members report age and race/ethnicity, it avoids the numerator–denominator mismatch problems that characterize official vital statistics mortality data. We restrict the analysis to persons who were between the ages of 45 and 84 at time of survey and who had complete data on the variables of interest. We also restrict the analysis to individuals who identified as Mexican Origin (of any race), Other Hispanic (of any race), Asian American, American Indian, black, or white. (Non-Hispanics who identified with multiple racial groups were also excluded.) This resulted in a data set of 509,621 individuals aged 45 to 84 years (276,479 women and 233,142 men), 103,495 (51,216 women and 52,279 men) of whom were identified as deceased between the time they were surveyed and the end of 2006.

We estimate race/ethnic differences in mortality in Table 9.4 using Cox proportional hazards models (Allison, 1984), separately for female and male adults. Our models specify race/ethnic differences in mortality in comparison to whites, while adjusting for demographic and socioeconomic covariates. Mortality differences across race/ethnic groups are expressed in the form of hazard ratios, with ratios above 1.0 indicating higher mortality during the follow-up period for a particular race/ethnic group than that of whites, and ratios below 1.0 indicating lower mortality during the follow-up period for a particular group compared to whites. Four different Cox proportional hazard models of mortality risk for each sex are shown, with the models becoming progressively more inclusive of demographic and socioeconomic characteristics that influence race/ethnic differences in U.S. adult mortality.

Model 1 for each sex shows that blacks and American Indians share the highest risk of mortality among U.S. adults aged 45 and above: each group exhibits about 30 percent higher mortality risk (i.e., hazard ratios of about 1.3) than whites, controlling for age. It is to be noted that these results for American Indians differ considerably from those reported above that used official U.S. vital statistics mortality data, with the key difference being that the survey-based data used in this section rely on self-reports of race/ethnicity. The results in Table 9.4 are also consistent with a theoretical perspective of historically based discrimination and continued social disadvantage in the U.S. context for blacks and American Indians relative to whites (Hummer & Chinn, 2011; Williams & Sternthal, 2010). In contrast, Model 1 shows that Mexican Origin, Other Hispanic, and Asian American adults for each sex each exhibit generally lower mortality than whites in the 45 and above age range. Consistent with vital statistics data presented above, Asian Americans display the lowest hazard ratios of mortality: 42% lower mortality for Asian American women compared to white women and 48% lower mortality for Asian American men compared to white men. The generally lower mortality risks for Mexican Origin and Other Hispanic women and men in Model 1 in comparison to whites and blacks (patterns which are also consistent with vital statistics data presented above) illustrates the *epidemiologic paradox*: relatively favorable mortality risks for Hispanics despite their disadvantaged socioeconomic status (Markides & Coreil, 1986; Markides & Eschbach, 2005, 2011). For example, the hazard ratio for Mexican Origin men is 0.85 and for Other Hispanic men is 0.84, each about 15 percent lower mortality than white men in this age range.

TABLE 9.4 Hazard Ratios for Race/Ethnic Differences in Mortality of U.S. Adults Aged 45+, 1989–2006

	FEMALES				MALES			
	Model 1	Model 2	Model 3	Model 4	Model 1	Model 2	Model 3	Model 4
Race/ethnicity/nativity (reference = whites)								
Non-Hispanic Black	1.29**	1.49**	1.49**	1.40**	1.34**	1.49**	1.50*	1.35**
Mexican Origin	0.94	1.00	1.09*	0.93*	0.85**	0.90**	0.99	0.83**
Other Hispanic	0.81**	0.84**	1.00	0.92	0.84**	0.86**	1.00	0.94
Asian/Pacific Islander	0.58**	0.58**	0.73**	0.73**	0.52**	0.54**	0.67**	0.71**
American Indian	1.32**	1.46**	1.46*	0.99	1.29*	1.42**	1.42**	1.27*
Age *(continuous in years)*	1.09**	1.10**	1.10**	1.09**	1.09**	1.10**	1.10**	1.09**
Age* Non-Hispanic Black		0.98**	0.98**	0.98**		0.98**	0.98**	0.98**
Age* Mexican Origin		0.99*	0.99*	0.99*		0.99*	0.99**	0.99**
Age* Other Hispanic		1.00	1.00	1.00		1.00	1.00	1.00
Age* Asian/Pacific Islander		1.00	1.00	1.00		1.00	0.99	0.99*
Age* American Indian		0.99*	0.99**	0.99*		0.98*	0.98*	0.97**
Nativity/duration (reference = U.S. born)								
Foreign born, <10 years in the United States			0.64**	0.60**			0.56**	0.53**
Foreign born, 10+ years in United States			0.77**	0.75**			0.78**	0.77**
Education (reference = 12 years)								
0–8 years				1.32**				1.30**
9–11 years				1.22**				1.19**
13–15 years				0.90**				0.93**
16+ years				0.73**				0.68**
Degrees of freedom	6	11	13	17	6	11	13	17
N	276,479	276,479	276,479	276,479	233,142	233,142	233,142	233,142

* $p < 0.05$; ** $p < 0.01$.

Data are weighted.

Source: National Health Interview Survey Linked Mortality File, 1989–2006 (Ingram et al., 2008; Lochner et al., 2008).

Model 2 for each sex additionally includes interaction terms between age and race/ethnicity to account for varying slopes of mortality by age for each group. That is, previous research strongly suggests that the mortality rates for blacks and Hispanics increase somewhat less steeply with age in comparison to whites (Hummer, Benjamins, & Rogers, 2004; Palloni & Arias, 2004; Preston & Elo, 2006). Indeed, Model 2 for both women and men shows that the age-by-race/ethnicity interactions are lower than 1.00 and statistically significant for blacks, Mexican Americans, and American Indians; for each group, the slope of mortality rises a bit less steeply with age in comparison to whites. Because we centered the age variable at 60 years in this and all subsequent models, the main effect coefficients for each race/ethnic group now reflect mortality differences at age 60 in comparison to whites. Thus, for example, the hazard ratio of 1.49 for black females in Model 2 exhibits 49 percent higher mortality for blacks than whites at age 60.

Because the inclusion of interaction effects make these models difficult to interpret using just the tables, Figures 9.1 and 9.2 graphically show the results of Model 2 for men and women, respectively. For both blacks and American Indians, the much higher mortality risk compared to whites at age 45 becomes less pronounced with age. For both black men and

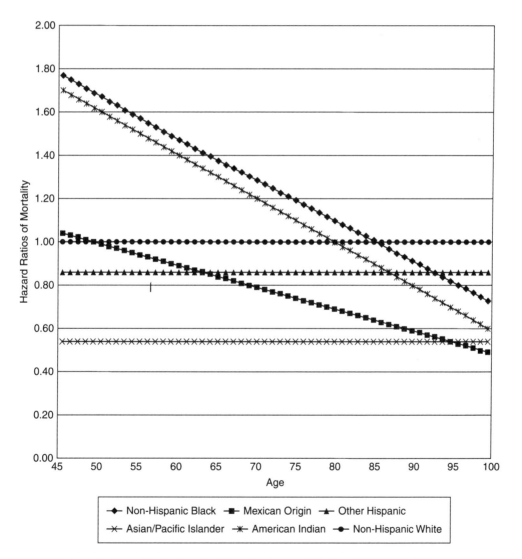

FIGURE 9.1 Predicted Race/Ethnic Mortality Disparities by Age, U.S. Men, NHIS 1989–2006.

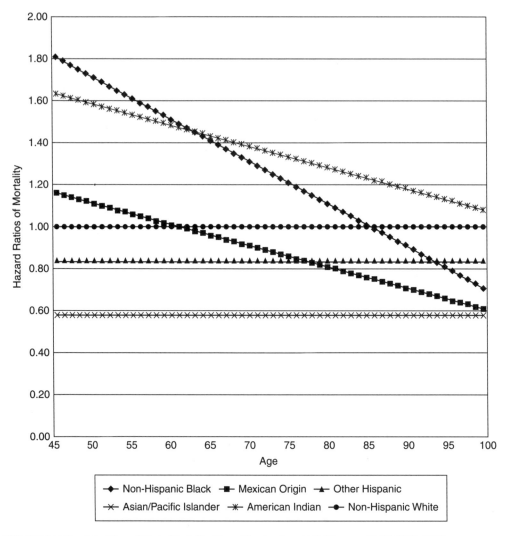

FIGURE 9.2 Predicted Race/Ethnic Mortality Disparities by Age, U.S. Women, NHIS 1989–2006.

women relative to white men and women, a mortality crossover is portrayed in these figures, with blacks exhibiting lower mortality than whites after about age 85 or so. A crossover is also documented for American Indian men relative to white men at about age 80. Again, though, it is easy to see in both figures that black and American Indian women and men exhibit much higher mortality than white women and men up through at least age 80.

Figures 9.1 and 9.2 also show that Mexican Origin adults experience increasingly favorable mortality risks compared to whites at older ages. For men (Figure 9.1), Mexican Origin adults exhibit equivalent mortality risk to whites at age 45 and substantially lower mortality risk than whites at the older ages. For women (Figure 9.2), modestly higher mortality risk for Mexican Origin adults relative to whites becomes a mortality advantage by age 70 and increasingly so at the oldest ages. Clearly, Figures 9.1 and 9.2 demonstrate that race/ethnic differences in U.S. adult mortality are dynamic with age. The two exceptions are that both Other Hispanic and Asian American adults exhibit consistently lower mortality than white adults at ages 45 and above.

Referring to Table 9.4 again, Model 3 for both women and men additionally includes a nativity variable to account for mortality differences between foreign- and U.S.-born adults. Official mortality rates documented by government reports do not differentiate the mortality patterns of the foreign- and U.S.-born subpopulations in these broad race/ethnic groups.

However, the immigrant subpopulation in each race/ethnic group has been shown to exhibit lower mortality than each U.S.-born subpopulation (Hummer et al., 1999; Singh & Miller, 2004; Singh & Siahpush, 2002). Moreover, given that 40% of the Hispanic population and 67% of the Asian American population is currently foreign-born (Grieco, 2009), lower mortality rates among the foreign-born population has the potential to significantly influence the overall mortality rates of each of these groups.

Clearly, Model 3 shows that both female and male foreign-born individuals are characterized by lower mortality than their U.S.-born counterparts; for example, foreign-born women who have been in the United States for less than 10 years exhibit 36 percent lower mortality risk than U.S.-born women, and foreign-born women who have been in the United States for 10 or more years exhibit 23 percent lower mortality than U.S.-born women. This control for nativity status also impacts race/ethnic mortality differences. Indeed, Model 3 for both women and men shows that the risk of mortality for the Hispanic groups is no longer lower than that of whites, net of nativity; in fact, Mexican Origin women exhibit 9 percent higher mortality than white women, net of nativity. Moreover, the hazard ratios for both Asian American women and men increase in Model 3 in comparison to Model 2 after nativity is controlled, illustrating that a sizable portion of their lower mortality relative to whites is due to low mortality among foreign-born individuals. On the contrary, there is no change in the hazard ratios for blacks or American Indians relative to whites after controlling for nativity, which makes sense given that there are relatively few foreign-born black or American Indian adults in this age range.

Clearly, then, low mortality among foreign-born individuals helps to explain some of the overall low adult mortality exhibited by both the Asian American and Hispanic populations (Hummer et al., 1999; Singh & Miller, 2004; Singh & Siahpush, 2001, 2002). Some related demographic work has delved into the question of why U.S. immigrants have lower mortality rates than their U.S.-born, counterparts. Three potential explanations are most prominent in the literature. First, immigrants have been shown to be healthier upon arrival than either the populations from their home countries who did not migrate or the population of their U.S.-born co-ethnics (Akresh & Frank, 2008; Jasso, Massey, Rosenzweig, & Smith, 2004). Such a pattern of "health selection" is probably the most powerful explanation for low mortality among U.S. immigrants. Second, some have argued that unhealthy immigrants leave the United States and die in their home countries, making the low mortality rates among U.S. immigrants largely a statistical artifact (Palloni & Arias, 2004). Subsequent analyses based on both infant mortality and adult mortality data, though, have largely quashed this potential explanation (Hummer, Powers, Pullum, Gossman, & Frisbie, 2007; Turra & Elo, 2008). Third, patterns of positive health behavior may also be, in part, responsible for the low mortality rates among U.S. immigrants (Hummer et al., 1999; Singh & Siahpush, 2002). Perhaps most important, low rates of cigarette smoking have recently been shown to be an important explanation for low immigrant mortality (Blue & Fenelon, 2011; see also Fenelon & Preston, 2012).

Finally, educational attainment is included in Model 4 for each sex to help determine the extent to which race/ethnic differences in mortality are attributable to socioeconomic differences across groups. We use educational attainment as our indicator of socioeconomic status because it is generally completed early in the life course, is less prone than income to misreports and non-response in surveys, and is much less volatile than income to changes in employment status and health at ages 45 and above (Hummer & Lariscy, 2011). Also, it is clear from Model 4 for both women and men that educational attainment is strongly related to adult mortality in a graded fashion. Relative to those with 12 years of schooling, individuals with lower levels of educational attainment exhibit 19 to 32 percent higher mortality risk during the follow-up period, while individuals with more than 12 years of schooling exhibit 7 to 32 percent lower levels of mortality risk across the follow-up period.

Controlling for educational attainment in Model 4 results in some sizable changes in race/ethnic differences in adult mortality compared to Model 3. Higher mortality for blacks and American Indians relative to whites is reduced with the inclusion of educational attainment in Model 4, illustrating that lower socioeconomic status accounts for at least some of the higher mortality experienced by blacks and American Indians in this age range. For example, the hazard ratio of 1.50 for black males in Model 3 is reduced to 1.35 in Model 4 once educational attainment is included. One may note as well that this simple control for educational attainment falls far short of controlling for the range of intergenerational and life course socioeconomic disadvantages experienced by blacks and American Indians relative to whites (Hummer & Chinn, 2011). Note as well that the hazard ratios for Mexican Origin females and males exhibit sizable declines in Model 4 once educational attainment is included in the models. This suggests that Mexican Origin adults would experience even lower mortality relative to whites if educational attainment between the populations were equalized. Clearly, Model 4 for both sexes helps illustrate the contemporary mortality impact of lower socioeconomic status for blacks, American Indians, and Mexican Americans relative to whites.

SCIENTIFIC AND POLICY IMPLICATIONS

This chapter has revealed mortality and longevity differences across U.S. race/ethnic groups using two national data sources, and has discussed key theoretical considerations related to the understanding of contemporary mortality differentials. Unfortunately, blacks and American Indians exhibit less favorable mortality and longevity patterns than other race/ethnic groups, reflecting their longstanding and continued social, economic, and political disadvantages in U.S. society. For each of these groups, their relatively higher mortality compared to whites becomes less pronounced at older ages, reflecting what appear to be the strong effects of mortality selection playing out across groups into old age. High rates of heart disease and cancer mortality among blacks play a significant role in their elevated rates of mortality in the 45- to 64-year range, while high rates of diabetes and chronic liver disease/cirrhosis mortality in this same age range are striking for American Indians. On the contrary, Hispanics and Asian Americans exhibit generally favorable mortality patterns compared to whites at ages 45 and above, with relatively low rates of heart disease and cancer mortality standing out among both groups, and particularly so for Asian Americans. Clearly, low mortality among foreign-born adults in the U.S. works to keep mortality rates among Hispanics and Asian Americans low in comparison to the other groups, while socioeconomic disadvantages among blacks, American Indians, and Mexican Americans works to keep their mortality levels higher than what would be the case if these groups achieved socioeconomic equality with whites.

This chapter contains implications that are important for future scientific work in this area. First, mortality researchers should continue to place very high value and invest substantial resources in accurately documenting patterns and trends of mortality and longevity across race/ethnic groups (Arias, 2010; Arias et al., 2008, 2010; Elo, 2001; Elo et al., 2004; Lauderdale & Kestenbaum, 2002; Preston & Elo, 2006; Turra & Elo, 2008). Such detailed and challenging demographic work is vitally important to "getting the facts right," as perhaps best illustrated by the vastly differing portrait of American Indian adult mortality this chapter documented, depending on which data source was being used. Continued challenges in this specific line of research includes shifting patterns of race/ethnic identification over time and the continued inconsistencies in numerator and denominator counts that have long characterized U.S. vital statistics data. Researchers should also attempt to specify mortality patterns and trends among specific ethnic subpopulations (e.g., Puerto Ricans, Cubans, Mexican Americans, Dominicans, etc., for Hispanics) and nativity subpopulations (e.g., immigrants and the native borns for each group) whenever data sets allow. Indeed, accurate descriptive work may necessarily rely on a combination of U.S. vital statistics data and survey-based mortality data sets such as the NHIS-LMF and the National Longitudinal Mortality Study (NLMS; e.g., Arias et al., 2008, 2010). Accurate description is a necessary precursor to in-depth explanation.

Second, it is clear from this chapter and previous work in the area that survey-based data sets such as the NHIS-LMF (Ingram et al., 2008; Lochner et al., 2008) and the NLMS (Sorlie, Backlund, & Keller, 1995) yield very valuable insights into U.S. mortality patterns and trends. The production of such data sets, in large part due to the extraordinary efforts of researchers at the National Center for Health Statistics and other federal agencies, is increasingly challenged by federal budget cuts and threats of cuts that have the potential to seriously undermine scientific progress in this area of study. Without continued production and refinement of these data sets, the public's understanding of mortality patterns, trends, and explanations suffers and policymakers will not have the information they need to make informed decisions about the public health of the population, including programs and policies specifically designed for improving the health and longevity of minority groups. We urge the general scientific community to strongly support the continued production of such valuable data sets and the governmental research community more specifically to continue to invest whatever funds they can allocate toward this effort.

Third, scientific progress in this area will depend on the refinement of explanations of mortality differentials across race/ethnic populations. This chapter outlined two key theoretical considerations—social/historical context and the life course—that researchers must take into consideration when aiming to explain mortality differences and trends by race/ethnicity. Attention to these two theoretical considerations is not easy when even the best data sets in the area are seriously limited in the range of variables that they have available. Thus, creativity is in order if data analysis is to approach the magnitude of theoretical considerations we discussed above. One example might involve the linkage of race/ethnic- and birth cohort-specific indicators of social advantage/disadvantage context to individually based mortality data sets such as the NHIS-LMF and NLMS. Such linked data sets would potentially allow for understanding the extent to which differential social and economic contexts of birth cohorts result in race/ethnic differences in mortality for the birth cohorts being considered.

Finally, the mortality and longevity differences we documented and discussed above have important policy implications, particularly if social policy is considered to be an important component of health policy (Schoeni, House, Kaplan, & Pollack, 2008). Consider from Table 9.4 the models showing that the statistical equalization of educational attainment across groups could significantly reduce the elevated levels of mortality risk for blacks and American Indians relative to whites. Yet the educational attainment of blacks and American Indians (along with Hispanics) remains considerably lower than that of whites (Everett, Rogers, Hummer, & Krueger, 2011) due to the continued social, economic, and generational disadvantages faced by these minority populations. Social policy can clearly make an impact through increased investments in teachers, schools, and students, if aimed specifically at increasing educational attainment for the populations in greatest need. Such contemporary investments could have major impacts on reducing or eliminating future race/ethnic differences in U.S. adult mortality. Our documentation and above discussion should help advance a social policy agenda that is geared toward the eventual closing of mortality and longevity differences and assurance of equally long and healthy lives for all U.S. race/ethnic groups.

ACKNOWLEDGMENTS

We are grateful for financial support from the MacArthur Foundation Research Network on an Aging Society: John W. Rowe, Columbia University (Chair) and by infrastructural research support (5 R24 HD042849) and training grant support (5 T32 HD007081) from the Eunice Kennedy Shriver National Institute of Child Health and Human Development to the Population Research Center at the University of Texas at Austin. We also thank the National Center for Health Statistics and the Minnesota Population Center for making the data available for this chapter, and Dustin Brown and Joseph Lariscy for helpful assistance regarding data and methods.

REFERENCES

Akresh, I. R., & Frank, R. (2008). Health selection among new immigrants. *American Journal of Public Health, 98*(11), 2058–2064.

Allison, P. (1984). *Event history analysis: Regression for longitudinal event data.* Beverly Hills, CA: Sage Publications.

Arias, E. (2010). United States life tables by Hispanic origin. *Vital and Health Statistics. Series 2, Data Evaluation and Methods Research*, (152), 1–33.

Arias, E. (2011). United States life tables, 2007. *National Vital Statistics Reports: From the Centers for Disease Control and Prevention, National Center for Health Statistics, National Vital Statistics System, 59*(9), 1–60.

Arias, E., Eschbach, K., Schauman, W. S., Backlund, E. L., & Sorlie, P. D. (2010). The Hispanic mortality advantage and ethnic misclassification on US death certificates. *American Journal of Public Health, 100*(S1), S171–S177.

Arias, E., Schauman, W. S., Sorlie, P. D., & Backlund, E. (2008). The validity of race and Hispanic origin reporting on death certificates in the United States. *Vital and Health Statistics, 2*(148), 1–24.

Blue, L., & Fenelon, A. (2011). Explaining low mortality among US immigrants relative to native-born Americans: The role of smoking. *International Journal of Epidemiology, 40*(3), 786–793.

Eberstein, I. W., Nam, C. B., & Heyman, K. M. (2008). Causes of death and mortality crossovers by race. *Biodemography and Social Biology, 54*(2), 214–228.

Elo, I. T. (2001). New African American life tables from 1935–1940 to 1985–1990. *Demography, 38*(1), 97–114.

Elo, I. T., Turra, C. M., Kestenbaum, B., & Ferguson, B. R. (2004). Mortality among elderly Hispanics in the United States: Past evidence and new results. *Demography, 41*(1), 109–128.

Everett, B. G., Rogers, R. G., Hummer, R. A., & Krueger, P.M. (2011). Trends in educational attainment by race/ethnicity, nativity, and sex in the United States, 1989–2005. *Ethnic and Racial Studies, 33*(7), 1168–1193.

Feliciano, C. (2005). Educational selectivity in U.S. immigration: How do immigrants compare to those left behind? *Demography, 42*(1), 131–152.

Fenelon, A., & Preston, S. H. (2012). Estimating smoking-attributable mortality in the United States. *Demography, 49*(3), 797–818.

Fischer, C. S., & Hout, M. (2006). *Century of difference: How America changed in the last one hundred years.* New York: Russell Sage Foundation.

Frisbie, W. P., Cho, Y., & Hummer, R. A. (2001). Immigration and the health of Asian and Pacific Islander adults in the United States. *American Journal of Epidemiology, 153*(4), 372–380.

Gates, Jr., H. L., Steele, C., Bobo, L. D., Dawson, M. C., Jaynes, G., Crooms-Robinson, L. et al. (Eds.). (2012). *The oxford handbook of African American citizenship, 1865-present.* Oxford: Oxford University Press.

Geronimus, A. T. (1992). The weathering hypothesis and the health of African-American women and infants: Evidence and speculations. *Ethnicity & Disease, 2*(3), 207–221.

Geruso, M. (2012). Black-white disparities in life expectancy: How much can the standard SES variables explain? *Demography, 49*(2), 553–574.

Grieco, E. M. (2009). *Race and Hispanic origin of the foreign-born population in the United States: 2007. American Community Survey Reports, ACS-11.* Washington, DC: U.S. Census Bureau.

Harper, S., Lynch, J., Burris, S., & Davey Smith, G. (2007). Trends in the black-white life expectancy gap in the United States, 1983–2003. *JAMA: The Journal of the American Medical Association, 297*(11), 1224–1232.

Harper, S., Rushani, D., & Kaufman, J. S. (2012). Trends in the black-white life expectancy gap, 2003–2008. *JAMA: The Journal of the American Medical Association, 307*(21), 2257–2259.

Heron, M. (2011). Deaths: Leading causes for 2007. *National Vital Statistics Reports: From the Centers for Disease Control and Prevention, National Center for Health Statistics, National Vital Statistics System, 59*(8), 1–95.

Hoyert, D. L. (2012). 75 years of mortality in the United States, 1935–2010. *NCHS Data Brief, (88),* 1–8.

Humes, K. R., Jones, N. A., & Ramirez, R. R. (2011). Overview of race and Hispanic origin: 2010. *2010 Census Briefs* (C2010BR-02). United States Census Bureau.

Hummer, R. A. (1996). Black-White differences in health and mortality: A review and conceptual model. *The Sociological Quarterly, 37*(1), 105–125.

Hummer, R. A., Benjamins, M. R. & Rogers, R. G. (2004). Racial and ethnic disparities in health and mortality among the U.S. Elderly population. In N. B. Anderson, R. A. Bulatao, & B. Cohen (Eds.). *Critical Perspectives on Racial and Ethnic Differences in Health in Late Life* (pp. 53–94). Washington, DC: The National Academies Press.

Hummer, R. A., & Chinn, J. J. (2011). Race/ethnicity and U.S. adult mortality: Progress, prospects, and new analyses. *Du Bois Review: Social Science Research on Race, 8*(1), 5–24.

Hummer, R. A., & Lariscy, J. T. (2011). Educational attainment and adult mortality. In R. G. Rogers & E. M. Crimmins (Eds.). *International Handbook of Adult Mortality* (pp. 241–261). New York: Springer.

Hummer, R. A., Powers, D. A., Pullum, S. G., Gossman, G. L., & Frisbie, W. P. (2007). Paradox found (again): Infant mortality among the Mexican-origin population in the United States. *Demography, 44*(3), 441–457.

Hummer, R. A., Rogers, R. G., Nam, C. B., & LeClere, F. B. (1999). Race/ethnicity, nativity, and US adult mortality. *Social Science Quarterly, 80*(1), 136–153.

Huyser, K. R., Sakamoto, A., & Takei, I. (2010). The persistence of racial disadvantage: The socioeconomic attainments of single-race and multiple-race native Americans. *Population Research and Policy Review, 29*(4), 541–568.

Ingram, D. D., Lochner, K. A., & Cox, C. S. (2008). Mortality experience of the 1986–2000 National Health Interview Survey linked mortality files participants. *Vital and Health Statistics, 2*(147), 1–45.

Jackson, J. S., Hudson, D., Kershaw, K., Mezuk, B., Rafferty, J., & Tuttle, K. K. (2011). Discrimination, chronic stress, and mortality among Black Americans: A life course framework. In R. G. Rogers & E. M. Crimmins (Eds.). *International Handbook of Adult Mortality* (pp. 311–328). New York: Springer.

Jasso, G., Massey, D. S., Rosenzweig, M. R., & Smith, J. P. (2004). Immigrant health: Selectivity and acculturation. In N. B. Anderson, R. A. Bulatao, & B. Cohen (Eds.). *Critical perspectives on racial and ethnic differences in health in late life* (pp. 227–267). Washington, DC: The National Academies Press.

Kaestner, R., Pearson, J. A., Keene, D., & Geronimus, A. T. (2009). Stress, allostatic load and health of Mexican immigrants. *Social Science Quarterly, 90*(5), 1089–1111.

Kochlar, R. (2004). *The wealth of Hispanic households: 1996 to 2002. Pew Hispanic Center Report.* Washington, DC: The Pew Research Center. Available at: www.pewhispanic.org.

Lauderdale, D. S., & Kestenbaum, B. (2002). Mortality rates of elderly Asian American populations based on Medicare and Social Security data. *Demography, 39*(3), 529–540.

Lochner, K., Hummer, R. A., Bartee, S., Wheatcroft, G., & Cox, C. (2008). The public-use National Health Interview Survey linked mortality files: Methods of reidentification risk avoidance and comparative analysis. *American Journal of Epidemiology, 168*(3), 336–344.

Lynch, S. M., Brown, J. S., & Harmsen, K. G. (2003). Black-White differences in mortality compression and deceleration and the mortality crossover reconsidered. *Research on Aging, 25*, 456–483.

Macinko, J., & Elo, I. T. (2009). Black-white differences in avoidable mortality in the USA, 1980–2005. *Journal of Epidemiology and Community Health, 63*(9), 715–721.

Markides, K. S., & Coreil, J. (1986). The health of Hispanics in the southwestern United States: An epidemiologic paradox. *Public Health Reports (Washington, D.C.: 1974), 101*(3), 253–265.

Markides, K. S., & Eschbach, K. (2005). Aging, migration, and mortality: Current status of research on the Hispanic paradox. *The Journals of Gerontology. Series B, Psychological Sciences and Social Sciences, 60* Spec No 2, 68–75.

Markides, K. S., & Eschbach, K. (2011). Hispanic paradox in adult mortality in the United States. In R. G. Rogers & E. Crimmins (Eds.). *International Handbook of Adult Mortality* (Chapter 14). New York: Springer.

Massey, D. S. (2007). *Categorically unequal: The American stratification system.* New York: Russell Sage Foundation.

Masters, R. M. (2012). Uncrossing the Black-White mortality crossover: The role of cohort forces in life course mortality risk. *Demography, 49*(3), 773–796.

Miniño, A. M., Murphy, S. L., Xu, J., & Kochanek, K. D. (2011). Deaths: Final data for 2008. *National Vital Statistics Reports: From the Centers for Disease Control and Prevention, National Center for Health Statistics, National Vital Statistics System, 59*(10), 1–126.

Murphy, S. L., Xu, J., & Kochanek, K. D. (2012). Deaths: Preliminary data for 2010. *National Vital Statistics Reports* 60(4), 1–68.

Nam, C. B. (1995). Another look at mortality crossovers. *Social Biology, 42*(1–2), 133–142.

National Center for Health Statistics. (2011). *2009 Mortality Multiple Cause Micro-Data Files.* Available at: http://www.cdc.gov/nchs/data/dvs/deaths_2009_release.pdf

National Research Council. (2001). *America becoming: Racial trends and their consequences*. In N. J. Smelser, W. J. Wilson, & F. Mitchell (Eds.). (Vol. 1). Washington, DC: National Academies Press.

National Research Council. (2006). *Multiple origins, uncertain destinies: Hispanics and the American future*. In M. Tienda & F. Mitchell (Eds.). Washington, DC: National Academies Press.

Norris, T., Vines, P. L., & Hoeffel, E. M. (2012). *The American Indian and Alaska native population: 2010. 2010 Census Briefs* (C2010BR-10). Suitland, MD: United States Census Bureau.

Palloni, A., & Arias, E. (2004). Paradox lost: Explaining the Hispanic adult mortality advantage. *Demography, 41*(3), 385–415.

Powers, D. A. (2013). Paradox revisited: A further investigation of racial/ethnic differences in infant mortality by maternal age. *Demography, 50*(2), 495–520.

Preston, S. H., & Elo, I. T. (2006). Black mortality at very old ages in official US life tables: A skeptical appraisal. *Population and Development Review, 32*(3), 557–565.

Preston, S. H., Elo, I. T., Rosenwaike, I., & Hill, M. (1996). African-American mortality at older ages: Results of a matching study. *Demography, 33*(2), 193–209.

Rogers, R. G. (1992). Living and dying in the U.S.A.: Sociodemographic determinants of death among blacks and whites. *Demography, 29*(2), 287–303.

Rogers, R. G., Hummer, R. A., & Nam, C. B. (2000). *Living and dying in the USA: Behavioral, health, and social differentials of adult mortality*. San Diego, CA: Academic Press.

Rosenberg, H. M., Maurer, J. D., Sorlie, P. D., Johnson, N. J., MacDorman, M. F., Hoyert, D. L. et al. (1999). Quality of death rates by race and Hispanic origin: A summary of current research. *Vital and Health Statistics, 218*(2), 1–13.

Saenz, R., & Morales, M. C. (2005). Demography of race and ethnicity. In D. L. Poston, & M. Micklin (Eds.). *Handbook of population* (Chapter 6) (pp. 169–206). New York: Kluwer Academic/Plenum Publishers.

Satcher, D., Fryer, G. E., McCann, J., Troutman, A., Woolf, S. H., & Rust, G. (2005). What if we were equal? A comparison of the black-white mortality gap in 1960 and 2000. *Health Affairs (Project Hope), 24*(2), 459–464.

Schoeni, R. F., House, J. S., Kaplan, G. A., & Pollack, H. (Eds.). (2008). *Making Americans healthier: Social and economic policy as health policy*. New York: Russell Sage Foundation.

Shapiro, T. M., Meschede, T., & Sullivan, L. (2010). *The racial wealth gap increases fourfold. Research and Policy Brief* (May). Waltham, MA: Institute on Assets and Social Policy, Brandeis University.

Singh, G. K., & Miller, B. A. (2004). Health, life expectancy, and mortality patterns among immigrant populations in the United States. *Canadian Journal of Public Health. Revue canadienne de santé publique, 95*(3), I14–I21.

Singh, G. K., & Siahpush, M. (2001). All-cause and cause-specific mortality of immigrants and native born in the United States. *American Journal of Public Health, 91*(3), 392–399.

Singh, G. K., & Siahpush, M. (2002). Ethnic-immigrant differentials in health behaviors, morbidity, and cause-specific mortality in the United States: An analysis of two national data bases. *Human Biology, 74*(1), 83–109.

Sloan, F. A., Ayyagari, P., Salm, M., & Grossman, D. (2010). The longevity gap between Black and White men in the United States at the beginning and end of the 20th century. *American Journal of Public Health, 100*(2), 357–363.

Sorlie, P. D., Backlund, E., & Keller, J. B. (1995). US mortality by economic, demographic, and social characteristics: The National Longitudinal Mortality Study. *American Journal of Public Health, 85*(7), 949–956.

Stehr-Green, P., Bettles, J., & Robertson, L. D. (2002). Effect of racial/ethnic misclassification of American Indians and Alaskan Natives on Washington State death certificates, 1989–1997. *American Journal of Public Health, 92*(3), 443–444.

Thornton, R. (1987). *American Indian holocaust and survival: A population history since 1492*. Norman: University of Oklahoma Press.

Turra, C. M., & Elo, I. T. (2008). The Impact of Salmon Bias on the Hispanic Mortality Advantage: New Evidence from Social Security Data. *Population Research and Policy Review, 27*(5), 515–530.

Williams, D. R., & Jackson, P. B. (2005). Social sources of racial disparities in health. *Health Affairs (Project Hope)*, 24(2), 325–334.

Williams, D. R., & Sternthal, M. (2010). Understanding racial-ethnic disparities in health: Sociological contributions. *Journal of Health and Social Behavior*, *51 Suppl*, S15–S27.

Xie, Y., & Goyette, K. A. (2005). A demographic portrait of Asian Americans. In R. Farley & J. Haaga (Eds.). *The American People: Census 2000* (pp. 415–446). New York: Russell Sage Foundation.

Xu, J., Kochanek, K. D., Murphy, S. L., & Tejada-Vera, B. (2010). Deaths: Final data for 2007. *National Vital Statistics Reports*, 58(19), 1–136.

CHAPTER 10

What Does Knowing About Genetics Contribute to Understanding the Health of Minority Elders?

Keith E. Whitfield, Marvella E. Ford,
and Christopher Edwards

BRIEF HISTORY OF GENES AND MINORITIES

Two arguments prevail in the field of aging about the source of racial disparities. One posits that health differentials across ethnic groups exist solely on the basis of genetic differences, whereas the other suggests that environmental factors alone will yield comprehensive identification of the mechanisms responsible for health disparities. Each of these perspectives has its own limitations. The genetically oriented perspective tends to include preconceived notions about genetically based racial inferiority and a lack of appreciation of variability within ethnic groups. The environmentally oriented perspective arises, in part, from trepidation by some social scientists and behavioral medicine researchers about the use of genetic approaches in the study of health (Whitfield, Brandon, & Wiggins, 2003). The apprehension may arise from previous research that used poorly or inappropriately defined phenotypes to make generalizations about group differences (Bowman, 1991; Gamble, 1993; King, 1992). Attempts to explain the differential health burden experienced by ethnic minorities relying solely on genetic explanations is illogical given that there are relatively small genome-wide genetic differences across racial groups than within each group, with respect to any particular disease or health-related phenotype. Overemphasis on genetics as the single major explanatory factor in health disparities could lead researchers to overlook factors that contribute to disparities in more substantial ways and may also reinforce the kind of racial stereotyping that contributed to disparities in the first place (Sankar et al., 2004). The role of genetic influences on health disparities, however, cannot be completely dismissed. Population differences can and do exist with respect to major disease-related loci (not only between majority and minority populations, but also between majority groups of different European origin).

Complementary, interdisciplinary approaches are needed to utilize information that has been obtained from the Human Genome Project so that informative explorations of the underlying causes of health and illness and the related psychosocial behaviors can be performed. The utility of the increasingly sophisticated statistical designs of structural equation models in quantitative genetics can be enormously amplified by incorporating measurements of theoretically relevant environmental variables, specific genetic loci, and physiological mediators of the causal nexus. Such programs of research will clearly require expertise of teams of scholars and deployment of considerable resources. There are at least two perspectives that have been taken that each provide different interesting but limited information about genetic influences on the health and behavior of ethnic minorities: molecular genetic investigations of inherited diseases and quantitative genetic examinations.

INHERITED DISEASES IN MINORITIES

Inherited diseases are those that show a clear pattern of transmission of risk within families. There are several inherited diseases that show high prevalence among ethnic minorities, but one of the best known is sickle cell disease (SCD) among African Americans. SCD does not only impact African Americans but the prevalence of the disease among this group makes it one of the clearer examples of an inherited disease that is related to a ethnic group. SCD is the most common genetic disease of the blood and represents a group of hematological disorders where hemoglobin (Hgb) ineffectively carries oxygen to tissues and organs and gaseous byproducts of metabolism to the lungs for expiration (Edwards et al., 2005). A mutation in the hemoglobin gene (*HbS*) causes glutamic acid (GAG) to be replaced with valine (GTG), and this deoxygenated polymer reduces cell membrane elasticity and distorts red blood cells into sickle-shaped cells that ineffectively carry blood gases (Pells et al., 2007). In other cases, the hemoglobin gene (*HBB*) can mutate to produce abnormal hemoglobin C (HbC), hemoglobin E (HbE), beta thalassemia, and hemoglobin S-beta thalassemia (HbSBetaThal). SCD is inherited in an autorecessive pattern where one *HBB* gene from a parent is mutated into *HbS*. In sickle cell anemia, the most common form of SCD, both parents contribute a mutated *HbS* gene.

One of the primary symptoms associated with SCD is the presence of pain. Pain is produced when sickle-shaped cells occlude small blood vessels, not in a thrombotic fashion, but due to surface adhesive properties and the shape of the cells (Edwards et al., 2005). SCD pain crises can be associated with longer term complications such as delayed growth, vascular damage, fatigue, neuropsychological deficits, and cerebral vascular events (CVEs; Ballas et al., 2010; Edwards et al., 2007; Feliu et al., 2011). Influenced, in part, by the presence of significant physical and psychological morbidities, median survival in years for patients with SCD has cohered in the forties, with some patients recently living into their sixties and seventies as a result of reduced disease burden and advances in treatment (Platt et al., 1994).

SCD, a genetic disorder, may serve as an optimal model for understanding issues of aging in minority populations. Research in SCD highlights the value of managing psychosocial factors toward better quality of life, even when many clinical indices of disease severity are primarily biological and in some cases subjective (pain). For example, adult men and women with SCD seem equally and negatively influenced by poor body image (Reddy et al., 2011), and psychological factors such as perceived racial discrimination are associated with increased health care utilization (Stanton et al., 2010). Adult patients often change their patterns of macronutrient consumption during periods of pain or psychological distress in a fashion that results in greater than expected rates of overweight and obesity (Pells et al., 2005). Furthermore, patients who somaticize and focus exclusively without distractions on health concerns tend to report greater pain and have greater psychopathology (Wellington et al., 2010). Adults with SCD may suffer high rates of depression and affective disturbance, with one third of patients having sustainable suicide ideation or attempts and few patients getting treatment (Edwards et al., 2009). Although religion and spirituality may assist some adult patients with SCD to cope with their pains and affective distress (McDougald et al., 2009; O'Connell-Edwards et al., 2009), only patients who are actively engaged in weekly religious activity seem to get quantifiable benefit (Harrison et al., 2005). Lastly, adult patients who are exposed to their parent's poor coping may be at greatest risk for poor clinical and psychiatric outcomes via social learning (Edwards et al., 2006).

SCD is an important model of multifactorial conceptualization of genetic-based chronic disease among aging populations. Whether the disease is a dementia that impairs cognition or an elevated risk for essential hypertension or diabetes, psychosocial interventions appear effective, relevant, and available (Edwards & Edwards, 2010; Heard et al., 2011; Surwit et al., 2002).

PRIMER ON GENETIC APPROACHES/METHODS

Generally, molecular genetic methodologies are called to mind when people consider the role of genetic factors in health and disease. Broadly, molecular genetics focuses on the role of an identified or suspected gene on the phenotype or disease of interests. The genetic dissection of traits has had a long history and recently has been applied to a number of complex traits: those with multiple genetic and environmental influences (Landers & Schork, 1994; McClearn, Vogler, & Plomin, 1996). For example, researchers have investigated the association of particular gene variants, such as angiotensinogen M235T in hypertension (Corvol & Jeunemaitre, 1997; Ferrario, 2003). The ultimate aim of molecular genetic studies is the identification, treatment, or prevention of disease based on genotype (Schork, 1997). Molecular genetic studies take a variety of methodological approaches in the examination of specific gene effects, such as linkage analysis or association studies (for further explanation see Landers & Schork, 1994; Risch & Merikangas, 1996). One of the most significant uses of molecular techniques to examine the role of genes in age-related processes has been the work on Alzheimer's disease. Although research on the role of Apolipoprotein E (APOE) in ethnic minority populations continues, one of the first reports was by Tang et al. (1996). They found that the age distribution of the proportion of Caucasians and Hispanics without AD was consistently lower for those with at least one copy of the APOE-epsilon 4 allele. In African Americans, this relationship was observed only in those with two copies of the APOE-epsilon 4 allele. The authors conclude that there is variability in genetic or environmental factors across groups, which may modify the effect of APOE-epsilon 4.

Recent advances in molecular genetics have significantly increased our ability to understand the contribution of genes to the study of health and health disparities. The National Human Genome Research Institute (NHGRI) of the National Institutes of Health (NIH) announced in June 2000 that they had developed a working draft of the human genome. This historic event places science on the doorstep of limitless possibilities, including new insights about diseases and how to treat and prevent them. The development and testing of explanatory hypotheses about the underlying mechanisms that involve genes and behavior/social environment that create health disparities among ethnic minorities will be crucial in identifying solutions for reducing the current differentials (Whitfield et al., 2003).

Behavioral genetic studies have a common historical origin with molecular genetic studies but differ substantially in approach (McClearn & Vogler, 2001; McClearn et al., 1996). Behavioral genetics can be defined as the application of quantitative genetic theories and principles to the study of behavior. According to quantitative genetic theory, observable traits or phenotypes such as behavior or health outcomes result from an amalgam of inherited genetic factors and environmental influences (McClearn & Vogler, 2001; McClearn et al., 1996). Furthermore, in a given population, variability in the value or quantity of a complex trait will vary among individuals due to differences in genetic and environmental influences (McClearn & Vogler, 2001). Thus, both genetic and environmental factors play a role in determining a given phenotype.

Quantitative genetics broadly and behavioral genetics specifically use various methods to assess the proportion of variability in a given trait that is attributable to genetic and environmental influences. The use of quantitative genetic designs is "an important first step in the direction of understanding the etiology of individual differences" (Plomin & McClearn, 1990). One of the most common quantitative genetic designs is the "classic twin design," a comparison of monozygotic twin pairs (MZ; produced from one egg) and dizygotic twin pairs (DZ; two eggs fertilized at the same time) using some measurement instrument. Because MZ twins share 100% of their genes and DZ twin pairs share on average 50% of their segregating genes, one can make assumptions about the amount of variance in a behavioral trait due to genetic and environmental sources (Plomin, DeFries, & McClearn, 1990). Heritability, the portion of observed variation due to genetic sources, can be computed by calculating twice the difference in correlations between MZ and DZ twins on a behavioral measurement (Plomin et al., 1990).

Furthermore, phenotypic variation can be modeled by decomposing the individual variation of a trait into genetic, shared environmental, and nonshared environmental sources. Thus, variance can be partitioned in the following way:

$$Pv = Gv + Cv + Ev$$

where Pv is equal to the total variance for a trait (phenotype), Gv reflects the genetic variance of the trait, Cv represents that part of environmental variance due to the twins sharing the same environment, and Ev reflects the variance due to the nonshared environment of each twin and measurement error (Plomin et al., 1990).

Other designs that include genetically informative samples are employed in quantitative genetic research (e.g., adoption, family, twins reared apart, co-twin control; see Neale & Cardon, 1992; Plomin et al., 1990). A simple extension of the classic twin design is to include a sibling in the assessment of each twin pair. Using this simple strategy, one can test within family environmental sources of variance because the siblings share the same family position (offspring) as both members of the twin pair. In addition, siblings are similar to the same degree as DZ twins but do not share the same prenatal environment at the same time. Thus, the addition of siblings to twin design allows for greater rigor in the assessment of shared environmental sources of variance without significantly increasing the number of subjects to be tested.

MOLECULAR AND BEHAVIORAL GENETICS AND THE STUDY OF ETHNICITY

One of the most significant contributions to behavioral medicine research that genetically informed studies can provide is to elucidate the impact of sociocultural influences on individual variability. For purposes of this discussion, we offer a working definition of sociocultural influences. Sociocultural influences are those environmental, contextual, and familial factors that make individuals of various racial and ethnic groups different from one another. These factors also make individuals in these racial/ethnic groups different from one another because of external pressures from the majority culture as well as historical and experiential dimensions common to individuals of a particular culture (Cauce, Coronado, & Watson, 1998). Sociocultural influences are the common beliefs, typical ways that people solve problems, laws and regulations, ideologies, and other factors that are shared by a group of people. Sociocultural influences are also the structural and institutional forces that affect development. These forces differentially affect people by race. In addition, the folkways and mores of a people serve as the behavioral guidelines for development and interactions with others. They also influence people's perceptions of the world. These forces can create very different environments in which minorities live. The sociocultural influences are not uniform for every member of any group of minorities living in the United States. These influences are particularly important because they can play a significant role in molding and shaping why people are different from one another within a race.

Of particular interest to the discussion in this chapter is the identification of individual differences in health behaviors and health status among minorities. Although there is a considerable void in our knowledge about the behavior and health interface of minorities, there now appears to be a concerted effort to enhance our knowledge about racial/ethnic minorities, which is supported by federal funding agencies. With this interest in enhancing our knowledge of the diversity of the various groups within America, we must begin to re-examine our conceptualizations in framing research questions, hypotheses, and theories on ethnically diverse populations. In addition, the use of research methodologies that can serve to enhance our knowledge about these populations must be integrated into this effort, regardless of past research that used the same methodologies wrongly to proliferate ideas of inequalities among races.

The current knowledge of minorities was largely developed through cross-ethnic research (see, Burton & Bengston, 1982; Jackson, 1985). Initially, social scientists argued that while ethnic minorities may, in fact, have some distinctive attributes by virtue of their language, lifestyle, socioeconomic status, and historical experiences in this country, that distinction was best captured in comparative research between groups. Contemporary researchers, however, argue that the cross-ethnic comparisons have several limitations that preclude a full appreciation for that distinctiveness (Markides, Liang, & Jackson, 1990). One limitation in past cross-ethnic studies involves the comparability of measures used. Quite often, measures are developed, refined, and validated within one group and then applied to other groups under the assumption that their validity and reliability are stable across groups.

One of the primary limitations of past cross-ethnic comparisons concerns a lack of attention to within-group variability. In much of the previous research, cross-ethnic comparisons tended to homogenize ethnic groups. Moreover, early comparative research often grouped certain ethnic groups together with little appreciation for subgroup differences. For example, a Hispanic group might include Mexican Americans, Latin Americans, and Puerto Ricans, all of whom reflect varying historical cultures and levels of assimilation. Since these individual subgroups are inherently different, by collapsing them under one ethnic umbrella and then comparing them to whites, important distinctions between the subgroups are lost. Of course, this approach also said little or nothing about the variability within each of the groups that arises from sociocultural influences.

While the validity of direct comparisons' heritable influences across cultural/ethnic groups requires significant attention, there are several studies that provide interesting comparisons to consider how genes and environmental factors work to impact phenotypes. For example, in a study by Lee et al. (2004), longevity was examined in Hispanics, whites, and African Americans. They found that in deceased relatives of probands, the heritabilities were dramatically different by ethnic group, ranging from 0.29 to 0.26 for Caribbean Hispanics and Caucasians to as low as 0.04 for African Americans. They also found that genetic influence on survival age did not differ between the three ethnic groups and ranged between 0.34 and 0.38. While estimates of genetic contribution to survival may not differ across groups, how genes and environments work in concert must account for the differences in population survival rates.

Behavioral genetic methods will be particularly useful if one begins studying minorities from the perspective that there is significant heterogeneity within populations of minorities. Conceptual and methodological discussions of heterogeneity within minority populations are particularly timely given the changing sociodemographic features of ethnic/racial populations related to health disparities (Whitfield & Hayward, 2003). Individual differences within these groups make it difficult to assess the "average" behavior without first knowing what variability exists as well as the sources of variability. Behavioral genetic studies can begin to untangle these complexities by decomposing individual variation into genetic and environmental sources. The particular importance this strategy has for the study of minorities is that the element in the human experience that typically accounts for a significant proportion of variability, namely the sociocultural environment, can be examined within the conceptualization of the heterogenous nature of minority populations.

GERO-GENETIC STUDIES

There are relatively few genetic gerontological (gero-genetic) studies (Whitfield, 1994). Most of the past and existing studies involve twin samples. The lack of gero-genetic studies, for the most part, is due to the lack of large established populations of elderly twins in geographically centralized areas. There have been successful efforts to establish registries of older twins and perform assessments. There are several gero-genetic studies of older twin pairs from the Scandinavian twin registries (Hauge, 1980; Kaprio, Sarna, Koskenvuo, & Rantasalo, 1978; Medlund, Cederlof, Floderus-Myrhed, Friberg, & Sorensen, 1977). Two of the main ongoing studies are the "Swedish Adoption/Twin Study of Aging" and the "Octogenarian Twins Study of the Oldest of Old."

Perhaps, the most impressive study of older twins is known as the Swedish Adoption/ Twin Study of Aging (SATSA). This ongoing series of investigations includes a unique sample of approximately 100 monozygotic twins reared apart, 150 monozygotic twins reared together, 200 dizygotic twins reared apart, and 200 dizygotic twins reared together. In the first phase of SATSA, a mailed questionnaire was used to collect data (in 1984) on a wide variety of psychological endpoints, including emotionality, activity level, sociability temperaments (Plomin, Pedersen, McClearn, Nesselroade, & Bergeman, 1988), neuroticism, extroversion, implusivity, monotony avoidance (Pedersen, Plomin, McClearn, & Friberg, 1988), social support (Bergeman, Plomin, Pedersen, McClearn, & Nesselroade, 1990), recollections of childhood environment (Plomin, McClearn, Pedersen, Nesselroade, & Bergeman, 1988), life events (Plomin, Lichtenstein, Pedersen, McClearn, & Nesselroade, 1990), and locus of control (Pedersen, Gatz, Plomin, Nesselroade, & McClearn, 1989). Subsequent waves of data collection have included in-person testing of cognition (Pedersen, Plomin, Nesselroade, & McClearn, 1992). At the time of initial data collection, the median age of the sample was 58.6 years. Follow-up work in this sample has included telephone interviews to assess cognitive ability (Nesselroade, Pedersen, McClearn, Plomin, & Bergeman, 1988) and forthcoming publications will examine physical functioning.

The Octogenarian-Twin study (OCTO-Twin) is a longitudinal study of like-sexed twin pairs 80 years and older identified from the population-based Swedish Twin Registry. The general aim of the study is to estimate the genetic and environmental sources of individual variability at each of three time points, examining continuity and change over time. The OCTO-Twin base sample comprises 856 pairs. In the first wave, 353 pairs have been investigated. The projection is 180 pairs for the second wave and 90 pairs for the third wave. Access to other ongoing studies, such as a study of the oldest of old singletons and younger old twins from the Swedish Adoption and Twin Study of Aging, will provide a rich context from which to interpret the data. By studying those 80 and older, we may enhance our knowledge of aging by identifying the factors involved in the behaviors of this rapidly growing segment of the population.

One of the greatest impediments to applying quantitative genetic models to study aging is identifying a statistically powerful and representative sample of twins. Most successful attempts at ascertaining and recruiting older twin samples have taken place in Scandinavian countries, but there are two large ongoing studies in the United States, the NAS-NRC and the Minnesota Twin Study of Adult Development and Aging.

The NAS-NRC Twin Studies in Gerontology is a national twin cohort of veterans in the United States. This valuable resource consists of male–male white twin pairs born between 1917 and 1927 with both brothers having served in the military during World War II or the Korean Conflict (Jablon, Neel, Gershowitz, & Atkinson, 1967). A subset of this sample (the NHLBI Twin Study of approximately 250 MZ and 250 DZ pairs) has been intensively studied for coronary disease (Feinlieb et al., 1977). As this population grows older, studies of gerontological health have become possible. The first of these studies, based on the NHLBI Twin Study third examination cycle in 1986, has been reported (Swan, Carmelli, Reed, Harshfield, Fabsitz, & Eslinger, 1990). This study examined the heritability of the Mini-Mental State Examination in an older population (mean age at examination was 63). Recently, a follow-up study of genetic and behavioral risk factors for cognitive decline has been published (Swan, LaRue, Carmelli, Reed, & Fabsitz, 1992).

During the past 10 years, a group of researchers at the University of Minnesota built a population twin registry (Lykken, Bouchard, McGue, & Tellegen, 1990). Currently, the Minnesota Twin Registry contains more than 10,000 pairs of like-sexed twins aged 11 to 86 years. Of particular relevance to the current project is the elderly twin sample ascertained and recruited as part of the Minnesota Twin Study of Adult Development and Aging (MTSADA, funded under AG06886; McGue, Lykken, & Hirsch, 1993). The current status of approximately 50% of these older twin pairs has been determined through use of public records (e.g., birth records, phone directories, driver registrations, marriage licenses). Of the located and living pairs, 67% agreed to complete the in-person MTSADA assessments. As of May 1993, 239 twin pairs meeting the requirements have completed the MTSADA assessments. The MTSADA assessment is a six-hour battery that includes measures of: (a) cognitive functioning (the WAIS-R, selected subtests of the Weschler Memory Scale, List Learning, and an inductive reasoning test), (b) personality and interests (the Multidimensional Personality Questionnaire, Leisure-Time Interests, Talents), (c) affect and life satisfaction (CES-D, Neugarten's LSI-A), (d) physiological functioning (blood pressure, pulmonary capacity, simple and choice reaction time), and (e) lifestyle factors (e.g., intellectual, social, and physical engagement).

One recent twin study of aging African Americans is the Carolina African American Twin Study of Aging (CAATSA; Whitfield, Brandon, Wiggins, Vogler, & McClearn, 2003). CAATSA was designed to examine health and psychosocial factors in older adult African American twins. Based on birth records from North Carolina, twins between 22 and 92 years were recruited for a 2.5-hour interview. The goal of CAATSA was to examine the proportion of genetic and environmental influences on health indices and psychosocial factors in relation to health in African American adults. The study included measures associated with chronic illness (e.g., hypertension, arthritis, cardiovascular disease), health behaviors, personality, stress, and memory. Results from the study have contributed to the literature on cognitive impairment (Whitfield, Kiddoe, Gamaldo, Andel, & Edwards, 2009), depression (Whitfield, Edwards, Brandon, & McDougald, 2008), stress and coping (Bennett, Merritt, Sollers, Edwards, Whitfield, & Brandon, 2004; Whitfield et al., 2006), smoking (Whitfield et al., 2007), hypertension (Brandon et al., 2003), lung function (Whitfield, Wiggins, Belue, & Brandon, 2004), obesity (Nelson, Brandon, Wiggins, & Whitfield, 2002), arthritis (Baker, Whitfield, & Edwards, 2012), and mortality (Whitfield et al., 2003) in African Americans. Taken together, this research shows significant contributions of genetics to behavioral phenomena and environmental influences to biological and health factors.

Gero-genetic studies have only begun to increase our understanding of the interindividual variability in older adults. This information is of great value in the effort to understand the forces that are involved in shaping the lives of older adults. While the previously discussed twin studies have significantly contributed to our knowledge of interindividual differences in aging, they do not include ethnically diverse samples. The study of ethnically diverse samples using a quantitative genetic approach is important for at least two reasons: (a) it allows a closer examination of how the environment, specifically sociocultural environments, affect patterns of aging; and (b) given these methods are designed and based on population statistics and theory, a diverse sample would provide a true assessment of the contributions of genetic and environmental influences on aging.

GENETIC AND ENVIRONMENTAL INFLUENCES ON AGING AND HEALTH

The complex interaction between genetic and environmental influences on aging becomes clearer when several facts are reviewed. First, it is now known that no racial group possesses a completely discrete set of genetic characteristics. Second, definite biologic links between racial group and disease have rarely been found. The genes associated with skin color are not typically associated with the genes responsible for disease. Third, the genetic variation in gene frequency is approximately 93% to 95% within racial group and about 3% to 5% between racial groups. Thus, greater genetic variation exists within racial groups than between them.

The interplay between race as a social and biologic construct is seen in the arena of prostate cancer, which, like many other cancer types, is diagnosed most frequently in men ages 50+ years. Although African American men have a higher risk of developing prostate cancer and higher mortality rates from this disease than European American men, the expression of current diagnostic and prognostic genetic markers is not significantly different between men in the two groups (Powell et al., 2010; Wallace et al., 2008). However, several genes related to metastasis or immune pathways are more highly expressed in prostate cancer tumors found in African American men. A two-gene tumor signature has been found to accurately predict whether prostate cancer tumors were from African American or European American men (Wallace et al., 2008; Figure 10.1).

As shown in Figure 10.1, using quantitative real-time reverse transcription polymerase chain reaction (RT-PCR), genes autocrine motility factor (AMFR), Chemokine C-X-C motif receptor 4 (CXCR4) , and matrix metallopeptidase 9 (MMP9) were found to be more highly expressed in the prostate tumors of African American men compared to European American men. CXCR4 and MMP9 are recognized to be related to metastasis of prostate cancer. Therapies to targeting CXCR4 pathway are currently being researched (Wallace et al., 2008).

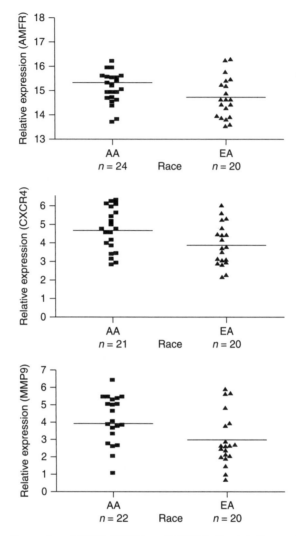

FIGURE 10.1 Higher Expression of AMFR, CXCR4, and MMP9 in Prostate Tumors in African American Men (Wallace et al., 2008). Used with Permission.

In addition to the impact of biologic factors on racial differences in prostate cancer mortality, social factors play a role as well. For example, although African American men are often diagnosed at a late stage of disease, they are also significantly less likely than European Americans to receive aggressive therapy, leading to lower likelihood of treatment success (Mutetwa et al., 2010; Pisu et al., 2010). Late stage at diagnosis is related to lack of access to adequate screening and treatment facilities, often as a result of economic barriers but also because of sociocultural barriers, such as fear and mistrust of the health care system and/or use of differential medical treatment strategies. To illustrate, Chu et al. (2012) examined retrospective data from 2,502 men in a Veterans Administration (VA) health care system in North Carolina. They found that even in a system in which financial access to care is equal among African Americans and European Americans, higher income level predicted better prostate cancer treatment outcomes, and race had a significant and independent effect on likelihood of poorer treatment outcomes even after adjustment for income level.

In breast cancer, while incidence rates are lower for African American women compared to European women, the mortality rates are much higher for African American women, particularly for those less than 50 years of age. The mortality rate of African American women less than 50 years of age with breast cancer is 77% higher than for European American women in the same age group (Adams et al., 2012; Carey et al., 2006; Odierna et al., 2011).

Basal-like breast cancer, linked to higher mortality rates, is more common in premenopausal African American women and was found to have a high frequency among breast cancer patients in Nigeria (Carey et al., 2006). Additionally, *p53* gene mutation, which is linked to basal-like breast cancer and more aggressive tumor characteristics, is associated with poorer prognosis among African American women and may be associated with low socioeconomic status. As such, the *p53* gene mutation may provide a molecular basis to understand poorer breast cancer outcome among women from economically disadvantaged communities (Baker et al., 2010; Dookeran et al., 2012). However, premenopausal African American women without basal-like breast cancer still have the worst survival rate, suggesting that other aspects of their cancer or social-environmental factors negatively impact their survival.Thus, the causes underlying the racial disparities in mortality rates in prostate and breast cancer are believed to be multifactorial. Race appears to be a predictor of exposure to external health risks, with resultant racial differences in health outcomes. Within the framework of race as a social-political construct, race is used to understand the health consequences of variations in factors that impact health outcomes such as health care quality and utilization, education, and nutrition. Race, in this sense, is a multidimensional construct and a predictor of exposure to external health risks posed by environmental, social, and behavioral factors. For example, Freeman (1998) argues that biologic expressions of race result in social interactions, which in turn produce racial and ethnic disparities in morbidity and mortality (i.e., discrimination). Ford and Kelly (2005) contend that the best way to understand race is to view it as a social construct that is influenced by social and political factors. For example, members of racial minority groups may have dietary and lifestyle habits that are associated with their socioeconomic status. These habits or behaviors influence disease susceptibility or risk. At the same time, socioeconomic factors such as lack of health insurance coverage negatively affect access to health care. Together, the factors in this model have significant contributions to health disparities. Thus, phenotypic genetic expressions of race affect social interactions and health outcomes.

As Pascoe and Richman (2009) note, perceived discrimination produces heightened stress response, which has a significant and deleterious impact on health. Similarly, Williams, Yu, Jackson, and Anderson (1997); Krieger et al. (2005); and (Pearlin et al. (2005) argue that over the life course, continued exposure to stressful social environmental interactions leads to susceptibility to disease that, coupled with low rates of access to health care, contributes to racial and ethnic disparities in health (Canetti, Bachar, & Berry, 2002; Dallman et al., 2003; Figure 10.2).

Coping strategies in the face of non-race and race-specific stressors may themselves be harmful to health (Jackson, Knight, & Rafferty, 2010). Stress-related precursors of serious mental health problems are more available to consciousness than are those of physical health problems. This psychological awareness motivates individuals to action. For example, Tomiyama et al. (2011) and Canetti et al. (2002) suggest that people eat comfort food to reduce activity in the chronic stress-response network. Other behaviors, such as smoking, alcohol, and drug use have similar, immediate, effects to reduce activation of the stress-response network.

Under chronic stress, negative feedback break down and there is continued release of corticotropin-releasing factor (CRF) and cortisol. Long-term chronic activation of hypothalamic-pituitary–adrenal (HPA) axis may be related to etiology of some mental disorders (Barden,

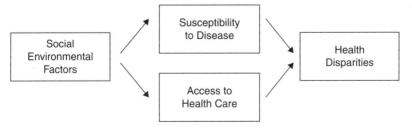

FIGURE 10.2 A Basic Model of Social and Environmental Drivers to Health Disparities That Includes Individual Susceptibility of Disease.

Source: Adapted from Dallman et al., 2003; Cannetti et al., 2002.

2004; Young, 2004). Comfort foods (high in fats and carbohydrates) may aid in shutdown of stress response by inhibiting release of CRF (e.g., Tomiyama et al., 2011). Alcohol, nicotine, and drug use stimulate release of dopamine and beta-endorphins, aiding in shutdown of stress response and leading to feelings of relaxation and calm (Filip et al., 2012; Wei et al., 2012). Paradoxically, these drugs may also further activation of the HPA axis—thus, individuals may be psychologically released from stress, but they are not physically released from the effects of stress (Tomiyama et al., 2011).

As Dallman et al. state, "Habitually attempting to relieve stress-induced dysphoric effects of the CRF-driven (neurons) central chronic stress-response network may make one feel better, but is likely to be bad for long-term health" (Dallman et al., 2003, p. 11700; Williams, Mohammed, Leavell, & Collins, 2010; Figures 10.3 and 10.4).

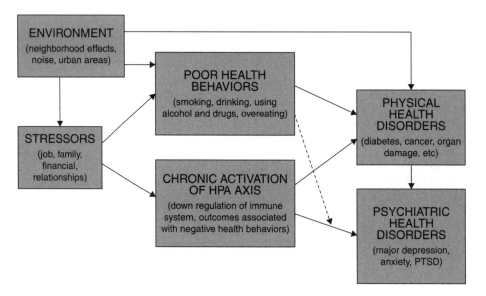

FIGURE 10.3 This Model Illustrates How Psychiatric and Physical Health Disorders Arise From Poor Health Behaviors and the Dysregulation of the Immune System. These Behaviors and Physiological Consequences Arise in Part from Contextual Environmental Factors Directly and Indirectly as a By-Product of Stressors.
Source: Adapted from Dallman et al., 2003.

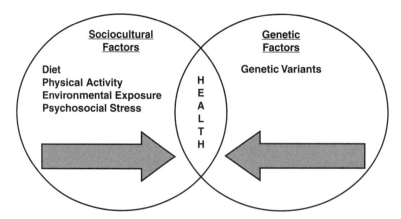

FIGURE 10.4 Health Outcomes Arise From the Intersection of Genetic Variants and a Myriad of Sociocultural Factors That Evince From Short-Term and Long-Term Exposures.
Source: Adapted from AACR Plenary Session, 2007. 2007 Cancer Health Disparities Conference November, 2007. Used with Permission.

MODEL OF GENES' IMPACT ON HEALTH

Health is commonly conceptualized by the medical community as the absence of disease. Studies of health include chronic conditions, precursors, and behaviors that are associated with or involved in the maintenance of good health as well as the development of diseases. There are three primary causes of mortality and morbidity observed among African Americans in late life: coronary heart disease, hypertension, and diabetes (see, Berkman, Singer, & Manton, 1989). Coronary heart disease is the leading cause of death in the United States (NHLBI, 1985). African Americans experience higher age-adjusted morbidity and mortality rates of both coronary heart disease and stroke (NHLBI, 1985). The number one health problem for African Americans is hypertension with a two-to-one prevalence ratio to Caucasians (Anderson, NcNeilly, & Myers, 1991). This disease affects approximately 65% of African American elderly between the ages of 65 and 74 (Wagner, Grothaus, Hect, & LaCroix, 1991). This condition is predictive of functional decline (Wagner et al., 1991). Another disease that is disproportionately experienced by African American elderly is diabetes mellitus (Kumanyika, 1990). The major risk factors associated with heart disease, diabetes mellitus, and hypertension include smoking, hypertension (for coronary heart disease), obesity, alcohol use, and physical activity level.

The incidence of obesity is substantially higher among African Americans and becomes exaggerated with increased age (Lackey, Kolasa, & Horner, 1992). Both poor diet and lack of physical exercise contribute to obesity. There is evidence to suggest that significant proportions of African Americans over the age of 65 (65% of men and 44% or women) lead sedentary lives and that sedentary behavior is linked to hypertension (Ainsworth, Keenan, Strogatz, Garrett, & James, 1991). In addition, it has also been noted that African American diets tend to be high in fat and low in fiber (Bal & Foerster, 1991). Therefore, the diet of African Americans may also be a risk factor for diseases like hypertension, heart disease, cancer, and diabetes (Kumanyika, 1990).

Sociodemographic factors have also been identified as risk factors for chronic illness. Socioeconomic status and education have been found to be important variables associated with the development of chronic illness. The importance of socioeconomic status (SES) factors in the study of chronic illness among African Americans increases when poverty rates are taken into account. The number of individuals living in poverty is twice as high in elderly African Americans as in older Caucasians (Manuel, 1988). Furthermore, in urban areas, 32% of African American elderly as compared to 11% of Caucasian elderly live in poverty (Harper & Alexander, 1990).

Previous research has examined the question of the heritability of hemodynamic indicies among African Americans. In a study of African American adult twins, systolic blood pressure was found to range between 44% and 52% for young and older adults, respectively. Diastolic pressure was found to have a heritability of 27% for younger twins and 36% for older twins. The results indicate that genetic factors are a significant source of variance in hemodynamic indexes and also suggest that, with advancing age, genetic factors play an increasing role in determining blood pressure and pulse pressure in this population.

While environmental and health behaviors impact hypertension, this is also a disease that demonstrates genetic patterns, and the Renin-Angiotensinogen System is an important biochemical pathway regulating blood pressure that has received much attention in recent years. Three genes in particular have been associated with an increased risk for hypertension: Angiotensinogen (AGT), Angiotensin Converting Enzyme (ACE), and Angiotensin II receptor 1 (AGT1R). AGT encodes the precursor protein that is proteolytically cleaved into Angiotensin 1 by renin. AGT has been associated with hypertension in some, but not all, studies in spite of the fact that alleles and haplotypes of the gene are consistently associated with plasma levels of AGT 14. In a recent analysis, various polymorphisms of the *ACE* gene were found to be related to variability in blood pressure among African Americans and supported previous evidence of associations between hypertension to the A allele of *ACE* (Whitfield et al., 2009). Although these results suggest significant genetic influence on hypertension, there is still variability unaccounted for in this analysis. One approach to better modeling hypertension in African Americans is to examine possible interactions between genes and environmental factors.

MODELS OF GENE X ENVIRONMENT INTERACTIONS

These findings also demonstrate that sources of individual differences may not be static across cultures and that further investigation of the environmental mediation of estimates of genetic and environmental influences is warranted. It also supports the notion that investigations of health differentials across ethnic groups, solely on the basis of genetic differences, will not yield accurate identification of the mechanisms responsible for health disparities. Instead, describing health differentials as arising from insults to a complex system represented by the interaction between genes and environments that creates excess burden of chronic illness and disease within some groups is a more accurate perspective (Whitfield & McClearn, 2005).

In addition, there are also growing examples of gene–gene and gene–environment interactions among various populations related to health outcomes (Lee et al., 2004). Gene–environment interactions provide perhaps the most reasonable and comprehensive way to consider the impact single nucleotide polymorphisms (SNPs) have on disease. Currently, there is much interest in alterations in DNA that are influenced by common DNA variants in the form of SNPs. These alterations in the DNA change the way important proteins are made and are thought to be primary sources of variability in an individual's susceptibility to diseases. These alterations can involve a single-base pair of DNA and can be shared by many people. These alterations are common, but minute, and occur at a frequency of 1 every 1,000 bases. These variations can be used to track inheritance in families.

One health condition that has been greatly researched, demonstrating both genetic and environmental influences, is hypertension. Hypertension is a major cause of death and functional decline. Race is a particularly important risk factor, with African Americans twice as likely to develop hypertension as Caucasians. By ages 51 to 61 (Hayward, 2000), over 50% of African Americans already report having a hypertensive diagnosis. African Americans tend to experience earlier onset and greater severity of the condition relative to Caucasians (Lang, de Gaudemaris, Chatellier, Hamici, & Diène, 2001). For example, previous research has shown that African Americans were nearly eight years younger on average for their diagnosis of hypertension in a comparison to Caucasians (Wilk et al., 2004). There is evidence that demonstrates genetic patterns in blood pressure regulation. The Renin-Angiotensinogen System is an important biochemical pathway regulating blood pressure that has received much attention in genetic investigation in recent years. Three genes in particular have been associated with an increased risk for hypertension: Angiotensinogen (AGT), Angiotensin Converting Enzyme (ACE), and Angiotensin II receptor 1 (AGT1R). AGT encodes the precursor protein that is proteolytically cleaved into Angiotensin 1 by renin. AGT has been associated with hypertension in some, but not all, studies despite the fact that alleles and haplotypes of the gene are consistently associated with plasma levels of AGT (Fejerman et al., 2004). While these genes have been indicated in individual variability in hypertension, environmental factors have also been shown to play a role.

A number of hypotheses have been put forward to attempt to explain why African Americans disproportionately experience hypertension (Anderson & Armstead, 1995; Kington & Nickens, 2001). For example, Clark, Anderson, Clark, and Williams (1999) proposed two hypotheses to help explain findings that the prevalence of hypertension and all-cause mortality were higher for African Americans than for European Americans, even at comparable levels of education (Bell, Adair, & Popkin, 2004). First, within-SES-group "protection" may not be comparable across ethnic groups (Anderson & Armstead, 1995; Williams & Collins, 1995). As such, attempts to compare African Americans and European Americans at any given educational level, for instance, would not take into account the observation that African Americans earn significantly less than their European American counterparts at every level of education attainment (Pamuk, Makuc, Heck, Reuben, & Lochner, 1998). Second, if African Americans disproportionately perceive their environments as threatening, harmful, or challenging as a result of ethnically specific stimuli (James, 1991; Krieger, 1990; Outlaw, 1993; Thompson, 1996; Williams et al., 1997), they may, relative to European Americans, be required to expend an inordinate amount of energy to cope with the psychological and physiological stress responses that follow these perceptions. Over time, the cumulative psychological and physiological effects associated with these added stressors have the potential to account, in part, for between- and within-group health disparities. These cumulative effects (also known as allostatic load) have been conceptualized as a marker for the wear and tear exacted on the body secondary to negotiating the daily events of life (McEwen & Seeman, 1999).

Socioecological conceptual frameworks of hypertension focus on a contextual model of hypertension in African Americans like the one presented in Macera, Armstead, and Anderson (2001). The socioecological stressors include urban/rural distinctions and poverty rates. This is based on research by Harburg et al. (1973) and Calhoun, Mutinga, Wyss, and Oparil (1994), who found that these environmental influences impact the development of hypertension.

Although both research identifying genetic markers and environmental risk factors contribute to our understanding of the etiology of hypertension, the addition of a synergistic perspective from these two perspectives will be useful in gaining a clearer picture of individual differences in blood pressure and hypertension, and in approaches to reduce health disparities. Some previous research suggests that it would be unlikely to find one major gene associated with hypertension. Instead, each gene polymorphism associated with hypertension probably accounts for about 2% to 10% of genetic variation in respect to hypertension. It is likely that all of these gene polymorphisms interact with the environment, making gene X environment studies extremely complicated. However, past research on gene X environment interactions have shown that the effect of a gene can be modulated by environmental factors (Hirvonen, 1995). It is likely that basing $G \times E$ examinations on well-known genetic markers and well-studied environmental risk factors could identify important effects.

THE INTERPLAY BETWEEN SOCIAL AND BIOLOGIC FACTORS AS CONTRIBUTORS TO HEALTH DISPARITIES

Current knowledge of the interplay between social and biologic factors in producing health disparities demonstrates that interventions to reduce disparities must be multifactorial, as the underlying causes of disparities are multifactorial. Interventions must address the social factors of lack of access to health care (whether due to financial or sociocultural barriers or both) and the biologic factors such as genetic markers of disease that could be addressed with targeted therapies. While the concept of individualized medicine at first seems to be an attractive solution to reducing health disparities, it warrants a second look. As Ward (2012) notes, if personalized therapeutics are used differentially for the benefit of the most socioeconomically advantaged groups in society, then the gap in health outcomes among wealthy individuals and those who are struggling economically will widen unless specific measures are taken. In addition, as Odierna et al. (2011) argue, widespread use of gene-expression profiling may not yet be adequately validated in racially and ethnically diverse populations, and further testing is needed to demonstrate the broad utility of these tests in different population groups.

In order for individualized medicine approaches to have the greatest utility, they must be employed in conjunction with interventions that address lack of access to health care. The Institute of Medicine report, *Unequal Treatment: Confronting Racial and Ethnic Disparities in Healthcare*, highlights three sets of psychosocial factors that contribute to racial and ethnic disparities in health outcomes: characteristics of health care systems, perceptions of/actual interactions with health care providers, and preferences/attitudes of patients (Smedley et al., 2003). Multilevel interventions that address each of these sets of factors could work to enhance the participation of racially and ethnically diverse populations in the delivery of health care. Only then, when they are full participants in these health care delivery systems, and have trusted relationships with clinicians in these systems, will racially and ethnically diverse patients be able to fully participate in individualized medicine approaches on a therapeutic level and help validate these approaches in diverse populations.

REFERENCES

Adams, S. A., Butler, W. M., Fulton, J., Heiney, S. P., Williams, E. M., Delage, A. F., . . . Hebert, J. R. (2012). Racial disparities in breast cancer mortality in a multiethnic cohort in the Southeast. *Cancer, 118*(10), 2693–2699.

Ainsworth, B. E., Keenan, N. L., Strogatz, D. S., Garrett, J. M., & James, S. A. (1991). Physical activity and hypertension in black adults: the Pitt country study. *American Journal of Public Health, 81*, 1477–1479.

Anderson, N. B., McNeilly, M. D., & Myers, H. (1991). Autonomic reactivity and hypertension in blacks: a review and proposed model, *Ethnicity and Disease, 1*, 154–170.

Anderson, N. B., & Armstead, C. A. (1995). Toward understanding the association of socioeconomic status and health: A new challenge for the biopsychosocial approach. *Psychosomatic Medicine, 57*(3), 213–225.

Baker, L., Quinlan, P. R., Patten, N., Ashfield, A., Birse-Stewart-Bell, L. J., McCowan, C., . . . Thompson, A. M. (2010). P53 mutation, deprivation and poor prognosis in primary breast cancer. *British Journal of Cancer, 102*(4), 719–726.

Baker, T. A., Whitfield, K. E., & Edwards, C. L. (2012). Heritability of arthritis in African American twins: Findings from the Carolina African American Twins Study of Aging. *Journal of the National Medical Association, 104*(9–10), 436–440.

Bal, D., & Foerster, S. (1991). Changing the American Diet. *Cancer, 67*, 2671–2680.

Ballas, S. K., Lieff, S., Benjamin, L. J., Dampier, C. D., Heeney, M. M., Hoppe, C., . . . Telen, M. J.; Investigators, Comprehensive Sickle Cell Centers. (2010). Definitions of the phenotypic manifestations of sickle cell disease. *American Journal of Hematology, 85*(1), 6–13.

Barden, N. (2004). Implication of the hypothalamic-pituitary-adrenal axis in the physiopathology of depression. *Journal of Psychiatry & Neuroscience, 29*(3), 185–193.

Bell, A. C., Adair, L. S., & Popldn, B. M. (2004). Understanding the role of mediating risk factors and proxy effects in the association between socio-economic status and untreated hypertension. *Social Science & Medicine, 59*, 275–283.

Bennett, G. G., Merritt, M. M., Sollers, J. J., Edwards, C. L., Whitfield, K. E., & Brandon, D. T. (2004). Stress, coping, and health outcomes among African-Americans: A review of the John Henryism hypothesis. *Psychology and Health, 19*(3), 369–383.

Berkman, L. F., Singer, & B., Manton, K. (1989). Black/white differences in health status and mortality among the elderly. *Demography, 26*(4):661–677.

Bergeman, C. S., Plomin, R., Pedersen, N. L., McClearn, G. E., & Nesselroade, J. R. (1990). Genetic and environmental influences on social support: The Swedish Adoption/Twin Study of Aging. *Journal of Gerontology, 45*, P101–P106.

Bowman, P. (1991). Race, class and ethics in research: Belmont principles to functional relevance. In R. L. Jones (Ed), *Black psychology* (3rd ed., pp. 747–766). Berkeley, CA: Cobb & Henry Publishers.

Brandon, D. T., Whitfield, K. E., Sollers, J. J., Wiggins, S. A., West, S. G., Vogler, G. P., . . . Thayer, J. F. (2003). Genetic and environmental influences on blood pressure and pulse pressure among adult African Americans. *Ethnicity & Disease, 13*(2), 193–199.

Burton, L. M., & Bengston, V. L. (1982). Research in elderly minority communities: Problems and potentials. In R. C. Manuel (Ed.), *Minority aging: Sociological and social psychological issues* (pp. 215–222). Westport, CN: Greenwood.

Canetti, L., Bachar, E., & Berry, E. M. (2002). Food and emotion. *Behavioural Processes, 60*(2), 157–164.

Calhoun, D. A., Mutinga, M. L., Wyss, J., & Oparil, S. (1994). Muscle sympathetic nervous system activity in Black and Caucasian hypertensive subjects. *Journal of Hypertension, 12*(11), 1297–1296.

Carey, L. A., Perou, C. M., Livasy, C. A., Dressler, L. G., Cowan, D., Conway, K., . . . Millikan, R. C. (2006). Race, breast cancer subtypes, and survival in the Carolina Breast Cancer Study. *JAMA: The Journal of the American Medical Association, 295*(21), 2492–2502.

Cauce, A. M., Coronado, N., & Watson, J. (1998). *Conceptual, methodological and statistical issues in culturally competent research.* In M. Hernandez & M. R. Isaacs (Eds.), *Promoting cultural competence in children's mental health services.* Baltimore, MD: Paul H. Brookes Publishing Co. pp. 305–331.

Chu, D. I., Moreira, D. M., Gerber, L., Presti, J. C., Aronson, W. J., Terris, M. K., . . . Freedland, S. J. (2012). Effect of race and socioeconomic status on surgical margins and biochemical outcomes in an equal-access health care setting: Results from the Shared Equal Access Regional Cancer Hospital (SEARCH) database. *Cancer, 118*(20), 4999–5007.

Corvol, P., & Jeunemaitre, X. (1997). Molecular genetics of human hypertension: Role of angiotensinogen. *Endocrine Reviews, 18*(5), 662–677.

Dallman, M. F., Pecoraro, N., Akana, S. F., La Fleur, S. E., Gomez, F., Houshyar, H.,…Manalo, S. (2003). Chronic stress and obesity: A new view of "comfort food." *Proceedings of the National Academy of Sciences of the United States of America, 100*(20), 11696–11701.

Dookeran, K. A., Dignam, J. J., Holloway, N., Ferrer, K., Sekosan, M., McCaskill-Stevens, W., & Gehlert, S. (2012). Race and the prognostic influence of *p53* in women with breast cancer. *Annals of Surgical Oncology, 19*(7), 2334–2344.

Edwards, C. L., Green, M., Wellington, C. C., Muhammad, M., Wood, M., Feliu, M.,…McNeil, J. (2009). Depression, suicidal ideation, and attempts in black patients with sickle cell disease. *Journal of the National Medical Association, 101*(11), 1090–1095.

Edwards, C. L., Scales, M., Loughlin, C., Bennett, G., Harris-Peterson, S., De Castro, L. M.,…Killough, A. (2005). A brief review of the pathophysiology, associated pain, and psychosocial issues associated with sickle cell disease (SCD). *International Journal of Behavioral Medicine, 12*(3), 171–179.

Edwards, C. L., Raynor, R. D., Feliu, M., McDougald, C., Johnson, S., Schmechel, D.,…Whitfield, K. E. (2007). Neuropsychological assessment, neuroimaging, and neuropsychiatric evaluation in pediatric and adult patients with sickle cell disease (SCD). *Neuropsychiatric Disease and Treatment, 3*(6), 705–709.

Edwards, C., Whitfield, K., Sudhakar, S., Pearce, M., Byrd, G., Wood, M.,…Robinson, E. (2006). Parental substance abuse, reports of chronic pain and coping in adult patients with sickle cell disease. *Journal of the National Medical Association, 98*(3), 420–428.

Edwards, L. Y., & Edwards, C. L. (2010). Psychosocial treatments in pain management of sickle cell disease. *Journal of the National Medical Association, 102*(11), 1084–1094.

Feinlieb, M., Garrison, M. J., Fabitz, R., Christian, J. C., Hrubec, Z., Borhani, N. O., Kannel, W .B., . . . Schwartz, J. O. (1977). The NHLBI twin study of cardiovascular disease risk factors: Methodology and summary of results. *American Journal of Epidemiology, 106*, 284–295.

Fejerman, L., Bouzekri, N., Wu, X., Adeyemo, A., Luke, A., Zhu, X.,…Cooper, R. S. (2004). Association between evolutionary history of angiotensinogen haplotypes and plasma levels. *Human Genetics, 115*(4), 310–318.

Feliu, M. H., Crawford, R. D., Edwards, L., Wellington, C., Wood, M., Whitfield, K. E., & Edwards, C. L. (2011). Neurocognitive testing and functioning in adults sickle cell disease. *Hemoglobin, 35*(5–6), 476–484.

Ferrario, C. M. (2003). Contribution of Angiotensin-(1–7) to cardiovascular physiology and pathology. *Current Hypertension Reports, 5*(2), 129–134.

Filip, M., Zaniewska, M., Frankowska, M., Wydra, K., & Fuxe, K. (2012). The importance of the adenosine A(2A) receptor-dopamine D(2) receptor interaction in drug addiction. *Current Medicinal Chemistry, 19*(3), 317–355.

Ford, M. E., & Kelly, P. A. (2005). Conceptualizing and categorizing race and ethnicity in health services research. *Health Services Research, 40*(5 Pt 2), 1658–1675.

Freeman, H. P. (1998). The meaning of race in science–considerations for cancer research: Concerns of special populations in the National Cancer Program. *Cancer, 82*(1), 219–225.

Gamble, V. N. (1993). A legacy of distrust: African Americans and medical research. *American Journal of Preventive Medicine, 9*(6 Suppl), 35–38.

Harburg, E., Erfurt, J. C., Hauenstein, L. S., Chape, C., Schull, W. J., & Schork, M. A. (1973). Socio-ecological stress, suppressed hostility, skin color, and black-white male blood pressure: Detroit. *Psychosomatic medicine, 35*(4), 276–296.

Harper, M. S., & Alexander, C. D. (1990). Profile of the black elderly. In M. S. Harper (Ed.), *Minority aging: Essential curricula content for selected health and allied health professions* (pp. 193–222). DHHS Publication No. HRS-P-DV 90-4.

Harrison, M. O., Edwards, C. L., Koenig, H. G., Bosworth, H. B., Decastro, L., & Wood, M. (2005). Religiosity/spirituality and pain in patients with sickle cell disease. *The Journal of Nervous and Mental Disease, 193*(4), 250–257.

Hauge, M. (1980). The Danish twin register. In S. A. Mednick & A. E. Baert (Eds.) *An empirical basis for primary prevention: Prospective longitudinal research in Europe.* Oxford, UK: Oxford University Press.

Hayward, M. D., Miles, T. P., Crimmins, E. M., & Yang, Y. (2000). The significance of socioeconomic status in explaining the racial gap in chronic health conditions. *American Sociological Review, 65*(6), 910–930.

Heard, E., Whitfield, K. E., Edwards, C. L., Bruce, M. A., & Beech, B. M. (2011). Mediating effects of social support on the relationship among perceived stress, depression, and hypertension in African Americans. *Journal of the National Medical Association, 103*(2), 116–122.

Hirvonen, A. (1995). Genetic factors in individual responses to environmental exposures. *Journal of occupational and environmental medicine, 37*(1), 37–43.

Jablon, S., Neel, J. V., Gershowitz, H., & Atkinson, G. F. (1967). The NAS-NRC twin panel: Methods of construction of the panel, zygosity diagnosis, and proposed use. *American Journal of Human Genetics, 19,* 133–161.

Jackson, J. J. (1985). Race, national origin, ethnicity, and aging. In R. H. Binstock & E. Shanas (Eds.), *Handbook of aging and social sciences* (pp. 264–303). New York, NY: Van Nostrand-Reinhold.

Jackson, J. S., Knight, K. M., & Rafferty, J. A. (2010). Race and unhealthy behaviors: Chronic stress, the HPA axis, and physical and mental health disparities over the life course. *American Journal of Public Health, 100*(5), 933–939.

James, G. D. (1991). Race and perceived stress independently affect the diurnal variation of blood pressure in women. *American Journal of Hypertension, 4,* 382–384.

James, G. D., Schlussel, Y. R., & Pickering, T. G. (1993). The association between daily blood pressure and catecholamine variability in normotensive working women. *Psychomatic Medicine, 55,* 55–60.

Kaprio, J., Sarna, S., Koskenvuo, M., & Rantasalo, I. (1978). Finnish twin registry: Formation and compilation, questionnaire study, zygosity determination procedures, and research program. *Progress in Clinical Biological Research, 24B,*179–184.

King, P. A. (1992). The dangers of difference. *Hastings Center Report, 22*(6), 35.

Kington, R. S., & Nickens, H. W. (2001). Racial and ethnic differences in health: Recent trends, current patterns, future directions. In N. J. Smelser, W. J. Wilson, & F. Mitchell (Eds.), *America becoming: Racial trends and their consequences* (Vol. 2, pp. 253–310; Commission on Behavioral and Social Sciences and Education, National Research Council). Washington, DC: National Academies Press.

Krieger, N. (1990). Racial and gender discrimination: Risk factors for high blood pressure? *Social Science and Medicine, 30,* 1273–1281.

Krieger, N., Smith, K., Naishadham, D., Hartman, C., & Barbeau, E. M. (2005). Experiences of discrimination: Validity and reliability of a self-report measure for population health research on racism and health. *Social Science & Medicine, 61*(7), 1576–1596.

Kumanyika, S. (1990). Diet and chronic disease issues for minority populations. *Journal of Nutrition Education, 22,* 89–96.

Lackey, C., Kolasa, K., & Horner, R. (1992). Nutrition education in a community cholesterol screening program. *Health Values, 16,* 39–47.

Lander, E. S., & Schork, N. J. (1994). Genetic dissection of complex traits. *Science-New York Then Washington-, 2037.*

Lang, T., de Gaudemaris, R., Chatellier, G., Hamici, L., & Diène, E. (2001). Prevalence and therapeutic control of hypertension in 30,000 subjects in the workplace. *Hypertension, 38*(3), 449–454.

Lee, J. H., Flaquer, A., Costa, R., Andrews, H., Cross, P., Lantigua, R.,…Mayeux, R. (2004). Genetic influences on life span and survival among elderly African-Americans, Caribbean Hispanics, and Caucasians. *American Journal of Medical Genetics, 128A*(2), 159–164.

Lykken, D. T., Bouchard, T. J., McGue, M., & Tellegen, A. (1990). The Minnesota Twin Family Registry: Some initial findings. *Acta Gemellogicae et Medicae, 39,* 35–70.

Manuel, R. C. (1988). The demography of older Blacks in the United States. In J. S. Jackson, P. Newton, A. Ostfield, D. Savage, & E. L. Schneider (Eds.), *The black American elderly* (pp. 25-49). New York, NY: Springer.

Macera, C. A., Armstead, C. A., & Anderson, N. B. (2001). Sociocultural influences on health. *Handbook of health psychology,* 427–440.

Markides, K. S., Liang, J., & Jackson, J. S. (1990). Race, ethnicity, and aging: Conceptual and methodological issues. *Handbook of Aging and Social Sciences.* (pp. 112–129). New York: Van Nostrand-Reinhold.

McClearn, G. E., & Vogler, G. P. (2001). The genetics of behavioral aging. In J. E. Birren & K. W. Schaie (Eds.), *Handbook of the psychology of aging* (5th ed., pp. 109–131). San Diego, CA: Academic Press.

McClearn, G. E., Vogler, G. P., & Plomin, R. (1996). Genetics and behavioral medicine. *Behavioral Medicine, 22*(3), 93–102.

McGue, M., Hirsch, B., & Lykken, D. T. (1993). Age and the self-perception of ability: A twin study analysis. *Psychology of Aging. 8*, 72–80.

McDougald, C., Edwards, C. L., Wood, M., Wellington, C., Feliu, M., O'Garo, K.,…O'Connell, C. (2009). Coping as predictors of psychiatric morbidity and pain in patients with sickle cell disease (SCD). *Journal of African American Studies, 13*(1), 47–62.

McEwen, B. S., & Seeman, T. (1999). Protective and damaging effects of mediators of stress. Elaborating and testing the concepts of allostasis and allostatic load. *Annals of the NY Academy of Sciences, 896*, 30–47.

Medlund, P., Cederlof, R., Floderus-Myrhed, B., Friberg, L., & Sorensen, S. (1977). A New Swedish Twin Registry. *Acta Medicae Scandinavia Supplementum, 600.*

Mutetwa, B., Taioli, E., Attong-Rogers, A., Layne, P., Roach, V., & Ragin, C. (2010). Prostate cancer characteristics and survival in males of African Ancestry according to place of birth: Data from Brooklyn-New York, Guyana, Tobago and Trinidad. *The Prostate, 70*(10), 1102–1109.

Neale, M. C., & Cardon, L. R. (Eds.). (1992). *Methodology for genetic studies of twins and families.* Dordrecht, Netherlands: Kluwer Academic.

Nelson, T. L., Brandon, D. T., Wiggins, S. A., & Whitfield, K. E. (2002). Genetic and environmental influences on body-fat measures among African-American twins. *Obesity Research, 10*(8), 733–739.

Nesselroade, J. R., Pedersen, N. L., McClearn, G. E., Plomin, R., & Bergeman C. S. (1988). Factorial and criterion validities of telephone-assessed cognitive ability measures: Age and gender comparisons in adult twins. *Res on Aging 10*, 220–233.

NHLBI. (1985). Hypertension prevalence and the status of awareness treatment and control in the U.S.: Final report of the subcommittee on definition and prevalence of the 1984 Joint National Committee. *Hypertension, 7*, 457–468.

O'Connell-Edwards, C., Edwards, C. L., Pearce, M., Wachholtz, A. B., Wood, M., Muhammad, M.,…Robinson, E. (2009). Religious coping and pain associated with sickle cell disease: Exploration of a non-linear model. *Journal of African American Studies, 13*(1), 1–13.

Odierna, D. H., Afable-Munsuz, A., Ikediobi, O., Beattie, M., Knight, S., Ko, M.,…Ponce, N. A. (2011). Early developments in gene-expression profiling of breast tumors: Potential for increasing black-white patient disparities in breast cancer outcomes? *Personalized Medicine, 8*(6), 669–679.

Outlaw, F. H. (1993). Stress and coping: the influence of racism on the cognitive appraisal processing of African Americans. *Issues in Mental Health Nursing, 14*, 399–409.

Pamuk, E., Makuc, D., Heck, K., Reuben, C., & Lochner, K. (1998). *Socioeconomic Status and Health Chartbook. Health, United States, 1998.* Hyattsville, MD: National Center for Health Statistics.

Pascoe, E. A., and Smart Richman, L. (2009). Perceived discrimination and health: A meta-analytic review. *Psychological Bulletin 2009, 135*, 531–534.

Pearlin, L. I., Schieman, S., Fazio, E. M., & Meersman, S. C. (2005). Stress, health, and the life course: Some conceptual perspectives. *Journal of Health and Social Behavior, 46*(2), 205–219.

Pedersen, N. L., Gatz, M., Plomin, R., Nesselroade, J. R., McClearn, G. E. (1989) Individual differences in locus of control during the second half of the lifespan for identical and fraternal twins reared apart and reared together. *Journals of Gerontology 44*, 100–105.

Pedersen N. L., Plomin R., McClearn G. E., & Friberg L. (1988). Neuroticism, extroversion, and related traits in adult twins reared apart and reared together. *Journal of Personal & Social Pathology, 55*, 950–957.

Pedersen, N. L., Plomin, R., Nesselroade, J. R., & McClearn, G. E. (1992). A quantitative genetic analysis of cognitive abilities during the second half of the life span. *Psychological Science, 3*, 346–353.

Pells, J., Edwards, C. L., McDougald, C. S., Wood, M., Barksdale, C., Jonassaint, J.,…Rogers, L. (2007). Fear of movement (kinesiophobia), pain, and psychopathology in patients with sickle cell disease. *The Clinical Journal of Pain, 23*(8), 707–713.

Pells, J. J., Presnell, K. E., Edwards, C. L., Wood, M., Harrison, M. O., DeCastro, L.,...Robinson, E. (2005). Moderate chronic pain, weight and dietary intake in African-American adult patients with sickle cell disease. *Journal of the National Medical Association, 97*(12), 1622–1629.

Pisu, M., Oliver, J. S., Kim, Y. I., Elder, K., Martin, M., & Richardson, L. C. (2010). Treatment for older prostate cancer patients: Disparities in a southern state. *Medical Care, 48*(10), 915–922.

Platt, O. S., Brambilla, D. J., Rosse, W. F., Milner, P. F., Castro, O., Steinberg, M. H., & Klug, P. P. (1994). Mortality in sickle cell disease. Life expectancy and risk factors for early death. *The New England Journal of Medicine, 330*(23), 1639–1644.

Plomin, R., DeFries, J. C., & McClearn, G. E. (1990). *Behavior genetics*. (2nd ed.). New York, NY: W. H. Freeman.

Plomin, R., Lichtenstein, P., Pedersen, N. L., McClearn, G. E., & Nesselroade, J. R. (1990). Genetic influences on life events during the last half of the lifespan. *Psychology and Aging 5*, 25–30.

Plomin, R., & McClearn, G. E. (1990). Human behavioral genetic and aging. In J. E. Birren & K. Warner Schaie (Eds.), *Handbook of The psychology of aging* (p. 77). San Diego, CA: Academic Press.

Plomin, R., McClearn, G. E., Pedersen, N. L., Nesselroade, J. R., Bergeman, C. S. (1988). Genetic Influences on childhood and family environment perceived retrospectively from the last half of the lifespan. *Developmental Psychology, 24*, 738–745.

Plomin R., Pedersen N. L., McClearn, G. E., Nesselroade, J. R., & Bergeman, C. S. (1988). EAS temperaments during the last half of the lifespan: Twin reared apart and twins reared together. *Psychology and Aging, 3*, 43–50.

Powell, I. J., Bock, C. H., Ruterbusch, J. J., & Sakr, W. (2010). Evidence supports a faster growth rate and/or earlier transformation to clinically significant prostate cancer in black than in white American men, and influences racial progression and mortality disparity. *The Journal of Urology, 183*(5), 1792–1796.

Risch, N., & Merikangas, K. (1996). The future of genetic studies of complex human diseases. *Science-AAAS-Weekly Paper Edition, 273*(5281), 1516–1517.

Reddy, S., Edwards, C. L., Wood, M., O'Garo, K., Morgan, K., Edwards, L.,...Whitfield, K. (2011). Body image and pain in adult patients with sickle cell disease (SCD). *Journal of African American Studies, 15*, 115–119.

Sankar, P., Cho, M. K., Condit, C. M., Hunt, L. M., Koenig, B., Marshall, P., ... & Spicer, P. (2004). Genetic research and health disparities. *Journal of the American Medical Association, 291*(24), 2985–2989.

Schork, N. J. (1997). Genetics of complex disease approaches, problems, and solutions. *American Journal of Respiratory and Critical Care Medicine, 156*(4), S103–S109.

Smedley, B. D., Stith, A. Y., & Nelson, A. R. (Ed.). (2003). *Unequal treatment: Confronting racial and ethnic disparities in healthcare*. Washington, DC: The National Academies Press.

Stanton, M. V., Jonassaint, C. R., Bartholomew, F. B., Edwards, C., Richman, L., DeCastro, L., & Williams, R. (2010). The association of optimism and perceived discrimination with health care utilization in adults with sickle cell disease. *Journal of the National Medical Association, 102*(11), 1056–1063.

Surwit, R. S., van Tilburg, M. A., Zucker, N., McCaskill, C. C., Parekh, P., Feinglos, M. N.,...Lane, J. D. (2002). Stress management improves long-term glycemic control in type 2 diabetes. *Diabetes Care, 25*(1), 30–34.

Swan, G. E., Carmelli, D., & LaRue, A. (1995). Performance on the digit symbol substitution test and 5-year mortality in the Western Collaborative Group Study. *American Journal of Epidemiology. 141*, 32–40

Swan, G. E., Carmelli, D., Reed, T., Harshfield, G. A., Fabsitz, R. R., Eslinger, P. J. (1990). Heritability of cognitive performance in aging twins: The NHLBI Twin Study. *Archives of Neurology, 47*, 259–262.

Tang, M. X., Maestre, G., Tsai, W. Y., Liu, X. H., Feng, L., Chung, W. Y.,...Mayeux, R. (1996). Relative risk of Alzheimer disease and age-at-onset distributions, based on APOE genotypes among elderly African Americans, Caucasians, and Hispanics in New York City. *American Journal of Human Genetics, 58*(3), 574–584.

Thompson, V. L. (1996). Perceived experiences of racism as stressful life events. *Community Mental Health Journal, 32*, 223–233.

Tomiyama, A. J., Dallman, M. F., & Epel, E. S. (2011). Comfort food is comforting to those most stressed: Evidence of the chronic stress response network in high stress women. *Psychoneuroendocrinology, 36*(10), 1513–1519.

Wagner, E. H., Grothaus, M. S., Hect, J. A., & LaCroix, A. Z. (1991). Factors associated with participation in a senior health promotion program. *Gerontologist, 3_1*, 598–602.

Wallace, T. A., Prueitt, R. L., Yi, M., Howe, T. M., Gillespie, J. W., Yfantis, H. G., . . . Ambs, S. (2008). Tumor immunobiological differences in prostate cancer between African-American and European-American men. *Cancer Research, 68*(3), 927–936.

Ward, M. M. (2012). Personalized therapeutics: A potential threat to health equity. *Journal of General Internal Medicine, 27*(7), 868–870.

Wei, Q., Fentress, H. M., Hoversten, M. T., Zhang, L., Hebda-Bauer, E. K., Watson, S. J., . . . Akil, H. (2012). Early-life forebrain glucocorticoid receptor overexpression increases anxiety behavior and cocaine sensitization. *Biological Psychiatry, 71*(3), 224–231.

Wellington, C., Edwards, C. L., McNeil, J., Wood, M., Crisp, B., Feliu, M., . . . Whitfield, K. E. (2010). Somatization in the conceptualization of sickle cell disease. *Journal of the National Medical Association, 102*(11), 1079–1083.

Whitfield, K. E. (1994). The use of quantitative genetic methodology to gain insights into the origins of individual differences in later life. *Experimental Aging Research, 20*(2), 135–143.

Whitfield, K. E., Brandon, D. T., & Wiggins, S. A. (2003). Genetics and health disparities: Fears and realities. *Journal of the National Medical Association, 95*(7), 539–543.

Whitfield, K. E., Brandon, D. T., Robinson, E., Bennett, G., Merritt, M., & Edwards, C. (2006). Sources of variability in John Henryism. *Journal of the National Medical Association, 98*(4), 641–647.

Whitfield, K. E., Brandon, D. T., Wiggins, S. A., Vogler, G., & McClearn, G. (2003). Does intact pair status matter in the study of African American twins?: The Carolina African American twin study of aging. *Experimental Aging Research, 29*(4), 1–17.

Whitfield, K. E., Edwards, C. L., Brandon, D., & McDougald, C. (2008). Genetic and environmental influences on depressive symptoms by age and gender in African American twins. *Aging & Mental Health, 12*(2), 221–227.

Whitfield, K. E., Grant, J., Ravich-Scherbo, I., Marytuina, T., & Iboutolina, A. (1999). Genetic and environmental influences on forced expiratory volume in midlife: A cross-cultural replication. *Experimental Aging Research, 25*(3), 255–265.

Whitfield, K. E., & Hayward, M. (2003). The landscape of health disparities in older adults. *Public Policy and Aging Report, 13*(3), 1–7.

Whitfield, K. E., Kiddoe, J. M., Gamaldo, A., Andel, R., & Edwards, C. L. (2009). Concordance rates for cognitive impairment among older African American twins. *Alzheimer's and Disease, 5*(3), 276–279.

Whitfield, K. E., King, G., Moller, S., Edwards, C. L., Nelson, T., & Vandenbergh, D. (2007). Concordance rates for smoking among African-American twins. *Journal of the National Medical Association, 99*(3), 213–217.

Whitfield, K. E., & McClearn, G. (2005). Genes, environment, and race: Quantitative genetic approaches. *The American Psychologist, 60*(1), 104–114.

Whitfield, K. E., Wiggins, S. A., Belue, R., & Brandon, D. T. (2004). Genetic and environmental influences on forced expiratory volume in African Americans: The Carolina African-American Twin Study of Aging. *Ethnicity & Disease, 14*(2), 206–211.

Whitfield, K. E., Yao, X., Boomer, K. B., Vogler, G. P., Hayward, M. D., & Vandenbergh, D. J. (2009). Analysis of candidate genes and hypertension in African American adults. *Ethnicity & Disease, 19*(1), 18–22.

Wilk, J. B., Djousse, L., Arnett, D. K., Hunt, S. C., Province, M. A., Heiss, G., & Myers, R. H. (2004). Genome-wide linkage analyses for age at diagnosis of hypertension and early-onset hypertension in the HyperGEN study. *American Journal of Hypertension, 17*(9), 839–844.

Williams, D. R., & Collins, C. (1995). US socioeconomic and racial differences in health: Patterns and explanations. *Annual Review of Sociology*, 349–386.

Williams, D. R., Mohammed, S. A., Leavell, J., & Collins, C. (2010). Race, socioeconomic status, and health: Complexities, ongoing challenges, and research opportunities. *Annals of the New York Academy of Sciences, 1186*, 69–101.

Williams, D. R., Yu, Y., Jackson, J. S., & Anderson, N. B. (1997). Racial differences in physical and mental health: Socio-economic status, stress and discrimination. *Journal of Health Psychology, 2*(3), 335–351.

Young, A. H. (2004). Cortisol in mood disorders. *Stress, 7*(4), 205–208.

CHAPTER 11

Minority Elders: Nutrition and Dietary Interventions

Maciej S. Buchowski, Mohamad A. Sidani,
and James S. Powers

NUTRITION, CULTURE, AND HEALTH

Cultural factors dramatically influence health behaviors and outcomes. They intersect issues of poverty, equity, disparities, access, beliefs, expectations, and both linguistic and numeracy literacy capabilities. For health care professionals, cultural competence is defined as a shared decision making between themselves and the patient, built on mutual trust, respect, and understanding of the patient's cultural orientation. These principles, used to create individualized patient-centered treatment plans, are ever so pertinent to nutritional care.

Ethnicity and Aging Epidemiology

In the United States, minority elderly (over age 65 years) populations have increased from 16% of the population in 1999 to a projected 25% by 2030. The Hispanic population is expected to increase by 328%; African Americans by 131%; and American Indians, Eskimos, Asians, and Pacific islanders by 285% (Aging, 2012). The United States will continue to be characterized as an increasingly diverse population. People of color is the term preferred by many when addressing issues that include simultaneously several ethnic groups. It is important to avoid stereotyping all individuals of similar cultural background (individualism vs. collectivism), as they may have quite different life styles, values, and adoption of traditional practices. Present-day ethnic groups residing in the United States may be removed from their homeland for several generations. Many cultural traditions are based on religious ceremonies, feasting, cooking, and raising food, but traditional habits and practices may have been modified, with younger generations tending to adopt more Western dietary influences (Sofianou, Fung, & Tucker, 2011).

Ethnicity and Health Disparities

Improved nutritional status is an important component of efforts to improve the health of older adults, whose ability to consume a healthy diet is affected by comorbidities and behavioral, cognitive, and psychological factors. Results of the second National Health and Nutrition Examination Survey (NHANES II), conducted from 1976 to 1980, showed the primary sources of energy for all people in the United States were white breads, cookies and donuts, and meat (McDowell et al., 1994). Dietary data from NHANES III, suggested that diets of all ethnic groups have become more healthful, that is, during the course of 30 years, the percentage of energy from fat dropped from 38% (NHANES I) to 34% (NHANES III; Popkin, Siega-Riz, & Haines, 1996). These changes, however, did not affect the prevalence of conditions integrally related to nutritional status. Using obesity and type-2 diabetes as examples, the prevalence of obesity in the United States is approximately 18.5% in Caucasians, 23.4% in Hispanics, and 29.3% in African Americans, with attendant proportionate increases in type-2 diabetes in these populations (Calzada & Anderson-Worts, 2009).

Ethnicity and Genetic Risk

Principle component analysis of food intake demonstrates strong associations with Western diets (higher in meats and refined grains) and type-2 diabetes, and obesity risks (Mokdad et al., 2001; Tucker, 2010). In addition, disparities in type-2 diabetes incidence rates across ethnic populations are linked, at least in part, to the differential frequencies of type-2 diabetes risk alleles. In particular, most type-2 diabetes risk alleles share a consistent pattern of decreasing frequencies along human migration into East Asia. In comparison to European populations, type-2 diabetes genetic risk is consistently higher for individuals in African populations (Palmer et al., 2012) and lower in Asian populations (Chen et al., 2012; Rees et al., 2011). It has also been documented that obesity and type-2 diabetes are closely correlated genetically (Zhou et al., 2012), and obesity is considered a risk factor for metabolic syndrome. Among obesity-related genes, the *FTO* gene has been consistently identified to be associated with obesity phenotypes (Fawcett & Barroso, 2010). More specifically, the *FTO* rs9939609 variant has been implicated with obesity and dietary intake in populations of European descent (Dina et al., 2007; Scuteri et al., 2007). In a biracial cohort of Caucasian and African American diabetic and nondiabetic adults, Bressler and colleagues showed that type-2 diabetes and obesity were differentially associated with the *FTO* variations (Bressler, Kao, Pankow, & Boerwinkle, 2010). Significant statistical interaction between race and the *FTO* variants suggested that the effect on diabetes susceptibility may be context dependent (Lear et al., 2011). In the multiethnic cohort study, Lear et al. (2011) showed that Aboriginal, Chinese, European, and South Asian populations living in Canada and having the *FTO* rs9939609 minor allele had greater percent body fat mass and relatively greater subcutaneous abdominal adipose tissue mass. In a study within Pima Indians, where the risk allele is the major allele, common variation in the *SIM1* gene was associated with BMI on a population level (Traurig et al., 2009). In another report, Puerto Rican and Hispanic older adults homozygous for the *FTO*-risk allele had a higher mean BMI than individuals with different genotypes, but only when they had a high intake of saturated fatty acids (SFA). The authors concluded that SFA intake modulates the association between *FTO* and BMI in American populations (Corella et al., 2011). Finally, Grau et al. suggested that the *FTO* rs9939609 may interact with the macronutrient composition in low- and high-fat weight loss diets in various ways affecting metabolic rate and insulin resistance (Grau et al., 2009).

Nutrition, Environment, and Ethnicity

In addition to genetics and nutrition intake, nutritional status of the elderly could be affected by socioeconomic factors, such as education and income levels, and environmental factors, such as proximity to stores and transportation, that can affect food variety and availability. For example, it has been documented that access to healthy foods can be challenging to older individuals with mobility and transportation limitations. Some older ethnic minority populations have reduced access to healthy foods because of unavailability of food outlets in their neighborhoods (Yamashita & Kunkle, 2012). Moreover, it has been shown in elderly from similar socioeconomic strata that particular groups consume certain foods in greater amounts. For example, total consumption of fruit, meat, and beans among African Americans, whole grains among African Americans and American Indians, milk among non-Hispanic whites, and energy from solid fat, alcohol, and added sugars among American Indians were higher when compared to Caucasian Americans (Hendrix et al., 2008; Vitolins et al., 2007). Other differences in food patterns were found between older men and women. For example, in a study of community-dwelling Kansans 80 years of age and older who participated in congregate meal programs, female participants were significantly more likely to consume more fruit servings than males. In addition, chronic health conditions and dietary supplement use were consistently predictive factors of the amount of each of five food groups (dairy, fruits, vegetables, protein foods, grains) consumed (Weeden & Remig, 2010). Behavioral risk factors continue to contribute to years of life lost, even in high-income countries, due to low vegetable and, high fat intake, and low levels of physical activity (Lopez, Mathers, Ezzati, & Jamison, 2006). There also remain continued self-reported health disparities among older Mexican-born Americans as they age (Villa, Wallace, Bagdasaryan, & Aranda, 2012).

There is also a disparity in dietary patterns and quality between older adults living in urban and rural areas (Savoca et al., 2009). In general, rural older adults are more likely to be obese or overweight, have high rates of chronic disease, and are less likely to access preventive health care (Casey, Thiede Call, & Klingner, 2001). This increases the likelihood that rural older adults will consume diets that fail to meet recommendations for the types and quantities of foods recommended. In a recent study of African and Caucasian American older adults in Mississippi, however, intakes of dark green and orange vegetables were adequate, and many participants complied with the added fat and sugar guidelines (Van Rompay et al., 2012).

CULTURAL INFLUENCE ON FOOD PATTERNS AND NUTRITION

Ethnic and religious customs are two of many factors that influence food preferences. Cultural variation is additionally influenced by regionalism and within-culture diversity.

African Culture

Some of the strongest influences on American cuisine came from African slaves. African American cooking, popularly termed "soul food" is diverse and flavorful with origins in Africa, the West Indies, and American southern states (Delisle, 2010). Soul food may refer to meals made with fried chicken, pork chops, chitterlings, grits, cornbread, macaroni and cheese, and hushpuppies. Dishes such as *hoppin' John* (rice, black-eyed peas, and salt pork), *gumbo*, *jambalaya*, *fried porgies*, and *potlikker* may all be considered soul food. Many African Americans eat foods such as greens, legumes, beans, rice, and potatoes, which are rich in nutrients. Some foods, however, are very low in fiber, calcium, and potassium and very high in fat content. Preparation of food often involves deep-frying, barbecuing, or serving heavy sauces or gravy. Still, the African American diet is characterized as high in fat and salt and low in fruits and vegetables (Kumanyika, 1993). For example, a study comparing diets of African Americans living in Harlem, New York City, indicated that diet of those born in the Southern states were less healthful than those born in other regions of the United States or in the Caribbean, who reported the lowest intake of fat (Greenberg, Schneider, Northridge, & Ganz, 1998).

Examples of more recent African influences on food patterns in some U.S. population segments are Somali and Ethiopian cultures. Traditional staples of the Somali and Ethiopian diets are rice, bananas, and the meat of sheep, goats, and cattle, with little fresh fruit or vegetables. All meat is ritually slaughtered according to Islamic law. Traditional Somali bread is similar to pita bread. Coffee and teas are preferred Somali drinks. According to custom, food is eaten with the right hand and men and women eat separately. *Qat* (also spelled *khat*, *chat*, *kat*), a mild stimulant used by some Somali men, is derived from fresh leaves of the *Catha edulis* tree. The Ethiopian diet includes various meats with different types of spicy sauce, peas, lentils, cabbage, and green beans—all eaten with *injera*, a pancake-like bread made of teff grain. *Injera* is a major food staple, and provides approximately two thirds of the diet in Ethiopia. Teff contains high levels of calcium, phosphorous, iron, copper, aluminum, barium, and thiamine.

Native American Culture

The traditional diet of American Indians was generally low in fat, moderate in carbohydrates, high in protein, and rich in antioxidants (Kattelmann, Conti, & Ren, 2010). The diet consisted mostly of large game from hunting and corn beans and squash from farming and gardening or from trade with neighboring tribes (Moore, Kruse, Tisdall, & Corrigan, 1946). Other gathered diet components were wild plants used for food, medicine and teas, and included the wild turnip, wild potato, onion, mushrooms, other roots, nuts and seeds, and a variety of berries (Nurge, 1970). The wild foods were slowly digested and absorbed, allowing blood sugar levels to be maintained in balance with insulin production (Brand, Snow, Nabhan, & Truswell, 1990). Alaska Native diet was primarily limited to protein from fish, moose, caribou, and marine mammals (Murphy et al., 1995). Working with the Sandy Lake Cree, Gittelsohn et al. (1998) found that local concepts of food and illness dichotomized into "Indian" and "white man's" groupings, with "Indian" foods perceived as healthful and "white man's" foods as unhealthful. A similar dichotomy of "white man" and "Indian" foods is part of the Dakota belief systems (Lang, 1990), as it is for the Pima (Williams et al., 2001). An example of a composite food that is a challenge for nutrition researchers is "fry bread," a food item pervasive among American Indians throughout North America (Smith & Wiedman, 2001). Ballew and colleagues (Ballew et al., 1997) report on the challenge of the Navajo Health and Nutrition Study's interviewers to elicit detailed descriptions of each reported Navajo taco. Indian fry bread, like pizza, is an example of emerging local foods that combine and recombine global food products into complex composite meals confounding nutritional surveys. Today's Native American typical diet is similar to that of the general U.S. population, although it is often poorer in quality; consists of high-fat, salty, and sugary foods; and lacks sufficient fruit, vegetables, grains, and dairy products (Berg et al., 2012; Supplee et al., 2011).

Mediterranean Culture

The traditional Mediterranean diet pattern is characterized by an abundance of plant foods and wine, usually with meals. The Mediterranean diet features vegetables and fruit selections including artichokes, avocados, apricots, tomatoes, and zucchini. Dairy selections include yogurt and ricotta and feta cheeses, and herbs and spices such as basil, oregano, and garlic are included. However, research interest in this field during the past years has been focused on estimating adherence to the whole Mediterranean diet rather than analyzing the individual components of the dietary pattern in relation to the health status of the population (Tangney et al., 2011). This happens because the analyses of single nutrients ignore important interactions between components of a diet and, more importantly, because people do not eat isolated nutrients. Hence, dietary scores estimating adherence to a Mediterranean diet, devised a priori based on the characteristic components of the traditional diet of the Mediterranean area, have been found to be associated with a reduction of overall mortality and mortality from cardiovascular diseases and cancer (Bach et al., 2006). The health benefits of this pattern are many and include reduced risk of ischemic heart disease (de Lorgeril & Salen, 2006; Fung et al., 2009), cancers (Dixon et al., 2007; Reedy et al., 2008), all-cause mortality (Knoops et al., 2004; Mitrou et al., 2007), and, more recently, Alzheimer's disease and cognitive decline (Féart et al., 2009; Scarmeas et al., 2009).

Latino Culture

Variations of the Latino diet have existed in parts of the United States where corn, potatoes, peanuts, and beans are grown. This diet is a blend of traditional diets of indigenous Central and South American Indians, Spaniards, and Africans. Fruit and vegetable examples include chard, carrots, bananas, papayas, melons, and yams. Meats include beef, goat, lamb, and pork. The diet of assimilated Hispanics/Latinos in the United States tends to be related to level of acculturation, nativity, and duration of residence in the United States. Sofianou et al. (2011) used principal components analysis on food frequency questionnaire data for all adult respondents of the National Health and Nutrition Examination Survey (NHANES III) from 2003 to 2006. Four dietary patterns were identified: Western, healthy, tomato/tortilla, and coffee/sugar. Mean score for each diet pattern did not differ significantly by duration of U.S. residence category in the Mexico-born Mexican American population. However, in comparison to all Mexico-born Mexican Americans, U.S.-born Mexican Americans had significantly lower scores for the tomato/tortilla pattern, and significantly higher scores for the Western pattern. Scores for the healthy pattern were relatively low in all Mexican American subgroups, indicating low adherence to the Healthy diet. The authors concluded that education and policy action promoting healthy food access in Hispanic neighborhoods could help limit consumption of Western and coffee/sugar diet patterns and promote healthier choices in the Mexican American population.

In a study that included Mexicans, Mexican Americans, and Non-Hispanic whites, Batis, Hernandez-Barrera, Barquera, Rivera, and Popkin (2011) found a mix of positive and negative aspects of food acculturation. The overall proportion of energy obtained from unhealthy foods was higher among the U.S. subpopulations than in those born outside the United States in both younger and older adults. Compared to Mexicans, the U.S. subpopulations had greater intakes of saturated fat, sugar, dessert and salty snacks, pizza and french fries, low-fat meat and fish, high-fiber bread, and low-fat milk, as well as decreased intakes of corn tortillas, low-fiber bread, high-fat milk, and Mexican fast food. The findings indicate that within one generation in the United States, the influence of the Mexican diet is almost lost.

Using a similar food pattern approach in a cohort of Puerto Rican older adults, Mattei et al. (2011) identified three major dietary patterns as "meat, processed meat, and french fries," "traditional (rice, beans, and oils)," and "sweets, sugared beverages, and dairy desserts." The meat and french fries pattern was associated with higher blood pressure and waist circumference, whereas the traditional pattern was associated with lower high-density lipoprotein (HDL) cholesterol and higher odds of metabolic syndrome. In this population, acculturation was associated with lower legume fiber and greater cereal fiber intake. Among those above the poverty threshold, acculturation was associated with lower dietary glycemic index and starch intake, and greater fruit and nonstarchy vegetable intake (Van Rompay et al., 2012). The authors concluded that their studies underscore the need to discourage critical unhealthful components of the American diet among Mexican Americans (Batis et al., 2011), Puerto Ricans (Van Rompay et al., 2012), and most likely other minority populations. Dietary recommendations should include maintenance of traditional, healthful dietary practices including consumption of legumes, but also reduction in refined grains and greater inclusion of fruit, nonstarchy vegetables, and whole grains. Interventions to improve access to better quality carbohydrate sources are necessary for this group disproportionately affected by diabetes.

Eastern and Central European Culture

Eastern Europe, mostly Russian and Ukrainian, and Central Europe-born Americans often maintain a diet high in fat, carbohydrates, and sodium, contributing to health problems that include diabetes, hypertension, and coronary and gastrointestinal diseases. During the early years of communism and food shortages in the Eastern Europe, the main concern was eating enough calories to stay alive. Meals were heavy, fatty, and salty, though otherwise bland. The ideal meal for a working peasant included boiled buckwheat with lard and a fermented drink made from dense, sour, black bread—food that would "hold you to the earth" and last a full working day. Conventional wisdom dictated that the richer and more fatty the food, the harder one would work. Traditional meal patterns in European Americans born in the United States, or whose ancestors came from the region, include pickled and dried meats, bread, potatoes, dumplings, porridge, cabbage and beet soup, and vegetables.

Asian Culture

Asian countries and regions have their own distinct food patterns and styles, but all share rice as a staple. There is generally high consumption of plant products including cabbage, bean sprouts, tofu, pineapple, and coconut. Fish and seafood are common ingredients in the diets of populations living close to coastlines or on islands. Vegetarian meals provide ample fruit and vegetables and dairy products and whole grains are main sources of protein. Vegans, who avoid all products of animal origin, may lack vitamin B12, iron, and calcium and may require supplements and addition of soy products as a protein source.

The Indian cuisine is characterized by the use of spices, herbs, vegetables, fruits, and a wide assortment of dishes that varies from region to region, reflecting the varied demographics of a large, ethnically diverse country. India's religious beliefs and culture, as well as exposure to the foods of Greece, the Middle East, and Asia have influenced its cuisine. Hinduism encourages a vegetarian diet. Staples include rice, whole-wheat flour, red lentils, peas, and seeds. Most Indian curries are cooked in peanut, mustard, soybean, or coconut oil. The most frequently used Indian spices are turmeric, chili pepper, black mustard seed, cumin, ginger, coriander, cinnamon, clove, and garlic. Popular spice mixes are *garam masala* and *goda masala*. In southern India, a banana leaf is used as a plate for celebrations. When hot food is served on banana leaves, it adds a particular aroma and flavor to the food. Food is most often eaten using two fingers of the right hand, with bread, such as *naan*, *puri*, or *roti*, to scoop the curry without letting it touch the hands. Pan, or beetle leaves, is often chewed after a meal to aid digestion.

A typical Vietnamese diet is generally healthy, with rice or noodles, fresh vegetables, and fish or meat. However, the diet also can be high in sodium from fish sauce and MSG, and low in fiber from lack of whole grains. Dairy and soy products are not part of a typical Vietnamese diet and adults are mostly lactose intolerant and thus may lack calcium.

Khmer often attribute good health to equilibrium, adopting the Chinese philosophy of balancing hot and cold. Food is deemed hot, cold, or neutral. For example, chicken is hot, vegetables are cold, and rice is neutral. Khmers in the United States who eat a traditional Cambodian diet eat rice at all three meals and prefer warm tea or water to drink. Most Khmer do not use ice and rarely consume dairy products because of lactose maldigestion and intolerance. Similarly, traditional staples of the Hmong diet are rice, noodles, fish, meat, and green vegetables with hot chili sauces. Hmong tend to eat the same types of food at each meal, with very little fruit or dairy products. Hmong people often prefer hot dishes and drink hot or warm water. Traditionally, a sick person must eat hot food with certain vegetables.

Middle Eastern Culture

Middle Eastern diet includes plant products such as olives, dates, beans, cucumbers, eggplant, spinach, and humus. Meats include poultry, lamb, and beef, sometimes prepared as kabob. Israeli and Jewish law requires food preparation according to kosher (pure) guidelines with dairy from kosher cattle. Only fish with scales are traditionally permitted. Several Middle Eastern African and Asian cultures observe Islam, which influence the kinds of food chosen and how the foods are combined. *Halal* is an Arabic word meaning lawful or permitted. The opposite of *halal* is haram, which means unlawful or prohibited. *Halal*, when applied to food, is a dietary set of guidelines for Muslims living an Islamic lifestyle. Lawful foods exclude alcohol, pork, meat from carnivorous animals, birds of prey, and certain other animals. *Halal* permits meat only from humanely slaughtered and blood-drained cattle and forbids any meat that has been slaughtered without mentioning God's name (http://www.faqs.org/nutrition/Foo-Hea/Greeks-and-Middle-Easterners-Diet-of.html). Foods containing ingredients such as gelatin, enzymes, emulsifiers, and flavors are questionable (mashbooh), because the origin of these ingredients is not known.

Caribbean Culture

Caribbean diet is a fusion of African, Amerindian, European, East Indian, and Chinese cuisine. Traditional dishes are important to regional culture, for example, goats stew or pelau. *Callaloo* is a dish containing leafy vegetables and sometimes okra amongst, others, widely distributed in the Caribbean, with a distinctively mixed African and indigenous character. Common ingredients are rice, plantains, beans, cassava, cilantro, bell peppers, chickpeas, tomatoes, sweet potatoes, coconut, and any of various meats (beef, poultry, pork, or fish), as well as curries. The variety of dessert dishes in the area also reflects the mixed origins of the recipes. The energy contribution of fat to the diet (30%–35%) mostly from rice and beans is similar to the current U.S. diet.

NUTRITION AND AGE-RELATED CHANGES

Nutrition and aging are connected inseparably because eating patterns affect progress of many chronic and degenerative diseases associated with aging. In turn, disease progression, health status, and ultimately quality of life may be adversely affected by a number of cultural and ethnic factors associated either directly or indirectly with nutrition and aging (Buchowski & Sun, 1996). These factors are particularly relevant to minority groups in which issues of poverty, equity, disparities, access, beliefs, expectations, and both linguistic and numeracy literacy capabilities and outcomes intersect. It is well documented that, in older adults, inadequate diet may cause malnutrition either in the form of undernutrition or overnutrition, both leading to body composition and physiological changes. Undernutrition, traditionally referred to as malnutrition, is associated with a decline in functional status, impaired muscle function, decreased bone mass, immune dysfunction, anemia, reduced cognitive function, poor wound healing, delay in recovering from surgery, and higher hospital and readmission rates and mortality. Overnutrition may lead to obesity, which is associated with higher risk for diabetes type 2, hypertension, hyperlipidemias, and some cancers.

Body Composition and Physiological Changes

The aging process is associated with a decline in vital physiological functions, such as reserve and storage capacity, recovery, and regulatory functions of several organs and systems (Ahmed & Haboubi, 2010). The most important physiological changes occur in body composition, cytokine and hormonal levels, delayed gastric emptying, alterations in fluid electrolyte regulation, and diminished sense of smell and taste (Table 11.1). In general, after the age of 50 years, body bone mass, lean mass, and water content decrease and body fat mass increases (Brownie, 2006). The major causes of changes in body composition are reduced total physical activity, reduced growth and sex hormones secretion, and decreased resting metabolic rate. Decline in skeletal muscle mass, known as sarcopenia (Candow, 2011; Cederholm et al., 2011; Muscaritoli et al., 2010), is defined as the age-related loss of muscle quantity and quality (Thompson, 2009), which subsequently has a negative effect on strength (Evans, 1995), muscle protein kinetics (Combaret et al., 2009), metabolic rate (Piers, Soares, McCormack, & O'Dea, 1998), and oxidative capacity (Roubenoff & Hughes, 2000). In turn, sarcopenia may lead to an increase in fat mass (Marzetti, Lees, Wohlgemuth, & Leeuwenburgh, 2009) and an impaired ability to perform tasks of daily living. It is estimated that skeletal muscle mass and strength decrease by approximately 1% to 2% per year after 50 years of age and affect approximately 25% of individuals greater than or equal to 70 years of age and 30% to 50% for individuals greater than or equal to 80 years of age. Fat mass increase is usually accompanied by a greater proportion of total body fat accumulating as intrahepatic and intraabdominal than subcutaneous fat stores, often associated with increased insulin resistance and higher risk of ischemic heart disease, stroke, and diabetes type 2 (Cree et al., 2004). Both environmental and genetic factors likely influence body composition and body fat distribution (O'Rahilly, Barroso, & Wareham, 2005; Tuomilehto et al., 2001).

TABLE 11.1 Major Physiological Changes Associated With Aging

SYSTEM	BIOMARKER/MEASURE	
	Decreased	Increased
Musculoskeletal	height; weight, especially after 75 years of age; lean body mass; intracellular and extracellular water volume; bone mass	fat mass
Cardiovascular	heart rate; lung vital capacity; decreased pO_2; maximal oxygen consumption (VO_2max)	systolic blood pressure; lung residual volume
Renal	glomerular filtration rate; urinary concentrating ability; sodium-conserving capacity; renal blood flow	
Hormonal	growth hormone; insulin growth factor; DHEA; calcitonin; aldosterone; renin	vasopressin; atrial natriuretic peptide; norepinephrine (but normal epinephrine); insulin; pancreatic polypeptide; parathormone
Immune	T-cell function; antibody response	
Gastrointestinal	esophageal motility; brush border enzyme; mucosal immune response	atrophic gastritis
Sensory	flavor detection (salty, sweet, sour, and bitter); taste perception; smell detection	

DIETARY GUIDELINES AND RECOMMENDATIONS

My Plate

My Plate is a USDA initiative with helpful culturally sensitive advice (ChooseMyPlate, 2011) and is replacing the food pyramid formerly used (Lichtenstein, Rasmussen, Yu, Epstein, & Russell, 2008). It gives a pictorial recommendation with easy-to-understand guidelines: (a) balance calories, enjoy eating food but eat less and avoid oversized portions, (b) make half the plate fruits and vegetables, make half of all grains whole grain, use fat-free or low-fat dairy products, and (c), compare sodium content in prepared foods, choose foods with lower sodium, and drink water rather than sugary beverages. A modified food guide for older adults based on MyPlate, has been recently released (MyPlate for Older Adults, 2011). MyPlate for Older Adults is intended to be a guide for healthy, older adults who are living independently and looking for examples of good food choices and physical activities. It provides examples of foods that contain high levels of vitamins and minerals per serving and recommends limiting foods high in transsaturated and saturated fats, salt, and added sugars, and emphasizes whole grains high in fiber. The Older American's Act nutrition programs have developed several culturally appropriate strategies to meet the needs of changing U.S. demographics.

Oldways®

Oldways, a nonprofit organization that promotes healthy eating based on regional diet pyramids, has developed four consumer-friendly pyramids, which display prudent food choices in a culturally sensitive manner (oldwayspt.org). These pyramids include Mediterranean, Latin American, Asian, and vegetarian alternatives to the USDA pyramid and reflect consistency with eating patterns of healthy populations around the world. Each pyramid stresses consumption of increased fruits and vegetables, fish twice weekly, and reduced total fat intake, while acknowledging the benefits of omega 3 and 6 fatty acids, as well as polyunsaturated fats and oils.

Healthy Eating Index

In recent years, a validated tool often used in assessing quality of diet in multiple populations is Healthy Eating Index (HEI), which reflects current increased emphasis on grains; dark-green and orange vegetables; certain oils; and energy from sweets, solid fats, and alcohol (Guenther, Reedy, & Krebs-Smith, 2008; Jill Reedy, Krebs-Smith, & Bosire, 2010).

ENERGY AND NUTRITIONAL REQUIREMENTS

Energy Requirements

Reduced basal metabolic rate in older adults reflects loss of lean body mass (Speakman & Westerterp, 2010). The basal metabolic rate is the principal determinant of total energy expenditure and age has been suggested to have a direct effect on tissue basal metabolic rate (Johnstone, Rance, Murison, Duncan, & Speakman, 2006; S. Roberts & Dallal, 1998; S. B. Roberts & Rosenberg, 2006; Vaughan, Zurlo, & Ravussin, 1991). Energy expenditure related to physical activity is the most variable component (Speakman & Westerterp, 2010) of total daily energy expenditure.

Macronutrient Requirements

The Food and Nutrition Board of the Institute of Medicine has developed macronutrient guidelines that recommend a culturally prudent diet, with 20% to 35% of energy as fat, and reduced intakes of cholesterol, saturated fat, and transfatty acids. Carbohydrates should constitute 45% to 65% of energy; complex carbohydrates are the preferred fiber source. The recommended fiber intake for those age 60 years or older is 30 g for men and 21 g for women. Protein intake is recommended at 0.8 g/kg/d, accounting for 10% to 35% of total energy. With stress or injury, protein requirements are usually estimated at 1.5 g/kg/d, but underlying renal or hepatic insufficiency may warrant protein restriction (Kukkonen-Harjula, Borg, Nenonen, & Fogelholm, 2005).

Micronutrient Requirements

Revisions of the Dietary Reference Intakes (RDIs) include recommended dietary allowances (formerly RDAs) with more specific guidelines for older adults (Dietary Reference Intakes for Energy, Carbohydrate, Fiber, Fat, Fatty Acids, Cholesterol, Protein, and Amino Acids [Macronutrients], 2005). The guidelines are designed no longer just to prevent deficiency diseases but to optimize the health of the population (Table 11.2). These recommendations can be adapted to culturally appropriate dietary instructions and food preparation methods.

Fluid and Electrolyte Needs

Normal aging is associated with a decreased perception of thirst, impaired response to serum osmolality, and reduced ability to concentrate urine after fluid deprivation. This impaired fluid and electrolyte balance is due to several factors, including reduced glomerular filtration rate, reduced ability to concentrate urine, less efficient sodium-conserving capacity, reduced ability to excrete water load, and altered thirst sensation (Baker, Munce, & Kenney, 2005; Kenney & Chiu, 2001). A decline in fluid intake can also result from disease states that reduce mental or physical ability to recognize or express thirst, or that result in decreased access to water. In general, fluid needs of older adults can be met with 30 ml/kg/day or 1 ml/kcal ingested. Fluid needs may be different during stress or illness. Dehydration is the most common fluid or electrolyte disturbance in older adults. Rehydration should be individualized and based on total body estimated fluid deficit, route of replacement, and patient-specific cardiac and renal function.

TABLE 11.2 Recommended Dietary Intakes of Micronutrients for Adults 71 Years Old and Older

NUTRIENT	RECOMMENDED DAILY ALLOWANCE	
	Male	Female
Calcium	1,200 mg*	1,200 mg*
Magnesium	420 mg	320 mg
Vitamin D	1,600 IU*	1,600 IU*
Thiamine	1.2 mg	1.1 mg
Riboflavin	1.3 mg	1.1 mg
Niacin	16 mg	14 mg
Vitamin B$_6$	1.7 mg	1.5 mg
Folate	400 mcg	400 mcg
Vitamin B$_{12}$	2.4 mcg	2.4 mcg
Pantothenic acid	5 mg*	5 mg*
Vitamin A	5,000 IU	4,000 IU
Vitamin K	120 mcg*	90 mcg*
Iron	10 mg	10 mg
Zinc	15 mg	15 mg
Vitamin C	90 mg	75 mg
α-Tocopherol	10 IU	10 IU
Selenium	55 mcg	55 mcg
Potassium	4,700 mg*	4,700 mg*

*Adequate intake, not recommended dietary allowance.

Sources: Data from Standing Committee on the Scientific Evaluation of Dietary Reference Intakes, Food and Nutrition Board, Institute of Medicine, Dietary Reference Intakes for Calcium, Phosphorus, Magnesium, Vitamin D, and Fluoride. Washington, DC: National Academy Press; 1997; Standing Committee on the Scientific Evaluation of Dietary Reference Intakes, Institute of Medicine, Dietary Reference Intakes for Thiamin, Riboflavin, Niacin, Vitamin B6, Folate, Vitamin B12, Pantothenic Acid, Biotin, and Choline. Washington, DC: National Academy Press; 1999; Standing Committee on the Scientific Evaluation of Dietary Reference Intakes, Food and Nutrition Board, Dietary Reference Intakes for Vitamin C, Vitamin E, Selenium, and Beta Carotene, and Other Carotenoids. Washington, DC: National Academy Press; 2000; Standing Committee on the Scientific Evaluation of Dietary Reference Intakes, Food and Nutrition Board, Dietary Reference Intakes for Vitamin A, Vitamin K, Arsenic, Boron, Chromium, Copper, Iodine, Iron, Manganese, Molybdenum, Nickel, Silicon, Vanadium, and Zinc. Washington, DC: National Academy Press; 2000; Standing Committee on the Scientific Evaluation of Dietary Reference Intakes, Institute of Medicine, Dietary Reference Intakes for Water, Potassium, Sodium, Chloride, and Sulfate. Washington, DC: National Academy Press; 2004; Dietary Reference Intakes for Calcium and Vitamin D (2011). Available at http://www.nap. edu (accessed April 2011).

NUTRITION SCREENING AND ASSESSMENT

Anthropometrics

Anthropometric measurements are often used for nutritional assessment of older adults and are reliable across ethnicities (Lustgarten & Fielding, 2011). An unintended weight loss of 10 pounds in the preceding 6 months is a useful indicator of morbidity; this degree of weight loss is predictive of functional limitations, health care charges, and the need for hospitalization. The Minimum Data Set (MDS-3) used by Medicare-certified nursing homes defines significant weight loss as more than or equal to 5% in the past month or more than or equal to 10% in the past 6 months. Body mass index (BMI) calculated as weight in kg divided by height in meters squared (kg/m^2) is a useful measure of body size and indirect measure of body fatness. The risk threshold for low BMI is set at 18.5 kg/m^2 but should be interpreted in the context of the individual's lifelong weight history. Skinfold and mid-arm circumference measurements have limited application because of the difficulty of achieving reliability in routine clinical use.

Nutritional Status Screening

Screening is vital in identifying and monitoring older adults. Three interdisciplinary tools to screen for nutrition risk were developed by the Nutrition Screening Initiative to aid in the evaluation of the nutritional status of older adults. The DETERMINE checklist (Posner, Jette, Smith, & Miller, 1993) is a self-report questionnaire comprising 10 items and is intended to identify potential risks but not to diagnose malnutrition. The Level I screen, intended for use by health care professionals, incorporates additional assessment items regarding dietary habits, functional status, living environment, and weight change, as well as measures of height and weight. The Level II screen, for use by more highly trained medical and nutrition professionals and suggested for use in the diagnosis of malnutrition, contains all the items from Level I with additional biochemical and anthropometric measures, as well as a more detailed evaluation of depression and mental status.

Mini-Nutritional Assessment (MNA)

The MNA tool (Guigoz, 2006) was developed to evaluate the risk of malnutrition among frail older adults. This assessment tool requires administration by a trained professional and consists of 18 items, including questions about BMI, mid-arm and calf circumferences, weight loss, living environment, medication use, dietary habits, clinical global assessment, and self-perception of health and nutrition status. A shortened screening version that contains only six items, the short-form Mini-Nutritional Assessment (MNA-SF; MNA® Mini Nutritional Assessment, 2009) is also now available. Another patient self-report nutritional assessment tool, the Simplified Nutrition Assessment Questionnaire (SNAQ) has a sensitivity and specificity of 88.2% and 83.5%, respectively, for identifying persons at risk for weight loss (Rolland, Perrin, Gardette, Filhol, & Vellas, 2012; M.-M. G. Wilson et al., 2005). Nutritional screening shows reduced nutritional status highly correlated to socioeconomic status, including higher prevalence of obesity in individuals under the age of 75 years.

Biochemical Markers of Nutritional Status

Serum proteins synthesized by the liver have been used as markers of nutrition albumin, transferrin, retinol-binding proteins, and thyroxin-binding prealbumin. Serum albumin has been recognized as a risk indicator for morbidity and mortality also associated with injury, disease, or inflammatory conditions. As a negative acute-phase reactant, albumin is subject to cytokine-mediated decline in synthesis and to increased degradation and transcapillary leakage. The prognostic value of hypoalbuminemia is largely associated with tissue injury, disease, or inflammation. In the ambulatory setting, hypoalbuminemia has been associated with functional limitation, sarcopenia, increased health care use, and mortality. In the hospital setting, it has also been associated with increased length of stay, complications, readmissions, and mortality. Prealbumin has a shorter half-life (48 hours) than albumin (18–20 days) and may, therefore, more adequately reflect short-term changes in protein status. Among serum lipids, cholesterol has been considered a marker of nutritional status in the elderly. Low cholesterol levels (less than 160 mg/dL) are often detected in adults with serious underlying disease, such as malignancy. Poor clinical outcomes have been observed among hospitalized and institutionalized older adults with hypocholesterolemia (Aslam, Haque, Lee, & Foody, 2009).

Micronutrient Deficiencies

The most valuable means of screening patients for vitamin and mineral deficiency (or toxicity) is a thorough nutrition-focused history and physical examination.

Iron deficiency anemia is a common clinical problem in older individuals and it is consistent with a hemoglobin concentration of less than 13 g/dL in men and less than 12 g/dL in women. The most prevalent anemias are those associated with blood loss, inflammation and chronic disease, and protein-energy malnutrition (Guralnik, Eisenstaedt, Ferrucci, Klein, & Woodman, 2004; Patel, 2008). Common causes of vitamin B12 deficiency are hypochlorhydria (decreased gastric acid production noted to occur in up to 15% of individuals older than age 65) and *Helicobacter pylori* infection of the stomach (Dali-Youcef & Andrès, 2009). Vitamin B12 deficiency can result in both, hematologic (e.g., anemia) and neurologic signs and symptoms such as nonspecific paresthesias (e.g., numbness) of the extremities and gait ataxia (Mold, Vesely, Keyl, Schenk, & Roberts, 2004). Neuropsychiatric symptoms may occur secondary to vitamin B12 deficiency, such as delirium manifesting as slowed thinking, confusion, memory loss, and depression, which may be difficult to differentiate from Alzheimer's disease (Mold, Lawler, & Roberts, 2008). Low serum folate levels have been associated with atrophy of the cerebral cortex, possible because of hyperhomocysteinemia (Scott et al., 2004). Although deficiencies of vitamin B12 and folic acid are common in frail older adults with cognitive impairment, supplementation with folic acid and vitamin B12 rarely alters the course of cognitive decline that is slowly progressive (Malouf, Grimley, & Areosa, 2008; Schneider, Tangney, & Morris, 2006). Low vitamin B6 concentrations are associated with inflammation, higher oxidative stress, and metabolic conditions in older Puerto Rican adults (Shen, Lai, Mattei, Ordovas, & Tucker, 2010). Approximately 90% of adults between the ages of 51 and 70 years do not get adequate vitamin D from their diet and often have minimal exposure to sunlight. Individuals with low vitamin D levels have lower bone density and are at risk for fractures as they age (Lai, Lucas, Clements, Roddam, & Banks, 2010). High-dose vitamin D supplementation (greater than or equal to 800 IU daily) was somewhat favorable in the prevention of hip fracture and any nonvertebral fracture in persons 65 years of age or older (Bischoff-Ferrari et al., 2012). Vitamin D deficiency causes osteomalacia in adults, which may cause bone pain and contribute to osteoporosis (Bhan, Rao, & Rao, 2010).

CHRONIC DISEASE AND AGING

Chronic illness is not part of normal aging; however, the risk and presence of disease and disability increases with age, with 40% of individuals aged 65 years reporting at least one disabling condition (Chalé, Unanski, & Liang, 2012). Nutritional management is closely related to the care of older individuals with many chronic illnesses, including diabetes, hypertension, congestive heart failure, chronic kidney disease, pressure ulcers, and obesity (Abaterusso et al., 2008; Aronow & Frishman, 2010; Dini, Bertone, & Romanelli, 2006; Han, Tajar, & Lean, 2011; Little, 2011; Rolland, Dupuy, Abellan van Kan, Gillette, & Vellas, 2011). It has been shown that socioeconomic disparities in functional limitations among older Americans exist independent of disease burden, whereas socioeconomic differences and disease burden account for racial disparities (Louie & Ward, 2011). Interestingly, pressure ulcers are more prevalent in African American nursing home residents, who have higher prevalence of risk factors for this condition (Fogerty, Guy, Barbul, Nanney, & Abumrad, 2009). It has been documented that differences in health behaviors may be important contributors to racial/ethnic disparities in the health status of older adults (August & Sorkin, 2011).

Recent genome-wide association (GWA) studies have provided compelling evidence of association between genetic variants and common complex diseases. Although differences in risk allele frequencies between populations are not unusually large and are thus likely not due to positive local selection, there is substantial variation in risk allele frequencies between populations, which may account for differences in disease prevalence among race/ethnic population groups (Myles, Davison, Barrett, Stoneking, & Timpson, 2008). Population differentiation can evidence environmental selection pressures. For example, such genetic information is limited in Puerto Ricans, the second largest Hispanic ethnic group in the United States, and a group with high prevalence of chronic disease. Minor allele frequency distributions for 45.5% of the SNPs assessed in Puerto Ricans were significantly different from those of Caucasians. Puerto Ricans carried risk alleles in higher frequency and protective alleles in lower frequency than Caucasians. Patterns of population differentiation showed that Puerto Ricans had SNPs with exceptional fixation index values in intronic, nonsynonymous, and promoter regions (Mattei et al., 2009). The differences in blood pressure levels and the prevalence of hypertension among the middle-aged and elderly between two East Asian populations, Bai Ku Yao and Han, might result from different dietary patterns, lifestyle choices, physical activity levels, sodium intake, and even genetic factors (Ruixing et al., 2008).

Malnutrition in Aging

Malnutrition is defined as a state in which a deficiency or surplus of energy, protein, and other nutrients causes adverse effects on body form, function, and clinical outcome (Chapman, 2006; Zeanandin et al., 2012). It is more common in the older population and predicted to rise dramatically in the next 30 years (WHO, 2006). Major risk factors for malnutrition are displayed in Table 11.3.

Undernutrition and Aging Epidemiology

Almost two thirds of general and acute hospital beds are occupied by people aged more than 65 years (Hickson, 2006). In developed countries, including the United States, approximately 15% of community-dwelling and homebound older adults, 20% to 60% of hospitalized patients, and 85% of nursing home residents suffer from undernutrition (Hajjar, Kamel, & Denson, 2004). Undernutrition is associated with a decline in functional status, impaired muscle function, decreased bone mass, immune dysfunction, anemia, reduced cognitive function, poor wound healing, delayed recovering from surgery, higher hospital and readmission rate, and higher mortality, and it is not related to ethnicity (Kyle, Unger, Mensi, Genton, & Pichard, 2002). The limited reliability of accurately assessing dietary intake measures is well known, so undernutrition is generally defined as average or usual intake of food groups, nutrients, or energy 25% to 50% below the RDI. In a study conducted by Kyle and coworkers, it was observed that energy intake was reduced in 21% of hospitalized older adults, in 5% to 18% of nursing home residents, and in 37% to 40% of community dwelling men and women 65 to 98 years old. Many reported skipping at least one meal each day. Estimated intakes by consumption surveys, however, may be unreliable because some studies suggest that older adults underreport energy intakes by 20% to 30%.

TABLE 11.3 Major Risk Factors for Poor Nutritional Status

MEDICAL/PHYSIOLOGICAL	ENVIRONMENTAL/BEHAVIORAL
Cognitive dysfunction	Low socioeconomic status
Medical problems, chronic diseases	Alcohol or substance abuse
Depression, poor mental health	Decreased physical activity level
Functional limitations	Limited education
Medications	Limited mobility, transportation
Poor dentition	Restricted diet, poor eating habits
	Social isolation
	Residence in location with restricted access to nutritious foods

Oral Nutrition

Preventing undernutrition is much easier than treating it. In an institutionalized setting, food intake can be enhanced by catering to individual and cultural food preferences as much as possible and by avoiding therapeutic diets unless their clinical value is certain. Patients should be prepared for meals with appropriate hand and mouth care, and they should be comfortably situated for eating. Assistance should be provided for those who need help. Placing two or more patients together for meals can increase sociability and food intake. Foods should be of appropriate consistency, prepared with attention to color, texture, temperature, and arrangement. The use of herbs, spices, and hot foods helps to compensate for loss of the sense of taste and smell often accompanying old age and to avoid the excessive use of salt and sugar. Hard-to-open individual packages should be avoided. Adequate time should be taken for leisurely meals. For the home-dwelling setting, the Title IIIC of the Older Americans Act has provided for congregate and home-delivered meals for older adults, regardless of economic status. This service is available in most parts of the country, albeit with a waiting list in some locations.

Enteral Feeding

In the nursing home setting, unacceptable weight loss is any loss more than or equal to 5% in the past month or more than or equal to 10% in the past six months. The Minimum Data Set (MDS) uses intake of less than 75% of food provided as the threshold to trigger nutrition assessment. Standards of care include acceptable parameters of nutritional status such as body weight and protein levels, and a modified (therapeutic) diet when a nutritional deficiency is present. Management involves treating pathological causes such as poor dentition and optimizing the management of chronic diseases. Patients with physical or cognitive impairment require special care and attention. Advance directives prohibiting the use of feeding tubes are honored unless there is compelling evidence that the individual would have changed his or her mind in the current situation. In incompetent adults without advance directives, the decision to start or to discontinue artificial feeding should be considered carefully with the surrogate, taking into account the risks and burdens of such an action, the risks and burdens of alternative actions, and the evidence to support likely benefits of the various actions. To date, evidence supporting the use of feeding tubes in patients with end-stage cancer, dementia, and chronic obstructive pulmonary disease (COPD) are lacking. Cultural and religious influences should always be present in decisions regarding artificial nutrition. All major religions permit withholding of nutrition and fluids when there is no benefit. Individuals and families may interpret futility quite differently, however, and the goals of care must be individualized. Culturally and racially motivated concerns regarding equitable care and treatment may also influence the decision. Supportive counseling from concerned physicians, patient education, family meetings, involvement of clergy, and translators all facilitate the development of an ethically acceptable and patient-centered treatment plan.

Pharmacological Treatment for Undernutrition Syndromes

Several agents have been suggested to treat sarcopenia and/or promote increased appetite or to serve as anabolic aids (Brass & Sietsema, 2011; Rolland et al., 2011). For example, appetite stimulants include the antidepressant mirtazapine, cyproheptadine, a serotonin, and a histamine antagonist, but there is the potential for confusion in older adults (Fox, Treadway, Blaszczyk, & Sleeper, 2009). Megestrol is a progestin that stimulates appetite, however, this weight gain is primarily fat, and clinical benefits to the patient have not been demonstrated (Yaxley, Miller, Fraser, & Cobiac, 2012). Megestrol acetate in nursing home populations can be associated with a higher risk of deep-vein thrombosis, fluid retention, edema, and exacerbation of congestive heart failure. Dronabinol, a cannabinoid, can stimulate appetite but it is associated with somnolence and dysphoria in older adults (M. Wilson, Philpot, & Morley, 2007). Cytokine-modulating agents are experimental in the treatment of undernutrition syndromes, although some anticytokines have been breakthrough treatments for selected forms of disease-related cachexia. Anabolic agents include human growth hormone, testosterone, and oxandrolone. While muscle mass has consistently improved with anabolic agents, significant improvements in strength, function, or a reduction in fractures have not been demonstrated.

Obesity and Aging Epidemiology

The growing prevalence of obesity in the United States extends to older adults in their sixties and seventies. According to National Health and Nutrition Examination Surveys (NHANES), the prevalence of obesity (BMI greater than or equal to 30 kg/m^2) has climbed from 14% to 33% between 1976 and 2011. Trends were similar for all ages, both genders, and all racial or ethnic groups; however, minority and lower socioeconomic status groups are disproportionally affected. The relationships among these risk factors are complex and dynamic (Wang & Beydoun, 2007). The aging of the U.S. society also affects the obesity epidemic in that aging adults have been obese in higher numbers and for longer periods of life than ever before (Hoffman, Lee, & Mendez-Luck, 2012). Additionally, their caregivers engage in poor health behaviors as a result of caregiving with increased smoking, sedentary behavior, regular consumption of high-sugar beverages, and high-energy and fat "fast" foods (Leveille, Wee, & Iezzoni, 2005).

Obesity and Health

Excess body weight and modest weight gain (greater than or equal to 5 kg) in middle age can be associated with medical comorbidities in later life that include hypertension, diabetes mellitus, cardiovascular disease, and osteoarthritis (Villareal, Apovian, Kushner, & Klein, 2005). Adverse outcomes associated with obesity include impaired functional status (especially with decreased muscle mass), increased use of health care resources, and increased mortality. The NHANES data suggest that measures of abdominal adiposity strongly and positively predict mortality, independent of BMI, among white and black adults (Reis et al., 2009). It has been shown that BMI greater than or equal to 35 kg/m^2 is associated with increased risk of functional decline among older adults (Rejeski, Marsh, Chmelo, & Rejeski, 2010). Of interest, poor quality of diet and micronutrient deficiencies are relatively common among obese older adults, especially obese older women living alone (Jensen, 2005). However, in older individuals, higher BMI may have a protective effect. In Finnish nonagenarians, waist circumference and BMI were positively correlated with survival (Lisko et al., 2011). Stevens et al. found that in persons 75 years of age or older, the mortality rate was lowest in people with BMIs of 27 to 29 (J. Stevens et al., 1998). Al Snih et al. found that in non-Hispanic white Americans, African Americans, and Mexican Americans 65 years of age or older, mortality was lowest in persons with BMIs 25 to 35 kg/m^2. However, the likelihood of disability during 7 years of follow-up was lowest in older adults with BMIs of 18.5 to 30 kg/m^2 (Al Snih et al., 2007).

MICRONUTRIENT AND DIETARY SUPPLEMENTATION

It has been estimated that 10% to 20% of the adult population in the United States regularly take an assortment of dietary supplements for a variety of reasons, including improving health, preventing disease, and feeling better (Park, Johnson, & Fischer, 2008; Sebastian, Cleveland, Goldman, & Moshfegh, 2007).

Vitamin and Mineral Supplements

The benefit of routine vitamin and mineral supplementation for healthy older adults is controversial; however, there is evidence that multivitamin/mineral supplements improve immune status in this population (Albright et al., 2012). Supplementation with a multivitamin containing at least the RDAs is recommended for seniors at risk for vitamin deficiency, since tests to diagnose early deficiencies can be difficult and expensive (Buhr & Bales, 2009).

To achieve optimal intakes of particular micronutrients, including vitamin B12, vitamin D, vitamin C, calcium, and magnesium, multivitamin–mineral supplements may be needed (McKay et al., 2000). Dietary preferences and/or sensitivities and intolerances to particular foods, such as dairy, may also necessitate the need for micronutrients. Despite the potential benefits associated with the use of multivitamin supplements, supplements providing high doses of antioxidants should be used with caution. In a meta-analysis (Bjelakovic, Nikolova, Simonetti, & Gluud, 2008), the use of antioxidant supplements for primary and secondary prevention was associated with an increase in mortality. Vitamins A and E ingested singly or combined with other antioxidants may increase mortality (Bjelakovic et al., 2008). Other micronutrients considered antioxidants, such as vitamin C and selenium, consumed singly, or in combination, had no significant impact on mortality risk (Bjelakovic et al., 2008). Several trials have reported that multivitamin–mineral use was associated with a higher risk for fatal prostate cancer when compared with no use of supplements (Lawson et al., 2007; V. L. Stevens et al., 2005; Watkins, Erickson, Thun, Mulinare, & Heath, 2000). Given the weight of this evidence and the associated increased risk in all-cause mortality with use of antioxidant supplements; they should be used judiciously in the older adult population (Miller et al., 2005).

Dietary Supplements

Supplements have been widely used in an effort to enhance nutrient intake, often when patients eat only small amounts. Standard supplements contain macro- and micronutrients. Many different oral formulations are available in both liquid and bar forms. They can be chosen based on patient preferences, chewing ability, or product cost. Oral formulas can also be selected based on their caloric density, osmolality, protein, fiber, or lactose content. Most formulas provide 1 to 1.5 kcal/mL and many are lactose- and/or gluten-free. However, it has yet to be demonstrated that any supplementation regimen is superior to regular food intake. Among supplements used, creatine has been shown to increase muscle mass and strength in older adults. However, the timing of creatine ingestion (e.g., 0.03–0.5 g per kg of body weight before and after resistance training sessions) may be more important than the quantity of creatine. These findings have immediate application for the design of optimal creatine application strategies for older individuals. For example, emphasizing commercial creatine or food products that contain dietary creatine (i.e., red meat, seafood) in close proximity to resistance training sessions may augment muscle mass and strength more largely than resistance training alone.

DIETARY PATTERNS AND BODY COMPOSITION

Dietary patterns may better capture the multifaceted effects of diet on body composition than individual nutrients or foods. Dietary pattern analysis examines the overall diet, and thus takes into account correlation among nutrient intakes as well as nutrient–nutrient interactions.

Dietary Patterns and Obesity

Several studies have examined dietary patterns of older adults and their associations with adiposity (Ryan, Martinez, Wysong, & Davis, 1989). For example, in a study of dietary patterns of rural men and women age 66 to 87 years in relation to weight, it was shown that those in a low-nutrient-dense cluster, with high intake of breads, sweet breads, and desserts, processed meats, eggs, and fats/oils, were twice as likely to be obese as those in a high-nutrient-dense cluster, with high intake of cereals, dark green/yellow vegetables, other vegetables, citrus/melons/berries, other fruits, milks, poultry, fish, and beans (Ledikwe, Smiciklas-Wright, Mitchell, Miller, & Jensen, 2004). A dietary pattern analysis of Mexican adults showed that diets with increased amounts of refined foods and dietary fat produced more obesity compared to the traditional Mexican diet (Denova-Gutiérrez et al., 2011; Flores et al., 2010). The

Baltimore Longitudinal Study of Aging (Newby, Muller, Hallfrisch, Andres, & Tucker, 2004) found a dietary pattern high in reduced-fat dairy products, fruit, and fiber to be inversely associated with annual change in BMI in women, and inversely associated with annual change in waist circumference in both sexes. Despite this evidence, the relationship between food intake patterns and obesity remains unclear. Diets characterized by more favorable dietary scores or indices are generally inversely related to BMI (Murtaugh et al., 2007). However, there is no clear relationship between food intake patterns and BMI or waist circumference in older adults. Limitations, including heterogeneity of food intake patterns and study populations, hinder the ability to make clear comparisons. It appears that a limited number of food groups predict diet quality and health outcomes in various population groups. In particular, fruit and vegetables, fish, whole-grain cereal, and legumes have protective effects; whereas sweets, processed meats, fried foods, fats and oils, and salty snacks have negative effect (Delisle, 2010).

Weight Management in Older Adults

The National Institutes of Health has suggested that "age alone should not preclude weight loss treatment for older adults." A careful evaluation of potential risks and benefits in the individual patient should guide management (Clinical Guidelines on the Identification, Evaluation, and Treatment of Overweight and Obesity in Adults: The Evidence Report, 1998). The focus must be on achieving a healthful weight to promote health, function, and quality of life. A combination of prudent diet, behavior modification, and activity or exercise may be appropriate for selected candidates. For frail, obese older adults, the emphasis may be better placed on preservation of strength and flexibility, rather than on weight reduction. Additionally, the American Diabetes Association has stated that the older patient who has good functional status is cognitively intact, and with significant life expectancy should have the same treatment goals as younger patients (Executive Summary: Standards of Medical Care in Diabetes—2012, 2012). Individuals not meeting these criteria should have treatment goals relaxed, using individualized criteria, and taking into account dexterity, frailty, and vision. Preventive strategies should be based on whether life expectancy is greater than the time-frame of the primary and secondary prevention goals (Executive Summary: Standards of Medical Care in Diabetes—2012, 2012) and any treatment that risks iatrogenic harm should be avoided. Involvement of the patient's social network reduces mortality and achieves better health outcomes.

CULTURALLY SENSITIVE NUTRITIONAL INTERVENTION TO OPTIMIZE HEALTH

Several factors influence the design of optimal nutritional intervention and may influence a person's ability to adopt and maintain new behavior. First, various psychological factors enable individuals to adopt as well as sustain new behaviors long term. In general, for initiating a behavior, persons' consideration of the anticipated benefits must compare favorably to their current situation, and they need to hold favorable expectancies regarding future outcomes (Rothman, 2000). The decision to maintain a behavior is dependent, at least in part, on whether the achieved outcomes associated with the new behavior pattern are sufficiently desirable to sustain the behavior (i.e., on the individual's perceived satisfaction with the outcomes of that behavior change; Artinian et al., 2010). Most individuals have clear expectations about what a new lifestyle will provide; if their experiences do not meet those expectations, they will be dissatisfied and less motivated to maintain it, particularly in cultural environments that are frequently not supportive of healthy choices. Other factors that may influence adoption and maintenance of new physical activity or dietary behavior include age, pain, depression, and comorbidities.

Aging and Cultural Barriers

Evidence suggests that older age per se does not significantly reduce the response to physical activity or dietary interventions. Older age may be associated with more healthful dietary patterns and better adherence, such as higher consumption of fruits (Howarth, Huang, Roberts,

Lin, & McCrory, 2007; Stables et al., 2002). In the Diabetes Prevention Program (DPP), the greatest risk reduction in response to the lifestyle intervention was seen in the oldest age group, suggesting better adherence and/or efficacy in this group. However, although older adults on average may have better adherence, some may have cultural barriers to overcome to achieve this adherence. For example, some older adults may be at particular risk for poor dietary habits, especially if they live alone and/or have low incomes. Although younger adults are more likely to cite time as the main constraint to exercise (Crespo, Ainsworth, Keteyian, Heath, & Smit, 1999; Marshall et al., 2007), older adults most frequently cite poor health, including pain, reduced mobility, and low endurance (Artinian et al., 2010).

Ethnicity and Race

Numerous racial and ethnic groups exist with diverse cultural norms, values, attitudes, beliefs, and lifestyle patterns in the United States. Interventions designed to change dietary and/or PA behavior in one population group may be less effective in another group, especially when the population is educationally or economically disadvantaged or differs in cultural health beliefs or practices from the population in which the intervention was initially tested. Optimally, methods to design or adapt interventions should be directly assessed in diverse populations and settings. For example, in a randomized controlled trial of weight reduction and exercise for diabetes management in older African American adults, Agurs-Collins and colleagues found that the intervention program focused on diet and physical activity was effective in improving glycemic and blood pressure control (Agurs-Collins, Kumanyika, Ten Have, & Adams-Campbell, 1997). In their study, the decrease in hemoglobin A1C values was generally independent of the relatively modest changes in dietary intake, weight, and activity and might have reflected indirect program effects on other aspects of self-care, including ethnicity.

Other studies showed that high-intensity progressive resistance training, in combination with moderate weight loss, was effective in improving glycemic control in older patients with type-2 diabetes (Dunstan et al., 2002). An interesting church-based intervention targeting metabolic risk for type-2 diabetes and cardiovascular disease was well received by participants and improved short-term metabolic control in older African American men and women (Samuel-Hodge et al., 2009). An adherence index based on the American Heart Association 2006 Diet and Lifestyle Recommendations was found to be associated with cardiovascular risk factors in older Puerto Ricans living in Massachusetts (Bhupathiraju, Lichtenstein, Dawson-Hughes, & Tucker, 2011).

Ethnicity and Diet Interventions

Relatively fewer studies evaluated samples other than white middle- or upper middle-class Americans. The most commonly studied minorities were African Americans and Hispanics. However, studies in Hispanic populations often did not adequately address linguistic competency. Although intervention studies have been conducted that included Asian American and Native American populations, in most, numbers were insufficient to conduct ethnic-specific subgroup analyses. It is important to recognize that additional diversity occurs within racial/ethnic groups, so that intervention designs should consider the potentially diverse values, beliefs, and socioeconomic characteristics within each group. Adhering to this notion, Schultz and colleagues (Schulz et al., 2006) reported that Pima Indians living in Mexico (traditional environments) have a much lower prevalence of type-2 diabetes and obesity than those living in the Westernized environment of the United States. Anecdotally, Northern Plains Indians have reported better control of their type-2 diabetes when following a diet that is higher in protein. A diet patterned after the historical hunter–gatherer type diet, or even the early reservation diet (with the higher proportion of energy being supplied from protein), may provide better blood glucose control and lower the circulating insulin levels in Northern Plains Indians with type 2 diabetes. Thus, the objective of the Kattelmann et al. study (Kattelmann, Conti, & Ren, 2010) was to determine whether Northern Plains Indians with type-2 diabetes exposed to a culturally based nutrition intervention would have better control of their type-2 diabetes and risk for cardiovascular disease. The participating adults were randomized to receive culturally adapted educational lessons based on the Medicine Wheel Model for Nutrition in addition to their usual dietary education and a nonintervention, or only the usual dietary education from their personal providers. The education group had a significant weight loss and decrease in BMI from baseline to completion. The usual care group had no change in weight or BMI. There were no between-group differences due to intervention in energy, carbohydrate, protein, and fat intake and physical activity. The culturally based nutrition intervention promoted small but positive changes in weight. The authors concluded that greater frequency and longer duration of educational support may be needed to influence blood glucose and lipid parameters (Kattelmann et al., 2010).

The Strong Heart Study, a longitudinal study of cardiovascular disease and its risk factors among 13 American Indian communities in four states (North Dakota, South Dakota, Oklahoma, and Arizona), examined the association between total physical activity (leisure-time plus occupational) and incident diabetes among 1,651 American Indians (Gilliland, Azen, Perez, & Carter, 2002). During 10 years of follow-up (from 1989–1999), it was observed that, compared with participants who reported no physical activity, those who reported any physical activity had a lower risk of diabetes after adjustment for age, sex, study site, education, smoking, alcohol use, and family history of diabetes. Further adjustment for body mass index and other potential mediators attenuated the risk estimates and suggested that physical activity is associated with a lower risk of incident diabetes among American Indians. This study identifies physical activity as an important determinant of diabetes and suggests the need for physical activity outreach programs that target inactive American Indians (Fretts et al., 2009).

In summary, for interventions in minority or socially and/or economically disadvantaged populations, an important consideration is identifying a setting to minimize barriers to accessing the intervention. Once access is established, interventions conducted in work sites, clinics, communities, and churches can lead to improved dietary intake and PA levels among minorities.

FOLK MEDICINE AND ILLNESS BELIEFS

Since ancient times, humans have known the healing power of certain plants. It is estimated that more than 25% of modern medicines come from plants and nature. Historically, populations with no access to physicians have relied on home remedies and folk healers (Newman, Cragg, & Snader, 2003). Even today, in some Asian and African countries, more than half of the population relies on folk healers. Belief in or preference for home remedies may persist and even conflict with modern medical practices.

Native American Culture

The five great values of Native American Indians include generosity and sharing, respect for elders and collective wisdom, harmony with nature, individual freedom, and courage (Sanchez, Plawecki, & Plawecki, 1996). Natural American pharmaceuticals include many botanical and herb compounds. U.S. Appalachian practices include use of barks, berries, and leaves in teas, as well as poultices made from plants and animal fat. Superstitions are also prevalent in mountain folk medicine (Fisher, 1997).

African American Culture

African American populations find spirituality an important source of emotional support during illness, and spiritual concerns greatly influence health care decisions (Polzer & Miles, 2005). A common belief among Ethiopian immigrants is that well-being is based on a balance of spiritual, physical, social, and environmental forces. Illness can be attributed to God, destiny, nature, demonic spirits, emotional stress, or a breach of social taboos or vows. Ethiopian medicine relies heavily on magical and supernatural beliefs, such as the belief that miscarriages are the result of demonic spirits (Ethiopians in Minnesota, 2012). Mental illness and some physical illnesses, such as epilepsy, are commonly attributed to evil spirits, with the view that these types of illnesses are a stigma. Many families do not disclose information to the community about family members with such illnesses for fear of being shunned. Men and women avoid marrying into families with members who are mentally ill or have other disabilities, and they generally resist psychiatric treatment for themselves and other family members. Ethiopians often use home-based therapies and herbal remedies to heal common ailments. They may use healing ingredients from animals, minerals, and plants, such as eucalyptus leaves, oil seeds, and spices.

There is no word for stress in the Somali language. Health prevention is practiced primarily through prayer and living a life according to Islam. Many Somalis believe that an individual cannot prevent illness, as the ultimate decision is in God's hands. They believe that illness may be caused by a communicable disease, by God, by spirit possession, or by the "evil eye." Mental illness is often believed to be caused by spirit possession or as a punishment from God (Fenta, Hyman, & Noh, 2007). Traditional spiritual healers use religious rituals for healing. Patients often wear amulets, believed to have medicinal value and to keep evil spirits away. Often, Somalis will not take medications such as anti-tubercular agents if they feel healthy.

Latino Culture

Many Latino immigrants believe in disease as destiny, fatalism, and often fear side effects of medications given to treat disease. Many expect the healer to cure the ailment, with difficulty comprehending the concept of chronic illness. This can greatly compromise the care of certain conditions such as diabetes. The hot and cold theory of disease traditionally held by Hispanic cultures is a continuing influence of ancient Greek and Arabic humoral pathology, which maintained that the four body "humors" regulated health and disease: blood, bile, and black and yellow bile, each characterized as warm or cold, wet or dry. Although disagreement exists within Latino populations, warm illnesses (kidney ailments, rashes, dysentery) are produced by the body and cold illnesses (pain, paralysis, stomachache) are produced by outside influences. Warm illnesses are treated by avoiding cold foods (vegetables, dairy products, tropical fruits), and cold illnesses treated by avoiding warm foods (lamb, beef, grains, temperate fruits; Cersosimo & Musi, 2011; Cusi & Ocampo, 2011).

Eastern European Culture

Immigrants from Eastern Europe may be distrustful of physicians and reject health recommendations, such as refusing to take medications as prescribed or combining medications and therapies with home remedies and treatments. Home remedies are often used before seeking medical attention, such as oil rubs, mud or steam baths, and exposure to fresh air and sunlight (Russians in Minnesota, 2012). The "*bonki*" is a cold and flu remedy where glass cups are pressed on a sick person's back and shoulders to ease symptoms. The *bonki* often leaves behind bruises and welts, which may be misinterpreted as a sign of physical abuse.

Asian Culture

Traditional East Asian health beliefs are often linked to Traditional Chinese Medicine (TCM), with 75% to 100% of Asian Americans reporting using TCM, primarily herbal medicine (Wu, Burke, & LeBaron, 2007). Approaches, in addition to various forms of herbal medicine, include acupuncture, massage (*Tui na*), exercise (*qigong*), and dietary therapy. The TCM is mainly concerned with the identification of functional entities (which regulate digestion, breathing, aging, etc.). While health is perceived as harmonious interaction of these entities and the outside world, disease is interpreted as a disharmony in interaction. Health concerns driving the use of TCM therapies are primarily those of chronic pain, musculoskeletal problems, and mood disturbances, including back and neck pain, joint pain and stiffness, headaches, anxiety, and depression (Manheimer, Wieland, Kimbrough, Cheng, & Berman, 2009).

Hindu immigrants mostly from India believe good health involves a balance between self-control and meditation in harmony with nature. Nutrition beliefs include classification of foods as *tamasic*: spoiled or left over, producing negative emotions; *rajasic*: strong emotions and passions, represented by eggs, fish, spices; and *sattvic*: most desirable, nonirritating, represented by fruits, whole grains, and vegetables. Indian immigrants may also use faith and spiritual healing, including ritual acts and reciting charms, and the belief that yoga eliminates certain physical and mental illnesses (Mahadevan & Blair, 2009). Hindus and Sikhs believe that disease is due to karma, the result of one's actions in past lives. They may also attribute illness to body imbalances, which create toxins that can accumulate in weaker areas of the body, resulting in conditions such as arthritis. Many older Indian immigrants use home remedies based on the Indian medicine system called Ayurveda (knowledge of life/health), which uses spices and herbs for cold, congestion, diabetes, and heart problems (Brar et al., 2012; Sridharan, Mohan, Ramaratnam, & Panneerselvam, 2011). Remedies may include turmeric paste as an antiseptic, ginger and lime juice for stomachache, and buttermilk stored in an iron utensil for anemia.

Khmer immigrants who subscribe to traditional beliefs attribute illness to natural or supernatural powers. Illness may be considered punishment for sins committed in a past life. Many believe that evil spirits or ancestors cause mental illness. Khmer may seek traditional practices before they seek Western medicine, and often hold traditional healing ceremonies in the home. They may reject or not appreciate the value of preventive care, screening, or early detection. Khmer are known for enduring pain stoically. Rather than asking general questions about pain or symptoms, clinicians should ask very specific questions. Common treatments for pain include herbal medicines, acupuncture, acupressure, cupping, coining, and use of Tiger Balm (Schattner & Randerson, 1996). In cupping and coining, cutaneous hematomas are made on the face and trunk by pinching and pulling the skin to release excessive air. Coining refers to rubbing oiled skin with a coin or spoon, and cupping refers to heating air in a cup with a flame, then placing the cup onto the skin. As the air in a cup cools, it contracts and pulls on the skin, leaving a purple mark.

Many Vietnamese immigrants believe that Asian people are different physiologically from white people. Western medicines are thought of as "hot" and too potent for their physiology. As a result, they may not take medicines as prescribed. Many people attribute symptoms to a physical weakness; for example, a weak heart is expressed by panic, palpitations, and dizziness; a weak kidney is expressed by impotence; a weak stomach or liver is expressed by indigestion; and a weak nervous system is expressed by headache or lack of concentration. Many elders do not trust Western medicine and use it only as a last resort (Najm, Reinsch, Hoehler, & Tobis, 2003). They use traditional remedies as well as Western medicines but may not reveal this to a provider. Vietnamese patients often resist invasive procedures and immunizations, and see a provider who does not intrude on the body as the best healer. Some patients believe a physician should be able to diagnose a problem by looking at them and feeling their pulse. Vietnamese also believe in the medicinal properties of specific foods, such as mung beans, green beans, and bitter melon, which are believed to help control high blood pressure. Acupuncture is used widely for arthritis pain, stroke, visual problems, and other ailments (Rich & Dimond, 2009).

Although Hmong immigrants to the United States have been exposed to Western medicine since the 1950s, they traditionally view illness from a holistic perspective, with perfect health being a balance between the spirit and the body. Good health comes from the souls living within each person. When a person is ill, they seek the help of a shaman to determine whether the cause of the illness is within the realm of the spirit. Spiritual causes require religious remedies. Traditional spiritual causes of illness may include evil spirits or because one's own spirit has left the body (Gerdner, Cha, Yang, & Tripp-Reimer, 2007). A person may be ill because an ancestor or evil spirit is unhappy with them or their family or because someone cursed the family or offended the family's ancestors or spirits. The sick person may accept either the appropriate Hmong medicine or treatment, or the Western approach. Some

Hmong people will not communicate dissatisfaction with the quality of health care they receive. If they are dissatisfied with their care, they may refuse care and turn to traditional treatments. Older Hmong may listen attentively to health professionals, but avoid direct eye contact, which is considered rude. Many Hmong practice spiritual healing, which involves retrieving the lost soul from another plane of existence. They may consider an illness or an invasive surgical procedure to be the cause of soul loss. Hmong may conduct healing ceremonies in the hospital or in the home. Herbal medicine and traditional healing practices are often widely used before a person seeks Western medical remedies (Srithi, Trisonthi, Wangpakapattanawong, & Balslev, 2012).

NUTRITION EDUCATION

Among the significant challenges that nutrition educators face today and are likely to face in the immediate future are the increasingly diverse population of older adults, and increased emphasis on individualized behavioral change as components of personalized health care. For example, a culturally based diabetes nutrition intervention promoted small but positive changes in weight among Northern Plains Indians (Kattelmann et al., 2010). Sensitivity to cultural differences in the United States and in those of different ethnic backgrounds is an important aspect of competence in reaching a diverse population. Nutrition educators would likely be evaluated on their ability to generate desirable behavioral changes in older patients from a variety of cultural backgrounds. In the current and future environment, multicultural competence in relation to food intake, attitudes, and behavior would be considered an important skill and perhaps a requirement (Sindler, 2001). Understanding the "culture" and its relationship to food preferences could help health professionals and nutrition educators improve the quality of their services to all populations, including older adults. Education should emphasize the health value of indigenous foods and take advantage of the growing interest in preserving traditional customs and skills.

Multicultural Nutrition Counseling

It occurs when a nutrition professional and client are from different cultures. Ethnicity, religion, group affiliation, socioeconomic status, and world-view may all influence clients' needs (Sindler, 2001). Gaining insight into what competencies are important for multicultural nutrition counseling can help ensure cultural proficiency in counseling. Harris-Davis and Haughton developed and tested a model for multicultural nutrition counseling competencies for registered dietitians (Harris-Davis & Haughton, 2000). From their model, 28 competencies emerged in three groups as summarized below:

Multicultural nutritional counseling skills:

- have ability to differentiate between individual and universal similarities;
- be experienced in application of medical nutrition therapy and nutrition-related health promotion/disease prevention strategies that are culturally appropriate;
- have ability to use cultural knowledge and sensitivity for appropriate nutrition intervention and materials;
- take responsibility of collectively working with community leaders or members about unique knowledge or abilities for benefit of the culturally different client; and
- be able to evaluate new techniques, research, and knowledge as to validity and applicability in working with culturally different populations.

Multicultural awareness:

- be aware of how one's own cultural background and experiences and attitudes, values, and biases influence nutrition counseling;
- be able to recognize limits of one's own cultural competencies and abilities;
- be able to value and respect cultural differences;
- have multicultural food and nutrition counseling knowledge;

- understand food selection, preparation, and storage within a cultural context;
- have knowledge of cultural eating patterns and family traditions such as core foods, traditional celebrations, and fasting; and
- familiarize self with relevant research and latest findings regarding food practices and nutrition-related health problems of various ethnic and racial groups.

Careful attention should also be paid to nutrition education materials. "Ideally, written materials in other languages should reflect the dialectic and cultural nuances of the target population" (Harris-Davis & Haughton, 2000). Nutrition education resources that reflect an awareness of these details and the educational and literacy level of the target audience require a more sensitive approach than mere text translation. The best process involves developing materials from scratch in the target language based on discussions with focus groups representing the target population. The material should reflect an appreciation of the cultural norms of that population, especially when used to motivate behavior change (Sindler, 2001).

CONCLUSIONS AND KEY POINTS

Life span is greatly influenced by lifestyle. Nutrition is integrally related to lifestyle and influences the age trajectory. Nutrition health disparities are growing and must be addressed as the diversity of the U.S. population increases and society ages. Positive dietary and physical activity behaviors should be promoted during critical preventive ages, when racial/ethnic disparities are large and the potential to prevent chronic disease is higher than later in life. There is a wealth of healthy culturally appropriate nutrition resources, which should be used to improve the health of the population. The influence of traditional beliefs and folk medicine is variable in different populations and may affect the outcome of standard of care treatments for many illnesses and chronic diseases. Nutritional supplementation and feeding modalities should be tailored to disease state, promote health, and be applied in accord with ethical principles in keeping with defined goals and informed patient choices.

Further research on dietary patterns and their healthfulness is in ethnic and cultural population groups. In general, traditional dietary patterns are healthier than the patterns that have evolved with globalization, urbanization, or acculturation, although micronutrient intakes need to improve. Additionally, healthy eating patterns are only feasible if access to food supply is adequate. Studies on the role of specific macronutrients, as well as longitudinal analysis on the change of dietary habits as related to development or progression of physiologic dysregulation, could help identify specific mechanisms by which nutrients affect physiology of aging. Genetic contributions to understanding nutrition and nutritional interventions may improve our ability to deliver personalized nutritional care.

REFERENCES

Abaterusso, C., Lupo, A., Ortalda, V., De Biase, V., Pani, A., Muggeo, M., & Gambaro, G. (2008). Treating elderly people with diabetes and stages 3 and 4 chronic kidney disease. *Clinical Journal of the American Society of Nephrology, 3*(4), 1185–1194.

Aging, A. O. (2012). Minority aging. http://www.aoa.gov/aoaroot/aging_statistics/minority_aging/Index.aspx. Retrieved May 31, 2012, from http://www.aoa.gov/aoaroot/aging_statistics/minority_aging/Index.aspx

Agurs-Collins, T. D., Kumanyika, S. K., Ten Have, T. R., & Adams-Campbell, L. L. (1997). A randomized controlled trial of weight reduction and exercise for diabetes management in older African-American subjects. *Diabetes Care, 20*(10), 1503–1511.

Ahmed, T., & Haboubi, N. (2010). Assessment and management of nutrition in older people and its importance to health. *Clinical Interventions in Aging, 5*, 207–216.

Al Snih, S., Ottenbacher, K. J., Markides, K. S., Kuo, Y. F., Eschbach, K., & Goodwin, J. S. (2007). The effect of obesity on disability vs mortality in older Americans. *Archives of Internal Medicine, 167*(8), 774–780.

Albright, C. L., Schembre, S. M., Steffen, A. D., Wilkens, L. R., Monroe, K. R., Yonemori, K. M., & Murphy, S. P. (2012). Differences by race/ethnicity in older adults' beliefs about the relative importance of dietary supplements vs prescription medications: Results from the SURE Study. *Journal of the Academy of Nutrition and Dietetics, 112*(8), 1223–1229.

Aronow, W. S., & Frishman, W. H. (2010). Management of hypercholesterolemia in older persons for the prevention of cardiovascular disease. *Cardiology in Review, 18*(3), 132–140.

Artinian, N. T., Fletcher, G. F., Mozaffarian, D., Kris-Etherton, P., Van Horn, L., Lichtenstein, A. H., . . . Burke, L. E. (2010). Interventions to promote physical activity and dietary lifestyle changes for cardiovascular risk factor reduction in adults: A scientific statement from the American Heart Association. *Circulation, 122*(4), 406–441.

Aslam, F., Haque, A., Lee, L. V., & Foody, J. (2009). Hyperlipidemia in older adults. *Clinics in Geriatric Medicine, 25*(4), 591–606.

August, K. J., & Sorkin, D. H. (2011). Racial/ethnic disparities in exercise and dietary behaviors of middle-aged and older adults. *Journal of General Internal Medicine, 26*(3), 245–250.

Bach, A., Serra-Majem, L., Carrasco, J. L., Roman, B., Ngo, J., Bertomeu, I., & Obrador, B. (2006). The use of indexes evaluating the adherence to the Mediterranean diet in epidemiological studies: A review. *Public Health Nutrition, 9*(1A), 132–146.

Baker, L. B., Munce, T. A., & Kenney, W. L. (2005). Sex differences in voluntary fluid intake by older adults during exercise. *Medicine and Science in Sports and Exercise, 37*(5), 789–796.

Ballew, C., White, L. L., Strauss, K. F., Benson, L. J., Mendlein, J. M., & Mokdad, A. H. (1997). Intake of nutrients and food sources of nutrients among the Navajo: Findings from the Navajo Health and Nutrition Survey. *The Journal of Nutrition, 127*(10 Suppl), 2085S–2093S.

Batis, C., Hernandez-Barrera, L., Barquera, S., Rivera, J. A., & Popkin, B. M. (2011). Food acculturation drives dietary differences among Mexicans, Mexican Americans, and Non-Hispanic Whites. *The Journal of Nutrition, 141*(10), 1898–1906.

Berg, C. J., Daley, C. M., Nazir, N., Kinlacheeny, J. B., Ashley, A., Ahluwalia, J. S., . . . Choi, W. S. (2012). Physical activity and fruit and vegetable intake among American Indians. *Journal of Community Health, 37*(1), 65–71.

Bhan, A., Rao, A. D., & Rao, D. S. (2010). Osteomalacia as a result of vitamin D deficiency. *Endocrinology and Metabolism Clinics of North America, 39*(2), 321–31, table of contents.

Bhupathiraju, S. N., Lichtenstein, A. H., Dawson-Hughes, B., & Tucker, K. L. (2011). Adherence index based on the AHA 2006 diet and lifestyle recommendations is associated with select cardiovascular disease risk factors in older Puerto Ricans. *The Journal of Nutrition, 141*(3), 460–469.

Bischoff-Ferrari, H. A., Willett, W. C., Orav, E. J., Oray, E. J., Lips, P., Meunier, P. J., . . . Dawson-Hughes, B. (2012). A pooled analysis of vitamin D dose requirements for fracture prevention. *The New England Journal of Medicine, 367*(1), 40–49.

Bjelakovic, G., Nikolova, D., Simonetti, R., & Gluud, C. (2008). Antioxidant supplements for preventing gastrointestinal cancers. *Cochrane Database of Systematic Reviews, 16*(3), CD004183.

Brand, J. C., Snow, B. J., Nabhan, G. P., & Truswell, A. S. (1990). Plasma glucose and insulin responses to traditional Pima Indian meals. *The American Journal of Clinical Nutrition, 51*(3), 416–420.

Brar, B. S., Chhibber, R., Srinivasa, V. M., Dearing, B. A., McGowan, R., & Katz, R. V. (2012). Use of Ayurvedic diagnostic criteria in Ayurvedic clinical trials: A literature review focused on research methods. *Journal of Alternative and Complementary Medicine, 18*(1), 20–28.

Brass, E. P., & Sietsema, K. E. (2011). Considerations in the development of drugs to treat sarcopenia. *Journal of the American Geriatrics Society, 59*(3), 530–535.

Bressler, J., Kao, W. H., Pankow, J. S., & Boerwinkle, E. (2010). Risk of type 2 diabetes and obesity is differentially associated with variation in *FTO* in whites and African-Americans in the ARIC study. *Plos One, 5*(5), e10521.

Brownie, S. (2006). Why are elderly individuals at risk of nutritional deficiency? *International Journal of Nursing Practice, 12*(2), 110–118.

Buchowski, M. S., & Sun, M. (1996). Nutrition in minority elders: Current problems and future directions. *Journal of Health Care For the Poor and Underserved, 7*(3), 184–209.

Buhr, G., & Bales, C. W. (2009). Nutritional supplements for older adults: Review and recommendations-part I. *Journal of Nutrition For the Elderly*, *28*(1), 5–29.

Calzada, P. J., & Anderson-Worts, P. (2009). The obesity epidemic: Are minority individuals equally affected? *Primary Care*, *36*(2), 307–317.

Candow, D. G. (2011). Sarcopenia: Current theories and the potential beneficial effect of creatine application strategies. *Biogerontology*, *12*(4), 273–281. doi: 10.1007/s10522–011–9327–6

Casey, M. M., Thiede Call, K., & Klingner, J. M. (2001). Are rural residents less likely to obtain recommended preventive healthcare services? *American Journal of Preventive Medicine*, *21*(3), 182–188.

Cederholm, T. E., Bauer, J. M., Boirie, Y., Schneider, S. M., Sieber, C. C., & Rolland, Y. (2011). Toward a definition of sarcopenia. *Clinics in Geriatric Medicine*, *27*(3), 341–353.

Cersosimo, E., & Musi, N. (2011). Improving treatment in Hispanic/Latino patients. *The American Journal of Medicine*, *124*(10 Suppl), S16–S21.

Chalé, A., Unanski, A. G., & Liang, R. Y. (2012). Nutrition initiatives in the context of population aging: Where does the United States stand? *Journal of Nutrition in Gerontology and Geriatrics*, *31*(1), 1–15.

Chapman, I. M. (2006). Nutritional disorders in the elderly. *The Medical Clinics of North America*, *90*(5), 887–907.

Chen, R., Corona, E., Sikora, M., Dudley, J. T., Morgan, A. A., Moreno-Estrada, A.,...Butte, A. J. (2012). Type 2 diabetes risk alleles demonstrate extreme directional differentiation among human populations, compared to other diseases. *Plos Genetics*, *8*(4), e1002621.

ChooseMyPlate. (2011). April 4, 2011, from http://www.choosemyplate.gov/healthy-eating-tips.html

Clinical Guidelines on the Identification, Evaluation, and Treatment of Overweight and Obesity in Adults: The Evidence Report. (1998). In N. H. L. a. B. Institute (Ed.), Obesity and Physical Activity-Guidelines (Vol. 98–4083). Bethesda, MD: National Institutes of Health. Retrieved from http://www.nhlbi.nih.gov/guidelines/obesity/ob_gdlns.htm

Combaret, L., Dardevet, D., Béchet, D., Taillandier, D., Mosoni, L., & Attaix, D. (2009). Skeletal muscle proteolysis in aging. *Current Opinion in Clinical Nutrition and Metabolic Care*, *12*(1), 37–41.

Corella, D., Arnett, D. K., Tucker, K. L., Kabagambe, E. K., Tsai, M., Parnell, L. D.,...Ordovas, J. M. (2011). A high intake of saturated fatty acids strengthens the association between the fat mass and obesity-associated gene and BMI. *The Journal of Nutrition*, *141*(12), 2219–2225.

Cree, M. G., Newcomer, B. R., Katsanos, C. S., Sheffield-Moore, M., Chinkes, D., Aarsland A.,...Wolfe, R. R. (2004). Intramuscular and liver triglycerides are increased in the elderly. *The Journal of Clinical Endocrinology and Metabolism*, *89*(8), 3864–3871.

Crespo, C. J., Ainsworth, B. E., Keteyian, S. J., Heath, G. W., & Smit, E. (1999). Prevalence of physical inactivity and its relation to social class in U.S. adults: Results from the Third National Health and Nutrition Examination Survey, 1988–1994. *Medicine and Science in Sports and Exercise*, *31*(12), 1821–1827.

Cusi, K., & Ocampo, G. L. (2011). Unmet Needs in Hispanic/Latino Patients with Type 2 Diabetes Mellitus. *The American Journal of Medicine*, *124*, S2–S9. doi: 10.1016/j.amjmed.2011.07.017

Dali-Youcef, N., & Andrès, E. (2009). An update on cobalamin deficiency in adults. *Qjm: Monthly Journal of The Association of Physicians*, *102*(1), 17–28.

de Lorgeril, M., & Salen, P. (2006). The Mediterranean-style diet for the prevention of cardiovascular diseases. *Public Health Nutrition*, *9*(1A), 118–123. doi: 10.1079/PHN2005933

Delisle, H. (2010). Findings on dietary patterns in different groups of African origin undergoing nutrition transition. *Applied Physiology, Nutrition, and Metabolism = Physiologie Appliquée, Nutrition Et Métabolisme*, *35*(2), 224–228.

Denova-Gutiérrez, E., Castañón, S., Talavera, J. O., Flores, M., Macías, N., Rodríguez-Ramírez, S., ...Salmerón, J. (2011). Dietary patterns are associated with different indexes of adiposity and obesity in an urban Mexican population. *The Journal of Nutrition*, *141*(5), 921–927.

Dietary Reference Intakes for Energy, Carbohydrate, Fiber, Fat, Fatty Acids, Cholesterol, Protein, and Amino Acids (Macronutrients). (2005). In F. a. N. B. Institute of Medicine (Ed.). Washington, DC: National Academy Press.

Dina, C., Meyre, D., Gallina, S., Durand, E., Körner, A., Jacobson, P.,...Froguel, P. (2007). Variation in *FTO* contributes to childhood obesity and severe adult obesity. *Nature Genetics*, *39*(6), 724–726.

Dini, V., Bertone, M., & Romanelli, M. (2006). Prevention and management of pressure ulcers. *Dermatologic Therapy, 19*(6), 356–364.

Dixon, L. B., Subar, A. F., Peters, U., Weissfeld, J. L., Bresalier, R. S., Risch, A.,...Hayes, R. B. (2007). Adherence to the USDA Food Guide, DASH Eating Plan, and Mediterranean dietary pattern reduces risk of colorectal adenoma. *The Journal of Nutrition, 137*(11), 2443–2450.

Dunstan, D. W., Daly, R. M., Owen, N., Jolley, D., De Courten, M., Shaw, J., & Zimmet, P. (2002). High-intensity resistance training improves glycemic control in older patients with type 2 diabetes. *Diabetes Care, 25*(10), 1729–1736.

Ethiopians in Minnesota. (2012). Retrieved June 25, 2012, from http://www.culturecareconnection.org/matters/diversity/ethiopian.html

Evans, W. J. (1995). What is sarcopenia? *The Journals of Gerontology, 50,* 5–8.

Executive Summary: Standards of Medical Care in Diabetes—2012. (2012). *Diabetes Care, 35,* S4–S10. doi: 10.2337/dc12-s004

Fawcett, K. A., & Barroso, I. (2010). The genetics of obesity: *FTO* leads the way. *Trends in Genetics, 26*(6), 266–274.

Féart, C., Samieri, C., Rondeau, V., Amieva, H., Portet, F., Dartigues, J. F.,...Barberger-Gateau, P. (2009). Adherence to a Mediterranean diet, cognitive decline, and risk of dementia. *JAMA, 302*(6), 638–648.

Fenta, H., Hyman, I., & Noh, S. (2007). Health service utilization by Ethiopian immigrants and refugees in Toronto. *Journal of Immigrant and Minority Health/Center for Minority Public Health, 9*(4), 349–357.

Fisher , P. (1997). Folk medicine. *West Virginia Historical Society Quarterly, 11*(1). Available from: http://www.wvculture.org/history/wvhssoc.html

Flores, M., Macias, N., Rivera, M., Lozada, A., Barquera, S., Rivera-Dommarco, J., & Tucker, K. L. (2010). Dietary patterns in Mexican adults are associated with risk of being overweight or obese. *The Journal of Nutrition, 140*(10), 1869–1873.

Fogerty, M., Guy, J., Barbul, A., Nanney, L. B., & Abumrad, N. N. (2009). African Americans show increased risk for pressure ulcers: A retrospective analysis of acute care hospitals in America. *Wound Repair and Regeneration, 17*(5), 678–684.

Fox, C. B., Treadway, A. K., Blaszczyk, A. T., & Sleeper, R. B. (2009). Megestrol acetate and mirtazapine for the treatment of unplanned weight loss in the elderly. *Pharmacotherapy, 29*(4), 383–397.

Fretts, A. M., Howard, B. V., Kriska, A. M., Smith, N. L., Lumley, T., Lee, E. T.,...Siscovick, D. (2009). Physical activity and incident diabetes in American Indians: The Strong Heart Study. *American Journal of Epidemiology, 170*(5), 632–639.

Fung, T. T., Rexrode, K. M., Mantzoros, C. S., Manson, J. E., Willett, W. C., & Hu, F. B. (2009). Mediterranean diet and incidence of and mortality from coronary heart disease and stroke in women. *Circulation, 119*(8), 1093–1100.

Gerdner, L. A., Cha, D., Yang, D., & Tripp-Reimer, T. (2007). The circle of life: End-of-life care and death rituals for Hmong-American elders. *Journal of Gerontological Nursing, 33*(5), 20–9; quiz 30.

Gilliland, S. S., Azen, S. P., Perez, G. E., & Carter, J. S. (2002). Strong in body and spirit: Lifestyle intervention for Native American adults with diabetes in New Mexico. *Diabetes Care, 25*(1), 78–83.

Gittelsohn, J., Wolever, T. M., Harris, S. B., Harris-Giraldo, R., Hanley, A. J., & Zinman, B. (1998). Specific patterns of food consumption and preparation are associated with diabetes and obesity in a Native Canadian community. *The Journal of Nutrition, 128*(3), 541–547.

Grau, K., Hansen, T., Holst, C., Astrup, A., Saris, W. H., Arner, P.,...Sørensen, T. I. (2009). Macronutrient-specific effect of *FTO* rs9939609 in response to a 10-week randomized hypo-energetic diet among obese Europeans. *International Journal of Obesity, 33*(11), 1227–1234.

Greenberg, M. R., Schneider, D., Northridge, M. E., & Ganz, M. L. (1998). Region of birth and black diets: The Harlem Household Survey. *American Journal of Public Health, 88*(8), 1199–1202.

Guenther, P. M., Reedy, J., & Krebs-Smith, S. M. (2008). Development of the Healthy Eating Index-2005. *Journal of The American Dietetic Association, 108*(11), 1896–1901.

Guigoz, Y. (2006). The Mini Nutritional Assessment (MNA) review of the literature–What does it tell us? *The Journal of Nutrition, Health & Aging, 10*(6), 466–85; discussion 485.

Guralnik, J. M., Eisenstaedt, R. S., Ferrucci, L., Klein, H. G., & Woodman, R. C. (2004). Prevalence of anemia in persons 65 years and older in the United States: Evidence for a high rate of unexplained anemia. *Blood*, *104*(8), 2263–2268.

Hajjar, R., Kamel, H., & Denson, K. (2004). Malnutrition in aging. *The Internet Journal of Geriatrics and Gerontology*, *1*(1).

Han, T. S., Tajar, A., & Lean, M. E. (2011). Obesity and weight management in the elderly. *British Medical Bulletin*, *97*, 169–196.

Harris-Davis, E., & Haughton, B. (2000). Model for multicultural nutrition counseling competencies. *Journal of the American Dietetic Association*, *100*(10), 1178–1185.

Hendrix, S. J., Fischer, J. G., Reddy, R. D., Lommel, T. S., Speer, E. M., Stephens, H., … Johnson, M. A. (2008). Fruit and vegetable intake and knowledge increased following a community-based intervention in older adults in Georgia senior centers. *Journal of Nutrition For the Elderly*, *27*(1–2), 155–178.

Hickson, M. (2006). Malnutrition and ageing. *Postgraduate Medical Journal*, *82*(963), 2–8.

Hoffman, G. J., Lee, J., & Mendez-Luck, C. A. (2012). Health behaviors among Baby Boomer informal caregivers. *The Gerontologist*, *52*(2), 219–230.

Howarth, N. C., Huang, T. T., Roberts, S. B., Lin, B. H., & McCrory, M. A. (2007). Eating patterns and dietary composition in relation to BMI in younger and older adults. *International Journal of Obesity*, *31*(4), 675–684.

Jensen, G. L. (2005). Obesity and functional decline: Epidemiology and geriatric consequences. *Clinics in Geriatric Medicine*, *21*(4), 677–687.

Johnstone, A. M., Rance, K. A., Murison, S. D., Duncan, J. S., & Speakman, J. R. (2006). Additional anthropometric measures may improve the predictability of basal metabolic rate in adult subjects. *European Journal of Clinical Nutrition*, *60*(12), 1437–1444.

Kattelmann, K. K., Conti, K., & Ren, C. (2010). The Medicine Wheel nutrition intervention: A diabetes education study with the Cheyenne River Sioux Tribe. *Journal of the American Dietetic Association*, *110*(5 Suppl), S44–S51.

Kenney, W. L., & Chiu, P. (2001). Influence of age on thirst and fluid intake. *Medicine and Science in Sports and Exercise*, *33*(9), 1524–1532.

Knoops, K. T., de Groot, L. C., Kromhout, D., Perrin, A. E., Moreiras-Varela, O., Menotti, A., & van Staveren, W. A. (2004). Mediterranean diet, lifestyle factors, and 10-year mortality in elderly European men and women: The HALE project. *JAMA*, *292*(12), 1433–1439.

Kukkonen-Harjula, K. T., Borg, P. T., Nenonen, A. M., & Fogelholm, M. G. (2005). Effects of a weight maintenance program with or without exercise on the metabolic syndrome: A randomized trial in obese men. *Preventive Medicine*, *41*(3–4), 784–790.

Kumanyika, S. K. (1993). Diet and nutrition as influences on the morbidity/mortality gap. *Annals of Epidemiology*, *3*(2), 154–158.

Kyle, U. G., Unger, P., Mensi, N., Genton, L., & Pichard, C. (2002). Nutrition status in patients younger and older than 60 y at hospital admission: A controlled population study in 995 subjects. *Nutrition*, *18*(6), 463–469.

Lai, J. K., Lucas, R. M., Clements, M. S., Roddam, A. W., & Banks, E. (2010). Hip fracture risk in relation to vitamin D supplementation and serum 25-hydroxyvitamin D levels: A systematic review and meta-analysis of randomised controlled trials and observational studies. *BMC Public Health*, *10*, 331.

Lang, G. (1990). *Talking about a new illness with the Dakota. Reflections on diabetes, food, and culture*. Lanham, MD: University Press of America.

Lawson, K. A., Wright, M. E., Subar, A., Mouw, T., Hollenbeck, A., Schatzkin, A., & Leitzmann, M. F. (2007). Multivitamin use and risk of prostate cancer in the National Institutes of Health-AARP Diet and Health Study. *Journal of the National Cancer Institute*, *99*(10), 754–764.

Lear, S. A., Deng, W. Q., Paré, G., Sulistyoningrum, D. C., Loos, R. J., & Devlin, A. (2011). Associations of the *FTO* rs9939609 variant with discrete body fat depots and dietary intake in a multi-ethnic cohort. *Genetics Research*, *93*(6), 419–426.

Ledikwe, J. H., Smiciklas-Wright, H., Mitchell, D. C., Miller, C. K., & Jensen, G. L. (2004). Dietary patterns of rural older adults are associated with weight and nutritional status. *Journal of the American Geriatrics Society*, *52*(4), 589–595.

Leveille, S. G., Wee, C. C., & Iezzoni, L. I. (2005). Trends in obesity and arthritis among baby boomers and their predecessors, 1971–2002. *American Journal of Public Health, 95*(9), 1607–1613.

Lichtenstein, A. H., Rasmussen, H., Yu, W. W., Epstein, S. R., & Russell, R. M. (2008). Modified MyPyramid for Older Adults. *The Journal of Nutrition, 138*(1), 5–11.

Lisko, I., Tiainen, K., Stenholm, S., Luukkaala, T., Hervonen, A., & Jylhä, M. (2011). Body mass index, waist circumference, and waist-to-hip ratio as predictors of mortality in nonagenarians: The Vitality 90+ Study. *The Journals of Gerontology, 66*(11), 1244–1250.

Little, M. O. (2011). Hypertension: How does management change with aging? *The Medical Clinics of North America, 95*(3), 525–537.

Louie, G. H., & Ward, M. M. (2011). Socioeconomic and ethnic differences in disease burden and disparities in physical function in older adults. *American Journal of Public Health, 101*(7), 1322–1329.

Lopez, A., Mathers, C., Ezzati, M., & Jamison, D. (2006). *Measuring the global burden of disease and risk factors in global burden of disease and risk*. Washington, DC: World Bank.

Lustgarten, M. S., & Fielding, R. A. (2011). Assessment of analytical methods used to measure changes in body composition in the elderly and recommendations for their use in phase II clinical trials. *The Journal of Nutrition, Health & Aging, 15*(5), 368–375.

Mahadevan, M., & Blair, D. (2009). Changes in food habits of south Indian Hindu Brahmin immigrants in State College, PA. *Ecology of Food and Nutrition, 48*(5), 404–432.

Malouf, M., Grimley, E., & Areosa, S. (2008). Folic acid with or without vitamin B12 for cognition and dementia. *Cochrane Database of Systematic Reviews, 4*(4), CD004514.

Manheimer, E., Wieland, S., Kimbrough, E., Cheng, K., & Berman, B. M. (2009). Evidence from the cochrane collaboration for traditional Chinese medicine therapies. *Journal of Alternative and Complementary Medicine, 15*(9), 1001–1014.

Marshall, S. J., Jones, D. A., Ainsworth, B. E., Reis, J. P., Levy, S. S., & Macera, C. A. (2007). Race/ethnicity, social class, and leisure-time physical inactivity. *Medicine and Science in Sports and Exercise, 39*(1), 44–51.

Marzetti, E., Lees, H. A., Wohlgemuth, S. E., & Leeuwenburgh, C. (2009). Sarcopenia of aging: Underlying cellular mechanisms and protection by calorie restriction. *BioFactors, 35*(1), 28–35.

Mattei, J., Noel, S. E., & Tucker, K. L. (2011). A meat, processed meat, and french fries dietary pattern is associated with high allostatic load in Puerto Rican older adults. *Journal of the American Dietetic Association, 111*(10), 1498–1506.

Mattei, J., Parnell, L. D., Lai, C. Q., Garcia-Bailo, B., Adiconis, X., Shen, J., ... Ordovas, J. M. (2009). Disparities in allele frequencies and population differentiation for 101 disease-associated single nucleotide polymorphisms between Puerto Ricans and non-Hispanic whites. *BMC Genetics, 10*, 45.

McDowell , M. A., Briefel, R. R., Alaimo, K., Bischof, A. M., Caughman, C. R., Carroll, M. D., ... Johnson, C. L. (1994). Energy and macronutrient intakes of persons ages 2 months and over in the United States: Third National Health and Nutrition Examination Survey, Phase 1, 1988–91. *Advance Data*, (255), 1–24.

McKay, D. L., Perrone, G., Rasmussen, H., Dallal, G., Hartman, W., Cao, G., ... Blumberg, J. B. (2000). The effects of a multivitamin/mineral supplement on micronutrient status, antioxidant capacity and cytokine production in healthy older adults consuming a fortified diet. *Journal of the American College of Nutrition, 19*(5), 613–621.

Miller, E. R., Pastor-Barriuso, R., Dalal, D., Riemersma, R. A., Appel, L. J., & Guallar, E. (2005). Meta-analysis: High-dosage vitamin E supplementation may increase all-cause mortality. *Annals of Internal Medicine, 142*(1), 37–46.

Mitrou, P. N., Kipnis, V., Thiébaut, A. C., Reedy, J., Subar, A. F., Wirfält, E., ... Schatzkin, A. (2007). Mediterranean dietary pattern and prediction of all-cause mortality in a US population: Results from the NIH-AARP Diet and Health Study. *Archives of Internal Medicine, 167*(22), 2461–2468.

MNA® Mini Nutritional Assessment. (2009). Nestle Health Svience. April, 2012.

Mokdad, A. H., Bowman, B. A., Ford, E. S., Vinicor, F., Marks, J. S., & Koplan, J. P. (2001). The continuing epidemics of obesity and diabetes in the United States. *JAMA, 286*(10), 1195–1200.

Mold, J. W., Lawler, F., & Roberts, M. (2008). The health consequences of peripheral neurological deficits in an elderly cohort: An Oklahoma Physicians Resource/Research Network Study. *Journal of the American Geriatrics Society, 56*(7), 1259–1264.

Mold, J. W., Vesely, S. K., Keyl, B. A., Schenk, J. B., & Roberts, M. (2004). The prevalence, predictors, and consequences of peripheral sensory neuropathy in older patients. *The Journal of the American Board of Family Practice/American Board of Family Practice, 17*(5), 309–318.

Moore, P., Kruse, H., Tisdall, F., & Corrigan, R. (1946). Nutrition Among the Northern Manitoba Indians. *Canadian Medical Association Journal, 54*(3), 223–233.

Murphy, N. J., Schraer, C. D., Thiele, M. C., Boyko, E. J., Bulkow, L. R., Doty, B. J., & Lanier, A. P. (1995). Dietary change and obesity associated with glucose intolerance in Alaska Natives. *Journal of the American Dietetic Association, 95*(6), 676–682.

Murtaugh, M. A., Herrick, J. S., Sweeney, C., Baumgartner, K. B., Guiliano, A. R., Byers, T., & Slattery, M. L. (2007). Diet composition and risk of overweight and obesity in women living in the southwestern United States. *Journal of the American Dietetic Association, 107*(8), 1311–1321.

Muscaritoli, M., Anker, S. D., Argilés, J., Aversa, Z., Bauer, J. M., Biolo, G., . . . Sieber, C. C. (2010). Consensus definition of sarcopenia, cachexia and pre-cachexia: Joint document elaborated by Special Interest Groups (SIG) "cachexia-anorexia in chronic wasting diseases" and "nutrition in geriatrics." *Clinical Nutrition, 29*(2), 154–159.

Myles, S., Davison, D., Barrett, J., Stoneking, M., & Timpson, N. (2008). Worldwide population differentiation at disease-associated SNPs. *BMC Medical Genomics, 1*, 22.

MyPlate for Older Adults. (2011). Retrieved March 25, 2011, from http://nutrition.tufts.edu/docs/pyramid.pdf

Najm, W., Reinsch, S., Hoehler, F., & Tobis, J. (2003). Use of complementary and alternative medicine among the ethnic elderly. *Alternative Therapies in Health and Medicine, 9*(3), 50–57.

Newby, P. K., Muller, D., Hallfrisch, J., Andres, R., & Tucker, K. L. (2004). Food patterns measured by factor analysis and anthropometric changes in adults. *The American Journal of Clinical Nutrition, 80*(2), 504–513.

Newman, D. J., Cragg, G. M., & Snader, K. M. (2003). Natural products as sources of new drugs over the period 1981–2002. *Journal of Natural Products, 66*(7), 1022–1037.

Nurge, E. (1970). *Dakota diet: Traditional and contemporary. The modern sioux: Social systems and reservation culture.* Lincoln, NE: University of Nebraska Press.

O'Rahilly, S., Barroso, I., & Wareham, N. J. (2005). Genetic factors in type 2 diabetes: The end of the beginning? *Science, 307*(5708), 370–373.

Palmer, N. D., McDonough, C. W., Hicks, P. J., Roh, B. H., Wing, M. R., An, S. S., . . . Sladek, R. (2012). A genome-wide association search for type 2 diabetes genes in African Americans. *PloS One, 7*(1), e29202.

Park, S., Johnson, M., & Fischer, J. G. (2008). Vitamin and mineral supplements: Barriers and challenges for older adults. *Journal of Nutrition For the Elderly, 27*(3–4), 297–317.

Patel, K. V. (2008). Epidemiology of anemia in older adults. *Seminars in Hematology, 45*(4), 210–217.

Piers, L. S., Soares, M. J., McCormack, L. M., & O'Dea, K. (1998). Is there evidence for an age-related reduction in metabolic rate? *Journal of Applied Physiology, 85*(6), 2196–2204.

Polzer, R., & Miles, M. S. (2005). Spirituality and self-management of diabetes in African Americans. *Journal of Holistic Nursing, 23*(2), 230–250; discussion 251.

Popkin, B. M., Siega-Riz, A. M., & Haines, P. S. (1996). A comparison of dietary trends among racial and socioeconomic groups in the United States. *The New England Journal of Medicine, 335*(10), 716–720.

Posner, B. M., Jette, A. M., Smith, K. W., & Miller, D. R. (1993). Nutrition and health risks in the elderly: The nutrition screening initiative. *American Journal of Public Health, 83*(7), 972–978.

Reedy, J., Krebs-Smith, S. M., & Bosire, C. (2010). Evaluating the food environment: Application of the Healthy Eating Index-2005. *American Journal of Preventive Medicine, 38*(5), 465–471.

Reedy, J., Mitrou, P. N., Krebs-Smith, S. M., Wirfält, E., Flood, A., Kipnis, V., . . . Subar, A. F. (2008). Index-based dietary patterns and risk of colorectal cancer: The NIH-AARP Diet and Health Study. *American Journal of Epidemiology, 168*(1), 38–48.

Rees, S. D., Islam, M., Hydrie, M. Z., Chaudhary, B., Bellary, S., Hashmi, S., . . . Jafar, T. H. (2011). An *FTO* variant is associated with Type 2 diabetes in South Asian populations after accounting for body mass index and waist circumference. *Diabetic Medicine: A Journal of the British Diabetic Association, 28*(6), 673–680.

Reis, J. P., Araneta, M. R., Wingard, D. L., Macera, C. A., Lindsay, S. P., & Marshall, S. J. (2009). Overall obesity and abdominal adiposity as predictors of mortality in U.S. white and black adults. *Annals of Epidemiology*, *19*(2), 134–142.

Rejeski, W. J., Marsh, A. P., Chmelo, E., & Rejeski, J. J. (2010). Obesity, intentional weight loss and physical disability in older adults. *Obesity Reviews*, *11*(9), 671–685.

Rich, N. M., & Dimond, F. C. (2009). Results of Vietnamese acupuncture seen at the Second Surgical Hospital. *Journal of Special Operations Medicine*, *9*(2), 102–104.

Roberts, S. B., & Dallal, G. E. (1998). Effects of age on energy balance. *The American Journal of Clinical Nutrition*, *68*(4), 975S–979S.

Roberts, S. B., & Rosenberg, I. (2006). Nutrition and aging: Changes in the regulation of energy metabolism with aging. *Physiological Reviews*, *86*(2), 651–667.

Rolland, Y., Dupuy, C., Abellan van Kan, G., Gillette, S., & Vellas, B. (2011). Treatment strategies for sarcopenia and frailty. *The Medical Clinics of North America*, *95*(3), 427–38, ix.

Rolland, Y., Onder, G., Morley, J. E., Gillette-Guyonet, S., Abellan van Kan, G., & Vellas, B. (2011). Current and future pharmacologic treatment of sarcopenia. *Clinics in Geriatric Medicine*, *27*(3), 423–447. doi: 10.1016/j.cger.2011.03.008

Rolland, Y., Perrin, A., Gardette, V., Filhol, N., & Vellas, B. (2012). Screening older people at risk of malnutrition or malnourished using the Simplified Nutritional Appetite Questionnaire (SNAQ): A comparison with the Mini-Nutritional Assessment (MNA) tool. *Journal of the American Medical Directors Association*, *13*(1), 31–34.

Rothman, A. J. (2000). Toward a theory-based analysis of behavioral maintenance. *Health psychology*, *19*(1 Suppl), 64–69.

Roubenoff, R., & Hughes, V. A. (2000). Sarcopenia: Current concepts. *The Journals of Gerontology*, *55*(12), 716–724.

Ruixing, Y., Weixiong, L., Hanjun, Y., Dezhai, Y., Shuquan, L., Shangling, P., … Yaju, D. (2008). Diet, lifestyle, and blood pressure of the middle-aged and elderly in the Guangxi Bai Ku Yao and Han populations. *American Journal of Hypertension*, *21*(4), 382–387.

Russians in Minnesota. (2012). Retrieved May 27, 2012, from http://www.culturecareconnection.org/matters/diversity/russian.html

Ryan, A. S., Martinez, G. A., Wysong, J. L., & Davis, M. A. (1989). Dietary patterns of older adults in the United States, NHANES II 1976–1980. *American Journal of Human Biology*, *1*(3), 321–330.

Samuel-Hodge, C. D., Keyserling, T. C., Park, S., Johnston, L. F., Gizlice, Z., & Bangdiwala, S. I. (2009). A randomized trial of a church-based diabetes self-management program for African Americans with type 2 diabetes. *The Diabetes Educator*, *35*(3), 439–454.

Sanchez, T. R., Plawecki, J. A., & Plawecki, H. M. (1996). The delivery of culturally sensitive health care to Native Americans. *Journal of Holistic Nursing*, *14*(4), 295–307.

Savoca, M. R., Arcury, T. A., Leng, X., Bell, R. A., Chen, H., Anderson, A., … Quandt, S. A. (2009). The diet quality of rural older adults in the South as measured by healthy eating index-2005 varies by ethnicity. *Journal of the American Dietetic Association*, *109*(12), 2063–2067.

Scarmeas, N., Luchsinger, J. A., Schupf, N., Brickman, A. M., Cosentino, S., Tang, M. X., & Stern, Y. (2009). Physical activity, diet, and risk of Alzheimer disease. *JAMA*, *302*(6), 627–637.

Schattner, P., & Randerson, D. (1996). Tiger Balm as a treatment of tension headache. A clinical trial in general practice. *Australian Family Physician*, *25*(2), 216–220.

Schneider, J. A., Tangney, C. C., & Morris, M. C. (2006). Folic acid and cognition in older persons. *Expert Opinion On Drug Safety*, *5*(4), 511–522.

Schulz, L. O., Bennett, P. H., Ravussin, E., Kidd, J. R., Kidd, K. K., Esparza, J., & Valencia, M. E. (2006). Effects of traditional and western environments on prevalence of type 2 diabetes in Pima Indians in Mexico and the U.S. *Diabetes Care*, *29*(8), 1866–1871.

Scott, T. M., Tucker, K. L., Bhadelia, A., Benjamin, B., Patz, S., Bhadelia, R., … Folstein, M. F. (2004). Homocysteine and B vitamins relate to brain volume and white-matter changes in geriatric patients with psychiatric disorders. *The American Journal of Geriatric Psychiatry*, *12*(6), 631–638.

Scuteri, A., Sanna, S., Chen, W. M., Uda, M., Albai, G., Strait, J.,…Abecasis, G. R. (2007). Genome-wide association scan shows genetic variants in the *FTO* gene are associated with obesity-related traits. *PLoS Genetics, 3*(7), e115.

Sebastian, R. S., Cleveland, L. E., Goldman, J. D., & Moshfegh, A. J. (2007). Older adults who use vitamin/mineral supplements differ from nonusers in nutrient intake adequacy and dietary attitudes. *Journal of the American Dietetic Association, 107*(8), 1322–1332.

Shen, J., Lai, C. Q., Mattei, J., Ordovas, J. M., & Tucker, K. L. (2010). Association of vitamin B-6 status with inflammation, oxidative stress, and chronic inflammatory conditions: The Boston Puerto Rican Health Study. *The American Journal of Clinical Nutrition, 91*(2), 337–342.

Sindler, A. (2001). Cultural Diversity as Part of Nutrition Education and Counseling. *Creative Solutions* Retrieved May 30, 2012, from http://nutritionandaging.fiu.edu/creative_solutions/nutrition_ed.asp

Smith, J., & Wiedman, D. (2001). Fat content of south Florida Indian frybread: Health implications for a pervasive Native-American food. *Journal of the American Dietetic Association, 101*(5), 582–585.

Sofianou, A., Fung, T. T., & Tucker, K. L. (2011). Differences in diet pattern adherence by nativity and duration of US residence in the Mexican-American population. *Journal of the American Dietetic Association, 111*(10), 1563–1569.e2.

Speakman, J. R., & Westerterp, K. R. (2010). Associations between energy demands, physical activity, and body composition in adult humans between 18 and 96 y of age. *The American Journal of Clinical Nutrition, 92*(4), 826–834.

Sridharan, K., Mohan, R., Ramaratnam, S., & Panneerselvam, D. (2011). Ayurvedic treatments for diabetes mellitus. *Cochrane Database of Systematic Reviews,* (12), CD008288

Srithi, K., Trisonthi, C., Wangpakapattanawong, P., & Balslev, H. (2012). Medicinal plants used in Hmong women's healthcare in northern Thailand. *Journal of Ethnopharmacology, 139*(1), 119–135. doi: 10.1016/j.jep.2011.10.028

Stables, G. J., Subar, A. F., Patterson, B. H., Dodd, K., Heimendinger, J., Van Duyn, M. A., & Nebeling, L. (2002). Changes in vegetable and fruit consumption and awareness among US adults: Results of the 1991 and 1997 5 A Day for Better Health Program surveys. *Journal of the American Dietetic Association, 102*(6), 809–817.

Stevens, J., Cai, J., Pamuk, E. R., Williamson, D. F., Thun, M. J., & Wood, J. L. (1998). The effect of age on the association between body-mass index and mortality. *The New England Journal of Medicine, 338*(1), 1–7.

Stevens, V. L., McCullough, M. L., Diver, W. R., Rodriguez, C., Jacobs, E. J., Thun, M. J., & Calle, E. E. (2005). Use of multivitamins and prostate cancer mortality in a large cohort of US men. *Cancer Causes & Control, 16*(6), 643–650.

Supplee, J. D., Duncan, G. E., Bruemmer, B., Goldberg, J., Wen, Y., & Henderson, J. A. (2011). Soda intake and osteoporosis risk in postmenopausal American-Indian women. *Public Health Nutrition, 14*(11), 1900–1906.

Tangney, C. C., Kwasny, M. J., Li, H., Wilson, R. S., Evans, D. A., & Morris, M. C. (2011). Adherence to a Mediterranean-type dietary pattern and cognitive decline in a community population. *The American Journal of Clinical Nutrition, 93*(3), 601–607.

Thompson, L. V. (2009). Age-related muscle dysfunction. *Experimental Gerontology, 44*(1–2), 106–111.

Traurig, M., Mack, J., Hanson, R. L., Ghoussaini, M., Meyre, D., Knowler, W. C., Kobes, S.,…Baier, L. J. (2009). Common variation in SIM1 is reproducibly associated with BMI in Pima Indians. *Diabetes, 58*(7), 1682–1689.

Tucker, K. L. (2010). Dietary patterns, approaches, and multicultural perspective. *Applied Physiology, Nutrition, and Metabolism = Physiologie Appliquée, Nutrition et Métabolisme, 35*(2), 211–218.

Tuomilehto, J., Lindström, J., Eriksson, J. G., Valle, T. T., Hämäläinen, H., Ilanne-Parikka, P.,…Uusitupa, M. (2001). Prevention of type 2 diabetes mellitus by changes in lifestyle among subjects with impaired glucose tolerance. *The New England Journal of Medicine, 344*(18), 1343–1350.

van Rompay, M. I., McKeown, N. M., Castaneda-Sceppa, C., Falcón, L. M., Ordovás, J. M., & Tucker, K. L. (2012). Acculturation and sociocultural influences on dietary intake and health status among Puerto Rican adults in Massachusetts. *Journal of the Academy of Nutrition and Dietetics, 112*(1), 64–74.

Vaughan, L., Zurlo, F., & Ravussin, E. (1991). Aging and energy expenditure. *The American Journal of Clinical Nutrition, 53*(4), 821–825.

Villa, V. M., Wallace, S. P., Bagdasaryan, S., & Aranda, M. P. (2012). Hispanic Baby Boomers: Health inequities likely to persist in old age. *The Gerontologist, 52*(2), 166–176.

Villareal, D. T., Apovian, C. M., Kushner, R. F., & Klein, S. (2005). Obesity in older adults: Technical review and position statement of the American Society for Nutrition and NAASO, The Obesity Society. *The American Journal of Clinical Nutrition, 82*(5), 923–934.

Vitolins, M. Z., Tooze, J. A., Golden, S. L., Arcury, T. A., Bell, R. A., Davis, C.,...Quandt, S. A. (2007). Older adults in the rural South are not meeting healthful eating guidelines. *Journal of the American Dietetic Association, 107*(2), 265–272.

Wang, Y., & Beydoun, M. A. (2007). The obesity epidemic in the United States–gender, age, socioeconomic, racial/ethnic, and geographic characteristics: A systematic review and meta-regression analysis. *Epidemiologic Reviews, 29*, 6–28.

Watkins, M. L., Erickson, J. D., Thun, M. J., Mulinare, J., & Heath, C. W. (2000). Multivitamin use and mortality in a large prospective study. *American Journal of Epidemiology, 152*(2), 149–162.

Weeden, A. M., & Remig, V. M. (2010). Food intake of Kansans over 80 years of age attending congregate meal sites. *Nutrients, 2*(12), 1297–1307.

WHO. (2006). World Population Prospects: The 2006 Revision, from http://www.un.org/esa/population/publications/wpp2006/wpp2006.htm

Williams, D. E., Knowler, W. C., Smith, C. J., Hanson, R. L., Roumain, J., Saremi, A.,...Nelson, R. G. (2001). The effect of Indian or Anglo dietary preference on the incidence of diabetes in Pima Indians. *Diabetes Care, 24*(5), 811–816.

Wilson, M. M., Thomas, D. R., Rubenstein, L. Z., Chibnall, J. T., Anderson, S., Baxi, A.,...Morley, J. E. (2005). Appetite assessment: Simple appetite questionnaire predicts weight loss in community-dwelling adults and nursing home residents. *The American Journal of Clinical Nutrition, 82*(5), 1074–1081.

Wilson, M. M., Philpot, C., & Morley, J. E. (2007). Anorexia of aging in long term care: Is dronabinol an effective appetite stimulant?–a pilot study. *The Journal of Nutrition, Health & Aging, 11*(2), 195–198.

Wu, A. P., Burke, A., & LeBaron, S. (2007). Use of traditional medicine by immigrant Chinese patients. *Family Medicine, 39*(3), 195–200.

Yamashita, T., & Kunkle, S. (2012). Geographic access to healthy and unhealthy foods for the older population in a US metropolitan area. *Journal of Applied Gerontology, 31*, 287–313.

Yaxley, A., Miller, M. D., Fraser, R. J., & Cobiac, L. (2012). Pharmacological interventions for geriatric cachexia: A narrative review of the literature. *The Journal of Nutrition, Health & Aging, 16*(2), 148–154.

Zeanandin, G., Molato, O., Le Duff, F., Guérin, O., Hébuterne, X., & Schneider, S. M. (2012). Impact of restrictive diets on the risk of undernutrition in a free-living elderly population. *Clinical Nutrition, 31*(1), 69–73. doi: 10.1016/j.clnu.2011.08.007

Zhou, D., Liu, H., Zhou, M., Wang, S., Zhang, J., Liao, L., & He, F. (2012). Common variant (rs9939609) in the *FTO* gene is associated with metabolic syndrome. *Molecular Biology Reports, 39*(6), 6555–6561.

CHAPTER 12

Two Approaches to Developing Health Interventions for Ethnic Minority Elders: From Science to Practice and From Practice to Science

Sue Levkoff, Hongtu Chen, and Martha Norton

THE COMPLEX CHALLENGE TO CULTURAL COMPETENCY IN HEALTH CARE SERVICES

According to the Pew Research Center, the population of the United States will increase from 309 million in 2010 (U.S. Census Bureau, 2010a) to 438 million in 2050 (Passel & Cohn, 2008). At this time, nearly one in five Americans (19%) will be an immigrant (Passel & Cohn, 2008), compared with over one in eight (12.5%) in 2010 (U.S. Census Bureau, 2010b). A large part of this increase (82%) will be due to the influx of new immigrants and their U.S.-born descendants, according to new projections developed by the Pew Research Center (Passel & Cohn, 2008). Thus, over the next 40 years, the United States is going to see a dramatic expansion in the proportion of its population that is over the age of 65 and non-White Hispanic (Passel & Cohn, 2008).

The changing demographic has led to complex challenges in the U.S. health care system. The impact of this diversity means that health care providers increasingly encounter, and must learn to manage, complex differences in communication styles, attitudes, expectations, and world views. The delivery of effective health care services hinges on health care professionals' ability to recognize varied understandings of and approaches to health care across cultures. According to various reviews, individuals of ethnic cultural backgrounds are typically influenced by a range of culture-related factors (see Table 12.1), which become a persistant challenge to health care organizations intending to serve a community with one or more ethnic minority groups.

In addition to the individual factors mentioned above that often serve as barriers to health care delivery, there are institutional barriers to health care services that affect ethnic minorities more generally. For instance, minority groups are manifestly under-represented in clinical trials—a phenomenon that predominantly stems from participant recruitment issues. Logistical barriers, such as transportation to clinical trials, the affordability of childcare, and lack of time off work, impact the ability of minority groups to participate in clinical trials.

TABLE 12.1 Cultural Characteristics That May Impact Care Decisions Among Racial/Ethnic Minority Individuals

	SOURCES
African Americans	
Historical segregation of and lack of access to health care & social services	Hargrave, R. (2010, p. 24).
Legacy of distrust due to abuse (e.g., Tuskegee Study)	Hargrave, R. (2010, p. 16).
Preference for remedies from nontraditional providers & folk remedies	Hargrave, R. (2010,p. 30).
Centrality of spiritual/religious faith & practice	Banks, A. M. (Jan. 2009).
Inter-generational family ties & supports	Taylor, R. J., & Chatters, L. M. (1991, pp. 103–111).
American Indians	
History of negative interactions with settlers & American institutions	Hendrix, L. (2010, p. 5).
Traditional spiritual belief in a higher power and creator and interconnectedness of all things	Hendrix, L. (2010, p. 24).
Importance of compassion, generosity, social justice, and self-sacrifice for the common good	Hendrix, L. (2010, p. 12).
Belief in deep connection between medical & spiritual healing	Hendrix, L. (2010, p. 12).
Respect for the wisdom & experience of elders	Hendrix, L. (2010, p. 19).
Importance of listening & displaying humility	Hendrix, L. (2010, p. 19).
Chinese Americans	
Cultural notions of health encompass the physical body, mental state, and social support	Dong, X., Chang, E., Wong, E., Skarupski, K., & Simon, M. (2010, p. 4).
Linguistic isolation	Dong, X., Chang, E., Wong, E., Skarupski, K., & Simon, M. (2010, pp. 4–7).
Traditional provision of care by family members	Dong, X., Chang, E., Wong, E., Skarupski, K., & Simon, M. (2010, pp. 5–8).
Korean Americans	
Family-based social bonds & care responsibilities	Jang, Y., Kim, G., Chiriboga, D., & Cho, S. (2008, pp. 110–117).
Linguistic challenges	Sohn, L., & Harada, N. D. (2004, pp. 1946–1950).
Reluctance to access health care	Sohn, L., & Harada, N. D. (2004, pp. 1946–1950).
Filipino Americans	
Linguistic isolation	McBride, M. (n.d.).
Strong Catholic religious beliefs	McBride, M. (n.d.).
Desire to act as own translator to English	McBride, M. (n.d.).
Southeast Asians (Cambodian, Laotian, Vietnamese, Hmong)	
Buddhist beliefs that illness is related to spiritual growth	Walsh, J. R., Salazar, R., Nguyen, T. T., Kaplan, C., Nguyen, L. K., Hwang, J.,...Pasick, R. J. (2010, pp. 1–14).
Linguistic isolation	Walsh, J. R., Salazar, R., Nguyen, T. T., Kaplan, C., Nguyen, L. K., Hwang, J.,...Pasick, R. J. (2010, pp. 1–14).
Indian Asians	
Use of Ayurvedic/Hindu medicines, diets, and treatments	Alagiakrishnan, K. (n.d.).
Linguistic barriers	Misra, R., Menon, U., Vadaparampil, S. T., & BeLue, R. (2011, pp. 787–792). Boxwala, F. I., Bridgemohan, A., Griffith, A., & Soliman, A. S. (2010, pp. 534–543).
Latinos	
Strong reliance on family, friends and the media for health care information	Livingston, G., Minushkin, S., & Cohn, D. (2008).

Furthermore, trials are often unequipped to manage the literacy issues and language barriers that accompany a diverse participation (Friedman, 2009). Effective minority recruitment requires an understanding of the interplay between individual- and institutional-level recruitment factors.

Health care providers may employ different strategies to increase participation of service users by bridging barriers to communication and understanding that stem from these racial, ethnic, cultural, and linguistic differences. One approach to manage these obstacles to recruitment is early outreach campaigns to screen potential participants for literacy issues. This evaluation process allows for a more thorough understanding of the needs and preferences of potential participants in order to accommodate these factors into the trial. With this information, researchers can develop translated materials and provide appropriate personnel to support participants with a conceptual understanding of the proposed research. Another approach health care providers can take is to invoke a sense of credibility in their study through the incorporation of familiar faces such as celebrities, local leaders, and patient spokesmen. As distrust of research is an oft-cited barrier according to minority interviewees, familiarity and ongoing exposure are important qualities of successful recruitment campaigns. Lastly, study funds can be set aside specifically for the transportation, childcare, and employment costs of participants. These "co-payments" provide incentives to participants who may not otherwise find value in clinical research (Stirland et al., 2011).

Researchers can attempt to work with minority populations in an open and honest manner to incorporate them into research more often. In addition, researchers should integrate an overall discussion of how researchers have misused minority research participants in the past, and give the community an ownership of the research project (Dancy, Wilbur, Talashek, Bonner, & Barnes-Boyd, 2004).

In general, these efforts represent a typical method of enhancing cultural competency of a service program by improving participation of, and outreach to, ethnic minority groups, after a clinical program is determined and implemented. Below, we summarize another method that focuses on developing a culturally competent health care intervention program before finalizing a clinical service program.

DEVELOPING CULTURALLY COMPETENT HEALTH INTERVENTIONS FOR ETHNIC MINORITY ELDERS

In the context of health or health care improvement, little debate exists concerning the recognized need to help ethnic minority patients maintain and restore health. At the core of the discussion is the question of whether health interventions intended for ethnic minority groups should differ from those that have been predominantly developed, and used by, nonminority populations. If such differences are considered necessary or favored, how should we determine the correct type of health intervention, and the correct approach to implementing this intervention for the target population?

This issue is key to the development of truly client-centered medicine, an agenda identified by the Institute of Medicine as the greatest challenge of 21st century health care (Committee on Quality of Health Care in America, Institute of Medicine, 2001). When serving ethnic minority patients, practitioners can misuse or oversimplify the client-centered approach in two ways. The first is founded upon the position that each client is uniquely different and, therefore, compels those serving ethnic minority communities to explore and develop solutions tailored to individual clients. The other outlook views each major ethnic minority group as uniquely different from both other ethnic groups and majority populations. This position identifies and promotes more generic intervention guidelines, which are applicable for each major ethnic group.

Both positions are problematic. The first position, which is more or less a postmodernist view, risks downplaying or ignoring the vast and fast expanding knowledge base accumulated from the mainstream medical world, thus ultimately transferring risk to patients. The second position, based on the stereotypic assumption that variation within each ethnic group is far smaller than the variation between ethnic groups, not only neglects the differences between the subgroups in any major ethnic minority group, but also exaggerates the gaps between ethnic minority health care and mainstream medicine. Both positions can promote the unfortunate separation of services between ethnic minorities and mainstream medicine.

TWO APPROACHES TO DEVELOPING HEALTH INTERVENTION PROGRAMS

In 2003, the Center for Mental Health Services within the U.S. Substance Abuse and Mental Health Service Administration launched a national project to expand behavioral health service capacity by encouraging the spread of evidence-based practice in mental health care for the elderly. The main goal of the project was to enhance mental health services for underserved ethnic minority communities by developing evidence-based, culturally competent intervention service programs at over forty clinics in nine participating states.

Recognizing the practical difficulties in implementing this scheme, the funding agency designated a national technical assistance center to be in charge of providing technical assistance and support to the service sites (two of the authors of this chapter, Drs. Sue Levkoff and Hongtu Chen, served as directors of the National Technical Assistance Center, which later was known as the Positive Aging Resource Center). Each site had originally selected some specific evidence-based practices that would guide their new project and address the identified service needs.

As the project started, it soon became clear that it was hard to judge how the identified needs, evidence-based practices, and proposed operational plans outlined in the proposals reflected the sites' operational realities and goals, besides that of obtaining funding. As a result of this realization, a systematic effort was exerted to assess the real needs for both service enhancement and technical assistance at each participating site. Through in-depth telephone interviews, site visits, and questionnaire surveys of the service administrators, we collected detailed data about each service site. Based on the data acquired, we identified experts in the fields of minority aging services, evidence-based mental health practice, and mental health service evaluation. The experts were assigned to the sites according to their specific needs and played the role of a "coach" to provide assistance and support tailored for the situation of each site.

A year into the efforts of redesign and implementation of the intervention plan, the sites began to show a variety of approaches to developing interventions for their target population. By reviewing each site's required process evaluation documentation, we noticed

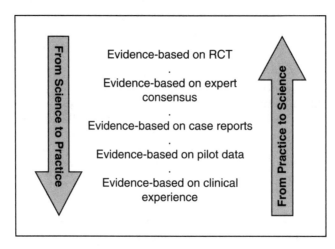

FIGURE 12.1 Two Approaches to Developing Culturally Competent Health Interventions (Adapted from Levkoff et al., 2006, pp. 67–91).

considerable variation in the pathways for achievement of the sites' intervention designs and implementation plans. These pathways could be sorted into two general approaches to developing culturally appropriate health interventions (these two approaches have been published in an edited volume, titled *Evidence-Based Behavioral Health Practice for Older Adults: A Guide to Implementation,* Levkoff, Chen, Fisher, and McIntyre, 2006) (see Figure 12.1). It should be noted that although examined as part of a project focused on mental health, we recognize the applicability of this model to all minority elderly health interventions, as will be discussed below.

In this chapter and other writings, we promote a more integrated approach or process for developing a health intervention for ethnic minority groups that incorporates accepted principles of medicine and scientific methodology. In addition to our own previous work on this subject, we also draw upon the empirical results of other relevant studies and datasets, such as the NHANES (National Health and Nutrition Examination Survey). We also incorporate the recommendations of major health organizations whose work is most relevant to elderly minority individuals, such as the American Cancer Society, American Diabetes Association, American Heart Association, and the Alzheimer's Association, and we have tracked the work and recommendations of the HSS's Office of Minority Health, the Indian Health Service, and the National Indian Health Board.

Approach 1: From Science to Practice

This is the most common strategy for developing an evidence-based intervention for ethnic minority communities. This approach is also called cultural adaptation or cultural tailoring of a health intervention. In the aforementioned project, after identifying specific needs or problems for the improvement of services for ethnic minority clients, sites employing this approach undertook the following five steps: (1) finding the best scientific evidence from available sources (e.g., published clinical guidelines, research literature of randomized controlled trials, or demonstration programs) that address the identified problem; (2) identifying the cultural characteristics of the target community that require modifications to the evidence-based intervention protocol and barriers that need to be addressed in order to implement an intervention; (3) adapting the evidence-based practice to the cultural and clinical service situation identified in Step 2, thus, forming a new, culturally qualified protocol; (4) implementing and adhering to the adapted protocol, with particular attention to changes in operational procedures and staff behaviors; and (5) confirming the effectiveness of the new intervention by collecting outcome data, and including feedback from the targeted population.

These steps broadly describe this science-driven approach to developing health interventions for ethnic minority communities. However, depending on the project, some steps are more emphasized than others. For instance, after reviewing various emerging cancer prevention and treatment demonstration projects for ethnic and racial minorities, researchers found that the top seven barriers to access and utilization of cancer programs are cultural attitudes, poverty, lack of transportation, language, mistrust of the medical system, lack of insurance, and lack of knowledge about cancer (Schneider Institute for Health Policy, Brandeis University, 2003). The top methods for cultural tailoring of implementation efforts were having people in the local community deliver interventions, holding group events at community settings, providing transportation and benefit counseling services, and focusing on positive health promotion rather than disease (negative) information.

In a recent article, Netto, Bhopal, Lederle, Khatoon, and Jackson (2010) reviewed numerous cases of adapting behavioral interventions for minority ethnic communities and identified five guiding principles: (a) use community resources to publicize the intervention and increase accessibility; (b) identify and address barriers to access and participation; (c) develop communication strategies that are sensitive to language use and information requirements; (d) work with cultural or religious values that either promote or hinder behavioral change; and (e) accommodate varying degrees of cultural identification (Netto et al., 2010).

Case Example 1: The Focus Project

In El Paso, Texas, the largest city along the U.S.-Mexico border, over 78% of residents are of Hispanic or Latino origins. For decades, the area supplied an abundance of unskilled workers for low-wage manufacturing jobs and served as a gateway for seasonal agricultural workers. Since the North American Free Trade Agreement (NAFTA), however, El Paso has lost over 15,000 manufacturing jobs, leaving behind mostly older, unskilled, Spanish-monolingual women unemployed in the area (The Final Progress Report to SAMHSA, 2003).

Despite the weakness of this economic situation and its associated impact on increased depression among elderly residents, El Paso has a successful elder service program, *Bienvivir Senior Health Services* (*"Bienvivir"*), established since 1986. *Bienvivir* is the first and only senior health service program in Texas that follows an evidence-based PACE (Program of All-Inclusive Care for the Elderly) protocol. As an alternative to confinement in a long-term care facility for the frail elderly, *Bienvivir* offers, at no expense to the participant or their family, a full spectrum of health and human services, including primary physician care; medical specialist care; hospitalization; physical, speech, and recreational therapy; pharmaceuticals; nursing care; transportation; meals; long-term care; hospice care; and a full array of social services. Since its inception, *Bienvivir* has grown from a small, leased site with less than 10 participants to two facilities to one that currently provide services to 587 frail elderly, financially disadvantaged El Pasoans (The Final Progress Report to SAMHSA, 2003, p. 3).

Although *Bienvivir* has clearly proven its effectiveness in addressing the medical and social needs of El Paso's physically frail Mexican American elderly, *Bienvivir,* like other PACE programs, has never formally enrolled any cases with mental health problems for treatment. Given that "Only a fraction (0.6%) of El Paso's elderly are receiving mental health treatment while a large number of individuals who might benefit from early treatment interventions end up either with a worsening condition leading to crisis intervention or are never served" (Excerpt from the Quarterly Report of the Focus Project, Bienvivir Senior Health Services, 2003, 6), the city of El Paso decided to support a new initiative (named "Focus Project") to find ways of using existing mental health resources to serve the elderly of the community. In general, the Focus Project aims to increase the accessibility of mental health services for the elderly by linking aging services (i.e., *Bienvivir*) to mental health services (i.e., El Paso Community Mental Health and Mental Retardation Center, or MHMR).

In implementing the project, the Focus Project leaders worked closely with a "coach" from a federally funded technical assistance center, of which the lead author of this chapter was the director. Together, they soon realized the following specific needs: (a) the identification of appropriate screening tools for assessing dementia and anxiety, since the screening tool for depression has already been found; (b) the identification of evidence-based clinical protocol for treating depression and anxiety in frail elderly; (c) the formulation of evidence-based recommendations for developing integration of services between a PACE program, such as *Bienvivir*, and a mental health service, such as MHMR (Excerpt from the Quarterly Report of the Focus Project, Bienvivir Senior Health Services, 2003, 8).

The Focus Project team indicated that they had limited access to relevant journals and publications, but given the technical assistance center's affiliation with academicians, team members were easily able to identify relevant evidence-based tools and protocols. More challenging, however, was the task of determining whether a particular tool should be used and/or modified.

Initial screening for depression was based on two questions taken from the Composite International Diagnostic Interview (CIDI). One question asks whether the respondent has felt sad, empty, or depressed nearly every day for 2 weeks or longer, and the other question asks about loss of interest in things usually enjoyed every day for 2 weeks or longer. Anyone responding with a "yes" to either question was to be further assessed for depression. Upon review of the first 92 screenings, it was determined that 46 (50%) of these individuals needed to be assessed. This number seemed too high and suggested false positive cases.

Project physicians felt that it would be beneficial to have an additional measure to assist in identifying who should be assessed. After studying the CIDI, they selected 13 questions to yield a Mental Health Index (MHI). When the results of the first 92 screenings were reviewed and ranked, according to this MHI, it was found that those individuals who responded with a "yes" to both screening questions had higher MHI scores, whereas the lower MHI scores correlated with "no" responses to the two screening questions. Based on the new criteria, 34 of the initial 46 positive screens had been assessed, 18 (19.6%) of which were determined to have a mental health problem. 12 of the 18 accepted services from the MHMR Center, and 6 decided to remain with the *Bienvivir* primary care physician currently treating their conditions (The Final Progress Report to SAMHSA, 2003, p. 15).

Comments

As an example of the "from science to practice" approach, the Focus Project case showed at least two interesting points. First, the steps summarized above (e.g., from "finding the best scientific evidence" to "cultural adaptation") constitute a circular or iterative process, rather than a linear sequence. Second, the project team proactively moved beyond the standard prescription of using two screening questions. Instead, team members used a scientific evaluation method to triangulate the screening data with the MHI and assessment data, creating an informed local adaptation/modification of the initial screening tool, which ultimately enhanced its effectiveness.

Case Example 2: La Diabetes y La Unión Familiar

The rate of type 2 diabetes among the Hispanic populations in communities along the border of the United States and Mexico is more than double that of non-Hispanic whites in the same communities. Research attributes this phenomenon partly to the influence of family members in the dietary management of individuals. The attitudes and perceptions of the family, as a whole, hinder the acceptance of any recommended diet or exercise changes of individual family members. Hispanics place a particularly strong emphasis on familial coherence, which impacts behavioral patterns of the unit and defines its conduct. Thus, changes in diet and exercise need to derive from a holistic approach to health education in the context of Hispanic culture and lifestyles (Teufel-Shone, Drummond, & Rawiel, 2005, p. 2).

Because of this public health issue, the University of Arizona and two community health organizations located along the Arizona–Mexico border, Campesinos Sin Fronteras and Mariposa Community Health Center, worked together to design and implement a pilot program for diabetes education. This project, *La Diabetes y La Unión Familiar,* employed a health care outreach worker to educate local families on risk factors, health implications, and preventive measures for diabetes. The intervention program was tailored to the preferences and needs of Hispanic families residing in the area. It addressed food selection, nutritional values, health communication, and familial support mechanisms in its diabetes education (Teufel-Shone, Drummond, & Rawiel, 2005, pp. 2–3).

More specifically, this program followed a total of 249 individuals from 72 families. Through preintervention and postintervention questionnaires, the researchers tracked the health education attainment of all adults involved in the study. The results of the intervention demonstrated a significant increase in participants' awareness of eight risk factors for diabetes. In addition, the study reported significant positive behavioral changes in food selection and physical activity (Teufel-Shone, Drummond, & Rawiel, 2005, p. 1).

Comments

The family intervention program, *La Diabetes y La Unión Familiar*, is a culturally adapted approach to diabetes management designed by clinicians familiar with the specific health issues common to the Hispanic population in the United States–Mexico border region. The researchers took conventional principles of diabetes management and applied them to a familial setting in order to optimally convey them, given the cultural context.

Case Example 3: Seamos Activas

On average, Latinos in the United States tend to be less physically active than the U.S. population in general, leading to higher rates of chronic diseases such as type-2 diabetes. Obesity is another negative repercussion of inadequate levels of physical activity, also more prevalent in Latinos than in non-Hispanic whites. Research on the subject attributes these health disparities to cultural and socioeconomic circumstances that limit access to critical health education programs for certain population groups (Pekmezi et al., 2009, p. 501).

For this reason, Pekmezi et al. (2009) designed a culturally and linguistically adapted intervention method customized to the individual needs of participants. The randomized clinical trial involved 93 overweight, low-income Latinos in the United States. Participants in the study were assigned, at random, to either a culturally and linguistically tailored physical activity intervention or a wellness contact control program (Pekmezi et al., 2009, p. 500).

Participants in the intervention reported a more significant rate of behavioral change in physical activity as well as a greater level of access to physical activity equipment in comparison to the control group. More precisely, physical activity of, at least, moderate intensity increased in the intervention group by about 130 minutes per week (from about 17 minutes/week to 147 minutes/week), while the physical activity of the control group was increased by 85 minutes per week (from about 12 minutes/week to about 97 minutes/week; Pekmezi et al., 2009, p. 500).

Comments

On the basis of empirically supported evidence, this study developed an intervention for Latinos to induce behavioral changes in the intensity and duration of physical activity. Educational materials were translated to Spanish, and participants conveyed their appreciation of the gesture, even citing that it encouraged their involvement in the trial.

Case Example 4: Telephone-Linked Care for Hypertension in African Americans

Hypertension is a medical condition found disproportionately among African Americans in the United States. While most African Americans with hypertension do, indeed, receive medical treatment and medication for their condition, only a slight majority (58%) are able to manage their blood pressure effectively through treatment. This is because medication and medical treatment cannot induce the lifestyle changes necessary to maintain healthy blood pressure levels. In-person outreach programs are effective in inducing the diet and exercise regimens necessary for reduced hypertension. However, this method is costly and unsustainable given the amount of resources needed to deliver such a service. For this reason, a most cost-effective approach is required to confront this public health challenge among African Americans (Migneault et al., 2012).

A randomized trial conducted by Migneault et al. (2012) developed a culturally adapted, computer-based intervention method for African Americans with hypertension residing in Boston, Massachusetts. The intervention was multibehavioral in its approach in that it addressed various health-related activities, not just hypertension. The researchers devised the study to evaluate the efficacy of this automated method on hypertension reduction. The intervention used an interactive phone-based counseling system to observe, educate, and advise African Americans with hypertension. The system compiled the user's responses to its inquiries and advice, and then transmitted the results to the patient's primary care physician (Migneault et al., 2012, p. 63).

The randomized control trial evaluated the outcomes of two groups of participants: an intervention group and a usual care control group. The study involved 337 African American hypertension patients over an 8-month period. The results indicated that the computer-based intervention induced behavioral change in the form of dietary improvements and increased energy expenditure—both of which reduce the negative effects of hypertension. The automated messages conveyed to the intervention participants were tailored to their cultural background. Presumably, the culturally adapted guidance accounted for at least part of the improvement recorded in the intervention group (Migneault et al., 2012).

Comments

This "science to practice" approach expanded upon previous automated intervention methods that addressed singular behavioral change by incorporating multiple health behaviors. This more comprehensive, cost-effective, and culturally adapted intervention method demonstrates the promises of technology and automation in health care management and lifestyle change. The approach's success is a testament to its translatability to various health conditions and scenarios, since it is a modification of models used in other health interventions.

Approach 2: From Practice to Science

In contrast to the first approach of cultural adaptation of the mainstream science-based intervention to ethnic minority populations, the second approach emphasizes the importance of developing a culturally grounded or rooted intervention, rather than transplanting and adapting an established evidence-based protocol to a new cultural setting. This approach is based on two main assumptions: first, service providers who are experienced in serving the local ethnic cultural community know the best way to serve that particular population; and, second, the cultural characteristics of individuals and their community settings are complex, such that it might be not wise or feasible to import an intervention protocol originated in another context.

Based on the authors' experience with the National Technical Assistance Center, and the assumption that service needs or problem areas have already been identified, this approach typically involves the following steps, (1) systematically documenting local experience and anecdotal evidence about best practices in delivering health services to ethnic minority communities; (2) summarizing the local evidence into a model by developing a service manual or protocol that may be supplemented with evidence-based principles from other sources (e.g., literature or other demonstration interventions); (3) refining the model to allow flexibility or versatility in serving different ethnic subgroups; (4) implementing the newly developed service manual and conducting a formative evaluation to ensure acceptance and feasibility of the model in the local community; and (5) conducting outcome evaluation studies to assess the effectiveness of the locally grown intervention model.

Pursuant to the anthropological tradition or a primarily qualitative methodology, this approach emphasizes the importance of cultural humility while cautioning against premature decisions or choices regarding intervention design or implementation strategy. In Step 1, for example, the documentation of local experiences and clinical cases of successfully serving a target population encourages triangulation of evidence by employing two or more methods (e.g., focus group, qualitative interview of multiple informants, survey, etc.) to crossexamine and confirm findings (Reynoso-Vallejo, 2009).

At the very least, one should question and re-examine any simple understanding of a culturally stereotypic concept, especially when this concept is critical in a health intervention design. In a recent review of health behavior theories and concepts applied to the breast cancer screening interventions for ethnic cultural groups, Pasick and Burke (2008) cited an example about fatalism as a key cultural belief that deters members of minority groups from engaging in cancer screening intervention (Pasick & Burke, 2008). A number of thoughtful researchers went beyond the widely accepted notion of fatalism as consisting of a cultural belief that the mysteriously predetermined course of fate is unchangeable and that life events are beyond one's control, and explored, using anthropological methods, the normative meaning of the concept among members of the cultural group (Abraído-Lanza et al., 2007). When fatalism is viewed simply as a culturally innate and unreasonable obstacle to health promotion, interventionists are likely to dismiss the belief or directly ask people to abandon it. However, after more intensive ethnographic investigation, when fatalism is viewed as a reasonable "cultural tool" providing a sense of predictability over that which is seemingly unpredictable and uncontrollable (Kagawa-Singer & Kassim-Lakha, 2003), a health intervention should focus on ways to increase the participants' self efficacy or sense of control and confidence in adopting health behavior.

This approach encourages the intervention model developer to have a more complex view of the psychosocial context of the health service delivery, ensuring that the intervention can flexibly serve a diverse range of ethnic subgroups, and employing formative evaluation to continuously improve the service model. In doing so, it values complexity, diversity, and the use of multiple data sources over simplicity and clarity.

Case Example 1: The Tiempo de Oro Program

Valle de Sol (VdS) is a company with years of experience providing prevention services for substance abuse and problems affecting youth and families in Guadalupe, Arizona, a Yaqui Native American and Hispanic community between Phoenix and Tempe at the base of South Mountain. In 2002, VdS, on the basis of their success in servicing local communities and families, decided to expand their services and launched a new program named "Tiempo de Oro (TdO)" to improve mental health conditions among elderly populations not only in Guadalupe but also in El Mirage, another city in the same county of Maricopa, Arizona. At the time, Guadalupe was a town with a Latino population of 72%; El Mirage had a Latino population of 50%. Both were among American cities that witnessed the fastest growth of Hispanic populations in the 1990s (Levkoff et al., 2006, pp. 67–91).

In numerous ways, the TdO program employs a novel approach to delivering behavioral health services to elderly Latinos. First, it uses prevention services as a "doorway" to reach ethnic Latinos whose needs for mental health support have gone unrecognized; second, the prevention services provided by local community health workers are culturally and linguistically appropriate, holistic, community centered, and reflect local needs as gauged through the input of local members; third, these community health workers function as a bridge between the formal service delivery system (e.g., primary health care) and the community's informal social support system. The prevention and outreach services include the following:

- Educational classes on topics such as changing roles, coping with loss, and healthy aging
- Educational workshops intended to help seniors improve their well-being by connecting them with others for support
- Educational sessions provided during home visits with seniors at risk
- Family education and counseling (in-home or office based) for people who care for seniors at risk
- Support for isolated seniors via telephone or visitation (Levkoff et al., 2006, pp. 67–91).

During the initial period of the TdO program, its parent organization, VdS, experienced a major transition. It expanded its previous focus on youth and families to include focus on the elderly and their families. To make sure that the new prevention services could serve their intended target, the VdS tasked a Consumer Advisory Committee to review the program's service model. This committee has gradually become a key driving force of organizational improvement. First, this committee recognized that the TdO service was built on two very general evidence-based notions: one, receiving social support is critical to positive functioning later in life (Silliman, 1985; Snow & Gordon, 1980) and inversely related to depression (Holahan & Holahan, 1987); and, two, a community health worker (i.e., *promotora/animadora*) familiar with the target ethnic community can play a central role in promoting the health of elderly members in this community. Recognizing these general principles can provide important guidance in concerning the overall program development, but they cannot constitute the evidentiary basis for a specific service model or protocol. The committee concluded that the

TdO's prevention-based mental health program for the ethnic Latino population represented an entirely novel approach.

Based on communications with coaches sent from the national technical assistance center to help with overall service implementation and evidence-based service enhancement, the committee and the TdO leaders were convinced that the documentation and manualization of these practices would serve as important first steps in making these practice methods accessible to other programs and to the larger evidence-based practice field.

After receiving the qualitative input from the consumer advisory committee, TdO initiated two quantitative evaluation activities focusing on areas of greatest concerns. One evaluated the impact of the prevention service activities by using pre-and post-test questionnaires. The overall impacts of the prevention service activities were generally positive, with participants showing increasingly less "apathy or lack of interest in things," less "difficulty with work" (e.g., completing tasks, performance level, finding or keeping a job), and increased interest in "developing independence or autonomy" and "pursuing leisure time or recreational activities" (Levkoff et al., 2006, pp. 67–91).

The second evaluation activity entailed the creation and distribution of a survey examining the program's outreach efforts. Because Valle de Sol had previously served the Guadalupe community but was new to the El Mirage community, prevention activities were expectedly successful in Guadalupe, but far more limited in El Mirage. TdO program leaders sought to determine the successful and unsuccessful components of their operations in El Mirage. Using qualitative input from various groups such as the Consumer Advisory Committee, selected VdS outreach workers, experts, and staff members at the national technical assistance center, the TdO leaders formulated an "Outreach Documentation Survey." This survey instrument was developed to assess three aspects of the outreach efforts: outreach knowledge and planning, outreach activities and strategies, and outreach evaluative activities (Levkoff et al., 2006, pp. 67–91).

The preliminary findings in the two cities indicated several major barriers to successful outreach. The Latino communities in El Mirage and Guadalupe were quite different, and TdO outreach workers were insufficiently knowledgeable about the cultures and traditions in the Guadalupe community. This finding demonstrated the necessity of collaboration between TdO workers and local partners in the El Mirage community. After this review, the TdO program successfully obtained further federal funding to establish permanent clinical treatment components for managing behavioral health problems (Levkoff et al., 2006, pp. 67–91).

Comments

The experience of the TdO program provides a new angle to the concept of "evidence-based practice." It demonstrates that, with the use of scientific methodology, evidence can be extracted from service experiences. Such learning can be critical for guiding service development. It also demonstrates that consumer advisory inputs and evaluation tools can proactively assist a service program to seek self-understanding and provide quality assistance to local communities.

Case Example 2: Barriers to Recruitment of African Americans

Despite the advancements of modern medicine for decreasing mortality and improving people's health statuses, health care disparities persist for certain population groups within the United States. For instance, African Americans experience health disparities in heart disease, cancer, pulmonary disease, sexually transmitted disease, and infant mortality, stemming from social inequalities in both the past and the present. The inequalities go beyond socioeconomic status, which is a primary determinant of health status. Institutionalized racism is also a factor in African American health disparities. African Americans not only face discrimination, but they also experience unequal access to education, accommodation, employment, and health services. The compounding effects of these factors result in overall health and quality of life disparities for the African American population (Dancy et al., 2004).

Another effect of health inequalities for African Americans is their underrepresentation in clinical trials. The distrust generated by institutionalized racism causes African Americans to doubt the benefits of medical research for their overall health. This distrust manifests in two forms of barriers to recruitment for clinical trials: power difference and conceptual barriers. Power differences occur when there is a perceivable inequality, whether it is economic, educational, or sociocultural, in the level of authority between the researcher and the participant. Conceptual barriers occur when the researcher is unable to develop a comprehensive understanding of an ethnic group. A study performed by Dancy et al. (2004) focused on developing a thorough understanding of these barriers in order to design culturally appropriate approaches to overcome them.

The study found that different strategies are needed to overcome the two different forms of recruitment barriers. For power-difference barriers, community advisory boards and research cooperatives between investigators and community members are optimal strategies. For conceptual barriers, researchers must identify and address cultural misperceptions held regarding a certain ethnic group by learning about the sociocultural context that binds them (Dancy et al., 2004).

Comments

This study's employment of the "from practice to science" approach emphasizes the role of data collection in the form of participant recruitment for clinical trials. Through practical experiences, researchers identified the deficiencies in their research design, as research outcomes systematically excluded certain population groups. Researchers identified the need to reformulate the scientific method used in clinical trials through observations made during practice, thus demonstrating the added value of this approach in certain circumstances.

Case Example 3: Community-Based Breast Cancer Intervention

The most prevalent form of cancer among women in the United States is breast cancer. Breast cancer also places second in terms of cancer-related deaths for women. African American women fare worse than their white counterparts in terms of breast cancer mortality, despite the lower prevalence of breast cancer in African American women overall. This is due to lower breast cancer screening rates and the resulting postponed treatment of breast cancer among African American women. African American women tend to visit their physicians less frequently than advised, and they are also less likely to obtain a referral for a mammogram. Both of these factors make it difficult for practitioners to reach African American women for breast cancer intervention (Forte, 1995).

In order to reach a greater number of African American women above the age of 50 for breast cancer education and screening, researchers devised a culturally appropriate intervention method. A study conducted by Deidra Forte identified beauty salons as a culturally familiar setting in which African American women could be targeted for breast cancer awareness. The study targeted about 250 low-income African American women over the age of 50 through local beauty salons over an 8-month period. The objective of this endeavor was to provide these targeted women with culturally sensitive breast cancer informational materials. The familiarity of beauty salons allows for the dissemination of sensitive health education information, such as instructions for self-examination. Approximately 125 of these women were granted free mammograms and clinical examinations on site or at a local clinic (Forte, 1995).

Comments

This community-based breast cancer intervention exposed the deficiencies in conventional intervention programs for reaching certain population groups. Mainstream approaches for preventive breast cancer care assume that women visit their physicians on a regular basis, and that breast cancer is a common enough phenomenon that most women are educated on the matter. Although breast cancer examinations can be performed at home, this does not mean that women know how to effectively perform such self-examinations. The approach used in the study followed the "practice to science" method of cultural intervention in order to reach a population group that would otherwise be overlooked in breast cancer intervention approaches that use science as a starting point.

Case Example 4: Save Our Sons

Preventable diseases afflict the African American population at an overwhelming rate, and lead to higher morbidity and mortality among African Americans than Caucasians in the United States. In fact, African Americans experience approximately 40% more deaths per year than the white population. African American men have a life expectancy of nearly 8 years below the national average, at 66.1 years of age. African American men, more than any other group in the United States, are susceptible to the ramifications of preventable diseases, particularly in terms of diabetes and obesity. Approximately 14.7% of all African Americans over the age of 20 suffer from diabetes, compared to just 8% of the total U.S. population. The rate of diabetes among African American men has doubled since 1980, and 80% to 90% of those diagnosed with type-2 diabetes are obese (Treadwell et al., 2010).

A study conducted by Treadwell et al. (2010) addresses preventive health care measures among African American males, specifically for diabetes and obesity. The location of focus for the study was Lorain county, Ohio, where 8% of the population is African American. The leading causes of death in the total population of Lorain county include cancer, heart disease, lung disease, stroke, diabetes, and preventable injury, while diabetes and the complicating factors associated with obesity are the leading causes of death for underserved African American men. A nonrandomized study of a small group of at-risk African American men (42 in total) was developed to help reduce the rate of diabetes and obesity among the participants (Treadwell et al., 2010).

Through group health education, increased access to health care resources, and enhanced community advocacy networks for health-related needs, this study achieved greater knowledge among its African American male participants of the prevention and management of diabetes and obesity. Moreover, participants reported increased levels of exercise and fitness training and correspondingly lower levels of blood pressure, weight, and body mass index (Treadwell et al., 2010).

Comments

The intervention model developed in this study was not only culture-specific, but it was also gender-specific. Since the diabetes epidemic among African Americans in the United States particularly affects men in this population group, a gender-specific approach was needed in addition to its cultural component. Camaraderie among the participants was an effective tactic for improving accountability within the group—an effect that may not have been achieved if both genders were involved in the intervention.

CONCLUDING REMARKS

In facing the complex challenge of improving cultural competency in health care services for ethnic minority groups, we have highlighted two general approaches that can be used to develop culturally competent interventions to effectively address chronic diseases among minority groups. Both high-reach approaches have great potential to affect public health positively and reduce health disparities. The "science to practice" approach allows for the guiding principles of heath care to be adapted to culture-specific scenarios for a more nuanced approach to health care delivery, while the "practice to science" approach fosters unique approaches to health-related scenarios by assuming that a range of frameworks may exist for developing health intervention for diverse groups, and that all frameworks may not be translatable to all cultural circumstances.

Either of these two approaches, which we have observed through numerous case examples, can lead to the successful development of culturally competent health service interventions for ethnic minority communities. They will also foster, which is perhaps more important, particularly for those devoted, innovative local service leaders, a meaningful course of learning about the best fit between scientific considerations and local practice improvements. In the age of rapid advances in both health sciences and multiculturalism in our society, the success of our attempts to reduce minority health disparities may very much depend on a persistent, conscious effort to seek a dynamic balance between scientific thinking and cultural humility (Reynoso-Vallejo, 2009), which seems to be key to achieving all other balances, such as those between dissemination and adaptation, effectiveness and acceptance, and verification and discovery.

REFERENCES

Abraído-Lanza, A. E., Viladrich, A., Flórez, K. R., Céspedes, A., Aguirre, A. N., & De La Cruz, A. A. (2007). Commentary: Fatalismo reconsidered: A cautionary note for health-related research and practice with Latino populations. *Ethnicity & Disease, 17,* 153–154.

Alagiakrishnan, K. (n.d.). Health and health care of Asian Indian American elders. Retrieved from http://www.stanford.edu/group/ethnoger/asianindian

Banks, A. M. Pew forum on religion & public life: African-Americans surpass others in religiosity. *Religion News Service,* 30 (Jan. 2009).

Boxwala, F. I., Bridgemohan, A., Griffith, A., & Soliman, A. S. (2010). Factors associated with breast cancer screening in Asian Indian women in metro-detroit. *Journal of Immigrant Minor Health, 12,* 534–543.

Brangman, S. (1995). African American elders: Implications for health care providers. *Clinics in Geriatric Medicine, 11,* 15–23.

Committee on Quality of Health Care in America, Institute of Medicine. (2001). *Crossing the quality chasm: A new health system for the 21st century.* Washington, DC: The National Academies Press.

Dancy, B. L., Wilbur, J., Talashek, M., Bonner, G., & Barnes-Boyd, C. (2004). Community-based research: Barriers to recruitment of African Americans. *Nursing Outlook, 52,* 234–235.

Dong, X., Chang, E., Wong, E., Skarupski, K., & Simon, M. (2010). Assessing the health needs of Chinese older adults: Findings from a community-based participatory research study in Chicago's Chinatown. *Journal of Aging Research,* (2010), 4.

Excerpt from the Quarterly Report of the Focus Project, Bienvivir Senior Health Services. (2003). El Paso, TX: Fall.

Forte, D. A. (1995). Community-based breast cancer intervention program for older African American women in beauty salons. *Public Health Report, 110,* 179–180.

Friedman, E. (2009). Supporting diversity in research participation: A framework for action. *Independent Health Policy and Ethics Analyst, CIRM.* Contract No. 2214.

Hargrave, R. (2010). Health and health care of older African American adults. *eCampus Geriatrics,* 16–30.

Hendrix, L. (2010). Health and health care of American Indian older adults. *eCampus Geriatrics,* (2010), 5.

Hendrix, L. (2010). Health and health care of American Indian older adults. *eCampus Geriatrics,* (2010), 12–24.

Holahan, C. K., & Holahan, C. J. (1987). Self-efficacy, social support, and depression in aging: A longitudinal analysis. *Journal of Gerontology, 42,* 65–68.

Jang, Y., Kim, G., Chiriboga, D., & Cho, S. (2008). Willingness to use a nursing home: A study of Korean American elders. *Journal of Applied Gerontology, 27.1*(2008), 110–117.

Kagawa-Singer, M., & Kassim-Lakha, S. (2003). A strategy to reduce cross-cultural miscommunication and increase the likelihood of improving health outcomes. *Academic Medicine, 78,* 577.

Levkoff, S. E., Chen, H., Fisher, J., and McIntyre, J. (2006) Evidence-Based Behavioral Health Practice for Older Adults: A Guide to Implementation. In H. Chen, R. Vega, J. E. Kirchner, J. Maxwell, & S. E. Levkoff (Eds.), Quality management in evidence-based service programs (pp. 67–91).

Livingston, G., Minushkin, S., & Cohn, D. (2008). Hispanics and health care in the United States: Access, information, and knowledge. Washington, DC: Pew Hispanic Center and Robert Wood Johnson Foundation (2008).

McBride, M. (n.d.). Health and health care of Filipino American elders. Retrieved from: http://www.stanford.edu/group/ethnoger/filipino.html

Migneault, J. P., Dedier, J. J., Wright, J. A., Heeren, T., Campbell, M. K., Morisky, D. E.,…Friedman, R. H. (2012a). A culturally adapted telecommunication system to improve physical activity, diet quality, and medication adherence among hypertensive African–Americans: A randomized controlled trial. *Annals of Behavioral Medicine, 43*, 62–63.

Misra, R., Menon, U., Vadaparampil, S. T., & BeLue, R. (2011). Age- and sex-specific cancer prevention and screening practices among Asian Indian immigrants in the United States. *Journal of Investigative Medicine, 59.5*(June 2011), 787–792.

Netto, G., Bhopal, R., Lederle, N., Khatoon, J., & Jackson, A. (2010). How can health promotion interventions be adapted for minority ethnic communities? Five principles for guiding the development of behavioural interventions. *Health Promotion International, 25*, 248–249.

Pasick, R. J., & Burke, N. J. (2008). A critical review of theory in breast cancer screening promotion across cultures. *Annual Review of Public Health, 29*, 351.

Passel, J., & Cohn, D. (2008). Immigration to play a lead role in future U.S. growth. Pew Research Center (February 2008).

Pekmezi, D. W., Neighbors, C. J., Lee, C. S., Gans, K. M., Bock, B. C., Morrow, K. M.,…Marcus, B. H. (2009). A culturally adapted physical activity intervention for Latinas: A randomized controlled trial. *American Journal of Preventive Medicine, 37*, 500–501.

Reynoso-Vallejo, H. (2009). Support group for Latino caregivers of dementia elders: Cultural humility and cultural competence. *Ageing International, 34*, 67–78.

Schneider Institute for Health Policy, Brandeis University. (2003). *Cancer prevention and treatment demonstrations for ethnic and racial minorities: Evidence report and evidence-based recommendations.* Rep. Baltimore, MD: Centers for Medicare and Medicaid Services.

Silliman, R. A. (1986). Social stress and social support. *Generations, 10*, 18–20.

Snow, D. L., & Gordon, J. B. (1980). Social network analysis and intervention with the elderly. *Gerontologist, 20*.

Sohn, L., & Harada, N. D. (2004). Time since immigration and health services utilization of Korean-American older adults living in Los Angeles County. *Journal of the American Geriatric Society, 52.11*(November 2004), 1946–1950.

Stirland, L., Halani, L., Raj, B., Netuveli, G., Partridge, M., Car, J.,…Sheikh, A. (2011). Recruitment of South Asians into asthma research: qualitative study of UK and US researchers. *Primary Care Respiratory Journal, 20*, 282–290.

Taylor, R. J., & Chatters, L. M. (1991). Nonorganizational religious participation among elderly black adults. *Journal of Gerontology, 46.2*(1991), 103–111.

Teufel-Shone, N. I., Drummond, R., & Rawiel, U. (2005). Developing and adapting a family-based diabetes program at the U.S.-Mexico border. *Preventing Chronic Disease, 2*, 1–3.

The Final Progress Report to SAMHSA: The Focus Project, Bienvivir Senior Health Services. (2003a). El Paso, TX, Fall.

Treadwell, H., Holden, K., Hubbard, R., Harper, F., Wright, F., Ferrer, M., & Kim, E. K. (2010a). Addressing obesity and diabetes among African American men: Examination of a community-based model of prevention. *Journal of the National Medical Association, 102*, 794–795.

U.S. Census Bureau, Profile of General Population and Housing Characteristics: 2010. (2010a). Demographic Profile Data.

U.S. Census Bureau. (2010b). Selected Social Characteristics in the United States 2010 American Community Survey 1-Year Estimates.

Walsh, J. R., Salazar, R., Nguyen, T. T., Kaplan, C., Nguyen, L. K., Hwang, J.,…Pasick, R. J. (2010). Healthy colon, healthy life: A novel colorectal cancer screening intervention. *American Journal of Preventive Medicine, 39.1*(July 2010), 1–14.

CHAPTER 13

Structural and Cultural Issues in Long-Term Services and Supports for Minority Populations

D. Imelda Padilla-Frausto, Steven P. Wallace, and A. E. Benjamin

Racial and ethnic minorities in the United States have historically been excluded from mainstream institutions, whether it is quality education, good jobs, or equitable access to health services. Formal (paid) long-term services and supports (LTSS) have often been seen as residual services, provided only when the family is unable to provide appropriate or adequate care. The original LTSS institutions were established in the late 1800s and early 1900s by religious orders and communities to care for those without family help, but stronger families and fewer alternative options in minority communities led to low levels of their use of "homes for the aged."

Public funding greatly expanded the availability of nursing homes starting in the 1960s; home care expanded greatly starting in the 1980s as a way to prevent or delay institutionalization (Wallace, Abel, Pourat, & Delp, 2007). Public funding to support home care for low-income seniors was a more acceptable option in minority communities and had a more equitable use, although some disparities continue. The growth of assisted living started in the 1990s and attracted mostly private-pay residents and is therefore disproportionately non-Latino white, reducing the proportion of whites in nursing homes at the same time African American institutionalization rates rose. The complex mix of services and funding makes it difficult to provide a comprehensive picture of LTSS use by minority elders, but it appears that the net result is that formal LTSS use overall continues to be lower for minority elders. This chapter examines the history of LTSS programs to document their racially and ethnically disparate impact, and explain the current research on the access and quality of LTSS used by older adults in communities of color.

MAJOR POLICIES SHAPING THE CURRENT U.S. LONG-TERM CARE SYSTEM AND INFLUENCING THE TRENDS IN USING LONG-TERM CARE SERVICES

LTSS are a set of health and social services delivered over a sustained period to people who have lost (or never acquired) some capacity for personal care. Ideally, LTSS enables recipients to live with as much independence and dignity as possible in the least restrictive environment that they desire. They can be provided in institutional, community, and home settings and can involve assistance with daily activities such as walking, bathing, cooking, managing medications, and overseeing finances. The focus of this chapter is formal (paid) LTSS because of their policy relevance, although all the research agrees that most LTSS is provided without pay by family and friends.

Overview of LTSS Polices in the Past Century

Over the last century, the long-term care system for older adults has evolved in ways that have impacted minority populations. The most widely known form of LTSS is the nursing home. During the late 1800s some of the first welfare policies were created to support and care for the impoverished immigrants, predominately southern and eastern Europeans. It was thought that providing aid to people in their homes promoted laziness and so institutions were established to provide for the poor and ill. This era led to the first widespread establishment of asylums for the mentally ill, homes for the aged, and poorhouses for the destitute (Katz, 1996). By 1910, poorhouses had also taken the role of old age homes for the destitute, especially for immigrants. Of the 92 million residents of the United States in 1910, 282,000 native born and 61,000 immigrants were in mental institutions, elder homes, poor houses, or other asylums (Table 13.1). Two thirds of immigrants and one third of the native born in poorhouses were aged 60 or older. The most common institutional location for older adults was old age homes, especially old soldier's homes for the native born. Mental institutions were also a common location to warehouse older adults who had nowhere else to go. Overall, 1.7% of the native born and 3.3% of immigrants lived in these institutional settings.

In addition to the poor houses, religious and ethnic organizations also established homes for the aged. During the early 1900s African Americans developed a number of these homes to serve the African American population since they were excluded from white homes. African American elders comprised 7.9% of the population aged 60 and over, but only 4.7% of elders in homes for the aged and 6.3% of elders in poorhouses. Jews also founded old age homes due to discrimination, and a number of Christian religious orders founded homes as part of their charity work (African American Registry, 1883, 1897). Support for the social welfare of older adults evolved over time due to many factors, including the Depression of the 1930s that led to the establishment of Old Age Assistance under the Social Security Act in 1935. Old Age

TABLE 13.1 Institutions Caring for Older Adults, U.S., 1910

		MENTAL INSTITUTION	ELDER HOMES	POOR HOUSES	ASYLUMS, OTHER	TOTAL IN INSTITUTIONS	TOTAL POPULATION
Immigrants	Under 60	78.2%	8.4%	33.4%	43.6%	47.7%	
		20,550	1,305	3,712	3,406	28,973	5,886,126
	60 & over	21.8%	91.6%	66.6%	56.4%	52.3%	
		5,712	14,236	7,411	4,409	31,768	968,383
	Total immigrants	100.0%	100.0%	100.0%	100.0%	100.0%	
		26,262	15,541	11,123	7,815	60,741	6,854,509
Native	Under 60	82.2%	10.2%	64.5%	83.4%	67.0%	
		115,022	5,115	26,976	41,929	189,042	80,192,170
	60 & over	17.8%	89.8%	35.5%	16.6%	33.0%	
		24,870	45,009	14,839	8,327	93,045	5,305,179
	Total native	100.0%	100.0%	100.0%	100.0%	100.0%	
		139,892	50,124	41,815	50,256	282,087	85,497,349

Source: Author's calculation from the 1910 U.S. Census. Ruggles, S., Alexander, J. T., Genadek, K., Goeken, R., Schroeder, M. B., & Sobek, M. (2010). Integrated Public Use Microdata Series: Version 5.0 [Machine-readable database]. Minneapolis: University of Minnesota.

Assistance provided very modest cash support for poor elders while Social Security, one of the first social insurance programs in U.S. history, founded a universal retirement benefit system for workers and their families. These programs marked a change in welfare policy from "indoor" relief to "outdoor" relief and led to the closure of poorhouses (Quadagno, 1988).

In 1965, two new health insurance programs were established to provide access to health care and some long-term care for many older adults—Medicare, a social insurance program, and Medicaid, a public assistance program. While Medicare was instrumental in desegregating hospitals, similar efforts were not made in nursing homes. Medicaid, like Old Age Assistance, helped primarily destitute older adults, while Medicare, like Social Security retirement benefits, was of most use to those who were better off. However, Medicare long-term care services are limited to only posthospitalization care and rehabilitation on a short-term basis. Even though Medicaid was originally designed for low-income families and children, it does cover many different LTSS, including nursing home care, with no time limit. The high costs of LTSS have led a smaller number of low-income older adults to consume a large share of Medicaid expenditures. High LTSS costs also result in a significant number of nonpoor older adults exhausting their resources and then becoming eligible for Medicaid.

The different models used for these programs established a two-class system of LTSS policies that still exists today: one set for better paid workers who receive universal, federally administered Social Security and Medicare, and the other set of policies for low-income and marginalized populations who receive means-tested, state administered, and politically vulnerable programs for income, housing, and health care (Wallace, 2012). This two-class system of LTSS has played an important role in LTSS use by older minority populations. While Medicaid has helped to reduce the financial barriers to long-term care for low-income populations, Medicaid recipients may continue to use fewer and less appropriate LTSS than their non-Medicaid counterparts (Niefeld & Kasper, 2005).

The shift in emphasis from nursing homes to home and community-based care was strongly supported in 1990 with the enactment of the Americans with Disabilities Act (ADA). The ADA was the basis for the 1999 Supreme Court's *Olmstead versus L.C.* ruling that persons receiving state assistance had the right to care in the least restrictive environment that they desire, if feasible. States have followed that ruling unevenly, with some states emphasizing consumer-directed care while others continue to have an institutional bias in their public programs (Reinhard, Kassner, Houser, & Mollica, 2011). Consumer-directed long-term care services are particularly pertinent to older minority populations because they allow care recipients the flexibility to hire, train, and supervise their own caregiver, such as a family member—which is allowed in some states (Benjamin, 2001)—and results in more positive outcomes for the care recipient (Benjamin, Matthias, & Franke, 2000; Foster, Dale, & Brown, 2007) and is a more preferred option among minority populations.

Trends in LTSS Use By Minority Populations

As older adults begin to lose their independence, many of them, and in particular minority populations, prefer family caregivers to provide assistance in their homes over care in an institutionalized setting such as a nursing home. The need for long-term care has been shaped in part by the aging of the population; the population aged 65 and over doubled from 20 million in 1970 to over 40 million in 2010, and those aged 85 and over grew from 7.6% of the elderly in 1970 to 13.8% in 2010. Minority elders have similarly increased from 11% of the population aged 65 and over in 1970 to 20% in 2010. In this next section trends in formal long-term care service use are explored to better understand the gaps in long-term care needs for minority populations.

Trends in Nursing Home Use

Over the past 30 years, studies have documented a shifting trend in nursing home use among older minority populations compared to older non-Latino whites. Historically, due in part to racism and segregation, nursing homes were predominantly used by and made for non-Latino white elderly populations (Borrayo, Salmon, Polivka, & Dunlop, 2002; Miller & Weissert, 2000).

Early studies on disparities in nursing home use were largely focused on differences between African Americans[1] and white populations. By and large these studies found that African Americans were less likely to use nursing homes than white populations, even after controlling for risk factors such as disability, comorbidities, and marital status (Coughlin, McBride, & Liu, 1990; Murtaugh, Kemper, Spillman, & Carlson, 1997; Wallace, Levy-Storms, Kington, & Andersen, 1998). The first studies that included Latino populations found inconsistent findings; one study found older Latinos were less likely to utilize nursing home care than their white counterparts (Mui & Burnette, 1994) and another found no statistically significant differences (Wallace et al., 1998).

Trends in institutionalization since 1970 from Census data show the basic patterns that research has tried to explain (Table 13.2). In 1970, just over 5% of all white older adults were in nursing homes. The proportion of white elders in nursing homes peaked in 1980 at 5.5%, and has fallen with the emphasis on diverting older adults to other settings since then. In 2010, the rate had fallen to 3.3%. In the 1970s, the institutionalization rate was substantially lower than the white rate for all racial/ethnic groups. While the rates for each group rose in the intervening years, especially for African Americans, they are higher than their 1970 rate only for African Americans. The institutionalization rate for those aged 85 and older is much higher than all those aged 65 and over, but it followed the same overall patterns (Table 13.2). The dropping institutionalization rates have been accompanied by increases in both the level of disability and the age of nursing home residents.

Similar to a century earlier, the use of nursing homes varies significantly between immigrants and native-born persons. The trends are clearest when examining rates for those aged 85 and over who are at the highest risk of institutionalization, as well as separately for men and women (Table 13.3). Immigrants and men are both less likely to be institutionalized, with white women aged 85 and over having the highest rate of all (14.7%). Both Latino and Asian immigrants have institutionalization rates about half that of whites. This may be due to greater family support, less access to insurance coverage, language barriers, and/or lower rates of disability. The lower rates for men are due in part to the higher rates of men being married, versus women being more often widowed.

While the trends in nursing home use among minority populations show some increased use, studies have documented lower levels of quality care for minorities in nursing homes. Compared to non-Latino whites, African American and Latino diabetic nursing

TABLE 13.2 Percent Population Institutionalized Age 65 and Over, and Age 85 and Over, by Race/Ethnicity, U.S., 1970 to 2010

	1970 (%)	1980 (%)	1990 (%)	2000 (%)	2010 (%)
Age 65+					
Latino	1.9	2.7	2.7	2.4	2.1
African American	3.2	3.8	4.7	5.1	4.3
Asian American	2.2	2.3	1.9	1.5	1.4
White	5.2	5.5	5.4	4.9	3.3
Age 85+					
Latino	7.0	10.4	12.6	9.7	7.4
African American	7.6	12.8	16.1	16.1	12.3
Asian American	6.8	9.8	13.0	7.5	6.3
White	19.5	24.4	25.0	19.2	11.7

Note: Latino may be of any race; all others are non-Latino.

Source: U.S. Census IPUMS. Ruggles, S., Alexander, J. T., Genadek, K., Goeken, R., Schroeder, M. B., & Sobek, M. (2010). Integrated Public Use Microdata Series: Version 5.0 [Machine-readable database]. Minneapolis: University of Minnesota.

TABLE 13.3 Institutionalized Population Age 85 and Over by Race/Ethnicity, Gender, and Nativity, U.S., 2010

	% OF MEN AGE 85+ IN INSTITUTIONS	% OF WOMEN AGE 85+ IN INSTITUTIONS	DISTRIBUTION OF RACE/ ETHNICITY AMONG ALL AGE 85+ INSTITUTIONALIZED
Latino, native	8.0	10.1	2.3
Latino, immigrant	3.7	6.3	2.6
Asian, native	6.3	10.7	0.7
Asian, immigrant	5.5	7.7	1.8
African American	10.5	13.8	7.0
White	8.0	14.7	84.8
Total[a]			100

Note: Latino may be of any racial group; all others are non-Latino.

[a]Includes races not shown.

Source: 2008–2010 American Community Survey. Ruggles, S., Alexander, J. T., Genadek, K., Goeken, R., Schroeder, M. B., & Sobek, M. (2010). Integrated Public Use Microdata Series: Version 5.0 [Machine-readable database]. Minneapolis: University of Minnesota.

home residents were less likely to receive antidiabetic medications (Allsworth, Toppa, Palin, & Lapane, 2005; Spooner, Lapane, Hume, Mor, & Gambassi, 2001), and African Americans, Latinos, and Asian and Pacific Islanders at risk for secondary stroke were less likely to receive anticoagulants (Christian, Lapane, & Toppa, 2003; Quilliam & Lapane, 2001). Similarly, studies have documented that African Americans and Latinos disproportionately reside in segregated nursing homes (Reed & Andes, 2001; Smith, Feng, Fennell, Zinn, & Mor, 2007) that are often of lower quality (Grabowski, 2004; S. C. Miller, Papandonatos, Fennell, & Mor, 2006; Mor, Zinn, Angelelli, Teno, & Miller, 2004) and lead to worse health outcomes (Fennell, Feng, Clark, & Mor, 2010). Many of the quality issues stem from structural issues of segregated nursing homes having high numbers of low-paying Medicaid patients. Decreasing Medicaid reimbursements have led to disparities in funding and resources for nursing homes that provide care predominately for low-income minority populations.

It is not entirely clear what factors are influencing the growing rate of minority residents and decreasing rate of white elderly in nursing home settings. Some speculate that the decreasing trend in nursing home use has been primarily among private payers who have opted to spend their money on preferred options such as assisted living facilities (Grabowski, 2001; Grabowski, Ohsfeldt, & Morrisey, 2003), which historically have been disproportionally non-Latino white (Spillman, Liu, & McGuilliard, 2002). Assisted living, also called residential care, has increased as a source of long-term care for older adults in recent years, but since they are mostly private pay, access will be limited for lower income and minority populations (Hernandez & Newcomer, 2007). One study comparing nursing home versus assisted living use found African Americans more likely to reside in nursing homes and more likely to be concentrated in smaller, lower quality assisted living facilities compared to non-Latino whites (Howard et al., 2002). Data from the 2010 National Center for Health Statistics survey of residential care facilities found that 89% of the residents were aged 65 and over, and that 84% to 94% of the residents were non-Latino white depending on age (Table 13.3). While 85% of nursing home residents aged 85 and over are white (Table 13.3), 95% of comparable residential care residents are non-Latino white (Table 13.4). The number of residents of each racial/ethnic group increases with age, but the non-Latino white group increases the fastest.

While these shifting trends may seem to be reducing disparities in long-term care for older minority populations, nursing home care is the least preferred long-term care option and is often seen as the last resort when functional disabilities are too severe for

TABLE 13.4 Residential Care Residents by Age and Race, U.S., 2010

		AGE GROUPS				TOTAL
		<65	65 TO 74	75 TO 84	85+	
Latino	Population estimate	2,340	2,528	5,770	10,351	20,989
	% of age group	3.0	4.0	2.9	2.6	2.9%
White	Population estimate	59,278	52,554	184,444	371,532	667,808
	% of age group	76.8	84.2	92.8	94.1	91.1%
African American	Population estimate	13,274	5,386	5,385	7,635	31,680
	% of age group	17.2	8.6	2.7	1.9	4.3%
Asian & other	Population estimate	2,326	1,956	3,212	5,338	12,832
	% of age group	3.0	3.1	1.6	1.4	1.7%
Total	Population estimate	77,218	62,424	198,811	394,856	733,309
	% of age group	100.0	100.0	100.0	100.0	100.0%

Note: Latino may be any race; each race group is non-Latino.

Source: National Center for Health Statistics. (2011). 2010 National Survey of Residential Care Facilities (NSRCF). Tabulations by author.

an older adult to stay in the community. This paradoxical increase in nursing home use among minority populations has left some researchers questioning if this shift reflects disparities in lower access to preferred options such as home- and community-based services and assisted living facilities (Akamigbo & Wolinsky, 2007; Feng, Fennell, Tyler, Clark, & Mor, 2011). The next section explores the trends in home- and community-based services among minority populations to better understand the context of this preferred location of care.

Trends in Community-Based LTSS

Almost all elders, independent of race and ethnicity, prefer to remain living in their own home rather than move to a nursing home if they become disabled. The complicated web of services that can help them achieve that goal includes services such as personal care (e.g., help with bathing), homemaker services (e.g., help with cooking, laundry), chore services (e.g., small home repairs), home-delivered meals, home modification (e.g., install grab bars), medical alert devices (e.g., calls 911 after a serious fall), transportation, case management, in-home nursing (e.g., for medication management, wound care), physical therapy, adult day care, and more (Kietzman et al., 2012). Untangling the use and access to community services by minority elderly is difficult due to this myriad of different possible services that may have different names in different communities. This is likely to contribute to the mixed set of findings about whether or not minority elders have higher, the same, or lower levels of use overall of community-based care. If their net use of paid help in the community is lower we then must ask if they are more dependent on informal caregivers, or disproportionally face greater amounts of unmet needs. The former suggests that communities of color shoulder a disproportionate share of the effort to maintain disabled older adults in the community, while the latter indicates inequity in the burden of disability on older adults.

For African American and Latino older adults, some studies have found no racial differences in community service use (Peng, Navaie-Waliser, & Feldman, 2003; Kirby & Lau, 2010), others have found higher use (Laditka, Laditka, & Drake, 2006; Wallace et al., 1998), and some found lower usage of services (Kemper, 1992) among older African Americans. When examining overall unmet needs, Casado et al. (2011) found that African American elders in the community had higher levels of unmet needs when considering a set of seven different community-based LTSS. Driving that unmet need was a lack of awareness of the services and programs that were available, a reluctance to use public services, and the lack of availability and affordability of needed services in their communities.

For Latino elderly, trends show lower service use (Crist, Woo, & Choi, 2007; Kemper, 1992; Wallace, Levy-Storms, & Ferguson, 1995), but subgroup analysis has found Mexican American elderly have lower usage compared to white elderly (Crist et al., 2007; Wallace & Lew-Ting, 1992), as well as lower usage compared to Puerto Ricans and Cuban elderly (Wallace & Lew-Ting, 1992) despite having similar or higher levels of need. Like Latinos, older Asians are a heterogeneous group, and when subgroups are lumped together, it appears that there are no racial disparities in using community-based LTSS among Asian elderly when compared to other racial and ethnic groups (Kirby & Lau, 2010; Peng et al., 2003). When subgroups are analyzed separately, however, lower trends in both awareness and use of services are seen among Korean Americans (Moon, Lubben, & Villa, 1998) and similarly for more recent Taiwanese immigrants (Kuo & Torres-Gil, 2001).

In contrast, the few studies on American Indian use of community services are more consistent. Rural American Indians living on a reservation were more likely to use community-based LTSS than white elderly living in a rural community (Goins et al., 2011) and nonreservation American Indians (Chapleski & Dwyer, 1995). The higher trends for American Indians living on reservations may be attributed to the organization of Indian health and tribal health services that provides long-term care services by American Indian peers, similar to promotoras, who provide a range of paraprofessional health assistance that is culturally sensitive and appropriate.

Unmet needs in the community may be patterned by race and ethnicity because each state varies in eligibility criteria for public programs and in the types of services they provide. Southern states, where over half of older African Americans live, have the least generous public programs for LTSS. Almost half of older Latinos are found in the Western states (e.g., California) and the West South Central region (e.g., Texas), which includes a mixture of relatively generous (California) and very meager (Texas) public LTSS programs (Reinhard et al., 2011). For those minority populations that do receive services, there are still barriers in care, such as many programs that do not provide enough hours of coverage, problems with the reliability and trustworthiness of the caregiver, and language and cultural barriers (Mullan et al., 2009).

FUTURE DIRECTION OF LTSS

Sociodemographic Shift of Older Adults

By 2030, the population aged 65 and over in the United States is estimated to double in size to 80 million, with the largest growth in those aged 85 and older—the age group with the highest LTSS needs (Federal Interagency Forum on Aging-Related Statistics, 2012). The older population is continuing to become more racially and ethnically diverse as well. It is estimated that racial/ethnic minorities will grow from 20% of the older population in 2010, to 41% by 2050. The total numbers of older adults will more than double in that time period; the number of older Latinos will increase six times to become the largest group after non-Latino whites. Asians will increase more than fivefold and African Americans will increase three times (Federal Interagency Forum on Aging-Related Statistics, 2012). It is important to highlight the demographic shift among older adults because the system of LTSS that exists today was historically created for and previously utilized by a predominately non-Latino white population who were monolingual English, and in comparison to minority elders, they were in better health and had more financial means to access these services. The increasingly diverse population of older minority adults are more likely to be in worse health than whites (Markides & Wallace, 2007), more disabled (Seeman, Merkin, Crimmins, & Karlamangla, 2010), and have fewer financial resources to access needed LTSS (Wallace & Villa, 2009).

Structural and Cultural Issues in LTSS for Minority Populations

Structural issues can be thought of as factors that are amenable to policy change, such as the way LTSS systems are organized, operated, and financed. For example, income levels and type of health insurance (e.g., Medicaid vs. private supplement to Medicare) are often identified as structural determinants and major predictors of the use of LTSS among minority populations (Wallace, Campbell, & Lew-Ting, 1994). Cultural issues can be thought of as unique characteristics belonging to a group of individuals such as beliefs about family responsibility to care for older adults as well as attitudes toward the use of health care services.

Structural Issues

One of the most significant structural issues that creates barriers to LTSS for all elders is that the fragmented and uncoordinated system of services is difficult for older adults and their families to navigate and access in an appropriate and timely manner (E. A. Miller, Allen, & Mor, 2008). The various eligibility criteria for LTSS under Medicare and Medicaid creates gaps in coverage and leaves access to LTSS largely dependent on an older adult's ability to pay for these services. The intersection of inadequate long-term care coverage and economic insecurity may be a particular structural issue for middle income minority populations. This group of minority older adults is most likely to be facing an income gap where they do not have enough income to pay for long-term services on their own and their income is not low enough to qualify for many services that use the Federal Poverty Level (FPL) guidelines to determine eligibility. For example, in California, minority elders are more likely to have incomes between 100% and 199% of the FPL (Figure 13.1) compared to non-Latino white elderly. However, even using an FPL cutoff of 199%, FPL does not mean that other older adults would be able to afford long-term care services, since the income needed to cover the basic average cost of living for an older adult, before LTSS costs, is already at 200% of the FPL (Wallace, Padilla-Frausto, & Smith, 2010) and long-term care expenses can double the amount of income an older adults needs to cover those costs (Wallace, Satter, Padilla-Frausto, & Peter, 2009). Nationally, the median cost of a shared nursing home room is $6,000/month, while a half-time personal care assistant in home would cost $1,440/month (Genworth Financial, 2012). A poll of California

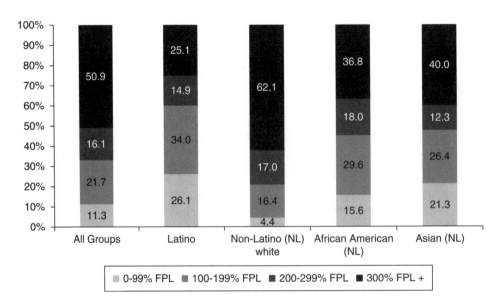

FIGURE 13.1 Federal Poverty Level by Race and Ethnicity, California Adults, Ages 65 and Over.

Source: Pooled 2007 and 2009 California Health Interview Survey (CHIS).

voters aged 40 and over found that 46% reported that they could not afford a single month of nursing home care, rising to 68% among Latinos (The SCAN Foundation & UCLA Center for Health Policy Research, 2012).

Minority elderly on average have lower educational attainment, lower incomes, and fewer assets, such as retirement benefits and homeownership, compared to their non-Latino white counterparts (Choudhury, 2002; Wallace & Villa, 2009), which are mainly due to historical and institutionalized racism and discrimination. As a result, minority elderly are more likely than non-Latino white elders to rely on Social Security as their primary source of income (Caldera, 2010). However, for many older adults residing in states such as California, where cost of living is above the national average, Social Security income barely covers half the cost of basic living expenses, much less the costs associated with their long-term care needs (Wallace et al., 2009). Affordable housing is another structural issue, since older adults prefer to age in place in their homes and in their communities (Kane & Kane, 2001). Policies that provide housing support can help offset the high cost of housing and free up some of their limited income to purchase in-home services and supports. Housing cost is one of the biggest expenses that older adults may have as they age and their incomes become relatively fixed. Higher housing costs are a particular problem for low-income minority populations who are more likely to be renters or homeowners still paying a mortgage. Among low-income older adults (less than 200% of the FPL), renters and homeowners with a mortgage are more likely found among Asians (49.6% and 22.5%, respectively), Latinos (41.5% and 23.6%, respectively), and African Americans (40.3% and 22.4%, respectively) compared to non-Latino white (24.2% and 16.7%, respectively; Table 13.5). In states such as California, rental costs far exceed housing costs for homeowners without a mortgage (Wallace & Molina, 2008).

Housing supports for current older minority groups could be in the form of providing more affordable housing or subsidized rental units. For frail low-income elderly populations, providing assisted living services would help meet their long-term care needs (Wilden, Redfoot, Institute, & AARP, 2002). According to the 2012 Current Population Survey, 7% of low-income (less than 200% FPL) older adults live in public housing and 2.5% receive rent subsidies. Public housing and rent subsidies are more common among older African Americans and rent subsidies are more common for older Latinos than average (King et al., 2010). When public housing for seniors includes enhanced services, such as a dining room or personal care assistance, it provides a context where aging in place is more likely. For the future generation of minority older adults, policies that promote homeownership before old age can influence usage in the least preferred option for long-term care—nursing homes. For example, in studies of homeownership and nursing home usage, one study found homeowners to have a lower probability of a permanent nursing home admission (Coughlin et al., 1990) and another found homeowners were more likely to be discharged alive (Greene & Ondrich, 1990) which suggests this type of usage is not by choice but due to a lack of options in aging and dying in one's home.

TABLE 13.5 Housing Type by Race/Ethnicity, Noninstitutionalized Population Ages 65 and Over With Household Income Less Than 200% FPL, U.S., 2008 to 2010

	ALL GROUPS	LATINO	NON-LATINO (NL) WHITE	AFRICAN AMERICAN (NL)	ASIAN (NL)
Renters	29.1	41.5	24.2	40.3	49.6
Owners, paying mortgage	18.4	23.6	16.7	22.4	22.5
Owners, mortgage paid off	48.9	31.9	55.4	33.9	23.7
No cash rent	3.6	3.1	3.7	3.4	4.1
Total	100	100	100	100	100

Source: 2008–2010 American Community Survey. Ruggles, S., Alexander, J. T., Genadek, K., Goeken, R., Schroeder, M. B., & Sobek, M. (2010). Integrated Public Use Microdata Series: Version 5.0 [Machine-readable database]. Minneapolis: University of Minnesota.

TABLE 13.6 Linguistic Isolation by Race and Ethnicity, Noninstitutionalized U.S., Older Adults, Ages 65 and Over

	ALL OLDER ADULTS	LATINO	NON-LATINO (NL) WHITE	AFRICAN AMERICAN (NL)	ASIAN (NL)
Linguistically isolated	4.5	30.7	1.5	1.0	30.3
Not linguistically isolated	95.5	69.3	98.5	99.0	69.7
Total	100.0	100.0	100.0	100.0	100.0

Source: 2008–2010 American Community Survey (ACS). Ruggles, S., Alexander, J. T., Genadek, K., Goeken, R., Schroeder, M. B., & Sobek, M. (2010). Integrated Public Use Microdata Series: Version 5.0 [Machine-readable database]. Minneapolis: University of Minnesota.

For minority populations, other structural issues can add further layers of complexity to meeting LTSS needs. For instance, the passage of the Patient Protection and Affordable Care Act (PPACA, P.L. 111–148; ACA) in 2010 offers a long awaited improvement in access to health care in the United States, in particular for low to middle-income populations, and incentivizes states to shift public funding from nursing homes to community-based care. While encouraging community-based care should be of particular benefit to communities of color, the ACA also excludes undocumented immigrants, which will continue inequities in some Latino and Asian communities. While few older adults lack the needed immigration documents, not providing health care to younger undocumented immigrants now will likely lead to a future older immigrant population with worse health, placing a greater demand on medical and long-term care systems.

Culturally Appropriate Outreach, Services, and Providers as a Structural Issue

Lack of awareness of all the various LTSS available and the eligibility criteria for programs that can pay for them is a barrier for many older adults (Tang & Pickard, 2008). These issues are a particular barrier to older minorities and their families who also face educational and linguistic barriers (Bradley et al., 2002; Crist, Kim, Pasvogel, & Velázquez, 2009; Moon et al., 1998; NAC, 2009). Language is not just an issue when it comes to increasing awareness, but it directly influences whether or not older minority populations and their family caregivers will decide to use long-term care services (Scharlach et al., 2006). This is particularly true for more recent immigrant populations such as Latinos and Asians, who are less likely to speak English and more likely to be isolated linguistically (Table 13.6). Linguistic isolation, where no one in the household speaks English well, makes it so that even when older adults have strong family support, the family is less likely to be able to help the elder learn about and navigate the complex systems needed to qualify for public LTSS programs.

While language is often treated as a cultural issue, it is also a structural barrier because institutional language barriers can be reduced with appropriate policies. These policies could include, but are not limited to, providing translation services, hiring and training a multilingual work force, promoting a more racially and ethnically diverse administration through incentives for higher education, and providing more resources to organizations already providing culturally sensitive and linguistically appropriate services to minority populations. Support for culturally tailored models such as those used on American Indian reservations could help increase the number of older minority adults who get their long-term care needs met (Chapleski & Dwyer, 1995; Goins et al., 2011).

Cultural Issues

Cultural issues, unlike structural issues, are less amenable to policy change, but are just as important to understand as they may also play a role in the lower usage trends seen among minority populations. Cultural beliefs about family responsibility to care for older adults (filial piety) as well as attitudes toward the use of formal and/or public health and long-term care services can shape older adults' use of LTSS.

Filial Piety and familism are terms given to belief systems that hold family members responsible for the care of their aging parents or relatives. While many cultural issues vary by race and ethnicity, one salient cultural issue that cuts across all minority populations is that of filial piety (Scharlach et al., 2006). For both the aging parent and the family caregiver, beliefs about family responsibility can play a role in the decision-making process to use formal long-term care services. However, while the desire to take care of an aging relative may be strong, the ability to carry out filial responsibilities may be influenced by other factors such as changing preferences in living arrangements, health conditions, and acculturation. For example, when older Latinos are asked about their preference in living arrangements, most say that they prefer to live with their spouse or if the spouse is deceased, with their children (Angel, Angel, McClellan, & Markides, 1996). Korean Americans often share in the same filial piety beliefs; however, in the case of dementia care, some elderly Korean Americans were more likely to report intentions to use formal long-term care services than to burden their children (Lee & Casado, 2011). Likewise, acculturation differences were seen among Korean Americans who prefer living on their own more than Koreans living in Korea, who prefer extended family living arrangements (Moon et al., 1998). There is also likely to be an interaction between culture and class, as in one study that found upwardly mobile Taiwanese immigrants feeling that they were being filial by paying for the LTSS that their elders in the United States needed rather than providing it themselves (Lan, 2002).

There can also be a difference between cultural intent and behavior. Younger Mexican American caregivers were less likely than older Mexican American caregivers to live with their care recipient and more likely to use formal long-term care services (Scharlach et al., 2006). Higher use of formal long-term care services was particularly more likely among Mexican American caregivers who were knowledgeable about long-term care resources or whose parent was covered by Medicaid (Herrera, Lee, Palos, & Torres-Vigil, 2008). This dynamic left older Mexican American caregivers concerned about the effect of acculturation and what filial beliefs their children will hold when they become the next generation of care recipients. These shifting trends in preferences and behavior may hint at what is to come for future generations of minority older adults who will have a greater need for formal LTSS.

Trust in the health care system and government agencies is by far one of the most challenging cultural issues that African American and American Indian populations face (Boulware, Cooper, Ratner, LaVeist, & Powe, 2003; Kramer, 1991; Musa, Schulz, Harris, Silverman, & Thomas, 2009). African Americans and American Indians have historically experienced abuse and discrimination by government institutions and society as a whole. African Americans are more likely to question the motives of the medical care system due to a long history of being subjected to medical experimentation and mistreatment (Gamble, 1997) and are currently still less likely to received adequate treatment for certain conditions (Musa et al., 2009). American Indians' distrust in government agencies is deeply rooted in a long history of being conquered, stripped of their land and relocated to desolate and barren parts of the country, and being subject to coerced "acculturation" (Sturtevant, 1988). Other minority groups have also expressed a mistrust in anyone outside of family being able to provide adequate care for their loved ones (Scharlach et al., 2006). To overcome the barrier of trust for minority groups, the importance of policies that would foster the training and hiring of more minority caregivers might help to create long-term care services provided by racial and ethnic peers.

SUMMARY

The current system of LTSS is complex and difficult to navigate, which limits access to appropriate and continuous services in a timely manner. The multiple funding streams and various eligibility criteria discourage older adults from accessing needed services, compounding barriers for minority elders who are more likely to rely on public services than non-Latino whites. While many erroneously believe that Medicare pays for the bulk of long-term care, the long-term care services covered by Medicare are limited to only posthospitalization care and rehabilitation on a short-term basis. For older adults who are eligible, Medicaid provides the bulk of funding for long-term care. However, there are some minority older adults who are not eligible for Medicaid—either because they are caught in the income gap where their income is too high to qualify for Medicaid but too low to purchase long-term care services, or they are ineligible due to their citizenship status. Additionally, while Medicaid has helped to reduce the financial barriers to long-term care for low-income populations, evidence suggests that other barriers to appropriate services exist for older adults who rely on Medicaid. In sum, to reduce the complexity of accessing long-term care services and supports and increase the usage trends in formal LTSS among minority populations, a universal program such as Medicare for LTSS funding and a single point of entry is needed.

The coming sociodemographic shift of older minority adults calls attention to other structural and cultural issues that facilitate or inhibit the appropriate use of LTSS. Many minority elderly on average face a lower socioeconomic status with lower educational attainment, lower incomes, and fewer assets, such as retirement benefits and homeownership compared to their non-Latino white counterparts. Income and housing supports can help offset two of the largest expenses in an older adult's budget—long-term care and housing.

Cultural beliefs about family responsibility to take care of their aging relative (filial piety) and mistrust in the health care system, government agencies, and nonfamily caregivers all play an important role in determining usage of long-term care services. Long-term care services such as consumer-driven home-based care could help foster the use of formal services that would benefit both the care recipient and the family caregiver. While the distrust in the health care system and in government agencies may be more challenging to overcome, policies that foster the training and hiring of more minorities throughout the LTSS workforce, especially in professional and administrative positions, might help to foster an LTSS system that is responsive to the needs of the rapidly diversifying population in ways that are accepted by those communities.

In sum, to meet the long-term care needs of a growing and increasingly diverse aging population, it is evident that the fragmented and uncoordinated long-term care services of today need restructuring. Salient structural issues facing minority populations such as health care coverage, income and housing supports, and language barriers must be addressed in the restructuring of the long-term care system. Additionally, cultural issues such as filial piety and trust must also be integrated in the design and delivery of long-term care services. Older minority adults are more likely to prefer family caregivers and both are more likely to have their long-term care needs met if long-term care services are affordable, culturally tailored, and linguistically appropriate.

NOTE

1. Early studies were limited to black–white differences, in large part because data on Hispanic ethnicity was not routinely collected and the numbers of older Asians and American Indians was small. Politically, the issue of health disparities for groups other than African Americans did not enter the political discourse until the 1970s and 1980s.

REFERENCES

African American Registry. (1897). *The Cleveland home for age colored people opens*. Retrieved September 15, 2012, from http://www.aaregistry.org/historic_events/view/cleveland-home-aged-colored-people-opens

African American Registry. (1883). *Lemington elder care, a First for African American*. Retrieved September 15, 2012, from http://www.aaregistry.org/historic_events/view/lemington-elder-care-first-african-america

Akamigbo, A. B., & Wolinsky, F. D. (2007). New evidence of racial differences in access and their effects on the use of nursing homes among older adults. *Medical Care, 45*(7), 672–679.

Allsworth, J. E., Toppa, R., Palin, N. C., & Lapane, K. L. (2005). Racial and ethnic disparities in the pharmacologic management of diabetes mellitus among long-term care facility residents. *Ethnicity & Disease, 15*(2), 205–212.

Angel, J. L., Angel, R. J., McClellan, J. L., & Markides, K. S. (1996). Nativity, declining health, and prefer-ences in living arrangements among elderly Mexican Americans: implications for long-term care. *The Gerontologist, 36*(4), 464–473.

Benjamin, A. E. (2001). Consumer-directed services at home: A new model for persons with disabilities. *Health Affairs (Project Hope), 20*(6), 80–95.

Benjamin, A. E., Matthias, R., & Franke, T. M. (2000). Comparing consumer-directed and agency models for providing supportive services at home. *Health Services Research, 35*(1 Pt 2), 351–366.

Borrayo, E. A., Salmon, J. R., Polivka, L., & Dunlop, B. D. (2002). Utilization across the continuum of long-term care services. *The Gerontologist, 42*(5), 603–612.

Boulware, L. E., Cooper, L. A., Ratner, L. E., LaVeist, T. A., & Powe, N. R. (2003). Race and trust in the health care system. *Public Health Reports (Washington, D.C.: 1974), 118*(4), 358–365.

Bradley, E. H., McGraw, S. A., Curry, L., Buckser, A., King, K. L., Kasl, S. V., & Andersen, R. (2002). Expanding the Andersen model: The role of psychosocial factors in long-term care use. *Health Services Research, 37*(5), 1221–1242.

Caldera, S. (2010). *Social security: A key retirement income source for minorities*. Washington, DC: AARP Public Policy Institute.

Casado, B. L., van Vulpen, K. S., & Davis, S. L. (2011). Unmet needs for home and community-based services among frail older Americans and their caregivers. *Journal of Aging and Health, 23*(3), 529–553.

Chapleski, E. E., & Dwyer, J. W. (1995). The effects of on- and off-reservation residence on in-home service use among Great Lakes American Indians. *The Journal of Rural Health: Official Journal of the American Rural Health Association and the National Rural Health Care Association, 11*(3), 204–216.

Choudhury, S. (2002). Racial and ethnic differences in wealth and asset choices. *Social Security Bulletin, 64*(4), 1–15.

Christian, J. B., Lapane, K. L., & Toppa, R. S. (2003). Racial disparities in receipt of secondary stroke pre-vention agents among US nursing home residents. *Stroke; A Journal of Cerebral Circulation, 34*(11), 2693–2697.

Coughlin, T. A., McBride, T. D., & Liu, K. (1990). Determinants of transitory and permanent nursing home admissions. *Medical Care, 28*(7), 616–631.

Crist, J. D., Kim, S. S., Pasvogel, A., & Velázquez, J. H. (2009). Mexican American elders' use of home care services. *Applied Nursing Research: ANR, 22*(1), 26–34.

Crist, J. D., Woo, S. H., & Choi, M. (2007). A comparison of the use of home care services by Anglo-American and Mexican American elders. *Journal of Transcultural Nursing: Official Journal of the Transcultural Nursing Society/Transcultural Nursing Society, 18*(4), 339–348.

Federal Interagency Forum on Aging-Related Statistics. (2012). *Older Americans 2012: Key indicators of well-being*. Retrieved September 15, 2012, from http://www.agingstats.gov

Feng, Z., Fennell, M. L., Tyler, D. A., Clark, M., & Mor, V. (2011). The Care Span: Growth of racial and ethnic minorities in US nursing homes driven by demographics and possible disparities in options. *Health Affairs (Project Hope), 30*(7), 1358–1365.

Fennell, M. L., Feng, Z., Clark, M. A., & Mor, V. (2010). Elderly hispanics more likely to reside in poor-quality nursing homes. *Health Affairs (Project Hope), 29*(1), 65–73.

Foster, L., Dale, S. B., & Brown, R. (2007). How caregivers and workers fared in cash and counseling. *Health Services Research, 42*(1 Pt 2), 510–532.

Gamble, V. N. (1997). Under the shadow of Tuskegee: African Americans and health care. *American Journal of Public Health, 87*(11), 1773–1778.

Genworth Financial (2012). *Cost of care*. Retrieved September 15, 2012, from http://www.genworth.com/costofcare

Goins, R. T., Spencer, S. M., McGuire, L. C., Goldberg, J., Wen, Y., & Henderson, J. A. (2011). Adult caregiv-ing among American Indians: the role of cultural factors. *The Gerontologist, 51*(3), 310–320.

Grabowski, D. C. (2001). Medicaid reimbursement and the quality of nursing home care. *Journal of Health Economics, 20*(4), 549–569.

Grabowski, D. C. (2004). The admission of blacks to high-deficiency nursing homes. *Medical Care, 42*(5), 456–464.

Grabowski, D. C., Ohsfeldt, R. L., & Morrisey, M. A. (2003). The effects of CON repeal on Medicaid nursing home and long-term care expenditures. *Inquiry: A Journal of Medical Care Organization, Provision and Financing, 40*(2), 146–157.

Greene, V. L., & Ondrich, J. I. (1990). Risk factors for nursing home admissions and exits: a discrete-time hazard function approach. *Journal of Gerontology, 45*(6), S250–S258.

Hernandez, M., & Newcomer, R. (2007). Assisted living and special populations: what do we know about differences in use and potential access barriers? *The Gerontologist, 47 Spec No 3*, 110–117.

Herrera, A. P., Lee, J., Palos, G., & Torres-Vigil, I. (2008). Cultural influences in the patterns of long-term care use among Mexican American family caregivers. *Journal of Applied Gerontology, 27*(2), 141–165.

Howard, D. L., Sloane, P. D., Zimmerman, S., Eckert, J. K., Walsh, J. F., Buie, V. C., ... Koch, G. G. (2002). Distribution of African Americans in residential care/assisted living and nursing homes: more evidence of racial disparity? *American Journal of Public Health, 92*(8), 1272–1277.

Kane, R. L., & Kane, R. A. (2001). What older people want from long-term care, and how they can get it. *Health Affairs (Project Hope), 20*(6), 114–127.

Katz, M. B. (1996). *In the shadow of the poorhouse: A social history of welfare in America.* New York, NY: Basic Books.

Kemper, P. (1992). The use of formal and informal home care by the disabled elderly. *Health Services Research, 27*(4), 421–451.

Kietzman, K. G., Wallace, S. P., Durazo, E. M., Torres, J. M., Choi, A. S., Benjamin, A. E. T., et al. (2012). A portrait of older Californians with disabilities who rely on public services to remain independent. *Home Health Services Quarterly, 31*(4), 317–336.

King, M., Ruggles, S., Alexander, J. T., Flood, S., Genadek, K., Schroeder, M. B., et al. (2010). *Current population survey. Integrated public use microdata series.* Current Population Survey: Version 3.0 [Machine-readable database].

Kirby, J. B., & Lau, D. T. (2010). Community and individual race/ethnicity and home health care use among elderly persons in the United States. *Health Services Research, 45*(5 Pt 1), 1251–1267.

Kramer, B. J. (1991). Urban American Indian aging. *Journal of Cross-Cultural Gerontology, 6*(2), 205–217.

Kuo, T., & Torres-Gil, F. M. (2001). Factors affecting utilization of health services and home- and community-based care programs by older Taiwanese in the United States. *Research on Aging, 23*(1), 14–36.

Laditka, S. B., Laditka, J. N., & Fisher Drake, B. (2006). Home- and community-based service use by older African American, Hispanic, and non-Hispanic white women and men. *Home Health Care Services Quarterly, 25*(3–4), 129–153.

Lan, P. C. (2002). Subcontracting filial piety. *Journal of Family Issues, 23*(7), 812–835.

Lee, S. E., & Casado, B. L. (2011). Attitudes toward community services use in dementia care among Korean Americans. *Clinical Gerontologist, 34*(4), 271–286.

Markides, K. S., & Wallace, S. P. (2007). Minority elders in the United States: Implications for public policy. In R. A. Pruchno & M. A. Smyer (Eds.), *Challenges of an aging society.* Baltimore, MD: The John Hopkins University Press.

Miller, E. A., Allen, S. M., & Mor, V. (2009). Commentary: navigating the labyrinth of long-term care: shoring up informal caregiving in a home- and community-based world. *Journal of Aging & Social Policy, 21*(1), 1–16.

Miller, E. A., & Weissert, W. G. (2000). Predicting elderly people's risk for nursing home placement, hospitalization, functional impairment, and mortality: a synthesis. *Medical Care Research and Review: MCRR, 57*(3), 259–297.

Miller, S. C., Papandonatos, G., Fennell, M., & Mor, V. (2006). Facility and county effects on racial differences in nursing home quality indicators. *Social Science & Medicine (1982), 63*(12), 3046–3059.

Moon, A., Lubben, J. E., & Villa, V. (1998). Awareness and utilization of community long-term care services by elderly Korean and non-Hispanic white Americans. *The Gerontologist, 38*(3), 309–16; discussion 317.

Mor, V., Zinn, J., Angelelli, J., Teno, J. M., & Miller, S. C. (2004). Driven to tiers: socioeconomic and racial disparities in the quality of nursing home care. *The Milbank Quarterly, 82*(2), 227–256.

Mui, A. C., & Burnette, D. (1994). Long-term care service use by frail elders: is ethnicity a factor? *The Gerontologist, 34*(2), 190–198.

Mullan, J. T., Grossman, B. R., Hernandez, M., Wong, A., Eversley, R., & Harrington, C. (2009). Focus group study of ethnically diverse low-income users of paid personal assistance services. *Home Health Care Services Quarterly, 28*(1), 24–44.

Murtaugh, C. M., Kemper, P., Spillman, B. C., & Carlson, B. L. (1997). The amount, distribution, and timing of lifetime nursing home use. *Medical Care, 35*(3), 204–218.

Musa, D., Schulz, R., Harris, R., Silverman, M., & Thomas, S. B. (2009). Trust in the health care system and the use of preventive health services by older black and white adults. *American Journal of Public Health, 99*(7), 1293–1299.

NAC. (2009). *Caregiving in the U.S.: A focused look at the ethnicity of those caring for someone age 50 or older.* Bethesda, MD: Author.

Niefeld, M. R., & Kasper, J. D. (2005). Access to ambulatory medical and long-term care services among elderly Medicare and Medicaid beneficiaries: Organizational, financial, and geographic barriers. *Medical Care Research and Review: MCRR, 62*(3), 300–319.

Peng, T. R., Navaie-Waliser, M., & Feldman, P. H. (2003). Social support, home health service use, and outcomes among four racial-ethnic groups. *The Gerontologist, 43*(4), 503–513.

Quadagno, J. (1988). *The transformation of old age security: Class and politics in the American welfare state.* Chicago, IL: University of Chicago Press.

Quilliam, B. J., & Lapane, K. L. (2001). Clinical correlates and drug treatment of residents with stroke in long-term care. *Stroke; A Journal of Cerebral Circulation, 32*(6), 1385–1393.

Reed, S. C., & Andes, S. (2001). Supply and segregation of nursing home beds in Chicago communities. *Ethnicity & Health, 6*(1), 35–40.

Reinhard, S. C., Kassner, E., Houser, A., & Mollica, R. (2011). *Raising expectations: A state scorecard on long-term services and supports for older adults, people with physical disabilities, and family caregivers.* Washington, DC: AARP, The Commonwealth Fund, and The SCAN Foundation.

Scharlach, A. E., Kellam, R., Ong, N., Baskin, A., Goldstein, C., & Fox, P. J. (2006). Cultural attitudes and caregiver service use: lessons from focus groups with racially and ethnically diverse family caregivers. *Journal of Gerontological Social Work, 47*(1–2), 133–156.

Seeman, T. E., Merkin, S. S., Crimmins, E. M., & Karlamangla, A. S. (2010). Disability trends among older Americans: National Health And Nutrition Examination Surveys, 1988–1994 and 1999–2004. *American Journal of Public Health, 100*(1), 100–107.

Smith, D. B., Feng, Z., Fennell, M. L., Zinn, J. S., & Mor, V. (2007). Separate and unequal: racial segregation and disparities in quality across U.S. nursing homes. *Health Affairs (Project Hope), 26*(5), 1448–1458.

Spillman, B. C., Liu, K., & McGuilliard, C. (2002). *Trends in residential long-term care: Use of nursing homes and assisted living and characteristics of facilities and residents.* Washington, DC. Prepared by The Urban Institute for the Office of Disability, Aging and Long-Term Care Policy, Office of the Assistant Secretary for Planning and Evaluation, U.S. Department of Health and Human Services under Contract #HHS-100–97-0010. Retrieved friom http://aspe.hhs.gov/daltcp/reports/2002/rltct.pdf

Spooner, J. J., Lapane, K. L., Hume, A. L., Mor, V., & Gambassi, G. (2001). Pharmacologic treatment of diabetes in long-term care. *Journal of Clinical Epidemiology, 54*(5), 525–530.

Sturtevant, W. C. (1988). *Handbook of North American Indians: History of Indian-white relations* (Vol. 4). Washington, DC: U.S. Government Printing Office.

Tang, F., & Pickard, J. G. (2008). Aging in place or relocation: Perceived awareness of community-based long-term care and services. *Journal of Housing for the Elderly, 22*(4), 404–422.

The SCAN Foundation & UCLA Center for Health Policy Research. (2012). *Findings from a new survey among California voters 40 and older on long-term care.* In Lake Research Partners (Ed.). Los Angeles, CA: UCLA Center for Health Policy Research.

Wallace, S. P. (2012). Long-term care policy and older Latinos. In J. L. Angel et al. (Eds.), *Aging, health and longevity in the Mexican-origin population.* New York, NY: Springer Science + Business Media.

Wallace, S. P., Campbell, K., & Lew-Ting, C. Y. (1994). Structural barriers to the use of formal in-home services by elderly Latinos. *Journal of Gerontology, 49*(5), S253–S263.

Wallace, S. P., Levy-Storms, L., & Ferguson, L. R. (1995). Access to paid in-home assistance among disabled elderly people: do Latinos differ from non-Latino whites? *American Journal of Public Health, 85*(7), 970–975.

Wallace, S. P., Levy-Storms, L., Kington, R. S., & Andersen, R. M. (1998). The persistence of race and ethnicity in the use of long-term care. *The Journals of Gerontology. Series B, Psychological Sciences and Social Sciences, 53*(2), S104–S112.

Wallace, S. P., & Lew-Ting, C. Y. (1992). Getting by at home. Community-based long-term care of Latino elders. *The Western Journal of Medicine, 157*(3), 337–344.

Wallace, S. P., & Molina, L. C. (2008). Federal poverty guideline underestimates costs of living for older persons in California. *Policy Brief (UCLA Center for Health Policy Research), (PB2008–1)*, 1–4.

Wallace, S. P., Padilla-Frausto, D. I., & Smith, S. E. (2010). Older adults need twice the federal poverty level to make ends meet in California. *Policy Brief (UCLA Center for Health Policy Research), (PB2010–8)*, 1–8.

Wallace, S. P., Abel, E., Pourat, N., & Delp, L. (2007). Long-term care and the elderly population. In R. Andersen, T. Rice, & G. Kominski (Eds.), *Changing the U.S. health care system: Key issues in health services policy and management* (3rd ed., pp. 341–362). San Francisco, CA: Jossey-Bass.

Wallace, S. P., Satter, D., Padilla-Frausto, D. I., & Peter, S. E. (2009). *Elder economic security standard index: Supplemental home and community-based long-term care service package costs, California 2007.* Los Angeles, CA: UCLA Center For Health Policy Research.

Wallace, S. P., & Villa, V. M. (2009). Healthy, wealthy, and wise? Challenges to income security for elders of color. In L. Rogne, C. E. Estes, B. Grossman, B. Hollister, & E. Solway (Eds.), *Social insurance and social justice: Social security, medicare, and the campaign against entitlements* (pp. 165–178). New York, NY: Springer.

Wilden, R., Redfoot, D. L., Institute, P. P., & AARP. (2002). *Adding assisted living services to subsidized housing: Serving frail older persons with low incomes.* Washington, DC: AARP Public Policy Institute.

CHAPTER 14

Does Health Care Quality Contribute to Disparities? An Examination of Aging and Minority Status Issues in America

Toni P. Miles and Matthew Lee Smith

The Patient Protection and Affordable Care Act of 2010 (ACA) has reformed the Medicare payment system and incorporated the voice of older minority adults in shaping the performance of their local health care delivery system. ACA transforms the health care system by linking payment to outcomes in Title III SEC. 3001. This section has the obscure heading of "Hospital Value-based Purchasing Program." Within this complex legislative, language is a reference to the Hospital Consumer Assessment of Healthcare Providers and Systems Survey (HCAHPS). (See https://www.cms.gov/Medicare/Quality-Initiatives-Patient-Assessment-Instruments/HospitalQualityInits/HospitalHCAHPS.html for survey details). This survey is the first national, standardized, publicly reported survey that captures patients' perspectives of hospital care. Pronounced "H-caps," this survey is a national standard for collecting and publicly reporting information about patients' experience of care. Data from this survey can be used to draw valid comparisons across hospitals locally, regionally, and nationally. The HCAHPS survey asks all discharged patients 27 questions about their recent hospital stay. It is administered to a random sample of adult patients across medical conditions between 48 hours and 6 weeks after discharge. The survey is not restricted to Medicare beneficiaries. The ACA includes HCAHPS among the measures to be taken to calculate value-based incentive payments in the Hospital Value-Based Purchasing program, beginning with discharges in October 2012. For the first time in the history of U.S. hospitals, patients rate the quality of care received during their treatment. Hospital payments are tied to standard performance criteria. Table 14.1 shows a side-by-side comparison of publically available patient assessment data for two sample hospitals, the state, and the U.S. national average for four sample items from the patient survey. Older minority adults and their families are able to view the results from their local hospitals at http://www.hospitalcompare.hhs.gov/. This website also includes other measures of health care quality, including the timeliness and effectiveness of care, hospital readmission rates, and use of medical imaging.

This chapter is a reflection on the changing health care policy climate. These changes can either reduce current barriers or create new challenges to health care. By all measures, older adults are the primary consumers of health care in the United States. Their experience with barriers is intensely personal. The setting for health care defines that experience. The sense

TABLE 14.1 Sample Items From the Hospital Consumer Assessment of Health Care Providers and Systems—Survey Items and National Results for the Period October 1, 2010 to September 30, 2011

	LOCAL HOSPITAL A	LOCAL HOSPITAL B	STATE AVERAGE	U.S. NATIONAL AVERAGE
Item: How often did nurses communicate well during your stay? Communicate well means nurses explained things clearly, listened carefully, and treated you with courtesy and respect.				
Patients who reported that their nurses "Always" communicated well	79%	81%	77%	77%
Patients who reported that their nurses "Usually" communicated well	17%	16%	17%	18%
Patients who reported that their nurses "Sometimes or Never" communicated well	4%	3%	6%	5%
Item: How often did doctors communicate well during your stay? Communicate well means doctors explained things clearly, listened carefully, and treated you with courtesy and respect.				
Patients who reported that their doctors "Always" communicated well	80%	83%	82%	81%
Patients who reported that their doctors "Usually" communicated well	16%	13%	14%	15%
Patients who reported that their doctors "Sometimes or Never" communicated well	4%	4%	4%	4%
Item: How often was your hospital room and bathroom kept clean?				
Patients who reported that their room and bathroom were "Always" clean	70%	74%	71%	72%
Patients who reported that their room and bathroom were "Usually" clean	20%	18%	19%	19%
Patients who reported that their room and bathroom were "Sometimes or Never" clean	10%	8%	10%	9%
Item: Was the area around your room quiet at night?				
Patients who reported that the area around their room was "Always" quiet at night	59%	69%	65%	59%
Patients who reported that the area around their room was "Usually" quiet at night	30%	26%	27%	30%
Patients who reported that the area around their room was "Sometimes or Never" quiet at night	11%	5%	8%	11%

This table contains four sample items from the Survey of Patient Experience. Data from all items are at http://www. hospitalcompare.hhs.gov. Including:

"How quickly were you helped when you used the call button or needed help in getting to the bathroom?"

"How often was your pain well controlled? Well controlled means that the hospital staff did everything they could to help you with your pain."

"If you were given medicine that you had not taken before, how often did the staff explain about the medicine? Explain means that the staff told *what the medicine was for* and *what side effects it might have* before giving it."

"Did the hospital staff discuss the help you could need at home when you were ready to leave the hospital? Did you receive written information about symptoms or health problems to watch for during your recovery?"

"Would you recommend the hospital to your friends and family?"

"On a scale of 0 to 10, where 0 is the lowest and 10 is the highest, how would you rate the hospital?"

of change is determined by local factors. The location of care can shift from an emphasis on prolonged hospital stay to treatment in an outpatient facility. Change can take the form of care from a primary care physician rather than a specialist. Ultimately, health care quality is defined by the experience. Medicare was enacted in 1964 to improve the access of older adults to local health care. (See the Kaiser Family Foundation for a timeline of key developments [http://www.kff.org/medicare/timeline/pf_05.htm]). The first disparity issue for older adults was access to hospitals. Before the enactment of Medicare, older adults were routinely denied treatment in the hospital. Why? Older adults were least likely to afford the cost of care. At the time of enactment, U.S. hospitals were segregated by race. The framers of Medicare explicitly addressed this issue for older minority adults. As a precondition for receipt of federal funds, hospitals were required to serve everyone. By targeting age-, race-, and income-related barriers, Medicare had a positive impact on access to care by older minority adults. In the 10-year period after the enactment of Medicare, mortality rates for minorities aged 65 to 74 years declined by 29% (National Center for Health Statistics [NCHS], 1975). Access to care, then, also improved mortality rates.

Why discuss disparities in a context of health care quality? Health care access inequity and policy-based remedies have historic roots in U.S. civil rights legislation. A brief history of public health insurance and delivery systems is needed to fully understand this point. Enacted in 1965, Medicare and Medicaid was the last major federal health care legislation. Its concept is based on the civil rights agenda of President Johnson's Great Society (Berkowitz, 2005). Health care policy in ACA is less like the Great Society programs of the 1960s. ACA is more like President Roosevelt's New Deal. New Deal programs were designed to provide household resources during a time of scarcity. Medicare's civil rights emphasis reflects deliberate planning by policymakers. Before 1964, the majority of older adults did not have health insurance. Without health insurance, most were denied access to hospital-based care. The civil rights of older adults and their access to health care were resolved through Medicare. Simply put, Medicare was enacted to remedy age-based health care inequity. With Medicare, all persons were guaranteed hospital care. To receive Medicare payments, hospitals were required to accept all patients regardless of race. Using financing as a tool, Medicare also forced the racial integration of hospitals across the United States for all groups (Berkowitz, 2005). Medicare continued a process of desegregation in hospitals, which began with the Hill-Burton Hospital Survey and Construction Act of 1946 (Public Law 79 -725). Before Hill-Burton, most U.S. communities had separate race-segregated hospitals. The Hill-Burton Act provided funds to upgrade the infrastructure of hospitals. To obtain these funds, hospitals were obligated to serve all patients. The framers of both Medicare and Hill-Burton understood that placement of federal dollars was a key strategy to improve access to hospital-based health care.

Inequity can be created by policy. Social Security was a New Deal program to provide financial resources for households. Farmers, domestics, and sharecroppers were specifically excluded when Social Security was enacted in 1935. Large numbers of blacks worked in these occupations. Social Security policy worsened income inequity in old age for these occupational groups. Subsequent amendments to Social Security law diminished this occupational inequity; however, extended discussion of this legislative history is beyond the scope of this chapter. Title II of ACA is focused on inequity created by the eligibility criteria for inclusion in public insurance plans—Medicare and Medicaid. Public plans are the primary source of health care and long-term care insurance for older minority adults.

Medicare policy evolves when Congress amends the law. Some amendments are small changes. In 2001, Medicare began covering people with Amyotrophic Lateral Sclerosis (ALS or "Lou Gherig's Disease"). ALS is a neurological disorder that can impact all racial and ethnic groups. ALS is a chronic, progressive disease that starts in middle age. This amendment removed an age-related barrier to care for persons with ALS. In 1972, the End Stage Renal Disease Program (ESRD) was enacted under Medicare. This program is nearly universal, covering more than 90% of all U.S. citizens with severe chronic kidney disease across all age groups. Again, age was the barrier being targeted. Hypertension and diabetes are the most common causes of chronic renal disease in the United States. These conditions disproportionately affect older minority adults. This is an example of how a health care policy improved access to care for older minority adults without explicitly targeting this subpopulation. (See https://www.cms.gov/Medicare/End-Stage-Renal-Disease/ESRDGeneralInformation/index.html for general information about this national insurance program for persons with ESRD [Centers for Medicare and Medicaid Services, 2012b]). The enactment of The Medicare Prescription Drug, Improvement, and Modernization Act of 2003 (Public Law 108–173) created a temporary prescription drug discount card and transitional assistance program. This amendment was created in response to the widespread need among older adults for support with the purchase of medications. In January 2006, the Medicare Drug Benefit went into effect. Medicare beneficiaries began receiving subsidized prescription drug coverage through Part D plans. All of these amendments to Medicare illustrate one point. Health care policy can change access to care without specific reference to race, ethnicity, gender, or other individual characteristics of older minority adults.

ACA is the largest shift in United States health care policy since the enactment of Medicare in 1964. For an extended discussion of ACA, policy, and disparities, see *Health Reform and Disparities* (Miles, 2012a). On June 28, 2012, the United States Supreme Court upheld the constitutionality of this new law (Miles, 2012b). The decision will force health care delivery systems to implement standard procedures. The policy underlying standardized health care delivery is the promotion of quality practice. ACA is an opportunity to measure change about older minority adults' lived experience with health care. Does the ACA influence this experience?

One measure of health care quality is patient safety (Aspden, Wolcott, & Erickson, 2004; Ginsburg & Ralston, 2008; Kohn, 2000). What kind of evidence do we have to state that older minority adults are less safe in the health care environment? In 2000, the Institute of Medicine (IOM) published the report *To Err is Human* (Kohn, 2000). This report explicitly discussed the issue of medical errors. This was a sentinel event in health care quality research. In it, safety for older adults was discussed within the context of long-term care. There was no discussion of linguistic factors contributing to errors. A national survey of health literacy connects safety with language (Kutner, Jin, Paulson, & White, 2006). Advanced age and use of a language other than English make it difficult to navigate the health care system (Fischer, Sauaia, & Kutner, 2007). How was Congress educated about the issue of patient safety in health care? Congressional awareness of safety was based on reports from the IOM. By law, the IOM develops reports to educate U.S. Congress. The IOM report "Patient Safety: Achieving a New Standard for Care" provided an extensive analysis for the development of health care legislation (Aspden et al., 2004; Institute of Medicine, 2006). This report neither contained an explicit discussion of linguistic barriers in health care, nor did any of its case studies highlight the contributions of language differences to medical errors.

Older adults are becoming increasingly diverse with respect to primary language (Vincent & Velkoff, 2010). This diversity presents a challenge when developing a process to enhance safety. Safe treatment requires close communication. Communication is influenced by the primary language used among all parties involved in the interaction. These factors influence safety whether you have cancer or a broken leg. Older minority adults are particularly vulnerable to errors attributable to communication barriers. Quality care is safe care. A new feature of the ACA is a requirement that all institutions collect data about the primary language spoken by the patient. Will this data policy influence the safety of older minority adults within health care?

The larger theme of this book is minority health and aging. Can we identify a policy that targets the barriers experienced by older minority adults? One example is an ACA policy currently being implemented by the Center for Medicare and Medicaid Services (CMS). CMS and 26 states are launching a large-scale managed care demonstration project potentially involving millions of the sickest and most expensive Medicare and Medicaid beneficiaries, the so-called *dual eligibles* (Hackbarth, 2010, Kaiser Commission on Medicaid and the Uninsured, 2012). This project is called *Money Follows the Person*. The 9.1 million dual-eligible beneficiaries represent just a small share of the 97 million beneficiaries served by either Medicare or Medicaid, but they account for approximately 35% of all dollars spent by these two big programs. As a group, these individuals are the most complex of Medicare beneficiaries. Half have three or more chronic conditions, and six in ten have cognitive limitations. Although most are aged 65 years and older, four in ten are younger with permanent disabilities. Two of three are women. A striking 56% have incomes of less than $10,000 per year. As Drew Altman, CEO of the Kaiser Family Foundation points out:

> Success in the dual eligibles demonstration could reduce federal and state health spending in both big health care entitlement programs and improve the health of a very needy population. But the pressure to save money always cautions prudence, patience, and in this case careful targeting and customization of services, when large numbers of low-income people with disabilities and serious illnesses are involved. (*Source*: http://www.kff.org/pullingittogether/dual-eligibles-health-reform.cfm)

The ACA broadly reforms the private health insurance markets and public health insurance plans like Medicare and Medicaid. These reforms have the largest impact on the experience of dual-eligible older minority adults. With its market focus, ACA policy creates an opportunity to reframe health disparities research as a consumer issue. However, the terms health disparities, older minorities, and barriers to care are not usually viewed as consumer issues. By emphasizing health care quality, the ACA incorporates consumer assessment of care into its mix of quality measures. For the first time since the enactment of Medicare, researchers will have standardized surveys capturing the hospital experiences of older minority adults. Hearing the voice of the consumer is a core component of ACA Title III. For those who are unfamiliar with the research, quality could be viewed as a generic and broad concept. Within health care delivery, it is a well-defined term associated with specific measures. To illustrate this concept and its application in the real world, we give examples of quality assessment and its application through ACA polices throughout this chapter. Health care quality is the idea that health care providers will be held accountable to a standard of care. The formal idea of quality only began to take shape in the 1990s with the work of the National Quality Care Forum. Tools used in clinical practice to measure quality of care are available through the National Quality Measures Clearinghouse (http://www.qualitymeasures.ahrq.gov). The clearinghouse is a public resource for evidence-based quality measures. In ACA, quality is more than just a good idea; it is a determinant of health care outcome.

WHAT IS HEALTH CARE QUALITY?

Quality refers to the timing and appropriateness of care. Do you get the correct treatment? Did that treatment conform to the standard of care? Quality in U.S. health care is the subject of serious scholarship. What does it take to improve care for chronic illness? By asking this question, a conceptual model with a larger point of view was created (Leveille & Davis 1998; Lorig & Steward, 1999; Wagner, 1998). The *Chronic Disease Model* created a new starting point to initiate health care change. The science of quality improvement evolved from this model. In a synthesis of this model, Galvin and McGlynn (2003) published their classic article—"Using Performance Measurement to Drive Improvement: A Road Map for Change." This road map created a process to assess the performance of health care delivery. ACA Title III, "Improving the Quality and Efficiency of Healthcare," translates 20 years of quality measurement research into law. Elizabeth McGlynn testified before Congress to make the case for quality health care and its role in cost control (McGlynn, 2008; McGlynn, Ringel, Price, & Girosi, 2010). The idea that poor quality care contributes to health outcome disparities is in its developmental stages for both researchers and practitioners.

Does poor health care quality contribute to observed health outcome gaps between demographic groups? These gaps include mortality rates, re-hospitalization rates, and treatment failure rates. We now know that age makes a difference in these rates. Medicare payment policy only recently began to include references to age when modifying payment. The specialty of Geriatric medicine evolved in response to the low quality of care experienced by older adults. It can be argued that increasing quality made a significant contribution to the improved care of older adults. A geriatrician from the University of California, Los Angeles,

David Ruben (Ory, Jordan, & Bazzarre, 2002), addressed the delivery system changes needed to improve outcomes for older persons:

> [we need component] interventions that include comprehensive geriatric assessment, acute care of the elderly units, hospital elder life programs, hospital in the home, self-management programs, disease management programs, and case / care management.

Can we extend our views of age-based quality improvement to an examination of care for older minority adults? The ACA gives social gerontologists two new tools to improve the discussion. First, ACA payment policy will require institutions participating in Medicare and Medicaid to report patient race, ethnicity, gender, and primary language. For the first time, we will be able to identify outcomes at the institution level. Second, ACA links payment to both outcome and quality. Patient satisfaction is a significant component of quality measurement. In the early 2000s, tests of these interventions were funded largely by organizations such as the Robert Wood Johnson Foundation, the John A. Hartford Foundation, and the California Healthcare Foundation (CHCF). Title III policy is based on the results of these early efforts to improve age-related outcomes in health care. In the United States, legislative change is achieved by restructuring finances. The interventions targeted age-related outcome disparities. These studies provide evidence for a positive effect of Medicare payment policy on outcomes for older adults. In ACA, examples of new Medicare policy include linking payment to outcome (Part I) and formal support for the development of new patient care models (Part III). In general, these interventions did not explicitly target minority older adults. There were some interventions, however, that targeted dually eligible older adults.

Financial resources are the criteria used to determine dual eligibility. It is beyond the scope of this chapter to discuss the details of these waivers. Waivers are administrative or regulatory structures that states can use to test new or existing ways to deliver and pay for health care services in Medicaid. There are four types of demonstration/waiver programs: Section 1115 Research and Demonstration Programs; Section 1915(b) Managed Care Waivers; Section 1915 (c) Home and Community-based Waivers; and Concurrent 1915 (b) and 1915(c) Waivers. Waiver and demonstration programs are a poorly understood but a significant component of health care access for older minority adults. The reader is directed to http://www.medicaid.gov/Medicaid-CHIP-Program-Information/By-Topics/Waivers/Waivers.html for a thorough discussion of this policy. The Kaiser Family Foundation commission on Medicaid and the uninsured also provide a detailed discussion about these policies at http://www.kff.org/about/kcmu.cfm.

For our discussion of quality and health disparities, it is useful to focus on federal laws with specific intent to reform our health care delivery system. Do these intentions align with current research describing the social determinants of health care disparities? What can we learn about prior federal legislative efforts targeting health care inequity across the age span? Do these federal laws improve the quality of care for older minority adults? Let us begin by asking who is the primary beneficiary of ACA policy. During the process of legislative development, there were different versions of the bill. Each version of the ACA had its own title, which reflected the intent of craftsmen. The final law is entitled "The Patient Protection and Affordable Care Act of 2010." This title suggests an emphasis on health care safety and cost. In the U.S. Senate, there were two committees involved in writing the legislation—the Health Labor, Education, and Pensions Committee (HELP) and the Finance Committee. HELP called their version the "Affordable Health Choices Act" (S. 1679). The Finance Committee's bill was entitled "American's Healthy Future Act" (S. 1796). The HELP Committee's title emphasizes cost and choice. The Finance Committee's title emphasizes a forward-looking emphasis on wellness. The House version of the bill was called "The Affordable Healthcare for America Act" (H.3962). If legislative nomenclature is any indication, cost control was the primary intent in health care reform for a sizable number of Senate and House members. In thinking through the legislation, cost control was somewhat tempered by the idea of public health (i.e., future health). The final version of the ACA, then, is consumer-focused, market-based legislation.

Most sections do not have explicit race- or ethnic-focused language. Will this market-based approach change our concept of health care outcome disparities for older adults?

HOW DO WE DISCUSS DISPARITIES WITHOUT A TRADITIONAL FOCUS ON RACE?

The United States has stark variation in its regional mortality and morbidity statistics. Consider the evidence for poor health care quality from the following recent reports. Schoenberg and colleagues (Schoenberg, Manchikanti, & Goodenow, 2011) conducted qualitative interviews among Appalachian residents with two or more chronic diseases requiring self-management. Disease self-management is a complex task. Strategies for self-management derived from studies about single diseases, which do not translate into effective approaches for multiple diseases. The interviews were designed to help explain the barriers preventing translation between single and multiple disease management. In addition to limited financial resources, these study participants lived in a federally defined mental health professional's shortage areas. To obtain a complete view, participants were also encouraged to describe assets available to help manage complex treatments. Among participant responses were kin support, cultural values of independence, hard work, local federally qualified health clinics, local health department programming, and medication assistance programs. Federal policy formally defines health profession shortage areas (Salinsky, 2010; U.S. Government, 2006). Regional variation in these shortage areas can be used to link disparities with measures of policy impact.

Rural areas are defined by population size and density. These demographic measures are tied to health care policy. Erwin and colleagues examined health disparities in rural areas (Erwin, Brown, Looney, & Forde, 2010). Their work highlights the interaction of race, socioeconomic status, and geography. Statistics from 16 counties in East Tennessee clearly show the expected excess mortality among blacks compared to whites living in the same area. There was, however, an unexpected interaction between the size of the black population and the extent of excess mortality. The counties with smaller proportions of blacks had smaller differentials between black and white mortality rates. Their results emphasize the idea that disparity is not just a racial issue; rather, race must be studied within the context of geography.

Rural areas are defined by population size and other measures that trigger federal health care policies. These policies include specific Medicare payments for rural *Critical Access Hospitals* (Centers for Medicare and Medicaid Services, 2012a). Cossman and colleagues described differences about a startling new trend in U.S. mortality for rural areas (Cossman, Cosby, & Cossman, 2010). Although rural areas have been associated with greater stroke mortality for the last 40 years, persons living in urban areas generally had higher rates of combined mortality for all causes when compared to rural areas. All-cause mortality rates in selected rural areas now exceed those of urban areas (Gamm, Hutchison, Dabney, & Dorsey, 2003). This change coincided with increases in heart disease deaths in rural areas. Excess cancer mortality in rural areas is also an emerging issue. The authors acknowledge that the underlying reasons for changes in mortality are not known. These data represent a reversal of a century-long trend in the association between rural residence and lower mortality risk. One explanation—regional variation in the use of advanced diagnostic procedures—may explain the emerging rural mortality penalty (Song, Bynum, Sutherland, Wennberg, & Fisher, 2010). Use of advanced diagnostic procedures is a quality measure (Centers for Medicare and Medicaid Services, CMS Slide Presentation, 2011). These data support the idea that place matters in the receipt of health care. Theories about the role of socioeconomics, race, or ethnicity alone cannot completely explain regional variation. Would a focus on health care delivery systems help us see the influence of quality within this complex environment of race and geography?

THE 8 AMERICAS AND ALIGNING FORCES FOR QUALITY (AF4Q)

Murray and colleagues use the term *8 Americas* to define regional differences in mortality (Murray et al., 2006). The 8 Americas are defined on the basis of race, location of the county of residence, population density, and race-specific county-level per capita income. The definition is further refined with the use of homicide rates. With this structure, Murray and his team were able to estimate life expectancy and other measures of socioeconomic inequity. Although 8 Americas is useful in understanding the relation between geography and race, there are no specific references to older minority adults. This limitation is solved by measurement of the performance of hospitals operating within defined regions across the United States by Fisher and the researcher at the Dartmouth Atlas Project (Fisher & Chandra, 2008). Together, these reports give us the combined race–geography model needed to study the association between quality and disparities for older minority adults. To social gerontologists, these are relatively new explanatory elements. With the advent of the ACA, quality performance data will become publically available to researchers. The Robert Wood Johnson Foundation partnered with the Dartmouth Atlas Project to develop the AF4Q Report (Fisher & Chandra, 2008). This report is organized around the idea that who you are and where you live determines the volume and quality of health care received. Quality refers to the timing and appropriateness of care. The report explores timing and appropriateness issues that contribute to variations within and across geographic regions. Based on Medicare data, this analysis divides the national mosaic of hospitals into 306 referral regions. The AF4Q Report identifies unwarranted variations in health care. In their discussion, unwarranted refers to variation in medical practice or spending that cannot be explained by illness, strong scientific evidence, or well-informed patient preferences. The analysis acknowledges variation due to excessive and deficient levels of service. Appropriate care matches the population's burden of illness. The AF4Q uses Dartmouth Atlas Project analyses to describe three categories of appropriate care—effective care, preference sensitive care, and supply-sensitive care. Effective care consists of evidence-based service. Variations in effective care often reflect failure to deliver service, and this means that a necessary treatment is not received. Preference-sensitive care encompasses treatment decisions, and patient and physician weigh options with different risks and benefits. Patient attitude toward these risks may vary. At the end of the discussion, however, patient preferences lead to a decision about treatment. Failure to include individual preference can lead to over- as well as undertreatment. There are also issues surrounding supply-sensitive care. The number of hospital beds, the frequency of physician visits, and the tendency to consult a specialist are examples of supply-sensitive resources. The supply of these resources has a major influence on the likelihood of actual use. Excess supply has a clearly demonstrated link to excessive use. Excessive use means the patient received a service where none was required. Since 2002, the Dartmouth Atlas Project has conducted analyses clearly showing the relation between spending across geographic areas and differences in the quality of supply-sensitive services. For example, regions differ dramatically in the use of the hospital. Hospital beds are a key indicator for supply-sensitive care. Areas with a large number of hospital beds tend to fill them. Blacks within a region are somewhat more likely than whites to be hospitalized for conditions that could also be treated outside of the hospital. In the Medicare data from 80 million beneficiaries, region is the most important determinant of utilization. Regional differences exceed the differences between racial groups living in the same region. Simply put, where you live determines the type and intensity of health care received. This simple observation underscores the importance of the local health care delivery system. These differences become clear when examining the following question: What is the predominant approach to selecting a site for care when a chronic disease needs treatment? Some local delivery systems emphasize acute, inpatient care, whereas others emphasize ambulatory, outpatient care. One indicator of poor quality care is the rate of hospitalization for conditions that are usually treated with an outpatient visit. One commonly encountered problem for older minority adults is illness caused by too many conflicting medications—polypharmacy. The American Geriatrics Society has recently updated its Beers Criteria for prescribing (American Geriatrics Society Updated Beers Criteria for Potentially Inappropriate Medication Use in Older Adults, 2012). Publishing criteria is one matter; uptake of these new procedures by prescribing providers is quite a different matter.

Place does matter. In the modern era of health care delivery, geography has emerged as a significant determinant of the observed gaps in health care outcomes among racial, ethnic, and socioeconomic groups of older adults. These disparities are particularly striking when examined across U.S. states and regions. It is not only who you are that matters, but also where you live. Indeed, many studies that report racial disparities based on national samples do not account for the tremendous variation across regions and procedures. For evidence-based services, such as screening mammography and appropriate testing for diabetes, disparities across regions are substantially greater than the differences by race. There are some regions where blacks receive equal or better care than non-Hispanic whites. In these regions, care for all patients is of low quality. Hemoglobin A1c is a measure that shows how well a diabetes treatment plan is working. The average annual percentage of Medicare beneficiaries with diabetes aged 65 to 74 years having A1c testing is as follows: total 84%, black 79.4%, and white 84.7%. Among the states, the overall rate of hemoglobin A1c testing was highest in Vermont (91.5%) and lowest in Alaska (70.9%). Limb loss is a devastating complication of poorly managed diabetes. Factors that increase the risk for limb loss are broad, including environmental, economic, social, and behavioral issues. The U.S. national rate of leg amputation is four times greater among blacks than among non-Hispanic whites, but rates of amputation vary almost tenfold across regions (See www.rwjf.org/qualityequality for a detailed copy of this analysis).

Researchers have begun to use this concept of combined quality and geography. Slack and Slack in a Mayo Clinical Proceedings commentary entitled "the United Countries of America" promoted benchmarking the quality of health care by using the experience of other states (Slack & Slack, 2011). Minnesota, as the authors indicate, has a large immigrant population of Hmong refugees, Native Americans, and others. Their commentary highlights positive impact of patient-centered care delivered in a linguistically comfortable setting. Lichtenberg examined the impact of medical care quality and its relationship to increases in longevity (Lichtenberg, 2011). He used three different measures of health care quality—advanced diagnostic imaging, quality of medical schools, and "vintage" of self- and provider-administered medications. Vintage refers to the year the Food and Drug Administration (FDA) approved a medication. Since 1991, the states where life expectancy increased most rapidly shared three characteristics: (a) states where the fraction of Medicare diagnostic imaging procedures were most "advanced"; (b) states where prescribers used medications with the latest FDA approval year; and (c) states with physicians from high-quality schools. The vintage of Medicaid prescriptions increased more slowly in states with polices imposing restricted access. Types of restrictions include "prior authorization" requirements. "Prior authorization" is a clear example of policy restricting access. Older adults who are dually eligible for Medicare and Medicaid are most likely to experience the prior authorization barrier. Preretirement minority adults with low-quality health insurance are also likely to experience this barrier. The extent of access restrictions vary across state Medicaid. Twelve states do not restrict, whereas five states restrict more than 47% of drugs. In Lichtenberg's analysis, the use of newer outpatient prescription drugs was associated with increases in life expectancy by 0.96 to 1.26 years. This is a significantly larger increase than the overall 2006 United States increase of 0.3 years (Arias, 2010). These differences in diagnostic quality, drugs, and physician quality were not associated with larger increases in per capita medical expenditure. Quality measured by technology, medications, and physician education is an important influence the geographic variation in life expectancy.

WHAT DO AMERICANS SAY ABOUT HEALTH CARE QUALITY?

Quality is an issue faced by all racial and ethnic groups. Chronic illness is the thread that links these groups in their experience with health care delivery. The National Committee for Quality Assurance (NCQA) discussed this issue in its 2010 State of Health Care Quality Report (NCQA, 2010). In spring 2012, Robert Wood Johnson Foundation, Harvard School of Public Health, and National Public Radio surveyed a nationally representative sample of Americans with severe medical problems. The interviews were conducted via telephone from March 5 through March 25, 2012, among a nationally representative sample of 1,508 adults aged 18 years and older. Of these, 516 respondents were defined as "sick," that is, those who had a serious illness, medical condition, injury, or disability requiring a great deal of medical care or who had been hospitalized overnight in the past 12 months. In this survey, a majority of the public believed many people are unable to access high-quality care (61%) and are not getting the drugs they need (53%). Nearly seven in ten Americans wanted their doctor to spend time with them discussing other, broader health issues that might affect their long-term health (68%), rather than just their specific medical problem. Despite increased health care expenditures in the United States, many sick Americans reported quality problems. Two thirds of sick Americans thought that there was a serious problem with the quality of the nation's health care. Sick Americans saw a wide range of issues that contribute to quality problems across the nation. These included problems related to insurance plan restrictions, lack of availability of quality services, and concerns about some aspects of the way care is provided. Close to eight in ten Americans believed that people being unable to afford the tests or drugs they need (78%) is a problem. They were concerned about the influence of health insurance plans on treatment decisions (64%). Many expressed concerns about being able to get access to the high-quality doctors and hospitals that exist (61%). Many sick Americans had experienced situations where they believe the care provided was not appropriate. These included instances where the wrong care (e.g., diagnosis, treatment, or test) was believed to be provided to them (one in eight Americans). There was also concern about some aspects of the medical care. About a quarter of sick Americans said their condition was not well managed. Some of these problems involved a lack of communication. For example, a quarter of sick Americans reported that a doctor, nurse, or other health professional did not provide them with all the needed information about their treatment or prescriptions. Participants in Medicaid programs reported the same communication and access issues (NCQA 2010). Whether an older minority adult has private or public health insurance plans, quality of care is an issue.

WHAT DOES RESEARCH TELL US ABOUT THE PROCESS OF QUALITY IMPROVEMENT?

If we accept the premise that poor quality contributes to some of the observed disparities in health care, then the obvious response is quality improvement. This is a complex undertaking. Manley calls it a negotiation (Manley, 2000). The negotiation begins with the recognition that standard operating procedures need to change. If outcome does not drive change, what then does drive change? ACA policy links quality improvement to two areas that do matter for health care business. One set of quality improvement tools are embedded within a process required for accreditation. Another set of quality improvement tools are linked to payment for services through customer satisfaction and health effectiveness measures. Interestingly, quality improvement—like much of social science research—requires a mixture of quantitative and qualitative methods to measure the phenomenon. Quality improvement involves measurement of introduction and impact. Successful implementation requires negotiations of existing formal and informal power relationships. Some employees and managers embrace quality management strategies, whereas others do not. Employees who resist quality improvement will sometimes use the language of quality to justify increased bureaucratic control. Research targeting health disparities would be improved with a specific focus on the implementation of quality improvement into health care delivery systems that serve minority older adults.

Standardized, evidence-based treatment in medical care is a relatively new idea. Selection of treatment by physicians based on systematic evaluation can be traced to the recent work of Gordon Guyatt of McMaster University (2012) (Guyatt & Busse, 2002). He writes the following history of the use of evidence in medical practice:

> In fewer than 20 years, evidence-based practice has gone from a tentative name of a fledgling concept to the fundamental basis for clinical practice that is used worldwide. The first history of the movement has already appeared in the form of an authoritative book (Guyatt & Busse, 2002). This second edition of the *User's Guide* reflects that history and the evolving conceptual and pedagogic-basis of the EBM movement. In 1981, a group of clinical epidemiologists at McMaster University, led by David Sackett,

published the first of a series of articles advising clinicians how to read clinical journals. Although a huge step forward, the series had its limitations. After teaching what they then called critical appraisal for a number of years, the group became increasingly aware of both the necessity and the challenges of going beyond reading the literature in a browsing mode and using research studies to solve patient management problems on a day-to-day basis.

> ....My mission...was to train physicians who would practice this new approach...I presented our plans for changing the program to members of the Department of Medicine, many of whom were not sympathetic. [Initially, we called...] the new approach scientific medicine. Those already hostile were incensed and disturbed at the implication that they had previously been 'unscientific'.... the name...evidence-based medicine turned out to be a catchy-one.

The evidence-based concept of practice to decrease health disparities is cultural competence in medicine (CCM; Hasnain-Wynia, 2006). CCM seeks to respect individuals' health beliefs, values, and behaviors. It started with rather simplistic attempts to teach doctors about population groups, their cultural norms, and especially cultural peculiarities regarding health and health care. It is still evolving and has not found its way into minority aging research.

Shortell and colleagues (2001) show the elements needed for coordinating structural change. These elements provide a starting point for social gerontology research. The policies act on multiple levels and outline the timing of financial incentives. These incentives are simultaneously applied to physician organizations, individual clinics, and specialties. Health care organizations must demonstrate the infrastructure to manage fiscal relationships. There are requirements for practice. Practices must also show strength and stability of their leadership. Evidence-based practice also requires accountability for making the needed changes. Performance feedback needs to be provided at all levels—individual physician, health care team, and individual clinical and practice group. These recommendations can be used to understand the complex structure of ACA. Title III of ACA contains policies for this process, and is worthy of its own book-length analysis. The core of this law is oversight of the business of health care. Is quality, equitable health care also profitable? A new volume, *Health Disparities and Reform* (Miles, 2012a), provides an extended discussion about health care business models illustrating potential impact. A race–county frame of reference is required to accurately measure the impact of these policies on health disparities.

The voice of the patient is an important part of the conversation about health care quality. Medicare utilization data clearly shows variation across regions. Is there regional variation in patient satisfaction with health care quality? Quality is a significant issue for mid-life adults with chronic diseases. Other than the ESRD program, there are no surveys of patient satisfaction for this demographic group. When we move out of the hospital environment and into the community, what does health care quality look like for community-dwelling adults aged 55 to 64 years? Adults in this age group are most likely to have employer-sponsored health insurance (U.S. Department of Labor, 2010). During the 2008 to 2009 recessions, workers aged 55 to 64 years had the highest rates of joblessness (7.2%) and the highest rates of being unemployed 27 weeks or longer (49.1%). Before the recession of 2008, 77% of workers aged 55 to 64 years had employer-sponsored health insurance (Medical Expenditure Panel Survey, 2006; http://www.meps.ahrq.gov).

Although support and guidance from national organizations are helpful, quality changes happen in institutions that are just down the street from your house. In the section below, we use survey data to give voice to persons with chronic diseases by documenting the community barriers they encounter in terms of effective self-management. In 2009, the National Council on Aging (NCOA) commissioned The NCOA Chronic Care Survey, a nationally representative probability survey of 1,000 community-dwelling adults aged 44 years and older with at least one chronic disease, with support from Atlantic Philanthropies and the CHCF (Re-forming health care: Americans speak out about chronic conditions and challenges to self-care: Findings from a national survey of Americans 44 years and older with chronic conditions, 2009). Using these data, we illustrate the prevalence of barriers to self-care behaviors and compare rates across geographic regions of the United States (i.e., Northeast, Midwest, South, and West). Of these 1,000 respondents, almost one in ten reported that they did not have the money to do things that would improve their health or condition (38.4%). Another 37.9% reported a wish that they could change and engage in things that are healthier, but that they lacked the confidence to do so. In this survey, over one third reported needing help to learn how to take better care of their health in a way that works for them and their life (35.5%), and another 30.3% reported needing help to learn what they should do to take better care of their health. When comparing these barriers to self-care by geographic region, no statistically significant variation was observed (see Table 14.2). As can be seen through this data-driven example, barriers to self-care behaviors among individuals with chronic disease are influenced by communication (i.e., learning about how and what to do to take better care of health conditions) and financial burden. Further, perceptions of pessimism or a lack of efficacy (i.e., wanting to change but not believing they can) is another barrier that shows people know healthier solutions exist, but require additional training, coaching, or communication to overcome these challenges. These self-reported barriers are consistent with the Robert Wood Johnson Foundation survey data discussed previously in this chapter. This indicates that a substantial number of American patients are hindered by communication issues with their health care providers. This is a barrier to better self-care for chronic conditions. These data suggest that it is reasonable to believe that health care providers have an opportunity to improve health care quality by providing information to patients during interactions in

TABLE 14.2 Self-Reported Barriers to Self-Care Behaviors Among a Nationally Representative Sample of Adults With One or More Chronic Conditions

	TOTAL (N = 1,000)	NORTHEAST (N = 190)	MIDWEST (N = 230)	SOUTH (N = 360)	WEST (N = 220)	N^2	P
I need help learning what I should be doing to take better care of my health						2.97	0.396
Disagree	69.7%	70.7%	71.7%	66.4%	72.2%		
Agree	30.3%	29.3%	28.3%	33.6%	27.8%		
I need help learning how to take better care of my health in a way that works for me and my life						6.52	0.089
Disagree	64.5%	68.4%	68.9%	59.9%	64.0%		
Agree	35.5%	31.6%	31.1%	40.1%	36.0%		
I don't have the money it takes to do things that will improve my health or condition						1.66	0.646
Disagree	61.6%	63.8%	63.0%	59.0%	62.4%		
Agree	38.4%	36.2%	37.0%	41.0%	37.6%		
I wish I could change and do things that are healthier, but I just don't think I can						0.63	0.890
Disagree	62.1%	63.6%	60.6%	61.4%	63.4%		
Agree	37.9%	36.4%	39.4%	38.6%	36.6%		

health care settings. Although appropriate solutions to close these barrier gaps exist for the provider and patient alike, a combined approach is needed to ensure helpful information, resources, and services fill this demand. Clinical interventions to modify provider behavior have shown to be effective; however, patients also have a responsibility to actively seek health care opportunities to improve their situation. Without a systems approach to addressing barriers to self-care (i.e., including health policy, health care settings, and interpersonal and individual aspects), we are destined to see persisting health disparities and associated negative health outcomes nationwide. These data were provided to the authors by Nancy Whitelaw and the NCOA.

WHAT'S NEXT FOR HEALTH POLICY, DISPARITIES, AND RESEARCH?

PLACE MATTERS is a major initiative of the Joint Center to build the capacity of community leaders to address social, economic, and environmental conditions in communities that shape health and health outcomes (http://www.jointcenter.org/hpi/pages/place-matters). PLACE MATTERS is a short-hand term designed to capture the idea that social determinants play a role in health. In this chapter, we will promote this concept because it links race with place (race-county) to measure mortality differentials and preventable risk factors (Danaei, Oza, Kulkarni, Murray, & Ezzati, 2010).

Geographic variations in health care quality are responsible for a substantial component of the observed racial disparity in care because demographic groups are clustered in areas with low-quality hospitals and providers. Hospitals and regions of the country also vary enormously in the extent to which disparities are present. Health care disparities are the result of unequal treatment within a hospital (or by a given provider) and unequal treatment because of where people live. These findings highlight the importance of understanding health and health care within a local context—and of efforts to explore and address the underlying causes of disparities within and across regions.

The ACA transforms the relationship between health care delivery and payment by increasing emphasis on *quality care*. The framers of this law intended to use evidence-based practice to increase the quality of health care regardless of race, ethnicity, primary language, gender, or disability. What's next? Research is needed to examine provider readiness to adopt evidence-based practice. In the British Journal *Quality and Safety in Healthcare,* Shekelle (2002) argued that the resistance of physicians to clinical governance will continue until they can see how a real program for measureable quality improvement operates. This article examined the beginning of the British National Health Service in 1945. The sentiment expressed by physicians at that time about the implementation of quality improvement in health care is descriptive of some provider attitudes in the United States today.

There are unintended consequences of provider resistance to the ACA. There are several physicians serving terms in both the U.S. House of Representatives and the U.S. Senate. In the Senate, these officials are Rand Paul (R-Kentucky, Ophthalmologist), Tom Coburn (R-Oklahoma, Family Practice), and John Barrasso (R-Wyoming, Surgeon). If Senator Paul were still in daily clinical practice, would he oppose the implementation of ACA-associated quality measures? What about Senators Coburn or Barrasso? Has anyone asked them about health care inequity in their states? Do they think about resistance to the ACA's implementation and the perpetuation of health care disparities? Senator Coburn's Oklahoma has an Indian Health Service facility in every county. There is clear evidence that the Indian Health Service has been consistently underfunded since its inception in 1832 (Walke, 2009). The ACA made major amendments to existing law governing the Indian Health Service by promoting a policy to support the continued existence of Indian Health Service facilities. This included allowing these facilities to accept payment for serving patients with Medicare, Medicaid, and the Children's Health Insurance Program. Prior to the ACA, the Indian Health Service could not participate in these public programs. This change improves access to the financial capital that Indian Health Service facilities need to implement quality care changes. The ACA contains provisions allowing tribal organizations to purchase coverage for their employees from the Federal Employees Health Benefits Program. This program provides health insurance to members of Congress. The ACA also allows tribes and tribal organizations to purchase insurance coverage to supplement Indian Health Service beneficiaries. Before the ACA, the Indian Health Service beneficiaries were not allowed to use supplemental health insurance. Supplemental health insurance has been a staple of Medicare beneficiary financing for many years. This means that Native Americans in the Indian Health Service can now purchase supplemental health insurance—just as Medicare beneficiaries have been able to do for years. The ACA authorizes the Indian Health Service to offer hospice, assisted living, long-term care, and community-based services to homebound persons. These benefits have been available in Medicaid for years and are considered an essential part of quality health care. By asking "what's next?" our goal is measuring readiness to adopt the quality policies of the ACA. Readiness to change practice involves hearing the voice of the patient and adapting one's practice style. The NCOA survey and others like it provide insight into the patient experience. The ACA has created formal linkage between patient satisfaction and financial incentives. Will these factors drive the changes that decrease health care inequity experienced by older minority adults?

One classic model for measuring attitudes and behaviors around the change process is the classic *Stages of Change* (Prochaska, DiClemente, & Norcross, 1983). Readiness to change is a concept commonly applied to diet, exercise, and smoking behaviors. Some individuals have never thought about changing or do not feel the need to do so. Others think about changing but do nothing about it. A final group has successfully adopted a good diet, regular exercise, and quit smoking. Some in this group have even maintained the change over long periods. Is provider readiness to embrace evidence-based practice an important but not well-measured social determinant of health care inequity? Recent political events notwithstanding, racism, classicism, gender bias, age bias, and xenophobia persist. Health care providers were human beings before they received their training. We all grew up in our local communities. Nothing in our training is explicitly designed to confront our own biases. Some of us believe that we have no biases. Does missing insight into one's own beliefs create paths to inequity in health care delivery for one's patients (Tatum, 1997)? Does this personal blind spot create access barriers for a broad spectrum of disadvantaged groups? By framing *provider attitudes* as a stage of change problem, we can systematically design interventions to influence variation in race-county disparities. Although many hope health care reform will address inequity, a hard look at stages of change would identify attitudes linked with illness and death for older minority adults.

One starting place for this analysis could be provider willingness to adopt the Cultural and Linguistically Appropriate Standards (CLAS) policy. CLAS is a set of 14 standards, of which 4 are mandated. The remaining 10 are either guidelines or recommendations. All institutions that receive federal funds must comply with the mandates. Hospitals that serve Medicare and Medicaid beneficiaries, for example, must comply. These four standards are based on Title IV of the Civil Rights Act of 1964. One example is Standard Four. It requires health care organizations to offer and provide assistance services, including bilingual staff and interpreter services, at no cost to each patient and consumer with limited English proficiency at all points of contact, in a timely manner during all hours of operation. Many providers express concerns about the cost of compliance with CLAS. During the health care debate, this objection was raised by the Mayo Foundation "… [this is an] *unreasonable burden in costs and resources… if applied literally, they would overwhelm most hospital and physician resources—both time and money*." Not all providers and institutions share this view. The National Business Group on Health offered this view about CLAS:"[CLAS-related changes can lead to]… *increased patient compliance and satisfaction… improved health outcomes. As employers respond to an increasingly consumer-driven health system, emphasis on cultural competence and assessment of what services are available and how they're delivered to a diverse workforce will become increasingly important*." The arguments for and against CLAS can be summed up with two general concepts. Arguments against CLAS emphasize the cost of change. The arguments in favor of CLAS emphasize patient communication and outcomes. CLAS in health care will be an emerging determinant of health disparity as the U.S. population becomes increasingly diverse, and providers and institutions with CLAS have the potential to diminish health care disparities.

Imagine four stages of readiness to adopt CLAS. A precontemplation stage provider might make the argument that if the patient learned English, then all of his or her problems would be solved. A contemplation stage provider might make the argument that CLAS is a good idea, but it costs too much. An implementation stage provider might say that he or she is trying to learn medical Spanish, but that everyone laughs when he or she attempts to use it conversationally. Finally, the maintenance stage provider has hired office staff who speak Spanish. The size of the patient panel in the local Latino community is growing. The Healthcare Effectiveness Data and Information Set (HEDIS) statistics for a maintenance stage provider gives researchers a measurement tool. The HEDIS is a tool used by more than 90% of America's health plans to measure performance on important dimensions of care and service. These dimensions include timely application of evidence-based therapy. (See http://www. ncqa.org for a detail description of HEDIS measures.) Pre-contemplation and contemplation stage providers might have a significantly lower proportion of patients with up-to-date prevention care and poorly controlled chronic conditions. The barrier for their patients is communication in the office. At these early change stages, providers might be inclined to attribute the missing preventive services to health illiteracy, willful noncompliance, or mistrust of the health care system. If we help the provider to advance a stage or two in the change model, perhaps patient outcomes will improve.

As director of a hospital, how could I use quality improvement measures in a stage of change model? Adoption of CLAS could influence my institution's Consumer Assessment of Healthcare Providers and Systems (CAHPS) scores. The term CAHPS refers to a comprehensive and evolving family of surveys that ask consumers and patients to evaluate the interpersonal aspects of health care. CAHPS surveys probe those aspects of care for which consumers and patients are the best and/or only source of information, as well as those that consumers and patients have identified as being important. (See http://www.cms.gov/Research-Statistics-Data-and-Systems/Research/CAHPS/index.html for a detailed description of measures available in CAHPS.) It is designed to support the consumer's information needs. The surveys are the results of more than 10 years of scientific testing. One item in particular asks, "*During this hospital stay, how often did doctors treat you with courtesy and respect?*" When providers are arrayed by stage of readiness to change, which stage would have the highest proportion rated as *usually* or *always*? Which stage is more likely to be rated as *sometimes* or *never*? How might CAHPS rating averages differ for institutions who serve patients with low literacy or low income? This is a critical period for measuring ACA's impact on access to health care. We have already seen resistance to ACA implementation. One casualty is the long-term care portion of the law. Carrying out of the Community Living Assistance Services and Supports Act was stopped. What does this retreat on long-term care financing mean for future cohorts of impoverished older adults? Currently, these adults are dependent on state Medicaid programs.

On June 28, 2012, the Supreme Court upheld the constitutionality of the ACA. For older minority adults, a critical component was the ruling on the Medicaid expansion. Medicaid is the public health insurance that supports both seniors and dependent children. Its expansion refers to the provision in the ACA to increase the number of eligible participants by setting income eligibility criteria at 133% of poverty. By redrawing the income line, the ACA Medicaid expansion creates coverage for working adults who fall at or below 133% of the federal poverty line. The court's decision endorses a state's right to make choices consistent with local needs and limits. That is, states can choose to participate in the expansion, or not. And, states (and their leaders) will manage the consequences of their choices. The law remains but the office coordinating its implementation was closed in November 2011. What happens after that? We do not know.

The expansion of Medicaid has a direct impact on state resources for the overall program. Dually eligible older minorities derive their sole long-term care support from state Medicaid programs. Medicaid is the only insurance plan in the United States that provides support for both ends of life. This support is particularly important in minority communities. According to the Kaiser Family Foundation, almost 60% of all children in the United States are born with the support of Medicaid. The health of pregnant women and their newborns is tied to

Medicaid. Also, in the United States, Medicaid is the primary source for financing long-term care for seniors. Before the enactment of Medicaid in 1965, seniors needing long-term care had no options if they had no family. Medicaid protects children as well as honors the contribution of our older adults. The program's expansion supports both of these commitments. It is not a permanent fix, though. The expansion buys the states time to address the need for long-term care financing. During the ACA expansion period, all states will need to design a response to the growth of the population requiring long-term care. While there will always be a need for institutional care, many people can be better served in their homes. Minority elders, like all Americans, want care in their homes. The results from ongoing Medicaid demonstration projects to deliver home-based care can lead to quality processes that meet the growing needs of minority elders.

SUMMARY

This chapter is a summary of the changing health care policy climate. These changes can either reduce current barriers or create new challenges to health care. The ACA is the largest legislative change in health care financing since the enactment of Medicare, and its provisions have been upheld by the U.S. Supreme court. Researchers can focus their attention to the process of implementation. The research underlying new ACA policy is based on a concept of health care quality. Quality health care is defined as timely, effective, and patient-centered. The ACA creates new opportunities to identify health care quality gaps at the level of the local delivery system. The law contains mechanisms to identify and mediate these gaps. (See Weissman et al. [2011] for a thorough discussion of health care disparities measurement.) The law also provides standardized protocols for obtaining consumer reports describing the quality of health care. Standardization of health care practice creates research opportunities for social gerontologists to evaluate policy and its impact on health care access disparities.

REFERENCES

American Geriatrics Society Updated Beers Criteria for Potentially Inappropriate Medication Use in Older Adults (2012). *Journal of the American Geriatrics Society, 60*(4), 616–631. doi: 10.1111/j.1532–5415.2012.03923.x

Arias, E. (2010). *United States life tables, 2006.* National Vital Statistics Reports. Vol. 58 no. 21. Hyattsville, MD: National Center for Health Statistics.

Aspden, P., Wolcott, J., & Erickson, S. M. (2004). *Patient safety: achieving a new standard for care.* Institute of Medicine, Committee on Data Standards for Patient Safety. ISBN 030909776.

Berkowitz, E. (2005). Medicare and Medicaid: The past is prologue. *Health Care Financing Review, 27*(2), 11–23.

Centers for Medicare and Medicaid Services (2011). *Advanced diagnostic imaging: education and outreach for contractors and suppliers.* Slide presentation. Retrieved from http://www.cms.gov/Medicare/Provider-Enrollment-and-Certification/MedicareProviderSupEnroll/downloads/SlidePresentationThuJune23ADI_Accred_ProviderCall.pdf

Centers for Medicare and Medicaid Services (2012a). *Critical access hospitals: rural health fact sheet.* Retrieved from https://www.cms.gov/Outreach-and-Education/Medicare-Learning-Network-MLN/MLNProducts/downloads/CritAccessHospfctsht.pdf

Centers for Medicare and Medicaid Services (2012b). *ESRD—General Information.* http://cms.gov/Medicare/End-Stage-Renal-Disease/ESRDGeneralInformation. Accessed July 19, 2012.

Cossman, J. S., Cosby, A. G., & Cossman, R. E. (2010). Underlying causes of the emerging nonmetropolitan mortality penalty. *American Journal of Public Health, 100*(8), 1417–1419.

Danaei, G., Oza, S., Kulkarni, S. C., Murray, C. L., & Ezzati, M. (2010). The promise of prevention: the effects of four preventable risk factors on national life expectancy disparities by race and county in the United States. *PLoS Medicine, 7*(3), e1000248. doi: 10.1371/journal.pmed.100248

Erwin, P. C., Brown, K. C., Looney, S., & Forde, T. (2010). Health disparities in rural areas: the interaction of race, socioeconomic status, and geography. *Journal Health of the Poor and Underserved, 21*, 931–945.

Fischer, S. M., Sauaia, A., & Kutner, J. S. (2007). Patient navigation: A culturally competent strategy to address disparities in palliative care. *Journal of Palliative Medicine, 10*(5), 1023–1028. doi: 10.1089/jpm.2007.0070

Fisher, E. S., & Chandra, A. (2008). Regional and racial variation in health care among Medicare beneficiaries: A brief report of the Dartmouth Atlas Project. In K. K. Bonner (Ed.), *Aligning forces for quality: Improving health and health care in communities across America* (A Dartmouth Atlas Project Report Commissioned for the Aligning Forces for Quality Program). Princeton, NJ: Trustees of Dartmouth College.

Galvin, R. S., & McGlynn, E. M. (2003). Using performance measurement to drive improvement: a road map for change. *Medical Care Supplement: The Strategic Framework Board's Design for a National Quality Measurement and Reporting System, 41*(1), I48–I60.

Gamm, L. D., Hutchison, L. L., Dabney, B. J., & Dorsey, A. M. (Eds.) (2003). *Rural healthy people 2010: A companion document to healthy people 2010* (Vol. 1). College Station, TX: The Texas A&M University System Health Science Center, School of Rural Public Health, Southwest Rural Health Research Center.

Ginsburg, J. A., & Ralston, J. F. (2008). Achieving a high performance health care system with universal access: what the United States can learn from other countries. *Annals of Internal Medicine, 148*(1), 55–75.

Guyatt G. H., & Busse, J. W. (2002.) The philosophy of evidence-based medicine. In V. M. Montori (Ed.), *Contemporary endocrinology: Evidence-based endocrinology* (Chapter 3). Rochester, MN: Mayo Foundation for Medical Research.

Hackbarth, G. M. (2010). Aligning incentives in medicare. *MEDPAC—Medicare Payment Advisory Commission*, 17.

Hasnain-Wynia, R. (2006). Is evidence-based medicine patient-centered and is patient-centered care evidence-based? *Health Services Research, 41*(1), 1–8. doi: 10.1111/j.1475–6773.2006.0054.x

Institute of Medicine (2006). Committee for Redesigning Health Insurance Performance and Performance Improvement Program. *Medicare's quality improvement organization program: maximizing potential.* National Academies.

Institute of Medicine (U.S.) Committee on Quality of Health Care in America., Kohn, L. T., Corrigan, J., & Donaldson, M. S. (2000). *To err is human: Building a safer health system.* Washington, DC: National Academy Press.

Kaiser Family Foundation (2011). Commission on Medicaid and the Uninsured. *Case Study: Georgia's Money Follows the Person Demonstration.* Publication 8262. http://www.keff.org

Kaiser Family Foundation (2012). *Medicare: A timeline of key development.* http://www.kff.org/medicare/timeline/pf_05.htm. Accessed July 17, 2012.

Kutner, M., Jin, Y., Paulson, C., & White, S. (2006). *The health literacy of America's adults: results from the 2003 National Assessment of Adult Literacy.* NECS 2006–483.

Leveille, S. G., & Davis, C. (1998). Preventing disability and managing chronic illness in frail older adults: a randomized trial of a community-based partnership with primary care. *Journal of American Geriatrics Society, 46*, 1191–1198.

Lichtenberg, F. (2011). The quality of medical care, behavioral risk factors, and longevity growth. *International J of Health Care Finance Economics, 11*, 1–34. doi: 10.1007/s10754–010-9086-y

Lorig, K. R., & Steward, A. L. (1999). Evidence suggesting that a chronic disease self-management program can improve health status while reducing hospitalization: a randomized trial. *Medical Care, 37*, 5–14.

Manley, J. (2000). Negotiating quality: total quality management and the complexities of transforming professional organizations. *Sociological Forum, 15*(3), 457–484.

McGlynn, E. A. (2008). *The case for keeping quality on the health reform agenda.* [Healthcare]. RAND Corporation Testimony Series, CT-306.

McGlynn, E. A., Ringel, J. S., Price, C. C., & Girosi, F. (2010). *Analysis of the affordable health care for America Act (H.R. 3962).* Santa Monica, CA: RAND Corporation.

Miles, T. P. (2012a). *Health reform and disparities: History, hype, hope.* Santa Barbara, CA: ABC-Clio.

Miles, T. P. (2012b). *Supreme court decision on medicaid honors the past, protects the future.* Retrieved from http://newamericamedia.org/2012/06/supreme-court-decision-on-medicaid-honors-the-past-protects-the-future.php

Miller E. G., & Carroll W. A. (2009). *Health insurance status of full time workers by demographic and employer characteristics, 2006* (Medical Expenditure Panel Survey, Statistical brief #234). Rockville, MD: Agency for Healthcare Research and Quality.

Murray, C. J. L., Kulkarni, S. C., Michaud, C., Tomijima, N., Bulzacchelli, M. T., Iandiorio, T. J., et al. (2006). Eight Americas: investigating mortality disparities across races, counties, and race-counties in the United States. *PLoS Medicine, 3*(9), e260–e260.

National Center for Health Statistics (NCHS) (1975). *Vital statistics of the United States.* Volume II—Mortality Part A. PHS 79–1114. Table 1–3: Death rates by Age, Color, and Sex, 1966–1975.

National Committee for Quality Assurance (NCQA) (2010). *The state of health care quality—reform.* The Quality Agenda and Resource Use.

National Council on Aging (NCOA) (2009). *Re-forming healthcare: Americans speak out about chronic conditions and challenges to self-care.* Findings from a national survey of Americans 44 years and older with chronic conditions. Retrieved July 14, 2012, from http://www.ncoa.org/improve-health/chronic-conditions/healthier-lives-a.html

Ory, M. G, Jordan, P. J., & Bazzarre, T. (2002). The behavior change consortium: Setting the stage for a new century of health behavior-change research. *Health Education Research, 17*(5), 500–511.

Prochaska, J. O., DiClemente, C. C., & Norcoss, J. C. (1983). Stages and processes of self-change of smoking: toward an integrative model of change. *Journal of Consulting and Clinical Psychology, 51*(3), 390–395. doi: 10.1037/0022–006X.51.3.390

Salinsky, E. (2010). Health care shortage designations; HPSA, MUA, and TBD. *National Health Policy Forum.* Background Paper No. 75. Washington, DC. http://www.nhpf.org

Schoenberg, N. E., Manchikanti, K. N., & Goodenow, S. (2011). Appalachian resident's experiences with and management of multiple morbidity. *Qualitative Health Research, 21*, 601–611. doi: 10.1177/1049732310395779

Shekelle, P. G. (2002). Why don't physicians enthusiastically support quality improvement programmes? *Quality & Safety In Health Care, 11*(1), 6–6.

Shortell, S. M., Burns, L. R., Alexamder, J. A., Gillies, R. R., Budetti, P. P., Waters, T. M., et al. (2001). Implementing evidence-based medicine: the role of market pressures, compensation incentives, and culture in physician organizations. *Medical Care Suuplement: Health Outcomes Methodology, 39*(7), I62–I78.

Slack, C. W., & Slack, S. W. (2011). Commentary: The United Countries of America - Benchmarking the quality of U.S. health care. *Mayo Clinical Proceedings, 86*(8), 788–790. doi: 10.4065/mcp.2011.0311

Song, Y., Bynum, S. J., Sutherland, J., Wennberg, J. E., & Fisher, E. S. (2010). Regional variations in diagnostic practices. *New England Journal of Medicine, 363*(1), 45–53.

Tatum, B. (1997). *Why are all the black kids sitting together?* Perseus Books.

U.S. Government. Government Accounting Office (2006). *Health professional shortage areas: problems remain with primary care shortage area designation system: report to congressional committees.* GAO-07–84. Washington, DC. http://www.gao.gov/cgi-bin/getrpt?GAO-07–84

U.S. Department of Labor (2010). Bureau of Labor Statistics. On benefits by wage level: survey finds that employer-provided benefits vary with earnings. *Program Perspectives* 2 No. 1. http://www.bls.gov/epub/perspectives/program_perspectives_vol2_issue1.pdf

Vincent, G. K., & Velkoff, V. A. (2010). *The next four decades: the older population in the United States 2010–2050.* Current Population Reports, P25–1138.

Wagner, E. H. (1998). Chronic disease management: what will it take to improve care for chronic illness? *Effective Clinical Practice, 1*, 2–4.

Walke, R. (2009). Indian health service: Health care delivery, status, funding and legislative issues. *Congressional Research Service,* R133022.

Weissman, J. S., Green, A. R., Meyer, G. S., Tan-McGrory, A., Nudel, J. D., Zeidman, J. A., et al. (2011). *Health disparities measurement.* National Quality Forum.

PART III

SOCIAL WORK AND MINORITY AGING

CHAPTER 15

Introduction: Social Work and Minority Aging

Philip A. Rozario and Letha A. Chadiha

Part III uses a social work lens to address seven pressing issues discussed in this book: end-of-life (EOL) care, aging in place, long-term care in residential and community settings, mental and developmental disabilities (DD), civic engagement, productive aging and the Older Americans Act (OAA). This part aims to provide the reader with state-of-the-art knowledge on these issues and implications for practice, policy, and research in the field of social work.

Social work is an applied discipline with a long tradition of using the theories and methods of social sciences to enhance practice, policy, and research. The field is at the forefront of addressing the opportunities and challenges emerging from a rapidly aging and more diverse ethnic and racial society. In their professional roles, social workers practice work with minority older adults and their families in diverse community-based and institutional settings that encompass social and health services. The professional practice of social workers in such settings is informed by a biopsychosocial perspective (sometimes referred to as a person-in-environment perspective), which considers the impact of the individual, social, and environmental contexts that "simultaneously affect how people age" as well as their aging experiences (Richardson & Barusch, 2006, p. 13). Indeed, Burnette, Morrow-Howell, and Chen (2003) argue that social workers bring their expert knowledge about eligibility, availability, quality, and barriers to health and social services in their delivery of these services.

The conduct of social work practitioners and researchers in working with human populations is guided by the Code of Ethics of the National Association of Social Workers. The Preamble to this code states: "The primary mission of the social work profession is to enhance human wellbeing and help meet the basic human needs of all people, with particular attention to the needs and empowerment of people who are vulnerable, oppressed, and living in poverty" (National Association of Social Workers, n.d., p. 2). This code is highly relevant to older adults and minority populations, particularly minority elders (commonly labeled Native American/Native Alaskan, Asian American, black or African American, Latino or Hispanic, and Native Hawaiian/Pacific Islander). These and all elders in the United States are living longer and healthier lives (Anderson, Bulatao, & Cohen, 2004). However, minority elders' unprecedented longevity, increasing numbers, continuing health disparities, persistent economic disadvantages, and increasing cultural, racial, and ethnic diversity arising from more recent immigration streams raise important concerns about how the social work field as a human service profession will address these trends (see Gardner & Rosenthal-Gelman, 2008;

Torres-Gil, & Bickson-Moga, 2002). According to Torres-Gil and Bickson-Moga (2002), such trends "will require social work to rethink issues of diversity, to move beyond generalized notions of race, and to have a greater understanding of population aging and its long term consequences" (p. 14). They further argue: "In fact, the reality of a nation becoming more diverse is that it creates complexities and conflicts as well as opportunities. Allocating finite public resources and addressing the economic and linguistic needs of minority and racial groups become problematic as their numbers and diversity increase" (p. 17).

As the social work profession prepares to work with a more aged and diverse minority population in light of the anticipated demographic revolution, the profession will also have to expand training and educational efforts to produce an adequate supply of trained, competent practitioners (Scharlach, Damron-Rodriguez, Robinson, & Feldman, 2000) and researchers (Morrow-Howell & Burnette, 2008). Morrow-Howell and Burnette (2008) found that social workers' knowledge production in multidisciplinary aging research lags behind their involvement in interdisciplinary practice. The majority of social workers are not trained in gerontology; only about 5% of social workers have undergone this training (Hudson, Gonyea, & Curley, 2003). The low availability of skilled workers and the high demands of an aging population have led some social work scholars to wonder whether the profession is ready to deal with the complexities of the needs of older adults and their families (Scharlach et al., 2000). Furthermore, some have opined that "the situation in social work with minority elders is bleak" (Min, 2005, p. 353). Over the years, a number of initiatives funded by the John A. Hartford Foundation have been undertaken to address this shortage (see Robbins & Rieder, 2008). These efforts were initially targeted at building capacity at institutions of higher learning with research grants for gerontological social work scholars and doctoral students, and subsequently led to curriculum development efforts as well. However, a more sustained and concerted effort is required to ensure that there is a sufficient supply of gerontologically trained social workers to meet the growing demands of a more aged and diverse society.

CHAPTER REVIEW

A few common themes emerge from the chapters grouped under Part III. Much of the research in the areas we cover has focused on the dominant racial and ethnic group, whites. When research is undertaken with elders of color, it is often cross-comparison research with whites as the comparison group. More recently, there has been an increase in research focusing exclusively on a single racial/ethnic minority group, though often some of these categories are so broad that they may confound national origin, social class, immigration status, and level of acculturation and assimilation. In some cases, namely with Native Americans, Asian Americans, and Pacific Islanders, research may not only be sparse but often nonexistent.

EOL Care

Increasingly, social workers are encountering "terminally ill older people in hospitals, hospices, private homes, nursing homes, and other alternative living situations" (Richardson & Barusch, 2006, p. 235). In their chapter on EOL care among racial and ethnic minority groups, Bullock, Hall, and Leach (Chapter 16) assert that the morbidity and mortality disparities experienced by these groups add to the saliency of the matter. They argue that the preterminal phases can critically influence the anticipation and expectations of as well as the preparedness for EOL care. Their review of the literature points to a consistent lack in access, use, and quality in EOL care for minority elders, which may result in a less than desirable dying experience. Interestingly, they reported an intervention study that did not alter African American participants' use of advanced care planning despite being provided with more information about it. Perhaps, their intransigence is the result of a history of discrimination by and distrust of the health care system. Bullock et al.'s inclusion of critical race theory (CRT) as a theoretical framework allows us to appreciate the sociohistorical contexts that might better explain the racial/ethnic differences in not only the meaning of death but also the experience of EOL care; we think CRT deserves closer examination in future research. Bullock et al. remind us that a lifetime of discrimination and unequal access to educational, health, and occupational opportunities may cause minority elders to view with suspicion any attempts to help them die better. Similar to other chapters in this part, the literature on EOL care for some racial and ethnic groups, namely Native Americans and Asian Americans, remains sparse.

Aging in Place

Housing and the living arrangement are very important for older people. In Chapter 17, McCallion highlights the preference of the majority of older people to age in place. This can be a challenge, especially if an older person begins to experience diminishing functional abilities in addition to chronic illness and normal aging. This is further complicated if there is a lack of financial resources to modify and adapt the physical environment based on a person's reduced physical capacity.

Nursing Homes

Nursing home placement remains an important, yet expensive, option in meeting the long-term care needs of elders with severe physical and cognitive impairments, although the number of available beds and occupancy rates have both steadily declined over the past years. Choi's chapter (Chapter 18) highlights the shift to an increased use of nursing homes by racial and ethnic minorities, in part due to the changing demographics and cultural norms as well as the increase in dementia care needs and economic pressures experienced by families; shifting patterns in long-term care use have also been seen among white elders. Choi reviews the state of the knowledge of access to and predictors of nursing home placements and the quality of care for African Americans, Latino/Hispanic Americans, Asian Americans, and Native Americans. For Native Americans, the unavailability of culturally appropriate and quality nursing homes remains a huge obstacle. Further, Choi highlights research that points to a pattern of delayed nursing home use among African Americans and Latino/Hispanic Americans and poorer services in nursing homes that serve predominantly people of color. In her recommendations, Choi examines the implications of culturally competent care. Her review of the literature on quality of care for Asian Americans highlights a gaping hole in our knowledge base. Researchers need to make a concerted effort to evaluate the implementation and effectiveness of culturally competent care to ensure greater access and improved care for racial and ethnic minority elders and their families.

Family Caregiving

In the United States, families remain very much at the foundation of the long-term care system and provide much of the informal care that allows the older adult to remain in the community. Although caregiving can provide some positive outcomes for family caregivers, caregiving presents challenges and stresses and is often associated with poorer health and well-being outcomes for the caregiver (Richardson & Barusch, 2006). The caregiving challenges are further exacerbated for racial and ethnic minority elders, as pointed out in the chapter by Rosenthal-Gelman, Tompkins, and Ihara (Chapter 19), who are more likely than their white counterparts to face poverty, poor health, barriers to service utilization, and discrimination. Caregivers may also subscribe to cultural values that underpin their role, and may, as such, not feel comfortable seeking help beyond their informal network. This review of the literature points to worse physical and mental health outcomes for racial and ethnic minority caregivers compared with their white counterparts, though there are nuances and slight differences in these findings. For example, the present literature indicates that African American caregivers might appraise their caregiving burden as being lower than white caregivers do, and may rely more heavily on spirituality and religiosity as ways to cope with caregiving demands. A better understanding of the caregiving experience and outcomes for racial and ethnic minority family caregivers can lead to the development of better caregiver interventions. Rosenthal-Gelman et al. (Chapter 19) review some of the caregiving interventions, highlighting the dearth of evidence of the efficacy of interventions designed to aid racial and ethnic minority caregivers, thus emphasizing the need for more research in this area.

DD and Serious Mental Health

The demographic revolution affects all groups, including those with DD and serious mental illness (SMI), who previously did not normally live into old age. People with DD may be at greater risk for certain chronic and debilitating conditions as they age, in comparison with the general aging population. In their chapter (Chapter 20) on aging with DD and serious mental health, Magaña and Ghosh underscore the lack of research that focuses exclusively on racial and ethnic minority elders with DD and/or SMI; in fact, research in this field for the dominant racial group is only currently emerging. As such, much of the evidence on disparities in service and treatment they draw upon in developing this chapter comes from racial and ethnic minority families with younger individuals with DD and SMI, which may provide us with tentative yet useful insights into the issues of disparities faced by minority elders with DD and SMI. In their review, Magaña and Ghosh provide evidence to illustrate that the disparities experienced by minority groups with DD and SMI are further complicated by the stigma of their diagnoses and their families' understanding of the causes of DD or SMI. Despite perceived and real cultural differences, service providers of people with DD and SMI bear the burden of ensuring services and programs are developed that are accessible, adequate, and acceptable. Indeed, research into the needs of older racial and ethnic minorities with DD and SMI need to address prevalence, needs, and the effectiveness of services.

Productive Aging

Richardson and Barusch (2006) contend that the incorporation of emancipatory agendas in social work practice models tends to "emphasize clients' strengths and suggest ways to enhance their resilience and coping strategies" despite the setbacks and challenges of experiencing lifelong inequities (p. 20). As such, Morrow-Howell and Wang (Chapter 21) argue that the productive aging perspective can potentially resonate with social work practice, as it emphasizes positive aspects about a rapidly aging population and reframes the experiences with elders as valuable for society. Morrow-Howell and Wang caution that those who have faced lifelong disadvantages may continue to experience limited access to or support for productive engagement. They present readers with a conceptual framework that considers the antecedents and outcomes of productive engagement as well as the influence of the sociocultural context and, where available, statistics on the engagement patterns of older racial/ethnic minority groups in the areas of employment, volunteerism, caregiving, and grandparenting. Another important area they review is the policy and programmatic interventions that can promote productive engagement among these groups. Indeed, they find that minority elders are well represented in certain federally supported initiatives such as Senior Corps programs. However, as readers will discover, a paucity of research exists on the effects of these policies and programs as well as the factors that influence engagement among some of these groups, especially Native Americans. There is a need for more scholarly attention to these groups.

OAA

In its enactment of the OAA in 1965, Congress set a bold and ambitious agenda of programs and services aimed at preserving and enhancing the inherent dignity of aging individuals in the United States. Richardson and Barusch (2006) argue that although "the goals of the law present a compelling mandate for professionals who work with the elderly," Congress did not match its intent with adequate federal resources, thus presenting a fundamental paradox—"wonderful (if unachievable) goals and paltry resources" (pp. 378–379). Despite this, in their chapter, Torres-Gil, Spencer-Suarez, and Rudinica (Chapter 22) briefly highlight the accomplishments of the OAA, which has provided an extensive array of home- and community-based services for older adults. They assert that the OAA has as exemplary record of developing culturally sensitive programs to serve a heterogeneous clientele of older adults and their caregivers. However, they contend that the OAA remains a secondary player in setting the national agenda for older people and their families. The OAA is presently due for reauthorization by Congress. Despite challenges presented by the contentious political climate and disconcerting economic situation, Torres-Gil et al. are hopeful that OAA could evolve into a piece of legislation that is responsive to the community-based, long-term care needs of a heterogeneous older population. In anticipation of greater diversity in the coming decades that will move beyond the current racial and ethnic categories, they argue for a new and inclusive conceptualization of need, which recognizes the aging-diversity nexus to help build intergenerational and interracial/ethnic coalitions.

LIMITATIONS

Our consideration of the needs of racial/ethnic minority elders in this part is not without its limitations, which perhaps deserve closer attention elsewhere. We are presented with five tensions in highlighting the current state of knowledge of the issues facing different racial and ethnic elders in the United States. First, in focusing on the disparities in experience and outcomes, we risk the "danger ... of adopting a 'victim-oriented' perspective that undervalues the significance and contributions of the struggle of minority ethnic people and their organizations" (Ahmad & Atkins, 1996, p. 5). Such a focus sometimes deflects attention from the mezzo- and macro-level influences and may lead minority elders and their families to ask themselves, to paraphrase DuBois (1903), "How does it feel to be a problem?" (p. 2).

Second, we did not directly address the conceptual complexities of terms such as *race* and *ethnicity* that have plagued scholars. For example, Bullock et al. (see Chapter 16 on EOL care) use The National Institutes of Health's (2001) definition of minority group that refers to "a readily identifiable subset of the U.S. population that is distinguished by racial, ethnic, and/or cultural heritage" (p. 10). This definition is vague, especially when we consider the category "Asian American," which serves as a catch-all category for people from the continent of Asia who may not have a shared history, language, religion, or even immigration pattern. Although race is frequently referred to in this part, race as a conceptual category remains contentious and problematic for various reasons (LaViest, 2004; Martin & Yeung, 2003). Still, many scholars have accepted it as a proxy of differential access to power and resources in a multicultural society (Williams, 2004), which Torres-Gil et al. briefly consider in their chapter on the OAA. LaViest (2004) asserts that not only does race lack a consensus in its definition, but our understanding of it has often been "confounded by social class, nationality, ethnicity, and social status" (p. 87).

Third, Martin and Yeung (2003) assert that "the repeated use of the conceptual category of race has the potential to restrict our understanding of actual social processes, because of the implication of homogenization within categories that is psychologically (even if not logically) implied by their continual use" (pp. 521–522). This homogenization is often seen in cross-comparative research that examines one or more groups with another. For example, when we compare caregiving outcomes between African American and white caregivers, we may fail to consider the structural heterogeneity that exists within both categories and potentially attribute these differences to culture. Indeed, as some authors in this part underscore, the within-group heterogeneity can be greater than the between-group differences.

A fourth tension we do not fully explore pertains to the dynamism of culture and within-group differences in allegiance to one's cultural heritage. Often, culture is presented as a homogeneously static phenomenon impervious to change. However, Atkin and Rollings (1996) challenge the assumption that Asians in the United Kingdom live in "self-supporting families" because of their cultural heritage as not only simplistic but one that does not consider "the changes in family structure, household structure, and geographical dispersal of close and extended kin" (p. 76). We sometimes forget that the countries of origin from which these immigrants come may have also undergone economic and cultural transformations. Further, like race, we sometimes conflate culture with class, educational level, and acculturation. In their review of attributions of DD and SMI, Magaña and Ghosh (see Chapter 20 on Developmental Disabilities and Serious Mental Illness) underscore this nuance. Still, as they point out, it is important for social workers to examine their preconceptions about cultural differences so as not to be the obstacle for their clients' service use.

Finally, we face a fifth tension. That is, it is expedient that social work researchers clarify the scientific utility of the racial and ethnic categories as well as the relevance and adequacy of various theoretical constructs for racial and ethnic minority elders that were developed for white elders (Burnette, 1998). Further, Martin and Yeung (2003) argue that simply treating race in a regression model as a control variable "implies that, while race makes a difference, it is not a very profound one, in that race does not affect the relationships between other variables" (p. 532). In a multicultural society like the United States, with a long history of institutionalized racism and segregation, "the problem of the color-line" (DuBois, 1903) will most likely linger on in the 21st century and beyond. As such, it is important for social workers to "identify and develop a conceptual framework for addressing race/ethnicity as a main focal point" (Min, 2005, p. 354). Although this is beyond the scope of this handbook, it remains an important area for further development.

WHAT'S NEXT IN THE FIELD?

Due to space constraints, we could not include other equally important issues in this part on social work. In our concluding remarks, we highlight topics social work researchers and practitioners should consider addressing next in the field of social work; this is not an exhaustive list.

While we consider the issue of aging in place in McCallion's chapter, we do not specifically address homelessness among racial and ethnic minority elders, which is especially important as affordable, quality housing stock has dwindled over the years. The current economic situation precipitated by the housing bust, global economic slowdown, and overextended financial institutions may have more than an immediate effect on publicly financed programs and services; it may also have long-term effects on government support for these programs. The economic downturn has hit racial and ethnic minority groups disproportionately harder than whites, and as such may have a greater negative impact on the overall well-being of current and future minority elders and their families. Social work researchers and practitioners will need to be responsive to the impact of government social spending cuts on the availability and delivery of services to their elderly clients who are most in need.

Regarding other issues deserving attention in the social work field, we do not specifically address transitions and adjustments across care settings (Morrow-Howell, Burnette, & Chen, 2005), although we do consider nursing home care in Choi's chapter. In their chapter on DD and SMI, Magaña and Ghosh allude to the effects of substance abuse in potentially complicating outcomes for persons with SMI, but we do not specifically address late-life substance abuse. As population aging affects every segment of society, there is currently increased attention given to the aging of long-term incarcerated individuals of color. We believe this is an issue that deserves attention for research in light of the inadequate health, mental health, and social services within prison systems related to privatization and cost-cutting initiatives at the federal and state levels. We do not consider HIV and AIDS among older adults, who have a high incidence rate in comparison to other age groups. Another important issue that we do not consider is the intersectionality that exists among racial/ethnic minority individuals. For example, we do not explore the challenges that older gay, lesbian, and transgendered persons of color face in their long-term care options or late-life financial well-being, especially those living in rural areas. Last but not least, we do not include a chapter on elder abuse, which may not be any more prevalent among racial and ethnic minority groups than whites but has received even less attention.

In terms of future direction for research with racial and ethnic minority groups, Morrow-Howell et al. (2005) found that social work researchers and practitioners rated highly the need to develop and test culturally appropriate and sensitive assessment tools and intervention programs. More importantly, we believe that social work researchers should make a special effort to ensure the inclusion of, if not focus solely on, racial and ethnic elders in their studies and pay closer attention to developing or refining explanatory frameworks on the effects and phenomena of race and ethnicity. While identifying differences in experiences and outcomes between racial and ethnic groups is important, Martin and Yeung (2003) also caution against ignoring commonalities between members of these groups.

REFERENCES

Ahmad, W. I. U., & Atkins, K. (1996). "Race" and community care: An introduction. In W. I. U. Ahmad & K. Atkins (Eds.), *"Race" and community care* (pp. 1–13). Buckingham, UK: Open University Press.

Anderson, N. B., Bulatao, R. A., & Cohen, B. (Eds.). (2004). *Critical perspectives on racial and ethnic differences in health in late life*. Washington, DC: The National Academies Press. Retrieved from http://www.nap.edu/openbook.php?record_id=11086&page=R1

Atkin, K., & Rollings, J. (1996). Looking after their own? Family caregiving among Asian and Afro-Caribbean communities. In W. I. U. Ahmad & K. Atkins (Eds.), *"Race" and community care* (pp. 73–86). Buckingham, UK: Open University Press.

Burnette, D. (1998). Conceptual and methodological considerations in research with non-white ethnic elders. *Journal of Social Service Review, 23*(3–4), 71–91.

Burnette, D., Morrow-Howell, N., & Chen, L. M. (2003). Setting priorities for gerontological social work research: A national Delphi study. *The Gerontologist, 43*(6), 828–838.

DuBois, W. E. B. (1903). *The souls of Black folk*. Lexington, KY: Tribeca Books. (Reprinted 2012)

Gardner, D., & Rosenthal-Gelman, C. (2008). Aging: Racial and ethnic groups. In T. Mizrahi & L. Davis (Eds.), *Encyclopedia of social work*. (20th ed.). New York: Oxford University Press.

Hudson, R. B., Gonyea, J. G., & Curley, A. (2003). The geriatric social work labor force: Challenges and opportunities. *Public Policy and Aging Report, 13*(2), 12–14.

LaViest, T. A. (2004). Conceptualizing racial and ethnic disparities in access, utilization, and quality of care. In K. E. Whitfield (Ed.), *Closing the gap: Improving the health of minority elders in the new millennium* (pp. 87–93). Washington, DC: Gerontological Society of America.

Martin, J. L., & Yeung, K. T. (2003). The use of the conceptual category of race in American sociology, 1939–99. *Sociological Forum, 18*, 521–543.

Min, J. W. (2005). Cultural competency: A key to effective future social work with racially and ethnically diverse elders. *Families in Society, 86*, 347–358.

Morrow-Howell, N., & Burnette, D. (2008). Gerontological social work research: Current status and future directions. *Journal of Gerontological Social Work, 36*(3–4), 63–79.

Morrow-Howell, N., Burnette, D., & Chen, L. M. (2005). Research priorities for gerontological social work: Researchers and practitioner perspective. *Social Work Research, 29*, 231–242.

National Association of Social Workers (N.D.). *Preamble to the code of ethics of the National Association of Social Workers*. Retrieved July 5, 2012, from http://www.socialworkers.org/pubs/code/code.asp

National Institute of Health. (2001). *NIH policy and guidelines on the inclusion of women and minorities as subjects in clinical research*. Amended October, 2001. Retrieved on May 8, 2012, from http://grants.nih.gov/grants/funding/women_min/guidelines_amended_10_2001.htm

Richardson, V. E., & Barusch, A. S. (2006). *Gerontological practice for the twenty-first century: A social work perspective*. New York, NY: Columbia University Press.

Robbins, L. A., & Rieder, C. H. (2008). The John A. Hartford Foundation geriatric social initiative. *Journal of Gerontological Social Work, 39*(1–2), 71–89.

Scharlach, A. E., Damron-Rodriguez, J., Robinson, B., & Feldman, R. (2000). Educating social workers for an aging society: A vision for the twenty-first century. *Journal of Social Work Education, 36*(3), 521–538.

Torres-Gil, F., & Bickson-Moga, K. (2002). Multiculturalism, social policy and the new aging. *Journal of Gerontological Social Work, 36*(3–4), 13–32.

Williams, D. R. (2004). Racism and health. In K. E. Whitfield (Ed.), *Closing the gap: Improving the health of minority elders in the new millennium* (pp. 69–80). Washington, DC: Gerontological Society of America.

CHAPTER 16

End-of-Life Care
Among Older Minorities

Karen Bullock, Jodi K. Hall, and Monica T. Leach

The fastest growing segment of the U.S. population is older adults. By the year 2030, they are expected to represent approximately 20% of the total population, and because approximately 70% of deaths in the United States are among people of advanced age (65+), the Centers for Disease Control and Prevention (2009) has issued statements regarding the need to understand end-of-life (EOL) care as a part of a health care paradigm. Hospice and palliative care are deemed to be the gold standard of care for persons faced with life-threatening and noncurable illnesses. However, minority older adults tend to underutilize these services (National Hospice and Palliative Care Organization [NHPCO], 2010). Of particular concern are the racial differences in EOL care decision making across groups.

In the following section of this chapter, we provide definitions and scope of the problem of eliminating disparities in EOL care. We then present research that examines the disparities in this area, in addition to outlining theories that are useful in understanding EOL care as a health behavior. Finally, we provide a translation of the theories and research that can be used to guide social work practice with minority older adults.

DEFINITIONS AND SCOPE

The term end-of-life care traditionally refers to the last phases of an illness before death; however, experiences across the earlier course of the illness (i.e., preterminal phases) are critical to shaping the anticipation, expectations, and preparedness for care during the terminal phases of illness. Although research into EOL care issues, including advance care planning and factors that influence decision making around the withdrawal and withholding of treatment, has grown exponentially during the past decade, knowledge about the reasons for differences in the use of the available care options remains vague. Several national consensus panels (National Consensus Project for Quality Palliative Care, 2009; NHPCO, 2010; National Institutes of Health [NIH], 2004) have outlined strategic initiatives to advance the state of the science, confirming the need for research into the experiences of individuals, families, and extended support systems of care for the dying (Tennstedt, 2002). One of the most important issues to address is the disparity in hospice and palliative care utilization among racial and ethnic minority older adults. The NIH (2001) defines minority groups as "a readily identifiable subset of the U.S. population that is distinguished by racial, ethnic, and/or cultural heritage" (p. 10). This definition applies to the following ethnic and racial categories: Hispanic or Latino American, Asian American, black or African American, American Indian or Alaskan Native Hawaiian, or Other Pacific Islander.

According to the Agency for Health Care Research and Quality (AHRQ; 2012), the elimination of health care disparities is a national priority, and simply addressing low socioeconomic status (SES) and financial vulnerability will not likely close the gap. Furthermore, we must link issues of health disparities with those of health care quality (AHRQ, 2012) because the two are inextricably related (Leach & Hall, in press). The quality of people's lives may influence how they die, and since the early 1970s, researchers and practitioners in the United States have focused on understanding how to help people die a good death (Altilio & Otis-Green, 2011; Blank, 2002; Bullock, McGraw, Blank, & Bradley, 2005; Byock, 1997; Fried & Gillick, 1994; Hill & Shirley, 1992; Jennings, Kaebnick, & Murray, 2005; Nuland, 1993).

Research has begun to examine EOL decision making as a health care behavior (Fried, Bullock, Iannone, & O'Leary, 2009). Although studies have documented improvements in EOL care for older adults and their family members (Bradley, Fried, Kasl, & Idler, 2001; Fried, Bradley, & Towle, 2003), the literature on patterns and types of EOL care for racial and ethnic minority persons reveals particular concerns (Carlisle, Leake, & Shapiro, 1995; Crawley et al., 2000; Gordan, 1995; Johnson et al., 2010; McKinley, Garrett, Evans, & Danis, 1996). As a group, minority older adults are less likely than white older adults to seek and to receive hospice and palliative care (NHPCO, 2010), less likely to receive adequate pain management (Green et al., 2004; Todd, Lee, & Hoffman, 1994), and more likely to experience poor physician–patient communication (Steinhauser et al., 2000; Welch, Teno, & Mor, 2005). These disparities are of concern because the absence of such care is linked to poor quality care (Commonwealth Fund, 2012). Furthermore, pain management and communication between physician and patient are key components of a good death, and any deficiency in either domain may characterize a less than desirable dying experience (Smith, 2000).

Several classic EOL texts have helped define key components of what might be termed a "good death" (Hill & Shirley, 1992; Nuland, 1993; Byock, 1997), but these scholarly works exclude the voice of racial and ethnic minorities in their definition. The following goals of care have often been used to characterize a good death: freedom from suffering, written directive about desired and undesirable medical intervention, individual/autonomous decision making, and a death that occurs at home. There is sufficient evidence to suggest that the views of what matters at EOL for racial and ethnic minority and nonminority groups may differ.

Use of medical treatment among minority elders is an important topic of research in light of health disparities among this population. It is well documented that minority older adults tend to have higher prevalence of certain diseases, such as hypertension, coronary heart disease, and diabetes compared to their white counterparts. Furthermore, members of these groups are at least twice as likely to die from cancer as are their white counterparts (U.S. Department of Health and Human Services [USDHHS], 2010), and they experience different physiological responses to various medical treatments than whites (Lavizzo-Mourey & Mackenzie, 1996). We argue that the morbidity and mortality rates alone provide justification for giving more attention to minority aging and EOL care.

WHAT WE KNOW ABOUT EOL CARE AMONG MINORITIES

Since the 1970s, when hospice developed in the United States as a grassroots movement to extend more humane care for dying people, the relief of pain and suffering has been paramount in acute care settings. Yet, according to the SUPPORT study (Support Principal Investigators, 1995), patients continue to receive care at EOL that is inappropriately invasive, prolonged, and inconsistent with their wishes. In recent years, there has been growing concern, supported by findings in the literature, about medical decision making among African Americans and Latinos at EOL and the factors that influence their preference for and against certain types of care (Crawley et al., 2000; Smith, Sudore, & Pérez-Stable, 2009). Moreover, studies (Hanson & Rodgman, 1996; Sachs, 1994) have documented that being white and affluent can be a predictor of the likelihood that one will engage in advance care planning to ensure a less protracted and more peaceful death than not.

NHPCO (2010) data document that more than 80% of hospice care recipients are white, with the vast majority of those individuals being older adults. Several studies examining differences by race in patient preferences for EOL treatments found that minority patients tend to prefer more life-sustaining treatments than their white counterparts (Blackhall et al., 1999; Caralis, Davis, Wright, & Marcial, 1993; Crawley et al., 2000). Overall, care for minority patients has been described as deficient in terms of the provision of palliation and hospice referrals (Gordan, 1995; Neubauer & Hamilton, 1990; NHPCO, 2010).

Hopp and Duffy (2000) identified racial differences in advanced care planning and EOL decision making between white and black older adults (aged 70+) by interviewing family members (proxy respondents) of 540 persons who died between the first and second waves of the study to understand decisions that family members made regarding a deceased member. They found that whites were significantly more likely than blacks to discuss treatment preferences before death, to complete a living will, and to designate a Durable Power of Attorney for Health Care. Further, the treatment decisions for whites were more likely to involve limiting and withholding treatment before death than was the case for blacks. Conversely, the treatment decisions for black participants were more likely to be based on the desire to provide all care options to prolong life. Race continued to be a significant predictor of differences in advance care planning and treatment decisions after controlling for sociodemographic factors, including age, gender, educational attainment, and marital status.

Crawley and colleagues (2000) argued that the underutilization of hospice and palliative care among African Americans has engendered much speculation and that there is limited data to explain these gaps in services. To expand our understanding of the experience of African Americans and EOL care, they undertook the Initiative to Improve Palliative and End-of-Life Care in the African American Community as a means for delineating historical, social, cultural, ethical, economic, legal, health policy, and medical factors that may affect African Americans' attitudes toward, acceptance of, access to, and utilization of palliative care. This report, produced by an interdisciplinary group of African American scholars and professionals, addressed barriers to palliative and EOL care for African Americans. They argued that lived experiences, values, and norms influence EOL decision making and care behaviors. More specifically, they pointed out that among African Americans, the identification of pain and suffering associated with death and dying is shaped by various historical and contemporary events, as well as by a range of sociocultural values and perspectives.

Five years later, Welch et al. (2005) systematically compared EOL medical care experiences of deceased white and African American patients and their family members. With a nationally representative sample of surrogate decision makers ($N = 1,447$), this retrospective study explored EOL care including symptom management, decision making, informing and supporting families, individualized care, coordination, service utilization, and financial impact. The research findings documented racial disparities that persist into EOL care, particularly regarding communication and family needs. Family members of African American patients were less likely than those of white patients to feel that the patient had received excellent or very good care at EOL. These family members were also more likely to identify problematic physician communication and informed consent than were family members of white patients. Moreover, fewer African Americans had expressed their EOL treatment wishes or had a written advance directive. These differences persisted when the sample was limited to those participants for whom the expectation for life-sustaining treatment matched the actual treatment that the patient received.

Scholars have argued that advance care planning and the completion of advance directives may be a key in eliminating such disparities (Smith et al., 2009). Latinos are a group with tremendous diversity, despite the commonalities of language, beliefs, attitudes, and behaviors. Differences by national origin, although important, are attenuated when we consider their immigrant status and experiences. Cultural misunderstandings can impede the care of dying Latino patients and their families. Thus, it is recommended that providers tailor their interventions and care plans to the specific needs of the individual, family, and members of the social support network as much as possible.

Relying on a culturally tailored research design, Bullock (2006) used a faith-based model to conduct research with 102 African Americans (aged 55 years or older). Study participants were recruited from local churches and community-based agencies to participate in a mixed-method pilot study to promote advance care planning. Focus groups were used to gather data on participants' preferences for care, desire to make personal choices, values and attitudes, beliefs about death and dying, and advance directives. There was also an education component to the study, in which participants were educated about advance care planning and advance directives. Three fourths of the participants refused to complete advance directives, despite receiving information and educational materials explaining advance directives and advance care planning. Consistent with the report from Crawley and colleagues (2002), participants identified spirituality; their view of suffering, death, and dying; social support networks; barriers to utilization; and mistrust of the health care system as factors that influence advance care planning behaviors and/or the lack thereof.

DECISION MAKING

EOL decision making is often difficult and one that many elderly persons and their families struggle with (Hansen, Cornish, & Kayer, 2000). Individuals, families, and health care providers are challenged when decisions need to be made regarding the use of treatment goals that affect the quality of life and death (Christ & Sormanti, 1999; Csikai, 2000). Although proactive planning for EOL care might be ideal, the decision-making process does not typically begin until late in the patient's dying trajectory. Furthermore, poorer physical and cognitive functioning, increasing age, and white ethnicity have been predictors of advance care planning for EOL and the use of treatment goals that affect the quality of life and death (Reese et al., 1999).

More than two decades ago, the Ethics Committee of the American Geriatrics Society (1995) identified 10 domains in which quality at the EOL might be measured. Advance care planning, which was listed as number 3, is an organized approach to initiating discussion, reflection, and understanding regarding an individual's current state of health, goals, values, and preferences for future treatment decisions (Field, Cassel, & IOM, 1997). It routinely includes assessment of and communication about an individual's understanding of his or her medical history and conditions; values; preferences; and personal, family, and community resources. Although the Patient Self-Determination Act of 1991 has resulted in more discussions of EOL wishes by providers, patients, and family members, as many as 80% of residents in long-term care facilities still do not have documented treatment wishes in their medical records (Lu & Johantgen, 2011). The omission of advance care planning significantly contributes to inadequate attention to and treatment of pain and symptom distress in patients. In contrast, research has documented the positive impact that advance care planning has on the dying and bereaved. These benefits include improved physical symptoms of depression (Lu & Johantgen, 2011), increased patient belief that the care team understands their preferences and cares more (Fried et al., 2003), and reduction in burden of those who provide social support (Hanson & Rodgman, 1996).

Hospice and palliative care are the means by which death with dignity is most likely to occur (Field et al., 1997). Among ethnic minority older adults, there is a much lower probability that they will receive this care at EOL than white older adults (Johnson et al., 2008). Knowledge, attitudes, and completion of advance directive may serve as barriers (Crawley et al., 2002). Tailoring care for patients and their families at the EOL is important. In a study on the difference in level of care at EOL (Johnson et al., 2010), data on demographics and level of care (full code, do not resuscitate, or withdrawal of life support) were collected on 1,072 patients, ranging in age from 62 to 78 years, who died in a hospital on a cardiac care unit. After controlling for age, sex, diagnosis, and lengths of stay in intensive care units and hospitals, blacks were 1.9 times more likely than whites to choose full code status, which means they have opted to have all attempts made to revive them, should the heart stop beating, rather than to have a Do Not Resuscitate (DNR) Order invoked at the time of death.

THEORETICAL UNDERSTANDING

Three frameworks that are particularly helpful in understanding the behaviors that produce racial differences in advance care planning and EOL care are the Theory of Planned Behavior (Azjen, 1991), Critical Race Theory (CRT; Delgado & Stefanic, 2001), and a Cultural

Competence perspective (National Association of Social Workers [NASW], 2007). Research on health practices and behaviors has applied Azjen's (1991) theory of planned behavior (TPB) in an attempt to understand individual-level health care decisions and actions. In social work, CRT is ideally suited to advance a social justice framework and the cultural competence perspective is well rooted in the literature on race, culture, and EOL care.

Theory of Planned Behavior

Advance care planning can be understood through the TPB. TPB proposes that a person's intention to perform a behavior is the key determinant of that behavior. Intention is determined by three factors. The first determinant is attitude, which is reflected in a positive or negative evaluation of performing the behavior. The second determinant is subjective norm, which reflects the perceived social pressure that individuals may feel to perform or not perform the behavior. The final determinant is planned behavioral control (PBC), which indicates the perceived ease or difficulty of performing the behavior. The summary proposition (Ajzen, 1991) of TPB is that individuals perform a behavior when they evaluate it positively, believe that important others think they should perform it, and perceive it to be under their control. When applied to understanding advance care planning among minority older adults, this may prove to be an excellent explanatory model (Garcia & Mann, 2003). In a qualitative, cross-sectional study to explore whether models of health behavior change can help to inform interventions for advance care planning, Fried et al. (2009) document that participants used a variety of processes of change to progress through stages of readiness, and advance care planning was only one of a broader set of behaviors in which participants engaged to prepare for declines in their health or for death. The study concluded that the variability in participants' readiness, barriers, benefits, perceptions of susceptibility, and use of processes to increase readiness for participating in each component of advance care planning may be linked to the utility of tailored, stage-specific interventions based on individualized assessments to improve this as a health care behavior (Fried et al., 2009). For example, when participants were given scenarios that mirrored EOL care situations that they had experienced or knew of someone who had experienced them, those participants identified levels of readiness that led them to respond more favorably about completing advance directives. Thus, they were more likely to say that they would complete a living will in response to that particular query than when they were asked about a scenario of less concern for them. Many of the African American participants in this study were not motivated to complete an advance directive when presented with the scenario that emphasized the lack of a support person that they could trust to make decisions on their behalf.

Critical Race Theory

CRT typically refers to a specific set of practices and ideologies advanced in the 1990s primarily by African American, Latino, and Asian American legal scholars (Delgado & Stefanic, 2012). A more expansive definition refers to a broad constellation of historical and contemporary notions that have actively engaged the prevailing racial theories of particular times and/or social contexts. In terms of EOL care decision making and the disparity in hospice utilization across racial groups, CRT offers insight for looking at race relations in a broader context than the traditional perspective (Hall, 2010). If, historically, people have had negative experiences with health care systems, which they felt were race-based, they may be hesitant to agree to withhold or withdraw care when people in their own communities or racial group are underrepresented as consumers of these types of care. Therefore, when exploring hospice and palliative care as alternatives to aggressive, life-prolonging interventions, people who feel that people of their own race have been denied treatment or care historically may be less inclined to sign documents to withdraw or withhold treatment when they are faced with a terminal illness. Furthermore, in contrast to more traditional perspectives on race relations, this framework provides a lens that draws upon various contextual and structural factors to explain the experiences of race/ethnic minorities.

CRT suggests that the ethical and practical questions about advance care planning and hospice care utilization that have dominated the national debate on EOL are not universal concerns (Fergus, Noguera, & Martin, 2010). Moreover, if social work practitioners were to focus on values and preferences of the minority groups, they may discover that the preferred standard of care may be culturally incongruent for many of those persons, although they may genuinely feel that they are providing their patients optimal care. For example, persons of Chinese and/or Korean descent may place a value on protecting the dying person from negative information (Hallenbeck, Goldstein, & Mebane, 1996), and therefore, may not want to discuss openly impending death with dying loved ones. Similarly, for family members who may have recently arrived from Mexico or Puerto Rico, there may be a rejection of the notion of individual autonomy in EOL decision making, which is preferred by persons of European descent who may have not recently immigrated (Field et al., 1997). (See Magaña and Ghosh's chapter [Chapter 20], a discussion on the cultural differences among the different racial/ethnic groups in the United States.) Furthermore, cultural and religious traditions are core values in many diverse groups and there is a need to discuss these topics with their clients and their families in hospital and other care settings, especially since cultural beliefs, attitudes, and practices are common sources of conflict and misunderstanding at EOL.

These cultural values may be centered on age, gender, communication styles, and even role definitions. In many minority cultures, older adults are viewed as chief decision makers, consultants, and even wise warriors of wisdom. In regards to gender, males may be deemed the primary communicator for the family and there may be an expectation that women rely on the authority and advice of male authorities (e.g., family members, professionals, etc.) for decision making. Scholars have noted that the deference that women show to men can be viewed as an expectation of women's self-sacrifice when women show signs of putting the needs of others before their own care needs (Braun, Pietsch, & Blanchette, 2000). When observed, it is important for social workers to engage the individuals and/or family members in a discussion about cultural norms and expectations to better understand the observed behaviors.

The manner in which one conveys sensitive messages around death and dying may well be rooted in cultural tradition. For example, in the tradition of Navajo Indians, planning for death and dying is contrary to their core values, particularly the value of "avoiding thinking or speaking in a negative way" (Carrese & Rhodes, 1995, p. 828). In this tradition, the discussion of negative information is believed to be harmful in that it may bring about a feared negative outcome. CRT posits that behaviors are influenced by contextual factors. As such, understanding historical and contemporary events, as well as a range of sociocultural values and experiences, may help to explain why it is that views of EOL care are perceived through seemingly contradictory perspectives. For example, death is seen by some as a home-going; something to look forward to, as the antithesis of the struggles "here on earth" (Johnson, 1992). Yet, given their struggle throughout life, when faced with a noncurable disease or illness, this is not a time to give up hope, but to opt for more aggressive, life-prolonging intervention. The legacy of slavery, abuses in medical experimentation, social and economic injustices, racial-profiling practices, migration, and other factors that shape the reality of oppressed groups may lead older minorities to seek aggressive treatment as opposed to electing to sign an advance directive, which would allow for the withdrawing and/or withholding of treatment when one has a terminal diagnosis.

Cultural Competence Framework

In the United States, the dominant discourse about illness, dying, and death focuses on autonomy, independence, self-control, and individual choice. Our health care system reinforces this autonomous decision making through the legal structures of advance directives. The focus on the individual and on planning for death presupposes the following elements: the individual is the primary decision maker; the individual has an interest in being in charge; typically, there is a clear communication and understanding between the individual and the medical team about diagnosis, prognosis, and options; the individual has equal financial access to the different options offered; and the individual has the power and sense of entitlement to make whatever choice is desired (Field et al., 1997).

There are many people in the United States, particularly minority older adults, for whom at least some of these conditions may be neither attainable nor desirable. In the absence of a cultural competence framework, this model of EOL care may be inadequate because it does not account for the experiences and values of persons who are in one way or another culturally different or socially disadvantaged. This includes ethnic and religious minorities for whom collective decision making may be a priority. Persons who are economically disadvantaged also may not access a range of different EOL care options that do not rely on informal support networks because of the cost of care.

Minority elders vary in regard to their beliefs and opinions about EOL decision making. This includes their views on the appropriateness of talking about and planning for death; truthtelling (Candib, 2002), which may take the form of advising persons that they are dying; and the roles of the collective family members and fictive kin in the decision-making process, as well as communicating with physicians regarding EOL decisions. These groups also may vary in even more basic dimensions (such as orientation to the future, the social construction of the self, and beliefs about who is in control of one's destiny and/or fate) that may have implications for EOL decision making (Bullock, 2011). In addition, within-group differences among racial/ethnic minority elders in their social support network and/or extended family system can be as great as, or greater than, between-group differences because individuals are often exposed to multiple and sometimes contradictory systems of values. To this point, it is worth acknowledging that not all Latinos/Hispanics will desire the same EOL care, and neither will all black or African Americans, Asians, nor any other racial/ethnic group members. Group experiences and the system of values affecting attitudes and behavior are not static. Although there are cultural values and norms that are helpful to be aware of and knowledgeable about, culturally appropriate assessments should be conducted to determine the extent to which one identifies with his/her cultural norms and their individual preferences at EOL (NASW, 2004).

Cultural competency practices have been widely accepted in social work as a means to decrease disparities in the quality of services delivered to ethnic minority groups. NASW (2007) Standards for Cultural Competence include guidelines that address several key areas of social work practice—including ethics and values, self-awareness, cross-cultural knowledge, cross-cultural skills, service delivery, empowerment and advocacy, workforce diversity, professional education, language diversity, and cross-cultural leadership.

Scholars have found that Latinos and African Americans are more likely than non-Hispanic white Americans to express a preference for life-sustaining treatment, regardless of the state of the disease and independent of educational level (Crawley et al., 2000). These preferences may be related to negative experiences with the medical system, leading to a lack of trust in formal care providers (Johnson, 1992). From the social work literature, we learn that Latinos/Hispanics may have a unique set of circumstances explored through the lens of language barriers (Colon, 2005). This may well be the case for non-Latino immigrant groups, especially older adults who might not have fluency in the English language.

To understand hospice services within the Latino community, Carrion (2010) undertook a qualitative study in Florida with hospice and nonhospice users. This research revealed cultural factors, including language, that contribute to the underutilization of hospice services by this population. The findings suggest that hospice users learned about their terminal diagnosis during a hospital admission from an attending physician and suggest that having information translated by family members is not necessarily an effective method of delivering medical information about terminal illness. Culturally, family members may not feel it is appropriate to tell older adults what they perceive to be bad news. Thus, according to Carrion's research, older Latino adults are not likely to receive a comprehensive diagnostic report if the family member feels it is not culturally appropriate to convey the information. However, when hospice services were offered, these individuals accepted the services. Similarly, the nonhospice users learned about their terminal diagnosis from a primary physician as well. The author suggested that the delivery of what is perceived to be bad news for older adults is not a culturally congruent behavior for Latinos. Therefore, it is culturally accepted to withhold this information in the interest of the individual. Yet, when the older persons did actually receive the information about noncurable disease and were offered hospice services, they refused the services. Family members were not likely to engage in discussions about diagnosis, advance directives, and/or planning for life's end.

Research on hospice use by minority older adults, although increasing since the late 1990s, remains sparse. To this end, Colon (2005) compiled a review of the available literature, which focused on Latino hospice use over a 15-year timeframe. The most important points were related to access to hospice care and various factors that researchers found to affect older Latinos' utilization of hospice care. These factors included beliefs about health care, death and EOL care, lack of insurance, lower referral rates by health care professionals, and the hospice caregiver requirement. Colon (2005) notes that Latinos underutilized hospice but did not offer reasons for their underutilization. There was no evidence of dissatisfaction reported by those who actually received hospice services. Furthermore, there was no evidence to suggest that persons who desired hospice services were unable to obtain services. One might conclude that Latinos who prefer to use hospice are not experiencing barriers to care. Crawley et al. (2002) concluded that even when minorities have access to hospice, they tend to underutilize it. Therefore, the issue of utilization may have less to do with access and more to do with preference for and/or against the hospice approach of care. More research is needed to compare and contrast access versus preference.

In the Midwestern region of the United States, researchers (Schroepfer et al., 2010) have made an effort to bridge two cultures: Hmong and non-Latino white populations. Given the disproportionately high incidence rate of cancer among Hmong patients with advanced stage disease, this research incorporated a community-based participatory approach to gain knowledge about the stages of illness and recommendations for effective intervention so that they could make informed decisions about treatment options. The tailored intervention, which they developed, enabled the research team to educate and reach out to people who tended to rely, primarily, on informal supports and who were being cared for by providers who were in need of knowledge and awareness about culturally specific formal EOL care. Research evidence indicates that informal supports and culturally specific care plans provide a valuable source of comfort over the life course for minority persons.

The health disparities, which can be seen at the beginning of life for Latinos, African Americans, Asians, and Native Americans (USDHHS, 2012) can also be seen at the EOL. High rates of chronic disease among these populations put them at risk for serious illnesses as they age. Suggestions to plan ahead for death and dying may not be appealing to people whose historical existence has been cultivated by resiliency, hope, and overcoming adversity in the United States. Furthermore, some religious beliefs and cultural values are present-rather than future-oriented. As such, some people are more focused on getting through their daily lives as opposed to planning for the end, and are more likely to make decisions collectively rather than autonomously (Bullock & Hall, 2012).

In EOL situations, minority elders tend to talk more about their belief in a "higher power" and "believing in miracles," whereas whites are more likely to express confidence in the medical team and health care system to address EOL and palliative care (Bullock, 2011). Whites tend to have far more favorable references about and experiences with EOL when making decisions about whether to use hospice care or not. Data from the white older adults revealed themes of social supports, symptom management, and comfort care during times of medical crisis and illness, and home as a preferred location of death (Bullock, 2011). Among black participants, the discussions about EOL experiences and hospice care suggested more negative experiences, such as having witnessed loved ones refuse nutrition and hydration by formal care providers, receive too much medication, or be denied inclusion of spiritual and community leaders in their care.

Furthermore, the notion of "giving up," withdrawing, and withholding treatment or intervention until the end, for many older adults, is considered to be inconsistent with their values of hope, belief in miracles, and suffering as justified, according to these research participants. Sometimes, the fear that one will not receive adequate care will result in request for the doctor "do all that is possible" to save a patient (Bullock, 2011). Older persons, women, religious and ethnic minorities, and sexual minorities who are seriously ill may be particularly likely to be perceived as burdensome by the medical system because their distinct cultural needs may not be understood. Certain behaviors, reactions, and responses to medical and treatment information may be perceived by the care team as problematic. For example, minority groups tend to have large extended family networks and may wish to involve many, if not all, of them in the care. They may decide that they cannot, adequately, engage in a care plan without certain family members being present. Furthermore, if they have limited resources, they may also have a lower sense of entitlement to optimal care, and thus feel that the treatment team views them as appropriate candidates for an accelerated death.

Social work practitioners should assess the cultural background of each patient using appropriate assessment tools that allow for the inclusion of values that may affect care at the EOL. We need to continuously educate ourselves about culturally specific beliefs and practices of the groups that we serve, as well as assess the degree to which the person and/or family adheres to the specific cultural beliefs and norms. The attention to cultural difference increases the likelihood that minority elderly will receive comprehensive and compassionate care at the EOL.

In conclusion, literature reviewed in this chapter suggests that when working with minority elderly, the psychosocial needs of the patient and family become even more critical in decisions that may affect the timing of death. There is a risk that regardless of how careful we are to be inclusive of differences, EOL care decisions occur in a national context of social inequality, bias, and unequal access to health care services. People who have felt discriminated against over the life course and denied equal social, economic, and health care access may not choose to participate in initiatives that are designed to help them to "die a good death." Their views of suffering and a gold standard of EOL care may be inconsistent with those of our U.S. health care system. CRT (Anderson & Collins, 2012) helps us to understand that a legacy of health disparities cannot be corrected at the EOL with the strategy of advance care planning and the completion of advance directives. Retrospective research with surviving family members and loved ones will provide much-needed data on EOL outcomes for older minorities. We need to know whether these individuals are actually receiving the care that they prefer and whether their loved ones feel that they died a good death. The fact that they tend not to engage in advance care planning and not complete advance directives is not necessarily an indication that they did not receive the care that they wanted or that they were not satisfied with the outcome.

In addition to this data, practice approaches that seek to understand patients' values and beliefs about EOL and palliative care are paramount. For those individuals who value collectivism and interdependence, practitioners should allow family and others to be involved in all aspects of the care plan as appropriate. We also need to respect cultural differences in how individuals and families make sense of issues related to death and dying (Stein, Sherman, & Bullock, 2009). For those patients and families who refer to God and wish to pray and hope for a miracle, creating a space for them to do so would be in keeping with a cultural competence model of care. Asking appropriate screening questions regarding culture, religion, and faith can be useful in developing the care plan. Incorporating members of the social support network and accommodating their involvement as much as possible without disruption to the care setting is recommended. Social workers are equipped with a set of skills that are ideally suited for the EOL care team. Our professional practice is guided by a core set of values and standards of care (NASW, 2004, 2007) that prepare us to work effectively with older minority populations.

REFERENCES

Agency for Health Care Research and Quality. (AHRQ). *Eliminating health care disparities*. Retrieved March 1, 2012, from http://www.ahrq.gov/qual/qsummit/qsummit5.htm#OMH

Altilio, T. & Otis-Green, S. (2011). Oxford textbook of palliative social work. New York, NY: Oxford University Press.

American Geriatrics Society Ethics Committee. (1995). The care of dying patients: A position statement from the American Geriatrics Society. *Journal of the American Geriatrics Society, 43*, 577–578.

Anderson, M., & Collins, P. H. (2012). Race, class & gender: An anthology (8th ed.). Belmont, CA: Cengage Learning.

Azjen, I. (1991). The theory of planned behavior. *Organizational Behavior and Human Decision Process, 50*(2), 179–211.

Blackhall, L. J., Frank, G., Murphy, S. T., Michel, V., Palmer, J. M., & Azen, S. P. (1999). Ethnicity and attitudes towards life sustaining technology. *Social Science & Medicine (1982), 48*(12), 1779–1789.

Blank, K. (2002). Respectful decisions at the end of life. *The American Journal of Geriatric Psychiatry: Official Journal of the American Association for Geriatric Psychiatry, 10*(4), 362–364.

Bradley, E. H., Fried, T. R., Kasl, S. V., & Idler, E. (2001). Quality-of-life trajectories of elders in the end of life. In M. P. Lawton (Ed.), *Annual review of gerontology and geriatrics* (Vol. 20, pp. 64–96). New York, NY: Springer.

Braun, K. L., Pietsch, J. H., & Blanchette, P. L. (2000). Cultural issues in end-of-life decision making. Thousand Oaks, CA: Sage.

Bullock, K. (2006). Promoting advance directives among African Americans: a faith-based model. *Journal of Palliative Medicine, 9*(1), 183–195.

Bullock, K. (2011). The influence of culture on end-of-life decision making. *Journal of Social Work in End-of-Life & Palliative Care, 7*(1), 83–98.

Bullock, K., & Hall, J. K. (2012). End-of-life care. In E. J. Clark & E. F. Hoffler (Eds.), *Social work matters: The power of linking policy and practice.* Washington, DC: NASW Press.

Bullock, K., McGraw, S. A., Blank, K., & Bradley, E. H. (2005). What matters to older African Americans facing end-of-life decisions? A focus group study. *Journal of Social Work in End-of-Life & Palliative Care, 1*(3), 3–19.

Byock, I. (1997). *Dying well: The prospect of growth at end of life.* Waterville, ME: Thorndike Press.

Candib, L. M. (2002). Truth telling and advance care planning at the end of life: Problems and autonomy in a multicultural world. *Family, Systems, & Health, 20*(3), 213–228.

Carlisle, D. M., Leake, B. D., & Shapiro, M. F. (1995). Racial and ethnic differences in the use of invasive cardiac procedures among cardiac patients in Los Angeles County, 1986 through 1988. *American Journal of Public Health, 85*(3), 352–356.

Carrese, J. A., & Rhodes, L. A. (1995). Western bioethics on the Navajo reservation. Benefit or harm? *JAMA: The Journal of the American Medical Association, 274*(10), 826–829.

Carrion, I. V. (2010). When do Latinos use hospice services? Studying the utilization of hospice services by Hispanics/Latinos. *Social work in health care, 49*(3), 197–210.

Centers for Disease Control and Prevention. (2009). Death: Preliminary data. Leading causes of death. Retrieved May 31, 2012, from http://www.cdc.gov/nchs/fastats/lcod.htm

Christ, G., & Sormanti, M. (1999). Advancing social work practice in end-of-life care. *Social Work in Health Care, 30,* 81–99.

Colon, M. (2005). Hospice and Latinos: a review of the literature. *Journal of Social Work in End-of-Life & Palliative Care, 1*(2), 27–43.

Commonwealth Fund (2012). *Hospice use at end of life.* Retrieved July 1, 2012, from http://mobile.commonwealthfund.org/Performance-Snapshots/Access-to-Hospice-Care/Hospice-Use-at-End-of-Life.aspx

Crawley, L. M., Marshall, P. A., Lo, B., & Koenig, B. A.; End-of-Life Care Consensus Panel. (2002). Strategies for culturally effective end-of-life care. *Annals of Internal Medicine, 136*(9), 673–679.

Crawley, L., Payne, R., Bolden, J., Payne, T., Washington, P., & Williams, S.; Initiative to Improve Palliative and End-of-Life Care in the African American Community. (2000). Palliative and end-of-life care in the African American community. *JAMA: the Journal of the American Medical Association, 284*(19), 2518–2521.

Csikai, E. L. (2000). The roles of values and experiences in determining social workers' attitudes toward euthanasia and assisted suicide. *Social Work in Health Care, 30,* 75–95.

Curd, P. R. (1999). Advance care planning reconsidered: Toward an operational definition of outpatient advance care planning. *Journal of Palliative Medicine, 2*(2), 157–159.

Delgado, R., & Stefanic, J. (2012). *Critical race theory: An introduction.* New York, NY: New York University Press.

Fergus, E., Noguera, P., & Martin, M. (2010). Construction of race and ethnicity for and by Latinos. In E. Murillo, Jr., S. A. Vilenas, R. T. Galavan, J. S. Munoz, C. Martinez, & M. Machedo-Casas (Ed.), *Handbook on Latinos and education: Theory, research and practice* (pp. 170–181). New York, NY: Routledge.

Field, M. J., Cassel, C. K., & Institute of Medicine (US) Committee on Care at End-of-Life (IOM). (1997). *Approaching death. Improving care at the end of life.* Washington, DC: National Academy Press.

Fried, T. R., & Gillick, M. R. (1994). Medical decision-making in the last six months of life: choices about limitation of care. *Journal of the American Geriatrics Society, 42*(3), 303–307.

Fried, T. R., Bradley, E. H., & Towle, V. R. (2003). Valuing the outcomes of treatment: do patients and their caregivers agree? *Archives of Internal Medicine, 163*(17), 2073–2078.

Fried, T. R., Bullock, K., Iannone, L., & O'Leary, J. R. (2009). Understanding advance care planning as a process of health behavior change. *Journal of the American Geriatrics Society, 57*(9), 1547–1555.

Garcia, K., & Mann, T. (2003). From "I Wish" to "I Will": Social-cognitive predictors of behavioral intentions. *Journal of Health Psychology, 8*(3), 347–360.

Gordan, A. K. (1995). Deterrents to access and service for blacks and Hispanics: The Medicare hospice benefit, healthcare utilization, and cultural barriers. *Hospice Journal, 19*(2), 65–83.

Green, C. R., Ndao-Brumblay, S. K., Nagrant, A. M., Baker, T. A., & Rothman, E. (2004). Race, age, and gender influences among clusters of African American and white patients with chronic pain. *The Journal of Pain: Official Journal of the American Pain Society, 5*(3), 171–182.

Hall, J. K. (2010). *African-American doctoral students at for-profit colleges and universities: A critical race theory exploration* (Doctoral dissertation). North Carolina State University. http://www.lib.ncsu.edu/resolver/1840.16/6211

Hallenbeck, J., Goldstein, M. K., & Mebane, E. W. (1996). Cultural considerations of death and dying in the United States. *Clinics in Geriatric Medicine, 12*(2), 393–406.

Hansen, P., Cornish, P., & Kayser, K. (1998). Family conferences as forums for decision making in hospital settings. *Social Work Health Care, 27*, 57–74.

Hanson, L. C., & Rodgman, E. (1996). The use of living wills at the end of life. A national study. *Archives of Internal Medicine, 156*(9), 1018–1022.

Hill, T. P., & Shirley, D. (1992). A good death: Taking more control at the end of your life. Reading, MA: Addison Wesley.

Hopp, F. P., & Duffy, S. A. (2000). Racial variations in end-of-life care. *Journal of the American Geriatrics Society, 48*(6), 658–663.

Jennings, B., Kaebnick, G. E., & Murray, T. H. (2005). Improving end-of-life care: Why has it been so difficult? Garrison, NY: The Hasting Center.

Johnson, J. W. (1992). Go down death. In M. G. Secundy (Ed.), *Trials and tribulations and celebrations: African American perspectives on health, illness, aging, and loss* (pp. 171–173). Yarmouth, ME: Intercultural Press.

Johnson, K. S., Kuchibhatla, M., & Tulsky, J. A. (2008). What explains racial differences in the use of advance directives and attitudes toward hospice care? *Journal of the American Geriatrics Society, 56*(10), 1953–1958.

Johnson, R. W., Newby, L. K., Granger, C. B., Cook, W. A., Peterson, E. D., Echols, M.,...Granger, B. B. (2010). Differences in level of care at the end of life according to race. *American Journal of Critical Care: An Official Publication, American Association of Critical-Care Nurses, 19*(4), 335–343; quiz 344.

Lavizzo-Mourey, R. J., & MacKenzie, E. (1996). Cultural competence–an essential hybrid for delivering high quality care in the 1990's and beyond. *Transactions of the American Clinical and Climatological Association, 107*, 226–235; discussion 236.

Leach, M. T. & Hall, J. K. (in press). Health disparities among older adults. In T. P. Gullotta & M. Bloom (Eds.), *Encyclopedia of primary prevention and health promotion*. Springer Publishers.

Lu, C. Y., & Johantgen, M. (2011). Factors associated with treatment restriction orders and hospice in older nursing home residents. *Journal of Clinical Nursing, 20*(3–4), 377–387.

McKinley, E. D., Garrett, J. M., Evans, A. T., & Danis, M. (1996). Differences in end-of-life decision making among black and white ambulatory cancer patients. *Journal of General Internal Medicine, 11*(11), 651–656.

National Association of Social Workers (NASW). (2004). NASW standards for palliative & end-of-life care. Washington, DC: Author.

National Association of Social Workers (NASW). (2007). Indicators for the achievement of the NASW standards for cultural competence in social work practice. Washington, DC: Author.

National Consensus Project for Quality Palliative Care. (2009). *Clinical practice guidelines for quality palliative care* (2nd ed.). Retrieved February 25, 2012, from http://www.nationalconsensusproject.org/guideline.pdf

National Hospice and Palliative Care Organization (NHPCO). (2010). Retrieved August 25, 2011, from http://www.nhpco.org/files/public/Statistics_Research/Hospice_Facts_Figures_Oct-2010.pdf

National Institute of Health. (2001). NIH policy and guidelines on the inclusion of women and minorities as subjects in clinical research. Amended October, 2001. Retrieved May 8, 2012, from http://grants.nih.gov/grants/funding/women_min/guidelines_amended_10_2001.htm

National Institutes of Health (NIH). (2004). State of the science conference statement: Improving end-of-life care, final report. Bethesda, MD: Author. Retrieved from http://consensus.nih.gov/2004/200 4EndOfLifeCareSOS024html.htm

Neubauer, B. J., & Hamilton, C. L. (1990). Racial differences in attitudes toward hospice care. *The Hospice Journal, 6*(1), 37–48.

Nuland, S. B. (1993). How we die: Reflections on life's final chapter. New York, NY: Knopf Publishers.

Reese, D. J., Ahern, R. E., Nair, S., O'Faire, J. D., & Warren, C. (1999). Hospice access and use by African Americans: Addressing cultural and institutional barriers through participatory action research. *Social Work, 44*(6), 549–559.

Sachs, G. A. (1994). Increasing the prevalence of advance care planning. *The Hastings Center Report, 24*(6), S13–S16.

Schroepfer, T. A., Waltz, A., Noh, H., Matloub, J., & Kue, V. (2010). Seeking to bridge two cultures: The Wisconsin Hmong cancer experience. *Journal of Cancer Education: The Official Journal of the American Association for Cancer Education, 25*(4), 609–616.

Smith, A. K., Sudore, R. L., & Pérez-Stable, E. J. (2009). Palliative care for Latino patients and their families: Whenever we prayed, she wept. *JAMA: The Journal of the American Medical Association, 301*(10), 1047–57, E1.

Smith, R. (2000). A good death. An important aim for health services and for us all. *British Medical Journal (Clinical Research ed.), 320*(7228), 129–130.

Stein, G. L., Sherman, P. A., & Bullock, K. (2009). Educating gerontologists for cultural proficiency in end-of-life care practice. *Journal of Educational Gerontology, 35*(11), 1008–1025.

Steinhauser, K. E., Christakis, N. A., Clipp, E. C., McNeilly, M., McIntyre, L., & Tulsky, J. A. (2000). Factors considered important at the end of life by patients, family, physicians, and other care providers. *JAMA: The Journal of the American Medical Association, 284*(19), 2476–2482.

Support Principal Investigators. (1995). A controlled trial to improve care for seriously ill hospitalized patients (SUPPORT). *JAMA, 274*, 1591–1598.

Tennstedt, S. L. (2002). Commentary on "Research Design in End-of-Life Research: State of Science." *The Gerontologist, 42*(Spec No 3), 99–103.

Todd, K. H., Lee, T., & Hoffman, J. R. (1994). The effect of ethnicity on physician estimates of pain severity in patients with isolated extremity trauma. *JAMA: The Journal of the American Medical Association, 271*(12), 925–928.

U.S. Department of Health and Human Services (USDHHS). (2010). *Healthy People 2020.* Retrieved February, 10, 2012, from http://www.health.gov/healthypeople

Welch, L. C., Teno, J. M., & Mor, V. (2005). End-of-life care in black and white: Race matters for medical care of dying patients and their families. *Journal of the American Geriatrics Society, 53*(7), 1145–1153.

CHAPTER 17

Aging in Place

Philip McCallion

In this chapter, aging in place is considered both within larger community and societal contexts as well as through description of the unique experiences of older Latinos or Hispanics, African Americans, Asian Americans, Native Americans, and Pacific Islanders. Future challenges and opportunities and implications for the social work field are also considered.

BACKGROUND

It is well established that a majority of older adults wish to remain in their own homes and communities and prefer to avoid movement to nursing homes and other long-term care options (Pynoos, Caraviello, & Cicero, 2009). On the one hand, there is ample evidence of the value of aging in place. For example, planning to remain often results in investment both in the physical stock of the home and in building community connections that will benefit the aging individual as well as the community in which s/he is located. Social connectedness within a neighborhood and community is also posited to increase informal supports likely to be critical to remaining there (Sabia, 2008). On the other hand, diminished and declining health and functioning, unavailability of family members (due to death or moving away), and increasing costs make aging in place more difficult. Such concerns are reported to be more likely experienced by older adults who are African American, Latino or Hispanic American, Asian American, Native American, and Native Hawaiian/Pacific Islander (Jacobsen, Kent, Lee, & Mather, 2011; Sabia, 2008; Weng & Nguyen, 2011).

In addition to racial and ethnic status, aging in place may also be influenced by changes in longevity, family demographics, caregiving, and household structures (Vasunilashorn, Steinman, Liebig, & Pynoos, 2012). These changing characteristics are influenced by (a) emigration and fertility, (b) changing family structures, and (c) economic preparedness.

Emigration and Fertility

The impact of immigration on the aging of the U.S. population is often underestimated. Although the typical immigrant to the United States is younger, there are important trends to consider. Mui and Shibusawa (2008) point out that more than 30% of Chinese, Korean, and Filipino immigrants and more than 40% of Vietnamese arrived in the United States after age 60 and the growth rate of this older age group is faster than in other Asian American age groups. Among Latinos, the impact of immigration is mostly manifested in a younger population, but projections are that immigrant and resident Latinos will be the largest group over 65 years by 2019 (NHCA, 2011), reflecting improved health and greater longevity among older Latinos. Such demographic gains are also to be found in older African, Asian, and Native Americans (Jacobsen et al., 2011; Ludtke & McDonald, 2002). Formal services are not prepared for this growing aging population. Not only are newer and growing populations of elders likely to desire different types of services than those historically served, but they may particularly need assistance in understanding what services are available and how to access these services. Further, they may require these services to be provided in languages other than English.

Higher fertility rates (as well as immigration) particularly among the U.S. Latino population will mean that by 2042 they will be the new majority population (Jacobsen et al., 2011). However, the overall, historically low fertility rates (U.S. Census, 2008) will challenge the ability of families to continue to provide the levels of support that are often critical to an older adult's ability to remain in the community. In addition, family caregiving is being further challenged by greater numbers of women in the workforce and by the greater care needs being presented by longer living older adults with multiple chronic conditions, who are often discharged from hospitals with considerable care challenges (NAC & AARP, 2008).

Changing Family Structures

The greater longevity among women and greater likelihood among widowed and divorced men to remarry have together contributed to greater numbers of women living alone in general, and these trends are becoming more pronounced in minority populations (Gallant, Spitze, & Grove, 2010; Jacobsen et al., 2011; Scharlach, Giunta, Chow, & Lehning, 2008). However, this is only part of the picture; fewer children will mean fewer opportunities for the widowed and divorced to live with another family member, and greater longevity will mean an independent living situation that is sustainable at age 65; given greater onset of chronic conditions, may be less viable at 75; and even more challenging at age 85 regardless of ethnicity.

Economic Preparedness

African American and Latino older adults are less likely to have participated in employer pension plans; while more recent older immigrants, including newly immigrated older Asian Americans, may also not have accumulated sufficient social security credits to receive the maximum benefits. All of these groups and Native Americans are not likely to have accumulated sufficient financial resources needed to support their retirement (McCallion & Ferretti, 2008). Some of these older adults may not be able to either afford insurance supplements to cover gaps in Medicare coverage and cover formal support services, or qualify for Medicaid benefits because their income and assets make them ineligible for assistance. Inadequate resources—including the lack of formal and informal support services, lack of one's own residence or a relative's home, and inadequate/inaccessible financial resources—present challenges to the ability to age in place.

THEORETICAL INFLUENCES ON OUR UNDERSTANDING OF AGING IN PLACE

Most considerations of aging in place emphasize the importance of the fit between the physical environment (usually best exemplified by one's home) and the individual to successfully age.

Moss and Lawton (1982) argued that as people get older they spend more time in their home and less time in work and social activities beyond its confines. However, the relationship is not fixed or static. The individual has the agency to take proactive steps and attitudes to increase the likelihood of success, that is, increase his or her competence in

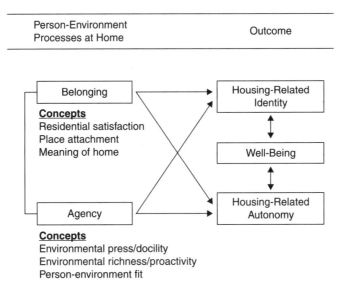

Person-Environment Processes at Home	Outcome

FIGURE 17.1 Conceptual Framework—Housing in Later Life (Oswald, Wahl, Martin, & Mollenkopf, 2003). Used with permission.

finding resources in the environment that are more likely to satisfy needs (Lawton, 1989). Such a view of aging and environments gives value to the physical and objective housing environment and neighborhood and to subjective impressions and coping styles in helping to understand how "fit" occurs and is sustained.

The Wahl and Oswald Conceptual Framework first presented in 2003 extends our understanding of "fit." Person-environment exchanges, how an individual is located within the place where they live, are seen as involving both subjective (housing-related identity) and objective (housing-related autonomy) outcomes. When applied to older adults, the framework also considers the individual's changing levels of independence, increases in functional and health-related needs, and challenges to connectedness to others (Oswald et al., 2003). Two key concepts of the framework are belonging and agency. There are three aspects to the concept of belonging: (a) satisfaction with one's living space (why would I leave, I like it here); (b) attachments one feels to that location on behavioral, cognitive, and emotional levels (I know every aspect of this house and how to manage it, I have so many good memories and I am able to manage in this house); and (c) the meaning the home has (this is where my children grew up). In an update to the model Wahl, Iwarsson, and Oswald (2012) make explicit that the sense of belonging is "driven" by experience. Taken together, these ideas contribute significantly to the creation of a housing-related identity (this house is part of who I am) and to some extent also speak to a sense of housing-related autonomy (I can manage my life and will be able to maintain quality of life if I remain here). More directly related to housing-related autonomy (but also to identity) are ideas of agency. Agency refers to the extent to which the home itself is perceived by the older adult to compensate for increasing functional declines in ways that maintain independence. There are three considerations: (a) environmental press (changing circumstances and declining functional abilities make independence and remaining in place more difficult); (b) environmental richness (people proactively arranging their day-to-day lives and acquiring personal and technological supports to not simply maintain but also increase their ability to remain within the home); and (c) person-environment fit (the congruence between the person's needs and the capacity of the home to support those needs). The examples provided here illustrate recent additions (see Figure 17.2) to the model (Wahl et al., 2012) to make explicit that as well as being influenced by experience-driven belonging, outcomes are enhanced by behavior-driven agency; that is, older adults are active participants in shaping their older age.

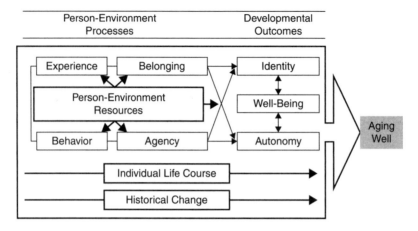

FIGURE 17.2 Revised Conceptual Framework—Housing in Later Life (Wahl et al., 2012).

Oswald et al., (2003) conceptualized well-being as the outcome of the person's success in meeting both identity and autonomy needs. This is a useful paradigm and for some older adults who are African American, Latino, Asian American, Native American, and Native Hawaiian/Pacific Islander, increased difficulty in finding environmental richness and even fit, given, for example, neighborhood challenges are certainly relevant. However, absent from the original model was detailed consideration of (a) what is gained by the individual in continuing within his or her home and neighborhood, (b) the impact of neighborhood factors such as the challenges when living in ethnically dissimilar neighborhoods (Yen, Shim, Martinez, & Barker, 2012), coupled with the importance of family members and inter-generational exchanges (McCallion, Janicki, Grant-Griffin, & Kolomer, 2000; Mui & Kang, 2006), and (c) the challenges to sense of home and autonomy posed by differential level of acculturation. The recent addition to the model of the individual life course and historical change now offers a means to recognize three particularly influential components of aging in place relevant for African Americans, Latinos, Asian Americans, Native Americans, and Native Hawaiian/Pacific Islanders: social capital, the impact of the social environment, and acculturation.

Social Capital

Social capital is the benefit to an individual (both psychosocial, and in some cases, tangible in terms of reciprocal support) that emerges from social connection and social relations with others formed through voluntarism and participation in supportive community activities (Cannuscio, Block, & Kawachi, 2003). Social capital offers older adults greater opportunities for independent and fulfilling lives (Tang & Lee, 2011), but these opportunities are currently challenged by changing demographics and community structures, for example, small families and other networks and the decline of local organizations and associations (Cannuscio et al., 2003). Nevertheless, it is argued that the opportunities for aging in place in terms of staying connected with one's communities and supports and engaging in roles that contribute to community building have many positive effects, including raising the significance for individuals of the experience of later life and contributing to the individual's better health (Martinson & Minkler, 2006; Scharlach, Graham, & Lehning, 2012; Vladeck & Segel, 2010; Yen et al., 2012). For African Americans, in particular, the opportunity to continue to be an active participant in faith-based activities has been recognized as an important contributor to their well-being in older age (Gallant et al., 2010).

Impact of the Social Environment

Aging in place in a community that is challenged by poverty and violence or where there are minimal opportunities to connect with others may not reap the benefits often associated with aging in place. Based on findings from a study of residents in a high-poverty, integrated urban area, Laveist, Pollack, Thorpe, Fesahazion, and Gaskin (2011) argued that place was more important in explaining health disparities than ethnic identity, highlighting whether aging in place is to be valued when that place itself "supports" poorer health. Informal supports are usually reported as more prevalent for African Americans, Latinos, Asian Americans, Native Americans, and Pacific Islanders (Gallant et al., 2010; Yee, Debaryshe, Yuen, Kim, & McCubbin, 2006). Conversely, for Native Americans, Pacific Islanders, and Asian Americans, the absence of local family members has been reported to have links to poorer outcomes in older age (Gallant et al., 2010; Ruthig, Hanson, Ludtke, & McDonald, 2009; Yee et al., 2006). Such absence may be because other family members have moved away or because the elder is an immigrant and therefore those family members were never present locally. Restricted social networks reflect a different and important form of impoverished "place" concerns (Goins et al., 2011; McCallion & Grant-Griffin, 2000; Mui & Kang, 2006).

Acculturation

To the extent that there is both possibility and reality of cultural congruence between the older adult, other family members, available social networks, current living situation, and the neighborhood in which one is located, it is likely that aging is place will be valued and successful. However, life for African, Latino, Asian, and Native Americans is more often marked by different levels of incongruence and pressures to conform to and/or to assimilate into more dominant cultures. The aging in place experience of racial/ethnic minority older adults, and more specifically immigrant elders, is likely to be influenced by their level of acculturation. Understanding the role of acculturation, defined as the process where a cultural group adopts a host group or community's beliefs and practices (Mills & Henretta, 2001), is fraught with difficulty given different levels of acculturation across generations and resulting expectations about the role of family members, position for older persons in society, and the types of support to be expected and actually offered (McCallion & Grant-Griffin, 2000; Mui & Kang, 2006; Weng & Nguyen, 2011). Aging in place may not be a positive experience to the extent that an older adult is not well acculturated and finds him- or herself in a community that does not meet his or her own cultural expectations, or where he or she continues to feel a stranger. Some have noted that for Native American nations that are situated near large cities, the acculturation among younger generations is likely to be higher and older adult expectations about family caregiving are less likely to be met (Goins et al., 2011). However, others have documented that for isolated rural nations, there is a greater likelihood that younger generations have moved away to find work, and it is also difficult to maintain traditions and a sense of community among those remaining for their elders to age in place meaningfully (McCallion & Grant-Griffin, 2000).

The literature on older Asian Americans discusses the challenges that many experience when they have immigrated to the United States later in life. These challenges include language difficulties, shorter connectedness to U.S. communities, and dramatically different levels of acculturation between generations around issues of the authority of elders and the obligations associated with filial piety, and lower likelihood of intergenerational living. The combination of these challenges may not only make successful aging in place more difficult, but may also add to the disease burden of these individuals, particularly to their depression levels (Mui & Kang, 2006). In their review of the literature on aging in place for African Americans and Latinos during the past 30 years, Yen et al. (2012) note that racial and ethnic minority elders who live in ethnically dissimilar neighborhoods are more likely to face obstacles in building the kind of social connectedness that supports aging in place, and may also experience it as a detrimental impact on their health. Instead of seeing acculturation as solely the concern for minorities and immigrants, there is also an acculturation challenge for others in the neighborhood to reflect in attitudes and inclusion the realities of diversity in neighbors. To the extent that different groups in neighborhoods do not acculturate, social connectedness is likely to suffer. Yet, all of these ideas should be approached with caution; no one is a cultural stereotype; each of the groups identified is made up of multiple ethnicities, cultures, and life experiences (McCallion & Grant-Griffin, 2000). These ideas should instead be seen as fluid influences on success in aging in place.

Systematic Efforts to Support Aging in Place

There is an emerging literature on aging in place options. Two longstanding aging in place options have been independent living and multigenerational households, where African, Latino, Asian, and Native American elders are well represented. Naturally Occurring Retirement Communities (NORCs) and age-integrated multiunit housing that have emerged also include many African American, Latino, and Asian American participants (Prosper, 2004; Valdeck & Segel, 2010). The very small numbers or the absence of identification of Native Hawaiian/Pacific Islanders in reported studies means that their experiences with these options are less known. The most recent models of aging in place, shared housing, villages, assisted living, retirement communities and livable communities, and home- and community-based services, represent further efforts to manage and facilitate aging in place but remain options where ethnic minorities are underrepresented among residents (Dietz & Wright, 2002). Action research work in developing aging-prepared communities (Bronstein, McCallion, & Kramer, 2006; McCallion, 2007) and in understanding supports for grand-parent caregivers (McCallion et al., 2000) included a series of focus groups and individual interviews with older adults seeking to age in place. Among the older adults were African Americans (14), Latinos (12), Asian Americans (9), and Native Americans (3) residing in a range of aging in place settings in Northeast New York. Quotes from these individuals are used here to help illustrate the characteristics of each setting and their potential to meet housing identity and autonomy in ways that will sustain and/or increase well-being among African Americans, Latinos, Asian-Americans, and Native Americans as they age.

Independent Living

In this case, individuals chose to remain in their own home, often an owned single family house. Success is often facilitated by a ground floor bedroom and bathroom, safety and security devices, and other features likely to prolong independence. However, there are many older adults who chose to continue living in less than optimal situations to be able to preserve "home." Two quotes from a Mexican American woman and an African American man help to illustrate the adaptations often made to preserve independent living.

> I can't get up the stairs anymore to the bathroom. My son put in a chemical toilet downstairs, we put a bed in the living room, I can wash up in the kitchen and I get meals on wheels.... It's not the same but I can manage and I would sooner be here,....

> We thought about this.... Added a bathroom downstairs years ago...I don't use as much of the house but it's comfortable and the grandkids still visit.... They use the upstairs...everyone is still here on the holidays...it still feels like home.

Multigenerational Household

There is evidence that, after declining over many years, the number of multigenerational households, defined as a household where three or more generations including an older generation are living together, are now increasing (Taylor et al., 2010). These increases among racial and ethnic minority groups reflect increases in immigrant populations, older age of first marriage, and grandparent caregiving. The number of Americans living in multigenerational households has grown 33% since 1980, with rates of multigenerational households higher among Latinos (22%), African Americans (23%), and Asian Americans (25%) than among whites (13%; Taylor et al., 2010). Others also report higher rates than whites among Native Americans and Pacific Islanders (Gallant et al., 2010; Yee et al., 2006). The generational composition of these homes and the sense of family ties and responsibilities (Taylor et al., 2010) have also been changing. Quotes from two African American women and a Chinese American woman help illustrate emerging differences in multigenerational households.

> I grew up in a home where my grandmother lived with us. She took care of me while my mother was at work. Then she got sick, my mother cared for her; sometimes I helped.... We were all there around her when she died.... Then it was my mother's turn....Now I'm that grandmother; I help where I can with the grandchildren and we now have a great grandchild in the house...it's such a blessing.... This is what I would have hoped for in my old age.... To have them all around me as my grandmother did,...I hope my daughter gets to live her older age supported by love....
>
> Well this wasn't how I thought my old age would be and my husband definitely didn't expect this. He thought after all his years of working we'd be moving to a little house in Florida, "No more shoveling snow" he said...they call it the Great Recession but there have been other problems too...we've lost a daughter to drugs...so we have two of our children and four grandchildren living with us...some will be here until they get on their feet...some will just be here...hopefully they will help more with shoveling snow...but we are making the best of it....I don't think I would have liked Florida...too humid and too many bugs.

And:

> It is as it should be. We are living with my son and his wife and she will take care of us. That is the tradition.

Naturally Occurring Retirement Communities

NORCs are geographically defined communities, usually consisting of neighborhoods or apartment complexes with a large proportion of older residents. Often these residences within the NORC and other community features were not purposefully designed to support its aging residents but there is an existing combination of community features (often easily maintained homes with close availability of faith communities, banks, libraries, doctors' offices, and public transportation) that have encouraged older adults to remain in residence. AARP estimates that between 17% and 36% of older adults live in NORC-like neighborhoods (Colello, 2007) and these communities include a cross section of socioeconomic, racial, and ethnic groups. (Some formally established NORCs make additional recreational, health, and social services available to older residents, forming partnerships between services providers and housing managers to develop a model of health and social services delivery described as supportive services programs [SSPs; Colello, 2007].) Services may include case management, health care management and prevention activities, recreational activities, transportation, and volunteer opportunities for older residents, helping to further reduce risk for institutional placement (Vladeck & Segel, 2010). The following quotes from a Puerto Rican woman and an African American man illustrate the emergence of NORCs in a neighborhood:

> It's strange now to think about. When we moved here I wasn't thinking about getting old. My husband got some of that GI help...we wanted our kids to have a better life, it was a nice neighborhood, we thought it would be tough but that we could afford it...I prayed a lot...my kids would be close to their schools and I liked living in a place with things close by. I never drove a car, never have either, and a bus stop at the end of the

> street, well I liked that too. We looked different from most families and I know you know what I mean...but there were enough of us and most lived and let live...the others...I had one neighbor who thought I'd be roasting pigs and keeping chickens in the backyard...well they're not here anymore...I think as much as anything there were a lot of families that moved here during that time that felt the same...the children are gone but we have all aged here together...we like this neighborhood and it likes us.

And:

> Our kids have grown up and moved away...they visit...but before we knew it was just us old folks. Then one day in church the priest told us we were a NORC and explained to us what that meant...also that there were some money, some grants he called them out there to make us a better NORC...and who wanted to be on a "committee"....
> We all groaned a little...he likes those committees...but he was right...this is where we live...it's a good neighborhood but now we need some different things. Some of my neighbors can't get out to the grocery store anymore, can't pick up their medicines...but we are a NORC...we talked to the supermarket and told them we are your customers...we got a free delivery service....We started a volunteer navigator program too...I'm a navigator...I help some of my neighbors who don't have good English with their doctor visits and when they come out of the hospital. We all want to stay in this neighborhood, in our NORC...we all want to help and we have ideas about what services will help...we don't want our homes to become nursing homes...we just need some changes.

Age-Integrated Multifamily Housing

Age-integrated multifamily housing may be public or private apartment and condominium settings that serve people of multiple ages and are designed to serve multiple age groups rather than older adults. Older adults are likely to have moved there in their earlier years (as in NORCs) and remained. Unlike NORCs, age-integrated multifamily housing units are not defined by the occurrence of aging among residents; age integration is just one of the features of the housing arrangement and it does not follow that there should be age-focused approaches to the management (Prosper, 2004). One African American woman explained the value of age-integrated multifamily housing and challenges this way:

> This is what they call low-income housing but it's a good apartment building. I've lived here almost 30 years. I've seen a lot of changes, a lot of families come through here. Some come only for a short time and others are here forever like me. There are some buildings that are only for old people but I've lived here a long time and I don't know [if] I would like being just with old people...how much bingo can you play...I go once a week and that's enough.... The manager doesn't really understand that there are old people in this building and that we need things to be a little different...you know he should think about is it a good idea to put noisy young people next to old people...that's been happening a lot.... I don't see the people I know as much...it's harder to get around and at night it's not always safe...maybe I should look at one of those old people buildings but it's nice to look out the window [at the] kids...brings back memories.

Shared Housing

There are no good estimates of the numbers of shared housing arrangements, as they are often private pay and unregulated. However, they are often inexpensive options, and longstanding examples of shared housing such as adult foster care are well documented

(Prosper, 2006). In shared housing, two or more unrelated people share a house or an apartment. Usually private sleeping quarters are available; the rest of the house is shared. Shared housing may occur naturally when a group of individuals decide to pool resources or may be agency-sponsored. In agency-sponsored arrangements, services such as meal preparation, housekeeping, shopping, and case management may be provided, but the primary purpose of shared housing is to better manage economic, physical, and social losses that may accompany aging. A Native American man describes the meaning of shared housing this way:

> I wonder sometimes if this is what the long houses were like…well there would have been parents and children living there too but there would have been a part of the long house where there were just the elders. Anyway, I live now in a house with two other elders. Usually you think of groups of older women not three older men living together. Jim had this big old house, he can't drive anymore and I still do although not at night, and John's eyesight is going but he has been our friend. Now we all help each other and the health services provides us with some help. We probably thought we would be in a long house with our families but children have moved away, some are dead…. Vietnam you know…. And so we have created our own long house. Sometimes we light a big fire in the backyard and children and their parents come over and bring food…we sit and talk about the old days and the old ways…yes, we are the elders in the long house.

Villages

Villages are grassroots membership organizations in communities and neighborhoods often with an annual fee in the $400 to 1,000 range, where neighbors and/or a paid staff help other neighbors access support and services to age in place, for example, rides to the doctor, home repair referrals, mail pickup, snow removal and lawn management services, and sometimes companionship and home care supports. Some Villages also offer social opportunities, such as clubs, classes, lectures, and cultural outings (Scharlach et al., 2012). A recently retired Korean American man explained his interest in a "village" this way:

> I've never been a traditional Asian-American, whatever that means. I was recruited as a student out of engineering school, worked for [a major U.S. company] and travelled the world with my home base here. If I think of anywhere as home, it's here. I don't expect my children to provide for me, I expect them to succeed. I will take care of myself. Where I live, there are a lot of professionals just like me, well maybe not Asian American but you know what I mean. So we have been looking at this "Village" idea. I think my wife and I can benefit but getting old is a business too and we need to be entrepreneurs…. Can't wait on the government…so we are looking at bylaws, non-profit status, fee structures and a marketing and business plan.

Assisted Living

The characteristics of assisted-living residences or assisted-living facilities vary across the United States, but in general they provide supervision or assistance with activities of daily living; coordinate services by outside health care providers; and monitor resident activities to help ensure their health, safety, and well-being, and often offer assistance with the administration or supervision of medication, and/or personal care services. Assisted-living facilities range in size from small residential homes for one resident up to facilities providing services to hundreds. Assisted living falls somewhere between independent living and a skilled nursing facility (NF) in terms of the level of care provided. Although largely private pay and still serving primarily a white population, the range of types and sizes of assisted-living facilities mean that many can afford this level of care and increasing use of assisted living has been documented among ethnic minorities (Perkins, Ball, Whittington, & Hollingsworth, 2012). A Mexican American woman explained her decision to enter assisted living in this way:

> I never thought I would move out of my home. My daughter was really helping me but between my asthma and after I fell and broke my hip...well it healed, the doctor says, but I never felt the same and I was afraid all the time, afraid I might fall again...didn't like the stairs in my house, didn't like those high cupboards, even felt dizzy when I cleaned...and I like a clean house.... But someone with my asthma shouldn't be cleaning.... It started to feel like I was a prisoner.... But I didn't want to go into a nursing home.... Oh no, not that.... This assisted living facility is in my neighborhood. I can still go to my church, my bank, and doctors are close by but I'm in a place where I can get the help that I need and where I feel safe.... There are no stairs and they keep it very clean.... My sister says it's a disgrace my daughter let me go somewhere like this and last time she was here she said the food is too anglo...it is...rice and beans once in a while wouldn't kill us...but I feel safer, I have some friends, I don't feel like a prisoner.... And my daughter visits and she sometimes cooks things I like in the little kitchen...my sister is wrong, but then, who can tell her anything.

Retirement Communities

A retirement community organized as apartments or condominiums with some shared amenities is housing designed for older adults who are generally able to care for themselves; however, assistance from home care agencies is sometimes available as well as activities and socialization opportunities. The community is often age-restricted and residents must be partially or fully retired. A recently retired African American woman described her choice of a retirement community this way:

> It was a big old house full of kids and then it was just me staring at the walls and wondering when they would tell me it was time for a nursing home. I was a professional, I had run a large bureau, I had earned my early retirement and I was going to enjoy it. I didn't need to be cleaning a big old place and I needed to be somewhere with a pool, where there were things going on. A 55+ community sounded just right. It's kinda like when I visit the grandkids—love to spoil 'em but then it's time to go home. In a 55+ community you get to go home and leave other parts of the world outside...you got people interested in what you're interested in and who have the time and money to travel, to do things. Around here 55+ is a pretty white world but then that was my work world too. I can handle that.... Yeah, it's a different kinda home.

Livable Communities

A livable community offers older adults affordable and appropriate housing, supportive services, and accessible transportation, which together facilitate an individual's independence (Bronstein, et al., 2006). The realization of a livable community often requires self-advocacy and leadership from older adults themselves, as one African American woman explained:

> I was so MAD.... Poor Mrs. W....yes she ran that red light but you can't see it because of the TREES growing over it...they changed the bus route because it didn't suit people who worked...what about old people going to the grocery store???...They've got working streetlights, delivery services, vans that will take you places in some parts of the city, but not in our neighborhood...we need CHANGE.... I talked to our city council person and said don't expect me to get the vote out if you aren't going to do something....

That's when I heard about livable communities....They did a survey...I helped...our neighborhood had the most needs and the least amount of services...it's still not much better but now we know what we need to do...I'm at the city council meetings, at the transportation authority stirring things up.... We got that bus to change its route and stop again at the apartments. They've promised to fix the lights and the sidewalks but we've got to do so much more.... Yes we.... This is our neighborhood.

Home- and Community-Based Services

Home- and community-based services include personal care and other formal services that support older adults continuing to live in a home setting rather than an NF or hospital. Often such services are delivered using staff from visiting nurse and home health care organizations, but participant-directed or consumer-directed approaches are growing where the individual is able to both choose and manage his or her own workers and train and supervise them to perform tasks that would otherwise require licensed staff. One Puerto Rican man explained how the opportunity to manage care was transformative.

We've been living in our home all these years and I need some help now. Social services said we could get 6 hours of personal care a week for my wife...good luck with that...I never knew one day to the next who was coming and when they would actually arrive...would they be gentle...do they speak any Spanish....It's not that we don't speak English, but this is our home...we speak Spanish here. Then they told me about the consumer-directed program...they made it sound hard...all these things like timesheets I would be responsible for...my wife and I hired a neighbor...someone who helped us anyway but now we could offer her some money...she speaks Spanish, she comes when she promises, she is gentle...we are not worried anymore about how long we can stay in our home.

FUTURE CHALLENGES AND OPPORTUNITIES FOR AGING IN PLACE

Well-being is a core outcome for aging in place. Given the increasing number of older adults and the dramatic growth being seen in African American, Latino, Asian American, and Native American and Native Hawaiian/Pacific Islander older populations, increased well-being is to be valued both to assure quality of life in a longer old age and to address society's concerns about the escalating costs, particularly health and long-term care costs as people age. There are serious challenges. The growing older racial and ethnic minority populations are likely to have fewer family resources to turn to; less than adequate financial resources sufficient for their daily living care needs, especially for an extended life span; and some may be living in neighborhoods that are detrimental to their health. However, to end the story, there is an underestimated desire for well-being and the power of aging in place to have older adults feel empowered to:

- Take steps to increase their autonomy within their homes,
- Extract value from the sense of identity that is preserved when continued living in valued places is possible, and
- Improve their communities in ways that will enhance their own ability to age in place.

Moreover, the example offered in so many of these population groups in their use of intergenerational household and age-integrated multihousing units, in particular, offers low-cost approaches for both the individual and society to address meeting what is a fundamental desire by most older adults regardless of ethnicity, to age in place.

Implications for Social Work

The United States is at an interesting moment of change as public policy must grapple with increased longevity and increased numbers of older adults, and in proposed Medicaid Rebalancing Initiatives, care transitions programs and use of evidence-based health promotion and participant-directed programs is increasingly moving from a focus on long-term care to one on long-term services and supports, responses to chronic conditions rather than acute illness, and increased self-management and reliance on informal and community supports (NYS4A, 2011). On the one hand, social workers should celebrate and advance an increasing emphasis on empowerment and choice for older adults and the opportunity to realize cherished goals of remaining in the community. However, on the other hand, social workers must be vigilant that choice is available to everyone, supports are adequate and equitably available, and informal and formal service provision builds upon strengths and desires within ethnic groups rather than uses cultural history to make demands on families and older adults that they are not in a position to honor (McCallion & Ferretti, 2008; McCallion, 2010; Mui & Kang, 2006; Yen et al., 2012).

The most pressing issue for all older adults is that neighborhoods and communities themselves become more aging prepared and livable for older adults (Bronstein et al., 2006). As was noted, efforts to date have been less likely to focus upon challenged neighborhoods or upon the unique needs of African American, Latino, Asian American, Native American, and Native Hawaiian/Pacific Islander older adults. Regardless of percentage of population, neglecting these issues is wrong for society. Yet, together, these racial and ethnic minority groups are about to become the majority of older adults in our society and the lack of attention to their needs and the challenges that they face must be addressed.

REFERENCES

Bronstein, L., McCallion, P., & Kramer, E. (2006). Developing an aging prepared community: Collaboration among counties, consumers, professionals and organizations. *Journal of Gerontological Social Work, 48*(1–2), 193–202.

Cannuscio, C., Block, J., & Kawachi, I. (2003). Social capital and successful aging: The role of senior housing. *Annals of Internal Medicine, 139*(5 Pt 2), 395–399.

Colello, K. J. (2007). Supportive services programs to naturally occurring retirement communities: CRS Report for Congress. Washington, DC: Congressional Research Service.

Dietz, T. L., & Wright, J. D. (2002). Racial and ethnic identity of older adults residing in assisted living facilities in central Florida. *Care Management Journals: Journal of Case Management; The Journal of Long Term Home Health Care, 3*(4), 185–191.

Gallant, M. P., Spitze, G., & Grove, J. G. (2010). Chronic illness self-care and the family lives of older adults: A synthetic review across four ethnic groups. *Journal of Cross-Cultural Gerontology, 25*(1), 21–43.

Goins, R. T., Spencer, S. M., McGuire, L. C., Goldberg, J., Wen, Y., & Henderson, J. A. (2011). Adult caregiving among American Indians: The role of cultural factors. *The Gerontologist, 51*(3), 310–320.

Jacobsen, L. A., Kent, M., Lee, M., & Mather, M. (2011). America's aging population. *Population Bulletin, 66*(1), 1–16.

Laveist, T., Pollack, K., Thorpe, R., Fesahazion, R., & Gaskin, D. (2011). Place, not race: Disparities dissipate in southwest Baltimore when blacks and whites live under similar conditions. *Health Affairs (Project Hope), 30*(10), 1880–1887.

Lawton, M. P. (1989). Environmental proactivity in older people. In V. L. Bengtson & K. W. Schaie (Eds.), *The course of later life* (pp. 15–23). New York, NY: Springer.

Ludtke, R. L., & McDonald, L. R. (2002). *Projections of long term care needs in Indian health service areas.* Grand Folks: National Resource Center on Native American Aging, Center for Rural Health, School of Medicine and Health Sciences, University of North Dakota.

Martinson, M., & Minkler, M. (2006). Civic engagement and older adults: A critical perspective. *The Gerontologist, 46*(3), 318–324.

McCallion, P. (2007). *Developing and aging prepared community in the Capital District: Final report*. Albany, NY: School of Social Welfare, University at Albany.

McCallion, P., & Ferretti, L. A. (2008). Retirement. In T. Mizrahi & L. E. Davis (Eds.), *Encyclopedia of social work* (pp. 533–536). Washington, DC: NASW Press.

McCallion, P., & Grant-Griffin, L. (2000). Redesigning services to meet the needs of multi-cultural families. In M. P. Janicki & E. Ansello (Eds.), *Aging and developmental disabilities* (pp. 97–108). Baltimore, MD: Paul Brookes.

McCallion, P., Janicki, M. P., Grant-Griffin, L., & Kolomer, S. R., (2000). Grandparent Caregivers II: Service needs and service provision issues. *Journal of Gerontological Social Work, 33*, 63–90.

Mills, T. L., & Henretta, J. C. (2001). Racial, ethnic, and sociodemographic differences in the level of psychosocial distress among older Americans. *Research on Aging, 23*, 131–152.

Moss, M. S., & Lawton, M. P. (1982). Time budgets of older people: A window on four lifestyles. *Journal of Gerontology, 37*(1), 115–123.

Mui, A. C., & Kang, S. Y. (2006). Acculturation stress and depression among Asian immigrant elders. *Social Work, 51*(3), 243–255.

Mui, A. C., & Shibusawa, T. (2008). *Asian American elders in the 21st century: Key indicators of psychosocial well-being*. New York, NY: Columbia University Press.

National Alliance for Caregiving (NAC) and AARP. (2008). *Caregiving in the U.S.* Bethesda, MD: AARP Public Policy Institute.

National Hispanic Council on Aging (NHCA). (2011). *A snapshot of Hispanic older adults: Economic security, demographics and voting trends*. Washington, DC: Author.

NYS4A (2011). *Area agencies on aging: Strategies to rebalance long term care and delay medicaid eligibility*. Retrieved May 2012, from http://www.nysaaaa.org/Legislative_/Fact%20Sheets,PolicyPaper/NYSAAAA%20policy%20paper,%20August%202011%20rev3.pdf

Oswald, F., Wahl, H.-W., Martin, M., & Mollenkopf, H. (2003). Physical environments and aging: Critical contributions of M. Powell Lawton to theory and practice. *Journal of Housing for the Elderly, 17*, 135–155.

Perkins, M. M., Ball, M. M., Whittington, F. J., & Hollingsworth, C. (2012). Relational autonomy in assisted living: A focus on diverse care settings for older adults. *Journal of Aging Studies, 26*(2), 214–225.

Prosper, V. (2004). Aging in place in multifamily housing. *Cityscape, 7*(1), 81–106.

Prosper, V. (2006). Adult foster care and adult family care. In B. Berkman & D'Ambruoso (Eds.), *Handbook of social work in health & aging* (pp. 685–692). New York, NY: Oxford University Press

Pynoos, J., Caraviello, R., & Cicero, C. (2009). Lifelong housing: The anchor in aging-friendly communities. *Generations, 33*(2), 26–32.

Ruthig, J. C., Hanson, B. L., Ludtke, R. L., & McDonald, L. R. (2009). Perceived barriers to health care and health behaviours: Implications for Native American elders' self-rated health. *Psychology, Health & Medicine, 14*(2), 190–200.

Sabia, J. J. (2008). There's no place like home. A hazard model analysis of aging in place among older homeowners in the PSID. *Research on Aging, 30*, 3–35.

Scharlach, A. E., Giunta, N., Chow, J. C., & Lehning, A. (2008). Racial and ethnic variations in caregiver service use. *Journal of Aging and Health, 20*(3), 326–346.

Scharlach, A., Graham, C., & Lehning, A. (2012). The "Village" model: A consumer-driven approach for aging in place. *The Gerontologist, 52*(3), 418–427.

Tang, F., & Lee, Y. (2011). Social support networks and expectations for aging in place and moving. *Research on Aging, 33*, 444–464.

Taylor, P., Passel, J., Fry, R., Morin, R., Wang, W., Velasco, G., et al. (2010). *The return of the multi-generational family household*. Philadelphia, PA: Pew Research Center.

U.S. Census (2008). *Population projections*. Washington, DC: Author.

Vasunilashorn, S., Steinman, B. A., Liebig, P. S., & Pynoos, J. (2012). Aging in place: Evolution of a research topic whose time has come. *Journal of Aging Research, 2012*, 120952.

Vladeck, F., & Segel, R. (2010). Identifying risks to healthy aging in New York City's varied NORCs. *Journal of Housing for the Elderly, 24*, 356–372.

Wahl, H. W., Iwarsson, S., & Oswald, F. (2012). Aging well and the environment: Toward an integrative model and research agenda for the future. *The Gerontologist, 52*(3), 306–316.

Weng, S. S., & Nguyen, P. V. (2011). Factors affecting elder caregiving in multigenerational Asian American families. *Families in Society, 92*, 329–335.

Yee, B. W. K., Debaryshe, B. D., Yuen, S., Kim, S. Y., & McCubbin, H. I. (2006) Asian American and Pacific Islander families: Resilience and life span socialization in a cultural context. In F. T. L. Leong, A. G. Inman, A. Ebreo, L. Yang, L. M. Kinoshita, & M. Fu (Eds.), *Handbook of Asian American psychology* (pp. 69–86). Thousand Oaks, CA: Sage.

Yen, I. H., Shim, J. K., Martinez, A. D., & Barker, J. C. (2012). Older people and social connectedness: How place and activities keep people engaged. *Journal of Aging Research, 2012*, 139523.

CHAPTER 18

Racial/Ethnic Minority Older Adults in Nursing Homes: Need for Culturally Competent Care

Namkee G. Choi

Despite the increasing number of assisted-living facilities as preferred choices of care, skilled nursing facilities remain the most important institutional long-term care settings, where older adults with severe functional and cognitive impairments receive help with their activities of daily living (ADL) and clinical needs in the last stage of their lives. In 2009, the United States had 15,700 nursing homes with 1,705,808 beds, down from 16,886 homes with 1,795,388 beds in 2000; and 1,401,718 people were nursing home residents, down from 1,480,076 residents in 2000 (U.S. Department of Health and Human Services [DHHS] Centers for Disease Control and Prevention, 2010). The nursing home occupancy rates decreased from 84.5% in 1995 to 82.2% in 2009, partly because many nursing home-eligible older adults who could afford private pay assisted living facilities (largely non-Hispanic whites) chose them as popular substitutes for nursing homes. Older adults and their families also prefer other formal home- and community-based long-term care services, where and when they are available, accessible, and affordable (Mui, Choi, & Monk, 1998).

This chapter is divided into three sections: First, it summarizes and discusses the findings of previous studies of the predictors of nursing home admissions and the issues regarding access among four groups of racial/ethnic minority older adults: blacks/African Americans; Hispanics/Latinos; Asians/Pacific Islanders; and American Indians/Native Americans. Second, findings on the quality of care that these minority older adults receive are summarized. The final section of the chapter provides a summary of the need for providing culturally competent nursing home care and future directions for alleviating racial/ethnic disparities and segregation in nursing home care.

Historically, racial/ethnic minority older adults were admitted to nursing homes at significantly lower rates than non-Hispanic whites, as they, especially Hispanics/Latinos and Asians/Pacific Islanders, utilized other formal long-term care services at a rate significantly lower than that of their non-Hispanic white counterparts (Dilworth-Anderson, Williams, & Gibson, 2002; Giunta, Chow, Scharlach, & Dal Santo, 2004; Mui et al., 1998). As a result, minority older adults were once disproportionately underrepresented among nursing home residents. However, in recent years, the racial/ethnic gap in access to nursing homes has been narrowing due to changing demographics and cultural norms, increasing dementia care demands, and family economic pressures, as well as to increased bed availability resulting from the declining occupancy rates. Analysis of 885,785 Minimum Data Set (MDS)[1] admission records between January 2003 and June 2004 found that 79.3% were non-Hispanic whites, 12.9% were non-Hispanic blacks, 5.3% were Hispanics/Latinos, 1.9% were Asians/Pacific Islanders, and 0.7% were American Indians/Alaska Natives (Buchanan, Rosenthal, Graber, Wang, & Kim, 2008). Between 1999 and 2008, the number of older blacks/African Americans, Hispanics/Latinos, and Asians/Pacific Islanders living in nursing homes increased 10.8%, 54.9%, and 54.1%, respectively, whereas the number of non-Hispanic white residents decreased 10.2% (Feng, Fennell, Tyler, Clark, & Mor, 2011).

Increased reliance on nursing home care among racial/ethnic minority older adults is in part due to changing demographics: growth in the number of older adults, stemming from greater longevity; lower fertility; increasing rates of female employment; decline in the two-parent family; long-distance migration by children in search of better occupational and other life opportunities; changes in hospital discharge practices attributable to the introduction of Medicare's prospective payment system based on diagnosis-related groups (DRGs); and other regulatory and structural changes affecting systems of health care (Angel, Angel, Aranda, & Miles, 2004; Smith, Feng, Fennell, Zinn, & Mor, 2008).

Along with these demographic changes, traditional cultural norms that emphasized family care of frail older parents and other relatives at home, usually in multigenerational households, have also been undergoing changes. The necessity and inevitability, if not embracement, of nursing home care as a last resort, has been accepted by both caregivers and older adults themselves (Lampley-Dallas, Mold, & Flori, 2001; Schoenberg & Coward, 1997). In Schoenberg and Coward's study (1997) of black/African American older adults' attitudes toward entering a nursing home, the most significant influence on their acceptance of nursing home care appeared to be their perceived or actual familial support. The older adults were willing to enter a nursing home if they perceived that they were too much burden on their loved ones with excessive care demand. Overall, however, family caregivers of racial/ethnic minority older adults still delay placing their loved ones in nursing homes, and as a result, minority older adults enter nursing homes more physically, functionally, and cognitively impaired and needing more services than their non-Hispanic white counterparts (Chiodo, Kanten, Gerety, & Mulrow, 1994; Davis, 2005; Davis & Lapane, 2004; Espino et al., 2001; Gaugler, Kane, Kane, & Newcomer, 2006; Stevens et al., 2004).

The surge in nursing home admissions among minority older adults may also stem from the introduction of DRGs and the Medicare prospective payment system in the 1980s, which encouraged hospitals to quickly discharge patients who were still sick and needed medical care. Hospitals hired discharge planners, whose responsibilities were to work with the patients and their caregivers to find appropriate home- and community-based care, including that in skilled nursing facilities (Smith et al., 2008). Other structural factors that may have contributed to minority older adults' nursing home entry are (a) the decline in state-operated chronic care hospitals (for psychiatric illness, developmental disability, and other chronic diseases) that disproportionately served blacks/African Americans; (b) as mentioned, the booming industry, since the 1990s, of assisted-living facilities that predominantly serve non-Hispanic white older adults; and (c) nursing homes struggling with declining occupancy rates have an incentive to admit minorities with higher resource utilization group (RUG) scores and greater impairment than their non-Hispanic white counterparts.

Economic pressures also play an important role in determining minority older adults' nursing home entry. Adult children and other relatives who struggle to meet their own basic needs lack financial means to deal with the increasing demand of caring for their severely ill and/or functionally and/or cognitively impaired parents/loved ones. The caregivers simply cannot reduce work hours or quit their jobs to meet the caregiving duties. For example, one study found that low-income family caregivers made decisions to place their older relatives in nursing homes when neither they nor the older relatives could afford life-saving medications and attendant care services that were not covered under Medicaid, and they were relieved that the older relatives could receive the needed care at a nursing home (Choi, Kim, & Asseff, 2009). This unequal access to home- and community-based alternatives for poor minorities and disparities in available options are likely push factors for their nursing home entry (Feng et al., 2011).

Unfortunately, increased access to and utilization of nursing homes among racial/ethnic minority older adults have not translated into improved quality of nursing home care for them. The consensus findings of previous studies are that minority older adults, compared with non-Hispanic white older adults, are concentrated in low-quality/lower tier nursing homes that have a record of more inspection deficiencies, including poor facility cleanliness, lighting, and maintenance; poor staffing; and poor financial viability (Fennell, Feng, Clark, & Mor, 2010; Grabowski & McGuire, 2009; Howard et al., 2002; Smith et al., 2008). Other studies of nursing home care quality also found that a concentration of blacks/African Americans or Hispanics/Latinos was associated with higher incidents of hospital admissions, higher prevalence of pressure ulcers, lower incidents of pharmacological and other treatments for their clinical conditions, and more health-related deficiencies (Buchanan et al., 2008; Christian, Lapane, & Toppa, 2003; Gerardo, Teno, & Mor, 2009; Gruneir, Miller, Feng, Intrator, & Mor, 2008; Mor, Zinn, Angelelli, Teno, & Miller, 2004; Mor, Papandonatos, & Miller, 2005; Sengupta, Bercovitz, & Harris-Kojetin, 2010; Yue, Jun, Xueya, Temkin-Greener, & Mukamel, 2011). The racial/ethnic segregation of nursing home residents and disparities in nursing home care are due to hospital discharge practices in which racial/ethnic minority older adults tend to be referred to minority-concentrated nursing homes; the types of nursing homes that are willing to admit poor minority older adults who are Medicaid-funded and/or highly impaired individuals; and the fact these nursing homes tend to be located in poor, minority-concentrated communities (Angelelli, Grabowski, & Mor, 2006; Howard et al., 2002; Mor et al., 2004). Grunier et al.'s (2008) study based on MDS and Online Survey Certification and Reporting System (OSCAR)[2] data in 2000 found that availability, or lack thereof, of facility resources (e.g., staffing and pay or mixes) was highly correlated with facility racial profiles.

Most poor-quality, understaffed, and underresourced nursing homes do not and cannot provide culturally competent care for racial/ethnic minority older adults (Gorek, Martin, White, Peters, & Hummel, 2002; Magilvy, Congdon, Martinez, Davis, & Averill, 2000). Cultural and language barriers are especially serious issues for Hispanic/Latino and Asian/Pacific Islander immigrant older adults and American Indian/Native American older adults with limited English proficiency when they are admitted to a nursing home that is not specially targeted to them (Guinta et al., 2004; Jervis, Jackson, & Manson, 2002; Kolb, 1999; Mercer, 1996). Minority nursing home residents are also often subjected to overt and/or indirect acts of discrimination from staff, administrators, and non-Hispanic white residents when they are placed in predominantly white-serving facilities, adding to the stress of adjusting to a new environment and to institutional living that has little respect for their own culture (Aeschleman, 2000).

ACCESS TO AND PREDICTORS OF NURSING HOME PLACEMENT

Blacks/African Americans

With more non-Hispanic white older adults choosing assisted-living facilities than nursing homes, blacks/African Americans are at a higher risk for nursing home placement than non-Hispanic white Americans (Ness, Ahmed, & Aronow, 2004). In 2000, their use of nursing homes was 14% higher than that of non-Hispanic whites, especially in the South and the West (Arizona, Delaware, Florida, North Carolina, and West Virginia; Smith et al., 2008). However, most previous studies that examined time to nursing home placements found that, compared with their non-Hispanic white counterparts with similar physical and cognitive conditions, black/African American older adults were less likely to use nursing homes and, when they entered one, they did so later (Akamigbo & Wolinsky, 2007; Stevens et al., 2004). Based on data derived from the three-year multiregional analysis of community-based long-term care for older adults with dementia and their family caregivers (Medicare Alzheimer's Disease Demonstration Evaluation [MADDE]), Gaugler, Leach,

Clay, and Newcomer (2004) found that blacks/African Americans suffering from dementia were less likely to use nursing homes than were their non-Hispanic white counterparts, and that they relied on informal and/or formal care or had no care for a longer duration. During the 3-year course of MADDE, 70% of the blacks/African Americans suffering from dementia did not enter a nursing home. Time to placement among blacks/African Americans was expedited by caregivers' emotional difficulty in adapting to caregiving demands; by care recipients being male, older, unmarried, Medicaid eligible, and having more severe instrumental activities of daily living (IADL) and cognitive impairment; and by caregivers being male or older (see also Miller & Prohaska, 1999; Kersting, 2001 for similar findings). These previous studies found that decisions about nursing home placement among black/African American older adults depend heavily on the availability of family caregivers and the extent of their caregiving burden. Black/African American caregivers of older adults with dementia, who were intent on respectful and dignified treatment of their loved ones, were generally disenchanted with nursing home care and did not believe nursing homes would be able to provide adequate care (Lampley-Dallas et al., 2001). The study also found that the low male census in most nursing homes made caregivers hesitant to place their male care recipients in them. One study of black/African American community-living older adults found that one third of the interviewed sample had a positive attitude toward a nursing home, stating that it would be a nice place for just resting and being fed, whereas one half of the interviewees had a negative attitude, stating that a nursing home would be a bad place to live, that it would require a big adjustment, and that it would be a place to go to die (Schoenberg & Coward, 1997). In general, compared to their non-Hispanic white counterparts, black/African American nursing home residents were less likely to have recovery stays, but more likely to have Medicaid-financed long-term stays, showing that their nursing home placement tended to be the last resort, permanent care arrangement (Pourat, Andersen, & Wallace, 2001).

Previous studies based on an analysis of MDS admissions and other resident data sets also found that, compared to their non-Hispanic white counterparts, black/African American residents were more likely to be unmarried, to have less external social support (family or friends), to be younger at time of admission, and to suffer from more severe functional and cognitive impairments and poorer mental health at admission (Buchanan, Martin, Zuniga, Wang, & Kim, 2004; Buchanan et al., 2008; Branco, 2007; Gaugler et al., 2004). The younger age of black/African American nursing home residents is likely due to their generally poorer health status, younger onset age of chronic illnesses, and shorter life expectancy compared with non-Hispanic whites.

Hispanics/Latinos

As in the case of black/African American families of older adults, Hispanic/Latino families try to take care of their disabled loved ones at home as long as possible. In Hispanic/Latino culture, the emphasis is on the family as a group rather than on individuals, and there is a deep sense of commitment, obligation, and responsibility for one another, especially for older adults (Garcia-Preto, 1996). Hispanic/Latino older adults and their family members tend to view nursing homes with mixed feelings, seeing them as places to be used only as a last resort and wishing that they would never have to place their loved ones in one or to be sent to one (Magilvy et al., 2000). Placement of their older-adult relatives in nursing homes goes against the cultural norms of the importance of family unity, respect for elders, and family obligations to care for aging parents, and it often creates serious disagreements/conflicts between some family members who propose/carry out a placement and others who oppose such a placement (Gorek et al., 2002; Kolb, 1999; Magilvy et al., 2000). The placement decision-making can also create strong disagreements between an older care recipient who does not want to move to a nursing home and his/her caregivers who feel that they can no longer care for him/her at home (Kolb, 1999). However, many families follow physicians' advice about and support for nursing home placement, as Hispanics/Latinos in general are more likely than non-Hispanic whites to defer to physicians' judgment when there is discord over treatment choices for their loved ones (Decourtney, Jones, Merriman, Heavener, & Branch, 2003; Gorek et al., 2002). For most Hispanic/Latino families, the placement of their loved one in a nursing home is their first such placement. Without professional help, families also may lack knowledge about how nursing homes work and how to choose a quality one.

Analysis of the Hispanic-Established Populations for the Epidemiologic Studies of the Elderly (EPESE) data showed that predictors of nursing home admissions among Hispanic/ Latino older adults were being male, being older, living alone, having no surviving child, and having ADL and cognitive impairments (Angel et al., 2004). The analysis of MADDE data found predictors of nursing home admissions among Hispanics/Latinos with dementia to be Medicaid eligible and have a higher level of ADL disability, higher caregiver income, and higher caregiver depressive symptoms (Gaugler et al., 2006). The study found that cognitively impaired Hispanics/Latinos who lived with their primary caregivers were more likely to have delayed nursing home placement than were non-Hispanic whites and blacks/ African Americans. Hispanic/Latino older adults who entered nursing homes were more disabled, depressed, and cognitively impaired, and more likely to have diabetes and stroke, but younger than their non-Hispanic white counterparts (Espino et al., 2001; Shetterly, Baxter, Morgenstern, Grigsby, & Hamman, 1998).

Especially for immigrants, the move into a nursing home can be particularly difficult as it is another transition into a new culture and environment into which they must once again adjust (Kolb, 1999). Older, recent immigrants also may not have a large social support network and caregivers since they have left their relatives behind in their country of origin. The low levels of education and assimilation among immigrant older adults are also often risk factors for cognitive decline and low psychosocial resource availability, which creates increased stress for caregivers (Espino et al., 2001). Limited English proficiency is a serious barrier to entering a nursing home, even when older adults and informal caregivers are willing to make the transition. Unless they are located in an area with a high concentration of Hispanics/Latinos, nursing homes may not have any Spanish-speaking staff in general or have only one Spanish-speaking staff person, who may be available only during specific shifts or who may not be specifically assigned to work with Spanish-speaking residents. The linguistic isolation is likely to make the adjustment to a new, unfamiliar institutional environment more difficult than it would be without such isolation.

American Indians/Native Americans

Although the number of American Indian/Native American older adults is increasing, they account for less than 1% of the residents in Medicare-/Medicaid-certified nursing homes nationwide (Buchanan et al., 2008). As such, they are often excluded from studies that examine nursing home residents' characteristics and nursing home-related issues. Thus, this section reviews a small number of studies that focused on American Indians/Native Americans rather than a comparison between them and any other racial/ethnic group.

American Indians/Native Americans, in general, experience some of the highest rates of chronic disease and disability in the country. The pace of aging among them appears to exceed that of other racial/ethnic groups, and they seem to experience expansion of morbidity rather than compression, which amplifies the need for long-term care services (Goins & Pilkerton, 2010). More than any other racial/ethnic groups, residential location of American Indians/Native Americans determines the availability of long-term care services. For those dwelling in urban, nonnative communities, nursing homes serving all racial/ethnic groups may be available. However, availability does not directly translate into accessibility for them, given their possible lack of awareness of the services, cultural and language/literacy barriers, different cultural expectations regarding formal and informal care of older adults, and mixed feelings about nursing homes (Jervis et al., 2002). Older Natives and their families tend to distrust and fear nursing home facilities and their services, believing that they would not help them. Other access barriers include a relatively low level of Medicare and Medicaid enrollment, lack of awareness or knowledge, mistrust of federal or state government, belief in the federal government's trust responsibility, welfare stigma, language/literacy problems, and minimization of the need for help among older Natives (Goins, Bogart, & Roubideaux, 2010; Jervis et al., 2002).

American Indians/Native Americans dwelling in rural areas, including tribal reservations, may rarely find a nursing home, although their need for long-term care services is likely to be greater than that of their urban-dwelling counterparts, given the higher rates of poverty; comorbidity and unmet needs; fewer social contacts; and greater environmental deprivation in many rural-area reservations that contributes to poor health and early onset of disability (Baldridge, 2001). Some tribes constructed their own nursing homes, but tribally operated nursing homes remain quite rare in native communities. A survey of 220 tribes and tribal consortia between 2005 and 2007 found that 15% (10%–21%, 95% confidence interval [CI]) of them had nursing homes, 16% (11–23%, 95% CI) had assisted-living facilities, 6% (4%–12%, 95% CI) had adult day services, and 33% (27–40%, 95% CI) had home health services. Among nursing homes, 52% (33%–71%, 95% CI) were tribally operated (Goins et al., 2010). The Indian Health Service (IHS), charged by the federal government with provision of health services for American Indians/Native Americans, focuses primarily on acute care. Congress has never appropriated funding for the IHS to provide long-term care. Provision of long-term care services in impoverished American Indian/Native American communities is a challenge because of lack of funding, excessive regulations and other bureaucratic requirements that tribes must meet, as well as a lack of trained staff (Goins et al., 2010).

Most rural, reservation-dwelling American Indians/Native Americans who require nursing home care must leave the reservation and their families to enter urban-area nursing homes that rarely employ American Indian/Native American staff, serve traditional food, or encourage traditional customs. When the nursing homes are located far from Native communities, family members are often not able to visit their elders because of transportation problems—lack of a means of transportation and/or transportation costs (Jervis et al., 2002). For American Indian/Native American older adults who remain in areas where nursing homes and other long-term care services are not available, family continues to be their most frequent source of long-term care services (Baldridge, 2001). However, American Indian/Native American families have been going through extensive changes due to the high rates of poverty, psychiatric disorders, and alcohol and other substance abuse. In fact, physical abuse of older adults by alcohol-abusing family members or alcohol abuse by the older adults themselves, along with the difficulty of family members' caring for older adults with cognitive impairment and/or psychiatric disorders, were often found to be reasons given for entering a tribally owned, reservation nursing home (Mercer, 1996; Jervis, 2006; Jervis & Manson, 2007).

Asians/Pacific Islanders

The Asian/Pacific Islander category includes people with origins in a wide variety of regions in the Far East Asia, Southeast Asia, Indian subcontinent, Hawaii, Guam, Samoa, or other Pacific Islands. Because of their heterogeneous national origins, cultures, and languages, it does not do justice to treat them as a homogeneous group. However, the Asian/Pacific Islander group, along with the Hispanic/Latino group, includes a large proportion of immigrants, and as a result, traditional values and beliefs from the country of origin, limited English proficiency, and the degree of assimilation are more likely to be factors in nursing home placement of these older adults than those of any other racial/ethnic minority. Traditional cultural values and health beliefs pertinent to elder care that tend to be common in most Asian/Pacific Islander groups include familism, filial piety, the importance of teaching children by being a good role model, and feeling proud of one's caregiving accomplishments in the eyes of other relatives (Chow, 2004; Lee, Farran, Tripp-Reimer, & Sadler, 2003). Overall, Asian/Pacific Islander cultures are collectivist, rather than individualist, placing emphasis on shared/family-centered medical and end-of-life care decision-making rather than individual autonomy and freedom (Kwak & Haley, 2005; Linda & Braun, 1998). However, with the growth of the Asian American population and dual-income families, the children of Asian American older adults often cannot find time and resources to provide in-home care for their functionally and/or cognitively impaired parents. Older parents also do not want to live with their busy adult children, imposing caregiving burden on them. As a result, the number of assisted-living facilities and nursing homes specifically catering to Asian Americans has been growing, and the presence of Asian Americans in general nursing homes has also increased. One study of older Korean Americans, all of whom were immigrants, found that 45% were willing to use a nursing home (Jang, Kim, & Cho, 2008).

An analysis of MDS admissions records between January 2003 and June 2004 found that Asians/Pacific Islanders accounted for 1.9% of new admissions (Buchanan et al., 2008). Between 1999 and 2008, the number of older Asians living in U.S. nursing homes grew by 54.1%, a rate almost identical to that for Hispanics/Latinos (Feng et al., 2011). Unfortunately, however, Asians/Pacific Islanders were largely excluded from previous research on nursing home access and quality care. Only a very limited number of studies examined Asian/Pacific Islander nursing home residents in conjunction with other racial/ethnic minority residents. A limited number of other studies examined caregivers' perceptions about nursing home placement of their loved ones or older adults' attitudes about long-term care among specific Asian/Pacific Islander groups. Based on a convenience sample of 118 South Asian households in Dallas-Fort Worth, Gupta (2002) found that an older adult's being female, having a greater degree of caregivers' role conflict, having a greater level of care recipient's confusion, and having lived in the United States for a greater number of years were associated with a greater likelihood of the nursing home care options being considered, while the level of caregivers' adherence to Asian cultural norms and the older adults' marital status were factors preventing nursing home placement. A study of 124 1.5- and second-generation Korean American adults regarding filial expectations and support for aging immigrant parents found that in addition to their strong sense of gratitude and responsibility toward their parents, the language barriers and lack of parental financial resources also motivated the adult children to prepare for future support of their parents' financial, health care, and long-term care needs (Yoo & Kim, 2010).

One study found that older Japanese Americans in the Northwest were using nursing home care at a rate (5%) similar to that of the general U.S. older population (McCormick et al., 1996). Further analysis comparing the attitudes of older Japanese Americans and older non-Hispanic white Americans toward long-term care found that the Japanese Americans were as likely as (in the case of hip fracture) or more likely than (in the case of dementia) their Caucasian counterparts to intend to use nursing home care. However, Japanese Americans also demonstrated more certainty than the non-Hispanic white Americans about the influences of others on their opinions. Significant correlates of Japanese Americans' intentions to enter nursing homes were lack of social support (including unmarried status), female gender, and high levels of assimilation into American society (never lived in Japan, English-speaking only; McCormick et al., 1996, 2002).

One of the few studies that examined Asian American nursing home residents focused on the sociodemographic and health status of older Chinese newly admitted to a New York City municipal nursing home near Chinatown between November 1992 and May 1997. A majority of 125 Chinese were first-generation immigrants with no or limited English proficiency. Compared with older non-Hispanic whites who were newly admitted, the Chinese were more likely to be married, less likely to have lived alone, more likely to be using Medicaid, less likely to make medical decisions alone, and more likely to have depended on family members for their care. A high rate of dementia, overall serious health problems, and severe dependence in ADLs were present among the Chinese residents, but fewer of them than the non-Hispanic whites were using psychotropic medications on admission (Huang et al., 2003). Other studies that examined women's health care needs and service utilization in nursing homes, however, found that although nursing home residents of color were, in general, more likely than non-Hispanic white residents to be bedfast and require ADL/IADL assistance; Asian/Pacific Islander female residents were the least impaired while American Indian/Native American female residents were the most impaired among racial/ethnic minority women (Davis & Lapane, 2004; Davis, 2005).

QUALITY OF CARE

Blacks/African Americans

Nursing homes are highly racially segregated. One study of 220 long-term care facilities (both assisted-living facilities and nursing homes) in Florida, Maryland, New Jersey, and North Carolina showed that a vast majority (93%–100%) of non-Hispanic whites lived in facilities that predominantly served non-Hispanic whites, and that a little more than half of blacks/African Americans lived in facilities that predominantly served blacks/African Americans (Howard et al., 2002). The same study also found that the facilities that predominantly served black/African Americans had poor facility cleanliness, lighting, and maintenance because such facilities were more likely to admit individuals who were bedfast, developmentally disabled, mentally ill, and/or substance abusing, as well as those who were low income and Medicaid financed. Moreover, those facilities were often located in low-income black/African American communities where only low-income black/African Americans would choose to enter.

Mor et al.'s studies (2004, 2005) on the quality of nursing home care, based on the MDS and OSCAR data, found a two-tiered nursing home system in which 85% of the homes in the lower quality tier were taking care of largely Medicaid-financed residents and had fewer nurses, lower occupancy rates, and more health-related deficiencies. Compared with others, these facilities were also more likely to be terminated from the Medicaid or Medicare programs, disproportionately located in the poorest counties, and more likely to serve blacks/African Americans. Only 9% of non-Hispanic whites, compared with 40% of blacks/African Americans, were in lower tier facilities. Analysis of the 2002 MDS also found that blacks/African Americans were significantly more likely than non-Hispanic whites to have been admitted to nursing homes in the lowest quality quartile. Individuals without a high school diploma, who were more likely to be blacks/African Americans than non-Hispanic whites, were also more likely to be admitted to a low-quality nursing home, possibly because of their greater difficulty in finding, interpreting, and acting on information about quality choices and because their choices, based on geography, were often limited (Angelelli et al., 2006).

One study, based on the 1998 to 2002 MDS, found disparities between African American residents and non-Hispanic white residents in the use of feeding tubes but not of physical restraints, catheters, and antipsychotics (Grabowski & McGuire, 2009). However, another study, based on the 2003 to 2008 MDS, OSCAR, and Area Resource Files, found that black/African American residents persistently showed higher pressure ulcer rates than their non-Hispanic white counterparts (16.8 vs. 11.4% in 2003 and 14.6 vs. 9.6% in 2008; Yue et al., 2011). The same study also found that in nursing homes with the highest percentage of black/African American residents (35%+), both black/African American and non-Hispanic white residents had higher rates of pressure ulcers than in nursing homes serving primarily white residents.

Another study, based on the 2000 MDS and OSCAR, found that, overall, 18.5% of non-Hispanic white and 24.1% of black/African American residents were hospitalized, and that residents in nursing homes with high concentrations of blacks/African Americans had 20% higher odds of hospitalization than those in nursing homes that had no black/African American residents (Gruneir et al., 2008). Also, $10 increments in Medicaid reimbursement rates reduced the odds of hospitalization by 4% for non-Hispanic white residents and 22% for black/African American residents. The higher rates of hospitalization in nursing homes that have black/African American residents may be due both to the lack of facility resources, such as staffing, that could have prevented hospitalizations and to blacks'/African Americans' preference for more aggressive care.

Another study of end-of-life hospitalization for nursing home residents also found that, in general, a significantly higher proportion of black/African American than non-Hispanic white residents were hospitalized and that older, more physically impaired, dying blacks/African Americans were more likely to be hospitalized than their non-Hispanic white counterparts (Mor et al., 2005). Moreover, regardless of race/ethnicity, nursing home residents in facilities having higher proportions of blacks/African Americans had greater odds of hospitalization, indicating that facilities serving more blacks/African Americans may have had fewer resources to prevent hospitalization and provide in-home end-of-life care for their residents.

In general, nursing homes serving a higher proportion of blacks/African Americans have fewer do-not-resuscitate directives (DNRs) living wills, and other end-of-life care decision-making processes established. This may be attributable to religious influence and the family-centered, authority-centered decision-making approach that many older black/African American nursing home residents prefer to use (Ott, 2008; Smith, 2004). In a qualitative study, Ott found that older black/African American nursing home residents were deferring to their families' and doctors' decision-making for their end-of-life care. In another study of families' perception of end-of-life care for their loved ones who lived in nursing homes, black/African American family members, compared with their non-Hispanic white counterparts, were less likely to report that the decedent had treatment wishes or written advance care planning documents; less likely to rate the care received as excellent or very good; and more likely to report absent or problematic physicians and lack of communication and information sharing (Welch, Teno, & Mor, 2005).

Hispanics/Latinos

Previous studies, based on MDS and OSCAR data, also found that older Hispanics/Latinos were more likely than their non-Hispanic white counterparts to live in poor-quality nursing homes, characterized by severe deficiencies in performance, staffing, care, and financial viability (Fennell et al., 2010; Gerardo et al., 2009). Compared with their non-Hispanic white, black/African American, and Asian/Pacific Islander nursing home resident counterparts, the Hispanics/Latinos were found to have poorer health and higher impairment, indicating that they are likely to require more care and assistance than the others (Buchanan et al., 2008; Fennell et al., 2010). Lack of access to and appropriate utilization of health and mental health services throughout their lives, due to poverty and low educational levels, are likely to have contributed to poorer health among both Hispanic/Latino and black/African American residents (Davis, 2005). As mentioned previously, nursing home placement among racial/ethnic minority older adults that is delayed until they are extremely frail physically, mentally, and cognitively further contributes to their need for an advanced care regimen and facility resources. However, compared with their non-Hispanic white counterparts, both Hispanic/Latino and black/African American residents tend to receive lower quality care in nursing homes that have fewer resources. For example, both groups of minority residents were found to have a higher prevalence of pressure ulcers than non-Hispanic whites. Moreover, a facility's concentration of Hispanic/Latino residents was associated with prevalent pressure ulcers after adjusting for other resident characteristics (Gerardo et al., 2009). At admission, both blacks/African Americans and Hispanics/Latinos also received, on average, significantly fewer medications and minutes of occupational and physical therapy than non-Hispanic whites (Buchanan et al., 2008). These disparities in nursing home care reflect or magnify underlying community segregation and disparities in physical and mental health services (Gruneir et al., 2008). The more segregated a state's nursing homes, the higher the nursing home use rates of non-Hispanic whites and the greater the disparities in quality of care between them and the minority residents (Smith et al., 2008).

Like black/African American nursing home residents, Hispanic/Latino nursing home residents are less likely than their non-Hispanic white counterparts to have advance directives and more likely to prefer aggressive treatment as opposed to palliative care. This reluctance to agree to withholding or withdrawing treatment may reflect religious influence. It may also stem from the fact that many of these older adults did not have health insurance when they were younger, but now finally have access to it through Medicare and/or Medicaid eligibility (Espino et al., 2001).

An important quality gap for Hispanic/Latino residents also stems from the lack of cultural competence in most nursing homes, especially in facilities that do not predominantly serve Hispanics/Latinos. As mentioned, linguistically isolated Hispanic/Latino residents experience significant barriers to expressing their needs. Even among Hispanic/Latino nursing home residents who are proficient in English, adjustment to a culture that is incongruent with their own in values/beliefs, norms, customs, religious practices/faith, and food is difficult. Although most family members try to maintain cultural norms and routines through frequent visits, monitoring care, and bringing ethnic food, but they often find that the nursing home staff does not show respect to their elders and ignores their Latino heritage and traditions (Gorek et al., 2002).

American Indians/Native Americans

Tribally operated nursing homes, compared to non-Native facilities, are more likely to provide culturally competent services in Native-member staffing, language, food, and respect for traditional values and customs. However, many tribal facilities lack sufficient resources to provide quality care for residents who are cognitively impaired or have other mental disorders. Notwithstanding the lack of resources, these tribal nursing homes have often become de facto mental health institutions given the lack of access, due to rurality, poverty, and dependence on the underfunded IHS, to mental health services. Statistics for tribal nursing homes show that the proportions of residents with dementia (64%), depression (29%), and alcoholism (27%) were significantly higher than those based on national nursing home surveys (Jervis & Manson, 2007). Lack of professional mental health service providers, a high rate of residents' resistance to care, and overall high employee turnover rates made it difficult for these facilities to provide quality services, especially behavioral interventions (Jervis, 2006; Jervis & Manson, 2007). One study found suboptimal pharmacological treatment of depression and psychotic/agitated symptoms to be especially common in a tribal nursing home. Although potential underuse of pharmacotherapy affected the largest proportion of residents, potential inappropriate use, especially of analgesics, psychotropics, and antihistamines, as well as overuse of anticonvulsant, antibiotic, cardiovascular, and psychotropic drugs were also quite common (Jervis, Shore, Hutt, & Manson, 2007).

Some Native families continue to care for their institutionalized older relatives, especially when they have had emotionally close relationships and live near the facility. However, for a large proportion of Native elders in nursing homes, families are either nonexistent or estranged. Families who are stigma avoidant, overburdened with their own problems, transportation-less or fuel-less, guilt ridden, or uninterested also do not visit their family members in nursing homes. Worse, some dysfunctional families visit only to access residents' money to obtain alcohol (Jervis, 2006).

American Indian/Native American older adults placed in non-Native community nursing homes face far more difficulty than those in tribal homes in adjusting to a new environment due to a myriad of cultural differences—language, food, music, dance, religion, conceptualization of disease and pain, practice of medicine—and, too often, facility staff's ignorance about Native cultures and stereotypical assumptions. This is especially true of Native older adults who leave their reservation to enter a nursing home that is a distance away; in this situation, cultural and linguistic barriers and various adjustment problems often lead to their isolation from other residents in facilities serving predominantly white or other racial/ethnic groups. They long for visits from family, news, and contacts from their reservation (Cooley, Ostendorf, & Bickerton, 1979). Lack of cultural competence among staff may also result in inappropriate care. For example, one study of Native cancer patients found that urban elders were more disadvantaged than their reservation peers in receiving critical linkage information about psychological and supportive services from their attending physicians. The study also found that medical providers' stereotypical perception of the stoic Indian resulted in insufficient provision of pain medication (Burhansstipanov & Hollow, 2001). The same study found that Natives tend to conceptualize pain (and other illness conditions) in circular, not linear, ways by holistically taking into account body, mind, emotion, and spirit; for this reason, pain scales did not appear to be working, as the patients chose favorite or sacred numbers on the scale rather than evaluating their pain levels on it. In some American Indian/Native American traditional beliefs, talking about death and dying is almost taboo, which leads to a lack of acceptance of advance directives (Mercer, 1996).

Asians/Pacific Islanders

A literature search did not yield a single study that examined the quality of care for Asian/Pacific Islander nursing home residents either in general nursing homes or those catering to specific Asian American groups. Only one study, based on 1992 to 1996 data, found that, compared with non-Hispanic white residents, non-white residents (including blacks/African Americans, Hispanics/Latinos, and Asians/Pacific Islanders) were less likely to receive secondary stroke-prevention agents (Christian et al., 2003). Future studies should examine the quality of care at Asian/Pacific Islander–serving nursing homes.

NEED FOR CULTURALLY COMPETENT CARE

With the demographic revolution among racial/ethnic minorities and older adults (U.S. Census Bureau, 2011), the number of racial/ethnic minority nursing home residents will continue to increase. Without concerted efforts, however, the nursing home quality gap between non-Hispanic white residents and racial/ethnic minority residents is also likely to continue.

According to long-term care policy expert Harrington (2007), three areas need to be improved, to enhance the quality of nursing home care: (a) better enforcement of regulation to ensure compliance; (b) improvement in staffing levels and quality along with raising payment rates to providers; and (c) greater financial accountability and streamlining of cost centers. In conjunction with improvement of nursing staffing levels, social work staffing levels also need to be improved, as social workers currently spend the bulk of their time doing the MDS assessment and not sufficient time on individual or group therapeutic interventions for mental health and other quality-of-life issues (Choi, Wyllie, & Ransom, 2009).

In 2009, the Centers for Medicare and Medicaid Services (CMS) issued clarifications and new guidance for nursing home surveyors, placing great emphasis on making the nursing home environment more homelike and on improving nursing home residents' quality of life and environment. Under these new guidelines, nursing home surveys are focused on several key areas. These include ensuring that residents live with dignity; offering choices in care and services; accommodating the environment to each residents' needs and preferences; and creating a more homelike environment, with increased access to visitors, meals no longer served on institutional trays, and elimination of noise from paging systems, alarms, and large nursing stations. More focus will be on individualizing care and building relationships with residents, who will now have the right to make choices concerning their schedules, such as daily walking, eating, bathing, and bedtime. The new guidelines are intended to be a road map for environmental and cultural change, and facilities are encouraged to be proactive in adopting them. However, the new guidance states that "many facilities cannot immediately make these types of changes, but it should be a goal for all facilities that have not yet made these types of changes to work toward them" (Allen, 2010, p. 72).

As reviewed in this chapter, improvement in the quality of nursing home care for racial/ethnic minorities also requires culturally competent care. Cultural competence has been defined in many ways. One widely adopted definition states that "cultural and linguistic competence is a set of congruent behaviors, attitudes, and policies that come together in a system, agency, or among professionals and enables that system, agency, or those professionals to work effectively in cross-cultural situations. 'Culture' refers to integrated patterns of human behavior that include the language, thoughts, communications, actions, customs, beliefs, values, and institutions of racial, ethnic, religious, or social groups. 'Competence' implies having the capacity to function effectively as an individual and an organization within the context of the cultural beliefs, behaviors, and needs presented by consumers and their communities" (Cross, Bazron, Dennis, & Isaacs, 1989). More specific to health care and its delivery, another definition states as follows: "cultural competence in health care describes the ability of systems to provide care to patients with diverse values, beliefs and behaviors, including tailoring delivery to meet patients' social, cultural, and linguistic needs" (Betancourt, Green, & Carrillo, 2002, p. v). From its roots in early models of cross-cultural health care primarily for immigrants in the late 1980s, cultural competence expanded through the 1990s in three important ways: (a) its application to essentially all minority groups, particularly those most affected by racial disparities in the quality of health care; (b) the encompassing of such issues as prejudice, stereotyping, and social determinants of health; and (c) inclusion of health systems and communities as well as the interpersonal domain of cross-cultural care (Saha, Beach, & Cooper, 2008). According to Saha et al., this expansion in the scope of culturally competent health care was largely driven by accumulated research demonstrating that racial/ethnic minority groups received lower quality health care than the majority population, even after accounting for differences in access to care. Cultural and linguistic barriers might be contributing to racial/ethnic disparities in health care quality, but other factors had to be considered under the conceptual purview of culturally competent care. These include historical and ongoing institutionalized discrimination against people of color, personal biases and prejudices, patients' distrust of health care providers and institutions, limited functional/health literacy stemming from low levels of education and overall low socioeconomic status, and a lower level of public health care resources allocated to the poor.

To provide a common understanding and consistent definitions of culturally and linguistically appropriate services in health care and to assist federally funded health organizations in the development of culturally competent services, the U.S. DHHS Office of Minority Health (OMH) published the National Standards for Culturally and Linguistically Appropriate Services in Health Care (CLAS standards) in the Federal Register on December 22, 2000. The CLAS standards have since become the basis for subsequent government and private sector activities defining, implementing, and evaluating cultural competence activities among health care providers. The 14 standards are organized by themes (see Figure 18.1): Culturally Competent Care (Standards 1–3); Language Access Services (Standards 4–7); and Organizational Supports for Cultural Competence (Standards 8–14). Standards 1–7 address interventions that have the most direct impact on clinical care, and Standards 8–14 address organizational structures, policies, and processes that support the implementation of Standards 1–7 (Fortier & Bishop, 2003, DHHS OMH, 2001). The standards are also categorized into three types of varying stringency. These mandates, guidelines, and recommendations are as follows: CLAS mandates are current federal requirements for all recipients of federal funds (Standards 4–7). CLAS guidelines are activities recommended by the OMH for adoption as mandates by federal, state, and national accrediting agencies (Standards 1–3 and 8–13). CLAS recommendations are suggested by the OMH for voluntary adoption by health care organizations (Standard 14). The CLAS standards have also become bases/models of cultural competence standards for health care professionals, including nurses and social workers (Douglas et al., 2009; National Association of Social Workers [NASW], 2001).

In sum, the goal of cultural competence is to create a health care system and workforce capable of delivering the highest quality care to every patient regardless of race/ethnicity, culture, language proficiency, or socioeconomic status and to eliminate racial/ethnic and SES-related disparities in health care (Betancourt, Green, Carrillo, & Park, 2005). It was reported that between the early 1990s and May 2007, the term cultural competence had been mentioned in more than 1,000 medical and nursing journal articles and that myriad programs and initiatives addressing cultural competence in health care had been developed (Saha et al., 2008; The Henry J. Kaiser Family Foundation, 2003). Indicators of cultural competence in health care delivery organizations have also been developed (DHHS Health Resources and Services Administration [HRSA], 2002).

Standard 1. Health care organizations should ensure that patients/consumers receive from all staff members effective, understandable, and respectful care that is provided in a manner compatible with their cultural health beliefs and practices and preferred language.

Standard 2. Health care organizations should implement strategies to recruit, retain, and promote at all levels of the organization a diverse staff and leadership that are representative of the demographic characteristics of the service area.

Standard 3. Health care organizations should ensure that staff at all levels and across all disciplines receive ongoing education and training in culturally and linguistically appropriate service delivery.

Standard 4. Health care organizations must offer and provide language assistance services, including bilingual staff and interpreter services, at no cost to each patient/consumer with limited English proficiency at all points of contact, in a timely manner during all hours of operation.

Standard 5. Health care organizations must provide to patients/consumers in their preferred language both verbal offers and written notices informing them of their right to receive language assistance services.

Standard 6. Health care organizations must assure the competence of language assistance provided to limited English-proficient patients/consumers by interpreters and bilingual staff. Family and friends should not be used to provide interpretation services (except on request by the patient/consumer).

Standard 7. Health care organizations must make available easily understood patient-related materials and post signage in the languages of the commonly encountered groups and/or groups represented in the service area.

Standard 8. Health care organizations should develop, implement, and promote a written strategic plan that outlines clear goals, policies, operational plans, and management accountability/oversight mechanisms to provide culturally and linguistically appropriate services.

Standard 9. Health care organizations should conduct initial and ongoing organizational self-assessments of CLAS-related activities and are encouraged to integrate cultural and linguistic competence-related measures into their internal audits, performance improvement programs, patient satisfaction assessments, and outcomes-based evaluations.

Standard 10. Health care organizations should ensure that data on the individual patient's/consumer's race, ethnicity, and spoken and written language are collected in health records, integrated into the organization's management information systems, and periodically updated.

Standard 11. Health care organizations should maintain a current demographic, cultural, and epidemiological profile of the community as well as a needs assessment to accurately plan for and implement services that respond to the cultural and linguistic characteristics of the service area.

Standard 12. Health care organizations should develop participatory, collaborative partnerships with communities and utilize a variety of formal and informal mechanisms to facilitate community and patient/consumer involvement in designing and implementing CLAS-related activities.

Standard 13. Health care organizations should ensure that conflict and grievance resolution processes are culturally and linguistically sensitive and capable of identifying, preventing, and resolving cross-cultural conflicts or complaints by patients/consumers.

Standard 14. Health care organizations are encouraged to regularly make available to the public information about their progress and successful innovations in implementing the CLAS standards and to provide public notice in their communities about the availability of this information.

FIGURE 18.1 National Standards for Culturally and Linguistically Appropriate Services (CLAS) in Health Care. *Source:* DHHS Office of Minority Health, 2001.

Despite the huge interest in and rise of culturally competent health care in general, there is a paucity of research on the impact and effectiveness of culturally competent nursing home care. This lack of research on culturally competent nursing home care may have been due to the underrepresentation of racial/ethnic minorities in nursing facilities and the profit-maximization emphasis of for-profit chain nursing home operations at the expense of quality of care improvement. Lack of resources, including staffing, in largely poor, minority-serving nursing homes and the absence of a financing/funding source considered sufficient to develop and implement new initiatives may also have been reasons for lack of culturally competent initiatives to improve quality of care (The Henry J. Kaiser Family Foundation, 2003). However, with the increasing share/number of racial/ethnic minority nursing home residents and the continuing disparities in quality of care between majority and minority residents, culturally competent care in nursing home settings needs to be developed, implemented, and evaluated.

In both definitions of culturally competent care and the CLAS standards summarized here, culturally competent care requires involvement of and interactions among all entities at the system, facility, provider/staff, community, and resident/family levels, and it encompasses policies, knowledge, skills, behaviors, and attitudes. Recommendations for the development and implementation of culturally competent care for racial/ethnic minority residents of nursing homes need to cover these entities and the relevant policies, knowledge, skills, behaviors, and attitudes.

System Level

The Institute of Medicine (IOM, 2001) identified five key agenda items[3] for narrowing quality chasms in the health care systems, which can also apply to reducing the quality gap in nursing home care. The key agendas for nursing home care should be (a) that all nursing home care constituents, including policymakers, federal and state regulators, public and private purchasers, nursing home staff/care providers, and the current and future consumers and their families, commit to a national standard of improving culturally competent nursing home care; (b) that these constituents agree to and adopt a new set of principles to guide the redesign of care process; (c) that the CMS and the state Medicaid offices identify a set of priority conditions on which to focus initial efforts, provide resources to stimulate innovation, and initiate the change process, and that Congress continue to authorize and appropriate funds for the innovation and change process; (d) that the CMS and the state Medicaid offices design and implement more effective organizational support processes to make change in the delivery of equitable care possible; and (e) that the CMS and the state Medicaid offices move forward expeditiously with the establishment of monitoring, tracking, and barrier-identification mechanisms and procedures in evaluating progress and the creation of an environment that fosters and rewards improvement.

Facility Level

At the specific nursing home facility level, where culturally competent care should be delivered to residents on a daily basis, the CLAS standards should provide the basis for culturally and linguistically competent services. As at the system level, the essential first step for each facility is to have a commitment to provide culturally competent care to every resident to ensure his/her safety, and to respect his/her cultural values and health beliefs, rights, and individual care preferences in the most effective and efficient manner possible. Delivery of culturally competent care at the facility level also requires goal-setting, policy-making, and organizational infrastructure, including financial resources, staff development, communication/information sharing systems, and technology for program planning, development, and implementation. Mechanisms of monitoring and evaluating the delivery should also be developed to identify barriers and further improve the services/care. The HRSA-developed indicators of cultural competence in health care delivery organization provide a detailed organizational cultural competence assessment profile (DHHS HRSA, 2002).

Provider/Staff Level

As described in CLAS Standards 2 and 3, each facility should implement strategies to recruit, retain, and promote at all levels of its organization a diverse staff and leadership that represent the demographic characteristics of the service area and ensure that staff at all levels and across all disciplines receive ongoing education and training in culturally and linguistically appropriate service delivery. Nursing home staff, including administrators, medical directors, nurses, social workers, certified nurse assistants, and housekeepers interact directly with residents and bear the largest share of responsibility for the clinical aspects of nursing home care. The IOM's (2001) recommendations for narrowing the quality chasm provide excellent guidelines for processes in general, and they can also apply to nursing home care. Working together with residents, staff members should adhere to the following: (a) care based on continuous healing relationships; (b) customization based on individual patient needs, values, and preferences; (c) the patient as the source of control; (d) shared knowledge and the free flow of information; (e) evidence-based and shared decision-making; (f) safety as a system property; (g) transparency with residents and families; (h) anticipation of needs; (i) continuous decrease in waste of resources and resident time; and (j) cooperation and communication among providers/staff to ensure an appropriate exchange of information and coordination of care.

Both nursing and social work staff should also adhere to their own profession's standards for culturally competent practice pertaining to knowledge, skills, and attitudes. These include (a) self-awareness/critical reflection of their own personal and cultural values and beliefs as a way of understanding and appreciating the importance of these qualities in the lives of people and their impact on provision of culturally competent care; (b) continuing development of specialized knowledge and understanding about the history, traditions, values, perspectives, and family systems of culturally diverse individuals, families, communities, and populations they serve; (c) use of cross-cultural practice skills, methodological approaches, and techniques that reflect the staff person's understanding of the role of culture in the helping process; (d) resident advocacy and empowerment, in which staff members recognize the effect of health care policies/programs, delivery systems, and resources on their diverse client populations and empower and advocate for and with residents; and (e) training in and exercise of cross-cultural leadership through which the staff members have the ability to communicate information about diverse resident groups and influence individuals, groups, and systems to practice and achieve the outcomes of culturally competent care for diverse populations (Dougals et al., 2009; NASW, 2001).

Community Level

In recent years, strategies to increase quality and years of life and to eliminate health disparities have emphasized a community-level focus. Healthy People 2010 strongly supports community-level efforts in which health promotion messages and materials reflect the principles and practices of cultural and linguistic competence at the community level (Bronheim & Sockalingam, 2003). The impetus of developing a community-oriented, culturally competent approach often originated with the need to define health in a more holistic manner (Betancourt et al., 2002). In providing culturally competent nursing home care, nursing home administrators and staff should involve community representatives from faith/spiritual communities and from civic and cultural organizations in the facility's planning, monitoring, and quality-improvement meetings. An inclusive process in which the experiences and perspectives of community leaders, stakeholders, and constituencies are solicited and valued can forge alliances and partnerships that would provide opportunities for mutual education, increase positive outcomes in nursing home care, and have long-lasting benefits for the health of the community. As in health promotions (Bronheim & Sockalingam, 2003), community partners in culturally competent nursing care play several key roles, including (a) providing the cultural perspectives of the target population groups; (b) providing credibility to the effort within the facility and at the system level; (c) bringing expertise (e.g., knowledge of health beliefs and practices, language, and preferred sources of information for the intended population groups); and (d) bringing community resources to support culturally competent health care (e.g., access to local media outlets or other dissemination points, or local financial or in-kind support for activities). Collaboration with community leaders representing the underserved racial/ethnic minority groups will also be helpful in reaching out to older adults and their families who need nursing home care but are not accessing it.

Resident/Family Level

Culturally competent nursing home care at the resident/family level means that the residents and their families should be able to have a voice/input in their care planning and implementation, with staff showing respect for their cultural values and health beliefs; to access and receive culturally congruent services; to be fully informed of their rights regarding routine health care procedures and end-of-life care choices; and to have opportunities to remain connected to religious/spiritual venues and other community functions and activities when residents are able and want to do so. A resident and his/her family (or an advocate) should be able to use a variety of avenues for involvement that respect cultural differences in expression of opinions and in decision-making processes and that maintain cultural norms and routines (e.g., through family visits and monitoring of care; Gorek et al., 2002; Magilvy et al., 2000). Respect for the residents' cultural values and routines is an important step in building their trust in the systems of care and the providers/staff and in improving their compliance in the course of treatment. In the absence of trained bilingual/bicultural staff, residents and family members with limited English proficiency should be informed of their rights to free interpretation and translation services, so that lack of English proficiency will not pose barriers to accessing necessary health care and participating in activities and social interactions. Nursing home care should be provided in the individual resident's preferred language in both oral communications and written materials, and policies should be in place to minimize the use of family members as interpreters (Magilvy et al., 2000; DHHS HRSA, 2002).

CONCLUSIONS

Changing demographics and cultural norms, increasing dementia care demands, and family economic pressures, as well as increased bed availabilities resulting from the declining occupancy rates have contributed to the narrowing racial/ethnic gap in access to nursing homes. However, increased access to and utilization of nursing homes among racial/ethnic minority older adults have not translated into improved quality of nursing home care for them. The consensus findings of previous studies are that minority older adults, compared with non-Hispanic white older adults, are concentrated in low-quality/lower-tier nursing homes with a record of more inspection deficiencies, including poor facility cleanliness, lighting, and maintenance; poor staffing; and poor financial viability. Studies have found that older minorities—blacks/African Americans and Hispanics/Latinos—enter nursing homes more disabled, depressed, and cognitively impaired than their non-Hispanic white counterparts, since family caregivers of these racial/ethnic minority older adults often delay their nursing home admissions due to cultural norms, linguistic isolation (especially among recent immigrants), and lack of knowledge about available resources. Nursing homes that are willing to admit highly disabled and cognitively impaired older adults tend to be low quality and are located in minority-concentrated areas. These quality gaps in nursing home care for racial/ethnic minority older adults are continuations of the racial/ethnic disparities in health and access to quality health care. With the increasing numbers of racial/ethnic minority older adults, the number of racial/ethnic minority nursing home residents will continue to increase in the future. Without concerted efforts, however, the nursing home quality gap between non-Hispanic white residents and racial/ethnic minority residents is likely to continue.

Review of previous research on nursing home care for racial/ethnic minority older adults also revealed the paucity of studies on American Indians/Native Americans and Asian/Pacific Islander Americans. There was not a single study of the quality of care for

Asian/Pacific Islander nursing home residents either in general nursing homes or in nursing homes catering to specific Asian American groups. More research on these minority nursing home residents is needed in the future.

Improvement in nursing home care quality requires better enforcement of regulations, increased staffing levels, financial accountability for Medicare and Medicaid funded facilities, individualized care, and creating a more homelike environment. In addition to these regulatory and environmental changes, improvement in quality of nursing home care for racial/ethnic minorities also requires culturally competent care. In reality, despite the huge interest in and rise of culturally competent health care in general, little systematic research has been done on culturally competent nursing home care. Applying the CLAS standards, the development and implementation of culturally competent care for racial/ethnic minority residents of nursing homes need to cover the system, facility, provider/staff, community, and resident/family levels and relevant policies, knowledge, skills, behaviors, and attitudes. Specific recommendations at each level are provided and discussed. Further research and resources are needed to improve the care of the most vulnerable older adults.

NOTES

1. MDS is part of the federally mandated Nursing Home Quality Initiative (NHQI) that began in November 2002 and is composed of a comprehensive assessment of all residents' physical and clinical conditions and abilities as well as their preferences and life care wishes in Medicare- or Medicaid-certified nursing facilities. The MDS assessment is conducted with the residents at admission to the nursing facility and then periodically, within specified intervals, during their stay. In most cases, assessors are licensed health care professionals (e.g., social workers) employed by the nursing facility. The MDS provides the foundation on which a resident's individual care plan is formulated. MDS information is transmitted electronically by nursing facilities to the MDS database in the resident's state, and the state MDS data is captured into the national MDS database at the Centers for Medicare & Medicaid Services (CMS). MDS information determines the Resource Utilization Group (RUG) category, which ultimately determines the per diem rate paid to the facility for a resident whose stay is covered under Medicare Part A. The MDS data also feeds into the facility's quality indicator and quality measure reports, some of which are publicly posted on the Nursing Home Compare website, and others of which are used by surveyors during the survey process.

2. OSCAR: Skilled nursing facilities (SNFs) and nursing facilities (NFs) are required to be in compliance with the requirements in 42 CFR Part 483, Subpart B, to receive payment under the Medicare or Medicaid programs. To certify an SNF or NF, a state surveyor completes at least a Life Safety Code survey and a Standard Survey. Each state conducts the survey, which is not announced to the facility, and has the responsibility for certifying an SNF's or NF's compliance and noncompliance. There is an exception in the case of state-operated facilities, but the state's certification for an SNF is subject to CMS approval. In addition to certifying a facility's compliance, the state recommends appropriate enforcement actions to the state Medicaid Agency for Medicaid and to the regional office for Medicare.

3. (1) That all health care constituencies, including policymakers, purchasers, regulators, health professionals, health care trustees and managers, and consumers, commit to a national statement of purpose for the health care system as a whole and to a shared agenda of six aims (safety, effectiveness, patient-centered care, timeliness, efficiency, and equity) for improvement that can raise the quality of care to unprecedented levels; (2) that clinicians and patients along with the health care organizations that support care delivery adopt a new set of principles to guide the redesign of care processes; (3) that the Department of Health and Human Services identify a set of priority conditions on which to focus initial efforts, provide resources to stimulate innovation, and initiate the change process; (4) that health care organizations design and implement more effective organizational support processes to make change in care delivery possible; and (5) that purchasers, regulators, health professionals, educational institutions, and the Department of Health and Human Services create an environment that fosters and rewards improvement by (a) creating an

infrastructure to support evidence-based practice, (b) facilitating the use of information technology, (c) aligning payment incentives, and (d) preparing the workforce to better serve patients in a world of expanding knowledge and rapid change (IOM, 2001).

REFERENCES

Aeschleman, H. K. (2000). The white world of nursing homes: the myriad barriers to access facing today's elderly minorities. *The Elder Law Journal, 8,* 367–391.

Akamigbo, A. B., & Wolinsky, F. D. (2007). New evidence of racial differences in access and their effects on the use of nursing homes among older adults. *Medical Care, 45,* 672–679.

Allen, J. E. (2010). Nursing home federal requirements: Guidelines for surveyors and survey protocols (7th ed.). New York, NY: Springer. (Also refer to State Operations Manual Appendix P - Survey Protocol for Long Term Care Facilities - Part I, Rev. 42, 04–24-2009 and Appendix PP - Guidance to Surveyors for Long Term Care Facilities, Rev. 70, 01–07-2011). Retrieved from http://www.cms.gov/manuals/Downloads/som107ap_p_ltcf.pdf & http://www.cms.gov/manuals/Downloads/som107ap_pp_guidelines_ltcf.pdf

Angel, J. L., Angel, R. J., Aranda, M. P., & Miles, T. P. (2004). Can the family still cope? *Journal of Aging & Health, 16,* 338–354.

Angelelli, J., Grabowski, D. C., & Mor, V. (2006). Effect of educational level and minority status on nursing home choice after hospital discharge. *American Journal of Public Health, 96,* 1249–1253.

Baldridge, D. (2001). Indian elders: Family traditions in crisis. *American Behavioral Scientist, 44,* 1515–1527.

Betancourt, J., Green, A., & Carrillo, E. (2002). Cultural competence in health care: Emerging frameworks and practical approaches. Field report. New York, NY: The Commonwealth Fund. Retrieved from http://www.commonwealthfund.org/usr_doc/betancourt_culturalcompetence_576.pdf

Betancourt, J., Green, A., Carrillo, E., & Park, E. R. (2005). Cultural competence and health care disparities: Key perspectives and trends. *Health Affairs, 24,* 499–505.

Branco, K. J. (2007). Religious activities, strength from faith, and social functioning among African American and White nursing home residents. *Journal of Religion, Spirituality & Aging, 19*(4), 3–20.

Bronheim, S., & Sockalingam, S. (2003). *A guide to…choosing and adapting culturally and linguistically competent health promotion materials.* Washington, DC: National Center for Cultural Competence, Georgetown University Center for Child and Human Development, University Center for Excellence in Developmental Disabilities. Retrieved from http://nccc.georgetown.edu/documents/Materials_Guide.pdf

Buchanan, R. J., Martin, R. A., Zuniga, M., Wang, S., & Kim, M. S. (2004). Nursing home residents with multiple sclerosis: Comparisons of African American residents to white residents at admission. *Multiple Sclerosis, 10,* 660–667.

Buchanan, R. J., Rosenthal, M., Graber, D. R., Wang, S., & Kim, M. S. (2008). Racial and ethnic comparisons of nursing home residents at admission. *Journal of the American Medical Directors Association, 9,* 568–579.

Burhansstipanov, L., & Hollow, W. (2001). Native American cultural aspects of oncology nursing care. *Seminars in Oncology Nursing, 17,* 206–219.

Chiodo, L. K., Kanten, D. N., Gerety, M. B., & Mulrow, C. D. (1994). Functional status of Mexican American nursing home residents. *Journal of the American Geriatrics Society, 42,* 293–296.

Choi, N. G., Kim, J., & Asseff, J. (2009). Self-neglect and neglect of older adults and poverty: Re-examination of etiology. *Journal of Gerontological Social Work, 52*(2), 1–17.

Choi, N. G., Wyllie, R. & Ransom, S. (2009). Risk factors and intervention programs for depression in nursing home residents: Nursing home staff interview findings. *Journal of Gerontological Social Work, 52,* 668–683.

Chow, N. (2004). Asian value and aged care. *Geriatrics & Gerontology International, 4,* S21–S25.

Christian, J. B., Lapane, K. L., & Toppa, R. S. (2003). Racial disparities in receipt of secondary stroke prevention agents among US nursing home residents. *Stroke, 34,* 2693–2697.

Cooley, R. C., Ostendorf, D., & Bickerton, D. (1979). Outreach services for elderly Native Americans. *Social Work, 24,* 151–153.

Cross, T. L., Bazron, B. J., Dennis, K. W., & Isaacs, M. R. (1989). Toward a culturally competent system of care (Vol. 1). Washington, DC: National Institute of Mental Health, Child and Adolescent Service System Program Technical Assistance Center. Georgetown University Child Development Center. Retrieved from http://www.culturediversity.org/cultcomp.htm

Davis, J. A. (2005). Differences in the health care needs and service utilization of women in nursing homes: Comparison by race/ethnicity. *Journal of Women & Aging, 17,* 57–71.

Davis, J. A., & Lapane, K. L. (2004). Do characteristics associated with nursing home residents vary by race/ethnicity? *Journal of Health Care Poor Underserved, 15,* 251–266.

Decourtney, C. A., Jones, K., Merriman, M. P., Heavener, N., & Branch, P. K. (2003). Establishing a culturally sensitive palliative care program in rural Alaska Native American communities. *Journal of Palliative Medicine, 6,* 501–510.

Dilworth-Anderson, P., Williams, I. C., & Gibson, B. (2002). Issues of race, ethnicity, and culture in caregiving research: A twenty-year review (1980–2000). *The Gerontologist, 42,* 237–272.

Douglas, M. K, Pierce, J. U., Rosenkoetter, M., Callister, L. C., Hattar-Pollara, M., Lauderdale, J., et al. (2009). Standards of practice for culturally competent nursing care: A request for comments. *Journal of Transcultural Nursing, 20,* 257–269.

Espino, D. V., Mouton, C. P., Del Aguila, D., Parker, R. W., Lewis, R. M., & Miles, T. P. (2001). Mexican American elders with dementia in long-term care. *Clinical Gerontologist: The Journal of Aging and Mental Health, 23*(3–4), 83–96.

Feng, Z., Fennell, M. L., Tyler, D. A., Clark, M, & Mor, V. (2011). The care span: Growth of racial and ethnic minorities in US nursing homes driven by demographic and psooible disparities in options. *Health Affairs, 30,* 1358–1365.

Fennell, M. L., Feng, Z., Clark, M. A., & Mor, V. (2010). Elderly Hispanics more likely to reside in poor-quality nursing homes. *Health Affairs, 29,* 65–73.

Fortier, J. P., & Bishop, D. (2003). Setting the agenda for research on cultural competence in health care: Final report (C. Brach, Ed.). Rockville, MD: U.S. Department of Health and Human Services Office of Minority Health and Agency for Health care Research and Quality. Retrieved from http://www.ahrq.gov/research/cultural.pdf

Garcia-Preto, N. (1996). Latino families: An overview. In M. McGoldrick, J. Giordano, & J. K. Pearce (Eds.), *Ethnicity and family therapy* (pp. 141–154). New York, NY: The Guilford Press.

Gaugler, J., Kane, R., Kane, R., & Newcomer, R. (2006). Predictors of institutionalization in Latinos with dementia. *Journal of Cross-Cultural Gerontology, 21*(3/4), 139–155.

Gaugler, J. E., Leach, C. R., Clay, T., & Newcomer, R. C. (2004). Predictors of nursing home placement in African Americans with dementia. *Journal of the American Geriatrics Society, 52,* 445–452.

Gerardo, M. P., Teno, J. M., & Mor, V. (2009). Not so black and white: Nursing home concentration of Hispanics associated with prevalence of pressure ulcers. *Journal of the American Medical Directors Association, 10,* 127–132.

Giunta, N., Chow, J., Scharlach, A. E., & Dal Santo, T. S. (2004). Racial and ethnic differences in family caregiving in California. *Journal of Human Behavior in the Social Environment, 9*(4), 85–109.

Goins, R. T., Bogart, A., & Roubideaux, Y. (2010). Service provider perceptions of long-term care access in American Indian and Alaska Native communities. *Journal of Health Care for the Poor and Underserved, 21,* 1340–1353.

Goins, R. T., & Pilkerton, C. S. (2010). Comorbidity among older American Indians: The Native Elder Care Study. *Journal of Cross-Cultural Gerontology, 25,* 343–354.

Gorek, B., Martin, J., White, N., Peters, D., & Hummel, F. (2002). Culturally competent care for Latino elders in long-term care settings. *Geriatric Nursing, 23,* 272–275.

Grabowski, D. C., & McGuire, T. G. (2009). Black-White disparities in care in nursing homes. *Atlantic Economic Journal, 37,* 299–314.

Gruneir, A., Miller, S. C., Feng, Z., Intrator, O., & Mor, V. (2008). Relationship between state Medicaid policies, nursing home racial composition, and the risk of hospitalization for Black and White residents. *Health Research and Educational Trust, 43,* 869–881.

Gupta, R. (2002). Consideration of nursing home care placement for the elderly in South Asian families. *Journal of Immigrant Health, 4,* 47–56.

Harrington, C. (2007). How to improve nursing homes—One expert's 30-year view. *Aging Today, 28*(5). Retrieved from http://www.agingtoday.org

The Henry J. Kaiser Family Foundation. (2003). *Compendium of cultural competence initiatives in health care.* Menlo Park, CA: Author. Retrieved from http:// www.kff.org/uninsured/6067-index.cfm

Howard, D. L., Sloane, P. D., Zimmerman, S., Eckert, J. K., Walsh, J. F., Buie, V. C., et al. (2002). Distribution of African Americans in residential care/assisted living and nursing homes: More evidence of racial disparity? *American Journal of Public Health, 92,* 1272–1277.

Huang, Z.-B., Neufeld, R. R., Likourezos, A., Breuer, B., Khaski, A., Milano, E., et al. (2003). Sociodemographic and health characteristics of older Chinese on admission to a nursing home: A cross-racial/ethnic study. *Journal of the American Geriatrics Society, 51,* 404–409.

Institute of Medicine (IOM). (2001). *Crossing the quality chasm: A new health system for the 21st century.* Washington, DC: The National Academies Press.

Jang, Y., Kim, G., & Cho, S. (2008). Willingness to use a nursing home: a study of Korean American elders. *Journal of Applied Gerontology, 27,* 110–117.

Jervis, L. L. (2006). The missing family: Staff perspectives on and responses to familial noninvolvement in two diverse nursing homes. *Journal of Aging Studies, 20,* 55–66.

Jervis, L. L., Jackson, M. Y., & Manson, S. M. (2002). Need for, availability of, and barriers to the provision of long-term care services for older American Indians. *Journal of Cross-Cultural Gerontology, 17,* 295–311.

Jervis, L. L., & Manson, S. M. (2007). Cognitive impairment, psychiatric disorders, and problematic behaviors in a tribal nursing home. *Journal of Aging and Health, 19,* 260–274.

Jervis, L. L., Shore, J., Hutt, E., & Manson, S. M. (2007). Suboptimal pharmacotherapy in a tribal nursing home. *Journal of the American Medical Directors Association, 8,* 1–7.

Kersting, R. C. (2001). Predictors of Nursing Home Admission for Older Black Americans. *Journal of Gerontological Social Work, 35,* 33–50.

Kolb, P. J. (1999). A stage of migration approach to understanding nursing home placement in Latino families. *Journal of Multicultural Social Work, 7*(3/4), 95–112.

Kwak, J. & Haley, W. E. (2005). Current research findings on end-of-life decision making among racially or ethnically diverse groups. *The Gerontologist, 45,* 634–641.

Lampley-Dallas, V. T., Mold, J. W., & Flori, D. E. (2001). Perceived needs of African-American caregivers of elders with dementia. *Journal of the National Medical Association, 93*(2), 47–57.

Lee, E. E., Farran, C. J., Tripp-Reimer, T., & Sadler, G. R. (2003). Assessing the cultural appropriateness of the Finding Meaning Through Caregiving Scale for Korean caregivers. *Journal of Nursing Measurement, 11,* 19–28.

Linda, A. M., & Braun, K. L. (1998). Asian and Pacific Islander cultural values: Considerations for health care decision making. *Health & Social Work, 23,* 116–126.

Magilvy, J. K., Congdon, J. G., Martinez, R. J., Davis, R., & Averill, J. (2000). Caring for our own: Health care experiences of rural Hispanic Elders. *Journal of Aging Studies, 14,* 171–190.

McCormick, W. C., Ohata, C. Y., Uomoto, J., Young, H. M., Graves, A. B., Kukull, W., et al. (2002). Similarities and differences in attitudes toward long-term care between Japanese Americans and Caucasian Americans. *Journal of the American Geriatrics Society, 50,* 1149–1155.

McCormick, W. C., Uomoto, J., Young, H., Graves, A. B., Vitaliano, P., Mortimer, J. A., et al. (1996). Attitudes toward use of nursing homes and home care in older Japanese-Americans. *Journal of the American Geriatrics Society, 44,* 769–777.

Mercer, S. O. (1996). Navajo elderly people in a reservation nursing home: Admission predictors and culture care practices. *Social Work, 41,* 181–189.

Miller, S. C., & Prohaska, T. R. (1999). Nursing home admission for African Americans with Alzheimer's disease. *Journals of Gerontology Series A: Biological Sciences & Medical Sciences, 54A,* M365-M369.

Mor, V., Papandonatos, G., & Miller, S. C. (2005). End-of-life hospitalization for African American and non-Latino White nursing home residents: Variation by race and a aacility's racial composition. *Journal of Palliative Medicine, 8,* 58–68.

Mor, V., Zinn, J., Angelelli, J., Teno, J. M., & Miller, S. C. (2004). Driven to tiers: Socioeconomic and racial disparities in the quality of nursing home care. *Milbank Quarterly, 82,* 227–256.

Mui, A. C, Choi, N. G. & Monk, A. (1998). *Long-term care and ethnicity.* Westport, CT: Auburn House.

National Association of Social Workers (NASW). (2001). NASW standards for cultural competence in social work practice. Washington, DC: NASW. Retrieved from http://www.socialworkers.org/practice/standards/NASWCulturalStandards.pdf

Ness, J., Ahmed, A., & Aronow, W. S. (2004). Demographics and payment characteristics of nursing home residents in the United States: A 23-year trend. *Journals of Gerontology Series A: Biological Sciences & Medical Sciences, 59A,* 1213–1217.

Ott, B. B. (2008). Views of African American nursing home residents about living wills. *Geriatric Nursing, 29,* 117–124.

Pourat, N., Andersen, R., & Wallace, S. (2001). Postadmission disparities in nursing home stays of whites and minority elderly. *Journal of Health Care for the Poor and Underserved, 12,* 352–366.

Saha, S., Beach, M. C., & Cooper, L. A. (2008). Patient centeredness, cultural competence and health care quality. *Journal of National Medical Association, 100,* 1275–1285.

Schoenberg, N. E., & Coward, R. T. (1997). Attitudes about entering a nursing home: Comparisons of older rural and urban African American women. *Journal of Aging Studies, 11,* 27–47.

Sengupta, M., Bercovitz, A., & Harris-Kojetin, L. D. (2010). Prevalence and management of pain, by race and dementia among nursing home residents: United States, 2004. NCHS Data Brief *(30),* 1–8. Retrieved from http://www.ncbi.nlm.nih.gov/pubmed/20353701

Shetterly, S. M., Baxter, J., Morgenstern, N. E., Grigsby, J., & Hamman, R. F. (1998). Higher instrumental activities of daily living disability in Hispanics compared with non-Hispanic whites in rural Colorado. The San Luis Valley Health and Aging Study. *American Journal of Epidemiology, 147,* 1019–1027.

Smith, D. B., Feng, Z., Fennell, M. L., Zinn, J., & Mor, V. (2008). Racial disparities in access to long-term care: The illusive pursuit of equity. *Journal of Health Politics, Policy and Law, 33,* 861–881.

Smith, S. H. (2004). End-of-life care decision-making processes of African American families: Implications for culturally-sensitive social work practice. *Journal of Ethnic & Cultural Diversity in Social Work, 13*(2), 1–23.

Stevens, A., Owen, J., Roth, D., Clay, O., Bartolucci, A., & Haley, W. (2004). Predictors of time to nursing home placement in White and African American individuals with dementia. *Journal of Aging and Health, 16,* 375–397.

U.S. Census Bureau (2011). Overview of race and Hispanic origin: 2010. 2010 Census Briefs. C2010BR-02. Retrieved from http://www.census.gov/prod/cen2010/briefs/c2010br-02.pdf

U.S. Department of Health and Human Services (DHHS) & Centers for Disease Control and Prevention. (2010). Health, United States, 2010. Hyattsville, MD: Center for Health Statistics. Retrieved from http://www.cdc.gov/nchs/data/hus/hus10.pdf

U.S. Department of Health and Human Services (DHHS) & Health Resources and Services Administration (HRSA). (2002). Indicators of cultural competence in health care delivery organizations: An organizational cultural competence assessment profile. Retrieved from http://www.hrsa.gov/CulturalCompetence/healthdlvr.pdf

U.S. Department of Health and Human Services (DHHS) & Office of Minority Health (OMH). (2001). National standards for culturally and linguistically appropriate services in health care: Final report. Retrieved from http://minorityhealth.hhs.gov/assets/pdf/checked/finalreport.pdf

Welch, L. C., Teno, J. M., & Mor, V. (2005). End-of-life care in black and white: Race matters for medical care of dying patients and their families. *Journal of the American Geriatrics Society, 53,* 1145–1153.

Yoo, G., & Kim, B. (2010). Remembering sacrifices: Attitude and beliefs among second-generation Korean Americans regarding family support. *Journal of Cross-Cultural Gerontology, 25,* 165–181.

Yue, L., Jun, Y., Xueya, C., Temkin-Greener, H., & Mukamel, D. B. (2011). Association of race and sites of care with pressure ulcers in high-risk nursing home residents. JAMA: *Journal of the American Medical Association, 306,* 179–186.

CHAPTER 19

The Complexities of Caregiving for Minority Older Adults: Rewards and Challenges

Caroline Rosenthal Gelman, Catherine J. Tompkins, and Emily S. Ihara

The population of Americans over 65 years of age is becoming increasingly heterogeneous in terms of socioeconomic status, wealth accumulation, health and disability, work situations, living arrangements, family life, and especially race and ethnicity. The percentage of racial and ethnic minority elders, currently about 20% of the older population, is expected to increase to 42% by 2050.[1] The dramatic growth in the heterogeneity of the older population over the following decades has important consequences for social work practice, policy, and research pertaining to older adults and their families. Medical advances and greater longevity point to healthier and longer lives for many, but both formal and informal caregiving remain a concern as individuals age and develop conditions that require care.

The focus of this chapter is on informal caregiving among minority groups. In 2009, approximately 42 million Americans (19% of all adults) provided unpaid care to an older family member or friend (National Alliance for Caregiving [NAC], 2009). This unpaid care represents an estimated economic value of $450 billion each year (Feinberg, Reinhard, Houser, & Choula, 2011). Informal caregivers are diverse in every sense, and include spouses, children, grandchildren, other relatives, neighbors, and friends. Caregiving is a "heterogeneous phenomenon" (Seltzer, 2006, p. 337); each situation is unique because of the interdependent nature of the caregiving dyad, including the historical relationship, cultural and societal expectations, the economic and financial situations of the caregivers and care receivers, other family members or caregivers involved, local versus long-distance caregiving, and the type of care needed.

Throughout this chapter, we use the broad racial and ethnic categories of African American, Hispanic or Latino, Asian American, Native Hawaiian or Pacific Islander, and American Indian. Ethnic groups share a collective cultural identity and patterns of language, family structures, and social and religious traditions based on presumed common history, geographic origins, or genealogy. Race, a term often used interchangeably with or encompassing ethnicity, emphasizes the notion of common ancestry based primarily on shared biological traits, in particular that of skin color, although race is widely recognized as primarily a social construct (Abizadeh, 2001). Despite these categorizations, there are significant differences with regard to country of origin, language, religion, education, income, duration of residency in the United States, level of acculturation, immigration status, living arrangements, social capital, family support, and access to resources within these groups.

This chapter is organized into three primary sections. After presenting an organizing theoretical framework, we describe the context of caregiving and discuss the various specific challenges caregivers of minority older adults face. Second, we summarize the literature on these caregivers, noting the dearth of research for older American Indians, Native Hawaiians and Pacific Islanders, and subgroups of Asian Americans, Latinos, and black Americans, reflecting both the limitations of existing data sources and the immediacy of need for future research to focus on these groups and subgroups. Finally, we examine some of the specific caregiving interventions tailored for families of color and discuss the implications for practice, policy, and research. The take-home message is that caregiving is complex and is best understood as the interaction of biological, psychological, cultural, economic, familial, and social factors across the life course that affect both the care receivers and caregivers. The lifetime psychosocial experiences of racial and ethnic groups provide multidimensional layers to the intricacies of caregiving, and interventions should address these complexities.

THEORETICAL FRAMEWORK

Pearlin, Mullan, Semple, and Skaff's (1990) stress process model has been very influential in understanding caregivers' varying experiences. The model suggests that caregiver well-being (the outcome in the model) is affected by both primary stressors originating directly from the illness and care of the recipient, as well as by secondary stressors (e.g., family conflict, financial concerns, constriction of social activities) arising as a consequence of caring for the recipient. Internal coping resources and quality and quantity of social supports mediate appraisal of stressors and may account for differences in caregiver experiences. This process occurs in the context of the caregiver's background, which includes race, ethnicity, culture, and socioeconomic status. Subsequent coping models have sought to bring such contextual factors to the forefront in an effort to understand the experiences of minority caregivers (Rozario & DeRienzis, 2008). In some models, culture is seen to affect caregiver outcomes by influencing appraisal of caregiving burden (Aranda & Knight, 1997). The more recent sociocultural stress and coping model provides a better fit with existing research by positing that cultural values play a role by influencing coping resources such as social support and coping styles (Knight & Sayegh, 2010). In addition, as we shall note, differences exist in income, education, family position, level of health and functioning, access to resources, and other contextual variables that are linked to race and ethnicity. Thus, these models help us understand the particular vulnerabilities and strengths experienced by different groups of minority caregivers.

CONTEXT OF CAREGIVING

Members of racial and ethnic minorities face lifelong oppression, racism, and social inequality. With the ageism experienced by many in later life, these elders of color experience what Stoller and Gibson (1994) have aptly labeled as "multiple jeopardy." This cumulative disadvantage over the life course can result in vulnerable, frail elders with decreased access to resources and services, which may further compound the complexity of their family caregivers' tasks.

Higher Rates of Poverty

Elders of color are more likely to live in poverty than white elders. In 2010, 18% of older African Americans, 18% of older Latinos, and 14% of older Asian Americans were poor, compared to 6.8% of older white Americans (Administration on Aging [AOA], 2011). Women, American Indians, and those living alone or with non-relatives are particularly vulnerable to poverty. American Indians are less likely to voice their economic hardships, but poverty is nonetheless a reality (Centers for Disease Control and Prevention [CDC], 2009).

Educational attainment is lower among elders of color than among whites, with the exception of Japanese, Chinese, and Cuban Americans. Poverty and inadequate education are associated with lack of health insurance and lack of accumulated wealth during the life course, which in turn impacts access to services (LaVeist, 2003). Age at immigration is an important consideration, and those who immigrate in later life with limited education and skills have fewer opportunities and less time to accumulate financial resources. For example, Mui and Shibusawa (2008) found that recent Asian American immigrants are more likely to live below the poverty level and are ineligible for Social Security benefits. Financial strain and poverty over the life course are key determinants of health inequalities in later life (Kahn & Pearlin, 2006).

Poorer Health

Over the past century or so, life expectancy has nearly doubled (Wolff & Kaspar, 2006). However, research has consistently shown that poverty, low socioeconomic status, income and wealth inequality, racism, and sexism have detrimental long-term effects on morbidity and mortality, with the most egregious inequities persisting for racial and ethnic minorities in the United States (Gee & Ford, 2011; Sondik, Huang, Klein, & Satcher, 2010). For example, from birth to death, African Americans experience much poorer health than their white counterparts; compared to whites, life expectancy for African Americans is 5.1 years shorter at birth and 1.5 years shorter at age 65 (Angel, 2009). Similarly, overall life expectancy for American Indians/Alaska Natives is approximately 4.6 years shorter than their white counterparts (Trahant, 2010).

Prevalence of disability and chronic illness are also important factors for understanding the health of older adults. For both men and women, American Indians and African Americans have the highest disability prevalence at selected age groups: 60–64, 70–74, and 80–84 (Hummer, Benjamins, & Rogers, 2004). An analysis of disability rates using data from Census 2000 found that among older adults, African Americans had the highest rates of disability, followed by Latinos, Asians and Pacific Islanders, and non-Hispanic whites. When data were disaggregated among the major Latino groups, Puerto Ricans had the highest rates of disability, followed by Mexican Americans, Cuban Americans, Central Americans, and South Americans (Markides & Wallace, 2007). Further, the prevalence of chronic illnesses, such as arthritis, hypertension, heart disease, cancer, and diabetes, is estimated to be twice as high among African Americans as among whites, with younger onset for African Americans (Agency for Healthcare Research and Quality [AHRQ], 2005). Elders of color (particularly African Americans, American Indians, Latinos, and Pacific Islanders) consistently have elevated prevalence and incidence of many chronic diseases, and worse health outcomes than their white counterparts (Bulatao & Anderson, 2004; CDC, 2009; Goins, Moss, Buchwald, & Guralnik, 2007). Older women of color are particularly vulnerable to heart disease, diabetes, and hypertension, and experience more comorbid conditions than white women (Leigh & Huff, 2006). Although the prevalence of severe functional limitations is higher among minority elders, the rate of institutionalization is lower (Dilworth-Anderson, Williams, & Gibson, 2002), underscoring the need for a better understanding of family caregiving among families of color.

Mental Health Risks

Approximately 20% of all persons over 55 years of age experience mental health problems: the three most common are mood disorders, anxiety disorders, and severe cognitive disorders such as Alzheimer's disease (AD; AOA, 2001). Earlier research had concluded that minority older adults, particularly those born outside the United States, have lower rates of psychiatric disorders than their white counterparts. However, a recent study comparing lifetime and 12-month prevalence of psychiatric disorders in a nationally representative sample of older Latino, Asian, African American, and Afro-Caribbean adults with that of older non-Latino white adults uncovered a mixed, complex picture (Jiménez, Alegría, Chen, Chan, & Laderman, 2010). Older whites and Latinos had similar lifetime prevalence rates of depressive disorders, anxiety disorders, and substance use disorders. Asians had significantly lower rates of substance use and psychiatric disorders than whites, and African Americans had significantly lower rates of depressive disorders than whites. Afro-Caribbean older adults did not differ in prevalence rates from white older adults. Latinos had significantly higher 12-month prevalence rates of depressive disorders than whites. Researchers also found that the protective effect of nativity varied according to age, disorder, and ethnicity (Jiménez et al., 2010).

An estimated 5.2 million people age 65 and older have AD (Alzheimer's Association, 2012). The risk of AD is two times higher for African Americans and 1.5 times higher for Latinos because of the prevalence of several known or suspected risk factors for AD, such as high blood pressure, diabetes, and vascular diseases; lower levels of education; and other socioeconomic characteristics (Haan et al., 2003; Kukull et al., 2002; Tang et al., 1998). Furthermore, the specific way that AD presents in minorities potentially increases the burden on caregivers. Dementia-related behaviors, such as combativeness, wandering, and hallucinations—often the most troubling to caregivers—are more likely seen in African Americans and Latinos than whites (Sink, Covinsky, Newcomer, & Yaffe, 2004). Latinos may develop Alzheimer's symptoms on an average nearly seven years earlier than their non-Latino counterparts (Clark et al., 2005), making it more likely that their caregivers will be younger, with multiple familial and work responsibilities to fulfill.

The stigma associated with mental illness, such as depression and AD, presents risks to minority elders, as they may be less likely to seek help than white elders. Underutilization of mental health services is a significant issue for some minority groups, and studies have shown that they tend to delay treatment until symptoms become severe (Ihara & Takeuchi, 2004; U.S. Department of Health and Human Services [DHHS], 1999, 2001). For example, using data from the National Latino and Asian American Study (NLAAS), Nguyen and Lee (2012) found that as Chinese and Vietnamese individuals aged, they were less likely than other Asian American groups to seek mental health services.

Underutilization of Formal Services

Despite significant need, disparities in the access to and utilization of the various health and mental health services have been documented for minority older adults. Research seeking to elucidate the disparity between need and use of services has drawn a complex picture involving socioeconomic, cultural, and structural factors, with patterns of service use varying among minority groups. For example, higher levels of education and income and increased social support seem to facilitate use of services among Latinos (Burnette & Mui, 1995). Conversely, poverty is a barrier to accessing community-based care among Latinos (Wallace, Campbell, & Lew-Ting, 1994). Lack of knowledge regarding existing resources is a significant reason for the underuse of formal services by Latino and African American elders (Burnette & Mui, 1999; Richardson, 1992). Minimal use of formal services may further increase the risk of poor health outcomes by delaying diagnosis and intervention, thus potentially increasing impairment as well as caregiver burden.

Lack of Knowledge Regarding Normal Aging

Lack of knowledge regarding what constitutes normal, healthy aging among minority older adults has been reported in the literature (Hinton, Franz, Yeo, & Levkoff, 2005; Mahoney, Cloutterbuck, Neary, & Zhan, 2005; Ortiz & Fitten, 2000; Rosenthal Gelman, 2010). For example, in a study comparing knowledge of AD among white, Latino, Asian, and African American elders, Latinos and Asians demonstrated the greatest gaps. While 78% of older whites answered at least half of the questions correctly, only 53% of the African Americans, 20% of Asian Americans, and 22% of Latino older adults did so (Ayalon & Arean, 2004). Whether the basis of this misinformation is cultural beliefs or low levels of education is unclear, but poor health literacy is often associated with minority status. Nevertheless, this lack of knowledge contributes to delays in help-seeking, compromised health status, and thus the need for complex caregiving.

Structural Barriers to Accessing Care

Structural barriers including language difficulties, low socioeconomic status, undocumented immigrant status, lack of health insurance, and unreliable transportation preclude some minority elders from receiving care. For example, in a study of over 700 patients presenting to a public hospital emergency room for nonurgent care, Derose and Baker (2000) found that Latino patients with limited English proficiency made significantly lower use of physician services. Minority elders, particularly Latinos, are less likely to have health insurance than white elders, and African Americans and Latino older adults are more likely to have Medicaid or to use Medicare as their only source of health insurance. Older adults of color are also less likely to have a usual source of health care and more likely to have fewer health care visits than white elders (Bulatao & Anderson, 2004).

Discrimination and Stigma

Some research document that minority populations receive poorer quality care, and that health care providers exhibit racial biases in medical diagnosis and treatment (AHRQ, 2005; Smedley et al., 2003; van Ryn & Burke, 2000), for example, by referring people of color less often for more aggressive treatments (Schulman et al., 1999). Stigma surrounding disease, especially mental illness, and fears of dependency prevalent in some racial and cultural groups, especially among older cohorts, may also present barriers to the use of physical and mental health services among minority elders (Conner et al., 2010).

CAREGIVERS

All of these characteristics of minority older adults combine to create a very complex caregiving picture, adding to the challenges of their caregivers' experiences. Compared to white caregivers, non-white caregivers are less likely to be a spouse and more likely to be an adult child, friend, or other family member. In addition, as a group, minority caregivers are more likely to be younger, caring for children under 18 as well as aging relatives; poorer; less educated; underemployed; and in worse mental and physical health than their white counterparts (NAC, 2009; Pinquart & Sörensen, 2005), further impacting the provision of care to older adults. Goins and colleagues (2011) found that within the American Indian population, caregivers also tend to be younger women with more people living in their households, underscoring minority caregivers' multiple caregiving roles. However, there are also minority older adults who are in the role of caregivers to grandchildren or adult children with physical and developmental disabilities. In the United States, 2.7 million families are maintained by a grandparent (U.S. Census Bureau, 2010), and African Americans are twice as likely to become custodial grandparents as other elders (Fuller-Thompson, Minkler, & Driver, 1997).

Given that women are most often assuming the role of informal caregiver, gender differences for caregiving and poverty are important to consider. In a meta-analysis of 229 studies on gender differences, female caregivers had higher levels of caregiver stress and depression, provided more hours of care, assisted with more caregiving tasks, and provided more personal care than male caregivers (Pinquart & Sörensen, 2006). Financially, caregivers are often forced to make difficult choices between work and caregiving responsibilities, which may affect their career trajectories and future retirement income. Women typically have less flexible jobs and make less money than men, which adds to stress at multiple levels. Care recipients are also affected by the labor force realities of their caregivers. For example, caregivers who are working full time provide fewer hours of care, which puts their care recipients at higher risk of unmet needs (Scharlach, Gustavson, & Dal Santo, 2007).

The effect of caregiving on lower income families is a particularly significant concern. In a national study of family caregivers, those with incomes of less than $25,000 per year experienced higher deleterious effects, both in terms of the number of hours of care they provided and the proportion of their income that was spent on care (Evercare, 2007). Caregivers who are women of color face multiple challenges in this role, which are exacerbated by structural societal inequities.

Some studies have shown that racial and ethnic minority elders are more likely to receive informal care from family and friends than non-Hispanic whites (Dilworth-Anderson et al., 2002; Mitchell, Matthews, & Hack, 2000). African American and Latino elders are more likely to live with family and less likely to live alone or in institutional settings than whites, regardless of health status (Angel, Angel, Aranda, & Miles, 2004; Johnson, 1999). For example, Latina dementia caregivers delay institutionalization of their loved ones significantly longer than female white caregivers (Mausbach et al., 2004; see Chapter 18). Within American Indian and Alaska Native families, the term "caregiver" is seldom used. Caring for an American Indian elder is continuing the ancient custom of lifelong care for family. Although many American Indian young adults move away from their tribes and reservations, they often return to provide care to an older family member. In addition to a preference for remaining within their tribes and reservations, American Indian elders are hesitant to leave in fear of losing the benefits they receive from living on the reservation (CDC, 2009).

Impact of Caregiving

Reviews of the substantial literature on the effects of caregiving have revealed that caregivers experience serious negative mental and physical health outcomes from the chronic stress of caring for relatives, including increased rates of depression and other psychological distress, role stress, family conflict, poorer self-rated health, alterations in immune functioning, and even increased mortality (Haley & Bailey, 1999; Ory, Yee, Tennstedt, & Schulz, 2000; Schulz & Sherwood, 2008). A meta-analysis of caregiving studies found that dementia caregivers and spouse caregivers are at particular risk of depression and poor health (Pinquart & Sörenson, 2003). Minority caregivers face increased challenges because of special vulnerabilities both they and their care recipients are likely to experience as a result of their social position (Aranda & Knight, 1997).

Minority Caregivers' Physical and Emotional Health

Minority caregivers' level of mental and physical well-being is an important outcome for understanding their experience and targeting appropriate interventions. A meta-analysis of caregiving studies involving ethnic or racial minorities found that all groups of ethnic minority caregivers reported worse physical health than whites (Pinquart & Sörensen, 2005). Mixed findings exist on minority caregivers' emotional and psychological health. For instance, African American caregivers report lower levels of depression than white caregivers. However, Latino and Asian American caregivers seem to be more depressed than their white counterparts (Harwood et al., 1998; Janevic & Connell, 2001; Pinquart & Sörensen, 2005). A study comparing white American, African American, Japanese American, and Mexican American spousal caregivers of persons with dementia found that the Mexican Americans reported significantly higher rates of depression than any of the other groups (Adams, Aranda, Kemp, & Takagi, 2002).

Another aspect of emotional well-being, sense of burden, presented mixed findings in the meta-analytic study. African American caregivers reported lower appraisal of burden than white caregivers, but differences were not significant between white caregivers and their Latino and Asian American counterparts (Pinquart & Sörensen, 2005). Two other studies reported lower appraisals of stress and greater self-efficacy and perceived benefits of caregiving by Latinos compared to whites (Coon et al., 2004; Depp et al., 2005).

Spirituality and Religiosity

Researchers have examined the role of spirituality and religiosity on the caregiving experience as a source of coping, meaning, and concrete assistance and emotional support from fellow members of religious or spiritual communities (Chang, Noonan, & Tennstedt, 1998; Nightingale, 2003). Studies indicate that religion and spirituality may play an especially important role as a resource in the lives of minority caregivers, particularly African Americans, in the context of multiple historical and sociocultural stressors (Levin, Taylor, & Chatters, 1994; Navaie-Waliser et al., 2001).

Studies of spirituality, aging, and health have shown that spirituality increases social support and promotes health behaviors (George, Larson, Koenig, & McCullough, 2000). Among African American caregivers, spirituality and religiosity are used to increase coping, render meaning, and provide support in the caregiving role (Picot, Debanne, Namazi, & Wykle, 1997). In one study, caregivers often regained a sense of connection to their family member with AD when the family member recited a familiar prayer or song during a religious service (Tompkins & Sorrell, 2008). In some cultures, spirituality is interwoven with a sense of wellness. For example, from a Pacific Islander perspective, the concept of wellness is holistic and reflects a complete state of spiritual, physical, mental, and social balance (Ihara & Vakalahi, 2011). Altogether, this literature suggests the potential significance of spiritual and religious beliefs for both the caregiver and the recipient, and it is important to consider this when working with families of color.

Familism and Social Support

Familism describes the "reliance on family for support, obligation towards family members, and the use of relatives as referents" (Magaña, 1999, p. 466), and is defined as honoring the family name, showing respect for elders, and prioritizing family over self (Schwartz, 2007). Although often considered a Latino cultural value (Sabogal, Marín, Otero-Sabogal, Marín, & Pérez-Stable, 1987), the concept has also been applied to other minority groups (Chamberlain, 2003; Youn, Knight, Jeong, & Benton, 1999). Among immigrant families, familism facilitates the intergenerational transmission of culture, traditions, and values (Sabogal et al., 1987) and has often been considered to provide a mechanism for family members to accept their caregiving role without complaint (Magaña, Schwartz, Rubert, & Szapocznik, 2006).

However, despite the long-held view that minorities' strong value of and reliance on family leads to greater actual involvement of extended family in the care of sick members and reduced perception of burden compared to white caregivers, more recent research has reported low levels of social support among ethnic minority caregivers. In a review of studies on the impact of familism on Latino, Korean, Korean American, Japanese American, and African American caregivers, Knight and his colleagues (2002) found that the expected relationship of higher familism with lower burden based on the idea that this value would indicate a willingness, desire, and expectation to provide care, was not always apparent; in some cases, higher familism was actually associated with higher distress. Further studies have replicated such findings (Kim, Knight, & Flynn Longmire, 2007). Rozario and DeRienzis (2008) also found that more traditional beliefs about caregiving were related to more depressive symptoms in female African American caregivers. In addition, studies of diverse caregivers have found that minority groups may not actually have more available support than their white counterparts (Janevic & Connell, 2001). For example, Valle, Yamada, and Barrio (2004) report that Latino caregivers of relatives with dementia, compared to their white counterparts, had smaller social support networks, engaged in less help-seeking, and reported higher distress. These findings refine our understanding of the varied impact of familism among minority groups, including the possibility that for some caregivers, it complicates rather than facilitates caregiving, particularly when support from extended family is not available.

Positive Aspects of Caregiving

Although many studies have focused on the burden to caregivers of providing care to an older adult, it is important to note that caregivers also report positive aspects to caregiving. These include feelings of usefulness and being appreciated, a sense of competence and fulfillment, and the opportunity of sharing feelings of love and empathy with their care recipient (Toseland & Smith, 2001). Caregivers who report more positive feelings are less likely to report depression, burden, or poor health (Cohen, Colantonio, & Vernich, 2002). Caregivers are often able to realize the positive aspects of caregiving when they are not struggling with financial or social support challenges (Lee & Bronstein, 2010). Research has found that some groups of minority caregivers may experience caregiving more positively than whites. For example, in one study, Latino caregivers reported greater perceived benefits of caregiving than their white counterparts (Coon et al., 2004). A study comparing African American and white caregivers found that African Americans reported lower anxiety, better well-being, greater religious coping and participation, and more perceived benefits of caregiving than whites (Haley et al., 2004). Acknowledging the complexity of caregiving, with both its challenges and satisfactions, is important, particularly in the development of supportive interventions for caregivers.

INTERVENTIONS FOR CAREGIVERS

Given the complexity of the caregiving situation and the significant strain that caregivers experience, a variety of interventions to assist caregivers as well as resources for their care recipients have been developed. These can be broadly classified as resources that provide psychoeducation to caregiver and care recipient dyads around issues of caregiving, information about particular conditions and relevant referrals, counseling interventions that support caregivers in their role, and different forms of respite care to reduce caregiver burden. Evidence from a systematic review study indicates that most interventions have not been tailored specifically to the needs of minority older adults and their caregivers, and studies that evaluate the impact of cultural tailoring of caregiver interventions are imperative (Nápoles, Chadiha, Eversley, & Moreno-John, 2010).

The Family Care Navigator (Family Caregiver Alliance, 2012), a state-by-state, online guide to government, nonprofit, and private caregiver support programs, is an example of a psychoeducational resource for caregivers. The navigator includes information on government health and disability programs, legal resources, living arrangements, and disease-specific organizations. Another example of a psychoeducational resource is Elderpedia, a wiki-format database of information regarding resources in northern Manhattan created for and by older adults and their caregivers (http://elderpedia.org/). The site is available in Spanish and is tailored to the needs of residents of this ethnically diverse neighborhood. For example, one can access Chinese and Korean-speaking geriatric specialists.

Reviews of the literature indicate that supportive interventions for caregivers (most of which target dementia caregiving) generally are effective in producing clinically meaningful improvements in psychological well-being, and that multifaceted, individualized interventions have the strongest impact (Bourgeois, Schulz, & Burgio, 1996; Pinquart & Sörensen, 2006; Schulz et al., 2002; Sörensen, Pinquart, & Duberstein, 2002). The Resources for Enhancing Alzheimer's Caregiver Health (REACH) initiative, a multicomponent intervention that has demonstrated the effectiveness of a range of methods, including didactic instruction, role-playing, skills training, stress management techniques, and telephone support, has been tailored to serve ethnically diverse caregivers (Belle et al., 2006; Schulz et al., 2003).

A range of respite services is available to provide primary caregivers with some relief from caring for their care recipient. It has been suggested that use of informal extended family and community volunteers is particularly common among minority groups, although research indicates that existing familial and social support may not be sufficient for these families. Respite can be provided in-home by personal care or skilled home health aides or outside the home in adult day programs or residential treatment facilities. Nevertheless, such respite services are often underutilized and providers are constantly challenged to encourage caregivers to use them. Montoro-Rodriguez, Kosoloski, and Montgomery (2003) found that a practice-oriented model can help us understand barriers to respite service use among white and Latino caregivers and thus allows us to enhance timely use of respite among these groups of caregivers. Unlike the behavioral model of service use focusing on caregiver characteristics, such as age, gender, ethnicity, education, and relationship to the care receiver, the practice-oriented model explores the caregiver's knowledge and access to available services. These factors can often be more easily adjusted to increase service use (Yeatts, Crow, & Folts, 1992).

A new model for how caregivers and care recipients manage their respite care needs is the Cash and Counseling Program, which has introduced participant-directed programs into the Medicaid programs of 15 states. This intervention provides people with disabilities and frail older adults the option to manage a flexible budget, choose a care provider, and decide what mix of interventions best meets their personal care needs (National Resource Center for Participant-Directed Services, 2012). It shows promise for positive outcomes for care recipients and their caregivers (Carlson, Foster, Dale, & Brown, 2007). Although evaluation studies are not yet prevalent, one finding suggests that African American and Latino consumers show substantially higher interest and slightly higher enrollment in the Cash and Counseling option compared to white consumers. This may be attributed to a strong family network, wanting to remain independent and in control, and bringing more needed jobs to the African American and Latino communities (Mahoney, Simon-Rusinowitz, Loughlin, Desmond, & Squillace, 2004).

IMPLICATIONS FOR SOCIAL WORK EDUCATION, PRACTICE, RESEARCH, AND POLICY

Over the last several decades, a substantial body of research has demonstrated that families of color and their caregivers are at high risk for a range of challenges related to physical and mental health, finances, employment, wealth accumulation, and retirement over the life course. Lifelong inequities among racial and ethnic minorities increase the vulnerabilities of both care receivers and caregivers, which are exacerbated by structural barriers within the service delivery system. These ubiquitous inequities contribute to the complexity of the caregiving experience for families of color, and highlight the urgency for social workers to address the many existing gaps through education, practice, research, and policy efforts.

Despite the vast literature on caregiving in general, research pertaining to the needs and experiences of racial/ethnic minority older adults and their caregivers is limited, particularly for American Indians, Pacific Islanders, specific Asian American and Latino subgroups, and religious minorities groups such as Muslim Americans. This lack of knowledge could be countered by a basic perspective in social work—person in environment—which stresses the importance of understanding the heterogeneity and complexity discussed throughout this chapter while also accounting for the specific context of an individual's life. Cultural efficacy may be an important mechanism in efforts toward more equitable access and utilization of services for older adults and their caregivers. For example, social workers who are working with immigrant families may encounter language issues, generational differences, differing cultural expectations, and varying communication styles within the same family. Such issues can be addressed within social work education and reinforced at the micro and macro levels within social work practice.

On the policy level, several federal programs and initiatives are in place that provide direct support to caregivers in the form of respite care, education and training, tax relief, unpaid job-protected leave, and cash assistance through laws such as the Lifespan Respite Care Act (P. L. 109–442), Part E of the Older Americans Act related to the National Family Caregiver Support Program (P. L. 109–365), new provisions under Title III, and the Family Medical Leave Act (P. L. 103–3). Other federal programs that provide home and community-based long-term care may help the care recipient and indirectly benefit caregivers. However, other recent attempts to pass legislation that would expand caregiver services and supports, increase flexible workplace accommodations and income security policies for employed caregivers, and provide additional tax credits for caregivers have been unsuccessful (Colello, 2009). Despite the growing need for such policies, the realities of the economic downturn, fears of the unsustainability of the national debt, and the current state of divisive and partisan politics continue to pose a challenge to the enactment of such policies. Caregiver-specific support services and policies, including those that address culturally specific preferences and needs, are crucial and should be expanded, particularly in light of the strain and long-term health and financial effects on families of color. Additionally, efforts to eliminate inequities in the workplace, particularly for women and people of color, and provide better health care coverage for all segments of the population will ultimately create better living and working conditions for the diverse caregivers in our society.

NOTE

1. The projected increase in the older population varies by group. The percentage of African Americans who are over 65 years of age is expected to grow from 9% in 2010 to 18% by 2050. The corresponding proportion for Latinos is expected to grow from 6% to 13% and for Asian Americans from 9% to 22%. The smallest racial groups are projected to see the largest proportional growth in their over-65 cohort. For example, the proportion of American Indians and Alaska Natives over 65 years is projected to more than double, from 7% in 2010 to 17% by 2050, and the corresponding proportion for Native Hawaiians and other Pacific Islanders is projected to nearly triple, from 7% to 18%, by 2050 (Vincent & Velkoff, 2010).

REFERENCES

Abizadeh, A. (2001). Ethnicity, race, and a possible humanity. *World Order, 33*(1), 23–34.

Adams, B., Aranda, M., Kemp, B., & Takagi, K. (2002). Ethnic and gender differences in distress among Anglo American, African American, Japanese American, and Mexican American spousal caregivers of persons with dementia. *Journal of Clinical Geropsychology, 8*, 279–301. doi:10.1023/A:1019627323558.

Administration on Aging (AOA). (2001). Older adults and mental health: Issues and opportunities. Washington, DC: U.S. Department of Health and Human Services. Retrieved from http://www.globalaging.org/health/us/mental.pdf

Administration on Aging (AOA). (2011). A profile of older Americans: 2011. Washington, DC: U.S. Department of Health and Human Services. Retrieved from http://aoa.gov/AoARoot/Aging_Statistics/Profile/2011/docs/2011profile.pdf

Agency for Healthcare Research and Quality (AHRQ). (2005). National healthcare disparities report, 2005 (AHRQ Publication No. 06–0017). Rockville, MD: U.S. Department of Health and Human Services. Retrieved from http://archive.ahrq.gov/qual/nhdr05/nhdr05.pdf

Alzheimer's Association. (2012). Alzheimer's Association Report: 2012 Alzheimer's disease facts and figures. *Alzheimer's & Dementia, 8*(2), 131–168.

Angel, J. L., Angel, R. J., Aranda, M. P., & Miles, T. P. (2004). Can the family still cope? Social support and health as determinants of nursing home use in the older Mexican-origin population. *Journal of Aging And Health, 16*(3), 338–354.

Angel, R. J. (2009). Structural and cultural factors in successful aging among older Hispanics. *Family & Community Health, 32*(1 Supplement), S46–S57.

Aranda, M. P., & Knight, B. G. (1997). The influence of ethnicity and culture on the caregiver stress and coping process: A sociocultural review and analysis. *The Gerontologist, 37*(3), 342–354.

Ayalon, L., & Areán, P. A. (2004). Knowledge of Alzheimer's disease in four ethnic groups of older adults. *International Journal of Geriatric Psychiatry, 19*(1), 51–57.

Belle, S. H., Burgio, L., Burns, R., Coon, D., Czaja, S. J., Gallagher-Thompson, D.,...Zhang, S. Resources for Enhancing Alzheimer's Caregiver Health (REACH) II Investigators. (2006). Enhancing the quality of life of dementia caregivers from different ethnic or racial groups: a randomized, controlled trial. *Annals of Internal Medicine, 145*(10), 727–738.

Bourgeois, M. S., Schulz, R., & Burgio, L. (1996). Interventions for caregivers of patients with Alzheimer's disease: A review and analysis of content, process, and outcomes. *International Journal of Aging & Human Development, 43*(1), 35–92.

Bulatao, R. A., & Anderson, N. B. (Eds.). (2004). Understanding racial and ethnic differences in health in late life: A research agenda (Panel on Race, Ethnicity, and Health in Later Life, Committee on Population, Division of Behavioral and Social Sciences and Education, National Research Council). Washington, DC: The National Academies Press.

Burnette, D., & Mui, A. C. (1995). In-home and community-based service utilization by three groups of elderly Hispanics: A national perspective. *Social Work Research, 19*(4), 197–206.

Burnette, D., & Mui, A. C. (1999). Physician utilization by Hispanic elderly persons: National perspective. *Medical Care, 37*(4), 362–374.

Carlson, B. L., Foster, L., Dale, S. B., & Brown, R. (2007). Effects of cash and counseling on personal care and well-being. *Health Services Research, 42*(1 Pt 2), 467–487.

Centers for Disease Control and Prevention (CDC), National Center for Chronic Disease Prevention and Health Promotion (Producer). (2009). Caregiving in Indian country [Transcript from audio podcast]. Retrieved from http://www2c.cdc.gov/podcasts/media/pdf/caregivingIndianCountry.pdf

Chamberlain, M. (2003). Rethinking Caribbean families: Extending the limits. *Community, Work & Family, 6*, 63–76. doi: 1080/1366880032000063905

Chang, B. H., Noonan, A. E., & Tennstedt, S. L. (1998). The role of religion/spirituality in coping with caregiving for disabled elders. *The Gerontologist, 38*(4), 463–470.

Clark, C. M., DeCarli, C., Mungas, D., Chui, H. I., Higdon, R., Nuñez, J., . . . van Belle, G. (2005). Earlier onset of Alzheimer disease symptoms in Latino individuals compared with Anglo individuals. *Archives of Neurology, 62*(5), 774–778.

Cohen, C. A., Colantonio, A., & Vernich, L. (2002). Positive aspects of caregiving: Rounding out the caregiver experience. *International Journal of Geriatric Psychiatry, 17*(2), 184–188.

Colello, K. J. (2009). Family caregiving to the older population: Background, federal programs, and issues for Congress (CRS Reports No. RL34123). Washington, DC: Congressional Research Service.

Conner, K. O., Copeland, V. C., Grote, N. K., Koeske, G., Rosen, D., Reynolds, C. F., et al. (2010). Mental health treatment seeking among older adults with depression: the impact of stigma and race. *The American Journal of Geriatric Psychiatry: Official Journal of the American Association for Geriatric Psychiatry, 18*(6), 531–543.

Coon, D. W., Rubert, M., Solano, N., Mausbach, B., Kraemer, H., Arguëlles, T., . . . Gallagher-Thompson, D. (2004). Well-being, appraisal, and coping in Latina and Caucasian female dementia caregivers: Findings from the REACH study. *Aging & Mental Health, 8*(4), 330–345.

Depp, C., Sorocco, K., Kasl-Godley, J., Thompson, L., Rabinowitz, Y., & Gallagher-Thompson, D. (2005). Caregiver self-efficacy, ethnicity, and kinship differences in dementia caregivers. *The American Journal of Geriatric Psychiatry: Official Journal of the American Association for Geriatric Psychiatry, 13*(9), 787–794.

Derose, K. P., & Baker, D. W. (2000). Limited English proficiency and Latinos' use of physician services. *Medical Care Research and Review: MCRR, 57*(1), 76–91.

Dilworth-Anderson, P., Williams, I. C., & Gibson, B. E. (2002). Issues of race, ethnicity, and culture in caregiving research: A 20-year review (1980–2000). *The Gerontologist, 42*(2), 237–272.

Evercare. (2007). Family caregivers—What they spend, what they sacrifice. Minnetonka, MN: Evercare and National Alliance for Caregiving. Retrieved from http://www.caregiving.org/data/Evercare_NAC_CaregiverCostStudyFINAL20111907.pdf

Family Caregiver Alliance. (2012). Family caregiver navigator: State-by-state help for family caregivers. Retrieved from http://caregiver.org/caregiver/jsp/fcn_content_node.jsp?nodeid=2083

Feinberg, L., Reinhard, S. C., Houser, A., & Choula, R. (2011). Valuing the invaluable: 2011 update: The growing contributions and costs of family caregiving. Washington, DC: AARP Public Policy Institute. Retrieved from http://assets.aarp.org/rgcenter/ppi/ltc/i51-caregiving.pdf

Fuller-Thomson, E., Minkler, M., & Driver, D. (1997). A profile of grandparents raising grandchildren in the United States. *The Gerontologist, 37*(3), 406–411.

Gee, G. C., & Ford, C. L. (2011). Structural racism and health inequities: Old issues, new directions. Du Bois Review, 8(1), 115–132. doi:10.10170S1742058X11000130

George, L. K., Larson, D. B., Koenig, H. G., & McCullough, M. E. (2000). Spirituality and health: What we know, what we need to know. *Journal of Social and Clinical Psychology, 19*(1), 102–116. doi:10.1521/jscp.2000.19.1.102

Goins, R. T., Moss, M., Buchwald, D., & Guralnik, J. M. (2007). Disability among older American Indians and Alaska Natives: An analysis of the 2000 Census Public Use Microdata Sample. *The Gerontologist, 47*(5), 690–696.

Goins, R. T., Spencer, S. M., McGuire, L. C., Goldberg, J., Wen, Y., & Henderson, J. A. (2011). Adult caregiving among American Indians: The role of cultural factors. *The Gerontologist, 51*, 310–320. doi:10.1093/geront/gnq101

Haan, M. N., Mungas, D. M., Gonzalez, H. M., Ortiz, T. A., Acharya, A., & Jagust, W. J. (2003). Prevalence of dementia in older latinos: The influence of type 2 diabetes mellitus, stroke and genetic factors. *Journal of the American Geriatrics Society, 51*(2), 169–177.

Haley, W. E., & Bailey, S. (1999). Research on family caregiving in Alzheimer's disease: Implications for practice and policy. In B. Vellas & J. L. Fitten (Eds.), *Research and practice in Alzheimer's disease* (Vol. 2, pp. 321–332). Paris, France: Serdi.

Haley, W. E., Gitlin, L. N., Wisniewski, S. R., Mahoney, D. F., Coon, D. W., Winter, L., . . . Ory, M. (2004). Well-being, appraisal, and coping in African-American and Caucasian dementia caregivers: Findings from the REACH study. *Aging & Mental Health, 8*(4), 316–329.

Harwood, D. G., Barker, W. W., Cantillon, M., Loewenstein, D. A., Ownby, R., & Duara, R. (1998). Depressive symptomatology in first-degree family caregivers of Alzheimer disease patients: A cross-ethnic comparison. *Alzheimer Disease and Associated Disorders, 12*(4), 340–346.

Hinton, L., Franz, C. E., Yeo, G., & Levkoff, S. E. (2005). Conceptions of dementia in a multiethnic sample of family caregivers. *Journal of the American Geriatrics Society, 53*(8), 1405–1410.

Hummer, R. A., Benjamins, M. R., & Rogers, R. G. (2004). Racial and ethnic disparities in health and mortality among the U.S. elderly population. In N. B. Anderson, R. A. Bulatao, & B. Cohen (Eds.), *Critical perspectives on racial and ethnic differences in health in late life* (pp. 53–94). Panel on Race, Ethnicity, and Health in Later Life, National Research Council, Committee on Population, Division of Behavioral and Social Sciences and Education. Washington, DC: The National Academies Press.

Ihara, E. S., & Takeuchi, D. T. (2004). Racial and ethnic minorities. In B. L. Levin, J. Petrila, & K. D. Hennessy (Eds.), *Mental health services: A public health perspective* (2nd ed., pp. 310–329). New York, NY: Oxford University Press.

Ihara, E. S., & Vakalahi, H. F. O. (2011). Spirituality: The essence of wellness among Tongan and Samoan elders. *Journal of Religion & Spirituality in Social Work: Social Thought, 30*, 405–421. doi:10.1080/15426432.2011.619916

Janevic, M. R., & Connell, C. M. (2001). Racial, ethnic, and cultural differences in the dementia caregiving experience: Recent findings. *The Gerontologist, 41*(3), 334–347.

Jiménez, D. E., Alegría, M., Chen, C. N., Chan, D., & Laderman, M. (2010). Prevalence of psychiatric illnesses in older ethnic minority adults. *Journal of the American Geriatrics Society, 58*(2), 256–264.

Johnson, C. L. (1999). Fictive kin among oldest old African Americans in the San Francisco Bay area. *The Journals of Gerontology. Series B, Psychological Sciences and Social Sciences, 54*(6), S368–S375.

Kahn, J. R., & Pearlin, L. I. (2006). Financial strain over the life course and health among older adults. *Journal of Health and Social Behavior, 47*(1), 17–31.

Kim, J. H., Knight, B. G., & Longmire, C. V. (2007). The role of familism in stress and coping processes among African American and White dementia caregivers: Effects on mental and physical health. *Health Psychology: Official Journal of the Division of Health Psychology, American Psychological Association, 26*(5), 564–576.

Knight, B. G., & Sayegh, P. (2010). Cultural values and caregiving: The updated sociocultural stress and coping model. *The Journals of Gerontology. Series B, Psychological Sciences and Social Sciences, 65B*(1), 5–13.

Knight, B. G., Robinson, G. S., Flynn Longmire, C. V., Chun, M., Nakao, K., & Kim, J. H. (2002). Cross cultural issues in caregiving for persons with dementia: Do familism values reduce burden and distress? *Ageing International, 27*(3), 70–94. doi:10.1007/s12126–003-1003-y

Kukull, W. A., Higdon, R., Bowen, J. D., McCormick, W. C., Teri, L., Schellenberg, G. D.,…Larson, E. B. (2002). Dementia and Alzheimer disease incidence: A prospective cohort study. *Archives of Neurology, 59*(11), 1737–1746.

LaVeist, T. (2003). Pathways to progress in eliminating racial disparities in health. *Public Policy and Aging Report, 13*(3), 19–22.

Lee, Y., & Bronstein, L. R. (2010). When do Korean-American dementia caregivers find meaning in caregiving?: The role of culture and differences between spouse and child caregivers. *Journal of Ethnic and Cultural Diversity in Social Work, 19*(1), 73–86. doi:10.1080/15313200903547756

Leigh, W. A., & Huff, D. (2006). *Women of color health data book* (3rd ed.). Bethesda, MD: Office of the Director, National Institutes of Health.

Levin, J. S., Taylor, R. J., & Chatters, L. M. (1994). Race and gender differences in religiosity among older adults: findings from four national surveys. *Journal of Gerontology, 49*(3), S137–S145.

Magaña, S. M. (1999). Puerto Rican families caring for an adult with mental retardation: Role of familism. *American Journal of Mental Retardation: AJMR, 104*(5), 466–482.

Magaña, S., Schwartz, S. J., Rubert, M. P., & Szapocznik, J. (2006). Hispanic caregivers of adults with mental retardation: importance of family functioning. *American Journal of Mental Retardation: AJMR, 111*(4), 250–262.

Mahoney, D. F., Cloutterbuck, J., Neary, S., & Zhan, L. (2005). African American, Chinese, and Latino family caregivers' impressions of the onset and diagnosis of dementia: Cross-cultural similarities and differences. *The Gerontologist, 45*(6), 783–792.

Mahoney, K. J., Simon-Rusinowitz, L., Loughlin, D. M., Desmond, S. M., & Squillace, M. R. (2004). Determining personal care consumers' preferences for a consumer-directed cash and counseling option: Survey results from Arkansas, Florida, New Jersey, and New York elders and adults with physical disabilities. *Health services Research, 39*(3), 643–664.

Markides, K. S., & Wallace, S. P. (2007). Minority elders in the United States: Implications for public policy. In R. A. Pruchno & M. A. Smyer (Eds.), Challenges of an aging society: Ethical dilemmas and political issues (pp. 192–216). Baltimore, MD: The Johns Hopkins University Press.

Mausbach, B. T., Coon, D. W., Depp, C., Rabinowitz, Y. G., Wilson-Arias, E., Kraemer, H. C.,…Gallagher-Thompson, D. (2004). Ethnicity and time to institutionalization of dementia patients: A comparison of Latina and Caucasian female family caregivers. *Journal of the American Geriatrics Society, 52*(7), 1077–1084.

Mitchell, J., Mathews, H. F., & Hack, K. A. (2000). Differences by race in long-term care plans. *Journal of Applied Gerontology, 19*, 424–440. doi:10.1177/073346480001900404

Montoro-Rodriguez, J., Kosloski, K., & Montgomery, R. J. (2003). Evaluating a practice-oriented service model to increase the use of respite services among minorities and rural caregivers. *The Gerontologist, 43*(6), 916–924.

Mui, A. C., & Shibusawa, T. (2008). Asian American elders in the twenty-first century: Key indicators of well-being. New York, NY: Columbia University Press.

Nápoles, A. M., Chadiha, L., Eversley, R., & Moreno-John, G. (2010). Reviews: Developing culturally sensitive dementia caregiver interventions: Are we there yet? *American Journal of Alzheimer's Disease and Other Dementias, 25*(5), 389–406.

National Alliance for Caregiving (NAC). (2009). Caregiving in the U.S. 2009. Washington, DC: National Alliance for Caregiving and AARP. Retrieved from http://www.caregiving.org/data/Caregiving_in_the_US_2009_full_report.pdf

National Resource Center for Participant-Directed Services. (2012). Cash & counseling. Retrieved from http://www.bc.edu/schools/gssw/nrcpds/cash_and_counseling.html/search?TextIndex=enrollment&start:int=110

Navaie-Waliser, M., Feldman, P. H., Gould, D. A., Levine, C., Kuerbis, A. N., & Donelan, K. (2001). The experiences and challenges of informal caregivers: Common themes and differences among whites, blacks, and hispanics. *The Gerontologist, 41*(6), 733–741.

Nguyen, D., & Lee, R. (2012). Asian immigrants' mental health service use: An application of the life course perspective. *Asian American Journal of Psychology, 3*(1), 53–63. doi:10.1037/a0026865

Nightingale, M. C. (2003). Religion, spirituality, and ethnicity: What it means for caregivers of persons with Alzheimer's disease and related disorders. *Dementia, 2,* 379–391. doi: 10.1177/14713012030023006

Ortiz, F., & Fitten, L. J. (2000). Barriers to healthcare access for cognitively impaired older Hispanics. *Alzheimer Disease and Associated Disorders, 14*(3), 141–150.

Ory, M., Yee, J. L., Tennstedt, S., & Schulz, R. (2000). The extent and impact of dementia care: Unique challenges faced by family caregivers. In R. Schulz (Ed.), *Handbook on dementia caregiving* (pp. 1–32). New York, NY: Springer.

Pearlin, L. I., Mullan, J. T., Semple, S. J., & Skaff, M. M. (1990). Caregiving and the stress process: An overview of concepts and their measures. *The Gerontologist, 30*(5), 583–594.

Picot, S. J., Debanne, S. M., Namazi, K. H., & Wykle, M. L. (1997). Religiosity and perceived rewards of black and white caregivers. *The Gerontologist, 37*(1), 89–101.

Pinquart, M., & Sörensen, S. (2003). Differences between caregivers and noncaregivers in psychological health and physical health: A meta-analysis. *Psychology and Aging, 18*(2), 250–267.

Pinquart, M., & Sörensen, S. (2005). Ethnic differences in stressors, resources, and psychological outcomes of family caregiving: A meta-analysis. *The Gerontologist, 45*(1), 90–106.

Pinquart, M., & Sörensen, S. (2006). Gender differences in caregiver stressors, social resources, and health: An updated meta-analysis. *The Journals of Gerontology. Series B, Psychological Sciences and Social Sciences, 61*(1), P33–P45.

Richardson, V. (1992). Service use among African American elderly people. *Social Work, 37*(1), 47–54.

Rosenthal Gelman, C. (2010). Learning from recruitment challenges: Barriers to diagnosis, treatment, and research participation for Latinos with symptoms of Alzheimer's disease. *Journal of Gerontological Social Work, 53,* 94–114. doi:10.1080/01634370903361847

Rozario, P. A., & DeRienzis, D. (2008). Familism beliefs and psychological distress among African American women caregivers. *The Gerontologist, 48*(6), 772–780.

Sabogal, F., Marín, G., Otero-Sabogal, R., Marín, B. V., & Pérez-Stable, E. J. (1987). Hispanic familism and acculturation: What changes and what doesn't? *Hispanic Journal of Behavioral Sciences, 9,* 397–412.

Scharlach, A. E., Gustavson, K., & Dal Santo, T. S. (2007). Assistance received by employed caregivers and their care recipients: Who helps care recipients when caregivers work full time? *The Gerontologist, 47*(6), 752–762.

Schulman, K. A., Berlin, J. A., Harless, W., Kerner, J. F., Sistrunk, S., Gersh, B. J., … Escarce, J. J. (1999). The effect of race and sex on physicians' recommendations for cardiac catheterization. *The New England Journal of Medicine, 340*(8), 618–626.

Schulz, R., & Sherwood, P. R. (2008). Physical and mental health effects of family caregiving. *The American Journal of Nursing, 108*(9 Supplement), 23–7; quiz 27.

Schulz, R., Burgio, L., Burns, R., Eisdorfer, C., Gallagher-Thompson, D., Gitlin, L. N., et al. (2003). Resources for Enhancing Alzheimer's Caregiver Health (REACH): overview, site-specific outcomes, and future directions. *The Gerontologist, 43*(4), 514–520.

Schulz, R., O'Brien, A., Czaja, S., Ory, M., Norris, R., Martire, L. M., … Stevens, A. (2002). Dementia caregiver intervention research: in search of clinical significance. *The Gerontologist, 42*(5), 589–602.

Schwartz, S. J. (2007). The applicability of familism to diverse ethnic groups: a preliminary study. *The Journal of Social Psychology, 147*(2), 101–118.

Seltzer, M. (2006). Family and intergenerational social work practice in special caregiving situations. In B. Berkman & S. D'Ambruoso (Eds.), *Handbook of social work in health and aging* (pp. 337–338). New York, NY: Oxford University Press.

Sink, K. M., Covinsky, K. E., Newcomer, R., & Yaffe, K. (2004). Ethnic differences in the prevalence and pattern of dementia-related behaviors. *Journal of the American Geriatrics Society, 52*(8), 1277–1283.

Smedley, B. D., Stith, A. Y., & Nelson, A. R. (Eds.). (2003). *Unequal treatment: Confronting racial and ethnic disparities in health care.* Washington, DC: The National Academies Press.

Sondik, E. J., Huang, D. T., Klein, R. J., & Satcher, D. (2010). Progress toward the healthy people 2010 goals and objectives. *Annual Review of Public Health, 31,* 271–814.

Sörensen, S., Pinquart, M., & Duberstein, P. (2002). How effective are interventions with caregivers? An updated meta-analysis. *The Gerontologist, 42*(3), 356–372.

Stoller, E., & Gibson, R. (1994). *Worlds of difference.* Thousand Oaks, CA: Pine Forge Press.

Tang, M. X., Stern, Y., Marder, K., Bell, K., Gurland, B., Lantigua, R.,...Mayeux, R. (1998). The APOE-epsilon4 allele and the risk of Alzheimer disease among African Americans, whites, and Hispanics. *JAMA: The Journal of the American Medical Association, 279*(10), 751–755.

Tompkins, C. J., & Sorrell, J. M. (2008). Older adults with Alzheimer's disease in a faith community. *Journal of Psychosocial Nursing and Mental Health Services, 46*(1), 22–25.

Toseland, R., & Smith, T. (2001). Supporting caregivers through education and training. A technical assistance monograph prepared for the National Family Caregiver Support Program Initiative of the U.S. Administration on Aging. Washington, DC: U.S. Department of Health & Human Services.

Trahant, M. (2010, May 4). Measuring the progress in native health life expectancy for Native Americans [Web log post]. Retrieved from the race-talk website, a blog hosted by the Kirwan Institute for the Study of Race and Ethnicity at The Ohio State University, http://www.race-talk.org/?p=4115

U.S. Census Bureau. (2010). Grandchildren under 18 years living with a grandparent household by grandparent responsibility and presence of parent (Table B10002). Retrieved from U.S. Census Bureau, 2010 American Community Survey website: http://factfinder2.census.gov/rest/dnldController/deliver?_ts=350840804039

U.S. Department of Health and Human Services (DHHS). (1999). Mental health: A report of the Surgeon General. Rockville, MD: U.S. Department of Health and Human Services, Substance Abuse and Mental Health Services Administration, Center for Mental Health Services, National Institutes of Health, National Institute of Mental Health. Retrieved from http://www.surgeongeneral.gov/library/mentalhealth/home.html

U.S. Department of Health and Human Services (DHHS). (2001). Mental health: Culture, race, and ethnicity—A supplement to mental health: A report of the Surgeon General. Rockville, MD: U.S. Department of Health and Human Services, Substance Abuse and Mental Health Services Administration, Center for Mental Health Services. Retrieved from http://www.surgeongeneral.gov/library/mentalhealth/cre/sma-01–3613.pdf

Valle, R., Yamada, A. M., & Barrio, C. (2004). Ethnic differences in social network help-seeking strategies among Latino and Euro-Aamerican dementia caregivers. *Aging & Mental Health, 8*(6), 535–543.

van Ryn, M., & Burke, J. (2000). The effect of patient race and socio-economic status on physicians' perceptions of patients. *Social Science & Medicine (1982), 50*(6), 813–828.

Vincent, G. K., & Velkoff, V. A. (2010). The next four decades: The older population in the United States: 2010 to 2050 (Current Population Reports No. P25–1138). Washington, DC: U.S. Census Bureau. Retrieved from http://www.census.gov/prod/2010pubs/p25–1138.pdf

Wallace, S. P., Campbell, K., & Lew-Ting, C. Y. (1994). Structural barriers to the use of formal in-home services by elderly Latinos. *Journal of Gerontology, 49*(5), S253–S263.

Wolff, J. L., & Kasper, J. D. (2006). Caregivers of frail elders: Updating a national profile. *The Gerontologist, 46*(3), 344–356.

Yeatts, D. E., Crow, T., & Folts, E. (1992). Service use among low-income minority elderly: Strategies for overcoming barriers. *The Gerontologist, 32*(1), 24–32.

Youn, G., Knight, B. G., Jeong, H. S., & Benton, D. (1999). Differences in familism values and caregiving outcomes among Korean, Korean American, and White American dementia caregivers. *Psychology and Aging, 14*(3), 355–364.

CHAPTER 20

Older Adults of Color With Developmental Disabilities and Serious Mental Illness: Experiences and Service Patterns

Sandy Magaña and Subharati Ghosh

People with developmental disabilities (DD) and serious mental illness (SMI) are now experiencing increased life expectancy (Janicki, Dalton, Henderson, & Davidson, 1999) due to improved medical and technological advances. They are living to ages 70 and above, and experiencing similar health challenges as the general aging population, though, often at an accelerated rate. Although some of these challenges can be attributed to the nature of the disability itself, other contributing factors may include medication side effects, substance abuse, lack of proper preventive checkups, and limited age-appropriate services or coordination between agencies serving older adults and people with DD and SMI. The goal of this chapter is to show how these factors intersect with race and ethnicity in shaping the experiences of families from racial and ethnic minority communities.

There is paucity of literature on the extent to which these demographic transitions are evident among aging individuals with DD and SMI from ethnic minority communities and the challenges experienced by their caregiving families. It is important to address their needs as the U.S. population is increasingly becoming "bigger, older and more diverse" (The Population Reference Bureau, 2004), and this diversity is reflected in an increase in the number of individuals with disabilities and their families from diverse racial and ethnic backgrounds (Aponte & Crouch, 1995; Fujiura & Yamaki, 2000).

However, understanding the needs of aging adults with DD and SMI from diverse communities in the United States and their caregiving families is particularly challenging, because historically, there have been racial and ethnic disparities in the use of specialty health care services (Braun & Browne, 1998; Cheung & Snowden, 1990; Heller, Markwardt, Rowitz, & Farber, 1999). Although some may attribute underutilization of services by racial and ethnic minorities to their own cultural norms and values, it is equally plausible that service providers do not take into account these values in designing service; thus reducing service use among these populations. For example, values such as filial piety, dominant in Asian cultures (Braun & Browne, 1998), sekentei among the Japanese in particular (Asai & Kameoka, 2005), and familism among

Latin American countries (Magaña, 1999), emphasize the importance of the family in the care-giving role. Many providers believe these values make ethnic minorities reluctant to seek help from outside agencies, when it may be that the way services are delivered discourages partici-pation of some families who find mainstream values inconsistent with their own.

Families from different racial and ethnic backgrounds may experience unique challenges given the lower levels of formal support they receive. This chapter provides a comprehensive review of issues, which have never been discussed together, such as, aging with DD and SMI, the role of race and ethnicity in shaping the experiences of individuals and their caregiving families, barriers to access services, and possible recommendations for research and practice.

Conceptual Framework

Older adults with DD and SMI from racial minority groups are disadvantaged on multiple domains. We provide a conceptual framework (Figure 20.1) using a Venn diagram to elucidate the complexity of the situation. Three important domains are identified as contributors to the complexity. The *first* domain involves specific aging concerns experienced by individuals with DD and SMI. The second domain includes limitations within the health care system, which has yet to adequately address the needs of aging adults with DD and SMI. The final domain involves the experiences of persons of color with DD and SMI and their families. We will briefly discuss the first two domains to give the reader a better idea of the issues of aging with a DD or SMI. The literature we discuss here is emerging and has not examined the experiences of people of color. However, we believe it will provide important background to the experi-ences of older adults with DD and SMI.

We will focus more on the third domain, the experiences of older adults of color with DD and SMI and their families. Here, we will discuss cultural illness attributions, culture, and the role of the family, caregiver adaptation, service patterns and disparities, and lastly best practices for addressing the needs of older adults of color with DD and SMI.

AGING WITH DD AND SMI: COMORBIDITY OF AGE-RELATED ILLNESSES

The first factor we will discuss is the experience of aging with a disability. DD and SMI are two etiologically different groups of disabilities or illnesses, with different ages of onset and illness course that distinctly shape the experience of the individual with disability as well as

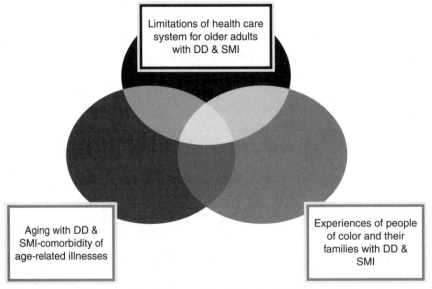

FIGURE 20.1 Conceptual Framework for Understanding Older People of Color With Developmental and Mental Disabilities.

his or her caregivers (Seltzer, Greenberg, Krauss, & Hong, 1997). The discussion that follows explores research on the experiences of older adults with DD and SMI.

Aging and DD

DDs are chronic conditions that are manifested before the age of 22, are likely to last a person's lifetime, and result in functional limitations in three or more major life activities (Beirne-Smith, Patton, & Ittenbach, 2002). Included in Figure 20.1 are disabilities, such as Down syndrome, cerebral palsy, intellectual disabilities (formerly known as mental retardation), and autism. Interest in aging issues in this population began in the 1980s, and several review studies have shown that some individuals with DD are at increased risk for various health problems, which are the primary predictor of their mortality (Fisher, 2004). For example, individuals with Down syndrome are predisposed to early onset of Alzheimer's compared to those with other forms of DD (Silverman, Zigman, Kim, Krinsky-McHale, & Wisniewski, 1998) and to the general population (Kozma, 2008). A study by Janicki and Dalton (2000) found that 22% of adults over 40 years and 56% for adults over age 60 have Alzheimer's disease. Further, adults with Down syndrome and those with any form of intellectual disability are four times and two-and-a-half times, respectively, more likely to experience extreme obesity than the general population (Janicki & Dalton, 2000). Also, there is a higher rate of occurrence of musculoskeletal conditions, such as scoliosis, hip displacement (Gajdosik & Cicirello, 2001), osteoarthritis, and osteoporosis (Janicki et al., 1999), which decrease mobility (Andersson & Mattsson, 2001), among those with DD compared to the general population. Finally, aging adults with intellectual disability, other than those with Down syndrome, experience significantly higher incidence of cardiovascular diseases, which is the leading cause of death in this population (Esbensen, Seltzer, & Greenberg, 2007). The early onset of age-related illnesses have important consideration for long-term care services, preventive care, and the need for early diagnosis.

Aging and SMI

SMI includes disorders such as schizophrenia, bipolar disorder, and major depression, among others. Most of our knowledge on people with SMI is restricted to adolescence and young adulthood. Research focused on older adults with severe and persistent mental illnesses is in its infancy (Barry, Blow, Dornfeld, & Valenstein, 2002). However, evidence from limited research suggests that older persons with SMI bear a disproportionate share of total health care costs, almost 27% greater than those below age 60 (Barry et al., 2002), and most of it attributed to comorbid health conditions such as hypertension, diabetes, heart disease (Barry et al., 2002), respiratory illnesses, neurological diseases, cancer (Lehmann, 2003), cognitive impairment, and dementia (Harvey, Leff, Trieman, Anderson, & Davidson, 1997). Furthermore, people with schizophrenia have a 20% shorter life expectancy (Newman & Bland, 1991). The emerging evidence suggests that older adults with SMI are equally, if not more, vulnerable to chronic illnesses than the general population.

LIMITATIONS OF THE HEALTH CARE SYSTEM FOR OLDER ADULTS WITH DD AND SMI

Despite this emerging evidence, it has only been within the past two decades that mental health practitioners and health care providers have come to realize that people with DD and SMI also experience the challenges of aging. While many comorbid conditions are preventable, health care providers are not prepared to address them among aging men and women with DD and SMI, and the comorbid health conditions have now been identified as a significant contributor to mortality in both the groups (Druss, Bradford, Rosenheck, Radford, & Krumholz, 2001).

Serious Mental Illness

Individuals with schizophrenia have a shorter life span than people in the general population, which can mostly be attributed to the side effects of medications, substance abuse, and nonadherence to prescribed medications (Newman & Bland, 1991). Substance use disorder, which is six times greater for patients with schizophrenia than for people without mental illness (Farris et al., 2003), contributes to medication nonadherence (Gilmer et al., 2004). Yet, patients with mental illnesses are less likely to be screened for drug and alcohol abuse (Dixon et al., 2001), and less likely to receive important general health checks than patients without schizophrenia (Roberts, Roalfe, Wilson, & Lester, 2007). Aging adults with SMI are further marginalized, as rates of participation in any psychotherapeutic interventions (Lehman & Steinwachs, 1998) or psychosocial rehabilitation programs (McQuaid et al., 2000) decline dramatically in this population. In addition, there are very few age-appropriate clinical, rehabilitative, or residential programs that exist for older chronic mental patients (Light & Lebowitz, 1991). These formal support deficits may be even more pronounced among minorities who, in general, receive worse medical and psychiatric treatment than their white counterparts (Lagomasino et al., 2005; Satre, Campbell, Gordon, & Weisner, 2010).

Developmental Disabilities

Similar health care disparities are also seen among aging adults with DD. The Office of the Surgeon General's (2002) report on health disparities and mental retardation concluded that there are disparities in health outcomes and health care between adults with DD and adults without disabilities. Families and persons with DD report that it is difficult to find health care providers who both understand how to work with persons with DD and that accept Medicaid, which is the form of insurance that most adults with DD have (Ward, Nichols, & Freedman, 2010). Due to these difficulties, many adults with DD remain with their pediatricians for health care (Ward et al., 2010). Review studies show that although people with DD have higher incidences of chronic health conditions, they are less likely to receive routine medical assessment compared to the general population, and even when detected, the conditions are not properly managed (Beange, McElduff, & Baker, 1992; Fisher, 2004; Janicki et al., 1999). There is a need for better screening to reduce the rate of mortality from preventable health conditions (Barr, Gilgunn, Kane, & Moore, 1999), yet the reality is far from perfect. An additional challenge faced by aging adults with DD and their families is permanency planning (planning for future residence and long-term care of the person with DD). Despite the fact that permanency planning has been identified as important to caregivers' well-being (Freedman, Krauss, & Seltzer, 1997), few families have developed long-term care plans, as many families face obstacles in doing so (Heller & Factor, 1991; Prouty & Lakin, 1997). Challenges are even greater for those from minority communities, as they are less connected to the service system (Heller & Factor, 1991).

In all, the discussion reveals that older adults with DD and SMI are vulnerable to chronic illnesses and experience systemic disparities and challenges in health care access and long-term planning. How these experiences play out for older adults from racial and ethnic minority backgrounds is extremely understudied.

EXPERIENCES OF PEOPLE OF COLOR WITH DD AND SMI AND THEIR FAMILIES

People with DD and SMI from minority backgrounds face all of the challenges of aging and service disparities described in the previous sections; however, these challenges may be compounded by cultural values, discrimination, and a lack of cultural competence among service providers. In this section, we review the literature on the experiences of minorities with DD and SMI and their families to better understand how these multiple challenges may manifest. We searched in various databases (i.e., Academic Search, ProQuest Research Library, and Web of Knowledge) for peer-reviewed articles using key terms such as mental illness or DD with minority, black, African American, Asian, American Indian, Native American, Latino, or

Hispanic to identify articles. We selected those articles that focused on empirical research of at least one under-represented minority group of adults with SMI or DD and/or their families. Our goal was to focus on the four main minority groups in the United States: blacks, Latinos, American Indians, and Asian Americans. Unfortunately, we were unable to find empirical studies on the experiences of American Indians with DD or SMI with respect to cultural attributions or the role of the family and caregiving; however, we did find some research on service use among American Indians with SMI.

These four racial and ethnic groups have within-group differences by country of origin or ancestry, as the countries are sociopolitically and culturally different as well as distinct historical experiences in the United States. In addition to cultural values, other factors such as acculturation are equally important in determining adaptation, as many immigrants are known to retain cultural beliefs from their home country for a few generations (Castles & Miller, 2003). Recognizing that American Indians are in their home country, and many Latinos, Asian Americans, and blacks have been in the United States for countless generations, acculturation and biculturalism can influence the extent to which their indigenous culture has an impact on the experiences of persons with SMI and DD and their caregiving families. The studies reported in the following section are a mix of qualitative and quantitative studies, some comparing between ethnicities and some within ethnic groups. We begin by exploring how culture shapes illness attribution, followed by how it shapes the family and caregiving role. We then discuss caregiver well-being, service patterns, and disparities of persons of color with DD and SMI, and lastly best practices for professionals working with people of color who have a DD or SMI.

Culture and Illness Attribution

Caregiving studies on ethnic minority groups show that culture plays a very important role in illness attribution. It provides a shared belief of values and attitudes about deviance and normative development, which ultimately determines health-seeking behavior among groups (Kleinman, 1980). It also shapes adaptation and availability of support from the family and the community at large.

Developmental Disabilities

It should be noted that beliefs described here are specific to the participants in the studies, and do not generalize for all members of the ethnic group under investigation. As will be evident, some of the themes are common across ethnic groups. Readers may also be cautioned that many studies cited in this section are from the literature on young children with DD. We cite these studies because the causal attributions may play an important role in what, when, and how care is sought, and how it shapes caregivers adaptation through life.

To begin, McCallion, Janicki, and Grant-Griffin (1997) used focus groups to understand how culture and acculturation shape the experiences of black, Chinese American, Hispanic/Latino American, Korean American, and selective Native American family caregivers for persons with DD. In explaining the cause of DD, respondents believed that the family member with a disability is a gift from God, or on the other extreme, a punishment from God. Among some of the cultural groups, disability represented shame and thereby the need to hide the person from everyone, whereas in other cultural groups there was a "soft spot" for the person with a disability, and he or she was accepted by the community. However, McCallion et al. (1997) have not indicated the extent to which these beliefs varied by ethnic group.

Studies focusing on specific ethnic groups provide evidence of a range of unique culturally specific attributions. For example, in a study of 30 Korean American women pursuing graduate studies in the United States, the participants were interviewed on their perspective about disability. The authors found that the women attributed the cause of disability to traditional beliefs, such as fate, punishment from God, or imbalance of the body (Erickson, Devlieger, & Sung, 1999), but were less likely to endorse these beliefs themselves. They rated mental retardation as the most severe form of disability from a list of 18 disabilities.

The authors interpreted this finding as an indication of the importance of soundness of mind among Koreans.

In a comparative qualitative study of 32 Korean and Korean American mothers caring for children with DD, Cho, Singer, and Brenner (2003) found that mothers in both groups held similar beliefs about the cause of disability, which ranged from believing that they were responsible for their child's disability due to poor prenatal practices (referred to as Tae Gyo) or early parenting practices. A few others attributed disability in a child to misfortune or to punishment for parental sins. Korean Americans Christians tended to believe that childhood disability was part of a divine plan that would benefit the family, a belief similarly shared by Latinos (Skinner, Rodriguez, & Bailey, 1999). The authors suggested that the Korean American mothers in the study held on to cultural beliefs because they only lived in the United States between 5 and 9 years and were therefore less acculturated (Cho et al., 2003).

Similar beliefs are also seen in a qualitative study of Chinese American mothers of children with DD (Shen-Ryan & Smith, 1989). Mothers blamed themselves for the child's disability or attributed disability to cultural beliefs such as fate, God's will, a bodily imbalance of the dual forces of Yin and Yang, or exposure of the pregnant woman to physical labor (Shen-Ryan & Smith, 1989). The authors found that of the 59 mothers interviewed, 53 were first-generation immigrants with limited fluency in English. Using English fluency and generational status as measures of acculturation, the authors attributed stronger adherence to traditional beliefs to low levels of acculturation.

Belief in reincarnation, karma, or the cycle of life was a dominant theme that was evident in a study of South Asian immigrants (Gabel, 2004). Gabel interviewed 20 Hindu Indian men and women about their perception of DD. All except one participant, who held a degree in psychology from a Western University, attributed DD in a child as a gift of God, or as a lesson for sins committed in a previous life. These causal beliefs were held irrespective of the number of years since the respondents have emigrated from India (Gabel, 2004).

Skinner et al. (1999) interviewed 250 Latinos of Mexican and Puerto Rican descent with young children with DD or mental retardation, to specifically explore religious interpretations of disability in the population. They found significant within-group variations in attribution to DD in that most of the parents believed in biomedical problems as a cause of their child's disability, but many simultaneously believed that God was involved in some way as well. Of those who attributed their child's disability to religious causes, three themes emerged. First, the child was a blessing or a gift, and the parents were chosen to take care of the child; second, the child was a test put forth by God; and third, the child with a disability was a punishment from God (Skinner et al., 1999). In another ethnographic study of 12 Puerto Rican American parents and their views on special education, Harry (1992) found that several causal themes emerged in the parents' explanation of the difficulties faced by their children with DD in school. A common theme was attributing disability to familial traits. For example, disability was thought to have come from the father's side of the family. For learning disabilities, parents often blamed the language barrier in the school and intolerance and unreasonable expectations by teachers as a causative factor (Harry, 1992).

Several studies have also sought to understand explanatory factors of mental illness among blacks, but to a lesser extent for DD within this community. In a study of black mothers of young children with DD, Harry (1992) noted that some mothers perceive the child as a "gift from God," which appears to be a common theme across cultures, particularly for people who believe in Christianity. It seems that with respect to attributions about DD, the more acculturated and perhaps more educated family members are, the more likely they will endorse medical causes; however, many families hold simultaneous beliefs in both medical and religious causes.

Serious Mental Illness

Similar to beliefs about DD, there is some evidence to show that some cultural groups attribute emotional and behavioral disturbance to biological and nonbiological factors, such as mystical beliefs and spiritual weakness (Schnittker, Freese, & Powell, 2000). Using data from the 1992 Social Survey, Schnittker et al. (2000) found that African Americans were more likely than whites to reject the idea that mental illness is caused by inherited genetic problems, chemical imbalances, or the way a person has been raised, but were more likely than whites to attribute mental illness to "bad character," and to some extent to the "will of God."

In contrast, in-depth interviews with African American, Hispanic, and white caregivers found that African American caregivers shared similar views with whites in that mental illness is a medical problem or resulted from negative personality traits (Guarnaccia & Parra, 1996; Milstein, Guarnaccia, & Midlarsky, 1995). However, African American caregivers were more likely than whites to attribute mental illness to religious and esoteric factors, such as demonic possessions (Milstein et al., 1995). In a qualitative study of Southern blacks, Morrison and Thornton (1999) interviewed African American mental health experts, people with mental illnesses, and nurses caring for persons with mental illness on their perceptions of mental illness. The authors found three dominant influences on mental illness attributions: black Voodoo, slave religion, and Evangelical Protestantism (Morrison & Thornton, 1999). The commonality between the groups was the belief that mental illness is caused by oppression of demonic spirits, and specific to Christians, the belief that mental illness is a punishment from God.

In a quantitative study designed to understand illness attributions for schizophrenia among 61 urban African Americans family members of 38 hospitalized patients with first-episode or acute schizophrenia, Esterberg and Compton (2006) found that the majority of the family members endorsed biological causes. A small number endorsed personality and societal factors; family crisis; and esoteric causes, such as punishment from God, possession by evil spirits, or unfavorable horoscopes. However, those with first-episode schizophrenia were more likely to endorse personality-related factors as causing schizophrenia, whereas those whose relatives had persistent schizophrenia were more likely to endorse biological causes. According to the authors, endorsement of biological causes may have resulted from continuous interaction with mental health professionals.

Compton, Esterberg, and Broussard (2008) replicated the same study with 127 urban African Americans from the general population using a brief self-administered survey. They found that the most commonly reported causes of mental illness were disturbances of brain biochemistry (49.6%), drug or alcohol abuse (42.5%), hereditary factors (40.9%), brain injury (42.2%), and avoiding problems in life (37.8%). Approximately 48% also listed esoteric factors as causes (e.g., possession by evil spirits, radiation, and punishment by God). However, attributing to esoteric factors was greatest among men with fewer than 12 years of education who never knew anyone with schizophrenia.

Using in-depth interviews of Korean American caregivers, Donnelley (2001, 2005) found that caregivers attributed mental illness to possession by Satan; an imbalance or the lack of Chi, a traditional view of health rooted in the Korean culture; or to self-blame, especially during the initial stages of the illness, which in turn influenced their help-seeking behaviors. In another study of 50 Korean clergymen, each of the clergymen was provided with vignettes of persons with mental illness and their causal attributions, along with their probability of referring the person to a psychiatrist (Kim-Goh, 1993). Kim-Goh (1993) found that 96% of the clergymen attributed depressive symptoms to biological causes, whereas 52% attributed severe psychotic symptoms with religious delusions to religious causes. Three quarters of the clergymen attributed persecutory delusions to spiritual conflict, fanaticism, demonic phenomenon, or not knowing God. Given that Koreans Americans often turn to the Church for services and support (Hurh & Kim, 1984), these attributions can shape the treatment and coping strategies of Korean American individuals with disabilities and their families.

Administering the Perceived Causes of Mental Illness Scale to a convenience sample of 30 Chinese American caregivers of adults with schizophrenia, Kung (2004) found the majority attributed the disease to biological causes, followed by stress, moral, and psychodynamic causes. The least causative factor subscribed to was supernatural causes. Biological attributions were higher among those who were better acculturated. Qualitative analysis suggested the same; however, interpersonal stresses were identified as more salient than biological factors. The author attributed the importance of interpersonal stress as a causative factor to the sociocentric nature and the centrality of the family among the Chinese in general.

Among Latino caregivers, Weisman, Gomes, and López (2003) interviewed 20 relatively unacculturated Latinos on causal attributions of schizophrenia and found three primary explanations associated with schizophrenia: (a) a legitimate illness; (b) caused by God; and (c) result of interpersonal and environmental stress. These explanations were often held simultaneously. For example, the majority of respondents (90%) indicated that schizophrenia is a form of illness, a genetic abnormality, mental disorder, or a physical condition. The same number of respondents also indicated that mental illness is a result of interpersonal problems, or environmental stressors, and 40% attributed mental illness to God (Weisman et al., 2003). In another qualitative study comparing 45 Latino (Puerto Rican and Cuban), 29 black (African American and West Indian), and 16 European American (South and East European) caregivers, researchers found that among the Latinos, concepts like nervios (nerves) and fallo mental (mental failure) shaped the concept of mental illness among Puerto Ricans as well as Cuban families caring for an adult with mental illness (Guarnacia, Para, Deschamps, Milstein, & Argiles, 1992).

Culture and the Role of the Family

Of significance to our current discussion are cultural values and the role of the family in caregiving. Cultural values play a very important role among families in determining how care should be provided and whether formal services will be used to care for the elderly and the disabled. The core of these values is the importance of family and community, and several studies show that these values are dominant among caregivers of color, compared to their white counterparts (Connell & Gibson, 1997), although acculturation is an important determinant of how strongly these beliefs were held. We discuss some of the common cultural values irrespective of the caregiving context.

Concepts common to Eastern belief systems are filial piety; respect for elders; social harmony; beliefs in past life; reincarnation and karma; and collectivism (Chun, Moos, & Cronkite, 2006), which prescribes how social relationships are to be fulfilled. The social construct of collectivism is common but not exclusive to Asian countries, and shared by those from Latin American countries as well. In individualistic societies, personal autonomy, individual rights, and concern for one's own self and one's family is emphasized, while in a collectivistic society there is greater emphasis on the common good of the group and fulfillment of societal roles (Chun et al., 2006). In general, research shows that European Americans are more individualistic compared to people from non-western and other less-developed countries (Oyserman, Coon, & Kemmelmeier, 2002). Individuals in non-western cultures fulfill their social relationships based on roles set by the social norms. In some East Asian societies, having a child with SMI or DD can result in the "loss of face" for the individual and his/her family. In several Asian societies, having a male child with a disability implies the end of a bloodline and the inability of the child to fulfill societal obligations. As a result, families are often alienated from sources of social support (see Magaña & Ghosh, 2010). Families in these societies may hide the disability and tend to provide care in the absence of any support. However, as children with disabilities live longer, caregivers often have to provide care for life. Long-term planning for older adults with DD or SMI can pose significant challenges, because the concept of filial piety calls for caregiving by family and kin. Families, therefore, struggle to maintain the fine balance between traditional and modern medicine or rehabilitative services for the cure of the disabled. For example, McCallion et al. (1997) found that Chinese and Korean participants rejected services that did not conform to their cultural norms. Most sought support from their community because they adhered to traditional values. However, they also realized that such adherence often led to barriers in accepting formal services, which in turn affected several aspects of their life. Much like the Chinese and Korean Americans, a culture-specific concept called sekentei (refers to social appearance, which causes an individual to worry about others' observations and evaluations of his or her behavior) dominates the caregiving activities of the Japanese (Asai & Kameoka, 2005). These sociocultural values can increase caregiving stress, as individuals are always under social scrutiny of how well they care for the older adults and persons with disabilities.

A cultural value common among Latinos is familism. It emphasizes feelings of loyalty, solidarity, and reciprocity among members (Marin & Marin, 1991), with the expectation that extended family will provide care (Cox & Monk, 1993). Three types of value orientations that constitute familism are: reliance on family members for support, obligation toward family members, and use of relatives as referents (Sabogal, Marin, Otero-Sabogal, Marin, Perez-Stable, 1987). An important underlying cultural construct is collectivism, which calls for willingness to sacrifice one's good for the greater good of the family or community (Marin & Marin, 1991). In a comparative study, Mary (1990) interviewed 20 Hispanics, 20 blacks, and 20 white mothers of young children with Down syndrome and found that of the three groups, Hispanic mothers were more likely to adopt an attitude of "self-sacrifice toward their young child with a disability" than white or black mothers. Familism may serve as a protective factor, as noted in a quantitative study of 72 Puerto Rican mothers of individuals with intellectual disabilities from Massachusetts (Magaña, 1999). The mothers in the study had low levels of acculturation, although they had been in the United States on average for 21 years. Measures of familism included mother's social support network, her satisfaction with social support, and her familial obligations. The study found evidence of the extensive family involvement (including husbands, other children, cousins, nephews, aunts, and mothers) in providing help to these women with their day-to-day activities. The majority (88%) of the mothers' social support network comprised family members, and 19% of the network members lived in Puerto Rico, providing long-distance support. Further, Magaña (1999) found that some aspects of familism were related to mother's emotional well-being, particularly lower depressive symptoms.

Several studies have shown that irrespective of taking on more caregiving duties, black caregivers tended to report lower levels of subjective burden than their white counterparts (Horwitz & Reinhard, 1995). Horwitz and Reinhard interviewed 78 parents and 70 siblings of black and white patients who were scheduled for release from psychiatric care and found that although black and white parents had similar levels of caregiving duties, the white parents reported higher levels of burden than the black parents. The authors attribute this to the importance of intergenerational caregiving among grandparents and extended kin among the blacks, where caregiving for a mentally ill relative may only seem normative, and thus less burdensome (Horwitz & Reinhard, 1995). Researchers have attributed lower burden among African Americans irrespective of their caregiver burden to their cultural traditions and strong sense of familial obligation to define their role as caregivers (Scharlach et al., 2006). These caregivers emphasized the role of family ties and the role of family members to provide care, irrespective of the caregiving circumstance, and that caregiving was an opportunity to get close to the individual with a disability.

This pattern of willingness to care is also evident in two studies that looked at permanency planning for adults with intellectual disabilities (Heller & Factor, 1988; McCallion et al., 1997). Compared to whites, Heller and Factor found that blacks were more likely to care for the person with DD in their home, that is, less likely to seek residential placements or have made financial plans for their relative. Similar unwillingness to seek residential settlement was also reported by blacks in McCallion et al.'s multiethnic group study. Further, their long-term care arrangements included their siblings or extended family.

Caregiver Adaptation

Family caregivers of adults with SMI and DD are most often the parents, who are themselves aging and facing challenges as older adults. As discussed earlier, in many cultures, caring for a person with the disability may be viewed positively and negatively; however, the challenges associated with caring for a person with DD and SMI can influence the health and well-being of older caregivers. Caregiving outcomes examined in the studies below include caregiving burden, depression, grief, and physical health. The studies show both between- as well as within-group differences in rates of physical and psychological health symptoms.

Serious Mental Illness

We begin with studies that specifically look at within-group differences. Magaña, Ramírez García, Hernández, and Cortez (2007) interviewed 85 Latino caregivers of adults with schizophrenia, particularly of Mexican descent, and found that 40% of the sample had rates of depressive symptoms that met the clinical cut-off for depression, compared to 12% to 18% among Mexican Americans in the general population. When compared across disabilities, Latina mothers of adults with schizophrenia showed lower psychological well-being than Latina mothers of youths/adults with autism (Magaña & Ghosh, 2010).

Most of the studies of black caregivers are comparative, and usually the comparison group is white caregivers. Black caregivers have more positive outcomes than white caregivers in studies that do not control for sociodemographic differences (Horwitz & Reinhard, 1995; Pickett, Vraniak, Cook, & Cohler, 1993; Pruchno, Hicks Patrick, & Burant, 1997; Valentine, McDermott, & Anderson, 1998). For example, Valentine et al. (1998) found black mothers of children with intellectual disabilities experienced a greater sense of caregiving gratification and intimacy compared to white mothers, but did not differ significantly in the caregiver burden. Similarly, a study of 24 black and 184 white parents of adults with SMI noted that black parents had higher levels of coping mastery and self-esteem and lower levels of depression than white Americans (Pickett et al., 1993). However, these authors also did not control for demographic factors. Another study that did account for demographic factors interviewed 103 low-income caregivers of adults with mental illness and initially found that there were no differences between white and black caregivers once maladaptive behaviors, residential status, gender, and social support were taken into account (Song, Biegel, & Milligan, 1997).

Magaña, Greenberg, and Seltzer (2004) argued that black–white comparative studies may not capture the toll caregiving has on black families, both because their different environmental and cultural contexts and measures of well-being may not have the same meaning across groups. When comparing health outcomes of black caregivers of adults with schizophrenia to a matched sample of noncaregiving blacks from the National Survey of Families and Households, Magaña et al. (2004) found that black mothers of adults with schizophrenia reported higher rates of chronic health conditions, such as high blood pressure, arthritis, and eye problems.

Studies that specifically examined burden and adaptive outcomes among Asian American caregivers reported that they experienced significant subjective and objective burden (Kung, 2003). In a study of 30 Chinese American caregivers of patients with schizophrenia, Kung found sources of subjective burden arose from worrying about the patient's future, being upset about changes in the patient, or feeling trapped in the caregiving role. Sources of objective burden included disruption in household routines, reduced leisure time, and changes in personal plans. Family conflict, a significant source of stress, arose from intense involvement in care by more than one caregiver, which led to disagreements on how care should be provided, often resulting in others feeling trapped. Disagreements also arose between the patient and the caregiver and also with those who did not understand the nature of the illness. Kung argues that this stress is exacerbated for Chinese immigrants who are socially stigmatized because of the "loss of face" from having a child with a disability, which further restricts their social life.

Developmental Disabilities

Much like mental illness, we see a significant number of studies that have looked at within-group differences in adaptive outcomes among Latino caregivers. Magaña, Seltzer, Krauss, Rubert, and Szapocznik (2002b) studied 44 Puerto Ricans and 49 Cuban American mothers of adults with intellectual disabilities using a structured interview schedule. They found no difference between the two groups on levels of depression, but the Cuban American mothers reported significantly higher burden. Predictors of depression for the entire sample included poor health, fewer years of education, and fewer years since emigrating from country of origin. Predictors of burden were poor maternal health, being married, and behavior problems. After family problems were taken into account, the differences in burden between the groups disappeared because the Cuban Americans reported more family problems. The authors attributed the higher level of family problems among Cuban Americans to the unique context in which they live in Miami where a high level of community involvement is expected by families, yet difficult to achieve when caring for an adult child with DD.

Similar to the study that examined health outcomes within a sample of black mothers, Magaña and Smith (2006) used data from the National Health Interview Survey to compare health outcomes of midlife and older Latina and black mothers who coresided with a son or daughter with DD to their noncaregiving counterparts. Controlling for demographic factors, they found Latina caregivers were more likely to be diagnosed with heart problems and arthritis that limited their physical activity and higher levels of depressive symptoms than Latina noncaregivers. Although depressive symptoms were not significantly higher for black Americans, they found similar results with respect to health conditions. Older black caregivers were also more likely to report limitations from arthritis and diabetes than noncaregivers. The authors attributed greater health limitations to greater vulnerability to chronic illnesses among blacks and Latinos in the general population, which likely is exacerbated due to caregiving.

Another study that examined the physical health of caregivers compared 71 black women to 71 white women age 50 and above, who were caring for an adult child with DD (Miltiades & Pruchno, 2002). The study found that black mothers rated their health as poorer than white caregivers, which significantly predicted higher depressive symptoms, an indication that caregiving may be more difficult for the black mothers (Miltiades & Pruchno, 2002). It is likely that these caregivers are providing care often at the cost of their own health and ignoring their health needs. This was noticed by Magaña and Smith (2008) using data from the National Health Interview Survey, who found that Latina and black DD caregivers were less likely to have seen a doctor for their own health care needs than their noncaregiving counterparts.

Service Patterns and Disparities

Services for Persons With DD

Children and adolescents with DD receive most of their disability-related services in the school systems through the federally mandated Individual Educational Plan (IEP) process. As persons with DD transition to adulthood, they typically work with their families and special education staff on creating a transition plan to arrange services they will need as adults. The main focus of adult services is on employment-related activities, social and recreational activities, and living independently (Blue-Banning, Turnbull, & Pereira, 2002). While living independently is a societal goal for young adults in the dominant U.S. population, many families from diverse backgrounds value having their son or daughter with DD living at home as adults (Blue-Banning et al., 2000; Magaña & Smith, 2006). In addition, some research shows a link between family low-income status and the family member with DD living at home, which may account for some of the racial/ethnic differences in living arrangements (Heller & Factor, 1988). Studies on patterns of service utilization among persons with DD show that aside from financial assistance through Supplemental Security Income (SSI), which is used by the majority of adults with DD (Magaña, Seltzer, & Krauss, 2002a), the most common services for adults with DD include vocational and day program services, health care, dental care, service coordination, transportation, and social and recreational services (Magaña et al., 2002a; Pruchno & McMullen, 2004). Factors related to greater service utilization can vary by the type of services, but most commonly include lower functioning levels, greater levels of disruptive behavior exhibited by the adult with DD (Magaña et al., 2002a; Pruchno & McMullen, 2004), and greater levels of caregiver burden and lower caregiver functioning (Pruchno & McMullen, 2004).

Racial or ethnic disparities in receipt of services among adults with DD may vary by living arrangements. Studies of Latino and black persons with DD who lived at home found that while there were some differences in service use between racial and ethnic minorities and whites, both blacks and Latinos with DD had higher levels of unmet service needs than whites (Magaña et al., 2002a; Pruchno & McMullen, 2004). Pruchno and McMullen (2004) reported that blacks with DD were more likely to use occupational therapy and psychological services than whites with DD. However, they were also more severely impaired and exhibited more disruptive behaviors, which were also related to greater service use. Differences in unmet service needs in this study were more glaring. For example, blacks with DD were more likely to have unmet service needs in dental services, vocational training, occupational therapy, and psychological services (Pruchno & McMullen, 2004). Magaña et al. (2002a) found that Puerto Rican adults with DD were less likely to use day programs, social and recreational services, and transportation services than whites with DD, and were more likely than whites to use personal care assistants, physical and occupational therapy, nursing services, and legal services. Similar to blacks with DD in Pruchno and McMullen's study (2004), the Puerto Rican adults with DD were more severely impaired than whites. Overall, there was no difference in the number of services used by each group on a bivariate level; however, when taking into account socioeconomic status and level of impairment, whites used more services than Puerto Ricans with DD. Consistent with Pruchno and McMullen's study (2004), differences in unmet service needs between Puerto Ricans and whites with DD were more striking. Puerto Ricans were more likely to have unmet needs in almost every service listed, including transportation, social and recreational services, psychological services, physical therapy, personal care assistants, occupational physical and speech therapies, legal services, and nutritional services (Magaña et al., 2002a).

Stancliffe and Lakin (2006) examined racial and ethnic differences in services among adults with DD living primarily in residential settings and found no differences between groups in some services and nonsignificant differences in others. These findings suggest that once individuals with DD live in a residential facility, their receipt of services is determined more by their disability status and residential facility access to services; subsequently, service use may in general become more equitable across racial and ethnic groups (Stancliffe & Lakin, 2006). Consistent with Magaña et al.'s study, Latinos and Asian Americans had lower levels of functioning than whites in the study. However, blacks were more similar to whites in adaptive functioning (Stancliffe & Lakin, 2006).

Because all of these studies examined racial and ethnic disparities among adults with DD who are already in the service system, we know very little about the racial and ethnic disparities between those who receive services and those who do not access the service system at all. In all of the above studies, the samples were recruited through the service system and for the most part the people of color with DD were more severely impaired than whites. This may reflect that persons of color with DD who have mild and moderate impairments are not being served to the same extent as whites with similar impairment levels. There is some evidence of racial and ethnic disparities in persons with DD who receive no versus some services (Hatton, 2002; Hewitt, Larson, & Lakin, 2000). Hewitt et al. (2000) found that minority groups were under-represented in receipt of home and community-based services. Getting at this information is challenging because most DD researchers find their samples with the help of the service system. Population-based studies on adults with DD are needed to determine to what extent persons with DD receive services at all and whether that varies by race and ethnicity. It should be noted that we found no empirical studies on service use and/or disparities among American Indian and Asian American adults with DD, which points to another tremendous gap in the literature.

The extent to which cultural beliefs and attitudes contribute to underutilization of services is difficult to determine. However, the number of unmet services in both of the home-based studies indicates that families are not rejecting the services. Both of these studies asked family caregivers whether a service was received, and if not, whether it was needed. Magaña et al. (2002a) found that the largest factor that contributed to why the service was not used among Puerto Rican families was the lack of knowledge of the availability of service or on how to access it. Cultural values were not a common response among caregivers. This may play out differently when considering the use of residential services. Some studies suggest a preference among many Latino families for the adult with DD to live at home (Magaña & Ghosh, 2010; Magaña & Smith, 2006). We also do not know whether cultural values or a lack of information and limited agency outreach contribute to why those with mild and moderate impairments are not in the service system. For immigrant families, one factor that could prove to be a barrier to service use is whether the person with DD has legal immigration documentation, especially for vocational services and programs, which require a U.S. Social Security number. Additionally, if the adult with DD is a citizen and his or her parents are not, parental caregivers may be fearful to seek services for their offspring with DD.

Services for Persons With Severe Mental Illness

People with SMI use a range of specialty mental health services in addition to general health care, such as counseling or psychotherapy with a mental health professional (that can include a social worker, counselor, psychologist, or psychiatrist), case management services, and medication treatment and monitoring.

Contrary to the research on service use among persons with DD, there are several studies that examine racial and ethnic disparities in mental health services using national probability samples. Alegría et al. (2002) used data from the National Comorbidity Study to examine differences in mental health disparity services across Latino, black, and white adults. They found that among adults who met diagnostic criteria for a psychiatric illness in the past year, there were no significant differences between the three groups in overall use of mental health, physical health, or human services. However, whites used more specialty care services (defined as treatment by mental health specialists) than Latinos or blacks.

Another study examined the use of case management services in a representative sample of people with schizophrenia who were receiving public mental health services in San Diego County, and found lower utilization among blacks and Latinos with schizophrenia than whites (Barrio et al., 2003). Interestingly, they found no difference among Latinos in case management use between those who lived with family and those who did not; however, whites who lived with family were less likely to use case management services. This contradicts the assumption that somehow culture and family prevent ethnic minorities from using services.

In a representative and comprehensive study of Latinos and mental health services, researchers found that rates of mental health service use have increased among Latinos compared to rates in the 1990s, and that service use varied by nativity, language, age at migration, and years living in the United States (Alegría et al., 2007b). However, they also found that rates of service use for those Latinos in the sample who met criteria for a mental health diagnosis were similar to those in the general population. Puerto Ricans had higher service use than three other Latino groups, indicating the importance of examining differences between countries of origin (Alegría et al., 2007b).

Blacks have been found to be overrepresented in some services, particularly psychiatric hospitalization (McGuire & Miranda, 2008). A study that examined disparities in the use of psychiatric inpatient care for persons with SMI found that, consistent with previous research, blacks were overrepresented in psychiatric hospitalization than non-Hispanic whites (Snowden, Hastings, & Alvidrez, 2009). These researchers also found that ethnicity matters. Caribbean-born blacks did not differ from whites in hospitalization; however, U.S.-born Caribbeans were more similar to African Americans and were more likely to have been hospitalized for psychiatric reasons (Snowden et al., 2009). These findings among Caribbean immigrants are similar to those found among Latino immigrants; the longer they are in the United States, the more likely they are to develop mental health problems (Alegría et al., 2007a). Distrust of the physical and mental health systems due to historical mistreatment may explain the overrepresentation of black hospitalizations; it is possible that they do not seek treatment until problems are severe.

A population-based study that examined mental health service use by Asian Americans found that they had lower use of mental health services than the general population; however, their rates of having a probable DSM IV diagnosis were similar if not slightly lower than the general population (Abe-Kim et al., 2007). Clearly, there is a gap between need for services and those receiving services among Asian Americans in this study. The study did not find significant differences in service use between four different Asian American groups; however, they found that U.S.-born Asian Americans had higher rates of service use than foreign-born Asian Americans. Furthermore, they found that second-generation Asian Americans were more similar to immigrants, and third generation were more similar to the general U.S. population, demonstrating a relationship between acculturation and service use (Abe-Kim et al., 2007).

While language is frequently a barrier to service use for immigrants, English language proficiency was not related to service use in this study, suggesting that there are other cultural and unmeasured influences.

In a report entitled, "Mental Health: Culture, Race, and Ethnicity," the Surgeon General indicated that research on mental health and American Indian populations was extremely limited (U.S. Department of Health and Human Services, 2001). Since that time there has been some effort to address this disparity in mental health research. Beals et al. (2005a) used a stratified random sample of adults from two tribes in the Northern Plains and one in the Southwest to examine prevalence of mental health disorders and mental health service utilization. This study compared rates of service use to the National Comorbidity Study (NCS) and found that American Indian men were less likely to use specialty or other medical providers for depressive or anxiety disorders than the NCS sample. However, they were more likely to use services for substance use disorders and had higher rates of these disorders than the NCS sample. American Indian women were comparable to women in the NCS sample in specialty service use for anxiety and depressive disorders, and similar to the American Indian men, the women were more likely to use services for substance use disorders than women in the NCS study. Both American Indian men and women had high rates of using traditional or spiritual healers (Beals et al., 2005b). In an article based on the same data, American Indians were found to have lower rates of major depressive episode than those in the NCS study, which was an unexpected finding, as previous research from nonrepresentative samples reported American Indians to be at a higher risk for this disorder (Beals et al., 2005a).

Barriers and Factors That Contribute to Low Service Use

Several factors may contribute to racial and ethnic disparities in mental health services, including discrimination by providers, which can occur through two mechanisms: provider bias and stereotyping and provider statistical discrimination (McGuire & Miranda, 2008). Provider bias occurs when a provider treats patients differently based on the provider's beliefs about the group; in the case of statistical discrimination, the provider may make decisions based on what they know about the probability of groups having certain problems (McGuire & Miranda, 2008). Furthermore, communication between provider and patients from different minority groups may be challenging due to language and culture, which could contribute to inadequate treatment. A study that examined service barriers for Asian Americans with disabilities identified communication difficulties due to language differences as a main barrier to services and a lack of knowledge about disabilities and services, which has been discussed previously as an important barrier for other immigrant groups (Choi & Wynne, 2000).

Additionally, the history of discrimination of a particular group may play an important role in determining whether services are used. For example, there is a cultural mistrust toward formal mental health care services among blacks, often based on their experiences with the mental health and health care system (Whaley, 2001). In a study of 154 black patients admitted to a state psychiatric hospital in New York, Whaley sought to explore the level of mistrust held by black persons with SMI toward mental health clinicians. Respondents were administered a structured questionnaire that included the Cultural Mistrust Inventory. The results from the study indicated that black participants with SMI favored someone from their own ethnic background to provide treatment. Ironically, however, participants were more likely to rate clinicians from their own background with higher levels of mistrust and believed that white clinicians received better training.

Culture-specific beliefs with regard to illness attributions may be more prevalent at the initial stages of the diagnosis or onset of the illness and may influence the use of culturally specific folk treatments (Helms & Cook, 1999), but many caregivers may later seek help from professional therapists or psychiatrists when the problem does not resolve (Donnelley, 2001). Donnelley found that Korean Americans caring for individuals with mental illness at the initial stages sought help from physicians trained in Traditional Chinese Medicine (TCM), acupuncturists, or ministers to chase away Satan, but moved on to western medicine and therapy when the problem did not dissipate. Participants in McCallion et al. (1997) study readily acknowledged that causality attribution of DD influenced both the level of services needed and a family's willingness to accept those services.

Stigma is another factor that may impede the use of services. As discussed earlier, among Asians, the potential loss of face associated with having mental illness or DD may result in closely guarding the disability as a secret (Kleinman & Kleinman, 1993) and may impede service use. Stigma in different communities may be perpetuated by a lack of knowledge about disabilities and their treatments. In an ethnographic study of black caregivers to persons with mental illness, Hines-Martin (1998) found that a lack of knowledge and prevalence of stigma among black clergies could result in caregivers feeling stigmatized, which may ultimately influence their help-seeking from mental health professionals.

The result of these factors may contribute to some people of color turning to informal sources, such as friends, family members, clergy, and indigenous healers. For example, among blacks, mental health care is often sought through the Church, since the Church has historically played a very important role in the lives of blacks (Aaron, Levine, & Burstin, 2003). Furthermore, the Church can be a positive influence for ensuring its constituencies receive adequate care and treatment. Using stratified sampling data, Aaron et al. (2003) conducted a quantitative study of 2,196 blacks from low-income communities and found that church attendance was associated with higher odds of positive health behavior and higher odds of seeking health services. Church is also the first point of contact to receive behavioral and emotional interventions (Blank, Mahmood, Fox, & Guterbock, 2002). Blank et al. (2002) interviewed 269 pastors from Southern churches to estimate the extent to which Southern churches were providing mental health services and had established a formal referral with the mental health system. The study found that black churches provided more services than white churches, regardless of racial composition or location in urban or rural areas.

In summary, this section discusses literature on older adults of color with DD and mental illness and their families, specifically focusing on cultural beliefs, help-seeking behaviors, adaption, and service use. We reviewed literature on causal attributions of DD and mental illnesses and found that certain attributions are very culturally specific, such as karma or the "cycle of life" prevalent among Hindus, whereas others are shared across ethnic groups, such as possession by evil spirits, or a birth of a child as a punishment or challenge from God, shared by African Americans, Latinos, and Korean Christians. It may be cautioned that individuals may endorse disability in a child to culture-specific beliefs and biological causes simultaneously. These causal attributions shape help-seeking behavior and also determine caregiver adaptation. However, it needs to be emphasized that these causal attributions are not true for every member of an ethnic group, as attributions vary by the levels of education, acculturation, stage of the illness, and interactions with physicians from the dominant culture.

We also discussed the role of the family in the life of an aging adult with DD and mental illness, and found that cultural values determine how care is to be given, who is to provide care, and what sort of care is sought. The values around caregiving ranged on a continuum, from those serving as protective factors for the caregiver, such as the cultural construct of familism among Latino caregivers, to those being a source of stress, such as identifying the mother or her poor prenatal practices as the cause of disability in the child, a belief prevalent among several East Asian communities. As such, the values determined caregiver adaptation. The review found both within- and between-group variations in caregiver well-being. The findings point to the heterogeneity in adaptive outcomes that arise from the age and health status of the caregiver, the type of illness and symptoms exhibited by the adult with DD or mental illness, years in the caregiving role, and role expectations of the caregiver within his or her community.

Finally, we discussed literature on service patterns and disparities in receipt of services. The DD research tends to find that among adults with DD living at home, there are distinct disparities between racial and ethnic minorities and whites in receipt of services. Whites receive some types of services more than minorities, and for other services it is the reverse. However, racial and ethnic minorities are consistently found to have higher unmet service needs than whites in most service categories. For those with DD living in residential facilities, the disparities are less apparent. Limitations of the DD service disparity research include the small number of studies, and that these studies are based on convenience samples of persons already in the system. Racial and ethnic minorities with DD tend to be in the system when their disability and functional status are more severe, which means that those with mild and moderate disabilities are likely underserved.

There is a larger body of research with diverse findings in the area of mental health service disparities, and many of these studies have used probability samples in which both prevalence of mental illness and service use are investigated. Research shows that Latinos, blacks, Asian Americans, and American Indians are less likely than whites to receive specialty mental health services. Studies also show that differences in service use between Latinos and whites are less pronounced than in the past, but differences in service use exist between Latino groups. Blacks have been found to be overrepresented in psychiatric hospitalization, and similar to Latinos, there are differences between U.S.-born and Caribbean-born blacks and between U.S.-born Asian Americans and foreign-born Asians, reinforcing the importance of within-group diversity. The limited research for American Indians suggests lower specialty mental health service use but higher use of substance abuse services compared to the general population.

Factors that may contribute to lower service use among racial and ethnic minorities include cultural attributions of illness, family cultural beliefs and practices, stigma, and discrimination and provider bias. These factors were discussed earlier in this section and will be discussed in more detail in the following section with respect to how to incorporate them into research policy and practice.

IMPLICATIONS FOR SOCIAL WORK RESEARCH, POLICY, AND PRACTICE

In developing programs and services for people of color with SMI and DD, service providers bear the burden of ensuring accessibility and quality of services. It is not acceptable to assume that individuals from specific cultures do not want or need services due to their own cultural orientations. Whitley and Lawson (2010) proposed four domains (i.e., discrimination, explanatory models, stigma, and family involvement) that should be considered for successful rehabilitation and interventions for African Americans with SMI. We argue that these domains are relevant for many of the groups we have discussed and could be considered for interventions with adults with DD as well.

To address provider bias, which may influence the quality and types of services received by persons of color (McGuire & Miranda, 2008), cultural competence training that emphasizes the importance of not stereotyping and making assumptions about clients may be important. Additionally, hiring clinicians who come from different racial and ethnic backgrounds that represent the patients served is an important way to ensure clinical staff understands the context, language, and experiences of people from different racial and ethnic backgrounds. Whitley and Lawson (2010) suggest that providers who work collaboratively with local ethnic organizations may lead to lower levels of mistrust among people of color and their families seeking care.

Often families maintain cultural explanations and attributions about the cause of mental illness and disabilities that are religiously based. We also learned that families frequently hold both cultural and medically based explanations about the illnesses. Interventions and providers that recognize and take these dual belief systems into account may be more successful. Providers need to be open to alternative worldviews and work in collaboration with churches, tribes, and other cultural organizations on programs that serve people with SMI and DD of different cultural groups (Grandbois, 2005; Whitley & Lawson, 2010).

Countering stigma should happen on the individual and macro levels. Although there is stigma toward persons with DD and SMI in the general population, it may play out differently or come about for different reasons depending on the group (Whitley & Lawson, 2010). Awareness campaigns about disabilities and mental illnesses that are culturally tailored for specific communities can help combat stigma on a macro level. These campaigns can utilize community leaders and organizations to promote more positive messages about these disorders (Whitley & Lawson, 2010). The first author of this chapter was involved in a community collaboration to create a radio novella for the Spanish-speaking community to reduce stigma and better understand DD. Many individuals internalize stigma and may need extra help in understanding that they can live normal lives and their disability does not have to define them.

As identified previously, many different cultural groups have closely knit families, and support often involves family members beyond the nuclear family. Whitley and Lawson (2010) make the point that the service systems do not foster family involvement because they are based on individualistic values versus collectivist ones that are held by many groups. As a result, adults with DD and SMI are encouraged to become independent from their families because that is considered normative (Magaña & Smith, 2006). Programs that encourage family involvement in treatment and recovery and provide education about the disabilities and services to family members beyond the parents are recommended.

CONCLUSION

People with DD and SMI are living longer and there is emerging research on their health and well-being throughout the life span. There is virtually no research on people of color with DD and SMI who are older adults. In this chapter, we presented a conceptual framework using a Venn diagram that shows the intersection between aging and having an SMI or DD, limited services for these aging populations, and being a person of color with SMI or DD. We discussed research on services and service disparities for adults with DD and SMI and found disparities in health care and services for people with DD and SMI compared to the general population, as well as disparities between people of color with DD and SMI and their white counterparts. This review suggests that for people of color with DD and SMI, the challenges in obtaining care and treatment are compounded and likely even more so for people of color with DD and SMI who are aging. We presented barriers to care and best practices for health and specialty care agencies to consider. Future research is needed to examine the experiences of older adults of color who have SMI and DD to understand the unique challenges they face and, more specifically, investigate the complexity of their needs to inform current practices and to make services culturally relevant, so that people with DD and SMI from ethnic minority communities have access to quality services that ensure healthy aging.

REFERENCES

Aaron, K., Levine, D., & Burstin, H. (2003). African American Church participation and health care practices. *Journal of General Internal Medicine, 18,* 908–913.

Abe-Kim, J., Takeuchi, D. T., Hong, S., Zane, N., Sue, S., Spencer, M. S.,...Alegría, M. (2007). Use of mental health-related services among immigrant and US-born Asian Americans: Results from the National Latino and Asian American Study. *American Journal of Public Health, 97*(1), 91–98.

Alegría, M., Canino, G., Ríos, R., Vera, M., Calderón, J., Rusch, D., et al. (2002). Inequalities in use of specialty mental health services among Latinos, African Americans, and non-Latino whites. *Psychiatric Services (Washington, D.C.), 53*(12), 1547–1555.

Alegría, M., Mulvaney-Day, N., Torres, M., Polo, A., Cao, Z., & Canino, G. (2007a). Prevalence of psychiatric disorders across Latino subgroups in the United States. *American Journal of Public Health, 97*(1), 68–75.

Alegría, M., Mulvaney-Day, N., Woo, M., Torres, M., Gao, S., & Oddo, V. (2007b). Correlates of past-year mental health service use among Latinos: Results from the National Latino and Asian American Study. *American Journal of Public Health, 97*(1), 76–83.

Andersson, C., & Mattsson, E. (2001). Adults with cerebral palsy: A survey describing problems, needs, and resources, with special emphasis on locomotion. *Developmental Medicine and Child Neurology, 43*(2), 76–82.

Aponte, J., & Crouch, R. (1995). The changing ethnic profile of the United States. In J. Aponte, R. Rivers, & J. Wohl (Eds.), *Psychological interventions and cultural diversity* (pp. 1–18). Needham Heights, MA: Allyn & Bacon.

Asai, M. O., & Kameoka, V. A. (2005). The influence of Sekentei on family caregiving and underutilization of social services among Japanese caregivers. *Social Work, 50*(2), 111–118.

Barr, O., Gilgunn, J., Kane, T., & Moore, G. (1999). Health screening for people with learning disabilities by a community learning disability nursing service in Northern Ireland. *Journal of Advanced Nursing, 29*(6), 1482–1491.

Barrio, C., Yamada, A. M., Hough, R. L., Hawthorne, W., Garcia, P., & Jeste, D. V. (2003). Ethnic disparities in use of public mental health case management services among patients with schizophrenia. *Psychiatric Services (Washington, D.C.), 54*(9), 1264–1270.

Barry, K. L., Blow, F. C., Dornfeld, M., & Valenstein, M. (2002). Aging and schizophrenia: Current health services research and recommendations. *Journal of Geriatric Psychiatry and Neurology, 15*(3), 121–127.

Beals, J., Manson, S. M., Whitesell, N. R., Mitchell, C. M., Novins, D. K., Simpson, S., et al. (2005a). Prevalence of major depressive episode in two American Indian reservation populations: Unexpected findings with a structured interview. *The American Journal of Psychiatry, 162*(9), 1713–1722.

Beals, J., Novins, D. K., Whitesell, N. R., Spicer, P., Mitchell, C. M., & Manson, S. M. (2005b). Prevalence of mental disorders and utilization of mental health services in two American Indian reservation populations: mental health disparities in a national context. *The American Journal of Psychiatry, 162*(9), 1723–1732.

Beange, J., McElduff, H., & Baker, A. (1992). People with mental retardation have an increased prevalence of osteoporosis: A Population study. *American Journal on Mental Retardation, 103*, 19–28.

Beirne-Smith, M., Patton, J., & Ittenbach, R. (1994). *Mental retardation* (4th ed.). New York, NY: Macmillan.

Blank, M. B., Mahmood, M., Fox, J. C., & Guterbock, T. (2002). Alternative mental health services: The role of the black church in the South. *American Journal of Public Health, 92*(10), 1668–1672.

Blue-Banning, M. J., Turnbull, A. P., & Pereira, L. (2000). Group action planning as a support strategy for Hispanic families: Parent and professional perspectives. *Mental Retardation, 38*(3), 262–275.

Braun, K. L., & Browne, C. V. (1998). Perceptions of dementia, caregiving, and help seeking among Asian and Pacific Islander Americans. *Health & Social Work, 23*(4), 262–274.

Castles, S., & Miller, M. (Eds.). (2003). *International population movements in the modern world: The age of migration.* New York, NY: The Guilford Press.

Cheung, F., & Snowden, L. (1990). Use of inpatient mental health services by members of ethnic minority groups. *American Psychologist, 45*, 347–355.

Cho, S., Singer, G. H., & Brenner, M. (2003). A comparison of adaptation to childhood disability in Korean Immigrant and Korean mothers. *Focus on Autism and Other Developmental Disabilities, 18*, 9–19.

Choi, K. H., & Wynne, M. E. (2000). Providing services to Asian Americans with developmental disabilities and their families: Mainstream service providers' perspective. *Community Mental Health Journal, 36*(6), 589–595.

Chun, C., Moos, R., & Cronkite, R. (2006). Culture: A fundamental context for the stress and coping paradigm. In P. Wong & L. Wong (Eds.), *Handbook of multicultural perspectives on stress and coping* (29–53). New York, NY: Springer-Verlag.

Compton, M. T., Esterberg, M. L., & Broussard, B. (2008). Causes of schizophrenia reported by urban African American lay community members. *Comprehensive Psychiatry, 49*(1), 87–93.

Connell, C. M., & Gibson, G. D. (1997). Racial, ethnic, and cultural differences in dementia caregiving: Review and analysis. *The Gerontologist, 37*(3), 355–364.

Cox, C., & Monk, A. (1993). Hispanic culture and family care of Alzheimer's patients. *Health & Social Work, 18*(2), 92–100.

Dixon, L., Green-Paden, L., Delahanty, J., Lucksted, A., Postrado, L., & Hall, J. (2001). Variables associated with disparities in treatment of patients with schizophrenia and comorbid mood and anxiety disorders. *Psychiatric Services (Washington, D.C.), 52*(9), 1216–1222.

Donnelley, P. (2001). Korean American family experiences of caregiving for their mentally ill adult children: An interpretive inquiry. *Journal of Transcultural Nursing, 12,* 292–301.

Donnelley, P. (2005). Multicultural health beliefs and help seeking behaviors of Korean American Parents of adult children with schizophrenia. *Journal of Multicultural Nursing & Health, 11,* 23–34.

Druss, B. G., Bradford, W. D., Rosenheck, R. A., Radford, M. J., & Krumholz, H. M. (2001). Quality of medical care and excess mortality in older patients with mental disorders. *Archives of General Psychiatry, 58*(6), 565–572.

Erickson, J., Devlieger, P., & Sung, J. (1999). Korean-American female perspectives on disability. *American Journal of Speech-Language Pathology, 8,* 99–108.

Esbensen, A. J., Seltzer, M. M., & Greenberg, J. S. (2007). Factors predicting mortality in midlife adults with and without Down syndrome living with family. *Journal of Intellectual Disability Research: JIDR, 51*(Pt 12), 1039–1050.

Esterberg, M. L., & Compton, M. T. (2006). Causes of schizophrenia reported by family members of urban African American hospitalized patients with schizophrenia. *Comprehensive Psychiatry, 47*(3), 221–226.

Farris, C., Brems, C., Johnson, M. E., Wells, R., Burns, R., & Kletti, N. (2003). A comparison of schizophrenic patients with or without coexisting substance use disorder. *The Psychiatric Quarterly, 74*(3), 205–222.

Fisher, K. (2004). Health disparities and mental retardation. *Journal of Nursing Scholarship: An Official Publication of Sigma Theta Tau International Honor Society of Nursing/Sigma Theta Tau, 36*(1), 48–53.

Freedman, R. I., Krauss, M. W., & Seltzer, M. M. (1997). Aging parents' residential plans for adult children with mental retardation. *Mental Retardation, 35*(2), 114–123.

Fujiura, G., & Yamaki, K. (2000). Trends in demography of childhood poverty and disability. *Exceptional Children, 66,* 187–199.

Gabel, S. (2004). South Asian Indian cultural orientations toward mental retardation. *Mental Retardation, 42*(1), 12–25.

Gajdosik, C. G., & Cicirello, N. (2001). Secondary conditions of the musculoskeletal system in adolescents and adults with cerebral palsy. *Physical & Occupational Therapy in Pediatrics, 21*(4), 49–68.

Ghosh, S., & Magaña, S. (2009). A Rich Mosaic: Emerging research on Asian families of persons with intellectual and developmental disabilities. *International Review of Research in Mental Retardation, 37,* 179–212.

Gilmer, T. P., Dolder, C. R., Lacro, J. P., Folsom, D. P., Lindamer, L., Garcia, P., et al. (2004). Adherence to treatment with antipsychotic medication and health care costs among Medicaid beneficiaries with schizophrenia. *The American Journal of Psychiatry, 161*(4), 692–699.

Grandbois, D. (2005). Stigma of mental illness among American Indian and Alaska Native nations: Historical and contemporary perspectives. *Issues in Mental Health Nursing, 26*(10), 1001–1024.

Guarnaccia, P. J., & Parra, P. (1996). Ethnicity, social status, and families' experiences of caring for a mentally ill family member. *Community Mental Health Journal, 32*(3), 243–260.

Guarnacia, P., Para, P., Deschamps, A., Milstein, G., & Argiles, N. (1992). Si Dios Quiere: Hispanic families' experiences of caring for a seriously mentally ill family member. *Culture, Medicine & Psychiatry, 16,* 187–215.

Harry, B. (1992). An ethnographic study of cross-cultural communication with Puerto Rican-American families in the special education system. *American Educational Research Journal, 29,* 471–494.

Harvey, P. D., Leff, J., Trieman, N., Anderson, J., & Davidson, M. (1997). Cognitive impairment in geriatric chronic schizophrenic patients: A cross-national study in New York and London. *International Journal of Geriatric Psychiatry, 12*(10), 1001–1007.

Hatton, C. (2002). Psychosocial interventions for adults with intellectual disabilities and mental health problems: A review. *Journal of Mental Health, 11,* 357–374.

Heller, T., & Factor, A. (1988). Permanency planning among black and white family caregivers of older adults with mental retardation. *Mental Retardation, 26*(4), 203–208.

Heller, T., & Factor, A. (1991). Permanency planning for adults with mental retardation living with family caregivers. *American Journal of Mental Retardation: AJMR, 96*(2), 163–176.

Heller, T., Markwardt, R., Rowitz, L., & Farber, B. (1994). Adaptation of Hispanic families to a member with mental retardation. *American Journal of Mental Retardation: AJMR, 99*(3), 289–300.

Helms, J., & Cook, D. (Eds.). (1999). *Using race and culture in counseling and psychotherapy and process.* Needham Heights, MA: Allyn & Bacon.

Hewitt, A., Larson, S., & Lakin, K. (2000). An independent evaluation of the quality of services and system performance of Minnesota's Medicaid Home and Community Based Services for persons with mental retardation and related conditions. Minneapolis: University of Minnesota, Research, and Training Center on Community Living.

Hines-Martin, V. P. (1998). Environmental context of caregiving for severely mentally ill adults: An African American experience. *Issues in Mental Health Nursing, 19*(5), 433–451.

Horwitz, A. V., & Reinhard, S. C. (1995). Ethnic differences in caregiving duties and burdens among parents and siblings of persons with severe mental illnesses. *Journal of Health and Social Behavior, 36*(2), 138–150.

Hurh, W., & Kim, K. (Eds.). (1984). *Korean immigrants in America.* Cranbury, NJ: Associated University Presses.

Janicki, M. P., & Dalton, A. J. (2000). Prevalence of dementia and impact on intellectual disability services. *Mental Retardation, 38*(3), 276–288.

Janicki, M. P., Dalton, A. J., Henderson, C. M., & Davidson, P. W. (1999). Mortality and morbidity among older adults with intellectual disability: Health services considerations. *Disability and Rehabilitation, 21*(5–6), 284–294.

Kim-Goh, M. (1993). Conceptualization of mental illness among Korean-American clergymen and implications for mental health service delivery. *Community Mental Health Journal, 29*(5), 405–412.

Kleinman A. (Ed.). (1980). *Patients and healers in the context of culture.* Berkeley, CA: University of California Press.

Kleinman, A., & Kleinman, J. (1993). Face, favor and families: The social course of mental health problems in Chinese and American societies. *Chinese Journal of Mental Health, 6,* 37–47.

Kozma, C. (2008). Down syndrome and Dementia. *Topics in Geriatric Rehabilitation, 24,* 41–53.

Kung, W. (2003). The illness, stigma, culture, or immigration? Burdens on Chinese American caregivers of patients with schizophrenia. *Families in Society, 84,* 547–557.

Kung, W. (2004). Causal attributions of Schizophrenia by Chinese American caregivers. *Journal of Ethnic and Cultural Diversity in Social Work, 13,* 37–57.

Lagomasino, I. T., Dwight-Johnson, M., Miranda, J., Zhang, L., Liao, D., Duan, N., et al. (2005). Disparities in depression treatment for Latinos and site of care. *Psychiatric Services (Washington, D.C.), 56*(12), 1517–1523.

Lehman, A. F., & Steinwachs, D. M. (1998). Translating research into practice: The Schizophrenia Patient Outcomes Research Team (PORT) treatment recommendations. *Schizophrenia Bulletin, 24*(1), 1–10.

Lehmann, S. W. (2003). Psychiatric disorders in older women. *International Review of Psychiatry (Abingdon, England), 15*(3), 269–279.

Light, E. & Lebowitz, B. (Eds.). (1991). *The elderly with chronic mental illness.* New York, NY: Springer.

Magaña, S. M. (1999). Puerto Rican families caring for an adult with mental retardation: Role of familism. *American Journal of Mental Retardation: AJMR, 104*(5), 466–482.

Magaña, S. M., Greenberg, J. S., & Seltzer, M. M. (2004). The health and well-being of black mothers who care for their adult children with schizophrenia. *Psychiatric Services (Washington, D.C.), 55*(6), 711–713.

Magaña, S. M., Ramírez García, J. I., Hernández, M. G., & Cortez, R. (2007). Psychological distress among latino family caregivers of adults with schizophrenia: The roles of burden and stigma. *Psychiatric Services (Washington, D.C.), 58*(3), 378–384.

Magaña, S., & Ghosh, S. (2010). Latina mothers caring for a son or daughter with Autism or Schizophrenia: Similarities, differences and the relationship between co-residency and maternal well-being. *Journal of Family Social Work, 13*(3), 227–250.

Magaña, S., & Smith, M. J. (2006). Health outcomes of midlife and older Latina and black American mothers of children with developmental disabilities. *Mental Retardation, 44*(3), 224–234.

Magaña, S., & Smith, M. J. (2008). Health behaviors, service utilization, and access to care among older mothers of color who have children with developmental disabilities. *Intellectual and Developmental Disabilities, 46*(4), 267–280.

Magaña, S., Seltzer, M., & Krauss, W. (2002a). Service utilization patterns of adults with intellectual disabilities: A comparison of Puerto Rican and non-Latino white families. *Journal of Gerontological Social Work, 37,* 65–86.

Magaña, S., Seltzer, M., Krauss, M., Rubert, M., & Szapocznik, J., (2002b). Well-Being and family role strains among Cuban American and Puerto Rican mothers of adults with mental retardation. *Journal of Human Behavior in the Social Environment, 5,* 31–55.

Marin, G., & Marin, B. (Eds.). (1991). *Research with Hispanic populations. Applied social research methods series* (Vol. 23). Thousand Oaks, CA: Sage.

Mary, N. L. (1990). Reactions of black, Hispanic, and white mothers to having a child with handicaps. *Mental Retardation, 28*(1), 1–5.

McCallion, P., Janicki, M., & Grant-Griffin, L. (1997). Exploring the impact of culture and acculturation on older families' caregiving for persons with developmental disabilities. *Family Relations, 46,* 347–357.

McGuire, T. G., & Miranda, J. (2008). New evidence regarding racial and ethnic disparities in mental health: Policy implications. *Health Affairs (Project Hope), 27*(2), 393–403.

McQuaid, J. R., Granholm, E., McClure, F. S., Roepke, S., Pedrelli, P., Patterson, T. L., et al. (2000). Development of an integrated cognitive-behavioral and social skills training intervention for older patients with schizophrenia. *The Journal of Psychotherapy Practice and Research, 9*(3), 149–156.

Milstein, G., Guarnaccia, P., & Midlarsky, E. (1995). Ethnic differences in the interpretation of mental illness: Perspectives of caregivers. *Research in Community Mental Health, 8,* 155–178.

Miltiades, H. B., & Pruchno, R. (2002). The effect of religious coping on caregiving appraisals of mothers of adults with developmental disabilities. *The Gerontologist, 42*(1), 82–91.

Morrison, E. F., & Thornton, K. A. (1999). Influence of southern spiritual beliefs on perceptions of mental illness. *Issues in Mental Health Nursing, 20*(5), 443–458.

Newman, S., & Bland, R. (1991). Mortality in a cohort of patients with schizophrenia: A record linkage study. *The Canadian Journal of Psychiatry, 36,* 239–245.

Office of the Surgeon General. (2002). *Closing the gap: A national blueprint to improve the health of persons with mental retardation: A report of the Surgeon General's Conference on Health Disparities and Mental Retardation.* Rockville, MD: U.S. Department of Health and Human Services. Retrieved from www.surgeongeneral.gov/topics/mentalretardation

Oyserman, D., Coon, H. M., & Kemmelmeier, M. (2002). Rethinking individualism and collectivism: Evaluation of theoretical assumptions and meta-analyses. *Psychological Bulletin, 128*(1), 3–72.

Pickett, S., Vraniak, D., Cook, J., & Cohler, B. (1993). Strength in adversity: Blacks bear burden better than whites. *Professional Psychology, Research and Practice, 24,* 460–467.

Prouty, R., & Lakin, K. (1997). Residential services for persons with developmental disabilities: Status and trends through 1996 (University of Minnesota Research and Training Center on Community Living Research Report No. 49). Retrieved March 26, 2012, from http://eric.ed.gov/PDFS/ED411653.pdf

Pruchno, R. A., & McMullen, W. F. (2004). Patterns of service utilization by adults with a developmental disability: Type of service makes a difference. *American Journal of Mental Retardation: AJMR, 109*(5), 362–378.

Pruchno, R., Hicks Patrick, J., & Burant, C. (1997). African American and white mothers of adults with chronic disablties: Caregiving burden and satisfaction. *Family Relations, 46,* 335–346.

Roberts, L., Roalfe, A., Wilson, S., & Lester, H. (2007). Physical health care of patients with schizophrenia in primary care: A comparative study. *Family Practice, 24*(1), 34–40.

Sabogal, F., Marin, G., Otero-Sabogal, R., Marin, B., & Perez-Stable, E. (1987). Hispanic familism and acculturation: What changes and what doesn't? *Hispanic Journal of Behavioral Sciences, 9,* 4397–4412.

Satre, D. D., Campbell, C. I., Gordon, N. S., & Weisner, C. (2010). Ethnic disparities in accessing treatment for depression and substance use disorders in an integrated health plan. *International Journal of Psychiatry in Medicine, 40*(1), 57–76.

Scharlach, A. E., Kellam, R., Ong, N., Baskin, A., Goldstein, C., & Fox, P. J. (2006). Cultural attitudes and caregiver service use: Lessons from focus groups with racially and ethnically diverse family caregivers. *Journal of Gerontological Social Work, 47*(1–2), 133–156.

Schnittker, J., Freese, J., & Powell, B. (2000). Nature, nurture, neither, nor: Black-White differences in beliefs about the causes and appropriate treatment of mental illness. *Social Forces, 78,* 1101–1132.

Seltzer, M., Greenberg, J., Krauss, M., & Hong, J. (1997). Predictors and outcomes of the end of co-resident caregiving in aging families of adults with mental retardation or mental illness. *Family Relations, 46,* 13–22.

Shen-Ryan, A., & Smith, M. (1989). Parental reactions to developmental disabilities in Chinese American families. *Child and Adolescent Social Work, 6,* 283–299.

Silverman, W, Zigman, W., Kim, H., Krinsky-McHale, S., & Wisniewski, H. (1998). Aging and dementia among adults with mental retardation and Down syndrome. *Topics in Geriatric Rehabilitation, 13,* 1–84.

Skinner, D., Rodriguez, P., & Bailey, Jr., D. (1999). Qualitative analysis of Latino parents' religious interpretations of their child's disability. *Journal of Early Intervention, 22,* 271–285.

Snowden, L. R., Hastings, J. F., & Alvidrez, J. (2009). Overrepresentation of black Americans in psychiatric inpatient care. *Psychiatric Services (Washington, D.C.), 60*(6), 779–785.

Song, L. Y., Biegel, D. E., & Milligan, S. E. (1997). Predictors of depressive symptomatology among lower social class caregivers of persons with chronic mental illness. *Community Mental Health Journal, 33*(4), 269–286.

Stancliffe, R. J., & Lakin, K. C. (2006). Longitudinal frequency and stability of family contact in institutional and community living. *Mental Retardation, 44*(6), 418–429.

The Population Reference Bureau. (2004). Retrieved February 10, 2012, from http://www.prb.org/Articles/2004/USGrowing BiggerOlderandMoreDiverse.aspx

U.S. Department of Health and Human Services. (2001). *Mental health: Culture, race, and ethnicity, a supplement to mental health: A report of the surgeon general.* Office of the Surgeon General, Center for Mental Health Services (US): National Institute of Mental Health (US).

Valentine, D. P., McDermott, S., & Anderson, D. (1998). Mothers of adults with mental retardation: Is race a factor in perceptions of burdens and gratifications. *Families in Society, 79,* 577–584.

Ward, R. L., Nichols, A. D., & Freedman, R. I. (2010). Uncovering health care inequalities among adults with intellectual and developmental disabilities. *Health & Social Work, 35*(4), 280–290.

Weisman, A. G., Gomes, L. G., & López, S. R. (2003). Shifting blame away from ill relatives: Latino families' reactions to schizophrenia. *The Journal of Nervous and Mental Disease, 191*(9), 574–581.

Whaley, A. (2001). Cultural mistrust: An important psychological construct for diagnosis and treatment of African Americans. *Professional Psychology: Research and Practice, 32,* 555–562.

Whitley, R., & Lawson, W. B. (2010). The psychiatric rehabilitation of African Americans with severe mental illness. *Psychiatric Services (Washington, D.C.), 61*(5), 508–511.

CHAPTER 21

The Productive Engagement of Older African Americans, Hispanics, Asians, and Native Americans

Nancy Morrow-Howell and Yi Wang

POPULATION AGING AND DEMAND FOR PRODUCTIVE ENGAGEMENT

Low birth and death rates are transforming the age structure of U.S. society, as described in other chapters of this handbook. The demographic and longevity revolutions in this country and across the world are indeed cause for concern as societies face tremendous challenges in providing economic support and health care to growing older populations. In most discussions of the aging population, age is viewed as a "problem," as an "age drain." These negative characterizations of age focus on functional dependency, chronic illness, cognitive impairment, and depression, and the discussion usually centers on how the older population will bankrupt the national budget, strain the health care system, and overburden the younger population.

The concerns are indeed serious, and we must shape our income support and health care policies in response. However, there is also the success story of population aging: most older adults are living longer, healthier lives with increased levels of education. In the United States, adults who reach the age of 65 years can expect to live another 20 years. Hence, there is another reality alongside the "age as problem" perspective—the human capital of the aging population is growing. This human capital must be considered in our discussions of population aging.

The productive aging perspective suggests that the growing capacity of older adults can be viewed as an asset, especially when they are engaged in activities that make economic and social contributions to society—working, volunteering, caregiving, and grandparenting—to address the problems associated with population aging (Morrow-Howell & Greenfield, 2010). This engagement may lead to several desired outcomes: offsetting the financial strains of an aging population, contributing to the betterment of society, and maintaining the health of older adults (Morrow-Howell, Hingterlong, & Sherraden, 2001).

However, there has also been widespread concern about the dangers of the concept. It is possible that older adults will be judged by their ability to be productive and expected to be productive. These expectations could differentially affect older adults with disabilities and lower socioeconomic status. Those older adults who have been disadvantaged across the life course will continue to be disadvantaged in later life when they still face discrimination in access to or support for productive engagement.

Thus, older ethnic adults who are more at risk for disadvantage across the life course should be a focus of concern as we develop programs and policies to support productive engagement. This is especially true given that the older population is becoming more racially and ethnically diverse. The productive aging agenda must pay close attention to the growing population of ethnic minorities in the older population and to the outcomes of engagement experienced by these subgroups. In this chapter, we will first review definitions and theoretical perspectives regarding the productive engagement of older adults. Second, we will review the productive engagement of four ethnic minority groups—African Americans, Hispanic Americans, Asian Americans, and Native Americans. We will describe programs and policies that will help increase the productive engagement of these older adults and conclude with ideas about going forward.

PRODUCTIVE ENGAGEMENT AMONG OLDER ADULTS: DEFINITIONS AND THEORETICAL PERSPECTIVES

In the mid-1980s, Robert Butler introduced the term productive aging to focus attention on the growing capacity of the older population and the contributions that they make to their families and communities (Butler & Gleason, 1985). This work challenged the negative images of aging and launched new research on productive engagement (Bass, Caro, & Chen, 1993; Hinterlong, Morrow-Howell, & Sherraden, 2001). Empirical work on the topic has been challenged by inconsistent definitions and conceptual frameworks. Sherraden, Morrow-Howell, Hinterlong, and Rozario (2001) offered the most stringent definition of productive engagement: engagement in activities that produced goods and services, whether paid for or not. These activities included working, volunteering, and caregiving—paid and nonpaid work. Formal volunteering refers to activities supported by a formal organization, whereas informal volunteering includes mutual aid within one's social network and neighborly assistance. Caregiving involves helping others who require assistance because of an illness or disability and includes spousal caregiving, caregiving to family members, or friends. Grandparenting, especially custodial grandparenting, has also been included under caregiving because of its high value to families and society. These activities—work, volunteering, and caregiving—can be assigned a dollar value. For example, in the United States, it has been estimated that $450 billion worth of care is provided by families in the United States (AARP, 2011b) and that the approximate value of older adults' formal volunteer activities is $44.3 billion per year (Johnson & Schaner, 2005). In sum, these activities have economic value that is quite easy to assess.

Several theoretical frameworks have been proposed to understand antecedents and outcomes of productive engagement (Bass et al., 1993; Sherraden et al., 2001; World Health Organization [WHO], 2002). Morrow-Howell and Wang (in press) combined elements of both the WHO (2002) and Sherraden et al. (2001) frameworks and proposed the following:

This framework consists of two parts: antecedents and outcomes. There are four types of antecedents—sociodemographic, economic, physical environment, and public policies and programs. These determinants influence the productive behaviors of working, volunteering, and caregiving. The activities are viewed as intermediate outcomes, which in turn affect the ultimate effects on the individual, families, communities, and society. There are many possible outcomes of engagement, and it would be advantageous to know the costs and benefits of seeking to change levels of engagement. Finally, the sociocultural context is included as a critical backdrop in understanding productive engagement within a diverse society. We posit that sociocultural contexts shape the antecedents as well as the specific productive activities of interest for ethnic minority populations.

Both definitions and theoretical perspectives are important to understanding the productive engagement of older racial/ethnic minorities. As will be reviewed later, ethnic minority older adults are more involved in informal volunteering and less involved in agency-based formal volunteering. If informal volunteering was not included as a productive activity, the productive contribution of these subpopulations of older adults would

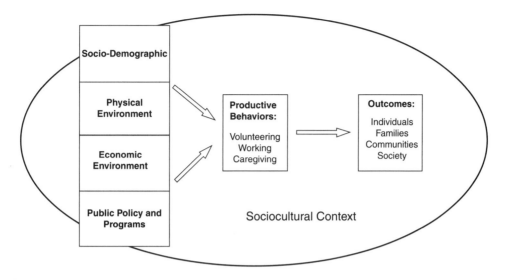

FIGURE 21.1 Antecedents and Outcomes of Productive Activities.
Source: Morrow-Howell and Wang, in press. Used with permission.

be discounted. This same argument can be applied to custodial grandparenting, where a growing number of ethnic older adults are providing primary parenting at a great benefit to society. The inclusion of this activity in discussions of productive engagement among older racial/ethnic minorities may help highlight the importance of programs and policies to support custodial grandparenting.

As suggested in Figure 21.1, many variables and contexts affect productive engagement. These factors may vary between minority and majority populations and within minority groups. Differential patterns and outcomes of engagement of ethnic minority groups can only be understood with a wide range of antecedents. For example, ethnicity status is related to living arrangements, which in turn affects demands for caregiving or grandparenting. Differences also exist between opportunities for work and volunteering as well as program supports for caregiving depending on neighborhood locations. Thus, opportunities and outcomes for productive engagement may vary by ethnicity status, and program and policy developments should be shaped accordingly.

OLDER AFRICAN AMERICANS

Working

According to the AARP Report prepared by the Urban Institute (2011), older African American men participate in the labor force at lower rates than their Hispanic and white counterparts. In 2008, labor force participation rates for 50- to 74-year-old African American, white, and Hispanic men were 55.9%, 64.9%, and 67.5%, respectively. Lower levels of education and poor health are factors associated with lower labor participation rates of older African American men. Older African American women participate in the labor force at the same rate as white women and higher rates than Hispanic women. It is interesting that the U.S. Department of Labor (2012) reported that older black workers (aged 55+) experienced an increase in labor force participation rate, from 35.3% in 2007 to 36.6% in 2011. At the same time, the participation rate of black teenagers and adults under the age of 55 declined.

Older African Americans are concentrated in the service sector of the labor market. The most common occupations for 50+ African American men are driver/sales worker, truck driver, janitor/building cleaner, security guard, hand laborer/mover, and bus driver. The most common occupations for older African American women are registered nurse, psych/home health aide provider, secretary/administrative assistant, elementary/middle school teacher, and maid/housekeeping/cleaner (AARP, 2011). When asked about reasons for staying in the workforce, 72% of African Americans aged 45 to 74 years said they "needed the money," 73% reported "needing to maintain health insurance," and 64% responded that they needed "to feel useful" (AARP, 2008).

Volunteering

African American older adults are under-represented among formal volunteer programs. Non-Hispanic whites have higher rates of volunteering than African Americans, about 28.2% compared to 20.3% (U.S. Department of Labor, 2011). Various barriers have been identified to explain this phenomenon, including disparities in economic and health resources and competing demands of caregiving and working (Center for Health Communication, Harvard School of Public Health, 2004; McBride, 2006–2007).

The African American community has a long history of mutual aid and civic engagement (Carlton-LaNey, 2006). African Americans are highly involved in neighboring and other forms of informal social assistance—described by Herd and Meyer (2002) as invisible civic engagement. Church-based volunteering and participation in mutual aid societies are traditional forms of participation in the black community (Carlton-LaNey, 2006). Further, when informal volunteering is included with formal volunteering, participation rates of blacks and whites are more comparable (AARP, 2003; Musick, Wilson, & Bynum, 2000).

Caregiving and Grandparenting

African American older women are heavily involved in caregiving activities (Chadiha, Adams, Biegel, Auslander, & Gutierrez, 2004). Carlton-LaNey, Hamilton, Ruiz, and Carleton (2001) discussed caregiving activities as "sitting with the sick" (2001, p. 447), which includes preparing meals, housekeeping, personal care, and visiting with individuals who are ill or grieving. Parental caregiving is less frequent among older African Americans because they are less likely to have living parents than non-Hispanic whites (AARP, 2011).

Grandparenting is prevalent among older African Americans. In the United States, there are more than 8 million African American custodial grandparents, six times more than whites (Watson, Randolph, & Lyons, 2005; Whitley, Kelley, & Sipe, 2001). Further, older African Americans are three times more likely to live with a grandchild than non-Hispanic whites (AARP, 2011). A typical African American grandparent is single, female, urban, and poor (Kelch-Oliver, 2008; Lee, Ensminger, & LaVeist, 2005). Rates of custodial grandparenting among African Americans, similar to all Americans, have increased in the last 20 years with increases in parental death, unemployment, and incarceration—particularly associated with the HIV/AIDS epidemic and illicit drug use (Burnette, Sun, & Sun, 2013; Henderson, 2006; Racicot, 2003).

OLDER HISPANICS

Working

Older Hispanics have levels of health comparable to their white counterparts and better than their black counterparts (AARP, 2009), and this may contribute to higher rates of labor force participation. According to the AARP Report "50+ Hispanic Workers: A growing segment of the U.S. workforce" (2009), employment rates of Hispanic men are comparable to those of older white men and higher than those of older black men. The trend is different for older Hispanic women who have employment rates below their white and black counterparts. As expected, labor force participation rates were lower for those who were older and those with lower education.

Despite relatively high levels of employment, the types of jobs and conditions of the work for Hispanic older adults are very challenging (AARP, 2009). They are more likely to be in physically challenging and low-skilled jobs, and these jobs are associated with lower wages, fewer benefits, and less job security. Older Hispanic men earn three fifths as much as their white counterparts and four fifths as much as their black counterparts, and only 38% have employee-sponsored retirement plans, almost 20% lower than other groups (The Urban Institute, 2011).

Low levels of education and lack of knowledge of English have limited employment prospects of Hispanic workers. Yet, as these factors change over time, it is estimated that the contributions of older Hispanic workers to the economy will triple by the year 2050 (AARP, 2009).

Volunteering

There is much literature on volunteering among Hispanics in the United States, but little on older Hispanics, specifically. Like most minority populations in the United States, Hispanics are highly involved in informal helping but less involved in formal volunteering than non-Hispanic whites (Musick & Wilson, 2007). The culture-specific values such as "collectivism" and "personalism" shape helping behaviors, and older Hispanics are more likely to participate in volunteer activities that are more personalized and less institutionalized than whites (National Hispanic Council on Aging [NHCOA], 2010). Similar to African American communities, faith-based networks in Hispanic communities are important sources of mutual aid for Hispanic families (NHCOA, 2010). AARP (2003) reported that 41% of Hispanics age 45 and older volunteered to help their community or someone who was in need, more than whites (36%) and Asian Americans (32%). Hispanics are more likely to provide service to extended family rather than assisting strangers (Musick & Wilson, 2007).

Caregiving and Grandparenting

Like all women in the United States, Hispanic women are greatly involved in family caregiving, although they are generally younger than caregivers from other ethnic groups (Magana, 2006). It is also documented that Hispanic spousal caregivers are more likely to be depressed than other ethnic caregivers (Adams, Aranda, Kemp, & Takagi, 2002). Magana (2006) describes how these higher rates of distress might be related to culture—Hispanic caregivers facing difficult family situations might have stronger negative reactions due to the values of familism and collectivism.

Of the 2.5 million custodial grandparents in the United States, 19% are Hispanics, with 24% being African American, 3% Asian American, and 2% American Indians (Fuller-Thomson, 2009). According to Fuller-Thomson and Minkler (2007a, b), 21% of Hispanic grandparents are caring for two grandchildren and 13% are caring for three or more. The high prevalence of grandparenting reflects the cultural value of familism, the importance of the grandparent role, and a sense of obligation to help extended family members (Burnette, 2009). Further, Hispanic grandparents pass on cultural traditions, values, and language to their grandchildren (Silverstein & Chen, 1999). It is significant that more than half of Hispanic grandparent caregivers are foreign-born. Many immigrated to the United States to take care of the children (Mutchler, Lee, & Baker, 2002).

High rates of grandparenting are related to family problems, including substance abuse, HIV/AIDS, and financial crisis (Burnette, 1997; Cox, Brooks, & Valcarcel, 2000; Goodman & Silverstein, 2002). In the face of high levels of teenage pregnancy, grandparenting is critical in supporting teen mothers (Fuller-Thomson & Minkler, 2007b). Studies conducted by Burnette (1997) and Cox et al. (2000) documented the high rates of poverty, poor health, and depression among Hispanic grandparents as well as barriers to service use, including lack of knowledge and limited English speaking abilities.

OLDER ASIAN AMERICANS

Working

Despite the rapid growth in the number of older Asian Americans, not much attention has been paid to older Asian American workers. According to The Urban Institute (2011), among workers age 50+, male Asian Americans had the highest labor force participation rates—85.1% for 50 to 61 year olds, 64.3% for 62 to 64 year olds, and 41.9% for 65 to 69 year olds. Only in the oldest age bracket, 70 years or older, did the rate for Asian men drop below the rate for Hispanic and white men. The labor force participation rate for older Asian American women is lower than the labor force participation rate for older white women. High rates of labor force participation among older Asian Americans can be explained by high levels of education.

Limited knowledge exists on the types of employment of older Asian workers in the United States. The Asian American Federation of New York (2005) considered Asian workers of all ages in New York and documented that the most common occupations are computer specialists; sales; administration and management; and textile, apparel, and furnishings workers (p. 24). The Urban Institute (2011) reported that in the age group of 50 to 61 years, the percentage of self-employment was highest among Asian Americans compared to whites and Hispanics. For full-time male workers age 50 to 61 years the 2009 median annual earnings were $50,000 for Asian Americans, $56,100 for non-Hispanic whites, $40,800 for African Americans, and $ 35,700 for Hispanics. For women, median earnings were $38,000 for Asian Americans, $40,800 for non-Hispanic Whites, $35,600 for African Americans, and $27,500 for Hispanics (Urban Institute, 2011).

Volunteering

Formal volunteering activities are less common among older Asian Americans compared to their white counterparts. Cultural factors, such as the centrality of the family and the relatively new concept of volunteerism, may explain this phenomenon. Cultural tradition in Asia does not support formal volunteering (Mui & Shibusawa, 2008). For example, a survey conducted in Hong Kong revealed that the vast majority of people (83%) thought that retired persons do not have a responsibility to serve the community (Mjelde-Mossey, Chi, & Chow, 2002). Such cultural attitudes may remain among older Asian Americans, although both in Asia and in America, new ideas and programs to engage Asian older adults are growing (Mui, 2010; Yang, 2013).

Older Asian Americans are similar to other ethnic minority groups in the cultural tradition of informal volunteering (Silva & Thomas, 2006). In the study conducted by Mui and Shibusawa (2008, p. 117), 44% of older Asian adults in New York reported that there was "a lot" of mutual support between neighbors, and 36% reported that they helped neighbors in emergencies. However, these rates differed by nationality, with mutual support being highest among Japanese and Indian older adults and lowest among Vietnamese. Only one quarter of Chinese elders reported that they assisted their neighbors.

Mui and Shibusawa (2008) compared volunteers and nonvolunteers among New York Asian older adults, and found that volunteers had better health, higher income, better English proficiency, higher rates of intergenerational exchanges, greater number of friends and neighbors, and higher life satisfaction. Further, they tended to be younger and more acculturated. It is interesting that the rate of volunteering was slightly higher among males than females (54.8% compared to 45.2%).

Caregiving and Grandparenting

Unlike volunteering, family caregiving and grandparenting is reported as a "welcome duty" by Chinese-Canadian grandparents (Fuller-Thomson, 2009). Mui and Shibusawa (2008) documented the heavy involvement of older adults in Asian American families: 61% raised a grandchild, 56% provided care to adult children when ill, 45% maintained the household, and

22% assisted the family financially. Grandparenting is a cultural expectation for Asian older adults. Interestingly, 92% of Asian grandparent caregivers in the United States are foreign-born and immigrated to help their children and grandchildren (Hooyman & Kiyak, 2008; Mutchler et al., 2002).

OLDER NATIVE AMERICANS

There is not much literature available that focuses on the productive engagement of older Native Americans. Caregiving and grandparenting are commonplace activities for older Native Americans, partly because intergenerational living is common (Polacca, 2001). In the history of Native American children and child welfare, it has been noted that as placement with extended families became preferred to non-American Indian foster care, grandparents became an important part of the Indian Child Welfare system; yet grandparenting is still challenged by high levels of functional limitations and poverty (Fuller-Thomson & Minkler, 2005). A disproportionate number of older Native Americans are custodial grandparents, and poverty levels are the highest among all other grandparenting groups (Mutchler et al., 2002).

High levels of unemployment, low-wage work, and poverty are ongoing problems for Native American elders, largely explained by low levels of education. Most have been employed in low-paying jobs that lacked both pension and health care coverage (Barusch, 2006; Polacca, 2001). It is notable that only 40% of older Native Americans receive Social Security benefits (Polacca, 2001).

There are high levels of informal volunteering in Native American communities, which is part of traditional community life (Silva & Thomas, 2006). Although not age-specific, Musick and Wilson (2007) report that American Indians' volunteer participation rate (31%) was slightly lower than non-Hispanic whites, but higher than non-Hispanic blacks, Hispanics, and Asians; however, American Indians reported volunteering fewer total hours than all other ethnic groups.

OUTCOMES OF PRODUCTIVE ENGAGEMENT

As depicted in Figure 21.1, productive engagement produces outcomes for the individual, family, community, and society. At the societal level, increasing the productive engagement of older adults, in general, may increase the supply of experienced employees, volunteers, and caregivers. In regards to working, one of the first gerontology scholars, Nathan Shock, commented in 1947 that the "The rapid increase in the proportion of older individuals in our society makes it imperative that plans be made for utilizing the capabilities of the older worker in our national economy" (Shock, 1947, p. 101). In fact, with the large numbers of baby boomers exiting the workforce, many scholars have expressed concern about the major loss of experience and historical knowledge. There are empirical demonstrations that longer working lives will mean reliance on postretirement income for the individual and less strain on public and private income support programs (Butrica, Smith, & Steuerle, 2006; Social Security Administration, 2011).

Older adults' volunteering is also valuable to society, measured both in economic terms and by the benefits to the recipients of older adults' services (Zedlewski & Butrica, 2007). There has been an emphasis on the development of intergenerational volunteer programs, with older adults tutoring and mentoring children and youth. The growth of these programs could foster more positive intergenerational relations and increase intergenerational reciprocity. Also, for many minority older adults, volunteering enables them to pass down cultural values to younger generations and preserve language and tradition (Yoshida, Gordon, & Henkin, 2008). Informal and formal volunteering are commonplace in the face of community problems, and such activities have enabled ethnic communities to survive (Carlton-LaNey, 2006; Hamilton & Sandelowski, 2003).

Increased involvement in caregiving and grandparenting can also strengthen intergenerational and family relationships. Many older Asian elders immigrate to assist their adult children in running households and taking care of their grandchildren (Min, Moon, & Lubben, 2005; Treas & Mazumdar, 2004). Older Chinese and Vietnamese immigrants have made major contributions in maintaining family households as well as grandparenting (Min, 1998; Yee, 1992).

In sum, increasing involvement of older adults as workers, volunteers, and caregivers may lead to stronger families and civic society. Yet, we need to be concerned about the effects of engagement on the individual older adults, and the extent to which individual outcomes vary by ethnicity needs to be fully understood.

Working not only provides older workers with more financial security; paid work has also been associated with reduced morbidity and improved mental health (Calvo, 2006; Kim & Moen, 2002). Employment may be health-producing because it keeps people physically and cognitively active, adds meaning and purpose, and maintains social engagement (Glass, Leon, Bassuk, & Berkman, 2006; Luoh & Herzog, 2002). Yet, certain subgroups of workers have less positive outcomes (Smith, 2007) given the demands of the working environment and their choices and preferences (Calvo, Haverstick, & Sass, 2009). Generally, workers with more education, higher salary, and more prestigious occupations tend to be more satisfied with their jobs; given the occupation types of African American and Hispanic workers, it is not surprising that job satisfaction ratings are low among these groups (Smith, 2007). Further, older employees reported to be "happy" if they had more choice and control over the retirement process (Calvo et al., 2009), and minority older workers may have less choice because they need to work for income and health insurance (AARP, 2008, 2009).

Volunteering in later life has been associated with improved physical, cognitive, and mental health (Carlson et al., 2009; Fried et al., 2004; Hong & Morrow-Howell, 2010). In a study that examined the relationship between informal volunteering (neighboring) and depressive symptoms among Hispanic older adults, the researchers concluded that higher levels of neighboring were related to lower levels of depressive symptoms, and they suggested that informal volunteering may be a protective factor against depressive symptoms (Brown et al., 2009). It is also documented that Asian elders who engage in volunteer work are more likely to be acculturated and socially involved as well as have a higher self-rated health (Mui & Shibusawa, 2008). Several studies have produced evidence that volunteering leads to better health outcomes for adults with lower socioeconomic status and for minority older adults (Morrow-Howell, Hong, & Tang, 2009). It is suggested that these differential benefits may be explained by a greater effect of the resources and status on volunteers in more disadvantaged situations (Morrow-Howell et al., 2009).

A large volume of literature documents that caregiving can negatively impact a person's physical health, mental health, and health habits (López, López-Arrieta, & Crespo, 2005; Pinquart & Sörenson, 2007). As mentioned above, Hispanic caregivers report higher levels of emotional distress than other ethnic caregivers. For those caregivers who are employed, caregiving is associated with reduced work hours and reduced work performance (MetLife Mature Market Institute [MMI], 1999). Family caregiving responsibility is the most common reason that older African American workers leave the labor force (AARP, 2011). Given the difficult circumstances that often accompany custodial grandparenting, it is not surprising that this productive activity is physically, psychologically, and financially challenging. African American grandparents are more likely to be depressed, have functional limitations, and live in poverty (Fuller-Thomson & Minkler, 2000).

Current research suggests that, in general, working and volunteering produce positive outcomes for older adults and that caregiving has both negative and positive effects. However, outcomes of working, volunteering, and caregiving vary by the context of the activity and individual attributes. For example, the negative outcomes of caregiving can be mediated by personal and social resources as well as policies that support caregiving activities (Greenfield, 2010). Hinterlong (2006) found that productive activities predict better functional status for both older African American and white adults, but higher self-rated health only among white adults. If productive engagement is important for society and, in many circumstances, good for older adults, researchers should seek to build knowledge about how to increase participation while increasing positive outcomes for individuals. Further, the effects of engagement on ethnic minority older adults should be explored more thoroughly, based on preliminary evidence that outcomes vary for these subpopulations. Given the dearth of research on older Native Americans, we especially need work in this area.

PROGRAMS AND POLICIES TO SUPPORT PRODUCTIVE ENGAGEMENT

Research has shown that the engagement in productive activities and outcomes associated with working, volunteering, and caregiving can be modified by program and policy interventions. In regards to working, there are federal programs aimed at workforce development and training. The Workforce Investment Act (WIA) is provided to individuals of all ages who seek to upgrade skills, but states can give priority to older workers and minority populations. For example, Indian and Native American Programs of the WIA are aimed at employment, training, and educational opportunities for this subpopulation (http://www.dol.gov/dol/topic/training/indianprograms.htm). The U.S. Department of Labor also runs the Senior Community Service Employment Program (SCSEP), which is aimed at training and placing low-income older adults. In 2011, the program served 105,851 enrolled participants, 51% of whom were ethnic minorities and 89% living below poverty level (http://www.doleta.gov/seniors/html_docs/AboutSCSEP.cfm). These are examples of two public programs that serve minority older adults in the workforce, but compared to the demographic situation, utilization of these programs is low (Washko, Schack, Goff, & Pudlin, 2011).

There is a growing movement to provide career counseling and job placement services to older workers. For example, Civic Ventures' Encore Careers program provides information, resources, and advice to mid-life and older individuals who are interested in working longer or switching careers (www.encore.org). However, these types of services have been primarily used by older adults with higher socioeconomic status, and inclusion remains more of a goal than a reality. Ongoing education is critically important in longer working lives, and older adults have not had easy access to skill development opportunities. The American Association of Community Colleges sponsors the Plus 50 Initiative to encourage innovative programming for older students, including career counseling and workforce training courses. Access and costs of community college are conducive to including diverse older adults.

As reviewed above, savings and income support programs differentially affect minority older adults. African American, Hispanic, and Native Americans are less likely to be in jobs with employment-sponsored retirement plans, and lower incomes across the life course lead to smaller Social Security payments. These ethnic groups are more vulnerable to negative effects of raising the eligible age for both early and full retirement benefits. Poorer health conditions and more physically demanding jobs threaten abilities to work longer, and debates on raising the retirement age need to consider the conditions of older ethnic minorities (Angel & Mudrazija, 2011).

Formal volunteering programs have traditionally involved older adults with higher education and income, and minority older adults have been underrepresented (Tang, 2006). Yet, there are programs where minority older adults are strongly represented. For example, the federal Senior Corps programs, Senior Companions and Foster Grandparents, solicit, train, and support older adults to work as tutors, coaches, and caregivers for children and youth in need and to provide supportive and companionship services to older adults in need. These programs provide stipends to cover the cost of volunteering, which may be an important component of increasing the diversity of the volunteer labor force (McBride, Gonzales, Morrow-Howell, & McCrary, 2011). There are volunteer programs geared specifically to older ethnic minorities. For example, Project Shine engages older immigrants transitioning to the United States in civic activities and workforce development programs. The project report, Community Treasures (Yoshida et al., 2008), documents the civic activities of elders from diverse ethnic communities and the important role of civic engagement in their lives and their communities.

In regards to caregiving, psychoeducational and support programs have flourished in attempts to support caregivers. The National Family Caregiver Support Programs, established in 2000 by Public Law 106–501, provides grants to states and area agencies to deliver information to caregivers about available services, assist caregivers in gaining access to services; provide individual counseling; and organize support groups, caregiver training, and respite care. However, it is known that minority caregivers are less likely to use services (Magana, 2006). The Case and Counseling program is particularly relevant to low-income ethnic minority caregivers. Through this Medicaid program, care recipients can decide how to use allocated funds to meet care needs and family caregivers can be paid to provide the necessary services (Mahoney, Simon-Rusinowitz, Loughlin, Desmond, & Squillace, 2004).

In the last decade, many programs have been implemented to serve the custodial grandparent. The National Caregiver Support Act includes grandparent caregivers and encourages communities to develop innovative programs to support them. The Grandparent Information Center, established by AARP, is a comprehensive source of information to assist caregivers in locating resources, both locally and nationally (http://www.aarp.org/families/grandparents/gic/). There is federal legislation (Grandparents Aiding Children and Youth Act of 2003) that supports housing developments (Smith & Beltran, 2003). There are also examples of intergenerational housing projects, like Grand Families in Boston and Grandparent Family Apartments in New York, where children and grandparents receive supportive services in an intergenerational-friendly environment (Burnette, 2009).

SUMMARY AND CONCLUSION

In sum, there are several trends that emerge across ethnic minority groups and engagement in productive activities. In regards to working, older Hispanics and African Americans are less likely to participate in the workforce and more vulnerable to unemployment compared with their Asian American and non-Hispanic white counterparts. Hispanic and African American older workers earn less, are less likely to be self-employed, and less likely to have employer-supported retirement plans (Urban Institute, 2011). There is limited research on older Native American workers, but high levels of unemployment, low wage, and lack of employment benefits had been identified as problems among Native American elders.

In regards to volunteering, minority older adults are more likely to engage in informal helping activities rather than formal volunteering services. Older African Americans are more likely to serve in faith-related activities, whereas older Hispanic and Asian Americans tend to focus helping efforts on extended families.

These minority groups engage in high levels of caregiving to families and friends, sometimes under difficult conditions. Grandparenting is prevalent among all minority groups, where intergenerational households are more common. The groups with the highest prevalence of custodial grandparenting are Native Americans, followed by African Americans and Latinos. Asian grandparents are unlikely to report main responsibility for a grandchild. In many African American and Hispanic families, grandparents are custodial because of family problems, like parental incarceration or substance abuse, whereas in Asian American families, grandparents are involved as parents are full-time employed (Hooyman & Kiyak, 2008; Mui & Shibusawa, 2008).

In recent years, there has been a focus on the productive engagement of older adults, as a response to population aging. The findings reviewed here about the productive activity of ethnic older adults show the value of unpaid and paid work to society. However, this review also confirms that we need to take seriously the concern that there will be an unequal burden on ethnic minorities when we strive to increase the involvement of older adults as workers, volunteers, and caregivers. Minority older adults perform these productive activities with certain vulnerabilities and accumulated disadvantages, whether it be lower education, worse health, language barriers, or race discrimination (in addition to age discrimination). For African Americans, Hispanics, and Native Americans, marginalization in the workforce will continue into later life unless programs and policies better support education and work across the life course. It is especially important to consider the effects of increasing the early and full retirement age for accessing Social Security—minority older adults who struggle more in the job market and who are more likely to be in physically demanding jobs will be disproportionately affected.

Minority older adults are less likely to be involved in agency-based volunteering, and it is in this formal volunteer role that older adults gain access to greater social capital, resources, knowledge, and recognition. Lower rates of participation limit the positive effects of formal volunteering on older ethnic minorities. Thus, programs and policies must support these groups in becoming more involved in civic activities. This review also reveals the importance of including informal volunteering, caregiving, and custodial grandparenting in any formal definitions of "productive behavior." These are critical activities to society, yet demanding on the individual older adults, especially those with fewer resources. If more value is assigned to these activities, older adults may be more recognized and supported in these roles.

Our conceptual model suggests that a wide range of factors are associated with engagement in productive behaviors, and this review indicates that many demographic and cultural factors are important to understand the engagement of ethnic older adults. Education, living arrangements, cultural expectations, and perspectives on help-giving differentially determine working, volunteering, and caregiving for these subgroups. Greater understanding of these contexts and how they affect engagement and outcomes associated with engagement is needed. The productive engagement of older adults in this society may be part of the solution to population aging, and we sorely need solutions. However, we must be vigilant about creating the conditions for participation that not only maximize engagement but produce more positive and less negative outcomes for ethnic older adults.

REFERENCES

AARP. (2003). *Multicultural study 2003: Time and money: An in-depth look at 45+ volunteers and donors.* Washington, DC: Author.

AARP. (2008). *Staying ahead of the curve 2007: The AARP work and career study.* Washington, DC: AARP.

AARP. (2009). *50+ Hispanic workers: A growing segment of the U.S. workforce.* Washington, DC: AARP.

AARP. (2011a). *50+ African American workers: A status report, implications, and recommendations.* Washington, DC: AARP.

AARP. (2011b). *Valuing the invaluable: 2011 update, the growing contributions and costs of family caregiving.* Washington, DC: AARP.

Adams, B., Aranda, M., Kemp, B., & Takagi, K. (2002). Ethnic and gender differences in distress among Anglo-American, African-American, Japanese-American and Mexican-American spousal caregivers of persons with dementia. *Journal of Clinical Geropsychology, 8,* 279–301.

Angel, J., & Mudrazija, S. (2011). Raising the retirement age: Is it fair for low-income workers and minorities? *Public Policy and Aging Report, 21,* 12–19.

Barusch, A. (2006). Native American elders: Unique histories and special needs. In B. Berkman (Ed.), *Handbook of social work in health and aging.* New York, NY: Oxford University Press.

Bass, S. A., Caro, F. G., & Chen, Y. P. (1993). *Achieving a productive aging society.* Westport, CT: Auburn House.

Brown, S.C., Mason, C. A., Perrino, T., Hirama, I., Verdeja, R., Spokane, A. R.,…Szapocznik, J. (2009). Longitudinal relationships between neighboring behavior and depressive symptoms in Hispanic older adults in Miami, Florida. *Journal of Community Psychology, 37*(5), 618–634.

Burnette, D. (1997). Grandparents raising grandchildren in the inner city. *Families in Society, 78,* 489–499.

Burnette, D. (2009). Grandparent caregiving in Caribbean Latino families: Correlates of children's departure from care. *Journal of Intergenerational Relationships, 7*(2), 331–343.

Burnette, D., Sun, J., & Sun, F. (2013). A comparative review of grandparent care of children in the U.S. and China. *Aging International, 36,* 43–57.

Butler, R. N., & Gleason, H. P. (1985). *Productive aging.* New York, NY: Springer.

Butrica, B., Smith, K. E., & Steuerle, C. E. (2006). Working for a good retirement. Retrieved April 18, 2012, from http://www.urban.org/UploadedPDF/311333_good_retirement.pdf

Calvo, E. (2006). *Does working longer make people healthier and happier? Work Opportunity Issue in Brief 2.* Chestnut Hill, MA: Center for Retirement Research at Boston College.

Calvo, E., Haverstick, K., & Sass, S. (2009). Gradual retirement, sense of control, and retirees' happiness. *Research on Aging, 31,* 112–135.

Carlson, M. C., Erickson, K. I., Kramer, A. F., Voss, M. W., Bolea, N., Mielke, M.,...Fried, L. P. (2009). Evidence for neurocognitive plasticity in at-risk older adults: the experience corps program. *The Journals of Gerontology. Series A, Biological Sciences and Medical Sciences, 64*(12), 1275–1282.

Carlton-LaNey, I. (2006). "Doing the Lord's work": African American elders' civic engagement. *Generations, 30*(4), 47–50.

Carlton-LaNey, I., Hamilton, J., Ruiz, D., & Carleton A. S. (2001). "Sitting with the sick": African American women's philanthropy. *Affilia, 16*(4), 447–466.

Center for Health Communication, Harvard School of Public Health. (2004). *Reinventing aging: Baby boomers and civic engagement.* Retrieved from http://www.hsph.harvard.edu/chc/reinventingaging/Report.pdf

Chadiha, L. A., Adams, P., Biegel, D. E., Auslander, W., & Gutierrez, L. (2004). Empowering African American women informal caregivers: a literature synthesis and practice strategies. *Social Work, 49*(1), 97–108.

Cox, C., Brooks, L., & Valcarcel, C. (2000). Culture and caregiving: A study of Latino grandparents. In C. Cox (Ed.), To grandmother's house we go and stay: Perspectives on custodial grandparents (pp. 215–233). New York, NY: Springer.

Fried, L. P., Carlson, M. C., Freedman, M., Frick, K. D., Glass, T. A., Hill, J.,...Zeger, S. (2004). A social model for health promotion for an aging population: Initial evidence on the Experience Corps model. *Journal of Urban Health: Bulletin of the New York Academy of Medicine, 81*(1), 64–78.

Fuller-Thomson, E. (2009, March). *The rich ethnic and racial diversity of grandparent caregivers: Portraits in resilience.* Presented at the 2nd Symposium on Grandparents Raising Grandchildren, National Center on Grandparents Raising Grandchildren at Atlanta, GA.

Fuller-Thomson, E., & Minkler, M. (2000). African American grandparents raising grandchildren: A national profile of demographic and health characteristics. *Health & Social Work, 25*(2), 109–118.

Fuller-Thomson, E., & Minkler, M. (2005). American Indian/Alaskan Native grandparents raising grandchildren: Findings from the Census 2000 Supplementary Survey. *Social Work, 50*(2), 131–139.

Fuller-Thomson, E., & Minkler, M. (2007a). Mexican American grandparents raising grandchildren: Findings from the Census 2000 American Community Survey. *Families in Society, 88*(4), 567–574.

Fuller-Thomson, E., & Minkler, M. (2007b). Central American grandparents raising grandchildren. *Hispanic Journal of Behavioral Science, 29*(1), 5–18.

Glass, T. A., De Leon, C. F., Bassuk, S. S., & Berkman, L. F. (2006). Social engagement and depressive symptoms in late life: Longitudinal findings. *Journal of Aging and Health, 18*(4), 604–628.

Goodman, C., & Silverstein, M. (2002). Grandmothers raising grandchildren: Family structure and well-being in culturally diverse families. *The Gerontologist, 42*(5), 676–689.

Greenfield, J. (2010). *An overview of informal caregiving among families in the U.S.: Who are the caregivers and how are they chosen? Working paper.* St. Louis, CA: Center for Social Development.

Hamilton, J. B., & Sandelowski, M. (2003). Living the golden rule: Reciprocal exchanges among African Americans with cancer. *Qualitative Health Research, 13*(5), 656–674.

Henderson, S. (2006). Parenting the second time around. *Ebony,* 104–108.

Herd, P., & Meyer, M. (2002). Care work: Invisible civic engagement. *Gender and Society, 16,* 665–688.

Hinterlong, J. E. (2006). Race disparities in health among older adults: Examining the role of productive engagement. *Health & Social Work, 31*(4), 275–288.

Hinterlong, J., Morrow-Howell, N., & Sherraden, M. (2001). Productive aging: Principles and perspectives. In N. Morrow-Howell, J. Hinterlong, & M. Sherraden (Eds.), *Productive aging: Concepts and challenges* (pp. 3–18). Baltimore, MD: Johns Hopkins University Press.

Hong, S. I., & Morrow-Howell, N. (2010). Health outcomes of Experience Corps: A high-commitment volunteer program. *Social Science & Medicine (1982), 71*(2), 414–420.

Hooyman, N., & Kiyak, A. (2008). *Social gerontology: A multidisciplinary perspective*. Boston, MA: Allyn & Bacon.

Johnson, R. W., & Schaner, S. G. (2005). *Value of unpaid activities by older Americans tops $160 billion per year*. Washington, DC: The Urban Institute.

Kelch-Oliver, K. (2008). African American grandparent caregivers: Stresses and implications for counselors. *The Family Journal, 16*(1), 43–50.

Kim, J. E., & Moen, P. (2002). Retirement transitions, gender, and psychological well-being: A life-course, ecological model. *The Journals of Gerontology. Series B, Psychological Sciences and Social Sciences, 57*(3), P212–P222.

Lee, R. D., Ensminger, M. E., & LaVeist, T. A. (2005). The responsibility continuum: Never primary, coresident and caregiver–heterogeneity in the African-American grandmother experience. *International Journal of Aging & Human Development, 60*(4), 295–304.

López, J., López-Arrieta, J., & Crespo, M. (2005). Factors associated with the positive impact of caring for elderly and dependent relatives. *Archives of Gerontology and Geriatrics, 41*(1), 81–94.

Luoh, M. C., & Herzog, A. R. (2002). Individual consequences of volunteer and paid work in old age: Health and mortality. *Journal of Health and Social Behavior, 43*(4), 490–509.

Magana, S. (2006). Older Latino family caregivers. In B. Berkman, & S. D'Ambruoso (Eds.), *Handbook of social work in health and aging* (pp. 371–380). Oxford University Press.

Mahoney, K. J., Simon-Rusinowitz, L., Loughlin, D. M., Desmond, S. M., & Squillace, M. R. (2004). Determining personal care consumers' preferences for a consumer-directed cash and counseling option: survey results from Arkansas, Florida, New Jersey, and New York elders and adults with physical disabilities. *Health Services Research, 39*(3), 643–664.

McBride, A. (2006–2007). Civic engagement, older adults, and inclusion. *Generations, 30*(4), 66–71.

McBride, A., Gonzales, E., Morrow-Howell, N., & McCrary, S. (2011). Stipended volunteer civic service: Inclusion, retention, and volunteer benefits. *Public Administration Review, 71*(6), 850–858.

MetLife Mature Market Institute (MMI, 1999). *The MetLife Juggling Act Study: Balancing caregiving with work and the costs involved*. Retrieved September 12, 2010, from http://www.metlife.com/assets/cao/mmi/publications/studies/mmi-studies-juggling-study-2007.pdf

Min, J. W., Moon, A., & Lubben, J. E. (2005). Determinants of psychological distress over time among older Korean immigrants and Non-Hispanic White elders: Evidence from a two-wave panel study. *Aging & Mental Health, 9*(3), 210–222.

Min, P. G. (1998). *Changes and conflicts: Korean immigrant families in New York*. New York, NY: Allyn & Bacon.

Mjelde-Mossey, L. A., Chi, I., & Chow, N. (2002). Volunteering in the social services: Preferences, expectations, barriers, and motivation of aging Chinese professionals in Hong Kong. *Hallym International Journal of Aging, 4*(1), 31–44.

Morrow-Howell, N., & Greenfield, J. (2010). Productive engagement of older Americans. *China Journal of Social Work, 3*(2/3), 153–164.

Morrow-Howell, N., & Wang, Y. (in press). Productive engagement of older adults: Elements of a cross-cultural research agenda. *Aging International*.

Morrow-Howell, N., Hingterlong, J., & Sherraden, M. (Eds.). (2001). *Productive aging: Concepts and challenges*. Baltimore, MD: John Hopkins University Press.

Morrow-Howell, N., Hong, S. I., & Tang, F. (2009). Who benefits from volunteering? Variations in perceived benefits. *The Gerontologist, 49*(1), 91–102.

Mui, A. C. (2010). Productive ageing in China: A human capital perspective. *China Journal of Social Work, 3*(2/3), 112–124.

Mui, A. C., & Shibusawa, T. (2008). *Asian American elders in the 21st century: Key indicators of psychological well-being*. New York, NY: Columbia University Press.

Musick, M. A., & Wilson, J. (2007). *Volunteers: A social profile*. Bloomington, IN: Indiana University Press.

Musick, M. A., Wilson, J., & Bynum, W. B. (2000). Race and formal volunteering: The differential effects of class and religion. *Social Forces, 78*(4), 1539.

Mutchler, J., Lee, S. A., & Baker, L. A. (2002). *Grandparent care in the United States: Comparisons by race and ethnicity.* Gerontology Institute Publications. Paper 24. http://scholarworks.umb.edu/gerontologyinstitute_pubs/24/

National Hispanic Council on Aging (NHCOA). (2010, August). *Volunteerism in the Hispanic community.* Retrieved from www.smpresource.org/ . . . /Helping_Others_Latinos_and_Volunteeris

Pinquart, M., & Sörensen, S. (2007). Correlates of physical health of informal caregivers: a meta-analysis. *The Journals of Gerontology. Series B, Psychological Sciences and Social Sciences, 62*(2), P126–P137.

Polacca, M. (2001). American Indian and Alaska Native elderly. In L. K. Olson (Eds.), *Aging through ethnic lenses: Caring for the elderly in a multicultural society.* Lanham, MD: Rowman & Littlefield.

Racicot, L. (2003, April). *Understanding the needs and issues of grandfamilies: A survey of grandparents raising grandchildren: A pilot study.* Paper presented at the biennial meeting of the Society for Research on Child Development, Tampa, FL.

Sherraden, M., Morrow-Howell, N., Hinterlong, J., & Rozario, P. (2001). Productive aging: Theoretical choices and directions. In N. Morrow-Howell, J. Hinterlong, & M. Sherraden (Eds.), *Productive aging: Concepts and challenges* (pp. 260–284). Baltimore, MD: Johns Hopkins University Press.

Shock, N. W. (1947). Older people and their potentialities for gainful employment. *Journal of Gerontology, 2*(2), 93–102.

Silva, P. & Thomas, C. (2006). Civic engagement and national service: Results from Senior Corps evaluations. In L. B. Wilson & S. P. Simson (Eds.), *Civic engagement and the baby boomer generation: Research, policy and practice perspectives* (pp. 43–60). New York, NY: Haworth Press.

Silverstein, M., & Chen, X. (1999). The impact of acculturation in Mexican American families on the quality of adult grandchild-grandparent relationships. *Journal of Marriage and the Family, 61*(1), 188–198.

Smith, C., & Beltran, A. (2003). The role of federal policies in supporting grandparents raising grandchildren families: *The case of the U.S. Journal of Intergenerational Relationships, 1,* 5–20.

Smith, T. W. (2007). *Job satisfaction in America: Trends and socio-demographic correlates.* Chicago, IL: University of Chicago. Retrieved from http://www-news.uchicago.edu/releases/07/pdf/070827.jobs.pdf

Social Security Administration, Office of the Chief Actuary. (2011). *Summary of provisions that would change the Social Security Program.* Retrieved April 18, 2012, from http://www.ssa.gov/OACT/solvency/provisions/retireage_summary.html

Tang, F. (2006). What resources are needed for volunteerism? *Journal of Applied Gerontology, 25,* 375–390.

Treas, J., & Mazumdar, S. (2004). Caregiving and kinkeeping; Contributions of older people to America's immigrant families. *Journal of Comparative Family Studies, 35,* 105–122.

U.S. Department of Labor. (2011). *Volunteering in the United States, 2011.* Retrieved from http://www.bls.gov/news.release/volun.nr0.htm

U.S. Department of Labor. (2012). *The African-American labor force in the recovery.* Retrieved from http://www.dol.gov/_sec/media/reports/BlackLaborForce/BlackLaborForce.pdf

Urban Institute (2011, August). *Employment and earnings among 50+ people of color. Retirement Security Data Brief, Number 4.* Washington, DC: Author. •

Washko, M. M., Schack, R. W., Goff, B. A., & Pudlin, B. (2011). Title V of the Older Americans Act, the Senior Community Service Employment Program: Participant demographics and service to racially/ethnically diverse populations. *Journal of Aging & Social Policy, 23*(2), 182–197.

Watson, J. A., Randolph, S. M., & Lyons, J. L. (2005). African-American grandmothers as health educators in the family. *International Journal of Aging & Human Development, 60*(4), 343–356.

Whitley, D. M., Kelley, S. J., & Sipe, T. A. (2001). Grandmothers raising grandchildren: Are they at increased risk of health problems? *Health & Social Work, 26*(2), 105–114.

World Health Organization (WHO). (2002). *Active ageing: A policy framework.* Retrieved from http://whqlibdoc.who.int/hq/2002/who_nmh_nph_02.8.pdf

Yang, P. S. (2013). Revitalizing roles of older adult citizens: Successful stories of Project History Alive. *Ageing International, 36,* 137–148.

Yee, B. W. K. (1992). Markers of successful aging among Vietnamese refugee women. In E. Cole, O. M. Espin, & E. D. Rothblum (Eds.), *Refugee women and their mental health: Shattered societies, shattered lives*. New York, NY: Haworth Press.

Yoshida, H., Gordon, D., & Henkin, N. (2008). *Community treasures: Recognizing the contributions of older immigrants and refugees*. Center for Intergenerational Learning, Temple University. Retrieved from http://www.projectshine.org/sites/default/files/Community%20Treasures.pdf

Zedlewski, S. R., & Butrica, B. A. (2007). *Are we taking full advantage of older adults' potential? The Retirement Project: Perspectives on productive aging*. The Urban Institute N.9 (December 2007).

CHAPTER 22

The Older Americans Act and the Nexus of Aging and Diversity

Fernando Torres-Gil, Kimberly N. Spencer-Suarez,
and Brittany Rudinica

This chapter examines the Older Americans Act (OAA) through the prism of the coming nexus of aging and ethnic/racial diversity. The United States is facing unprecedented demographic changes and challenges to the programs and public policies designed to serve an older population. With the rapid growth of minority and immigrant groups, the pending aging of baby boomers and the continuing debates about the sustainability of entitlement programs and the fiscal crisis facing federal and state budgets, the OAA may not only be at risk for funding limitations, but it also presents a potential solution for responding to the aging and growing diversity of the United States. This chapter posits that the OAA can serve as a foundation for building a home- and community-based set of services for all older adults and persons with disabilities and for addressing aging in the 21st century. The authors suggest that the OAA and its aging network must confront several challenges if it is to remain a relevant force in the new aging: integrating resources with the large income transfer programs (e.g., Medicare), broadening its definition of racial and ethnic minority groups, and expanding its aging network to a broader home- and community-based system of services. If done successfully, the OAA and its aging network can be an important policy and public influence on how the United States responds to the aging of baby boomers and to increasing diversity.

SETTING THE STAGE

The fact that the United States and much of the world is aging is not new. That the United States is becoming more diverse is also not new. But together, this nexus of aging and racial and ethnic diversity (commonly understood as black, Hispanic, Asian and Pacific Islander, and Native American identities) lends itself to a new politics of aging and diversity—one where the OAA and its aging network are impacted but can influence how we respond to this nexus. One example is the broad domain of long-term care, caregiving, and the public demands for home- and community-based programs and services. Older persons prefer community-based services and tend to loath the prospect of entering a nursing home or medical facility (the institutionalized bias of Medicare and Medicaid); racial and ethnic minority elders prefer culturally relevant services. Apropos of this fact, the long-term care workforce is increasingly composed of minorities and immigrants. Long-term care issues exemplify how our views of ethnicity and race have evolved since the passage of the OAA in 1965, and how the new demographics of the 21st century will require that the OAA's lead agency, the Administration on Aging (AOA), and its aging network rethink their approaches to targeting national minority groups and defining "those with the greatest economic and social need."

Despite its relatively small budget size, the OAA and its state and local network of agencies have the potential to be the "bellwether" for how we reshape the nation's response to aging and diversity. To do so, however, will require a rethinking of what we mean by diversity and how we shape the national agenda as the United States becomes older and more diverse. The traditional public entitlement programs of Social Security, Medicare, and Medicaid, which together command inordinate attention vis-à-vis their income transfers, will need to give greater credence to the home- and community-based approach of the OAA—an approach more in line with the interests of aging baby boomers, minority groups, and immigrants. In turn, the need to be more efficient with limited public dollars may reinforce the important role that the OAA, its aging network, and advocacy efforts of minority and immigrant groups can play in educating the public about program innovations and investing in diverse populations. To illustrate how these complex issues come together, the conceptual framework below renders the nexus of aging and diversity and offers a redefinition of diversity.

Figure 22.1 demonstrates that we are moving from a 20th century view of diversity, that assumed that four national minority groups (black, Hispanic/Latino, Native American, and Asian-Pacific Islanders) would be the beneficiaries of targeting OAA funds (and that would be the basis of affirmative action/civil rights policies), to one where the "New Diversity" in the 21st century requires that we diversify our client base to one that includes women; the lesbian, gay, bisexual, and transgender (LBGT) community; the younger disabled; the vulnerable; and immigrants (legal and illegal) among the various groups comprising a new majority–minority

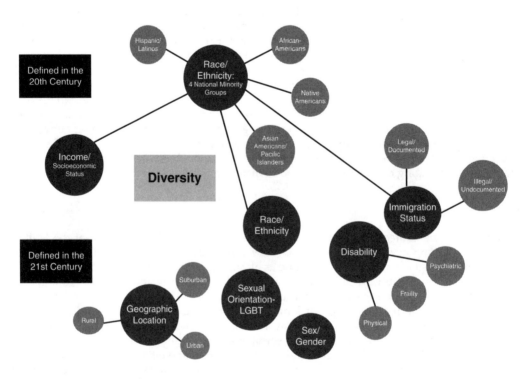

FIGURE 22.1 American Diversity Conceptual Framework: National Minority Groups in the 20th Century & New Diversity in the 21st Century.

nation. Parallel to this more sophisticated and contemporary understanding of "minority status" is a hopeful policy move toward an expansion of home- and community-based services that will enable aging baby boomers, minority elders, and those serving the elderly (e.g., family caregivers) to have more choices about remaining in their homes and communities (and a more influential role by the OAA and the aging network in national policy setting vis-à-vis the Medicare/Medicaid/Social Security Policy axis). A brief history of the OAA exemplifies these changing trends and the potentialities of aging in the 21st century.

THE OAA

The OAA is the primary federal program providing a host of services that enable older persons (60 years of age and over) and their families to live in their homes and communities with a measure of dignity and independence. Its lead agency, the AOA, is housed within the U.S. Department of Health and Human Services (DHHS) and relies on an "aging network" of 56 state and territorial units on aging (SUAs), 629 area agencies on aging (AAAs), 244 tribal organizations, 2 Native Hawaiian organizations, and nearly 20,000 direct service providers and hundreds of thousands of volunteers to provide home- and community-based services for older persons, their families, and caregivers (DHHS, 2010). Its budget of roughly $2 billion is dwarfed by the budgets of Social Security ($89.7 billion, FY 2011), Medicare ($295 billion, 2011), and Medicaid ($557 billion, 2011). But unlike those large-scale entitlement programs, which deliver crucial income and health supports, the OAA with its aging network is the only federal program that enables a nationwide system of programs, services, and assistance at the local and community levels. Thus, for older persons and their families who need direct, hands-on assistance to remain in their homes—even with frailties and chronic and disabling conditions—the AAAs and SUAs are the frontline for such programs and services. In 2010, approximately 11 million seniors and their caregivers benefited from the OAA (DHHS, 2010).

HISTORY: THE BEGINNINGS OF THE OAA AND THE AGING NETWORK

The OAA was passed in 1965, alongside the passage of Medicare and Medicaid. Its original intent was "to help older people maintain maximum independence in their homes and communities and to promote a continuum of care for the vulnerable elderly." Since 1965, a series of amendments, funding, and legislative changes have amplified and expanded the programs and services provided through the OAA (National Health Policy Forum, 2011). Figure 22.2 depicts the 45-year trajectory of changes and growth of the aging network and its programs, including the addition of congregate nutrition programs in 1972, home delivered meals in 1978, a Long-Term Care Ombudsman program in 1987, a family caregiver support program in 2000, and home- and community-based LTSS development activities in 2006. The OAA, AOA, and aging network today provide five major categories of services: access to social and legal services, nutrition, home- and community-based long-term social and supportive services, disease prevention and health promotion, and vulnerable elder rights protections.

MINORITIES AND TARGETING

An outgrowth of 20th century social policy and civil rights was a focus on racial and minority groups and devising policy and regulatory preferences toward such groups. Affirmative action, busing, racial quotas, and set-asides to minority small businesses manifested a sense that race is an accurate proxy for disadvantaged status. The 1965 OAA was influenced by this approach and, since then, legislation, regulations, and funding have targeted services to "individuals with the greatest economic or social needs, with particular attention to low-income minority individuals" (Moody, 2010). Much of the focus during the early decades of the OAA was on formulating this definition as a concentration on four national minority groups: black, Hispanic, Asian, and Native Americans. This led to special funding to national minority groups (e.g., the National Center and Caucus on the Black Aged, La Asociacion Nacional

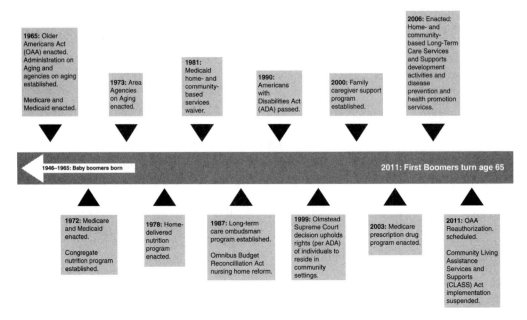

FIGURE 22.2 Timeline of Major Older Americans Act (and related) Legislation, 1965 to 2011.
Source: National Health Policy Forum (2011), Background Paper No. 38.

Pro Personas Mayores, the National Indian Council on Aging, the Asian American/Pacific Islander Resource Center). Much of the lobbying and advocacy around the use of limited OAA funds has been aimed at ensuring that these organizations receive a proportion of those dollars. Today, state units are held accountable by the AOA through the Intrastate Funding Formula (IFF) and must demonstrate that their allocation of funds give appropriate attention to blacks, Hispanics/Latinos, Asian Americans/Pacific Islanders, and Native Americans.

Is this targeting relevant to the growing diversity of the 21st century and the increasing social and economic disparities of the current recession? Can the OAA and AOA continue to narrowly define groups of greatest need? How do we account for the growing differences in the aging population—differences not just in terms of race but also of income, disability, frailty, sexual orientation, lifestyle choices, geographic location, isolation, and risk? Given the limited funding to the OAA, how can we efficiently and effectively target limited resources for a multifariously diverse population?

The World Changes: 1965 to 2010

Much changed demographically between 1965 and 2010. As Figure 22.3 illustrates (U.S. Census Bureau, 2011), the proportion of older persons in the United States increased dramatically between 1900 and 2010. The years between 1960 and 2010 reveal the greatest growth. That period witnessed a doubling of the 65-and-over population. Of course, the overall budget of the OAA did not grow commensurately.

More relevant still is the growth of racial and ethnic minority populations since 1965. Census data in the 1960s did not specify Hispanic and Asian American/Pacific Islander groups, but they did show that the black population grew by more than 130%, from 15 million to 35 million between 1950 and 2000 (Stanford Center on Longevity, 2010).

Before the 1970s, the minority population in the United States was almost entirely black. Only in the last 40 years have minority groups become increasingly diverse. In the second half of the last century, the non-black, non-white population grew from 1 million to 35 million, primarily due to expansion of the Asian/Pacific Islander and Hispanic populations. In sum,

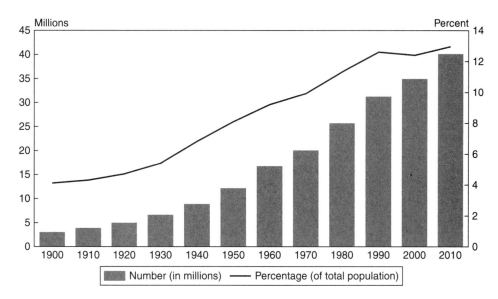

FIGURE 22.3 1900 to 2010 Population 65 Years and Older, Size and Percent of Population.

Source: U.S. Census Bureau, decennial census of population, 1900 to 2000; 2010 Census Summary File 1.

Chart Source: U.S. Census Bureau, The Older Population: 2010; 2010 Census Briefs.

the 1950 census showed that 11% of the U.S. population belonged to some minority group(s). By 2000, that proportion had grown to 25%. The passage and implementation of the OAA were predicated on what the nation looked like in the 1950s and 1960s. Clearly, the American population has transformed radically since then.

In the 1960s, with the passage of the Civil Rights Act and growing empowerment among racial groups (e.g., Latinos, blacks), there was a general consensus that minority status constituted an accurate predictor of a group's problems. Thus, affirmative action for minorities was established based on the assumption that all minorities were disadvantaged and needed special provisions. Today, while discrimination and educational and economic barriers remain extant, especially for young black and Hispanic males, we can no longer assume that all members of specific minority/racial groups (e.g., Asian American/Pacific Islander groups like Chinese and Japanese, and Hispanic subgroups like Cubans) need targeting provisions. This does not detract from the current economic recession that has placed all groups, including those with insufficient education or technical skills, in an even more precarious position. But if the United States is becoming a majority/minority nation, can we assume that all minorities making up that majority require targeted services?

As Figures 22.3 and 22.4 demonstrate, ethnic diversity will continue to increase among the general population (U.S. Census Bureau, 2011, 2012), as well as among older adults. By 2060, Hispanics/Latinos will be the nation's largest minority group.

Of course, the public policy approach has changed since 1965. At that time, older adults were portrayed as the "deserving poor," and there was little public opposition to expanding benefits (e.g., cost-of-living adjustments for Social Security), creating new entitlement programs (e.g., Medicare, Medicaid), specific legislative focus (e.g., U.S. House Select Committee on Aging), building new federal agencies (e.g., National Institute on Aging), encouraging volunteer programs and preferences (e.g., Retired Senior Volunteer Program [RSVP] and senior discounts), and otherwise responding to the interest-group politics of old-age organizations (e.g., National Council on Aging, AARP, Gray Panthers). However, the world began to change in the 1980s and 1990s, with increasing public attention paid to the growing disparities between young and old. Poverty rates had fallen for the elderly and risen for children. The "generational conflict" phobia of the 1990s, portraying young versus old, has matured into

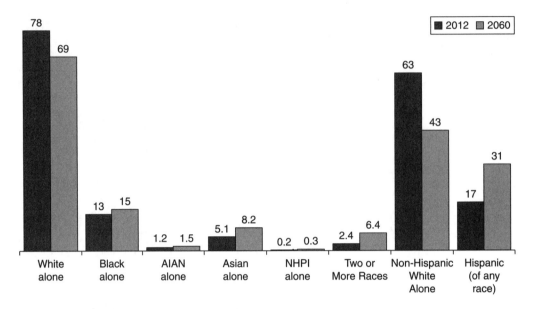

FIGURE 22.4 Increasing Racial/Ethnic Diversity of U.S. Population.

AIAN, American Indian and Alaska Native; NHPI, National Hawaiian and Other Pacific Islander.

Source: U.S. Census Bureau, 2012 National Population Projections: Summary Tables.

Chart Source: U.S. Census Bureau. Retrieved from http://www.census.gov/newsroom/releases/img/racehispanic_graph.jpg

a growing public perception that the elderly are doing well and are protecting their benefits (e.g., Social Security, retiree health care, pensions) at the expense of other social needs (e.g., public infrastructure, municipal finances, education). This has led to political pressures to scale back entitlement programs (e.g., privatizing Medicare), increase cost sharing (e.g., co-pays), and raise eligibility early- and full-retirement ages for Social Security.

So what might this mean as we aim to serve minority elderly as we look ahead to the role of the OAA in responding to the aging of the U.S. population and its growing diversity?

THE OAA: RESPONDING TO THE NEW AGING

The OAA and its aging network have become the one nationwide, community-based system of programs and services for those older persons (and caregivers) who reside in their homes and neighborhoods. Small though it might be in terms of federal funding, it has a long reach. Much like Social Security district offices and U.S. Postal Service offices, every city and county has an area agency on aging and a plethora of senior citizen centers, ombudsman programs, legal assistance, congregate meal sites, and the gamut of OAA funded programs. In addition, the OAA requires citizen participation, which is ensured by the advisory councils.

Congruent with its longstanding commitment to diversity and its targeting provisions toward national minority groups, the OAA has a long and exemplary record of serving diverse older persons and caregivers and promoting culturally competent practices (e.g., bilingual programs, ethnic-specific food). Yet, the OAA and the AOA remain secondary players in national agenda setting for an aging population. Public attention, debates, and policy setting revolve around the large income-transfer programs: Social Security, Medicare, and Medicaid. The latter two, in particular, account for the largest segment of the U.S. DHHS. Its operation division, the Center for Medicare and Medicaid Services (CMS), dwarfs the AOA. This reality is perhaps its chief weakness: the OAA, AOA, and the aging network are what consumers prefer in terms of services, and these programs' attention to diversity reflects a recognition of the needs of minority elders. Yet, the politics of aging and the legislative and policy debates over entitlement reform, budgetary deficits, and partisan battles about national priorities (e.g., the dilemma about whether we can afford to sustain Medicare and Social Security as baby boomers age) give CMS and these programs inordinate attention.

But if we were to ask: What might aging baby boomers and growing ethnic, minority, and immigrant groups prefer in terms of how they want to live in old age, the answer (at least according to various surveys) would be: "Let us live in our homes and neighborhoods, and if we need assistance, make those services available where we age in place." They might likely add: "Don't force us into a nursing home!" Of course, these groups would also want to know that their Social Security checks will continue uninterrupted and that Medicare will continue to pay for their medical care. The reality is that nursing homes, long-term care facilities, and life-care retirement communities can present viable options for a significant segment of the aging and diverse populations. But on a visceral level, what the OAA currently provides, and what the aging network delivers, is much more in line with what Americans want for themselves in old age and for their aging loved ones.

REAUTHORIZATION AND NEW OPPORTUNITIES

Notwithstanding the small size (with respect to budgets) of the OAA compared with the large entitlement programs, and despite its secondary role in national agenda setting for older persons, the OAA, AOA, and its aging network may be poised to serve as the template for how this nation responds to the aging of baby boomers and its growing diversity. Two developments may set the stage for new opportunities: the pending reauthorization of the OAA and an organizational change elevating the AOA mission.

Like most federal programs, the OAA must periodically be "re-legislated" to continue its mission and statutory requirements. Reauthorization of the initial legislation perpetuates its work but also allows for changes to the policy's original version. Since 1965, the OAA has been "amended" through reauthorizations, which has enabled it and its aging network to evolve with the changing times. As Figure 22.2 illustrates, earlier reauthorizations added a long-term care ombudsman program and home-delivered meals (in line with cost-of-living adjustments to Social Security and home and community-based services [HCBS] waivers in Medicaid), elder rights protections, a family caregiver support program (in line with the Olmstead Supreme Court decision) and, most recently, a home- and community-based LTSS set of activities, as well as disease prevention and health promotion initiatives (on the heels of the Medicare prescription drug program). Thus, just as other federal legislation has evolved during the last 50 years to account for public and political initiatives to serve the elderly and disabled, so has the OAA and the AOA added new programs for an aging population.

The next reauthorization is scheduled in 2013; but given the presidential election of 2013 and continuing budget debates, we are not likely to see legislative action until 2014. Legislative and executive branch deliberations will continue through 2013 and 2014, and a set of principles has been established between public officials (DHHS and AOA) and the many stakeholders who are concerned about the continuation and expansion of the OAA. A consensus exists among relevant parties that the OAA has, in fact, been a successful social policy and that it works well. It responds to individual and community needs, whether in rural, suburban, or urban areas; its aging network serves as a glue that holds together a variety of programs; it meets the Congressional intent to avoid premature institutionalization; and it has adequate flexibility to evolve to meet the needs of an increasingly diverse population.

A list of principles by advocates recommends that reauthorization add "parent caregiver" to the National Family Caregiver Support Program, allow for greater cost-sharing, utilize incentive payments for high performance, expand eligibility for long-term care ombudsman services, expand the legal assistance programs, transfer the Title V Older American Community Service Employment programs to the AOA (currently with the Department of Labor), and promote evidence-based disease prevention and health promotion services. What do these admittedly technical and program-oriented principles imply vis-à-vis the trends of diversity and the role of the OAA in responding to the aging of the baby boomers? It demonstrates the incremental nature of the legislative process (i.e., get *what* you can *while* you can), builds upon small-scale programs popular at the local level, and continues to be increasingly important at the executive level.

The AOA and its reauthorization recommendations recognize the proliferating hetero-geneity of the country's diverse population. In addition to its continued targeting of funds toward national minority groups, the AOA proposes new initiatives for vulnerable (e.g., at-risk) elderly and the poor, those threatened by elder abuse and neglect, persons with dis-abilities, caregivers, individuals with Alzheimer's disease and other dementias, and those of varying sexual orientations. In this respect, the AOA and its leadership recognize that "diver-sity" is no longer just about race and minority status and that, with an aging population, espe-cially the baby boomer cohort, we must augment definitions of diversity to facilitate greater efficiency and effectiveness in targeting limited resources.

NEW DEVELOPMENTS IN LEADERSHIP: DISABILITY AND LONG-TERM SERVICES AND SUPPORTS

The year 2012 witnessed a new development that may portend a more significant role for the OAA and for responding to growing differences within the aging population. In 2012, Secretary Kathleen Sibelius announced the creation of a new agency with the DHHS: the Agency for Community Living (ACL). For the first time at the federal level, programs serv-ing older persons and younger disabled would fall under a single administrative umbrella. The ACL would include the AOA, the Administration for Developmentally Disabled (ADD), and the Office on Disability. Many years of attempts to bring together advocacy groups for the elderly and the disability rights movement culminated in this new agency. Long-standing categorical programs, including a proliferation of group-specific public policies (e.g., OAA for the elderly, ADA for the disabled, senior centers for older adults, independent living centers for young disabled) and differences in expectations (discomfort, differing modalities of care), previously kept the elderly and the disabled apart. Yet, both groups realized two essential facts:

1. The elderly are living longer but would eventually face disabilities and chronic conditions.
2. The young disabled are living longer and would eventually be eligible for old-age programs.

This common consensus that both would benefit from home- and community-based services and supports (LTSS) gave rise to a coalition that successfully pressured Congress and the White House to include the Community Living Assistance Services and Supports (CLASS) Act in the Affordable Care Act (ACA). The CLASS Act would, for the first time, create a federal, public long-term care program benefiting all workers, regardless of age or disability. Unfortunately, Congress and the executive branch, fearful of a new entitlement program that might not prove financially self-sustaining, put the CLASS Act in abeyance. Nonetheless, this coalition came together as an effective advocacy group and the ACA marked a major mile-stone in consolidating programs for the elderly, the younger disabled, and inclusion of long-term care in policy at the federal level (a development already occurring in many states).

And what relevance might this have for minority aging? Minority, ethnic, and immi-grant groups demonstrate a general proclivity for remaining in their communities with their families. So they too benefit from this development, especially as we transform into a majority/minority nation. And longevity benefits all minorities. Second, and ironically, long-term care programs and services increasingly rely on minorities and immigrants as affordable labor. Evidence indicates that long-term care facilities, particularly those funded heavily through Medicaid (with its minimal reimbursements), rely on first-generation pop-ulations that are willing to work long hours in low-status jobs for minimum wage and few benefits. These groups increasingly include immigrants from the Philippines, India, Thailand, and Mexico, as well as low-income minorities, especially black and Hispanic women (Wallace, 2012).

Simultaneously—and this reflects socioeconomic disparities along lines of race, ethnicity, and immigration status, as well as increasing diversity—nursing homes and long-term care facilities are populated primarily by white, English-speaking, elderly women receiving care from a population of workers who may not have been a part of their lives when they were younger. Lest minorities, especially minority baby boomers, assume they will neither need long-term care nor reside in nursing homes given the cultural norms of "we take care of our own." Data now show that in nursing homes, we are witnessing an increase of minority elderly and a willingness of second- and third-generation minorities and immigrants to use institutional care for their elders (Fennel et al., 2012). In the long-term care arena, we can begin to see the nexus of aging and diversity and the age-race-stratification of an aging nation. So what might this mean for the OAA and minority aging?

THE POLITICS OF AGING AND DIVERSITY

The need to broaden our definition and understanding of diversity and the common stake that aging baby boomers, white elderly retirees, minority elderly, young minorities, and immigrants of all ages and legal status (e.g., legal permanent residents, illegal immigrants, refugees, asylum seekers, those seeking temporary work visas) share in finding a 21st century application of aging and diversity is perhaps best summed up by Ron Brownstein. Brownstein (2010, 2011), noted writer for *The National Journal*, published prescient articles about "The Gray and the Brown: the Generational Mismatch" (2010) and "The Great Divide" (2011). These admittedly provocative titles illustrate the new demographic realities facing the United States in this century. Between now and 2030, for example, the United States will have a largely white older retiree population supported by an increasingly young, immigrant, and largely Hispanic workforce. Yet, that older population, the dominant force in the electorate (because older persons vote more consistently than younger persons and much more than young minorities), tends to vote on their primary concerns: preserving property values, safe streets, protecting Social Security and Medicare, low taxes, and minimal government intrusions. The younger minority and immigrant population, like younger baby boomers in the previous century, tend to be most concerned about employment, educational and training opportunities, affordable housing, and government protections and supports (e.g., civil rights, a social safety net). The Gray versus Brown thesis, according to Brownstein, is a shot across the bow of what may become intergenerational and interracial tensions if we fail to find common cause among older whites and younger minorities. We can see this "cultural and generational divide" in places like Arizona, where a large, white retiree population of snowbirds relies on a young, low-wage, Hispanic population for supportive services (e.g., cleaning yards, maintaining their homes, washing their cars, helping with personal assistance).

The examination of the politics of aging and late-life diversity highlights three important areas that could potentially impact the opportunities of older adults in general and older racial/ethnic minorities in particular:

1. We need to be concerted in avoiding potential generational, racial, and ethnic cleavages in American society and find common ground. To this end, it would be paramount that we develop intergenerational and interracial coalitions and move beyond the current mode of organizing within racial/ethnic minority groups. No longer can we assume that minority organizations for blacks, Hispanics, Asian Americans/Pacific Islanders, and Native Americans will suffice. Advocates for the elderly, LBGT, caregivers, and rural elderly can be most influential in public policy. Intergenerational coalitions (e.g., Generations United) have the potential to mitigate tensions between young and old, especially during the heated debates around entitlement reform.
2. We need to develop a new paradigm where older whites and young immigrants and minorities can realize their "vested self-interest" in maintaining programs and services for today's elderly, and not at the expense of the interests of the latter

group. Indeed, we need to find ways to convince older and conservative elderly (e.g., Tea Party members) that it is in their self-interest to support immigration reform, including the Dream Act and a path to citizenship. Such immigration measures will allow for a young and industrious immigrant population to achieve the educational and professional opportunities that in turn will allow them to be productive taxpayers with a willingness to pay the Federal Insurance Contributions Act (FICA) and Income taxes that support public benefits such as Social Security and Medicare.

3. We need to reconceptualize and reoperationalize eligibility requirements by moving from race as a proxy for need to a more inclusive definition of targeting. Given that there have been social, educational, and economic advancements for important segments of blacks, Hispanics, and Asians, perhaps it is time to seek another definition for targeting limited public resources. Not all Hispanic, black, and Asian elderly or young persons are poor. New measures and proxies may prove more suitable in the 21st century. For example, definitions that include "at-risk, poverty status, disability, activities of daily living (ADLs) and disability status, geography (rural service deficiencies vs. service-rich urban areas), and social isolation (one in three baby boomers is now single) may be more accurate measures of who will most need OAA programs. And utilizing a conceptual framework of "the Nexus of Aging and Diversity" moves us away from pressuring the OAA, AOA, and the aging network to do more for minority aging and toward an approach that is more about how the OAA and its important programs can enable the nation to address growing diversity, increasing economic and social disparities, and the competing needs of vulnerable elderly and poor ethnic and minority groups. How this is to be operationalized remains uncertain. Yet, the need to reconfigure our targeting approach will be increasingly crucial if we are to address these changing demographics.

OAA, DIVERSITY, AND NEW OPPORTUNITIES

In sum, this article attempts to address several elements that are germane to minority aging and the OAA. The OAA and its aging network are the foundation upon which the nation can build a system of home- and community-based services that may enable all persons growing old to have choices about where and how they want to live. Notwithstanding its small budget, the OAA can grow in influence and impact vis-à-vis the large entitlement programs, particularly as aging baby boomers make their preferences known regarding where and how they want to grow old. At the same time, the OAA has shown its sensitivity to the importance of race and minority status. It has shifted toward a more comprehensive view of diversity. Continuing that march, it may generate new definitions of "minority and racial status" that are more representative of and responsive to increasing differences within a diverse population. The potential for age/race/immigration-based tensions, Brownstein indicates, can be mitigated, if we find ways to integrate the generational and racial/ethnic differences that are byproducts of a national population becoming majority/minority. The great test of how we address these complex changes will come in the next 20 to 30 years.

Aging baby boomers will grow old while society advances through this demographic transformation. Aging baby boomers will find that, as they move toward the latter stages of life, they will live through our nation's attempts to reconcile its new diversity. Adding to this, the current debates about the future of Social Security, Medicare, and Medicaid, the continued demise of other social safety nets, the real possibility of privatizing or scaling back entitlement programs and the potential for greater poverty and vulnerability among baby boomers means that boomers are likely to confront great challenges in their old age. Their parents and grandparents faced this test of adversity in their youth during the Great Depression, World War II, and the Cold War. Will aging baby boomers, minorities, and immigrants negotiate their pending tests as successfully? Herein lies the central question of aging and diversity in the next 20 to 30 years.

REFERENCES

Brownstein, R. (2010, July 24). The gray and the brown. *National Journal,* 14–29.

Brownstein, R. (2011, November 12). The great divide. *National Journal,* 46–50.

Fennel, M., Clark, M., Feng, Z., Mor, V., Smith, D., & Taylor, D. (2012). Separate and unequal access and quality of care in nursing homes: Transformation of the long-term care industry and implications of the research program for aging Hispanics. In J. Angel, F. Torres-Gil, & K. Markides (Eds.), *Aging, health and longevity in the Mexican-origin population* (pp. 207–225). New York, NY: Springer-Verlag.

Moody, H. R. (2010). *Aging: Concepts and controversies* (6th ed.). Thousand Oaks, CA: Pine Forge Press.

National Health Policy Forum. (2011, December 13). *The aging services network: Serving a vulnerable and growing elderly population in tough economic times* (Background Paper No. 83). Washington, DC: O'Shaughnessy, C.V. (Principal Policy Analyst).

Stanford Center on Longevity. (2010). *New realities of an older America.* Stanford, CA: Stanford University, Center on Longevity.

U.S. Census Bureau. (2011). *The older population: 2010* (2010 Census Briefs). Washington, DC.

U.S. Census Bureau. (2012). *2012 National population projections: Summary tables.* Washington, DC.

United States Department of Health and Human Services (DHHS). (2010). *Department of health and human services, administration on aging: FY 2010 report to congress.* Washington, DC: U.S. Government Printing Office.

Wallace, S. P. (2012). Long-term care policy and older Latinos. In J. Angel, F. Torres-Gil, & K. Markides (Eds.), *Aging, health and longevity in the Mexican-origin population* (pp. 243–257). New York, NY: Springer-Verlag.

PART IV

SOCIOLOGY OF MINORITY AGING

CHAPTER 23

Introduction: Sociology of Minority Aging

Roland J. Thorpe, Jr., and Jacqueline L. Angel

The populations of developed nations are aging rapidly with implications for all social institutions. The Census Bureau projects that by the year 2030 one in five Americans will be 65 years and older. This population is expected to nearly double between 2010 and 2050 (U.S. Census Bureau, 2008). The aging of the baby boomers is a driving force behind this phenomenon (U.S. Census Bureau, 2004). The fastest growing segment of the population consists of individuals over 85 years, a group expected to increase to 6.6 million by the year 2020, comprising 19% of the elderly population (U.S. Administration on Aging, 2011). As the population ages, the nation will also become more culturally and linguistically diverse. The U.S. Census Bureau forecasts that the United States will be a "majority–minority" country in barely three decades (Shrestha & Heisler, 2011). Population projections consistently indicate that the proportion of older adults who are non-Hispanic white will decline substantially, whereas that of older blacks, Asians, and especially Hispanics will increase (Federal Interagency Forum on Aging-Related Statistics, 2010). As a result, this expanding segment of the U.S. population will be more highly diverse than in the past, which will create both opportunities and challenges for sociologists and policy makers (Angel & Angel, 2006).

All the chapters in this volume examine the current and future challenges posed by this important societal change. Population aging is clearly a dynamic process that is heavily conditioned by sociocultural factors and brings significant consequences for social life and for family, education, religion, public economies, and political institutions alike (Angel & Settersten, 2011). As a result of high rates of immigration from Latin America and Asia and changing patterns of fertility, the "gerontological explosion" of older minorities will directly impact the experiences and meanings of aging for individuals, their families, and our society. There can be little doubt that the changes in diversity of aging and its relation to physical, mental, and social health will dramatically alter the life chances and life course of older individuals (Shrestha & Heisler, 2011).

All the authors in this section of the book have included in their work a sociological perspective on minority aging. The chapters cover the following topics: demography, gender, age at diagnosis/onset of cardiovascular disease (CVD), Medicare usage, work and retirement, social support, social context and neighborhoods, ethnography of families, qualitative research, and social policy. These topics constitute some of the key areas that should be the focus of future research on the sociology of minority aging.

Gerst and Burr begin this part with a demographic overview and portrait of the older minorities that include the five major U.S. racial groups examined throughout the volume (Office of Management and Budget, 2012). The chapter provides a rich description of trends in the ethnic (Hispanic) and racial composition of older cohorts to illustrate the dramatic changes that have taken place in the United States in the past century. The chapter also highlights the various ways in which the "graying of America" will be affected by this demographic fact.

Ajrouch and Abdulrahim present a concise argument for examining aging in the United States. In their argument, they discuss the social construction of age, gender, and race/ethnicity. This is followed by a conceptual overview of intersectionality as it relates to minority health and highlights its strengths and challenges. The authors' work represents the most current thinking on social, environmental, and methodological approaches to understanding the intersection of gender and minority health across the life course. Findings from the literature review indicate that intersectionality theory has provided new directions for identifying the importance of gender as a key element for predicting health. The authors conclude that additional research should seek to better understand gender and minority aging over the life course. Moreover, they recommend that research would benefit from expanding in four areas: comparative analysis, representative samples, diversity within larger groups, and meanings. Addressing issues in these areas using an intersectionality approach would offer a more comprehensive framework to understanding minority aging experiences in the United States.

Rooks and Thorpe systematically review the literature on age at onset/diagnosis and self-care/management as a potential contributor to CVD disparities among middle- to old-age minority adults. These authors also discuss key theories that might serve as frameworks for addressing CVD disparities in this segment of the population. A key insight is that earlier age at onset of CVD leads to worse self-care/management, and shorter trajectories of decline to death for racial and ethnic minorities. This is particularly the case for those of lower socio-economic status. The authors also note that the literature on age at onset/diagnosis is sparse, particularly for Asian Americans, Pacific Islanders, and Latinos/Hispanics, and is often based on regional samples. The authors conclude by underscoring the importance of focusing on addressing social determinants of health through health prevention and intervention efforts, and policy changes to minimize risk factors.

Weech, Pradhan, and Powell provide a historical perspective on Medicare and its development from 1965 to the present era, as well as the important role it plays in ensuring health care access for the older poor and minority adults. Given the rising costs of health care and the increasing older minority population, additional reform will be needed to maintain the sustainability of the program. There is an undeniable need to reform Medicare to ensure its future financial viability while at the same time preserving the extraordinary role it plays in ensuring access to medical care for older adults, particularly the poor and minorities. However, the contours of those reforms are important, as they may affect the most vulnerable of Americans and compromise hard-earned gains in addressing racial/ethnic disparities in the U.S. health care system.

Saad-Lessler, Ghilarducci, and Richman focus on older minorities and retirement. The authors' objective is to understand the main reasons why older minorities are less prepared to retire than older whites. Employing Census Bureau data, the analyses reveal that minority older adults are less likely to participate in a retirement plan when one is available, contribute less when they do participate, and more likely to take hardship withdrawals from their pension plans relative to white older adults. They conclude that an unacceptable number of minorities will face poverty in old age.

Although informal social support networks are critical for individuals of all ages, they are especially important for older adults who are dealing with difficult life circumstances. Taylor, Hernandez, Nicklett, Taylor, and Chatters provide a selective review of research on the informal social support networks among older African Americans, Hispanics, Asian Americans, and Native Americans. The authors highlight the importance of understanding informal social support networks among minority groups, and also address the paucity of research focusing on minority older adults. Two key areas discussed include the impact of major life events, such as widowhood on social support networks. These authors recommend that future research should seek to understand the effect social capital has on social support. They also suggest that new data will become available which will contain a sufficient number of older minorities with measures that are sensitive to challenges seen in these groups. Finally, research on effective culturally sensitive practices that improve the quality of life of older minorities merits attention.

Kelley-Moore and Thorpe examine the role of "place" in the aging experience of minority older adults. Decades of research in sociology, geography, and urban studies have documented the changes in patterns and trends in the racial and ethnic makeup of neighborhoods. The factors for these changes include segregation (Massey & Denton 1988), demographic shifts in race/ethnic composition (Deskins & Bettinger, 2002), and immigrant settlement (Alberts, 2005). There has been a simultaneous stream of literature focused on older adults and neighborhoods, examining issues such as aging in place (Rosel, 2003), age-friendly cities (Stafford, 2009), and later-life relocation (Longino, Bradley, Stoller, & Haas, 2008). Yet, there is a handful of research that examines the intersection of race/ethnicity, aging, and urban neighborhoods. They provide a fresh meta-analysis of the dynamic and multiethnic contexts of urban areas and highlight implications for minority older adults: (a) cohort replacement in transitioning neighborhoods; (b) age stratification in new ethnoburbs; (c) elders as new immigrants; and (d) hyper-segregation of the very old and very poor. The discussion offers new and critical insights into the intersection of ethnic geography and aging that have heretofore received little systematic attention.

Marta Rodríguez-Galán examines the sociological literature related to the ethnography of family structures of minority older adults. She succinctly address key sociological questions such as the importance of kin ties, including those that are "fictive" for the well-being of minority older adults, the role of older family members in social reproduction and in the transmission of ethnic identity and culture, changes in intergenerational family relationships in a globalized economy, and the relationship between cumulative disadvantage in families and later life health issues. She concludes that ethnographic research is much needed to enrich the understanding of the sociology of ethnic minority families, and that social and biomedical scientists turn to ethnography for a contextualized understanding of health issues and family life in life course perspective (Burton & Bromell, 2010).

Dilworth-Anderson and Hillard address how sociology, which has a broad range of conceptual frameworks and theories in which it grounds itself, is a ripe field for the use of qualitative studies of social networks in ethnically diverse populations in different contexts. The authors' primary aim is to describe how taking a qualitative research approach as opposed to reliance on numerical data allows for a nuanced and detailed understanding of the complex nature and structure of social relationships in late adulthood. Toward that end, they illustrate the numerous ways in which qualitative analysis can illuminate social processes by which the lives of aging minorities, and in particular African American caregivers, are created and changed (Maynes, Pierce, & Laslett, 2008).

Ronald Angel ends this section of the book with a description of how minority aging in the United States will impact the social contract between generations. A demographic portrait of the workforce and retirement population will look much different than it did in the past. Because of high fertility and immigration, racial and ethnic minority groups—particularly Hispanics and those of Mexican heritage—comprise an even larger share of the economically active population. Although the working-age population is becoming increasingly minority, the older retired population is predominantly non-Hispanic and white. This situation is particularly pronounced in states like Texas, where by the year 2040, well over half of the labor force will be Hispanic. A failure to address the importance of race and ethnicity will bring strife and only heighten the potential of serious age-based conflicts in the decades ahead, given that racial and ethnic minority populations are also younger. A system in which minority workers are largely taxed to support nonminority seniors undermines its political legitimacy and survival. Understanding the sort of social structures to be put in place for both the old and the young, as well as the poor, and the nature of what consequences arise over commitments when resources are limited (e.g., intergenerational conflict) deserves empirical analysis.

The implications of the ethnic-age grading and the New Social Contract are profound. For example, it is necessary to address difficult issues related to the rationing of care and the control of health care budgets. And yet, doing so will mean that the groups with the weakest political power become most vulnerable. Vital issues like these require a renewed understanding of the combined effects of minority group status, occupational disadvantage, and population change on the carrying capacity of the labor force, as well as the sources of support for older Americans.

In summary, during the past three decades there has been an enormous amount of descriptive work examining minority aging issues. Population projections suggest that we will become a nation where the minorities are the majority in the very near future. Yet, little progress has been achieved in understanding the mechanisms that underlie these issues. The chapters in this part succinctly address key topics using a sociological perspective that minority populations face. Future work should include a life course approach that involves a focus on early life conditions to help understand the minority aging experience. Also a mixed methods approach would allow us to further enrich the quantitative analyses. Data that is essential to understanding minority aging issues needs to be collected with a sufficient number of older minorities. Additional work examining within-race group differences is key to understanding minority aging issues given the large amount of cultural diversity in the United States.

REFERENCES

Alberts, H. C. (2005). Changes in ethnic solidarity in Cuban Miami. *The Geographical Review, 95*, 231–248.

Angel, J. L., & Settersten, R. A. Jr. (2011). Sociology in the decades ahead. In R. A Settersten & J. L. Angel (Eds.), *Handbook of sociology of aging* (pp. 661–672). New York, NY: Springer Sciences.

Angel, R., & Angel, J. (2006). Diversity and aging. In R. Binstock, & L. George (Eds.), *Handbook of aging and the social sciences* (6th ed., pp. 94–110). San Diego, CA: Elsevier Science.

Burton, L. M., & Bromell, L. (2010). Childhood illness, family comorbidity, and cumulative disadvantage. An ethnographic treatise on low-income mothers in later life. *Annual Review of Gerontology and Geriatrics, 30*(1), 233–265.

Deskins, D. R. Jr., & Bettinger, C. (2002). Black and White spaces in selected metropolitan areas. In K. A. Berry & M. L. Henderson (Eds.), *Geographical identities of ethnic America: Race, space, and place* (pp. 38–63). Reno, NV: University of Nevada Press.

Federal Interagency Forum on Aging-Related Statistics. (2010). *Older Americans 2010: Key indicators of well being*. Retrieved from http://www.forefrontaustin.com/sites/www.forefrontaustin.com/files/olderamericans_2010.pdfhttp://www.forefrontaustin.com/sites/www.forefrontaustin.com/files/olderamericans_2010.pdf

Longino, C. F., Bradley, D. E., Stoller, E. P., & Haas III, W. H. (2008). Predictors of non-local moves among older adults: A prospective study. *Journal of Gerontology: Social Sciences, 63*, S7–S14.

Massey, D., & Denton, N. (1988). The dimensions of residential segregation. *Social Forces, 67*, 281–315.

Maynes, M. J., Pierce, J. L., & Laslett, B. (2008). *Telling Stories: The use of personal narratives in the social sciences and history*. Ithaca, NY: Cornell University Press.

Office of Management and Budget. (2012). Revisions to the Standards for the Classification of Federal Data on Race and Ethnicity. *Federal Register* Notice October 30, 2007. Retrieved from http://www.whitehouse.gov/omb/fedreg_1997standardshttp://www.whitehouse.gov/omb/fedreg_1997standards

Rosel, N. (2003). Aging in place: Knowing where you are. *International Journal of Aging and Human Development, 57*, 77–90.

Shrestha, L. B., & Heisler, E. J. (2011). *The changing demographic profile of the United States. 7–5700*. Washington, DC: Congressional Research Service. Retrieved from www.crs.govhttp://www.fas.org/sgp/crs/misc/RL32701.pdfwww.crs.govhttp://www.fas.org/sgp/crs/misc/RL32701.pdf

Stafford, P. B. (2009). *Elderburbia: Aging with a sense of place in America*. Santa Barbara, CA: Praeger.

U.S. Administration on Aging. (2011). *Profile of older Americans*. Washington, DC: U.S. Department of Health and Human Services. Retrieved from http://www.aoa.gov/aoaroot/aging_statistics/Profile/2011/docs/2011profile.pdfhttp://www.aoa.gov/aoaroot/aging_statistics/Profile/2011/docs/2011profile.pdf

U.S. Census Bureau. (2004). *Global population at a glance: 2002 and beyond*. Washington, DC: Demographic Programs, International Population Reports. Retrieved from http://www.census.gov/ipc/prod/wp02/wp02-1.pdf

U.S. Census Bureau. (2008). *Table 2a. Projected population of the United States, by age and sex: 2000 to 2050*. Retrieved from http://www.census.gov/population/www/projections/usinterimproj/

CHAPTER 24

The Demography of Minority Aging

Kerstin Gerst-Emerson and Jeffrey A. Burr

Minority elders[1] represent the fastest growing segment of the older population in the United States, and as a result, the older adult population is becoming racially and ethnically more diverse. The goal of this chapter is to provide an overview of recent population estimates, trends, and projections of older adults, with a specific focus on minority populations. We highlight aging trends among several specific minority groups and discuss their different profiles in general demographic terms. In addition, we dedicate space to the special issue of foreign-born older adults in the United States. We review limitations of the available data and include a discussion of issues that require additional research.

DATA SOURCES AND METHODS

In this chapter, most of the population estimates, historical trends, immigration estimates, and projections of minority elders are based on data collected by the U.S. Census Bureau. These data sources include decennial censuses, Current Population Surveys (CPS), and American Community Surveys (ACS). When possible, we report statistics from published reports. In other instances, we report statistics based on our analyses of data from the combined 2006 to 2010 American Community Surveys (Ruggles et al., 2010).

We follow the U.S. Census Bureau's approach to the definition of race groups and Hispanic ethnicity, which are set forth by the Office of Management and Budget (1997). The Census Bureau asks individuals to self-report their race using various options: white, black or African American (hereafter, black), American Indian or Alaska Native (AIAN; hereafter, American Indian), Asian, Native Hawaiian or Other Pacific Islander (ANHPI; hereafter, Asian, unless otherwise noted).

For those who do not identify with any of the listed categories, the Census Bureau reports data using another category, "some other race," which encompasses all other race groups not included in the listed categories. Among persons aged 65 and older, 1.7% reported "some other race" (authors' calculation from 2006 to 2010 ACS data). The U.S. Census Bureau permits persons to identify more than one race. We do not report statistics for this group in this chapter. Among persons aged 65 and older, 0.9% report more than one race (authors' calculation from 2006 to 2010 ACS data). The reporting of more than one race is most common for younger adults and children.

The Census Bureau also provides individuals with the opportunity to self-report Hispanic ethnicity, which is considered separate from the self-report of race. Hispanic or Latino (hereafter, Hispanic) ethnicity refers to persons of Mexican, Cuban, Puerto Rican, South American, Central American, and other Spanish culture or origin (Humes, Jones, & Ramirez, 2011). Unless otherwise noted, we report statistics for non-Hispanic whites, blacks alone, Asians alone, American Indians alone, and Hispanics (of any race). Statistics based on data from the ACS follow the U.S. Census Bureau rules.

It is noteworthy that these broad race and Hispanic ethnicity categories conceal significant differences within groups. For instance, the "Asian" category lumps together persons who have origins from different countries, such as India, Vietnam, China, Japan, Korea, and the Philippines, among others. Among those persons aged 65 and older who self-identify with a single Asian group, the rank-order distribution is Chinese (27.8%), Filipino (22.1%), Japanese (13.8%), Indian (12.3%), Korean (10.5%), Vietnamese (9.9%), and "other Asian" (3.6%; authors' calculation from the 2006 to 2010 ACS). These groups have different cultures, histories, political economies, and population characteristics. In addition, within the American Indian group there are important cultural differences, with over 560 federally recognized tribes speaking more than 200 languages (Goins & Spencer, 2005). Although Hispanics are unified by a common language and often have similar cultural traditions, there are significant differences across these groups, as well. Among those persons aged 65 and older who self-identify with a specific Hispanic group, the rank-order distribution is Mexican (51.4%), Puerto Rican (11.6%), Cuban (11.4%), and "other Hispanic" (25.6%; authors' calculation from the 2006 to 2010 ACS). The diversity of experiences and levels of and paths to incorporation into American society across each of these unique race and Hispanic ethnic groups is impactful, and when possible, should not be ignored by researchers and policy makers. Nevertheless, a majority of research reports use these large race and ethnic groupings for ease of reporting. This chapter follows this strategy, with the cautionary note that these broad categories obfuscate intra-category heterogeneity. An analysis of other specific race and Hispanic groups is beyond the scope of this chapter.

In addition to race and ethnic minority classifications, persons immigrating to the United States may be considered a minority group. Over the next half century, immigration is projected to continue to be a key component in U.S. population growth (Passel & Cohn, 2008), contributing to increasing race and ethnic diversity among all age groups. This chapter focuses on older immigrants from Latin America and Asia (we use the terms immigrant and foreign-born interchangeably), although there are significant streams of immigration from Europe, the Middle East, Africa, and other regions of the world.

POPULATION SIZE AND COMPOSITION OF U.S. RACE AND ETHNIC GROUPS: ESTIMATES AND PROJECTIONS

According to the 2010 U.S. Census, there are more than 40 million adults aged 65 and older living in the United States, comprising approximately 13% of the total population (Werner, 2011). This is an increase of over 5 million older persons since the 2000 U.S. Census (Werner, 2011). The growth of the older population was faster than the growth of the total population, and is expected to continue to increase at a rapid pace in large part because of the aging of the baby boom cohorts and immigration trends (Vincent & Velkoff, 2010).

According to recent reports, a substantial majority (80.4%) of the current older adult population in the United States is non-Hispanic white (see Figure 24.1; Federal Interagency Forum on Aging-Related Statistics, 2010). Blacks are the second largest race group among elders, constituting 8.5% of the population. Asian elders represent 3.3% of all older adults, whereas all other races (alone or in combination) represent only 1.3% of older Americans. Hispanics, of any race, comprise about 7% of the population of older adults.

Population projections consistently indicate that the proportion of elders who are non-Hispanic white will decline substantially, leading to increased diversity among elders (Angel & Hogan, 1992; Federal Interagency Forum on Aging-Related Statistics, 2010). By

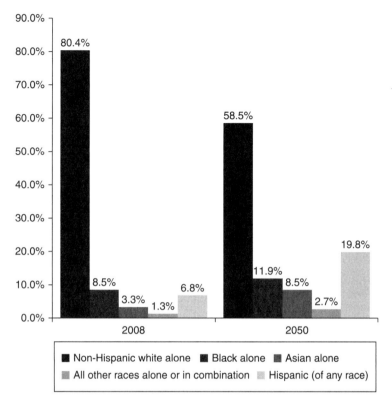

FIGURE 24.1 Population Projections for Persons 65 and Older by Race and Hispanic Ethnicity, 2000–2050.
Source: Federal Interagency Forum On Aging-Related Statistics (2010).

2050, more than 4 of 10 older adults will be from a minority group, which has significant social and policy implications. According to projections, the proportion of non-Hispanic whites will decline to 58.5% by 2050, while Blacks will increase to 11.9% and Asians to 8.5% of the older population (Federal Interagency Forum on Aging-Related Statistics, 2010). During this same time period, older Asians will increase from about 1 million persons (3.3% of the older population) to more than 7 million persons (8.5% of the older population). Hispanic elders are expected to show the most dramatic increase during the next 40 years, moving from about 2.6 million (6.8% of the older population) in 2008 to over 17.5 million persons (19.8%) in 2050, which is more than a sixfold increase (Federal Interagency Forum on Aging-Related Statistics, 2010). By 2050, Hispanics will be the largest elderly minority group in the United States.

One of the key drivers of this increased diversity is immigration. Although most immigrants are younger adults, the population of immigrants aged 65 and older represents 12% of immigrants living in the United States (U.S. Census Bureau, 2011a). Although the majority of immigrants arrive in the United States as working-age adults or children, approximately 10% arrive in later life (Terrazas, 2009). Understanding the differences between those immigrants who are aging in place and those who come to the United States to find a place to age is important because elders arriving late in life have less time to assimilate to the U.S. context, including less time to learn the English language, to accumulate work credits for receipt of Social Security retirement benefits, and to learn how to navigate federal, state, and local government and private, social, and health care service systems.

Historically, immigration to the United States was dominated by persons arriving from European countries. This was, in large part, due to national origin quotas that heavily favored northern and western European immigrants and restricted immigration from other parts of the world (He, 2002; Kandel, 2011). However, in 1965 the legislation effectively ended the quota system and unintentionally and dramatically shifted the immigration flow toward Asia and Latin America (Kandel, 2011). Currently, the largest share of immigrants regardless of age arrives in the United States from countries in Asia and Latin America (Kandel, 2011). In 2010, 2 of 3 immigrants aged 65 and older were born in a Latin American or an Asian country (U.S. Census Bureau, 2011b, authors' calculations), contributing significantly to the diversification of the older adult population.

AGE COMPOSITION AND STRUCTURE

Age composition varies by race and ethnic group, as shown in Table 24.1, where there are dramatic differences in median age across groups (U.S. Census Bureau, 2008a). Non-Hispanic whites have the highest median age at 41.3 years. The median age for Asians is 36 years (for Native Hawaiian and other Pacific Islanders, the median age is 30.5 years), for blacks it is 31.7 years, and for American Indians the figure is 29.9 years. The median age for Hispanics was 27.5 years. Projections indicate that the large gap in median age among blacks, Asians, and whites will decrease by 2050. However, Hispanics are expected to continue to be a relatively young population due to continued high fertility and immigration.

The foreign-born population is older than the U.S.-born population (Congressional Budget Office, 2004); this is, in part, due to the fact that a majority of persons who immigrate to the United States do so during their young adult years. In addition, these younger immigrants give birth to their children while living in the United States, resulting in fewer foreign-born children (children born to immigrant parents are considered U.S. citizens by law and thus are not considered foreign-born). For example, in 2003 only 9% of the foreign-born population was under age 18, compared to 28% of the U.S.-born population (Congressional Budget Office, 2004). The median age also varied considerably by global geographic region and country of birth. In 2003, the median age of European immigrants was 50, which is substantially higher than the total U.S.-born population, with a median age of 35 (Congressional Budget Office, 2004). However, Asian and Latin American immigrants were younger than their European immigrant counterparts, with median ages of 40 and 35.5 years, respectively (Congressional Budget Office, 2004). To summarize, while all race, ethnic, and immigrant groups will experience increased aging in the coming decades, there is wide variability in the degree of aging projected for specific race and ethnic groups (Vincent & Velkoff, 2010).

The older population itself is also growing older; the fastest rate of growth is found among those aged 90 and older. This "oldest-old" population is particularly important to consider because this population consumes resources at disproportionate rates, which has significant social and policy consequences, including implications for social support in later

TABLE 24.1 Median Age by Race and Hispanic Ethnicity in the United States: 2010 to 2050

	2010	2030	2050
Non-Hispanic white	41.3	43.7	44.6
Asian alone	36.0	41.1	43.4
Black alone	31.7	36.6	38.9
Native Hawaiian or other Pacific Islander alone	30.5	35.1	36.8
American Indian Alaskan Native	29.9	33.8	34.9
Hispanic	27.5	29.2	31.2

The U.S. Census Bureau allows for respondents to identify with more than one race. In this table only persons selecting one of the race categories are presented.

Source: U.S. Census Bureau (2008a).

life and resources spent on late-life medical care and long-term care (He & Muenchrath, 2011). According to a recent U.S. Census report (He & Muenchrath, 2011), the proportion of persons aged 90 and older nearly tripled between 1990 and 2010, with 1.9 million elders aged 90 and older living in the United States (slightly less than 5% of the total older population). This rapid growth is expected to continue, with a projected quadrupling during the next 40 years, compared to a doubling of the population aged 65 to 89 during that same time period (He & Muenchrath, 2011). Statistics show that by 2050 there will be well over 8 million persons aged 90 and older (He & Muenchrath, 2011). The current cohort of the oldest old is predominantly white (88.1% of all persons aged 90 and older). Blacks comprise 7.6% of the oldest old and Asians make up 2.2%. Only 0.3% of those aged 90 and older are American Indian and approximately 4% are Hispanic (He & Muenchrath, 2011). Statistics show that even among the oldest old age category, race and ethnic diversity is increasing rapidly (Vincent & Velkoff, 2010).

GENDER COMPOSITION

Gender composition, often evaluated by demographers with the sex ratio (number of males per 100 females), is useful to consider because imbalances reflect long-term demographic, immigration, and health processes that yield variability in social support options in later life, including implications for caregiving and care receipt among family and other social network members. Regardless of race or ethnic status, women outnumber men in old age because mortality risk at every age is higher for men than women (Howden & Meyer, 2011). According to results from the 2010 U.S. census, among persons aged 65 and older, the sex ratio was 76 (76 men for every 100 women), and for those 85 years old and older, the sex ratio was 48 (48 men for every 100 women; Werner, 2011, authors' calculations). This gap is expected to narrow, however, with projections of more rapid increases in life expectancy among men relative to women (Vincent & Velkoff, 2010).

The sex ratio among minority elders differs substantially from that of the total population, due to gender imbalances in immigration patterns and variability in the female survivorship advantage across groups. According to recent U.S. Census Bureau population estimates, the sex ratio was lowest among blacks for each adult age category (U.S. Census Bureau, 2011c; see Table 24.2). Among young old persons (aged 65–74), the sex ratio was 74 for blacks, 83 for Asians, and 81 for Hispanics, as compared to 89 for non-Hispanic whites. The larger imbalanced sex ratio for blacks is due to the higher rate of mortality among black men at earlier ages. Among the oldest old (persons aged 85 and older), the sex ratio followed similar patterns, although the differences among minority groups narrow at older ages.

LIFE EXPECTANCY

Life expectancy estimates inform us about the overall well-being of a population, and can be used effectively to demonstrate relative advantage and disadvantage (e.g., health disparities) at all stages of the life course. Life expectancy is affected by many factors, including socioeconomic opportunities, access to health care, exposure to disease, lifestyle differences, and in the case of immigrant populations, conditions experienced while living in the sending country.

TABLE 24.2 Sex Ratio by Age Groups for Race and Hispanic Ethnicity in the United States

	65–74	75–84	85+
Non-Hispanic White	89	74	49
Black	74	59	39
Asian	83	69	59
Hispanic	81	69	54

Source: U.S. Census Bureau (2011c).

TABLE 24.3 Projected Life Expectancy at Birth by Race and Hispanic Ethnicity in the United States: 2010 to 2050

	2010	2030	2050
Non-Hispanic white	78.7	80.9	83.1
Black alone	73.8	78.1	81.8
American Indian alone	79.1	81.3	83.4
Asian alone	78.8	81.1	83.3
Native Hawaiian and Pacific Islander alone	79.2	81.2	83.4
Hispanic	81.1	82.6	84.1

Source: U.S. Census Bureau (2008b).

Life expectancy at birth varies by race and ethnic group (see Table 24.3). Currently, Hispanics have the highest life expectancy at birth (81.1 years), despite being at a socioeconomic disadvantage relative to whites (this phenomenon is known as the Hispanic or Latino paradox and is discussed in detail in Chapter 5). While non-Hispanic whites, American Indian, Native Hawaiian and Pacific Islanders, and Asian groups all have relatively similar life expectancies at birth (approximately 79 years), blacks have a notably lower life expectancy at birth of only 73.8 years (U.S. Census Bureau, 2008b).

As people age, differences in life expectancy by race and ethnicity increase due to variability in mortality rates throughout the life course. Therefore, another measure of life expectancy captures average life expectancy for those who survive to old age. Life expectancy at older ages is particularly informative from a policy perspective, since many policies are age-based, and the need for assistance increases with age. For example, increases in life expectancy among persons who reach eligibility age for programs such as Social Security and Medicare result in the need for additional public resources. Currently, life expectancy at age 65 is 17.2 for men and 19.9 for women, regardless of race (U.S. Census Bureau, 2012). For those who live until age 85, the average life expectancy for men is 5.8 years and for women it is 6.8 years. Race and ethnic disparities persist in life expectancy among older adults (see Chapter 9).

DEPENDENCY RATIOS

An even more direct method for evaluating caregiving and care receipt potential is through an examination of dependency ratios. Although these measures have limitations, they provide a reasonable approximation of the size of the population that *may* need assistance as compared to the size of the population that *may* be asked to provide such assistance (Vincent & Velkoff, 2010). One way to quantify this is with an old age dependency ratio (population 65 and over divided by the population 18 to 65 per 100 total population), where the higher the old age dependency ratio, the higher the potential resource consequences for society. In 2010, the old age dependency ratio was 22, which is projected to increase to 35 in 2030 due to the aging of the boomer birth cohort (Vincent & Velkoff, 2010). This means that in 2010 for every 100 persons in the working-age population, there were 22 persons aged 65 and older, and in 2030 there will be 35 persons aged 65 and older for 100 persons in the working-age population.

After observing differences in age structure among the largest race and ethnic groups, it is not surprising that old age dependency ratios vary considerably among whites and minority groups (see Table 24.4). For non-Hispanic whites, the old age dependency ratio is 25, whereas for blacks and Asians it is only 14 (U.S. Census 2011c). Reflecting the relative youth of the Hispanic and the American Indian population, the old age dependency ratios are 10 and 12, respectively. However, this suggests that among minority families, the issues associated with old age dependency may be less severe than among non-Hispanic whites. On the contrary, the child dependency ratio represents a larger concern for some minority groups, especially for

TABLE 24.4 U.S. Dependency Ratios by Race and Hispanic Ethnicity

	OLD AGE DEPENDENCY RATIO (#65/#18–64)	CHILD DEPENDENCY RATIO (#<18/#18–64)	OLDEST OLD SUPPORT RATIO (#>85/#50–74)
Non-Hispanic white	25	32	8
Black	14	45	4
American Indian	12	48	4
Asian	14	35	5
Hispanic	10	58	5

Source: U.S. Census Bureau (2011c).

black and Hispanic groups, which often have fewer economic resources. Although the child dependency ratio was 32 per 100 adults aged 18 to 64 years old for non-Hispanic whites and 35 for Asians, it was 45 for blacks and 58 for Hispanics (U.S. Census 2011c, authors' calculations).

The dependency ratios reported here measure the potential support available from working-aged persons and are useful for public program planning. However, these support ratios do not consider the projected increase in the oldest old, who have the highest risk of frailty, and when needed, require more care for longer periods of time (Robine, Michel & Herrmann, 2007; Tsai, 2010). Therefore, the standard old age dependency ratio does not adequately estimate potential need for informal care (Tsai, 2010). To consider this issue more carefully, researchers have proposed a complement to the old age dependency ratio, sometimes called the "oldest old support ratio." This measure is calculated as the ratio of the number of persons in the oldest old age group (defined here as 85 years old and older) per 100 persons in the typical caregiving ages (50–74 years old; Robine, Michel & Herrmann, 2007). Because this ratio captures the balance between potential caregivers and the oldest persons in a population, it provides a more accurate indicator of informal care resources available for the oldest old (Robine, Michel, & Herrmann, 2007).

In 2009, the oldest old support ratio was 8 for non-Hispanic whites; that is, there were about 8 persons aged 85 and older for every 100 persons in the potential caregiving ages of 50 to 74 (U.S. Census 2011c, authors' calculations). Considering the demographic profile of the oldest old, it is not surprising that whites have the highest oldest old support ratio among race and ethnic groups. For the black and American Indian populations, the oldest old support ratio was 4. The ratio was slightly higher for the Hispanic and Asian populations at 5, but this was still substantially lower than the oldest old support ratio for non-Hispanic whites. Much like the old age dependency ratio, these ratios reflect the relative youth of minority groups.

EDUCATION

Education is an important resource for narrowing inequality in the United States. Education levels vary more for older persons than for younger persons, especially among blacks and Hispanics, due in part to cohort effects associated with changes in legislation meant to overcome historically lower access to this resource. Overall, minority elders have lower educational levels compared to non-Hispanic whites, with a few notable exceptions. Recent data show that in 2008, more than three quarters (77%) of all elders had a high-school degree and one in five (21%) of all elders obtained a bachelor's degree or higher (AOA, 2010a). Older blacks have a much lower level of education, although as noted, the past few decades have seen a significant increase in educational attainment among younger blacks (AOA, 2010a). In 2008, less than two thirds (60%) of blacks aged 65 and older had completed high school and approximately 12% of black elders had earned a bachelor's degree or higher. Although these levels are lower compared to the overall population of elders, they have improved dramatically during the past 40 years. For example, in 1970 only 9% of black elders had completed high school (AOA, 2010a). Hispanic elders also have lower education levels compared to non-Hispanic white elders. High-school completion rates were less than half (46%) among the older Hispanic population and only 9% completed a bachelor's degree or higher (AOA, 2010b). Data from the 2006 to 2010 ACS show that approximately 58% of American Indian elders achieved at least a high-school degree and 10.6% held at least a bachelor's degree.

However, Asian elders, like younger Asians, have an overall better profile regarding their educational status, emphasizing once again the heterogeneity among minority groups. Overall, Asian elders have rates of high-school graduation similar to those of the general population of elders. Perhaps most notable, Asians had a significantly higher rate of completing college; nearly 1 of 3 (32%) Asian elders hold a bachelor's degree or higher (AOA, 2010c). Despite this generally positive education profile among older Asians, it is important to note that there is substantial variability in education levels across the specific Asian groups, and thus variability in economic well-being is present within the Asian population (Sakamoto, Goyette, & Kim, 2009).

MARITAL STATUS AND LIVING ARRANGEMENTS

Marital status and living arrangements are informative, in part, because they indicate whether older persons are independent or dependent, and whether they have the support they need if and when they experience illness, functional limitations, and disability. Living arrangements and marital status among older adults vary by gender, as well as by race and ethnic group status, due in large part to variation in life expectancy, availability of kin (especially adult children), socioeconomic resources, and cultural norms. In addition, living arrangements are molded by the immigration experience, where combining households with others may be a strategy to offset the immediate needs for shelter, food, and information about employment and services. Combining households across generations may also be a strategy that helps some older immigrants maintain a transnational lifestyle (Treas, 2008).

Data from the 2006 to 2010 ACS (see Table 24.5) indicate that 56.6% of non-Hispanic whites are married, a figure similar to that of Asians (56.4%). Only about one third of blacks are married, whereas 4 of 10 American Indians are married. Widowhood is highest among older blacks (35.9%). The prevalence of marriage for older Hispanics (47.3%) is somewhat higher than that for American Indians (43.9%) and the widowhood rate (27.5%) is somewhat lower than that for non-Hispanic whites (28.8%). The group most likely to live alone is black elders (32.9%), followed by non-Hispanic whites (29.7%), and American Indian elders (27.6%). Older Asians have a very low prevalence of living alone (14.0%).

Regardless of race or ethnic group status, older women are far more likely to be widowed compared to men (Federal Interagency Forum on Aging-Related Statistics, 2010). Conversely, due to differences in life expectancy, older men are more likely to be married, and thus benefit disproportionately from having a spouse for companionship and social support. Thus, older women are more likely to live alone than older men. Data from the ACS show that among non-Hispanic white females aged 65 and older, 38.6% live alone compared to 18.3% of males. For elderly black females, 37.2% live alone and among older Asians, the group least likely to live alone among females, the figure is 18.1% (8.6% of Asian males live alone). American Indian and Hispanic females fall between non-Hispanic Whites and Asian females for this living arrangement type (31.9 and 24.0%, respectively). Living alone is even more prominent among the oldest old (defined here as 85 years old and older). Non-Hispanic whites report the highest levels of living alone in the oldest old age group (50.0%), whereas Asians report the lowest rate at 21.6%. The largest differences are for non-Hispanic white females, where 6 of 10 live alone, and Asian males, where only 1 in 10 live alone.

Headship status is another indicator of independence, but may also be culturally defined. We measure headship through the ACS survey question identifying who is regarded as the householder (i.e., person whose name is on the mortgage, title, or rental agreement); if the respondent is the householder or if the spouse of the householder, that individual is considered the head of the household. More than 9 of 10 older non-Hispanic whites are heads of household, whereas at the other end of the spectrum, only 6 of 10

TABLE 24.5 Marital Status and Living Arrangements by Race and Hispanic Ethnicity in the United States (%)

	NON-HISPANIC WHITE	BLACK	ASIAN, NATIVE HAWAIIAN, PACIFIC ISLANDER	AMERICAN INDIAN, ALASKA NATIVE	HISPANIC
Marital Status					
Married	56.6	34.4	56.4	43.9	47.3
Divorced/separated	11.7	21.8	13.0	19.1	19.1
Widowed	28.2	35.9	27.1	31.7	27.5
Never married	3.5	7.9	3.5	5.3	6.0
Lives Alone					
Both sexes 65+	29.7	32.9	14.0	27.6	19.9
Females 65+	38.6	37.2	18.1	31.9	24.0
Males 65+	18.3	26.1	8.6	22.2	14.3
Both sexes 85+	50.0	40.2	21.6	36.6	25.8
Females 85+	59.4	43.4	26.4	41.7	29.9
Males 85+	31.9	31.6	13.9	25.2	17.9
Headship Status					
Head of household	92.3	84.4	63.9	86.1	72.9
N (unweighted)[a]	1,855,894	163,743	65,924	11,983	123,570
Group Quarters Population					
Institutions	3.6	4.5	1.5	3.1	2.2
Other	0.7	0.7	0.5	0.6	0.5
N (unweighted)	1,938,876	174,564	67,512	12,393	127,634

[a] Community-residing population only.

Source: American Community Survey, 2006–2010.

older Asians report being heads of household. This is consistent with Asian elders' lower prevalence of living alone.

INSTITUTIONALIZATION

Approximately 3 of 4 caregivers providing long-term care to elders are family members (Albert & Freedman, 2010). When this care is not available or when the older person's needs become so great, one option is to enter a nursing home or an assisted living facility. The U.S. Census Bureau collects information on group quarters. There are two broad types of group quarters typically reported, institutions (e.g., nursing homes, in-patient hospice facilities, military treatment facilities) and other group quarters (e.g., prisons and other correctional facilities, college dormitories, military barracks). While at any point in time the population of elders living in nursing homes is relatively low (between 4 and 5%), the lifetime risk of living in a skilled nursing facility for at least some period time is more than 40% (Spillman & Lubitz, 2002). Nursing home utilization differs by gender, where the projected lifetime risk of entering a nursing home is higher for women. Additionally, the length of stay in facilities is longer for women compared to men (Spillman & Lubitz, 2002).

Rates of nursing home residence vary greatly by age, gender, and race. In 2004, the rate of nursing home use was 34.8 per 1000 persons aged 65 and older (Federal Interagency Forum on Aging-Related Statistics, 2008). The likelihood of residing in a nursing home increases significantly with age; the rate of persons residing in nursing homes was nearly four times as high for those aged 85 and older (138.7 per 1000 persons). At all ages, women had higher rates of nursing home residence compared to men, reflecting in part the higher life expectancy of women. Until relatively recently, whites reported a higher rate of institutionalization. However, in 2004, the rate of nursing home use was 34 per 1000 for whites and 49.9 for black persons aged 65 and older (Federal Interagency Forum on Aging-Related Statistics, 2008).

We calculate group quarters residency by race group and Hispanic ethnic group from the 2006 to 2010 ACS (see Table 24.5). We find among older persons living in all types of institutions (not just nursing homes but primarily this type of residence among this age group) that blacks had the highest (4.5%) and Asians had the lowest (1.5%) prevalence rate. Variability in utilization rates is based on a complex set of factors, including uneven access to alternatives to long-term care institutions, variability in group health and disability, and cultural norms regarding long-term care support options.

GEOGRAPHIC DISTRIBUTION AND GEOGRAPHIC MOBILITY

The place where older people reside geographically affects their quality of life and impacts the areas in which they live. America's race and ethnic groups are not distributed evenly across regions, states, metropolitan versus nonmetropolitan areas, or urban versus rural areas. Based on our search of the scholarly literature, in the last 10 years there has been relatively little research effort applied to questions surrounding the geographic distribution of older persons among the general population and even less attention has been given to their internal migration patterns. When race and ethnic diversity are considered, the absence of research on this subject is even more astounding.

According to data from the ACS, the south has the highest proportion of older adults, as more than one third (36.3%) of elders live in a southern state (see Table 24.6). Disaggregating geographic residence by race and Hispanic ethnicity shows different patterns of regional distribution. Elderly non-Hispanic whites are more evenly dispersed throughout the four census regions of the United States than any of the elderly minority groups. Black elders are heavily concentrated in the south (54.4%), whereas Asians are concentrated in the west (58.3%) along with American Indian elders (47.3%). Hispanics are concentrated in the south (39.6%) and west (38.6%). At a smaller level of geographic detail, the south Atlantic division (Georgia, South Carolina, Florida) and the Pacific division (California, Hawaii, Oregon, Washington) represent some of the most diverse areas of the country.

Where minority elders are concentrated has implications for state and local governments, especially with regards to providing services to the more vulnerable among these groups. Table 24.7 provides details on the top five states with the largest percentages of older persons for each race group, as well as for Hispanics. The states with the highest population of elderly blacks are New York, Florida, and Texas. Asians and Pacific Islanders are highly concentrated in California, Hawaii, New York, Texas, and New Jersey. Nearly half of all American Indian elders live in 1 of 5 states: California, Oklahoma, Arizona, New Mexico, and Texas. Hispanic elders are also geographically concentrated, where nearly three quarters live in California, Texas, Florida, New York, Arizona, or New Jersey.

Generally, older persons are not highly geographically mobile (Wolf & Longino, 2005). Results from the ACS show that among all elders combined only 5.3% change residences (either within their current state or across states) within the year prior to the survey (see Table 24.7). For all race and ethnic groups, most of the movement is within states: only about 1% moved across state lines or abroad. The most active minority elders to move within their state of residence are Hispanics and Asians, although the proportion of movers is low even for

TABLE 24.6 Geographic Distribution and Migration Rates for Persons Age 65 and Older in the United States by Race and Hispanic Ethnicity (%)

	NON-HISPANIC WHITE	BLACK	ASIAN, NATIVE HAWAIIAN, PACIFIC ISLANDER	AMERICAN INDIAN, ALASKA NATIVE	HISPANIC
Region and division					
Northeast	*20.3*	*18.6*	*17.5*	*6.9*	*15.5*
New England	5.8	2.0	2.6	2.1	2.0
Middle Atlantic	14.5	16.6	14.8	4.8	13.5
North Central	*25.1*	*18.2*	*8.1*	*13.4*	*6.3*
East north central	16.9	15.4	6.4	6.5	5.0
West north central	8.2	2.8	1.7	7.0	1.2
South	*35.6*	*54.4*	*16.1*	*32.3*	*39.6*
South Atlantic	19.9	33.1	10.0	11.7	18.9
East south Central	6.5	9.5	0.9	2.66	0.6
West south Central	9.2	11.8	5.2	18.1	20.0
West	*19.0*	*8.8*	*58.3*	*47.3*	*38.6*
Mountain	6.8	1.6	4.0	25.7	10.2
Pacific	12.2	7.2	54.4	21.5	28.5
Migration last year					
Stayed	94.1	93.2	91.5	93.0	92.5
Within state	4.6	5.7	5.6	5.6	5.7
Across states	1.1	0.9	1.1	1.1	1.0
Abroad	0.1	0.2	1.9	0.2	0.8
N (unweighted)	1,938,876	174,564	67,512	12,393	127,634

Source: 2006–2010 American Community Survey.

these groups. While approximately 5% of Hispanic and 5% of Asian elders move within their state, only 3.7% of older non-Hispanic whites move within their state.

Demographers have recently reported that immigrants of all ages, especially Hispanics but other groups as well, are redistributing themselves away from traditional gateway receiving metropolitan areas and states toward nontraditional destinations, such as small cities and towns and to the mid-west and south central states (Massey, 2008). The likely reasons for this are manifold, and include changes in employment opportunities, reactions to real and perceived hostilities toward immigrants in traditional receiving areas, and the hardening of traditional border crossing areas. Research on this topic is new. We are not aware of any research that examines this issue for older immigrants. It may be that older immigrants are not moving to these new destinations to any appreciable degree or they may be moving to be with family members.

TABLE 24.7 Population Distribution for the Top Five States Among Persons Age 65 and Older by Race and Hispanic Ethnicity (%)

NON-HISPANIC WHITE	BLACK	ASIAN, NATIVE HAWAIIAN, PACIFIC ISLANDER	AMERICAN INDIAN, ALASKA NATIVE	HISPANIC
CA (8.2)	NY (9.3)	CA (40.8)	CA (12.4)	CA (27.0)
FL (7.8)	FL (7.2)	HI (9.2)	OK (10.9)	TX (19.2)
NY (6.1)	TX (6.4)	NY (9.2)	AZ (10.3)	FL (15.9)
TX (5.7)	GA (6.1)	TX (4.4)	NM (8.2)	NY (9.1)
PA (5.6)	NC (5.6)	NJ (3.9)	TX (5.2)	AZ/NJ (3.4)

Source: 2006–2010 American Community Survey.

DISCUSSION

Race and Ethnic Diversity and the Boomer Cohort

A major driving force behind rapid population aging in the United States is the aging of the baby boom birth cohorts. The baby boom generation is defined as persons born between 1946 and 1964, and this demographic phenomenon represents a dramatic increase the U.S. birth rate following World War II. By 2030, all of the 78 million boomers will have moved into old age, resulting in 19% of the population being an older adult (Mutchler & Burr, 2009; Vincent & Velkoff, 2010). The boomer generation will be the largest cohort of older adults ever, and will also be the most racially diverse cohort of elders in the history of the United States (Mutchler & Burr, 2009). As increasing numbers of boomers hit retirement age, more and more are facing the economic pressures of work cessation at a time of national economic uncertainty (Gassoumis, Lincoln, & Vega, 2011; Gassoumis, Wilber, Baker, & Torres-Gil, 2010). At the same time, this diverse population of elders is continuing to face economic and health disparities that often started much earlier in the life course (Gassoumis et al., 2010; Gassoumis et al., 2011; Villa, Wallace, Bagdasaryan, & Aranda, 2012). A clearer understanding of the demographic characteristics of this diverse population will help policy makers better anticipate the needs of boomers, and help scholars understand how boomers are likely to age in very different ways from earlier cohorts.

Based on data from the ACS, Figure 24.2 displays the race and ethnic composition of the boomer generation (aged 46–64 in 2010). The boomer generation was majority (73%) non-Hispanic white. Non-Hispanic black boomers made up 11% and Hispanic boomers made up another 10% of this cohort, whereas Asian boomers comprise 5% and boomers from all other race groups include 1%. In part, the diversity among the boomer cohorts is due to immigration; approximately 1 in 7 boomers were born in a foreign country. Although only about 4% of non-Hispanic white boomers are immigrants, nearly 9 of 10 (85%) Asian boomers, and over half (58%) of Hispanic boomers were born abroad.

Currently, relatively little research investigates issues facing minority boomers, although this will certainly be a driving force in demographic shifts in the United States in the near future (for exceptions, see Gassoumis et al., 2010; Mutchler & Burr, 2009; Villa et al., 2012). The research that does examine boomers by race suggests that there is a substantial difference in socioeconomic standing across groups, especially in terms of education, wealth, and assets (Mutchler & Burr, 2009). However, 93% of white boomers have at least a high-school diploma, yet less than two thirds (61%) of Hispanic boomers achieved this level of education. Asian and black boomers, on the contrary, had 85% and 84% high-school diploma completion rates. The differences are even more pronounced for persons graduating with a college degree. Whereas nearly one third (32%) of non-Hispanic white boomers earned a college degree or higher, only 19% of blacks and only 14% of Hispanics achieved a higher level of education. However,

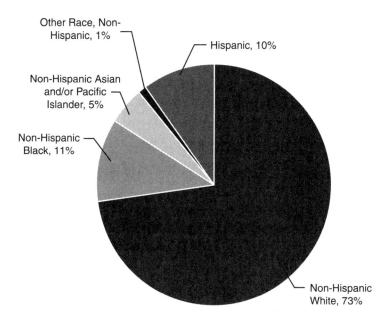

FIGURE 24.2 Boomers by Race and Hispanic Ethnicity.
Source: 2010 American Community Survey, Resticted to Persons Aged 46–64.

Asian boomers were far more likely to receive a bachelor's degree or higher, with nearly half (46%) reporting higher education (Mutchler & Burr, 2009).

In part, reflecting this disparity in education levels, there is a substantial gap in earnings among minority boomers. While non-Hispanic white and Asian boomers have similar median earnings (US$46,687 and US$44,272 annually, respectively), black and Hispanic boomers make substantially less; blacks had a median income of US$35,217 and Hispanics had a median income of US$30,186 annually (Mutchler & Burr, 2009). Similar gaps exist in pension availability to boomers nearing retirement. Projections indicate that about half of boomers will have employer-sponsored retirement benefits available to them once they reach age 62 (Moore, 2006). However, despite projected future increases in eligibility rates, private pension eligibility will still be significantly lower for blacks and Hispanics (Moore, 2006). Additionally, the amount of income from these pensions is projected to be lower for these groups. This suggests that as boomers are nearing retirement, minority boomers find themselves in a more precarious economic situation compared to non-Hispanic white boomers.

Data Quality and Availability

As previously discussed, this chapter focuses on large groups of minority elders, and due to space limitations does not take into consideration the substantial heterogeneity within these groups. Research on these smaller groups is relatively sparse due in large part to the lack of datasets available for such analyses, especially at the national level (Angel & Hogan, 1992). Smaller community and regionally based studies are more common. While data from the U.S. decennial census, Current Population Survey, and the American Community Survey provide researchers with the ability to identify specific race and Hispanic ethnicity groups, the range of information collected on these groups is limited.

Other studies provide detailed behavioral, social, economic, and health information, especially for whites and two of the largest minority groups: blacks and Hispanics. These data files are available as part of the National Archive of Computerized Data on Aging (NACDA). This data inventory is funded by the National Institute on Aging "to advance research on aging by helping researchers to profit from the underexploited potential of a broad range of datasets." NACDA preserves and maintains datasets relevant to gerontological research and is the largest library of electronic data available in the United States (for more information, see www.icpsr.umich.edu/icpsrweb/NACDA).

Useful studies housed at NACDA include Health and Retirement Study (HRS), Study of Assets and Health Dynamics Among the Oldest Old (AHEAD), Panel Study of Income Dynamics, Midlife in the United States, National Health and Nutrition Examination Survey, and National Health Interview Survey. The HRS and AHEAD allow investigators to examine the impact of individuals' economic situations in the years before retirement on their welfare and health in their postretirement years. The most recent version of the National Health and Nutrition Examination Survey (NHANES III) serves as a particularly useful source of information on the incidence and prevalence of type-2 diabetes among Mexican Americans.

There are a few notable exceptions where researchers have conducted data collection efforts focused on specific subpopulations of minority in subnational geographic areas. One well-known dataset is the Hispanic Established Populations for the Epidemiologic Study of the Elderly (HEPESE), which provides a prime example of how resources may be deployed to study specific groups of minority elders. There are additional datasets researchers may rely on to examine older Hispanics, including the Border Epidemiologic Study of Aging (BESA) and the Hispanic Community Health Study/Study of Latinos (HCHS/SOL). The BESA is a panel study of middle-aged and older Mexican Americans living along the Texas/Mexico border, and allows for an examination of the unique situation of the border region. The HCHS/SOL is conducted in four cities, Chicago, the Bronx area of New York, Miami, and San Diego, and enables researchers to identify the prevalence and development of disease among middle-aged and young old Hispanic adults.

Even with large national datasets, such as the U.S. Census Bureau, caution regarding the accuracy of the estimates and projections of smaller groups should be applied. Historically, the U.S. Census has been faced with undercounts from subpopulations, including members of minority groups (Government Accountability Office, 2008). One example of a historically undercounted minority group is American Indians, especially those who live on reservations. This results in limited information regarding the social, economic, and health status of such groups, restricting the in-depth demographic profiles of older Americans. The U.S. Census Bureau also provides projections of populations, although caution should be taken when considering estimates for minorities. Although there is error in all projections, this is particularly a problem when projecting small minority group population characteristics. Thus, demographic processes for these groups are often not well understood.

CONCLUSIONS AND FUTURE RESEARCH DIRECTIONS

The United States is one of the most heterogeneous nations in the world, and this is the case for its older population as well. With an increasing number of boomers entering old age, the United States will have the most diverse cohort of elders in its history (Mutchler & Burr, 2009). This has substantial implications for all aspects of society, including public health, social support systems, and public policy. Future research questions focusing on the impact of this increasingly diverse group of elders should be addressed. Public policy research questions will likely include the impact of future demographic changes on health care and entitlement programs. For instance, what are the implications of possible reductions in Social Security or changes in Medicaid or Medicare programs on the health and disability profiles of older minority groups? This chapter has shown that certain minority groups have a poorer socioeconomic profile and are, therefore, most likely to be impacted by any changes in such programs. This is especially pertinent in light of projections that suggest an increase in the absolute size of such minority groups (Mutchler & Burr, 2009).

Future research should also explore the impact of increased diversity on social support systems and public health. For instance, what will be the impact of the decline in average family size among many minority groups on the availability of social support in later life? As immigrants are increasingly shifting away from traditional gateway cities toward nontraditional destinations, will there be sufficient support for immigrants to successfully age in place in these new areas? What will be the impact of aging immigrants on the receiving areas?

Although it was beyond the scope of this chapter to go into depth about specific group differences, such analyses are vital for future research. Broad racial/ethnic groupings mask important differences across groups and obscure important differences within vulnerable subpopulations. For example, the experiences of Vietnamese refugee elders are likely vastly different from Japanese elders born in the United States, yet both groups are often combined under the heading of "Asian."

This is particularly important when examining the newest cohort of older adults, the boomers. The boomer cohort is commonly seen as healthier, better educated, and more financially prepared for retirement than earlier cohorts (Mutchler & Burr, 2009). However, such an optimistic vision would not be accurate for some subgroups of boomers, where pervasive inequalities remain (Villa et al., 2012). Research on diversity among boomers is relatively new and additional research is needed to generate more in-depth knowledge about this population and the differences within subpopulations. It is, therefore, imperative that researchers consider subpopulations of minority elders in the design and execution of future research endeavors. Resources should be spent on generating high-quality data on specific subpopulations to better prepare policymakers and service providers for an increasingly diverse older population.

NOTE

1. While the definition of older adult varies across the literature, for the purposes of this chapter, an elder will be considered anyone age 65 and older, unless otherwise noted.

REFERENCES

Albert, S. M., & Freedman, V. A. (2010). *Public health and aging: Managing function and well-being.* (2nd ed.). New York: Springer Publishing Company.

Angel, J. L., & Hogan, D. P. (1992). The demography of minority aging populations. *Journal of Family History,* 17(1), 95–115.

AOA (2010a). *A statistical profile of black older Americans aged 65+.* Retrieved February 2012, from http://www.aoa.gov/aoaroot/aging_statistics/minority_aging/Facts-on-Black-Elderly-plain_format.aspx

AOA (2010b). *A statistical profile of Hispanic older Americans aged 65+.* Retrieved February 2012, from http://www.aoa.gov/aoaroot/aging_statistics/minority_aging/Facts-on-Hispanic-Elderly.aspx.

AOA (2010c). *A statistical profile of Asian older Americans aged 65+.* Retrieved February 2012 from: http://www.aoa.gov/aoaroot/aging_statistics/minority_aging/Facts-on-API-Elderly2008-plain_format.aspx

Congressional Budget Office (2004). *A description of the immigrant population.* Retrieved April 2012, from http://www.cbo.gov/sites/default/files/cbofiles/ftpdocs/60xx/doc6019/11-23-immigrant.pdf

Federal Interagency Forum on Aging-Related Statistics (2008). Older Americans 2008: Key indicators of well-being. Washington, DC: U.S. Government Printing Office.

Federal Interagency Forum on Aging-Related Statistics (2010). *Older Americans 2010: Key indicators of well-being.* Washington, DC: U.S. Government Printing Office.

Government Accountability Office (2008). *2010 Census: The bureau's plans for reducing the undercount show promise, but key uncertainties remain.* Retrieved February 2012, from http://www.gao.gov/assets/130/121234.pdf

Gassoumis, Z. D., Lincoln, K. D., & Vega, W. A. (2011). *How low-income minorities get by in retirement: Poverty levels and income sources.* Los Angeles, CA: USC Edward R. Roybal Institute on Aging.

Gassoumis, Z. D., Wilber, K. H., Baker, L. A., & Torres-Gil, F. (2010). *Latino baby boomers: A demographic and economic profile.* Los Angeles, CA: UCLA Center for Policy Research on Aging, USC Ethel Percy Andrus Gerontology Center, & UCLA Chicano Studies Research Center.

Goins, R. T., & Spencer, S. M. (2005). Public health issues among older American Indians and Alaska Natives. *Generations*, XXIX(2), 30–35.

He, W. (2002). *The Older Foreign-Born. Population in the United States. 2000.* Washington, DC: U.S. Census Bureau.

He, W., & Muenchrath, M. N. (2011). *90+ in the United States: 2006–2008.* Washington, DC: U.S. Government Printing Office.

Howden, L. M., & Meyer, J. A. (2011). *Age and sex composition: 2010.* Retrieved March 2012, from http://www.census.gov/prod/cen2010/briefs/c2010br-03.p

Humes, K. R., Jones, N. A., & Ramirez, R. R. (2011). *Overview of race and Hispanic origin: 2010.* Census Briefs: U.S. Census Bureau.

Kandel, W. A. (2011). *The U.S. foreign-born population: Trends and selected characteristics.* Washington, DC: Congressional Research Service.

Massey, D. (2008). *New faces in new places: The changing geography of American immigration.* New York: Russell Sage.

Moore, J. H. (2006). Projected pension income: Equality or disparity for the baby-boom cohort? *Monthly Labor Review*, 129(3), 58–67.

Mutchler, J., & Burr, J. (2009). Boomer diversity and well-being: Race, ethnicity and gender. In R. Hudson (ed.), *Boomer or bust: Economic and political issues in the graying society* (pp. 23–45). Westport, CN: Praeger.

Office of Management and Budget (1997). *Revisions to the standards for the classification of federal data on race and ethnicity.* Retrieved April 2012, from http://www.Whitehouse.gov/omb/fedreg_1997 standards

Passel, J., & Cohn, D. (2008). *U.S. population projections: 2005–2050.* Washington, DC: Pew Hispanic Research Center.

Robine, J.M., Michel, J.P., & Hermann, F. R. (2007). Who will care for the oldest people in our aging society? *British Medical Journal*, 334, 570–571.

Ruggles, S., Alexander, J. T., Genadek, K., Goeken, R., Schroeder, M. B. & Sobek, M. (2010). *Integrated public use microdata series: Version 5.0 [Machine-readable database].* Minneapolis: University of Minnesota.

Sakamoto, A., Goyette, K., & Kim, C.H. (2009). Socioeconomic attainments of Asian Americans. *Annual Review of Sociology*, 35, 255–276.

Spillman, B. C., & Lubitz, J. (2002). New estimates of lifetime nursing home use: Have patterns of use changed? *Med Care*, 40(10), 965–975.

Terrazas, A. (2009). *Older immigrants in the United States.* Retrieved February 2012, from http://www.migrationinformation.org/U.S.focus/display.cfm?id=727#4

Treas, J. (2008). Transnational older adults and their families. *Family Relations*, 57, 468–478.

Tsai, T. (2010). *More caregivers needed worldwide for the 'oldest old'* Population Reference Bureau. Accessed April 2012, from http://www.prb.org/Articles/2010/oldestold2050.aspx

U.S. Administration on Aging (2010). *Projected future growth of the older population.* Retrieved March 2012, from http://www.aoa.gov/aoaroot/aging_statistics/future_growth/future_growth.aspx#hispanic

U.S. Census Bureau (2008a). *Table 14. Projections of the population by age and sex for the United States: 2010 to 2050 Tables 14–20.* Retrieved March 2012, from http://www.census.gov/population/www/projections/summarytables.html

U.S. Census Bureau (2008b). *Table 10. Projected life expectancy at birth by sex, race, and Hispanic origin for the United States: 2010 to 2050.* Washington, DC: U.S. Census Bureau.

U.S. Census Bureau (2011a). *Current population survey—March 2010: Characteristics of the foreign-born population by nativity and U.S. citizenship status (Table 1.1).* Retrieved March 2012, from http://www.census.gov/population/foreign/data/cps2010.html

U.S. Census Bureau (2011b). *Table 41: Foreign-born population: Selected characteristics by region of origin: 2010.* Retrieved March 2012, from http://www.census.gov/compendia/statab/2012/tables/12s0042.pdf

U.S. Census Bureau (2011c). *National intercensal estimates (2000–2010).* Retrieved February 2012, from http://www.census.gov/popest/data/intercensal/national/nat2010.html

U.S. Census Bureau (2012). *The 2012 statistical abstract*. Retrieved April 2012, from http://www.census. gov/compendia/statab/cats/births_deaths_marriages_divorces/life_expectancy.html

Villa, V. M., Wallace, S. P., Bagdasaryan, S., & Aranda, M. P. (2012). Hispanic baby boomers: Health inequities likely to persist in old age. *Gerontologist*, 52(2), 166–176.

Vincent, G. K., & Velkoff, V. A. (2010). *The next four decades: The older population in the United States: 2010 to 2050*. Retrieved March 2012, from http://www.census.gov/prod/2010pubs/p25–1138.pdf

Werner, C. A. (2011). *The Older Population: 2010*. Retrieved March 2012, from http://www.census.gov/prod/cen2010/briefs/c2010br-09.pdf

Wolf, D. A., & Longino, C. F. (2005). Our "increasingly mobile society"? The curious persistence of a false belief. *Gerontologist*, 45(1), 5–11.

CHAPTER 25

Social Networks and Minority Elders

Peggye Dilworth-Anderson and Tandrea S. Hilliard

The social networks of older adults provide them with the greatest amount of care and support. Therefore, understanding the working of these social networks in enhancing the health and well-being of our older adult population is central to the field of aging. More specifically, research studies on the role of social networks in maintaining or improving quantity and quality of life among minority elders offer vital contributions that inform both interventions to ensure adequate and culturally appropriate care and support for older minorities, and discussions on readiness to meet future health care challenges and demands. This chapter seeks to provide new insights, direction, and applicability of qualitative research methods in social network analysis, with special emphasis on the minority elder population. The objectives for this chapter are as follows:

1. To define and describe social networks.
2. To describe the importance and nuances of social network analysis with the minority elder population.
3. To describe how specific qualitative approaches may be applied and contribute to increased understanding in social network analysis.
4. To provide a list of suggested future directions to address issues that are void in the literature on social networks and minority elders.

DEFINING SOCIAL NETWORKS

Formally, a social network may be defined as any bounded set of connected social units (Streeter & Gillespie, 1993), or as the web of social relationships surrounding an individual, in particular, structural features, such as type and strength of each social relationship (Umberson & Montez, 2010). Simply stated, social networks represent ties between individuals or other meaningful units of analysis. Social networks have three key characteristics: (a) boundaries—at least one criterion to determine membership in the network; (b) connectedness—inclusion in a social network relies on actual or potential direct or indirect links among members; and (c) social unit—the analysis of support networks may be applied to a variety of social units (e.g., individuals, social institutions in communities, or nations; Streeter & Gillespie, 1993).

Although the distinction between social support and social networks has historically been blurred (traditionally, most studies of social network effects on health actually focused on social support [Smith & Christakis, 2008]), these concepts are interrelated, but indeed unique. Social support studies typically assess the quality or quantity of an individual's social ties, whereas social network studies treat those ties themselves as objects of study that may influence outcomes (Dykstra, 2007). By characterizing the web of social relations around an individual, social network studies focus explicitly on the specific network links and associated outcomes (Smith & Christakis, 2008).

Additionally, any definition of social networks needs to be grounded in both micro-structural and macro-structural perspectives. Such perspectives provide the conceptual opportunity to examine and understand a group's, in this case older minority elders, micro-structural cultural norms and beliefs that shape their social networks and the pathways of social support that impact health and well-being. A macro-structural perspective provides the opportunity to understand and examine how a group's social network is shaped by social location or position in society (e.g., minority group), and where members of the group fit within the larger societal social structure by such factors as age, gender, and socio-economic status (Angel, Angel, & Henderson, 1997; Dykstra, 2007). For example, although Angel and colleagues (1997) emphasize the importance of contextualizing social support in relation to gender, race, culture, and ethnicity, their views are very applicable to the larger discussion on social networks. They note, "From the perspective of social support, then, one's individual demographic history is important because it influences the amount and sources of social support available in later life, at the same time that it influences one's economic status" (p. 93).

SOCIAL NETWORKS AND MINORITY ELDERS

Central to social network analysis research with minority elders is the goal of understanding how cultural norms and values, as well as structural barriers within a society, help shape the ties that exist within this population. These factors are important elements in the overall understanding of health disparities, and in understanding how to effectively address them among older minority adults in American society.

Culture

Consideration for the critical role of culture in the development, composition, and maintenance of social networks among minority elders is essential. The social networks of minority elders are uniquely shaped by the cultural norms and values associated with the diverse racial and ethnic groups with which they identify. Social networks provide a *structure* by which the flow of resources (e.g., social support, access to material goods) to individuals is shaped. These resources may enable or constrain behaviors that affect one's health; thus, the flow of these resources via the social networking structure is a key determinant of health outcomes. It is important to note that the types of social networks and resources to which one has access are not only influenced by cultural factors, but also societal factors. These societal factors may come in the form of structural barriers, as discussed in the following section, or macro-level processes that directly impact cultural expression, social networks, and health. Nonetheless, culture is integral to the creation, composition, and function of social networks among minority elders. Generally, family members are an essential component of the social networks of older adults. However, in minority populations the ways in which family members participate in social networks may be culturally specific.

Although the Native American population consists of more than 500 federally recognized tribes, wherein each tribe has its own distinct identity, they all operate within a collectivist-centered way of life (Swisher & Pavel, 1994). This way of life is characterized by sharing, cooperation, noninterference, modesty, harmony with nature, time orientation toward living in the present, a preference for the explanation of natural phenomena according to spiritual beliefs, and a deep respect and reverence for elders (Garrett, 1999). For example, the cultural norms of living in the present, and avoiding negative thinking and speaking among Native Americans, help shape access to and utilization of services for elders. Carrese and Rhodes (1995) found that Navajo Indians did not accept advance directives because advance care planning would violate their cultural values of avoidance of negative thinking and speaking. The cultural norms of reverence and deep respect for elders observed among Native Americans also influence seeking support outside the family and limits "outsiders" as a part of their social network (Connell & Gibson, 1997). Additionally, other deeply rooted values, such as the importance of community contribution and sense of responsibility to the extended family, help to characterize social networks that structurally consist of other members of the tribe, and function to preserve cultural traditions, ancestry, beliefs, and medical practices. The care of elders, therefore, among Native Americans, is an expected obligation, duty, and rite of passage for middle-aged and younger generations who use and adhere to cultural values and beliefs in their caregiving.

Similarly, African Americans operate within a collectivist-centered way of life, where the family serves as the core of social networks for elderly family members. However, unlike other cultural groups, African Americans seek and receive help from friends and fictive kin who are often considered "family." Cultural values and beliefs about duty, respect, and sense of obligation in the care of the elderly among African American families have influenced the use of formal services in caring for dependent elders. Evidence shows, however, that family caregivers from minority groups, such as African Americans, tend to provide more care than their white counterparts, even after adjusting for health risk (Kirby & Lau, 2010). Culturally, among African Americans, this care reflects a high level of cultural reasons and meaning. Furthermore, this care provision can be justified through values and beliefs that center around duty, obligation, giving back to the culture, serving as an example to other members of the culture to influence its "legacy," and adhering to religious views that help shape the culture (Dilworth-Anderson et al., 2005; Dilworth-Anderson, Goodwin, & Williams, 2004).

The cultural norm of filial piety among Asian Americans, which is a concept that is associated with Confucianism, emphasizes that care of the elderly is part of the moral order of the society (Hashimoto & Ikels, 2005). Therefore, adult children and younger family members among Asians are expected to show respect for elders, have an obligation to their care, and are expected to be responsible for their general well-being (Hashimoto & Ikels, 2005). This cultural norm among Asian American families is an example of how norms can influence access to support, resources, and the availability of helpers that form the structure and function of the social network of elderly Asians. For example, the use of nursing home care in Asian cultures is viewed as a failure within the immediate family and among extended family members to meet an elder's needs based on filial piety. In this case, cultural norms may conflict with seeking outside support through institutions and agencies (e.g., nursing homes, hospice), thereby resulting in lower utilization of support outside the family unit, but at the same time reflect maintaining cultural expectations in the care the elderly.

There is also evidence in the literature of social networks, as influenced by culture, of having an effect on personal views about aging. In a study of Korean Americans, one of the fastest growing ethnic minority groups in the United States, Kim, Jang, and Chiriboga (2012) found that along with better physical health and higher levels of acculturation, larger social networks were significant contributors to more positive views about aging. The authors concluded that among older immigrant minority populations, promoting better physical health, acculturation, and greater social connectedness may positively impact attitudes toward aging (Kim et al., 2012). Here, the context of culture is critical in discussions of ways to improve and maintain improved attitudes about the aging process, as better attitudes toward aging can lead to better quality and quantity of life. Levy, Slade, Kunkel, and Kasl (2002) found that among persons aged 50 and older in the Ohio Longitudinal Study of Aging and Retirement, those with more positive self-perceptions of aging lived 7.5 years longer than those with less positive self-perceptions of aging. This effect was partially mediated by one's will to live (Levy et al., 2002). These findings provide strong evidence on the importance of self-perceptions about aging and its effects. Social environments may influence these perceptions and studies of social networks, with specialized emphasis on the role of culture, and are critical to the development of tailored approaches to delivering care to and improving care for minority elder populations.

Structural Barriers

Structural barriers within the American society, both historical and contextual, have an impact on and shape the social networks that are needed to survive within diverse groups. Structural barriers, including racial oppression and discrimination, have created socioeconomic inequities in education, health, housing, income, and occupation, resulting in barriers to accessing support and care outside of the family network (Bookman & Kimbrel, 2011). As previously discussed, some older minorities operate within collectivist cultural groups that emphasize intergenerational support, filial piety and duty, and obligation to others. They have spent a lifetime relying on family, friends, and their communities to provide many of the services and support that whites generally have had access to throughout their lifetime. Historically, this lack of access to formal support has been linked to racism and distrust in the health care system and its services (LaVeist, 2005). In particular, nursing homes have remained segregated by race and ethnicity, where marginal-quality care has been provided to minority elders (Feng, Fennell, Tyler, Clark, & Mor, 2011; Smith, Feng, Fennell, Zinn, & Mor, 2007). For example, among African Americans, structural barriers have resulted in reduced nursing home care use, as compared to their white counterparts, and higher levels of family care (Konetzka & Werner, 2009). Paradoxically, however, African American caregivers provide care to elderly family members who have higher medical needs and require greater assistance with activities of daily living (ADL) before being institutionalized (Connell & Gibson, 1997; Fennell, Feng, Clark, & Mor, 2010). Similarily, Hispanic elders have a greater rate of disability, and are more likey to need assistance with daily activities compared to whites (Angel & Whitfield, 2007); however, nursing home use among elderly Hispanics is low compared to many other groups. Further, nursing homes in communities with a high poverty rate and large proportions of Hispanic elders are more likely to be terminated from the Medicaid and Medicare programs and are at risk of closure (Fennell et al., 2010; Smith et al., 2007).

The above discussion on the role of culture and structural barriers in influencing the social networks of minority elders conceptually relates to what Dilworth-Anderson, Pierre, and Hilliard (2012) described as the "conundrum of health disparities." Dilworth-Anderson et al. (2012) originally described the interaction of health disparities, justice, and cultural interpretation of disease (i.e., Alzheimer's disease) as the "conundrum of health disparities"—the intricate and difficult problem of distinguishing between disparity in diagnosis and treatment based on need, and the role that cultural perception and normalization of disease play in racial and ethnic minorities being less likely than white families to receive and utilize services. The authors suggest that this conundrum takes into account the relationship between disparities, cultural beliefs and perceptions, and a lack of social justice in diagnosis, access to care, and screening of health problems among minority older groups. The roots of health disparities are multifactorial. Multiple factors work both independently and collectively to create the existing gaps in health status that currently plague the nation. Therefore, in discussions on the social networks of minority elders, it is important to understand that cultural values and beliefs, and structural barriers, independently influence social networks. Equally, it is important to seek to understand how these two factors intersect in this process.

CONCEPTUALIZING THE USE OF QUALITATIVE RESEARCH IN SOCIAL NETWORK ANALYSIS WITH MINORITY ELDERS

Several theories offer conceptual guidance for understanding the structure and function of social networks among minority elders, such as the sociocultural perspective, constructivism, and a life course approach. The sociocultural perspective suggests that human beings are not limited to their biological inheritance, as other species are, but are born into an environment that is shaped by the activities of previous generations and that higher order functions develop from social interaction (Dilworth-Anderson, 1997). This perspective also notes that meaningful experiences are interpreted within the human sphere of one's own culture and that individuals cannot be understood apart from their embeddedness in social and symbolic systems in their culture (Vygotsky, 1986). Thus, a sociocultural perspective allows for contextualizing how and why social networks form, which provides information on both the structure and function of social networks for minority elderly. These contextual factors may include, but are not limited to, history, place or geography, immigrant status, socioeconomic status, cultural beliefs, and values. Similarly, a constructivist approach suggests that the human experience emphasizes meaningful action by developing the self in complex and unfolding relationships, which take place within a cultural and social context (Kukla, 2000). It also places emphasis on how groups, minority elders in this instance, culturally create social order in their day-to-day experiences and interactions by giving culturally acceptable meanings to them. Therefore, meanings given to the social networks of elders must fit within their cultural frame of values, beliefs, and customs (i.e., nursing home vs. family care).

The conceptual guidance from the life course perspective can also inform understanding the structure and function of social networks among minority elders. The life course perspective also emphasizes the transactional influence between economic, political, social, and cultural developments and individuals' reactions to them.

It looks at the distinctive series of roles and experiences through which the individual passes from birth to death and provides direction for understanding the impact of various changes on these roles and experiences (Bengtson & Allen, 1993). Other aspects of this perspective that emphasize both context and time are important in the discussion of social networks and older minorities. Societal laws and policies within the United States, which upheld and enforced racial segregation as the current cohort of elders developed, influenced their life course choices and primarily restricted them from having access to basic needs, such as adequate education and health care. The family and the community became the core of most social support and the central core of their social networks. It is here that one could argue that the seed for the "conundrum of health disparities" was developed and fostered; thus, the intersection of cultural values (e.g., cultural obligation to take care of and be available to members of your cultural group) and societal structural barriers that prohibited access to care, services, and support. This type of information should be used in developing better and more inclusive conceptual models to address understanding the structure and function of social networks among minority elders and health disparities across the life cycle.

APPLICATION OF QUALITATIVE APPROACHES TO THE STUDY OF SOCIAL NETWORKS AMONG MINORITY ELDERS

Several qualitative approaches may be applied in the context of social network analysis among older minorities. Social network analysis has been traditionally associated with quantitative methods due to its obvious links with sociometrics and statistical measures; quantitative research obtained through questionnaires or other means provide data relating to the connectedness of individuals (Bloor & Wood, 2006). However, qualitative researchers may use data derived from a variety of qualitative methods (e.g., interviews, observations) to intensively analyze the subjective meanings that the individuals under study attach to their social relations and the variety of purposes implied in their social networks (Bloor & Wood, 2006). Therefore, qualitative approaches to social network analysis may help to uncover meanings and mechanisms attached to key social ties that contribute to the overall health and well-being of older minorities. The application of qualitative approaches in social network analysis is discussed next.

Ethnography

Ethnography is defined as the study of social interactions, behaviors, and perceptions that occur within groups, teams, organizations, and communities (Reeves, Kuper, & Hodges, 2008). The primary goal of ethnographic research is to provide rich, holistic insights into people's views and actions, as well as the nature of the location they inhabit, through the collection of detailed observations and interviews (Reeves et al., 2008). Several key characteristics of ethnographic research include (Hammersley & Atkinson, 1995; Reeves et al., 2008):

1. A strong emphasis on exploring the nature of a specific social phenomenon, rather than setting out to test hypotheses about it;
2. A tendency to work primarily with "unstructured data" (i.e., data that have not been coded at the point of data collection as a closed set of analytical categories);
3. Investigation of a small number of cases (or even one case) in detail;
4. Analysis of data that involves explicit interpretation of the meanings and functions of human actions (the research product is usually in the form of verbal descriptions and explanations).

The integration of ethnographic study in social network analysis, which explicitly seeks to understand the complex patterns of social ties, may help to explain why such ties exist. The context in which older minorities live is heavily dependent on culture, values, and beliefs, all of which work in unison to shape social connections and dependencies. Ethnographic methods, which focus attention on beliefs, values, rituals, customs, and behaviors of individuals interacting within socioeconomic, religious, political, and geographic environments, can inform understanding how the "conundrum of health disparities" pertains to social networks of older adults. In particular, ethnographic study of social networks within the caregiving realm may help to identify whether and how older minorities can access larger societal support. In that, participant observations and interviews are the typical modes of data collection in ethnography, and advanced interaction with participants through these methods would allow social network researchers to become fully immersed in the environments in which the social connections under study operate. For example, rather than simply asking a participant to complete a questionnaire purposed to gather specific information on their social connections to others, a researcher might instead observe that participant in their home for a period of time before administering the questionnaire to assess who comes in contact with the participant, their roles and responsibilities, cultural nuances of those relationships, and how their interactions impact the participant's understanding, health, and/or access to health care. Furthermore, such an approach would enable a researcher to examine perceived versus actual meanings of social interactions. This approach would generate a richer understanding of any key differences in the social networks of older minorities, given the influential contexts in which they live.

Grounded Theory

Grounded theory, which was first introduced by Glaser and Strauss (1967; Strauss, 1987), can also be used to study the social networks of older minority elders. Grounded theory takes an emic understanding of the world, whereby categories of information drawn from respondents themselves help make implicit belief systems explicit. It involves using an inductive process to collect, analyze, and interpret information gathered from cases (Glaser & Strauss, 1967; Strauss & Corbin, 1998). The use of grounded theory is most appropriate when the study of social interactions or experiences aims to explain a process, not to test or verify an existing theory (Lingard, Albert, & Levinson, 2008). Rather, theory emerges upon careful examination and analysis of collected qualitative data. Using the grounded theory approach to understand the "conundrum of health disparities" will also help identify traditional themes and concepts that emerge and new or different ones that are culture-specific versus those that are central to societal barriers regarding providing a viable social network that helps provide support in the care of minority elders.

Some key features of the grounded theory approach include its iterative study design, purposive sampling, and system of analysis (Lingard et al., 2008). Each of these features render grounded theory as an acceptable and useful approach to understanding the social networks of minority elders. An iterative study design means that data are collected and analyzed, and these findings then inform the next cycle of data collection (Lingard et al., 2008). For example, a researcher might conduct open-ended interviews (i.e., no choice responses are provided) with older minorities and ask them about their various social connections, allowing the participants to provide as much detail as they would like about the existence and dynamics of each identified relationship. Preliminary analysis of these interviews might suggest a common theme such as "extended family" within social networks. A next iteration from this initial work would be to delve deeper into the meaning of "extended family" and their roles within the social networks of minority elders, as defined by culture, through additional qualitative data collection. These efforts would ideally contribute to the development of theory regarding expansive social network relationships. Purposive sampling, as opposed to random sampling, allows social network researchers to recruit minority elders specifically as a means of addressing the proposed research questions. Lack of and underrepresentation of minorities is a common problem in clinical studies (Moreno-John et al., 2004). As such, qualitative research allows researchers to directly address this problem and enhance research by targeting marginalized groups. Having a system or process of analysis enables researchers interested in the social networks of minority elders to engage in comparative analysis and make connections in the wealth of data collected that would otherwise be lost without such broad examinations.

Some common methods of data collection in grounded theory research include focus groups and interviews. Focus groups are a form of group interview that capitalizes on communication between participants to generate rich data (Kitzinger, 1995). Generally, such interviews are viewed as a useful method for collecting data in a simple and convenient manner from multiple participants concurrently (Kitzinger, 1995). Focus groups rely heavily on interactions among participants. In the context of social network research, this method of gathering qualitative data would prove extremely useful for understanding this phenomenon within a specific culture. Focus groups can help to identify the types of network ties that are shared among minority elders and identify where key differences lie. In a safe, communal setting, focus group participants are encouraged to engage in an extensive dialogue in which they may ask questions of each other, share anecdotes, and build on the experiences of others in ways that contribute to advanced knowledge of the issue at hand. Focus groups are especially useful for exploring people's knowledge, understanding and experiences, as well as why they think or feel the way that they do (Kitzinger, 1995). In that, social network analysis recognizes that such networks are embedded within a larger social system, and focus groups may offer a mechanism for determining the effects of macro social factors on a group of persons who may have similar views and experiences. Undoubtedly, the lives and health of older minorities have been affected by historical shifts in societal views and actions. The shared, realized effects of these shifts may emerge during open conversations about the critical impacts of larger society on social ties and, subsequently, health.

Another form of qualitative research data collection is qualitative interviewing. There are three major forms of qualitative interviews: structured, semistructured, and in-depth (Britten, 1995). Structured interviews involve administering structured questionnaires, with interviewers trained to ask primarily fixed choice questions in a standardized fashion (Britten, 1995). Semistructured interviews consist of both open-ended questions surrounding an area to be explored as well as more structured questions (Britten, 1995). Semistructured interviews facilitate the exploration of ideas in both a broad and specific manner. In-depth interviews are typically less structured, and may only cover a couple of issues in extreme detail (Britten, 1995). Such interviews are typically directed by participant responses, as one response may lead the interviewer into a new and different line of inquiry. Conducting interviews is quite common in qualitative research. Qualitative interviews use a beneath-the-surface approach, exploring participant responses in detail to uncover new ideas that were not initially anticipated (Britten, 1995). As with ethnographic research, interviews are useful in the exploration of culturally driven perceptions of social networks. Depending on the level of detail desired, interviewing offers a direct method for engaging participants in discussions of their social interactions. The flexibility of qualitative interviews is a key strength that would render it a highly appropriate method for collecting data from minority elders. Minority elders may be more likely to harbor reservations for participating in research due to past societal wrongs, such as the Tuskegee Syphilis Study. A real and ever-present barrier to participation in research among African American, Latino, and American Indian older adults is mistrust of the scientific community and institutions (Moreno-John et al., 2004). Direct interviewing gives researchers an opportunity to establish a positive rapport with the participant and adapt the interview to that individual's level of comfort, with regard to setting or dialogue.

Using in-depth qualitative interviewing, Dilworth-Anderson and Gibson (2002) provided a much needed understanding in the literature on the cultural meanings caregivers use to interpret and perceive what is clinically described as "dementing" behaviors among older people with Alzheimer's disease and related dementias. Their findings show that cultural values and beliefs about illness and disease among different ethnic groups can shape the meanings they assign to dementia and, therefore, influence who gives care and why, as well as whether caregivers seek help outside the family system. Building from this research, Dilworth-Anderson and colleagues are conducting an ongoing study on the cultural context of dementia care. Preliminary findings from this ongoing qualitative study that includes in-depth interviews with 25 families (10 African American, 10 white, 5 American Indian; $N = 80$) entitled, "Perceiving and Giving Meaning to Dementia," show that family caregivers construct dementia in four different ways: contextually, situationally, culturally, and personally. The implications of this study are important in understanding how and when to intervene in the lives of minority elders and their caregivers using a culturally competent approach (Dilworth-Anderson et al., 2012).

Dilworth-Anderson and colleagues used both focus group data and semistructured qualitative interviews to develop a scale to assess cultural meanings and reasons for family caregiving to older African Americans. Both forms of qualitative data collection allowed the researchers to identify and discuss issues with African American adult children and spouses providing care to an older family member. The focus group meetings and subsequent semistructured qualitative interviews provided data on salient cultural, social, and historical information on African American family life regarding cultural justifications for caregiving to older family members. Using these data, Dilworth-Anderson and colleagues (2004) developed a 10-item culturally based justification for caregiving scale, "The Justification for Caregiving Scale (CJCS)," which is designed to assess caregivers' cultural reasons and expectations for providing care and increasingly being used in caregiving research (e.g., Romero-Moreno, Márquez-González, Losada, & López, 2011; Sayegh & Knight, 2011; Siegler et al., 2010).

Phenomenology

Phenomenology represents another qualitative approach that may be applied in examining social networks among minority elders. The goal of this approach is to identify phenomena through how they are perceived by the actors in a situation (Lester, 1999). More specifically, phenomenology often involves gathering "deep" information and perceptions through inductive qualitative methods such as interviews, discussions, and participant observation, and representing it from the perspective of the research participants (Lester, 1999). Phenomenology is based on a paradigm of personal knowledge and subjectivity, and emphasizes the importance of personal perspective and interpretation (Lester, 1999). This is yet another powerful approach to uncovering individual motivations and actions. As with other qualitative approaches, phenomenology is purposed to commence sans assumptions or preconceptions (Lester, 1999). Social network researchers may use this approach to examine subjective differences in the identification and usefulness of social connections. In the case of minority elders, instead of drawing blanket inferences regarding social networks for minority groups, researchers could instead apply this approach to uncover minority group-specific differences in social networks.

Community-Based Participatory Research

The use of the community-based participatory research (CBPR) approach, coupled with qualitative methods such as focus groups, is another methodological approach that informs conducting social network research, as well as creating and expanding theoretical thinking about culturally diverse older populations. This is a collaborative approach to research that equitably involves all partners in the research process and recognizes the unique strengths that each brings. Community members (in this instance, culturally diverse communities) can also contribute their expertise and share responsibility and ownership of the research project. The CBPR approach promotes co-learning, involves a cyclical and iterative process, disseminates findings to all partners, and involves a long-term commitment by all partners (Israel, Schulz, Parker & Becker, 1998). CBPR can help establish a framework of reference from which to think about and better understand the "conundrum of health disparities." Researchers using participatory methods have found community input invaluable in the design and adaptation of research instruments to make the tools user-friendly, applicable, and culturally appropriate (Andrews et al., 2007). Therefore, research questions need to be framed and developed in the context of other social constructs (i.e., age, gender, sexual orientation, disability, social class, language barriers, and religious and spiritual orientations) that require examining the multiple concerns of various cultural groups (Dilworth-Anderson & Boswell, 2006).

Dilworth-Anderson and her research team have employed a modified CBPR model to provide a dementia care intervention to a diverse group of caregivers in counties across North Carolina. The researchers collaborated with community members and state organizations and agencies to design and implement the intervention. Each community partner was involved in various degrees of intervention development, recruitment, and the training and certification of the dementia care trainers. The initial phase of the study resulted in the identification of gaps in knowledge about symptom recognition and dementia, access to care, and caregiver support. Further, while all caregivers involved in the intervention may have limited information, results from this CBPR study suggest that the need for a dementia care intervention may be greatest among minority populations, namely African American and American Indian caregivers. A dementia care training was then coconstructed with community partners on the areas in which knowledge gaps were identified (i.e., knowledge about symptom recognition and dementia, access to care for older people with dementia, and caregiver support). Through further collaborative efforts with study participants, both community partners and caregivers, the intervention team also developed and disseminated educational and informational resources that are being used by caregivers and their family members in the care of their older family members with Alzheimer's' disease and related dementias. These results underscore the need for dementia care training in low-income rural communities where caregivers have limited exposure to information and educational resources. Without the use of CBPR, Dilworth-Anderson and her colleagues would not have used the most culturally appropriate interventions to address the informational and educational needs of the participants in their study.

FUTURE DIRECTIONS

On the basis of the discussions in this chapter, a list of suggested future directions that have not been adequately addressed in the literature is provided:

- Additional research geared toward understanding the social networks of minority elders within cultural context and the broader macro-societal structures;
- Additional integration of qualitative methods in social network analysis research; and
- The development and use of more robust conceptual theories and models for understanding the multifactorial nature of social networks.

CONCLUSION

All of the previously discussed qualitative approaches grant social network researchers an opportunity to cushion their explicit studies of network ties in an understanding of why and how those ties are created and exist. Minority elders are a growing segment of the population, with growing needs. Social network researchers should have special consideration for the social networks of older minorities and the utilization of qualitative methods to advance our understanding of them.

Advancing this understanding can be significantly improved when methods and conceptualization are linked. Without inclusive conceptualization, as discussed in this chapter, we may fail to capture meanings and reasons that cultural groups use to structure and function within their social networks. As discussed, sociocultural and constructivist perspectives can help inform and guide research and understanding on the social networks of minority elders. The conceptual ideas of these perspectives emphasize the importance of environment, particularly the complexities of relationships and social interaction, on the beliefs, values, attitudes, and behaviors of individuals within cultural groups. Most importantly, these two perspectives help us understand how people exist and grow in living webs of relationships that define and give meaning to their experiences. Using such perspectives can provide conceptual guidance on the structure and functions of social networks among minority elderly. The life course perspective, as discussed in this chapter, can also expand the cultural understanding of social networks among minority elders by providing the lenses (long and short) on how societal factors, for example, coupled with the flow of historical time and context, shape social networks over the life cycle. From a life course perspective, the social networks of elders today speak to their networks in the earlier years of their lives.

Furthermore, studies are needed that address how structural barriers, cultural norms, and beliefs intersect. This new line of research should include social network analyses that incorporate qualitative methods to improve understanding of: (a) how different racial and ethnic groups define, describe, give meaning to, frame, and live by their cultural norms and beliefs; and (b) how these aspects of their cultures interact with larger societal views, practices, and access to care for providing support and resources in the care of minority elders. Mixed methods (i.e., joint qualitative and quantitative methods) may also prove to be a helpful approach.

Ultimately, understanding and researching the social networks of minority elders will require good theory and conceptualization, and the integration of qualitative methods, to better capture the reality of social networks among minority elders.

ACKNOWLEDGMENTS

The project described was supported by the National Center for Research Resources and the National Center for Advancing Translational Sciences, National Institutes of Health, through Grant Award Number TL1TR000085. The content is solely the responsibility of the authors and does not necessarily represent the official views of the NIH.

REFERENCES

Administration on Aging (AOA). *A profile of older Americans: 2011.* Retrieved October 11, 2012, from http://www.aoa.gov/aoaroot/aging_statistics/Profile/2011/docs/2011profile.pdf

Angel, J. L., & Whitfield, K. E. (Eds.). (2007). *The health of aging Hispanics: The Mexican-origin population.* New York, NY: Springer.

Angel, J. L., Angel, R., & Henderson, J. (1997). Contextualizing social support and health in old age: Reconsidering culture and gender. *International Journal of Sociology and Social Policy, 17*(9/10), 83–116.

Bengtson, V. L., & Allen, K. R. (1993). The life course perspective applied families over time. In P. G. Boss, W. J. Doherty, R. LaRossa, W. R. Schumm, & S. K. Steinmetz (Eds.), *Sourcebook of family theories and methods: A contextual approach* (pp. 469–504). New York, NY: Plenum.

Berkman, L. F., & Glass T. (2000). Social integration, social networks, social support, and health. In L. F. Berkman & I. Kawachi (Eds.), *Social epidemiology* (pp. 137–173). New York, NY: Oxford University Press.

Bloor, M., & Wood, F. (2006). *Social network analysis. Keywords in qualitative methods* (pp. 158–159). London: Sage. Retrieved October 11, 2012, from http://srmo.sagepub.com/view/keywords-in-qualitative-methods/n51.xml

Bookman, A., & Kimbrel, D. (2011). Families and elder care in the twenty-first century. *The Future of Children/Center for the Future of Children, the David and Lucile Packard Foundation, 21*(2), 117–140.

Boswell, G., Kahana, E., & Dilworth-Anderson, P. (2006). Spirituality and healthy lifestyle behaviors: Stress counter-balancing effects on the well-being of older adults. *Journal of Religion and Health, 45*(4), 587–602.

Britten, N. (1995). Qualitative interviews in medical research. *BMJ (Clinical Research ed.), 311*(6999), 251–253.

Carrese, J. A., & Rhodes, L. A. (1995). Western bioethics on the Navajo reservation. Benefit or harm? *JAMA: The Journal of the American Medical Association, 274*(10), 826–829.

Connell, C. M., & Gibson, G. D. (1997). Racial, ethnic, and cultural differences in dementia caregiving: review and analysis. *The Gerontologist, 37*(3), 355–364.

Dilworth-Anderson, P. (1997). Emotional well-being in adult and later life among African American: A cultural and socio-cultural perspective. In K. W. Schaie & M. P. Lawton (Eds.), *Annual review of gerontology and geriatrics* (Vol. 17, pp. 282–303). New York, NY: Springer.

Dilworth-Anderson, P., & Gibson, B. E. (2002). The cultural influence of values, norms, meanings, and perceptions in understanding dementia in ethnic minorities. *Alzheimer Disease and Associated Disorders, 16*(Supplement 2), S56–S63.

Dilworth-Anderson, P., Brummett, B. H., Goodwin, P., Williams, S. W., Williams, R. B., & Siegler, I. C. (2005). Effect of race on cultural justifications for caregiving. *The Journals of Gerontology. Series B, Psychological Sciences and Social Sciences, 60*(5), S257–S262.

Dilworth-Anderson, P., Goodwin, P. Y., & Williams, S. W. (2004). Can culture help explain the physical health effects of caregiving over time among African American caregivers? *The Journals of Gerontology. Series B, Psychological Sciences and Social Sciences, 59*(3), S138–S145.

Dilworth-Anderson, P., Pierre, G., & Hilliard, T. S. (2012). Social justice, health disparities, and culture in the care of the elderly. *The Journal of Law, Medicine & Ethics: A Journal of the American Society of Law, Medicine & Ethics, 40*(1), 26–32.

Dykstra, P. (2007). Aging and social support. In G. Ritzer (Ed.), *Blackwell encyclopedia of sociology online*. Retrieved October 24, 2012, from http://www.sociologyencyclopedia.com/subsciber/uid=834/tocnode

Feng, Z., Fennell, M. L., Tyler, D. A., Clark, M., & Mor, V. (2011). The care span: Growth of racial and ethnic minorities in US nursing homes driven by demographics and possible disparities in options. *Health Affairs (Millwood), 30*(7), 1358–1365.

Fennell, M. L., Feng, Z., Clark, M. A., & Mor, V. (2010). Elderly hispanics more likely to reside in poor-quality nursing homes. *Health Affairs (Project Hope), 29*(1), 65–73.

Garrett, M. T. (1999). Understanding the "medicine" of Native American traditional values: An integrative review. *Counseling and Values, 43*(2), 84–98.

Hammersley, M., & Atkinson, P. (1995). *Ethnography: principles in practice* (2nd ed.). London, UK: Routledge.

Hashimoto, A., & Ikels, C. (2005). Filial piety in changing Asian societies. In M. L. Johnson, V. Bengtson, P. Colman, & T. B. L. Kirkwood (Eds.), *The Cambridge handbook of age and ageing* (pp. 437–442). Cambridge, UK: Cambridge University Press.

HealthyPeople.gov. (2012). *Healthy people 2020. Older adults.* Retrieved on October 11, 2012, from http://www.healthypeople.gov/2020/topicsobjectives2020/overview.aspx?topicid=31

Kim, G., Jang, Y., & Chiriboga, D. A. (2012). Personal views about aging among Korean American older adults: the role of physical health, social network, and acculturation. *Journal of Cross-Cultural Gerontology, 27*(2), 139–148.

Kirby, J. B., & Lau, D. T. (2010). Community and individual race/ethnicity and home health care use among elderly persons in the United States. *Health Services Research, 45*(5 Pt 1), 1251–1267.

Kitzinger, J. (1995). Qualitative research. Introducing focus groups. *BMJ (Clinical Research Ed.), 311*(7000), 299–302.

Kukla, A. (2000). *Social constructivism and philosophy of science.* New York, NY: Routledge.

LaVeist, T. (2005). *Minority populations and health.* San Francisco, CA: Jossey-Bass.

Lester, S. (1999). *An introduction to phenomenological research.* Taunton, UK: Stan Lester Developments. Retrieved October 13, 2012, from www.sld.demon.co.uk/resmethy.pdf

Levy, B. R., Slade, M. D., Kunkel, S. R., & Kasl, S. V. (2002). Longevity increased by positive self-perceptions of aging. *Journal of Personality and Social Psychology, 83*(2), 261–270.

Lingard, L., Albert, M., & Levinson, W. (2008). Grounded theory, mixed methods, and action research. *BMJ (Clinical Research Ed.), 337,* a567.

Moreno-John, G., Gachie, A., Fleming, C. M., Nápoles-Springer, A., Mutran, E., Manson, S. M., et al. (2004). Ethnic minority older adults participating in clinical research: developing trust. *Journal of Aging and Health, 16*(5 Supplement), 93S–123S.

Reeves, S., Kuper, A., & Hodges, B. D. (2008). Qualitative research methodologies: Ethnography. *BMJ (Clinical Research Ed.), 337,* a1020.

Romero-Moreno, R., Márquez-González, M., Losada, A., & López, J. (2011). Motives for caring: Relationship to stress and coping dimensions. *International Psychogeriatrics/IPA, 23*(4), 573–582.

Sayegh, P., & Knight, B. G. (2011). The effects of familism and cultural justification on the mental and physical health of family caregivers. *The Journals of Gerontology. Series B, Psychological Sciences and Social Sciences, 66*(1), 3–14.

Scott, J. (1988). Trend report social network analysis. *Sociology, 22*(1), 109–127.

Siegler, I. C., Brummett, B. H., Williams, R. B., Haney, T. L., & Dilworth-Anderson, P. (2010). Caregiving, residence, race, and depressive symptoms. *Aging & Mental Health, 14*(7), 771–778.

Smith, D. B., Feng, Z., Fennell, M. L., Zinn, J. S., & Mor, V. (2007). Separate and unequal: racial segregation and disparities in quality across U.S. nursing homes. *Health Affairs (Project Hope), 26*(5), 1448–1458.

Smith, K. P. & Christakis, N. A. (2008). Social networks and health. *Annual Review Sociology, 34,* 405–429.

Stone, R., Cafferata, G. L., & Sangl, J. (1987). Caregivers of the frail elderly: A national profile. *The Gerontologist, 27*(5), 616–626.

Streeter, C. L., & Gillespie, D. F. (1993). Social network analysis. *Journal of Social Service Research, 16*(1–2), 201–222.

Umberson, D., & Montez, J. K. (2010). Social relationships and health: A flashpoint for health policy. *Journal of Health and Social Behavior, 51*(Supplement), S54–S66.

Vincent, G. K., & Velkoff, V. A. (2010). *The next four decades, the older population in the United States: 2010 to 2050* (Current Population Reports, P25–1138). Washington, DC: U.S. Census Bureau. Retrieved October 11, 2012 from http://www.census.gov/prod/2010pubs/p25–1138.pdf

Vygotsky, L. (1986). *Thought and language.* Cambridge, MA: The MIT Press.

CHAPTER 26

Informal Social Support Networks of African American, Latino, Asian American, and Native American Older Adults

Robert Joseph Taylor, Elise Hernandez, Emily J. Nicklett,
Harry Owen Taylor, and Linda M. Chatters

Informal social support networks are critical for individuals of all ages but especially for older adults who are dealing with difficult life circumstances. Research has shown that support is important both in daily life as well as in coping with issues such as poverty, serious health problems, depression, anxiety and other mental health issues, and the death of loved ones (Angel & Angel, 1997). The goal of this chapter is to provide a selective review of research on social support among older African American, Hispanic, Asian American, and Native American adults. Other chapters in this book focus on the influence of social support on mental and physical health, including the role of social support in the stress and coping process (see Lincoln, Chapter 3) and in caregiving (see Dilworth-Anderson and Hilliard, Chapter 25). This chapter focuses on social support as a dependent variable in relation to different sources and types of aid provided to older African American, Hispanic, Asian American, and Native American adults.

INFORMAL SUPPORT NETWORKS OF AFRICAN AMERICAN OLDER ADULTS

Older African Americans depend on informal social support networks of family and friends for assistance in emergency situations, as well as for help with various tasks of daily life. Older African Americans are involved in reciprocal support exchanges as both recipients (e.g., transportation and companionship) as well as providers (e.g., housing, child care, and financial assistance). This section highlights findings in three specific areas: (a) marriage and romantic relationships, (b) extended family and non-kin as sources of informal social support, and (c) black–white differences in informal social support.

Marital Relationships and the Decline in Marriage Among African Americans

The decline in marriage among black Americans documented during the last 40 to 50 years (Amato, 2010; Burton & Tucker, 2009; Cherlin, 2010; Goodwin, Mosher, & Chandra, 2010) has several important implications for family social support networks, social ties, living arrangements, and income adequacy. First, spouses are critical sources of informal support and provide a large share of caregiving responsibilities to the marital partner, as well as other family members. Also, marital dissolution can lead to a rapid decline in social ties (particularly difficult for men) and financial resources (particularly difficult for women). The loss of social support is a major reason why the dissolution of marriage and widowhood are such stressful life events.

Unfortunately, there is very little research on marriage and older adults. In fact, one of the major national surveys on marriage and married life (the National Survey of Family Growth) has a sample size of more than 12,500 respondents but only interviews persons between the ages of 15 and 44 (Goodwin et al., 2010). The implication being that marriage, cohabitation, and romantic relationships are only important for individuals who are younger than 45 years of age. The lack of research on marriage is particularly apparent for older African Americans. Accordingly, the following general conclusions concerning elderly blacks are drawn from a relatively small body of empirical research.

Black men as compared to black women have a higher likelihood of being married (Goodwin et al., 2010; Tucker & Taylor, 1989), especially among the elderly (Tucker, Taylor, & Mitchell-Kernan, 1993). Second, higher income is associated with marriage among men, indicating that the provider role among black husbands is a pivotal link to marriage (Tucker & Taylor, 1989; Tucker, Taylor, & Mitchell-Kernan, 1993). Despite the fact that unmarried elderly black women have very limited incomes, they indicate that one reason for their lack of romantic involvement is due to the fear that elderly black men are mainly after their economic resources (Tucker et al., 1993). Third, for elderly blacks who are married or who have a main romantic involvement, having a mate for financial security was more important for women, whereas for men, having a mate for a good love life (sex, companionship) was more important (Engram & Lockery, 1993). Fourth, the decline of marriage among blacks is not indicative of a reluctance to enter into intimate relationships. With the exception of elderly women, romantic involvement among unmarried blacks is quite high (Lincoln, Taylor, & Jackson, 2008; Tucker & Taylor, 1989). Additionally, many nonmarried romantic relationships can be quite lengthy. Lincoln et al. (2008) found that about one out of three nonmarital romantic relationships among African Americans and black Caribbeans lasted for at least five years.

Fifth, being female and older is associated with a decreased likelihood of romantic involvement among single African Americans (Tucker & Taylor, 1997). Such overall patterns of romantic involvement would be expected given that the black population has a shortage of males generally, and one's ability to compete for mates declines at the oldest ages. Sixth, widowhood is associated with a greater likelihood of romantic involvement among the young, but less involvement among persons who are middle age and older (Tucker & Taylor, 1997). Among both African Americans and black Caribbeans who were currently involved in a nonmarital romantic relationship, age was negatively associated with the expectations of marriage. This is consistent with the notion that older adults, who have considerable experience in relationships, are content with their current situation and do not want to have the legal and social obligations of marriage. Lastly, despite the possible structural impediments to relationship formation (e.g., unfavorable economic circumstances, sex ratio imbalance) and low rates of marriage, the majority of African Americans have a strong belief in the importance of marriage (Lincoln, et al., 2008; Tucker & Mitchell-Kernan, 1995).

Being unmarried in older age has implications for informal social support networks, living arrangements, and income adequacy. Unmarried older blacks tend to have smaller informal support networks, are more likely to live alone (which is a critical indicator of nursing home utilization), and have higher levels of poverty (see Tucker et al., 1993). Lower rates of marriage coupled with higher rates of marital disruption, increased longevity, and differential patterns of mortality of men and women ensure that the population of unmarried elderly black women will continue to grow (Worobey & Angel, 1990). Consequently, an increase in the percentage of single women among future cohorts of older blacks may signal corresponding decreases in the size of informal support networks, and increases in poverty, living alone, and nursing home utilization.

Family and Non-Kin Sources of Informal Social Support

Given the significant growth of research in this field, we provide a selective review of the literature on family and non-kin sources of support. Taken as a whole, this literature discusses supportive ties and networks within black families and communities that involve a diverse group of individuals (e.g., extended family, friends, church members). Several general conclusions can be drawn from this research.

Despite major demographic changes in family structure in the last 25 years, the informal social support networks of black Americans remain secure and viable. Taylor, Chatters, and Jackson's (1997) investigation of changes in support using the National Survey of Black Americans Panel data indicated that the majority of respondents received assistance from their support networks across all waves of the survey. Relatively small decreases in network involvement were found over time, but were offset by comparable increases in involvement with family, friends, and church members.

The composition of informal social support networks reflects a diverse group of individuals such as extended family members (Chatters, Taylor, & Neighbors, 1989; Lincoln, Taylor, & Chatters, 2003), best friends (Taylor & Chatters, 1986; Taylor et al., 1997), fictive kin (Chatters, Taylor, & Jayakody, 1994), and church members (Chatters, Taylor, Lincoln, & Schroepfer, 2002; Krause, 2002; Taylor & Chatters, 1988; Taylor, Lincoln, & Chatters, 2005). Older blacks were less likely to have a fictive kin and are generally less likely to have a best friend than their younger counterparts (Taylor, Chatters, & Jackson, 1997). This is probably due to the high rates of mortality among black Americans and the fact that best friends are not easy to replace. Church members are a critical source of informal assistance among black Americans and provide mainly socioemotional support (e.g., companionship, prayer) and cognitive aid (e.g., advice and encouragement), along with more modest amounts of instrumental aid (Taylor & Chatters, 1986, 1988; see Chapter 4, by Chatters et al., for more information on Church support networks).

Intergenerational family ties are of critical importance in the receipt of assistance from informal support networks. Although elderly black adults rely on a variety of kin and non-kin in their support networks, those with adult children possess a definite support advantage in comparison to their childless counterparts. Having an adult child and a pool of relatives who resided in close proximity facilitated the emotional and social integration of older blacks in family networks (Chatters, Taylor, & Jackson, 1985, 1986). Chatters and Taylor (1993) found that black adult children provide assistance to their parents on a fairly frequent basis and that the predictors of support to parents varied by gender.

Black adults with no surviving family members or who were estranged from their family relied on non-kin for assistance to a greater extent than others (Taylor, Hardison, & Chatters, 1996). Non-kin are particularly important for older black adults who are not married or who do not have adult children (Chatters et al., 1985, 1986). Although the majority of black adults received assistance from extended family, friends, or church members, a small minority were socially isolated and without a viable support network (Chatters et al., 2002; Taylor & Chatters, 1986).

Network variables were critical indicators of support from family members. Black adults who had more frequent contact with family members, resided in close proximity to their family, and whose families displayed high levels of affection, were more likely to receive assistance from their extended family. Network variables are important for support among single mothers (Jayakody, Chatters, & Taylor, 1993), elderly adults (Chatters et al., 1985, 1986; Lincoln et al., 2003), adults in general (Taylor et al., 1996), and both the receipt of support (Chatters et al., 2002) and provision of support to older parents by adult children (Chatters & Taylor, 1993). An analysis of family relationships among a national sample of three-generation black American families (Taylor, Chatters, & Jackson, 1993) found that the grandparent generation consistently reported the highest levels of familial closeness and satisfaction, followed by the parent generation, and lastly, the child generation.

Differences in the types of support received from family, generally, reflect the needs and challenges facing a specific subpopulation (Hatchett, Cochran, & Jackson, 1991; Jayakody et al., 1993; Taylor et al., 1993). Younger black adults indicate that advice/help with problem solving, encouragement, and child care were the most important types of assistance that they received. Older adults were more likely to indicate that goods and services (e.g., cooking, housekeeping, grocery shopping, small repairs), companionship, help during an illness, and transportation assistance were the most important types of help they received (Hatchett et al., 1991; Taylor et al., 1993).

When confronted with a serious problem (physical health, monetary problems, death of a loved one), older black adults are more likely to seek assistance from informal networks than formal service providers or to seek assistance from both informal and professional service providers (Woodward, Chatters, Taylor, Neighbors, & Jackson, 2010). Woodward et al. (2010) found that older African Americans were more likely than older non-Hispanic whites to *not* receive help from either informal or formal support networks. This difference, however, was ameliorated when controlling for experiences of discrimination. Woodward et al.'s (2008) study of formal and informal support among African Americans and black Caribbeans who had a lifetime mood, anxiety, or substance use disorder found that 41% used both professional services and informal support, 14% relied on professional services only, 23% used informal support only, and 22% did not seek help. Although there were no significant age or ethnicity differences (African American, black Caribbean), having more people in the informal helper network, being female, and having co-occurring mental and substance use disorders significantly increased the likelihood of using professional services and informal supports.

Black–White Differences in Informal Social Support Networks

Findings for black–white differences in social support from family are mixed (Sarkisian & Gertsel, 2004). One set of studies indicates that blacks are more likely than whites to give and receive assistance from their support networks (e.g., Benin & Keith, 1995; Hogan, Hao, & Parish, 1990), whereas another indicates that whites are more likely to give and receive support than blacks (e.g., Hogan, Eggebeen, & Clogg, 1993; Jayakody, 1998). Finally, a third set of studies found either no black–white differences in kin support networks or that race differences in levels of involvement in kin networks depended upon the measure used (Sarkisian & Gertsel, 2004; Silverstein & Waite, 1993). For instance, a recent study found that white middle-aged adults provided more support to grown children, whereas black middle-aged adults provided more support to elderly parents (Fingerman et al., 2011)

Discrepant findings for black–white differences in support networks are attributable to several factors (Sarkisian & Gertsel, 2004), including differences in: (a) the age of the populations studied (e.g., adolescent mothers, elderly adults), (b) the life circumstances of study populations (e.g., poverty, single mothers, diabetics), (c) whether support was examined in relation to crisis (e.g., emergencies, caregiving) versus noncrisis situations (e.g., advice), (d) the types of support examined (e.g., instrumental, emotional), (e) the specific kin groups studied (e.g., adult children, grandparents, other relatives), and (f) methodological issues including differences in the conceptualization and measurement of social support. Consequently, it is critical not to overgeneralize the results of one study.

Research on non-kin sources of support and social networks is extremely limited for black Americans of all ages. Research on black–white differences in friendship networks are mixed, but the preponderance of evidence seems to indicate that whites are more involved in friendship networks than are African Americans. Research on the composition of support networks indicates that in comparison to whites, African Americans have more kin than friends in their networks (Ajrouch, Antonucci, & Janevic, 2001; Keith, Kim, & Schafer, 2000) and rely more on kin-centered networks (Peek, Coward, & Peek, 2000). In the only major race comparative study of support from congregation members, Krause (2002) found that among elderly adults, blacks were more involved in activities with their church networks and significantly more likely than whites to give and receive assistance from church members.

INFORMAL SUPPORT NETWORKS OF LATINO OLDER ADULTS

Familismo, commonly defined as the central and prioritized role of the "family" in an individual family member's life (Lopez, 2006), is a tradition that motivates and guides social support and interpersonal interaction for Latino older adults. Familismo is a code of conduct that embodies an individual's commitment to the well-being of everyone in the family, which can be understood structurally, behaviorally, and attitudinally (Landale, Oropesa, & Bradatan, 2006). It is divided into three interrelated tenants: family cohesion with immediate, extended, and fictive kin family members, promotion of *respeto* (respect) within the family, and obligation to self-sacrifice for others. Within Latino families, *respeto* involves showing and maintaining respect for individuals in positions of authority (especially elders) and is a value commonly taught to young Latinos that they hold throughout their lives (Cauce & Domenech-Rodriguez, 2002; Steidel & Contreras, 2003). These values extend beyond the nuclear family to members of the extended family and close friends (Landale et al., 2006).

Latino culture embodies a strong emphasis on family and community. Although family cohesion is one of the most important features in Latino older adults' lives, cultural identification facilitates the social integration necessary to achieve this cohesion (Rivera et al., 2008). Culturally based expectations regarding social contact and informal support may explain why Latino older adults wish to remain physically close to family and friends.

Living Arrangements

Living arrangements are one avenue through which older Latinos maintain social connectedness. Older Latinos who live in close proximity to one another are more likely to have daily contact with social network members than those who live farther apart (Freidenberg & Hammer, 1998). Compared to white older adults, elderly Mexican Americans are more likely to live in the same household or in close proximity to their nuclear and extended families (Sarkisian, Gerena, & Gerstel, 2007). Language proficiency and age also play a role, irrespective of country of origin, as those Latino older adults who are less proficient in English and those who are older prefer to coreside (Zsembik, 1996).

Living with family members poses benefits and barriers alike. Some Latino older adults living in overcrowded homes desire more privacy but are willing to make sacrifices if it means they are closely connected to family (Becker, Beyene, Newsom, & Mayen, 2003). Similarly, many Latino older adults live with family because availability of tangible support is limited (Burr, Mutchler, & Gerst, 2011). Declining *familismo* among second- and third-generation Latinos has evidenced a gradual decrease in intergenerational coresidence (Landale et al., 2006), which may pose challenges and conflict for older Latinos' social integration in the future. Alternatively, this indication of acculturation may not induce familial conflict but may, in fact, improve family dynamics by encouraging culture-of-origin participation in other aspects of social support (Smokowski, Rose, & Bacallao, 2008).

Reasons for multigenerational living arrangements are often financial as well as sociocultural. For example, Mexican American older adults with limited wealth are less likely to own their own home (Burr et al., 2011). Similarly, many Latino older adults coreside with children and other family members because of the challenges associated with migration and resettlement (Van Hook & Glick, 2007); it also is not uncommon for adult children to live with elder parents because of life events (e.g., divorce, death of a loved one; Martinez, 2002). Furthermore, taking in adult children is more likely in older Latino households with higher incomes (Gonzales, 2007). This suggests that the cultural motivation for coresidence and values such as *familismo* are manifested within advantageous socioeconomic conditions.

Contextual Factors Influencing Informal Support

Beyond the home, Latino older adults live within broader social environments (enclave neighborhoods and communities) that provide many sources of social capital and social ties (Almeida, Kawachi, Molnar, & Subramanian, 2009). Latino elders who perceive their cultural enclave neighborhood as having a positive environment report greater perceived social support and less psychological distress (Brown et al., 2009). The positive relationship between neighborhood climate and perceived social support may be due to the tendency for Latinos and their immediate and extended families to live in close proximity to one another.

The economic and social resources with which older Latinos arrive to the United States influences their adaptation process and have implications for their health and well-being (Angel & Angel, 1992). In addition to assistance with self-care, Latino older adults receive social support from family members for emotional and financial needs. Nativity status is also influential for social support. Mexican American older adults who are born in the United States report lower levels of perceived social support than those born in Mexico (Almeida et al., 2009). Furthermore, generational status often determines what kind and how much social support Latinos receive. For example, first-generation Latinos rely on family and friends already established in the United States to help with migration and settlement processes, whereas second-generation Latinos rely on social network members to maintain and reinforce their cultural identity and sense of belonging (Viruell-Fuentes & Schulz, 2009).

Family and Non-Kin Sources of Informal Social Support

Nuclear and extended family networks of Latino older adults consist of a variety of individuals who provide social support (Gaugler, Kane, Kane, & Newcomer, 2005). Latino older adults have social networks that are composed of roughly half kin and half non-kin (Freidenberg & Hammer, 1998). This is not surprising given that well-established friends known as *comadres* and *compadres* represent fictive kin and are invested in the well-being of the family, oftentimes taking on supportive roles for older adults (Lopez, 1999; also see discussion of fictive kin among Puerto Rican families in Chatters et al., 1994). Cousins, in-laws, and godparents are almost always as important as other family members and are sometimes more frequently contacted for social support (Brown et al., 2009; Martinez, 2002).

Specific characteristics of Latino older adults and the contextual situation within which they seek and receive material, emotional, and informational support influences their expectations and perceptions of care from adult children (Kaniasty & Norris, 2000). Among elderly Latinos, those who have adult children and are recent arrivals to the United States have higher expectations of support. In contrast, language acquisition, education, and employment status are not associated with expectations for support (Kao & Travis, 2005).

The breadth of Latino social networks and differences in migration experiences and economic circumstances are contextual factors influencing who provides aid to Latino older adults. Interestingly, both Latino and African American older adults are more likely than non-Hispanic whites to receive multiple types of social support from extended family and fictive kin, as well as from nuclear family members (Chow, Auh, Scharlach, Lehning, & Goldstein, 2010). Mexican American older adults report more contact with and help from their adult children than do black Americans or whites, give more financial assistance than they receive, and are more likely than other groups to be involved in support exchanges with extended family members (Dietz, 1995).

Country of origin and generational status are both important in shaping social support within the broader Latino culture. Cuban Americans look to friends for emotional support, whereas Mexican Americans and Puerto Ricans seek family members (Angel & Angel, 1992). Latino older adults also emphasize the importance of connections to their extended families for a sense of well-being and having younger-generation family members (e.g., grandchildren, nieces, and nephews) as sources of emotional social support (Becker et al., 2003; Beyene, Becker, & Mayen, 2002). Like many other older adults, Latinos are both recipients and providers of social support who contribute to their families by participating in family functions, loaning money, and giving advice. Mexican American adult children report relying heavily on their parents for advice on financial, personal, and health problems (Markides, Boldt, & Ray, 1986). Similarly, Mexican American older adults give more financial assistance than they receive, and are involved with extended family to a greater extent than other groups. In contrast, older Cuban Americans express disappointment that younger generations do not ask for their advice on major decisions (Martinez, 2002). Social support also comes in the form of child care for both immediate and extended family members (Dietz, 1995) and in health care decision-making, where younger family members defer to older family members' wishes and wisdom (Calzada, Fernandez, & Cortes, 2010). Social support seems to contribute to intergenerational solidarity, although this connection is less apparent for grandparent and grandchildren generations (Markides et al., 1986) supporting the idea that *familismo* may decline among future generations of Latinos.

Finally, Latino older adults also provide assistance outside the home through activities such as church functions, babysitting, and volunteering in their broader cultural enclave communities (Wallace, 1992). Providing informal support to adult children and grandchildren can provide solace and sense of purpose in the face of declines in other social relationships (such as friendships). Furthermore, some Latinos who help with caring for grandchildren receive monetary compensation or gifts in kind and report a high sense of well-being and emotional reward (Martinez, 2002). However, given the significant psychological, physical, and time demands of childcare responsibilities, older adult immigrants can also feel more socially isolated (Treas & Mazumdar, 2002).

Limitations of Social Support

The realities of living in the United States place limitations on fulfillment of social support and caregiving expectations among Latino older adults. Immigrants are often faced with financial challenges that force families to relocate to places where work opportunities arise, often leaving aging parents behind in the process (Treas & Mazumdar, 2002). Although Cuban American older adults report a sense of disappointment regarding younger generations' lack of contact (Martinez, 2002), they also acknowledge the importance of letting their younger-generation family members live their own lives. Puerto Rican older adults indicate that the younger generation's unwillingness to provide care and lack of a sense of responsibility to them is attributable to changes in cultural beliefs (Delgado & Tennstedt, 1997). Others suggest (Padilla & Villalobos, 2007) that unfulfilled informal support expectations among Latinos may occur because maintaining traditional cultural values is not a realistic priority for family members in difficult health and financial circumstances.

Finally, some older Latinos are dissatisfied with the informal support they receive or reject outright assistance from their families. The concept of interdependency within Latino families creates a contradiction between *respeto* and *sacrifcio*, whereby younger generations may take advantage of their aging parents' and grandparents' vulnerable position. Some older adults resist this subordinate position by relying on their own resources or referencing the cultural value that supports elders' authority (Treas & Mazumdar, 2002). In sum, informal social support transactions within families are not always positive and simple, even when supported by cultural values and traditions. Instead, they require constant negotiation between interdependent participants, understanding of the changing cultural context, and appreciation of the costs and benefits of providing support.

SOCIAL SUPPORT AND INTERGENERATIONAL RELATIONSHIPS AMONG ASIAN ELDERS

Among many Asian families, family interconnectedness and cohesion are important cultural values and beliefs. Additionally, it is a cultural tradition and expectation to care for the elderly in the family. These expectations and values, often referred to as filial piety (Yee, Debaryshe, Yuen, Kim, & McCubbin, 2006; Kamo & Zhou, 1994; Nadan, 2007), are important for elderly Asians living in the United States, especially because many elderly Asians have emigrated from their former countries to live with their families in the United States (Mui, Nguyen, Kang, & Domanski, 2006; Nadan, 2007). The transition to the United States is often very stressful, involving hardships such as having less prestigious occupations and a lowered social status in comparison to their country of origin (Lee & Chan, 2009; Nadan, 2007). The impact of these hardships, however, may be mitigated with social support from families (Lee & Chan, 2009; Nadan, 2007; Tummala-Nara, 2001; Yee et al., 2006; Zhang & Ta, 2009). This brief section on social support and intergenerational relationships among Asian elders will discuss multigenerational families and households, address issues regarding filial piety, and provide examples from the research literature on social support and intergenerational relationships among Asian elders.

Living Arrangements

Asian Americans, and in particular, recent Asian immigrants to the United States, are more likely to live in intergenerational and multifamily households compared to their Caucasian American counterparts (Kamo & Zhou, 1994; Nadan, 2007; Yee et al., 2006). One reason for this phenomenon is the strong value of family interdependence, family interconnectedness, and filial piety seen in many Asian families. Both married and unmarried elderly Asians are more likely to live in extended family households, as opposed to living in a nuclear family or living alone (Kamo & Zhou, 1994). Filial piety and family responsibility among Asian families often vary depending on the level of acculturation and length of stay in the United States, which influences whether the adult children decide to let their parents (or even grandparents) live in their household (Kamo & Zhou, 1994).

Some elderly Asians move closer to their adult children as they age. Asian Indian elderly may move into the home of their adult children, or at least move to the same city/town, as their health declines (Nadan, 2007). One study found that 62% of elderly Asians decided to immigrate to the United States because they already had family members living in the United States (Mui et al., 2006).

Asian children living in multigenerational and multifamily households often have multiple parental figures (e.g., older siblings, aunts, uncles, older cousins, and grandparents) and are socialized at a young age to value family interdependence and family connectedness (Koh, Shao, & Wang, 2009; Yee et al, 2006).

Filial Piety and Familial Responsibility

Filial piety is a very common and important cultural value in many Asian countries, cultures, and families (Nadan, 2007; Yee et al., 2006; Zhang & Ta, 2009). Zhang and Ta (2009) note that "Asian Americans have strong familistic attitudes and behaviors, and are more likely to use kin for emotional or instrumental support compared to other ethnic groups." Within the filial piety virtue, adult children have a moral obligation to take care of their parents once they become aged and frail, and the oldest son should live with his parents until he gets married (Kamo & Zhou, 1994). Asian American families holding more traditional Asian cultural values often see it as their responsibility to take care of their aging family members (Yee et al., 2006). Asian Indian elders are often venerated by younger family members, children are expected to respect their elders and care for them when they reach old age (Nadan, 2007), and elders are asked for their blessings for important life events (i.e., weddings, birthdays, the birth of a child; Nadan, 2007). Yee and colleagues (2006) identify four common cultural values that are present among many Asian American and Pacific Islander families—collectivism, relational orientation, familism, and family obligation—that help promote family interdependence. In return for their care and support, Asian elders may provide support to children in the family, perform domestic tasks, and help younger family members complete mundane everyday tasks and household chores (Lee & Chan, 2009; Nadan, 2007).

Confucianism and Asian American Families

Park and Chesla (2007) note that "Confucianism is considered by many to be a form of religion, a branch of ethics, or a school of philosophy." Confucianism is important in many Asian American families and has had a profound influence on Asian societies (Park & Chesla, 2007; Yee et al., 2006). The family is viewed as the fundamental unit and base for society, and both the community and society are extensions of the family (Park & Chesla, 2007). Filial piety is an important virtue within Confucianism, which informs how Asian families should respect and care for relatives, and in particular the elderly (Kamo & Zhou, 1994; Park & Chesla, 2007). Many of the social support networks found among Asian elders and their families are based in Confucian cultural values and beliefs.

One of the five basic relationships in Confucianism is the relationship between parent and child. In regards to this relationship (and all familial relationships), the most important aspect is having respect for one's parents and grandparents (Park & Chesla, 2007). Children are expected to obey their parents and grandparents, while family elders are expected to offer their children guidance and discipline along with affection and love (Park & Chesla, 2007). One study found that elderly Chinese were happy to teach their younger relatives about Confucianism and other traditional Chinese cultural values (Park & Chesla, 2009).

Confucianism and other Asian cultural values retain their significance for elderly Asians who migrate to the United States (Lee & Chan, 2009). Lee and Chan (2009) found that the majority of elderly Chinese in their sample still maintained important Chinese cultural traditions; additionally, one third of the sample retained their Chinese values and faith systems as opposed to converting to Christianity (Lee & Chan, 2009). Participants also used traditional Chinese value systems to share religious affirmations with their family members, which in turn strengthened intergenerational familial relationships.

Social Support Among Elderly Asians

Elderly Asians often utilize kin and social support networks for a variety of reasons. Asian adult children are the most likely family relatives to provide support and assistance to their elderly parents (Han, Kim, Lee, Pistulka, & Kim, 2007). Han and colleagues (2007) found that Korean adult children were the primary support for urgent medical care, long-term medical care, financial needs, and emotional care. Among Chinese, Japanese, and Korean adult children, proximity to their elderly parents increases the amount of financial support that is provided (Ishii-Kuntz, 1997).

Comparisons across Asian subgroups indicate that Korean American elderly are more likely to be embedded in more social networks and are more likely to need more support than their Chinese and Japanese counterparts (Ishii-Kuntz, 1997). Furthermore, Korean elderly are more likely to receive help from other children besides the first-born child; Korean adult children are more likely to provide support to their elderly relatives as compared to Chinese and Japanese adult children (Ishii-Kuntz, 1997).

Tsai and Lopez (1997) found that Chinese elderly were most likely to rely on social support from their children and thought that social support from their family was adequate or good (Tsai & Lopez, 1997). Most of the elderly Chinese also relied on formal supports, including social security, recreational activities, housing assistance, and educational programs/ workshops (Tsai & Lopez, 1997). Interestingly, those who lived with their children were less likely to use social services, whereas elderly Chinese with lower incomes were more likely to utilize social services (Tsai & Lopez, 1997). Mui (1998) suggests that compared to their families, Chinese elderly may have higher expectations of family support because of differences in levels of acculturation to the United States.

Asian American family ties and supports may be an especially protective buffer against particular risk factors, including for Asian subgroups and families living in poverty, social isolation, discrimination, and traumatic experiences (Tummala-Nara, 2001; Yee et al., 2006; Zhang & Ta, 2009). Asian family members also provide their elderly relatives with transportation and translation/interpretation assistance in health care settings (Ruiz, 2007) and help with the planning and delivery of health services (Nadan, 2007).

AMERICAN INDIAN AND ALASKA NATIVE INFORMAL SOCIAL SUPPORT NETWORKS

Although American Indian and Alaska Natives (AI/ANs) comprise only about 1% of the overall U.S. population. Yet the growth rate for the AI/AN elderly population exceeds that of both white and African American elderly (Sandefur, Rindfuss, & Cohen, 1996; U.S. Census Bureau, 2004) and this trend is expected to increase dramatically over time (Garrett, Menke, Baldridge, & Inglis, 2002). Despite the small size of this population, AI/AN experience a disproportionate burden of chronic disease, with the highest rates of heart disease, diabetes, and arthritis among racial/ethnic groups in the United States (Gallant, Spitze, & Grove, 2010). Furthermore, AI/AN populations face a disproportionate risk of suffering from multiple chronic conditions and associated complications, as well as experiencing income inequalities and poverty that limits the availability of necessary formal resources and services. Given these circumstances, AI/AN elderly are in need of informal social supports and tangible assistance (Administration on Aging [AOA], 2001; Simmons & Lawler Dye, 2003). To fully understand the prevalence and correlates of social support among elderly AI/AN, it is critical to examine the cultural and historical contexts of AI/AN populations.

Historical Framework and Cultural Context

The AI/AN population comprises more than 564 federally recognized tribes (and over 200 Alaska Native Villages), each with unique organizations, languages, and historical experiences. Given this diversity, there is no monolithic "Native American culture" or identity (Indian Health Service, 2010). Despite the heterogeneity in tribal cultures and languages, there are several shared meanings that maintain Native culture. The concept of "seven generations" is a shared cultural view of reflecting on one's life and behavior within the context of preceding and subsequent generations (Kawamoto & Cheshire, 2004). These and other shared meanings have maintained Native culture despite attempts to disrupt cultural continuity and community cohesion (Rogers, 2001).

The U.S. government's policies and efforts at the internal colonization of AI/AN populations are an important historical framework for understanding how current-day elders interact with systems of formal and informal support. These government attempts included "pro-assimilation" policies in the latter half of the 19th century to promote a nuclear family structure, privatize lands, and the education of Native youth in boarding schools emphasizing white European American values (Glenn, 2010; Hoxie, 2001). These policies and programs aimed to disrupt traditional Native family organizations and the cultural emphasis on community and multigenerational interdependence (including childrearing and elder care). Although generally viewed as unsuccessful, these policies and programs resulted in migration of Native peoples to urban areas (approximately 60% of the AI/AN population live in urban areas), decentralization of Native communities, and a cultural shift to focusing on smaller family units (Duran & Duran, 1995; Scharlach et al., 2006). The lack of social support and cultural resources in urban areas are some of the lasting legacies from these colonialist policies.

Household and Family Living Arrangements

American Indian households tend to be multigenerational with many AI/AN elders (66%) residing with extended family members (Manson & Callaway, 1990). Households headed by an AI/AN elder tend to be larger than comparable African American or non-Hispanic white households. Overall, AI/AN and non-Hispanic white households are roughly similar in average household size (2.9 vs. 2.5 people, respectively). However, AI/AN households are more likely to be overcrowded and more than 15% of Indian households have four or more persons, compared with less than 4% for non-Hispanic white households (John & Baldridge, 1996).

Although geographic proximity is important in support exchanges, informal family support to elders is provided both within and across households. Among Prairie Band Potawatomi elderly, availability, proximity, and the actual number of available kin predicted the extent to which support was received. A female elder described the relationship between proximity and assistance: "My sons are pretty good about getting wood, and mowing, and would do more if they were closer" (John, 1991; p. 55). Family situations in which tangible supports are routinized and extended family members are in agreement regarding responsibilities tend to have the greatest success in informal support and caregiving situations (Hennessy & John, 1996).

Informal support situations in AI/AN populations have also been more successful when respite services are available (Hennessy & John, 1996). AI/AN elders tend to need formal services in addition to the informal assistance provided in the home. However, the lack of culturally appropriate programs, cultural concerns with institutionalizing the elderly, and distrust of government programs results in underutilization of such services when available (Manson, 1989; Scharlach et al., 2006). Finally, patterns of geographic mobility among AI/AN are particularly important for the elderly. For example, AI/AN who migrated to urban areas following World War II as young adults are now older and in need of tangible care and social support. In a study of 353 elders in Los Angeles, more than 80% stated that they did not plan to return to the reservation (Weibel-Orlando & Kramer, 1989). However, the present migration of AI/AN youth to urban centers from reservations and rural areas leaves behind elders who are without adequate social and tangible support. Moreover, because the likelihood of remaining in urban areas increases with age (Kramer, 1991), AI/AN elders will have continuing informal support and caregiving needs.

Roles of AI/AN Elders

American Indian culture emphasizes a community orientation exemplified by tribal structures that comprises extended families and their important role within tribal cultures. Extended families, as well as the interactions among constituent extended families, have an important influence on the nature of tribal culture and decisions within the tribe (Gallant et al., 2010; Smyer & Stenvig, 2007; Stubben, 2001). Red Horse, Lewis, Feit, and Decker observed that "American Indian family networks assume a structure which is radically different from other extended family units in Western society" (1978, p. 67). Historically, Native elders held prominent positions in institutions related to medicine and religion. For example, historical studies such as *Folk Medicine in the Mammoth Cave Area* (1876) describe the important role of elders in upholding these cultural traditions. These practices continue to be observed and elders occupy strong and central roles within American Indian families and communities as both cultural caretakers and support providers.

Native grandparents provide tangible support to younger generations and promote youth well-being. In particular, the cultural significance of the grandmother as tradition-keeper and teacher cannot be understated. Elders often provide direct care to grandchildren due to parental migration and distant employment, adult morbidity and mortality, substance abuse, child maltreatment, and the increase in female incarceration (Cross, Day, & Farrell, 2011; Fuller-Thomson & Minkler, 2005; Letiecq, Bailey, & Kurtz, 2008). The number of children in AI/AN communities being raised in "grandfamilies"—a type of structure where grandparents are the primary caregiver for their grandchildren—is increasing as indigenous communities face adversity (Cross et al., 2011). According to 2004 U.S. Census Bureau data, approximately 7% of the AI/AN population aged 30 and older were grandparents living in the same household with grandchildren under the age of 18. Among these grandparents, over half (58%) were responsible for the care of their grandchildren (U.S. Census Bureau, 2004).

Although caring for grandchildren demonstrates the strength of AI/AN familial and cultural bonds, it also indicates personal sacrifice and high financial, physical, and emotional burdens (Bahr, 2007; Letiecq et al., 2008). AI/AN grandparent caregivers in the 2000 Census experienced higher rates of poverty (32%), more physical limitations (34%), and crowded living conditions as compared to white grandparent caregivers (Fuller-Thomson & Minkler, 2005; Mutchler, Baker, & Lee, 2007). Furthermore, Native elders often share their limited resources (such as Social Security and housing support) with extended and immediate family members (Bahr, 2007; Letiecq et al., 2008). These forms of "downward assistance" are widespread, with many elders putting the needs of their family above their own (Gallant et al., 2010). This is a particular concern as approximately 20% of the AI/AN population aged 65 and older live below the poverty level, compared with 7% for non-Hispanic whites (U.S. Census Bureau, 2004).

Prevalence of Social Support

Within an AI/AN cultural framework, the provision of social support and health practices can be viewed as an extension of the family system (Hennessy & John, 1996; Red Horse, 1980). Among elders and their extended family, identification with tribal culture and traditions is predictive of social support. In particular, attendance and participation in indigenous events and involvement in traditional healing practices is positively associated with provision of support (Goins et al., 2011). Furthermore, because elders are revered in American Indian cultural traditions, honoring elders is symbolic of preserving American Indian culture. Qualitative research on social support among American Indian groups underscores this point, in which one family member remarked: "As you grow up you learn to respect your elders...they took care of you when you used to be younger, so you sort of have the obligation inside of you to where you should take care of them. And I think that follows for all Indians" (Hennessy & John. 1996, p. 279). These findings suggest that elders will be more likely to receive social and tangible support if they are integrated in a family system that maintains strong cultural traditions. Often, by providing support to elders, AI/AN families emphasize to youth the cultural value of age and provide the means for transmitting traditions and values from one generation to the next (Scharlach et al., 2006).

CHAPTER CONCLUSION AND DIRECTIONS FOR FUTURE RESEARCH

This chapter reviewed research on the informal social support networks of minority elderly. Despite growth in the quantity of work and improvements in the quality of research on minority elderly, the body of information is still limited when compared to what is available for elderly whites. Even a cursory review of *The Journals of Gerontology: Social Sciences*, *The Journal of Gerontology: Psychological Sciences*, and *The Gerontologist* demonstrates a paucity of work on minority elders. Although there are many significant gaps in the literature, a few areas of inquiry deserve special attention.

One area where research is clearly warranted concerns the impact of the death of family and non-kin network members on social support networks. Given the high rates of mortality among African Americans, Hispanic, and Native Americans, it is not unusual for many minority elders to have several members of family and non-kin networks die within a short period of time. A related topic deserving more study is widowhood. For instance, African American women become widows at much earlier ages and are less likely to remarry than their white counterparts (Taylor, Tucker, Chatters, & Jayakody, 1997). Currently, little work focuses on minority elders who are widowed and the resultant changes in their support networks after the death of a spouse.

Future research on minority elders may consider utilizing the impact of social capital on the receipt and provision of social support. Researchers have conceptualized social capital as resources embedded in social networks and measured it using the educational levels or occupational levels of the members of an individual's network (Song, 2011). This type of research may further assist our understanding of the strengths and limitations of the support networks of minority elders.

Although research on the informal support networks of minority elders has grown significantly, there are many issues that have yet to be explored. It is critical that new data sources become available that contain both significant numbers of minority elders and measures that are sensitive to the issues and concerns that confront these groups. Furthermore, it is important to remember that the primary goal of this research is to understand these social processes within the context of the broader social and economic circumstances facing minority elders. In order to fully realize the potential of these efforts, research should always be sensitive to issues of effective and culturally sensitive practice and social policy that improves the quality of life of minority elders.

REFERENCES

Administration on Aging (AOA). (2001). *A guidebook for providers of services to the older Americans and their families*. Washington, DC: Department of Health and Human Services Administration on Aging.

Ajrouch, K. J., Antonucci, T. C., & Janevic, M. R. (2001). Social networks among blacks and whites: The interaction between race and age. *The Journals of Gerontology. Series B, Psychological Sciences and Social Sciences, 56*(2), S112–S118.

Almeida, J., Molnar, B. E., Kawachi, I., & Subramanian, S. V. (2009). Ethnicity and nativity status as determinants of perceived social support: Testing the concept of familism. *Social Science & Medicine (1982), 68*(10), 1852–1858.

Amato, P. R. (2010). Research on divorce: Continuing trends and new developments. *Journal of Marriage and Family, 726*, 50–66.

Angel, J. L., & Angel, R. J. (1992). Age at migration, social connections, and well-being among elderly Hispanics. *Journal of Aging and Health, 4*(4), 480–499.

Angel, R. J., & Angel, J. L. (1997). *Who will care for us? Aging and long-term care in a multicultural America*. New York, NY: New York University Press.

Bahr, K. S. (2007). The strengths of Apache grandmothers: Observations on commitment, culture, and caretaking. In S. Ferguson (Ed.), *Shifting the center: Understanding contemporary families* (3rd ed., pp. 487–503). New York, NY: McGraw-Hill.

Becker, G., Beyene, Y., Newsom, E., & Mayen, N. (2003). Creating continuity through mutual assistance: intergenerational reciprocity in four ethnic groups. *The Journals of Gerontology. Series B, Psychological Sciences and Social Sciences, 58*(3), S151–S159.

Benin, M., & Keith, V. M. (1995). The social support of employed African American and Anglo mothers. *Journal of Family Issues, 16*(3), 275–297.

Beyene, Y., Becker, G., & Mayen, N. (2002). Perception of aging and sense of well-being among Latino elderly. *Journal of Cross-Cultural Gerontology, 17*(2), 155–172.

Brown, S. C., Mason, C. A., Spokane, A. R., Cruza-Guet, M. C., Lopez, B., & Szapocznik, J. (2009). The relationship of neighborhood climate to perceived social support and mental health in older Hispanic immigrants in Miami, Florida. *Journal of Aging and Health, 21*(3), 431–459.

Burr, J., Mutchler, J., & Gerst, K. (2011). Home ownership among Mexican-Americans in later life. *Research on Aging, 33*(4), 379–402.

Burton, L. M., & Tucker, M. B. (2009). Romantic unions in an era of uncertainty: A post-Moynihan perspective on African American women and marriage. *Annals of the American Academy of Political and Social Science, 621*, 132–149.

Calzada, E. J., Fernandez, Y., & Cortes, D. E. (2010). Incorporating the cultural value of respeto into a framework of Latino parenting. *Cultural Diversity & Ethnic Minority Psychology, 16*(1), 77–86.

Cauce, A. M., & Domenech-Rodriguez, M. (2002). Latino families: Myths and realities. In J. Contreras, K. Kerns, & A. Neal-Barnett (Eds.), *Latino children and families in the United States: Current research and future directions* (pp. 3–15). Westport, CT: Praeger.

Chatters, L. M., & Taylor, R. J. (1993). Intergenerational support: The provision of assistance to parents by adult children. In J. Jackson, L. Chatters, & R. J. Taylor (Eds.), *Aging in Black America* (pp. 69–83). Newbury Park, CA: Sage.

Chatters, L. M., Taylor, R. J., & Jackson, J. S. (1985). Size and composition of the informal helper networks of elderly Blacks. *Journal of Gerontology, 40*, 605–614.

Chatters, L. M., Taylor, R. J., & Jackson, J. S. (1986). Aged blacks' choices for an informal helper network. *Journal of Gerontology, 41*(1), 94–100.

Chatters, L. M., Taylor, R. J., & Jayakody, R. (1994). Fictive kinship relations in Black extended families. *Journal of Comparative Family Studies, 25*, 297–312.

Chatters, L. M., Taylor, R. J., & Neighbors, H. W. (1989). Size of informal helper network mobilized during a serious personal problem among Black Americans. *Journal of Marriage and Family, 51*, 667–676.

Chatters, L. M., Taylor, R. J., Lincoln, K. D., & Schroepfer, T. (2002). Patterns of informal social support from family and church members among African Americans. *Journal of Black Studies, 33*, 66–85.

Cherlin, A. (2010). Demographic Trends in the United States: A Review of Research in the 2000s. *Journal of Marriage and the Family, 72*(3), 403–419.

Chow, J. C., Auh, E. Y., Scharlach, A. E., Lehning, A. J., & Goldstein, C. S. (2010). Types and sources of support received by family caregivers of older adults from diverse racial and ethnic groups. *Journal of Ethnic & Cultural Diversity in Social Work: Innovation in Theory, Research & Practice, 19*(3), 175–194.

Cross, S., Day, A., & Farrell, P. (2011). American Indian and Alaska Native grandfamilies: The impact on child development. In P. Spicer, P. Farrell, M. Sarche, & H. Fitzgerald (Eds.), *American Indian and Alaska Native children and mental health: Development, context, prevention, and treatment* (pp. 43–62). Santa Barbara, CA: Praeger.

Delgado, M., & Tennstedt, S. (1997). Making the case for culturally appropriate community services: Puerto Rican elders and their caregivers. *Health & Social Work, 22*(4), 246–255.

Dietz, T. L. (1995). Patterns of intergenerational assistance within the Mexican-American family. *Journal of Family Issues, 16*, 344–356.

Duran, E., & Duran, B. (1995). *Native American postcolonial psychology.* Albany, NY: State University of New York Press.

Engram, E., & Lockery, S. A. (1993). Intimate partnerships. In J. Jackson, L. Chatters, & R. J. Taylor (Eds.), *Aging in Black America* (pp. 84–97). Newbury Park, CA: Sage.

Fingerman, K. L., Pitzer, L. M., Chan, W., Birditt, K., Franks, M. M., & Zarit, S. (2011). Who gets what and why? Help middle-aged adults provide to parents and grown children. *The Journals of Gerontology. Series B, Psychological Sciences and Social Sciences, 66*(1), 87–98.

Freidenberg, J., & Hammer, M. (1998). Social networks and health care: The case of elderly Latinos in East Harlem. *Urban Anthropology and Studies of Cultural Systems and World Economic Development, 27*(1), 49–85.

Fuller-Thomson, E., & Minkler, M. (2005). American Indian/Alaskan Native grandparents raising grandchildren: findings from the Census 2000 Supplementary Survey. *Social Work, 50*(2), 131–139.

Gallant, M. P., Spitze, G., & Grove, J. G. (2010). Chronic illness self-care and the family lives of older adults: a synthetic review across four ethnic groups. *Journal of Cross-Cultural Gerontology, 25*(1), 21–43.

Garrett, M., Menke, K., Baldridge, D., & Inglis, M. (2002). American Indians and Alaska natives in the 2000 U.S. Census Part 1. *NICOA's Monograph Series, 3*(3), 1–11.

Gaugler, J. E., Kane, R. L., Kane, R. A., & Newcomer, R. (2005). Unmet care needs and key outcomes in dementia. *Journal of the American Geriatrics Society, 53*(12), 2098–2105.

Glenn, E. (2010). *Forced to care: Coercion and caregiving in America.* Cambridge, MA: Harvard University Press.

Goins, R. T., Spencer, S. M., McGuire, L. C., Goldberg, J., Wen, Y., & Henderson, J. A. (2011). Adult caregiving among American Indians: the role of cultural factors. *The Gerontologist, 51*(3), 310–320.

Gonzales, A. M. (2007). Determinants of parent-child coresidence among older Mexican parents: The salience of cultural values. *Sociological Perspectives, 50*(4), 561–577.

Goodwin, P. Y., Mosher, W. D., & Chandra, A. (2010). Marriage and cohabitation in the United States: A statistical portrait based on cycle 6 (2002) of the National Survey of Family Growth. *Vital and Health Statistics. Series 23, Data From the National Survey of Family Growth*, (28), 1–45.

Han, H. R., Kim, M., Lee, H. B., Pistulka, G., & Kim, K. B. (2007). Correlates of depression in the Korean American elderly: focusing on personal resources of social support. *Journal of Cross-Cultural Gerontology, 22*(1), 115–127.

Hatchett, S. J., Cochran, D. L., & Jackson, J. S. (1991). Family life. In J. Jackson (Ed.), *Life in Black America* (pp. 46–83). Thousand Oaks, CA: Sage.

Hennessy, C. H., & John, R. (1996). American Indian family caregivers' perceptions of burden and needed support services. *Journal of Applied Gerontology, 15*, 275.

Hogan, D. P., Eggebeen, D. J., & Clogg, C. C. (1993). The structure of intergenerational exchanges in American families. *American Journal of Sociology, 98*(6), 1428–1458.

Hogan, D. P., Hao, L., & Parish, W. L. (1990). Race, kin networks, and assistance to mother-headed families. *Social Forces, 68*(3), 797–812.

Hoxie, F. E. (2001). *A final promise: The campaign to assimilate the Indians, 1880–1920.* Lincoln, NE: University of Nebraska Press.

Indian Health Service. (2010). *HIS fact sheet: Indian health service.* Retrieved from http://info.ihs.gov/Population.asp

Ishii-Kuntz, M. (1997). Intergenerational relationships among Chinese, Japanese, and Korean Americans. *Family Relations, 46*(1), 23–32.

Jayakody, R. (1998). Race differences in intergenerational financial assistance: The needs of children and the resources of parents. *Journal of Family Issues, 19*(5), 508–533.

Jayakody, R., Chatters, L. M., & Taylor, R. J. (1993). Family support to single and married African American mothers: The provision of financial, emotional, and child care assistance. *Journal of Marriage and the Family, 55*, 261–276.

John, R. (1991). Family support networks among elders in a Native American community: Contact with children and siblings among the Prairie Band Potawatomi. *Journal of Aging Studies, 5*(1), 45–59.

John, R., & Baldridge, D. (1996). *The National Indian Council on Aging report: Health and long-term care for Indian elders.* Washington, DC: National Indian Policy Center.

Kamo, Y., & Zhou, M. (1994). Living arrangements of elderly Chinese and Japanese in the United States. *Journal of Marriage and Family, 56*(3), 544–558.

Kaniasty, K., & Norris, F. H. (2000). Help-seeking comfort and receiving social support: the role of ethnicity and context of need. *American Journal of Community Psychology, 28*(4), 545–581.

Kao, H. F., & Travis, S. S. (2005). Effects of acculturation and social exchange on the expectations of filial piety among Hispanic/Latino parents of adult children. *Nursing & Health Sciences, 7*(4), 226–234.

Kawamoto, W. T., & Cheshire, T. C. (2004). A seven-generation approach to American Indian families. In M. Coleman & L. Ganong (Eds.), *Handbook of contemporary families* (pp. 385–393). Thousand Oaks, CA: Sage.

Keith, P. M., Kim, S., & Schafer, R. B. (2000). Informal ties of the unmarried in middle and later life: Who has them and who does not? *Sociological Spectrum, 20*(2), 221–238.

Koh, J. B. K., Shao, Y., & Wang, Q. (2009). Father, mother and me: Parental value orientations and child self-identity in Asian American immigrants. *Sex Roles, 60*, 600–610.

Kramer, B. J. (1991). Urban American Indian aging. *Journal of Cross-Cultural Gerontology, 6*, 205–217.

Krause, N. (2002). Exploring race differences in a comprehensive battery of church-based social support measures. *Review of Religious Research, 44*(2), 126–149.

Landale, N. S., Oropesa, R. S., & Bradatan, C. (2006). Hispanic families in the United States: Family structure and process in an era of family change. In M. Tienda & F. Mitchell (Eds.), *Hispanics and the future of America* (pp. 138–178). Washington, DC: National Academies Press.

Lee, E. K., & Chan, K. (2009). Religious/spiritual and other adaptive coping strategies among Chinese American older immigrants. *Journal of Gerontological Social Work, 52*(5), 517–533.

Letiecq, B. L., Bailey, S. J., & Kurtz, M. A. (2008). Depression among rural Native American and European American grandparents rearing their grandchildren. *Journal of Family Issues, 29*, 334–356.

Lincoln, K. D., Taylor, R. J., & Chatters, L. M. (2003). Correlates of emotional support and negative interaction among older Black Americans. *The Journals of Gerontology. Series B, Psychological Sciences and Social Sciences, 58*(4), S225–S233.

Lincoln, K. D., Taylor, R. J., & Jackson, J. S. (2008). Romantic relationships among unmarried African Americans and Caribbean Blacks: Findings from the National Survey of American Life. *Family Relations, 57*(2), 254–266.

Lopez, R. A. (1999). Las comadres as a social support system. *Affilia, 14*(1), 14–21.

Lopez, T. (2006). Familismo. In Y. Jackson (Ed.), *Encyclopedia of multicultural psychology* (p. 212). Thousand Oaks, CA: Sage.

Manson, S. M. (1989). Long-term care in American Indian communities: issues for planning and research. *The Gerontologist, 29*(1), 38–44.

Manson, S. M., & Callaway, D. G. (1990). Health and aging among American Indians. In *U.S. Department of Health and Human Services, minority aging.* Washington, DC: U.S. Public Health Service.

Markides, K. S., Boldt, J. S., & Ray, L. A. (1986). Sources of helping and intergenerational solidarity: A three-generations study of Mexican Americans. *Journal of Gerontology, 41*(4), 506–511.

Martinez, I. L. (2002). The elder in the Cuban American family: Making sense of the real and ideal. *Journal of Comparative Family Studies, 33*(3), 359–375.

Mui, A. C. (1998). Living alone and depression among older Chinese immigrants. *Journal of Gerontological Social Work, 30*(3/4), 147–166.

Mui, A. C., Nguyen, D. D., Kang, D., & Domanski, M. D. (2006). Demographic profiles of Asian immigrant elderly residing in metropolitan ethnic enclave communities. *Journal of Ethnic and Cultural Diversity in Social Work, 15*(1–2), 193–214.

Mutchler, J. E., Baker, L. A., & Lee, A. (2007). Grandparents responsible for grandchildren in Native-American families. *Social Science Quarterly, 88*(4), 990–1010.

Nadan, M. (2007). "Waves" of Asian Indian elderly immigrants: What can practitioners learn? *Journal of Cross Cultural Gerontology, 22,* 289–404.

Padilla, Y. C., & Villalobos, G. (2007). Cultural responses to health among Mexican American women and their families. *Family & Community Health, 30*(1 Supplement), S24–S33.

Park, M., & Chesla, C. (2007). Revisiting Confucianism as a conceptual framework for Asian family study. *Journal of Family Nursing, 13*(3), 293–311.

Peek, M. K., Coward, R. T., & Peek, C. W. (2000). Race, aging, and care: Can differences in family and household structure account for race variations in informal care? *Research on Aging, 22*(2), 117–142.

Red Horse, J. G. (1980). American Indian elders: Unifiers of Indian families. *Social Casework, 61,* 490–493.

Red Horse, J. G., Lewis, R., Feit, M., & Decker, J. (1978). Family behavior of urban American Indians. *Social Casework, 59,* 67–72.

Rivera, F. I., Guarnaccia, P. J., Mulvaney-Day, N., Lin, J. Y., Torres, M., & Alegria, M. (2008). Family cohesion and its relationship to psychological distress among Latino groups. *Hispanic Journal of Behavioral Sciences, 30*(3), 357–378.

Rogers, B. (2001). A path of healing and wellness for Native families. *American Behavioral Scientist, 44,* 1512–1514.

Ruiz, M. E. (2007). Familismo and filial piety among Latino and Asian elders: Reevaluating family and social support. *Hispanic Health Care International, 5*(2), 81–89.

Sandefur, G. D., Rindfuss, R. R., & Cohen, B. (1996). *Changing numbers, changing needs: American Indian demography and public health.* Washington, DC: National Academies Press.

Sarkisian, N., & Gerstel, N. (2004). Kin support among blacks and whites: Race and family organization. *American Sociological Review, 69,* 812–837.

Sarkisian, N., Gerena, M., & Gerstel, N. (2007). Extended family integration among Euro and Mexican Americans: Ethnicity, gender, and class. *Journal of Marriage and Family Relations, 69,* 40–54.

Scharlach, A. E., Kellam, R., Ong, N., Baskin, A., Goldstein, C., & Fox, P. J. (2006). Cultural attitudes and caregiver service use: lessons from focus groups with racially and ethnically diverse family caregivers. *Journal of Gerontological Social Work, 47*(1–2), 133–156.

Silverstein, M., & Waite, L. J. (1993). Are blacks more likely than whites to receive and provide social support in middle and old age? Yes, no, and maybe so. *Journal of Gerontology, 48*(4), S212–S222.

Simmons, T., & Lawler Dye, J. (2003). *Grandparents living with grandchildren: 2000-Census 2000 Brief* (Brief No. C2KBR-31). Washington, DC: U.S. Census Bureau.

Smokowski, P. R., Rose, R., & Bacallao, M. L. (2008). Acculturation and Latino family processes: How cultural involvement, biculturalism, and acculturation gaps influence family dynamics. *Family Relations, 57*(3), 295–308.

Smyer, T., & Stenvig, T. E. (2007). Health care for American Indian elders: An overview of cultural influences and policy issues. *Home Health Care Management & Practice, 20,* 27–33.

Song, L. (2011). Social capital and psychological distress. *Journal of Health and Social Behavior, 52*(4), 478–492.

Steidel, A. G. L., & Contreras, J. M. (2003). A new familism scale for use with Latino populations. *Hispanic Journal of Behavioral Sciences, 25*(3), 312–330.

Stubben, J. D. (2001). Working with and conducting research among American Indian families. *American Behavioral Scientist, 44*, 1466–1481.

Taylor, R. J., & Chatters, L. M. (1986). Patterns of informal support to elderly Black adults: Family, friends, and church members. *Social Work, 31*, 432–438.

Taylor, R. J., & Chatters, L. M. (1988). Church members as a source of informal social support. *Review of Religious Research, 30*, 193–203.

Taylor, R. J., Chatters, L. M., & Jackson, J. S. (1993). A profile of familial relations among three generation Black families. *Family Relations, 42*, 332–341.

Taylor, R. J., Chatters, L. M., & Jackson, J. S. (1997). Changes over time in support network involvement among Black Americans. In R. J. Taylor, J. Jackson, & L. Chatters (Eds.), *Family life in Black America* (pp. 293–316). Newbury Park, CA: Sage.

Taylor, R. J., Hardison, C. J., & Chatters, L. M. (1996). Non-kin as informal sources of social support to Black Americans. In H. Neighbors & J. Jackson (Eds.), *Mental health in Black America* (pp. 130–145). Newbury Park, CA: Sage.

Taylor, R. J., Lincoln, K. D., & Chatters, L. M. (2005). Supportive relationships with church members among African Americans. *Family Relations, 54*, 501–511.

Taylor, R. J., Tucker, M. B., Chatters, L. M., & Jayakody, R. (1997). Recent demographic trends in African American family structure. In R. J. Taylor, J. Jackson, & L. Chatters (Eds.), *Family life in Black America* (pp. 14–62). Thousand Oaks, CA: Sage.

Treas, J., & Mazumdar, S. (2002). Older people in America's immigrant families: Dilemmas of dependence, integration, and isolation. *Journal of Aging Studies, 16*, 243–258.

Tsai, D. T., & Lopez, R. A. (1997). The use of social supports by elderly Chinese immigrants. *Journal of Gerontological Social Work, 29*(1), 77–94.

Tucker, M. B., & Mitchell-Kernan, C. (1995). *The decline in marriage among African Americans: Causes, consequences, and policy implications.* New York, NY: Russell Sage Foundation.

Tucker, M. B., & Taylor, R. J. (1989). Demographic correlates of relationship status among Black Americans. *Journal of Marriage and the Family, 51*, 655–666.

Tucker, M. B., & Taylor, R. J. (1997). Gender, age and marital status as related to romantic involvement among African American singles. In R. J. Taylor, J. Jackson, & L. Chatters (Eds.), *Family life in Black America* (pp. 79–94). Thousand Oaks, CA: Sage.

Tucker, M. B., Taylor, R. J., & Mitchell-Kernan, C. (1993). Marriage and romantic involvement among aged African Americans. *Journal of Gerontology, 48*(3), S123–S132.

Tummala-Nara, P. (2001). Asian trauma survivors: Immigration, identity, loss, and recovery. *Journal of Applied Psychoanalytic Studies, 3*, 243–258.

U.S. Census Bureau (2004). *The American community-American Indians and Alaska natives.* Retrieved from http://www.census.gov/prod/2007pubs/acs-07.pdf

Van Hook, J., & Glick, J. E. (2007). Immigration and living arrangements: Moving beyond economic need versus acculturation. *Demography, 44*(2), 225–249.

Viruell-Fuentes, E. A., & Schulz, A. J. (2009). Toward a dynamic conceptualization of social ties and context: Implications for understanding immigrant and Latino health. *American journal of public health, 99*(12), 2167–2175.

Wallace, S. P. (1992). Community formation as an activity of daily living: The case of Nicaraguan immigrant elderly. *Journal of Aging Studies, 6*(4), 365–383.

Weibel-Orlando, J., & Kramer, B. J. (1989). *Urban American Indian elders outreach project.* Final report for the Administration of Aging, Grant #90 AMO273: County of Los Angeles, CA.

Woodward, A. T., Chatters, L. M., Taylor, R. J., Neighbors, H. W., & Jackson, J. S. (2010). Differences in professional and informal help seeking among older African Americans, Black Caribbeans and non-Hispanic Whites. *Journal of the Society for Social Work and Research, 1*(3), 124–139.

Woodward, A. T., Taylor, R. J., Bullard, K. M., Neighbors, H. W., Chatters, L. M., & Jackson, J. S. (2008). Use of professional and informal support by African Americans and Caribbean blacks with mental disorders. *Psychiatric Services (Washington, D.C.), 59*(11), 1292–1298.

Worobey, J. L., & Angel, R. J. (1990). Functional capacity and living arrangements of unmarried elderly persons. *Journal of Gerontology, 45*(3), S95–S101.

Yee, B. W. K., Debaryshe, B. D., Yuen, S., Kim, S. Y., & McCubbin, H. I. (2006). Asian American and Pacific Islander families: Resiliency and life-span socialization in a cultural context. In F. Leong, A. Inman, A. Ebreo, L. Yang, L. Kinoshita, & M. Fu (Eds.), *Handbook of Asian American psychology* (2nd ed., pp. 69–86). Thousand Oaks, CA: Sage.

Zhang, W., & Ta, V. M. (2009). Social connections, immigration-related factors, and self-rated physical and mental health among Asian Americans. *Social Science & Medicine (1982), 68*(12), 2104–2112.

Zsembik, B. A. (1996). Preference for coresidence among older Latinos. *Journal of Aging Studies, 10*(1), 69–81.

CHAPTER 27

The Ethnography of Ethnic Minority Families and Aging: Familism and Beyond

Marta B. Rodríguez-Galán

Scholarship on ethnic minority families and aging has wrestled implicitly or explicitly with the understanding of a theoretical dichotomy not uncommon in the field of sociology as a whole: the role that culture plays as either an epiphenomenon and/or as an integral element of the social structure. The literature has exposed a series of social and cultural factors that shape the experiences of aging and access to services for older minority elders. Is older African American and Hispanic families' lower use of nursing homes the result of a cultural preference or of institutional barriers? Are multigenerational living arrangements an expression of an ethnic identity or is this a survival strategy for minority families? These are some of the issues I will be discussing in this chapter. Interpretations of that basic structural versus cultural duality may derive from broader ideological perspectives, such as conservative and progressive leanings, but they may also reflect a superficial framing of the concept of culture in scholarly analyses of ethnic minority families. In his study of the Puerto Rican "underclass," *La Vida,* Oscar Lewis articulated the basic tenet of the culture of poverty hypothesis, often employed by conservative pundits: that poor ethnic communities develop a way of life and subculture that is at odds with the mainstream American values of competitive individualism and ultimately reproduces their disadvantageous socioeconomic position (Lewis, 1966). Absent from this perspective, however, are the structural barriers commonly faced by minority individuals and the role that ethnic culture has always played in helping minority and immigrant families adapt to the challenges of living on the margins of American society. When examining differences in the use of elder services by minority elders it is often stated that this is the result of a cultural preference among many ethnic groups for "taking care of their own," but many studies are also pointing to factors such as fear of discrimination and quality of formal services as influencing families' caregiving decisions.

Although the above-described debate exceeds the scope of this chapter, here I find it necessary to state three basic theoretical premises that will guide my review and analysis of the literature: (a) that the "culture" of ethnic minority families is constantly evolving and being redefined; (b) that this culture is both a phenomenon and epiphenomenon, that is, simultaneously shaping and being shaped by other structural forces; and (c) that ethnic minority cultures are transforming the cultural landscape and the experiences of growing old among North American families.

Zinn (1994) averred that the combined forces of increasing attention to race/ethnic issues in women's studies and developments in racial/ethnic studies could potentially transform social science perspectives on family life. Thus, both gender and ethnic/racial analyses can help us shed light on the experiences and coping strategies of aging minority families. According to Zinn (1994), this transformation in Western feminist thinking was grounded on a gender analysis of the institution of the family around three major themes: (a) "the family is socially constructed"—not just a biological arrangement, but shaped by social structure; (b) the institution of the family is closely intertwined with other societal structures and social institutions; and (c) structural conditions make family life difficult. As a result of these processes, in comparison to Anglo/white families, racial/ethnic minority families share common characteristics that can be attributed to social and economic conditions that created the so-called "alternative" family arrangements. These characteristics include extended kin structures, reliance on informal social support networks and family units extended across multiple households (Zinn, 1994), and, for African Americans and Latinos especially, resorting to various forms of "fictive" kinship. In this author's own words:

> As social and economic changes produce new family arrangements, some alternatives become more tolerable. Race plays an important role in the degree to which alternatives are deemed acceptable. When alternatives are associated with subordinate social categories, they are judged against "the traditional family" and found to be deviant. (Zinn, 1994, p. 24)

Other scholars have argued that minority families exhibit ingenuity in establishing family structures that respond to their social realities and, historically, they have often been at the vanguard of contemporary trends in families. For instance, during the nineteenth century African American couples were pioneers of the modern "dual-career" marriage. Indeed, African American activist women were afforded a great deal of respect and admiration from their communities and support from their husbands, whereas the feminist white women of this period struggled with the dilemma of having to choose between a career and a family (Franklin, 2010). Similarly, some scholars note that the tradition of "fictive kinship," more commonly seen in African American and Latino populations, is now a growing phenomenon among white families, and will likely constitute an important resource to aging individuals in the future (Allen, Blieszner, & Roberto, 2011).

In the following sections, I offer a review of ethnographic literature on minority families and aging that is grounded in both racial/ethnic and feminist perspectives. Because the field of aging is not only multidisciplinary but also conspicuous for its interdisciplinary research, I draw on studies that are closely aligned to the sociology of aging, such as anthropology, family studies, and nursing. Moreover, given the dearth of sociological literature in the ethnography of ethnic minority families, I will argue for the expansion of research in areas of sociological significance to this subfield. I have thematically organized the chapter around three major topics that emerged as most salient in recent ethnographic studies: (a) the concepts of familism, family obligations, and filial piety; (b) the role of living arrangements, urban/rural space, and the neighborhood context on family experiences; and (c) intergenerational relations, health, and caregiving. I also include a table to help illustrate the chronological evolution of scholarship during the past decade (see Table 27.1). This is arranged by author, discipline/department, sample used, ethnographic methods employed, and main findings. In this regard, in determining the disciplinary home of a study, I have used the principal author's discipline and/or department and the theoretical framework used in the study as criteria. Finally, the chapter concludes by examining the major research findings for each ethnic group (Asian/Pacific Islanders, Hispanic/Latinos, African Americans/black, and Native American), identifying gaps in sociological knowledge for each, and offering suggestions and directions for future research on the ethnography of ethnic minority families.

(text continues on page 442)

TABLE 27.1 Selected Ethnographic Studies on Ethnic Minority Families and Aging 2000–2013

STUDY	PURPOSE	DEPARTMENT/ DISCIPLINE	SAMPLE	METHOD	FINDINGS
Freidemberg (2000)	Explores socioeconomic and cultural factors related to experiences of growing old in El Barrio (Spanish Harlem).	Anthropology	Puerto Rican elders in NYC.	Life history narratives of selected key informants. Both qualitative and quantitative methods. Five years of data collection and fieldwork.	Older Puerto Ricans in El Barrio develop community networks that serve as support systems when facing adversity. Those with stronger social ties tend to have fewer medical problems. Religion also plays a significant role in the elders' lives.
Magilvy et al. (2000)	Examines the health experiences of rural Hispanic elders.	Nursing	Hispanic elders of Spanish, Mexican, and Native American origin in the Southern Colorado San Luis Valley. Purposive snowball sample.	Based on one longitudinal and three companion ethnographic studies of rural aging and health care. Open-ended interviews, minimally structured.	Three themes emerged: (a) "taking care of our own," or how Hispanic families meet obligations to elders; (b) spirituality as an important dimension in life and health; and (c) acceptance or prejudice: how cultural differences are understood. The study also describes observed patterns of utilization of various health care services by Hispanic elders and their families.
Klinenberg (2001)	Sociological and cultural factors associated with death rates among seniors during the Chicago Heat Wave of 1994.	Sociology	Urban seniors of various ethnicities (white, black, Hispanic) in Chicago.	Field work. Ethnographic interviews.	The degradation of public spaces, the culture of fear, and reduction in supportive state programs contributed to isolation among seniors. Older Latinos were more connected to extended family and community networks and, thus, less likely to die during the disaster.
Pierce (2001)	Explores African American family caregiver's expressions of coherence.	Nursing	Midwest, inner-city location. Low-income urban, African American family caregivers who take care of a stroke patient. Sample of 8 key and 16 general informants, the majority were women.	Ethnographic qualitative research design. Use of focused unstructured interviews and an open-ended questionnaire.	The author identified two patterns: (a) mutuality and (b) difference in filial functioning.

(Continued)

TABLE 27.1 Selected Ethnographic Studies on Ethnic Minority Families and Aging 2000–2013 *(Continued)*

STUDY	PURPOSE	DEPARTMENT/ DISCIPLINE	SAMPLE	METHOD	FINDINGS
Gerdner et al. (2002)	Describes the experiences of African American adults who provide in-home care for a family member who suffers from chronic confusion.	Nursing	Mississippi Alluvial Plain in Arkansas. Rural and small towns of the Arkansas "Delta." African American family caregivers (11 females and 4 males).	Ethnographic study over 14-month period. Participant observation in community settings, in-depth interview with caregivers.	Caregivers attributed their family member's confusion to: 1. Emotional stress. It was associated with having had a difficult life and working at very low paying, hard jobs. 2. Old age. They believed that this was a natural consequence of old age or a self-fulfilling prophecy. 3. Heredity. 4. Other. Such as an "spirit possession." Caregiving was experienced as an expression of love and devotion. It also required a personal sacrifice.
Martínez (2002)	Examines the differences between the ideal and the real Cuban American family intergenerational arrangements.	Anthropology	Cuban elders in Miami, FL.	Individual and focus group interviews were conducted in a senior center over a 14-month period. Snowball sample. Video and audio recordings and field notes were taken during and after each session.	In the interviews, the majority of respondents lived alone and preferred this type of living arrangement. However, in the focus groups Cuban elders were less likely to state their preference for living alone. There were a variety of strategies of living arrangements, such as living in a duplex or a two-family home or in an efficiency apartment next to other members of the family. Temporary arrangements were also common. Being childless and having limited availability of caregivers was a problem.
Treas and Mazumdar (2002)	An exploratory study about older people who migrate to the United States to be close to their children.	Sociology	Seniors from a variety of countries, mostly from Asia and Latin America. Most came to the United States later in life through the family reunification provisions of the U.S. immigration law, others came as refugees.	Twenty-eight intensive interviews conducted in 1998 and 1999. Interviewers were ethnically matched with elders and asked to recruit elders from their own ethnic networks.	Sending societies are often characterized as being more familistic. In spite of being integrated in family networks, many experienced loneliness, boredom and isolation. Several felt isolated because they lived in suburban neighborhoods with very few attractions in walking distance. Others lived in crime-infested neighborhoods and substandard housing conditions.

Becker (2003)	Explores the meanings of place among older immigrants in three ethnic groups.	Anthropology	Sample of three ethnic groups: Latinos, Filipino American, and Cambodian Americas living in an inner city.	Multiple interviews with 211 individuals 50+ years old. Participants were interviewed three times in a 1-year period.	The living conditions of these elders were very marginal, e.g., rooms without kitchens or bathrooms and overcrowded apartments. Many elders were also forced to move frequently. Economic need leads to sharing space, which may result in discontent. For some, overcrowding in family settings was preferable to living by oneself.
Johnson and Barer (2003)	Presents a contextualized portrait of the lives of aging African Americans in an urban area.	Anthropology	Draws on data from two prior research projects conducted in the San Francisco area: (a) 129 African American adults and (b) a longitudinal study of the oldest old, including 122 blacks over 85 years old.	1. Open-ended interviews. 2. Longitudinal methods, participants were interviewed several times to examine their life histories.	There were a range of experiences of aging among African American elders in the sample. Most had strong ties to family (both kin and fictive kin), friends, neighbors, and the "Church family." Many elders were childless, but they were still well integrated within their families and communities.
Weibel-Orlando (2003)	Examines the Lakota ceremony of "Hunka Lowanpi," or the making of relatives and the meanings of Lakota elderhood.	Anthropology	Data collected in 1989, case study of one Lakota-speaking elder.	Participant observation, use of video recordings.	There are two modes of aging recognized in the Lakota language: "elderlies" are seen as dependent, socially marginal, and fragile, whereas "elders" are seen as knowledgeable of the traditions, wise, active, and respected members of the community. The ceremony of "Hunka Lowanpi" publicly recognizes a special relationship between an elder and a child/children. During the ceremony these children receive their Indian names.
Burton, Winn, Stevenson, and Clark (2004)	Examines the use of the concept of "homeplace" in marriage and family therapy with African American clients.	Human development and family studies/multidisciplinary.	African Americans in urban and rural settings.	Draws on ethnographic and clinical research with African American families.	Participants defined "home place" as a physical space that evokes feelings of empowerment, ownership, rootedness, safety, and renewal. Key elements of home place include a sense of social and cultural identity. The author also explores experiences of "yearning" for a home place.

(Continued)

TABLE 27.1 Selected Ethnographic Studies on Ethnic Minority Families and Aging 2000–2013 *(Continued)*

STUDY	PURPOSE	DEPARTMENT/ DISCIPLINE	SAMPLE	METHOD	FINDINGS
Limpanichkul and Magilvy (2004)	Examines the caregiving experiences of Thai-speaking family caregivers providing in-home care.	Nursing	Thai-speaking adult caregivers, two men and five women ages 48–65.	Qualitative descriptive design and ethnography using a small sample of Thai-speaking adult caregivers. Data was collected using semi-structured interviews, observations, field notes, and memoranda.	Caregivers drew on Hinduism to interpret their caregiver role. Caregiving was willingly accepted as a burden and unavoidable duty. However, it was also based on love and attachment. There were negative and positive consequences of caregiving. Participants reported psychological and physical stress, suffering, difficulty sleeping, and less personal time. However, all participants found meaning through the experience.
Turner, Wallace, Anderson, and Bird (2004)	Examines the role of the caregiver, the family, and professionals in making decisions about the provision of care.	Family studies	African Americans from Northern, Southern, and Midwestern United States. Stratified purposeful sampling strategy.	In-depth ethnographic interviews and focus groups.	Caregivers believed that older persons deserve respect and that elders are the bulwark of the family. Various family members collaborated in providing different forms of care and support to elders "like a well-oiled machine."
Jett (2005)	Explores cultural and linguistic differences in how dementia is defined, explained, and experienced among African Americans.	Nursing	Recruited at three senior centers, key community leaders, a local clinic, and a church. Small town in East coast of Florida.	Ethnographic approach, participant observation, and guided conversations with 14 African Americans who had "lost their minds."	There were cultural and linguistic differences in how dementia was defined and experienced. Families are reluctant to use day care, and prefer to rely on the help from family and the spontaneous help of members of their immediate community. However, for those without close family or neighbors, spontaneous forms of care may be difficult to obtain before a crisis occurs.
Herbert et al. (2008)	Purpose was to find out what questions family members want to talk about with health care providers as they prepare for the death of a loved one.	Medicine/ gerontology	Thirty-three bereaved caregivers of terminally ill patients. Purposeful sampling strategy, oversampled African Americans. Palliative care consulting service and community-based hospice in Western Pennsylvania.	Ethnographic interviews and focus groups, held at the caregivers' location of preference.	Caregivers sometimes wrestle with questions of religious/spiritual nature. Obtaining answers for their questions may bring an enormous sense of relief.

Peters (2010)	The old head/young person dyad as a cultural African American tradition as an example of the making of "fictive kinship." Examines the socialization of young tap dancers by "old heads."	Sociology	African American tap dancers in an urban community.	Ethnographic field work from 1992–2001. Uses in-depth interviews. Case study.	The old head/younger dancer relationship fostered warm and caring friendships, and intergenerational loyalty. Older tap dancers were considered "artistic father figures."
Burton and Bromell (2010)	Explores how childhood illness, family comorbidity, and cumulative disadvantage affect social and behavioral environments for young mothers' physical and mental health as they age.	Sociology	Low-income families in Boston, Chicago, and San Antonio. Six-year longitudinal data from the Three-City Study ethnography, which studied the lives of 256 low-income Latino, African American, and white mothers and their children ($N = 685$).	Method of "structured discovery" for analyzing the data. Use of semi-structured interviews, and participant observation. In 92% of cases, ethnographers were ethnically matched with participants. Field notes were the main source of data for this article.	There was a high prevalence of physical and mental health problems among mothers and children. The mothers' current illness was associated with childhood health problems, and cumulative disadvantages related to their educational histories and unsteady low-wage employment. Mothers often neglected their own health while taking care of others in the family. Caregiving for ill dependents also interfered with keeping a job and providing for the family.
Rodríguez-Galán (2013)	Explores the meanings of the grandmother and great-grandmother role among Puerto Rican women in the United States from a life-course perspective.	Sociology	Puerto Rican grandmothers raising grandchildren in the Boston metro area.	Builds upon previous fieldwork experience. Semi-structured ethnographic interviews with 14 grandmothers and great-grandmothers.	Puerto Rican grandmothers have fluid definitions of their role, and often see themselves as both mothers and grandmothers. Although several women experienced role strain, for many it helps to combat loneliness, find meaning, and other forms of support. Public housing policies at times interfere with caregiving.

FAMILISM, FAMILY OBLIGATIONS, AND FILIAL PIETY

Sociologists and other social gerontologists have long speculated about the differences and similarities in family obligations and intergenerational family dynamics among white and ethnic minority populations (Gratton, 1987). Ethnic minority families are typically characterized as being more "familistic," that is, as placing greater value on family and having higher expectations of obligations toward elders. Generally, the term *familism* (or its Spanish equivalent "familismo") is associated with Hispanic/Latino populations to describe an idiosyncratic ethnic form of family orientation based on age hierarchy and respect for elders, which is assumed to be beneficial for aging individuals (Cortes, 1995; Montoro-Rodriguez & Koloski, 1998; Ruiz, 2007; Schwartz, 2007; Valle & Cook-Gait, 1998). However, the relationship between familism and well-being is still poorly understood (Losada et al., 2008). Moreover, some scholars are beginning to problematize the notion that familism itself is a desirable coping strategy for aging ethnic minority families. Empirical studies show that Hispanic women provide the bulk of caregiving for their aging relatives, thus resulting in higher emotional strain and higher levels of stress among these women (Falcón, Todorova, & Tucker, 2009), and quite likely in opportunity costs for Hispanic women more generally, as many sacrifice their own aspirations in exchange for providing informal and, typically, unpaid care and support for aging family members. Another question that is still relatively unexplored is whether or not the construct of familism is different across the various ethnic groups or generally more characteristic of Hispanics only. In this regard, Schwartz (2007) found that the factor structure of familismo, as captured by the Attitudinal Family Scale, did not significantly differ between Hispanics and non-Hispanics. However, it was also observed that *familismo* is still more common among Hispanics, followed by blacks, than among non-Hispanic whites (Schwartz, 2007).

Although recent ethnographic work largely corroborates some of these earlier findings, family scholars have described a broader social trend in North America toward moving beyond the nuclear modal family norm, in which contemporary families must adapt to new social and economic structural changes. Bengtson (2001) argues that family relationships in American society are increasingly more diverse in both structure and function. Moreover, multigenerational relationships will be more important in the 21st century due to several factors: (a) the demographic aging in the population resulting in "longer years of shared life"; (b) the growing importance of grandparents and other kin in performing key family functions; and (c) the endurance of intergenerational solidarity over time (Bengtson, 2001). Relationships across multiple generations within the family are also increasingly diverse because of changes in family structure, especially through divorce and stepfamily relationships; an increase in life expectancy of kin; and the diversity of forms of intergenerational relationships. In Bengtson's (2001) own words: "... for many Americans, multigenerational bonds are becoming more important than nuclear family ties for well-being and support over the course of their lives" (p. 14). Similarly, other scholars have noted a decline of the nuclear family structural model comprising two parents and their offspring or Standard North American Family (SNAF). As a result, extended family and fictive kin are increasingly playing more important roles for all aging individuals (Allen et al., 2011), not just ethnic minority families. Thus, many older persons now engage in some form of "kin reinterpretation," for example: substituting primary kin for fictive kin; upgrading a family role (a grandson is "like a son"); or defining a non-kin relationship as family, among others. On the basis of these findings, the authors conclude that, "the majority of middle-aged and older adults practiced at least one type of kin reinterpretation" (Allen et al., 2011, p. 1, 171).

Ethnic minority families are not a static social reality either (Martínez, 2002). The "traditional" extended family structure of ethnic minority families is simultaneously being transformed in the North American context by the confluence of these and other unique factors. However, among all ethnic minority groups (African American, Hispanic, Asian American, and Native American), the emphasis on respect for elders and family obligations represents a core belief that is often invoked in opposition to what is perceived to be the mainstream American culture with its more individualistic orientation.

Among rural Mexican Americans in the Southern Colorado San Luis Valley, the notion of "taking care of our own" remains a strongly held belief among Hispanic families (Magilvy,

Congdon, Martínez, Davis, & Averill, 2000). As Magilvy and colleagues observe, although Hispanics are a relatively young population as a whole, in many parts of rural America— especially the Southwest—a higher percentage of the adult population is Hispanic. Such is the case of the Southern Colorado San Luis Valley where Hispanics comprise more than 40% of the population; rich Spanish, Mexican, and Native American cultures exist, and Spanish is the preferred language for many older adults. In this study, close family maintained daily contact either by phone or visiting, and individuals expressed deep concern for family and a clear sense of family obligation. Moreover, older adults in these rural communities were treated with *respeto*[1] and valued for their wisdom (Magilvy et al., 2000).

In contrast to rural Hispanic populations in the Southwest, Cuban Americans in the Miami area have had to adapt to structural changes brought by immigration and acculturation to mainstream U.S. culture. In her ethnographic work, Martínez (2002) examined the differences between the ideal and the real among Cuban American families. Her study showed that, in contrast to the ideal traditional multigenerational living arrangements, many Cuban seniors are opting for independent living arrangements. This change is largely explained by lower fertility rates among Cubans and family separation due to migration—in comparison to other Hispanic groups—as well as new living arrangements. Having devoted most of their energies to providing opportunities for their children, many Cuban elders must adapt to the new reality of living alone. Other alternative living arrangements for Cubans included:

> Living in the same apartment building where other relatives live, renting a room from a sibling next door, efficiency apartments created out of old duplex homes, or owning a home on the same street as a brother, for example. Choices of living arrangements may be limited by economic resources and other resources such as the skills needed to manage instrumental daily tasks on one's own. (Martínez, 2002, p. 368)

However, family contact and a strong family orientation are still observed among Cuban families.

If notions of familismo pervade the literature on Hispanic families, the disorganization versus superorganization perspectives (Sarkisian & Gerstel, 2004) underlies much of the scholarship on African American families and aging. According to this binary, families are either portrayed monolithically as lacking a clear structure and being unable to meet the needs of individuals, or as heroically adaptable and functional. In their study of African American families in the San Francisco area, Johnson and Barer (2003) showed that neither of these views accurately reflected their ethnographic observations. Among African American elders in the San Francisco Bay area, although diversity in family experiences is evident, multifunctional extended families and community networks were most common and contributed to the elders' overall life satisfaction (Johnson & Barer, 2003). Indeed, these elders often showed pride in their role as progenitors' of the family, as implied in the following quote by one of the study's participants, "I am a six times great great grandmother" (Johnson & Barer, 2003, p. 112). As was the case for Hispanics, black elders relied on both close kin and extended and fictive kin for various forms of material and emotional support and sociability, and their relationships with relatives were meaningful and satisfactory (Johnson & Barer, 2003). Although elders in this San Francisco-area study resided in impoverished neighborhoods that were plagued by social problems—which may affect their own families—the majority lived purposeful and connected lives. Many in this sample were in fact childless, but still maintained close family relationships with nieces, nephews, neighbors, fictive kin, and other relatives. Moreover, they also enhanced their sociability, positive attitude, and meaning through their involvement in churches and with the Church "family."

As mentioned earlier, African Americans, Hispanics, and Native Americans are proportionally more likely than whites to count non-kin or "fictive kin" as family. In urban black communities, the old head/young person dyad is a common cultural practice that exemplifies the tradition of the "fictive" making of relatives, which can be traced back to the days of slavery. An old head is a black elder who plays a supportive family-like role in relation to a younger person, and contributes to the transmission of ethnic culture to younger generations. Peters (2010), a cultural sociologist, studied elder tap dancers' key role in passing the history, the steps, and the values associated with this art form. Between 1992 and 2001, Peters studied the socialization of younger tap dancers by old heads and showed this to be a mutually beneficial relationship: older dancers felt useful and needed and younger dancers reaped the rewards of having an "artistic father figure" to encourage and guide them. Peters observes that,

> Unlike many elders in our society, who are discarded as a result of old age, and wind up alone and bereft of community, mentoring and the opportunity to dance gave these older dancers a sense of being needed—compelling them to remain active and engaged for a lifetime. When they experienced medical problems, the social support network they had developed with the younger dancers helped them to cope with them. Overall, their high level of physical activity and emotional engagement contributed to their physical and emotional health, and helped them to age successfully. (Peters, 2010, p. 442)

Native American families also place high value on the indigenous cultural and social capital of elder members of the community. Among the Lakota nation, a linguistic and sociological distinction is drawn between "elderlies" and "elders." The former tend to be frail and relatively marginal; the latter are deemed in very high esteem for their service to community, self-esteem, sense of dignity, and sagacity. Elders speak the Lakota language, are knowledgeable of the powwow traditions, the traditional crafts, and try to pass on this cultural knowledge to the younger generation (Weibel-Orlando, 2003). A key ritual ceremony among the Lakota is the "hunka lowampi" or the making of relatives. During the ceremony a young boy or girl "hunka" (person, human, relative) is sponsored by an "ate" (sponsor, advisor, adoptive parent) and given his or her Indian name. A Shaman explained this special family bond as follows: "when one's heart is good towards another, let them be as one family" (Weibel-Orlando, 2003, p. 41). Thus, through this ceremony, a formerly unrelated adult and a child express in public a relationship that is stronger than family or friendship. Similarly, the roles of grandparent, foster grandparent, and cultural conservator are highly praised among Lakota and other Native American nations, and a sense of kinship often extends to the entire tribe, where elders receive their due appreciation (Weibel-Orlando, 2003). Not surprisingly, Jervis (2006), in her institutional ethnographic work in a tribal nursing home, found that even when marginal Native American elderly are confined to the institution and find themselves relatively isolated from the family, American Indian staff acted as family to the residents. The author explains that, at this tribal nursing home, the staff and residents were not related just metaphorically but also by language and culture, which helped them "relate" to the patients. Moreover, when the actual families of the residents were perceived to be uninterested in visiting the elders, the staff attributed noninvolvement to the detrimental influence of American mainstream culture, and accused these Indian relatives of "acting like whites" (Jervis, 2006).

The role of grandparent, especially grandmother, raising a grandchild represents another "especial" form of family relationship, which is proportionally more common in communities of color. In my own ethnographic work with Puerto Rican grandmothers who are raising grandchildren I have found that the definition of this role among Puerto Rican women is fluid and at times problematic, especially when grandmothers do not have legal custody. These women see themselves as both (social) mothers and grandmothers, and in fact, many state that they play multiple family roles in relation to their grandchildren. Often, low-income Puerto Rican women's life histories have shaped a social identity that is tied to "mothering," because they have raised or helped raise their own children, other relatives, and sometimes foster or non-kin children. Although they see themselves as mothers first, Puerto Rican grandmothers also believe that the grandchild must know who the biological mother is and pay her "respeto." In this way, these grandmothers attempt to reconcile their expanded grandmother role while adhering to the cultural ideals of "motherhood" within their Hispanic heritage (Rodríguez-Galán, 2013).

INTERGENERATIONAL FAMILY RELATIONSHIPS, HEALTH, AND CAREGIVING

For many family caregivers the decision to take care of one's own aging family member may be both a response to a culturally normative expectation as well as to perceived institutional barriers to formal care. In this context, the field of nursing has been relatively more prolific in presenting ethnographic testimonies of family caregiver's experiences. Discussions of *familism* among Asian American families usually revolve around the notion of "filial piety," a Confucian-based concept defined as the virtue of respect, obedience, and obligation to care for one's parents. Limpanichkul and Magilvy (2002), in a study of a small sample of Thai-adult caregivers, found that they drew on Hinduism, particularly the law of Karma and Bunkhun system, to interpret their caregiver role. Based on these beliefs, caregiving was willingly accepted as a burden and unavoidable duty. However, it was also accepted on the basis of love and attachment for the frail elder. Moreover, although there were several negative consequences of caregiving, such as reported psychological and physical stress, suffering, difficulty sleeping, and less personal time, all participants found meaning through the caregiving experience. Because of this, the authors conclude that among Thai family caregivers "Buddhism seemed to provide a means of coping with the stressful caregiving role" (Limpanichkul & Magilvy, 2002, p. 22).

Religion and spirituality also play a prominent role in the lives of aging African Americans, and are a common coping mechanism exercised by family caregivers (Gerder, Tripp-Reimer, & Simpson, 2002; Herbert, Schulz, Copeland, & Arnold, 2008). Gerder and colleagues (2002) conducted an ethnographic study over a 14-month period in the Arkansas Delta, a site noted for its role in slavery, and where 34% of the population today is of African American descent. These authors maintain that religion is a central protagonist in enabling family to cope. Caregivers typically receive emotional support from other family members—especially adult siblings—and the decision to become caregivers is an expression of love and devotion reflected in their personal sacrifice (Gerder et al., 2002). Caregivers in the Arkansas Delta believed that a history of arduous, low-paying jobs, racism, discrimination, and general life hardship had contributed to their family member's confusion; as one daughter put it: "People in the Delta were raised in fear" (Gerder et al., 2002, p. 361). Because of these negative experiences, distrust in biomedicine was prevalent, as was the family's reluctance to seek formal assistance in many cases. They feared that their loved ones would not be treated with respect in long-term care facilities or even that they could be physically or emotionally harmed. However, home health services were preferred, and several caregivers participated in a service that allowed the hiring of relatives and friends.

Jett (2005) found a similar disposition toward taking care of a family member with dementia among African Americans in a small town in the East Coast of Florida. Consider the following quote from one of the study's participants:

> We don't go outside for day care. That is not what we do. We support each other. It's just like a village. The concept of village. I see you can't do it, if you need something I am there for you, whether it is to baby sit or to watch your mom…and it's still functional, even though communities have changed. (Jett, 2005, p. 6)

In close-nit ethnic communities such as this, the neighborhood itself allows for spontaneous forms of support upon which family caregivers may rely (Jett, 2005).

The reluctance among ethnic minority families to seek formal care can also be interpreted as a personal/cultural barrier. In the San Luis Valley study of Hispanic caregivers, the key informants believed that the traditional orientation toward caring for one's own aging family members may at times interfere with obtaining adequate care. It was reported that Hispanic families wait too long to seek assistance with caregiving. Yet, in the participants' own view, caregiving was not perceived as a burden. In its recent past, however, a conflict began to emerge between traditional values and changing attitudes as difficult economic conditions forced the young to leave the community in search for jobs in the cities. But even in those cases, strong family connections were reportedly maintained (Magilvy et al., 2000).

Similarly, Radina (2007), in a qualitative study about the process of preparing for parent care-giving among Mexican American adult siblings in Missouri, found that caregiving by chil-dren is a normative expectation. The notions of "respeto" and "machismo" and "marianismo" were also likely to strongly influence the selection of a caregiver. Sometimes, the decision of who becomes the main caregiver was a factor of a natural extension of an existing role, an expressed personal choice, a parent's expressed wish, or a combination of these. More gener-ally, however, it was believed that all children should be involved in the caregiving, that older children should bear most of the responsibility, and that for some specific tasks caregivers and care recipients should be of the same sex (Radina, 2007).

All these studies suggest that ethnic minority families tend to view family and infor-mal or home care for frail elders as preferable and qualitatively better to formal institutional services. However, research has also shown that the demands of caregiving can have a very taxing effect on the caregiver and possibly the entire family, particularly among the poor. The complex tangle of social reproduction of ill health among poor families was superbly investi-gated in Burton and Bromell's (2010) ethnographic study of childhood illness, family comor-bidity, and cumulative disadvantage among low-income mothers in later life. Using data from the "Three City Study," which included Hispanic, African American and white low-income families, the authors found a pattern of "family co-morbidity" among participants. This pat-tern refers to families in which two or more individuals have concurrent health problems, including physical and mental health issues. The ethnographic methodology offers a unique tool for understanding how this pattern unfolds:

> Mothers often neglected their own physical health and mental health needs to meet the eco-nomic and health care needs of their children and other family members .... Their health is weathering as a function of sustained biomedical and social conditions. (Burton & Bromell, 2010, p. 255)

In Burton and Bromell's view, it is only through sustained ethnographic fieldwork that social and biomedical scientists may be able to access sensitive information and contextual data to advance our understanding of social inequalities and health in families.

LIVING ARRANGEMENTS, URBAN SPACE, AND THE NEIGHBORHOOD CONTEXT

A burgeoning number of studies in the sociology of aging have examined the impact of the physical and social characteristics of the neighborhood and housing context on the well-being of older individuals (Balfour & Kaplan, 2002; Young, Russell, & Powers, 2004). In his ground-breaking social "autopsy" of the 1995 Chicago *Heat Wave*, Klinenberg (2001, 2003) employed ethnographic methods to examine a compounding set of social factors linked to the dispro-portionate death rates among isolated elderly, particularly white and black males. According to this author, key social conditions contributed to the social disaster, namely: (a) a rise in the number of people living alone and, in particular, a rise in levels of isolation and reclu-siveness among seniors; (b) real and "perceived" fear of crime among elders living in urban neighborhoods, who in many cases reside in high crime areas, and are also influenced by the media fueled "culture of fear"; (c) the deterioration of urban public spaces, which lim-its opportunities for spontaneous leisure and socializing activities in the neighborhood; and (d) the dysfunctions of social service programs, which having increasingly adopted the con-sumer model of social service delivery, failed to address the needs of the most isolated seniors (Klinenberg, 2001, 2003).

Klinenberg's social autopsy of vulnerability is not a new sociological endeavor. Throughout the history of sociological theorizing, many scholars have been preoccupied with the effects of the sharp decline in levels of social integration of individuals, especially in the context of urbanization and rapid social change (Durkheim, 1979; Putnam, 2001). Similarly, social gerontologists have also attempted to explicate the gradual "social disengagement" that is apparently likely to occur as individuals grow older (Cumming, Henry, & Parsons, 1961). Moreover, the possession of *social capital* becomes particularly crucial for aging individuals in the United States, who more than ever before will spend their later years alone and away from their families, and who simultaneously are opting for *aging in place*. Although independent living is for many seniors a deliberate choice, and possibly a symbol of "successful" independent aging in the United States, many would concur with Klinenberg's assessment that "when someone dies alone and at home the death is a powerful symbol of social abandonment and failure" (Klinenberg, 2001, p. 503).

Equally intriguing to elders' risk of death in the face of a natural disaster is Klinenberg's analysis of resiliency among disadvantaged urban seniors. In this context, the positive effects of possessing social capital, including family ties, were evident among the elderly survivors of the heat wave. A seemingly paradoxical finding was that—among the elderly—Latinos were found to be the least likely to die, a phenomenon that can be partly attributed to Hispanic "familismo" or Latinos' stronger ties to their families in the neighborhoods where they resided. Indeed, this "Latino" or "Hispanic Paradox" is an interesting epidemiological phenomenon that has been analyzed and debated by scholars during the last few decades. Many epidemiological studies have consistently documented the—surprisingly—positive health outcomes among recent immigrant Latinos, despite their socioeconomically disadvantageous position (Markides & Eschbach, 2005). It is important to caution that the "Hispanic paradox" is more characteristic of Mexican populations and may not necessarily reflect the experiences of Hispanics of Caribbean origin, particularly Puerto Ricans who have lower life expectancy and poorer health outcomes than other Hispanic subgroups.

Freidemberg (2000) wrote a fascinating urban ethnography of older Puerto Ricans who migrated to New York City during the 1950s and 1960s and settled in El Barrio (East Harlem). This author explored a series of connected factors that have negatively impacted the lives of Puerto Rican elders, such as poverty, lack of English proficiency, discrimination, underemployment, and high mobility and family separation, among others. However, she also described the importance her informants placed on connections to family, both in the mainland and in Puerto Rico, as well as to the community. Consider the following author's field note observation:

> People come in and out of her house—real and fictive kin, neighbors, friends, home attendants—asking for her *bendición [blessing that is asked of a mother or older family member in Puerto Rican culture. Requesting the "bendición" also signifies respect.]* while Radio WADO paints the world in Spanish. Emiliana tells me that it is important to have people coming and going, that silence is no good. (Freidemberg, 2000, p. 153)

Freidemberg observes that, among Puerto Rican elders living in the barrio, social connectedness and the feeling of being needed promote a healthier mode of aging for many.

As immigrants acculturate to life in the United States they are likely to rely on government services for elders, increase their prevalence of independent living, and even adopt some of the "mainstream" cultural orientation toward autonomy in old age (Lamb, 2002), such as living apart from children. Since the 1990s, there has been an increase in independent living among unmarried elderly Hispanic females (Burr & Mutchler, 1992). More generally, foreign individuals who become citizens are similar in their living arrangements and receipt of supplemental security income (SSI) to native born (Lee & Angel, 2002). However, regardless of living arrangements, older Hispanics—especially females—are still more likely to interact with children and relatives than non-Hispanic whites (Rodríguez-Galán & Falcón, 2010).

Maintaining intergenerational support can be more difficult for minority seniors living alone in subsidized and senior housing. In my fieldwork with Puerto Rican grandmothers raising grandchildren, I have found that the type of housing—the majority of them live in subsidized housing—and neighborhood context often pose obstacles for intergenerational exchanges, particularly child rearing. For example, grandmothers who do not have custody of their grandchildren are not allowed to let their grandchildren stay overnight, thus they must circumvent housing policies that are based on the normative model of U.S. nuclear family and the cultural ideal of independence between older adults and their offspring. This phenomenon applies particularly to Puerto Rican populations who, because of their U.S. citizenship, are eligible for subsidized senior or low-income housing. In my investigation in the Boston area, many middle-age and senior Puerto Ricans live alone or with grandchildren in public housing, but in close proximity (sometimes the same building) to children, siblings, partners, ex-spouses, and other extended family members. Therefore, constraining housing policies have important implications for the availability of informal and intergenerational social support to Hispanic seniors and their families. Older Puerto Rican grandmothers and great grandmothers who reside in senior living arrangements face additional challenges in carrying out their caregiving duties. Accommodating grandchildren is often challenging, because these buildings are not designed to house children, and grandmothers must deal with problems such as cramped spaces and the prohibition against school buses making a stop at their building. Moreover, when Puerto Rican grandmothers need a larger apartment for their children and themselves, they may be reluctant to move to a different apartment complex because they have already developed supportive relationships with other Spanish-speaking seniors living in the same building. Those who live in communities that are majority English-speaking often experience greater social and linguistic isolation (Rodríguez-Galán, 2013).

Unlike most Latinos elders, the majority of immigrant older Indians come largely from the well-educated social classes. Lamb (2002) studied transnational aging among Indian elders living in the San Francisco, San Jose, and Boston areas. Geographically, Indian elders move frequently between India and the United States, and many maintain residency in both nations. Culturally, they must make adaptations to a very different mode of aging and to differing expectations of intergenerational dynamics in America. For example, intergenerational reciprocity is often reversed in the U.S. context, as Indian seniors frequently provide "services of caring" for their children, such as cooking, cleaning, and babysitting—rather than being on the receiving end of services as is normally the case in India. Although this role reversal may seem difficult at first, many elders find purpose in helping their children and grandchildren in the United States (Lamb, 2002).

Although most Indian children provide the bulk of the material support for their parents, Indian seniors are increasingly willing to accept the use of government resources, such as SSI benefits, Medicare, and subsidized housing for seniors. In fact, thanks to their reliance on government services, a significant portion of Indian seniors enjoy the ability to become more independent from family and even take up jobs to earn their own pocket money (Lamb, 2002). It seems that, in comparison to Latino immigrant populations, Indian seniors benefit from high levels of English proficiency and the cultural and social capital associated with their own, and their children's, middle-class status. In these urban areas, Indian seniors easily navigate the resources available to elders, resorting to use of discount bus passes, senior centers, and free lunches. Nonetheless, in Lamb's (2002) study, Indian seniors also lamented the fast-paced urban lifestyle of the United States. Particularly, they complain that their children do not have enough time to spend with them, that they do not receive the same amount of respect and honor as in India, and are unable to practice elaborate dying and funeral rituals in the more medicalized American setting (Lamb, 2002).

Treas and Manzundar (2002) conducted a notable exploratory in-depth interview study of foreign elderly from various countries, mainly from Asia and Latin America. Most of these seniors lived in suburban neighborhoods with their children and came to the United States later in life through the family reunification provisions of the U.S. immigration law, although some came as refugees. The authors found that, in spite of being integrated in family networks, many of these elders experienced loneliness, boredom, isolation, and general dissatisfaction with their lives in the United States. Although married couples tended to be relatively more satisfied, many elders in this sample felt isolated because the suburban neighborhoods where they lived had very few attractions within walking distance. As the authors indicate, "outside ethnic enclaves, not speaking English increased social isolation and dependence on kin" (Treas & Mazundar, 2002, p. 249). Indeed, not speaking English also undermined communication with younger members of the family. Some did not have any social ties outside of their kinship network, and family obligations, such as cleaning, cooking, and childcare in their children's home, could be so time consuming that many had little spare time or energy for socialization outside of the family. In essence, the companionship from family was not always sufficient to keep off feelings of loneliness and boredom: "Families sometimes seemed to fold in on older people, simultaneously ignoring, indulging, and isolating them. The very solidarity and integration of families could contribute to loneliness and boredom" (Treas & Mazundar, 2002, p. 250). Many seniors bemoaned many aspects of America life style, such as the weaker family ties, its fast pace, and high demands of work and school on the young. Thus, they willingly provided help for their children with household and child care to allow them to concentrate their energies on getting ahead in the United States through work and study.

In contrast to the above-described suburban setting, Becker (2003) employed ethnographic interviewing in a study of meanings of place and displacement in three groups of older immigrants: Latinos, Filipino American, and Cambodian American, the majority of whom lived in run-down, crime-infested inner city neighborhoods. The living conditions of these elders were extremely marginal, which included rooms without kitchens or bathrooms and overcrowded apartments. Many elders were forced to move frequently due to the precariousness of their living situations, substandard housing, and the likelihood of rent to rise. Not surprisingly, elders were generally demoralized about their living situations but still preferred to live among co-ethnics and extended family networks. In this study, Latinos lived in predominantly Spanish-speaking neighborhoods, and in a range of living conditions due to several factors, such as length of stay in the United States and whether or not they had family in the United States (some had been live-in nannies and were not able to bring their families with them to the United States). Overcrowding was also common for many of them, but for some overcrowding in family settings was preferable to living by oneself. Often, Latinos expressed a longing to return to their old homes in their country of origin, but few actually had the assets to do so. With respect to Asian elders in the sample, Filipino Americans who have migrated in the last 10 years were likely to live in single-occupancy rooms (SROs), with as many as five men in each, and without legal access to kitchen and bathroom facilities. Some men liked these overcrowded living conditions because they were seen as a substitute for extended family. Cambodians similarly experienced overcrowding. In both Asian groups, economic need led to sharing space which could result in discontent (Becker, 2003).

Without a doubt, the physical, social, and cultural context of the neighborhood and community where elders dwell in their older years plays an enormous role in their quality of life and modes of aging. The studies reviewed in this section show that minority elders are frequently more constrained in their options for living arrangements and must negotiate a space that poses many hurdles for them. In contrast, advantaged nonminority seniors often have the ability to occupy spaces that are designed to meet theirs and their family's needs, generally at the expense of excluding minority populations. In his ethnographic review of Sun Belt retirement communities, McHugh (2000), a critical social geographer, stresses the power of *place* and the "emplacement of identities" in the marketing strategies of retirement communities. Building upon Glenda Laws' (1995) notion of aging as an emplaced process, he argues that the retirement community industry constructs and promotes images of seniors as affluent and actively enjoying their "golden years." Based on his own ethnographic work, the author further suggests that for these advantaged nonminority elderly—whose lives were often built around careerism, change, and mobility—the busy work ethic remains for as long as they can in these communities. However, in creating this ideal space for an "ageless" active self, many are consciously engaging in the exclusion of people of color and younger residents.

CONCLUSIONS AND DIRECTIONS FOR FUTURE RESEARCH

It is fair to say that sociological literature is yet to fully engage in the use of ethnographic methods to address the questions of most significance to this subfield. Ethnography, even in its more focused and applied form typically used today in the study of U.S. populations, requires a tremendous amount of time investment, whereas ethnographers have fewer options for sources of funding and support for their research, especially when conducting stand-alone studies. For scholars investigating populations that are non-English speaking, the additional challenge is the difficulty in finding bilingual assistants. Despite these challenges, a few scholars and researchers during this past decade have begun to address some key sociological questions in gerontology: the importance of kin ties, including those that are "fictive," for the well-being of seniors; the roles of older family members in social reproduction and in the transmission of ethnic identity and culture; changes in intergenerational family relationships in a globalized economy; and the relationship between cumulative disadvantage in families and later life health issues.

Given the more professionally institutionalized ethnographic tradition for which anthropology is known, it was not a surprise to find that most of the studies on aging minority families come from this discipline. Collectively, anthropologists have examined the impact of the geographical, local, and spatial contexts on family dynamics; changes in family living arrangements brought by immigration; cultural norms and ideals; an institutional ethnography of perceived family involvement in a nursing home; and the depiction of an almost extinct age family rite of passage. In addition to these topical areas, the work of Sarah Lamb offers a unique cross-national analysis of the Indian aging diaspora. Finally, those working from the fields of nursing and family studies have made a significant contribution to the literature on caregiving, especially in the areas of family members as informal caregivers; barriers to formal care; and cultural coping mechanisms.

A close examination of the ethnic groups in this chapter would reveal some significant points of conversion and diversion. Scholarship on Asian and Pacific Islander families has addressed research questions related to intergenerational relations, migration, urban space, and the caregiving experience. This body of literature has sampled several nationalities. However, scholars examining Hispanic populations have addressed similar topics and focused their research on the three major Latino ethnic groups: Mexican, Cuban, and Puerto Rican. In addition to underscoring the importance of the local context, the literature on African American families has also highlighted the centrality of religion/spirituality and the decision-making process regarding caregiving. All the studies available used samples of African American families in several regions of the country. However, to my knowledge, there is no ethnographic literature on other black populations, such as Afro-Caribbean and African groups. Similarly, very little is known about Native American families and aging. In general, much ethnographic work is needed for each and all of these ethnic minority populations.

Future research may also need to explore in more depth the roles of elders in the family, not only as potential care recipients but also as care givers. Most of the scholarship on grandparents raising grandchildren is primarily quantitative, with some qualitative studies, but ethnographic approaches regardless of their research design and methods are practically nonexistant. More work is needed in this area, as well as on the role of elders as family mentors and "fictive kin." Likewise, ethnographies detailing kin networks of support and intergenerational solidarity would be especially beneficial to our understanding of the experiences of growing old in ethnic minority families.

More sociological studies of family caregiving are also needed. Sociology could strengthen this body of research by offering a more defined gender lense, looking at both male and female family caregivers and definitions of the caregiver role. Although some qualitative studies in sociology have examined this issue, an ethnographic approach would offer a more contextualized, reliable, and richer description. Sociology may also offer a unique perspective on institutional ethnographies with a focus on family inclusion in a range of long-term care settings, such as nursing homes, adult day care, assisted living, and hospice. This kind of work would expand gerontological understanding of how organizations approach family involvement, how ethnic minority families navigate institutional settings from which they have historically been excluded, and how they advocate for their loved ones. Finally, the work of Burton and Bromell (2010) encourages social and biomedical scientist to turn to ethnography for a contextualized understanding of health issues and family life in life course perspective.

It is crucial that ethnographic research finds its deserved place in the sociology of ethnic minority families. Only then may we discover the most important questions we need to ask. In the final analysis, it is through the investigation of these particular ethnic groups that we would be better positioned to comprehend how aging functions among all human beings.

NOTE

1. Respect that includes deference and obedience to an elder's higher authority.

REFERENCES

Allen, K. R., Blieszner, R., & Roberto, K. (2011). Perspectives on extended family and fictive Kin in the later years: Strategies and meanings of Kin reinterpretation. *Journal of Family Issues, 32*(9), 1156–1177.

Balfour, J. L., & Kaplan, G. A. (2002). Neighborhood environment and loss of physical function in older adults: evidence from the Alameda County Study. *American Journal of Epidemiology, 155*(6), 507–515.

Becker, G. (2003). Meanings of place and displacement in three groups of older immigrants. *Journal of Aging Studies, 17,* 129–149.

Bengtson, V. L. (2001). The burgess award lecture: Beyond the nuclear family: The increasing importance of multigenerational bonds. *Journal of Marriage and Family, 63*(1), 1–1.

Burr, J. A., & Mutchler, J. E. (1992). The living arrangements of unmarried elderly Hispanic females. *Demography, 29*(1), 93–112.

Burton, L. M., & Bromell, L. (2010). Childhood illness, family comorbidity, and cumulative disadvantage. An ethnographic treatise on low-income mothers in later life. *Annual Review of Gerontology and Geriatrics, 30*(1), 233–265.

Burton, L. M., Winn, D. M., Stevenson, H., & Clark, S. L. (2004). Working with African American clients: considering the "homeplace" in marriage and family therapy practices. *Journal of Marital and Family Therapy, 30*(4), 397–410.

Cortes, D. E. (1995).Variations in familism in two generations of Puerto Ricans. *Hispanic Journal of Behavioral Sciences, 17*(2), 249–255.

Cumming, E., Henry, W. E., & Parsons, T. (1961). *Growing old, the process of disengagement.* New York, NY: Basic Books.

Durkheim, E. (1979). *Suicide: A study in sociology.* New York, NY: The Free Press.

Falcón, L. M., Todorova, I., & Tucker, K. (2009). Social support, life events, and psychological distress among the Puerto Rican population in the Boston area of the United States. *Aging & Mental Health, 13*(6), 863–873.

Franklin, D. L. (2010). African Americans and the birth of modern marriage. In B. Risman (Ed.), *Families as they really are* (pp. 63–74), New York, NY: W.W. Norton.

Freidemberg, J. N. (2000). *Growing old in El Barrio.* New York, NY: New York University Press.

Gerder, L. A., Tripp-Reimer, T., & Simpson, H. C. (2002). Hard lives, god's help, and struggling through: Caregiving in Arkansas Delta. *Journal of Cross-Cultural Gerontology, 22,* 355–374.

Gratton, B. (1987). Familism among the Black and Mexican American elderly: Myth or reality. *Journal of Aging Studies, 1*(1), 19–32.

Herbert, R. S., Schulz, R., Copeland, V., & Arnold, R. M. (2008). What questions do family caregivers want to discuss with health care providers in order to prepare for the death of a loved one? An ethnographic study of caregivers of patients at the end of life. *Journal of Palliative Medicine, 11*(3), 476–483.

Jervis, L. L. (2006). The missing family: Staff perspectives on and responses to familial noninvolvement in two diverse nursing homes. *Journal of Aging Studies, 20,* 55–66.

Jett, K. F. (2005). Mind-loss in the African American community: Dementia as a normal part of aging. *Journal of Aging Studies, 20,* 1–10.

Johnson, C. L., & Barer, B. M. (2003). Family lives of aging Black Americans. In J. F. Gubrium & J. A. Holstein (Eds.), *Ways of aging* (pp. 111–131). Malden, MA: Blackwell.

Klinenberg, E. (2001). Dying alone: The social production of urban isolation. *Ethnography, 2*(4), 501–531.

Klinenberg, E. (2003). *Heat wave: A social autopsy of disaster in Chicago.* Chicago, IL: University of Chicago Press.

Lamb, S. (2002). Intimacy in a transnational era: The remaking of aging among Indian Americans. *Diaspora, 11*(3), 299–330.

Laws, G. (1995). Embodiment and emplacement: Identities, representation and landscape in sun city retirement communities. *International Journal of Aging and Human Development, 40*, 253–280.

Lee, G.-Y., & Angel, R. J. (2002). Living arrangements and supplemental security income use among elderly Asians and Hispanics in the United States: The role of nativity and citizenship. *Journal of Ethnic and Migration Studies, 28*(3), 553–563.

Limpanichkul, Y., & Magilvy, K. (2004). Managing caregiving at home: Thai caregivers living in the United States. *Journal of Cultural Diversity, 11*(1), 18–24.

Losada, A., Knight, B. G., Márquez-González, M., Montorio, I., Etxeberría, I., & Peñacoba, C. (2008). Confirmatory factor analysis of the familism scale in a sample of dementia caregivers. *Aging & Mental Health, 12*(4), 504–508.

Magilvy, J. K., Congdon, J. G., Martínez, R. J., Davis, R., & Averill, J. (2000). Caring for our own: Health care experiences of rural Hispanic elders. *Journal of Aging Studies, 14*(2), 171–190.

Markides, K. S., & Eschbach, K. (2005). Aging, migration, and mortality: current status of research on the Hispanic paradox. *The Journals of Gerontology. Series B, Psychological Sciences and Social Sciences, 60*(Spec No 2), 68–75.

Martínez, I. L. (2002). The elder Cuban American Family: Making sense of the real and ideal. *Journal of Contemporary Family Studies, 33*(3), 359–375.

McHugh, K. E. (2000). The "Ageless Self"? Emplacement of identities in sun belt retirement communities. *Journal of Aging Studies, 14*(1), 103–115.

Mitchell, B. A. (2006). The boomerang age from childhood to adulthood: Emergent trends and issues for aging families. *Canadian Studies in Population, 33*(2), 155–178.

Montoro-Rodriguez, J., & Koloski, K. (1998). The impact of acculturation on attitudinal familism in a community of Puerto Rican Americans. *Hispanic Journal of Behavioral Sciences, 20*(3), 375–390.

Peters, D.-M. (2010). Passing on: The old head/younger dancer mentoring relationship in the cultural sphere of rhythm rap. *The Western Journal of Black Studies, 34*(4), 438–446.

Pierce, L. L. (2001). Coherence in the urban family caregiver role with African American stroke survivors. *Top Stroke Rehabil, 8*(3), 64–72.

Putnam, R. (2001). *Bowling alone: The collapse and revival of American community*. New York, NY: Simon & Schuster.

Radina, M. E. (2007). Mexican American siblings caring for aging parents: Processes of caregiver selection/designation. *Journal of Comparative Family Studies, 38*(1), 143–168.

Rodríguez-Galán, M. B. (2013). Grandmothering in life course perspective: A study of Puerto Rican grandmothers raising grandchildren in the United States. In K. Lynch & J. Danely (Eds.), *Transitions and transformations: Cultural perspectives on the life course* (pp. 173–191). New York, NY: Bherghan Books.

Rodríguez-Galán, M. B., & Falcón, L. (2010). Patterns of social activity engagement among older Hispanics and its relationship with socio-demographic and health variables. *Activities, Adaptation and Aging, 34*(4), 251–275.

Ruiz, M. E. (2007). Familismo and filial piety among Latino and Asian elders: Reevaluating family and social support. *Hispanic Health Care International, 5*(2), 81–89.

Sarkisian, N. & Gerstel, N. (2004). Kin support among Blacks and Whites: Race and family organization. *American Sociological Review, 69*(6), 812–837.

Schwartz, S. J. (2007). The applicability of familism to diverse ethnic groups: a preliminary study. *The Journal of Social Psychology, 147*(2), 101–118.

Treas, J., & Mazumdar, S. (2002). Older people in America's immigrant families dilemmas of dependence, integration, and isolation. *Journal of Aging Studies, 16*, 243–258.

Turner, W. L., Wallace, B. R., Anderson, J. R., & Bird, C. (2004). The last mile of the way: Understanding caregiving in African American families at the end of life. *Journal of Marital and Family Therapy, 30*(4), 427–438.

Valle, R., & Cook-Gait, H. (1998). *Caregiving across cultures*. Oxford: Routledge.

Weibel-Orlando, J. (2003). Elderhood in contemporary Lakota society. In J. F. Gubrium & J. A. Holstein (Eds.), *Ways of aging* (pp. 36–57). Malden, MA: Blackwell.

Young, A. F., Russell, A., & Powers, J. R. (2004). The sense of belonging to a neighbourhood: can it be measured and is it related to health and well being in older women? *Social Science & Medicine (1982), 59*(12), 2627–2637.

Zinn, M. B. (1994). Feminist rethinking from racial-ethnic families. In M. B. Zinn & B. T. Dill (Eds.), *Women of color in U.S. society*. Philadelphia, PA: Temple University Press.

CHAPTER 28

Intersections Among Gender, Race, and Ethnicity: Implications for Health

Kristine J. Ajrouch and Sawsan Abdulrahim

OVERVIEW

The sociological study of gender and minority aging benefits from an approach that privileges "social things" as the lens through which an understanding of men and women, who are members of minority groups, experience the aging process. The sociological literature is replete with writings on the constructed nature of gender and race/ethnicity. Racialized science, which has advanced that social and economic differences between groups are based on immutable biological factors, has long been discredited. Moreover, feminist scholarship has exposed flaws in biological explanations for women's subordination and economic dependence on men. Feminist writings have critiqued ways that race/ethnicity and gender have been examined as independent axes or through models that emphasized the additive influence of the two (Collins, 1989; Glenn, 1999). The critique of this approach and the conceptual shift in feminist approaches to examining how racial and gender inequalities intersect has expanded to include other axes of inequality, such as social class, sexuality, age, and citizenship status (Purkayastha, 2012).

In this chapter, we present a case for examining aging in the United States through an intersectionality lens. We begin by presenting age, gender, and race/ethnicity as social constructions, followed by a conceptual overview of intersectionality to highlight strengths as well as challenges in this approach, particularly as it relates to health. We then show demographics of aging by gender and race/ethnicity to draw attention to intersections. We review the most current thinking on gender and minority health, with special attention to social roles and contextual factors, and methodological approaches. Similarities and differences between racial/ethnic groups are discussed. Finally, we end with a brief list of future directions not yet addressed in the literature.

Social Constructions

The social construction of reality involves attention to how the definition of a situation(s) comes to represent daily life, and leads to the structures that shape, constrain, and enable individual action. This approach permits the identification of assumptions behind social facts that describe individuals and groups in a society. For the purposes of this chapter, we present age, gender, race/ethnicity, as social constructions.

Age is a construct usefully understood through its social characteristics, as opposed to a biological certainty. Age as a social construction first and foremost must acknowledge the roles of political economy and governing laws that shape a society, understanding of who is young and who is old (Estes, 2001; Hendricks, 2004; Walker, 2006). Chronological age has historically been the basis upon which one is evaluated as being "old enough" for certain rights and privilege as a member of society. For instance, by law, in many states one must reach the age of 16 to drive, 18 to vote, and 21 to drink alcohol. Perhaps, more significant for the study of aging is the age at which one is considered eligible to receive benefits through the age-based social insurance programs in the United States, including Social Security and Medicare; the former provides financial resources and the latter health care. Decisions on the age at which one becomes eligible for full benefits have changed over time, from 65 to 67, indicating that definitions of being old are situated in a particular historical moment. Moreover, age norms dictate our definitions of old age, with informal rules and widely held expectations of appropriate roles, activities, and social engagement in later life (Riley, Kahn, & Foner, 1994). For instance, role transitions into grandmother or great-grandmother status that are not on time, and deviate from expected age in the life course, may make women feel old before their time (Burton, 1996). Finally, identifiers of old age also include definitions given to physical characteristics such as gray hair, wrinkled or sagging skin (Calasanti & Slevin, 2001), as well as functional disability including challenges in walking long distances, climbing stairs, or lifting objects. Regardless of chronological age, these attributes often define being old, and hence illustrate the multiple dimensions that indicate old age, which together derive from a socially constructed notion of age.

The social construction of gender has been widely addressed in the sociological literature, with identified insights for better understanding health and the aging process. Gender refers to ideals of masculinity and femininity, each of which provide distinguishing characteristics believed appropriate and core to being a man or a woman (Phillips, Ajrouch, & Hillcoat-Nalletamby, 2010). Gender constitutes a critical social force in the experience of aging, and is considered a pervasive marker of inequality. Though gender issues may vary depending on the social, cultural, and political context in which people grow older, research suggests that areas where older men and women differ include life expectancy, health, social relations, and socioeconomic resources. One of the most consistently observed gender differences in aging experiences around the world is that women live longer than men, yet report higher prevalence of chronic illness and disability (Barer, 1994; Knodel & Ofstedal, 2003; Verbrugge, 1985). Moreover, roles, expectations, and social network characteristics vary depending on whether one is a man or woman (Ajrouch, Blandon, & Antonucci, 2005; Moen, 2001). Finally, men accumulate financial resources over the life course that often exceeds levels earned by women (Hartmann & English, 2009). Some argue that with age, differences that distinguished men and women earlier in life tend to disappear, and therefore inequalities based on gender diminish. For instance, gender gaps in depressive symptoms documented during earlier parts of the life course diminish in old age so that men's and women's experience of depressive symptoms do not vary greatly from one another (Akiyama & Antonucci, 2002). Nevertheless, men and women often differ with regard to earlier life course opportunities and encounters, which then shape situations during later life. Gender may be especially key to understanding race/ethnic differences in multiple areas of social life such as work (Read, 2004), family organization (Saraksian & Gerstel, 2004), and the immigrant health advantage (Read & Reynolds, 2012).

The aging of men and women may vary by race and ethnicity. In this chapter, we use race and ethnicity interchangeably, but recognize that whereas each emphasizes different aspects of a minority group identity, racial hierarchies also influence understandings about and expressions of ethnicity (Ford & Harawa, 2010). Omi and Winant (1986, p. 55) define racial formation as the "sociohistorical process by which racial categories are created, inhabited, transformed, and destroyed." We use race to reference people's physical traits including skin color, facial features, and hair texture, as the basis upon which differences and ideological inferiority/superiority between groups are indicated (Cornell & Hartmann, 1998; Lewis, 2002). As such, race must be understood as a social construction, a reality that does not exist unless it is defined as such. The taxonomy of five major race groupings: white/Caucasian, black/African American, Asian American, Native American, and Pacific Islander, may be traced back to folk classifications established centuries ago by Europeans (Harawa & Ford, 2009; Jaret, 1995). Though "race as biology is fiction," racism is a worldwide social problem (Smedley & Smedley, 2005); as a social fact, race is, and has been, an important organizing principle of social relations in the United States. In the United States, race has historically played a crucial role as an important orga- nizing principle of social relations, maintained through the competitive interactions between state agencies and minority groups agitating for social change (Omi & Winant, 1986). While ideas of race structure individual experiences and interactions, definitions of race are also sub- ject to renegotiations, drawing simultaneously from present day and historical predicaments (Ajrouch & Kusow, 2007). Race categories are unstable and fluctuating, as may be seen with the case of Arab Americans, who are legally defined as white, yet can select to be white or non- white (Abdulrahim, 2008) and are perceived by members both inside and outside of that group as non-white (Ajrouch, 2004; Ajrouch & Jamal, 2007; Cainkar, 2010). The significance of race to understanding gender, aging, and health includes the historical legacy of race-based discrimi- nation, which affects men and women differently over the life course.

We use ethnicity to reference cultural traits, emphasizing common shared values, beliefs, and lifestyles, which serve to identify a social group both by in-group and out-group members (Phillips et al., 2010). The rise of immigration over the past 50 years has paralleled an inter- est in the role of ethnicity in the aging process, in part because of the growing diversity that comes with immigration (Angel & Angel, 2006). The importance of ethnicity corresponds to links between meaning and experience of aging with diverse cultural codes and priorities, all of which occur over the life course. Cultural codes may be particularly influential on gendered aspects of aging and well-being. For instance, Wray (2003) suggested that women in various national origin groups more likely feel older at younger chronological ages because of cultural life course patterns such as marrying and having children at young ages. Timing of childbirth and family responsibilities constitute two examples of social roles that inform identification of one as old. The timing of old age is of particular relevance with regard to ethnicity. Ethnicity provides a lens through which to understand cultural aspects of gender and minority aging. Next, we turn to a conceptual overview of intersectionality.

Conceptual Overview of Intersectionality

Development of the intersectionality paradigm emerged as an interdisciplinary project that builds from notions that race and gender as social constructions are made meaningful within specific contexts through social relationships. Its roots lay in black feminist thought (Collins, 1989), which advanced that gender interacts with other forms of oppression (race and social class) to influence the experiences of women of color and working women. The intersectionality lens suggests that race, class, and gender are "mutually constitutive and interconnected" in the ways that they influence health and determine health disparities (Mullings & Schulz, 2006, p. 3). This perspective moves beyond the notion that advantages or disadvantages associated with race, class, and gender simply accumulate. Instead, inter- sectionality advocates for understanding how such factors operate in tandem, each influ- encing and interacting with the other (Mullings & Schulz, 2006; Stoller & Gibson, 2000; Thornton Dill & Zambrana, 2009). For example, the meaning of manhood and womanhood may vary by racial/ethnic group, and vice versa, the meaning of being black, Asian, Latino, Native American, or Arab may depend on whether one is a man or woman. The strength of the intersectionality framework lies in the attention it draws to traditionally marginalized (minority) groups, focusing on multiple identities (e.g., gender and race/ethnicity) and mul- tiple dimensions of social organization (e.g., power dynamics), simultaneously (Thornton Dill & Zambrana, 2009).

We propose to apply this framework with the added variable of age. In other words, we advance that the experience of old age varies depending on gender and race/ethnicity and, simultaneously, manhood and womanhood are shaped by age, as is race/ethnicity. As is now widely understood, men and women are perceived to be old at different ages (Toothman & Barrett, 2011). Moreover, the meaning of being old and the role of an older adult varies across racial/ethnic groups. For example, Native Americans view older adults as important cultural conservators (Weibel-Orlando, 2000), whereas African Americans often admire those who survive into old age (Stoller & Gibson, 2000). More centrally, health status in later life will vary by both gender and race/ethnicity, and each dimension of difference shapes experiences in mutually reinforcing ways over the life course. It is now clear that racial/ethnic health inequalities emerge at all points in the life course, not simply during old age (Ferraro, 2007). This chapter aims to review the latest research in the areas of gender, age, and race/ethnicity to highlight strengths as well as challenges in this approach, particularly as it relates to health. We begin with a demographic overview of older adults by race/ethnicity.

DEMOGRAPHIC OVERVIEW

We provide an updated overview of key minority groups according to age and gender using demographic data available from the U.S. Census Bureau. The population distributions have been calculated using 2010 Census data, with the exception of Arab Americans. Because Arab Americans are legally considered white, recent data (after the 2000 census) for this ethnic group are available only through the American Community Survey, where the ethnic ancestry question is asked. Any person who listed ancestry to an Arabic speaking country was counted as Arab American[1] (U.S. Census Bureau, 2008–2010 American Community Survey). In this demographic overview, we also include numbers and proportions of those who identify as some other race to illustrate the fluidity of racial categories, as well as demonstrate the growing numbers for whom traditional racial categories do not apply. First, we show the total population for each group, followed by a presentation of the overall population of more than 65 years, and then reveal proportions of men and women aged 65 years or older, within each racial/ethnic group (see Table 28.1).

In terms of total population, those who identify as Hispanic/Latino report the largest numbers, at more than 50 million, followed by African Americans at slightly less than 40 million persons. Asian Americans follow as the third largest minority group, with almost 15 million people, followed by Native Americans at just less than 3 million persons. Arab Americans number at just over 1.5 million, followed by Pacific Islanders at just over a half million people. Almost 20 million Americans identified as Some Other Race.

In examining the proportions of minority group elders who are aged 65 or above, African Americans report the highest numbers at almost 4 million, and well as the highest proportion of their population at 10%. Asian Americans report the next highest proportion of their population at 9.4%, followed by Arab Americans at 7.5%, and Native Americans at 7.1%. Pacific Islander and Hispanic/Latinos report 5.8% and 5.5%, respectively. Those who identified as Some Other Race report 3.5% of their population, more than 6 million persons, who are aged more than 65 years.

TABLE 28.1 U.S. Census Bureau, 2010, Population Distribution by Racial/Ethnic Group

	TOTAL POPULATION	65+ POPULATION		MEN 65+		WOMEN 65+	
	N	*N*	%	*N*	%	*N*	%
Asian Americans	14,674,252	1,386,626	9.4	598,140	43.1	788,486	56.9
Pacific Islander	540,013	31,213	5.8	14,193	45.5	17,020	54.5
African Americans	38,929,319	3,949,389	10.0	1,350,829	34.2	2,398,560	65.8
Native Americans	2,932,248	207,059	7.1	92,470	44.7	114,589	55.3
Hispanic/Latino	50,477,594	2,781,624	5.5	1,181,882	42.5	1,599,742	57.5
Arab Americans[a]	1,597, 385	119,788	7.5	59,535	49.7	60,253	50.3
Some Other Race	19,107,368	665,994	3.5	290,139	43.6	375,855	56.4

[a]*Source*: 2008–2010 American Community Survey.

For all racial/ethnic categories, women outnumber men among those aged 65 years and over. Most striking, perhaps, is the extent to which women outnumber men among African Americans, almost two to one, where women constitute almost 66% of those aged more than 65 years and men roughly one third at 34%. Among Arab Americans, the gender distribution is almost exactly even with women constituting 50.3% of the population aged 65 years and more, and men 49.7%. Among the remaining, the population distribution reflects parallel patterns, with women constituting between 54% and 57% of the population aged 65 years and older and men comprising between 43% and 46%.

The demographic profiles presented above provide population-level data on aging and gender among minority groups in the United States. The comparative approach allows for a more detailed understanding of demographic similarities and differences among minority groups in the United States. Although population size varies, women nevertheless comprise the majority of those aged more than 65 years, regardless of race/ethnicity. It should be noted, however, that within-group diversity is great, yet often obscured when for research purposes groups are bundled for ease of identification (Thornton Dill & Zambrana, 2009). We next turn to a review of the literature concerning gender and minority health.

GENDER AND MINORITY HEALTH DEBATE

The importance of gender to aging and minority health has been widely understood through the triple jeopardy framework. The premise of triple jeopardy rests on the belief that being old, a member of a minority racial/ethnic group, and being a woman, each constitutes risk factors for a poor quality of life (Phillips et al., 2010). This framework originally derived from the double jeopardy hypothesis, which suggested the experience of growing old as a racial/ethnic minority incurs numerous social experiences where poor treatment and access to fewer resources accumulate to yield poorer health among minority group members compared to members of dominant society (National Urban League, 1964). Later, the inclusion of gender as a key stratifying factor was included to advance the notion of triple jeopardy. The social norms that have traditionally guided women's life trajectories, including marital and employment trajectories, along with extended life expectancies and higher rates of chronic illness, put women at heightened risk of a poor quality of life in old age (Hartmann & English, 2009). Women, it seems, are far more likely to incur living in poverty in old age than are men, particularly older ethnic minority women (Minkler & Stone, 1985). Living in poverty is frequently included as an additional "jeopardy" (Manthorpe & Hettiaratchy, 1993). Triple jeopardy advances the belief that the additive effects of being old, being a racial/ethnic minority, and being a woman combine to produce challenges in old age.

The counterthesis to double or triple jeopardy, called the age-as-leveler hypothesis (Kent, 1971), suggested that aging in and of itself constitutes a universal human problematic experience, and hence supersedes any effects due to social stratification (i.e., racial/ethnic, gender) that may occur earlier in the life course. More specifically, biological and social processes are thought to intervene. House et al. (1994) indicate that increasing inequality occurs with age until early old age when biological processes experienced by all as well as social insurance programs that provide age-based resources in later life serve to flatten out any differences from earlier in the life course.

Research over the last decades has shown evidence to support the theoretical specifications of the fact that either double or triple jeopardy is mixed. Hence, three caveats to the jeopardy hypothesis include awareness of an ontogenetic fallacy, the assumption of discrimination, and selective mortality (Ferraro & Farmer, 1996). Awareness of the ontogenetic fallacy means rejecting the presumption of aging to be a self-contained process, and instead understands aging as one shaped by social and contextual factors. For example, the chronological age at which one is considered "old" must be acknowledged, particularly given that life expectancies vary by racial/ethnic group. The second caveat involves an assumption of race and age effects due to discrimination. To better specify this effect, it is suggested that discrimination be directly measured. As Ferraro and Farmer point out, the differential health effects may be due to health behavior differences, variations in efficacy, or cultural practices. The final caveat concerns selective mortality. Ferraro and Farmer caution that any exploration of a jeopardy hypothesis must consider not only health but also survival over the life course, hence the need for longitudinal data. In particular, attention must be paid to the racial-mortality crossover effect illustrating that black men have lower life expectancies than whites, but if they reach age 75, they have a better chance of outliving their white counterparts. Of course, women in general have longer life expectancies than men, though they are more likely to report living with a chronic illness.

The intersectionality framework addresses the shortcomings of triple jeopardy. According to this approach, race/ethnicity and gender are not considered additive factors, but instead are mutually reinforcing to dictate life experiences and resource access (Mullings & Schulz, 2006; Stoller & Gibson, 2000; Thornton Dill & Zambrana, 2009). Though social class is often included as a key stratifying characteristic, it has been increasingly conceptualized as a life course resource that is (a) influenced by race/ethnicity and gender, and (b) having a similar effect regardless of race/ethnicity or gender; in other words, it does not vary in its influence on health depending on those stratifying factors in any systematic way (Warner & Brown, 2011). Indeed:

> Within intersectional analyses, unveiling the workings of power, which is understood as both pervasive and oppressive, is vitally important. It reveals both the sources of inequality and its multiple and often conflicting manifestations...in different historical and geographical contexts. (Thornton Dill & Zambrana, 2009, p. 11)

As such, the intersectionality of gender and race/ethnicity to better understand health in later life will constitute the approach taken. In the section below, we review recent findings to highlight similarities and differences across racial and ethnic groups with regard to how research on the intersections of race/ethnicity and gender signify interlocking hierarchies that ultimately inform mental and physical health outcomes in later life.

Mental Health

Research on how gender and race intersect to influence health outcomes in old age has been limited in its examination of mental health. Some recent work addressed gender and race patterns, analyzing each separately to predict depressive symptoms by age and cohort. Yang and Lee (2009) analyzed the Americans' Changing Lives longitudinal data of a nationally representative sample to investigate age and cohort patterns of depressive symptoms, comparing blacks and whites as well as men and women. Ten-year birth cohorts were operationalized, including those born before 1905, 1905 to 1914 (Young Progressives); 1915 to 1924 (Jazz Age Babies); 1925–1934 (Depression Kids); 1935 to 1944 (War Babies); 1945 to 1954; and 1955 to 1964 (Baby Boomers) to specify cohort-specific age trajectories. They found that more recent cohorts of older adults reported higher levels of depressive symptoms than did earlier cohorts, especially among blacks and women. Such cohort differences are attributed to changes in women's roles and situations that increase stress, as well as continuing racial discrimination. Interestingly, Yang and Lee find that gender differences do diminish over the life course, substantiating earlier cross-sectional research suggesting similar trends with age (Akiyama & Antonucci, 2002). Socioeconomic status (SES) and functional limitations may represent important contexts for better understanding racial difference in depressive symptoms differentially for blacks and whites by gender. More specifically, it appears that among low SES elders, African Americans, particularly men, reported less depressive symptoms in the face of functional limitations than whites overall, while among high SES elders, African American men and women as well as white men incur more depressive symptoms than white women (Schieman & Plickert, 2007). Such findings demonstrate that race and gender intersect in unique ways so that contexts such as SES and physical health differentially influence mental health outcomes among African Americans and whites.

Although some research suggested that blacks and Hispanics report lower incidence of mental health problems than whites (Thoits, 2010), this does not seem to hold in old age (Russell & Taylor, 2009; Yang & Lee, 2009). Indeed, Russell and Taylor (2009) found that older

Hispanic immigrants who lived alone were far more likely to report depressive symptoms than were African Americans. Cultural preferences for living arrangements may explain why. Hispanic men, in particular, were more prone to depression when living alone than were Hispanic women, most likely because women perceived more social support available to them (Russell & Taylor, 2009). Such gender differences were not found among non-Hispanic whites or blacks.

The Hispanic subgroup of Mexican American represents the most often researched group concerning matters of aging and health, likely due the fact that they are the most numerous and oldest Hispanic group in the United States (Rumbaut, 2006). From research conducted on Mexican Americans, it has been suggested that understanding how emotions relate to psychological distress may vary by culture. Chiribiga, Jang, Banks, and Kim (2007) found that less acculturated Mexican American elders reacted more to interpersonal problems than to feeling depressed, suggesting the need for a culturally sensitive approach to the study of mental health. In a study that focused only on Mexican American elders, women reported more depressive symptoms than men. Moreover, among married couples in the same study, husband's well-being (depressive symptoms) predicted wives well-being, but not vice versa (Peek, Stimpson, Townsend, & Markides, 2006). Such findings suggest that Mexican American women may be uniquely vulnerable to depressive symptoms in later life and also highlight the utility of an intersectionality approach to show that ethnicity may matter with regard to gender and mental health in later life. Contrary to findings reported by Akiyama and Antonucci (2002), gender differences in depressive symptoms appear prominent in later life among Mexican elders.

Far less research addresses how gender may influence the mental health of Asian/Pacific Islander, Native American, and Arab American elders. Though Mui and Kang (2006) found high levels of depressive symptoms (indicating clinical depression) among a diverse group of Asian immigrants (Chinese, Korean, Indian, Filipino, Vietnamese, and Japanese) living in New York City, no gender differences were detected. Furthermore, gender differences in mental health are inconclusive when examining older Arab Americans. For instance, Wrobel, Farrag, and Hymes (2009) found that women reported more depressive symptoms than did men in a community sample of older Arab Americans, whereas Ajrouch (2007a) found no gender differences in reports of feeling down. Research on these populations is much less prevalent than that carried out on African Americans and Latinos, lessening our understanding of how gender intersects with ethnicity and age to shape mental health outcome in these minority groups.

Physical Health

Research on gender and physical health outcomes draws much greater scholarly attention than mental health in later life. The outcome most studied involves functional health and disability, with attention to the age as leveler framework, the role of SES, and immigration experiences.

Once again, the better part of research in this area focuses on blacks and Latinos, often comparing their trajectories to whites. Warner and Brown (2011) use the Health and Retirement Study to examine intraindividual trajectories, comparing men and women across three groups: non-Hispanic white, black, and Mexican Americans. Findings illustrate that men overall have less disability than women in all groups, and gender gaps are wider among minorities than whites. Furthermore, black and Mexican women report the greatest number and similar prevalence of functional limitations. Yet, it may be that black women have differential rates of change in disability (Fuller-Thomson, Nuru-Jeter, Minkler, & Guralnik, 2009; Kim & Miech, 2009). Indeed, Warner and Taylor (2011) show unique experiences among black women, who experience accelerated functional limitations from mid-fifties to mid-sixties, but then slower rates after that, what the authors term accelerated disability or accelerated aging. Additionally, the "weathering hypothesis" advances that, due to structural discrimination, which exerts negative health outcomes on women's bodies, the optimal fertility timing for African American women in the United States is earlier than white women (Geronimus, Hicken, Keene, & Bound, 2006). Due to coping with structural insults, such as stress responses to discrimination and poverty, it has been suggested that African American women experience accelerated biological aging compared to white women in the United States (Geronimus et al., 2010).

The age-as-leveler explanation nevertheless continues to be a viable explanation for health outcomes between racial groups in later life (Quinones, Liang, Bennett, Xu, & Ye, 2011; Yang & Lee, 2009). Warner and Brown (2011) suggest that age as leveler may play a role after the age of 75, but not in middle and young-old age. Yet, recent work suggested a gendered experience. Kim and Miech (2009) found that differences in functional health between black and white men remain constant over time and into old age. Among women, however, the rate of disability slows among black women in young-old age and converges in later-old age. As a result, the age as leveler notion may be specific to women only, challenging the notion that biological processes alone or social insurance programs that provide age-based resources in later life (House et al., 1994) are the mechanism since only women are affected. Kim and Miech (2009) furthermore illustrated that SES differences did not explain the racial convergence, and given that panel data were analyzed, cohort experiences of racial discrimination were ruled out.

It is now understood that some minority groups experience more SES disadvantage over the life course than others. For instance, Mexican men and women report more disadvantaged early life SES than black men and women, regardless of gender (Warner & Taylor, 2011), whereas Asian and Arab Americans seem to live in households with higher than average income and education levels (Read, 2004). SES differences explain racial difference in health differentially for men and women. More specifically, it appears that SES played a lesser role in explaining racial inequalities for women than for men. For instance, Fuller-Thomson et al. (2009) used 2003 American Community Survey data and found that SES (education and poverty levels) explained 90% of the racial difference in disability (functional limitation and activities of daily living [ADL]) prevalence among men, but only 75% among women between the ages of 55 to 64, which become even more apparent among those aged 65 to 74, where SES explained only 50% of racial difference exacerbated among women aged 65 to 74. Furthermore, Warner and Taylor (2011) found that SES explained racial differences in health among men in early old age, but not among women. These findings on aging and functional disability point to the complex pathways through which gender, SES, and race interact over the life course.

Native American functional health tends to be poorer than any other racial/ethnic group (Altman & Rasch, 2000). On a national adult sample, women reported higher levels of functional limitations than Native American men, as well as higher levels than women in other groups, including African Americans (Altman & Rasch, 2000). Furthermore, findings from a representative sample of Native American elders living in all 12 Indian Health Service regional areas in the United States showed that women reported more functional limitations than men in later life (Ruthig & Allery, 2008). Gender differences were moderated, however, by health outlook. Ruthig and Allery found that men and women reported no differences in functional health when they were realistic about their good health, yet women who were pessimistic about their good health reported more functional difficulties than men who were pessimistic about their good health. It is not clear, however, whether gender differences vary by tribe in later life. Among older Navajos living in Arizona, functional health status appeared not to differ by gender (Fitzpatrick, Alemán, & Tran, 2008). Interestingly, even while health outcomes among younger samples may vary for Native Americans depending on place and/ or tribe, gender differences are not always obvious (Sprague et al., 2010).

The role of immigration must also be recognized. Immigration is a growing area in need of better understanding with regard to gender differences in physical health outcomes as people age. Immigrant women appear to be less "selected" on health when they immigrate, as they are more likely to leave their homelands for family reasons as opposed to economic opportunity (Cerrutti & Massey, 2001; Purkayastha, 2005). Indeed, the immigrant physical health advantage among adults appears to be driven by men, and the gender gap in health outcomes is greater among immigrants than the U.S.-born (Read & Reynolds, 2012; Wakabayashi, 2010), though such differences seem to vary by whether immigration occurred in early or late life and which health outcome was examined. For instance, Wakabayashi (2010) examined a longitudinal sample of older adults from the Health and Retirements Study, and found that later-life immigrant women reported worse ADL limitations over time than U.S.-born women, yet earlier life immigrant men reported worse ADL limitations over time than U.S.-born men. Both gender and immigrant differences, however, may reflect not only socioeconomic disparities, but also incidence of doctor visits. In an examination of Mexican and Middle Eastern adult immigrants from the National Health Interview Survey, Read and Reynolds (2012) found that knowing one has an illness, for example, having been diagnosed by a physician, reflected differences identified along both gender and immigrant dimensions. Moreover, gender patterns in immigrant health trajectories over the life course seemed to stem from access to socioeconomic resources rather than ethnic cultural factors (Wakabayashi, 2010). National origin, however, may indicate key differences in how gender patterns vary with regard to physical health.

Research on the physical health of Asian Americans and Arab Americans is growing, though gender patterns across the life course are difficult to identify. Recent evidence shows the utility in disaggregating groups from these larger pan-ethnic categories. One mounting effort has been the intent to separate Native Hawaiian and Pacific Islanders from the broad categorization of Asian Americans. Native Hawaiians are found to resemble African Americans in their mortality patterns (Panapasa, Mau, Williams, & McNally, 2010), though whether or not Native Hawaiian women face similar patterns as African American women has not yet been determined. A comparative examination of morbidity, however, showed that Native Hawaiian women reported greater rates of cancer than Caucasian, Japanese, or Filipino women in Hawaii (Johnson, Oyama, LeMarchand, & Wilkens, 2004). Furthermore, a health advantage may not reflect the situation of all immigrants. In particular, evidence on Arab Americans, in general, runs in contrast to the immigrant health literature where evidence shows no advantage (Ajrouch, 2007b), or that U.S.-born Arab Americans report better health than Arab immigrants (Abdulrahim & Baker, 2009). This pattern extended to a national sample of older adults identified from the 2000 U.S. census. Analysis revealed that immigrant Arab American elders had a higher sex- and age-adjusted prevalence of having a physical (limited in one or more basic physical activities such as walking, climbing stairs, reaching, lifting, carrying) or self-care (dressing, bathing, or getting around inside the home) disability compared to U.S.-born Arab Americans (Dallo, Al-Snih, & Ajrouch, 2009). Advantages in health appear accounted for by the U.S.-born generation's possession of more human capital, specifically higher education levels, and better English language skills. National origin diversity also arose as an important factor for health status among Arab American elders. Dallo and colleagues showed that older adults from Iraq and Syria reported the highest estimates of having a physical disability compared to individuals from other Arab countries. Individuals from Iraq and Lebanon reported the highest estimates of having a self-care disability compared to other countries. Although gender differences did not constitute the focus of the above analysis, findings showed that foreign-born Arab American women reported higher levels of physical disability but lower prevalence of self-care disability than their U.S.-born counterparts. Furthermore, Ajrouch (2007b) found that educational level, more than gender or immigrant status, was a most important influence on health as indicated by self-ratings, chronic illness count, and functional ability on an older sample of Arab Americans. In sum, the available research on Asian and Arab Americans focused on adult samples, documenting patterns overall with preliminary attention to gender.

The minority health debate plays out differentially, depending on health outcome examined and minority groups compared. The study of minority health must carefully delineate an approach to recognize its multidimensional nature. Furthermore, understanding gendered dimensions of the minority experience is imperative, with a need to look more at within-group patterns (are there heterogeneous age trajectories of disabilities within groups), and widen the groups studied by disaggregating pan-ethnic categories. The accumulating research does suggest that origins of racial/ethnic health disparities appear to be gendered (Warner & Taylor, 2011).

GENDERED LIFE COURSE IN RACIAL AND ETHNIC PERSPECTIVE

Although gender structures life course trajectories, the unique experiences by virtue of racial/ethnic group membership must be considered. Gender roles are most commonly explained within the context of family relations (Hill, 2002; Read & Oselin, 2008; Parrado et al., 2005), but contexts of migration heavily influence gender experiences. For instance, colonization weighs on Native Americans and Native Hawaiians (Panapasa et al., 2010; Walters & Simoni, 2002), nonvoluntary migration on African Americans (Collins, 1990), and voluntary migration on others (Paraddo, Flippen, & McQuiston, 2005; Read & Reynolds, 2012). We describe the importance of each mode of entry (colonization, nonvoluntary, and voluntary) to the United States for "doing gender" and then consider how such experiences inform intersections between gender and race/ethnicity in mental and physical health over the life course.

Colonization constitutes the means by which Native Americans became a minority group in the United States. The end results of colonization included not only land confiscation and genocide, but also a concerted effort to eradicate the culture of Native Americans among those who survived, including the powerful and central role of women (LaFromboise, Heyle, & Ozer, 1990; Walters & Simoni, 2002). Such injustices have yielded historical trauma that continues today. The stress of such trauma has been introduced as key to better understanding mental and physical health outcomes over the life course, though little attention has focused on comparative research in the areas of gender and health patterns. We now know that exposure to stress is unequally distributed in populations, and that accumulation of stress is greatest among racial/ethnic minorities, who incur an additional level of stress via acts of discrimination (Thoits, 2010). Yet, the historical circumstances of that stress may reveal key insights into the roles of women and men, and how such expectations and experiences inform health outcomes.

The nonvoluntary migration and the enslavement of African Americans suggests that traditional masculine and feminine ideals prominent in middle-class white America have not described African American men's or women's experiences. Due to the legacy of slavery and pervasive discrimination that followed, men have historically been denied opportunities to assume the bread winner role and women have taken to the expectation that they should be financially independent and strong (Collins, 1990). A rising middle class following the Civil Rights Movement has led to variations in gender expectations, and a growing recognition that the meaning of gender equality among African Americans may not necessarily reflect the traditional role of homemaker as gender oppression. For instance, Hill (2002, p. 502) explored gender socialization in socioeconomically diverse families and found that masculine and feminine ideals were shaped by class and family structure, so that the "practical realities of everyday life shape how gender gets done in the family" regardless of gender ideals. The plethora of research that addresses African American health over the life course, and new findings suggesting the centrality of gender, may benefit from considering African American men's and women's roles historically, and how they are changing. A promising future direction, for example, includes direct examination of masculinity ideals (Griffith, Gunter, & Watkins, 2012). Moreover, consideration of how health behaviors, mental health, and physical health inform one another may provide a deeper understanding of health trajectories among minority groups (Jackson, Knight, & Rafferty, 2010). Explicit attention to how African American men and women "do gender" across the life course, including in middle and old age, may provide new insights into racial/ethnic health disparities.

Voluntary migration influences men's and women's power in various ways. Much of the literature has focused on women, however. Migration sometimes undermines a woman's power if she becomes more dependent on a spouse given her limited human capital (Parrado et al., 2005) or enhances it due to her central and contiguous role in family matters (Yee, 1989), or if the woman assumes the role of bread winner post-migration. A mounting set of literature also suggests that first- and second-generation immigrant women are given the responsibility of carrying on homeland culture, and hence often find their movements and opportunities restricted in the United States as they symbolize the homeland culture through their actions, attitudes, and behaviors (Ajrouch, 2004; Espiritu, 2001; Parrado et al., 2005). Comparative research has provided the most telling information on gender and health (hypertension and self-rated health), suggesting that the immigrant advantage is driven by men (Read & Reynolds, 2012), though still needed are longitudinal panel studies to better identify whether such patterns hold over time and in late life.

FUTURE DIRECTIONS

The intersectionality paradigm has provided new directions for identifying the importance of gender as a key element for predicting health across the life course. Research that seeks to better understand gender and minority aging over the life course would benefit from expanding four areas: comparative analysis, representative samples, diversity within larger groups, and meanings.

Comparative analysis is in advanced form when considering African American and Hispanic populations. Representative and longitudinal samples are available, advancing our knowledge about the role of gender and minority aging. Severely lacking, however, are representative and longitudinal samples of other minority groups. Comparative gender and aging research on understudied groups of Asian Americans, Native Americans, and Arab Americans would move the field forward in important ways. Moreover, the U.S. census identifies a growing racial category termed "some other race." Attention to the fluid and changing nature of race and ethnicity must be researched to better understand the diversity of aging experiences. Given that "doing" gender appeared to reflect mode of entry to the United States, the ways in which gendered life experiences play out for those who do not readily identify with accepted racial categories needs more attention. Furthermore, the pan-ethnic or umbrella terms used to categorize racial and ethnic groups in the United States serve to homogenize experiences of diverse groups of people, leading to the potential for misleading conclusions. For instance, the Hispanic subgroups of Mexican, Puerto Rican, and Cuban each invoke unique historical circumstances in relations with the United States, conditions of immigration, and racial classifications. Disaggregating the Hispanic/Latino umbrella group to identify subgroups would improve our understandings of how gender/race/ethnicity intersections account for distinct experiences in later life and over the life course. Finally, meanings attributed to aging, gender, and health through qualitative approaches would elaborate cultural aspects of aging and health, and in comparative perspective provide unprecedented knowledge about the life course.

Some suggest that changing roles of women and men, for example, higher prevalence of women working outside of the home, as well as a globalizing economy may reflect more equal opportunities in gendered life course experiences (Moen & Spencer, 2006). Yet, African American women have historically assumed public roles of work (Collins, 1990; Hill, 2002). Women and men from immigrant cultures incur an added layer of difference in experiences due to competing norms and expectations from both homeland and host country cultures. Delineating processes by which groups become a minority yield important insights for better identifying the importance of gender to health and well-being. Application of the intersectionality framework in future studies of minority aging would enrich both theoretical as well as practical understandings of links between gender and health/well-being across the life course.

NOTE

1. Includes those who listed their ancestry as an Arabic-speaking country, including Arab, Arabic, and Middle East, but excluding those who listed Assyrian, Chaldean, or Syriac.

REFERENCES

Abdulrahim, S. (2008). "White" or "Other": Racial subjectivity and the Arab immigrant experience in the United States. In A. Jamal & N. Naber (Eds.), *Race and Arab Americans before and after 9/11: From invisible citizens to visible subjects*. Syracuse, NY: Syracuse University Press.

Abdulrahim, S., & Baker, W. (2009). Differences in self-rated health by immigrant status and Language preference among Arab Americans in the Detroit metropolitan area. *Social Science and Medicine, 68*(12), 2097–2103.

Ajrouch, K. J. (2004). Gender, race, and symbolic boundaries: Contested spaces of identity among Arab-American adolescents. *Sociological Perspectives, 47*, 371–391.

Ajrouch, K. J. (2007a). Resources and well-being among Arab-American elders. *Journal of Cross-Cultural Gerontology, 22*(2), 167–182.

Ajrouch, K. J. (2007b). Health disparities and Arab American elders: Does intergenerational support buffer the inequality-health link? *Journal of Social Issues, 63*(4), 745–758.

Ajrouch, K. J., Blandon, A., & Antonucci, T. C. (2005). Social networks among men and women: The effects of age and socioeconomic status. *Journal of Gerontology: Social Sciences, 60B*, 311–317.

Akiyama, H., & Antonucci, T. C. (2002). Gender differences in depressive symptoms: Insights from a life span perspective on life stages and social networks. In J. A. Levy & B. A. Pescosolido (Eds.), *Social networks and health* (Vol. 8, pp. 343–358). Oxford, UK: Elsevier Science.

Altman, B. M., & Rasch, E. K. (2000). Disability among Native Americans. In B. Altman, S. N. Barnartt, G. E. Hendershot, & S. A. Larson (Eds.), *Using survey data to study disability: Results from the National Health Survey on disability* (Vol. 3, pp. 299–326). Bingley, UK: Emerald Group.

Angel, R. J., & Angel, J. L. (2006). Diversity and aging in the United States. In R. H. Binstock & L. K. George (Eds.), *Handbook of aging and the social sciences* (6th ed., pp. 94–110). London, UK: Elsevier.

Barer, B. M. (1994). Men and women aging differently. *International Journal of Aging and Human Development, 38*, 29–40.

Burton, L. M. (1996). Age norms, the timing of family role transitions, and intergenerational caregiving among aging African American women. *The Gerontologist, 36*(2), 199–208.

Calasanti, T. M., & Slevin, K. F. (2001). *Gender, social inequalities, and aging.* New York, NY: Alta Mira Press.

Chiribiga, D. A., Jang, Y., Banks, S., & Kim, G. (2007). Acculturation and its effect on depressive symptom structure in a sample of Mexican American elders. *Hispanic Journal of Behavioral Sciences, 29*(1), 83–100.

Cornell, S., & Hartmann, D. S. (1998). *Ethnicity and race: Making identities in a changing world.* Thousand Oaks, CA: Pine Forge Press.

Collins, P. H. (1989). The social construction of Black feminist thought. *Signs: Journal of Women in Culture and Society, 14*(4), 745–773.

Dallo, F., Al-Snih, S., & Ajrouch, K. J. (2009). The prevalence of disability among US- and foreign-born Arab Americans: Results from the 2000 US Census. *Gerontology, 55*(2), 153–161.

Espiritu, Y. L. (2001). "We don't sleep around like White girls do": Family culture and gender in Filipina American lives. *Signs, 26*(2), 415–440.

Estes, C. (2001). *Social policy and aging.* Thousand Oaks, CA: Sage.

Ferraro, K. F. (2007). The gerontological imagination. In J. M. Wilmoth & K. F. Ferraro (Eds.), *Gerontology: Perspectives and issues* (3rd ed., pp. 325–342). New York, NY: Springer.

Fitzpatrick, T. R., Alemán, S., & Tran, T. V. (2008). Factors that contribute to levels of independent activity functioning among a group of Navajo elders. *Research on Aging, 30*, 318–333.

Ford, C. L., & Harawa, N. T. (2010). A new conceptualization of ethnicity for social epidemiologic and health equity research. *Social Science & Medicine, 71*, 251–258.

Fuller-Thomson, E., Nuru-Jeter, A., Minkler, M., & Guralnik, J. M. (2009). Black-White disparities in disability among older Americans: Further untangling the role of race and socio-economic status. *Journal of Aging and Health, 21*(5), 677–698.

Geronimus, A. T., Hicken, M., Keene, D., & Bound, J. (2006). "Weathering" and age patterns of allostatic load scores among blacks and whites in the United States. *American Journal of Public Health, 96*(5), 826–833.

Geronimus, A., Hicken, M., Pearson, J., Seashols, S., Brown, K., & Cruz, T. (2010). Do US Black women experience stress-related accelerated biological aging?: A novel theory and first population-based test of Black-White differences in telomere length. *Human Nature, 21*(1), 19–38.

Glenn, E. N. (1999). The social construction and institutionalization of gender and race: An integrative framework. In M. M. Ferree, J. Lorber, & B. B. Hess (Eds.), *Revisioning gender*. Walnut Creek, CA: Alta Mira Press.

Griffith, D. M., Gunter, K., & Watkins, D. C. (2012). Measuring masculinity in research on men of color: Findings and future directions. *American Journal of Public Health, 102*(S2), S187–S194.

Harawa, N. T., & Ford, C. L. (2009). The foundation of modern racial categories and implications for research on black/white disparities in health. *Ethnicity and Disease, 19*, 209–217.

Hartmann, H., & English, A. (2009). Older women's retirement security: A primer. *Journal of Women, Politics, & Policy, 30*(203), 109–140.

Hendricks, J. (2004). Public policies and old age identity. *Journal of Aging Studies, 18*(3), 246–260.

Hill, S. A. (2002). Teaching and doing gender in African American families. *Sex Roles, 47*(11/12), 493–506.

House, J. S., Lepkowski, J. M., Kinney, A. M., Mero, R. P., Kessler, R. C., & Herzog A. R. (1994). The social stratification of aging and health. *Journal of Health and Social Behavior, 35*(3), 213–234.

Jackson, J. S., Knight, K. M., & Rafferty, J. A. (2010). Race and unhealthy behaviors: Chronic stress, the HPA axis, and physical and mental health disparities over the life course. *American Journal of Public Health, 100*(5), 933–939.

Jaret, C. (1995). *Contemporary racial and ethnic relations*. New York, NY: Harper Collins College.

Johnson, D. B., Oyama, N., LeMarchand, L., & Wilkens, L. (2004). Native Hawaiians mortality, morbidity, and lifestyle: Comparing data from 1982, 1990, and 2000. *Pacific Health Dialog, 11*(2), 120–130.

Kent, D. P. (1971). The elderly in minority groups: Variant patterns of aging. *The Gerontologist, 11*, 26–29.

Kim, J., & Miech, R. (2009). The Black-White difference in age trajectories of functional health over the life course. *Social Science & Medicine, 68*, 717–725.

Knodel, J., & Ofstedal, M. B. (2003). Gender and aging in the developing world: Where are the men? *Population and Development Review, 29*(4), 677–698.

LaFromboise, T. D., Heyle, A. M., & Ozer, E. J. (1990). Changing and diverse roles of women in American Indian Cultures. *Sex Roles, 22*(7/8), 455–476.

Lewis, A. E. (2002). Whiteness studies: Past research and future directions. *African American Research Perspectives, 8*(1), 1–16.

Manthorpe, J., & Hettiaratchy, P. (1993). Ethnic minority elders in the UK. *International Review of Psychiatry, 5*, 171–178.

Minkler, M., & Stone, R. (1985). The feminization of poverty and older women. *The Gerontologist, 25*(4), 351–357.

Moen, P. (2001). The gendered life course. In R. H. Binstock & L. K. George (Eds.), *Handbook of aging: Social sciences* (pp. 179–196). San Diego, CA: Academic Press.

Moen, P., & Spencer, D. (2006). Converging divergences in age, gender, health and well-being: Strategic selection in the third age. In R. H. Binstock & L. K. George (Eds.), *Handbook of aging and the social sciences* (6th ed., pp. 127–144). London, UK: Elsevier.

Mullings, L., & Schulz, A. J. (2006). Intersectionality and health: An introduction. In L. Mullings & A. J. Schulz (Eds.), *Gender, race, class, and health: An intersectional approach* (pp. 3–17). San Francisco, CA: John Wiley & Sons.

National Urban League (1964). *Double jeopardy: The older Negro in American today*. Washington, DC: Library of Congress.

Omi, M., & Winant, H. (1986). *Racial formation in the United States*. New York, NY: Routledge.

Panapasa, S. V., Mau, M. K., Williams, D. R., & McNally, J. W. (2010). Mortality patterns of Native Hawaiians across their lifespan: 1990–2000. *American Journal of Public Health, 100*(11), 2304–2310.

Paraddo, E. A., Flippen, C. A., & McQuiston, C. M. (2005). Migration and relationship power among Mexican women. *Demography, 42*(2), 347–372.

Peek, M. K., Stimpson, J. P., Townsend, A. L., & Markides, K. S. (2006). Well-being in older Mexican American Spouses. *The Gerontologist, 46*(2), 258–265.

Phillips, J., Ajrouch, K. J., & Hillcoat-Nalletamby, S. (2010). *Key concepts in social gerontology*. London, UK: Sage.

Purkayastha, B. (2005). Skilled migration and cumulative disadvantage: The case of highly qualified Asian Indian immigrant women in the U.S. *Geoforum, 36*(2), 181–196.

Purkayastha, B. (2012). Patricia Hill Collins symposium: Intersectionality in a transnational world. *Gender & Society, 26*(1), 55–66.

Quinones, A. R., Liang, J., Bennett, J. M., Xu, X., & Ye, W. (2011). How does the trajectory of multimorbidity vary across black, white, and Mexican Americans in middle and old age? *The Journals of Gerontology, 66B*(6), 739–749.

Riley, M. W., Kahn, R. K., & Foner, A. (Eds.). (1994). *Age and structural lag.* New York, NY: Wiley.

Read, J. G. (2004). *Culture, class and work among Arab American women.* New York, NY: LFB Scholarly Publishing.

Read, J. G., & Reynolds, M. M. (2012). Gender differences in immigrant health: The case of Mexican and Middle Eastern immigrants. *Journal of Health and Social Behavior, 53*(1), 99–123.

Read, J. G., & Oselin, S. (2008). Gender and the education-employment paradox in ethnic and religious contexts: The case of Arab Americans. *American Sociological Review, 73*, 296–313.

Rumbaut, R. G. (2006). The making of a people. In M. Tienda & F. Mitchell (Eds.), *Hispanics and the future of America. Panel on Hispanics in the United States.* National Research Council Committee on Population, Division of Behavioral and Social Sciences and Education. Washington, DC: The National Academies Press.

Russell, D., & Taylor, J. (2009). Living alone and depressive symptoms: The influence of gender, physical disability, and social support among Hispanic and non-Hispanic older adults. *The Journals of Gerontology: Psychological Sciences and Social Sciences, 64B*(1), 95–104.

Ruthig, J. C., & Allery, A. (2008). Native American elders' health congruence: The role of gender and corresponding functional well-being, hospital admissions, and social engagement. *Journal of Health Psychology, 13*(8), 1072–1081.

Saraksian, N., & Gerstel, N. (2004). Kin support among blacks and whites: Race and family organization. *American Sociological Review, 69*(6), 812–837.

Schieman, S., & Plickert, G. (2007). Functional limitations and changes in levels of depression among older adults: A multiple hierarchy stratification perspective. *Journal of Gerontology, 62B*(1), S36–S42.

Smedley, A., & Smedley, B. D. (2005). Race as biology is fiction, racism as a social problem is real: Anthropological and historical perspectives on the social construction of race. *American Psychologist, 60*(1), 16–26.

Sprague, D., Bogart, A., Manson, S., Buchwald, D., & Goldberg, J.; the AI-SUPERPFP Team (2010). The relationship between post-traumatic stress disorder, depression, and lung disorders in Northern Plains and Southwest American Indians, *Ethnicity & Health, 15*(6), 569–579.

Stoller, E. P., & Gibson, R. C. (Eds.) (2000). *Worlds of difference: Inequality in the aging experience.* London, UK: Pine Forge Press.

Thoits, P. A. (2010). Stress and Health: Major findings and policy implications. *Journal of Health and Social Behavior, 51*(S), 541–553.

Thornton Dill, B., & Zambrana, R. E. (2009). Critical thinking about inequality: An emerging lens. In B. Thornton Dill & R. E. Zamrana (Eds.), *Emerging intersections: Race, class and gender in theory, policy, and practice* (pp. 1–21). Piscataway, NJ: Rutgers University Press.

Toothman, E. L., & Barrett, A. E. (2011). Mapping midlife: An examination of social factors shaping conceptions of the timing of middle age. *Advances in Life Course Research, 16*, 99–111.

U.S. Census Bureau (2010). "Census." Retrieved March 15, 2012 from http://factfinder2.census.gov/faces/nav/jsf/pages/searchresults.xhtml?refresh=t

Verbrugge, L. M. (1985). Gender and health: An update on hypotheses and evidence. *Journal of Health and Social Behavior, 26*, 56–82.

Wakabayashi, C. (2010). Effect of immigration and age on health of older people in the United States. *Journal of Applied Gerontology, 29*(6), 697–719.

Walker, A. (2006). Aging and politics: An international perspective. In R. H. Binstock & L. K. George (Eds.), *Handbook of aging and the social sciences* (6th ed., pp. 339–359). London, UK: Elsevier.

Walters, K. L., & Simoni, J. M. (2002). Reconceptualizing Native women's health: An 'indigenist' stress-coping model. *American Journal of Public Health, 92*(4), 520–524.

Wray, S. (2003). Connecting ethnicity, agency and ageing. *Sociological Research Online, 8*(4). Retrieved March 5, 2009 from http://www.socresonline.org.uk/8/4/wray.html

Wrobel, N. H., Farrag, M. F., & Hymes, R. W. (2009). Acculturative stress and depression in an elderly Arabic sample. *Journal of Cross-Cultural Gerontology, 24*(3), 273–290.

Yee, B. W. K. (1989). Loss of one's homeland and culture during the middle years. In R. A. Kalish (Ed.), *Coping with the losses of middle age*. Newbury Park, CA: Sage.

CHAPTER 29

Understanding Age at Onset and Self-Care Management to Explain Racial and Ethnic Cardiovascular Disease Disparities in Middle- and Older-Age Adults

Ronica N. Rooks and Roland J. Thorpe, Jr.

What we have to do is to find a way to celebrate our diversity and debate our differences without fracturing our communities. Hillary Rodham Clinton

We are motivated to understand why African American and other racial and ethnic minority adults experience higher rates of cardiovascular diseases (CVD), often leading to faster disease declines, higher rates of comorbidity and disease-related disability, and earlier deaths from these diseases than white adults (Bulatao & Anderson, 2004; Ferraro & Farmer, 1996; Martin & Soldo, 1997; Whitfield, Thorpe, & Szanton, 2011; Williams & Collins, 1995). Our research has led us to investigate racial health disparities in chronic conditions among older adults and explanations as to why they exist (Rooks & Whitfield, 2004; Rooks et al., 2002, 2008; Thorpe, Brandon, & LaVeist, 2008a; Thorpe et al., 2008b, 2011, 2012). This research has culminated in our desire to prevent and intervene on chronic conditions across racial and ethnic minorities. However, we have come to the conclusion that if we want to prevent or intervene on racial and ethnic CVD disparities, we need to follow younger cohorts over time to understand the natural history of these diseases.

We need to better understand how social and behavioral determinants contribute to CVD development, self-care/management, and subsequent health disparities earlier in adulthood. Middle-age and older age racial and ethnic minorities with lower socioeconomic status (SES) spend fewer years managing disease (i.e., the time after CVD diagnosis and before death spent accessing health care and/or using self-care practices) compared to white adults (Bahrami et al., 2008; Herd, Robert, & House, 2011; Jackson, Govia, & Sellers, 2011; Shantsila, Lip, & Gill, 2011; Williams & Collins, 1995; Zhang et al., 2008). Thus, the focus for this chapter is to (a) examine conceptual frameworks and theories on racial and ethnic health disparities that can apply to CVD among middle-age and older age adults; (b) investigate age at onset/diagnosis of CVD as it varies by race and ethnicity, with some explanations as to why these disparities exist; (c) understand difficulties with CVD self-care/management by race and ethnicity, with some explanations as to why these disparities exist; and (d) discuss future directions, considering data, prevention, and intervention, and policy needs.

CONCEPTUAL MODELS AND THEORIES

Several conceptual models and theories can address racial and ethnic CVD disparities among middle-age and older age adults, including the social determinants of health (SDOH) model, the social-ecological model, and life course theory. The SDOH perspective broadly focuses on any nonmedical factors influencing health, including upstream (i.e., fundamental causes that initiate causal pathways leading to health effects through downstream factors) and downstream (i.e., factors that are temporally and spatially close to health effects but are influenced by upstream factors) determinants (Braveman, Egerter, & Williams, 2011). Examples of upstream determinants include neighborhood conditions, occupation and work conditions, education, income, wealth, racial, and other types of discrimination, which then shape downstream determinants, such as health-related knowledge, attitudes, beliefs, or behaviors.

Although the SDOH model does not exclusively focus on middle-age and older age adults, it may be especially pertinent to these age groups. Earlier onset of chronic conditions and poor disease self-management for racial and ethnic minorities could be associated with their higher likelihood of living in disadvantaged neighborhoods, experiencing poor work conditions, low educational attainment and quality, and high chronic stress related to racial and ethnic bias (Braveman et al., 2011). These exposures may also change, improving or worsening over time, during different life course stages. Furthermore, when considering that middle-age and older age adults have lived with these SDOH exposures longer than children or younger adults, the possibility of experiencing earlier onset of chronic conditions, with poor disease self-management, becomes more plausible.

The social-ecological model is defined as a multidisciplinary conceptual framework focusing on individual and environmental determinants of behavior, with intrapersonal, interpersonal, organizational, community, and public policy levels of influence (Richard, Gauvin, & Raine, 2011). This model views multilevel interventions, evaluation, interaction, reciprocal causation, environmental changes, and individual support as various ways to address health issues. It includes key assumptions about developing effective strategies to promote personal and collective well-being through the social and physical environments (Stokols, 1992, 1996). These environments are characterized by their objective and subjective qualities and proximal or distal scale to individuals and groups. Additionally, these environments have multiple levels of analysis, using diverse methodologies to assess the healthiness of settings and the well-being of individuals and groups.

Of particular relevance to middle-age and older age adults are changes that may occur with aging as they interact with the physical environment and experience difficulties in managing and maintaining their independent, personal health. Physical environments may become more difficult as middle-age and older age adults (a) encounter increased limitations in mobility and housing options (Carp, 1986); (b) spend more time throughout the day in their communities than those in the labor force, because they are often no longer employed; and (c) experience a stronger attachment to place as they grow older, providing a sense of continuity through other changes in the life course (Krause, 2003). These links between the physical environment and older adults likely vary by race and ethnicity and differentially influence the disablement process (Kaplan, 1997; Verbrugge & Jette, 1994). Personal health management, including health behaviors, resources, and beliefs (Meyers, 2007), may also change for aging racial and ethnic minorities as physical environments, mobility, and dependency changes occur.

Racial and ethnic health disparities in middle and older adulthood develop over the life course. Life course theory states that an individual's health is influenced by personal biography, sociocultural factors, and sociocultural times—where both macro and micro factors throughout one's life influence health (Stoller & Gibson, 1997). It suggests that health and disease are influenced by social factors that are accumulated as people move through various life stages and social institutions into older age (Dannefer & Uhlenberg, 1999). As we approach middle and older age these cumulative factors are associated with advantages and disadvantages for health. Jackson, Govia, & Sellers et al. (2011) also suggest that life course models reflecting aging and health disparities among racial and ethnic minorities in the United States must address dynamic intersections of age-, period-, and cohort-related phenomena (e.g., shifting sex ratios, increased longevity as evidenced by increasing numbers of centenarians and growing biomedical technologies, shifting immigration policies related to family reunification, etc.), social identities (e.g., shifting family structures and intergenerational relationships, changing role opportunities, within-group attitudes and behaviors, etc.), and other social and psychological statuses (e.g., gender, SES, and discrimination). This intersectional model discusses the multiple factors that accumulate over time to produce racial and ethnic health disparities from development in the uterus to late life.

Three variants of life course theory exist. The "weathering" hypothesis states that African Americans experience premature health deterioration or accelerated aging over their lifetimes in response to social and economic adversity, as well as related psychosocial stressors such as discrimination (Geronimus, 2001; Geronimus, Bound, Keene, & Hicken, 2007). As a result, African Americans may be biologically older than the same chronologically aged whites due to their chronic and cumulative exposure to stressors, as well as high-effort coping. In a population-based, cohort study of middle-age women, African American women were 7.5 years biologically older than the same chronically aged white women based on shortened telomere length (i.e., the stabilizing caps on chromosomes that are essential to genetic stability and cell functioning; Geronimus et al., 2010). Scientists know that telomeres are shortened by oxidative stress linked to aging, psychosocial stress, biological stress activation, inflammation, and disease development, but in this research, racial differences in telomere length were associated with racial differences in perceived stress, poverty, and waist–hip ratio.

The second variant of life course theory is cumulative (dis)advantage (CDA) theory. It posits that early advantage or disadvantage is essential to how cohorts differ over time. Early life experiences set in motion a chain of risk or protective factors for short- and long-term outcomes. CDA emphasizes that the effects of earlier life experiences accumulate over the life course, which subsequently increase heterogeneity in later life (Dannefer, 1987, 2003; Ferraro, 2006; Ferraro & Kelley-Moore, 2003; O'Rand, 1996). For example, some people are advantaged in their early years, and this advantage may compound over time to produce health benefits. Others are disadvantaged because of social or environmental factors, and these disadvantages also accumulate over time to produce poor health outcomes (Preston, Hill, & Drevenstedt, 1998). Because inequalities typically develop earlier in the life course for most racial and ethnic minorities compared to whites, it is likely that there will be an increase in the variation in health trajectories due to the accumulation of risk factors among minorities (Ferraro, Farmer, & Wybraniec, 1997; Verbrugge & Jette, 1994).

The third variant of life course theory is cumulative inequality theory, proposed as a new way of thinking about how inequality accumulates over the life course (Ferraro & Shippee, 2009). This theory can be viewed as an interdisciplinary approach to the study of aging, including social sciences, biology, epidemiology, and immunology perspectives in five axioms. The first axiom states that social systems generate inequality over the life course, manifested by demographic and developmental processes over time where early life events shape late-life health outcomes. Second, advantages should be viewed as exposures to opportunities, whereas disadvantages should be viewed as exposures to risk, with conceptual and measurement attention given to the magnitude, onset, and duration of advantage and disadvantage exposures. Third, life course trajectories are shaped and modified by the accumulation of risk, available resources, and human agency, leading to differences in how social adversity translates physiologically in individuals. Fourth, people's perceptions of their life trajectories influence their subsequent trajectories, where an individual's subjective views of his/her positions and resources may have more of a health impact than his/her objective positions and resources. And, finally, cumulative inequality may lead to premature mortality, giving the appearance of decreasing inequalities in later life for the remaining cohort.

Thus, cumulative inequality leads to long-term biological changes in humans commonly associated with chronic stressors and the aging process, creating socially stratified groups with different health outcomes and mortality onset. By middle age cumulative inequality processes are well underway. But, a take-away message from this theory is that simply examining older racial and ethnic minorities in prospective cohort studies limits our understanding of the everyday experiences contributing to their survival prior to entry into these studies. Also, these existing cohort studies on older adults state nothing about the many racial and ethnic minorities who did not survive into older age.

The earlier conceptual models and theories provide background support for our literature review on disparities in CVD age at onset/diagnosis and self-care/management practices. Our literature review addresses two of the three phases of health disparities research identified by Kilbourne, Switzer, Hyman, Crowley-Matoka, and Fine (2006), including (a) detecting health disparities among vulnerable groups and (b) understanding and identifying determinants and pathways connecting these groups to poorer health outcomes. In this chapter, we provide insight into the commonalities across racial and ethnic groups for the third phase, assisting with future interventions to reduce and eliminate health disparities. A brief synopsis of the original research reviewed in this chapter can be found in the Appendix table at the end of this chapter.

RACIAL AND ETHNIC VARIATION IN CVD AGE AT ONSET/DIAGNOSIS

An argument emphasizing the importance of determining trends in age at onset/diagnosis in CVD was found in research examining differences between middle age versus older age at onset of diabetes, to assess participants' burden and control of cardiovascular complications (Selvin, Coresh, & Brancati, 2006). Using the 1999 to 2002 National Health and Nutrition Examination Survey (NHANES) data, it was determined that those who had middle-age diabetes onset had a greater burden of micro-vascular disease and poorer glycemic control compared to those who had older age onset. The authors found that these two groups represented distinctly different groups regarding their disease burdens and possible treatment needs. The middle-age onset adults were more likely to be treated for hypertension and high cholesterol, but the older-age onset adults had similar systolic blood pressure and total cholesterol levels, suggesting that the latter group may require less treatment for CVD risk factor control. Thus, research examining the age at onset/diagnosis of CVD by racial and ethnic groups may provide broader insight into premature aging trends in CVD risk factors and outcomes, despite the limited amount of research in this area.

One explanation for racial and ethnic CVD disparities, explored mainly among African Americans compared to whites, is the concept of premature or accelerated aging (Geronimus et al., 2007; Jones, 1994, 2000). This research states that African Americans experience earlier onsets of CVD and faster declines, leading to sicker and shorter lives, often due to SDOH, such as economic adversity and discrimination. In Geronimus' (2007) research, using the NHANES III and IV, she found that African American women experienced a faster increase in hypertension prevalence in young to middle adulthood, reaching a peak high by age 40 years, compared to white women, white men, and African American men. She found inconsistent results when considering explanations of poverty, where lower SES was significantly associated with increased odds of hypertension among the total and white men samples.

In a predominately white sample, Lloyd-Jones, Leip, Larson, Vasan, and Levy (2005) found that the standard age at onset/diagnosis of hypertension in the Framingham Heart Study (FHS) was age 55 years for men and 59 years for women. Compared with white adults, black adults develop hypertension earlier in life and their average blood pressure is much higher (Roger et al., 2012). As a result, black adults have a greater risk of developing more progressive and health-damaging CVD, such as non-fatal and fatal stroke and end-stage kidney disease. The earlier compared to later onset of diabetes and hypertension described by Selvin and colleagues (2006) and Geronimus et al. (2007), respectively, may relate to the chronic burden of coping with accumulated disadvantages for more years in the life course, which is asserted across each of the variants of life course theory.

Using the Health and Retirement Survey, Glymour, Avendaño, Haas, and Berkman (2008) showed that older African Americans compared to white adults, at a mean age of 63.0 versus 64.6 years at study enrollment, had higher unadjusted stroke incidence rates (i.e., the number of new cases per population in a given time period) over a little more than nine years of follow-up (14.2 vs. 10.6 per 1,000 person years). They found that racial differences in stroke incidence were largely explained by low childhood and adult SES and Southern birth state. Glymour and colleagues speculated that their findings were related to the majority of older African Americans being born in southern states, where older African Americans were likely exposed to greater amounts of segregation, poverty, and discrimination in their education and medical care in early life, with detrimental impacts on their health in later life. These findings highlight contextual risk factors embedded within the culture of a geographic region, emphasizing SDOH and the social-ecological models, at each stage of the life course.

Statistics from the 2010 Behavioral Risk Factor Surveillance Survey in the United States showed that the percentage of adults aged more than 18 years with a stroke history by race and ethnicity was 2.4% for non-Hispanic whites; 4.0% for non-Hispanic blacks; 1.4% for Asian and Pacific Islanders; 2.5% for Hispanics; 5.8% for American Indian and Alaska Natives; and 4.1% for other races or multiracial people (Roger et al., 2012). The prevalence of stroke-related symptoms was found to be relatively high in a general population free of a prior diagnosis of stroke or transient ischemic attack (TIA). About 18% of the population aged more than 45 years reported at least one symptom, and stroke symptoms were more likely among black than white adults, those with lower income and educational attainment, and those with fair to poor perceived health status.

In the Coronary Artery Risk Development in Young Adults (CARDIA) study, Bibbins-Domingo et al. (2009) found incident heart failure to be more common among black compared to white participants during a 20-year follow-up. The average age at onset for incident heart failure in black adults was 39 years, and it was predicted by hypertension, obesity, chronic kidney disease, depressed systolic function, and left ventricular hypertrophy 10 to 15 years earlier. Additionally, 87% of the black participants who developed heart failure had untreated or poorly controlled hypertension. The rate of incident heart failure before age 50 years was 20 times greater in black compared to white participants. These results and other research on middle age and older age adults (Bahrami et al., 2008; Loehr, Rosamond, Chang, Folsom, & Chambless, 2008; Kalogeropoulos et al., 2009) have implications for changing the target age of CVD prevention and intervention among African Americans to younger ages in the twenties and thirties.

At age 40 years, the lifetime risk of developing heart failure for both men and women is one in five (Roger et al., 2012). By age 80 years, remaining lifetime risk for development of new heart failure was 20% for men and women, despite a much shorter life expectancy. However, African Americans have a higher prevalence of heart failure than other racial and ethnic groups in the United States (Hunt et al., 2005; Yancy, 2005). Based on the Multi-Ethnic Study of Atherosclerosis (MESA) research, the highest prevalence of heart failure in African Americans is followed by Hispanic, white, and Chinese Americans (Roger et al., 2012).

Among the Native Americans who participated in the Strong Heart Study (SHS), the age-adjusted stroke incidence rate varied by sex (Zhang et al., 2008). Men compared to women had a rate of 707 versus 653 per 100,000 person years. The mean age at first stroke onset was 66.5 years, where the rate for men compared to women was similar (66.2 vs. 66.7). At baseline, those who suffered from incident stroke were more likely to be older; have higher blood pressure, triglycerides, fasting glucose, hemoglobin A1c, insulin, and 2-hour glucose levels; have lower high-density lipoprotein (HDL, "good") cholesterol levels; be less physically active at baseline than those who remained stroke-free; and be past alcohol users. For all strokes, Zhang and colleagues found age, diastolic blood pressure, fasting glucose, smoking, and albuminuria as risk factors for stroke incidence. Their analyses show negative health behaviors contributing to the higher incidence of stroke among Native Americans, which are related to the SDOH model. Compared to data pooled from the Atherosclerosis Risk in Communities Study (ARIC), the Cardiovascular Health Study (CHS), and the FHS, incidence and case-fatality rates (i.e., the ratio of the number of deaths caused by a specified disease to the number of diagnosed cases of that disease) for stroke in this study were higher than those of comparably aged white and black populations in the United States.

Also in the SHS, Best and Colleagues (2011) found that the mean age at onset for an acute myocardial infarction (MI) was 69 years. Making comparisons across similar data, the authors found the mean age at onset of acute MI among Native Americans was older than the mean age of 61 to 62 years in three intervention studies focused on multiple racial and ethnic groups, and similar to a mean age of 66 years in the National Registry of MI. Another comparison of national statistics from the American Heart Association (Lloyd-Jones et al., 2009) shows the mean age for a first heart attack at age 65 and 70 years for men and women, with the mean age at onset for acute MI in the Strong Heart study falling in the middle. Based on prior comparisons, the age at onset of acute MI among Native Americans does not appear to be premature, unlike stroke, among this racial group in the United States.

With regard to Asians, Shantsila and colleagues (2011) conducted a systematic review and found that systolic heart failure among South Asians (i.e., those originating from India, Pakistan, and Bangladesh) tends to manifest earlier in life with a higher prevalence of coronary artery disease and more frequent hospital admissions. Heart failure incidence rates were 56 versus 44 among South Asian compared to white men and 43 versus 41 among South Asian compared to white women, for first hospital admission related to heart failure in the United Kingdom (Blackledge, Newton, & Squire, 2003). South Asians were on average eight years younger than whites at their first hospital admission. Despite their younger age, South Asians compared to whites also had more risk factors, such as lower levels of hemoglobin, higher levels of urinary albumin, and higher prevalence of type II diabetes at hospital discharge. Similar results of higher hospitalizations for heart failure and younger age for South Asians compared to whites were found in Canada (Singh & Gupta, 2005). However, South Asians have greater survival from heart failure than whites, which may be associated with lower rates of left ventricular systolic dysfunction (Shantsila et al., 2011).

Contrary to what is known about the age at onset/diagnosis of CVD in the previous racial groups, Latinos tend to have older onset unless they are compared to whites. Lisabeth, Smith, Brown, Uchino, and Morgenstern (2005) found the age at stroke onset with and without a family history was 71.4 versus 73.9 years in a population surveillance study in Texas, with a majority of Mexican Americans (56%) and non-Hispanic white adults. Another regional examination of stroke found significant differences in the mean age at onset of stroke for Hispanics compared to whites, 61 versus 69 years, and for Native Americans (56 years) compared to Hispanics and whites (Frey, Jahnke, & Bulfinch, 1998). Hemorrhage strokes were also significantly more prevalent among Hispanics than Native Americans or whites, which may reflect a combination of risk factors among Hispanics, including lower blood pressure control, sensitivity to the effect of hypertension because of relative arterial wall thinness, and alcohol intake.

Significant risk factors for stroke in Frey et al.'s (1998) study included hypertension, found to be more prevalent among Hispanics than whites; type II diabetes, more prevalent among Native Americans than Hispanics and whites; smoking, more prevalent among whites than Hispanics and Native Americans; cardiac disease, more prevalent among whites than Hispanics; and heavy alcohol intake, more prevalent among Native Americans than Hispanics and whites. The lower age at stroke onset was consistent with prior stroke studies, showing a younger age at onset in Hispanics compared to whites in the northern Manhattan (67 vs. 80 years) and San Diego (60 vs. 63 years) studies. In addition, negative health behaviors, as part of the SDOH model, were consistently mentioned as relevant stroke risk factors among Hispanics and Native Americans.

In summary, previous research shows the greatest disparities in age at onset/diagnosis among African American and Native Americans for stroke and among African Americans and South Asians for heart failure. While there is little information on the age at onset/diagnosis of acute MI by race and ethnicity, available data show that Native Americans have a moderate risk of acute MI compared to other existing studies on multiple racial and ethnic groups. Racial and ethnic comparisons for the age at onset/diagnosis for hypertension could not be made due to the lack of literature on the topics. However, the literature is clear that African Americans experience disparities in hypertension, as they often have a younger age at onset/diagnosis, with higher prevalence rates, than other racial and ethnic groups. Finally, across this literature on the various types of CVD, common risk factors from our conceptual models and theories mention SES at different stages of the life course, geographic region, and health behaviors.

RACIAL AND ETHNIC VARIATION IN CVD SELF-CARE/MANAGEMENT

An earlier age at onset/diagnosis of CVD for racial and ethnic minorities potentially leads to earlier health declines and earlier death because of access to care and self-management difficulties. For example, among hypertensive adults, 80% are aware of their condition, 71% are using antihypertensive medication, and only 48% of those who are aware of their hypertension have it controlled (Roger et al., 2012). CVD self-management difficulties across middle-age and older age racial and ethnic minorities may be related to (a) not recognizing CVD symptoms; (b) patient–provider communication difficulties; and (c) self-care practices. These may also be secondary and tertiary prevention points.

Not Recognizing CVD Symptoms and Delaying Medical Care

A detrimental consequence of not recognizing CVD symptoms is delayed medical care. Ferris, Robertson, Fabunmi, and Mosca (2005) found racial and ethnic differences in stroke risk awareness among women, where more Hispanics and blacks compared to white adults were likely to report not being informed about stroke, warning signs or symptoms, or treatment. White compared to Hispanic and black women were more likely to identify sudden weakness/numbness of the face or a limb on one side, difficulty talking or understanding speech, sudden dimness or loss of vision, often in one eye, and dizziness as warning signs of stroke. Also, more white women were aware that at the onset of a stroke, treatment could be given to break up blood clots compared to Hispanic and black women. Similarly, in a focus group study of Samoans' and Native Hawaiians' perspectives on heart failure, Keawe'aimoku Kaholokula, Saito, Mau, Latimer, & Seto (2008) found many SDOH and social-ecological model barriers to heart failure care. These barriers included poor knowledge of heart failure, lack of trust in physicians' care (Native Hawaiians only), poor physician–patient communication, financial burden, difficulty in making dietary changes, and competing demands on time, such as childcare, work, and family obligations.

Ting et al. (2008) found that a combination of risk factors for MI, including those who were aged more than 70 years, black or Hispanic race or ethnicity, female sex, and had type II diabetes, represented a vulnerable subgroup. This subgroup had larger delays compared with patients who had a single risk factor for delay. The authors believe that improving patient responsiveness and access to care in this subgroup represents an important opportunity to improve quality of care and minimize health disparities. In particular, knowledge improvements about symptoms and treatment for stroke and MI could contribute to reduced racial and ethnic disparities in CVD morbidity and subsequent mortality.

Among Native American women, Struthers, Savik, and Hodge (2004) asked participants what they would do if they experienced crushing pain in their chest that lasted longer than 15 minutes, possibly indicating a heart attack. Over two thirds of the women responded that they would take an active response and either immediately go to a medical facility or call an ambulance. The remainder of women indicated passive responses (31.2%), that they would sit down and wait until it passed (23.3%), go to a medical facility when it becomes convenient (3.2%), continue doing what they were doing and hope it went away (2.1%), do something else, responding as "other" (2.6%), or go to a traditional healer (0.1%), while others would not answer the question (2.0%). Comparisons between the passive and active groups showed the passive group was younger in age (less than 45 years) and less educated (less than a high school graduate). Thus, the challenge in addressing racial and ethnic CVD disparities may be in education. Specific cardiovascular education may help people recognize symptoms of cardiovascular events and what to do in response to them, particularly discussing complications resulting from inaction.

Patient–Provider Communication Difficulties

Previous research has shown that among those who seek and use health information, African Americans and Latinos are more likely than whites to use health information outside of the medical encounter, often in self-care practices (Rooks, Wiltshire, Elder, BeLue, & Gary, 2012). African Americans and Latinos compared to whites are also more likely to use health information to change their approach to maintaining their health and better understand how to treat illnesses. These populations may also be more likely to use health information for self-care practices in lieu of seeking health care due to racial and ethnic disparities in SDOH such as health insurance (Town, Wholey, Feldman, & Burns, 2007), access to care difficulties (Haas et al., 2004), and/or perceived discrimination attributed to cultural and communication barriers (Blanchard, Nayar, & Lurie, 2007; Collins et al., 2002; Johnson, Roter, Powe, & Cooper, 2004). Additionally, Greer (2010) found that hypertensive African American patients who faced overt and subtle racial discrimination had negative emotional reactions, mistrust of their providers, decided not to return for follow-up appointments or did not schedule their next appointments, and did not trust prescriptions or referrals from these providers. Her research suggests that African Americans may turn to self-care after experiencing negative medical encounters.

Self-Care Practices

Complementary and alternative medicines (CAM) are a type of self-care practice. Asian American older adults are more likely to use CAM, followed by Hispanic, white, and African American older adults (Arcury et al., 2006). Research on CAM use, such as prayer, meditation, diet-based therapies, and natural products like herbal medicines and teas, is often associated with lack of health insurance, complaints of expensive medical care, difficulties with medical professionals diagnosing or treating health problems, and treating illnesses rather than prevention (Arcury et al., 2006; Graham et al., 2005; Trangmar & Diaz, 2008). Keawe'aimoku Kaholokula et al. (2008) also found that Native Hawaiians believed traditional Hawaiian healing methods, including Hawaiian therapeutic massage and medicinal herbs, might be as or more effective in treating heart failure than Western medicine. Therefore, racial and ethnic minorities may use CAM instead of or in supplement to medical care to reduce expenses or to avoid poor quality health care.

Elaborating on one aspect of poor quality of care, Shippee, Schafer, and Ferraro (2012) found an association between discrimination and CAM use in self-care practices. Experiencing racial discrimination within and outside of medical encounters was associated with greater CAM use and more types of CAM in black adults. The authors suggest that CAM use is a way for those experiencing racial discrimination to reassert control over their health. However, a drawback to using CAM is the possibility of patients, when they do seek medical care, of not informing their providers of CAM use and its potential negative interactions with prescription drugs.

Another issue associated with self-care is the possibility that older compared to middle-age and younger adults are more likely to use self-care effectively to control their health. Among first-generation Korean American immigrants, Kim et al. (2010) found that participants who were older compared to middle-age were more likely to be compliant (i.e., if they had transmitted greater than or equal to 24 weeks of home blood pressure monitoring recordings) with home blood pressure monitoring instruction. Participants who were more compliant were four times more likely than those who were not compliant to achieve blood pressure control by the end of the intervention period.

Similarly, Warren-Findlow and Seymour (2011) found that older compared to younger African Americans with hypertension were more likely to use self-care effectively to control their blood pressure. For four of the six recommended Joint National Committee on Prevention, Detection, Evaluation, and Treatment of High Blood Pressure (JNC7) guidelines for hypertension self-care activities, the authors found acceptable prevalence rates: 58.6% for adherence to hypertension medications, 52.2% for engaging in physical activity most days of the week, 75% for not smoking, and 66% for not drinking alcohol. However, for a low-salt diet and weight management activities, adherence was lower at 22% and 30.1%, respectively. Older average age was significantly associated with a few of the self-care activities, such as medication adherence versus nonadherence (mean age 55.8 vs. 49.0 years), not smoking versus smoking (mean age 54.9 vs. 47.3 years), and not drinking alcohol versus drinking (mean age 57.2 vs. 45.2 years). Warren-Findlow, Seymour, and Shenk's (2011) research also found that older African American parents were more compliant to hypertension medication adherence than their adult children. They found evidence of an intergenerational transfer of hypertension self-care knowledge from older parent to adult child, influencing their children's medication adherence.

Social isolation may also play a role in self-care practices. Hinojosa, Haun, Hinojosa, and Rittman (2011) found high reports (44%–55%) of social isolation among Veteran stroke survivors of various racial and ethnic backgrounds, but racial and ethnic differences in social isolation were not significant. Over a 1-year rehabilitation period, about 61% of stroke survivors reported no change in social isolation. During this period, those who were socially isolated had a decreased ability to manage daily domestic, leisure/work, and outdoor activities associated with instrumental activities of daily living. Thus, social isolation impaired stroke survivors' activity functioning and likely their self-care abilities.

In summary, the prior research on racial and ethnic variation in CVD self-care/management in middle- and older-age minorities shows some guidelines for future prevention and intervention. While having health insurance and access to care may account for some CVD health disparities attributed to management difficulties, self-care practices may play an equal role in managing CVD. Improved and culturally sensitive, patient education on CVD risk factors, symptom recognition, and medical adherence, as well as provider discussions on CAM and potential prescription drug interactions, are common themes across racial and ethnic groups. Another barrier to managing CVD, social isolation, could be improved through social support provided by family and/or friends. Finally, improved provider education is needed, such as improving patient–doctor communication, building trust, and reducing discrimination to avoid patients' not adhering to their provider's treatment advice or avoiding medical care altogether.

FUTURE DIRECTIONS AND CONCLUSIONS

Data on the age at onset/diagnosis of CVD by race and ethnicity is sparse, but we need to better understand common risk factors and contexts across racial and ethnic groups that are associated with and/or precursors to a younger age at onset/diagnosis of CVD. Hopefully, as these shared issues emerge we can better address the third phase of health disparities research (Kilbourne et al., 2006), which focuses on interventions to reduce CVD disparities and its associated risk factors across these groups. First, while the literature we found on mean age at onset/diagnosis focused on hypertension, acute MI, stroke, and heart failure, a broad spectrum of early to later stage CVD development, we need better and consistent CVD data across the range of racial and ethnic groups. There was a particular dearth of age at onset/diagnosis CVD data on Latinos, Pacific Islanders, and Asian Americans, where the existing data was on South Asians in countries outside of the United States. Improving and understanding this information on all of these groups will decrease CVD morbidity and mortality, thereby improving overall population health. Second, we need this data to be based on national, not just regional, studies with large enough samples within racial and ethnic subgroups to understand if there are possible differences within the same racial and ethnic group across geographic regions, SES, and other SDOH (Holland & Palaniappan, 2012; Mensah, 2005; Yancy, Benjamin, Fabunmi, & Bonow, 2005).

Third, although many of the data cited are from cohort studies, additional longitudinal data needs should include repeated survey and qualitative measurements of SDOH (e.g., SES, health behaviors, discrimination, social isolation or support, etc.) associated with CVD. Longitudinal mixed methods data combine contextual and life course trends from survey questions with more in-depth, qualitative methods, such as focus groups or interviews. This combination of data can elucidate the SDOH that influence CVD directly and indirectly and subsequently impact aging in different ways across racial and ethnic groups. Research on one particular SDOH, the place or geographic area where people live, related to racial and ethnic CVD disparities among middle-age and older age adults seems to be limited (Diez Roux, Borrell, Haan, Jackson, & Schultz, 2004; LaVeist, Thorpe, Galarraga, Bower, & Gary-Webb, 2009; Mujahid, Diez Roux, Cooper, Shea, & Williams, 2011; Thorpe et al., 2008a). Minorities typically live in distinctly different communities which influence the resources and opportunities that are critical to reducing and eliminating disparities. Understanding how and when SDOH influence CVD across the life course are important for identifying solutions to reduce and eliminate health disparities and improve minority aging (Thorpe et al., 2011; Whitfield et al., 2011).

Fourth, one of the purposes in examining research on age at onset/diagnosis was to focus on similar characteristics across racial and ethnic groups for prevention and intervention needs. Prevention and intervention efforts to reduce racial and ethnic health disparities need to focus on common CVD risk factors, such as SES, geographic area, hypertension, obesity, quality of care, discrimination and other stressors, social support or social isolation, and health behaviors (e.g., smoking and alcohol intake). For health care management issues, we need to improve patient education to recognize CVD symptoms and when to seek medical care, possibly through multidisciplinary medical teams (Peterson et al., 2008); patient–provider communication, by investing in culturally competent, patient-centered care, building trust and satisfaction; and patient education on CAM, where providers inquire about and better communicate possible negative interactions of CAM practices with Western medicine.

Fifth, more consideration in our research should be given to social and economic policies for older adults, such as Social Security, Supplemental Security Income (SSI), the Older Americans Act (OAA), and food stamps for their assistance in reducing health disparities among low income and/or racial and ethnic minority adults. Social Security accounts for 40% of the annual income of older Americans aged more than 65 years, and SSI, for those ineligible for Social Security or with incomes below the poverty threshold, subsidizes about 6% of older Americans' incomes (Herd et al., 2011). Both of these programs have been effective at reducing poverty among older adults, and SSI has had a positive benefit on the health of older adult beneficiaries. However, older, racial and ethnic minority adults tend to have lower skills, lower income work during their life course, and typically work in more hazardous and physically demanding conditions associated with more health risks (Brown, 2010). Thus, older racial and ethnic minority adults may qualify for and rely on benefits from the OAA and food stamps programs earlier in their lives. The OAA is a universal program for all those aged more than 60 years, while food stamps are means-tested programs for adults and families (i.e., eligibility is based on low income and need). These two programs focus on addressing SDOH at a population level, such as housing, employment, community services, adequate nutrition, health promotion and restorative services, and protection against abuse, neglect, and exploitation (Wacker & Roberto, 2011). All of these programs are likely helping to reduce SES and racial and ethnic health disparities in the United States.

Advocating for policy changes to address racial and ethnic health disparities related to obesity, a common risk factor for CVD and other chronic diseases, Smith et al. (2005) make some suggestions. These include (a) advocating for research funding to train obesity researchers who are recruited from racial and ethnic minority populations; (b) lobbying the food and entertainment industries for conduct standards to limit their aggressive targeted marketing of high-calorie, low-nutrient-density products to racial and ethnic minority communities; (c) lobbying for the Centers for Disease Control and Prevention research funding to study ways to stimulate grassroots advocacy of policy and environmental changes that will reduce characteristics of daily living environments related to obesity; and (d) advocating for obesity treatment as a reimbursable service in health insurance policies. Their suggestions connect policy needs to people's everyday environments, such as work places, retail and health care industries, and social and physical environments in their communities, as with the social-ecological model, to impact individual health. We should also consider the need for long-term policy evaluation with a life course perspective, reducing CVD risk and making management improvements to benefit health early in adulthood that have subsequent impacts into middle and older adulthood.

Finally, while the Patient Protection and Affordability Care Act of 2010 elevated the National Center for Minority Health and Health Disparities to institute status; created provisions to improve data collection on sociodemographic characteristics and provide cultural competency training; and reauthorized the Indian Health Care Improvement Act, aimed at improving American Indian health care, with greater tribal autonomy in providing health programs (Bleich, Jarlenski, Bell, & LaVeist, 2012), other needs should be considered to reduce racial and ethnic health disparities. Instead of focusing primarily on medical care to reduce health disparities, which plays a proportionately small role in preventing the onset of chronic diseases but a larger role in self-care/management practices (Herd et al., 2011), efforts to reduce CVD will require a broader focus on preventing and intervening on risk factors by addressing SDOH.

In conclusion, progress toward understanding CVD disparities among middle- to older-age racial and ethnic minorities has improved. The next steps will require a shared understanding of how SDOH affect age at onset/diagnosis and self-care/management practices across these groups. Interventions targeting CVD risk factors that are culturally tailored toward common concerns of SES across the life course, geographic regional differences, social support or isolation, and health behaviors may prove to be the most valuable in helping us decrease CVD morbidity and mortality.

ACKNOWLEDGMENT

We wish to thank Ms. Anastasia Wynn for her assistance with the Appendix for this chapter.

REFERENCES

Arcury, T. A., Suerken, C. K., Grzywacz, J. G., Bell, R. A., Lang, W., & Quandt, S. A. (2006). Complementary and alternative medicine use among older adults: Ethnic variation. *Ethnicity & Disease, 16*(3), 723–731.

Bahrami, H., Kronmal, R., Bluemke, D. A., Olson, J., Shea, S., Liu, K.,...Lima, J. A. (2008). Differences in the incidence of congestive heart failure by ethnicity: The multi-ethnic study of atherosclerosis. *Archives of Internal Medicine, 168*(19), 2138–2145.

Best, L. G., Butt, A., Conroy, B., Devereux, R. B., Galloway, J. M., Jolly, S.,...Kedan, I. (2011). Acute myocardial infarction quality of care: The Strong Heart Study. *Ethnicity & Disease, 21*(3), 294–300.

Bibbins-Domingo, K., Pletcher, M. J., Lin, F., Vittinghoff, E., Gardin, J. M., Arynchyn, A.,...Hulley, S. B. (2009). Racial differences in incident heart failure among young adults. *The New England Journal of Medicine, 360*(12), 1179–1190.

Blackledge, H. M., Newton, J., & Squire, I. B. (2003). Prognosis for South Asian and white patients newly admitted to hospital with heart failure in the United Kingdom: Historical cohort study. *BMJ (Clinical Research Ed.), 327*(7414), 526–531.

Blanchard, J., Nayar, S., & Lurie, N. (2007). Patient-provider and patient-staff racial concordance and perceptions of mistreatment in the health care setting. *Journal of General Internal Medicine, 22*(8), 1184–1189.

Bleich, S. N., Jarlenski, M. P., Bell, C. N., & LaVeist, T. A. (2012). Health inequalities: Trends, progress, and policy. *Annual Review of Public Health, 33*, 7–40.

Braveman, P., Egerter, S., & Williams, D. R. (2011). The social determinants of health: Coming of age. *Annual Review of Public Health, 32,* 381–398.

Brown, E. (2010). Work, retirement, race, and health disparities. In T. C. Antonucci & J. S. Jackson (Eds.), *Annual review of gerontology and geriatrics: Life-course perspectives on late-life health inequalities* (Vol. 29, pp. 233–249). New York, NY: Springer.

Bulatao, R. A., & Anderson, N. B. (Eds.) (2004), for the Committee on Population, Division of Behavioral and Social Sciences and Education, National Research Council. *Understanding racial and ethnic differences in health in late life: A research agenda.* Washington, DC: National Academies Press.

Carp, F. M. (1986). Neighborhood quality perception and measurement. In R. J. Newcomer, M. P. Lawton, & T. O. Byerts (Eds.), *Housing and aging society: Issues, alternative, and policy.* New York, NY: Van Nostrand Reingold.

Collins, K. S., Hughes, D. L., Doty, M. M., Ives, B. L., Edwards, J. N., & Tenney, K. (2002). *Diverse communities, common concerns: Assessing health care quality for minority Americans. Findings from the Commonwealth Fund 2001 Health Care Quality survey.* Publication no. 523. New York, NY: Commonwealth Fund.

Dannefer, D. (1987). Aging as intracohort differentiation: Accentuation, the Matthew effect, and the life course. *Sociological Forum, 2,* 211–236.

Dannefer, D. (2003). Cumulative advantage/disadvantage and the life course: Cross-fertilizing age and social science theory. *The Journals of Gerontology. Series B, Psychological Sciences and Social Sciences, 58*(6), S327–S337.

Dannefer, D., & Uhlenberg, P. (1999). Paths of the life course: A typology. In V. L. Bengtson & K. W. Schaie (Eds.), *The handbook of theories of aging* (pp. 306–326). New York, NY: Springer.

Diez Roux, A. V., Borrell, L. N., Haan, M., Jackson, S. A., & Schultz, R. (2004). Neighbourhood environments and mortality in an elderly cohort: Results from the cardiovascular health study. *Journal of Epidemiology and Community Health, 58*(11), 917–923.

Ferraro, K. F. (2006). Health and aging. In R. H. Binstock & L. K. George (Eds.), *Handbook of aging and the social sciences* (6th ed., pp. 238–256). San Diego, CA: Academic Press.

Ferraro, K. F., & Farmer, M. M. (1996). Double jeopardy, aging as leveler, or persistent health inequality? A longitudinal analysis of white and black Americans. *The Journals of Gerontology. Series B, Psychological Sciences and Social Sciences, 51*(6), S319–S328.

Ferraro, K. F., & Kelley-Moore, J. A. (2003). Cumulative disadvantage and health: Long-term consequences of obesity? *American Sociological Review, 68*(5), 707–729.

Ferraro, K. F., & Shippee, T. P. (2009). Aging and cumulative inequality: How does inequality get under the skin? *The Gerontologist, 49*(3), 333–343.

Ferraro, K. F., Farmer, M. M., & Wybraniec, J. A. (1997). Health trajectories: Long-term dynamics among black and white adults. *Journal of Health and Social Behavior, 38*(1), 38–54.

Ferris, A., Robertson, R. M., Fabunmi, R., & Mosca, L.; American Heart Association; American Stroke Association. (2005). American Heart Association and American Stroke Association national survey of stroke risk awareness among women. *Circulation, 111*(10), 1321–1326.

Frey, J. L., Jahnke, H. K., & Bulfinch, E. W. (1998). Differences in stroke between white, Hispanic, and Native American patients: The Barrow Neurological Institute stroke database. *Stroke; A Journal of Cerebral Circulation, 29*(1), 29–33.

Geronimus, A. T. (2001). Understanding and eliminating racial inequalities in women's health in the United States: The role of the weathering conceptual framework. *Journal of the American Medical Women's Association, 56*(4), 133–136, 149–150.

Geronimus, A. T., Bound, J., Keene, D., & Hicken, M. (2007). Black-white differences in age trajectories of hypertension prevalence among adult women and men, 1999–2002. *Ethnicity & Disease, 17*(1), 40–48.

Geronimus, A. T., Hicken, M. T., Pearson, J. A., Seashols, S. J., Brown, K. L., & Cruz, T. D. (2010). Do US black women experience stress-related accelerated biological aging?: A novel theory and first population-based test of black-white differences in telomere length. *Human Nature (Hawthorne, N.Y.), 21*(1), 19–38.

Glymour, M. M., Avendaño, M., Haas, S., & Berkman, L. F. (2008). Lifecourse social conditions and racial disparities in incidence of first stroke. *Annals of Epidemiology, 18*(12), 904–912.

Graham, R. E., Ahn, A. C., Davis, R. B., O'Connor, B. B., Eisenberg, D. M., & Phillips, R. S. (2005). Use of complementary and alternative medical therapies among racial and ethnic minority adults: Results from the 2002 National Health Interview Survey. *Journal of the National Medical Association, 97*(4), 535–545.

Greer, T. M. (2010). Perceived racial discrimination in clinical encounters among African American hypertensive patients. *Journal of Health Care for the Poor and Underserved, 21*(1), 251–263.

Haas, J. S., Phillips, K. A., Sonneborn, D., McCulloch, C. E., Baker, L. C., Kaplan, C. P.,…Liang, S. Y. (2004). Variation in access to health care for different racial/ethnic groups by the racial/ethnic composition of an individual's county of residence. *Medical Care, 42*(7), 707–714.

Herd, P., Robert, S. A., & House, J. S. (2011). Health disparities among older adults: Life course influences and policy solutions. In R. H. Binstock & L. K. George (Eds.), *The handbook of aging and the social sciences* (7th ed., pp. 121–134). San Diego, CA: Academic Press.

Hinojosa, R., Haun, J., Hinojosa, M. S., & Rittman, M. (2011). Social isolation poststroke: Relationship between race/ethnicity, depression, and functional independence. *Topics in Stroke Rehabilitation, 18*(1), 79–86.

Holland, A. T., & Palaniappan, L. P. (2012). Problems with the collection and interpretation of Asian-American health data: Omission, aggregation, and extrapolation. *Annals of Epidemiology, 22*(6), 397–405.

Hunt, S. A., Abraham, W. T., Chin, M. H., Feldman, A. M., Francis, G. S., Ganiats, T. G.,…Riegel, B.; American College of Cardiology; American Heart Association Task Force on Practice Guidelines; American College of Chest Physicians; International Society for Heart and Lung Transplantation; Heart Rhythm Society. (2005). ACC/AHA 2005 Guideline Update for the Diagnosis and Management of Chronic Heart Failure in the Adult: A report of the American College of Cardiology/American Heart Association Task Force on Practice Guidelines (Writing Committee to Update the 2001 Guidelines for the Evaluation and Management of Heart Failure): Developed in collaboration with the American College of Chest Physicians and the International Society for Heart and Lung Transplantation: Endorsed by the Heart Rhythm Society. *Circulation, 112*(12), e154–e235.

Jackson, J. S., Govia, I. O., & Sellers, S. L. (2011). Racial and ethnic influences over the life course. In R. H. Binstock & L. K. George (Eds.), *The handbook of aging and the social sciences* (7th ed., pp. 91–103). San Diego, CA: Academic Press.

Johnson, R. L., Roter, D., Powe, N. R., & Cooper, L. A. (2004). Patient race/ethnicity and quality of patient-physician communication during medical visits. *American Journal of Public Health, 94*(12), 2084–2090.

Jones, C. P. (1994). *Methods for comparing distributions: Development and application exploring "race"- associated differences in systolic blood pressure* [dissertation]. Baltimore, MD: Johns Hopkins School of Hygiene and Public Health.

Jones, C. P. (2000). *The impacts of racism on health.* Presentation at the 2000 Summer Public Health Research Videoconference on Minority Health at the University of North Carolina's School of Public Health.

Kaholokula, J. K., Saito, E., Mau, M. K., Latimer, R., & Seto, T. B. (2008). Pacific Islanders' perspectives on heart failure management. *Patient Education and Counseling, 70*(2), 281–291.

Kalogeropoulos, A., Georgiopoulou, V., Kritchevsky, S. B., Psaty, B. M., Smith, N. L., Newman, A. B.,…Butler, J. (2009). Epidemiology of incident heart failure in a contemporary elderly cohort: The health, aging, and body composition study. *Archives of Internal Medicine, 169*(7), 708–715.

Kaplan, G. A. (1997). Behavioral, social and socio-environmental factors adding years to life and life to years. In T. Hickey, M. A. Speers, & R. E. Prohaska (Eds.), *The role of public health in an aging society.* Baltimore, MD: The Johns Hopkins University Press.

Kilbourne, A. M., Switzer, G., Hyman, K., Crowley-Matoka, M., & Fine, M. J. (2006). Advancing health disparities research within the health care system: A conceptual framework. *American Journal of Public Health, 96*(12), 2113–2121.

Kim, J., Han, H. R., Song, H., Lee, J., Kim, K. B., & Kim, M. T. (2010). Compliance with home blood pressure monitoring among middle-aged Korean Americans with hypertension. *Journal of Clinical Hypertension (Greenwich, Conn.), 12*(4), 253–260.

Krause, N. (2003). Neighborhoods, health, and well-being in late life. In H. Wahl, R. Scheidt, & P. Windley (Eds.), *Annual review of gerontology and geriatrics, Volume 23, 2003, Aging in context: Socio-physical environments*. New York, NY: Springer.

LaVeist, T. A., Thorpe, R. J., Galarraga, J. E., Bower, K. M., & Gary-Webb, T. L. (2009). Environmental and socio-economic factors as contributors to racial disparities in diabetes prevalence. *Journal of General Internal Medicine, 24*(10), 1144–1148.

Lisabeth, L. D., Smith, M. A., Brown, D. L., Uchino, K., & Morgenstern, L. B. (2005). Family history and stroke outcome in a bi-ethnic, population-based stroke surveillance study. *BMC Neurology, 5*, 20.

Lloyd-Jones, D. M., Leip, E. P., Larson, M. G., Vasan, R. S., & Levy, D. (2005). Novel approach to examining first cardiovascular events after hypertension onset. *Hypertension, 45*(1), 39–45.

Lloyd-Jones, D., Adams, R., Carnethon, M., De Simone, G., Ferguson, T. B., Flegal, K.,…Hong, Y.; American Heart Association Statistics Committee and Stroke Statistics Subcommittee. (2009). Heart disease and stroke statistics–2009 update: A report from the American Heart Association Statistics Committee and Stroke Statistics Subcommittee. *Circulation, 119*(3), e21–181.

Loehr, L. R., Rosamond, W. D., Chang, P. P., Folsom, A. R., & Chambless, L. E. (2008). Heart failure incidence and survival (from the Atherosclerosis Risk in Communities study). *The American Journal of Cardiology, 101*(7), 1016–1022.

Martin, L. G., & Soldo, B. J. (Eds.), for the Committee on Population, Commission on Behavioral and Social Sciences and Education, National Research Council (1997). *Racial and ethnic differences in the health of older Americans*. Washington, DC: National Academy Press.

Mensah, G. A. (2005). Eliminating disparities in cardiovascular health: Six strategic imperatives and a framework for action. *Circulation, 111*(10), 1332–1336.

Meyers, K. S. H. (2007). *Racial and ethnic health disparities: Influences, actors, and policy opportunities*. Oakland, CA: Kaiser Permanente Institute for Health Policy.

Mujahid, M. S., Diez Roux, A. V., Cooper, R. C., Shea, S., & Williams, D. R. (2011). Neighborhood stressors and race/ethnic differences in hypertension prevalence (the Multi-Ethnic Study of Atherosclerosis). *American Journal of Hypertension, 24*(2), 187–193.

O'Rand, A. M. (1996). The precious and the precocious: Understanding cumulative disadvantage and cumulative advantage over the life course. *The Gerontologist, 36*(2), 230–238.

Peterson, E. D., Albert, N. M., Amin, A., Patterson, J. H., and Fonarow, G. C. (2008). Implementing critical pathways and a multidisciplinary team approach to cardiovascular disease management. *The American Journal of Cardiology, 102* (supplement), 47G–56G.

Preston, S. H., Hill, M. E., & Drevenstedt, G. L. (1998). Childhood conditions that predict survival to advanced ages among African-Americans. *Social Science & Medicine (1982), 47*(9), 1231–1246.

Richard, L., Gauvin, L., & Raine, K. (2011). Ecological models revisited: Their uses and evolution in health promotion over two decades. *Annual Review of Public Health, 32*, 307–326.

Roger, V. L., Go, A. S., Lloyd-Jones, D. M., Benjamin, E. J., Berry, J. D., Borden, W. B.,…Turner, M. B.; American Heart Association Statistics Committee and Stroke Statistics Subcommittee. (2012). Heart disease and stroke statistics–2012 update: A report from the American Heart Association. *Circulation, 125*(1), e2–e220.

Rooks, R. N., & Whitfield, K. E. (2004). Health disparities among older African Americans: Past, present, and future perspectives. In K. E. Whitfield (Ed.), *Closing the gap: Improving the health of minority elders in the new millennium* (pp. 45–54). Washington, DC: The Gerontological Society of America.

Rooks, R. N., Simonsick, E. M., Klesges, L. M., Newman, A. B., Ayonayon, H. N., & Harris, T. B. (2008). Racial disparities in health care access and cardiovascular disease indicators in Black and White older adults in the Health ABC Study. *Journal of Aging and Health, 20*(6), 599–614.

Rooks, R. N., Simonsick, E. M., Miles, T., Newman, A., Kritchevsky, S. B., Schulz, R. et al. (2002). The association of race and socioeconomic status with cardiovascular disease indicators among older adults in the health, aging, and body composition study. *The Journals of Gerontology. Series B, Psychological Sciences and Social Sciences, 57*(4), S247–S256.

Rooks, R. N., Wiltshire, J. C., Elder, K., BeLue, R., & Gary, L. C. (2012). Health information seeking and use outside of the medical encounter: Is it associated with race and ethnicity? *Social Science & Medicine (1982), 74*(2), 176–184.

Selvin, E., Coresh, J., & Brancati, F. L. (2006). The burden and treatment of diabetes in elderly individuals in the U.S.. *Diabetes Care, 29*(11), 2415–2419.

Shantsila, E., Lip, G. Y., & Gill, P. S. (2011). Systolic heart failure in South Asians. *International Journal of Clinical Practice, 65*(12), 1274–1282.

Shippee, T. P., Schafer, M. H., & Ferraro, K. F. (2012). Beyond the barriers: Racial discrimination and use of complementary and alternative medicine among Black Americans. *Social Science & Medicine (1982), 74*(8), 1155–1162.

Singh, N., & Gupta, M. (2005). Clinical characteristics of South Asian patients hospitalized with heart failure. *Ethnicity & Disease, 15*(4), 615–619.

Smith, S. C., Clark, L. T., Cooper, R. S., Daniels, S. R., Kumanyika, S. K., Ofili, E.,…Tiukinhoy, S. D.; American Heart Association Obesity, Metabolic Syndrome, and Hypertension Writing Group. (2005). Discovering the full spectrum of cardiovascular disease: Minority Health Summit 2003: Report of the Obesity, Metabolic Syndrome, and Hypertension Writing Group. *Circulation, 111*(10), e134–e139.

Stokols, D. (1992). Establishing and maintaining healthy environments. Toward a social ecology of health promotion. *The American Psychologist, 47*(1), 6–22.

Stokols, D. (1996). Translating social ecological theory into guidelines for community health promotion. *American Journal of Health Promotion: AJHP, 10*(4), 282–298.

Stoller, E. P., & Gibson, R. C. (1997). *Worlds of difference: Inequality in the aging experience* (2nd ed.). Thousand Oaks, CA: Pine Forge Press.

Struthers, R., Savik, K., & Hodge, F. S. (2004). American Indian women and cardiovascular disease: Response behaviors to chest pain. *The Journal of Cardiovascular Nursing, 19*(3), 158–163.

Thorpe, R. J., Brandon, D. T., & LaVeist, T. A. (2008a). Social context as an explanation for race disparities in hypertension: Findings from the Exploring Health Disparities in Integrated Communities (EHDIC) Study. *Social Science & Medicine (1982), 67*(10), 1604–1611.

Thorpe, R. J., Kasper, J. D., Szanton, S. L., Frick, K. D., Fried, L. P., & Simonsick, E. M. (2008b). Relationship of race and poverty to lower extremity function and decline: Findings from the Women's Health and Aging Study. *Social Science & Medicine (1982), 66*(4), 811–821.

Thorpe, R. J., Koster, A., Bosma, H., Harris, T. B., Simonsick, E. M., van Eijk, J. T.,…Kritchevsky, S. B.; Health ABC Study. (2012). Racial differences in mortality in older adults: Factors beyond socioeconomic status. *Annals of Behavioral Medicine: A Publication of the Society of Behavioral Medicine, 43*(1), 29–38.

Thorpe, R. J., Koster, A., Kritchevsky, S. B., Newman, A. B., Harris, T., Ayonayon, H. N.,…Simonsick, E. M.; Health, Aging, and Body Composition Study. (2011). Race, socioeconomic resources, and late-life mobility and decline: Findings from the Health, Aging, and Body Composition study. *The Journals of Gerontology. Series A, Biological Sciences and Medical Sciences, 66*(10), 1114–1123.

Ting, H. H., Bradley, E. H., Wang, Y., Lichtman, J. H., Nallamothu, B. K., Sullivan, M. D.,…Krumholz, H. M. (2008). Factors associated with longer time from symptom onset to hospital presentation for patients with ST-elevation myocardial infarction. *Archives of Internal Medicine, 168*(9), 959–968.

Town, R. J., Wholey, D. R., Feldman, R. D., & Burns, L. R. (2007). Hospital consolidation and racial/income disparities in health insurance coverage. *Health Affairs (Project Hope), 26*(4), 1170–1180.

Trangmar, P., & Diaz, V. A. (2008). Investigating complementary and alternative medicine use in a Spanish-speaking Hispanic community in South Carolina. *Annals of Family Medicine, 6*(Suppl 1), S12–S15.

Verbrugge, L. M., & Jette, A. M. (1994). The disablement process. *Social Science & Medicine (1982), 38*(1), 1–14.

Wacker, R. R., & Roberto, K. A. (2011). "Aging social policy (ch. 2)" and "Aging social policy challenges (ch. 10)." *Aging social policies: An international perspective*. Thousand Oaks, CA: Sage.

Warren-Findlow, J., & Seymour, R. B. (2011). Prevalence rates of hypertension self-care activities among African Americans. *Journal of the National Medical Association, 103*(6), 503–512.

Warren-Findlow, J., Seymour, R. B., & Shenk, D. (2011). Intergenerational transmission of chronic illness self-care: Results from the caring for hypertension in African American families study. *The Gerontologist, 51*(1), 64–75.

Whitfield, K. E., Thorpe, R., & Szanton, S. (2011). Health disparities, social class, and aging. In W. Schaie & S. Willis (Eds.), *The handbook of the psychology of aging* (7th ed., pp. 207–218). Burlington, MA: Elsevier.

Williams, D. R., & Collins, C. (1995). U.S. socioeconomic and racial differences in health: Patterns and explanations. *Annual Review of Sociology, 21,* 349–386.

Yancy, C. W. (2005). Heart failure in African Americans. *The American Journal of Cardiology, 96*(7B), 3i–12i.

Yancy, C. W., Benjamin, E. J., Fabunmi, R. P., & Bonow, R. O. (2005). Discovering the full spectrum of cardiovascular disease: Minority Health Summit 2003: Executive summary. *Circulation, 111*(10), 1339–1349.

Zhang, Y., Galloway, J. M., Welty, T. K., Wiebers, D. O., Whisnant, J. P., Devereux, R. B., ... Lee, E. T. (2008). Incidence and risk factors for stroke in American Indians: The Strong Heart Study. *Circulation, 118*(15), 1577–1584.

APPENDIX: Literature Review

CITATION	DATA/POPULATION	METHOD(S)	OUTCOME MEASURE	MAJOR FINDINGS
Bahrami et al. 2008	—MESA—a prospective, observational study of individuals aged 45–84 without baseline CVD. —6,814 total participants —4 major racial/ethnic groups: 1. Chinese Americans (11.8%) 2. African Americans (27.8%) 3. Hispanics (21.9%) 4. Whites (38.5%)	—Cox proportional hazards models —Telephone interview for follow up every 6–9 months.	The relationship between incident CHF and race/ethnicity, as well as racial/ethnic differences in the mechanisms leading to CHF.	African Americans had the highest incidence rate of CHF, followed by Hispanics, whites, and Chinese Americans. Adding hypertension and/or diabetes mellitus to models including ethnicity eliminated statistical ethnic differences in incident CHF. African Americans had the highest proportion of incident CHF not preceded by clinical MI (75%) compared to other ethnic groups.
Best et al., 2011	—The Strong Heart Study, a population based cohort study of CVD and its risk factors in 13 tribes and communities across southwestern OK, central AZ, and North and South Dakota begun in 1989 among American Indians aged 45–74. —The largest longitudinal, population-based study of cardiovascular disease and its risk factors in a diverse group of American Indians —Acute MI cases (72) occurring between January 1, 2001, and December 31, 2006, were identified from a cohort of 4,549.	At baseline and 2 subsequent follow-up periods ~4 and 8 years from baseline, a physical examination, fasting venipuncture, standardized blood pressure measurements, and electrocardiograms were obtained.	The proportion of cases that were provided standard quality of care therapy, as defined by the Healthcare Financing Administration (now the Center for Medicare/Medicaid Services) and other organizations.	Administration of aspirin on admission and at discharge, reperfusion therapy within 24 hr, prescription of beta blocker medication at discharge, and smoking cessation counseling were found to be 94%, 91%, 92%, 86%, and 71%, respectively. Unadjusted 30 d mortality rate was 17%.
Bibbins-Domingo et al., 2009	—CARDIA study—a multicenter study used to investigate the development of coronary disease in young adults. —5,115 blacks and whites of both sexes who were aged 18–30 at baseline.	Prospectively assessed the incidence of HF over 20 yrs.	Examined predictors of hospitalization or death from HF	HF developed in 27 participants, all but 1 were black. Cumulative incidence of HF before the age of 50 years was 1.1%. Among blacks, independent predictors at 18–30 yrs of age of HF occurring 15 y, on average, later included higher diastolic blood, higher BMI, lower high-density lipoprotein cholesterol and kidney disease.

(*Continued*)

CITATION	DATA/POPULATION	METHOD(S)	OUTCOME MEASURE	MAJOR FINDINGS
				Three quarters of those in whom HF subsequently developed had hypertension by the time they were aged 40. Depressed systolic function was independently associated with the development of HF 10 yrs, on average, later. MI, drug use, and alcohol use were not associated with the HF risk.
Blackledge et al., 2003	—United Kingdom district health information service —5,789 consecutive patients newly admitted w/HF. —South Asians of Indian subcontinent origin and whites —patients aged 40+, admitted with HF for the first time between April 1, 1998 and March 31, 2001	—Chi-square tests —Cox proportional hazards models	Population admission rates, incidence rates for first admission with HF, survival, and readmission rates	Compared with the white population, South Asian patients had significantly higher age-adjusted admission and hospital incidence rates. South Asian patients were younger and more often male than white patients. South Asian patients were also more likely to have previous MI or concomitant MI or diabetes. A trend was shown to longer unadjusted survival for both sexes among South Asian patients. After adjustment for covariates, South Asian patients had a significantly lower risk of death and a probability of death or readmission compared with white patients.
Ferris et al., 2005	—1,024 women, aged 25+ —68% white, 12% black, 12% Hispanic	—Telephone survey using a standardized questionnaire about heart disease and stroke risk. —Chi-square tests	The purpose of this study was to assess knowledge and awareness about stroke in a nationally representative sample of women.	Only 26% of women 65+ reported being well informed about stroke, even though this group carries the highest incidence of stroke. Overall, 20% of women stated that they worried a lot about stroke. Among women aged 25–34 years, 37% stated that they were not at all informed about stroke, which was significantly higher than for women 45–64 years and those 65+. More Hispanics reported being not at all informed about stroke compared with whites and blacks. Correct identification of the warning signs of stroke was low among all racial/ethnic and age groups. More white respondents correctly identified sudden one-sided weakness or numbness of the face or a limb and difficulty talking or understanding speech as warning signs of stroke versus Hispanics.

Study	Sample/Data	Purpose	Statistical methods	Findings
Frey et al., 1998	—Data were collected on 1,716 subjects admitted to the Barrow Neurological Institute of St Joseph's Medical Center, Phoenix, AZ, with stroke or TIA from 1990–1996. —Patients were identified through emergency department admission logs, and data were collected from concurrent and retrospective chart review and interviews with patients or families. —1,290 WHI, 242 HIS, 83 NA, and 101 other stroke and TIA patients hospitalized.	Identification of specific features of stroke in minority populations should lead to more effectively focused treatment and prevention.	Chi-square tests	Stroke types—lacunes more prevalent in NA than WHI and HIS (30% vs. 16% and 15%); cardioembolic more prevalent in WHI than HIS (16% vs. 9%, NA 14%); and hemorrhages more prevalent in HIS than WHI and NA (48% vs. 37% and 27%). There were no significant outcome differences between races for any stroke type. A significantly lower mean age at stroke onset in NA than HIS and WHI (56 vs. 61 and 69 years) was detected.
Geronimus et al., 2007	—1999–2002 NHANES IV and data from the first phase of 1988–1991 NHANES III, a stratified, multistage probability sample of the civilian noninstitutionalized population of the United States. —5,501participants aged 15–65 —1,803 white men, 1,681 white women, 1,047 black men, and 970 black women	Systolic blood pressure ≥140 or diastolic blood pressure ≥90 or reporting current use of anti-hypertensive medications to be hypertensive	—descriptive statistics —logistic regression —predicted probability of hypertension	The black/white disparity in hypertension prevalence in the United States widened over the reproductive and working ages (15–65 years). The largest black/white gap exists among women, largely due to the rapid increase in hypertension prevalence among black women from young to middle adulthood. Study findings refute the cohort effects hypothesis. At younger ages women were less likely than men to be hypertensive, but the reverse was true at older ages. By the age of 40 black women had the highest hypertension risk and the highest age-gradient increase through middle age.
Glymour et al. 2008	—HRS, a longitudinal survey of a national sample of U.S. adults aged 50+ and their spouses. —Black and white adults —20,661 participants aged 50+ were followed on average 9.9 yrs for self or proxy reported first stroke (2,175 events).	Assess the role of life course SES in explaining stroke risk and stroke disparities	Childhood social conditions (southern birth state, parental SES, self-reported fair/poor childhood health, and attained height), adult SES (education, income, wealth, and occupational status) and traditional cardiovascular risk factors were used to predict first stroke onset using Cox proportional hazards models.	Blacks had 48% higher risk of first stroke incidence than whites (95% CI: 1.33, 1.65). Childhood conditions predicted stroke risk in both blacks and whites, independently of adult SES. Adjustment for both childhood social conditions and adult SES measures attenuated racial differences to marginal significance (HR = 1.13; 1.00, 1.28).

(Continued)

APPENDIX: Literature Review (Continued)

CITATION	DATA/POPULATION	METHOD(S)	OUTCOME MEASURE	MAJOR FINDINGS
Greer et al., 2010	—A random sample of African American hypertensive patients was identified and recruited by querying a local outpatient medical clinic's electronic medical records system in central South Carolina. —The clinic served as the site for focus-group recruiting, averaging over 35,000 patient visits per year. —Approximately 70% of the patients are African American.	—Six focus groups, with 37 African American hypertensive patients, were conducted. —Transcribed sessions were analyzed using content analysis.	African American patient perceptions of racial discrimination in clinical encounters and general barriers to hypertension management were also investigated.	Patients valued providers who shared information regarding self-care behaviors to manage hypertension and those who provided information regarding treatment options. Provider assumptions about patient inability to afford services, and provider apathy in reaching services were perceived as racially discriminatory. Patients discussed providers' avoidance of touch during physical exams as overtly discriminatory. Patients reacted to discriminatory experiences by not keeping appointments with providers perceived as racially discriminatory. Barriers to hypertension management were associated with family responsibilities and lifestyle factors, but were not attributed to provider racial biases.
Hinojosa et al., 2011	—A longitudinal study of culturally sensitive models of stroke recovery and care giving among veterans. —Stroke survivors were identified from 5 geographically and ethnically diverse Department of Veterans Affairs Medical Centers in Florida and Puerto Rico by sampling persons whose stroke events occurred from 2003–2006. —77 male veterans, aged 41–88 enrolled prior to discharge: 18 African Americans, 29 Puerto Rican Hispanics, and 30 non-Hispanic whites	—ANOVA, Chi-square, and Fisher exact tests —multilevel hierarchical linear models —In-home face-to-face semi-structured interviews using a ground theory method —self-report measures of recovery and functioning at 1, 6, 12, 18, and 24 months after hospital discharge	Examined the relationship between social isolation, race/ethnicity, functional dependence, and depressive symptoms, as well as the ability to manage activities of daily living post stroke	Veterans who were socially isolated during the first year of post-stroke recovery reported higher levels of depressive symptoms and a decreased ability to manage daily activities. Social isolation was evenly distributed among white, African American, and Puerto Rican stroke survivors, but the numbers were large ranging from one third to over half the stroke survivors who were socially isolated. Additionally, social isolation trends did not change over the 1-year rehabilitation period.

Kalogeropoulos et al., 2008	—Health ABC study is a population-based study of 3,075 community-dwelling men and women aged 70–79 years at enrollment. —Participants had to report no difficulty in walking one-quarter mile or climbing 10 stairs without resting. —Participants were identified from a random sample of white Medicare beneficiaries and all age-eligible black community residents in designated zip codes areas surrounding Pittsburgh and Memphis.	They studied 2,934 participants without HF enrolled in the Health ABC study and assessed incidence of HF, PAR of independent risk factors for HF, and outcomes of incident HF.	Race- and gender-specific incident HF	During a median follow-up of 7.1 years, 258 (8.8%) participants developed HF. Men and blacks were more likely to develop HF. No significant sex differences were observed in risk factors. Coronary heart disease and uncontrolled BP carried the highest PAR in both races. Participants who developed HF had a higher annual mortality (18.0% vs. 2.7%). No racial differences in survival after HF were noted; however, rehospitalization rates were higher in blacks (62.1 vs. 30.3/100 person-years, $P < .001$).
Keawe'aimoku Kaholokula et al., 2008	—The study used open-ended questions to probe participants' health beliefs and attitudes, self-care practices, barriers to adherence, and the role of family and social supports in managing their HF. —36 Native Hawaiians and Samoans from rural and urban communities with HF	—4 focus groups were convened with participants and their family caregivers. —Thematic data analysis was used to categorize data into four domains: health beliefs and attitudes, preferred health practices, family and social support systems, and barriers to HF treatment.		Common coping styles and emotional experiences of HF equaled avoidance or denial of illness, hopelessness and despair, and reliance on spiritual/religious beliefs as a means of support. Among study participants, more Samoans preferred to be treated by physicians whereas more Native Hawaiians preferred traditional Hawaiian methods of healing. Two types of social support (informational and tangible-instrumental) were identified as important in heart failure care. Barriers to HF care included poor knowledge of HF, lack of trust in physicians' care, poor physician-patient relations, finances, dietary changes, and competing demands on time.
Kim, et al., 2010	—Baseline data on 377 middle-aged 40–64 year old individuals with high BP from a pool of 445 Korean Americans —Participates were a part of a community-based HBPM intervention trial in which year-long HBPM was integrated as an intervention component	The intervention focused on structured behavioral education, participants measured their BP 3 times in a row upon waking and thrice again at bedtime, at least 2 or more times a week for 48 weeks.	The factors affecting the level of compliance of HBPM and its relation to BP control among hypertensive adults in a community setting.	Older participants were more compliant with the HBPM instruction than were younger participants. Participants who were more compliant to HBPM instruction were 4 times more likely than those who were noncompliant to have controlled their BP by the end of the intervention period. These results suggest that the participants who checked their BP regularly at home had a stronger tendency to achieve BP control.

(Continued)

APPENDIX: Literature Review (Continued)

CITATION	DATA/POPULATION	METHOD(S)	OUTCOME MEASURE	MAJOR FINDINGS
Lisabeth et al., 2008	—BASIC-population-based stroke surveillance study conducted in the bi-ethnic community of Nueces County, Texas —NHW comprise 38% of the population, and Mexican Americans MA comprise 56% —Completed ischemic strokes ($n = 400$) were identified among patients 45+ seen at hospitals in the county between January 1, 2000 and December 31, 2002	—A random sample of ischemic stroke patients underwent an in-person interview and detailed medical record abstraction —Chi-square tests —Multivariable logistic and linear regression	Association between family history of stroke among a first degree relative and the following outcomes: initial stroke severity (NIH stroke scale), age at stroke onset, 90-day mortality, and functional outcome (modified Rankin scale ≥ 2).	The study population was 53.0% MA and 58.4% female. Median age was 73.2 yrs. 40% reported a family history of stroke among a first degree relative. Family history of stroke was borderline significantly associated with stroke subtype ($P = .0563$). Family history was associated with poor functional outcome in the multivariable model (OR = 1.87; 95% CI: 1.14–3.09). Family history was not significantly related to initial stroke severity, age at stroke onset, or 90-day mortality.
Loehr et al., 2008	—The ARIC cohort is a population-based study from four U.S. communities between 1987–2002. —The sample of 1,282 HF cases includes men and women and white and black participants.	—Prevalent HF cases were identified by self-report and were excluded. —Incident HF was defined by the International Classification of Diseases codes for HF (428.0 to 428.9, I50) from hospitalization ($n = 1,206$) or death certificate ($n = 76$)	Race and gender differences in HF incidence rates and case fatality	The age-adjusted incidence rate (per 1,000 person-years) for white women, 3.4, was significantly less compared with all other groups (white men, 6.0; African American women, 8.1; African American men, 9.1). Age-adjusted HF incidence rates were greater for African Americans than whites, but adjustment for confounders attenuated the difference. The adjusted African American-to-white hazard ratio was 0.86 (95% CI, 0.70 to 1.06) for men, and similarly, 0.93 (95% CI, 0.46 to 1.90) for women during the second half of follow-up. African Americans had a greater 5-year case fatality compared with whites ($P < .05$).
Peterson, et al., 2008	—Post-MI patients, especially those with left ventricular dysfunction and HF	—A literature review focused on multi-disciplinary, clinical approaches, using proven therapies, to provide better care to hospitalized cardiovascular patients and ultimately resulting in reduced morbidity and mortality		There is a need to improve the care of post-MI patients, especially those with left ventricular dysfunction and HF. This can potentially be achieved by implementing disease management programs which include critical pathways, patient education, and multidisciplinary hospital teams. Reductions in all-cause hospitalizations and medical costs as well as improved survival rates have been observed when multidisciplinary teams (a cardiologist, a nurse, a pharmacist, and a hospitalist) are engaged in patient care.

Selvin et al., 2006	—1992–2002 The NHANES, a cross-sectional nationally representative survey of the civilian noninstitutionalized population of the United States —Oversamples of Mexican American and non-Hispanic black adults —The eligible study sample consisted of 2,809 individuals aged 65+ who were not missing information on diabetes status.	ANOVA and Chi-square tests	—Assess the prevalence of diabetes for elderly with diabetes diagnosed in middle age ("middle age-onset diabetes") vs. elderly with recently diagnosed diabetes ("elderly onset diabetes") —Assess the burden of complications and control of cardiovascular risk factors in these groups	Among adults aged 65+ the prevalence of diagnosed diabetes was 15.3%, representing 5.4 million individuals in the United States. The prevalence of undiagnosed diabetes was 6.9% or 2.4 million individuals. Elderly individuals with middle age–onset diabetes had a much greater burden of microvascular disease but have a similar burden of macrovascular disease compared with individuals with elderly onset diabetes. Elderly individuals with middle age-onset diabetes had substantially worse glycemic control vs. either elderly with older age-onset or nonelderly individuals with diabetes. Individuals with elderly onset diabetes were also less likely to be taking glucose-lowering medications.
Shantsila et al., 2011	South Asians including: "India," "Indian," "Pakistan," "Pakistani," "Bangladesh," and "Bangladeshi"	—Literature review on HF and left ventricular systolic dysfunction, respectively, and South Asians —Published data for this review were identified by searches of PUBMED from 1980 to the present	Systolic HF in South Asians	Systolic HF tends to manifest earlier among South Asians and with frequent hospital admissions. However, survival for such patients appears to be significantly better compared with the white group, which might be associated with different patterns of HF. A high prevalence of hypertension and diabetes mellitus among South Asians may predispose them to diastolic HF with preserved systolic function. Also, because South Asians are under-represented in clinical trials, little data exist on optimal management for this ethnic group.
Shippee et al., 2012	—National Survey of MIDUS —Sample limited to black adults aged 25+ at baseline ($n = 201$)	—Analyses account for multiple forms of discrimination: major lifetime discriminatory events and everyday discrimination —Logistic and negative binomial regression	—Whether self-reported racial discrimination is associated with greater use of CAM among black adults —Whether reported racial discrimination specific to the setting in which the unfair treatment occurred (i.e., medical or nonmedical settings) is associated with CAM among black adults	Racial discrimination was associated with a higher likelihood of using any type of CAM as well as using more modalities of CAM. Discrimination in health care and in nonmedical contexts predicted greater use of CAM. The experience of racial discrimination among black people is associated with greater use of alternative means of health care, as a way to cope with the barriers they experience in institutional settings in the United States.

(Continued)

CITATION	DATA/POPULATION	METHOD(S)	OUTCOME MEASURE	MAJOR FINDINGS
Singh & Gupta, 2005	A retrospective, sequential chart review of South Asian and non-South Asian white patients hospitalized with a primary diagnosis of HF between 1997–1999 at two Toronto-area community hospitals in Canada	—Student *t*-test —Cox proportional hazard models	Ethnic variations in prevalence, presentation characteristics, and mortality in Canadian patients with coronary artery disease with respect to HF	South Asians were significantly younger, of lower BMI, were more often diabetic, and were less often smokers. In-hospital mortality was not different between groups, although South Asians were more likely to experience ventricular arrhythmias. Despite presenting at a younger age, South Asians had more high-risk features at hospital discharge.
Struthers et al., 2004	—The original data consisted of an age stratified, random sample of 1,376 adult American Indian participants aged 22+ from 3 participating rural, geographically isolated reservations from 1992–1994 —63% of the participants were women (*n* = 866) and 37% were men (*n* = 510) —This research targets the 866 women participants of the Inter-Tribal Heart Project in Minnesota and Wisconsin	—A comprehensive survey was administered during a face-to-face interview conducted by an Inter-Tribal Heart Project staff —Topic areas included medical history, family history, biological factors (e.g., blood pressure, weight, and cholesterol levels), psychosocial factors (e.g., stress), behavioral factors (e.g., diet, physical activity levels, and tobacco use), and individual responses to chest pain	Response behaviors to chest pain in a group of American Indian women	68% of women would actively seek health care immediately if experiencing crushing chest pain that lasted longer than 15 minutes. 32% would take a passive action to crushing chest pain, with 23% reporting they would sit down and wait until it passed. Women reporting a passive response were younger in age (under age 45) and had less education (less than a high school education).
Ting et al., 2008	—Patients enrolled in the National Registry of Myocardial Infarction in the United States, a voluntary prospective registry of patients with acute MI between January 1, 1995, and December 31, 2004 —Patients who also had ST-elevation MI, including: white, black, Hispanic, and other patients	—They studied risk factors individually and in combination to determine the cumulative effect on delay times in 482,327 patients with ST-elevation MI	Factors associated with longer time from symptom onset to hospital presentation for patients with ST-elevation MI	The mean delay time was 114 minutes, with a decreasing trend from 123 minutes in 1995 to 113 minutes in 2004 (*P* < .001). Nearly half of the patients (45.5%) presented more than 2 hours and 8.7% presented more than 12 hours after the onset of symptoms. Compared with the reference group (those < 70 years, men, white, and did not have DM), subgroups with longer delay times (*P* < .01 for all) included

			those < 70 years, men, black, and had DM (+43 minutes); those < 70 years, women, black, and had DM (+55 minutes); those 70+, men, black, and had DM (+60 minutes); and those 70+, women, black, and had DM (+63 minutes).
		—They analyzed patient subgroups with the following risk factors in combination: younger than 70 yrs vs. 70+, race/ethnicity, men vs. women, and nondiabetic vs. diabetic	
Warren-Findlow, et al., 2011	—The CHAAF study, is a cross-sectional study designed to examine intergenerational transfer of self-care among African Americans. —It was conducted at the University of North Carolina at Charlotte from September 2008 to August 2010. —Eligible participants were African American, at least 21 years old, diagnosed with BP months, and were prescribed hypertensive medications. —95 African American older parent-adult child dyads with hypertension were recruited.	This study examined whether intergenerational transmission of hypertension knowledge and self-efficacy would affect hypertension self-care (medication adherence) of older parents and their adult children. —Separate logistic regression models for older parents and adult children with medication adherence as the outcome —Each model included individual demographic and health characteristics, the partner's knowledge, and self-efficacy to manage hypertension and dyad-related characteristics	Parents were more adherent with medication than adult children (67.4% vs. 49.5%, $P < .012$). There were no significant factors associated with parent medication adherence. In adjusted models for adult children, medication adherence was associated with child's gender (OR = 3.29, 95% CI = 1.26–8.59), parent beliefs that the child had better hypertension self-care (OR = 4.36, 95% CI = 1.34–14.17), and child reports that the dyad conversed about hypertension (OR = 3.48, 95% CI = 1.18–10.29). Parental knowledge of hypertension and parent's self-efficacy were weakly associated with adult children's medication adherence (OR = 1.35, 95% CI = 0.99–1.84 and OR = 2.59, 95% CI = 0.94–7.12, respectively).
Warren-Findlow & Seymour, 2011	—CHAAF study —186 interviews with diagnosed hypertensive African Americans	This study examines a new self-report measure to assess hypertension self-care activities recommended by the medical community for optimal control of BP. This measure is the H-SCALE, assessing 6 prescribed self-care activities. Adherence to six clinically prescribed hypertension self-care behaviors: adherence to medication, weight loss or maintenance of ideal body weight, adoption of a low-salt diet, regular physical activity for 30 min most days of the week, limiting alcohol intake, and ceasing tobacco use	58.6% and 52.2% of participants reported adhering to medication recommendations and prescribed physical activity levels. Following practices related to weight management (30.1%) and adherence to low-salt diet recommendations (22.0%) were lower. Three fourths were nonsmokers and 65% abstained from alcohol. Across the self-care activities, adherers were more likely to be older and female. Nonadherers were more likely to be uninsured.

(Continued)

APPENDIX: Literature Review *(Continued)*

CITATION	DATA/POPULATION	METHOD(S)	OUTCOME MEASURE	MAJOR FINDINGS
Zhang et al., 2008	The Strong Heart Study	—Person-time incidence rates of stroke calculated in male, female, and both sex participants for 3 study centers —Age-specific rates and age-adjusted rates with 95% CIs, using the U.S. 1990 population as the standard population in all age-adjustments —Chi-square tests —Cox proportional hazards models	The aims were to determine the incidence of stroke and to understand stroke risk factors among American Indians.	At baseline examination in 1989 to 1992, 42 participants (age- and sex-adjusted prevalence proportion 1,132/100,000) had prevalent stroke. Through December 2004, 306 (6.8%) of 4,507 participants without prior stroke suffered a first stroke at a mean age of 66.5 years. The age- and sex-adjusted incidence was 679/100,000 person-yrs. Nonhemorrhagic cerebral infarction occurred in 86% of participants with incident strokes; 14% had hemorrhagic stroke. The overall age-adjusted 30-day case-fatality rate from first stroke was 18%, with a 1-year case-fatality rate of 32%. Age, diastolic blood pressure, fasting glucose, hemoglobin A1c, smoking, albuminuria, hypertension, prehypertension, and diabetes mellitus were risk factors for incident stroke.

Abbreviations: ARIC = Atherosclerosis Risk in Communities; BP = blood pressure; BMI = body mass index; BASIC = Brain Attack Surveillance in Corpus Christi; CARDIA = Coronary Artery Risk Development in Young Adults; CHAAF = Caring for Hypertension in African American Families; CAM = complementary and alternative medicine; CHF = congestive heart failure; CI = Confidence interval; CVD = cardiovascular disease; DM = diabetes mellitus; HRS = Health and Retirement Study; Health ABC = Health, Aging, and Body Composition; HF = heart failure; HBPM = high blood pressure monitoring; H-SCALE = Hypertension Self-Care Activity Level Effects; HIS = Hispanic; MA = Mexican Americans; MESA = Multi-ethnic study of Atherosclerosis; MI = Myocardial infarction; MIDUS = Midlife Development in the United States; NA = Native Americans; NHANES = National Health and Nutrition Examination Survey; NHW = non-Hispanic whites; OD = odds ratio; PAR = population attributable risk; SES = socioeconomic status; TIA = transient ischemic attack; WHI = white.

CHAPTER 30

Age in Place and Place in Age: Advancing the Inquiry on Neighborhoods and Minority Older Adults

Jessica A. Kelley-Moore and Roland J. Thorpe, Jr.

There has been a long tradition of work on the role of neighborhoods for minority older adults, ranging from their health-protective elements (e.g., Satariano et al., 2012) to their challenges for older adults (e.g., Clark et al., 2009). The recent explosion of new studies that have multidimensional measurement of both neighborhood characteristics and individual well-being have significantly advanced our understanding of these interactive dynamics between minority older adults and their neighborhoods. This volume brings together scholarship from diverse disciplines and perspectives to advance our state of knowledge on minority aging. In the company of this excellent work, we take the opportunity to set a new challenge for scholarship on minority aging and neighborhoods, namely through the stronger integration of perspectives from ethnic geography and sociology of age.

Decades of research in geography and urban studies have documented race/ethnic residential patterns in neighborhoods, including segregation (Massey & Denton, 1988); shifts in race/ethnic composition (Deskins & Bettinger, 2002); and immigrant settlement (Wen, Lauderdale, & Kandula, 2009). Simultaneously, there has been a stream of literature focused on older adults and neighborhoods, examining issues such as aging in place (Rosel, 2003); age-friendly cities (Phillipson, 2011; Stafford, 2009); and later-life migration (Longino, Bradley, Stoller, & Haas, 2008). While there has been a consistent call for researchers to synthesize research on *age* and *place* (e.g., Rowles, 1993), we argue that much of this work has been focused, somewhat narrowly, in two important ways. First, researchers typically examine *aging* as an individual process rather than age as a structural characteristic of society. Second, neighborhoods are often categorized either as socially meaningful enclaves or as objective environmental space irrespective of the sociopolitical context of the space.

As we expand this inquiry, there needs to be more systematic consideration of *age in studies of place* and *place in studies of age* to advance research on minority older adults and neighborhoods. In this chapter, we have two goals. First, we explicate both of these perspectives, to provide a framework for understanding as to how further integration of work on the sociology of age and ethnic geography can provide greater context and explanatory power. Second, we present illustrative examples that represent new frontiers of research that exist at the nexus of these streams of inquiry.

Sociology of Age

As introduced above, research on neighborhood context for minority older adults could benefit from an expanded view of *age in studies of place*. Traditionally, this work has focused on individual-level issues that may affect older adults, such as walkability (Brown et al., 2011) or perceived safety (Roh et al., 2011). Largely framed by the press-competence framework (Lawton & Nahemow, 1973), this work informs questions about the dynamic balance between environmental demands and the individual's ability to deal with those challenges, heavily focused on aging in place and later-life residential relocation (Glass & Balfour, 2006). In the past several decades, researchers have integrated urban sociology and social geography (e.g., Rowles, 1983), which helped inform work on identity and place attachment (Phillipson, 2007) and increase attention to *aging* in place (Rowles, 1993).

Yet, individual-level processes of aging are only one aspect when considering the role of *age* in *place*. Sociologists have long argued that age is a culturally powerful organizing criterion that channels resource allocation and social dynamics (Walker, 2006). Careful attention to structural elements such as age stratification within and across urban areas and cohort replacement within neighborhoods may provide more insight into the lived experiences of race/ethnic minority elders beyond individual-level competence and identity. While research has often used demographic shifts such as the aging population or in-migration of specific ethnic groups as a starting point for inquiry (e.g., Alba, Logan, & Stults, 2000), little work has integrated structural forces associated with age into analysis, greatly limiting its contributions to questions of age, race/ethnicity, and neighborhoods. To illustrate such potential explanatory power from an expanded focus on age in place, we provide two examples in the section Age in Studies of Place: (a) cohort replacement in transitioning neighborhoods; (b) hypersegregation of the very old and very poor in senior-dedicated public housing.

Ethnic Geography

Research on minority older adults and neighborhoods could also benefit from an expanded focus on *place in studies of age*, namely integrating research from ethnic geography. Rich work has examined subpopulations of race/ethnic minority older adults, yielding significant insights into the diversity of lived experience (e.g., Angel, Torres-Gil, & Markides, 2011; Jackson, Newton, Ostfield, Savage, Schneider, & 1988). Given the distinctive racial/ethnic residential patterning in the United States, such work has necessarily paid attention to environment and context. However, this work could benefit from a stronger connection to research in human and social geography, such as the social construction of communities (Hunter, 1974; Suttles, 1972); urban change (Phillipson, 2011); and country-of-origin patterns of immigrant settlement in urban areas (Price, Cheung, Friedman, & Singer, 2005).

Ethnic geography has traditionally focused on ethnic settlement patterns, migration, as well as the social and spatial integration of race/ethnic minorities (Li, 1998). Wen, Lauderdale, and Kandula (2009) emphasized that this work is crucial for understanding race relations, opportunity structures, and social inequality for race/ethnic minorities. While some exemplary work has successfully integrated ethnic geography into studies of older adults (cf., Ward, 2007), the field could generally benefit from greater systematic attention to the sociopolitical and structural dynamics of place. This can deepen our understanding of minority aging by providing explanations for within-ethnic group variation between regions or differential attachment and well-being across groups in the same geographic area. To illustrate the potential gain from the stronger synthesis of these elements of *place* research into aging studies, we provide two examples: (a) meaning of place for new older immigrants; and (b) older adult migration patterns to and from ethnoburbs.

AGE IN STUDIES OF PLACE

Cohort Replacement in Transitioning Neighborhoods

Many urban and suburban neighborhoods have been subject to racial, sometimes accompanied by socioeconomic, turnover in the latter half of the 20th century and first part of the 21st century. Demographers have documented white flight and stages of neighborhood succession (Massey & Denton, 1988; Park Burgess, & McKenzie, 1925), and this work has been foundational in our understanding of racial residential segregation. However, this rich literature has been critiqued for using decennial snapshots of neighborhood racial composition to draw subtle conclusions about neighborhood succession and group mobility, mainly because they are drawn solely from measures of the minority group's proportional gain in a geographic area over time (Logan, Zhang, & Alba, 2002; Reibel & Regelson, 2007). One classic example is the index of dissimilarity measured at sequential census points and used to document stages of ecological succession in urban areas (cf., Massey & Denton, 1988). These critiques of static composition measures have been largely focused on the risk of using crude composition measures as indicators of dynamic and nuanced processes of neighborhood succession and group mobility.

We argue that the limitations of the decennial snapshot measurement of neighborhood composition further extend to issues of age. First, traditional indicators of residential segregation or succession tend to be *ageless* in their measurement, whereby all persons aged 18 or above are counted solely by their race/ethnicity. This obscures the fact that birth cohorts are frequently confounded with race/ethnicity and social class in transitioning neighborhoods, neglecting the dynamic processes associated with cohort replacement within a neighborhood over time.

Second, this approach conflates age stratification in a neighborhood with cohort replacement processes. Geographic research emphasizes age stratification as an important characteristic of bounded space (e.g., Meade & Earickson, 2000), but often delinks the age distribution from indicators of neighborhood transition. Some empirical work on transitioning neighborhoods has noted social dynamics associated with differential age stratification patterns between neighborhoods. For example, older adults are widely acknowledged to be stable features of transitioning neighborhoods since they are generally long-time residents and homeowners (Stafford, 2009). At the other end of the age spectrum, some research noted the increased demand for schools and day cares that accompanies the in-migration of younger families (Galster, 2011). However, these observations are frequently based on comparative work between neighborhoods at a given time point, and fail to observe the within-neighborhood changes that occur over time.

It is quite interesting to note that some work in urban sociology has followed individual neighborhoods over time, documenting the dynamics of transition and stability within a small bounded space and this has yielded insights into neighbor relations, social participation, and safety (e.g., Hunter 1974; Taylor, 2001). Yet, in this literature, there is virtually no mention of cohort replacement as a feature of transitioning neighborhoods. This cohort replacement can represent shifts in neighborhood socioeconomic status, shared values, or culture, creating tension between cohorts of older long-term residents and younger cohorts of recent transplants. Once such transition reaches a tipping point, many older adults can feel disenfranchised in their own neighborhood.

Researchers have largely focused on these older isolates, framing them as either under siege or stalwart holdouts (Rubinsten, Kilbride, & Nagy, 1992). However, a recent exemplary ethnography of a single neighborhood over two decades demonstrates that the relationships between cohorts in a neighborhood are much more nuanced. Woldoff (2011) traced the transition from an all-white, predominantly Jewish neighborhood through the first and second waves of black residents. She found that the neighborhoods undergoing such a transition may be composed of *stayers*, who are older white adults, and *pioneers* who are middle-class black families with young children.

Popular characterizations of conflict between the long-time homeowners and newly transplanted residents in transitioning neighborhoods (one may recall the iconic scene in *Gran Torino* when Clint Eastwood, an older Irish Catholic homeowner, aims a shotgun at a gang of Vietnamese young men ordering them to "Get off my lawn!"), reflect the bias in empirical research that presumes such conflict is axiomatic. Yet, Woldoff (2011) demonstrates the positive aspects of these multiethnic neighborhoods, specifically the opportunity to learn about another race/ethnic group through benign surveillance and active neighboring. Older white residents may be the recipients of cross-ethnic caregiving and care-neighboring, such as receiving help with snow removal. These same residents, many of whom are retired, are also able to keep watch over the neighborhood during the day or when children are out playing (Rosel, 2003).

Further, elderly white stayers and black middle-class pioneers may forge a bond through a shared desire to invest in the neighborhood, keep it safe, and protect its socioeconomic standing. These residents may share similar angst when a second wave of black residents appear, who tend to be younger and have more children than the pioneer black families, whose own children may already be nearly grown. As Woldoff (2011) demonstrated in her own study, this second wave of black families may be of lower socioeconomic status, be variably employed, and more likely to rent rather than have self-owned homes. For these new arrivals, the neighborhood does not represent the same hope for social mobility and middle-class lifestyle. Thus, the social tension may develop, not between the elderly white neighbors and the first wave of black residents, but *between first and second waves of black residents*.

Since race, ethnicity, and immigrant status are measured in the U.S. Census, it is no surprise that the concept of transitioning neighborhoods is predominantly applied to shifts in the racial/ethnic composition over time (Massey & Denton, 1988). However, there are myriad other transitions in neighborhoods that are not easily captured or completely obscured in administrative data. One such example is cohort replacement in a neighborhood that is homogenously composed of a particular race/ethnic minority group. In the case of Cuban neighborhoods in or near Miami, FL, census measures of Cuban proportional composition have remained extremely high and stable for more than 40 years (Wen et al., 2009). Yet, it is widely understood that more recent waves of immigrants do not share the socioeconomic status or political orientation of early Cuban immigrants (Alberts, 2005; Borjas, 1994). Thus, while the neighborhoods remain predominantly Cuban in composition over time, there have been significant shifts in culture, shared history, and even socioeconomic status that create tension between birth cohorts and threaten the sense of bounded solidarity that had governed politics, economics, and the social life of the neighborhood (Portes & Sensenbrenner, 1993).

Many of the early exiles from Cuba (ca. 1959–1962), who are now elderly, express concern that these shifts in Cuban immigration will damage their image as a model minority (Alberts, 2005). These older adults cite the cessation of character loans to residents within the Cuban neighborhoods and the fact that Cuban employers are showing less preference for hiring fellow Cubans. These older Cubans remember a different ethnic culture, with a stronger informal economy and a shared political ideology that was focused on a pro-Cuban agenda. Although these neighborhoods are still predominantly Cuban in composition, the culture and within-group composition has shifted radically enough that the older adults may be somewhat adrift in the space they had helped build. This is not unique to Cubans. Similar cohort tensions have been found in black middle-class neighborhoods (Patillo, 2005), Polish neighborhoods in Chicago (Erdmans, 2009), and agribusiness cities with Mexican immigrant labor (Jimenez, 2009).

In sum, attention to the dynamics of cohort replacement in neighborhoods, which can be accompanied by transitions in race/ethnic or socioeconomic composition, allows us to contextualize the lived experiences of older adults in urban areas. Many studies that focus on individual-level characteristics such as engagement in healthy behaviors (Osypuk, Diez Roux, Hadley, & Kandula, 2009), perceived safety (Roh et al., 2011), and walkability (e.g., Brown et al., 2011) fail to consider the dynamic within-neighborhood context that may have developed over many decades. Further, the substantial literature on the health-protective effects of living in ethnic enclaves frequently fails to consider such potential cultural or economic shifts in neighborhoods that, by the numbers, remains ethnically homogenous over time (e.g., Aranda, Ray, Al Snih, Ottenbacher, & Markides, 2011; Kang, Domanski, & Moon, 2009). More systematic consideration of within-neighborhood dynamics could help to sort out the mixed findings that appear in this literature.

Hypersegregation of the Old and Poor in Senior-Dedicated Public Housing

It is widely recognized that the most extreme concentrations of urban poverty in the United States are found in public housing developments. Originally constructed as temporary housing for lower and working-class families, urban spatial and employment shifts in the 1960s and 1970s created circumstances where public housing became permanent enclaves of poverty and violence for generations of low-income, predominantly black/African American families (Popkin, Cunningham, & Burt, 2005). Today, many of these metropolitan housing authorities are facing a surge of older adults who have aged through the system and now qualify for senior-dedicated housing (typically ages 55 or older). Yet, due to national policy priorities focused on housing opportunities for working-age adults and children, these older adults receive far fewer resources and are typically housed in the oldest and largest buildings in the metro housing systems.

With the launch of HOPE VI (Housing Opportunities for People Everywhere) program in 1992, there have been nationwide initiatives to create mixed-income developments in place of high-density concentrations of public housing. This place-based strategy to poverty has been designed to improve access to information, economic opportunity, and collective efficacy for residents, primarily through proximity to higher income neighbors who bring greater levels of economic and political power. Although critiques of the HOPE IV framework exist (Briggs, 1997; Patillo, 2007), there has been virtually no criticism for its hyperfocus on young families to the neglect of older residents. Programs such as Moving to Opportunity (see Gennetian, Sanbonmatsu, & Ludwig, 2011, for review) emphasize the long-term goals of improving "the well-being of families and their children, including their housing conditions, mental and physical health, employment and earning, receipt of social program assistance and income, education, and delinquent or risky behavior of children" (Gennetian et al., 2009. p. 163). In other words, the funding priority in public housing reform is concentrated on young families and employment-age adults. Thus, older adults are increasingly segregated and isolated from the geographic areas of priority development.

Employment and self-sustainability are anticipated outcomes of a mixed-use housing strategy, making a focus on families as logical use of resources. This is generally defended as a long-term strategy to reduce the need for public housing assistance by moving people toward independence (Joseph, 2011). Since age integration in the residential areas has not been a priority of the HOPE IV program, the net effect has been the increasing concentration of older adults in residential units that have the lowest priority for demolition and reconstruction into mixed-income residences. Although senior-dedicated housing began in the 1970s, it has only been in the past 15 years that older adults have been increasingly concentrated in the huge high-rise buildings as a low-cost solution for the increasing premium of defensible space (Briggs, 1997; Newman, 1972).

Eligibility criteria for public housing that prioritize age creates socially imposed stratification and inequality for older adults, predominantly black Americans. Policies and programs that systematically exclude older adults are not new, nor are exclusionary policy practices that differentially affect minority elders (Wallace & Villa, 1999). Our emphasis here, however, is that some policy priorities and economic initiatives use age as a criterion for allocation of resources such as housing, and these can disproportionately disadvantage minority older adults who may then be hypersegregated by age and socioeconomic status. Research on individual-level well-being, such as aging in place, optimization, and residential choice, could be significantly improved with the integration of critical policy perspectives on age. In other words, we need a stronger integration of *age* in studies of *place*.

PLACE IN STUDIES OF AGE

Older New Immigrants

The recent climate in the United States regarding immigration has largely centered on contentious debates about border control, documentation, and allocation of economic (e.g., health insurance) and political (e.g., driver's licenses) resources. Notably, these debates focus on working-age immigrants and their children, while a substantial wave of older immigrants has been quietly resettling in the United States over the past several decades. Today, one in eight foreign-born older adults in the United States is a new immigrant (Treas, 2009) and middle-aged and older parents make up 7.5% of all legal immigrants annually (Treas & Batalova, 2007). A distinctive feature of recent older immigrants is their substantial diversity. Mexicans and Chinese account for nearly one quarter of all recent older immigrants (Leach, 2009), but other key contributors include Cuba, El Salvador, Korea, and Eastern Europe. While there are often strong pull factors that bring older adults to the United States, including grandchild care needs and diminishing health of the older adult, a significant driver in the boon of older immigrants is the U.S. policy priority to reunite families (Alberts, 2005).

Given this growing population of older-aged newcomers to the United States, one may be surprised to learn that there is little systematic research on this subset of immigrants. In the opening essay of a Special Issue of *Generations*, Torres-Gil and Treas (2009) state: "The fields of gerontology and geriatrics have generally ignored discussions of immigration and, with rare exceptions, have made few sustained intellectual and theoretical contributions to our understanding of the nexus of aging and immigration" (p. 6). While we concur generally, we extend this critique to traditional studies of aging and neighborhoods. Many of these studies focus on the structural or social features of the neighborhood that are considered to be assets for aging in place (e.g., Stafford, 2009), but tend to neglect subgroup differences among older adults, such as new older immigrants.

Since older immigrants are very likely to be joining other family in the United States, much of the research on this population has focused on living arrangements and inter-generational relations (e.g., Treas & Mazumdar, 2002). Hispanic and Asian/Pacific Islander older immigrants, for example, are overwhelmingly more likely to live with other family, generally adult children (Angel, Angel, Lee, & Markides, 1999; Wilmoth, 2001). Some work has focused on adjustment issues such as initial difficulty accessing services in the United States (Jang, Chiriboga, Kim, & Rhew, 2010).

There is a substantial literature on the mental and physical health benefits for older immigrants living in an ethnic enclave (e.g., Kim, 2009; Osypuk et al., 2009). Although there is an active debate regarding selection effects into and out of ethnic enclaves (Eschbach, Ostir, Patel, Markides, & Goodwin, 2004; Johnston, Poulsen, & Forrest, 2008), it has significantly informed our understanding of the social and physical assets of these types of neighborhoods. However, an increasing proportion of new older immigrants are likely to settle with or nearby their adult children who hold professional jobs and live outside of ethnic enclaves. Located in car-dependent suburbs with English-speaking neighbors, older immigrants often report substantial social isolation and loneliness (Ajrouch, 2008; Treas & Mazumdar, 2002).

This residential pattern can create a contradiction whereby the objectively safe, amenity-rich neighborhood is actually intimidating, inaccessible, and hyperisolating for the new immigrant who may be limited in English proficiency, does not drive, and is adjusting to a new culture of consumerism and service provision. Considering this extreme mismatch between a destination neighborhood and the new older immigrant sharpens the debate about the value of objective versus subjective perceptions of neighborhoods in predicting well-being. Researchers must consider how characteristics of *place* interact with the specific population under study when asked, "What makes a 'good' neighborhood?"

Elder Migration Patterns to and From Ethnoburbs

The ethnic geography literature has proffered three frameworks to explain the residential clustering and segregation along racial/ethnic lines in urban neighborhoods—assimilation, stratification, and resurgent ethnicity. It is this third framework that represents an emerging area of inquiry and could provide a rich opportunity to consider issues of minority aging. As part of the suburban sprawl around large global cities, a new type of neighborhood is developing—the *ethnoburb*. Li (2006, p. 12) defines the ethnoburb as an, "ethnic cluster of residential areas and business districts in a large metropolitan area." This is not a particularly new phenomenon, but such purposeful ethnic settlement in resource-rich neighborhoods has been growing in recent decades (Wen et al., 2009). Today, in the United States, ethnoburbs are most common for Asian Indian, Cuban, Filipino, and Vietnamese immigrant groups (Wen et al., 2009).

These ethnoburbs have characteristics of traditional ethnic enclaves, such as shared language, availability of goods from the home country, and culturally sensitive medical and social services, representing intention to preserve ethnic identity (Logan et al., 2002; Price et al., 2005). Ethnoburbs are distinctive, however, from traditional enclaves for two key reasons. First, the design of an ethnoburb is more closely related to a destination suburb, with low-density new housing subdivisions, shopping centers, medical services, and schools (Li, 2006). By creating culturally distinctive architectural and design components, these ethnoburbs succeed in distinguishing their space from other, multiethnic and middle-class suburbs that offer the same amenities. These are visually, spatially, and socioeconomically distinctive from other types of ethnic settlements such as *colonias*, that often develop in peri-urban areas as informal homesteads for economically marginalized groups (Ward, 2007), or economically segregated ethnic enclaves in urban centers with high poverty rates and concentrations of elderly residents (Loo & Mar, 2010). In these latter ethnic settlements there is a distinct lack of appropriate services and transportation, creating significant challenges for those aging in place relative to ethnoburbs.

Second, affluent areas that emphasize ethnic solidarity and cultural distinctiveness provide counter-data to the widely accepted model of immigrant assimilation, whereby socioeconomic mobility is generally expected to lead to spatial diffusion for an ethnic group (Wen et al., 2009). Indeed, English-language proficiency, which is generally understood to be an indicator of assimilation since it is tied closely to locational flexibility and socioeconomic opportunity, is essentially unrelated to the settlement patterns of ethnoburbs (Logan et al., 2002). In other words, immigrants with limited English proficiency in ethnoburbs are more capable of owning a home, securing employment, and receiving services than residents of traditional ethnic enclaves (Ward, 2007).

Demographers and sociologists who have studied migration patterns of older adults have documented later-life residential moves to amenity destinations, and then return migration following widowhood or a health decline (Longino, 1990). This literature has been critiqued for its overemphasis on choice and upper socioeconomic bias (Phillipson & Biggs, 1998). In response, some work has examined migration patterns of specific race or ethnic groups such as black older adults (Longino et al., 2008). Generally speaking, however, there has been little integration of race/ethnic settlement patterning in research on older adult migration and residential location.

Research on ethnoburbs has typically focused on immigrant settlement patterns, ethnic heterogeneity and mixing within and between geographic areas, and socioeconomic stratification. We posit here that, with the rise of ethnoburbs, and its counterfactual of the persistence of high-density, poorer ethnic enclaves in and near the city, we have a unique opportunity to examine patterns of migration among minority older adults. For example, although these areas have been dominated by young professionals and families (Price et al. 2005), is it possible that the ethnoburbs may represent an amenity move for older adults of that particular ethnic group? Poorer ethnic enclaves often develop informal caregiving networks to help older adults maintain residence, but do the economic and structural amenities in ethnoburbs such as transportation, long-term care, and social activities eliminate the need for such informal care? Integrating this emerging work in ethnic geography could inform potential relocation patterns and preferences of older adults into ethnoburbs, or out of ethnic enclaves.

CONCLUSION

The purpose of this chapter has been to consider potential new lines of inquiry that emerge from the synthesis of research in ethnic geography, urban studies, race/ethnicity, and age/life course. We illustrate four examples that rise from this nexus, compelling us to ask questions about the role of neighborhoods in the lived experience of race/ethnic minority elders.

In the section Age in Studies of Place, we emphasize that, while aging is an individual-level process, much can be learned by considering age as a structural characteristic of a particular place. We first considered cohort replacement in transitioning neighborhoods. The social and economic shifts in a neighborhood over time are influenced directly by the distributional age of residents and their collective history with a particular area. Thus, older adults may represent a particular attachment or investment in a neighborhood that changes over time as newer transplants replace the stayers as the oldest residents. We then addressed the issue of hyper-segregation of the very old and very poor in senior-dedicated housing. Once again, age is a structural feature, used to organize people and allocate resources. The use of age in programs and policies to justify differential access is so common in U.S. society that it has been woefully neglected in research.

In Place in Studies of Age, we shift focus to emphasize the importance of integrating work from ethnic geography into studies of minority older adults and their neighborhoods. Expanding our perspective of *place* may help us understand in a more effective manner the lived experience of minority older adults in ways that no treatment—or a generic treatment—of neighborhood may not. Our first example was the potential challenges of Americanized affluent suburbs for new older immigrants. Typically characterized as amenity-rich, these neighborhoods could make elderly newcomers feel isolated and disenfranchised. Our second example is the rise of ethnoburbs and its growing potential as a destination location for older adults of particular ethnic groups. Traditional work on older adult migration and residential relocation has documented patterns of race/ethnicity (e.g., Longino, 1990) but has not tapped the burgeoning literature on ethnic settlement and creation of resource-rich places of choice.

Integrating research from multiple levels of context, ranging from cross-national migration to attachment to place, opens a new vista of inquiry on minority aging and neighborhoods. As we become an increasingly global, and a notably aging society, we must consider how age influences the structure of opportunity within particular geographic areas and how the ethno-political context of space can influence the aging experience of individuals.

REFERENCES

Ajrouch, K. J. (2008). Social isolation and loneliness among Arab American elders: Cultural, social, and personal factors. *Research In Human Development, 5*, 44–59.

Alba, R. D., Logan, R. J, & Stults, J. B. (2000). The changing neighborhood contexts of the immigrant metropolis. *Social Forces, 79*, 587–621.

Alberts, H. C. (2005). Changes in ethnic solidarity in Cuban Miami. *The Geographical Review, 95*, 231–248.

Angel, J. L., Torres-Gil, F., & Markides, K. (Eds.). (2011). *Aging, health, and longevity in the Mexican-origin population*. New York, NY: Springer.

Angel, R. J., & Angel J. L., Lee G.-Y., & Markides K. (1999). Age at migration and family dependency among older Mexican immigrants: Recent evidence from the Mexican American EPESE. *The Gerontologist, 39*, 59–65.

Aranda, M. P., Ray, L. A., Al Snih, S., Ottenbacher, K. J., & Markides, K. (2011). The protective effect of neighborhood composition on increasing frailty among older Mexican Americans: A barrio advantage? *Journal of Aging and Health, 23*, 1189–1217.

Borjas, G. (1994). The economics of immigration. *Journal of Economic Literature, 32*, 1667–1717.

Briggs, X. (1997). Moving up versus moving out: Neighborhood effects in housing mobility programs. *Housing Policy Debate, 8*, 195–234.

Brown, S. C., Huang, S., Perrino, T., Surio, P., Borges-Garcia, R., Flavin, K., Brown, . . . Szapocznik, J. (2011). The relationship of perceived neighborhood social climate to walking in Hispanic older adults: A longitudinal, cross-lagged panel analysis. *Journal of Aging and Health, 23*, 1325–1351.

Clark, C. R., Kawachi, I., Ryan, L., Ertel, K., Fay, M. E., & Berkman, L. F. (2009). Perceived neighborhood safety and incident mobility disability among elders: The hazards of poverty. *BMC Public Health, 9*, 162.

Deskins, D. R., Jr., & Bettinger, C. (2002). Black and White spaces in selected metropolitan areas. In K. A. Berry & M. L. Henderson (Eds.), *Geographical identities of ethnic America: Race, space, and place* (pp. 38–63). Reno, NV: University of Nevada Press.

Eschbach , K., Ostir, G. V., Patel, K. V., Markides, K., & Goodwin, J. S. (2004). Neighborhood context and mortality among older Mexican Americans: Is there a barrio advantage? *American Journal of Public Health, 94,* 1807–1812.

Erdmans, M. P. (1998). *Opposite Poles: Immigrants and ethnics in Polish Chicago, 1976–1990.* University Park, PA: Pennsylvania State University Press.

Galster, G. (2011). Changing the geography of opportunity by helping poor households move out of concentrated poverty: Neighborhood effects and policy design. In H. B. Newburger et al., (Eds.), *Neighborhood and life chances* (pp. 221–236). Philadelphia, PA: University of Pennsylvania Press.

Gennetian, L. A., Sanbonmatsu, L., & Ludwig, J. (2011). An overview of moving to opportunity: A random assignment housing mobility study in five U.S. cities. In H. B. Newburger et al., (Eds.), *Neighborhoods and Life Chances* (pp. 163–178). Philadelphia, PA: University of Pennsylvania Press.

Glass, T., & Balfour, J. (2006). Neighborhoods, aging, and functional limitations. In I. Kawachi & L. Berkman (Eds.), *Neighborhoods and health* (pp. 303–334). Oxford, UK: Oxford University Press.

Hunter, A. (1974). *Symbolic communities: The persistence and change of Chicago's local communities.* Chicago, IL: University of Chicago Press.

Jackson, J. S., Newton, P., Ostfield, A., Savage, D., & Schneider, E. L. (Eds.). (1988). *The black American elderly.* New York, NY: Springer.

Jang, Y., Chiriboga, D. A., Kim G., & Rhew, S. (2010). Perceived discrimination, sense of control, and depressive symptoms among Korean American older adults. *Asian American Journal of Psychology, 1,* 129–135.

Jimenez, T. R. (2009). What different generations of Mexican Americans think about immigration from Mexico. *Generations, 4,* 93–96.

Johnston, R., Poulsen, M., & Forrest, J. (2008). Asians, Pacific Islanders, and Ethnoburbs in Auckland, New Zealand. *The Geographical Review, 98,* 214–241.

Joseph, M. L. (2011). Reinventing older communities through mixed-income development: What are we learning from Chicago's public housing transformation? In H. B., Newburger et al. (Eds.), *Neighborhood and life chances* (pp. 122–139). Philadelphia, PA: University of Pennsylvania Press.

Kang, S.-Y., Domanski, M. D., & Moon, S. S. (2009). Ethnic enclave resources and predictors of depression among Arizona's Korean immigrant elders. *Journal of Gerontological Social Work, 52,* 489–502.

Kim, S. H. (2009). Health literacy and functional health status in Korean older adults. *Journal of Clinical Nursing, 18,* 2340–2343.

Lawton, M. P., & Nahemow, L. (1973). Ecology of the aging process. In C. Eisdorfer & M. P. Lawton (Eds.), *Psychology of adult development and aging* (pp. 619–624). Washington, DC: American Psychological Association.

Leach, M. (2009). America's older immigrants: A profile. *Generations, 32,* 34–39.

Li, W. (1998). Anatomy of a new ethnic settlement: The Chinese ethnoburb in Los Angeles. *Urban Studies, 35,* 479–501.

Li, W. (2006). Asian immigration and community in the Pacific rim. In W. Li. (Ed.), *From urban enclave to ethnic suburb: New Asian communities in Pacific Rim countries* (pp. 1–22). Honolulu, HI: University of Hawaii Press.

Logan, J. R., Zhang, W., & Alba, R. D. (2002). Immigrant enclaves and ethnic communities in New York and Los Angeles. *American Sociological Review, 67,* 299–322.

Longino, C. F. (1990). Geographical distribution and migration. In R. H. Binstock & L. K. George (Eds.), *Handbook of aging and the social sciences* (3rd ed.). San Diego, CA: Academic Press.

Longino, C. F., Bradley, D. E., Stoller, E. P., & Haas, W. H. III. (2008). Predictors of non-local moves among older adults: A prospective study. *Journal of Gerontology: Social Sciences, 63,* S7–S14.

Loo, C., & Mar, D. (2010). Desired residential mobility in a low income ethnic community: A case study of Chinatown. *Journal of Social Issues, 38,* 95–106.

Massey, D., & Denton, N. (1988). The dimensions of residential segregation. *Social Forces, 67,* 281–315.

Meade, M. S. & Earickson, R. J. (2000). *Medical geography.* New York, NY: Guilford Press.

Newman, O. (1972). *Defensible space.* New York, NY:Macmillan.

Osypuk, T. L., Diez Roux, A. V., Hadley, C., & Kandula, N. R. (2009). Are immigrant enclaves healthy places to live? The multi-ethnic study of atherosclerosis. *Social Science and Medicine, 69,* 110–120.

Park, R. E., Burgess, E. W., & McKenzie, R. D. (1925).*The city.* Chicago, IL: Chicago University Press.

Patillo, M. (2005). Black middle-class neighborhoods. *Annual Review of Sociology, 31,* 305–329.

Patillo, M. (2007). *Black on the block: The politics of race and class in the city.* Chicago, IL: University of Chicago Press.

Phillipson, C. (2011). Developing age-friendly communities: New approaches to growing old in urban environments. In J. R. A. Settersten & J. L. Angel (Eds.), *Handbook of sociology of aging* (pp. 279–296). New York, NY: Springer.

Phillipson, C. (2007). The "elected" and the "excluded": Sociological perspectives on the experience of place and community in old age. *Ageing and Society, 27,* 321–342.

Phillipson, C., & Biggs, S. (1998). Modernity and identity: Themes and perspectives in the study of older adults. *Journal of Aging and Identity, 3,* 11–23.

Portes, A., & Sensenbrenner, J. (1993). Embeddedness and immigration: Notes on the social determinants of economic action. *American Journal of Sociology, 98,* 1320–1350.

Popkin, S. J., Cunningham, M., & Burt, M. (2005). Public housing transformation and the hard-to-house. *Housing Policy Debate, 16,* 1–24.

Price, M., Cheung I., Friedman, S., & Singer, A. (2005). The world settles in: Washington, D.C. as an immigrant gateway. *Urban Geography, 26,* 61–83.

Reibel, M., & Regelson, M. (2007). Quantifying neighborhood racial and ethnic transition clusters in multiethnic cities. *Urban Geography, 28,* 361–376.

Roh, S., Yuri, J., David, A. C., Hwa Kwag, K., Cho, S., & Bernstein, K. (2011). Perceived neighborhood environment affecting physical and mental health: A study with Korean American older adults in New York city. *Journal of Immigrant and Minority Health, 13,* 1005–1012.

Rosel, N. (2003). Aging in place: Knowing where you are. *International Journal of Aging and Human Development, 57,* 77–90.

Rowles, G. D. (1983). Place and personal identity in old age: Observations from Appalachia. *Journal of Environmental Psychology, 3,* 299–313.

Rowles, G. D. (1993). Evolving images of place in aging and "aging in place." *Generations, 17,* 65–70.

Rubinsten, R. L., Kilbride, J. C., & Nagy, S. (1992). *Elders living alone.* New York, NY: Aldine de Gruyter.

Satariano, W., Guralnik, J. M., Jackson, R. J., Marottoli, R. A., Phelan, E. A., & Prohaska, T. R. (2012). Mobility and aging: New directions for public health action. *American Journal of Public Health, 102,* 1508–1515.

Stafford, P. B. (2009). *Elderburbia: Aging with a sense of place in America.* Santa Barbara, CA: Praeger.

Suttles, G. D. (1972). *The social construction of communities.* Chicago, IL: University of Chicago Press.

Taylor, R. (2001). *Breaking away from broken windows.* Boulder, CO: Westview Press.

Torres-Gil, F., & Treas, J. (2009). Immigration and aging: The nexus of complexity and promise. *Generations, 32,* 6–10.

Treas, J. (2009). Four myths about older adults in America's immigrant families. *Generations, 32,* 40–45.

Treas, J., & Batalova, J. (2007). Older immigrants. In K. W. Schaie & P. Uhlenberg (Eds.), *Social structures: The impact of demographic changes on the well-being of older persons* (pp 1–24). New York, NY: Springer.

Treas, J., & Mazumdar, S. (2002). Older people in America's immigrant families: Dilemmas of dependence, integration, and isolation. *Journal of Aging Studies, 16,* 243–258.

Walker, A. (2006). Reexamining the political economy of aging: Understanding the structure/agency tension. In J. Baars et al. (Eds.), *Aging, globalization, and inequality* (pp. 81–102). Amityville, NY: Baywood.

Wallace, S. P., & Villa, V. M. (1999). Caught in hostile cross-fire: Public policy and minority elderly in the United States. In M. Minkler & C. L., Ested (Eds.), *Critical Gerontology* (pp. 237 –256). New York, NY: Baywood.

Ward, P. (2007). *Colonias,* informal homestead subdivisions, and self-help care for the elderly among Mexican populations in the United States. In J. L., Angel & K. E., Whitfield (Eds.) *The health of aging Hispanics; The Mexican-origin population* (pp. 141–162). New York, NY: Springer.

Wen, M., Lauderdale, D. S., & Kandula, N. R. (2009). Ethnic neighborhoods in multi-ethnic America, 1990–2000: Resurgent ethnicity in the ethnoburbs? *Social Forces, 88,* 425–460.

Wilmoth, J. M. (2001). Living arrangements among older immigrants in the United States. *The Gerontologist, 41,* 228–238.

Woldoff, R. A. (2011). *White light/black flight: The dynamics of racial change in an American neighborhood.* Ithaca, NY: Cornell University Press.

CHAPTER 31

Work and Retirement

Joelle Saad-Lessler, Teresa Ghilarducci,
and Karen Richman

Many minorities in the United States will not have adequate income in retirement, such that an unacceptably large number of American minority workers will face poverty in their old age. Though many white workers face economic hardship in retirement, the retirement readiness of near retiree minority workers is worse. Minorities save less for retirement than their white peers primarily because minorities have less income, and also, surprisingly, have less access to the most convenient way workers save consistently for retirement—having a retirement plan or pension plan sponsored at work—when most factors predicting access to an employer-sponsored retirement plan are considered. We have used data from the Bureau of Labor Statistics, the Current Population Survey (CPS), to identify several reasons of the workplace experience that adversely affect the relative retirement income insecurity of minorities. Minorities have lesser access to employer-sponsored retirement plans because they are particularly affected by the substitution of defined benefit (DB) plan coverage for less secure and less comprehensive defined contribution (DC) plans. Also, minorities have inaccurate estimates about their average expected life span and thus have reduced incentive to save for their retirement in voluntary plans.

This chapter provides new data and a critical look at the comparative assessment of different ethnic groups' overall levels of savings given their different experiences in the labor market. We add insight about how employers differentially treat minorities to their disadvantage with a multiple regression analysis that identifies the independent negative impact of being a minority on retirement sponsorship and pension plan participation.

MINORITIES AND RETIREMENT INCOME INSECURITY

Research on the standard of living and social life of the minority elderly population in the United States has advanced recently as the ethnic diversity of the nation's elderly population has grown. At the same time, American employers' commitment to providing retirement plans, including 401(k) and traditional pensions for workers has fallen. As a result, aging is unfortunately still a gateway to poverty especially for minority workers (Banerjee, 2012).

Using the poverty threshold levels from the U.S. Census Bureau (2013), researchers have confirmed what we have always known. Elderly whites have a much lower poverty rate than blacks or Hispanics. In 2011, the difference in poverty rates by ethnic group was large—19.3% of black seniors (aged 65 and older) and 19.0% of Latino seniors have incomes below the federal poverty line—as compared to 7.4% for the white senior population (Rhee, 2012; see Table 31.1).

The economic conditions for older workers are often fragile so that the poverty rates for elderly blacks and whites generally fall and their economic status actually improves the few years after collecting Social Security. But, a people get older, the expenses rise while wage and other income fall, increasing the chances of being poor. The poverty risks are especially high after the age of 85. In 2007, 9.8% of people aged 50 to 64 were poor, whereas the poverty rate among people aged 65 to 74 fell to 8.2% (mainly due to receiving Social Security benefits), then rose to 13.7% after the age of 85, as more people lost income and buying power due to the death of a spouse and inflation[1] (Banerjee, 2012).

Not surprisingly, the poverty rates for all age groups increased in the recession that began in 2008: The poverty rates were 12.3% for people aged 50 to 64, fell to 9.4% for those aged 65 to 74 (when they first became eligible for Social Security), and rose sharply to 14.6% for the oldest of the old (those aged 85 and above). The poverty standards are quite low, they provide for $5 a day for food (Borrowman, 2012).

THE ROLE OF SOCIAL SECURITY

Social Security recipiency reduces poverty rates not only from what they would have been without the program but also reduces poverty rates of older people who are just too young to receive Social Security. Social Security is an important source of retirement income for all Americans (Laursen, 2012). However, it is particularly important for minority workers. Sixty-three percent of all single Hispanic retirees and 40% of Hispanic married couples receive 90% or more of their retirement income from Social Security as compared to 46% for all singles and 23% for all couples (Table 31.2) .

TABLE 31.1 **Poverty Rates of the Elderly by Ethnic Group and Age, 2011**

ETHNIC CATEGORY	OVER AGE 65
White	7.4
Black	19.3
Hispanic	19.0

Source: Rhee (2012) from the American Community Survey 2009–2011, 3-year estimates.

TABLE 31.2 **Minorities Receive a Substantial Share of Their Retirement Income From Social Security**

PERCENTAGE OF PEOPLE RECEIVING OVER 90% OF RETIREMENT INCOME FROM SOCIAL SECURITY		
Ethnic Category[a]	Single (%)	Married Couple (%)
All[b]	46	23
Black	57	28
Hispanic	63	40
Asian and Pacific Islander	53	31

Source: [a]Social Security Factsheet for Demographic Groups. http://www.ssa.gov/pressoffice/factsheets/demographic.htm. U.S. Social Security Administration (2012; 2013)

[b]Social Security Basic facts Factsheet for Demographic Groups. http://www.ssa.gov/pressoffice/basicfact.htm

Because minorities are more likely to be in lower wage jobs throughout their lifetime, Social Security's progressive benefit structure[2] helps keep aged and disabled minorities and their dependents and survivors out of poverty. The value of the life insurance provided to survivors of a typical covered family is over $433,000 and the disability insurance is worth slightly less (Rockeymoore & Lui, 2011). Even though African American men have a lower life expectancy than whites, which may mean that they do not gain as much out of Social Security old age benefits relative to whites, they have higher rates of disability benefit receipt from the program. As Social Security is so effective in raising incomes for the poor elderly, who are disproportionately minority, the 2011 Commission to Modernize Social Security recommended raising revenues for Social Security to restore a long-term fiscal balance to the program and finance benefit increases for the very lowest income recipients.

In the late 1980s, research using the Retirement History Study concluded that the racial and ethnic income disparities that develop in the labor market and through people's working lives are somewhat reversed in retirement as a result of the progressive redistributive structure of Social Security benefits (Ozawa & Kim, 1989).

However, voluntary retirement assets that are derived from tax-deductible contributions to voluntary, individually directed, and commercial-retirement accounts such as 401(k)s and Individual Retirement Accounts (IRAs) magnify racial and ethnic income disparities in retirement income (Hogan, Kim, & Perrucci, 1997; Hogan & Perrucci, 1998; Smith, 1995). In addition, minorities' lack of inherited assets, which perpetuates itself across generations, exacerbates racial income differences that Social Security income can only partially reverse. Intergenerational bequests tracked by the Survey of Consumer Finances indicate that transfers among blacks and Latinos have consistently been at much lower levels than among whites. In 2001, average gifts and inheritances transferred between black generations totaled US$2,365, between Latinos $385, and between whites $20,685 (Conley, 1999; Robles, 2006) implying that socioeconomic class and property ownership are the most important determinants of racial income and wealth inequality in retirement.

Our analysis concurs that differences in accumulated financial assets are a major determinant of the difference in retirement readiness among ethnic groups, but we emphasize the workplace effect on retirement insecurity and disparity. We find that because older workers are not equally distributed across industries and occupations in the crucial period before retirement, earnings before retirement as well as unequal retirement account coverage greatly affect inequality in the adequacy of retirement income after people stop working.

CAUSES OF RETIREMENT INCOME DISPARITIES ACROSS RACIAL GROUPS

Retirement income insecurity for all American workers is growing as a result of two major trends. First, fewer and fewer employees have access to retirement savings plans through their employer. Less than 59% of white workers nearing retirement (age 55–64) work for employers who sponsor any sort of pension plan, and the sponsorship rate for minority workers nearing retirement is even lower. Second, employers who do sponsor any kind of retirement pension plan are likely to offer DC plans rather than DB plans (Ghilarducci, 2008). DC plans are more risky and more insecure for workers than DB plans.[3]

The Racial Disparity in Employer-Sponsored Retirement Accounts

The probability of an employee being offered a retirement account plan at work depends on a person's type of firm and employer and the worker's employment status and characteristics. Minorities are disproportionately employed in lower-paid industries and occupations, which have lower rates of retirement account coverage. As a result, while white workers (as a group) are most likely to be sponsored for a pension plan at work, and black workers follow close behind, the retirement account sponsorship of Asians and Hispanic workers lags by 6% to 18% (see Table 31.3).

TABLE 31.3 Minorities Near Retirement Are Less Likely to Work for Employers Who Sponsor a Retirement or Pension Planning 2010

ETHNIC CATEGORY OF WORKERS AGE 55–64	PEOPLE WHO WORK FOR AN EMPLOYER WHO SPONSOR A PENSION PLAN OR 401(K) TYPE RETIREMENT ACCOUNT (%)
White	58
Black	57
Hispanic	40
Asian	52

Source: Authors' tabulation of CPS data. Data includes the retirement account sponsorship of people ages 55–64 who worked in the preceding calendar year.

Sponsorship rates for younger workers are even lower, but minorities are consistently less likely to work for an employer who offers a retirement account plan at work, regardless of their age.

Increased Prevalence of DC Plans: Financial Literacy and Minorities

The erosion of employer-sponsored DB pensions and the rise of voluntary, employee-directed DC plans raised a host of new research questions. Under DB plans, the employer is responsible for investing pension money. The employer hires an experienced plan administrator to make financial decisions. Under DC retirement account plans, the employee is responsible for allocating contributions and making all the investment decisions. What happens when employees do not have the capacity to make informed investment choices?

This concern has fueled many studies of the status of *financial literacy* across various demographic groups. Lusardi and Mitchell (2004), Choi, Laibson, and Metrick (2001), Bernheim (1998), and other economists explored financial literacy and retirement savings decision making using national data sets. Their research revealed that most people were financially illiterate—which means respondents did not understand the difference between stocks and bonds, or that inflation erodes investment returns. The National Endowment for Financial Education (NEFE) funded much financial education research. Richman, Barboza, Ghilarducci, and Sun (2008) explored Latinos' low use of financial education and revealed that Latinos' lack of financial literacy compromised their already tenuous connection to the retirement system.

Though the research implies that improving financial literacy will improve retirement income security, knowing the difference between a stock and a bond will not help workers persuade their employers to sponsor a retirement plan, to provide automatic enrollment, to raise their incomes, lower investment fees, or find a low-cost annuity. Nor will financial literacy persuade policy makers to expand Social Security, which is the major source of retirement income among minorities.

Retirement Account Plan Participation Rates Among Minorities

An additional concern with DC pension plans is that participation in them is voluntary (participation in DB pension plans, on the other hand, is mandatory). Research on minorities' rates and levels of participation in voluntary DC plans has shown that with the exception of Asians, minorities' pension participation lags far behind whites. Scholars have documented the factors contributing to the relatively high participation of Asian workers, and the low participation of black workers. Latinos, now the largest minority population, have the lowest retirement account participation rates, a looming crisis in light of Latinos' relatively young age and their longer life expectancy (Bulanda & Zhang, 2009). Ghilarducci and colleagues (Ghilarducci & Richman 2008; Sun & Ghilarducci, 2004) have explained the causes of Latinos' lower participation in DC plans relative to any other group. Latino workers are less likely to work for employers who sponsor retirement accounts, and even when Latino employees are working for an employer who sponsors a retirement account plan, they are less likely than Asians, whites, and blacks to be included and more likely to opt not to participate. Fontes (2011) presents encouraging evidence that settlement or nativity correlates with increasing retirement savings participation—Latinos born in the United States have a higher propensity to save for retirement than the foreign born.

Retirement Account Plan Contributions Among Minorities

Once a worker is sponsored for a DC pension plan at work, and if the worker chooses to partic-ipate in the plan, there is still the question of how much to contribute to the plan. Research has revealed that minority workers who do participate in a pension plan contribute to those plans differently from their nonminority peers. The Ariel-Hewitt study (Ariel Education Initiative & Aon-Hewitt Associates [Ariel-Hewitt], 2009), *401(K) in Living Color,* surveyed the DC practices of three million workers. The study found that for those workers who save, Asians have the highest average contribution rate of 9.4%; whites have an average contribution rate of 7.9%, African Americans, 6.0%, and Hispanics 6.3%.

Retirement Account Plan Withdrawals Among Minorities

Another significant finding was the tendency of blacks and Latinos to deplete their savings through hardship withdrawals that are only possible in DC plans (hardship withdrawals are not allowed in traditional DB pension plans). African Americans were 167% more likely than whites, and Hispanics 50% more likely to take a hardship withdrawal (Ariel-Hewitt, 2009). Miranda (2009) analyzed the Ariel-Hewitt study focusing on Latinos and concluded that 401(k) employer-sponsored retirement plans do not serve Latino workers well. She also predicted that the adverse trend would worsen as recession and high unemployment con-tinues. The 2012 update by Ariel-Hewitt of its study nonetheless found a positive trend in participation rates as a consequence of the widespread implementation of automatic enroll-ment by employers, which requires workers to opt out rather than sign up for the program (Ariel-Hewitt, 2012).

A 2012 study by ING of 4,050 workers with a minimum income of US$40,000 confirmed most of Ariel-Hewitt's findings. Culture complex showed that Asians are less likely than other groups to formally plan for retirement, but more likely to have the highest retirement and other savings. African Americans report that debt is their greatest barrier to saving for retire-ment and they are more likely to use life insurance as a savings instrument. Hispanics admit feeling "more unsure" about retirement savings decisions and less prepared for retirement than any other cohort (ING Research Institute, 2012).

WHY DO MINORITIES SAVE LESS FOR RETIREMENT?

Interdisciplinary research involving anthropologists, economists, psychologists, and soci-ologists is emerging to explain why minorities save less than their white peers. Richman, Ghilarducci, Knight, Jelm, and Saad-Lessler (2012) describe how Latinos' collectivist values— investing in social wealth—provide a bulwark against poverty in retirement, but these same collectivist norms undermine an individual worker's retirement savings. As younger Latinos integrate into American culture, they become less collectivist than their parents. This leaves older Latinos vulnerable, because they may find that their children are not willing to support them in old age. Their findings echo the work of Freidenberg (2006) and of Angel and Angel (1997), who have documented the psychological and sociological consequences of the inevi-table abandonment and isolation of the Latino elderly in the United States.

The descendants of Asian immigrants are facing similar challenges. Yoo and Kim (2010) describe how Asian second-generation workers are reinterpreting cultural norms of filial obligation to justify deviating from the patriarchal and patrilineal norm, which previously required daughters-in-law to care for their husband's parents. Adult daughters are shifting their allegiance to support their own elderly parents. At the same time, however, the individualistic norms of American society create pressure on the second generation to want to withdraw from these obligations. Asians' high participation rate in DC plans as well as the relative magnitude of their savings suggests that they are indeed moving toward a more individualistic approach to retirement.

DIFFERENCES IN RETIREMENT EXPECTATIONS AMONG MINORITIES

Starting in the early 2000s, foundations and other organizations funded an addition to the Retirement Confidence Survey sponsored by the Employee Benefit Research Institute (EBRI), which oversampled African Americans, Hispanics, and Asians in order to make comparisons between these groups (Employee Benefit Research Institute, 2007). The latest report available for the Minority Retirement Confidence Survey was from 2007. It found that about half (48%) of African American workers and only 41% of Hispanics said they saved for retirement, compared to 66% of American workers who reported that they saved for retirement. These savings rates are far lower than they were in 2003, when 62% of blacks and 60% of Hispanic workers reported they saved money for retirement.

Doubtless perceptions about retirement can affect retirement planning, and there are key differences in retirement expectations across ethnic and racial groups. The stark difference is that minority groups are extreme in their expectations. Blacks and Hispanics are more likely to say they will be well-off in retirement and more likely to say they will be struggling (see below). When asked their expectations about retirement, 6% of all workers said they would be well-off in retirement. On the other hand, twice as many black and Hispanic workers (12%) said they would be well-off (Table 31.4). Whites were less confident about their retirement security even though they had more assets, saved more, and, though we are not making claims about the causality, they were much more likely to participate in an employer retirement account plan.

The overconfidence displayed in the first column among blacks and Hispanics seems unwarranted compared to their lower savings rates and access to assets for retirement (reported in the next section, Assessing Retirement Readiness Among Minorities).

In 2007, more than half of African Americans and Hispanics reported having less than US$15,000 in savings and investments, compared to approximately one third of all workers. On the other hand, the pessimistic expectations of blacks and Hispanics displayed in the second column are compatible with the present-day reality of minorities' relative income, labor force experience, predicted retirement income, and life spans.

Fifteen percent of Hispanics said their spending in the first five years of their retirement will be higher than in the five years right before retirement, compared to 10% of blacks and 11% of all workers (Minority Retirement Confidence Survey, 2007). This makes sense if Hispanics have relatively low-paying and unstable jobs and they expect to get steady Social Security. Furthermore, approximately 70% of respondents said that they will live comfortably

TABLE 31.4 Minority Workers' Confidence About Retirement Security is More Polarized Than Average

ETHNIC CATEGORY OF WORKERS	PEOPLE WHO SAY THEY WILL BE WELL-OFF IN RETIREMENT (%)	PEOPLE WHO SAY THEY WILL BE STRUGGLING (%)
All Workers	6	10
Black	12	20
Hispanic	12	19

Source: Employee Benefit Research Institute, 2007 Minority Retirement Confidence Survey. Used with permission.

throughout their retirement years, and among those with household incomes of US$25,000 or less, minority workers are considerably more likely than workers overall to feel confident (perhaps because they anticipate a steady source of Social Security income).

A significant source of mismatches between expectations and reality for African Americans may be coming from overconfidence in employer pensions. African Americans are more likely than workers overall to say that a DB pension plan will be a major source of funding for their retirement, even though private-sector pension coverage is declining among these groups, as we illustrate below. Hispanics may also be overconfident about their probable participation in a traditional pension plan. According to the 2007 survey, more than a third of African Americans and Hispanics reported that they expected to receive a DB plan from a future employer, compared to less than a quarter of all workers.

The mismatch between expectations and reality is not limited to retirement income. Using the survey of minorities about their retirement confidence, we compare the retirement expectations, the observed retirement ages, and the expected longevity across racial groups. We confirm what others have found, that Hispanics at the age of 65 have a higher life expectancy than whites or blacks. Yet, the survey reveals that blacks expect to live longer; 47% say they will make it to 85 years, whereas only 32% of whites do, when in fact the average longevity for those who reach the age of 65 is 82 for blacks, and 83.5 for whites. Hispanic workers have the longest longevity—85.6 years of age, but they are the least likely to say they will live until age 85; only 27% say they will (see Table 31.5). Hispanics may not be preparing enough for retirement.

There is a pressing need for workers to have an accurate knowledge of their expected longevity, the value of the Social Security benefits, and the safety and adequacy of their retirement assets.

If people expect to die sooner, denial and complacency about the lack of retirement income may be expected, but people who expect to live longer would ideally take concrete personal and collective political actions to ensure more income in old age, including working longer, saving more, demanding or seeking jobs with pension plans, and advocating for Social Security stability and retirement account reform.

Another area of ill-preparedness for retirement is the lack of health insurance before retirement and the lack of Medicare supplements after the age of 65. Between 1997 and 2008, the percentage of employers offering health insurance to retirees younger than 64 fell from over 21% to 11%. Yet more than half of African Americans, compared to 40% of all workers, expect to have access to retiree health insurance through an employer (Gould, 2010). Among those who are elderly but younger than the eligibility age for Medicare (age 55–64), Gould and Hertel-Fernandez (2010) found that Hispanics aged 50 to 64 are most likely not to be insured; 29.4% are uninsured as compared to whites at 11.7%, blacks at 14.9%, and Asians at 20.8%. Health care costs are a significant source of expenditures for elderly workers and Medicare recipients because of co-pays, deductibles, and uncovered services. The new health care bill will not affect the provision of retiree health care supplements for those eligible for Medicare.

Policy makers will have to contend with constituents' expectations when forming retirement policy. Americans' confidence in their ability to retire comfortably dipped to historically low levels in 2012. As a result, policy makers wanting to take bold steps to shore up the

TABLE 31.5 African Americans Overestimate and Hispanics Underestimate Their Mortality at Age 65

CATEGORY	PEOPLE WHO SAID IT IS LIKELY THAT THEY WILL LIVE UNTIL 85[a](%)	CATEGORY	AGE PROFESSIONALS EXPECT PEOPLE WILL LIVE AT AGE 65[b]
Other	32	White	83.5
Black	47	Black	82.0
Hispanic	27	Hispanic	85.6

Source: [a]Minority Retirement Survey. Used with permission.

[b]Arias E. United States life tables by Hispanic origin. National Center for Health Statistics. Vital Health Stat 2(152), 2010.

retirement security of lower income workers, by extending Social Security or mandating employer retirement account plans, may find that voters are receptive to bold reform ideas. Below, we aim to assess retirement readiness by ethnic and racial category. We also connect labor market experience to differences in readiness.

ASSESSING RETIREMENT READINESS AMONG MINORITIES

Government-supported, national surveys focused on retirement, combined with increasing attendance to racial and ethnic variables, facilitated the development of a research agenda to understand trends in minorities' income, savings, and pension participation. Research and scholarship on minorities and retirement has mushroomed since the 1980s, becoming more nuanced and attentive to the heterogeneity of the minority populations in the United States. The availability of large data sets facilitated increasingly sophisticated quantitative analysis. Qualitative research and interdisciplinary collaborative studies of minority retirement behavior have emerged (Fry & Keith, 1986). Unfortunately, the steady evisceration of workers' entitlement to a decent life in retirement has continued apace. As a result, recent research has been limited to illuminating the increasingly precarious state of minority retirement in the United States.

The Social Security administration sponsored one of these major surveys. The Retirement History Study interviewed 11,153 seniors between the ages of 58 and 63 during the decade of the 1970s. Belated recognition of the inadequacy of a survey that overrepresented white males, and largely ignored blacks, Hispanics, and women, brought the project to an end in 1979. A new panel survey, which addresses the under-sampling of minorities, was therefore started in 1992. The Health and Retirement Study (HRS) interviews heads of households of the age of 50 and above and has sampled 26,000 individuals every two years. The funding for the University of Michigan's HRS comes from the National Institute on Aging and is the most comprehensive national survey of older Americans.

Meanwhile, the U.S. Census Bureau created the Survey of Income and Program Participation (SIPP), a multipanel, nationally representative data set that follows the same individuals over time and collects detailed information on workers' retirement plans. The SIPP survey includes individuals who are aged 15 and higher. The first major rollout of the SIPP was in 1996; the 2001–2004 SIPP covered 36,700 households.

National survey data on retirement, though at a more general level of detail, is also provided annually by the long-standing CPS, a joint project of the U.S. Census Bureau and Bureau of Labor Statistics. Finally, statistical research on retirement has also been facilitated by EBRI, a nonprofit organization, which has, since 1991, sponsored the above described Retirement Confidence Survey. This random, nationally representative annual survey covers 1,000 individuals of the age of 25 and over. Like the Social Security Administration, the U.S. Census Bureau, and the Bureau of Labor Statistics, EBRI has published numerous internal studies and made their data available to researchers.

We use the SIPP and the CPS to identify how much people have saved for retirement. We do this, in particular, for workers[4] aged 55 to 64, who are nearing retirement. The SIPP is used rather than the HRS because of its larger sample size. The data are drawn from the 2008 panel of the SIPP, from Waves 3 and 4, which were fielded in 2009.[5]

We find that in 2009, among workers near retirement age who have some retirement savings, that white workers had the most assets which can be used in retirement (not including Social Security or DB assets), followed by Asians, Hispanics, and blacks. The disparity in financial savings between the racial groups is quite large. White workers had US$363,527 in total assets as compared to black workers who had the lowest level of assets US$197,725. However, white workers only had 3% more cumulative savings than Asian workers. The same trends held for retirement savings as for cumulative savings. White workers accumulated 75% more in retirement savings than black workers, 71% more than their Hispanic counterparts, and 24% more than Asian workers (see Table 31.6).

Since a large percentage of workers who are nearing retirement age have *no* assets for retirement, we recalculate the differences in retirement assets by ethnic group, including workers who have zero balances in their retirement accounts, or no retirement accounts altogether.

The difference in retirement readiness is wide; 32% of white near retirees have nothing in their retirement accounts; 55% of blacks aged 55 to 64 have nothing; 61% of Hispanics aged 55 to 64 have nothing; and 43% of Asians aged 55 to 64 have nothing.

With respect to savings, whites had the highest level of savings at US$298,370, followed by Asians at US$255,273 (14% less than whites), blacks at US$140,657 (53% less), and Hispanics at US$135,456 (55% less; see Table 31.7).

TABLE 31.6 Among Workers With Positive Retirement Account Balances, White Workers Have More Assets Than Other Groups

ASSETS OF NEAR RETIREES AGE 55–64 WITH POSITIVE VALUES IN RETIREMENT ACCOUNTS				
	White (US$)	Black (US$)	Hispanic (US$)	Asian (US$)
Retirement Accounts				
401K, 403b, Thrift plan, KEOGH and IRA Accounts	95,605	54,620	55,997	77,277
Other Assets				
Investments, Business Equity, and Non-Residential Real Estate	181,956	87,484	126,969	150,763
Home Equity*	92,257	61,255	73,648	128,399
Debt	6,291	5,634	7,495	3,718
TOTAL	363,527	197,725	249,119	352,721
TOTAL Without Home Equity	271,270	136,470	175,471	224,322

Note: *Includes the value of a mobile home.

Source: Authors' tabulation using data from the SIPP, 2008 Panel, Waves 3 and 4.

TABLE 31.7 White Workers Have More Assets Than Other Groups When We Include People With No Retirement Savings

ASSETS OF NEAR RETIREES AGED 55–64 WITH POSITIVE VALUES IN RETIREMENT ACCOUNTS				
	White (US$)	Black (US$)	Hispanic (US$)	Asian (US$)
Retirement Accounts				
401(k),403b,Thrift plan, KEOGH and IRA Accounts	64,719	24,461	21,882	44,041
Other Assets				
Investments, Business Equity, and Non-Residential Real Estate	156,935	74,023	68,779	119,634
Home Equity*	83,114	46,898	50,783	96,162
Debt	6,398	4,725	5,988	4,564
TOTAL	298,370	140,657	135,456	255,273
TOTAL Without Home Equity	215,256	93,759	84,673	159,111
Share of Group Who Have Zero Retirement Assets (%)	32	55	61	43

Note: *Includes the value of mobile home.

Source: Authors' tabulation using data from the SIPP, 2008 Panel, Waves 3 and 4.

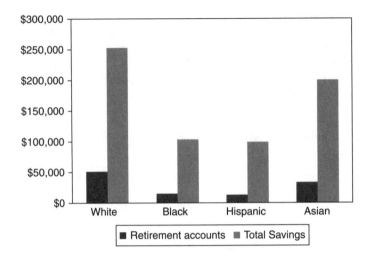

FIGURE 31.1 Whites Have More Assets than Other Groups, When We Include Non-Workers, and People With No Retirement Savings.

Source: Authors' tabulation using data from the SIPP 2008 Panel, Waves 3 and 4.

When we examine the composition of savings, we find that for white workers, most of their savings are in financial investment vehicles, followed by home equity, retirement accounts, real estate, and business equity. Black workers have a similar distribution of savings to that of their white counterparts, but Hispanic and Asian workers have most of their savings locked up in home equity, followed by investments. For Asians, the next place they put their savings is retirement accounts, followed by real estate investments and business equity. Hispanic workers put the balance of their savings into real estate before putting it away in retirement accounts.

So far, we have only looked at workers. What about nonworkers? What are average savings when we look at the whole population of near retirees, regardless of their employment status? Unsurprisingly, the situation looks much worse when we include nonworkers, both for retirement savings and for the overall level of savings; 44% of near-retiree whites have no retirement savings, whereas among near-retiree minorities, 71% of blacks, 76% of Hispanics, and 57% of Asians have no retirement savings at all. Looking at the overall level of savings, whites have 156% more assets than Hispanics, and 144% more than blacks, but only 26% more assets than Asians (see Figure 31.1).

EMPLOYMENT AND EARNINGS DIFFERENTIALS FOR WORKING MINORITIES NEARING RETIREMENT

Why do minorities accumulate so little in the way of savings? Obvious reasons, as mentioned earlier, are that minorities have different labor market experiences than whites. Minority workers more often find themselves in industries and occupations that pay less and have shorter job tenure (see Table 31.8). As they earn less, minority workers cannot afford to save as much as their white peers. Their shorter job tenure also contributes to a reduced sense of job security, which makes it more likely that they will need cash to survive spells of unemployment. These factors reduce the likelihood that they will put money away in accounts that are illiquid, and have barriers to withdrawal (see Table 31.8A).

Compared to other groups, Asian workers have the highest average earnings, so they should be able to save the most for retirement. However, their job tenure is much lower than that of white workers, and this fact must explain why they still lag behind their white counterparts, though they are doing better than black and Hispanic workers are. Black workers have

TABLE 31.8 Minority Near Retirees Have Lower Tenure and Work in Jobs With Lower Earnings (shown in Table 31.8A)

Industry Classification	WHITE		BLACK		HISPANIC		ASIAN	
	Male	Female	Male	Female	Male	Female	Male	Female
Average Job Tenure, in months	176.1	155.7	158.8	149.1	131.9	137.3	152.8	140.8
Average Earnings (US$)	8,005	41,801	46,134	34,279	43,877	27,412	63,063	38,347

Source: Authors' tabulation using data from the SIPP 2008 Panel, Wave 3.

TABLE 31.8A Job Tenure and Earnings of Minority Near-Retirees, By Industry and Occupation

Industry Classification	WHITE		BLACK		HISPANIC		ASIAN	
	Male	Female	Male	Female	Male	Female	Male	Female
Manufacturing	16.3	6.2	17.1	7.7	18.8	11.0	16.0	12.0
Education, Health Care, Social Assistance	15.0	43.6	18.7	43.3	9.7	39.4	13.2	33.8
Professional, Scientific, Management	11.4	8.1	8.0	7.4	9.4	5.6	8.9	3.8
Retail Trade	9.4	9.9	7.1	6.9	9.8	5.5	8.8	13.9
Transport, Warehousing, Utilities	9.0	2.9	15.7	3.3	7.3	4.1	7.3	0.8
Construction	8.8	1.6	6.2	0.8	12.7	0.5	6.7	1.1
Public Administration	7.2	6.9	6.3	12.5	4.2	9.3	3.0	6.1
Finance, Insurance, Real Estate and Rental	5.7	7.5	5.0	6.6	4.9	3.0	7.2	6.9
Other Services (excl. public)	4.8	3.7	8.3	5.6	3.4	3.7	3.1	9.1
Wholesale Trade	3.9	2.2	0.5	0.9	5.6	2.2	6.9	2.5
Arts, Entertainment, Recreation, Accommodation, Food	3.4	4.1	4.1	3.4	8.5	13.7	15.1	7.8
Information Services	2.5	2.6	1.7	1.3	1.5	0.6	2.5	1.4
Mining	1.2	0.2	0.9	-	0.8	-	0.2	-
Agriculture, Forestry, Fishing, Hunting	1.0	0.4	0.3	-	2.9	1.3	1.1	-
Military	0.3	0.0	0.1	0.4	0.4	-	-	0.8
Occupational Classification								
Management and Professionals	44.5	47.4	28.3	34.3	15.1	30.8	43.5	31.0
Service, Sales, Office Occupations	8.1	12.7	18.5	30.3	23.6	35.0	18.1	26.8
Farming, Fishing, and Forestry	16.8	35.4	13.0	25.4	16.2	22.0	17.9	30.8
Construction, Extraction, Maintenance	14.1	0.6	14.4	0.8	15.6	-	6.4	1.4
Production, Transportation, Machine Operation	16.5	4.0	25.9	9.3	29.5	12.3	14.2	10.1

Note: Authors' tabulation using data from the SIPP, 2008 Panel, wave 3.

lower average earnings and lower job tenure than white workers, and Hispanic workers have the lowest average earnings and the shortest job tenures of all workers.

DO EMPLOYERS OFFER LESS RETIREMENT ACCOUNTS TO MINORITIES? REGRESSION ANALYSIS

An earlier section of this chapter described the disparities in pension plan sponsorship and participation between minorities near retirees. However, we just learned that minority groups have different experiences because their members are in different types of jobs. Knowing that a minority group faces lower rates of sponsorship or participation does not necessarily imply that there is any discrimination if we do not control for differences in worker choices and productivity; even when we control for observed differences between workers, unexplained differences in sponsorship or participation rates may persist. These can be attributed to discrimination, or to uncontrolled-for factors.[6]

We find evidence for discrimination. Using Wave 3 of the SIPP 2008 panel to regress pension sponsorship and participation rates on all the measurable characteristics known to affect the coverage rates we can isolate the effects of being in an ethnic group category. Using what is called a *Probit* regression analysis,[7] we find that minorities are less prepared for retirement, even controlling for income, as well as other factors explaining employer pension plan sponsorship and participation rates. The negative effects of being black and Hispanic, independent of other factors, on pension and retirement account provision were strongly significant.

We controlled for most factors affecting retirement savings accumulation and coverage and considered the effect of being a minority independently. A Probit regression decomposes the factors that affect the probability of having an employer who sponsors a retirement account plan at work (or of participating in such a plan) into explanatory variables, such as a worker's gender, race, age, and other observed characteristics. The estimated coefficient on each characteristic reflects the impact that a change in such a characteristic implies for the person's sponsorship (participation) rate. Once we have these estimated coefficients, we can predict the sponsorship (participation) rate for any ethnic/racial group, using the average characteristics of members of that ethnic/racial group.

Among the explanatory variables, we included a worker's gender, race, citizenship status, education level, age, occupation, industry, firm size, union status, full-time/part-time status, whether the worker was an hourly wage worker, sector of employment, nativity, marital status, household income, and length of their tenure at their current employer. The variables included in the model explained 27% of the variation in pension sponsorship rates across individuals, but only 18% of the variation in participation rates, meaning that the model was better at explaining differences in a person's likelihood of being sponsored for a pension plan at work than in explaining whether they participate in a pension plan.

After controlling for all the observed determinants of pension plan sponsorship and participation, ethnic/racial differences still had a measurable impact on the likelihood of a person being sponsored for a pension plan at work, and the likelihood that the person participated in a plan when one was available. In fact, being black reduced one's likelihood of being sponsored for a retirement account plan at work by nine percentage points relative to a comparable white worker; being Hispanic lowered one's likelihood of being sponsored by 37%, and Asian workers suffered a drop in pension sponsorship of 13%. These are differences in predicted sponsorship rates that cannot be explained by observed differences in worker characteristics. In other words, these differences may be interpreted as measures of discrimination in the labor market and other uncontrolled-for factors

Predicted retirement account participation rate for black workers is 9% lower than for white workers, while the participation rate of Hispanic workers is 15% lower, and that of Asians is 1% higher (see Table 31.9). Again, these differences in participation rates already control for differences in observed worker characteristics, meaning that they stem from unobserved influences, such as cultural factors or institutional factors that are at play among black and Hispanic workers, holding them back from fully participating in their pension plans at

TABLE 31.9 Being a Minority Reduces the Probability of Working for an Employer Sponsoring a Retirement Account or Pension and Participating in a Retirement Account

	EFFECT OF BEING IN ETHNIC GROUP ON SPONSORSHIP, (COMPARED TO WHITES; %)	EFFECT OF BEING IN ETHNIC GROUP ON PARTICIPATION, (COMPARED TO WHITES; %)
Black	-9	-9
Hispanic	-37	-15
Asian	-13	1
Pseudo R-squared	27	18

TABLE 31.10 Black and Hispanic Workers Will Likely Be Poor Retirees Even if They Have Retirement Assets

LIFETIME MONTHLY INCOME AFTER AGE 65	WHITE	BLACK	HISPANIC	ASIAN
Poor (Less than or Equal to FPL)	9.6%	21.7%	27.2%	14.7%
Near Poor (100–200% of FPL)	21.1	31.5	34.4	20.1
Adequate Income (More than 300% FPL)	49.8	29.0	23.2	43.0

Source: Authors' tabulation using data from the SIPP, 2008 Panel, Waves 3 and 4.

work when those are available. An example of cultural factors is Latinos' reliance on collectivism in lieu of individual saving for retirement; institutional factors may include instances when an employer discourages workers from participating.

DISCUSSION

What Are the Implications of Low Levels of Retirement Savings?

Using the level of overall savings for all[8] workers aged 55 to 64, we project what each worker's savings will be when they reach the age of 65. We then convert that level of overall savings into a monthly lifetime income, using standard assumptions about life expectancy by gender. We also add in each person's expected monthly Social Security benefit, using the person's earnings and age. This tells us how much each person should expect to receive in monthly income once they retire at the age of 65. This level of lifetime monthly income is then compared with the federal poverty level to analyze how workers will fare when they reach retirement. The findings are astounding. Among white workers aged 55 to 64 in 2009, 9.6% will be poor when they retire at the age of 65, and a further 21% will be near poor, living on less than twice the federal poverty level (see Table 31.10, above). For other racial groups, the situation is worse! Among black workers, 21.7% can expect to be poor, while an additional 31.5% will be near poor. 14.7% of Asian workers will be poor, and an additional 20.1% will be near poor, despite their relatively high levels of savings. And finally, Hispanic workers are the worst off, with 27.2% poor when they retire, and an additional 34.4% near poor. In fact, less than 30% of blacks and 23% of Hispanics will live comfortably in retirement—this is defined as having a monthly income at three times the federal poverty level or greater.

These numbers are very worrisome and they indicate that the country faces a looming poverty crisis when the current generation of near retirees reaches retirement age.

CONCLUSIONS AND POLICY IMPLICATIONS

Our findings on minority retirement saving accumulations are very worrisome because they indicate that the country faces a looming poverty crisis when the current generation of near retirees reaches retirement age. However, we are experiencing a decline in the retirement security of all but the most affluent Americans. Whites today face a greater likelihood of poverty in retirement than in the previous 40 decades, while for minorities, the precariousness of old age continues unabated.

Our chapter finds that minorities are less ready for retirement than their white peers and explains why minorities are less prepared to retire with adequate income. The causes include the role of differential retirement account sponsorship at work among racial groups, as well as the impact of steady erosion of DB plans in favor of DC plans. Minorities are less likely to participate in a retirement plan when one is available and they contribute less when they do participate. Minorities are more likely to take hardship withdrawals from their retirement account plans. When we compared minorities' overall savings with those of white workers, we found that even after accounting for nonretirement assets, minorities are less ready for retirement than white workers. We found evidence of a connection between the work experience of older minority workers and the likely adequacy of their retirement income. Minority expectations about their future retirement adequacy diverge sharply with the likely reality of their financial futures. On the one hand, minority workers about to retire are more confident than white workers on the likelihood that they will have adequate retirement income, while on the other hand, a greater share of minorities report more pessimism, which is appropriate.

Finally, the multiple regression analysis shows that even after controlling for observed differences across individuals, members of minority groups are less likely to have access to a retirement plan at work and they are less likely to participate in such a plan when it becomes available. As a result of low levels of overall savings, and of retirement savings in particular among near retiree minorities, we project that an unacceptable number of minorities will face poverty in old age. These results ought to serve as a wake-up call to policy makers that the situation among minority elderly is a crisis that will soon be upon us.

Despite its alarming implications, the retirement income security crisis is not an anomaly, but rather a predictable outcome of the structuring of the system of retirement in the United States. Unlike in comparable societies, lifelong employment in the United States no longer ensures a decent quality of life in old age (Angel & Angel, 2009). The erosion of employer-based defined pensions means that the workplace with a retirement plan no longer provides annuity income. The voluntary, individual DC plans offered by employers are insufficient, and less than 50% of employees even have access to these savings plans.

The DC plans were invented in 1978 as a way for the affluent set-aside pre-tax income as a supplement to their retirement savings. What was once a *supplement* that was most beneficial to the wealthy has become the *only* retirement savings option for those eligible workers. As Ghilarducci (2008) has shown, the stock market and the mutual fund industry benefitted greatly from the infusion of employees' contributions, but ordinary employees, with the exception of investment experts, are utterly unprepared to make retirement investment decisions. Ghilarducci (2012) argued that "this do-it-yourself pension system expects individuals without investment expertise to reap the same results as professional investors and money managers. What results would you expect if you were asked to pull your own teeth or do your own electrical wiring?" Indeed, Ted Benna, the inventor of the 401(k), has disavowed his own creation. Reflecting on the development of the model over three decades, he called the 401(k) "a monster" and exclaimed to Jeremy Olshan, "I would blow up the system and restart with something totally different" (Olshan, 2011).

Unless and until "something totally different" replaces the 401(k) system, the system of Social Security is even more essential to keeping elders, and especially minority elders, out of extreme poverty.

Unfortunately, in 2013, Social Security remains under threat of attack. The U.S. government lags behind other comparable states to ensure the welfare of elders when they stop working (Angel & Angel, 2009). Mounting debt and deficient resources, especially since the financial crisis of 2007, are the commonly cited reasons that explain why government programs are not willing to do more to keep seniors out of poverty. But, a broader, concomitant trend also accounts for the crisis in retirement, namely, a cultural shift toward individual self-reliance and away from communal welfare. Ironically, the emphasis on the rhetoric of individual independence and self-reliance is expanding in inverse relation to the security and retirement assets of most current and future retirees, as these numbers show. When individual privacy, independence, and freedom are hailed as the highest moral precepts, these notions deflect attention away from the structural patterning and inevitability of the retirement crisis. The belief in individual self-reliance suggests that individuals are primarily responsible for their own ability or inability to prepare for retirement and that collective solutions are neither warranted nor possible.

NOTES

1. Inflation erodes all sources of retirement income except Social Security benefits, which are indexed to inflation.
2. It replaces a larger share of lower earners' preretirement earnings.
3. The employer decides whether to sponsor a DB and/or DC retirement plan. A DB plan uses a formula that typically credits every year of service with a certain percentage of pay to determine lifetime pension benefits. The employer invests the assets and guarantees the pension, and the worker implicitly pays for the DB plan with reduced take-home earnings. The worker has no choice with a DB plan about whether to participate and at what level. With DC plans—most are 401(k)s—the employer provides a tax-advantaged savings account that employees can contribute to on a voluntary basis. The amount of workers' contribution is a matter of choice, as is participation in the plan altogether. The worker, not the employer, invests the assets.
4. Workers are defined as individuals who had a job in the reference period, had positive earnings, were not unpaid family workers, and were not in the armed forces or in the agricultural sector.
5. Tabulation of retirement savings and total assets required the use of both Wave 3 and Wave 4 data, because the former has information on retirement savings while the latter has information on assets. Characteristics of workers, and regressions of sponsorship and participation only used data from Wave 3.
6. Unobserved differences across workers, for example.
7. A Probit model is a type of regression where the dependent variable can only take two values, 0 or 1. This model is most often estimated using standard maximum likelihood procedure. In the present case, the dependent variable is whether the worker is sponsored for as pension plan at work (1) or not (0), or whether the worker participates in the pension plan (1) or not (0).
8. This is done for all workers, whether they have positive retirement savings or not.

REFERENCES

Angel, R. J., & Angel, J. L. (2009). *Hispanic families at risk: The new economy, work, and the welfare state.* New York, NY: Springer.

Angel, J., & Angel, R. (1997). *Who will care for us?: Aging and long-term care in multicultural America.* New York, NY: New York University Press.

Ariel Education Initiative & Aon-Hewitt Associates (Ariel-Hewitt). (2009). *401(k) plans in living color: A study of 401(k) savings disparities across racial and ethnic groups.* Chicago, IL: Ariel Education Initiative.

Ariel Education Initiative & Aon-Hewitt Associates (Ariel-Hewitt). (2012). *401(k) plans in living color: A study of 401(k) savings disparities across racial and ethnic groups.* Chicago, IL: Ariel Education Initiative.

Banerjee, S. (2012, April). Time trends in poverty for older Americans between 2001–2009. *Employee Benefit Research Institute ebri.org Notes, 33*(4), 10. Retrieved from http://ebri.org/pdf/notespdf/EBRI_Notes_04_Apr-12.CDHP-EldPovty.pdf

Borrowman, M. (2012). *Understanding elderly poverty in the United States: Alternative measures of elderly deprivation* (Working Paper SCEPA). Retrieved from https://docs.google.com/file/d/0B35bSCEPA WORKING PAPER 2012–3

Bernheim, D. (1998). Financial illiteracy, education, and retirement saving. In S. M. Olivia & J. S. Sylvester (Eds.), *Living with defined contribution pensions*. Philadelphia, PA: University of Philadelphia Press.

Bulanda, J., & Zhang, Z. (2009). Racial-ethnic differences in subjective survival expectations for the retirement years. *Research on Aging, 31*, 688–709.

Choi, J., Laibson, D., Madrian, B., & Metrick, A. (2001). *Defined contribution pensions: Plan rules, participant decisions, and the path of least resistance* (NBER Working Paper Series, w8655). Cambridge, MA: National Bureau of Economic Research.

Conley, D. (1999). Getting into the Black: Race, wealth, and public policy. *Political Science Quarterly, 114*, 595–612.

Employee Benefit Research Institute (EBRI). (2007, June). *2007 Minority Retirement Confidence Survey* (Issue Brief #306).

Fontes, A. (2011). Differences in the likelihood of ownership of retirement saving assets by the foreign and native-born. *Journal of Family and Economic Issues*, 1–13.

Freidenberg, J. (2006). Elderly Latinos of Langley Park: Understanding retirement issues. *Journal of Latino-Latin American Studies, 2*, 112–124.

Fry, C. L ., & Keith, J. (Eds.). (1986). *New methods for old-age research: Strategies for studying diversity*. South Hadley, MA: Bergin and Garvey.

Ghilarducci, T. (2012, July 21). Our ridiculous approach to retirement. *New York Times*.

Ghilarducci, T. (2008). *When I am sixty four: The plot against pensions and the plan to save them*. Princeton, NJ: Princeton University Press.

Ghilarducci, T., & Richman, K. (2008). Latinos' retirement income security. *Business Journal of Hispanic Research, 2*(2), 50–63.

Gould, E., & Hertel-Fernandez. A. (2010). Early retiree and near-elderly health insurance in recession (Special issue: Retirement security in the great recession). *Journal of Aging & Social Policy, 22*(2), 172–187.

Hogan, R., & Perrucci, C. (1998). Producing and reproducing class and status differences: Racial and gender gaps in U.S. employment and retirement income. *Social Problems, 45*, 528–549.

Hogan, R., Kim, M., & Perucci, C. (1997). Racial inequality in men's employment and retirement earnings. *Sociological Quarterly, 38*, 431–438.

ING Research Institute. (2012) *Culture complex: Insights from ING's Retirement Revealed Study*. Vernon, CA: ING Retirement Research.

Laursen , E. (2012). *The people's pension: The struggle to defend social security since Reagan*. Oakland, CA: AK Press.

Lusardi, A., & Mitchell, O. (2004). Saving and the effectiveness of financial education. In O. Mitchell & S. P. Utkus (Eds.), *Pension design and structure: New lessons from behavioral finance*. New York, NY: Oxford University Press.

Miranda, L. (2009). *Insecure retirements: Latino participation in 401(k) plans*. Washington, DC: National Council of La Raza.

Minority Retirement Confidence Survey. (2007). *Fact sheet expectations about retirement*. Retrieved from http://www.ebri.org/files/MRCS07.FS2_Final.pdf

Olshan, J. (2011, November 22) Father of the 401(k)'s tough love. *The Wall Street Journal*.

Ozawa, M., & Kim, T. (1989). Distributive effects of social security and pension benefits. *Social Service Review, 63*, 335–358.

Rhee, N. (2012). *Black and Latino retirement (in)security*. Berkeley, CA: University of California, Center for Labor Research and Education.

Richman, K., Barboza, G., Ghilarducci, T., & Sun, W. (2008). *La tercera edad: Latinos, pensions, retirement and impact on families*. Notre Dame, France: University of Notre Dame, Institute for Latino Studies.

Richman, K., Ghilarducci, T., Knight, R., Jelm, E., & Saad-Lessler, J. (2012). *Confianza, savings, and retirement: A study of Mexican immigrants*. Notre Dame, France: University of Notre Dame, Institute for Latino Studies.

Robles, B. (2006). Wealth creation in Latino communities: Latino families, community assets, and cultural capital. In J. Nembhard & N. Chieji (Eds.), *Wealth accumulation and communities of color in the United States: Current issues* (pp. 241–266). Ann Arbor, MI: University of Michigan Press.

Rockeymoore, M. M., & Lui, M. (2011). *Plan for a new future: The impact of social security reform on people of color*. Washington, DC: Commission to Modernize Social Security.

Smith, J. (1995). Racial and ethnic differences in wealth in the health and retirement study. *Journal of Human Resources, 30*, 158–183.

Sun, W., & Ghilarducci, T. (2004). *Latinos' low pension coverage and disenfranchisement from the US financial system*. NotreDame, IN: University of Notre Dame, Institute for Latino Studies.

U.S. Social Security Administration (2012). *Factsheet for Demographic Groups.* Retrieved from http://www.ssa.gov/pressoffice/factsheets/demographic.htm

U.S. Social Security Administration (2013). *Social Security Basic Facts.* Retrieved from http://www.ssa.gov/pressoffice/basicfact.htm

U.S. Census Bureau (2013). *How the Census Bureau Measures Poverty.* Retrieved from www.census.gov/hhes/www/poverty/methods/measure.html

Yoo, G., & Kim, B. (2010). Remembering sacrifices: Attitude and beliefs among second-generation Korean Americans regarding family support. *Journal of Cross-Cultural Gerontology, 25*(2), 165–181.

CHAPTER 32

Public Policy, the Welfare State, and Older Minority Americans

Ronald J. Angel

THE WELFARE STATE AND MINORITY AMERICANS

The welfare state represents a relatively late development in human social, economic, and political history (Esping-Andersen, 1990; C. Pierson, 2007; Sigerist, 1999). Although humans have always been interdependent and reliant on the tribe or community for support, it was only during the 19th Century when Chancellor Otto Von Bismarck of Germany first introduced old-age pensions, sickness, and accident insurance, and other aspects of the welfare state that citizens of industrializing nations began to expect the state to guarantee their basic material security (Esping-Andersen, 1990; Palier, 2010; Sigerist, 1999). The welfare state is clearly the result of capitalist industrialization and the social and political relations it brings about (C. Pierson, 2007). It has evolved in unison with capitalist economies to mitigate the serious human suffering that an unfettered market would bring about (Baldwin, 1990; Marshall, 1950). The modern welfare state with which we are familiar today took shape after World War II as part of the rebuilding of a war-torn Europe. In 1942, English economist William Beveridge proposed the basics of the British social guarantees in a report entitled "Social Insurance and Allied Services" (Beveridge, 1942). That report marked the beginning of the National Health Service and the rest of the British welfare state.

In the United States the welfare state has remained much more limited than in Europe, and yet it is vitally important for low-income families, the elderly, and minority Americans (R. J. Angel & J. L. Angel, 1997; R. J. Angel & J. L. Angel, 2009; Hacker, 2002; Weir, Orloff, & Skocpol, 1988). Social Security and Medicare represent the only support programs that are universal citizenship rights, and those benefit only retired individuals and those above 65 years of age. Even if President Obama's health care reform package, the Patient Protection and Affordable Care Act, is implemented, the United States will still not have universal health care coverage. Beyond that, Workers Compensation and unemployment insurance are available to some workers, but for the most part social welfare programs remain means-tested and targeted to the poor. Medicaid, food stamps, housing assistance, and other means-tested programs, such as the Earned Income Tax Credit (ETIC) are vitally important to those with limited resources, but for the most part programs for the poor remain stigmatized and stigmatizing. Explanations for the limited welfare state in the United States are beyond the scope of this chapter and focus on political, cultural, and historical differences between Europe and the United States, as well as on institutional factors related to the timing and ways in which such programs as old-age pensions and health care coverage were introduced (Béland & Hacker, 2004).

This chapter provides a review of public policy and public programs related to important aspects of the welfare state in the United States, with particular attention to the impact of various policies and programs related to income support, health care, and housing on low-income and minority Americans. Although the focus is primarily on programs that provide support to older individuals, it is necessary to understand the system more completely since programs for different age groups compete for the same limited resources. In addition, the economic and social situations, as well as the health of older minority group members, are determined by life-long factors that influence their level of wealth and their health in later life. There are, of course, hundreds of specific governmental and nongovernmental programs that affect minority and low-income Americans, from assistance with home repairs to meals on wheels.

The discussion focuses on the major aspects of the labor force that affect wealth accumulation and income over the life course, and that determine one's economic security in old age. Also reviewed are policies related to health care and housing, two major aspects of overall well-being. Rather than going into excessive detail concerning specific programs, this chapter focuses more on the guiding principles that motivate the various parties in today's welfare state debates and investigate how the basic structure of the way social welfare, broadly defined, is guaranteed in the United States affects low-income and minority individuals. Such guiding principles inform policy and reflect a nation's political culture, as well as the nature of the historical and political processes that have structured competition among various racial and ethnic groups, as well as different social classes in the past and that continue influencing policy today. Ultimately, the major question that must be addressed is how low-income minority Americans will be affected by the end of the post–World War II economic boom. The world has entered what some have described as a period of protracted or permanent austerity in which competition for scarce resources could have serious negative implications for those individuals most dependent on public programs (Pierson, 2001).

Before proceeding to a discussion of specific policies and social programs, it is necessary to frame the discussion of U.S. exceptionalism in terms of universal guarantees of social rights. The limited welfare state in the United States has always left many vulnerable individuals without an adequate safety net, and those with inadequate support have never been a cross-section of the population; they have always been disproportionately African American, Native American, and Latino. Educational and labor market disadvantages have left large numbers of minority individuals and families at risk of poverty, ill health, and premature death. Many older minority group members enter the later years of life with little wealth and inadequate retirement incomes. Left with few options, they find themselves dependent on children for support and assistance (J. L. Angel, Angel, Aranda, & Miles., 2004; R. J. Angel & Angel, 1997).

The neoliberal political economics and an intensified assault on welfare state principles that have influenced social policy in recent years have particularly serious implications for minority group individuals and families. The 2008 recession and the collapse of the housing bubble that fueled it provide examples of the serious negative impact that even well-meaning policies can have. In a desire to increase home ownership among less affluent groups, policies that privileged the market over government-sponsored housing resulted in lending practices that placed many minority families and single women at serious risk of foreclosure and the trauma that entails (Ashton, 2010; Erickson, 2009; Immergluck, 2011; Rugh & Massey, 2010).

Why public policy looked to the real estate market over public housing is an important part of the story and reminds us that although the welfare state is a core aspect of modern capitalist societies, it has always been contested (Hayek, 1944, 1976). It remains the target of criticism from conservative critics who advocate a limited role for government in providing for the material welfare of the population (Etzioni, 1993, 2000, 1995; L. M. Mead, 1986, 1997; Murray, 1994, 1996, 1999, 2006). These critics believe that social welfare programs create dependency and contribute to the decline of the family and community, as well as the growth of an underclass. Conservatives are not the only critics.

Those on the left fault the welfare state for its limited coverage and see it as depoliticizing the debate over the distribution of wealth and undermining more radical structural solutions (Dwyer, 2004; C. Pierson, 2007).

In the United States, the term *welfare* has a negative connotation. Middle-class Americans do not see themselves as dependent on the welfare state, yet they are. In fact, real social welfare expenditures in the United States account for as much of gross domestic product (GDP) as is the case in the more developed welfare states of Europe (Gilbert & Gilbert, 1989; Gottschalk, 2000; Hacker, 2002; Howard, 1997; Stevens, 1988). Retired Americans rely on Social Security and Medicare; tax incentives for pension and health plans, credit subsidies, and other indirect transfers for the middle-class represent foregone tax revenues and account for a major component of economic productivity (Hacker, 2002). The fact that a large fraction of total social spending in the United States is indirect and subsidizes benefits for the middle class has major distributional implications, but they do not benefit the poor. As Jacob S. Hacker notes, " it matters fundamentally whether a nation's social welfare framework is characterized by low public spending, low taxes, and high private spending, on the one hand, or high public spending, high taxes, and low private spending, on the other; and this is true even if after-tax spending is identical" (Hacker, 2002, p. 23). The first scenario characterizes the United States; the second, the more egalitarian societies of Europe that have far less income inequality and lower rates of poverty than the United States (Smeeding, 2000; Smeeding, Rainwater, & Burtless, 2001).

Of course, even in our free-market economy the state plays a major role in economic activity. The federal government regulates interstate commerce, it insures the safety of food and drugs, it regulates securities markets, if not always effectively, and at the state level it regulates the insurance and health care industries. As more of the total health care bill is paid by federal and state programs such as Medicaid and Medicare, we are moving toward even more governmental control of health care. Yet in the United States the state's role in regulating the market, regulating labor contracts, and assuring a more equal distribution of wealth remains far more limited than that of European governments (Hacker, 2002; King & Wood, 1999). The United States has never had parties with the Social Democratic or Christian Democratic orientations of many European political parties. The Democratic party has traditionally represented labor but in the United States labor has often been unsupportive of, and at times even hostile, to such core aspects of the welfare state as universal health care (Hoffman, 2001; Numbers, 1978; Quadagno, 2005; Starr, 1982a).

The fiscal crises that mature welfare states face in dealing with aging population and costly welfare programs during a period of serious globalized financial crises have led to attempts to decrease the state's role in social insurance (Palier, 2010; C. Pierson, 2007). Yet, despite its growing cost, in developed nations the belief that the state should provide a minimal level of security against material want persists. The ongoing debate centers on what that minimal level of security consists of and what responsibilities those who receive it bear. In a period of economic retrenchment in which attacks on welfare state programs are increasing, and in which the need to control the rising costs of public programs are unavoidable, low-income individuals, among whom minorities are overrepresented, face particular risks. Reductions in Medicare reimbursements, for example, may mean that many older low-income minority elders may not be able to find a physician that will accept them. Even supposedly positive policy changes could have unintended effects. The extension of Medicaid coverage to low-income childless adults that is part of the new health care law, a clearly laudable step toward reducing the number of uninsured Americans, could potentially reduce funding for long-term care for disabled minority elders. Policies that affect the private sector can also have serious negative effects for minority elders. Policies and laws that regulate retirement plans are one example. Today employers are shifting their retirement plans from defined benefit to defined contribution plans (Hardy, 2011). This means that even among those minority workers who participate in an employer sponsored plan, their accumulated savings may be insufficient to guarantee an adequate income in old age.

Policies, Programs, and Minority Americans

This somewhat lengthy introduction to the welfare state is necessary to set the stage for a closer examination of the specific government-sponsored social welfare programs on which minority Americans, and especially elderly minority group members, rely. Although the focus of the chapter is on government programs, the devolution of government functions from Washington to more local levels of government requires some mention of the role of nongovernmental organizations (NGOs), including faith-based organizations (FBOs) in social welfare. As part of the neoliberal rejection of the welfare state, more responsibility for addressing human needs has been relegated to such organizations. The question that immediately arises, though, is whether the nongovernmental sector is up to the task or whether a focus on the nongovernmental sector is merely a retreat of the federal government from its responsibility for the welfare of the population (R. J. Angel, Bell, Beausoleil, & Lein, 2012). I will return to the potential role of NGOs and FBOs at the end of the chapter. First, though, let us examine the factors that determine the economic situation of minority Americans throughout life and that affect their ability to save, invest, and accrue wealth with which they can support themselves in retirement, in addition to assisting their children.

Wealth and Income

One's economic welfare in old age, just like one's health, depends on what has come before. Economic security depends on savings, either one's own or someone else's. Americans over the age of 65 have three potential sources of material security: (1) Wealth in the form of cash savings, real property, stocks, bonds, etc.; (2) income from a defined benefit or a defined contribution (401K) plan; and (3) Social Security. In terms of wealth, measured either in terms of housing equity or in terms of savings or securities, blacks and Hispanics enter retirement with far fewer assets than non-Hispanic whites (Flippen, 2001). This situation is particularly serious for minority women who suffer the combined effects of gender and race in lowering rates of retirement savings (Brown, 2011). A lifetime of employment in a low-wage occupation, in which minority men and women tend to work, then means that black and Hispanic retirees frequently have little or no accumulated wealth and are dependent solely on Social Security for survival (R. J. Angel & Angel, 1997).

In addition to savings, true financial security in old age depends on an adequate income from an employment-based retirement plan. The definition of a good job or career has come to include not only more than just an adequate salary, but also access to health insurance and a retirement plan. Not all employers offer health coverage or retirement plans to their employees, and not all of those to whom they are offered participate. In 2009, 64.6% of white, 55.7% of black, and 38.4% of Hispanic wage and salary workers were offered retirement coverage by their employers (Butrica & Johnson, 2010). Data from the 2006 Current Population Survey illustrate the seriousness of the problem for Mexican-origin Hispanics, the largest Hispanic subgroup. In that year while 60.1% of non-Hispanic white males and 58% of African American males reported participating in an employer sponsored retirement plan, only 31.5% of Mexican-origin men reported participating in such a plan (R. J. Angel & Angel, 2009). From the beginning, then, the majority of Mexican-origin men have lacked this important third component of retirement security. The problem is more serious, though, given changes in retirement plan funding. Increasingly private and even some government employers who offer retirement plans are shifting from defined benefit plans that offer some percentage of one's earnings as a guaranteed income for life to defined contribution plans, in which the worker contributes part of his or her earnings, perhaps with an employer match, to an investment plan that provides income in retirement (R. J. Angel & Angel, 2009). If a worker does not save enough or if he or she invests unwisely, the eventual savings will be inadequate to guarantee financial security for a long retirement.

Given life-long labor force disadvantages, low incomes, the inability to save and invest, and incomplete employment-based retirement coverage, elderly minority group members enter the later years of life with fewer assets, less income, and are at higher risk of poverty than non-Hispanic white elders (Choudhury, 2001/2002; Gassoumis, Lincoln, & Vega, 2011; Williams & Wilson, 2001). Low-income minority group workers face other serious obstacles to financial security in retirement even if they have a retirement plan. In order for the savings to grow to a level that allows one to live on the principle and interest for a significant number of years, one cannot use the money for other purposes. Given their lower incomes, less wealth, and frequent family financial emergencies, Hispanics and blacks with 401K plans not only contribute too little to guarantee an adequate retirement income, they are more likely than non-Hispanic white workers to withdraw money from their plans in times of economic strain, a practice that depletes the amount available and that can incur penalties for early withdrawal (Ariel/Hewitt Study, 2009).

Another major problem with combined contribution retirement plans for minority workers, even when they are offered them, is the need to become at least minimally financially sophisticated. Unfortunately, individuals with lower incomes and education, as well as minority individuals, tend to lack basic knowledge of optimal investment strategies (Korniotis & Kumar, 2010). A typical 401K plan offers a number of different investments, including mutual funds, bond funds, and other instruments usually offered though a major brokerage firm. The employee is responsible for choosing the investments into which his or her contributions are placed, along with whatever match the employer offers. Choosing wisely requires education and knowledge of such investment vehicles. Even understanding the advice one might receive from a fund representative requires more knowledge of financial instruments than what the poorly educated workers possess. There is also an element of luck to investing, which means that individuals who invest the same amount of money but who retire at different times can obtain very different returns depending on economic conditions at retirement (Burtless, 2010). As the current economic crisis has demonstrated, even sophisticated advisors cannot guarantee a high rate of return, or even guarantee that the employee will not suffer a major loss. It seems clear that the shift to defined contribution retirement plans requires an active program of investor education to assist individuals who have little experience with saving and investing to preserve and grow whatever assets they have. Experiments with such educational initiatives have been attempted in other countries (Lusardi & Mitchell, 2007). The possibility of providing useful advice to minority group members, single women, and others throughout life should be considered. Of course, if one makes too little to save, all of the investment sophistication in the world will do little good.

Social Security

Since it was introduced in 1935, Social Security has served as the third rail of old-age income support along with personal savings and private retirement plans. The program has been a major success in reducing rates of poverty among the elderly (Engelhardt & Gruber, 2004). Given their low levels of savings and private retirement plan participation, Social Security is particularly important for minority Americans (Furman, 2005; Martin, 2007). Although Social Security is regressive in the taxation of workers, in that those with high incomes pay Social Security taxes only on a portion of their earnings, low-income workers receive a higher percentage relative to their contributions (Spriggs & Furman, 2006). This aspect of Social Security is clearly a positive feature for workers with low lifetime earnings. Despite its importance, though, Social Security was never intended to serve as a retiree's sole source of income, yet for many individuals that is what it has become. Social Security provides half or more of total income to the majority of individuals over 65 (Furman, 2005). Over a quarter of older African Americans and Hispanics depend on Social Security for more than 90% of their family income. The importance of the program is revealed by the fact that Social Security lifts 30% of older African Americans and Hispanics and 19% of older Asians out of poverty (Caldera, 2010).

The designers of Social Security wished to avoid portraying it as a welfare program, but they realized that many individuals who needed immediate assistance would never contribute. To address this problem, Title 1 of the Social Security Act established Old Age Assistance (OAA), a means-tested program administered by the states (R. J. Angel & Angel, 1997). In 1974, this program was replaced by a federally funded and administered program called

Supplemental Security Income (SSI), which provides income support to disabled children and adults who meet certain income requirements and elderly individuals with limited incomes. It is particularly important for minority Americans who are disproportionately dependent on SSI, again because of their lower incomes in old age (Martin, 2007).

Since one pays a portion of one's salary as Social Security tax, which appears as FICA (Federal Insurance Contributions Act) on one's wage statement, many people think of it as a savings plan in which one receives income in retirement from what one contributed while working. In reality Social Security is a pay-as-you-go arrangement, which means that current retirees receive payments directly from the contributions of current workers. In effect, the system is a transfer from the working population to the retired population. The growing number of retired Americans means that some adjustments will have to be made, since at current funding and payment levels, the Social Security trust fund will be depleted rapidly after 2014 when the baby boom generations retire (Social Security Administration, 2011). As the retired population grows which will increasingly be made up of African Americans and Hispanics, the tax burden will grow to unsupportable levels. The situation is even more dire for Medicare, for which expenditures are projected to soar as the baby boomers age (Social Security Administration, 2011).

In response to this supposed funding crisis, proposals for the partial privatization of Social Security have been put forward (Markham, 2001). There are various specific recommendations, but the essence of privatization would be to make Social Security more like the defined contribution private retirement plans mentioned earlier, in which a part of one's contribution would be placed in private investments. Unfortunately, such reforms would introduce the same sorts of risks associated with private defined contribution plans, and they would place minority retirees at particularly serious risk of the loss of their principle (Moore, 2000). The post 2008 recession has perhaps dampened some of the enthusiasm for privatization, since it showed clearly just how precarious investments in securities and other investment vehicles can be. Financially unsophisticated individuals are in no position to weight the relative risks of bonds, stocks, mutual funds, and so on, and it is unclear who else might make those decisions for them. The neoliberal philosophy that privileges the market over a paternalistic state ignores the real situation of many citizens who are dependent on the direction that only a benevolent and enlightened government can provide.

Even a cursory examination of defined benefit retirement plans and reflection on the risks to low-income and minority citizens of the complete or even partial privatization of Social Security makes the option unappealing. Yet the crisis in Social Security funding is real and political forces will demand some solution. Already, the age at which one can receive full benefits is increasing incrementally to 67. Another possibility would be to reduce benefits for future retirees. This solution, though, could have serious negative consequences for low-income minority retirees unless they were specifically exempted from cuts. Advocates of the interests of minority Americans must seek other solutions that would have less of a negative effect on low-income individuals. One obvious way to increase Social Security revenues would be to raise the cap on FICA contributions. Currently one pays Social Security tax on the first $110,100 of earnings. Above that there is no tax. Removing the cap would greatly increase revenues and place more of the burden on high-income earners.

Health Care and Health Care Reform

The United States is unique among developed nations in not providing access to health care to all citizens as a basic right (Reid, 2009). In this country health care financing has been based on an insurance model in which adequate coverage depends on access to an employer-sponsored group health plan (Starr, 1982b). The fact that health insurance, like a retirement plan, is provided as an employment benefit means that those individuals employed in low-wage service sector jobs, and those who are unemployed or underemployed, do not have access to a group plan. The result is what can only be considered a crisis in health care coverage. In 2006, while 14.6% of non-Hispanic white adults had no health insurance, 24.4% of African Americans, 22.8% of Puerto Ricans, 28.2% of Cuban origin Hispanics, and 45.3% of Mexican-origin

Hispanics lacked any form of coverage (R. J. Angel & Angel, 2009). Coverage rates are low for Native Americans/Alaskan natives as well (H. Mead et al., 2008). Among children, Hispanics, and especially those of Mexican origin, are at particularly elevated risk of lacking private insurance or Medicaid (R. J. Angel & Angel, 2009).

The implications are serious, since a large body of research clearly shows that individuals with health insurance have greater access to health care and have better health outcomes (Institute of Medicine, 2001), and that entire communities are harmed by low rates of coverage (Institute of Medicine, 2003). Although there have been recurring attempts to introduce insurance pool models that are not employer based, they have not been successful. President Bill Clinton's attempt to introduce health cooperatives and other reforms quickly lost public support (Blendon, Brodie, & Benson, 1995). President Obama's health reform legislation faced equally energetic opposition, although it was finally passed and upheld by the Supreme Court.

Although the United States does not have a universal health care system for everyone, for the population of above 65 years of age, near-universal coverage is a reality and nearly all citizens, including older minority group members, participate (R. J. Angel & Angel, 1997; R. J. Angel, Angel, & Markides, 2002). Yet for low-income and minority elders the safety net is not complete. Low-income, very old, and chronically ill elders pay a substantial fraction of their limited incomes to cover health care costs that Medicare does not pay (Briesacher et al., 2010; Fishman, Tamang, & Shea, 2008). Traditional Medicare consists of Part A, hospital insurance, which includes a monthly premium of $451, and does not cover all hospital costs. In 2012, Part A included a $1,156 deductible per benefit period and a copayment of $289 per day for stays of 61 to 90 days, and $578 per day after that. If one is discharged to a skilled nursing facility, one gets 20 days at no cost and then must pay $144.50 for days 21 to 100, after which all coverage ends (Center for Medicaid and Medicare Services, 2012). Part B, which pays for physician services, has a basic monthly premium of $99.90, which increases with income. In addition there is a $140 annual deductible and coinsurance for various other services, including 40% for all Medicare-approved outpatient mental health services (Center for Medicaid and Medicare Services, 2012). Medicare also includes optional coverage for medication, Part D, the cost of which varies with income. Part D includes a low-income subsidy to provide some relief to low-income elders. Medicare Part C, known as Medicare Advantage, combines aspects of the other three parts and is of use to individuals in certain areas.

One major problem with Medicare is that there is no limit on out-of-pocket expenditures, so that the costs that an individual can incur can be rather high, far more than a low-income or even a middle-income person can pay. Given these high costs, various options have been introduced to help low-income elders with the premiums and cost-sharing expenses (Zuckerman, Shang, & Waidmann, 2012). The most important is Medicaid, the program for low-income and disabled individuals, which is available to individuals who are deemed to be *dual eligible,* a term that refers to those who receive both Medicare and Medicaid. For these elderly individuals, Medicaid pays for Part A and B premiums and all cost-sharing expenses for individuals designated as qualified Medicare beneficiaries (QMBs). Two other programs, the Specified Low-income Medicare Beneficiary (SLMB) and Qualified Individual (QI) pay Part B premiums. Given the high cost of drugs, Part D—prescription drug coverage—includes a low-income subsidy to help individuals who might otherwise simply do without the medications they need.

Given the fact of higher rates of poverty and lower incomes among minorities, these low-income subsidies are particularly important for African American and Hispanic elders. In general those who are dual eligible are more likely than nondual eligible Medicare beneficiaries to be female, disabled, minority group members or residents of long-term care facilities. In 2006, while 7% of nondual eligible Medicare recipients were African American, 19% of the dual-eligible population was African American. Hispanics comprised 5% of the nondual Eligible Medicare population but 17% of the dual-eligible population (Jacobson, Neuman, Damico, & Lyons, 2011).

In light of problems with Medicare coverage, such as the lack of limits on out-of-pocket expenditures, various reforms and options—many of a technical sort—have been proposed (Zuckerman et al., 2012). These are too extensive to be discussed in detail here but the objective is to make the system work more efficiently and limit the costs that elderly individuals on limited incomes must pay. Given the serious limitations in assets and income among minority elderly populations, reforms of this sort are welcome. Unfortunately, given Medicare's impending funding crisis, major reforms, such as covering all medical and prescription drug expenses for low-income individuals, seem unlikely. What is particularly worrisome is that attempts to reduce the federal deficit will result in cuts to state Medicaid programs, to which the federal government is a major contributor. Such cuts could have serious negative effects for the dual-eligible population, which has high levels of need and consists disproportionately of minority group elders.

Housing and Long-Term Care

For the majority of Americans their home represents their largest asset and homeownership represents the American dream. Until 2005, as the result of initiative such as the Home Mortgage Disclosure Act of 1975 (HMDA) and the Community Reinvestment Act of 1977 (CRA), legislation that addressed practices such as redlining, a practice in which lenders would not provide mortgages for purchases in certain neighborhoods, homeownership rose rapidly among minority Americans (Kochhar, Gonzalez-Barrera, & Dockterman, 2009). In 2005, the housing bubble began to burst and since then homeownership rates among African Americans and Latinos have dropped. In 2008, 74.9% of non-Hispanic whites and 59.1% of Asians owned a home, while only 48.9% of Hispanics and 47.5% of blacks did so (Kochhar, et al., 2009). The housing bust was caused largely by subprime lending based on complex mortgages to individuals who in reality could not afford them. These products were particularly expensive, about 2.5 to 3 percentage points higher than conventional mortgages, and African Americans and Hispanics were seriously victimized. In 2007, while only 10.5% of white borrowers received these risky mortgages, 27.6% of Hispanic and 33.5% of black borrowers were sold subprime loans (Kochhar et al., 2009).

The foreclosure crisis was particularly serious for minority Americans and it had particularly serious consequences for minority neighborhoods (Rugh & Massey, 2010). The serious deterioration in housing values that resulted from the collapse of the housing market reduced the equity that individuals nearing retirement could draw upon. The National Council on Aging reports that in the current foreclosure crises homeowners aged 50 and older represent 28% of all delinquencies and foreclosures, and that three out of five senior households of color use more than 30% of their income to pay housing costs, which is the U.S. Department of Housing & Urban Development's definition of unaffordable housing. In addition, 44% of African American and 37% of Latino seniors either rent or have no home equity (National Council on Aging, 2012). While the loss in home equity affects everyone to some degree, for those with little else the consequences are serious.

Although one's home is one's castle, at some point declines in health make it difficult or impossible for certain older adults to live at home without at least some assistance. Historically, impoverished older individuals had no choice but to live with their children, since there were few options. Changes in marital patterns, fertility, and migration have changed the options dramatically. Today, Hispanics continue to use nursing homes at very low rates. Given their higher fertility and the tendency for children to remain close to their parents' homes, older Hispanics have more family care available in the event of poor health (J. L. Angel et al., 2004; R. J. Angel & Angel, 1997). As a consequence, their use of nursing homes and long-term care facilities has remained below that of non-Hispanic whites, although it has increased in recent years (Fennell, Feng, Clark, & Mor, 2010). African Americans enter nursing homes at higher rates than whites, who prefer and are able to afford more desirable long-term care arrangements, such as assisted living facilities. In general, the quality of the facilities that African American and Hispanic seniors enter is inferior (Fennell, et al., 2010; Smith, Feng, Fennell, Zinn, & Mor, 2008).

One major barrier to the use of nursing homes, of course, is the cost and one reason for the increase in the use of such facilities by minority elders is the availability of Medicaid financing. Medicare, the program for the elderly, pays for only a limited amount of post–acute care in skilled nursing facilities but does not pay for long-term custodial care. Unlike Medicare, Medicaid represents one of the major expenditures on state budgets, since it is a joint federal/ state program. States set reimbursement levels to facilities and the requirements for participation, resulting in large variation among states (Miller, Mor, Grabowski, & Gozalo, 2009). In order to qualify for Medicaid coverage, an individual has to be or become destitute. Given the undesirability of low-quality Medicaid, mill-type nursing facilities and the clear desire of older individuals and their families to have elderly parents remain in the community, several community-based options have been proposed and attempted. These are far too numerous and complicated to describe here, but it is clear that in the future new options in community care will be developed. Given the aging of the population and the inevitable increase in the dependency of the baby boom cohorts, more cost-effective methods of providing long-term care will become imperative.

NGOs and the Promise of Civil Society

Let me end this discussion by returning to the nongovernmental possibilities I mentioned at the beginning. My discussion has of necessity focused heavily on the labor market, and formal aspects of the welfare state, as it affects older minority Americans. These are the sectors of the economy and aspects of formal programs that we think of when we discuss policy. It is important to remember, though, that informal organizations and social movements have always been important in further the well-being of individuals (R. J. Angel, 2011). Religious groups have historically assumed caring for the poor and infirm (Idler, 2006). International Faith-Based Organizations (FBOs), such as *CARITAS, Catholic Charities,* and *Lutheran Social Services* provide assistance to the elderly as part of their general missions. There are far too many NGOs involved in eldercare to mention, but I mention some as illustration.

The *Meals on Wheels Association of America* (http://www.mowaa.org) is the oldest nutrition program for the elderly in the country. It was founded during World War II and has contributed significantly to insuring that isolated elders receive the nutrition they need. *Little Brothers—Friends of the Elderly (LBFE;* http://www.littlebrothers.org) is an international network of volunteer organizations with branches in the United States that provides companionship to reduce isolation and loneliness. The network is part of a larger international organization, the Fédération Internationale des petits frères des Pauvres (International Federation of Little Brothers of the Poor, http://www.petitsfreres.org). Another international organizations is the *Fédération Internationale des Associations de Personnes Agées* (International Federation of Associations of Older Persons, FIAPA: http://www.fiapa.org) headquartered in Paris. Its mission is also to reduce isolation and improve the quality of life for isolated older individuals.

A quick internet search reveals many other examples of NGOs involved in eldercare activities, in the United States and other nations. In India NGOs are playing an important role as advocates for providers of services to the elderly (Sawhney, 2003). *Dignity Foundation* (http://www.dignityfoundation.com), a member of the American Association of Retired Persons (AARP) Global Network, provides housing, companionship, recreation and other services to elderly individuals in several Indian cities. *HelpAge India* (http://www.helpageindia.org) provides financial, medical, and emotional support to poor elderly Indians. These are examples of eldercare NGOs filling voids in which formal supports are rare. Such organizations might fill the void in resource-poor communities in more developed nations, including the United States.

One example in the United States is named *On Lok*, a Cantonese term that means *peaceful, happy abode,* that began in San Francisco in the 1970s to provide services to frail Asian elderly individuals in certain Bay area communities so that they could remain in their own homes (http://www.onlok.org; Bodenheimer, 1999). The success of this program led to its formal adoption by Congress as a model for the *PACE* program (Program of All-Inclusive Care for the Elderly; http://www.cms.hhs.gov/pace), which provides comprehensive services paid for primarily by Medicare and Medicaid to high-need frail elderly individuals (Gross, Temkin-Greener, Kunitz, & Mukamel, 2004).

Such civil society organizations hold great promise for providing assistance and services that formal organizations may not be well suited to provide. We must be careful though not to expect that such organizations can replace the government in providing such basic services and education and medical care, and more. At most, civil society organizations can complement the government and help put a human face on the response to disasters and the alleviation of human suffering (R. J. Angel et al., 2012). Hostility toward big government and the welfare state has led to a widespread desire to devolve what are federal government responsibilities to local government or nongovernmental and faith-based organizations. Such a desire is probably expecting too much of organizations and groups that can assist and provide valuable local knowledge if their efforts are sought out and coordinated, but will likely fail if given tasks that even the federal government has difficulty dealing with.

CONCLUSION: A POLICY AGENDA

This chapter began by mentioning *guiding principles* that inform public policy as it related to elderly minority group members. Space limitations prevented a detailed description of specific groups and several programs. There are simply too many policies and programs that have some important impact on older minority Americans, as well as low-income majority Americans. This chapter focused primarily on the general features of our economic, political, and social systems that place minority Americans at serious risk of poverty and ill health throughout life, including its waning years. We end with suggestions for a research and policy agenda that could guide investigation, as well as advocacy in the coming years. As mentioned at the beginning, the arrival of what may be a protracted or even a permanent era of fiscal austerity presents serious problems for defenders of the welfare state and advocates for minority Americans. For all of the reasons discussed in this chapter, low-income Americans are not in a powerful position from which to defend their rights and entitlements. Austerity measures and the desire to reduce government spending and debt strike hardest at those programs upon which minority children, adults, and elders depend most. Medicaid, Food Stamps, Housing assistance, and the rest of the welfare state provide the basis of a dignified and healthy life, and their existence may well be imperiled.

The vulnerability of minority families and their elderly parents is clear. Between 2005 and 2009, while the median net worth of non-Hispanic white households dropped by 16%, Hispanic households lost 66% of their net worth and African American households lost 53% (Taylor, Kochhar, Fry, Velasco, & Motel, 2011). This disproportionate loss was from a far smaller base. Data from the Survey of Income and Program Participation (SIPP), an ongoing government survey that is a major source of information on minority Americans, show that the median household wealth of non-Hispanic white households is 18 times greater than that of Hispanic households and 20 times greater than that of African American households (Taylor et al., 2011).

What is clear from this review of policies and policy proposals is that the economic opportunities available to an individual earlier in life and those economic choices he or she makes are clearly influenced by race and ethnicity, as well as social class. Minority Americans, and especially certain Hispanic groups, have extremely low levels of education and high school dropout rates (R. J. Angel & Angel, 2009). This fact places them in a poor position in the labor market relative to those with more education. This fact also places them in a disadvantageous position in terms of financial planning. With limited resources, sophistication is even more important, but it is rare among individuals with low levels of education. As I have discussed, defined contribution retirement plans require much more informed involvement by a worker than do defined benefit plans. As of yet there is little research on the use of other financial instruments, such as reverse mortgages by minority elders, but one fears that they may not have the financial sophistication to choose wisely and to decide whether such products make sense for them.

The future presents a complex picture. The post–World War II economic boom that propelled Japan, Europe, and the United States to historically unprecedented levels of wealth is over and probably for good. At the same time the populations of the developed and even of the developing world are aging rapidly at a time when Keynesian expansionary economic policies are out of favor. All over the world, including the United States, inequality is increasing and the have-nots are gaining less. How nations, including the United States, will insure equity in the distribution of resources and how the elderly will be guaranteed a dignified existence remains unclear. What is much clearer is that the debates will be heated and the outcomes of vital importance to elderly minority Americans.

REFERENCES

Angel, J. L., Angel, R. J., Aranda, M. P., & Miles., T. P. (2004). Can the family still cope? Social support and health as determinants of nursing home use in the older Mexican-origin population. *Journal of Aging and Health, 16*, 338–354.

Angel, R. J. (2011). Civil society and eldercare in post traditional society. In R. A. Settersten & J. L. Angel (Eds.), *Handbook of sociology of aging* (pp. 549–581). New York, NY: Springer.

Angel, R. J., & Angel, J. L. (1997). *Who will care for us? Aging and long-term care in multicultural America.* New York, NY: New York University Press.

Angel, R. J., & Angel, J. L. (2009). *Hispanic families at risk: The new economy, work, and the welfare state.* New York, NY: Springer.

Angel, R. J., Angel, J. L., & Markides, K. S. (2002). Stability and change in health insurance among older Mexican Americans: Longitudinal evidence from the Hispanic established populations for epidemiologic study of the elderly. *American Journal of Public Health, 92*, 1264–1271.

Angel, R. J., Bell, H., Beausoleil, J., & Lein, L. (2012). *Community lost: The state, civil society and displaced survivors of Hurricane Katrina.* New York, NY: Cambridge University Press.

Ariel/Hewitt Study. (2009). 401(k) Plans in Living Color: A Study of 401(k) Savings Disparities Across Racial and Ethnic Groups. Retrieved April 18, 2012, from http://www.arielinvestments.com/images/stories/PDF/arielhewittstudy_finalweb_7.3.pdf

Ashton, P. (2010). CRA's "blind spots": Community reinvestment and concentrated subprime lending in Detroit. *Journal of Urban Affairs, 32*(5), 579–608.

Baldwin, P. (1990). *The politics of social solidarity: Class bases of the European welfare state, 1875–1975.* New York, NY: Cambridge University Press.

Béland, D., & Hacker, J. S. (2004). Ideas, private institutions and American welfare state "exceptionalism": The case of health and old-age insurance, 1915–1965. *International Journal of Social Welfare, 13*, 42–54.

Beveridge, S. W. (1942). *Social insurance and allied services.* London, England: H.M. Stationary Office.

Blendon, R. J., Brodie, M., & Benson, J. (1995). What happened to Americans' support for the Clinton health plan? *Health Affairs, 14*(2), 7–23.

Bodenheimer, T. (1999). Long-term care for frail elderly people—The On Lok model. *The New England Journal of Medicine, 341*(17), 1324–1328.

Briesacher, B. A., Ross-Degnan, D., Wagner, A. K., Fouayzi, H., Zhang, F., Gurwitz, J. H., & Soumerai, S. B. (2010). Out-of-pocket burden of health care spending and the adequacy of the Medicare Part D low-income subsidy. *Medical Care, 48*(6), 503–509.

Brown, T. (2011). The intersection and accumulation of racial and gender inequality: Black women's wealth trajectories. *The Review of Black Political Economy, 1–20.*

Burtless, G. (2010). Lessons of the financial crisis for the design of national pension systems. *CESifo Economic Studies, 56*(3), 323–349.

Butrica, B. A., & Johnson, R. W. (2010). Racial, ethnic, and gender differentials. in Employer-Sponsored Pensions, Testimony before the ERISA Advisory Council U.S. Department of Labor. Retrieved March 18, 2012, from http://www.urban.org/UploadedPDF/901357-racial-ethnic-gender-differentials.pdf. Washington, DC: Urban Institute.

Caldera, S. (2010). *Social Security: A Key Retirement Income Source for Minorities.* Retrieved April 20, 2012, from http://assets.aarp.org/rgcenter/ppi/econ-sec/fs201-economic.pdf Washington, DC: AARP Public Policy Institute.

Center for Medicaid and Medicare Services. (2012). *Medicare Costs.* Retrieved April 21, 2012, from http:// www.medicare.gov/cost/

Choudhury, S. (2001/2002). Racial and ethnic differences in wealth and asset choices *Social Security Bulletin, 64*(4), 1–15.

Dwyer, P. (2004). *Understanding social citizenship.* Bristol, England: The Policy Press and the Social Policy Association.

Engelhardt, G. V., & Gruber, J. (2004). *Social security and the evolution of elderly poverty.* Retrieved April 20, 2012, from http://www.nber.org/papers/w10466. Cambridge, MA: National Bureau of Economic Research.

Erickson, D. J. (2009). *The Housing policy revolution: Networks and neighborhoods.* Washington, DC: Urban Institute Press.

Esping-Andersen, G. (1990). *The three worlds of welfare capitalism.* Princeton, NJ: Princeton University Press.

Etzioni, A. (1993). *The spirit of community: Rights, responsibilities, and the communitarian agenda.* New York, NY: Crown.

Etzioni, A. (2000). *The third way to a good society.* London, England: Demos.

Etzioni, A. (Ed.). (1995). *New communitarian thinking: Persons, virtues, institutions, and communities.* Charlottesville, VA: University Press of Virginia.

Fennell, M. L., Feng, Z., Clark, M. A., & Mor, V. (2010). Elderly Hispanics more likely to reside in poor-quality nursing homes. [Comparative Study Research Support, N.I.H., Extramural]. *Health affairs, 29*(1), 65–73.

Fishman, E., Tamang, S., & Shea, D. (2008). *Medicare out-of-pocket costs: Can private savings incentives solve the problem?* Retrieved March 18, 2012, from http://www.thecommonwealthfund.com/~/media/Files/Publications/Fund%20Report/2008/Mar/Medicare%20Out%20of%20Pocket%20Costs%20%20Can%20Private%20Savings%20Incentives%20Solve%20the%20Problem/Fishman_Medicareout%20of%20pocketcosts_1113%20pdf.pdf. New York, NY: The Commonwealth Fund.

Flippen, C. A. (2001). Racial and ethnic inequality in homeownership and housing equity. *Sociological Quarterly, 42*(2), 121–149.

Furman, J. (2005). *Top ten facts on social security's 70th anniversary.* Retrieved April 20, 2012, from http:// www.cbpp.org/files/8–11-05socsec.pdf. Washington, DC: Center on Budget and Policy Priorities.

Gassoumis, Z. D., Lincoln, K. D., & Vega, W. A. (2011). *How low-income minorities get by in retirement: Poverty levels and income sources.* Los Angeles, CA: USC Edward R. Roybal Institute on Aging.

Gilbert, N., & Gilbert, B. (1989). *The enabling state: Modern welfare capitalism in America.* Oxford, England: Oxford University Press.

Gottschalk, M. (2000). *The shadow welfare state: Labor, business, and the politics of health care in the United States.* Ithaca, NY: ILR Press.

Gross, D. L., Temkin-Greener, H., Kunitz, S., & Mukamel, D. B. (2004). The growing pains of integrated health care for the elderly: Lessons from the expansion of PACE. *The Milbank Quarterly, 82*(2), 257–282.

Hacker, J. S. (2002). *The divided welfare state.* New York, NY: Cambridge University Press.

Hardy, M. (2011). Rethinking Retirement. In R. A. Setterstein, Jr. & J. L Angel (Eds.), *Handbook of Sociology of Aging* (pp. 213–227). New York, NY: Springer.

Hayek, F. A. (1944). *The road to serfdom.* Chicago, IL: University of Chicago Press.

Hayek, F. A. (1976). *Law, legislation, and liberty, volume 2: The mirage of social justice.* Chicago, IL: University of Chicago Press.

Hoffman, B. R. (2001). *The wages of sickness: The politics of health insurance in progressive America.* Chapel Hill, NC: University of North Carolina Press.

Howard, C. (1997). *The hidden welfare state: Tax expenditures and social policy in the United States.* Princeton, NJ: Princeton University Press.

Idler, E. (2006). Religion and aging. In R. H. Binstock & L. K. George (Eds.), *Handbook of aging and the social sciences* (6 ed., pp. 277–300). New York, NY: Academic Press.

Immergluck, D. A. N. (2011). The local wreckage of global capital: The subprime crisis, federal policy and high-foreclosure neighborhoods in the US. *International Journal of Urban and Regional Research, 35*(1), 130–146.

Institute of Medicine. (2001). *Coverage matters: Insurance and health care*. Washington, DC: National Academy Press.

Institute of Medicine. (2003). *A shared destiny: Community effects of uninsurance*. Washington, DC: National Academy Press.

Jacobson, G., Neuman, T., Damico, A., & Lyons, B. (2011). *The role of Medicare for the people dually eligible for Medicare and Medicaid*. Washington, DC: The Henry J. Kaiser Family Foundation.

King, D., & Wood, S. (1999). The political economy of neoliberalism: Britain and the United States in the 1980s. In H. Kitschelt, P. Lange, G. Marks & J. D. Stephens (Eds.), *Continuity and change in contemporary capitalism* (pp. 371–397). Cambridge, England, and New York, NY: Cambridge University Press.

Kochhar, R., Gonzalez-Barrera, A., & Dockterman, D. (2009). *Through boom and bust: Minorities, immigrants and homeownership*. Washington, DC: Pew Hispanic Center.

Korniotis, G. M., & Kumar, A. (2010). Do older investors make better investment decisions? *Review of Economics and Statistics, 93*(1), 244–265.

Lusardi, A., & Mitchell, O. (2007). Financial literacy and retirement preparedness: Evidence and implications for financial education. *Business Economics, 42*(1), 35–44.

Markham, J. W. (2001). Privatizing social security. *San Diego Law Review, 38*(3), 747–816.

Marshall, T. H. (1950). *Citizenship and social class: And other essays*. Cambridge, England: Cambridge University Press.

Martin, P. P. (2007). Hispanics, social security, and supplemental security income. *Social Security Bulletin, 67*(2), 73–100.

Mead, H., Cartwright-Smith, L., Jones, K., Ramos, C., Woods, K., & Siegel, B. (2008). *Racial and ethnic disparities in U.S. health care: A chartbook*. Washington, DC: The Commonwealth Fund.

Mead, L. M. (1986). *Beyond entitlement*. New York, NY: The Free Press.

Mead, L. M. (1997). Citizenship and social policy: T. H. Marshall and poverty. *Social Philosophy and Policy, 14*(2), 197–230.

Miller, E. A., Mor, V., Grabowski, D. C., & Gozalo, P. L. (2009). The devil's in the details: Trading policy goals for complexity in Medicaid nursing home reimbursement. [Comparative Study Research Support, Non-U.S. Government]. *Journal of Health Politics, Policy and Law, 34*(1), 93–135.

Moore, K. L. (2000). Partial privatization of social security: Assessing its effect on women, minorities, and lower-income workers. *Mossouri Law Review, 65*, 342–403.

Murray, C. (1994). *Losing ground: American social policy 1950–1980* (10th Anniversary ed.). New York, NY: Basic Books.

Murray, C. (1996). *Charles Murray and the underclass: The developing debate*. London, England: The IEA Health and Welfare Unit.

Murray, C. (1999). *The Underclass Revisited*. Washington, DC: AEI Press.

Murray, C. (2006). *In our hands: a plan to replace the welfare state*. Blue Ridge Summit, PA: AEI Press.

National Council on Aging. (2012). *Economic security*. Retrieved April 22, 2012, from http://www.ncoa.org/assets/files/pdf/FactSheet_EconomicSecurity.pdf. Washington, DC: Author.

Numbers, R. L. (1978). *Almost persuaded: American physicians and compulsory health insurance, 1912–1920*. Baltimore, MD: Johns Hopkins University Press.

Palier, B. (Ed.). (2010). *A long goodbye to Bismark? The politics of welfare reform in Continental Europe*. Amsterdam, Netherlands: Amsterdam University Press.

Pierson, C. (2007). *Beyond the welfare state? The new political economy of welfare* (3 ed.). University Park, PA: The Pennsylvania State University Press.

Pierson, P. (2001). Coping with permanent austerity: Welfare state restructuring in affluent democracies. In P. Pierson (Ed.), *The New Politics of the Welfare State*. Oxford, England and New York, NY: Oxford University Press.

Quadagno, J. (2005). *One nation, uninsured: Why the U.S. has no national health insurance*. New York, NY and Oxford, England: Oxford University Press.

Reid, T. R. (2009). *The Healing of America: a global quest for better, cheaper and fairer health care*. New York, NY: The Penguin Press.

Rugh, J. S., & Massey, D. S. (2010). Racial segregation and the American foreclosure crisis. *American Sociological Review, 75*(5), 629–651.

Sawhney, M. (2003). The role of non-governmental organizations for the welfare of the elderly: The case of HelpAge India. In P. S. Liebig & S. I. Rajan (Eds.), *An aging India: Perspectives, prospects, and policies*. Binghamton, NY: The Hayworth Press.

Sigerist, H. E. (1999). From Bismarck to Beveridge: Developments and trends in social security legislation. *Journal of Public Health Policy, 20*(4), 474–496.

Smeeding, T. M. (2000). Changing income inequality in OECD countries: Updated results from the Luxembourg income study (LIS). In R. Hauser & I. Becker (Eds.), *The personal distribution of income in an international perspective*. Berlin, Germany: Springer-Verlag.

Smeeding, T. M., Rainwater, L., & Burtless, G. (2001). U.S. poverty in a cross-national context. In S. H. Danziger & R. H. Haveman (Eds.), *Understanding poverty* (pp. 162–189). New York, NY, and Cambridge, MA: Russell Sage Foundation and Harvard Univ. Press.

Smith, D. B., Feng, Z., Fennell, M. L., Zinn, J., & Mor, V. (2008). Racial disparities in access to long-term care: The illusive pursuit of equity. *Journal of Health Politics, Policy and Law, 33*(5), 861–881.

Social Security Administration. (2011). A summary of the 2011 annual reports social security and medicare boards of trustees, Retrieved April 22, 2012, from http://www.ssa.gov/oact/TRSUM/index.html. *Status of the Social Security and Medicare Programs*.

Spriggs, W., & Furman, J. (2006). *African Americans and social security: The implications of reform proposals*. Retrieved April 20, 2012, from http://www.cbpp.org/cms/?fa=view&id=885. Washington, DC: Center on Budget and Policy Priorities.

Starr, P. (1982a). *The social transformation of American medicine*. New York, NY: Basic Books.

Starr, P. (1982b). *The social transformation of American medicine: The rise of a sovereign profession and the making of a vast industry*. New York, NY: Basic Books.

Stevens, B. (1988). Blurring the Boundaries: How the federal government has influenced welfare benefits in the private sector. In M. Weir, A. S. Orloff & T. Skocpol (Eds.), *The politics of social policy in the United States*. Princeton, NJ: Princeton University Press.

Taylor, P., Kochhar, R., Fry, R., Velasco, G., & Motel, S. (2011). Wealth gaps rise to record highs between whites, blacks and Hispanics. Washington, DC: Pew Research Center.

Weir, M., Orloff, A. S., & Skocpol, T. (1988). *The politics of social policy in the United States*. Princeton, NJ: Princeton University Press.

Williams, D. R., & Wilson, C. M. (2001). Race, ethnicity, and aging. In R. H. Binstock & L. K. George (Eds.), *Handbook of aging and the social sciences* (5 ed., pp. 160–179). San Diego, CA: Academic Press.

Zuckerman, S., Shang, B., & Waidmann, T. (2012). *Policy options to improve the performance of low income subsidy programs for Medicare beneficiaries*. Washington, DC: Urban Institute.

CHAPTER 33

Medicare and Health Care Utilization

Robert Weech-Maldonado, Rohit Pradhan, and M. Paige Powell

In this chapter, we examine the role of Medicare and its influence on health care utilization among the elderly, particularly minority aging. The sections in this chapter will (a) discuss the history, organization, development, and the future of Medicare; (b) apply Andersen's Behavioral Model of Health Services Use to understand utilization among the elderly and conduct a systematic literature review; (c) analyze racial/ethnic disparities in health care utilization among the elderly using Andersen's model; and (d) discuss the implications of the current proposals for changes in Medicare for health care utilization especially among minority aging.

MEDICARE: HISTORY AND ITS ROLE IN ACCESS TO CARE

In this section we offer a historical perspective on Medicare and its development from 1965 to the present era, and the increasingly important role it plays in ensuring health care access for the elderly, particularly among racial/ethnic minorities.

Medicare History

The Medicare and Medicaid programs were signed into law on July 30, 1965, under the Lyndon B. Johnson Administration (Starr, 1982). These programs were part of the *Great Society*, the anti-poverty agenda championed by President Johnson. Medicare and Medicaid received the largest share of budgetary resources of all social programs initiated during the Great Society (Davis & Reynolds, 1976).

Medicare had significant implications for access to care for the aged, especially among low-income and racial/ethnic minorities. According to Long and Settle (1984), the impetus for Medicare was in large part a result of increasing societal awareness of inequities among certain subgroups within the elderly population, such as the poor, racial minorities, rural dwellers, and the very old. Prior to Medicare and Medicaid, the only option available to poor seniors needing medical care was charity.

The next significant legislation, the Medicare Prescription Drug, Improvement and Modernization Act of 2003, usually referred to as the Medicare Modernization Act (MMA), was designed to provide prescription drug coverage to Medicare beneficiaries. When Medicare was passed in 1965, prescription drug use was relatively minor, and therefore not covered. Meara, White, and Cutler (2004) estimate that per person prescription drug costs in 1963 for the over-65 age group were approximately $207 in 2002 inflation-adjusted dollars, compared to

$1,250 per capita in 2000. The growth in both use and price of prescription drugs led to a need for coverage for seniors who did not have retiree plans (Meara et al., 2004). The MMA created Medicare Part D, the Medicare Prescription Drug Benefit, which took effect in 2006. Private insurance plans compete to provide prescription drug coverage to Medicare beneficiaries.

Medicare Benefits

Medicare has benefits under four "parts": A, B, C, and D. Part A covers hospitalization, skilled nursing services, home health care services, and hospice care. Part B covers medically necessary services such as physician services, outpatient care, home health services, durable medical equipment, and other medical services. While there are no premiums for Part A coverage, premiums are required under Part B. Beneficiaries are also required to pay deductibles, coinsurance, and copayment amounts. Table 33.1 details Medicare benefits, what it pays, and what beneficiaries pay out of pocket.

Part C or Medicare Advantage (MA) offers private plans to Medicare beneficiaries. MA is currently offered as an alternative to the conventional fee-for-service (FFS) Medicare program; the program is voluntary and the private insurance market is utilized to offer managed care coverage. According to a U.S. Government Accountability Office (GAO; 2009) report, 11 million beneficiaries were enrolled in MA plans in 2009, whereas government payment to MA organizations totaled approximately $110 billion. The essential idea behind MA is that by leveraging market forces, more choice can be provided to consumers at an affordable price. The Centers for Medicare and Medicaid Services (CMS) annually contracts with MA organizations and it pays them a monthly amount determined by plan bids. The bid amount is guided by a preset benchmark, which is the maximum amount Medicare will pay MA plans in a given locality. If the bid amount is less than the benchmark, the excess may be used to offer additional benefits or reduce premiums for beneficiaries. MA benefits include Parts A and B services. These plans may require additional premiums. Beneficiaries are also responsible for cost sharing, which may include deductibles or copayments as imposed by individual MA plans. However, CMS may act to limit the maximum permissible out-of-pocket expenditures allowed (Government Accountability Office, 2009). MA plans also frequently cover medical services that are not covered by Parts A and B, acting as another form of supplemental insurance.

Part D covers prescription drugs. Congress outlined three structures for the prescription drug benefit: a standard defined benefit, a basic alternative, and an enhanced alternative. In 2012, the standard benefit has a $320 deductible, and then pays 75% of drug costs up to $2,930. If a beneficiary has total drug spending that exceeds $2,930, that patient pays 100% of the cost up to a catastrophic threshold of $6.657.50 (or $4,700 total out-of-pocket spending; Figure 33.1). This is often referred to as the donut hole. After reaching the catastrophic limit, beneficiaries pay $2 for generics, $5 for brand name drugs, or 5% of the cost, whichever is greater. However, the Patient Protection and Affordable Care Act (ACA) signed into law by President Obama in 2010 put in provisions to close the donut hole. Now, once a beneficiary enters the coverage gap or donut hole, the beneficiary will only pay 86% of the cost of a generic drug and 50% of the cost of a brand name drug. The ACA increases the subsidies each year. By 2020, Medicare Part D beneficiaries should only pay 25% of their total drug costs (Kaiser Family Foundation [KFF], 2011).

Part D plans can also structure benefits differently, as long as they are actuarially equivalent (both the plan and the beneficiary pay the same amounts as they would under the standard benefit), and they can offer enhanced alternative plans that provide coverage that exceeds the standard benefit. Plans vary in formularies and in premium prices. The average monthly premium is approximately $40, but premiums range from $14 to $131 per month (KFF, 2011).

Medicare does not provide coverage for many services and products typically needed by beneficiaries such as long-term care, eyeglasses, hearing aids, and routine dental care. The combination of cost-sharing requirements and limited benefits leaves about 45% of Medicare beneficiaries' costs uncovered. As a result, about 80% of Medicare beneficiaries receive some type of private supplemental coverage to limit their exposure; 11% receive their supplemental coverage through Medicaid (Ryan & Super, 2003).

TABLE 33.1 Medicare Benefits, What Medicare Pays, and What Beneficiary Pays

SERVICES	BENEFIT	MEDICARE PAYS	BENEFICIARY PAYS
PART A			
Hospitalization: semi-private rooms, meals, general nursing, and drugs as part of your inpatient treatment, and other hospital services and supplies	First 60 days 61st to 90th day 91st to 150th day Beyond 150 days	All but $1,156 All but $289 a day All but $578 a day Nothing	Deductible of $1,156 $289 a day $578 a day All costs
Skilled Nursing Facility: semi-private rooms, meals, skilled nursing and rehabilitative services, and other services and supplies	First 20 days Additional 80 days Beyond 100 days	100% of approved amount All costs but $144.50 a day Nothing	Nothing $144.50 per day All costs
Home Health Care: part-time or intermittent skilled nursing care; and/or physical therapy, speech-language pathology services; and/or services for people with a continuing need for occupational therapy	Unlimited as long as you meet Medicare requirements for home health care benefits	100% of approved amount; 80% of approved amount for durable medical equipment	Nothing for services; 20% of approved amount for durable medical equipment
Hospice Care: pain relief and symptom management; medical, nursing, and social services; certain durable medical equipment and other covered services for the terminally ill	For as long as doctor certifies need	All but limited costs for outpatient drugs and inpatient respite care	Limited cost sharing for outpatient drugs ($5 per prescription) and inpatient respite care (5%)
PART B			
Medical Expenses: doctor services that are medically necessary (includes outpatient and some doctor services you get when you are a hospital inpatient) or covered preventive services	Unlimited if medically necessary	80% of approved amount	Except for certain preventive services (for which you pay nothing), you pay 20% of the Medicare-approved amount, and the Part B $120 deductible applies
Clinical Laboratory Services: blood tests, urinalysis, and some screening tests	Unlimited if medically necessary	100% of approved amount	Nothing
Home Health Care: part-time or intermittent skilled nursing care; and/or physical therapy, speech-language pathology services; and/or services for people with a continuing need for occupational therapy	Unlimited if medically necessary	100% of approved amount; 80% of durable medical equipment	20% of durable medical equipment after $120 Part B deductible
Outpatient Hospital Treatment: diagnostic and treatment services in participating hospital outpatient departments	Unlimited if medically necessary	Medicare payment based on hospital costs	20% of billed amount after $120 Part B deductible

Source: 2012. CMS: Medicare & You.

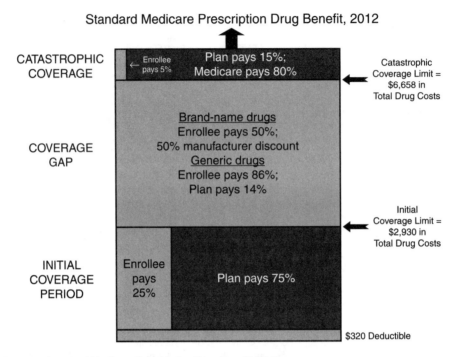

FIGURE 33.1 Standard Medicare Prescription Drug Benefit, 2012.

Source: Kaiser Family Foundation Illustration of standard Medicare drug benefit for 2012 (standard benefit parameter update from Centers for Medicare & Medicaid Services, April 2010). Amount rounded to nearest dollar. Used with permission.

Medicaid and Medicare

Medicaid is a federal-state health care financing program that covers certain low-income groups. Though adopted together, Medicare had strong public approval from its very beginning, while Medicaid was "burdened by the stigma of public assistance," as it was meant primarily for low-income Americans who fall into certain eligible groups such as the elderly and pregnant women (Starr, 1982).

There are several Medicaid programs that can assist seniors in covering the gaps in the Medicare program; these individuals are considered *dual eligibles*. First, full Medicaid benefits are available to seniors that meet income and asset guidelines and are eligible for Supplemental Security Income (SSI) or are deemed medically needy. For these individuals, the Medicaid program assumes out-of-pocket expenses associated with Medicare coinsurance and entitles beneficiaries to comprehensive acute and long-term care benefits. However, the scope of Medicaid coverage depends on the state, with some states providing more comprehensive eligibility and benefits than others (Ryan & Super, 2003). Second, there are Medicaid programs to assist Medicare beneficiaries with incomes too high to qualify for full Medicaid but considered too low to afford private health insurance. In 1986, Congress enacted several Medicaid programs to help these individuals with Medicare cost sharing (Ryan & Super, 2003): Qualified Medicare Beneficiaries (QMBs); Specified Low-Income Medicare Beneficiaries (SLMBs); Qualifying Individuals (QIs); and Qualified Disabled Working Individuals (QDWIs). The generosity of these programs again varies based on income guidelines (Table 33.2). Finally, Medicaid recipients may simply age into Medicare coverage once they cross the age of 65.

Prior research shows that only about half of all Medicare beneficiaries with incomes below the federal poverty line (FPL) are enrolled in Medicaid (Pezzin & Kasper, 2002; Ryan & Super, 2003). Reasons for the relatively low take-up rate include lack of information about program and eligibility criteria and welfare stigma. In addition, only a handful of states have extended coverage up to 100% of the FPL (Ryan & Super, 2003), though they are required to meet the

TABLE 33.2 Medicaid Programs for Medicare Beneficiaries

	ELIGIBILITY REQUIREMENTS	BENEFITS
Full Medicaid	SSI Medically needy Limited assets[a]	Medicaid program assumes out-of-pocket expenses associated with Medicare coinsurance and entitles beneficiaries to acute and long-term care benefits
Qualified Medicare Beneficiaries (QMBs)	Income at or below 100% of the FPL and limited assets[a]	Medicare Part A and B premiums, deductibles, and coinsurance, but does not have access to other Medicaid benefits
Specified Low-Income Medicare Beneficiaries (SLMBs)	Incomes between 100% and 120% of the FPL and limited assets[a]	Medicare Part B premium
Qualifying Individuals (QIs)	Incomes between 120% and 135% of the FPL and limited assets[a]	Assistance with Part B premium only
Qualified Disabled Working Individuals (QDWIs)	Incomes up to 200% of the FPL and limited assets[a]	Have not worked enough quarters to qualify for Medicare benefits without paying a premium. Medicaid pays the Part A premium only

[a]Assets—no more than $4,000 (for a couple $6,000). Lower threshold for full Medicaid.

Source: Adapted from Ryan and Super (2003).

minimum federal guidelines. There are large state variations in take-up rates (Pezzin & Kasper, 2002). Similar take-up rates have been observed for QMBs and SLMBs.

The total number of individuals who are considered to be dual eligible is estimated at approximately 9 million and fully 31% of all Medicare expenses and 39% of Medicaid spending is attributable to them (Jacobson, Neuman, & Damico, 2012). The vast majority of Medicaid spending on the dual eligibles is on two types of expenses: Long-term care (69%) and Medicare premiums and cost sharing (25%; Young et al., 2012). Dual eligibles are more likely than other Medicare beneficiaries "to be frail, live with multiple chronic conditions and have functional or cognitive impairments" (Jacobson et al., 2012, p.1); they are also likely to be poorer than the average Medicare beneficiary. As the program is likely to attract people with the greatest medical needs, this group is among the most costly of populations being served by public funds (Ryan & Super, 2003), with average spending 1.8 times higher than other Medicare beneficiaries (Jacobson, et al., 2012). Dual eligibles are also more likely to reside in a nursing home or other long-term facility. Pezzin and Kasper (2002) found that over 40% of dual eligibles are from minority populations.

Dual eligibles may also face access issues. Since each program (Medicare and Medicaid) has strong incentives to shift financial responsibilities to the other, care is rarely coordinated. Furthermore, dual eligibles rarely fully understand their coverage and how their benefits should be coordinated. However, there has been limited research examining access issues among dual eligibles. Using 1996 Medicare Current Beneficiary Survey (MCBS) data, Pezzin and Kasper (2002) found that the observed positive effect of dual enrollment on service use (physician visits and prescription medicines) was primarily accounted for by observed and unobserved characteristics of Medicaid enrollees (for instance, need factors). McCall and colleagues (2004) found racial/ethnic differences in preventive care (annual HbA1c, biennial eye test, and biennial lipid test) among dual-eligible diabetics in Colorado. Black dual eligibles were less likely to receive a yearly HbA1c test, a lipid test over the 2-year period, and the combined tests, than whites. Hispanics were less likely to receive eye and lipid tests over the 2-year period and the combined tests than whites.

The ACA has created a Medicare–Medicaid Coordination Office to better coordinate care for the dual eligibles. As an initial step, this new office has attempted to address coverage differences between Medicare and Medicaid, such as coverage of services for home health care and durable medical equipment. It has also developed and funded pilot projects to demonstrate the benefits of better coordination for the dual eligibles (Robert Wood Johnson Foundation [RWJF], 2012).

Medicare and Access to Care

Early studies examining the impact of Medicare showed that it had a positive impact on seniors' health care utilization and physical functioning (Davis, Gold, & Makuc, 1981; Davis & Reynolds, 1976). Andersen and colleagues (1972) found that 65% of low-income persons in 1970 saw a physician sometime in the year 1969, compared to just 56% in 1963 before the advent of Medicare. Similarly, data from the National Health Surveys showed that the elderly experienced hospitalization rates that increased from 11% in 1962 to 16% in 1968 (Schultze et al., 1972). With respect to physical functioning, Friedman (1976) found that the elderly had fewer days of restricted activity since implementation of Medicare, and that this decline was inversely related to the level of personal health care expenditures by the aged. Finally, Davis and Schoen (1978) found that the limitation of activity caused by chronic conditions in the aged declined from 1964 to 1973, and the number of restricted activity days fell by 15% during the same period.

Income and Medicare Access to Care

Notwithstanding the increased access provided by Medicare and Medicaid for the elderly population, there were still observed differences in access by income in the late 1960s. For example, an analysis of 1969 Health Interview Survey data showed that among seniors, high-income elderly persons made 60% more physician visits than low-income elderly without Medicaid, after adjusting for health status and other determinants (Davis, 1975; Davis & Reynolds, 1976). The gap was reduced to 27% when high-income seniors were compared to low-income elderly with Medicaid (Davis & Reynolds, 1976). Similarly, the Medicare average reimbursement per physician visit was 50% higher for higher income seniors than for lower income persons. With respect to hospitalizations, there was a gap of 45% in terms of hospital days between the highest and lowest income groups, after adjusting for health status and other determinants (Davis, 1975; Davis & Reynolds, 1976). These income gaps in health care utilization were attributed to financial barriers arising from the cost-sharing provisions (deductibles and coinsurance) in the Medicare program. These early findings also showed that the elimination of cost sharing for dual eligibles brought their utilization up to par with that of middle-income elderly.

Link, Long, and Settle (1982) found that income disparities were a less significant factor by the mid-1970s. Yet income was still responsible for statistically significant variations in the use of ambulatory health services among elderly with no chronic health problems. Among this group, the highest income seniors made 32% more visits than those in the lowest income group. On the other hand, there was no significant difference for those with chronic conditions.

Race/Ethnicity and Medicare Access to Care

Racial/ethnic differences in seniors' use of medical care were sizable before the Medicare program (Escarce & Kapur, 2003). For example, in 1964, white seniors used 42% more physicians per capita than blacks and other minorities (Davis, et al., 1981). Similarly, the probability of an elderly white person receiving inpatient care was nearly double that of a non-white elderly person, even when non-whites had greater medical needs (Long & Settle, 1984).

While the removal of racial disparities in access to medical care was not a primary goal for Medicare initially, it subsequently became an important consideration due to the shifting political and social environment (Long & Settle, 1984). In particular, Medicare was required to enforce Title VI of the Civil Rights Act of 1964, which required institutional providers such as hospitals to furnish services without discrimination (Davis, 1975).

While early Medicare studies did not show significant differences in health care utilization between whites and blacks, there were substantial racial differences in the South (Davis, 1975; Davis & Reynolds, 1976). Although elderly Southern blacks had lower health status than the population as a whole, they received fewer ambulatory services than any income group. For example, low-income elderly blacks with average health in the South without Medicaid made half as many visits as other persons aged 65 and above (Davis & Reynolds, 1976). Similar differences were observed for hospitalization, with elderly Southern blacks of average health having 2.8 days in the hospital compared to 4.6 days for other elderly. However, there were no significant racial differences outside of the South in terms of physician visits and hospitalizations.

Racial disparities in physician and hospital utilization in the early years of the Medicare program have been attributed to discriminatory practices in the South during this period. The Medicare program did not enforce nondiscriminatory practices among physicians as it did with hospitals, arguing that Medicare "merely reimburses patients for services received and does not enter into contractual agreements with physicians" (Davis & Reynolds, 1976, p. 414). Furthermore, study findings suggest that hospital policies were only partially successful in curbing discrimination.

As Davis and Reynolds (1976, p. 409) have indicated, "It was originally hoped that the removal of financial barriers to medical care would enable all elderly persons to receive medical care services largely on the basis of medical need. Yet, those elderly population groups with the poorest health [were] the lowest utilizers of medical care services under the program—the poor, blacks, rural residents, and residents of the South."

However, subsequent studies of the Medicare program showed that by the 1970s the racial disparities in care in the South started to diminish. Link, Long, and Settle (1982) analyzed the Health Interview Survey data for 1974 and 1976, and found that racial differences in the utilization by physician services in the South had disappeared completely. There were, however, still significant differences in the rates at which Southern blacks were hospitalized, even when the differences had narrowed between 1969 and 1976. Elderly Southern blacks utilized 65% as many hospital days as elderly Southern whites in 1976 compared to 54% in 1969, after controlling for differences in health status. In a related study, Long and Settle (1984) analyzed 1977 MCBS data and found that the likelihood of being admitted to a hospital was almost twice as high for whites than for non-whites in the South. These racial differences in inpatient care in the South were attributed to racial discrimination, and a greater tendency for whites to acquire some form of supplementary health insurance coverage (Long & Settle, 1984).

Nevertheless, it should be acknowledged that Medicare has played an important role in ensuring access to care for the elderly, particularly minorities. However, other factors apart from race may dictate health services utilization. In the next section, we use Andersen's Behavioral Model of Health Services Use to understand the various factors that may influence the utilization of various types of health services by racial/ethnic minorities.

MEDICARE AND HEALTH SERVICES UTILIZATION: APPLICATION OF ANDERSEN'S BEHAVIORAL MODEL OF HEALTH SERVICES USE

The Andersen (1995) Behavioral Model of Health Services Use is one of the most frequently applied models to explain factors influencing an individual's health care utilization. Factors that affect health care use include health system characteristics and individual characteristics. Health system characteristics include factors such as nurse-to-patient ratios, bed-to-patient ratios, and availability and proximity of services. Individual characteristics are classified as predisposing, enabling, and need based. Predisposing characteristics are those that make a person more likely to use health care and are mostly unchangeable, and include age, race, sex, marital status, education, occupation, and health care beliefs, attitudes, and behaviors. Enabling factors help people to gain access to health care and include income, insurance status, rural–urban residence, having a regular source of care, convenience of care, literacy, transportation, and other factors that help individuals obtain care. All Medicare beneficiaries by definition have at least some level of health insurance coverage. However, the coverage available to beneficiaries may vary according to individual circumstances—for instance, some may be dual eligible, while others have access to retiree coverage through a former employer that may supplement their Medicare benefits. In general, those with more generous insurance, higher income, urban residence, and a usual source of care will use more services. Finally, need is the most important indicator of use of health care (Andersen, 1995). It simply refers to whether a person is ill or not and can be classified as perceived need (symptoms) or evaluated need (diagnosis). Need should be the primary driver of health care use.

When examining access to care among minority elders, it is important to recognize the role of discrimination stemming directly or indirectly from racism (Williams, 1999). Within the Andersen model, perceived discrimination can be viewed as an important barrier to care (non-enabling factor). In their comprehensive review of literature, Williams and colleagues (2003) report that perceived discrimination is associated with poorer physical and mental health. In an updated literature review, Williams and Mohammed (2009) note that perceived discrimination is linked to multiple adverse health outcomes including cardiovascular diseases, mental disorders, and substance abuse.

LaVeist and colleagues (2003), in a study of the prevalence of discrimination in the U.S. health care system, showed that minorities (blacks and Hispanics) perceive more race discrimination than whites. In their study on perceived discrimination and adherence to medical care, Casagrande and colleagues (2007) show that for both black and white patients, lifetime experience of discrimination was associated with delay in seeking medical care and poor adherence.

In this section, we examine how individual determinants of the Andersen model may affect use of health care services among elderly minorities on Medicare.

Preventive Care

Predisposing and enabling determinants have been shown to be associated with minorities' use of preventive services. Resistance to vaccination is a health belief, which is a predisposing factor. Believing that the vaccine causes influenza and worrying about perceived side effects were the largest factors for individuals of all races who resisted vaccinations. However, there was an 11.8 percentage point difference in vaccination rates between whites and blacks attributable to resistance to vaccines (Hebert, Frick, Kane, & McBean, 2005).

Jerant and colleagues (2008) examined factors that affected racial/ethnic differences in colorectal cancer screening rates using the MEPS (2001–2005) and National Health Interview Survey (2000–2004), and found overall that screening was lower for Asians and Hispanics. After they adjusted for demographics, socioeconomic factors, language and access, differences between blacks and whites, and Hispanics and whites, disappeared from the models. However, the differences persisted between Asians and whites. Those who had a usual source of care, who were born in the United States, and who spoke English at home, were more likely to receive screening. These three factors may be classified as enabling factors.

Acute Care and Surgical Procedures

Using the Andersen model as a framework, Clay and colleagues (2011) examined differences between black and white Medicare beneficiaries in Alabama of overnight hospital admissions. They did not find any differences for surgical admissions, but did find that blacks had fewer nonsurgical admissions than whites. In terms of enabling determinants, they found that those who had perceived discrimination in the past were less likely to have a nonsurgical inpatient admission.

Skinner and colleagues (2003) showed that the incidence of knee arthroplasty was consistently higher for whites compared to Hispanics and blacks. Similar findings were reported by Hanchate et al. (2008); in their study using the Health and Retirement Study survey data, racial/ethnic disparities for knee arthroplasty remained significant for black men compared to whites even after controlling for economic factors. On similar lines, Cisternas and colleagues (2009) report significant disparities between black and white beneficiaries in the incidence of total knee replacement. Focusing on certain complex surgical procedures, Jha and colleagues (2005) report sharp differences among blacks for nine surgical procedures including hip replacement and coronary artery bypass graft (CABG). Jha et al. (2005, 683) conclude that "for the decade of the 1990s, we found no evidence, either nationally or locally, that efforts to eliminate racial disparities in the use of high-cost surgical procedures were successful." It is possible that while Medicare has been able to address racial/ethnic disparities on routine care, disparities persist for more complex and expensive procedures.

Joynt and colleagues (2011), analyzing national Medicare data, report that hospitals serving disproportionately black patients had worse quality for three common diseases (myocardial infection, congestive heart failure, and pneumonia), while blacks overall had higher 30-day readmission rates than whites across both minority and nonminority-serving hospitals. It appears that racial disparities were related to both race as well as the site of care.

Miles and Washington (2011) point out that quality of care received by elderly hospital patients may be influenced by their ethnicity as well as their need for language assistance. Diamond et al. (2010) report that only 13% of hospitals nationwide met all the federal regulations requiring provision of language services as measured by the Culturally and Linguistically Appropriate Services (CLAS) standards.

Prescription Drugs

Predisposing, enabling, and need variables all play a role in the elderly prescription drug use. Using data from the 1999 MCBS, Gaskin and colleagues (2006) found that whites used more prescription drugs than blacks (9%) and Hispanics (5%), and had higher levels of total drug spending. Minorities also spend much less on prescription drugs in their last year of life compared to white beneficiaries even when enrolled in a Medicare managed care plan. In the last year of life, minorities had, on average, eight fewer prescriptions than white enrollees, $381 less in total drug spending by the managed care plan, and $151 less in out-of-pocket spending on prescription drugs.

The cost of prescriptions can often lead people to forego purchasing medications, especially if they lack Part D coverage or have high coinsurance rates. Frankenfield and colleagues (2010) examined differences in cost-related nonadherence to medications between Hispanic and non-Hispanic Medicare beneficiaries using the Consumer Assessment of Healthcare Providers and Systems (CAHPS) Survey. A significantly larger proportion of Hispanics reported cost-related nonadherence to medications than non-Hispanics. Hispanic beneficiaries with a Part D low-income subsidy reported less likelihood of cost-related nonadherence than those without Part D.

Cost-related issues may not be the only factor explaining the observed racial/ethnic differences in prescription drug spending. As Gaskin and colleagues (2006, p. 10) argue, disparities in prescription drug spending by race/ethnicity "may reflect patients' skepticism about medicine and medical care in general, patients' adherence to medical advice, patient–physician communication, physicians' prescribing habits, and usual source of care."

Recent research has also shown disparities in patient experiences among Medicare beneficiaries with Part D prescription drug coverage. Using Medicare CAHPS data, Haviland and colleagues (2012) found disparities for Hispanic, black, and Asian/Pacific Islanders (APIs) on obtaining needed prescription drugs and information regarding coverage relative to non-Hispanic whites, with the greatest disparities observed for Spanish-preferring Hispanics and API beneficiaries, especially those with low income.

Subacute and Long-Term Care

Subacute care relates to skilled nursing care and therapy services associated with a hospital inpatient discharge. On the other hand, long-term care includes a range of services, otherwise known as "custodial care," that address the health, personal care, and social needs of individuals who lack some capacity for self-care (Kane & Kane, 1982). Subacute and long-term care settings include nursing homes, home health agencies, and hospice. While Medicare is a major payer of subacute care, Medicaid is the principal payer of long-term care.

The nursing home industry has been more segregated than other similarly located health care facilities such as hospitals (Angelelli, Grabowski, & Mor, 2006; Smith et al., 2007). Mor and colleagues (2004) have pointed out that nursing home quality is essentially a two-tiered system with the lower tier consisting of facilities with high Medicaid census; these facilities are located in the poorest communities, disproportionately treat minority patients, and are likely to report worse outcomes of care. Smith and colleagues (2007) affirm these findings, reporting that blacks are more likely than whites to be located in nursing homes that have serious deficiencies, lower staffing ratios, and greater financial vulnerability.

Although Hispanics and Asians are less likely to reside in nursing homes, this pattern has been changing in recent years. Feng et al. (2011) point out that between the years 1999 and 2008, the number of elderly Hispanics and Asians in nursing homes increased by approximately 55% each, while the number of elderly black residents increased by 11%. White residents actually declined by 0.2%. The authors attribute these findings to demographic shifts, with an increase in the number of minority elderly as well as inferior access to home and community-based services (HCBS) services for minority patients.

Yeboah-Korang and colleagues (2011) examined Outcome and Assessment Information Set (OASIS) data to determine if there were differences in the provision of home health care services among Medicare beneficiaries by race/ethnicity. They found that blacks and Hispanics were less likely than whites to receive physical therapy services, while Hispanics were less likely to use Home Health Aide visits than whites.

Hospice use tends to be much lower among blacks compared to whites, except in the case of cancer. Kwak et al. (2008) examined hospice use and in-hospital death for black and white dual-eligible beneficiaries in Florida, and found that, even after controlling for predisposing, enabling, and need variables, blacks were still less likely to use hospice and significantly more likely to die in the hospital. The authors posit that the observed racial differences may be due to a cultural preference among blacks for more aggressive treatment toward the end of life. Prior studies suggest that black attitudes toward hospice care differ significantly from those of other races. Blacks are more likely to prefer hospitalization at the end of life and require mechanical ventilation, and to eschew palliative care drugs that might shorten their lives compared to Hispanics and non-Hispanic whites (Barnato et al., 2009). A particularly striking reason for the preference for mechanical ventilation among blacks has been the belief that most people who are ventilated are able to successfully recover. Many black surrogates also believe that their parents or spouses should receive all medical care possible to prolong life. In one study using multiple focus groups, black surrogates who had to make end-of-life decisions for Medicare beneficiaries reported that "doing 'everything' was the 'right' thing to do." For many of the respondents, this was a matter of religious faith (Braun et al., 2008).

SUMMARY

This section explored the various types of health care services in which there have been differences between white and minority Medicare beneficiaries and also in which other individual determinants of the Andersen Behavioral Model of Health Services Use have played a role. Most prior literature has focused on white-black differences in health care use among the elderly Medicare beneficiaries. However, Hispanics and Asians constitute rapidly growing segments of the aging population, and further research is needed to examine the access issues of these ethnic groups.

MEDICARE ADVANTAGE AND THE ROLE OF MARKET IN MEDICARE

In this section, we discuss the Medicare Advantage (MA) program in detail, including a discussion of its evolution over the years. We believe that MA and what it represents—an increasingly important role for the market even within government insurance programs—are illustrative of the directions in which entitlements programs including Medicare may be structured in the future.

Background

In its various iterations, managed care has been an integral part of Medicare since its inception in 1965. Initially, Medicare accommodated prepaid plans by allowing them to be paid on a reasonable cost basis for services in contrast to the reasonable charges model it generally favored; this allowed private plans greater flexibility in designing their programs. Subsequently, the Social Security Act was amended in 1972 and it introduced health maintenance organization (HMO) enrollment and contracting to the Medicare program. The amendments also defined the performance standards for HMOs including the requirement to have an open enrollment season, and to provide the full range of Medicare services (Zarabozo, 2000). The program also introduced economic incentives for HMOs; costs incurred by contracting HMOs were compared to the average Medicare beneficiary costs, and savings, if any, were split equally between the HMO and the government.

The next major milestone in the Medicare HMO program was the enactment of the Tax Equity and Fiscal Responsibility Act in 1982. Under its provisions, a full-fledged risk-sharing model labeled the Medicare risk program was launched. Medicare entered into risk contracts with HMO plans paid at the rate of 95% of the adjusted per capita cost (APCC). The plans were allowed normal profit levels while any excessive savings were either returned to the beneficiaries or to the federal government (Zarabozo, 2000). The program was designed to yield cost savings to Medicare while expanding the options available to the beneficiaries. Despite initial hiccups, the HMO model gained market share in 1980s and 1990s, with enrollment increasing from 498,000 in 1985 to about 5.2 million beneficiaries by 1997 (Government Accountability Office, 2009). However, as risk-based programs were paid on the basis of Medicare FFS expenditures, they were generally concentrated in urban areas where such expenditures were higher (Riley & Zarabozo, 2006)

Congress next passed the Balanced Budget Act (BBA) of 1997. The BBA retired the Medicare risk program and formally introduced a new risk program called Medicare+ Choice (M+C; Rossiter, 2001). Under the M+C model, new provider organization forms like preferred provider organizations (PPO) and private FFS plans were allowed to enter into risk contracts (Riley & Zarabozo, 2006). It also introduced major reforms to the reimbursement mechanism: national/local blended rates, a payment floor for the lowest-paid counties, and a minimum update payment with plans guaranteed a 2% increase in reimbursement rates every year designed to increase the availability of private plans in rural/underrepresented areas. However, partially, as a result of these reforms, many health plans withdrew from the program, arguing that the reimbursement rates set by Medicare were financially unsustainable. M+C allowed enrollment in and out of plans every 30 days, which promoted adverse selection.

Faced with a sharp decline in the enrollment in the M+C program, Congress enacted the Medicare Prescription Drug, Improvement, and Modernization Act (MMA) of 2003. While the MMA was primarily focused on introducing the prescription drug benefit to Medicare, it also renamed the M+C program as MA and provided increases to MA plan payment rates and other program changes, such as removing the ability for MA enrollees to switch plans monthly. MMA also introduced two special categories of plans: regional plans that were to be offered in 26 designated regions and special needs plans that could restrict their availability to certain classes of Medicare beneficiaries (e.g. dual eligible; Riley & Zarabozo, 2006).

The MMA also permitted MA plans to offer prescription drug benefits in addition to their Parts A and B coverage. These are known as Medicare Advantage-Prescription Drug

Plans. Furthermore, the MMA also provides a Low-Income Subsidy (LIS) automatically to dual eligibles, QMBs, SLMBs, QIs, and SSI-only beneficiaries. Other beneficiaries can qualify under an income and asset test, but it is estimated that approximately 2 million beneficiaries who are eligible for the LIS do not receive it (Summer et al., 2010).

MA has been particularly attractive to racial/ethnic minorities. As of 2010, 29% of blacks, 33% of Asian Americans, and 36% of Hispanic Medicare beneficiaries were enrolled in MA plans compared to 25% of whites (America's Health Insurance Plans [AHIP], 2012). The popularity of MA care among racial/ethnic minorities may be due to the relatively lower out-of-pocket costs of managed care (especially HMOs) compared to the traditional FFS program. This may be particularly appealing to racial/ethnic minorities because they tend to be over-represented among the lowest income groups. However, the higher proportion of minority enrollment may be concerning because it appears that, at least in some metrics, traditional Medicare performs better than MA. For instance, in a recent study using the national representative Commonwealth Fund 2012 Health Insurance Survey, Davis and colleagues (2012) report that 6% of the elderly with traditional Medicare gave their insurance a fair or poor rating compared to 15% of MA enrollees.

MA and Racial/Ethnic Disparities

MA was designed as a mechanism to introduce market competition in Medicare. The essential argument is that contrary to the one-size-fits-all approach of the traditional Medicare program, the market friendly features of MA would allow for improved quality at a lower cost. For instance, it was hypothesized that some features of managed care such as a designated primary care physician and case-management programs for patients with chronic conditions would improve quality of care. On the other hand, as most managed care organizations are profit driven, they may introduce barriers of care through "gatekeepers," which may disproportionately affect racial/ethnic minorities, which are frequently socially and economically disadvantaged.

Schneider et al. (2002) examined white–black differences between beneficiaries enrolled in MA plans across four quality measures in the Health Plan Employer Data and Information Set (HEDIS): rates of breast cancer screening, eye examinations for patients with diabetes, β-blocker use after myocardial infarction, and follow-up after hospitalization for mental illness. They report that even after adjusting for potential confounding factors, significant white-black differences persisted for multiple measures including β-blocker use after myocardial infarction and follow-up after hospitalization for mental illness. Utilizing nine HEDIS quality measures, Trivedi and colleagues (2005) assessed changes over time in the overall quality of care and in the magnitude of racial disparities. While they report that quality improved across all nine measures for both white and black beneficiaries, racial disparities continue to persist, with blacks consistently reporting worse quality than whites. In another study, Trivedi and colleagues (2006) examined the relationship between quality of health plan and racial difference across four HEDIS outcome measures. They report that clinical performance on HEDIS outcomes measures was consistently lower for black enrollees compared to white enrollees, with more than 70% of these disparities explained by within-plan differences rather than between-plan differences. It appears that blacks were not enrolling in plans of lower quality—rather, they suffered from poorer clinical outcomes even when enrolled in a higher quality plan.

Several studies have examined racial/ethnic differences in Medicare managed care using CAHPS data (Elliott et al. 2011; Fongwa et al., 2006; Lurie et al., 2003; Weech-Maldonado et al., 2008). A study conducted by Lurie and colleagues (2003) found that, compared with whites, Hispanics had less positive assessments of getting needed care, timeliness of care, and staff helpfulness, but higher ratings for their health plans. Weech-Maldonado et al. (2008) report that Hispanics in Medicare managed care faced barriers to care; however, their experiences with care vary by language and region. Spanish speakers have less favorable experiences with provider communication and office staff helpfulness than their English-speaking counterparts, suggesting language barriers in the clinical encounter. Finally, Elliott et al. (2011) show that compared to the traditional Medicare FFS plans, MA beneficiaries report higher disparities for vulnerable populations including minorities; these differences were highest for Part D.

Health Policy and Minority Aging

Wallace and Villa (1997) argue that the voice of the minority elderly is largely missing from the health care debate. The lack of the representation for the minority elderly may be due to multiple factors. First, the elderly in the United States are still less diverse than the general population; therefore, policymakers are less likely to be cognizant of the concerns of the minority elderly. Second, even among minorities, the voice of the elderly is often ignored as the population is heavily skewed toward the young. For instance, among the Hispanic population, there are six youths for every elderly person. Third, in many minority cultures, the family assumes primary responsibility for elderly care. The overt emphasis on family as the primary caregiver makes it harder to advocate for health and social policy changes designed to aid the minority elderly.

The unfortunate absence of minority elderly from the health policy debate arrives at a particularly pivotal time in U.S. history. After the financial collapse of 2008 and the election of President Obama, the political debate in the United States has been dominated almost entirely by economic concerns aligned with a clash over the proper place of government in the American society (Starr, 2012). Essentially, fiscal deficits and the mounting national debt have become prime drivers of public policy. The passage of the ACA of 2010 has further crystallized opposition among those who believe that the government is increasingly dominant in American society and is exceeding its traditional and even "constitutional" bounds.

The focus on deficits and controlling the cost of government has in turn increased the focus on health care and entitlement programs like Medicare. Mandatory spending constitutes nearly 60% of the total budget in FY 2013; Medicare alone consumes nearly $600 billion and it has been growing at the rate of 7% each year (Office of Management & Budget, 2012). With the sharp rise in the number of the elderly and an aging workforce, Medicare's reliance on general revenues as a source of funding is only likely to increase in the future. Therefore, reforming entitlement programs like Medicare have been emphasized as essential to controlling the red ink in the federal budget. Even President Obama has acknowledged the need for Medicare reforms; some of which have been incorporated in the ACA, including the creation of an Independent Payment Advisory Board (IPAB) to control Medicare's increasing health care costs. The IPAB would have the powers to structure Medicare to achieve cost savings. Congress would have three choices: it can accept IPAB recommendations, propose its own plans to achieve the same cost savings, or allow Medicare to grow at a larger rate than permitted by law; however, the last option would require the approval of three-fifths support in the Senate. Despite the supervisory powers available to Congress, IPAB would mark an important shift in the balance of power, with the board becoming the primary driver of Medicare payment policy. Critics on the other hand argue that the IPAB would introduce rationing and reduce access to health care for particularly needy elderly who may require experimental and extraordinarily expensive care. Provider groups argue that because IPAB by law does not have the authority to restrict benefits or change eligibility criterion, it has few tools available but to cut payment rates; this may further reduce access for Medicare beneficiaries.

The chairman of the House Budget Committee, Representative Paul Ryan (R) has recently offered market-driven solutions to control Medicare costs. Representative Ryan's 2012 budget proposal—the so-called Path to Prosperity—has the potential to fundamentally restructure Medicare by terminating its status as an entitlement with a much greater role for the market in the program. Ryan's Medicare proposals have the following important features: First, the age of eligibility for Medicare would be gradually increased to 67 by the year 2034. Second, it would cap Medicare spending growth at gross domestic product (GDP) growth plus 0.5%; it is sharply lower than historical trends where medical inflation has typically exceeded GDP growth by 2%. Third, it would provide a set amount of money—premium support—for Medicare beneficiaries to purchase either a private health plan or the traditional government-provided Medicare. The government would pay the premium for the second lowest Medicare bid; beneficiaries would have the freedom to buy a more expensive plan but they would have to cover the additional premium from personal funds (Serafini, 2012). Representative Ryan has also emphasized that the cost to the beneficiaries would be determined purely by competitive market pressures and not set by the government. In order to allay the concerns of the current beneficiaries and minimize political backlash, Ryan's plan would be implemented only from the year 2024, preserving Medicare as it currently exists for anyone over 55 (Serafini, 2012).

Representative Ryan's proposal has set off a political firestorm with critics alleging that the proposal would "destroy" Medicare, replacing it with an essentially privately run system. They also argue that traditional Medicare may be saddled with the sickest patients, which may render the program noncompetitive and nonsolvent in a short order (Serafini, 2012). Finally, the proposal is said to transform Medicare from a defined benefit plan to a defined contribution plan, as it would not control costs per se but simply shift them to the beneficiaries, particularly if the increase in the voucher payments trailed medical inflation. However, supporters of the Ryan plan argue that it will control Medicare costs while offering beneficiaries greater choice and autonomy. They believe that market discipline is superior to government controls in cutting costs as well as improving quality and patient satisfaction.

Nevertheless, considering the importance of Medicare to minority elderly, it is disconcerting that their voice has not been heard in this important debate. In particular, despite assurances to the contrary, premium support is likely to adversely affect the poor who are disproportionately minority (Center for Budget & Policy Priorities, 2012). For instance, minorities may be forced to enroll in the cheapest plan as they may not have the resources to meet the extra premium of a higher cost plan. Therefore, Representative Ryan's proposal may result in a two-tiered Medicare system, with the poor and minorities restricted to cheaper plans with potentially lower quality. These concerns are further exacerbated by the overt cost control measures in the Ryan proposal, which may result in physicians and hospitals simply refusing to accept Medicare. This may affect access for the minority elderly who already face difficulty in meeting essential health care needs.

CONCLUSIONS

Medicare is important to ensure access to health care for the elderly, particularly the poor and minorities. It has substantially improved access to medical care for the poor and minority to the extent that overt racial/ethnic disparities have largely disappeared. However, racial/ethnic disparities continue to persist in access to more specialized care particularly surgical and advanced procedures as well as quality of care with minority elderly generally reporting poorer access and quality than whites.

In addition to race and ethnicity, many other factors influence differences in health care utilization between whites, blacks, Hispanics, Asians, and American Indians. Although we cannot, from a policy standpoint, counter differences in predisposing factors, there are many enabling determinants could be influenced to narrow the differences in use. Health policy has traditionally focused on enabling resources. Having a usual source of care, providing interpretation services, reducing discrimination or perceived discrimination, providing better insurance coverage, and providing better social support and resources to beneficiaries may all be mechanisms by which we can improve care for older minorities. Patient-centered medical homes and accountable care organizations may help increase access to a usual source of care. Some evidence indicates that discrimination may be declining; however, it is still present and needs to be addressed. An increased emphasis on cultural competency training in the health professions may reduce this barrier to care. Ultimately, though, need should dictate who receives which services. Fortunately, many studies show that need is a very good predictor of those who are using health care services after controlling for other predisposing and enabling determinants.

Medicare has undergone many changes since its inception in 1965. Market forces are increasingly important within the Medicare program, while it offers additional benefits including Part D—the largest expansion of entitlement program in the United States since the original enactment of Medicare and Medicaid in 1965. However, with the rising health care costs and changing demographics, it is clear that Medicare needs some type of reform to ensure its continuing viability. In their 2012 report, trustees report that by 2024 the Medicare Hospital insurance (HI) trust would be "exhausted," at which point it is projected to meet 87% of HI costs; the actuarial imbalance is projected to expand substantially over the next few decades requiring general revenues for Medicare to meet its shortfalls (Social Security Administration, 2012). There is an undeniable need to reform Medicare to ensure its future financial viability while at the same time preserving the extraordinary role it plays in ensuring access to medical care for the elderly, particularly the poor and minorities.

However, the contours of those reforms are important as they may affect the most vulnerable of Americans and compromise hard-earned gains in addressing racial/ethnic disparities in the U.S. health care system. It is important, therefore, to ensure that the minority elderly are part of this important conversation and their requirements and needs are included in any discussion on Medicare's future especially as the United States is increasingly becoming a more diverse country (Dougherty, 2008). The Census Bureau (2011) estimates that by 2042, the United States will be a "minority–majority" country with the proportion of non-Hispanic whites falling to 46%. Similar to the general population, the elderly population will gradually become more diverse; the U.S. Census Bureau estimates that by 2050, the proportion of the non-Hispanic elderly would decrease from 84% in 2000 to 64% in 2050. Therefore, the reforms introduced in the early years of 21st century may affect an America that differs substantially from how it looks now.

The elderly are a powerful voting block and no politician can afford to antagonize them. Paradoxically, the dominating voice of the elderly in the health care debate may have potential negative implications for the minority elderly due to their lagging diversity vis-à-vis the general population. Because racial/ethnic minorities tend to be younger and due to high rates of Hispanic and Asian immigration, the diversity among the elderly still lags the dramatic shifts in the racial composition of the general U.S. population. The policymakers face a significant challenge in addressing this power gap and in ensuring that the minorities and other vulnerable groups are equal participants in any debate over Medicare.

REFERENCES

America's Health Insurance Plans (AHIP) Centers for Policy and Research. (2012). *Low-income & minority beneficiaries in Medicare advantage plans, 2010.* Retrieved on April, 30, 2012, from www.ahip.org/MALowIncomeMinorityReport2012/

Andersen, R. M. (1972). *Health service use. National trends and variations—1953–1971.* Rockville, MD: National Center for Health Services Research and Development.

Andersen, R. M. (1995). Revisiting the behavioral model and access to medical care: Does it matter? *Journal of Health and Social Behavior, 36*(1), 1–10.

Angelelli, J., Grabowski, D. C., & Mor, V. (2006). Effect of educational level and minority status on nursing home choice after hospital discharge. *American Journal of Public Health, 96*(7), 1249.

Barnato, A, Anthony, D., Skinner, J., Gallagher, P., & Fisher, E. (2009). Racial and ethnic differences in preferences for end-of-life treatment. *Journal of General Internal Medicine, 24*(6), 695–701.

Braun, U. K., Beyth, R. J., Ford, M. E., & McCullough, L. B. (2008). Voices of African American, Caucasian, and Hispanic surrogates on the burdens of end-of-life decision making. *Journal of General Internal Medicine, 23*(3), 267–274.

Casagrande, S. S., Gary, T. L., LaVeist, T. A., Gaskin, D. J., & Cooper, L. A. (2007). Perceived discrimination and adherence to medical care in a racially integrated community. *Journal of General Internal Medicine, 22*(3), 389–395.

Center for Budget Policy & Priorities. (2012). Chairman Ryan gets nearly two-thirds of his huge budget cuts from programs for lower-income Americans. Retrieved on April, 20, 2012, from http://www.cbpp.org/files/4–5-11bud2.pdf

Centers for Medicare & Medicaid. (2012). *Medicare & You.* Retrieved on April, 30, 2012, from http://www.medicare.gov/publications/pubs/pdf/10050.pdf

Cisternas, M. G., Murphy, L., Croft, J. B., & Helmick, C. G. (2009). Racial disparities in total knee replacement among Medicare enrollees—United States, 2000–2006. *Morbidity and Mortality Weekly Report, 58*(6), 133–138.

Clay, O. J., Roth, D. L., Safford, M. M., Sawyer, P. L., & Allman, R. M. (2011). Predictors of overnight hospital admission in older African American and Caucasian Medicare beneficiaries. *The Journals of Gerontology Series A: Biological Sciences and Medical Sciences, 66A*(8), 910–916.

Davis, K. (1975). Equal treatment and unequal benefits: The Medicare program. *The Milbank Memorial Fund Quarterly. Health and Society, 53*(4), 449–488.

Davis, K., Gold, M., & Makuc, D. (1981). Access to health care for the poor: Does the gap remain? *Annual Review of Public Health, 2*(1), 159–182.

Davis, K., & Reynolds, R. (1976). The impact of Medicare and Medicaid on access to medical care. In N. R. Rosset, (Ed.) *The role of health insurance in the health services sector.* Washington, DC: National Bureau of Economic Research.

Davis, K., & Schoen, C. (1978). *Health and the war on poverty: a ten-year appraisal.* Washington, DC: The Brookings Institution.

Davis, K., Stremikis, K., Doty, M. M., & Zezza, M. A. (2012). Medicare beneficiaries less likely to experience cost-and access-related problems than adults with private coverage. *Health Affairs, 31*(8), 1866–1875.

Diamond, L. C., Wilson-Stronks, A., & Jacobs, E. A. (2010). Do hospitals measure up to the national culturally and linguistically appropriate services standards? *Medical Care, 48*(12), 1080.

Dougherty, C. (2008). Whites to lose majority status in US by 2042. *The Wall Street Journal.* Retrieved on April, 30, 2012, from http://online.wsj.com/article/SB121867492705539109.html

Elliott, M. N., Haviland, A. M., Orr, N., Hambarsoomian, K., & Cleary, P. D. (2011). How do the experiences of Medicare beneficiary subgroups differ between managed care and original Medicare? *Health Services Research, 46*(4), 1039–1058.

Escarce, J. J., & Kapur, K. (2003). Racial and ethnic differences in public and private medical care expenditures among aged Medicare beneficiaries. *Milbank Quarterly, 81*(2), 249–275.

Escarce, J. J., & Puffer, E. W. (Eds.). (1997). *Racial and ethnic differences in the health of older Americans.* Washington, DC: National Academies Press.

Feng, Z., Fennell, M. L., Tyler, D. A., Clark, M., & Mor, V. (2011). Growth of racial and ethnic minorities in US nursing homes driven by demographics and possible disparities in options. *Health Affairs, 30*(7), 1358–1365.

Fongwa, M. N., Cunningham, W., Weech-Maldonado, R., Gutierrez, P. R., & Hays, R. D. (2006). Comparison of data quality for reports and ratings of ambulatory care by African American and white Medicare managed care enrollees. *Journal of Aging and Health, 18*(5), 707–721.

Frankenfield, D., Wei, I., Anderson, K., Howell, B., Waldo, D., & Sekscenski, E. (2010). Prescription medication cost-related non-adherence among Medicare CAHPS respondents: Disparity by Hispanic ethnicity. *Journal of Health Care for the Poor and Underserved, 21*(2), 518–543.

Friedman, B. (1976). *Mortality, disability, and the normative economics of Medicare.* New York, NY: National Bureau of Economic Research. Retrieved on May 13, 2013, from http://www.nber.org/chapters/c3823.pdf

Gaskin, D. J., Briesacher, B. A., Limcangco, R., & Brigantti, B. L. (2006). Exploring racial and ethnic disparities in prescription drug spending and use among Medicare beneficiaries. *The American Journal of Geriatric Pharmacotherapy, 4*(2), 96–111.

Government Accountability Office. (2009). *Relationship between benefit package designs and plans. Average beneficiary health status.* Washington, DC: Author.

Hanchate, A. D., Zhang, Y., Felson, D. T., & Ash, A. S. (2008). Exploring the determinants of racial and ethnic disparities in total knee arthroplasty: Health insurance, income, and assets. *Medical Care, 46*(5), 481.

Haviland, A. M., Elliott, M., Weech-Maldonado, R., Hambarsoomian, K., Orr, N., & Hays, R. D. (2012). Racial/ethnic disparities in Medicare Part D experiences. *Medical Care 50*(Suppl), S40–S47.

Hebert, P. L., Frick, K. D., Kane, R. L., & McBean, A. M. (2005). The causes of racial and ethnic differences in influenza vaccination rates among elderly Medicare beneficiaries. *Health Services Research, 40*(2), 517–538.

Jacobson, G., Neuman, T., & Damico, A. (2012).*Medicare's role for dual eligible beneficiaries.* Retrieved on April, 30, 2012, from http://www.kff.org/medicare/upload/8138–02.pdf

Jerant, A. F., Fenton, J. J., & Franks, P. (2008). Determinants of racial/ethnic Colorectal cancer screening disparities. *Archives of Internal Medicine, 168*(12), 1317–1324.

Jha, A. K., Fisher, E. S., Li, Z., Orav, E. J., & Epstein, A. M. (2005). Racial trends in the use of major procedures among the elderly. *New England Journal of Medicine, 353*(7), 683–691.

Joynt, K. E., Orav, E. J., & Jha, A. K. (2011). Thirty-day readmission rates for Medicare beneficiaries by race and site of care. *The Journal of the American Medical Association, 305*(7), 675.

Kaiser Family Foundation (KFF). (2011) *The Medicare prescription drug benefit—An updated fact sheet.* Retrieved on April, 30, 2012, from http://www.kff.org/medicare/upload/7044–12.pdf

Kane, R. and Kane, R. (1982). *Values and long-term care.* Lexington, MA: Lexington Books.

Kwak, J., Haley, W. E., & Chiriboga, D. A. (2008). Racial differences in hospice use and in-hospital death among Medicare and Medicaid dual-eligible nursing home residents. *The Gerontologist, 48*(1), 32–41.

LaVeist, T. A., Rolley, N. C., & Diala, C. (2003). Prevalence and patterns of discrimination among US health care consumers. *International Journal of Health Services, 33*(2), 331–344.

Link, C. R., Long, S. H., & Settle, R. F. (1982). Equity and the utilization of health care services by the Medicare elderly. *Journal of Human Resources, 17*(2), 195–212.

Long, S. H., & Settle, R. F. (1984). Medicare and the disadvantaged elderly: Objectives and outcomes. *The Milbank Memorial Fund Quarterly. Health and Society, 62*(4), 609–656.

Lurie, N., Zhan, C., Sangl, J., Bierman, A. S., & Sekscenski, E. S. (2003). Variation in racial and ethnic differences in consumer assessments of health care. *American Journal of Managed Care, 9*(7), 502–509.

McCall, D. T., Sauaia, A., Hamman, R. F., Reusch, J. E., & Barton, P. (2004). Are low-income elderly patients at risk for poor Diabetes care? *Diabetes Care, 27*(5), 1060–1065.

Meara, E., White, C., & Cutler, D. M. (2004). Trends in medical spending by age, 1963–2000. *Health Affairs, 23*(4), 176–183.

Miles, T. P., & Washington, K. T. (2011). Physical health problems: Shaping transitions of care. *Annual Review of Gerontology and Geriatrics, 31*(1), 65–91.

Mor, V., Zinn, J., Angelelli, J., Teno, J. M., & Miller, S. C. (2004). Driven to tiers: Socioeconomic and racial disparities in the quality of nursing home care. *Milbank Quarterly, 82*(2), 227–256.

Office of Management & Budget (2012) *Fiscal year 2013 budget of the us government.* Retrieved on April, 30, 2012, from http://www.whitehouse.gov/sites/default/files/omb/budget/fy2013/assets/budget.pdf

Pezzin, L. E., & Kasper, J. D. (2002). Medicaid enrollment among elderly Medicare beneficiaries: Individual determinants, effects of state policy, and impact on service use. *Health Services Research, 37*(4), 827–847.

Riley, G., & Zarabozo, C. (2006). Trends in the health status of Medicare risk contract enrollees. *Health Care Financing Review, 28*(2), 81.

Robert Wood Johnson Foundation (RWJF). (2012). *Care for dual eligible.* Princeton, NJ: Author.

Rossiter, L. F. (2001). *Understanding Medicare managed care: Meeting economic, strategic, and policy challenges.* Chicago, IL: Health Administration Press.

Ryan, J., & Super, N. (2003). *Dually eligible for Medicare and Medicaid: Two for one or double jeopardy.* Retrieved April, 30, 2012, from http://ww.nhpf.org/library/issue-briefs/IB794_Duals_9–30-03.pdf

Schneider, E. C., Zaslavsky, A. M., & Epstein, A. M. (2002). Racial disparities in the quality of care for enrollees in Medicare managed care. *The Journal of the American Medical Association, 287*(10), 1288–1294.

Schultze, C. L., Fried, E. R., Rivlin, A. M., & Teeters, N. H. (1972). *Setting national priorities: The 1973 budget.* Washington, DC: The Brookings Institution.

Serafini, W. M. (2012). *New Ryan budget would transform Medicare and Medicaid.* Washington, DC: Kaiser Health News.

Skinner, J., Weinstein, J. N., Sporer, S. M., & Wennberg, J. E. (2003). Racial, ethnic, and geographic disparities in rates of knee arthroplasty among Medicare patients. *New England Journal of Medicine, 349*(14), 1350–1359.

Smith, D. B., Feng, Z., Fennell, M. L., Zinn, J. S., & Mor, V. (2007). Separate and unequal: Racial segregation and disparities in quality across US nursing homes. *Health Affairs, 26*(5), 1448–1458.

Social Security Administration. (2012). *A summary of 2012 annual reports.* Washington, DC: Author.

Starr, P. (1982). *The social transformation of American medicine.* New York, NY: Basic Books.

Starr, P. (2012) *Remedy and reaction: The peculiar American struggle over health care reform.* New Haven, CT: Yale University Books.

Summer, L., Hoadley, J. & Hargrave, E.(2010).*The Medicare part d low-income subsidy program experience to date and policy issues for consideration.* Retrieved on April, 30, 2012, from http://www.kff.org/medicare/upload/8094.pdf

Trivedi, A. N., Zaslavsky, A. M., Schneider, E. C., & Ayanian, J. Z. (2005). Trends in the quality of care and racial disparities in Medicare managed care. *New England Journal of Medicine, 353*(7), 692–700.

Trivedi, A. N., Zaslavsky, A. M., Schneider, E. C., & Ayanian, J. Z. (2006). Relationship between quality of care and racial disparities in Medicare health plans. *The Journal of the American Medical Association, 296*(16), 1998–2004.

U.S. Census Bureau. (2011). Washington, DC: Author.

Wallace, S. P., & Villa, W. M. (Eds.). (1997). *Caught in hostile cross-fire: Public policy and minority elderly in the United States.* Thousand Oaks, CA: Sage.

Weech-Maldonado, R., Fongwa, M. N., Gutierrez, P., & Hays, R. D. (2008). Language and regional differences in evaluations of Medicare managed care by Hispanics. *Health Services Research, 43*(2), 552–568.

Williams, D. R. (1999). Race, socioeconomic status, and health: The added effects of racism and discrimination. *Annals of the New York Academy of Sciences, 896*(1), 173–188.

Williams, D. R., & Mohammed, S. A. (2009). Discrimination and racial disparities in health: Evidence and needed research. *Journal of Behavioral Medicine, 32*(1), 20–47.

Williams, D. R., Neighbors, H. W., & Jackson, J. S. (2003). Racial/ethnic discrimination and health: Findings from community studies. *American Journal of Public Health, 93*: 200–208.

Yeboah-Korang, A., Kleppinger, A., & Fortinsky, R. H. (2011). Racial and ethnic group variations in service use in a national sample of Medicare home health care patients with type 2 Diabetes Mellitus. *Journal of the American Geriatrics Society, 59*(6), 1123–1129.

Young, K., Garfield, R., Musumeci, M., Clemans-Cope, L., & Lawton, E. (2012). *Medicaid's role for dual eligible beneficiaries.* Washington, DC: The Kaiser Family Foundation

Zarabozo, C. (2000). Milestones in Medicare managed care. *Health Care Financing Review, 22*(1), 61–68.

Index